World Almanac of Islamism 2011

World Almanac of Islamism 2011

American Foreign Policy Council

ROWMAN & LITTLEFIELD PUBLISHERS, INC.
Lanham • Boulder • New York • Toronto • Plymouth, UK

Published by Rowman & Littlefield Publishers, Inc.
A wholly owned subsidiary of The Rowman & Littlefield Publishing Group, Inc.
4501 Forbes Boulevard, Suite 200, Lanham, Maryland 20706
www.rowmanlittlefield.com

Estover Road, Plymouth PL6 7PY, United Kingdom

British Library Cataloguing in Publication Information Available

Library of Congress Cataloging-in-Publication Data

World almanac of Islamism 2011 / American Foreign Policy Council.
   p. cm.
Includes bibliographical references and index.
  ISBN 978-1-4422-0713-4 (cloth : alk. paper)—ISBN 978-1-4422-0715-8 (electronic : alk. paper)
  1. Islam and world politics. 2. World politics—1989– 3. Radicalism—Religious aspects—Islam. 4. Islamic fundamentalism. 5. Religious awakening—Islam. I. American Foreign Policy Council.
  BP173.5.W66 2011
  297.2'72—dc23   2011031627

Printed in the United States of America

TABLE OF CONTENTS

ACKNOWLEDGEMENTS

The *World Almanac of Islamism* has been a massive intellectual and organizational undertaking, several years in the making. This, the *Almanac's* inaugural edition, would not have been possible without the dedication and assistance of a number of talented researchers, including Matthew Brodsky, Amanda Lamb, Michelle Hong, Zachary Young, Mary DePuglio, Lisa Aronson and Adam Schusterman.

Special thanks also go to AFPC Special Projects Coordinator Elizabeth Wood, for her assistance in the copy-editing of the project's numerous chapters; to AFPC Research Associate Amanda Pitrof, for her extensive work on the layout and design of the *Almanac's* print and online editions; to AFPC Junior Fellow Micah Levinson, for his role in fact-checking and copy-editing selected chapters of this collection; and to AFPC Research Fellow and Program Officer Rich Harrison for spearheading the creation and design of the *Almanac's* digital edition.

Finally, AFPC President Herman Pirchner deserves special recognition for his vision in conceiving of this project, and for his encouragement and guidance throughout its development.

Ilan Berman
Chief Editor

Jeff M. Smith
Managing Editor

Washington, DC
July 2011

A WORD ABOUT DEFINITIONS

For the purposes of this collection, the term ISLAMIST is used to describe movements, groups and individuals which harness religious values and ideals to serve a larger political agenda aimed at spreading or imposing Islamic law, either locally, regionally or internationally.

GLOBAL OVERVIEW

Summary

In 2010-2011, Islamism remained a prominent political force worldwide, and in select countries and regions charted some significant advances.

In North America, Islamism remains a phenomenon that is poorly understood and largely unaddressed. Islamist activity in the United States is dominated by grassroots groups associated with Egypt's Muslim Brotherhood and Pakistan's Jamaat-e Islami, which have erected an elaborate web of professional activist organizations involved in local, state, and national politics over the past five decades. In Canada, meanwhile, lax oversight and law enforcement historically have allowed Salafist, Shi'a and Palestinian Islamist groups to use the country as a safe haven, although Ottawa has taken significant steps in recent years to reverse that trend.

There is considerable evidence that Islamist groups and movements have begun to make significant inroads in Latin America as well, operating among the local Muslim communities that dot the countries of the region. This includes groups such as Hezbollah and al-Qaeda, which have deftly exploited the large ungoverned areas and widespread anti-American sentiment of Central and South America to set up financing, fundraising and logistics hubs there.

In the Middle East and North Africa, the political ferment surrounding the Arab Spring has injected new dynamism into historically-stagnant regional politics. In the process, it also has provided Islamists with significant opportunities to advance their position, and expand their political voice. The withdrawal of U.S. forces from Iraq, now underway, likewise has made that country an intellectual battleground for the insurgent Islamism advocated by Iran and affiliated Shi'a militias and the nationalism promoted by the Iraqi government and its related forces.

In Sub-Saharan Africa, weak governance and corruption among regional states has allowed Islamist ideas and political parties to take root. Somalia and Sudan have been the countries hardest hit by Islamic radicalism, but significant instability likewise can bee seen in the Sahel region abutting Mali and Mauritania--an area where al-Qaeda's regional franchise, al-Qaeda in the Islamic Maghreb, has emerged as a serious challenge to security and stability.

In Europe, steady immigration from the Middle East and North Africa, coupled with stagnant demographic trends among native Europeans, has made Islamism an increasingly prevalent--and potent--political force. Most countries on the Continent have sought to accommodate their increasingly vocal Muslim minorities, even as they engage in counterterrorism operations to neutralize violent Islamist groups and activities. Nevertheless, a growing undercurrent of opposition to Islamism can be seen in places such as the Netherlands, Denmark and France, often finding its expression in nationalist and protectionist sentiment.

Eurasia likewise remains a locus of resilient Islamist activity, with corruption and authoritarian governments providing added legitimacy to the Islamist opposition in Azerbaijan and the "Stans" of Central Asia. Particularly hard hit in this regard is Russia, where Islamic militancy is no longer localized to its turbulent North Caucasus region, but is expanding into the country's traditionally moderate Muslim heartland.

South Asia's political environment is dominated by the ripple effects of the Islamic radicalism that is endemic to the state of Pakistan. India has been most directly impacted by this phenomenon, long grappling with Islamic terrorism engineered in Pakistan and carried out by Pakistani proxy groups. The ongoing war in Afghanistan has also served as a major cause of regional instability, with the pending withdrawal of the U.S. troops raising questions about the future stability of the country, and the role the Taliban and other Islamist groups will play there.

East Asia likewise faces a growing problem with Islamist extremism, which has taken different forms and seen varying degrees of success across the region. In Thailand, the Philippines, and China, Islamist activism has largely paralleled ethno-religious separatism, while other states, such as Indonesia and Malaysia, have grappled with powerful domestic Islamist political groups seeking the implementation of *sharia* law. Violent, transnational Islamist groups, most notably Jemaah Islamiyaa, are also present in the region, although significant counterterrorism efforts on the part of regional states have blunted their capabilities in recent years.

North America

Regional Summary

The terrorist attacks of September 11, 2001 brought new attention and urgency to popular discussions of Islamic terrorism in North America, and touched off a wide-ranging global campaign on the part of the United States and its allies to target al-Qaeda and associated groups. Yet a decade later, the larger political phenomenon of Islamism, as well as its manifestations in North America, remains poorly understood and largely unaddressed by governments on the continent.

In the United States, five-plus decades of activity and organization by grass-roots groups associated with Egypt's Muslim Brotherhood and Pakistan's Jamaat-e Islami have yielded an elaborate web of professional activist organizations involved in local, state and national politics. This network operates on a variety of levels; some of its constituent organizations seek to influence attitudes towards (and discourse about) Islam and Islamism among elected officials and the general public. Others have historically worked through schools, universities, and educational institutions to promote Islamist ideas and values. Still others serve as economic conduits and repositories for wealth and holdings associated with the Brotherhood and Jamaat-e Islami. All have a considerable degree of overlap in terms of associated individuals and boast close associations with both the Brotherhood and Jamaat-e Islami, although those relationships are not commonly known. To a lesser extent, organizations and/or activists affiliated with other Islamist movements (such as Hizb-ut Tahrir) also exist on U.S. soil. And radical Islamist groups such as Hamas and Hezbollah are known to have used the United States as a significant financing hub. The joint organizations of the Brotherhood and Jamaat-e Islami, however, are far and away the most influential, and even have attracted American Muslims who do not espouse or adhere to Islamist ideas or beliefs.

While the threat from this "soft" Islamist activity—which is designed to promote Islamist ideas and policies, as well as to alter popular perceptions toward Islamic law and a range of religio-political issues—can be characterized as pervasive, it has largely been ignored by the United States government. Rather, federal authorities remain focused on the threat posed by Islamic terrorist groups, chief among them al-Qaeda. An estimated thirty-two separate terrorist attacks on the U.S. homeland have been successfully thwarted over the past decade, highlighting that the United States remains an active target. The U.S. law enforcement community remains preoccupied with such plots, as well as with the comparatively new phenomenon of "lone wolf" terrorism—terrorism autonomously perpetrated by American Muslims inspired to violence by *jihadist* ideology. The most prominent such incident was the November 2010 massacre at Fort Hood, Texas, in which a Muslim-American serviceman opened fire on soldiers and civilians after being radicalized through his communications with al-Qaeda-affiliated cleric Anwar al-Awlaki.

Canada has historically served as more hospitable soil for Islamist groups and movements. For decades prior to the September 11th attacks, the absence of comprehensive counterterrorism laws and lax oversight on the part of national law enforcement authorities allowed a range of Islamist groups to proliferate. These elements historically have fallen into three broad categories: Salafists (such as al-Qaeda and Algeria's Armed Islamic Group), Shi'ites (Hezbollah) and Palestinians (including Hamas and the Palestinian Islamic Jihad). In recent years, however, a new focus on counterterrorism on the part of the government in Ottawa has made Canada less attractive to terrorist groups and their sympathizers. Nevertheless, a number of Islamist groups—including al-Qaeda and Hezbollah—continue to operate and fundraise within the country. Like in the U.S., Canada is also home to a range of Islamist community organizations, which seek to alter the national debate over Islam, Islamism and Middle Eastern politics. And, as in the United States, these organizations—as well as their linkages with larger Islamist movements active worldwide—remain only sporadically acknowledged and poorly addressed by the government.

CANADA

In the last three decades, Canada has earned the reputation of being a terrorist haven. A succession of terrorist groups flocked to Canada in the decades prior to Canada's post-9/11 enactment of anti-terrorism laws. They flourished amid Canada's immigrant communities—including its nearly 600,000-person Muslim population. Although there are signs that the Canadian Muslim community is better integrated than many of its counterparts in Europe, Islamist groups nevertheless are known to have penetrated the community and established terrorist cells, fundraising operations, communal organizations, mosques, and schools. Comparatively recently, the Canadian government has strengthened its response to these developments through legislation (including Canada's Anti-Terrorism Act and hate crimes laws) that has created new tools to fight terrorism and the ideology responsible for it.

ISLAMIST ACTIVITY

Exploiting the lack of anti-terrorism legislation that existed until 2001, terrorist groups traditionally used Canada's immigrant communities as safe havens and, occasionally, as bases of operations. These groups included, *inter alia*, the Armenian Secret Army for the Liberation of Armenia (ASALA),[1] Sri Lanka's Liberation Tigers of Tamil Eelam (LTTE),[2] and Sikh extremists.[3] More recently, these organizations and groups have been joined by radical Islamic elements of various political and ideological stripes.

Canada's Islamic terrorists fall into three broad camps: (1) Salafist, (2) Shi'ite, and (3) Palestinian. The Salafists belong primarily to al-Qaeda and the Armed Islamic Group (GIA), an Algerian group striving to turn Algeria into a theocratic Islamic state. As the Islamist insurgency in Algeria subsided, the remaining GIA members increasingly collaborated with al-Qaeda in waging a global *jihad*. That collaboration has translated into greater overlap between the personnel of al-Qaeda and the GIA in Canada. The Lebanese Shi'ite militia Hezbollah raises funds, buys equipment, and hides wanted terrorists in Canada. The Islamist Palestinian group Hamas confines itself mainly to raising money on Canadian soil.

Al-Qaeda

Al-Qaeda in Canada has several loci. Perhaps the most prominent is the Khadr family, headed by patriarch Ahmed Said Khadr (1948-2003). A Palestinian whose family moved to Egypt when he was an infant, Ahmed immigrated to Canada in 1975 and studied computer programming at the University of Ottawa.[4] While a student, Ahmed joined his university's chapter of the Muslim Student's Association, which introduced him to political Islam. By the time he graduated, Khadr was advocating the institution of *sharia* in his native Egypt.[5] In the 1980s, Ahmed traveled to Pakistan and Afghanistan for ostensibly humanitarian purposes. He headed the Peshawar office of the Ottawa-based charity Human Concern International (HCI), which is alleged to have provided funds to Osama bin Laden.[6] A 1996 CIA report connected HCI to an outfit smuggling arms to the *mujahideen* in Bosnia, the GIA, and the radical Egyptian group *Al-Gama'a Al-Islamiyya*.[7] While in Peshawar, Ahmed befriended Abdullah Azzam, Osama bin Laden's mentor and the intellectual godfather of al-Qaeda, and Ayman al-Zawahiri, who would later become Osama bin Laden's deputy. In 1994, Khadr sent his two older sons, Abdullah Khadr, 13, and Abdurahman Khadr, 12, to the Khalden training camp in Afghanistan, which was run by the Taliban.[8] Pakistani authorities arrested Khadr pere in connection with the 1995 attack on the Egyptian embassy in Pakistan but released him after the intervention of Canadian Prime Minister Jean Chretien.

Khadr returned to Canada frequently to raise money for al-Qaeda. In response, the UN flagged him pursuant to Security Council Resolution 1267, which created a blacklist of individuals and entities associated with al-Qaeda, Osama bin Laden, and the Taliban. Ahmed died in a 2003 confrontation with the Pakistani military,[9] but his Islamist legacy lives on through his children. Two sons, Omar and Abdul Rahman, fought for the Taliban (Omar killing an American medic) and were sent to Guantanamo. In 2003, the U.S. released Abdul Rahman and he returned to Canada.[10]

Another locus of al-Qaeda activity in Canada is the Montreal Cell, a group of Algerians connected to the GIA. This cell is best known for its involvement in the Millennium Plot, a plan by al-Qaeda to attack targets all over the world between Christmas 1999 and Christmas 2000. Abu Zubaydah, the plan's coordinator and then the third highest-ranking member of al-Qaeda, directed the Montreal Cell to attack the Los Angeles International Airport. The plan was foiled when American authorities arrested Algerian-born bomber Ahmed Ressam in December 1999 with 70 kilograms of explosives in his car.[11] Fateh Kamel headed another al-Qaeda-GIA band. Originally from Algeria, Kamel fought with the *mujahideen* in Afghanistan in the 1980s and then relocated to Montreal.[12] In 1993, he fought with the *mujahideen* in Bosnia under the command of the Algerian Abdelkader Mokhtari. At this time he also established contacts with future members of the violent French *jihadist* Roubaix Gang. In 1996, he joined Osama bin Laden in Khartoum where served as liaison between al-Qaeda and the GIA.[13] He returned to Montreal to raise money and forge documents for al-Qaeda, the GIA, and the Roubaix Gang. He was subsequently arrested in Jordan and extradited to France for his support for the Roubaix Gang. Following his release, he returned to Montreal.[14]

In recent years, al-Qaeda cells in Canada have graduated from planning attacks in Canada to planning attacks against Canada. In 2006, the Royal Canadian Mounted Police (RCMP) arrested eighteen people plotting to bomb the Toronto Stock Exchange, a military base located off Highway 401 between Toronto and Ottawa, and Front Street offices of CSIS, Canada's spy agency.[15] They also intended to storm the Canadian Broadcasting Center and Canadian Parliament, decapitate the Prime Minister, take hostages, and demand that Canada withdraw her troops from Afghanistan.[16] The group set up a camp in Orilla, Ontario, where they trained for their mission and watched taped lectures by radical cleric Anwar al-Awlaki.[17]

Hezbollah

Canada has been an important source of financing and equipment for Hezbollah. In 1998, the RCMP uncovered a car theft ring run by members of the group to raise money for the organization.[18] Mohamed Dbouk managed one of the most lucrative Hezbollah cells. After seeking refugee status in Canada, he raised cash through credit card and banking scams,[19] as well as cigarette smuggling, and used the proceeds to purchase high-tech military supplies and ship them to Lebanon. After Canada indicted Dbouk, he fled to Lebanon.[20] In June 2002, Israeli authorities arrested Fawzi Ayoub, a 39-year-old Lebanese-born Canadian, who used a fake American passport to enter Israel. Israel accused him of being a Hezbollah fighter and of training Palestinian militants in the West Bank in Hezbollah bomb-making techniques.[21] Hezbollah also hides terrorists wanted by other countries in Canada. Hani Abd al-Rahim al-Sayegh, a leader of Saudi Hezbollah involved in the 1996 Khobar Towers bombing that killed nineteen American Air Force personnel, made a refugee claim in Canada using a bogus name and settled in Ottawa, where he was arrested a year later.[22]

Palestinian Islamists

Hamas, the most influential Palestinian Islamist group, has a history of using Canada as a fundraising base, even after the government designated it a terrorist organization in November 2002.[23] A May 2000 Privy Council Office memo to Prime Minister Jean Chretien identified The Jerusalem Fund for Human Services (Jerusalem Fund) as a fundraiser for Hamas.[24] The Canadian Coalition for Democracies alleges that the Jerusalem Fund responded to the flagging by merely changing its name to the International Relief Fund for the Afflicted and Needy (IRFAN) in 2001-2002. The *Canadian Jewish News* discovered that the Jerusalem Fund and IRFAN shared a mailing address in Mississauga, as well as a fax number.[25] Hamas also has raised hundreds of thousands of dollars in Canada through the Texas-headquartered Holy Land Foundation (HLF).[26] The U.S., which designated Hamas a terrorist organization in 1995, shut down HLF in 2008 and, in 2009, sentenced five of its leaders to prison terms ranging from 15 to 65 years.[27]

Additionally, Hamas is known to have recruited Canadians to commit attacks in Canada herself. In 2003, for example, Israel arrested a Canadian in Gaza who pled guilty to conspiracy and illegal military training for planning attacks on Jews in Canada and the U.S.[28] Hamas denied recruiting him, claiming that they limit their attacks to Middle Eastern targets.[29]

The smaller Palestinian Islamic Jihad (PIJ) has also tried to penetrate Canada—albeit on a much more modest scale. The group is known to have long collected and laundered money in Canada, and even attempted to acquire a fraudulent visa so that its treasurer, Muhammed Tasir Hassan Al-Khatib, could visit Canada.[30] Additional details of PIJ activity inside Canada remain spotty, but the country's intelligence service has warned that the group could expand its current, minimal activity in the years ahead; a confidential 2003 CSIS report notes that the discovery of a PIJ fundraising network in Florida "raises the possibility of PIJ elements crossing the border to develop a similar infrastructure in Canada."[31] To date, however, here is no evidence that the PIJ has done so. Like Hamas, PIJ was designated a foreign terrorist organization by the Canadian government in November 2002.[32]

Islamist community organizations

A number of radical Islamic communal organizations are active in Canada as well. The most prominent of these is the Canadian Islamic Congress (CIC), which calls itself "Canada's largest national non-profit and wholly independent Islamic organization."[33] The CIC has a history of demonizing Israel and apologizing for Islamist groups that wage war against it.[34] This incitement foments anti-Semitism and justifies the violence committed by Islamist groups against Israel. The CIC's leadership has further validated terrorism by denouncing the Canadian government's decision to designate Hamas and Hezbollah as terrorist groups, calling it an "unconscionable act of hypocrisy and a mockery of justice."[35]

In December 2001, in response to 9/11, Tarek Fatah founded the Muslim Canadian Congress (MCC) to provide an alternative to the CIC. The MCC opposes political Islam, supporting the "separation of religion and state in all matters of public policy."[36] The MCC has also advocated Canada banning the *burka*,[37] applauded the conviction of terrorists,[38] and condemned Hamas's cynical use of civilians as human shields.[39]

The Islamist Muslim Student's Association (MSA) has chapters at many Canadian universities. Muslim Brotherhood activists founded the MSA in 1963 at the University of Illinois Urbana-Champaign[40] to help Muslims "practice Islam as a complete way of life."[41] Chapters of the MSA have raised funds for the Hamas-linked Holy Land Foundation,[42] as well as the Benevolence International Foundation and the Global Relief Foundation (both of which were later outlawed by the U.S. government for their links to al-Qaeda).[43]

Radicalism can be found in Canadian places of worship as well, with certain mosques and Islamic schools indoctrinating their parishioners and students. The Salaheddin Islamic Center and Al-Rahman Islamic Centre, each in Toronto, are examples of this trend. The Khadr family frequented the former, and six of the terrorists in the cell that planned to storm parliament and decapitate the Prime Minister prayed at the latter.[44] The Salaheddin Islamic Center's imam, Aly Hindy, refused to join 120 other Canadian imams and condemn the London Transit Bombings.[45] He also directs his parishioners not to cooperate with Canadian authorities, and officiates at illegal polygamous weddings.[46] Additionally, a former principal of the Salaheddin Islamic Center's school, Mahmoud Jaballah, was a member of Egyptian Islamic Jihad and involved in the 1998 attacks on the U.S. embassies in Kenya and Tanzania.[47]

The problem, moreover, is not confined to Toronto. A former teacher at the Almadina Language Charter Academy in Calgary reported that, when she joined the faculty, she received a pamphlet outlining the school's ideology. Along with furnishing an overview of Islam, it "took pains to justify Palestinian suicide bombers and called upon Muslims to take up arms against any group that was perceived as a threat to their religious beliefs." She claims that many of her coworkers said that America deserved the September 11th attacks.[48] Such experiences, however, remain the exception rather than the norm in terms of public expression of Muslim attitudes.

ISLAMISM AND SOCIETY

The most recent official census of Canada, which took place in 2001, recorded 579,640 Muslims, equaling 2.0 percent of the total population.[49] At that time, most Canadian Muslims were immigrants, over 60 percent having immigrated in the previous twenty years.[50] A majority of Muslim-Canadians live in the province of Ontario (352,530), and most of those are located in the city of Toronto (254,110). The province of Quebec hosts the second largest Muslim community (108,620), 100,185 of whom live in Montreal, and is home to many immigrants from the former French colonies of Algeria and Lebanon. Sizeable Muslim populations also reside in the provinces of British Columbia (56,215) and Alberta (49,045).

Continued immigration and a high birth rate is rapidly increasing those numbers, making Islam Canada's fastest growing religion. Between 1991 and 2001, for example, Islam registered 128.9 percent growth.[51] Although the breakdown between Sunnis and Shi'ites is unknown, approximately 65,000-75,000 Canadian Muslims are Ismai'ilis.[52] The community is very ethnically diverse: 36.7 percent are South Asian, 21.1 percent are Arab, 14.0 percent are West Asian, and 14.2 percent are part of other minority groups.[53] This population, however, compares negatively with the larger Canadian public on a number of levels. As of 2001, for example, the Muslim community suffered a 14.4 percent unemployment rate, almost double the national rate of 7.4 percent.[54] However, despite the disproportionately high unemployment rate, according to a 2007 Environics poll, 81 percent of Canadian Muslims "felt satisfied with the way things were going in their country," clocking in significantly higher than comparable statistics in Britain, Germany, and France (51 percent, 44 percent, and 33 percent respectively).[55] Unfortunately, the same Environics poll highlighted a troubling propensity for radicalism among respondents, with about 12 percent of Canadian Muslims polled saying that the terrorist plot to storm Parliament and behead the Prime Minister was justified.[56]

Perhaps that often-vocal minority explains why a 2010 Leger Marketing poll found that 55 percent of Canadians disagreed when asked whether "Muslims share our values."[57] A subsequent 2009 Angus Reid Strategies poll uncovered similar opinions, with only 28 percent of Canadians polled viewing Islam favorably, compared with 72 percent approval for Christianity and 53 percent approval for Judaism.[58]

Nevertheless, Islamic law has made at least a limited mark in certain locales and sectors of Canadian society. When first passed, Ontario's Arbitration Act of 1991 permitted people to submit civil disputes to arbitration panels whose decisions, if the parties consented, could deviate from Canadian civil law as long as they did not breach the criminal code.[59] Controversy erupted in 2003 when the Islamic Institute for Civil Justice broadcast its intention to establish panels that would use *sharia*. The fierceness of the debate prompted Ontario's government to ask Marion Boyd, a former attorney general of Ontario, to study the proposal for *sharia*-influenced arbitration panels. Although Boyd concluded that the Arbitration Act should remain in force so long as several new safeguards were added,[60] Ontario's Premier Dalton McGuinty decided to scrap the arbitration panels altogether. In 2006, Ontario's legislature amended the Arbitration Act to require that arbitration be "conducted exclusively in accordance with the law of Ontario or another Canadian jurisdiction."[61]

ISLAMISM AND THE STATE

Canada passed its first anti-terrorism legislation, the Canadian Anti-Terrorism Act (Bill C-36), in the wake of the September 11th terrorist attacks on the United States. Before the Anti-Terrorism Act received the Royal Assent on December 18, 2001, the Canadian criminal code did not even formally define "terrorist activity." The Anti-Terrorism Act rectified this deficiency, providing a definition of both "terrorist activity" and "terrorist group,"[62] and authorizing the Governor in Council, on the recommendation of the Solicitor General, to designate an entity as a terrorist group.[63] The law mandates that:

> "No person in Canada and no Canadian outside Canada shall knowingly
> (a) deal directly or indirectly in any property that is owned or controlled by or on behalf of a terrorist group;
> (b) enter into or facilitate, directly or indirectly, any transaction in respect of property referred to in paragraph (a); or
> (c) provide any financial or other related services in respect of property referred to in paragraph (a) to, for the benefit of or at the direction of a terrorist group."[64]

The Anti-Terrorism Act's prohibition of providing financial services to terrorist groups represented Canada's first measure aimed at curbing terrorist financing. Before that, people could legally raise money for terrorist groups in Canada and the Crown could only prosecute people for directly funding a terrorist attack. However, as a practical matter, because of the opaque nature with which terrorist groups utilize banks and financial markets, it had proved to be almost impossible to connect donors to attacks.[65]

The Anti-Terrorism Act equipped authorities with several new tools to fight terrorism, including investigative hearings, preventive arrests, and new rules concerning information disclosure and rescinding a group's charity status. However, in 2007 the House of Commons voted 159-124, along party lines, against extending the investigative hearing and preventive arrest provisions of the Act (neither of which had ever been used).[66]

Anti-Terrorism Act provisions still in place authorize the Attorney General to issue a certificate prohibiting the disclosure of information that would normally be disclosed under an act of parliament if that information could jeopardize national defense or national security.[67] The Act amended the Proceeds of Crime (Money Laundering) Act to provide authorities with a scheme for monitoring suspicious financial transactions that could be tied to terrorism. The Act also established a mechanism for rescinding organizations' charitable status if there are reasonable grounds to believe that it has or will fund a terrorist group.[68]

A number of hate crimes laws on the books in Canada likewise could potentially be used to confront Islamist incitement. Sections 318 and 319 of the Canadian Criminal Code identify the following as indictable offences: (1) advocating or promoting genocide, (2) communicating statements in any public place or inciting hatred against any identifiable group where such incitement is likely to lead to a breach of the peace, and (3) willfully promoting hatred of any identifiable group outside of private conversation. The code defines "identifiable group" as "any section of the public distinguished by colour, race, religion, ethnic origin or sexual orientation."[69]

Lamentably, Islamists have on occasion abused these laws to squelch debate about Islamism and influence Canadian public discourse. Perhaps the most famous incident occurred in 2007, when the CIC filed complaints against *Maclean's* magazine with the Ontario Human Rights Commission, British Columbia Human Rights Tribunal, and Canadian Human Rights Commission, accusing the magazine of violating Muslims' civil rights by publishing an excerpt from Mark Steyn's book *America Alone*, which discussed the ramifications of larger Muslim populations in Europe and Canada, and for refusing to publish a rebuttal of length equal to that of the excerpt. Although the Ontario Human Rights Commission declined to hear the complaint, stating that it did not have jurisdiction, it subsequently released a statement condemning the original excerpt.[70] The British Columbia Human Rights Tribunal took a sterner stance, dismissing the complaints and concluding that the "complainants have not established that the Article is likely to expose them to hatred or contempt on the basis of their religion."[71] The Canadian Human Rights Commission came to the same conclusion.[72] However, *Maclean's* had to endure a taxing legal process throughout the proceedings—a process that invariably served as a warning to other writers.

ENDNOTES

[1] Andrew Millie and Dilip K. Das, *Contemporary Issues in Law Enforcement and Policing* (Boca Raton: CRC Press, 2008), 88.

[2] Stewart Bell, *Cold Terror: How Canada Nurtures and Exports Terrorism Around the World* (Ontario: Wiley, 2005), 42.

[3] "In Depth: Air India, The Victims," *CBC News*, March 16, 2005, http://www.cbc.ca/news/background/airindia/victims.html.

[4] "Khadr Family," *Global Jihad*, September 15, 2010, http://www.globaljihad.net/view_page.asp?id=902.

[5] Michelle Shephard, *Guantanamo's Child: The Untold Story of Omar Khadr* (Ontario: Wiley, 2008).

[6] Burnett et al. v. al Baraka Investment and Development Corp. et al., United States District Court for the District of Columbia, January 18, 2005, http://fl1.findlaw.com/news.findlaw.com/hdocs/docs/terrorism/burnettba81502cmp.pdf.

[7] U.S. Central Intelligence Agency, *International Islamic NGOs And Links To Terrorism*, 1996.

[8] "Khadr Family," *Global Jihad*.

[9] Ibid.

[10] Anti-Defamation League, "Canada And Terrorism," January 2004, http://www.adl.org/terror/tu/tu_0401_canada.asp.

[11] "Ahmed Ressam," *Global Jihad*, September 15, 2010, http://www.globaljihad.net/view_page.asp?id=281.

[12] Bell, Cold Terror, 140.

[13] "Fateh Kamel," *Global Jihad*, September 15, 2010, http://www.globaljihad.net/view_page.asp?id=294.

[14] Bell, Cold Terror, 140.

[15] "Toronto 18 Bomb Plot Chief' Jailed," *Al-Jazeera* (Doha), September 28, 2010, http://english.aljazeera.net/news/americas/2010/01/201011935438946391.html.

[16] "Another 'Toronto 18' Member Pleads Guilty," *CBC News*, September 28, 2010, http://www.cbc.ca/canada/toronto/story/2010/01/20/toronto-18-plea941.html.

[17] Michelle Shephard, "The Powerful Online Voice Of Jihad," *Toronto Star,* October 18, 2009, http://www.thestar.com/news/world/article/711964--the-powerful-online-voice-of-jihad.

[18] Bell, Cold Terror, 108-9.

[19] Paul Nowell, "Hezbollah In North Carolina?" Associated Press, March 28, 2001.

[20] Tony Locy, "U.S. Looks at Potential Danger from Hezbollah," *USA Today*, May 13, 2003, http://www.usatoday.com/news/nation/2003-05-13-hezbollah-usat_x.htm.

[21] Anti-Defamation League, "Canada and Terrorism."

[22] Bell, *Cold Terror*, 107.

[23] Public Safety Canada, "Currently Listed Entities," October 20, 2010 http://www.publicsafety.gc.ca/prg/ns/le/cle-eng.aspx#Hamas.

[24] Paul Lungen, "Group Claims Hamas Raising Funds In Canada," *Canadian Jewish News* November 22, 2004, http://www.cjnews.com/index.php?option=com_content&task=view&id=5971&Itemid=86.

[25] Bell, *Cold Terror*, 107.

[26] Anti-Defamation League, "Canada And Terrorism," January 2004, http://www.adl.org/terror/tu/tu_0401_canada.asp.

[27] Anti-Defamation League, "Backgrounder: The Holy Land Foundation For Relief And Development," May 28, 2009, http://www.adl.org/main_Terrorism/backgrounder_holyland.htm.

[28] "Canadian Pleads Guilty In Plot To Kill Jews," *CBC News*, November 24, 2004, http://www.cbc.ca/world/story/2004/11/24/akkal-israel041124.html.

[29] Rami Amichai, "Israel Remands Canadian In Alleged Attack Plot," *The Age* (Melbourne), December 16, 2003, http://www.theage.com.au/articles/2003/12/15/1071336890251.html.

[30] Stewart Bell, "The Holy War Comes To Canada," *National Post*, October 23, 2003, http://archive.frontpagemag.com/readArticle.aspx?ARTID=15775.

[31] Ibid.

[32] Public Safety Canada, "Currently Listed Entities."

[33] Canadian Islamic Congress, "Facts About the CIC," September 10, 2010, http://www.canadianislamiccongress.com/cicfacts.php.

[34] Wahida Valiante, "The New Syndrome - F.e.a.r. -- Fear Everything Anxiety Reaction," *Friday Magazine 9*, iss. 60 (2006), http://www.canadianislamiccongress.com/opeds/article.php?id=2840; Canadian Islamic Congress, "Islamic Congress And Arab Federation Call On All Canadians To Condemn Continuing Israeli War Crimes In Gaza," January 21, 2008, http://www.canadianislamiccongress.com/mc/media_communique.php?id=985.

[35] Canadian Islamic Congress, "Islamic Congress Urges Government To Take Hezbollah And Hamas Off Terrorist' List," August 22, 2006, http://www.canadianislamiccongress.com/mc/media_communique.php?id=814.

[36] Muslim Canadian Congress, "MCC Mission," September 29, 2010, http://www.muslimcanadiancongress.org/mission.html.

[37] Muslim Canadian Congress, "Muslim Canadian Congress Wants Canada To Ban The Burka," October 9, 2009, http://www.muslimcanadiancongress.org/20091008.html.

[38] Muslim Canadian Congress, "MCC Welcomes Conviction: Acquittal Would Have Been Huge Victory for Jihadis," September 26, 2008, http://www.muslimcanadiancongress.org/20080926.html.

[39] Muslim Canadian Congress, "MCC Calls For End To Bombing: Condemns Hamas For Inciting Hostilities," December 28, 2008,

http://www.muslimcanadiancongress.org/20081228.html.

[40] The Investigative Project on Terrorism, "Muslim Student's Association," January 1, 2008 http://www.investigativeproject.org/profile/166.

[41] Muslim Student's Association, "Constitution/Bylaws," October 25, 2010, http://www.msanational.org/about/constitution.

[42] Jonathan Dowd-Gailey, "Islamism's Campus Club: The Muslim Students' Association," *Middle East Quarterly* 11, no. 1 (2004), 63-72.

[43] Ibid.

[44] Anthony DePalma, "Six of 17 Arrested In Canada's Antiterror Sweep Have Ties To Mosque Near Toronto," *New York Times*, June 5, 2006.

[45] "Mohammed Adam, Fundamentalist And Proud Of It," *Ottawa Citizen*, August 13, 2005, http://www.truthandgrace.com/clericscarborough.htm.

[46] Noor Javed, "GTA's Secret World of Polygamy," *Toronto Star*, May 24, 2008, http://www.thestar.com/News/GTA/article/429490.

[47] "Case Against Jaballah Upheld in Court," *CanWest News Service*, October 17, 2006, http://www.canada.com/nationalpost/news/story.html?id=09d4191f-c688-41ec-af5f-10b73031c72e&k=46026.

[48] Shafer Parker, "Terror In The Heartland?" *Western Standard*, May 3, 2004, http://www.westernstandard.ca/website/article.php?id=80&start=3.

[49] Statistics Canada, "2001 Census: Selected Religions, For Canada, Provinces And Territories," n.d., http://www12.statcan.ca/english/census01/products/highlight/Religion/Page.cfm?Lang=E&Geo=PR&View=1a&Code=01&Table=1&StartRec=1&Sort=2&B1=Canada&B2=1.

[50] Jennifer Selby, "Islam In Canada," EuroIslam.info, September 21, 2010, http://www.euro-islam.info/country-profiles/canada/.

[51] Statistics Canada, "2001 Census: Selected Religions, For Canada, Provinces And Territories."

[52] Ibid.

[53] Selby, "Islam In Canada."

[54] Statistics Canada, "2001 Census: Selected Cultural And Labour Force Characteristics (58), Selected Religions (35A), Age Groups (5A) And Sex (3) For Population 15 Years And Over, For Canada, Provinces, Territories And Census Metropolitan Areas," n.d., http://www12.statcan.ca/english/census01/products/standard/themes/RetrieveProductTable.cfm?Temporal=2001&PID=67773&APATH=3&GID=517770&METH=1&PTYPE=55496&THEME=56&FOCUS=0&AID=0&PLACENAME=0&PROVINCE=0&SEARCH=0&GC=0&GK=0&VID=0&VNAMEE=&VNAMEF=&FL=0&RL=0&FREE=0.

[55] "Canada's Muslims: An International Comparison," *CBC News*, February 13, 2007, http://www.cbc.ca/news/background/islam/mus-

lim-survey.html.

[56] David B. Harris, "Is Canada Losing The Balance Between Liberty And Security?" in Alexander Moens and Martin Collacott, eds., *Immigration Policy and the Terrorist Threat in Canada and the United States* (Vancouver: Fraser Institute, 2008), 137.

[57] Elizabeth Thompson, "Canadians Don't Believe That Muslims Share Their Values," *National Post*, September 10, 2010, http://www.nationalpost.com/Canadians+believe+Muslims+share+their+values+poll/3508281/story.html.

[58] John Geddes, "What Canadians Think Of Sikhs, Jews, Christians, Muslims," *Maclean's*, April 28, 2009, http://www2.macleans.ca/2009/04/28/what-canadians-think-of-sikhs-jews-christians-muslims/.

[59] Anthony Bradney, *Law and Faith in a Skeptical Age* (New York: Routledge, 2009), 49.

[60] Marion Boyd, "Dispute Resolution In Family Law: Protecting Choice, Promoting Inclusion," December 20, 2004, http://www.attorneygeneral.jus.gov.on.ca/english/about/pubs/boyd/.

[61] *Arbitration* Act, 1991, S.O. 1991, c. 17 (version in force between 22 June 2006 and 29 April 2007), http://www.canlii.org/en/on/laws/stat/so-1991-c-17/1917/so-1991-c-17.html#history.

[62] Ibid., C-36 83.01 (1).

[63] Ibidem, C-36 83.05 (1).

[64] Ibidem, C-36 83.08 (1).

[65] Bell, *Cold Terror*, 97.

[66] "MPs Vote Against Extending Anti-Terrorism Measures," *CBC News*, February 27, 2007, http://www.cbc.ca/canada/story/2007/02/27/terror-vote.html.

[67] Ibid., 14-15.

[68] Ibidem, 19.

[69] "What Is A Hate Crime?" *CBC News*, June 2004, http://www.cbc.ca/news/background/hatecrimes/.

[70] Ontario Human Rights Commission, "Commission Statement Concerning Issues Raised By Complaints Against Maclean's Magazine," April 9, 2008, http://www.ohrc.on.ca/en/resources/news/statement.

[71] British Columbia Human Rights Tribunal, "Elmasry and Habib v. Roger's Publishing and MacQueen (No. 4), 2008 BCHRT 378," October 10, 2008, 37, http://www.bchrt.bc.ca/decisions/2008/pdf/oct/378_Elmasry_and_Habib_v_Rogers_Publishing_and_MacQueen_%28No_4%29_2008_BCHRT_378.pdf.

[72] Canadian Human Rights Commission, "Special Report To Parliament: Freedom Of Expression And Freedom From Hate In The Internet Age," June 2009, 31, http://www.chrc-ccdp.ca/pdf/srp_rsp_eng.pdf.

UNITED STATES

QUICK FACTS

Population: 310,232,863

Area: 9,826,675 sq km

Ethnic Groups: white 79.96%, black 12.85%, Asian 4.43%, Amerindian and
Alaskan native 0.97%, native Hawaiian and other Pacific Islander 0.18%, two or
more races 1.61% (a separate listing for Hispanic is not included because the US
Census Bureau considers Hispanic to mean persons of Spanish/Hispanic/Latino
origin including those of Mexican, Cuban, Puerto Rican, Dominican Republic,
Spanish, and Central or South American origin living in the US who may be of
any race or ethnic group; about 15.1% of the total US population is Hispanic)

Religions: Protestant 51.3%, Roman Catholic 23.9%, Mormon 1.7%, other
Christian 1.6%, Jewish 1.7%, Buddhist 0.7%, Muslim 0.6%, other or unspecified
2.5%, unaffiliated 12.1%, none 4%

Government Type: Constitution-based federal republic; strong democratic
tradition

GDP (official exchange rate): $14.43 trillion

Map and Quick Facts courtesy of the CIA World Factbook (Last Updated June
2010)

---

*The American public appears to remain largely unaware of and/or unin-
terested in Islamist groups in the U.S. unless they can somehow be linked to
al-Qaeda and/or terrorist attacks in the West. The largest terrorism financing
case in American history – which prosecuted individuals and groups linked to
Hamas in 2007-2008 – attracted little media coverage and even less public
interest, despite the fairly explosive information that came out in the course
of the trial about some of the most influential American Islamic civil society
groups. Several Islamist organizations have successfully framed themselves as
"moderate," "mainstream," and representative American Muslim religious
and civil rights organizations – a rebranding that has allowed them to avoid*

---

widespread public distrust and condemn criticism as "Islamophobia."

The U.S. government is, on the whole, only slightly more interested than the general public in the Islamist groups active within its borders. Due to official apathy and ignorance, civil society groups linked to the Muslim Brotherhood dominate governmental "outreach" to the American Muslim community. While recent events have jeopardized government relations with some groups, others remain active partners of various departments and agencies. U.S. law enforcement agencies, however, still aggressively target homegrown jihadist plots as well as some civil society groups that fund and support proscribed groups such as Hamas and Hezbollah.

ISLAMIST ACTIVITY

Contemporary Islamist activity in the United States can be understood in the context of five loose conceptual groupings:

The Ikhwan-Jama'at duopoly[1]

The Ikhwan-Jama'at duopoly is the largest and most influential grouping of organized Islamist activism in the United States. In the 1950s and 1960s, Muslim Brotherhood activists fled repression in Egypt to find a home and largesse in Saudi Arabia. Wahhabi[2] authorities took advantage of their organizational experience, placing them in key positions at major Islamic quasi-NGOs. With Saudi backing, these Brotherhood activists, joined by Jama'at-e Islami[3] cadres, propagated Islamist thought and institutions all over the world, including the United States and the larger West.[4]

The structure of the U.S.-based Ikhwan-Jama'at duopoly can be understood on three levels – *a covert vanguard, professional activist organizations* with formalized membership schemes, and the related grassroots they seek to mobilize. The vanguard consists of Brotherhood and Jama'at leaders in North America who hold key leadership positions in a series of activist organizations. These activist organizations are the most prominent Islamic groups in American civil society. They are influential in local, state, and national politics and have established relationships with editorial boards and news producers at media outlets throughout the country. The fact that they are linked to the Brotherhood and Jama'at-Islami is not commonly known, even though this information is readily available. This can perhaps be attributed to pervasive political correctness about matters concerning religion and ethnicity as well as a related lack of interest from mainstream and credible media outlets.

Internal U.S. Brotherhood records released as evidence in the terrorism financing trial of the Holy Land Foundation for Relief and Development (HLF) reveal that a covert vanguard of Muslim Brotherhood activists founded and directed the most influential Muslim-American civil society groups in the United States, including the Muslim Students' Association (MSA) the Islamic Society of North America (ISNA), the North American Islamic Trust (NAIT), the International Institute of Islamic Thought (IIIT), the Council on American-Islamic Relations (CAIR) and the Muslim American Society (MAS).[5] The Islamic Circle of North America (ICNA) similarly is a "front" for Jama'at-i-Islami.[6] The public faces of these groups are professionally-led activist organizations concerned with civil rights, religious education, political awareness, grass-roots organization, and other seemingly benign activities.[7] However, internal Brotherhood documents reveal another side to these organizations.

The strategy of the Muslim Brotherhood in the West is carried out largely through front groups coordinated by the covert Brotherhood vanguard. In an effort to establish Islamic governance, the Brotherhood seeks to manipulate and subvert local power structures by positioning themselves as the gatekeepers to the Muslim community, infiltrating civil society and state structures, and creating parallel ones. In practice, this involves establishing close contacts with editorial boards of newspapers; news producers; prominent journalists; government, law enforcement, defense, and intelligence officials; prominent academics; civil society groups, such as the American Civil Liberties Union; and others.

An internal document of the Muslim Brotherhood network in the U.S. states that "the main goal of Islamic activism" is: "establishing the nation of Islam, the rule of God in the lives of humans, making people worship their Creator and cleansing the earth from the tyrants who assault God's sovereignty, the abominators in His earth and the suppressors of His creation."[8] Brotherhood officials have done so by promoting the creation of civic organizations with a covert – and occasionally an overt – political agenda, an activity described by one Brotherhood official in the 1980s as "energizing political work fronts."[9] Such groups include:

The Muslim Student Association (MSA). Founded in 1963 by Brotherhood activists at the University of Illinois Urbana-Champaign, the MSA served as a coordinating committee for Brotherhood activities during the organization's formative years in the United States. During this early era, all Brotherhood activists in the U.S. had to be active in the MSA.[10] Now a national organization, the MSA has about 150 affiliated university chapters in the United States and Canada. In the U.S., the MSA is divided into East Zone, Central Zone, and West Zone. It is a 501(c)4 tax exempt organization, and claims to refuse foreign funding.[11]

Like all member organizations of the Ikhwan-Jama'at duopoly, the MSA proclaims "moderation," but public statements by MSA activists reveal an Islamist agenda and ideology. For instance, MSA officials have espoused the desire "to restore Islam to the leadership of society" and to be working toward "the reestablishment of the Islamic form of government."[12] They have likewise emphasized the importance of *dawah* (propagation of faith) as a vehicle for the spread of Islam in the United States, with the ultimate goal of making America "a Muslim country."[13]

The North American Islamic Trust (NAIT). NAIT was founded in 1973 as a *waqf* (trust) for the MSA and other Islamic institutions, including the Islamic Society of North America (ISNA).[14] NAIT is a non-profit 501(c)3 and holds the titles to hundreds of Islamic institutions – including mosques and schools – across the U.S., making it – according to some analysts – a holding company and financial hub for various Muslim Brotherhood-tied groups in North America.[15] It also manages the Iman Fund, a no-load mutual fund, and runs American Trust Publications (which publishes Islamic literature, including the works of Brotherhood luminary Yusuf al Qaradawi[16]) and the Islamic Book Service.[17] A 1987 FBI investigation of NAIT concluded that the organization supported the "Islamic Revolution." "Their support of JIHAD (a holy war) in the U.S. has been evidenced by the financial and organizational support provided through NAIT from Middle East countries to Muslims residing in the U.S. and Canada," it continued. The countries named as providing this support were Iran, Libya, Kuwait, and Saudi Arabia. "The organizational support provided by NAIT includes planning, organizing, and funding anti-U.S. and anti-Israel demonstrations, pro-PLO demonstrations and the distribution of political propaganda against U.S. policies in the Middle East and in support of the Islamic Revolution as advocated by the [Government of Iran]. NAIT also supports the recruitment, training and funding of black Muslims in the U.S. who support the Islamic Revolution."[18]

The Islamic Society of North America (ISNA). ISNA, which emerged out of the MSA in 1981, was named as an unindicted co-conspirator in the Hamas financing trial against the Holy Land Foundation.[19] Like NAIT, ISNA is included among the "individuals/entities who are and/or were members of the US Muslim Brotherhood."[20]

There is no evidence that ISNA currently provides material support to terrorist organizations. However, to this day, key U.S. Brotherhood activists hold leadership positions in ISNA. ISNA's twenty-two member board of directors includes the chairman of NAIT, the president of the MSA, and the heads of ISNA's other "constituent organizations:" the Association of Muslim Scientists and Engineers, the Islamic Medical Association of North America, the Association of Muslim Social Scientists (AMSS), the Canadian Islamic Trust, Muslim Youth of North America, the Council of Islamic Schools of North America, and the Islamic Media Foundation – some of which are explicitly named as Brotherhood-allied groups in internal Brotherhood documents.[21]

The Islamic Circle of North America (ICNA). ICNA is the successor to the Pakistani-American organization Halaqa Ahbabe Islami, which sought to recruit "Islamic movement oriented Urdu speaking Muslims and to strengthen the Jama'at-e-Islami Pakistan."[22] In 1977, Halaqa Ahbabe Islami formally changed its name to ICNA.[23] Today, ICNA holds conferences throughout the U.S. and states that its goal is "to seek the pleasure of Allah… through the struggle of Iqamat-ud-Deen (establishment of the Islamic system of life) as spelled out in the Qur'an and the Sunnah of Prophet Muhammad…"[24]

ICNA has three separate wings: the ICNA Sisters Wing, Young Muslims Sisters and Young Muslims Brothers.[25] It also runs the New York-based Islamic Learning Foundation, which is aimed at "enriching the lives of Muslims in general and Muslim Youth in particular by educating their minds and affecting their hearts with sound knowledge of Islamic Shariah."[26] Notably, these steps are in keeping with the strategy of Abdul A'la Maududi, the founder of Jama'at-e-Islami. In his book *The Process of Islamic Revolution*, Maududi calls for indoctrinated Islamic cadres as a foundation for revolution. To Maududi, the Islamic state begins with good Muslims, who would in turn create a "system of education to train and mould the masses in the Islamic pattern of life."[27]

The Council on American-Islamic Relations (CAIR). The idea for CAIR emerged out of a 1993 meeting in Philadelphia of the Muslim Brotherhood's Palestine Committee in the United States. Participants spoke of the need for a lobbying and public affairs group to promote the Islamist point of view in the U.S. The short-term goal was to serve as a spoiler for the Oslo Accords, but the long-term goal was to manipulate the public discourse in America on issues related to Islam and the Muslim world.[28] Three IAP officials founded CAIR several months later. CAIR portrays itself as a civil rights group, and has since become the most influential and pervasive Muslim civil society group in the United States.[29] They have been heavily involved in "sensitivity training" and other briefings on Islam and the Muslim community for U.S. law enforcement officers. However, in the last two years, CAIR has been increasingly challenged, largely as a result of the HLF case, in which it was named an unindicted co-conspirator.[30] CAIR is currently led by a five-person board.[31]

The Muslim American Society (MAS). The Northern Virginia-based MAS was founded in 1993. Among its founding members was Ahmed Elkadi, who supposedly led the Brotherhood in the U.S. from 1984 to 1994.[32] Mohammad Mehdi Akef, the Supreme Guide of the global Muslim Brotherhood in Egypt from 2004 to 2010, claims to have played a role in founding MAS in a push for more "openness" in the Brotherhood's activities in the U.S.[33] MAS is open about its lineage in the U.S., lauding older Brotherhood-affiliated groups such as MSA, ISNA, and NAIT.[34]

MAS claims to promote understanding between Muslims and non-Muslims, "encourage the participation of Muslims in building a virtuous and moral society," "offer a viable Islamic alternative to many of our society's prevailing problems," and "foster unity among Muslims and Muslim organizations."[35] The MAS Freedom Foundation is perhaps the most active and public part of the organization. It engages in and coordinates grassroots activism, including voter registration, civil rights work, lobbying Congress, and protesting.[36] Other departments include the Council of Imams (coordinated with ICNA), the National Council of Islamic Centers (also coordinated with ICNA), the Tarbiyya (religious educational) program, the *dawah* (propagation) program, Islamic American University, and the Muslim Youth Program.[37] Yusuf al-Qaradawi, often referred to as the Muslim Brotherhood's spiritual leader, is on the Islamic American University's Board of Trustees.[38]

The International Institute of Islamic Thought (IIIT). Conceived at a 1977 Islamic conference in Lugano, Switzerland, IIIT was founded four years later in Pennsylvania as "a private, non-profit, academic and cultural institution dedicated to promoting research, publications and conferences related to Islamic thought and contemporary social sciences."[39] It is now based in Herndon, Virginia. IIIT ostensibly "promotes academic research on the methodology and philosophy of various disciplines, and gives special emphasis to the development of Islamic scholarship in contemporary social sciences."[40] However, IIIT has been accused by the U.S. government of contributing funds to the World and Islam Studies Enterprise (WISE), which was founded to support the Palestinian Islamic Jihad.[41] IIIT is a part of a network of companies and not-for-profit organizations based in Northern Virginia known as the SAAR Network or the Safa Group, which has been under investigation by the U.S. Justice Department since at least 2003.[42] In May 2009, Ishaq Farhan, a trustee of IIIT, was chosen to head the Islamic Action Front – the Jordanian Muslim Brotherhood political party – a post he had held before.[43] Farhan had long been associated with the IAF and is said to be one of the key figures behind its formation.[44]

Jamaat al Fuqra

Jama'at al Fuqra (JF, Arabic for "Community of the Impoverished") was founded in New York in 1980 by the Pakistani religious leader, Sheikh Mubarak Ali Gilani.[45] JF has been described as a splinter group of Jaish-e-Mohammad (JeM).[46] Daniel Pearl, the late *Wall Street Journal* reporter, was on his way to interview Gilani in 2002 when he was kidnapped in Pakistan and subsequently beheaded.

In the U.S., JF is a loosely structured movement primarily composed of African-American converts to Islam. JF functions officially through Muslims of the Americas, a non-profit organization, and the International Quranic Open University.[47] JF also operates a news publication called *The Islamic Post*. JF runs a network of rural compounds in New York, Maryland, Pennsylvania, Arizona, Oregon, South Carolina, California and Colorado. Members of the group were involved in a wave of violent crime and fraud – including murder and arson – in the 1980s and 1990s.[48] Some members have also been known to attack Hindu places of worship.[49] Over the past decade, the group has been fairly quiet in the U.S. It received some attention in 2008 and 2009 as a result of a documentary on the group produced by the controversial Christian Action Network entitled *Homegrown Jihad*.[50]

Hizb ut-Tahrir

Hizb ut-Tahrir in America (HTA) has been led by Middle Eastern activists who moved the U.S. in the 1980s. For most of its history, it has met with little success in expanding its native activist base. This has been attributed to competition from other Islamist groups (mainly the Brotherhood); the limited ability of an older leadership to connect with the younger generation; and a level of paranoia and secrecy among the leadership that have limited outreach efforts, hindered online interaction, and may have turned off potential recruits – particularly in the pre-9/11 era.[51]

The HTA website states that the organization's aim is "to resume the Islamic way of life and to convey the Islamic *da'wah* to the world."[52] HTA is currently well-networked and connected with the larger global presence of HuT. Their three-stage methodology for taking power is the same as that promoted by the global movement:

> The First Stage: The stage of culturing to produce people who believe in the idea and the method of the Party, so that they form the Party group.
> The Second Stage: The stage of interaction with the Ummah (global Muslim community), to let the Ummah embrace and carry Islam, so that the Ummah takes it up as its issue, and thus works to establish it in the affairs of life.
> The Third Stage: The stage of establishing government, implementing Islam generally and comprehensively, and carrying it as a message to the world.[53]

In the West, HuT seeks to foster a mass movement toward revolution, while in Muslim-majority countries it attempts to recruit members of the military for the purpose of carrying out a military coup.[54] According to one specialist, HTA "counts well-educated professionals who are influential in their communities among their members" and in recent years the group has expanded beyond their main hubs of activity in New York, Orange County (California), Chicago, and Milwaukee.[55]

The jihadist-activist milieu

There are a number of small U.S.-based formal and informal groups and networks that support violent jihad in America and elsewhere, but do not necessarily engage in it themselves. Most of their activities are political and social in nature, consisting of provocative public statements and demonstrations. Two particularly prominent groups deserve mention in this regard.

Al Muhajiroun is a Britain-based Islamist movement founded in 1996 by former HuT activist Omar Bakri Mohammad. The Islamic Thinkers Society, or ITS, is the New York-based U.S. branch of al Muhajiroun. The organization's objective is "to resume the Islamic way of life which will fulfil the purpose of the aim... to bring back the apparatus that was destroyed in 1924, i.e. Khilafah."[56] Like HuT, al-Muhajuroun is opposed to democracy, free-market capitalism, and secular governance. However, al-Muhajiroun's ideology differs from HuT's on a few crucial issues. The latter limits its efforts to establish the Caliphate to select countries where it believes it will be more successful. Al-Muhajiroun, by contrast, insists that Muslims everywhere should strive to establish the Caliphate wherever they live. Al-Muhajiroun also prescribes a more aggressive public approach through demonstrations, marches, and public outreach, while HuT is more insular.[57]

ITS's activities primarily consist of aggressive pamphleteering and provocative demonstrations in which they call for the implementation of Islamic law globally – including in the United States – and condemn those they view as enemies of Islam. They also condemn Islamic scholars who do not conform to their interpretation of Islam.[58] According to a report by New York Police Department, ITS is largely made up of 2nd and 3rd generation young Muslim-Americans of South Asian and Middle Eastern background. The report describes ITS and likeminded groups as "indoctrination accelerants due to their ability to act as both incubators and proliferators of radicalization."[59] ITS' methodology largely promotes non-violent means for change, such as conferences, lectures, demonstrations, marches, rallies, and strikes; however, it also calls for "the physical action of the Muslims in the army who had pledged their support beforehand... and the authority to Muslims to appoint a leader... to implement the whole of Islam immediately, comprehensively, and exclusively."[60]

Revolution Muslim is another New York-based jihadist-activist group. Founded in 2007 "to invite people to proper Islam... and command the good... while forbidding the falsehood," RM's mission "is to one day see the Muslims united under one Khalifah and under the commands of Allah."[61] RM sometimes cooperates with ITS.

RM maintains an active blog and website, which serves as a forum for a dissemination of its views, proselytization, condemnation of U.S. policies, and even support for violence. For example, RM has expressed admiration for Major Nidal Malik Hasan, who was responsible for the shooting at Fort Hood (see below), and called his victims "slain terrorists."[62] According to the Anti-Defamation League, RM's non-virtual activities primarily consist of pamphleteering and demonstrating outside mosques on Fridays.[63]

Homegrown jihadist cells and networks
There were a number of Islamist terrorist plots in the U.S. that were thwarted or uncovered in 2009, many of which were planned by cells of Muslims who were either born in the U.S. or lived there for many years. There were also episodes of Americans planning attacks against U.S. interests abroad and/or going to fight with foreign Islamist movements. These included:

- Five American citizens of Middle Eastern and African origin who travelled from their homes in Virginia to Pakistan. They reportedly were trying to get to North Waziristan in order to train with al-Qaeda and the Taliban and then fight American troops in Afghanistan. The 'Sargodha five' were arrested in Pakistan.[64]
- Daniel P. Boyd, an American convert to Islam, has been accused of heading a seven-man North Carolina-based cell that allegedly planned to provide material support to al-Qaeda, murder, kidnap, maim and injure persons in Israel and elsewhere, and kill U.S. military personnel stationed at Quantico, Virginia.[65]
- In May 2009, James Cromitie, David Williams, Onta Williams, and Laguerre Payen were arrested in New York and charged with conspiring to bomb synagogues in the Bronx and shoot down military aircraft at the New York Air National Guard Base at Stewart Airport in Newburgh, New York with a surface-to-air missile.[66]
- Tarek Mehanna and Ahmad Abousamra of Massachusetts were arrested and charged with conspiring to provide material support to al-Qaeda.[67] The two are accused of aspiring to launch attacks in the U.S., including on a local shopping mall.[68] According to the superseding indictment, Mehanna and Abousamra went to Yemen to receive militant training in order to fight U.S. troops in Iraq. As of 2006, Mehanna allegedly saw himself as part of the "media wing" of al-Qaeda in Iraq.[69]
- David Coleman Headley (AKA Daood Gilani) of Chicago has been charged with providing crucial assistance for the 2008 Laskhar-e-Taiba (LeT) attack in Mumbai, India. Headley allegedly attended LeT training camps in 2002 and 2003. Beginning in 2006, Headley allegedly carried out extensive surveillance of possible targets in Mumbai on behalf of LeT. He is charged with aiding and abetting the murders of six U.S. citizens who were killed in the Mumbai attack. Headley is also accused of conspiring with LeT members and Ilyas Kashmiri, the head of the Kashmiri militant group Harakat ul Jihad al Islami (HUJI), to carry out attacks in Denmark against *Jyllands Posten*, the newspaper that published the Mohammad cartoons that led to the 2006 Danish Cartoons Crisis.

- Headley allegedly carried out surveillance in Denmark for that planned attack.[70]
- Najibullah Zazi, who drove an airport shuttle bus in Denver, and, before that, lived in Queens, has been accused of conspiring to use explosives in an attack thought to have been planned for New York City. Zazi was born in Afghanistan and raised in Pakistan. Zazi is thought to have travelled to the Federally Administered Tribal Areas in Pakistan where he received training from al-Qaeda.[71]
- Bryant Neal Vinas, an American convert to Islam, who has been charged with participating in and supporting terrorist attacks against U.S. persons and facilities in Afghanistan in 2008. He is accused of firing rockets at a U.S. military base in Afghanistan and providing "expert advice and assistance" to al-Qaeda about the New York transit system and Long Island Railroad.[72]
- Hosam Maher Husein Smadi, a Jordanian national, is charged with planning to blow up the Fountain Place office complex in downtown Dallas with a vehicle bomb. He also reportedly considered attacking a National Guard Armory and the Dallas Airport.[73]
- Michael Finton (AKA Talib Islam), an American who converted to Islam while in prison, has been charged with planning to detonate a van filled with explosives outside the Federal Building in Springfield, Illinois. He also reportedly considered going to fight in Afghanistan, Somalia, and Pakistan, but had reservations about al-Qaeda's targeting of civilians.[74]
- On Christmas day, a young Nigerian man tied to al-Qaeda on the Arabian Peninsula tried and failed to set off an explosive device on a transatlantic airline flight as it was landing in Detroit.[75]

There was also a "lone wolf" Islamist terrorist attack launched at Fort Hood, Texas on November 5th by Major Nidal Malik Hasan, a U.S. Army psychiatrist, who had been in regular contact with Anwar al-Awlaki, an American-born imam of Yemeni descent currently residing in Yemen. Hasan opened fire on base, killing thirteen people and wounding 31 others. Hasan was shot multiple times, but survived.[76]

ISLAMISM AND SOCIETY

The U.S. has the most diverse Muslim population in the Western world – indeed, maybe in the entire world. Half of America's estimated 2 to 3 million Muslims identify themselves as Sunnis, 16 percent as Shi'a, and 22 percent say they are just Muslim without affiliation. Twenty-three percent are converts.[77] A large proportion of Muslims in the U.S. are immigrants (65 percent), and slightly over a third are native-born, with one-fifth of them second generation.[78] A third of Muslim immigrants to the United States come from the Arab world (Middle East and North Africa), 27 percent from South Asia (including Afghanistan), 12 percent come from Iran, eight percent come from Europe, and six percent come from Africa (not including North Africa). Almost two-thirds of all Muslim immigrants have come to the U.S. since 1990 and 28 percent have come since 2000. Three-quarters of all Muslim-Americans are U.S. citizens.[79] At 35 percent, African-Americans make up the largest proportion of Muslims in America.[80] Muslims in America, as a group, are younger than other major religious groups in the U.S.[81]

The extent to which Muslim-Americans support U.S. Islamist organizations and movements is unclear and contentious. It does seem evident that support for al-Qaeda remains low, but significant enough. While only one percent of Muslim Americans expressed a very favorable view of al-Qaeda and four percent expressed a favorable view, that still means 25,000 and 100,000 people respectively (assuming a Muslim-American population of 2.5 million). As far as support for other Islamist groups is concerned, no reliable polling or studies have been carried out. While information on the membership levels of some groups – particularly CAIR – has made it into the public domain, some of it must be viewed with scepticism given the nature of the sources. Claims of foreign funding for Ikwhan-Jama'at groups are pervasive. While there are some examples of such funding available in the public domain, there has not been a comprehensive investigation or account of this issue that has been made public.

Nor are civil society, media institutions, and the public at large generally informed about Islamist groups in the U.S. and Islamism generally, beyond the occasional terrorist plots that are routinely disrupted every year. 2009 was no different in terms of limited public and media interest in the subject, although the attempted Christmas Day bombing of a Delta-Northwest airliner as it landed in Detroit reinvigorated public interest in terrorism against the U.S. homeland and kicked off renewed debate about intelligence coordination and airline security.

The fact that the most influential and well-resourced Muslim-American civil society groups are, in a very concrete sense, affiliated with the Muslim Brotherhood and Jama'at-e-Islami is not widely held knowledge. While "anti-Islamist" groups do exist – mostly on the right side of the American political spectrum – their efforts to call attention to U.S. networks tied to the Muslim Brotherhood and Jama'at-e-Islami have not gained much traction, and are often dismissed, particularly on the left, as "Islamophobic" in nature. This is partially because Islamist organizations have successfully framed themselves as "moderate," "mainstream," and representative American Muslim religious and civil rights organizations. This has allowed them to avoid widespread public distrust and frame criticism of them as "Islamophobia" targeting the Muslim-American community rather than criticism of the organizations themselves.

However, 2009 brought with it a significant victory for anti-Islamist groups. As a result of the revelations of the Hamas-financing trials against the Holy Land Foundation and the ensuing pressures from the aforementioned anti-Islamist groups and some members of the House and Senate, the FBI has ceased cooperation with CAIR.[82] Despite this step forward, it seems that ISNA is among those groups that have seen their influence increase as they step into the vacuum left by CAIR and assume a larger role in advising and training U.S. government and military officials.[83]

ISLAMISM AND THE STATE

The relationship between the state and Islamist groups can only be described as schizophrenic. There does not seem to be any detailed U.S. government policy on choosing appropriate partners in the Muslim community. As a result, we have seen parts of the U.S. government working with Islamist groups for community outreach and security service recruitment while other parts of the government – often in the same executive department – have investigated and prosecuted *the same groups* for a wide variety of suspected criminal activity, including financial crimes and material support of pro-scribed terrorist organizations.

In December 2009, Daniel Benjamin, the State Department's Coordinator for Counterterrorism, announced a planned policy called Countering Violent Extremism (CVE) that seems, at least at this nascent stage, to share some similarities with Britain's Preventing Violent Extremism strategy. This policy was not articulated in any detailed way prior to the end of 2009, but Benjamin explained that CVE would "focus on local communities most prone to radicalization," "address underlying conditions for at-risk populations," and "improve the ability of moderates to voice their views and strengthen opposition to violence." Benjamin likewise explained that "a tailored-approach to CVE requires identifying which of these problems are driving radicalization and are amenable to change with the help of local governments and leaders who understand the problems best."[84] It should be noted, however, that in Britain, the implementation of such an approach has empowered local authorities and funded various Muslim community organizations – including many Islamist and Salafist organizations – to engage with Muslim youth.

ENDNOTES

[1] This term was coined in Kalim Siddiqui, *Stages of Islamic Revolution* (London: The Open Press, 1996). It refers to groups tied to the Muslim Brotherhood (Al-Ikhwan al-Muslimeen) and the Pakistani Islamist party, Jama'at al-Islami.

[2] Wahhabi here is understood as the Saudi brand of Salafism, which is a movement within Islam that seeks to practice Islam in the fashion of the pious ancestors – namely the Prophet Muhammad and his Companions. Wahhabism derives from Muhammad ibn abd al Wahhab, who introduced a form of Salafism to the Arabian peninsula in alliance with the House of Saud in the early 20th Century.

[3] Jama'at-e Islami is a Pakistani Islamist party founded in 1941 by Syed Abul A'ala Maududi, who was perhaps the most influential Islamist thinker of the 20th Century.

[4] Giles Kepel, *The War for Muslim Minds: Islam and the West* (Cambridge, MA: Belknap Press, 2006); Lorenzo Vidino, *The New Western Brothers* (New York: Columbia University Press, forthcoming 2010); Lorenzo Vidino, "Aims and Methods of Europe's Muslim Brotherhood," *Current Trends in Islamist Ideology* 4 (2006); Allison Pargeter, *The New Frontiers of Jihad: Radical Islam in Europe* (Philadelphia: University of Pennsylvania Press, 2008), 20.

[5] "Elbarasse Search 1," *U.S. v. Holy Land Foundation et al*, 3:04-CR-240-G (Northern District TX, 2008), http://www.txnd.uscourts.gov/judges/hlf2/09-25-08/Elbarasse%20Search%201.pdf; "Elbarasse Search 3," *U.S. v. Holy Land Foundation et al*, http://www.txnd.uscourts.gov/judges/hlf2/09-25-08/Elbarasse%20Search%203.pdf; "Elbarasse Search 19," *U.S. v. Holy Land Foundation et al*, http://www.txnd.uscourts.gov/judges/hlf2/09-29-08/Elbarasse%20Search%2019.pdf; "Elbarasse Search 2," *U.S. v. Holy Land Foundation et al*, http://www.txnd.uscourts.gov/judges/hlf2/09-25-08/Elbarasse%20Search%202.pdf; Esam Omeish, Letter to the Washington Post, September 16, 2004, http://www.masnet.org/pressroom_release.asp?id=1664; Noreen S. Ahmed-Ullah et al, "A Rare Look at the Secretive Brotherhood in America," *Chicago Tribune*, September 19, 2004, http://www.chicagotribune.com/news/watchdog/chi-0409190261sep19,0,3008717.story.

[6] Stephen P. Cohen, *The Idea of Pakistan* (Washington, DC: Brookings Institution, 2004), 348 n. 7; Vali Reza Nasr, *The Vanguard of the Islamic Revolution: The Jama'at-I Islami of Pakistan* (Berkeley: University of California Press, 1994).

[7] See, for example: Esam Omeish, "MAS President Letter to the Washington Post," Muslim American Society Website, September 16, 2004, http://www.masnet.org/pressroom_release.asp?id=1664

[8] "Exhibit 0003918-0003919," (Letter from "The Political Office" re:

the founding of the Islamic Association for Palestine by "the Group"), US v. HLF, 5.

[9] Zeid al-Noman, as quoted in "Elbarasse Search 2," *U.S. v. Holy Land Foundation et al.*

[10] "Elbarasse Search 2," *U.S. v. Holy Land Foundation et al.*

[11] "Frequently Asked Questions About the MSA of the US & Canada," MSA National Website, n.d., http://www.msanational.org/about/faq/.

[12] Ahmed Shama, Speech before the 7th Annual MSA West Conference, University of Southern California, January 2005.

[13] Shah Imam, Speech before the MSA 2006 East Zone Conference, University of Maryland, March 2006.

[14] North American Islamic Trust Website, http://www.nait.net/.

[15] "The North American Islamic Trust – NAIT," North American Islamic Trust Website, n.d., http://www.nait.net/NAIT_about_%20us.htm; See also John Mintz and Douglas Farah, "In Search of Friends Among the Foes," *Washington Post*, September 11, 2004, http://www.washingtonpost.com/ac2/wp-dyn/A12823-2004Sep10?language=printer; Zeyno Baran, "The Muslim Brotherhood's U.S. Network," *Current Trends in Islamist Ideology* 6 (2008); Steven Merley, "The Muslim Brotherhood in the United States," Hudson Institute *Research Monographs on the Muslim World* Series no. 2, Paper no. 3, April 2009.

[16] Qaradawi is often described as the spiritual leader of the Muslim Brotherhood. He is based in Doha, Qatar and hosts the popular Al-Jazeera television show Sharia and Life. For more, see Husam Tammam, "Yusuf al-Qaradawi and the Muslim Brothers: The Nature of a Special Relationship," in Jakob Skovgaard-Petersen and Bettina Graf, eds., *Global Mufti: The Phenomenon of Yusuf al-Qaradawi* (London: Hurst & Co, 2009), 55-84.

[17] Ibid.

[18] Federal Bureau of Investigation, Indianapolis, Indiana, "North American Islamic Trust (NAIT)," December 15, 1987, http://www.investigativeproject.org/documents/misc/148.pdf.

[19] " List of Unindicted Co-Conspirators and Joint Venturers," *U.S. v. Holy Land Foundation et al*, http://www.investigativeproject.org/documents/case_docs/423.pdf.

[20] Ibid.

[21] "ISNA Board of Directors (Majlis Ash-Shura)," ISNA Website, n.d., http://www.isna.net/ISNAHQ/pages/Board-of-Directors.aspx; "Elbarasse Search 3," *U.S. v. Holy Land Foundation et al*

[22] Zaheer Uddin, "ICNA: A Successful Journey and a Promising Road Ahead." *The Message International* 23, no. 8 (1999), 24.

[23] Ibid.

[24] "About ICNA", ICNA Website, n.d., http://www.icna.org/about-

icna/.
[25] "Divisions," ICNA Website, n.d., http://www.icna.org/divisions/.
[26] "Education," ICNA Website, n.d., http://www.icna.org/education/.
[27] Sayyid Abdul A'la Mawdudi, *Process of Islamic Revolution* (New Delhi: Markazi Maktaba Islami, 1998), 3.
[28] See, for example, "Government's Trial Brief," *U.S. v. Holy Land Foundation et al*; Excerpts of the FBI transcripts of this meeting are available at http://www.investigativeproject.org/documents/case_docs/836.pdf and http://www.investigativeproject.org/documents/case_docs/720.pdf.
[29] "Our Vision, Mission, and Core Principles," CAIR Website, n.d., http://www.cair.com/AboutUs/VisionMissionCorePrinciples.aspx.
[30] "List of Unindicted Co-Conspirators and/or Joint Venturers," *U.S. v. Holy Land Foundation et al.*
[31] "About Us," CAIR Website, n.d., http://www.cair.com/AboutUs/CAIRNationalBoardandStaff.aspx
[32] Ahmed-Ullah, Roe and Cohen, "A rare look at secretive Brotherhood in America."
[33] Ibid.
[34] "About MAS," MAS Website, n.d., http://www.masnet.org/aboutmas.asp.
[35] Ibid.
[36] "Freedom Foundation," MAS Website, n.d., http://www.masnet.org/index_publicaffairs.asp.
[37] "Departments," MAS Website, n.d., http://www.masnet.org/index_depts.asp.
[38] "Departments – University," MAS Website, n.d., http://www.masnet.org/university.asp.; On Qaradawi's relationship with the Muslim Brotherhood, see: Husam Tammam, "Yusuf al-Qaradawi and the Muslim Brothers: The Nature of a Special Relationship," in Jakob Skovgaard-Petersen and Bettina Graf (eds.), *Global Mufti: The Phenomenon of Yusuf al-Qaradawi* (London: Hurst & Co, 2009), pp. 55-84.
[39] "About IIIT," IIIT Website, n.d., http://www.iiit.org/AboutUs/AboutIIIT/tabid/66/Default.aspx.
[40] Ibid.
[41] "Affidavit of SA David Kane," *In the Matter Involving 555 Grove Street, Herndon, Virginia, and Related Locations, 02-MG-114* (ED VA, March 2002), 49–50. (Hereinafter Kane Affidavit).
[42] Kane Affidavit.
[43] John Mintz and Douglas Farah, "In Search Of Friends Among The Foes," *Washington Post*, September 11, 2004; "Jordan's Islamic Action Front picks up New Leadership," Duetsche Press-Agentur, May 31, 2009.

[44] Syed Saleem Shahzad, "Jordan's Islamic Front rallies Muslims," *Asia Times Online*, March 7, 2003, http://www.atimes.com/atimes/Middle_East/EC07Ak01.html.

[45] "Jamaat ul-Fuqra," South Asia Terrorism Portal (SATP), n.d., http://www.satp.org/satporgtp/countries/pakistan/terroristoutfits/jamaat-ul-fuqra.htm.

[46] Richard Sale, "Pakistan ISI link to Pearl kinap probed," United Press International, January 29, 2002, http://www.upi.com/Business_News/Security-Industry/2002/01/29/Pakistan-ISI-link-to-Pearl-kidnap-probed/UPI-22581012351784/. JeM is designated as a Foreign Terrorist Organization by the U.S. government. JeM seeks to liberate Kashmir and reunite it with Pakistan.

[47] "Welcome to the International Quranic Open University," International Quranic Open University Website, n.d., http://www.iqou-moa.org/.

[48] Colorado Attorney General Press Release, "Attorney General Salazar announces 69 Year Sentence for 'Fuqra' defendant convincted of racketeering and conspiracy to commit murder," March 16, 2001.

[49] "United States: The Jamaat al-Fuqra Threat," Stratfor, June 2, 2005, http://www.stratfor.com/memberships/61912/united_states_jamaat_al_fuqra_threat

[50] "'Homegrown Jihad: The Terrorist Camps Around U.S.' Hits Cable TV," Christian Action Network Website, n.d., http://www.christianaction.org/can-events/homegrown-jihad-hits-cable-tv.aspx.

[51] Madeleine Gruen, "Hizb ut Tahrir's Activities in the United States," Jamestown Foundation *Terrorism Monitor* 5, no. 16 (August 22, 2007), http://www.jamestown.org/single/?no_cache=1&tx_ttnews[ttnews]=4377.

[52] "Hizb ut Tahrir," Hizb ut Tahrir America Website, n.d., http://www.hizb-america.org/about-us/hizb-ut-tahrir.

[53] Ibid.

[54] Houriya Ahmed and Hannah Stuart, *Hizb ut Tahrir: Ideology and Strategy* (London: Centre for Social Cohesion, 2009).

[55] Gruen, "Hizb ut Tahrir's Activities in the United States."

[56] "About Us," Islamic Thinkers Society Website, http://www.islamicthinkers.com/index/index.php?option=com_content&task=view&id=5&Itemid=57

[57] Quintan Wiktorowicz *Radical Islam Rising: Muslim Extremism in the West* (Boulder, CO: Rowman & Littlefield, 2005), pp. 6-11 The Khalifah, or Caliphate refers to the historical Islamic Empire that Islamists seek to revive.

[58] "Current Issues," Islamic Thinkers Society Website, n.d., http://www.islamicthinkers.com/index/index.php?option=com_content&task=blogcategory&id=0&Itemid=73; "Scholars of Batil," Islamic Thinkers Society Website, n.d., http://www.islamicthinkers.com/

index/index.php?option=com_content&task=blogcategory&id=86&I temid=74.

[59] Mitchell D. Silber and Arvin Bhatt, *Radicalization in the West: The Homegrown Threat* (New York: NYPD, 2008), 22

[60] "Khilafah: The Mother of All Obligations. The Evidences for Establishing Khilafah and the Method (Minhaj)," *Islamic Revival* 9, (2006), 7.

[61] "Mission Statement," Revolution Muslim Website, n.d., http://www.revolutionmuslim.com/index.php?option=com_content&view=article&id=3&Itemid=17.

[62] "An Officer & a Gentleman," Revolution Muslim Website, n.d., http://www.revolutionmuslim.com/index.php?option=com_conte nt&view=article&id=519:an-officer-a-a-gentleman&catid=1:yous efalkhattab&Itemid=4; "Fort Hood," Revolution Muslim Website, n.d., http://www.revolutionmuslim.com/index.php?option=com_c ontent&view=article&id=1608:fort-hood&catid=11:revolutionary-media&Itemid=15.

[63] Anti-Defamation League, "Backgrounder: Revolution Muslim," December 15, 2009, http://www.adl.org/NR/exeres/48925123-070C-411E-A42F-E23160C76E5D,DB7611A2-02CD-43AF-8147-649E26813571,frameless.htm.

[64] Jane Perlez, Salman Masood and Waqar Gillani, "5 U.S. Men Arrested in Pakistan Said to Plan Jihad," *New York Times,* December 10, 2009.

[65] U.S. Dept of Justice Press Release, "Seven Charged with Terrorism Violations in North Carolina," July 27, 2009; U.S. Dept of Justice Press Release, "Superseding Indictment in Boyd Matter Charges Defendants with Conspiring to Murder U.S. Military Personnel, Weapons Violations," September 24, 2009.

[66] "Sealed Complaint," *U.S. v. Cromitie et al,* (SD NY, May 19, 2009).

[67] "Superseding Indictment," *U.S. v. Mehanna and Abousamra.*

[68] "Government's Motion for Detention," *U.S. v. Mehanna,* 09-0017-GAO (D MA, November 2009).

[69] "Superseding Indictment," *U.S. v. Mehanna and Abousamra.*

[70] "Indictment," *U.S. v. Headley,* 09-CR-830 (ED IL, December 7, 2009).

[71] "Indictment," *U.S. v. Najibullah Zazi,* 09-CR-663 (ED NY, September 24, 2009); "Memorandum of Law in Support of the Government's Motion for a Permanent Order of Detention," *U.S. v. Najibullah Zazi;* U.S. Dept of Justice Press Release, "Three Arrested in Ongoing Terror Investigation," September 20, 2009, http://www.fbi.gov/pressrel/pressrel09/zazi_092009.htm.

[72] "Superseding Information," *U.S. v Bryan Neal Vinas,* 08-823 (ED NY, July 22, 2009).

[73] "Criminal Complaint," *U.S. v. Smadi*, 3:09-MT-286 (ND TX, September 24, 2009).

[74] "Criminal Complaint," *U.S. v. Michael C. Finton*, 09-2048-M (CD IL, September 24, 2009)

[75] Peter Walker and Chris McGreal, "Al-Qaida links to Christmas Day plane bomb plot investigated," The Guardian, December 28, 2009, http://www.guardian.co.uk/world/2009/dec/27/christmas-plane-bomber-al-qaida

[76] Philip Sherwell and Alex Spillius, "Fort Hood shooting: Texas army killer linked to September 11 terrorists," Telegraph, November 7, 2009

[77] *Muslim Americans: Middle Class and Mostly Mainstream*, Pew Research Center, May 22, 2007, 21-22, http://pewresearch.org/assets/pdf/muslim-americans.pdf.

[78] Ibid., 15.

[79] Ibidem, 15-16.

[80] *Muslim Americans: A National Portrait, The Muslim West Facts Project* (Gallup and the Coexist Foundation, 2009), 10.

[81] Ibid., 20.

[82] See, for example, James E. Finch, letter to MCOP Invitee, October 8, 2008, http://www.investigativeproject.org/documents/misc/238.pdf; Congressman 'Deeply Disappointed' By FBI's Lack of Answers on CAIR's Questionable Ties," FoxNews.com, March 11, 2009, http://www.foxnews.com/politics/2009/03/11/congressman-deeply-disappointed-fbis-lack-answers-cairs-questionable-ties/; Charles Schumer, Tom Coburn, and Jon Kyl, letter to Robert Mueller, February 24, 2009, http://www.investigativeproject.org/documents/misc/242.pdf

[83] See, for example, Erick Stakelbeck, "Controversial Islamic Speaker Welcomed at Ft. Hood," Christian Broadcasting Network, December 9, 2009, http://www.cbn.com/cbnnews/us/2009/December/Controversial-Speaker-Welcomed-at-Ft-Hood/. The paucity of sources that have reported on this issue indicate the extent to which basic information about Islamist groups in the U.S. outside mainstream discourse. The outlets that have addressed Louay Safi's work at Fort Hood include the Christian Broadcasting Network, the website Jihad Watch, the Investigative Project on Terrorism, a series of right-wing blogs, and other similar organizations.

[84] Daniel Benjamin, "International Counterterrorism Policy in the Obama Administration," Speech at the Jamestown Foundation, Washington, DC, December 9, 2009, http://www.state.gov/s/ct/rls/rm/2009/133337.htm.

LATIN AMERICA

COUNTRIES

Nicaragua

Bolivia

Venezuela

Regional Summary

At just six million people, Latin America's Muslim population represents only 1.2 percent of the region's total of 568 million. Yet, despite this modest size, there is considerable evidence that Islamist groups and movements have begun to make significant inroads there, operating among the local Muslim communities that dot the region's countries.

Most directly, there is growing awareness among policymakers and experts alike that Islamic terrorist organizations have succeeded in creating extensive economic and operational networks throughout the Americas. Currently, no fewer than six such groups—including Hezbollah and al-Qaeda—have been identified as being active in the region. These organizations have managed to exploit the area's large ungoverned spaces and lack of governmental oversight to erect a range of lucrative illicit enterprises, as well as to establish at least some level of operational capability. The U.S. military now estimates that Islamist groups raise between $300 and $500 million dollars annually as a result of their activities in areas such as the Tri-Border Region (where Argentina, Paraguay and Brazil intersect) and the free trade zones of Colon, Maicao and Margarita Island.

In their activities in the region, Islamist groups have been greatly aided by widespread anti-Americanism and vestiges of leftist revolutionary fervor. These attitudes can be seen most visibly in Venezuela, where the regime of Hugo Chavez has spearheaded efforts to erect an anti-American coalition with like-minded states under the banner of a new social movement termed "Bolivarianism" (referring to the 19th century Venezuelan-born independence hero Simón Bolívar). Significantly, these political proclivities have translated into warmth for Islamist causes and organizations. Thus Venezuela, under Chavez' leadership, has forged a broad-ranging political, economic and military partnership with the Islamic Republic of Iran over the past decade. This relationship encompasses not only extensive bilateral economic ties and cooperation on oil and natural gas, but also shared opposition to the West—as manifested by Venezuela's support for Iran's nuclear program and its offer to help the Iranian regime circumvent international sanctions.

Chavez' sympathetic attitude toward Islamism extends beyond cooperation with Iran, however. On his watch, Venezuela has emerged as a major "way station" and fundraising for Islamist groups, chief among them Hezbollah. So pervasive has Hezbollah's influence become that it has led to the creation of an indigenous group among the region's Wayuu Indian population which has pledged allegiance to—and support for—both the Lebanese militia and its chief sponsor, Iran.

Bolivia has likewise drifted toward partnership with the Iranian regime, although as of this writing—and despite positive pronouncements from both Tehran and La Paz—that relationship remains largely unconsummated. Nevertheless, the government of president Evo Morales appears to have positioned itself as a "bridge" to the Muslim world, and places considerable emphasis on its relationship with Islamic nations. Given the small size of the country's Muslim population and its integration into Bolivian society at large, this focus appears to reflect a governmental—rather than popular—priority.

NICARAGUA

QUICK FACTS

Population: 5,995,528

Area: 130,370 sq km

Ethnic Groups: Mestizo (mixed Amerindian and white) 69%, white 17%, black 9%, Amerindian 5%

Religions: Roman Catholic 58.5%, Evangelical 21.6%, Moravian 1.6%, Jehovah's Witness 0.9%, other 1.7%, none 15.7%

Government Type: Republic

GDP (official exchange rate): $6.372 billion

Map and Quick Facts courtesy of the CIA World Factbook (Last Updated July 2010)

Islam has had a presence in Nicaragua since the late 19th century, when Muslims from the territories of what was then known as Palestine placed a particular focus on Central America as an emigration destination. According to one author, as many as 40 families from Palestine settled in Nicaragua during this period.[1] This first wave of Muslim immigration, and a subsequent second wave that took place in the 1960s, did little to establish Islam in Nicaragua, however. The most recent group of emigrants arrived in the early 1990s, and while not a large number, helped establish what is today a small but thriving Islamic community.

Nicaragua's Islamic community, numbering well over 1,000 according to one source, largely resides in the capital city of Managua, but prayer centers have been established in private residences located around the country, including Granada, Masaya, and Leon.[2] The community consists of Muslim descendants of Arab emigrants from the Palestine territories and Lebanon. There are a relatively small number of Nicaraguan nationals who have converted.

In 1999, the country's first mosque was constructed with funding from local sources, as well as a delegation of Panamanian Muslims. Construction on a second mosque began in 2009. In January 2007, Iranian President Mahmoud Ahmadinejad visited the country's first mosque, signaling a growing international recognition of Nicaragua's Islamic community. The assumption of power by Daniel Ortega in 2006 brought with it a positive change in the relationship between Nicaragua's Muslim community and the government, including considerably better treatment than past governments when Muslims were forced into hiding or made to convert to Christianity.

ISLAMIST ACTIVITY

Nicaragua's Islamic Cultural Association in Managua serves as the focal point of the country's Muslim population. Run by Fahmi Hassan and his staff, the center also operates the country's first mosque. Apart from traditional prayer activities, the center maintains an office, a library, a children's area, and a school. Religious seminars are available for men and women and Spanish-language literature is made available for the community and visitors.

Hassan arrived in Nicaragua in 1960 and has remained in the country since, with one exception. During the Sandinista Revolution, he lived in Saudi Arabia and Jordan, but as he explains in an interview, he left for business reasons.[3]

A second mosque was under construction in June 2009, and Mr. Hassan had planned for the mosque to be ready in time for the period of Ramadan, which began on August 20 in 2009. Yusef Mohammed, a Honduran businessman with Pakistani roots, financed over half of the U.S. $500,000 price tag for the new mosque. Mr. Hassan has plans to purchase land nearby where he would like to construct an athletic center and another library.[4]

At the time, he admitted that there are about 200 committed members in regular attendance at Nicaragua's mosque.[5]

In 2007, the Cultural Center of Nicaraguan Islam opened with the sole purpose of spreading Islamic teachings.[6] Run by Carlos Arana, a Palestinian descendent, the center organizes seminars, and operates a library and website. There is no indication at this point that the Cultural Center is used for anything other than non-radical Islamic teaching. However, given the rising influence of Iran in the country and the growing presence of Iranian diplomats and businessmen, and the fact that most of the Muslims in Nicaragua are Shi'ite, the situation should be watched carefully.

ISLAMISM AND SOCIETY

Throughout much of Nicaragua's history, Islam has been a victim off-and-on government repression, largely rejected by the country's dominant Catholic society. The peak of this repression occurred just before the beginning of the Sandinista Revolution, in the late 1970s.

During the Revolution, however, Nicaragua's Government treated the Muslim community exceptionally well, especially the Palestinian Arabs.[7] Most men and women who immigrate to Nicaragua from the Middle East choose to settle in the country, and leave only when they are old because they would prefer to die in their homeland.[8] This trend suggests a high level of acceptance of Islam within Nicaraguan society.

Another indication of Islamic acceptance is Managua's Arabic business district. All along a road known *Casa de los Encajes*, in the *Ciudad Jardin* section of the capital, there is concentration of Arabic stores, most of them owned by Palestinians who sell Arabic rugs, home decoration, clothing, and fabrics. Mr. Hassan owns a rug store located in this small district, which by 2003 had been in place for "many years."[9]

As of 2009, historical pressures have all but disappeared as President Daniel Ortega, now in his second term of office, has focused on bringing the Central American country closer to Middle Eastern states, especially Iran.

ISLAMISM AND THE STATE

Nicaragua's first involvement with the Islamic world was perhaps in the 1940s, when the young Somoza dictatorship used a Nicaraguan-flagged vessel to ship weapons to Jewish guerrillas fighting in Palestine. The political tide turned when Daniel Ortega lead the Sandinistas to power in 1979, ushering in a new relationship with the Islamic world, one that embraced Islamic countries, and specifically the Palestine Liberation Organization, whose fighters had trained Sandinista guerrillas before Sandinista Revolution. Once the Sandinistas seized power, the PLO sent a 25-man team to train Sandinista soldiers in the use of Eastern-bloc weapons, and provided a U.S. $12 million loan. And by 1982, some 70 PLO officers with ranks from colonel to major and captain were assisting with special infantry training for the Nicaraguan army.[10] In return, Ortega and the Sandinistas granted the PLO full diplomatic status. Then-PLO leader Yasser Arafat visited Managua in 1980.

Once in power, the Sandinistas viewed Israel as an enemy. In 1983, Israel shipped hundreds of weapons to Nicaraguan Contras, in rebellion against

Ortega's Sandinista government. These weapons included 2,000 Kalashnikov AK-4 rifles and well over a hundred RPG 7 anti-tank rockets that the Israelis had recovered from PLO camps during a 1982 invasion.[11] Nicaragua's dwindling Jewish community provided further evidence of the Sandinista's disdain for Israel; by 1981, most of Nicaragua's Jews had emigrated to Israel – declining from some 50 members in 1976 to only a few by 1981.[12]

By 1985, the Reagan administration and many in Washington viewed Nicaragua as a regional trouble spot, largely due to the country's close ties to the USSR, as well as proven links to the PLO, Libya, and Iran. A 10-page study prepared by the U.S. State Department suggested that Libya had sent pilots, military advisors, and millions of dollars in financial assistance. Libya also tried to send a shipment of 84 tons of military equipment to Nicaragua in April 1983; it was seized, however, during a refueling stop in Brazil.[13] Ties to Iran were less explicit at the time, but Nicaragua and Iran inked a U.S. $23 million trade deal in 1984.[14] By 1985, Iran had entered into an agreement with Nicaragua to supply fuel to the Central American nation. Then Iranian Prime Minister Mir Hussein Moussavi signed the contract during a two-day visit to Managua, where he met with Sandinista leader and president Daniel Ortega. At the time, Iran produced over one million barrels of oil a day, and Nicaragua's need averaged 15,000 barrels of oil daily.[15]

In 1989, Ortega visited Europe and the Middle East in search of support, with stops in Qatar, Kuwait, and Bahrain. During a layover in Newfoundland, he announced that significant financing and aid had been secured for his country, presumably from patrons in the Middle East.[16]

When Ortega unexpectedly lost the historic elections of 1990 to Violeta Chamorro, the Nicaraguan attitude toward the Islamic world changed dramatically. One of the first things the Chamorro government did was close the Iranian embassy in Managua as well as the Nicaraguan embassy in Tehran. In addition, she renewed relations with Israel and significantly reduced the presence of the PLO and Libya in Nicaragua. This policy of refocusing Nicaraguan attention on Latin America and the United States continued until Ortega's re-election in November 2006.

During his second term as president, Daniel Ortega has welcomed Islam into Nicaragua through increasingly close ties with Iran. Among his first official acts were reestablishing diplomatic ties with Iran, waiving visa requirements for Iranian travelers and authorizing Iran to re-open its embassy in Managua. In a sign of this growing warmth, Iranian President Mahmoud Ahmadinejad attended Daniel Ortega's inauguration ceremony in January 2007 before visiting the country's mosque. President Ortega himself has also visited

Iran, where on June 10, 2007 he met with Supreme Leader Ali Khamenei to mutually criticize American imperialism, and secure Iranian support for a raft of foreign direct investment projects. While in Tehran, Ortega declared the Iranian revolution and Nicaragua's Sandinista revolution were "practically twins" because they shared not only the same year of triumph (1979) but the same goals of "justice, self-determination and the struggle against imperialism."[17] The meeting yielded concrete dividends. Later that year, in August, Iran's Deputy Minister of Energy, Hamid Chitchian, visited Nicaragua with a delegation of 21 businessmen. President Ortega presented the delegation with a long list of discussed projects: a deep-water port, a wharf at Port Corinto and another at Monkey Point, a 70-kilometer highway on the Caribbean coast, improvements to Managua's drinking water system, six hydraulic plants, a plan for the mechanization of the country's agricultural sector, assembly plants for tractors and other agricultural machinery, five milk processing plants, ten milk storage centers, and a health clinic in Managua. In exchange, Ortega offered in exchange meat, plantains, and coffee exports to Iran.[18]

Iran has moved forward on studies for a U.S. $350 million deep-water port, but construction on the project has yet to begin. And of the six hydroelectric plants, Iran has agreed to assist with four, but had the funding to invest only in one. Construction on the U.S. $120 million hydroelectric plant remains delayed.

Rumors of Iran operating the largest embassy in Central America in Managua have also recently been refuted.[19] And while Iran will not pardon Nicaragua's U.S. $160 million dollar debt, the country has followed through with some initial investments.[20] At least 1,000 of the 10,000 promised "social housing" units have been slated for construction, according to an agreement signed between President Ortega and Deputy Energy Minister, Hamid Chitchian.[21]

Nicaragua, however, does have plans to open an embassy in Iran, and through President Ortega's efforts, the Central American country continues to be an international partner for the Middle Eastern nation's non-aligned regime. Nicaragua's contact with Lebanon, Libya, and the Palestinian Territories – where most of the country's Muslim population retains some connection – is limited.

ENDNOTES

[1]Roberto Marín Guzmán, *A Century of Palestinian Immigration Into Central America: A Study of Their Economic and Cultural Contributions* (XXXX: Editorial Universidad de C.R., 2000), 49–59.

[2] International Religious Freedom Report, United States Department of State, 2008

[3] Edwin Sanchez, "El Ramadan de un musulman en El Oriental," *El Nuevo Diario*, October 9, 2005, http://impreso.elnuevodiario.com.ni/2005/10/09/nacionales/2967 .

[4] Mauricio Miranda, "La primera mezquita en Nicaragua," *El Nuevo Diario*, June 3, 2009, http://tinyurl.com/ybuoet3.

[5] Ibid.

[6] Doren Roa, "Inaguran Centro Cultrual Islámico," *El Nuevo Diario*, September 15, 2007, http://tinyurl.com/yeqmsnu.

[7] Sanchez, "El Ramadan de un musulman en El Oriental," *supra*.

[8] Ibid.

[9] Eduardo Tercero Marenco, "La defensa de Irak es obligatoria y necesaria," *La Prensa*, April 6, 2003, http://tinyurl.com/yzjhlp3 .

[10] George Gedda, "Administration Worried About Sandinista Ties to Middle East 'Radicals,'" Associated Press, July 10, 1985.

[11] Robert Fisk, "Long link with Middle East / Nicaraguan involvement in US-Iran arms deal," *Times of London*, November 28, 1986.

[12] Nicaragua did appear to make an attempt at improving relations in 2003, when Nicaraguan Foreign Minister, Norman Caldera Carnenal, visited Israel in August 2003. Minister Caldera did not visit with Yasser Arafat or any other Palestinian Authority leaders. This was the first such state visit between the two countries since 1966.

[13] George Gedda, "Administration Worried About Sandinista Ties to Middle East 'Radicals,'" *supra*.

[14] Ibid.

[15] Reuters, "Iran-Nicaragua Oil Pact Reported," *New York Times,* February 14, 1985.

[16] "Nicaragua Ortega on results of Middle East tour," Voz de Nicaragua, October 20, 1989.

[17] "Nicaragua e Iran: 'Union Invencible,'" BBC Mundo.com, June 11, 2007, http://news.bbc.co.uk/hi/spanish/latin_america/newsid_6741000/6741829.stm

[18] Revista Envio, "Nicaragua Briefs," Number 313, August 2007. Accessed via: http://www.envio.org.ni/articulo/3628 .

[19] Anne-Marie O'Connor and Mary Beth Sheridan, "Iran's Invisible Nicaraguan Embassy," *Washington Post*, July 13, 2009, http://tinyurl.com/knfpyt .

[20] Ludwin Lopez Loaisiga, "Iran sin perdonar US$160 millones," La Prensa, February 7, 2009, http://tinyurl.com/yj79tcr .

[21] Ludwin Loaisiga Lopez, "Iran have promses de ayudas millonarias," *La Prensa*, August 2007, http://tinyurl.com/yg28z9z .

BOLIVIA

QUICK FACTS

Population: 9,947,418

Area: 1,098,581 sq km

Ethnic Groups: Quechua 30%, mestizo (mixed white and Amerindian ancestry) 30%, Aymara 25%, white 15%

Religions: Roman Catholic 95%, Protestant (Evangelical Methodist) 5% Government Type: Republic (the new constitution defines Bolivia as a "Social Unitarian State")

GDP (official exchange rate): $17.76 billion

Map and Quick Facts Courtesy of the CIA World Factbook (Last Updated June 2010)

The practice of Islam in Bolivia remains small and dispersed predominantly between La Paz and Santa Cruz, with some 2,000 members scattered between eight different organizations with both Shi'a and Sunni sects.[1] There are also small Islamic organizations in Sucre and Cochabamba.

Bolivia's Muslim population counts among its members descendants from Bangladesh, Pakistan, Palestine, Syria, and Lebanon. The Islamic League for Latin America, the Muslim World League, and the World Assembly of Muslim Youth are among the top funders of Islamic activity in Bolivia. There is no history of persecution of Muslims in Bolivia, and since President Evo Morales entered office, Bolivia's official posture toward Islam has opened significantly.

ISLAMIST ACTIVITY

The Bolivian Islamic Center, based in Santa Cruz, claims to have founded Bolivia's first mosque in 1994; it serves some 50 congregants. The organization's current president, Mahmud Amer Abusharar, arrived in Bolivia in 1974 from the Palestinian Territories, and founded the organization so he would not "lose his faith" while abroad. In 2009, the center spread to Sucre, La Paz, and Cochabamba. The BIC claims to support "open-mindedness and peace," but does appear to espouse an anti-U.S. political position closely aligned with the Bolivian government.[2]

The Islamic Organization for Latin America and the World Islamic League both fund the BIC, and the BIC receives some support from the World Assembly of Muslim Youth, acting as this organization's Bolivian headquarters.

Also connected with the World Islamic League is the Bolivian Muslim Cultural Association, located in Sucre. A Palestinian doctor and lawyer, Fayez Rajab Khedeer Kannan, runs the organization. In 1998, he received a 30-year grant to use five acres of land in Sucre for his organization. Funding from the World Islamic League and the Islamic Development Bank helped with the construction of an educational center and clinic.

The Bolivia Islamic Cultural Foundation, based in La Paz, is a small organization founded in August 2007 by Roberto Chambi Calle, a Bolivian who converted to Islam in 1996. The organization's goals are to deepen the understanding of Islam in Bolivia and spread Islamic culture.[3] Chambi and his wife actively promote an Islamic message through the organization of seminars and small meetings. They have invited imams from other Latin American countries, such as Argentina and Uruguay, to speak at their events. In 2004, Chambi became the director of the At-Tauhid Mosque in Buenos Aires, Argentina, after its former director Mohsen Rabbani was implicated in the 1994 bombing of the Argentine-Jewish Mutual Association Building in Buenos Aires.[4]

Another La Paz-based organization is the Association of the Islamic Community of Bolivia. A Bolivian convert, Gerardo Cutipa Trigo, a.k.a. Ahmad Ali, is president of the organization, and claims that between 10 and 30 people regularly attend service at the organization's mosque. The organization's stated goals include strengthening the understanding of Islam in Bolivia, to coordinate and organize Islamic activities and projects in Bolivia, and to strengthen relations between Islamic organizations across the country and in neighboring countries.[5]

The Islamic Association of Bolivia operates the As-Salam mosque in La Paz. Mahmud Ali Teheran is the director of the organization and oversees the mosque, which counts a congregation of some 70 individuals, many of whom are young Bolivians.

The Shi'a Islamic Community of Bolivia, based in La Paz, counts some 13 members. Tommy Nelson Salgueiro Criales, a.k.a. Husayn Salgueiro, founded the organization in March 2006.

ISLAMISM AND SOCIETY

Mahmud Amer Abusharar of the Bolivian Islamic Center recently commented that his organization does not discriminate against anyone. He laughed at the indication of reports outlining Bolivia as a center of radical Islam in Latin America.[6] Apart from these isolated reports, there is no indication that Bolivian Muslims have any significant conflict with the rest of Bolivian society. Indeed, Bolivian President Evo Morales' continued good will towards Iran and other Middle Eastern countries indicates that, for the time being at least, political priorities will help maintain Bolivia as an Islam-friendly country.

ISLAMISM AND THE STATE

Bolivia's contemporary relationship with Islam is dominated by the growing political and strategic ties between La Paz and Tehran. Bolivian President Evo Morales first met Iranian President Mahmoud Ahmadinejad at the inauguration of Ecuadorian President Rafael Correa in mid-January 2007. At the time, the two leaders showed unprecedented interest in bringing their respective countries closer together politically, culturally, and economically. Ahmadinejad focused on agriculture, gas, and oil, referring to "academic potentials" in Iran for "improving the technical knowledge of Bolivia experts... in accordance with our Islamic teachings and duties."[7]

Months later, in September 2007, Bolivia's Foreign Minister, David Choquehvanca, visited Tehran to meet with his counterpart, Manuchehr Mottaki, and build upon the January meeting with firm commitments outlined in a signed agreement to broaden political and economic relations. During the same month, Morales signed an agreement with Iranian diplomat Abdulat Zisan to implement the importation and installation of six Iranian milk-processing plants in Bolivia. At the conclusion of the meeting, Morales noted: "we are interested in broadening relations with Iran, starting in the trade area with a view to continuing and consolidation relations of friendship, understanding and diplomacy." [8]

Iran's ties with Bolivia tightened upon Ahmadinejad's arrival in Bolivia at the end of September 2007, when the two countries officially announced an established diplomatic relationship during the Iranian president's short stay in La Paz after signing a raft of agreements in the oil and gas sectors. In the wake of this meeting, news surfaced that Morales might supplant investments from a number of international gas companies with Iranian funds. There was also suspicion that Bolivia might approach Libya as a new political and economic partner.[9]

By March 2008, Iran's relationship with Bolivia had developed a cultural facet. News sources out of Tehran reported that Iran had signed with Bolivia joint projects worth some U.S. $1 billion.[10] Some of this money was directed towards establishing an Iranian television network in Bolivia, ultimately to be integrated with the satellite-based Telesur television network established by Venezuelan President Hugo Chavez. The Republic of Iran Broadcasting (IRIB) planned to establish three television stations in Bolivia, and while announcing the new television stations to a group of coca growers in Bolivia's Chapare region, Morales stated that Iran would "support the peasant struggle here in Latin America."[11]

Morales finally reciprocated Ahmadinejad's Bolivian visit when he arrived in Tehran on September 1, 2008. Brief meetings with the Iranian president and the Minister of Mining and Industry punctuated his short stay in the Islamic Republic, where he focused on persuading Ahmadinejad to accelerate payments under Iran's promise to invest U.S. $1 billion in Bolivia.

Reflecting on Morales' visit to Iran, one columnist observed that the Bolivian president's visit to the Middle Eastern country "can provide a linking bridge between Bolivia as well as other Latin American states with other parts of the world, in particular the 57 Islamic nations. That will most certainly entail great gains for Latin America."[12] And within a week of his visit, Morales announced that Bolivia would move its lone Middle Eastern embassy from Cairo to Tehran.

By the end of September 2008, however, Bolivia and Iran had not yet exchanged ambassadors. The two countries had, however, exchanged technical delegations, with one Hojatollah Soltani emerging as Iran's business attaché to Bolivia. Soltani pledged that, apart from the promised investment of U.S. $1 billion, Iran would also invest some U.S. $230 million in a cement factory and another U.S. $3 million to build dairy farms.[13] Just under a month later, Soltani announced that Iran would use Bolivia as the base for a planned Red Crescent health clinic expansion across Latin America.[14] Two Iranian-funded health clinics have been planned for Bolivia.

By February 2009, pledges from Iran to support Bolivia's efforts to further exploit the country's natural gas fields had yet to materialize, but the milk processing plants were already under construction. Some Iranian funding had found its way to Bolivia, but the majority of what was promised had not yet been delivered. This gap between rhetoric and action, however, does not appear to have dampened relations between the two countries.

Money again headlined the Bolivian-Iranian relationship in July 2009, when Bolivia announced that it would receive a U.S. $280 million loan from the Middle Eastern state. Iran's top diplomat in Bolivia, Masoud Edrisi, stated at the time that the money was to be used as President Morales saw fit.[15] As long as Ahmadinejad remains the president of Iran and Morales the president of Bolivia, relations between the two countries will likely continue to grow, facilitating the spread of Islam in Bolivia.

ENDNOTES

[1] "Global Muslim Population: A Report on the Size and Distribution of the World's Muslim Population," Pew Research Center, October 2009.

[2] "Bolivia – Key Muslim Converts Assert Local Peril, Ally With Zealots Abroad," Open Source Center, May 12, 2009.

[3] Carillo, Liliana, "La comunidad musulmana de Bolivia," *La Razon* (La Paz), February 24, 2008, http://www.webislam.com/?idn=11654.

[4] "Bolivia – Key Muslim Converts…" Open Source Center, *supra*.

[5] Accessed via organization's website, http://www.geocities.com/asocisbol/.

[6] Devin Beaulieu, "Alarmismo por Bolivia y el Islam," CounterPunch, September 10, 2009, http://www.webislam.com/?idn=15078.

[7] "Presidents of Iran, Bolivia ask for higher level ties," IRNA (Tehran), January 16, 2007.

[8] "President Makes Agreement with Iran Official," *La Razón* (La Paz), September 9, 2007.

[9] Franz Chavez, "Bolivia: Morales Established Diplomatic Ties with Iran," BBC (London), September 28, 2007. Morales did finally visit Libya in September 2008, when the two countries formally established diplomatic ties.

[10] At the time, Morales announced that Bolivia would remove visa restrictions for Iranian nationals traveling to Bolivia. See John Kiriakou, "Iran's Latin America Push: As the U.S. ignores its neighbors to the south, Tehran has been making friends and influencing nations," *Los Angeles Times*, November 18, 2008.

[11] "Iran's Bolivian TV venture to 'interface' with Venezuela's Telesur," Fars (Tehran), March 19, 2008.

[12] Faramarz Asghari, "Iran-Bolivia strategic interaction," *Siyasat-e Ruz* (Tehran), September 1, 2008.

[13] "Iran, Bolivia State TVs Set To Co-op," Moj News Agency (Tehran), September 30, 2008.

[14] "Iran to open two clinics in Bolivia," Moj News Agency (Tehran), October 11, 2008, http://www.presstv.com/Detail.aspx?id=71865&sectionid=351020706.

[15] "Iran approves US$280 million loan for Bolivia," Associated Press, July 29, 2009.

VENEZUELA

QUICK FACTS

Population: 27,223,228

Area: 912,050 sq km

Ethnic Groups: Spanish, Italian, Portuguese, Arab, German, African, indigenous people

Religions: Nominally Roman Catholic 96%, Protestant 2%, other 2%

Government Type: Federal Republic

GDP (official exchange rate): $357.6 billion

Map and Quick Facts courtesy of the CIA World Factbook (Last Updated June 2010)

The regime of Hugo Chavez in Caracas long has sent the message to Islamist groups that their propaganda, recruitment and fundraising activities are welcome in Venezuela. Chavez exhibits strong sympathies for Islamic groups, and uses his regime to provide a safe haven for financial activities that benefit Islamic terrorist organizations. The roots of this affinity stretch back to Chavez's years as a revolutionary in the 4-F guerilla group, during which time the future Venezuelan president fell under the sway of individuals with a sympathetic view of a variety of "non-aligned" Middle Eastern rogues, among them Libyan dictator Muammar Qadhafi, Iraqi strongman Saddam Hussein, and the leaders of the Iranian revolution.[1] These early lessons provided the basis of the foreign policy that Chavez has pursued since taking power in 1998—a policy which has made his country a close ally of the Islamic Republic of Iran and radical Islamist groups, chief among them Hezbollah.

ISLAMIST ACTIVITY

Venezuela is an attractive way-station for Islamist groups, which have a quiet but longstanding and profitable presence there. It is a historically significant fund-raising and organizational base, and the U.S. Southern Command estimates that "Islamist terrorist groups raise between three hundred million and five hundred million dollars per year in the Triple Frontier and the duty-free zones of Iquique, Colon, Maicao, and Margarita Island, Venezuela."[2] The basic model is said to be a simple "pay to play" system, in which Lebanese Shi'a merchants are persuaded by Hezbollah agents and financiers, through varying degrees of coercion, to "tithe" to Hezbollah.[3]

As in most of Latin America, Hezbollah, Iran's chief terrorist proxy, is the primary Islamist force in Venezuela. Capitalizing on the network of enterprising Lebanese Shi'a merchants throughout the larger cities, it uses the South American country for fundraising and various forms of money-laundering, smuggling, and fraud. Apart from illicit financial business, however, there have been few overt signs of Hezbollah activity in Venezuela—save for the occasional Hezbollah propaganda that has periodically surfaced on the Internet or airwaves.[4]

ISLAMISM AND SOCIETY

While an acknowledged threat-finance concern, because there are no reports of organized al-Qaeda presence or activity, Venezuela is "off the map" for operations-based counterterrorism watchers. The country's Muslim population remains small. According to the U.S. State Department's 2007 *International Religious Freedom Report*, there were approximately 100,000 Muslims in Venezuela, forming 0.4 percent of the nation's population.[5] While Margarita Island's Muslim population is almost entirely Lebanese Shi'a, there are Sunni Muslims elsewhere in the country, and Caracas has a largely Sunni population of 15,000 which is served by the largest mosque in Latin America, built by the Saudis as a sister mosque to the Sheikh Ibrahim Al-Ibrahim mosque in Gibraltar.[6] There are other mosques in major cities of Maracaibo, Valencia, Vargas, Punto Fijo, and Bolivar. Local cable television outlets in Margarita carry *al-Jazeera* and the Lebanese Hezbollah outlet LBC, while on the mainland the Saudi Channel is available via satellite as well.[7]

The picture of Islamism and society in Venezuela resembles that of much of Latin America. This is to say that while there is a vague anti-globalist sense that pervades society, actual friendship with Islamist aims is at the political and not the social level.[8] While the Latin American left at times can sound Islamist in its politics and its understanding of who the "enemy" is, there appears to be no sizeable conversion to Islam taking place in Venezuela—or, indeed, in the region. To the contrary, in the past 150 years of immigration from the Middle East to the New World, the opposite trend has held sway.

A large number of prominent *turcos* (immigrants and their descendants from the Middle East) originally were Muslim, but have been genuine *conversos* (converts to Christianity) for generations. Thus, the presence in Caracas of the largest mosque in the New World reflects Venezuela's cosmopolitan self-image more than it serves as evidence of an Islamist trajectory. Finally, as in most of Latin America, birth rates among Venezuelan Muslims, who tend to be considerably wealthier than the population at large, are equal to or lower than the modal birth-rate of the population. New Muslim immigration, meanwhile, is understood to be minimal (although detailed statistics are hard to come by). The picture of Islamism in Venezuela, therefore, is decidedly a still-frame.

ISLAMISM AND THE STATE

Ever since Hugo Chavez took his first trip to Iran in 2001, upgraded relations with the Islamic Republic have become a cardinal tenet of Venezuelan foreign policy.[9] In October 2010, Chavez announced an initial study of a nuclear capacity for his country, a move analysts believe could be largely one of cover for Iran's program which Venezuela has been supporting for several years.[10]

In November 2008, Iranian and Venezuelan officials signed a secret "science and technology" agreement formalizing cooperation "in the field of nuclear technology."[11] As part of that outreach, Iranian Minister of Science, Research and Technology Mohammad-Mehdi Zahedi led a delegation to hold talks with Venezuelan high-ranking officials in Caracas. The delegation visited the Venezuelan Foundation for Seismological Research, Caracas Central University, the Simon Bolivar University, and the Venezuelan Institute for Scientific Research.[12] During the visit, Chavez promised to provide the Islamic Republic with 20,000 barrels of petrol a day, despite the sanctions on Iran's economy being contemplated by much of the responsible world and in spite of Venezuela's own problems in supplying its domestic markets with fuel.[13]

A whirlwind visit to Iran by Chavez in September 2009 yielded a new deal on nuclear cooperation.[14] The agreement was the most recent addition to a rapidly growing list of bilateral pacts between Caracas and Tehran. The mutual benefits of such cooperation are undeniable: helping Venezuela develop its oil industry could ensure an important source of supply for Iran, which lacks refinery capacity despite being a major oil producer. And, at least on paper, many of these projects appear benign. Upon closer inspection, however, the commercial links between Venezuela and Iran provide reason for considerable concern. An example is the Venezuelan-Iranian joint venture tractor company "VenIran." Ostensibly founded so that poor Venezuelan farmers could take advantage of Iranian technological advances, the firm has in fact been implicated in the supply of bomb-making materials. In 2008, Turkish customs inspectors intercepted, in containers bound for Venezuela and labeled "tractor parts," a bomb-making lab and all the nitrate and sulfite chemicals that needed to stock it.[15] Other joint ventures in oil exploration, petrochemicals, steel and auto manufacturing are under ever-increasing scrutiny.

It is clear that Iran sees its Venezuelan connection as an important means to render international sanctions impotent. The joint ventures erected between Caracas and Tehran, and the purchase of Venezuelan enterprises, allow Iran to do business with U.S. companies and even within the United States itself. Because of the direct connection between Caracas and Tehran, efforts to contain trade with Iran are futile without cutting off the billions of dollars of legitimate U.S. trade with Venezuela, according to Manhattan District Attorney Robert Morganthau.[16] These ties, moreover, are expanding; in April 2009, the two countries launched a bi-national bank with $200 million of initial capital—with each country contributing half—and a final goal of $1.2 billion.[17] The bank is supposed to finance projects of mutual benefit to the two countries. Based in Venezuela, it will offer a convenient channel for Iran to sidestep U.S.-led sanctions along with the several branches of Iran's Saderat Bank already open there.[18]

Although the greatest fears of the Iranian-Venezuelan relationship relate to Iran's looming nuclear weapons capability, the strategic partnership between Tehran and Caracas runs deeper. Since Iran's fraudulent June 2009 elections, Chavez has taken pains to express his affinity for the Iranian regime. He has offered "total solidarity" to Iranian president Mahmoud Ahmadinejad, equating attacks on him as an assault by "global capitalism,"[19] and condoned the brutal tactics of Iran's domestic militia, the *basij*, in their crackdown on opposition protesters.[20] Iran has reciprocated these friendly feelings. When he decorated Hugo Chávez with the Higher Medal of the Islamic Republic of Iran in 2008, Mahmoud Ahmadinejad called Chávez "my brother... a friend of the Iranian nation and the people seeking freedom around the world. He works perpetually against the dominant system. He is a worker of God and servant of the people."[21]

What all this may mean, in the longer term, may best be considered in light of the curious 2006 case of the rise—and apparent fall—of a group advertising itself as "Hezbollah in Venezuela." Though it was largely eclipsed in the news media by the U.S. 2006 mid-term elections, Hezbollah en América Latina's failed attempt in October 2006 to bomb the U.S. (and perhaps Israeli) embassy in Caracas was a significant event. The group, based within the country's Wayuu Indian population, boasts of activity in Argentina,

Chile, Colombia, El Salvador and Mexico on their website,[22] which is written in Spanish and Chapateka (a combination of the Wayuu language and Spanish). However, the backbone of the organization is located in Venezuela on the western border with Colombia. The members of this group are locals and not Muslim in origin despite their tenuous claim to be Shi'ite supporters of Hezbollah and Iran.[23]

In its manifesto, the organization asserted that Venezuelan society, with its interest in sex, money, industry and commerce, has become a "swamp of immorality and corruption."[24] In response, it claimed that political movements and parties cannot provide an answer to these problems because they are also part of the problem. Thus, only "a theocratic, Political-Islamic force can liberate society from this situation."[25] Hezbollah Latin America "respect[ed] the Venezuelan revolutionary process, and support[ed] its social policies as well as its anti-Zionism and anti-Americanism," even as it rejected socialism in favor of an Islamic order. Tellingly, the group urged everyone to vote for and support Chavez.[26]

It is not coincidental that this phenomenon occurred at precisely the moment when Hugo Chavez and Iranian President Mahmoud Ahmedinejad became close allies. It does, however, point to an alarming possibility: that Hezbollah and radical Islamist groups need not import Islamists from the Muslim world to Latin America. Rather, they can be "home-grown" in the region, because the social and emotional conditions provide fertile ground. Furthermore, this new available human capital does not need previous connection to Islam; it can be converted to Islam, because Islamism is not merely a religion but also a political movement.

This principle helps explain the near-perfect symbiosis of the "Bolivarian" Revolution promoted by Chavez with the aims of Hezbollah: "Hezbollah Latin America respects the Venezuelan revolutionary process and supports the policies of this process that have to do with social benefits for the poor, as well as the anti-Zionist and anti-imperialist policies of the revolution. It does not, however, support the socialist ideology. This is not because we are opposed to it but because we are theocrats and we obey a divine prerogative."[27]

While the incident could easily have been a one-off propaganda campaign, it will be important to watch, over the longer term, for this sort of cultural and ideological solidarity at the popular level between the traditional leftist, anti-globalist, and anti-Semitic forces of nominally Catholic Venezuela with the radical Islamists of the Middle East.

ENDNOTES

[1] Alberto Garrido, *Las Guerras de Chavez* (Rayuela: Taller de Ediciones, 2006), 17.

[2] Paul D. Taylor, ed., "Latin American Security Challenges: A Collaborative Inquiry from North and South," Naval War College *Newport Paper* no. 21, 2004.

[3] U.S. Department of the Treasury, Office of Public Affairs, "Treasury Designates Islamic Extremist, Two Companies Supporting Hezbollah in Tri-border Area," June 10, 2004, http://www.treas.gov/press/releases/js1720.htm.

[4] Mark S. Steinitz, "Middle East Terrorist Activity in Latin America," Center for Strategic & International Studies Policy Papers on the Americas XIV, Study 7, July 2003; *United States of America v. Mohamad Youssef Hammoud, aka Ali Abousaleh, aka Ali Albousaleh*, United States Court of Appeals for the Fourth District, 405 F.3d 1034, April 27, 2005.

[5] "Venezuela" in U.S. Department of State, Bureau of Democracy, Human Rights and Labor, *2007 Report on International Religious Freedom*, September 2007, http://www.state.gov/g/drl/rls/irf/2007/90271.htm.

[6] Ibid.

[7] Ibidem.

[8] For evidence of this claim, one need look at a few of the overwhelmingly negative comments on Hezbollah Venezuela's website: http://hezboallahpartidoislamico.blogspot.es/1149260280/hezboallah-grupo-islamico-venezolano/ (in Spanish).

[9] "Hugo Chávez de visita en Irán hasta el lunes," *El Universal* (Caracas), May 18, 2001.

[10] Roger F. Noriega, "Chávez's Secret Nuclear Program" *Foreign Policy*, October 5, 2010.

[11] Ibid; Documentation cited can be found at http://www.foreignpolicy.com/files/fp_uploaded_documents/101004_0_Acuerdos_Ciencia_y_Tecnologia.pdf.

[12] "Iranian Delegation In Venezuela," *Mathaba* (London), November 17, 2008, http://mathaba.net/news/?x=611701.

[13] Robert M. Morgenthau, "The Emerging Axis Of Iran And Venezuela," *Wall Street Journal*, September 8, 2009, http://online.wsj.com/article/SB10001424052970203440104574400792835972018.html.

[14] "Venezuela's President Wants To Marshal The Forces Of Anti-Imperialism," *The Economist*, September 15, 2009, http://www.economist.com/displayStory.cfm?story_id=14444403.

[15] U.S. Department of State, Office of the Coordinator for Counterterrorism, *Country Reports on Terrorism 2008* (Washington: U.S. Department of State, April 2009), 105, www.state.gov/documents/

organization/122599.pdf.

[16] Robert M. Morgenthau, "The Link between Iran and Venezuela: A Crisis in the Making?" Briefing before the Brookings Institution, Washington, DC, September 8, 2009.

[17] Ibid.

[18] "Iran Raises Profile In Latin America," *Washington Post*, November 22, 2008.

[19] "Iran-Venezuela Ties Serve Strategic Aims," United Press International, August 14, 2009, http://www.upi.com/Top_News/Special/2009/08/14/Iran-Venezuela-ties-serve-strategic-aims/UPI-91201250266165.

[20] Ibid.

[21] Chávez decorated in Iran; initials cooperation pacts," *El Universal* (Caracas), July 31, 2006.

[22] The organization's website was previously located at http:/groups.msn.com/AutonomiaIslamicaWayuu. It currently appears to be housed at http://autonomiaislamicawayuu.blogspot.com/.

[23] Manuel Torres Soriano, "La Fascinación por el éxito: Hezbollah en América Latina," *Jihad Monitor*, October 17, 2006.

[24] Ibid, 2.

[25] Gustavo Coronel, "Chávez Joins the Terrorists: His Path to Martyrdom," *Venezuela Today*, September 2, 2006.

[26] Gustavo Coronel, "The Hezbollah Venezuelan Metastasis," *Venezuela Today*, September 4, 2006, 3.

[27] Ibid; See also Hezbollah Venezuela, "Comunicado De Hezbollah Venezuela a Centro Simón," August 22, 2006, http://comunicadohezbollahacentrosimon.blogspot.com/2006/08/comunicado-de-hezbollah-latino-amrica.html.

MIDDLE EAST AND NORTH AFRICA

COUNTRIES

Iran
Iraq
Syria
Lebanon
Israel
Palestinian Authority
Jordan
Saudi Arabia
Bahrain
Qatar
United Arab Emirates
Kuwait
Yemen
Egypt
Libya
Tunisia
Algeria
Morocco

Regional Summary

For the Middle East and North Africa, arguably the global epicenter of Islamist activity, the past year has been one marked by dramatic change. Since the start of 2011, the so-called "Arab Spring" has fundamentally altered the region, injecting dynamism into its traditionally-stagnant politics. In the process, however, it also has presented heretofore unimagined opportunities for Islamist groups and political parties to expand their popularity and gain power.

Practically all regional regimes have been affected by this trend, albeit in different ways. The twenty-three-year rule of Tunisian strongman Zin el-Abidine Ben Ali in Tunisia was the first to end as a result of sustained domestic pressure, in the process providing inspiration to opposition forces elsewhere. Egypt was the next to follow suit, with the three-decade-long regime of

Hosni Mubarak coming to an end in February 2011 as a result of widespread anti-regime ferment. Notably, in both countries, ascendant Islamist forces (Tunisia's *al-Nadha* and Egypt's Muslim Brotherhood, respectively) are now gaining greater prominence in national politics, aided by the political disorder that has followed the overthrow of the old regimes.

To a lesser extent, the countries of Kuwait, Bahrain, Saudi Arabia, the United Arab Emirates, Jordan and Morocco have all been impacted by the "Arab Spring" as well, as both religious and secular opposition forces—inspired by the Tunisian and Egyptian examples—have increased their pressure on sitting regimes. Bahrain and Saudi Arabia have chosen to employ domestic and regional security forces to secure their respective monarchies and squelch serious anti-regime activism, at least temporarily. Others (in particular Jordan and Morocco) have responded to the challenge posed by reinvigorated domestic opposition in more measured fashion. All, however, have shown new willingness, in the face of this domestic ferment, to enact political and social reforms. Over time, the resulting changes—now being formulated by the respective governments—are likely to provide greater voice and political participation to Islamist opposition groups and political factions in local politics.

Not all regional states have sought to weather the "Arab Spring" peaceably, however. In Libya, domestic upheaval in the spring of 2011 was met by a harsh governmental response on the part of the Gadhafi regime, resulting in a civil war and subsequent international intervention, both of which are currently ongoing. Domestic conditions in Yemen likewise have deteriorated as a result of ongoing pitched fighting between the government of Ali Abdullah Saleh and assorted Islamist rebels. Similarly, broad-based and resilient grassroots opposition to the regime of Bashar al-Assad in Syria has led to significant domestic loss of life, with the Assad regime spearheading a clampdown on dissent that so far has left over a thousand dead. Notably, Syria has been aided in its repression by the Islamic Republic of Iran, which itself continues to weather significant grassroots discontent and sporadic anti-regime activism stemming from the controversial re-election of current president Mahmoud Ahmadinejad in June 2009.

Iran, which remains the world's most active sponsor of international terrorism, also has attempted to use the "Arab Spring" to expand its influence in the region, both ideologically (as in the case of Bahrain's Shi'a community) and operationally (through increases in its funding and political support for Islamist groups in Lebanon and the Palestinian Territories). Radical Islamist forces active in the region have sensed opportunity in the "Arab Spring" as well. In particular, the Bin Laden network's two regional franchises, al-Qaeda in the Arabian Peninsula (AQAP) and al-Qaeda in the Islamic Maghreb (AQIM), have shown signs of attempting to take advantage of the regional disorder to improve their geopolitical position and increase the pace of their activities in the Persian Gulf and North Africa.

Beyond the "Arab Spring," regional politics continue to be shaped by the ongoing post-9/11 Coalition campaign in Iraq. There, a U.S. withdrawal already underway has progressively handed over security to the Iraqi military and Shi'ite-dominated coalition government in Baghdad. For the most part, this transfer of power has occurred smoothly to date. However, Islamist groups—in particular, Shi'a militias supported by neighboring Iran—remain a significant threat to the country's stability. So do Iran's attempts, working through militias and the country's Shi'ite political parties, to surreptitiously influence national politics and bring Iraq more closely into its geopolitical orbit.

ISLAMIC REPUBLIC OF IRAN

In its most recent report on global terrorism trends, known as the Country Reports on Terrorism, the U.S. Department of State confirmed once again that Iran remains the world's "most active state sponsor of terrorism." It is a title that the Iranian regime has held consistently since the U.S. government began keeping track of terrorist trends nearly three decades ago. Its support for terrorism is rooted in the foundational tenets of the Ayatollah Ruhollah Khomeini's Islamic Revolution, which espoused the need to "export" Iran's successful religious revolution the world over—a priority that continues to animate the current Iranian leadership. Over the past two years, that support—ranging from economic aid to logistics to training—"had a direct impact on international efforts to promote peace, threatened economic stability in the Gulf and undermined the growth of democracy."[1]

ISLAMIST ACTIVITY

The Iranian regime's support for international terrorism predates the establishment of the Islamic Republic itself. In the 1960s and 1970s, while in exile in Iraq and in France, the Ayatollah Ruhollah Khomeini formulated his ideas about the need for a radical Islamic transformation in his home country, Iran, and of subsequently "exporting" this system of government throughout the Middle East and beyond.[2] In keeping with this thinking, Khomeini's manifesto, Islamic Government, extolled the virtues of "a victorious and triumphant Islamic political revolution" that would go on "to unite the Moslem nation, [and] to liberate [all] its lands."[3]

When the Ayatollah and his followers swept to power in Tehran in the spring of 1979, this principle became a cardinal regime priority. The preamble of the country's formative constitution, adopted in October 1979, outlines that the country's military henceforth "be responsible not only for guarding and preserving the frontiers of the country, but also for fulfilling the ideological mission of jihad in God's way; that is, extending the sovereignty of God's law throughout the world."[4] These words were backed by concrete regime action, with Khomeini consolidating the country's various radical militias into an ideological army known as the Islamic Revolutionary Guard Corps (IRGC, or *Pasdaran*), tasked with promoting his revolutionary message abroad, with violence if necessary.

The three-plus decades since have seen a consistent regime commitment to international terrorism. In the early years of the Islamic Republic, Iran is known to have ordered, orchestrated or facilitated a series of terrorist attacks in the Middle East, among them the 1983 U.S. Embassy and Marine Barracks bombings in Beirut, Lebanon; as well as abortive coup attempts and bombings in Bahrain, the United Arab Emirates and Kuwait.[5] These activities, and the rationale behind them, were reinforced by the outcome of the country's bloody eight-year war with Iraq, which strengthened its belief that radical proxies could serve as an attractive, low-cost substitute for direct military action. As a result, the principle of "exporting the revolution" remained a vibrant element of regime policy following the death of Khomeini in 1989. In the decade that followed Khomeini's death, the Islamic Republic bankrolled assassinations and terrorist acts on foreign soil, aided the infiltration of countries in Europe, Africa and Latin America by radical Islamic groups, and assisted irregulars in international conflict zones.[6]

In the aftermath of the September 11, 2001 terrorist attacks, the Islamic Republic chose to dramatically strengthen its links to international terrorism, redoubling its support for Hezbollah in Lebanon and Palestinian rejectionist groups, expanding its footprint in the Palestinian territories, maintaining at least low-level links to the al-Qaeda network, and becoming heavily involved in the bankrolling of radical militias (both Shi'ite and Sunni) in post-Saddam Iraq.

This support for terrorism, while ideologically driven, is rooted in pragmatism. While Khomeini's Islamic Revolution was a distinctly Shi'a one, in the more-than-three decades since its establishment, the Islamic Republic has embraced a more universalist conception of its international role, aspiring to serve as the vanguard of Islamic revolution worldwide.[7] The Iranian regime today funds a broad range of both Sunni and Shi'a groups throughout the greater Middle East and beyond. The critical determinant appears to be the degree to which these movements and organizations can reinforce Iran's leading role in the "Shi'a revival" now taking place in the Muslim world, and their shared animosity toward the West, most directly Israel and the United States.

The scope of this investment is enormous. U.S. officials have estimated that the Islamic Republic boasts "a nine-digit line item in its budget for support to terrorist organizations."[8] Before the outbreak of the "Arab Spring" in early 2011, that figure is believed to include more than $200 million per year for its principal terrorist proxy, Hezbollah;[9] $20 million to $30 million annually for Hamas, $2 million a year for the Palestinian Islamic Jihad, and, at least until recently, upward of $30 million a year for Iraqi insurgents.[10] These sums encompass direct financial assistance, training, logistics, arms and political support. (It is not yet apparent what effect, if any, the recent "Arab Spring" fervor has on Iran's budgeting for support of international terrorism).

The scope of Iran's support of violent Islamism is global in nature, and so is its reach. In recent years, it has included:

- *Rebuilding Hezbollah in Lebanon.* The month-long war between Hezbollah and Israel that took place in the summer of 2006 marked a turning point in the relationship between the Islamic Republic and its principal terrorist proxy. The Lebanese militia emerged from the conflict intact, but with a decimated arsenal and depleted military capability, and the Iranian regime has made reconstitution of the group a major priority. Today, as a result of this assistance, Hezbollah is estimated to possess some 50,000 artillery rockets and short-range missiles, making it the gravest immediate threat to the security of the State of Israel.[11]
- *Interference in Iraq.* In the wake of Saddam Hussein's overthrow in 2003, Iran made a major effort to expand its influence on the territory of the former Ba'athist state. It did so directly, through political support and funds to major Iraqi Shi'a political parties, and indirectly via the creation of an elaborate network of training compounds, safe houses and transit routes that have been used by the Iranian regime to train, equip and insert Iraqi militants into the fight against Coalition forces.[12] Since

2008, however, this effort has suffered significant setbacks, as the Iraqi government has moved against Iranian-supported Shi'a militias (such as the al-Mahdi Army of firebrand cleric Moqtada al-Sadr).[13] None of this, however, means that Tehran has ceased its involvement on Iraqi territory—or halted its attempts to alter Baghdad's political trajectory. U.S. officials have noted that Iranian activities in Iraq, although now more sporadic and indirect, remain a source of serious concern to the Iraqi government and other regional neighbors.[14]

- *Suporting insurgent activity in Afghanistan.* As Iranian activity in Iraq has diminished, its activism in Afghanistan has risen. Currently, the Islamic Republic serves as a significant source of support for the Taliban in Afghanistan in their fight against the U.S.-led Coalition and the fragile government of Hamid Karzai in Kabul. According to the U.S. Department of State, the IRGC Qods Force, Iran's premier paramilitary organization, in the past provided elements of the Taliban with training in "small unit tactics, small arms, explosives, and indirect fire weapons."[15] The Iranian regime also is implicated in the provision of Iranian-made armaments such as antipersonnel and anti-tank mines.[16] Through these avenues, analysts say, the Islamic Republic is attempting to exert leverage over the West as the United States and Europe contemplate more serious penalties for the Iranian regime's nuclear effort.[17] This activity is so pervasive that Britain's Foreign Office Minister, Alistair Burt, publicly condemned it as "hypocritical, two-faced and highly dangerous."[18]

- *Influencing Palestinian politics.* The unexpected electoral victory of the Hamas movement in the Palestinian Authority (PA) in January 2006 ushered in a new era for Iranian influence in the Palestinian Territories. Iran was instrumental in assisting the group's subsequent hostile takeover of the Gaza Strip in June 2007, and continues to provide the group with "training, weapons, and money," expanding its ability to strike Israel and facilitating the further radicalization of Palestinian politics.[19] Iran is also known to support other Palestinian rejectionist groups, such as the Palestinian Islamic Jihad (PIJ) and (to a lesser extent) the Popular Front for the Liberation of Palestine-General Command (PFLP-GC).[20] Most recently, as the Palestinian Authority government of Mahmoud Abbas moves toward a unilateral declaration of independence, the Iranian regime has accorded the PA much-sought-after international recognition, even as it has pressed for a continuation of resistance against Israel.[21]

- *Foreign subversion.* The overthrow of Saddam Hussein's regime in 2003 removed the Islamic Republic's chief conventional adversary and provided the Iranian regime with unexpected opportunities to project influence into the Persian Gulf. The years since have seen a steady growth in Iranian religious and sectarian activism, spurring mounting fears among

Iran's Sunni neighbors of the emergence of a destabilizing "Shi'a crescent" with Iran at its helm. Iran's influence has been amplified by the steady advances of its nuclear program, broadening the Islamic Republic's strategic reach and ideological appeal among the Middle East's Shi'ite communities. Over the past four years, Iran has waged an intensifying campaign of foreign subversion in Egypt,[22] Morocco,[23] and Yemen,[24] among other places.

Since January 2011, with the onset of the so-called "Arab Spring," Iranian activity in this sphere has intensified. Iranian officials have been quick to take credit for the anti-regime sentiment sweeping the region, and have depicted it as the belated product of the Ayatollah Khomeini's successful Islamic revolution in 1979. As a result, they have said, the "Arab Spring" marks the start of an "Islamic awakening" in which the Islamic Republic will inevitably play a leading role.[25] And Iran has backed these words with concrete action. Ongoing unrest among Bahrain's majority-Shi'ite population—and allegations of Iranian complicity—elicited a crackdown by Bahrain's ruling al-Khalifa family,[26] culminating in the mid-March incursion by a Saudi-led Gulf Cooperation Council security force intended in part as a hedge against Iran's asymmetric influence.[27] Iran likewise has been accused of aiding the regime of Bashar al-Assad in Damascus in suppressing the domestic protests currently underway in Ba'athist Syria.[28] Overall, observers say, a new "Cold War" is now underway between Riyadh and Tehran, as each country struggles to achieve ideological primacy in the shifting geopolitics of the region.[29]

ISLAMISM AND SOCIETY

While "exporting the revolution" was and remains a persistent regime objective, involvement and investment on the part of the Iranian population in this pursuit is far from universal. There is little empirical data to suggest that ordinary Iranians share the depth of their regime's commitment to the exportation of radical Islam. To the contrary, terrorism funding in Iran remains an elite—rather than popular—undertaking, directed through state institutions rather than non-governmental organizations, and overseen at an official, not a grassroots, level.

At times, Iran's involvement in the support of radical groups abroad has served as a significant bone of contention between the Iranian regime and its population. In the wake of Hezbollah's summer 2006 war with Israel, for example, Iran's extensive financial support for Lebanon's Shi'ites became a domestic flashpoint, with ordinary Iranians publicly questioning—and condemning—their government's skewed strategic priorities.[30]

Nevertheless, certain issues remain popular rallying points for the regime, chief among them the Israeli-Palestinian conflict. In a June 2007 survey of popular opinion within the Islamic Republic carried out by the polling group Terror Free Tomorrow, nearly two thirds of Iranians surveyed support financial assistance to Hamas and the Palestinian Islamic Jihad, although a far smaller number deemed this to be an important regime priority.[31] Hezbollah receives the same level of identification on the Iranian "street," as do Shi'a militias in Iraq.[32] This support, however, appears to be more rhetorical than operational, with little or no direct involvement of ordinary Iranian citizens in either the financing or operations of these groups, or of the governmental agencies that aid and abet them.

Support for radical Islamic causes is eroded by Iran's complex ethno/religious composition. Although the country is overwhelmingly (98 percent) Muslim and predominantly (89 percent) Shi'a, ethnically Persians hold only a razor-thin majority (51 percent) in Iran's population of almost 78 million. The remainder is Azeri (24 percent), Gilaki and Mazandarani (8 percent), Kurdish (7 percent), Arab (3 percent), Luri (2 percent), Baluchi (2 percent), Turkmen (2 percent), and a range of other minorities,[33] many of whom are systematically discriminated against by the Islamic Republic and feel little or limited allegiance to it. The base of support for Islamic radicalism—and other governmental priorities—in Iranian society is further eroded by the regime's persecution of religious minorities, which according has created "a threatening atmosphere for nearly all non-Shi'a religious groups" in the Islamic Republic.[34]

Social and economic malaise has similarly served to dilute identification with regime ideals and principles. The Islamic Republic was severely impacted by the 2008-2009 global economic crisis, and has since been burdened by unsustainable federal spending. Inflation remains severe, currently pegged at some 14.2 percent.[35] Unemployment is likewise rampant, officially estimated at 10 percent[36] but unofficially estimated at close to double that figure.[37] This has been compounded by widespread and severe underemployment in various sectors, caused by a chronic shortage of viable job opportunities—and an acute failure on the part of the Iranian government to create more. Related social indicators present an equally bleak picture. According to the United Nations, a fifth or more of Iran's population of nearly 78 million currently lives under the poverty line.[38] Prostitution is similarly out of control, forcing Iranian authorities to contemplate a range of remedial measures, from "temporary marriages" to sanctioned brothels known as "chastity houses."[39] Drug addiction is also rampant, fueled by the widespread opium trade taking place in neighboring Afghanistan; in 2005, the United Nations estimated Iran to have the highest rate of addiction in the world, with nearly three percent of the country's population addicted to opiates.[40] These factors have contributed to increasingly vocal discontent with the regime on the part of ordinary Iranians. In a 2008 opinion survey of Iranian attitudes, the Foundation for the Promotion of Democracy in Iran found that nearly 60 percent of all respondents believed Iran to be headed in the "wrong direction."[41]

That discontent found its expression in dramatic fashion in the summer of 2009, in the largest episode of unrest in the Islamic Republic's thirty-year history. The mass protests were catalyzed by the appearance of blatant institutional fraud in the re-election of Mahmoud Ahmadinejad in the country's June 2009 presidential election. In the weeks after the election, opposition to the Iranian regime gathered momentum, growing to encompass significant cracks in the previously-sound ideological consensus among Iran's clerical elites regarding the institutions and policies of Khomeini's Islamic Republic.

The Iranian regime responded with a major campaign to dominate the domestic media, intimidate regime opponents, and purge ideological dissent. These efforts included: tightening of already-strict controls over the Internet;[42] targeting of opposition leaders, both secular and religious;[43] and intimidation of Iranian opposition activists living abroad.[44] Since then, the Iranian government continues to suppress signs of domestic dissent. It has clamped down on independent journalists and bloggers, and shuttered numerous opposition media outlets.[45] It has floated proposals for the creation of a separate, Iran-centric World Wide Web.[46] Between March 2010 and 2011, the Iranian regime arrested more than 1,250 people "for participating in protests or for their political views."[47] And it has intensified its campaign of executions of domestic prisoners, including those incarcerated on political grounds, garnering the dubious distinction of becoming the world's most active executioner.[48]

Nevertheless, for the moment, the "Green Movement" appears to remain viable, if beleaguered. An official policy of persistent persecution directed at Green Movement activists—most prominently its titular leaders, former Prime Minister Mir Hossein Mousavi and former *majles* speaker Mehdi Kharroubi—strongly suggests that the Iranian government still believes its opposition to be a viable political force, as well as a threat to the integrity of the clerical state.[49] This anti-regime current, moreover, appears to have gained in intensity in recent months as a result of the "Arab Spring," with thousands of protestors demonstrating anew in Tehran and other major cities.[50] It is unclear as of this writing, however, whether this fervor can and will be sustained in coming months.

ISLAMISM AND THE STATE

Iran's support for Islamism is channeled through an elaborate infrastructure of institutions and governmental bodies tasked with the promotion of radical Islamic thought and action. These include:

The Islamic Revolutionary Guard Corps (IRGC, or Pasdaran). At home, the *Pasdaran*, in addition to its professional military duties, has become the guardian of the regime's ballistic missile and weapons of mass destruction programs.[51] The agenda of Iran's ideological army, however, is global in scope, and so is its reach. Over the past three decades, the *Pasdaran* has emerged as the shock troops of Iran's Islamic Revolution, training terrorist organizations both within Iran and in specialized training camps in places like Lebanon and Sudan, as well as providing assistance to radical movements and terrorist proxies throughout the Middle East, Africa, Europe and Asia via specialized paramilitary units.[52] The most notorious of these is the Qods Force, a crack military battalion formed in 1990 and dedicated to carrying out "extra-regional operations of the Islamic Revolutionary Guard Corps"—namely, terrorism and insurgency in the name of the Islamic Republic.[53] Since the 2003 ouster of Saddam Hussein, this unit has played a leading role in Iraq as part of what analysts have characterized as an "open-ended, resilient, and well-funded" covert effort on the part of the Iranian regime to extend its influence into the former Ba'athist state.[54] The Pasdaran also boasts a dedicated intelligence service, the Protection and Intelligence Department, or *Hefazat va Ettelaat-e Sepah-e Pasdaran.* Founded in 1980, it encompasses three main functions: intelligence in support of *Pasdaran* military operations; political operations at home and abroad; and support to the foreign terrorist operations of the Qods Force.[55]

Ministry of Intelligence and Security (MOIS). Controlled directly by Supreme Leader Ali Khamenei, the MOIS is used by Iran's ruling clergy to quash domestic opposition and carry out espionage against suspect members of the Iranian government.[56] Abroad, the MOIS plays a key role in planning and carrying out terrorist operations on foreign soil, using Iranian embassies and diplomatic missions as cover.[57] MOIS operatives are also known to operate abroad under unofficial identities—for example, as employees of Iran Air, Iran's official airline.[58] The MOIS conducts a variety of activities in support of the operations of Tehran's terrorist surrogates, ranging from financing actual operations to intelligence collection on potential targets. The Ministry also carries out independent operations, primarily against dissidents of the current regime in Tehran living in foreign countries, at the direction of senior Iranian officials.[59]

Ministry of Foreign Affairs. Iran's Foreign Ministry serves as an important enabler of the Iranian regime's international terrorist presence. Agents of the *Pasdaran* and MOIS often operate out of Iranian missions abroad, where they are stationed under diplomatic cover, complete with blanket diplomatic immunity. These agents—and through them Iranian foreign proxies—use the Ministry's auspices to untraceably obtain financing, weapons and intelligence from Tehran (for example, via diplomatic pouch).[60]

Cultural Affairs Ministry. Supplementing the role of the Foreign Affairs Ministry in exporting terrorism is Iran's Ministry of Culture and Guidance. Tasked with overseeing the cultural sections of Iranian foreign missions, as well as free-standing Iranian cultural centers, it facilitates *Pasdaran* infiltration of—and terrorist recruitment within—local Muslim populations in foreign nations.[61] The Ministry is particularly influential among majority Muslim countries like the former Soviet Republics, many of which share substantial cultural, religious and ideological bonds with Tehran. Between 1982 and 1992, the official in charge of the Ministry—and of its role in support of Iranian terror abroad—was Mohammed Khatami, Iran's future "reformist" president.

Basij. Formed during the early days of the Islamic Republic and trained by the *Pasdaran*, this militia represents the Iranian regime's premier tool of domestic terror. During the eight years of the Iran-Iraq war, the organization's cadres were the Islamic Republic's cannon fodder, selected to clear minefields and launch "human wave" attacks against Iraqi forces.[62] With the end of the conflict with Iraq, the role of the *Basij* was reoriented, and the organization became the watchdog of Iranian society. Today, it is used by the ayatollahs to quell domestic anti-regime protests and eradicate "un-Islamic" behavior. Their role ranges from enforcing modest dress to gathering intelligence on university students, which is handed over to the regime's undercover police.[63] There are reported to be as many as 10 million registered *Basij* members, though not all are on active service.[64] The *Basij* also plays an important supporting role in Iran's state sponsorship of terror. It is known to be active in training anti-Israeli forces, including carrying out maneuvers designed to ready Hezbollah and assorted Palestinian militants for guerrilla warfare. One such exercise, in the fall of 2000, reportedly involved some 90,000 men and 20,000 women.[65]

Domestic paramilitaries (guruh-I fishar). Supplementing the role of the *Basij* are the numerous vigilante or "pressure" groups that are harnessed by the Iranian government. Though officially independent, these gangs actually operate under the patronage of government officials, the *Pasdaran* or the MOIS, and target internal opposition to the clerical regime.[66] The most famous is the *Ansar-i Hezbollah*, which was responsible for fomenting the July 1999 crisis at Tehran University that led to the bloody governmental crackdown on student opposition forces.

Bonyads. These sprawling socio-religious foundations, which are overseen only by Iran's Supreme Leader, serve as conduits for the Islamic Republic's cause of choice. Arguably the most important is the *Bonyad-e Mostazafan* (Foundation of the Oppressed), a sprawling network of an estimated 1,200 firms created in 1979 with seed money from the Shah's coffers.[67] Another is the Bonyad-e Shahid (Martyrs' Foundation), an enormous conglomerate of industrial, agricultural, construction and commercial companies with some 350 offices and tens of thousands of employees.[68] The sums controlled by these organs are enormous: more than 30 percent of Iran's national GDP, and as much as two-thirds of the country's non-oil GDP.[69] And while many of their functions are legitimate, they are also used by Iran's religious leaders to funnel money to their pet causes, from financing domestic repression to arming radical groups abroad.

Notably, however, even as Iran remains complicit in the sponsorship of international terrorism, it is itself the target of violent activity by two separate and distinct groups. The first is the *Mujahideen e-Khalq* (MeK or MKO), also known as the People's Mujahideen Organization of Iran, or PMOI. The MeK is the most prominent and well-organized opposition group to the ruling Iranian government in existence today.[70] A guerrilla group of radical Marxist-Islamist ideology, the MeK was established in the 1960s in opposition to the government of Shah Mohammed Reza Pahlavi.[71] Following the overthrow of the Shah, however, the MeK found itself shut out of the Iranian regime's power structures. By the early 1980s, the organization moved into opposition, and became an active target of the Iranian security forces. As a result, it relocated to neighboring Iraq, which subsequently became its principal source of financial and political support, as well as the organization's major base of operations in its periodic attacks against the Iranian regime.[72] According to the U.S. Department of State, the MeK also assumed a domestic role, assisting the Iraqi government in "suppressing the Shia and Kurdish uprisings in northern and southern Iraq" in 1991 and thereafter playing a part in Iraq's internal security services.[73] In exchange, the regime of Saddam Hussein became the source of all of the MeK's military assistance, and the bulk of its economic revenue—a situation that would endure until the overthrow of the Iraqi regime by Coalition forces in the Spring of 2003.[74] During the 1990s, this support was estimated to be some $7 million monthly.[75] The extent of this support was made public in January 2004, when the Iraqi daily *Al-Mada* published a list of 270 beneficiaries of oil allocations from the regime of Saddam Hussein.[76] That list revealed that the MeK had been a major recipient of oil vouchers from the Iraqi government.[77] All told, the MeK is believed to have received more than 38 million barrels of oil from the Iraqi government in the four years before the U.S.-led invasion of Iraq—theoretically generating profits of more than $16 million.[78] Since the overthrow of the Saddam Hussein regime, the MeK has occupied a unique role. The group, while still listed as a Foreign Terrorist Organization by the U.S. State Department, signed a voluntary disarmament agreement with Coalition forces in July 2004, in exchange for which the organization has been granted the status of "protected persons" under the Geneva Conventions by the United States.[79] As a result of that arrangement, its roughly 3,000 members are now sequestered at the group's Camp Ashraf base in Iraq's Diyala province, under protection by Coalition forces and subsequently Iraqi military units.

The second, smaller group is the Free Life Party of Kurdistan, or PJAK. Led by Iranian-born German national Abdul Rahman Haji Ahmadi, PJAK is a violent Kurdish nationalist group which has carried out attacks on Iran from strongholds in neighboring Iraq since its formation in 2004. Among the most prominent of these were the organization's raids on Iranian military installations in March 2006, which cumulatively claimed the lives of some 24 Iranian soldiers.[80] As of 2008, the organization was estimated to have killed more than 100 Iranian soldiers as a result of its activities.[81] PJAK claims to seek "democratic change" and characterizes its actions as a "defense" against Iranian state repression of its Kurdish minority.[82]

The Iranian regime has sought to actively combat both of these entities. Regime security forces have clashed repeatedly with members of PJAK, arresting multiple group members as part of ongoing counterterrorism operations.[83] They have also actively sought to persecute individuals thought to be affiliated with the MeK, including through the arrest and detention of family members of those now resident in Camp Ashraf in Iraq.[84] And with the United States now withdrawing from Iraq, Iran has seized the opportunity to press the Shi'a-dominated government in Baghdad for the rendition of MeK members, or at least their ouster from the country. These efforts have met with some success; in April 2011, apparently at Iran's behest, the government of Iraqi prime minister Nouri al-Maliki launched a major crackdown on the group.[85] It is currently unclear whether this pressure will result in the lasting eviction of the MeK from Camp Ashraf, where it has been based since the 1980s.

ENDNOTES

[1] "Chapter 3: State Sponsors of Terrorism," in U.S. Department of State, Office of the Coordinator for Counterterrorism, *Country Reports on Terrorism 2009* (Washington, DC: U.S. Department of State, August 5, 2010), http://www.state.gov/s/ct/rls/crt/2009/140889.htm.

[2] Emmanuel Sivan, *Radical Islam: Medieval Theology and Modern Politics* (New Haven: Yale University Press, 1985), 188–207.

[3] Ruhollah Khomeini, *Islamic Government* (New York: Manor Books, 1979).

[4] Preamble of the Constitution of the Islamic Republic of Iran, http://www.oefre.unibe.ch/law/icl/ir00000_.html.

[5] Robin Wright, *Sacred Rage: The Wrath of Militant Islam* (New York: Simon & Schuster, 1986), 111–21.

[6] "Iranian Terrorism in Bosnia and Croatia," *Iran Brief*, March 3, 1997, http://www.lexis-nexis.com; Mike O'Connor, "Spies for Iranians Are Said to Gain a Hold in Bosnia," *New York Times*, November 28, 1997, 1.

[7] Vali Nasr, *The Shi'a Revival: How Conflicts within Islam will Shape the Future* (New York: W.W. Norton & Company, 2006), 137.

[8] Under Secretary of the Treasury for Terrorism and Financial Intelligence Stuart Levey, Remarks before the 5th Annual Conference on Trade, Treasury, and Cash Management in the Middle East, Abu Dhabi, United Arab Emirates, March 7, 2007, http://uae.usembassy.gov/remarks_of_stuart_levey_.html.

[9] "Chapter 3: State Sponsors of Terrorism" in U.S. Department of State, Office of the Coordinator for Counterterrorism, *Country Reports on Terrorism 2008* (Washington, DC: U.S. Department of State, April 30, 2009), http://www.state.gov/s/ct/rls/crt/2008/122436.htm.

[10] Rachel Ehrenfeld, *Funding Evil: How Terrorism Is Financed—And How To Stop It* (Chicago: Basic Books, 2003), 125; "Hamas," Council on Foreign Relations *Backgrounder*, June 8, 2007, http://www.cfr.org/publication/8968/; Program on Humanitarian Policy and Conflict Research, Harvard University, "Palestinian Islamic Jihad of Islamic Jihad Movement in Palestine (PIJ) (Harakat al-Jihad al-Islami fi Filastin)," n.d., http://www.armed-groups.org/6/section.aspx/ViewGroup?id=69; Joshua Partlow, "U.S.: Iran, Hezbollah Training Iraqi Militants," *Washington Post*, July 2, 2007, A08; "Chapter 3: State Sponsors of Terrorism" in U.S. Department of State, *Country Reports on Terrorism 2008*.

[11] "Hezbollah has 50,000 Rockets: Report," Agence France Presse, December 7, 2010, http://www.spacewar.com/reports/Hezbollah_has_50000_rockets_report_999.html.

[12] Joseph Felter and Brian Fishman, "Iranian Strategy in Iraq: Politics and 'Other Means,'" Combating Terrorism Center at West Point

Occasional Paper, October 13, 2008, http://ctc.usma.edu/Iran_Iraq/CTC_Iran_Iraq_Final.pdf.

[13] For a detailed review of this trend, see the *Almanac's* chapter on Iraq.

[14] "Petraeus Says Iran Still Supporting Iraqi Militants," *WashingtonTV*, June 1, 2009, http://televisionwashington.com/floater_article1.aspx?lang=en&t=3&id=10873&tr=y&auid=4924033.

[15] "Chapter 3: State Sponsors of Terrorism" in U.S. Department of State, *Country Reports on Terrorism 2008*.

[16] Ron Synovitz, "Afghanistan: Official Says Iranian Mines Found in Taliban Commander's House," *Radio Free Europe/Radio Liberty*, January 25, 2008, http://www.rferl.org/content/article/1079394.html.

[17] Ben Farmer, "Iranian Weapons Getting Through to Taliban," *Telegraph* (London), June 8, 2009, http://www.telegraph.co.uk/news/worldnews/asia/afghanistan/5477283/Iranian-weapons-getting-through-to-Taliban.html.

[18] Allan Urry, "Iran's Illegal Arms Trade: 'Hypocritical and Dangerous,'" BBC (London), June 7, 2011, http://www.bbc.co.uk/news/world-13545621.

[19] "Chapter 3: State Sponsors of Terrorism" in U.S. Department of State, *Country Reports on Terrorism 2008*.

[20] Ibid.

[21] On recognizing a Palestinian state, see "Palestinians Ask Iran to Open Embassy in Gaza," Fars News Agency (Tehran), May 11, 2011, http://english.farsnews.com/newstext.php?nn=9002211125; On Iran's continued support for Palestinian rejectionism, see "Iran Renews Call for Free Referendum in Palestine," Fars News Agency (Tehran), June 7, 2011, http://english.farsnews.com/newstext.php?nn=9003174296.

[22] The historically-tense relations between Iran and Egypt deteriorated precipitously during 2008-2010, spurred in large part by Egyptian fears of Iranian internal meddling. These worries were showcased in spring of 2009, when Egyptian authorities arrested a total of twenty-six individuals suspected of carrying out espionage for Hezbollah, and of plotting to carry out terrorist attacks within Egypt. The suspects were subsequently formally charged with plotting subversion against the Egyptian state. "Egypt Charges 26 'Hizbullah Spies,'" *Jerusalem Post*, July 26, 2009, http://www.jpost.com/servlet/Satellite?cid=1248277893866&pagename=JPost%2FJPArticle%2FShowFull.

[23] The same period (2008-2010) saw a steep decline in diplomatic relations between Iran and Morocco, with the Moroccan government formally severing ties in the spring of 2009 over allegations that the Islamic Republic was using its diplomatic mission in Rabat to spread Shi'a Islam in the North African state. (Economic relations between the two countries have continued, however.) "Morocco Severs Relations with Iran," *Al-Jazeera* (Doha), March 7, 2009, http://eng-

lish.aljazeera.net/news/africa/2009/03/2009370303221419.html; "Morocco to Continue Iranian Oil Imports," *Alexander's Gas & Oil Connections* 14, iss. 8 (May 26, 2009), http://www.gasandoil.com/goc/news/nta92197.htm.

[24] Iran has been accused for years of aiding Yemen's al-Houthi rebels in their separatist struggle against the government of Ali Abdullah Saleh in Sana'a, with at least circumstantial evidence to that effect. For an in-depth overview of the al-Houthi secessionist struggle (and Iran's role in it), see Ian Illych Martinez, "The Yemeni Vortex," *The Journal of International Security Affairs* no. 19, Fall/Winter 2010, http://www.securityaffairs.org/issues/2010/19/martinez.php.

[25] See, for example, "Lawmaker: Uprisings in Region Promising Birth of Islamic Middle-East," Fars News Agency (Tehran), February 5, 2011, http://english.farsnews.com/newstext.php?nn=8911161168.

[26] Simeon Kerr, "Police Crack Down on Bahrain's 'Day of Rage,'" *Financial Times*, February 14, 2011, http://www.ft.com/cms/s/db18b6aa-3836-11e0-8257-00144feabdc0,Authorised=false.html?_i_location=http%3A%2F%2Fwww.ft.com%2Fcms%2Fs%2F0%2Fdb18b6aa-3836-11e0-8257-00144feabdc0.html&_i_referer=http%3A%2F%2Fcachef.ft.com%2Fcms%2Fs%2F0%2F090f291a-3f92-11e0-a1ba-00144feabdc0%2Cs01%3D1.html#axzz1ErCyxIfm.

[27] Bill Spindle and Margaret Coker, "The New Cold War," *Wall Street Journal*, April 16, 2011, http://online.wsj.com/article/SB1000142405274870411640457626274410648816.html.

[28] Amro Ahmad, "Iranian Forces in Syria to Help al-Assad – Opposition," *Al-Sharq al-Awsat* (London), May 15, 2011, http://www.asharq-e.com/news.asp?section=1&id=25193.

[29] Spindle and Coker, "The New Cold War."

[30] See, for example, Azadeh Moaveni, "The Backlash against Iran's Role in Lebanon," *Time*, August 31, 2006, http://www.time.com/time/world/article/0,8599,1515755,00.html.

[31] Terror Free Tomorrow, "Polling Iranian Public Opinion: An Unprecedented Nationwide Survey of Iran," July 2007, http://www.terrorfreetomorrow.org/upimagestft/TFT%20Iran%20Survey%20Report.pdf.

[32] Ibid.

[33] U.S. Central Intelligence Agency, "Iran," *World Factbook*, May 26, 2011, https://www.cia.gov/library/publications/the-world-factbook/geos/ir.html.

[34] U.S. Department of State, Bureau of Democracy, Human Rights and Labor, *International Religious Freedom Report 2008*, n.d., http://www.state.gov/g/drl/rls/irf/2008/108482.htm.

[35] "Inflation Rate Hits 14.2%," *Tehran Times*, June 6, 2011, http://www.tehrantimes.com/index_View.asp?code=241940.

[36] "Iran's Unemployment Rate Hits 10%: Labor Minister,"

Zawya, April 1, 2011, http://www.zawya.com/Story.cfm/sidZA-WYA20110402053101/Iran%27s%20unemployment%20rate%20h its%2010%25%3A%20Labor%20minister.

[37] "Conflicting Reports on Iran's Unemployment Rate," *Radio Zamaneh*, April 7, 2011, http://www.payvand.com/news/11/apr/1062.html.

[38] United Nations Childrens' Fund, "At a Glance: Iran, Islamic Republic Of," n.d., http://www.unicef.org/infobycountry/iran.html.

[39] Ibid.; Nazila Fathi, "To Regulate Prostitution, Iran Ponders Brothels," *New York Times*, August 28, 2002, http://query.nytimes.com/gst/fullpage.html?res=9404E0DE1F3CF93BA1575BC0A9649C8B63.

[40] As cited in Karl Vick, "Opiates of the Iranian People," *Washington Post*, September 23, 2005, A01; See also "US to Reverse Afghan Opium Strategy," *Al-Jazeera* (Doha), June 28, 2009, http://english.aljazeera.net/news/asia/2009/06/200962815525664398.html.

[41] "Quarterly Iran General Population Poll," Foundation for the Promotion of Democracy, June 13-17, 2008, Excerpts available at http://www.ffpd.org/The_Work_Of_FPD.html.

[42] "Iran to Monitor Cyberspace to Fight Offenses," *Press TV* (Tehran), July 20, 2009, http://edition.presstv.ir/detail/101138.html.

[43] See, for example, Human Rights Watch, "Iran: Stop 'Framing' Government Critics," July 21, 2009, http://www.hrw.org/en/news/2009/07/21/iran-stop-framing-government-critics.

[44] Farnaz Fassihi, "Iran's Crackdown Goes Global," *Wall Street Journal*, December 3, 2009, http://online.wsj.com/article/SB125978649644673331.html.

[45] Kaveh Ghoreishi, "No Newspapers Left for Banning," *Rooz* (Tehran), May 5, 2011, http://www.roozonline.com/english/news3/newsitem/article/no-newspapers-left-for-banning.html.

[46] "Iran: Tehran announces new 'halal' Islamic internet," AKI (Rome), April 15, 2011, http://www.adnkronos.com/IGN/Aki/English/CultureAndMedia/Iran-Tehran-announces-new-halal-Islamic-internet_311908244227.html.

[47] "'More Than 1,000 Political Arrests in Iran' in Past Year," *Radio Free Europe/Radio Liberty*, March 23, 2011, http://www.rferl.org/content/more_than_1000_political_arrests_iran/2347174.html.

[48] "Amnesty: Iran has most Executions," United Press International, March 28, 2011, http://www.upi.com/Top_News/Special/2011/03/28/Amnesty-Iran-has-most-executions/UPI-39721301330385/.

[49] For an in-depth analysis, see Ilan Berman, "Iran's Die-Hard Democrats," *Wall Street Journal Europe*, January 11, 2011, http://online.wsj.com/article/SB10001424052748703779704576073682934244852.html.

[50] Farnaz Fassihi, "Tehran Beats Back New Protests," *Wall Street Jour-*

nal, February 15, 2011, http://online.wsj.com/article/SB1000142405
274870358480457614379235177466.html.

[51] Mohammad Mohaddessin, *Islamic Fundamentalism: The New Global Threat* (Washington: Seven Locks Press, 1993), 132-136.

[52] See, for example, Michael Eisenstadt, *Iranian Military Power: Capabilities and Intentions* (Washington: Washington Institute for Near East Policy, 1996), 70-72.

[53] Mohaddessin, *Islamic Fundamentalism*, 102.

[54] Michael Knights, "Iran's Ongoing Proxy War in Iraq," Washington Institute for Near East Policy *Policywatch* 1492, March 16, 2009, http://www.washingtoninstitute.org/templateC05.php?CID=3029.

[55] "Rev. Guards Intelligence," *Iran Brief*, January 6, 1997, http://www.lexis-nexis.com.

[56] "Ministry of Intelligence and Security [MOIS]: Vezarat-e Ettela'at va Amniat-e Keshvar VEVAK," globalsecurity.org, February 19, 2006, http://www.globalsecurity.org/intell/world/iran/vevak.htm.

[57] Eisenstadt, *Iranian Military Power*, 70.

[58] Federation of American Scientists, "Ministry of Intelligence and Security [MOIS]: Organization," http://www.fas.org/irp/world/iran/vevak/org.htm.

[59] See, for example, "Khamene'i Ordered Khobar Towers Bombing, Defector Says," *Iran Brief*, August 3, 1998, http://www.lexis-nexis.com; American intelligence officials have long maintained that Iranian terrorism is authorized at the highest official levels. See, for example, CIA Director R. James Woolsey, "Challenges to Peace in the Middle East," remarks before the Washington Institute for Near East Policy's Wye Plantation Conference, Queenstown, Maryland, September 23, 1994, http://www.washingtoninstitute.org/templateC07.php?CID=66.

[60] Eisenstadt, *Iranian Military Power*, 71.

[61] Ibid.; Mohaddessin, *Islamic Fundamentalism*, 101-102.

[62] Drew Middleton, "5 Years of Iran-Iraq War: Toll May Be Near a Million," *New York Times*, September 23, 1985, 4.

[63] Geneive Abdo, "Islam's Warriors Scent Blood," *Observer* (London), July 18, 1999, 26.

[64] Angus McDowall, "Tehran Deploys Islamic Vigilantes to Attack Protesters," *Independent* (London), July 11, 2003, 12.

[65] "Iran Trains Palestinians, Hizbullah in Military Drills," Jerusalem Post, October 20, 2000, 6A.

[66] For more on the guruh-i fishar, see Michael Rubin, *Into the Shadows: Radical Vigilantes in Khatami's Iran* (Washington: Washington Institute for Near East Policy, 2001).

[67] Robert D. Kaplan, "A Bazaari's World," *Atlantic Monthly* 277, iss. 3 (1996), 28.

[68] Wilfried Buchta, *Who Rules Iran? The Structure of Power in the*

Islamic Republic (Washington: Washington Institute for Near East Policy – Konrad Adenauer Stiftung, 2000), 75.

[69] Ibid.; See also Kenneth Katzman, Statement before the Joint Economic Committee of the United States Congress, July 25, 2006.

[70] Since October 1997, pursuant to the *Anti-Terrorism and Effective Death Penalty Act of 1996*, it has also been a designated Foreign Terrorist Organization under U.S. law.

[71] International Policy Institute for Counterterrorism, "Mujahedin-e Khalq Organization (MEK or MKO)," no date given. Available online at http://www.ict.org.il/.

[72] United States Department of State, Office of the Coordinator for Counterterrorism, *Patterns of Global Terrorism 2003* (Washington, DC: U.S. Department of State, June 2004), 129.

[73] United States Department of State, Office of the Coordinator for Counterterrorism, *Patterns of Global Terrorism 2001* (Washington, DC: U.S. Department of State, May 2002), 101. The MeK has publicly denied these charges.

[74] U.S. Department of State, Office of the Coordinator for Counterterrorism, *Country Reports on Terrorism 2004* (Washington, DC: U.S. Department of State, April 2005), 105.

[75] Cited in Charles Recknagel, "Iran: Washington Says Iranian Opposition Helping with Iraqi Security Operations," *Radio Free Europe/Radio Liberty*, May 23, 2002, http://www.rferl.org/features/2002/05/23052002084552.asp.

[76] *Al-Mada* (Baghdad), as cited in "The Beneficiaries of Saddam's Oil Vouchers: The List of 270," Middle East Media Research Institute *Inquiry and Analysis* no. 160, January 29, 2004 http://memri.org/bin/articles.cgi?Page=countries&Area=iraq&ID=IA16004.

[77] Ibid.

[78] Ibidem.

[79] Scott Peterson, "Why the US Granted 'Protected' Status to Iranian Terrorists," *Christian Science Monitor*, July 29, 2004, 7.

[80] "Tehran Faces Growing Kurdish Opposition," *Washington Times*, April 3, 2006, http://www.washingtontimes.com/news/2006/apr/3/20060403-125601-8453r/.

[81] Stefan Buchen, John Goetz and Sven Röbel, "Germany Concerned About PJAK Activities," *Der Spiegel* (Hamburg), April 18, 2008, http://www.spiegel.de/international/germany/0,1518,547211,00.html.

[82] "Tehran Faces Growing Kurdish Opposition," *Washington Times*, April 3, 2006, http://www.washingtontimes.com/news/2006/apr/3/20060403-125601-8453r/.

[83] See, for example, "4 Members of PJAK Terrorist Group Arrested in Iran," Fars News Agency (Tehran), November 30, 2010, http://english.farsnews.com/newstext.php?nn=8909091200.

[84] Amnesty International, "Iran: Arbitrary Arrests, Torture and Executions Continue," May 20, 2011, http://www.amnesty.org/en/library/asset/MDE13/051/2011/en/ad9b1ffd-7c9f-475c-9ace-c1e712a29f60/mde13051201 1en.html.

[85] "Iraq Forces Attack Iranian PMOI Rebels at Camp Ashraf," BBC (London), April 8, 2011, http://www.bbc.co.uk/news/world-middle-east-13011469.

IRAQ

QUICK FACTS

Population: 29,671,605

Area: 438,317 sq km

Ethnic groups: Arab 75-80%, Kurdish 15-20%, Turkoman, Assyrian, or other 5%

Religions: Muslim 97% (Shi'a 60-65%, Sunni 32-37%), Christian or other 3%

Government type: parliamentary democracy

GDP (official exchange rate): $70.93 Billion

Map and quick facts courtesy of the CIA World Factbook (last updated June 2010)

Iraq has a history of both secular and Islamist currents. Shi'a and Sunni Islamist movements formed in Iraq largely in response to Saddam Hussein's secular nationalist Ba'athist regime. Though many of these Islamist parties existed in exile or in hiding for much of 1980s and 1990s, they re-emerged after the fall of Saddam in 2003. Since that time, both Sunni and Shi'a Islamist parties have played an important role in Iraq's political system, though the 2010 parliamentary election saw the rise of dramatic secular political coalitions. Both Sunni and Shi'a radical Islamist militant groups are also active in Iraq, and have fueled insurgent activity and sectarian violence there, although operations by U.S. and Iraqi forces since 2007 have dramatically reduced their capabilities. As Iraq's nascent democratic system evolves, these secular and Islamist forces continue to vie for influence and power.

ISLAMIST ACTIVITY

Islamist activity in Iraq today takes three distinct forms, defined along both ethnic and confessional lines.

Shi'a Groups

The main Shi'a parties in Iraq are the *Dawa* Party (also known as *Dawa Islamiya*, or the Islamic *Dawa* Party), the Sadrist Trend, and the Islamic Supreme Council of Iraq (ISCI, formerly the Supreme Council for the Islamic Revolution in Iraq). Smaller Islamist groups include the National Reform Trend (led by former Prime Minister Ibrahim al-Jaafari); the *Fadhila* (Islamic Virtue) Party; and *Dawa Tanzim* (an offshoot of the main Dawa party).

The *Dawa* Party is the oldest Shi'a Islamist party in Iraq, having emerged in the late 1950s or early 1960s in response to the spread of Arab socialist and communist movements.[1] Grand Ayatollah Mohammed Baqir al-Sadr, a distinguished Shi'a scholar, is widely credited as being *Dawa's* founder.[2] *Dawa* emphasizes the promotion of Islamic values and ethics, but believes the right to govern was distinct from the juridical function of religious authorities, and that both should be subsumed under constitutional mechanisms.[3] *Dawa* was the leading Shi'a Islamist opposition party of the 1970s and 1980s, and was, therefore, fiercely persecuted by Saddam Hussein's Ba'athist regime. Throughout this time, members of *Dawa* remained active either in exile or in hiding. The main branches of *Dawa* existed in Syria, Iran, and the United Kingdom. Since 2003, *Dawa* has re-emerged as one of the main Shi'a political groups in Iraq, and prominent members include Prime Minister Nuri al-Maliki. Unlike its main Shi'a rivals, however, *Dawa* does not have its own militia and was therefore seen as a weaker party. Rather, from 2006, when he was selected as a compromise candidate for Prime Minister, until 2008, Maliki relied heavily on other Shi'a factions such as ISCI and the Sadrists for political support.[4] In recent years, however, Maliki and his allies have used the position and resources of the Prime Minister's office to greatly expand *Dawa's* influence in Iraqi politics and society, much to the alarm of rival groups.[5]

The Sadrist Trend is a nationalist religious movement founded by the Shi'a cleric Mohammed Sadeq al-Sadr in the 1990s. The movement gained widespread support from the poor Shi'a communities across southern Iraq and in Baghdad, which were drawn to its emphasis on economic and social relief for the poor and a return to traditional Islamic law and customs.[6] The Sadrists believe that religious leaders should take an active role in political and social affairs—a position that is closely aligned with the current Iranian regime, but distinguished by the desire for an Iraqi Supreme Leader (rather than simply allegiance to the Iranian Supreme Leader, Ayatollah Ali Khamenei).[7] Sadeq al-Sadr was assassinated by Saddam Hussein's regime in 1999 and much of the movement's leadership went into hiding, but the Sadrist Trend re-emerged after the 2003 invasion of Iraq under the leadership of his son, Muqtada al-Sadr. The Sadrists have vehemently opposed the presence of U.S. forces in Iraq. The Sadrist Trend and its *Jaysh al-Mahdi* (JAM) militia were a powerful force at the height of sectarian violence in Iraq from 2004 to 2007. The movement lost considerable influence as U.S. and Iraqi forces significantly degraded JAM during security offensives in 2007 and 2008, after which time Muqtada al-Sadr announced that JAM would formally be disbanded and his movement reorganized.[8] Since that time, the Sadrists have restructured the movement, emphasizing its political and social programs.[9] This has allowed them to win significant representation in the national government, as well as in key provincial governments in southern Iraq. The Sadrists nevertheless maintain a militant wing, called the Promised Day Brigade, which receives Iranian support and targets U.S. forces in Iraq.[10]

Until early 2007, ISCI was known as the Supreme Council for the Islamic Revolution in Iraq (SCIRI).[11] SCIRI and its militia, the Badr Corps, were founded in Iran in the early 1980s as an Iraqi umbrella group to fight with Iran against Saddam's regime.[12] SCIRI was led by Ayatollah Baqir al-Hakim until his assassination by al-Qaeda in August 2003. Subsequently, from 2003 to 2009, the organization was led by the Abd al-Aziz al-Hakim, Baqir's brother, and ISCI was a dominant political force in Iraq during this time. Under pressure to disband its militia in 2003, SCIRI announced that the Badr Corps would be transformed into a political entity known as the Badr Organization.[13] Still, many Badr members were incorporated into the Iraqi Security Forces, where they retained a lethal capability.[14] The group has been closely aligned with Iran, and as a result does not enjoy broad support from Iraqis. In an effort to distance itself from Iran, the organization changed its name to ISCI in 2007 and shifted its primary religious allegiance to Grand Ayatollah Ali al-Sistani.[15] Sistani, a quietist who believes religious leaders should not be involved in the administration of the state, is the most revered Shi'a cleric in Iraq and is the head of the Najaf hawza, or seminary. After the death of Abd al-Aziz al-Hakim in August 2009, his son, Ammar al-Hakim, assumed control of the movement.[16] As discussed below, despite a growing divergence between ISCI and Iran, ISCI has seen its political influence wane in recent years, largely on account of the continued perception of close ties with the Iranian regime, its rejection of Iraqi Islamist exile parties, and the group's inability to broaden its constituency and check the power of its political rivals.

The Shi'a political parties differ in their views of the role of federalism in Iraq. Prime Minister Maliki and his Dawa party have favored the creation of a strong central government in Baghdad. Like Dawa, the Sadrist Trend supports a strong central Iraqi government, but opposes an American presence in Iraq. ISCI has generally favored a weaker central government, with power diffused at the provincial or regional level. Though ISCI had previously pushed for the creation of a southern Shi'ite federation, it is no longer a vocal advocate of such a measure, perhaps because of its waning influence within the southern provincial governments.

Dawa and the Sadrist Trend have emerged from the 2009 provincial elections and the 2010 parliamentary elections as the predominant Shi'a political forces in Iraq. This has come at the expense of ISCI/Badr, which played a dominant role in the Iraqi government from 2003 to 2008 but has seen much of its influence and political power eroded in recent years. In response to growing popular sentiment, other Shi'a parties, including *Dawa* and ISCI, sought to style themselves as nationalist, secular, cross-sectarian movements.[17] This was particularly evident during the formation of electoral coalitions in the lead-up to the 2010 parliamentary election. Notably, Prime Minister Maliki's Dawa Party abstained from joining the main Shi'a coalition, the Iraqi National Alliance, and instead created a separate electoral list, the State of Law Coalition.[18] Despite secular and nationalist rhetoric surrounding the 2010 parliamentary vote, sectarian identity still plays an important role in Iraqi politics. During the prolonged negotiations to form the government, the desire to maintain unity among the Shi'a Islamist parties trumped efforts to create meaningful cross-sectarian or secular alliances.

In addition to the Sadrists' Promised Day Brigade, two other Iranian-backed Shi'a militant groups are also active in Iraq. They are Kataib Hezbollah (KH, or the Hezbollah Brigades) and Asaib Ahl al-Haq (AAH, or the League of the Righteous). KH emerged in 2007, and since that time has conducted numerous attacks on U.S. and Iraqi forces.[19] While little is known of the KH leadership, one known adviser is Abu Mahdi al-Muhandis, who is closely aligned with Iran's Islamic Revolutionary Guard Corps-Qods Force (IRGC-QF), and who has operated militant networks in Iraq and elsewhere for decades.[20] KH is the most elite of the Iranian-backed groups in Iraq, and has used advanced tactics and systems, including Improvised Rocket-Assisted Mortars (IRAMs).[21] AAH is an offshoot of JAM, which was formed following the split between Muqtada al-Sadr and several of his deputies, most notably Qais Khazali.[22] Khazali, who was captured by Coalition forces in March 2007 but released as part of a prisoner exchange in January 2010, is the leader of AAH.[23] Both AAH and KH are known to have received extensive support from Iran's IRGC-QF, including training, funding, and supplies.[24]

Sunni Groups
The Sunni political landscape has also shifted dramatically since 2009, as the influence of Islamist parties has waned in favor of more secular, nationalist groups.

The primary Sunni Islamist political party has been the Iraqi Islamic Party (IIP). The IIP has its earliest roots in mid-1940s or early 1950s, when Mohammed al-Sawwaf, an Iraqi studying in Egypt, met Muslim Brotherhood founder Hassan al-Banna.[25] Upon his return to Iraq, al-Sawwaf and another activist, Amjad al-Zahawi Mahmood, founded an Iraqi organization modeled on the Muslim Brotherhood, known as the Islamic Brotherhood

Society.[26] Later, in 1960, the Iraqi Islamic Party was formally established following the decision by Abdul-Karim Qassem's government to allow the formation of political parties in Iraq.[27] Following the overthrow of Qassem's government by the Ba'ath Party in 1963, the IIP was violently suppressed but continued its operations clandestinely and in exile.[28] Ayad al-Samarraie, who had been the Secretary General of the IIP since 1970, fled Iraq in 1980.[29] Following the fall of Saddam Hussein's Ba'athist regime in 2003, many IIP leaders, including al-Samarraie, returned to Iraq and the party re-emerged. In the December 2005 parliamentary election, the IIP ran as the leading party of a Sunni coalition known as *Tawafuq* (Iraqi Accord Front) and won 44 seats in the 275-member parliament. From 2005 to early 2009, *Tawafuq* (and therefore the IIP) was the dominant Sunni political presence in the parliament, though it was seen by many Sunni Iraqis as an exile party that did not represent their interests. By early 2009, *Tawafuq* began to disintegrate as its constituent parties left the coalition during the debate over the selection of the parliamentary speaker.[30] The IIP is currently led by Osama al-Tikriti, with Ayad al-Samarraie as his deputy.

In recent years, the IIP has seen its influence wane as a variety of other Sunni political parties have emerged. In the 2010 parliamentary election, the vast majority of Sunni political entities joined the *Iraqiyah* List, a secular nationalist coalition led by former Prime Minister Ayad Allawi. The IIP was the only political party that ran under the *Tawafuq* banner, and it saw its representation in the parliament shrink from 44 to just 6 seats. Today, most Sunnis are turning to secular (rather than Islamist) parties for political expression.

While Sunni Islamist political groups have seen their influence decline, a few Sunni Islamist militant groups remain active in Iraq. These militant groups have been largely degraded since 2007, as many Sunni resistance groups renounced violence and entered the political process. Still, a few groups retain a limited capability to conduct attacks. These groups include al-Qaeda in Iraq (AQI) and the *Jaysh Rajal al-Tariqah al-Naqshabandia* (JRTN).

AQI is a terrorist group that aims to overthrow the current government of Iraq and establish an Islamic state in its place. According to the U.S. military, AQI is comprised primarily of indigenous Sunni Iraqis and elements of the Kurdish Islamist group *Ansar al-Islam*.[31] AQI has been responsible for some of the deadliest car bomb and suicide bomb attacks in Iraq, as well as sectarian violence. AQI lost many of its strongholds in northern and western Iraq following the security offensives that began in 2007; however, it still operates in areas of northern Iraq, especially the city of Mosul. Though AQI leaders professed their allegiance to the global al-Qaeda movement in 2004, the group is no longer able to retain operational links with al-Qaeda leaders based in the tribal areas of Pakistan.[32] AQI's external support networks, largely located in Syria, have also been degraded by U.S. and Iraqi operations.

JRTN is a Sunni extremist group that was founded in December 2006 in response to the execution of Saddam Hussein.[33] JRTN is linked to former Iraqi Ba'athist officials now living in Syria, including Izzat Ibrahim al-Duri, one of Saddam's closest deputies.[34] A main goal of the group is the return of the Ba'ath Party in Iraq.[35] Although the group's name indicates a link with the Sufi Naqshabandia order, this connection is largely perfunctory.[36] JRTN operates primarily in the northern Iraqi provinces of Ninewah, Kirkuk, Salah ad-Din, and Diyala, where it conducts attacks against U.S forces.

Sunni Arabs have largely rejected both Islamist political parties and extremist groups. Yet, with U.S. forces scheduled to withdraw from Iraq by the end of 2011 and a growing disenchantment with the Iraqi government's ability to provide for its citizens, there is concern that these Sunni extremist groups will be able to regenerate and expand their operations.

Kurdish Groups

The largest Kurdish Islamist political groups are the Kurdistan Islamic Union (KIU) and the Kurdistan Islamic Group (KIG).[37] The KIU, also known as *Yekgirtu*, was established in 1994. Principally an adherent to Sunni Islam, the group was closely aligned with the Muslim Brotherhood. The group describes itself as "an Islamic reformative political party that strives to solve all political, social, economic and cultural matters of the people in Kurdistan from an Islamic perspective which can achieve the rights, general freedom, and social justice."[38] It is currently led by Secretary General Sheikh Salah ad-Din Muhammad Baha-al-Din. The KIU has no armed forces of its own, and is most active in charity work.

The KIG was established in 2001 as a splinter faction of the KIU. It is led by Mala Ali Bapir. KIG is believed to have close ties with extremist Islamist armed groups, such as *Ansar al-Islam*, which has been involved in attacks against leaders of the predominant political parties in Kurdistan, the Kurdistan Democratic Party (KDP) and the Patriotic Union of Kurdistan (PUK).[39] Bapir claims his group has abandoned violence and instead has said that "[the KIG's] policy is that we enter into fraternity and cooperation with all Islamic groups. We seek such fraternal relations with Islamic parties and organizations, Islamist figures, and groups that follow a Salafi tradition or a Sufi or a scientific tradition. In the Komele Islami, we believe that the group must be open-minded and seek fraternity with all those who call or act for Islam. If we see a mistake, we will try to correct it through dialogue and by creating a fraternal atmosphere."[40]

The political influence of the KIU and KIG is overshadowed by the KDP and the PUK, who have dominated Kurdish political and social life for decades. Of the 111 seats in the Kurdish parliament, the KIU and KIG have only four seats apiece.[41] At the national level, the influence of the Kurdish Islamist parties is even further diminished. The KIU has four seats in the 325-seat Iraqi parliament, while the KIG has only two seats. The emergence of the Change List (*Gorran*), a breakaway faction of the PUK, has shifted the balance of power slightly in the Kurdistan Regional Government, and has given the KIU and KIG another ally in the KRG parliament with which to challenge the dominant Kurdish parties. Still, the Kurdish Islamist parties remain only marginal actors in Iraqi political life.

ISLAMISM AND SOCIETY

Iraq is comprised of several ethnic and religious groups. Of Iraq's more than 30 million citizens, 75-80 percent are Arabs; 15-20 percent are Kurds; and Turkmen, Chaldeans, Assyrians, Armenians, and other minority groups comprise the remaining five percent.[42] The vast majority of Iraqis (97 percent) are Muslims. Of that number, 60-65 percent of Iraqi Muslims are adherents to the Shi'a tradition.[43] Iraqi Shi'a primarily live in central and southern Iraq, though there are Shi'a communities in the north. Thirty-two to thirty-seven percent of Iraqi Muslims are Sunnis, and they are concentrated mainly in central and northern Iraq.[44] Religious minorities, such as Christians, Mandeans, and Yazidis, comprise the remaining three percent of Iraq's population; however, the Christian population in Iraq has declined dramatically since 2003.[45] The Jewish community in Iraq has also all but disappeared.

Divergent trends of secularism and Islamism also exist in Iraqi society. Following the fall of Saddam Hussein's secular regime in 2003, both Sunni and Shi'a Iraqis were able to openly express their Islamic faith in ways that they had not been able to do under Saddam. This was especially true for Shi'a Iraqis, who for the first time in decades could take part in the religious pilgrimages to the holy cities of Najaf and Karbala in southern Iraq. Exiled Sunni and Shi'a Islamist parties and movements returned to Iraq, where they played key roles in shaping Iraq's emerging political system. Movements like the Sadrist Trend also found a broad following amongst Iraqi Shi'a, particularly those in urban and poor areas, by providing essential services such as water, electricity, and gasoline.

As security deteriorated from 2004 to 2006 and the Iraqi state proved unable to capably govern, Shi'a and Sunni Islamist militant groups (such as JAM and AQI, respectively) grew in strength, and they increasingly and violently imposed their strict interpretations of Islamic law. AQI established strongholds in the predominantly Sunni areas of northern and western Iraq, such as Anbar and Ninewah provinces. There, AQI brutally imposed harsh rules, including banning smoking and singing, prohibiting men to shave their beards, forcing marriages between local women and al-Qaeda fighters, forcing women to wear strict Islamic dress, and maiming or killing anyone caught violating their radical laws.[46] Shi'a militia groups like JAM also enforced similarly strict rules in the areas of Baghdad and southern Iraq that were under their control. Sectarian violence soared during this time, as Sunni and Shi'a extremist groups also violently cleansed mixed areas of Baghdad. According to the U.S. military, more than 77,000 Iraqis were killed during the height of sectarian violence from 2004 to 2008; Iraqi government statistics put that number at more than 85,000. [47]

By 2008, Iraqis of all sects and ethnicities had grown frustrated and fed up with the years of sectarian strife, during which time Islamist parties and militias dominated. Even as early as late 2006, Sunni tribal leaders in Anbar province rejected AQI rule and took arms against Sunni extremists, in a movement that became known as the Anbar Awakening. Awakening movements spread across Sunni areas from 2007 to 2008.[48] This, coupled with the security offensive during the Surge that first cleared Baghdad and later the provinces surrounding the capital, significantly degraded AQI's capabilities and networks. During the Surge, U.S. and Iraqi forces also targeted Shi'a militia groups in Baghdad and throughout central and southern Iraq. This culminated in the Iraqi-led operations in Basra and Baghdad, which dealt a significant blow to JAM and culminated in Sadr's announcement he was disbanding his once-fearsome militia.[49]

The 2009 and 2010 elections saw the reorientation of Iraqi politics that reflected changes in society away from Islamism. Islamist exile parties like ISCI and the IIP had their influence wane.[50] New political realities emerged in Iraq, and there was widespread anti-incumbent sentiment and a growing demand for secular, nationalist, and technocratic government that could preserve security, provide essential services, and reduce corruption.[51] These themes played an important role in the provincial and parliamentary elections.

Nonetheless, Iraqi society remains heavily fragmented and sectarian divisions still exist, providing an opening for Islamist groups.[52] During the prolonged negotiations to form a governing coalition after the 2010 parliamentary vote, many politicians turned to identity politics to garner support. At the same time, Dawa and the Sadrist Trend, the main Shi'a political groups in Iraq today, retain their Islamist character. Moreover, many Iraqis are discouraged by the inability for the Iraqi government to provide basic services and reduce unemployment.[53] This may create a dynamic whereby disenchanted Sunnis are drawn to the rhetoric of extremist Sunni militant groups, while Shi'ites are drawn to organizations like the Sadrist Trend to provide social services.

ISLAMISM AND THE STATE

Iraq is a parliamentary democracy and not a theocratic republic like its eastern neighbor, Iran. The Iraqi Constitution guarantees the democratic rights of all Iraqi citizens as well as "full religious rights to freedom of religious belief and practice of all individuals."[54] Still, the Iraqi Constitution stipulates Islam as the official religion of the state and makes clear that no law may be enacted that contradicts the establish provisions of Islam. The ambiguities inherent in these provisions have led to challenges in interpretation and meaning. In some areas of Iraq, local governments have adopted stricter interpretations of Islamic law. The provincial councils in Basra and Najaf, for instance, have banned the consumption, sales, or transit of alcohol;[55] and in November 2010, the Baghdad provincial council, which is dominated by Dawa, used a resolution from 1996 to similarly ban the sale of alcohol in a move that was seen as targeting Iraq's Christian minority, members of which are the primary merchants of alcohol in Iraq.[56] Recent months have also seen a number of violent raids or attacks on venues believed to be selling alcohol.[57] These events have prompted growing fears of a rollback of freedoms and a return to the days when militias violently enforced strict interpretations of Islam in their neighborhood strongholds.

The Iraqi government's response to radical Islamist militant groups has also varied. Islamist parties dominated provincial and national governments from 2004 to 2008. During that time, the state was unwilling or incapable of challenging the Islamist militant groups that threatened its legitimacy. Shi'a militia groups penetrated elements of the Iraqi Security Forces, and certain paramilitary and police units were accused of perpetrating brutal sectarian violence.[58] The threat from extremist groups ultimately jeopardized the functioning of the Iraqi state by late 2006. Several months later, in early 2007, U.S. forces announced a change of strategy in Iraq and the deployment of 20,000 additional troops, in what became known as the Surge. As the counterinsurgency offensives unfolded, the Iraqi state also became more willing and able to challenge Sunni and Shi'a extremist groups, as the influence and capability of these groups waned.[59] U.S. support during this time was critical in giving the Iraqi Security Forces, and even Iraq's political leadership, the confidence to move against these extremist groups as well as to prevent the manipulation of the security forces for political ends. U.S. and Iraqi leaders also worked to professionalize the Iraqi Security Forces, expand their capabilities, and root out corrupt or sectarian elements.[60] U.S. and Iraqi operations from 2007 to the present significantly degraded both Sunni and Shi'a extremist groups and reduced violence by over 90 percent.[61]

Today, the Iraqi forces continue to robustly target Sunni extremist groups, such as al-Qaeda in Iraq. With the growing influence of the Sadrist Trend in the government, however, the concomitant targeting of Shi'a militant groups has become less certain. Indeed, in an effort to garner Sadrist political backing during government formation, Prime Minister Maliki secured the release of hundreds of Sadrist detainees, many of whom were members of JAM.[62] Given the scheduled withdrawal of U.S. forces by the end of 2011, it is unclear whether the Iraqi state will maintain the political will to sufficiently check radical Shi'a militant groups (many of whom continue to receive Iranian assistance), or whether the political interests of dominant Shi'a parties will enable such groups to expand.

ENDNOTES

[1] Vali Nasr, *The Shia Revival: How Conflicts within Islam will Shape the Future* (New York: Norton, 2006), 117.

[2] Patrick Cockburn, *Muqtada* (New York: Scribner, 2008), 31; Faleh Jabar, *The Shi'ite Movement in Iraq* (London: SAQI, 2003), 78-80.

[3] Jabar, *The Shi'ite Movement in Iraq*, 78-80; Islamic Dawa Party, "Party History," n.d., http://www.islamicdawaparty.com/?module=home&fname=history.php&active=7&show=1.

[4] Richard Oppel, Jr., "Shiites Settle on Pick for Iraqi Premier," *New York Times*, April 22, 2006, http://www.nytimes.com/2006/04/22/world/middleeast/22iraq.html.

[5] Jeremy Domergue and Marisa Cochrane Sullivan, "Balancing Maliki," Institute for the Study of War *Iraq Report 14*, June 26, 2009, http://www.understandingwar.org/files/IraqReport14.pdf; Michael S. Schmidt and Jack Healy, "Maliki's Broadened Powers Seen as a Threat in Iraq," *New York Times*, March 4, 2011, http://www.nytimes.com/2011/03/05/world/middleeast/05iraq.html?_r=1.

[6] Jabar, *The Shi'ite Movement in Iraq*, 272-273.

[7] Marisa Cochrane Sullivan, "The Fragmentation of the Sadrist Movement," Institute for the Study of War *Iraq Report 12*, January 2009, http://www.understandingwar.org/files/Iraq%20Report%2012.pdf.

[8] Ibid.

[9] Ibidem.

[10] Michal Harari, "Status Update: Shi'a Militias in Iraq," Institute for the Study of War *Backgrounder*, August 16, 2010, http://www.understandingwar.org/files/Backgrounder_ShiaMilitias.pdf.

[11] "Shiite Politics in Iraq: The Role of the Supreme Council," International Crisis Group *Middle East Report* Number 70, November 15, 2007, 15, http://www.crisisgroup.org/~/media/Files/Middle%20East%20North%20Africa/Iraq%20Syria%20Lebanon/Iraq/70_shiite_politics_in_iraq___the_role_of_the_supreme_council.ashx.

[12] Joseph Felter and Brian Fishman, "Iranian Strategy in Iraq: Politics and 'Other Means,'" Combating Terrorism Center at West Point *Occasional Paper Series*, October 13, 2008, 19-20, http://www.ctc.usma.edu/Iran_Iraq/CTC_Iran_Iraq_Final.pdf.

[13] "Shiite Politics in Iraq: The Role of the Supreme Council," 10-11.

[14] Ibid.

[15] Felter and Fishman, "Iranian Strategy in Iraq: Politics and 'Other Means,'" 20.

[16] Ma'ad Fayad, "Ammar al-Hakim Appointed New Leader of Supreme Islamic Iraqi Council," *Ash-Sharq al-Awsat* (London), September 1, 2009, http://www.aawsat.com/english/news.asp?section=1&id=17965.

[17] Marisa Cochrane Sullivan, "Iraq's Parliamentary Election," Institute

for the Study of War *Backgrounder*, October 20, 2009, http://www. understandingwar.org/files/IraqsParliamentaryElection.pdf.

[18] Rahma al-Salim, "Al Maliki Announces Break With Iraqi National Alliance," *Ash-Sharq al-Awsat* (London), September 25, 2009, http:// www.aawsat.com/english/news.asp?section=1&id=18246.

[19] U.S. Department of State, Bureau of Public Affairs, "Media Note: Designation of Kata'ib Hezbollah as a Foreign Terrorist Organization," July 2, 2009, http://www.state.gov/r/pa/prs/ps/2009/july/125582. htm.

[20] U.S. Department of the Treasury, "PRESS RELEASE: Treasury Designates Individual, Entity Posing Threat to Stability in Iraq," July 9, 2009, http://www.treasury.gov/press-center/press-releases/Pages/ tg195.aspx; Felter and Fishman, "Iranian Strategy in Iraq: Politics and 'Other Means,'" 24.

[21] U.S. Department of the Treasury, "Treasury Designates Individual, Entity Posing Threat to Stability in Iraq."

[22] Karin Bruilliard, "Ex-Sadr Aide Held in American Deaths," *Washington Post*, March 23, 2007, http://www.washingtonpost.com/wp-dyn/content/article/2007/03/22/AR2007032200261.html; Felter and Fishman, "Iranian Strategy in Iraq: Politics and 'Other Means,'" 35; Sullivan, "The Fragmentation of the Sadrist Movement."

[23] Yusif Salman, "Leading Figure in the Al-Sadr Trend to Al-Mashriq: Al-Sadr Met Asa'ib Ahl al-Haq Leader in Qom," *Al-Mashriq* (Iraq), January 18, 2010; Martin Chulov, "Qais al-Khazali: from Kidnapper and Prisoner to Potential Leader," *Guardian* (London), December 31, 2009, http://www.guardian.co.uk/world/2009/dec/31/iran-hostages-qais-al-khazali.

[24] Sullivan, "The Fragmentation of the Sadrist Movement."

[25] Basim Al-Azami, "The Muslim Brotherhood: Genesis and Development," in Faleh A. Jabar, ed., *Ayatollahs, Sufis and Ideologues: State, Religion and Social Movements in Iraq* (London: Saqi, 2002), 164.

[26] Ibid.; Graham Fuller and Rend Rahim Francke, *The Arab Shi'a: The Forgotten Muslims* (Basingstoke, UK: Palgrave Macmillan, 2000); "Iraqi Islamic Party," globalsecurity.org, n.d., http://www.globalsecurity.org/military/world/iraq/iip.htm; Iraqi Islamist Party, "History," n.d., http://www.iraqiparty.com/page/who-are-we/.

[27] Thabit Abdullah, *A Short History of Iraq: From 636 to the Present* (London: Longman, 2003).

[28] "Iraqi Islamic Party"; Iraqi Islamic Party, "History."

[29] Ibid.

[30] Domergue and Sullivan, "Balancing Maliki."

[31] United States Forces-Iraq, "The Insurgency," July 31, 2009, http:// www.usf-iraq.com/?option=com_content&task=view&id=729&Item id=45.

[32] Kenneth Katzman, "Al Qaeda in Iraq: Assessment and Outside

Links," Congressional Research Service Report for Congress, August 15, 2008, http://www.fas.org/sgp/crs/terror/RL32217.pdf; DoD News Briefing with Commander, U.S. Forces-Iraq, Gen. Raymond Odierno from the Pentagon, June 4, 2010.

[33] United States Forces-Iraq, "The Insurgency"; Geoff Ziezulewicz, "Insurgent Group Looks to Future Without U.S.: Former Saddam Loyalists Work to Return Baath Party to Power," *Stars and Stripes,* April 3, 2009.

[34] Ziezulewicz, "Insurgent Group Looks to Future Without U.S."

[35] Ibid.

[36] United States Forces-Iraq, "The Insurgency"; Ziezulewicz, "Insurgent Group Looks to Future Without U.S."

[37] Rafid Fadhil Ali, "Kurdish Islamist Groups in Northern Iraq," Jamestown Foundation *Terrorism Monitor* 6, iss. 22, November 25, 2008, http://www.jamestown.org/single/?no_cache=1&tx_ttnews[tt_news]=34176.

[38] Qassim Khidhir Hamad, "Kurdish Election Lists," *Niqash* (Baghdad), June 30, 2009.

[39] Kathleen Ridolfo, "A Survey of Armed Groups in Iraq," Radio Free Europe/Radio Liberty *Iraq Report* 7, no. 20, June 4, 2004.

[40] Ibid.

[41] "The Kurdistan Parliament," krg.org, November 30, 2006, http://www.krg.org/articles/detail.asp?rnr=160&lngnr=12&smap=04070000&anr=15057; "The Members of the Parliament for Third Term 2009," krg.org, April 24, 2011, http://www.perleman.org/Default.aspx?page=Parliamentmembers&c=Presidency-Member2009&group=40.

[42] "Iraq," CIA *World Factbook*, April 6, 2011, https://www.cia.gov/library/publications/the-world-factbook/geos/iz.html; U.S. Department of State, Bureau of Near Eastern Affairs, "Background Note: Iraq," September 17, 2010, http://www.state.gov/r/pa/ei/bgn/6804.htm.

[43] Ibid.

[44] Ibidem.

[45] Ibidem.

[46] Rod Nordland, "Despite Gains, Petraeus Cautious About Iraq," *Newsweek*, August 21, 2008, http://www.newsweek.com/2008/08/20/avoiding-the-v-word.html; "Marriages Split al Qaeda Alliance," *Washington Times*, August 31, 2007, http://www.washingtontimes.com/news/2007/aug/31/marriages-split-al-qaeda-alliance/?page=all#pagebreak; "Severe Islamic Law Which Banned 'Suggestive' Cucumbers Cost Al Qaeda Public Support in Iraq," *Daily Mail* (London), August 10, 2008, http://www.dailymail.co.uk/news/worldnews/article-1043409/Severe-Islamic-law-banned-suggestive-cucumbers-cost-Al-Qaeda-public-support-Iraq.html.

[47] "US Military Says 77,000 Iraqis Killed Over 5 Years," Associated

Press, October 15, 2010, http://www.post-journal.com/page/content. detail/id/120540/US-military-says-77-000-Iraqis-killed-over-5-years-.html?isap=1&nav=5030.

[48] John A. McCary, "The Anbar Awakening: An Alliance of Incentives," *The Washington Quarterly* 32, no. 1, January 2009, http://www. twq.com/09winter/docs/09jan_mccary.pdf.

[49] Sullivan, "The Fragmentation of the Sadrist Movement," 37-38.

[50] Iraqi High Electoral Commission, "Iraqi CoR Election Results," n.d., http://ihec-iq.com/en/results.html.

[51] Sullivan, "Iraq's Parliamentary Election."

[52] Marisa Cochrane Sullivan and James Danly, "Iraq on the Eve of Elections," Institute for the Study of War *Backgrounder*, March 3, 2010, http://www.understandingwar.org/files/IraqEveofElections.pdf.

[53] Iraqi discontent is most evident in the widespread protests witnessed in February and March 2011. See Michael S. Schmidt and Duraid Adnan, "Protests Spread to More Iraqi Cities," *New York Times*, February 17, 2011, http://www.nytimes.com/2011/02/18/world/middleeast/18iraq.html; Jack Healy and Michael S. Schmidt, "Demonstrations Turn Violent in Iraq," *New York Times*, February 25, 2011, http://www.nytimes.com/2011/02/26/world/middleeast/26iraq.html.

[54] Iraqi Constitution, Section One, Article Two.

[55] "Alcohol Banned in Iraq holy Shiite City of Najaf," *Middle East Online*, October 11, 2009, http://www.middle-east-online.com/english/?id=34869.

[56] John Leland, "Baghdad Raids on Alcohol Sellers Stir Fears," *New York Times*, January 15, 2011, http://www.nytimes.com/2011/01/16/world/middleeast/16iraq.html.

[57] Ibid.; "Kurdish Club Scene Booming as Baghdad Bans Alcohol," Associated Press, January 11, 2011.

[58] Lionel Beehner, "Shiite Militias and Iraq's Security Forces," Council on Foreign Relations *Backgrounder*, November 30, 2005, http://www.cfr.org/iraq/shiite-militias-iraqs-security-forces/p9316; "Iraq 'Death Squad Caught in Act,'" BBC, February 16, 2006, http://news.bbc.co.uk/2/hi/middle_east/4719252.stm; Steve Inskeep, "Riding Herd on the Iraqi Police's Dirty 'Wolf Brigade,'" National Public Radio, March 28, 2007, http://www.npr.org/templates/story/story.php?storyId=9170738.

[59] Sullivan, "The Fragmentation of the Sadrist Movement," 22.

[60] For more information on the growth and professionalization of the Iraqi Security Forces during the Surge, see LTG James Dubik, "Building Security Forces and Ministerial Capacity: Iraq as a Primer," Institute for the Study of War *Best Practices in Counterinsurgency Report* 1, August 2009, http://www.csmonitor.com/World/Middle-East/2011/0208/US-reports-20-percent-drop-in-Iraq-violence.

[61] Scott Peterson, "US Reports 20 Percent Drop in Iraq Violence,"

Christian Science Monitor, February 8, 2011, http://www.csmonitor. com/World/Middle-East/2011/0208/US-reports-20-percent-drop-in-Iraq-violence.

[62] Kholoud Ramzi, "After Months of Negotiations, Maliki Holds on to Power," *Niqash* (Baghdad), December 25, 2010, http://www.niqash. org/content.php?contentTypeID=75&id=2755&lang=0.

SYRIA

QUICK FACTS

Population: 22,198,110

Area: 185,180 sq km

Ethnic Groups: Arab 90.3%, Kurds, Armenians, and other 9.7%

Religions: Sunni Muslim 74%, other Muslim (includes Alawite, Druze) 16%, Christian (various denominations) 10%, Jewish (tiny communities in Damascus, Al Qamishli, and Aleppo)

Government Type: Republic under an authoritarian military-dominated regime

GDP (official exchange rate): $54.99 billion

Map and Quick Facts courtesy of the CIA World Factbook (Last Updated June 2010)

For the past five decades, Syria has used terrorist tactics to advance its goals internally and throughout the Middle East. The methods have varied according to needs and circumstances, however. In the past, Syria has used both its own agents and proxy organizations to launch terrorist attacks. While the regime continues to seek a balance between the promotion of secularism domestically and Islamism abroad, Syrian President Bashar al-Asad has not limited his support to specific ideological strains of Islam. His government, working in tandem with the Islamic Republic of Iran, supports the Shi'a Hezbollah militia in Lebanon, even as it offers varying degrees of assistance to the Sunni Salafist Fatah al-Islam in northern Lebanon. Syria similarly supports and hosts the external leadership of the Sunni Palestinian Hamas movement (an outgrowth of Egypt's Muslim Brotherhood), while clamping down on the Sunni Muslim Brotherhood within Syria. Since the fall of Saddam Hussein's Iraq in 2003, Syria also has served as the primary gateway for foreign jihadists entering Iraq.

ISLAMIST ACTIVITY

Organized and effective Islamist opposition in Syria ceased to exist after President Hafiz al-Asad's brutal crackdown on the Syrian branch of the Muslim Brotherhood in 1982. Nevertheless, several groups—notably *Jund al-Sham* (the Army of the Levant) and *Ghuraba al-Sham* (Strangers of the Levant)— remain active in Syria.[1]

Jund al-Sham is an amorphous Islamic militant organization, and it remains unclear whether it is the creation of Syrian intelligence or of the late al-Qaeda lieutenant in Iraq, Abu Musab al-Zarqawi, or both. Yet the Syrian regime has claimed that the group carried out several attacks in 2005 and 2006, and that their security services managed to foil several terror attacks at its hands within Syria.[2]

The official stance toward *Ghuraba al-Sham* is similarly muddled, as it is difficult to ascertain whether the organization is truly independent or an invention of the government to provide an outlet for Sunni Islamist tendencies.[3] For example, in June 2006 Syrian security services clashed with terrorists who were allegedly planning an operation in Umayyad Square in Damascus. Those killed and apprehended were found in possession of CDs with sermons from the preacher of the Ash-Sharour mosque in Aleppo, Mahmoud al-Aghasi, also known as Abu Qaqa.[4] Known for his anti-American sermons and calls for the creation of an Islamist state in Syria based on *sharia*, he preached under the banner of *Ghuraba al-Sham*, albeit with a contradictory message.[5] In one television interview, he credits *Jund al-Sham* with the attack while at the same time denouncing the Muslim Brotherhood. In another interview he calls for working with the government to "achieve national unity in an Islamic manner."[6]

The protests that have swept over the region since the start of 2011 have touched Syria as well. On March 6, 2011, security forces arrested 15 teenagers for spraying anti-regime graffiti on a wall in the southern city of Deraa.[7] Their continued detention sparked massive demonstrations in the city, which in turn were met by a brutal regime crackdown using live fire and tear gas. Asad's heavy-handed response led to the protests that spread across the country and continue as of this writing.[8] As in other Middle East states experiencing the "Arab Spring," the protests were not designed to bring about a greater role for Islam in the government. Nevertheless, Islam still played in a role in them, to the extent that the mosque is where people congregate for Friday afternoon prayers and the largest protests have come on Friday afternoons, following prayers.

ISLAMISM AND SOCIETY

Given the high degree of repression inside Syria, it has been difficult for opposition activists to organize within the country. This trend has continued throughout the 2011 protests as well. One observer in Syria noted in April 2011, "There is almost no organization inside Syria among the protesters... As I told my friend, the problem is that unlike Cairo's Tahrir Square, all the demonstrators are dispersed across the country and do not have enough time to talk to each other to decide what they wanted."[9] Nevertheless several dissident groups operate abroad, notably in Western Europe. The former Syrian Vice President, Abd al-Halim Khaddam, formed the National Salvation Front (NSF) with the London-based leader of the Syrian Muslim Brotherhood, Sadr al-Din Bayanuni, in March 2006.[10] The NSF is an amalgam of both secular and Islamist opposition groups outside Syria and they held regular meetings with Bush administration officials in 2007 to discuss democracy promotion in Syria.[11] By 2009, the Muslim Brotherhood left the NSF, as differences in the approach to regional issues came to the fore, highlighting the fact that what had unified those in the NSF was opposition to the Asad regime, not the role of Islam in society or manner in which *muqawama*—resistance—should be practiced. For example, Bayanuni supported Hamas during Israel's Operation Cast Lead at the end of 2008 and supported the Asad regime in its efforts to reclaim Lebanon, whereas Khaddam opposed Hamas and supported Lebanon's secular and pro-freedom March 14 coalition.[12]

In recent years, Sunni Islamism has become more pronounced, especially in Syria's larger cities. However, civil society's ability to extend external support to Islamist groups, or the ability of those groups to form an internal base within Syria itself, is nearly nonexistent, given the authoritarian nature of the regime. Instead, such Islamic fervor is harnessed and driven outward to neighboring countries to serve the needs and wishes of the Syrian regime. Even with the current uprising during the "Arab Spring," most of the Salafist groups within Syria have been penetrated by the regime and focused against its enemies in Iraq and Lebanon.[13]

While Shi'a Muslims currently constitute only around two percent of Syria's 18 million people, their numbers have grown considerably from 1953, when they numbered no more than 0.4 percent of the Syrian population. Official and reliable statistics pertaining to the birthrates among confessional groups in Syria are tightly regulated by the regime, but an increase in conversions from Sunni to Shi'a can be clearly observed. This increase is, first, the consequence of geography and history. The Shi'a of Syria possess a considerable number of institutions and shrines in the country, such as the tomb of Sayyida Zaynab and the Mosque of the Drop in Aleppo. Numerous pilgrims who help disseminate Shi'ite ideas and doctrines visit these sites. The Shi'a also build houses of study next to their shrines and establish religious authorities there, which has given them more independence with respect to religious rulings. When tallied in 2009, more than 500 *husayniyyas* (Shi'a houses of prayer) were said to be under construction in Syria; according to other sources, that number refers to *husayniyyas* in Damascus alone.[14]

A drift toward greater expression of Islamic sentiment within Syrian society has received extensive coverage in the media in recent years. More women wear the *hijab* while more men have grown beards and declined to wear wedding rings.[15] There has also been an increase in the number of Islamic book shops and Islamist sayings that have replaced Ba'ath Party slogans.[16] Additionally, numerous nightclubs and restaurants that serve alcohol have been shut down.[17]

The regime's ability to channel Islamic fervor is best demonstrated by Syria's harsh response to the Danish cartoon episode of September 2005, when the newspaper, *Jyllands-Posten*, published the likeness of the Prophet Muhammad. At least a thousand people held a demonstration outside the Danish embassy in Damascus where dozens then stormed and burned the embassy and replaced the Danish flag with the Saudi flag that reads, "There is no god but Allah and Muhammad is his Messenger."[18] At the same time, demonstrations in support of Hezbollah and Hamas were also organized.[19] Such behavior does not ordinarily occur in Syria, and should be viewed as a governmental decision to allow Islamists and their sympathizers to direct their anger externally rather than against the regime.

The 2011 uprising provided a unique glimpse into some of the tensions that exist within Syrian society. During the initial uprising in Deraa, in which the 15 teenagers were arrested, the usual response from the affected families would have been to quietly seek the intervention of religious and tribal leaders. However, the continued detention of the protesters sparked massive demonstrations focusing on the Deraa's historic Omari mosque, where even the state-vetted Sunni preachers were swept up by popular passions.[20] By the time the teenagers were released, the clashes between the Syrian security services and the protesters had already claimed many lives. This began a cycle of funerals, which themselves became rallying points for further protests—much like in Iran's anti-Shah student movement in 1979.[21]

By March 15th, the demonstrations had swept across the county. Syria specialist Gary Cambill described the revealing disparity: "Secular liberal dissidents took to the streets in relatively small numbers and avoided confrontations with the police, while Kurdish groups largely abstained. In contrast, the demonstrations in Deraa and other predominantly Sunni flashpoints were 20 to 30 times larger, organized under the semi-inviolable protection of mosques and clearly intended to provoke the security forces. While it is premature to characterize the protests as an Islamist uprising, there is little doubt that those most eager to risk death or severe bodily harm are overwhelmingly Sunni and deeply religious."[22]

ISLAMISM AND THE STATE

Syria has been a stronghold of Arab secularism since the Ba'ath Party seized power in 1963. As scholar Eyal Zisser observed, "The Regime forbade preaching and religious education outside the mosques, increased its involvement in the appointment of clerics to religious institutions in the country, took over the management of the Waqf institutions, and did not hesitate to arrest or even execute clerics who demonstrated against it."[23] The chief political and economic casualty from the rise of this coalition was the urban class in which the Muslim Brotherhood was grounded.

Following the rise to power of Hafiz al-Asad in November 1970, the regime attempted to improve its relations with Islamic elements within the state. Softening the anti-Islamic line held by his predecessors, Asad began to participate in prayers at Sunni mosques in Damascus, made a pilgrimage to Mecca, raised the salaries of clerics, and actively tried to gain religious sanction for his minority Alawi community.[24] The result was a 1973 *fatwa* handed down by Musa al-Sadr, the leader of the Lebanese Shi'a community, which legitimized the Alawis, declaring them to be lawful Shi'a and therefore Muslim in all respects.

Nevertheless, in 1976, Islamic militants, some of whom were former Muslim Brotherhood activists, rose up in a violent struggle against Hafiz al-Asad's regime with the goal of toppling the government and replacing it with an Islamic state. The Muslim Brotherhood joined this struggle soon thereafter, drawing their support from the urban Sunni middle class, especially in the northern region of the country. While the Sunnis represented 60 percent of Syria's population (today they represent closer to 70 percent), half the number lived in rural areas and the periphery and did not support the Muslim Brotherhood's vision.

The Islamic Revolt lasted from 1976 until 1982, reaching its peak in 1980. It ended in February 1982, when Asad quashed the Muslim Brothers in Hama, the state's fourth-largest town, obliterating the movement as an organized and active force. Tens of thousands were killed and many more were forced to serve long prison sentences. The group's leaders were forced into exile.[25]

According to the Brotherhood, some 17,000 party members are either missing or detained inside Syria.[26]

The 1990s saw an improvement in the regime's relations with Islamic circles both inside and outside of Syria. The new direction was aimed at endowing Syria with an Islamic look and feel, but stopping short of full religious substance. Official Syrian sponsorship of Islam had the express purpose of preventing the mosque from becoming a source of rebellion. This was manifested through greater official openness to demonstrations of religious faith among Syrian citizens, and the release many members of the Muslim Brotherhood who had been held in Syrian prisons since the suppression of the Islamic Revolt.[27] Nevertheless, the regime continued to repress the Brotherhood, refusing to allow it to resume its activities in Syria. It became clear that Asad's conditions for reconciliation—namely, for the Brotherhood's leaders to repent, confess guilt, and express contrition over the Islamic Revolt and commit not to renew their political activity as an organized movement in Syria—were too difficult for the group to accept.

Bashar al-Asad became president after his father's death on June 10, 2000, and he continued efforts to promote an Islamic posture, including further efforts to Islamize the Alawi community. The Muslim Brotherhood, for its part, tried to forge a relationship with the regime in Damascus following Hafiz al-Asad's death, driven by hopes that the organization—whose leaders had become increasingly irrelevant after years of exile—could again become a player in Syria's political scene. These aspirations proved futile, however; the regime under Bashar showed little readiness for compromise.

Other Islamist groups have fared little better. The regime's decision to promote a state-sponsored version of Islam has left no alternative means to express any other form of political Islam. The only other prominent Islamic party is the Islamic Liberation Party (*Hizb al-Tahrir al-Islami*), and its members are subject to frequent arrests by Syrian authorities. The group, which calls for restoring the Islamic caliphate, is banned in most countries and has only a small following in Syria. Asad's regime remains vigilant in arresting and detaining those suspected of Islamist activities with ties to the Muslim Brotherhood.[28]

While the 2011 Syrian uprising has been largely free of Islamist overtones, the Syrian Muslim Brotherhood still seeks a more prominent role and has capitalized on the opportunity to reinvent itself as a street movement. Zuhair Salim, a London-based spokesman for the Syrian branch of the Brothers explained, "We have a desire to coordinate the position of the opposition." Nevertheless, he declined to assume credit for the protests: "We are supporters, and not creators. The voice of the street is a spokesperson for itself."[29] Salim has become more visible in Arabic-language television programs since April 2011, when the Brotherhood decided to back the protest movement, or what the group refers to as a "peaceful, popular intifada," or resistance.[30]

The Muslim Brotherhood's attempts to steer the opposition, however, has been hampered as a result of several factors. Since 1980, membership in the brotherhood has been a capital offense and after the brutal crackdown in 1982, most of its leaders were sent into exile. The devastation wrought upon the party also made other anti-government figures wary of political Islam as an effective tool to challenge the regime and unsure of how to engage the group that has had no operational base within Syria for decades. The Brotherhood left the NSF in 2009, and there has been a power struggle for leadership in exile, with Muhammad Riad al-Shakfa replacing Bayanuni as head of the organization in the summer of 2010. Failed alliances coupled with brief overtures to the Asad regime have raised doubts over their ability to even lead the anti-regime movement from abroad, let alone within Syria.[31] As one Paris-based opposition member and scholar of contemporary oriental studies, Burhan Ghalioun, explains, "Those 30 years destroyed their organization, and they lost their legitimacy because they changed positions so much without explanation over the past five years."[32]

Nevertheless, those gathered in Syria's streets have not yet coalesced around a central ideology or political platform. And as of yet, the Brothers do not possess anything tangible to offer the secular protesters. However, the longer the protests remain in a stalemate, the more appealing the Muslim Brotherhood's organization skills and funding may become. After all, despite the Brothers limited organizational ability, it remains one of the oldest anti-government movements in Syria with loose, external affiliations with other Arab Muslim Brotherhood movements.[33] They will likely continue to try to create an organized front with the secular protesters on the streets. The longer the uprising drags on, the larger the role the Brotherhood may play in the future of Syrian politics if the Asad regime falls.

If the Syrian government has long succeeded in co-opting Islamism at home, it has been active in the promotion of it abroad as a tool to increase its geopolitical standing in the region. The careful promotion and regulation of Islam pursued by Asad *pere* and *fils* were a clear departure from the traditional policy of the Ba'ath regime, which had sought to deprive Islam of any role or influence.

Lebanon
Syria's relationship with Lebanon's Shi'a militia, Hezbollah, dates back

to the group's inception in 1982, when Damascus allowed the Iranian regime to send around 1,000 members of the Revolutionary Guards to the Beka'a Valley of eastern Lebanon, an area occupied by Syrian forces. At the time, Syria was also vying for influence over its smaller neighbor in the Levant. In the years that followed, Syria came to view Hezbollah as an integral tool in its struggle against Israel, as well as a means by which to project its influence onto the world stage.

By 1991, Damascus had become Lebanon's *de facto* overlord. This was the result of Syria's participation in the coalition to oust Saddam Hussein from Kuwait. In return, Asad was given *carte blanche* to act against General Michael 'Awn, the pro-Iraqi General who stood as an obstacle to achieving Syrian hegemony in Lebanon. The signing of the "Agreement of Fraternity and Cooperation" in May 1991 granted the Asad regime unprecedented control over Lebanon's political system, and allowed it to help shape Hezbollah's role in the country.

Relations between Syria and Hezbollah in the 1990s were a marriage of convenience. Syria had a clear interest in continuing to sponsor paramilitary attacks against Israel so long as the Jewish state retained the Golan Heights, and it permitted Hezbollah alone to serve as its chosen proxy. Although there were other militant groups that were allowed to launch occasional small-scale attacks, only Hezbollah was allowed the full range of terrorist activities, from recruiting and training, to deploying a sophisticated resistance apparatus. As such, Hezbollah represented Syrian interests in applying pressure on Israel, which in turn served as Hezbollah's main source of support and legitimacy from within Lebanon. Yet Hafiz al-Asad always applied strict political and military constraints on the group's operations.

The subsequent assumption of power by his son Bashar in the year 2000, coupled with Israel's withdrawal from southern Lebanon the same year, significantly altered the relationship between Damascus and Hezbollah. Whereas Hafiz al-Asad had maintained a measure of distance from Hezbollah's leadership, Bashar sought a more intimate connection. By 2001, Hezbollah's unqualified support for Syria's occupation of Lebanon—at a time when opposition to Damascus had been growing among most sectarian communities in Lebanon—elicited an unprecedented degree of support for the militia from the Syrian regime.

Under Bashar al-Asad's direction, Syria has increased its support of Hezbollah in several spheres. It has provided direct military support to the militia, complementing the massive support it already receives from Iran. In the years leading up to the 2006 summer war between Hezbollah and Israel, Syria gave Hezbollah 200mm rockets with 80-kilogram (176 lb) warheads with a range of 70 kilometers (almost 44 miles), and 302mm rockets with 100-kilogram (220 lb) warheads with a potential range of about 100 kilometers (about 62 miles).[34] In addition, Syria gave Hezbollah advanced anti-tank rockets and missiles and quite probably anti-aircraft missiles as well.[35] According to some estimates, 80 percent of the 4,000 rockets fired at Israeli targets by Hezbollah during that conflict came from Syria.[36]

Although the flow of weapons from Syria to Lebanon has continued for decades, recent reports indicate that both the quantity and sophistication of the weapons systems has grown. Reports surfaced in 2010 that Syria is transferring Syrian-made M-600 missiles (a Syrian variant of the Iranian Fateh-110 missile) to Hezbollah.[37] Media reports also claimed that Syria transferred Scud D missiles to the Lebanese terrorist group as well.[38] Additionally, in March 2010, Israeli Brig. Gener. Yossi Baidatz told the Knesset's Foreign Affairs and Defense Committee that Syria had transferred the *Igla-S* portable air defense system to the terrorist group.[39] Estimates of Hezbollah's current arsenal, acquired overwhelmingly thanks to Syria and Iran, is estimated at between 40,000 and 60,000 rockets.[40]

Syria continues to reassure Hezbollah that it is committed to their relationship. In a September 2008 interview with Hezbollah's *Al-Manar* television, Asad explained Syrian policy: "We don't see an interest in abandoning the resistance [i.e., Hezbollah]… Our clear position remains in all our political discourse—our steadfast position for resistance" in Iraq, Lebanon and Palestine.[41] One month later, Syrian Ambassador to Washington Imad Mustapha referred to Hezbollah as a "close ally" which his country regarded with pride.[42]

Hezbollah is not the only Islamist force in Lebanon that Syria supports, however. Following the February 14, 2005 assassination of former Lebanese premier Rafiq Hariri, both Lebanese outrage and diplomatic pressure compelled Damascus to withdraw its military presence after their 30-year occupation. Rather than allowing the Lebanese government to go its own way, the Syrian regime exerted pressure by sponsoring radical, Sunni terrorist movements. This has had the added effect of providing insurance against an ascendant Hezbollah, should a rift between the group and Damascus ever develop.

Several Sunni Islamist groups are active today in Lebanon. Much like Syria's porous border with Iraq, the regime allows certain *jihadists* free passage into Lebanon and assists Salafi Islamist parties there.[43] Sources in Beirut have accused Syrian intelligence of helping to strengthen the Salafi fundamentalist group *Fatah al-Islam*, a splinter group of the Syrian-created *Fatah al-Intifada* (established in 1983 to challenge Yasser Arafat's *Fatah* movement in Lebanon).[44] Reports in the Arab press suggested that Damascus provided weapons to *Fatah al-Islam* and used the group to assassinate thirty-six people in Lebanon opposed to the Syrian regime.[45]

Fatah al-Islam was named by the U.S. as a Specially Designated Global Terrorist entity on August 13, 2007.[46] Its leader, Shaker al-Absi, had been acting as a Syrian agent since 1983. In 2003, Absi joined the insurgency in Iraq, where he worked with Abu Musab al-Zarqawi, then the leader of Al

Qaeda in Iraq. Absi was also wanted in Jordan for the October 2002 murder of U.S. diplomat Lawrence Foley—a murder planned by the network set up in Syria by Zarqawi between May and September 2002.[47]

Nevertheless, in working to promote Salafist (Sunni) Islamism abroad when it suits the needs of the regime in Damascus, Asad has created a problem for himself. Sensing the recent weakness of the regime in light of the recent 2011 protests, *Fatah al-Islam* called for *Jihad* in Syria in a statement disseminated on *jihadist* websites. The statement was signed by Abu Huraira al-Badawi also known as Khattab al-Maqdisi and it urged Sunnis to awaken and come to the aid of their brothers in Daraa. It also called Muslims in Syria and Lebanon to come to the aid of *Fatah al-Islam* in their fight against the Shi'ite encroachment from Iran and the "Party of the Devil" (*Hizb al-Shytan*)—the term used to mock Hezbollah. It should be noted that the statement was not disseminated through an accredited account on *jihad* forums but rather by members who posted it on behalf of *Fatah al-Islam*.[48] It is therefore difficult to tell with certainty if this was a true declaration from the terrorist group purely independent of Syrian instructions or whether it was ordered by the Asad regime in its early and ongoing effort to cast the blame for the protests on Islamist elements.

Israel and the Palestinian Authority

Syria has provided training, weapons, safe haven and logistical support to both secular leftist and Islamist Palestinian hardliners. Damascus is the headquarters for Hamas' external leadership and for the far-left Popular Front for the Liberation of Palestine-General Command. It also hosts the headquarters of the fundamentalist Palestinian Islamic Jihad (PIJ), which draws support directly from the Syrian government.[49]

Syria provides both direct and indirect sponsorship and support for Hamas, the main Palestinian Islamist movement. The leading authority of the movement is its "external" leadership, headed by Politburo chief Khalid Mishaal, which currently resides in Damascus with the permission of the Syrian regime. Damascus directs and supports Hamas by political and operational instructions, the transfer of millions of dollars per year, the training of operatives, and the provision of funds for purchasing weapons that are later smuggled into the Palestinian Authority and the Arab states.[50] This connection enables Damascus to directly influence Palestinian politics, from Palestinian Authority reconciliation efforts to the adoption of ceasefires. Moreover, in recent years, Damascus' ability to exercise direct control over the group is said to have increased.[51]

The Asad regime was quite happy with the results of the Palestinian Legislative Council elections in January 2006, which saw a Hamas victory and the formation of a Hamas-led government.[52] Since that time, Syrian activity in the Palestinian arena has increased significantly. On the political level, Damascus has stepped up its coordination with several Hamas representatives, including numerous meetings with Khalid Mishaal and meetings between Asad and senior members of the Palestinian government.[53] According to the U.S. State Department's *Country Reports on Terrorism 2008*, Mishaal's "use of the Syrian Ministry of Information as the venue for press conferences this year could be taken as an endorsement of HAMAS's message."[54]

Syria helped Hamas more directly as well. Media reports indicate that Hamas used Syrian soil to train its militant fighters.[55] The Syrian government also facilitated Palestinian conferences organized by Hamas, the PFLP-GC, and PIJ in January 2008, and another conference organized by Hamas and funded by Iran in November. With Mishaal's April 2009 reelection as leader of Hamas' Political Bureau, more Hamas leaders from Gaza traveled to Damascus for meetings and the election of a new politburo.[56]

The 2011 uprising in Syria has strained the Syrian-Hamas relationship. Reports surfaced in early May that Hamas might be seeking another home.[57] The apparent spat came as a result of Hamas refusing to publicly condemn the protests. A senior Hamas official at a Palestinian camp near Damascus explained, "The Syrian government said to us, 'Whoever is not with us is against us.' It wants us to express clearly our position over what is going on in Syria. It wants us to be against the Syrian demonstrations. We told them we are neutral. We said to them we are living in the country as visitors and we have no right to comment or interfere in the country's problems."[58] Khalid Mishaal later dismissed rumors that Hamas was seeking to move to Qatar. Whether it is true or not, Hamas has been unwelcome in most Arab capitals and previously had little choice but to accept Syrian patronage. The "Arab Spring" opens up the possibility of creating new bases in Egypt and beyond. This would have grave consequences for the Asad regime, which views Hamas as an asset to balance the more moderate forces of Fatah and the Palestinian Authority. Since Asad's regional value comes from his ability cause mischief throughout the Middle East, losing control over Hamas or Hezbollah weakens his political hand and his ability to project power across the region.

Iraq

Syria has armed, trained, financed, encouraged, and transported foreign *jihadists* to fight against Coalition forces in Iraq and against the emerging Iraqi government since Saddam Hussein's regime was toppled in 2003.[59] In Syrian terms, assisting the insurgency in Iraq is not regarded as terrorism but as legitimate resistance to U.S. occupation, and is supervised by Syria's intelligence services.[60]

The Syrian trafficking system, which accounts for a large part of the foreign *jihadist* industry, "is organized into independent rings of smugglers, generally transportation specialists who operate within a given territory and pay an established tribute to one of several officials with authority in that area."[61] The hand of the Syrian state is present throughout.

From 2003 to 2007, Syria facilitated both components of the Sunni Iraqi insurgency: the Iraqi Ba'athists and al-Qaeda in Iraq. The "New Regional Command" that was formed by former members of Hussein's regime received finances and directions from Syria.[62] According to estimates in 2004, Syrian financing of insurgents in Ramadi reached $1.2 million per month.[63] Signs of direct Syrian operational presence were also abundant; "U.S. troops in Fallujah, for example, found a GPS system in an explosives production facility that showed routes originating in western Syria. Coalition forces also captured a GPS system that showed waypoints in Western Syria."[64] The following year, Iraq's defense minister charged that 400 detainees had trained in Syria.[65]

The foreign fighter network in Syria represented a major contributor to ongoing instability and violence in Iraq. As early as 2004, General Richard Myers, then-chairman of the U.S. Joint Chiefs of Staff, said at a press conference in Baghdad, "There are other foreign fighters. We know for a fact that a lot of them find their way into Iraq through Syria for sure."[66] Other estimates suggest that as much as 80 percent of the foreign fighters who have infiltrated Iraq have come through Syria and are responsible for the most lethal suicide bombings in Iraq.[67] Indeed, an Italian investigation of foreign fighter recruitment in Italy found that "Syria has functioned as a hub for an Al-Qaeda network."[68] A large number of these foreign fighters arrived in Syria via the Damascus International Airport.[69] The flow of foreign fighters through Syrian territory reached a high of 80 to 100 a month in mid-2007 and despite repeated appeals Syria did not stem the flow of Sunni suicide bombers into Iraq.[70] 2008 showed a significant drop in the number of jihadists allowed into Iraq, but American sources claim this was the result of Iraqi and Coalition forces operating along the Syrian border—that is to say, not a result of Syrian actions.[71] Despite the short respite, in May 2009, terrorist traffic from Syria spiked again.[72] Examples of Syria's facilitation of terrorist movement into Iraq continued throughout 2010, but have dropped off substantially in 2011.[73]

This activity has created a causal connection between the Asad regime and al-Qaeda. Documents seized in a September 2007 raid on an al-Qaeda in Iraq (AQI) safe house in the border village of Sinjar in Western Iraq revealed that from August 2006 until August 2007 the Syrian city of Dayr al-Zawr along Iraq's border was an active and important logistics hub for fighters en route to Iraq. According to the documents, "AQI has relied on at least 95 different Syrian 'coordinators' to provide such services. Illustrating a sense of how well organized this system was, the coordinators appeared to specialize in working with prospective foreign fighters and suicide bombers from specific locales."[74] It appears from the 606 captured personnel records that all of the listed jihadists entered Iraq from Syria and Syrians comprised the third largest nationality of foreign fighters, behind only Saudis and Libyans.[75] Indeed, the Syrians coordinated the insertion into Iraq of almost all the foreign fighters listed in the Sinjar records.[76]

Syria also allowed key al-Qaeda activists in Iraq to use its territory for weapons, supplies, and financing. This came to light in the wake of a U.S. special forces operation in the Syrian village of Sukkariyeh near the Iraq border on October 26, 2008. Abu Ghadiyah, a senior al-Qaeda operative was killed in the raid. American intelligence sources claim he had operated in Syria on behalf of Abu Musab al-Zarqawi where he smuggled money, weapons, and fighters into Iraq and he continued to do so after Zarqawi was killed in 2006.[77] "U.S. intelligence indicates that Abu Ghadiyah supplied foreign *jihadists* with false passports, trained them, provided them with safe houses, and supplied them with weapons and other supplies. The volunteers came from many countries in the region—Morocco, Libya, Algeria, Egypt, Sudan, Saudi Arabia, and Turkey. Abu al-Ghadiyah made housing arrangements for them in Damascus and in the port city of Latakia with the help of Syrian intelligence officers. After moving the volunteers into Iraq, Abu Ghadiyah would continue to see to their logistical needs."[78]

American military sources further claimed that Syria has allowed al-Qaeda operatives to train in Syria since 2003.[79] Senior American officials also claim that Syria supplies al-Qaeda in Iraq with bomb-making materials to improve the lethality of their explosives.[80]

ENDNOTES

[1] Seth Wikas, "Battling the Lion of Damascus: Syria's Domestic Opposition and the Asad Regime," Washington Institute for Near East Policy *Policy Focus* 69, May 2007, 24.

[2] "A Look at the Terror Group Jund al-Sham," *Washington Post*, September 12, 2006, http://www.washingtonpost.com/wp-dyn/content/article/2006/09/12/AR2006091200844.html; "Jund al-Sham," globalsecurity.org, n.d., http://www.globalsecurity.org/security/profiles/jund_al-sham.htm; "Jund al-Sham," globaljihad.net, n.d., http://globaljihad.net/view_page.asp?id=230; "Qassioun Shootout," globaljihad.net, n.d., http://globaljihad.net/view_page.asp?id=1269.

[3] Wikas, "Battling the Lion of Damascus," 24.

[4] Chris Zambelis, "Violence in Syria Points to Growing Radical Islamist Unrest," Jamestown Foundation *Terrorism Focus* 4, iss. 3, June 13, 2006, http://www.jamestown.org/programs/gta/single/?tx_ttnews[tt_news]=800&tx_ttnews[backPid]=239&no_cache=1; Andrew McGregor, "Controversial Syrian Preacher Abu al-Qaqa Gunned Down in Aleppo," Jamestown Foundation *Terrorism Focus* 4, iss. 33, October 16, 2007, http://www.jamestown.org/single/?no_cache=1&tx_ttnews[tt_news]=4481.

[5] Sami Moubayed, "Terror within Syria," *Al-Ahram Weekly* (Cairo), June 14, 2006, http://weekly.ahram.org.eg/2006/798/re83.htm.

[6] Nicholas Blandord, "In Secular Syria, an Islamic Revival," *Christian Science Monitor*, October 3, 2003, http://www.csmonitor.com/2003/1003/p06s01-wome.html/%28page%29/2.

[7] Leila Fadel, "Syria' Bashar al-Assad Faces Most Serious Unrest of his Tenure," *Washington Post*, March 24, 2011, http://www.washingtonpost.com/world/syrias-bashar-al-assad-faces-most-serious-unrest-of-his-tenure/2011/03/24/ABmKANRB_story.html

[8] Leila Fadel, "Protesters Shot as Demonstrations Expand Across Syria," *Washington Post*, March 25, 2011, http://www.washingtonpost.com/world/protesters-shot-as-demonstrations-expand-across-syria/2011/03/25/AFTnewWB_story.html

[9] "Raw Intelligence Report: A View from Syria," *STRATFOR*, April 25, 2011, http://www.stratfor.com/analysis/20110425-raw-intelligence-report-view-syria

[10] Eli Lake, "Syrian Opposition to Open Washington Office," *New York Sun,* October 20, 2006, http://www.nysun.com/foreign/syrian-opposition-to-open-washington-office/42005/; Phil Sands, "Syrian Opposition Group Collapses," *The National* (Abu Dhabi), April 21, 2009, http://www.thenational.ae/article/20090422/FOREIGN/704219850/1135.

[11] National Salvation Front in Syria, "NSF delegation meets US officials, announces opening of Washington DC office," April 19, 2007,

http://www.savesyria.org/english/releases/2007/04/001.htm.

[12] "Syrian Muslim Brotherhood Withdraws from Opposition Group," *Al-Sharq Al-Awsat* (London), April 6, 2009, http://www.aawsat.com/english/news.asp?section=1&id=16306.

[13] Lee Smith, "Crack-up," *Tablet Magazine*, April 28, 2011, http://www.tabletmag.com/news-and-politics/65981/crack-up/.

[14] Khalid Sindawi, "The Shiite Turn in Syria," *Hudson Institute Current Trends in Islamist Ideology* 8 (2009), 89.

[15] Eyal Zisser, "Syria, the Ba'th Regime and the Islamic Movement: Stepping on a New Path," *The Muslim World*, January 2005, 60-62.

[16] Ibid.

[17] Ibidem.

[18] "Uproar at Syrian cartoon protests," BBC (London), February 5, 2006, http://news.bbc.co.uk/2/hi/middle_east/4682388.stm; "Rice: Syria, Iran Inflamed Violence," *Fox News*, February 8, 2006, http://www.foxnews.com/story/0,2933,184203,00.html.

[19] Ibid.

[20] Gary Gambill, "Assad's Survival Strategy," *Foreign Policy*, April 6, 2011, http://www.foreignpolicy.com/articles/2011/04/06/assads_survival_strategy?page=full.

[21] Ibid.

[22] Ibidem.

[23] Zisser, "Syria, the Ba'th Regime and the Islamic Movement," 45.

[24] Ibid.

[25] Thomas Mayer, "The Islamic Opposition in Syria, 1961-1982," Orient 24 (1983); Patrick Seale and Maureen McConville, *Asad of Syria: The Struggle for the Middle East*, (London: I.B. Tauris, 1988), 320-338.

[26] Jared A. Favole, "Brotherhood Raises Syria Profile: Islamist Group Tries to Organize Opposition to Assad Regime, as Protests Waiver," *Wall Street Journal*, May 17, 2011, http://online.wsj.com/article/SB10001424052748703509104576327212414590134.html.

[27] They were released in several presidential amnesties in December 1991 (2,864 prisoners), March 1992 (600 prisoners), November 1993 (554 prisoners), November 1995 (1,200 prisoners), and 1998 (250 prisoners).

[28] Wikas, "Battling the Lion of Damascus," 25.

[29] Favole, "Brotherhood Raises Syria Profile.".

[30] Ibid.

[31] Ibidem.

[32] Ibidem.

[33] Ibidem.

[34] Reuven Erlich, "Syria as a Strategic Prop for Hezbollah and Hamas," Intelligence and Terrorism Information Center at the Center for Special Studies, August 3, 2006, 4, http://www.terrorism-info.org.

il/malam_multimedia/English/eng_n/pdf/syria_strategy_e.pdf.

[35] Ibid.

[36] Yaakov Amidor, "Misreading the Second Lebanon War," Jerusalem Center for Public Affairs *Jerusalem Issue Brief* 15, No. 16, January 16, 2007, http://www.jcpa.org/JCPA/Templates/ShowPage.asp?DBID=1&LNGID=1&TMID=111&FID=283&PID=1844&IID=1485.

[37] "Report: Hizbullah Deployed Syrian-Made Missiles Capable of Destroying Israel," *Naharnet*, January 14, 2010, http://www.naharnet.com/domino/tn/NewsDesk.nsf/getstory?openform&057481A277A7B06FC22576AB00215DC5.

[38] Yaakov Katz, "Barak: Syria-Lebanon Arms Transfer Violates UN resolutions," *Ha'aretz* (Tel Aviv), April 13, 2010, http://www.jpost.com/Israel/Article.aspx?id=173033.

[39] Andrew Tabler, "Inside the Syrian Missile Crisis," *Foreign Policy*, April 14, 2010, http://www.foreignpolicy.com/articles/2010/04/14/inside_the_syrian_missile_crisis; Frederick Deknatel, "Roadblocks to Damascus," *The Nation*, July 2, 2010, http://www.thenation.com/article/36846/roadblocks-damascus; Katherine Zimmerman, "Arming Hezbollah: Syria's Alleged Scud Missile Transfer," *AEI Critical Threats*, May 11, 2010, http://www.criticalthreats.org/lebanon/arming-hez-bollah-syrias-alleged-scud-missile-transfer.

[40] Simon McGregor-Wood, "Missiles on Menu as Hezbollah, Iran and Syria Dine," *ABC News*, February 26, 2010, http://abcnews.go.com/International/nasrallah-dines-assad-ahmadinejad-damascus/story?id=9953472; "How the Tehran/Damascus Terror Axis Targets Israel," Investigative Project on Terrorism *IPT News*, January 13, 2011, http://www.investigativeproject.org/2493/how-tehran-damascus-ter-ror-axis-targets-israel.

[41] "Al Asad lil Manar: Mowqifna min al muqawama thabit was lam yataghayir [Al-Asad to Al-Manar: Our Position On The Resistance Remains Steadfast And Unchanged]," *Al Manar* (Beirut), September 4, 2008, http://www.almanar.com.lb/newssite/newsdetails.aspx?id=55724&language=ar.

[42] "Syria Envoy: Future Generations Will Pay If Israel Scuttles Peace Talks," *Ha'aretz* (Tel Aviv), October 22, 2008, http://www.haaretz.com/hasen/spages/1030438.html.

[43] "Lebanese Salafism: Between Global Jihad and Syrian Manipulation," *NowLebanon*, n.d., http://www.nowlebanon.com/Library/Files/EnglishDocumentation/Other%20Documents/salafist%20english1.pdf.

[44] Benny Avni, "Syrian Intelligence Linked to Terrorist Group," *New York Sun*, October 25, 2007, http://www.nysun.com/foreign/syrian-intelligence-linked-to-terrorist-group/65202/.

[45] "Militant Mastermind Flees from Lebanon to Syria," *Ya Libnan* (Beirut), June 5, 2007, http://yalibnan.com/site/archives/2007/06/

militant_master.php; Michael Young, "Syria's Useful Idiots," *Wall Street Journal*, June 3, 2007, http://www.opinionjournal.com/extra/?id=110010161.

[46] "Individuals and Entities Designated by the State Department Under E.O. 13224," in U.S. Department of State, Office of the Coordinator For Counterterrorism, *Terrorism Designations*, June 23, 2010, http://www.state.gov/s/ct/rls/other/des/143210.htm; "U.S. Designates Fatah al-Islam 'Terrorist' Group," *Reuters*, August 13, 2007, http://www.reuters.com/article/idUSN1334969020070813.

[47] For more on Shaker al-Absi, see "The Inside Story of Fatah al Islam's Leader Shaker al-Absi," *Ya Libnan* (Beirut), June 16, 2007, http://yalibnan.com/site/archives/2007/06/lebanon_the_ins_1.php; Dani Berkovich, "The Stand-off Between the Lebanese Army and 'Fatah al-Islam': A Test of the Siniora Government's Determination," Tel Aviv University Institute for National Security Studies *Tel Aviv Insight* no. 19, June 3, 2007, http://listserv.tau.ac.il/cgi-bin/wa?A3=ind0706&L=tau-inss-il&P=131425&E=2&B=-------_%3D_NextPart_001_01C7A5E9.842FB7D2&N=Berkovich+19.doc&T=application%2Fmsword; "The Truth About the Assault on Fatah al-Islam in Syria," NEFA Foundation, November 29, 2008, www.nefa-foundation.org/miscellaneous/nefafatahislam1208.pdf.

[48] "Fath Al-Islam Calls for Jihad in Syria," Middle East Media Research Institute *Special Dispatch* no. 3709, March 28, 2011, http://www.memri.org/report/en/0/0/0/0/0/0/5140.htm.

[49] "Anti-Israeli Terrorism, 2006: Data, Analysis and Trends," Intelligence and Terrorism Information Center at the Center for Special Studies, March 2007, 91, http://www.terrorism-info.org.il/malam_multimedia/English/eng_n/pdf/terrorism_2006e.pdf.

[50] Ibid.

[51] Kifah Zaboun, "Hamas: Who is in Charge?" *Al-Sharq al-Awsat* (London), February 14, 2009, http://www.aawsat.com/english/news.asp?section=3&id=15728.

[52] George Baghdadi, "Syria Congratulates Hamas on Gaza 'Victory,'" *CBS News*, January 24, 2009, http://www.cbsnews.com/8301-503543_162-4750858-503543.html; "Assad: Hamas Win Decreases Int'l Pressure on Damascus," *Ha'aretz* (Tel Aviv), March 6, 2006, http://www.haaretz.com/print-edition/news/assad-hamas-win-decreases-int-l-pressure-on-damascus-1.181897; Ibrahim Hamidi, "Was Syria Right to Hail Hamas' Victory?" *Daily Star* (Beirut), March 20, 2006, http://www.dailystar.com.lb/article.asp?edition_id=10&categ_id=5&article_id=23080#axzz0vZxHbkyH.

[53] "Chapter 3: State Sponsors of Terrorism, Syria," in U.S. Department of State, Office of the Coordinator For Counterterrorism, *Country Reports on Terrorism 2008* (Washington, DC: U.S. Department of State, April 30, 2009), http://www.state.gov/s/ct/rls/crt/2008/122436.

htm; David Schenker, "Syria, Hamas, and the Gaza Crisis," Washington Institute for Near East Policy *PolicyWatch* no. 1121, July 10, 2006, http://www.washingtoninstitute.org/templateC05.php?CID=2486; Jack Khoury, "Assad to Meshal: Syria Stands By Hamas," *Ha'aretz* (Tel Aviv), January 9, 2010, http://www.haaretz.com/hasen/spages/1141356.html.

[54] "Chapter 3: State Sponsors of Terrorism, Syria," in *Country Reports on Terrorism 2008*.

[55] Ibid.

[56] "Masha'al Reelected as Hamas Leader," *Al Bawaba*, April 27, 2009, http://www.albawaba.com/en/news/244533.

[57] Ethan Bronner, "Tensions Rise as Hamas Refuses to Take Sides in Syria," *New York Times*, May 2, 2011, http://www.nytimes.com/2011/05/03/world/middleeast/03hamas.html?_r=4&hp&tr=y&auid=8272696.

[58] Ibid.

[59] "Engaging Syria? U.S. Constraints and Opportunities," International Crisis Group *Middle East Report* no. 83 (February 11, 2009), 3.

[60] "Syrian President Bashar Assad Meets Iran's Supreme Leader," Iranian Student News Agency (ISNA), August 20, 2009, http://payvand.com/news/09/aug/1183.html; See also *Al-Ba'ath* (Damascus), January 17, 2009: Asad defined resistance as "a way to achieve peace," explaining that "peace without resistance is surrender."

[61] Brian Fishman, ed., *Bombers, Bank Accounts & Bleedout: Al-Qa'ida's Road In And Out Of Iraq* (West Point, New York: Harmony Project, 2008), 3, http://ctc.usma.edu/harmony/pdf/Sinjar_2_July_23.pdf; Joseph Felter and Brian Fishman, "Becoming a Foreign Fighter: A Second Look at the Sinjar Records," in Fishman, *Bombers, Bank Accounts & Bleedout*, 32.

[62] Ryan Mauro, "Has Damascus Stopped Supporting Terrorists?" Middle East Quarterly, Summer 2009, pp. 61-67, http://www.meforum.org/2406/damascus-supporting-terrorists; Thomas E. Ricks, "General: Iraqi Insurgents Directed from Syria," Washington Post, December 17, 2004, A29, http://www.washingtonpost.com/wp-dyn/articles/A5886-2004Dec16.html.

[63] Mauro, "Has Damascus Stopped Supporting Terrorists?"; Thomas E. Ricks, *Fiasco: The American Adventure in Iraq, 2003 to 2005* (New York: Penguin Press, 2006), 409.

[64] Mauro, "has Damascus Stopped Supporting Terrorists?"; See also Nicholas Blanford, "More Signs of Syria Turn up in Iraq," *Christian Science Monitor*, December 23, 2004, http://www.freerepublic.com/focus/f-news/1308234/posts.

[65] "180 Terrorists Escape to Syria at Start of Operation Steel Curtain," KUNA (Kuwait City), November 5, 2005.

[66] "Coalition Provisional Authority Briefing," Baghdad, Iraq, April

15, 2004.

[67] "Jihadist Blowback?" *The Economist* (London), October 2, 2008; Fishman, *Bombers, Bank Accounts & Bleedout*, 6.

[68] Sebastian Rotella, "A Road to Ansar Began in Italy," *Los Angeles Times*, April 28, 2003, http://articles.latimes.com/2003/apr/28/news/war-probe28; Matthew Levitt, "Foreign Fighters and Their Economic Impact: A Case Study of Syria and Al-Qaeda in Iraq (AQI)," paper presented at the "Foreign Fighter Problem" conference, Foreign Policy Research Institute, Washington, DC, July 14, 2009.

[69] Joseph Lieberman, "Al Qaeda's Travel Agent," *Wall Street Journal*, August 20, 2007, http://www.opinionjournal.com/editorial/?id=110010496.

[70] Karen DeYoung, "Terrorist Traffic Via Syria Again Inching Up: Pipeline to Iraq Back In Business After Lull." *Washington Post*, May 11, 2009, http://www.washingtonpost.com/wp-dyn/content/article/2009/05/10/AR2009051002242.html.

[71] Ibid.

[72] Ibidem.

[73] Robert Burns, "Syrian Envoy Denies Aiding Insurgency in Iraq," *Seattle Times*, November 11, 2009, http://seattletimes.nwsource.com/html/politics/2010251915_apussyriairaq.html; Leila Fadel, "Mosul Struggles with Ethnic Divides, Insurgency," *The Washington Post*, July 24, 2010, http://www.washingtonpost.com/wp-dyn/content/article/2010/07/23/AR2010072305604.html.

[74] Joseph Felter and Brian Fishman, *Al-Qaida's Foreign Fighters in Iraq: A First Look at the Sinjar Records*, (West Point, New York: Harmony Project, Combating Terrorism Center at West Point, December 19, 2007), www.ctc.usma.edu/harmony/pdf/CTCForeignFighter.19.Dec07.pdf.

[75] Ibid.

[76] Fishman, *Bombers, Bank Accounts & Bleedout*, 3, 32, 36; The insertion of the Saudi terrorists is especially instructive as Saudi Arabia shares a lengthy and porous border with Iraq. The Saudi *jihadists* presumably choose to travel to Iraq through Syria because Asad tolerates what the Saudi leadership will not. It is also possible that the total Syrian numbers are underrepresented, since Syrians formed a majority of the detainees held at Camp Bucca, the main U.S. detention camp in Iraq.

[77] Amir Kulick and Yoram Schweitzer, "Syria and the Global Jihad: A Dangerous Double Game," Institute for National Security Studies *Strategic Assessment* 11, no.3, January 2009, 67; See also Mark Hosenball, "Targeting a 'Facilitator:' A Commando Raid into Syria Aimed at Al Qaeda in Iraq," *Newsweek*, October 27, 2008, http://www.newsweek.com/id/166039; Felter and Fishman, Al-Qaida's *Foreign Fighters in Iraq*, 4–6.

[78] Amir Kulick and Yoram Schweitzer, "Syria and the Global Jihad: A Dangerous Double Game," *Strategic Assessment*, Institute for National Security Studies, Vol. 11, No.3, January 2009, 67.

[79] "Department of Defense News Briefing with Maj. Gen. Kelly from Iraq," Baghdad, Iraq, October 23, 2008, http://www.defense.gov/transcripts/transcript.aspx?transcriptid=4309.

[80] See federal district court ruling in Washington, D.C., *Francis Gates, et al., v. Syrian Arab Republic, et al.*, Civil Action No. 06-1500 (RMC) https://ecf.dcd.uscourts.gov/cgi-bin/show_public_doc?2006cv1500-42.

LEBANON

QUICK FACTS

Population: 4,125,247

Area: 10,400 sq km

Ethnic Groups: Arab 95%, Armenian 4%, other 1%

Religions: Muslim 59.7% (Shi'a, Sunni, Druze, Isma'ilite, Alawite or Nusayri), Christian 39% (Maronite Catholic, Greek Orthodox, Melkite Catholic, Armenian Orthodox, Syrian Catholic, Armenian Catholic, Syrian Orthodox, Roman Catholic, Chaldean, Assyrian, Copt, Protestant), other 1.3%

Government Type: Republic

GDP (official exchange rate): $33.04 billion

Map and Quick Facts courtesy of the CIA World Factbook (last updated July 2010)

Lebanon was created in 1943 on the basis of a pact between Muslims and Christians, whereby Beirut would serve as a crossroads between East and West. This pact was institutionalized into a democratic, confessional system that distributed power along religious lines. This political system encouraged the creation of diverse social and political groups, reinforcing democracy in the short term but simultaneously laying the groundwork for the proliferation of Islamist groups inimical to the ruling order. These forces presented Islam as the solution to the ills of Lebanese –and indeed, larger Arab – society, especially in the wake of the Arab defeat in the 1967 War with Israel. Iran's 1979 Revolution and Israel's subsequent invasion of Lebanon in 1982 changed the socio-political dynamics in Beirut, leading Iran and Syria to support the creation of Hezbollah, a Shi'ite jihadi organization dedicated to fighting Israel and its allies in Lebanon. Hezbollah, in turn, erected an expansive social, political and military infrastructure in Lebanon, ensconcing itself as a key arbiter of power. Sunni Islamist forces, by contrast, mobilized later—in reaction to the U.S. invasion of Iraq in 2003 and the murder of former Prime Minister Rafik Hariri in 2005. Hezbollah's seizure of West Beirut in May 2008 intensified sectarian tensions and deepened the activity of Islamist forces. Since then, the political discourse of the country has been polarized further, while Hezbollah has continued its drive to control the state and "Islamize" Lebanon's society and collective identity.

ISLAMIST ACTIVITY

Though the seeds of political Islam were sown in Lebanon in the aftermath of the 1948 War, the Arab defeat in the 1967 War and the failure of nationalist regimes to address the socio-political ills of Arab society provided the environment for the growth of Islamist movements, which asserted that "Islam" is the solution. Lebanon's confessional system and quasi-democracy allowed the Islamists to freely operate and to try to affect society and politics by expanding their popular base of support. No less significant, the same confessional system that favored one community over another provided the Islamists the political tool to rail against the system's intrinsic socio-political and administrative inequalities. The call to abolish political sectarianism, which favored the Christian community, became a rallying cry for Islamists and pan-Arabists alike. But it was the fight against the "Zionist entity" (the Islamists' designation of Israel) that served as a means for the Islamist movements, especially the Shi'a Islamist movement, to redress their socio-political marginalization and to mobilize and polarize Lebanon's communities.

Al-Jama'a al-Islamiyah and the Jabhat al-Amal al-Islami (Islamic Action Front)
The Islamic Association (*al-Jama'a al-Islamiyah*), an offshoot of the Muslim Brotherhood and Lebanon's first Sunni Islamist movement, had its origins in the Association of the Worshippers of the Compassionate (*Jama'at Ubad al-Rahman*) founded by Muhammad Umar al-Da'uq in the 1950s.
Distressed by the Arab defeat in Palestine in 1948, al-Da'uq fled to Beirut, where he established the Association, which reflected his belief that the loss of Palestine was linked to the distance of Muslims from their religion. He strove to bring Muslims back to "Islam as a faith, dogma [and] way of life" and to inculcate a "spirit of *Jihad* and sacrifice."[1] He based his proselytizing (*da'wa*) on the educational, cultural, ethical, and spiritual tenets of Islam. By the early 1950s, his *da'wa* activity reached many Sunni-majority cities and towns, including Tripoli (the capital of North Lebanon), where a center for *Jama'at Ubad al-Raham* was opened. It was in Tripoli that the future leaders of today's Islamic Association, including its co-founder, Fathi Yakan, joined the center.
Around the same time, Mustafa al-Siba'i, the superintendent of the Muslim Brotherhood in Syria, moved to Beirut following the outlawing of his group and the arrest of many of its members by the Syrian regime.[2] Invited

by Muslim associations to Tripoli, al-Siba'i organized a series of well-received lectures and forums there. Yakan and his colleagues were moved by al-Sibai's ideology, as well as his dedication to "liberating the Islamic nation from foreign rule" and "establishing a free Islamic state."[3] No sooner did they become familiar with the works of the Brotherhood ideologues Hassan al-Banna and Sayyid Qutb than they decided to move beyond mere cultural and educational activism. The resulting Islamist organization, *al-Jama'a al-Islamiyah*, was officially licensed by Lebanon's Interior Ministry on June 18, 1964.[4]

Following the Arab defeat in 1967, *al-Jama'a* and other Islamist movements gained momentum. During Lebanon's initial civil war years (1975-1976), the Islamic Association founded a militia, *al-Mujahiddin*, which fought alongside the pan-Arab, leftist National Movement against the Maronite Christians. Following the entry of Syrian troops into Lebanon in the summer of 1976, the Islamic Association dismantled its militia. But in the 1980s, *Al-Jama'a* founded a new armed corps, *Quwat Fajr* (the Fajr Brigades), to resist the 1982 Israeli invasion of Lebanon. Throughout the mid- to late-1980s, it supported Hezbollah's *jihad* against Israeli occupation of southern Lebanon.[5]

Following the end of the civil war in 1990, *al-Jama'a* supported Lebanon's resulting political system and participated in municipal and parliamentary elections. It has pursued an opportunistic electoral policy of cooperating with leaders and parties that enhance its chances of winning. Yet *al-Jama'a* has had uneasy relations with other Islamist parties and political actors. Specifically, *al-Jama'a* tried to strike a balance between supporting Hezbollah (the country's radical Shi'ite militia) and maintaining some sort of a political alliance with the Sunni community leadership of the al-Hariri family, which has been the leader of the U.S.-backed March 14th Forces.

The internal conflict within the Islamic Association came to a head in 2006, when the co-founder of the organization, Fathi Yakan, resigned over his objections to *al-Jama'a's* alliance with al-Hariri's *Mustaqbal* Party and the alliance's antagonistic stand toward Hezbollah. Yakan also fervently opposed *al-Mustaqbal's* close relationship with Washington, as he unequivocally supported the "resistance camp" of Iran, Syria, Hezbollah and Hamas.[6] Subsequently, Yakan recruited a number of Islamist groups and personalities and founded the *Jabhat al-Amal al-Islami* (The Islamic Action Front) in August 2006.[7] In its founding statement, the Islamic Action Front described its mission as "an affirmation of Islamic and national unity, protecting the Resistance and defending the unity of Lebanon...confronting sectarian and ethnic strife...and rejecting Western and American threats to Arab and Muslim countries."[8]

Hizb ut-Tahrir (Party of Liberation)
   Hizb ut-Tahrir was founded in Jordan by Sheikh Taqi al-Din al-Nabhani,

a Palestinian who studied at al-Azhar University, in the early 1950s. Following the 1948 War, he moved to Beirut, then to Jerusalem whence he moved to Jordan to become an instructor at the Islamic College in Amman. *Hizb al-Tahrir* in Lebanon was established in October of 1959.[9] The group describes itself as "a political party with Islam as its ideology."[10] It attributes the Islamic world's decline to irreligiouslity and seeks to resurrect Islam's golden age by reviving the Islamic way of life by establishing an Islamic State that implements Islam and carries its *da'wa* (call to Islam) to the world.[11] Strategically, it plans to institute Islamic law in one or more countries as a steppingstone to creating the greater Islamic state, the Caliphate, over all Islamic lands.[12]

However, the party did not fare well in Lebanon, or in any other Arab country. The organization consequently went underground, re-emerging in Lebanon only after the U.S.-led invasion of Iraq in 2003, when it organized anti-American demonstrations in Tripoli.[13] In 2005, Lebanese authorities indicted members of the group *in absentia* for their role in planning terror attacks in Iraq.[14] Though the party is still publicly committed to non-violence, and has vowed not to participate in Lebanese elections, it was officially banned for a time from operating in Lebanon. It remained active on an unofficial level, however; for example, in its organization of a demonstration in Beirut in September 2005 to commemorate the 81st anniversary of the Caliphate's abolition. In 2006, Ahmad Fatfat, the interior minister of the Hariri-backed Siniora government, permitted the party to renew its activity as a licensed political party. The party, in turn, has used its newfound legitimacy to stress that Lebanon's problems could only be addressed by turning Lebanon into an Islamic nation. And while it still maintains that such a transformation should come by peaceful means, the organization has supported violence elsewhere in the region; At the party's annual conference in 2009, its leader, Sheikh Adnan Mizyan, proclaimed that, "In light of the fact that many countries of Muslims are today under occupation, including Palestine, Iraq, Cyprus, the Balkans, the Caucasus, Afghanistan, and Kashmir, the Islamic Ummah must take Jihad measures in order to free them."[15] Official membership in the party is difficult to approximate; however, it is not implausible to estimate the number of its members and supporters to be in the several hundred on the basis of the number of attendees at the party's annual conferences and the number of protesters participating in its demonstrations.

Salafists

The return to Lebanon of the Afghan *mujahideen* in the late 1970s and early 1980s, following the end of the Soviet occupation of Afghanistan, contributed to the emergence of Salafist *jihadi* movements in under-developed and poor Sunni areas there.[16]

Salafi *jihadis* constitute a minority among the Salafists. Their activities can be traced to Lebanese Afghan veteran Bassam Kanj, also known as Abou Aisha. Kanj reportedly fought alongside bin Ladin in Afghanistan in the 1980s. During his stay in Peshawar, Pakistan, in 1988, he forged close relationships with a number of *mujahideen* who would later form the nucleus of the group he founded in 1996 in Northern Lebanon, *al-Takfir wal-Hijra.* This group also became known as the Dinniyeh Group, after the town where they had been active. In December 1999, the Dinniyeh group clashed with the Lebanese army. Kanj was killed and more than two dozen other members of the group were either killed or captured. Subsequently, in July 2000, the Mount Lebanon Criminal Court indicted 120 men for their alleged connection with the Dinniyeh group and the aforementioned clashes.[17]

Another *jihadist* group, *Isbat al-Ansar* (Band of Partisans), emerged in the Palestinian refugee camp of Ain al-Hilweh near the southern city of Sidon. The group was founded by Hisham Shridi, a former Palestinian leader of *al-Jama'a al-Islamiyah* who had gained notoriety fighting Israeli forces in South Lebanon. In December 1991, Shridi was assassinated by the PLO's Fatah movement in an attempt to re-impose its authority in the largest Palestinian refugee camp. Shridi was succeeded by his closest aide, Muhammad Abd al-Karim al-Saadi, also known as Abu Muhjin. During the 1990s, Abu Muhjin's group, in an attempt to assert its radical ideology, carried out a number of attacks on Christian religious targets and liquor stores. In 1995, his group assassinated Shaykh Nizar al-Halabi, the leader of *al-Ahbash* (see below). Lebanese authorities executed three members of the group for their participation in the plot, and issued a death sentence *in absentia* against Abu Muhjin. Another participant, Yasir Izzat Saud, was sentenced to death, but his sentence was later commuted.[18]

Since then, Abu Muhjin has disappeared from public view and *de facto* leadership of the organization passed to his brother, known as Abu Tarik. In June 1999, the group assassinated three Lebanese judges and the chief prosecutor for southern Lebanon at the Justice Palace in Sidon in an act of revenge for the execution of three of their colleagues. The group has taken pride in participating in the *jihad* against U.S. troops in Iraq.[19] It remains active mainly in the Ain al-Hilweh camp, and is estimated to command the loyalty of between 100 and 300 fighters.[20]

But the deadliest manifestation of Salafi *jihadism* in Lebanon is embodied by *Fatah al-Islam.* The organization emerged in November 2006, when it split from *Fatah al-Intifada* (Fatah Uprising), a Syrian-backed Palestinian group based in Lebanon. Its main founder was Shaker al-Absi, a Jordanian-Palestinian best known for organizing the 2002 assassination of U.S. diplomat Lawrence Foley in Amman. Gradually, Absi's motley group seized control of the Palestinian Nahr al-Bared refugee camp near Tripoli. The Lebanese government linked it to deadly bus bombings in Ain Alaq, Lebanon, on February 13, 2007, which killed three people.   On May 20, 2007, a battle between *Fatah al-Islam* and Lebanese troops erupted in Nahr al-Bared following a police search for suspects in a bank robbery. The fighting lasted until September 2, 2007 and claimed the lives of over 160 Lebanese soldiers. The Lebanese government initially claimed that the Salafi *jihadist* organization was the creation of Syrian intelligence. Damascus, however, denied any relationship with *Fatah al-Islam*. Later on, Lebanese authorities discovered that the group had links to al-Qaeda.[21]

Al-Ahbash

The Association of Islamic Philanthropic Projects (*Jam'iyyat al-Mashari' al-Khairiyya al-Islamiyya*) is a comparatively moderate Islamist force supported by Syria as a counterweight to radical Islamist forces in Lebanon. It is a Sufi movement that devoutly follows the teachings of its founder Sheikh Abdallah Ibn Muhammad Ibn Yusuf al-Hirari al-Shi'bi al-Abdari, also known as Abdallah al-Habashi. Al-Habashi, born in 1920 in al-Hirara, Ethiopia, migrated to Beirut in the 1950s and became a lecturer at al-Azhar University's Lebanese branch. His school of thought mixes elements of Sunni and Shi'a theological doctrines with Sufi spiritualism. The group's website and journal, *Manar al-Huda*, emphasize Islam's pluralistic nature; oppose the use of violence against the ruling authorities; accept the legitimacy of the Imam Ali (the Shi'a doctrine of legitimacy) and of his sons Hassan and Hussein; uphold the teachings of Hussein's son, Zayn al-Abidin; and defend many Sufi beliefs and practices condemned by Islamists as heresies.[22]

Tensions between *al-Ahbash* and Salafi *jihadis* in Lebanon peaked in 1995, when members of the radical group *Isbat al-Ansar* assassinated *al-Ahbash's* leader, Sheikh Nizar Halabi. In April 2001, *al-Ahbash* supporters took the streets in Beirut chanting pro-Syrian slogans while brandishing clubs and knives.[23] Moreover, following the murder of Hariri in 2005 and the withdrawal of Syrian troops from Lebanon thereafter, *al-Ahbash* took to the streets in Beirut, along with other pro-Syrian parties and groups, in a show of solidarity with Syria. This created friction between the government and *al-Ahbash* supporters—tension which played out in sporadic street fighting in West Beirut.

Notably, however, *al-Ahbash's* pro-Syrian stance has not translated into support for Hezbollah, especially following Hezbollah's takeover of West Beirut in 2008. Communal and personal tensions between Hezbollah and *al-Ahbash* erupted in deadly skirmishes in Burj Abi Haydar, the stronghold of *al-Ahbash* in West Beirut, in August 2010.[24] Syria did not take sides in the conflict, preferring to try and tamp down tensions.

Hezbollah

The ideological foundations of what would come to be known as Hezbollah were laid in the 1960s and 1970s in Lebanon by three religious scholars: the Ayatollahs Muhammad Hussein Fadlallah and Muhammad Mahdi Shamseddine and Imam Musa al-Sadr. The party embraced the Ayatollah Ruhollah Khomeini's revolutionary doctrine of *Velayat e-Faqih* (Guardianship of the Jurisconsult), which would come to dominate in Iran in 1979. Neglected by the Lebanese government and underrepresented in the country's confessional political system, these religious scholars sought to empower and unify Lebanon's Shi'a community.

Their efforts were greatly aided by Israel's 1982 invasion of Lebanon. The Shi'a community, which had initially welcomed the Israeli troops, quickly mobilized against the "occupation" forces. The reason had to do with the connection made by many Shi'ites between Israel's invasion and Iran's successful model of Islamic revolution, which convinced them that armed struggle could be a vehicle for achieving political dominance.[25]

The seeds for a fundamentalist movement were thus sown in Lebanon. The *jihadi* program proved to be popular, offering an outlet for some Shi'ites unhappy with what they considered the progressive taming of their community's main political movement, *Amal*. A breakaway faction of *Amal* led by Hussein Mussawi was the first to join the nascent Islamist movement. Before long, other Shi'ite fundamentalists from the Beka'a Valley, the south of Lebanon and the Beirut suburb of Dahiyeh followed. The result was the coalescence of the Party of God, or Hezbollah.

Iran's religious establishment immediately perceived the movement as a vehicle by which to expand its revolutionary principles to the Lebanese Shi'a community and become a player in the Arab-Israeli conflict. Tehran deployed its crack Revolutionary Guard Corps (IRGC, or *Pasdaran*) to train and indoctrinate Hezbollah's cadres. Tehran, however, could not do this on its own. Given Syria's border with Lebanon and the latter's considerable troop presence there (a product of the Lebanese civil war), Iran also needed the blessing of Damascus. This was not difficult to obtain, however. Adamant about preventing Israel and its Lebanese allies from controlling Lebanon, Syrian President Hafez al-Assad blessed the Iranian infiltration so long it did not affect Syrian attempts at controlling Lebanon.

Throughout the 1980s, militants associated with Hezbollah launched a campaign of terror targeting both the Multinational Forces sent in 1982 to oversee the evacuation of the PLO from Beirut and Westerners residing in the capital. Suicide bombers attacked the U.S. Embassy and the U.S. Marines barracks in April and October of 1983, respectively. They took dozens of Americans and Europeans hostage and hijacked TWA flight 847 in 1985. Though the Iranian government denied all involvement, enough circumstantial evidence pointed to involvement by high-ranking members of the regime in Tehran.[26]

Over time, Assad would come to see Hezbollah not only as a "resistance movement" but also as a potential Lebanese political force. The status quo was altered in 1989 with the death of the Ayatollah Ruhollah Khomeini and the ensuing shift in political focus that took place in Tehran. At the same time, Syria, assisted by Saudi and Algerian mediation, brokered the Taif Accord, ending Lebanon's civil war. Signed by a majority of Lebanese deputies on October 22, 1989, the accord amended the Lebanese constitution, conferring roughly equal powers on the country's three main communities, the Maronites, Sunnis, and Shi'a. The accord also recognized Syria's "special relationship" with Lebanon, a trusteeship subsequently cemented by the May 20, 1991 *Treaty of Brotherhood, Cooperation, and Coordination* and the September 1, 1991 *Lebanon-Syria Defense and Security Agreement.*[27] As a result, Hezbollah entered Lebanon's political realm as a political party, while at the same time it was allowed by Damascus, unlike any other party, to keep its weapons and continue its *jihadi* activities against Israel in South Lebanon. Supported by Iran and Syria, Hezbollah emerged as a strong, multi-pronged force, whose image as a "resistance" movement was enhanced following the withdrawal of Israeli troops from Lebanon in 2000.

The Hezbollah-Iranian-Syrian relationship grew stronger after the United States launched military operations against Iraq in March 2003, thereby shattering the regional *status quo*. Both Iran and Syria sought to prevent the United States from creating a new regional order that could threaten their rejectionist regimes. Thus, they supported Hezbollah not only as a deterrent force against the U.S. and Israel, but also as a military and political force against the pro-Western March 14 movement that was created following the murder of Hariri.[28]

It is in this context that the summer 2006 war erupted between Hezbollah and Israel. The hostilities ended on the basis of a seven-point plan and UNSCR 1701, which increased the number of United Nations Interim Force in Lebanon (UNIFIL) troops in southern Lebanon and called for the dismantling and disarming of all militias. Despite the destruction wrought upon Lebanese infrastructure and Hezbollah's cadres, the group's secretary general, Hassan Nasrallah, declared a "divine" victory and called for a national unity government and a new electoral law, asserting that the resistance had dealt a blow to American Middle East strategy.[29]

Whatever semblance of national unity Lebanon exhibited during the 2006 Lebanon War dissipated quickly. Recriminations and counter-recriminations have become a staple of Lebanese politics. A struggle for control of the state reemerged, with the March 14 Forces attempting to implement UN Security Council resolutions and support the Special Tribunal for Lebanon, created by the UN Security Council to investigate and prosecute the culprits of Hariri's assassination. Hezbollah, meanwhile, has sought veto power over government decisions under the pretext of national unity, with an eye toward changing the political structure in Lebanon so as to make it commensurate with Shi'a numbers.

ISLAMISM AND SOCIETY

While the roots of Islamism in Lebanon can be traced to the late 1940s, the phenomenon first gained traction politically in the late 1960s and 1970s, in response to domestic and regional failures. Key among them were the humiliating defeat of the Arab states in the 1967 War and the inability of the region's autocratic regimes to sustain economic growth for a growing Arab population. Islamists professed that Islam is the solution.

While Lebanon's confessional political system allowed the Islamists considerable room to operate, it simultaneously circumscribed their political development. Lebanon's Sunni leadership, acting in concert with the country's main religious establishment (*Dar al-afta*), managed to maintain its primacy at the expense of Islamist forces. Hezbollah, the Shi'ite militia, succeeded over time in reversing this trend, thanks in no small part to the support of Iran and Syria, especially since the 1990s when the movement became a political party. In fact, Hezbollah used its *Jihad* against Israel to enhance its political image as a patriotic party to put on the defensive those who questioned its actions, be they Christians or Muslims.

Both Shi'a and Sunni Islamists abhorred Maronite political power. Even when Nasserite pan-Arab nationalists were targeting Islamists in the 1950s, the Islamists sided with the pan-Arabists and leftists during Lebanon's civil strife in 1958.[30] Moreover, when the civil war erupted in 1975, Sunni Islamists, led by the Islamic Association, founded a militia to fight alongside the pan-Arabists and leftists against the Maronites. Fathi Yakan, the secretary general of the Islamic Association in the 1970s and 1980s, recommended that Lebanon merge with Syria as a solution to its confessional problems.[31]

Similarly, Hezbollah, until it became a political party and launched its *Infitah* (opening up) policy, acted not only to defeat the Maronite regime but also to turn Lebanon's multi-confessional society into an Islamic state.[32] Despite ideological differences between Sunni Islamism and Shi'a Islamism as expressed by Ayatollah Khomeini, Sunni Islamist movements, particularly the Islamic Unity Movement, accepted Iranian leadership and their policies. More so, the Islamic Unity Movement during its short rule over Tripoli imposed *sharia* law there and enforced strict Islamic behavior in the city regardless of sect. Christian women had to wear the veil and liquor stores, clubs, and churches were vandalized or bombed.

The U.S. invasion of Iraq and especially the murder of Hariri served to mobilize Sunni Islamists, particularly the Salafists, who were theretofore largely apolitical, weak or restricted in their movements by Lebanese and Syrian authorities. Moreover, sectarian tensions heightened following the summer

2006 war between Hezbollah and Israel and the seizure of Beirut in May 2008 by Hezbollah. As a result, the heightened political discourse sharpened sectarian tension across Lebanon's communities and society. Whereas some Sunni movements, such as the Islamic Action Front, supported Hezbollah, Salafists denounced the Shi'a community as heretical and deplored Hezbollah as the party of Satan. Even sectarian tension between two pro-Syrian groups, *al-Ahbash* and Hezbollah, degenerated into deadly street fighting in West Beirut.

Nevertheless, Hezbollah now is trying to make "resistance" against Israel the basis of Lebanese identity.[33] To a large extent, the Islamic Association has shared Hezbollah's vision of a society of resistance, despite some reservations about the Shi'a Islamist party. The Islamic Association's Political Manifesto underscores that "confronting this [Zionist] project requires great responsibilities on the part of the Islamic Association. The Ummah [community of believers] should be mobilized and made aware of the Zionist danger, which threatens its existence...and that a resistance society should be built in theory and practice."[34]

ISLAMISM AND THE STATE

Until the end of Lebanon's civil war in 1990, Islamist movements tended to shy away from national politics, focusing instead on their *da'wa* (proselytization) and the "Islamization" of Lebanese society. Both the Islamic Association and Hezbollah were forced to justify their participation in national politics on ideological grounds, the former going so far as to carry out a study of Islamic law which justified participation on the grounds "that to participate in parliamentary sessions does not mean approving any legislative position contradicting Islamic law... to participate in parliament sessions is a gateway to *Da'wa*... and to participate in parliament activities is to provide opportunities to realize peoples' interest and block vices, as well as achieve a balanced economic development."[35] Hezbollah's decision to enter Lebanese politics, by contrast, was sanctioned by none other than Iran's supreme leader, the Ayatollah Khamenei (although ideological questions over the group's participation were thrashed out by the party's Lebanese leadership).[36]

Today, although they ostensibly support pluralism in Lebanon, both the Islamic Association and Hezbollah remain steadfast in calling for the abolishment of the state's confessional system.[37] Christians and other minorities, however, fervently oppose such changes, fearing that they would be politically marginalized as a result. While the Islamic Association lacks the political capital to bring about such a fundamental change in the state's system, Hezbollah does not; rather, it has been using a dual policy of *Infitah* (opening up) and political coercion backed by military power to progressively control the Lebanese state. Since its participation in the first parliamentary elections in the 1990s, Hezbollah's *infitah* policy has sought to engage all communities in Lebanon, especially Christians. In theory, the party has shed its radical objective to turn Lebanon into an Islamic state, supporting pluralism. Yet, it has not relinquished its desire that Lebanon's non-Muslims convert to Islam. The Shi'a Islamist party uses political coercion whenever it faces pressure from the majority. In addition to seizing Beirut in May 2008 to force the government to repeal decisions considered hazardous to its security, Hezbollah has introduced the novel concept of consensual democracy, whereby a majority cannot make any decision or pass legislation without the consent of the minority. In fact, Hezbollah, in the name of national unity and co-existence, has succeeded in making this governing mode the dominant one in Lebanese politics.[38]

At the same time, however, Hezbollah has pursued a divisive political agenda that has deepened the sectarian and political rifts in Lebanese politics. The militia recently brought down the pro-Western Hariri government, following abortive attempts to force the government to forsake the Special Tribunal for Lebanon (STL). At the same time, fearing the indictment of its members for the murder of prime minister Rafiq Hariri, Hezbollah has raised the specter of sectarian strife should charges materialize. These moves have polarized an already-charged political climate riven by sectarian grievances.

The Lebanese state has maintained its policy of distinguishing between what it considers "resistance" movements, such as Hezbollah, and Islamist terrorist organizations, especially Sunni Salafist groups with links to al-Qaeda. In fact, since the Dinniyeh clashes in December 1999, and in particular in the aftermath of the September 11th terror attacks, Lebanese authorities have pursued and arrested many Sunni extremists. In October 2002, Interior Minister Elias Murr publicly stated that his government had arrested hundreds of suspected militants,[39] many of whom continue to be held on tenuous grounds. Following the battle of Nahr al-Bared, this campaign against Sunni extremism has evolved into a concerted counterterrorism effort, one supported and assisted by the United States. Specifically, Washington's aid to Beirut significantly increased since 2007 in the form of U.S. security assistance to the Lebanese armed forces and Internal Security Force.[40] Significantly, in October 2007, the U.S. and Lebanese governments signed a Letter of Agreement on Law Enforcement to strengthen "the capacity of the Internal Security Force to enforce the rule of law in Lebanon, cement sovereign Lebanese government control over its territory and protect the Lebanese people by training police."[41]

In addition to security cooperation with the United States, Lebanese authorities have tried to combat Islamic extremism domestically by supporting a dialogue with religious scholars and activists in Northern Lebanon, and endorsing a program by Dar al-Ifta', a scholarly religious institution, for supervising Islamic schools, colleges and institutes. In much the same spirit, parliamentary majority leader Saad Hariri launched a major developmental program in 2008 focusing on underdeveloped areas in northern Lebanon, where Islamic extremism has been spreading.

However, notwithstanding these efforts, Lebanese authorities have remained indecisive about entering Palestinian refugee camps, some of which have become safe havens for criminals and militants. Rather, they have been cooperating with the PLO in the hopes that the latter will re-impose its authority in the camps. Significantly, Lebanese-American cooperation has come under intense criticism by Hezbollah deputies and other pro-Hezbollah parties, who have urged the cessation of cooperation with the United States.[42] This has further blurred the lines between "terrorism" and "resistance" in the eyes of the official bureaucracy, and complicated official counterterrorism efforts.

ENDNOTES

[1] "al-Harakat al-Islamiyah fi Lubnan (Islamic Movements in Lebanon)," and "al-Jama'a al-Islamiyah (Islamic Association), in *al-Harakat al-Islamiyah fi Lubnan* (Beirut: al-Markaz al-Arabi lil-Ma'lumat, 2007), 110.

[2] Robert G. Rabil, "The Syrian Muslim Brotherhood," in Barry Rubin, ed., *The Muslim Brotherhood: The Organization and Policies of a Global Movement* (New York: Palgrave Macmillan, 2010).

[3] For details on the Muslim Brotherhood's doctrine and objectives see "Introducing the Muslim Brotherhood, Part One," Information Center of the Muslim Brotherhood in Syria, January 29, 2007, http://www.ikhwansyria.com/index.php?option=com_content&task=view&id=19&Itemid=114, and "Introducing the Muslim Brotherhood, Part Two," Information Center of the Muslim Brotherhood in Syria, February 7, 2007, http://www.ikhwansyria.com/index.php?option=com_content&task=view&id=218&Itemid=114.

[4] See *al-Harakat al-Islamiyah fi Lubnan*, 111; See also Ibrahim Bayram, "al-Jama'a al-Islamiyah min Ubad al-Rahman ila al-Intikhabat al-Niabiyah," (The Islamic Association from Ubad al-Rahman to Parliamentary Elections), *an-Nahar* (Beirut), April 1, 1997. At the time, Kamal Jumblat was the Minister of Interior. Based on the official license, the founders were Fathi Yakan, Sheikh Faisal Mawlawi, Zuhair al-Abidi, and Ibrahim al-Misri.

[5] Hassan Fadlallah, *Harb al-Iradat: Sira' al-Muqawamah wa al-Ihtilal al-Israeli fi Lubnan* 3rd edition (The Battle of Wills: The Struggle of the Resistance and the Israeli Occupation in Lebanon) (Beirut: Dar al-Hadi, 2009).

[6] For ideological and political details on Fathi Yakan, see Robert G. Rabil, *Religion, National Identity, and Confessional Politics in Lebanon: The Challenge of Islamism* (New York: Palgrave Macmillan, 2011).

[7] For details on the founding of the Islamic Action Front, including a list of its members, see "Tashkil Jabhat al-Amal al-Islami," (Forming of the Islamic Action Front), *al-Mustaqbal* (Beirut), August 3, 2006.

[8] Ibid.

[9] "Hizb al-Tahrir: Nakhbawi wa Sirri wa Yatmah li-Iqamat al-Khilafah," (Hizb al-Tahrir: Selective and Secret and Aspires to Create the Caliphate) *al-Diyar* (Beirut), December 3, 2001.

[10] "Concepts of Hizb ut-Tahrir," 1953, http://english.hizbuttahrir.org/.

[11] Ibid.

[12] Ibidem.

[13] "Hizb al-Tahrir: Min al-Sir ila al-'Alan," (Hizb al-Tahrir: From Secrecy to the Open) *as-Safir* (Beirut), July 24, 2004.

[14] "Khamsat Kawader fi Hizb al-Tahrir al-Islami Yuhadirun li-Haja-

mat fi al-Iraq bil-Tansiq Ma'a Isbat al-Ansar" (Five Cadres from Hizb al-Tahrir Plan in Coordination with Isbat al-Ansar Attacks in Iraq), *al-Mustaqbal* (Beirut), August 27, 2005.

[15] "Speaker at Hizb al-Tahrir Conference in Lebanon Calls for Jihad in Cyprus, Balkans, Caucasus," *as-Safir* (Beirut), July 20, 2009, http://www.thememriblog.org/blog_personal/en/18360.htm.

[16] Fida' 'Itani, *Al-Jihadiyun fi Lubnan: Min Quwat Fajr ila Fath al-Islam* (The Jihadists in Lebanon: From Fajr Brigades to Fath al-Islam) (Beirut: Dar al-Saqi, 2008); see also Bilal Y. Saab and Magnus Ranstorp, "Securing Lebanon from the Threat of Salafist Jihadism," *Studies in Conflict and Terrorism* 30 (2007).

[17] See Amnesty International, *Lebanon: Torture and Unfair Trial of the Dhiniyyah Detainees*, May 6, 2003, http://www.amnesty.org/en/library/asset/MDE18/005/2003/en/8d446494-d72e-11dd-b0cc-1f0860013475/mde180052003en.pdf.

[18] "Halabi's Killer Gets Sentence Commuted," *Daily Star* (Beirut), July 28, 2000.

[19] See Thair Abbas, "Al-Qaeda in Lebanon," *Ash-Sharq al-Awsat* (London), March 19, 2006.

[20] U.S. Department of State, Office of the Coordinator for Counterterrorism, *Country Reports on Terrorism 2009* (Washington, DC: U.S. Department of State, August 2010), 244.

[21] On nuanced details on Fath al-Islam, see 'Itani, *Al-Jihadiyun fi Lubnan*, 230-297; Gary C. Gambill, "Salafi-Jihadism in Lebanon," *Mideast Monitor* 3, January-March 2008; Saab and Ranstorp, "Securing Lebanon from the Threat of Salafist Jihadism."

[22] See www.aicp.org; and www.al-ahbash.org; See also Hamzeh and Dekmejian, "A Sufi Response to Political Islamism."

[23] Daniel Nassif, "Al-Ahbash," *Middle East Intelligence Bulletin* 3, no. 4, April 2001.

[24] Wassam Saade, "Harb al-Shaware' Khuruj 'an al-Qanun," (Street Fighting Is Outside the Law), *al-Mustaqbal* (Beirut), August 27, 2010.

[25] For details, see Robert G. Rabil, *Embattled Neighbors: Syria, Israel and Lebanon* (Boulder, CO: Lynne Rienner Publishers, 2003), 43-80; See also Rabil, *Religion, National Identity and Confessional Politics in Lebanon*.

[26] For more on this episode, see Augustus Richard Norton, "Walking between Raindrops: Hizballah in Lebanon," *Mediterranean Politics* 3, no. 1 (Summer 1998), and Magnus Ranstorp, *Hizb'allah in Lebanon: The Politics of the Western Hostage Crisis* (New York: St. Martin's Press, 1997).

[27] For more details, see Rabil, *Embattled Neighbors: Syria, Israel, and Lebanon*, 127-132.

[28] For more details, see Rabil, *Religion, National Identity and Confessional Politics in Lebanon: The Challenge of Islamism*; See also Robert

Rabil, *Syria, the United States and the War on Terror in the Middle East* (Connecticut: Praeger Security International, 2006).
[29] Nasrallah's speech was aired on the party's television station, *al-Manar* on September 22, 2006.
[30] For details see Rabil, *Religion, National Identity and Confessional Politics in Lebanon.*
[31] Fathi Yakan, *al-Masa'la al-Lubnaniyah min Manthur Islami* (The Lebanese Question from an Islamic Perspective) (Beirut: Mu'assassat al-Risalah, 1979), 126-128.
[32] See the text of the Open Letter addressed by Hezbollah to the oppressed in Lebanon and the world, February 16, 1985, as reprinted in Joseph Alagha, *The Shifts in Hizbullah's Ideology: Religious Ideology, Political Ideology, and Political Program* (Amsterdam: Amsterdam University Press, 2006), 223-238.
[33] Naim Qassem, *Hizbullah: al-Manhaj, al-Tajribah, al-Mustaqbal* (Hezbollah: The Curriculum [program], the Experience, the Future) (Beirut: dar al-Hadi, sixth edition, 2009), 275-276.
[34] "The Political Vision of the Islamic Association," June 24, 2010, http://www.al-jamaa.org/play.php?catsmktba=1484.
[35] See the full text of the Islamic Association's study in Fathi Yakan, *Adwa' 'ala al-Tajribah al-Niyabiyah al-Islamiyah fi Lubnan: Al-ida' al-Niyabi bayn al-Mabda' wa al-Tatbiq* (Lights on the Islamic Parliamentary Experience in Lebanon: The Parliamentary Performance Between Principle and Practice) (Beirut: Mu'assassat al-Risalah, 1996), 179-198.
[36] Qassem, *Al-Manhaj, al-Tajribah, al-Mustaqbal*, 338-339.
[37] See the Association's Political Manifesto.
[38] See details in "Political Manifesto of the Party of God," *al-Intiqad* (Beirut), November 30, 2009, http://www.alintiqad.com/essaydetailsf. php?eid=22807&fid=43.
[39] *as-Safir* (Beirut), October 28, 2002.
[40] The total of U.S. regular and supplemental foreign operations and defense appropriations from 2007 to 2011 (as requested) amounted to $860.12 million. Casey L. Addis, *U.S. Security Assistance to Lebanon* (Washington, DC: Congressional Research Service, January 2011), 3.
[41] "Letter of Agreement on Law Enforcement between the Government of the United States of America and the Government of Lebanon" n.d., http://www.state.gov/documents/organization/130486. pdf.
[42] In June 2010, parliament speaker Nabih Berri sent a letter to then Prime-Minister Saad Hariri and President Michel Suleiman calling the security agreement unconstitutional. Berri and Hezbollah deputies have argued that the security agreement is unconstitutional because it was surreptitiously concluded and signed by General Director of the Internal Security Force Achraf Rifi.

ISRAEL

QUICK FACTS

Population: 7,353,985

Area: 22,072 sq km

Ethnic Groups: Jewish 76.4% (of which Israel-born 67.1%, Europe/America-born 22.6%, Africa-born 5.9%, Asia-born 4.2%), non-jewish 23.6% (mostly Arab)

Religions: Jewish 76.4%, Muslim 16%, Arab Christians 1.7%, other Christians 0.4%, Druze 1.6%, unspecified 3.9%

Government Type: Parliamentary democracy

GDP (official exchange rate): $194 billion

Map and Quick Facts courtesy of the CIA World Factbook (last updated June 2010)

Although there was a strong Islamist current in the Palestinian national movement of the British Mandate Period, the Israeli War of Independence (1947-49) and subsequent policies adopted by the Israeli government kept Islamism largely at bay until the 1970s. Islamism regained popularity in the wake of Iran's 1979 Islamic Revolution, spreading to the Palestinian Territories and even into Israel itself. Today, the phenomenon is manifested most concretely in the Islamic Movement of Israel. In recent years, however, Israeli Arabs have shown increasing identification with their Palestinian cousins in the West Bank and Gaza Strip, as well as an affinity for participation in jihad abroad, and as a result have become more and more susceptible to Islamist ideology. Within Israel, Islamism is expressed in multiple ways, and is framed in nationalist, religious and even human rights terms. Islamism and secular Palestinian nationalism in Israel and the Palestinian Territories act in a synergistic manner to the same end: to undermine the identity and security of the State of Israel.

ISLAMIST ACTIVITY

Islamism, usually fused with Arab nationalism, was prevalent in the British Mandate of Palestine. The most powerful religious and political leader of the Palestinian community during that time, Mohammad Amin al-Husayni (Grand Mufti of Jerusalem from 1921-36 and chairman of the Arab Higher Committee) promoted an Islamist Palestinian national identity at odds with religious coexistence. A popular slogan among al-Husayni's supporters during the 1936-39 Arab Revolt, which was aimed at expelling the British and Jews from Palestine, was "after Saturday, Sunday;" that is, after the Palestinian national movement drives out the Jews, it will turn on the Christian Arabs.[1]

Soon after fleeing Palestine in 1937 to avoid arrest, al-Husayni began advocating for a transnational *jihad* against the British presence in the Islamic world. When Iraqi officers launched a pro-Axis coup in 1941 against Iraq's pro-British monarchy, al-Husayni called upon all Muslims to wage *jihad* against Britain, which he accused of launching an all-out war on Islam.[2] Al-Husayni then travelled to Berlin to cement an alliance with the Third Reich, where he recruited Bosnian Muslims for the SS and disseminated Islamist Nazi propaganda on Berlin Radio. After World War II, al-Husayni returned to Palestine and resumed his influential role in Palestinian politics, playing a leading role in the Israeli War of Independence and becoming the face of Palestinian nationalism until the formation of the PLO in 1964.

Despite Islamism's prevalence during the Mandate Period, however, a combination of factors served to marginalize the ideology for considerable time after World War II. The first was the exodus of most of the Palestinian population of what would become Israel during the Israeli War of Independence. The second was the subjection of those who remain to military rule until 1966. (Until then, Israeli Arabs were deemed a security threat and lived under military control, which restricted their mobility and citizenship roles. That year, however, Israeli Arabs were placed under civil government authority.[3]) Cumulatively, these trends prevented the organization of Israeli-Arab Islamist groups until the late 1970s, when Iran's Islamic Revolution gave new impetus to Islamism.

Following the Israeli War of Independence, Israeli authorities sought to suppress Islamism and craft an Israeli-Arab identity. To encourage Israeli-Arabs to identify with Israel, David Ben-Gurion, Israel's first Prime Minister, sponsored the creation of Arab political parties that espoused Jewish-Arab unity (e.g., the Democratic List of Nazareth in the 1st Knesset and the Democratic List for Israeli Arabs in the 2nd and 3rd Knessets) and were aligned with his own *Mapai* party. Ben-Gurion included those Arab parties in his government, with considerable effect. While most Muslim Israelis did not completely abandon their Palestinian identity, their inclusion in the political process and isolation from the rest of Palestinian and Muslim world facilitated assimilation. However, in the wake of the 1967 Six Day War, Israeli Arabs were reunited with their Palestinian relatives in the West bank and the Gaza Strip and became eligible for the *Hajj*.[4] Muslim preachers from the West Bank and Gaza Strip started imbuing Israeli-Muslims with a more conservative strain of Islam[5] and Israeli Muslims began studying in Islamic institutions in those territories. Soon, Israeli Muslims began calling anew for gender segregation in their schools and other conservative practices that had been on the wane since 1949. While the simultaneous re-exposure of the Israeli-Muslim community to the wider Muslim world and end of military rule over Israeli-Arabs contributed a drift towards Islamism, the radicalism did not reach threatening levels until after the 1979 Islamic Revolution in Iran.

In 1979, Farid Ibrahim Abu Mukh founded Israel's first violent Islamist group, *Usrat al-Jihad* (the Family of *Jihad*). Born in 1937, Abu Mukh grew more religious at the age of 40 under the direction of Sheikh Abdullah Nimar Darwish, who would later found the Islamic Movement in Israel. Influenced by the ideology of the Muslim Brotherhood, Abu Mukh raised a band of 60-70 *Usrat al-Jihad* fighters and they trained with weapons in the "Triangle" area (a concentration of Israeli Arab towns and villages located in the eastern Sharon plain). The group sought to destroy Israel and forcibly impose Islamic mores on Israel's Muslim population. To this end, they burned Israeli forests and orchards[6] and burned down a cinema in Umm al-Fahm for screening inappropriate films.[7] However, the group was short-lived; in 1981, Israeli authorities arrested its leadership—including Darwish—forcing it to cease operations.

Upon his release, Darwish and some of his *Usrat al-Jihad* colleagues chose to pursue their Islamist goals peacefully. Although Darwish claims that the Islamic Movement dates back to the following he acquired in the early 1970s through preaching, the organization as it exists today actually emerged from the Muslim Youth Movement created after Darwish was released from prison in 1983.[8] Darwish's movement rejected violence and commanded its members to obey Israeli law. It prioritized bringing secular Muslims back to Islam and providing public services, ranging from building schools to bus stop shelters, which the Israeli government did not provide.[9] Since the Israeli government largely neglected the Arab sector, the Islamic Movement's provision of public services made it very popular over time.

In the 1970s and 1980s, the Israeli government deemed secular Palestinian nationalism, as represented by Yasser Arafat's Fatah and George Habash's Popular Front for the Liberation of Palestine (PFLP), the greatest threat to the peace. Increasingly, therefore, Israel's political establishment grew to view Islamism as an advantageous distraction from secular Palestinian nationalism. As a result, the Israeli government consistently overlooked the growth of Islamism within and beyond Israel's Green Line. In the 1970s, over the objections of moderate Palestinians,[10] the Israeli government permitted Sheikh Ahmed Yassin, the leader of the Muslim Brotherhood in the Gaza Strip, to register an Islamist group called *Mujama al-Islamiya*, first as a charity and then, in 1979, as an association.[11] At first, the group devoted itself primarily to building schools, clinics, libraries, and an Islamic University. However, although *Mujama al-Islamiya* refrained from anti-Israel violence in its early years, its members sometimes clashed violently with members of the PLO. When the first *intifada* erupted in December of 1987, Yassin and some of his *Mujama al-Islamiya* colleagues founded the militant Hamas movement. In addition to promoting Islamic mores, such as the wearing of the *hijab* and polygamy, Hamas committed itself in its charter to waging an armed struggle to obliterate Israel. In 1989, an Israeli court convicted Yassin of ordering Hamas militants to kidnap and kill two Israeli soldiers. Then, in 1994, Hamas launched a wave a suicide bombings that would last, off and on, until 2005.[12]

Hamas's uncompromising approach, especially after the 1993 signing of the Oslo Accords, split the Islamic Movement of Israel. While the Islamic Movement's founder, Abdullah Darwish, supported the accords, a hard-line faction within the group identified with Hamas and consequently rejected the Accords. Sheikh Salah Raed and Sheikh Kemal Khatib, the mayors of Umm al-Fahm and Kafr Kanna, respectively, led the hard-line faction, which was called the "Northern Branch" because its leaders came disproportionately from the Triangle region in Northern Israel.[13] Darwish and Sheikh Ibrahim Sarsour led the more moderate Southern Branch.

This schism led to serious internal divisions within the movement. In 1996, Sheikh Ra'ed Salah advocated that all Arab citizens of Israel boycott elections.[14] By contrast, Sheikh Ibrahim Sarsour of the Southern Branch ran for elections together with the Arab Democratic Party (now known as the "United Arab List"). Both Salah and Sarsour have been reported to support the eventual establishment of an Islamic Caliphate.[15] Yet when Sarsour sought to run for the Knesset in the March 2006 elections, he argued that he was misquoted, and the Central Elections Committee permitted his list to participate.[16] Conversely, Sheikh Salah has confidently declared that Israel "will not survive another 20 years," and that Jerusalem will soon be transformed into the world capital of Islam.[17] Sheikh Kamal Khatib, his second in command, has publicly wished that Israel would soon be replaced by an Arab state run by Islamic law (*sharia*) as part of a greater Islamic Caliphate.[18] Nevertheless, the leaders of the Northern Branch of the Islamic Movement deny that they break the law and demand that the Israeli government accord them all their rights of citizenship.

Yet, during the 1990s, the Israeli Security Agency (GSS or Shin Bet) continuously closed down Northern Branch front organizations that were disguised as charities for transferring funds to Hamas. Salah himself was arrested in 2003 and imprisoned for two years for raising millions of dollars for Hamas.[19] He served another five months in prison for assaulting a policeman in 2007 at one of his many rallies against a notional Israeli plot to demolish the Al-Aqsa Mosque and Dome of the Rock.[20] In 2011, he was arrested again, this time for setting trees on fire in protest of Jewish National Fund policies.[21]

During the first intifada, the IM established the "Islamic Relief Committee," the stated purpose of which was assistance to injured Palestinians. However, experts have pointed out that this and other initiatives by the movement serve a larger strategic objective. "This is the way they work, from [providing] medical services to religious services to even soccer teams," Yitzhak Reiter of Hebrew University has noted. "If the government doesn't give enough money for sports activities or sports facilities, they will construct them by donations and provide the services. By so doing, they will attract particularly the poor – those that don't have enough money to pay."[22] Islamist civil society, in other words, has attempted to use civil society as a way to influence Israeli Arabs.

Today, that influence is extensive—and growing. Orna Simchon, director of the Israeli Education Ministry's Northern District, told a June 2010 Knesset Education committee hearing that out of approximately 500 recognized unofficial schools and preschools operating in the northern district, approximately 100 are operated by the Islamic Movement, with students subjected to Islamist indoctrination.[23]

On April 5, 2011, the Northern and Southern branches of the Islamic Movement signed a reunification deal and agreed to resume collaborating on projects and coordinate their positions on various issues.[24] It is not yet clear whether the coordinated positions will follow the Southern Branch's more moderate line or the rejectionist line of the Northern Branch.

ISLAMISM AND SOCIETY

At the end of 2009, the State of Israel's Central Bureau of Statistics (CBS) reported an Israeli population of 7.55 million. About 20 percent of that population was Arab[25] and about 17 percent was Muslim.[26] Muslim Israelis have the highest birthrate of any group: 4.0 children per woman, as opposed to

2.7 for Jewish Israelis, and a natural reproduction rate of 3 percent, as compared to 1.5 percent. And, according to forecasts, the Muslim population will grow to over two million people, or 24-26 percent of the total population, by 2020. Around 25 percent of the children born in Israel today are Muslim. The Muslim population is mostly young: 42 percent of Muslims are children under the age of 15, compared with 26% of the Jewish population.[27] The median age of Muslim Israelis is 18, while the median age of Jewish Israelis is 30. The percentage of people over 65 is less than 3 percent for Muslims, compared with 12 percent for the Jewish population.[28]

These demographic changes are taking place as Israeli Arabs become increasingly alienated from the state. Seemingly indicative of this shift, a University of Haifa study conducted in May 2009 found that only 41 percent of Israeli Arabs recognize Israel's right to exist as a Jewish and democratic state; in 2003, 65.6 percent had. It also noted that Holocaust denial cuts across all class sectors, with 40.5 percent of respondents believing that the Holocaust did not take place. In 2003, 28 percent made the same claim.[29] The study's author suggested that through denying the Holocaust, many Israeli Arabs believe they are expressing opposition to Israel's existence.[30]

Similarly, according to a poll conducted by Effi Ya'ar and Efrat Peleg of Tel Aviv University, the 2006 war in Lebanon had a negative effect on Israeli Arab patriotism. Eighty-five percent of Israeli Arabs view their primary patriotic identity as "Arab," followed by 52 percent whose primary patriotic identity is "Palestinian," and 32 percent whose primary patriotic identity is "Israeli."[31] Yet a June 2008 poll by Harvard University's Kennedy School of Government found that 77 percent of Israeli Arabs surveyed would rather remain in their native land as Israeli citizens than in any other country in the world.[32] These figures demonstrate that social and economic disparities do not adequately explain the causes of the latent hostility of Israeli Arabs toward the State of Israel. It does, however, showcase the susceptibility of the Israeli Arab population to outside influences—such as those of foreign Islamists.

There are many cases of Israeli Arabs being radicalized by Islamism abroad, and by events in the nearby Gaza Strip. Islamist groups are able to tap the vulnerability of Israeli Arabs to tensions that occur both within and outside the State of Israel. Thus, incitement by the Islamic Movement played a part in perpetuating violence following the start of the second *intifada* in September 2000. Specifically, incitement by the group helped instigate clashes between Israeli Arabs and police in the Wadi Ara region in October 2000—clashes which left 13 protesters dead.[33] The Islamic Movement was also instrumental in encouraging the *intifada* itself, with Sheikh Ra'ed Salah declaring that "the time has come [for us] to start an Islamic Muslim Intifada."[34] More recently, global *jihadism* has had a similar polarizing effect on some Israeli Arabs. In 2010, four Israeli Arabs were among those charged by Israeli authorities with establishing a terror cell and killing a taxi driver.[35] The accused had watched speeches of Osama bin Laden, and subsequently sought to join the fight against Jewish and Christian "infidels." Two of the plaintiffs had trained at an al-Qaeda camp in Somalia.[36]

Linkages between Israeli Arabs and Palestinian terror groups likewise abound. In 1996, an Israeli Police anti-fraud unit discovered that two Israeli-Arab charities, one in Nazareth and the other in East Jerusalem, were distributing funds collected abroad to the families of Hamas suicide bombers.[37] Then, in the summer of 1999, Hamas recruited Israel Arabs to bomb two buses in northern Israel.[38] In May 2011, the Haifa District Court sentenced an Israeli Arab to five years imprisonment for conspiring with his brother-in-law to gather an arms cache in Green Israel for Hamas.[39] Around the same time, Israeli authorities arrested two Arab residents of East Jerusalem holding Israeli citizenship who were planning to attack Jerusalem's Teddy Stadium during a Premier League soccer match. Authorities divulged that the two men had longstanding ties with Hamas.[40] Israeli Arabs have also collaborated with the smaller Palestinian Islamic Jihad (PIJ). In August 2008, Israeli authorities arrested a five-man PIJ cell, which included two Israeli Arabs, accused of planning an attack on an army checkpoint near Ramallah and of planning to assassinate Israeli pilots, scientists and university professors.[41] Then, in April 2011, an Israeli-Arab lawyer from Acre, Suhir Ayoub, was arrested for passing messages on two occasions between prisoners and the Gaza-based leader of *Mahajat El Kuds*, a group with close ties to PIJ.[42]

Israeli Arabs likewise have proven susceptible to external influence from radical regimes and Islamist groups. During the reign of Saddam Hussein, for example, numerous Israeli Arabs received military training in Iraq, having travelled there via Jordan right before the second *intifada*.[43] In February 2002, the head of Israel's General Security Service reported to the Knesset's Foreign Affairs and Defense Committee that Iran had succeeded in penetrating a minority of Israel's Arab population.[44] Following Israel's withdrawal from Lebanon in 2000, Hezbollah has also focused upon penetrating the Israeli Arab sector. According to ISA assessments, Hezbollah finds Israeli Arabs attractive because of "their ability to attain highly appreciated intelligence for both Iran and Hezbollah, which constitutes an Iranian front in the Middle East."[45] Hezbollah sees Israeli Arabs as advantageous operatives because they have the advantage of "being Israeli citizens, who enjoy freedom of movement and accessibility to targets, including security targets; they are familiar with the language and culture, hold social and economic contacts with Israelis, and also have access to both the Territories and abroad."[46] Most of the infrastructure operated by the group exists in the West Bank and, to a lesser degree, in the Gaza Strip. While the majority of its activities are affiliated with Fatah's Al Aqsa Martyrs Brigades, Hezbollah also cooperates with Hamas, the Palestinian Islamic Jihad and the Popular Front for the Liberation of Palestine (PFLP).[47] Even al-Qaeda has attempted to penetrate Israel; according to the IDF's Southern Command, the bin Laden network has attempted to penetrate the Egyptian border in order to establish terrorist cells in Israel.[48] In July 2008, Israeli Police and the Shin Bet arrested six Israeli-Arabs, two of whom were students at Hebrew University of Jerusalem, with alleged links to the al-Qaida terror network who planned to assassinate U.S. President George W. Bush during his trip to Israel.[49] The conspirators had been in contact with al-Qaeda over the Internet with the purpose of establishing a terror cell in Israel.[50] There likewise have been cases where Israeli Arabs have aligned themselves with global *jihad* after exposure to Islamist material on the Internet.[51]

This trend has generated growing worries among Israeli policymakers. In 2007, Yuval Diskin, the head of Israel's General Security Service (GSS), was reported to have warned the Prime Minister's Office that Israeli Arabs were rapidly becoming a "strategic threat."[52] The GSS report said that "the threat of Arab irredentism exceeded that of any external danger including Iran,"[53] and that Israel's Arab population was a "genuine long-range danger to the Jewish character and very existence of the State of Israel."[54]

ISLAMISM AND THE STATE

A number of former Israeli cabinet ministers, among them former Defense Minister Moshe Arens and Infrastructure Minister Benjamin Ben-Eliezer, have echoed the findings of the Orr Commission, a panel of inquiry established by the Israeli government to investigate the events surrounding clashes that precipitated the second *intifada*. The Commission report stated that successive governments have neglected the Israeli-Arab sector, and Ben-Eliezer has warned that a continuation of this policy may lead to an "internal *intifada*," or uprising against Israel.[55] Similarly, Mohammad Darawshe, Co-Executive Director of the Abraham Fund Initiatives, has advocated greater integration and equality for Israeli-Arabs.[56] To date, however, the Israeli government has not done so; although it has invested economically in the Israeli-Arab sector, it has yet not begun a coordinated approach of integrating Israeli-Arabs into Israeli civil society.[57] More significantly, in recent years, in parallel with the rise of "post-Zionist thought" in Israeli society, successive governments have flagged in their defense of the compatibility between Judaism and democracy. As a result, the state has failed to provide an ethos to rally its Israeli Arab minority, and unite it with the Jewish majority.

Israel has failed to factor in Islamism when formulating its strategic policies. Officially, Israel sees the issue of the political-legal status of Israeli-Arabs as a purely domestic matter without strategic implications. At the same time, however, it has traditionally refused to recognize Israeli Arabs as a national minority possessing collective rights apart from specific cases (such as in the education system and family law, each religious community being subject to its own clerical elite). This opening in the education system has enabled Israeli Arabs to cultivate a separate national identity—and created an ideological space in which Islamism can increasingly take root.

The education system in Israel has emerged as a notable ideological battleground in this regard. The country's Education Ministry has attempted to counter Islamism by banning the teaching of the *Nakba* ("catastrophe," the common Arabic reference for the establishment of Israel in 1948) in schools; by forcing students to sing *Hatikva* (the Israeli national anthem); and by encouraging military and national service as a criterion for rewarding schools and staff. (As yet, however, it has not allocated funds to effectively advance an educational curriculum that does not undermine the Jewish character of the State of Israel.) In response, the Higher Arab Monitoring Committee has sought an autonomous administration for Arab education—a step that, if implemented, would effectively put the education of Israel's Arabs outside of the purview of the Jewish state.[58] Israeli Arab leaders have also voiced opposition to the campaign to promote Israeli-Arab participation in national service, terming it a veiled attempt by the government to erode the community's sense of unity.[59]

Informing this friction is a persistent failure on the part of Israeli policymakers to account for Islamism as a discrete threat. Officially, the Israeli government has long viewed the political and legal status of Israeli Arabs as purely a domestic matter, and believed that Islamist tendencies among Israeli Arabs would be mitigated by the liberal-democratic culture of the state. Today, that assumption is being sorely tested, as Israeli Arabs become increasingly receptive to—and involved in—Islamist activities, both within Israel and abroad.

ENDNOTES

[1] Benny Morris, *1948: A History of the First Arab-Israeli War* (New Haven: Yale University Press, 2008), 13.

[2] Joseph E. Katz, "Summons to a Intifada Against Britain: A 'Fatwa' Issued by Haj Amin al-Husseini," Eretzyisroel.org, May 7, 2011, http://www.eretzyisroel.org/~jkatz/fatwa.html.

[3] Gerald B. Bubis, "Israeli Arabs: Expectations and Realities," Jerusalem Center for Public Affairs *Jerusalem Viewpoints* no. 478, May 15, 2002, http://www.jcpa.org/jl/vp478.htm.

[4] "The Islamic Movement," *Global Jihad*, May 9, 2011, http://www.globaljihad.net/view_page.asp?id=1780.

[5] Jacob M. Landau, *The Arab Minority in Israel: 1967-1991, Political Aspects* (Oxford: Clarendon Press, 1993), 37.

[6] Ibid., 39.

[7] Alisa Rubin Peled, *Debating Islam in the Jewish State: The Development of Policy Toward Islamic Institutions in Israel* (Albany: State University of New York, 2001), 130.

[8] Muhammad Hasan Amara, "The Nature of Islamic Fundamentalism in Israel," in Bruce Maddy-Weitzman and Ephraim Inbar, eds., *Religious Radicalism in the Greater Middle East* (London: Routledge, 1997), 161.

[9] Ibid., 162.

[10] Anat Kurz and Nahman Tal, "Hamas: Radical Islam in a National Struggle," Tel Aviv University Jaffee Center for Strategic Studies *Memorandum* no. 48, July 1997.

[11] Andrew Higgins, "How Israel Helped to Spawn Hamas," *Wall Street Journal*, January 24, 2009, http://online.wsj.com/article/SB123275572295011847.html.

[12] Peter Wilkinson, "Timeline: The Evolution of Hamas," CNN, December 30, 2008, http://articles.cnn.com/2008-12-30/world/hamas.profile_1_hamas-claims-responsibility-rantisi-hamas-leader?_s=PM:WORLD.

[13] Hillel Frisch, "Israel and Its Arab Citizens," in *Israeli Democracy at the Crossroads* (New York: Routledge, 2005), 216.

[14] "Israeli Arab Bought Weapons for Hamas Terrorists," IsraelNationalNews.com, August 13, 2007.

[15] Yoav Stern, 'Islamic Movement Head: J'lem Destined Capital of Caliphate," *Ha'aretz* (Tel Aviv), September 15, 2006, http://www.haaretz.com/news/islamic-movement-head-j-lem-destined-capital-of-caliphate-1.197342.

[16] Barak M. Seener, "Israeli Arabs between Palestinization and Islamism," Jerusalem Center for Public Affairs *Jerusalem Viewpoints* no. 560, January 1, 2008, http://www.jcpa.org/JCPA/Templates/ShowPage.asp?DRIT=2&DBID=1&LNGID=1&TMID=111&FID=443

&PID=0&IID=2019&TTL=Israeli_Arabs_between_Palestinianiza-tion_and_Islamism.

[17] Ilene R. Prusher, "Israeli Arab's Rising Voice of Opposition," *Christian Science Monitor*, October 26, 2006.

[18] "Muslim Leader Calls for Sharia in Israel," IsraelNationalNews.com, October 21, 2007, http://www.israelnationalnews.com/News/Flash.aspx/135024.

[19] "Sheikh Raed Salah Arrested for Allegedly Attacking Cops in Jerusalem," *Jerusalem Post*, March 23, 2009, http://www.jpost.com/Israel/Article.aspx?id=136848.

[20] Hassan Shaalan, "Sheikh Salah Released from Jail," *Yediot Ahronot* (Tel Aviv), December 12, 2010, http://www.ynetnews.com/articles/0,7340,L-3997799,00.html.

[21] "Salah Nabbed Again on Suspicion of Setting Fires in South," *Jerusalem Post*, February 22, 2011, http://www.jpost.com/Headlines/Article.aspx?id=209365.

[22] As cited in Brenda Gazzar, "Israel's Islamic Movement: Filling the Vacuum, Aiming for a Caliphate," *Jerusalem Post*, August 3, 2008.

[23] Rebecca Ann Stoil, "MKs: Islamists infiltrating Arab Schools," *Jerusalem Post*, June 30, 2010, http://www.jpost.com/Israel/Article.aspx?id=179949.

[24] Jack Khoury, "Israel's Islamic Movement Reunites after Rift Over Role in Knesset," *Ha'aretz* (Tel Aviv), May 4, 2011, http://www.haaretz.com/news/national/israel-s-islamic-movement-reunites-after-rift-over-role-in-knesset-1.359844.

[25] State of Israel, Central Bureau of Statistics, "Population by Population Group," *Statistical Abstract of Israel 2010*, May 10, 2011, http://www1.cbs.gov.il/reader/shnaton/templ_shnaton_e.html?num_tab=st02_01&CYear=2010.

[26] State of Israel, Central Bureau of Statistics, "Population by Religion," *Statistical Abstract of Israel 2010*, May 10, 2011, http://www1.cbs.gov.il/reader/shnaton/templ_shnaton_e.html?num_tab=st02_02&CYear=2010.

[27] "Israeli Muslim Birth Rate is Double that of Jews," *Yediot Ahronot* (Tel Aviv), February 13, 2003, http://www.jewishvirtuallibrary.org/jsource/Society_&_Culture/muslimpop.htm.

[28] "Table B/1.-Population, By Population Group," Central Bureau of Statistics *Monthly Bulletin of Statistics* 52, April 2001, http://www.cbs.gov.il/yarhon/b1_e.htm.

[29] Brenda Gazzar, "Arabs Slam Bill to Criminalize 'Nakba,'" *Jerusalem Post*, May 17, 2009, http://www.jpost.com/Israel/Article.aspx?id=142571v.

[30] Cited in Seener, "Israeli Arabs between Palestinization and Islamism."

[31] Yaniv Salama-Scheer, "Poll: Lebanon War was 'Breaking Point' for

Arab Israeli Patriotism," *Jerusalem Post*, January 18, 2007, http://www.jpost.com/Israel/Article.aspx?id=48476.

[32] Hillel Fendel, "Why Israeli-Arabs Don't Want to Live in a PA State," Israelnationalnews.com, April 29, 2010.

[33] Jonathan Lis, "Salah Calls for 'Intifada' against Temple Mount Excavation," *Ha'aretz* (Tel Aviv), March 7, 2007.

[34] Ibid.

[35] "Israeli Arabs 'Inspired by Global Jihad' Charged with Taxi Driver Murder," *Ha'aretz*, June 28, 2010.

[36] "Shin Bet Arrests Eight Israeli Arabs for Illicit Arms Trading," *Ha'aretz* (Tel Aviv), July 15, 2010.

[37] Matthew Levitt, *Hamas: Politics, Charity, and Terrorism in the Service of Jihad* (New Haven: Yale University Press, 2006), 115.

[38] Jonathan Schanzer, *Hamas vs. Fatah: The Struggle for Palestine* (New York: Palgrave Macmillan, 2008), 47.

[39] "Israeli Arab Gets 5 Years for Hamas Plot," UPI, May 11, 2011, http://www.upi.com/Top_News/World-News/2011/05/11/Israeli-Arab-gets-5-years-for-Hamas-plot/UPI-54921305125753/.

[40] Ibid.

[41] Jack Khoury and Yuval Azoulay, "Two Israeli Arabs Arrested over Suspected Jihad Plot to Kill Pilots, Scientists," *Ha'aretz* (Tel Aviv), August 28, 2008, http://www.haaretz.com/news/2-israeli-arabs-arrested-over-suspected-jihad-plot-to-kill-pilots-scientists-1.252814.

[42] Ron Friedman, "Lawyer Indicted for Passing Information to Islamic Jihad," *Jerusalem Post*, April 20, 2011, http://www.jpost.com/NationalNews/Article.aspx?id=217270.

[43] State of Israel, Ministry of Foreign Affairs, "Iraq's Involvement in the Palestinian Terrorist Activity against Israel," January 25, 2003.

[44] Bubis, "Israeli Arabs: Expectations and Realities."

[45] Israel Security Agency, "Terror Data and Trends: Hizballa Activity Involving Israeli Arabs," n.d., http://www.shabak.gov.il/English/EnTerrorData/Reviews/Pages/HizballaActivity.aspx.

[46] Ibid.

[47] See, for example, Emily Yoffe, What Are Hamas and Hezbollah?" *Slate*, October 17, 2000, http://www.slate.com/id/1006301/.

[48] Hana Levi Julian, "Al Qaeda Planned Karni Crossing Attack," IsraelNationalNews.com, February 12, 2010, http://www.israelnationalnews.com/News/News.aspx/135985.

[49] Amos Harel, "Six Arrested in Israel for Allegedly Plotting Attack on Bush," *Ha'aretz* (Tel Aviv), July 18, 2008, http://www.haaretz.com/news/six-arrested-in-israel-for-allegedly-plotting-attack-on-bush-1.249974.

[50] Israeli Security Agency, "A Review of Al Qaeda and the Diffusion of its Ideas in Israel and the Palestinian Authority," n.d., http://www.shabak.gov.il/SiteCollectionImages/

[51] Jonathan Fighel, "The Involvement of Israeli Arabs in Global Jihad Activity," *The Shilouv Project* blog, September 14, 2010, http://www.shilouv.org/2010/09/the-involvement-of-israeli-arabs-in-global-jihad-activity-by-jonathan-fighel-ict-senior-researcher/.

[52] Hillel Fendel, "GSS: Israeli Arabs Are Existential Danger to Israel," IsraelNationalNews.com, November 12, 2007.

[53] "Israeli Intel Terms Israeli Arabs a Greater Strategic Threat than Iran, WorldTribune.com, March 21, 2007, http://www.worldtribune.com/worldtribune/07/front2454181.0083333333.html.

[54] Fendel, "GSS: Israeli Arabs Are Existential Danger to Israel."

[55] Yoav Stern, "Ben-Eliezer: Continued neglect of Israeli Arabs may spark 'internal Intifada,'" *Ha'aretz* (Tel Aviv), September 9, 2007.

[56] For more, see Seener, "Israeli Arabs between Palestinianization and Islamism."

[57] Ibid.

[58] Abe Selig, "Sa'ar Drops 'Nakba' From Arab Textbooks," *Jerusalem Post*, August 31, 2009, http://www.jpost.com/Israel/Article.aspx?id=153344.

[59] "Israeli Arab Volunteers Rising," JTA, August 27, 2009, http://www.jta.org/news/article/2009/08/27/1007492/israeli-arab-volunteers-rising.

PALESTINIAN AUTHORITY

QUICK FACTS

Population: West Bank: 2,514,845 Gaza Strip: 1,604,238

Area: West Bank: 5,860 sq km Gaza Strip: 360 sq km

Ethnic Groups: West Bank: Palestinian Arab and others 83%, Jewish 17% Gaza Strip: Palestinian Arab

Religions: West Bank: Muslim 75% (predominately Sunni), Jewish 17%, Christian and other 8% Gaza Strip: Muslim (predominately Sunni) 99.3%, Christian 0.7%

Government Type: PLO/Fatah (contested)

GDP (official exchange rate): $6.641 billion

Map and Quick Facts courtesy of the CIA World Factbook (last updated June 2010)

Islamism in the Palestinian Authority is in many ways analogous to global Islamism, boasting the same broad totalitarian ideology, strategies, tactics, and ultimate goals. There is, however, one major exception: while the enemy of the latter is more general (the "infidel" West, apostate regimes, etc.), Islamism in the Palestinian Authority is primarily dedicated to the annihilation of the State of Israel.

The various Islamist groups within the Palestinian Authority have their counterparts among other international Islamist forces. Hamas has its roots in, and is akin to, the international Muslim Brotherhood, particularly with regard to its approach to propaganda and indoctrination. Organizations such as the Palestinian Islamic Jihad, which have deemed Hamas not to be violent enough, find their counterparts in other radical splinters of the Brotherhood, such as Ayman Zawahiri's Egyptian Jihad. Other ultra-violent jihadist organizations operating out of PA territory—among them Jund Ansar Allah, Jaysh al-Umma, and Jaysh al-Islam—are identical to al-Qaeda in outlook and strategy, and even claim affiliation. Even secular Fatah and its military wing exhibits Islamist elements not unlike those found among various moderate Muslim organizations in the West.

ISLAMIST ACTIVITY

The Palestinian National Authority (PA or PNA) was created by the Palestine Liberation Organization as a five-year interim body in accordance with the 1994 Gaza-Jericho agreement that followed the Oslo Accords. Under the Oslo process, the PA assumes the responsibilities of Israeli military administration in parts of the West Bank and Gaza Strip ("Area A") until final status negotiations. The PA includes a Palestinian Legislative Council (PLC), a legislative body with 132 seats elected from Gaza and the West Bank. Since 2006, Hamas has been the largest faction in the PLC, with 72 seats; following its 2007 clash with rival Fatah, Hamas also seized control of all PA facilities in the Gaza Strip. Within the jurisdiction of the PA, Hamas is the most influential Islamist movement, followed by the Palestinian Islamic Jihad and lesser known ultra-radical *jihadist* organizations.

Hamas

"Hamas" means "zeal" in Arabic and is an Arabic acronym for *harakat al-muqawamah al-islamiyyah* (the Islamic Resistance Movement). The group is primarily concentrated in the Gaza Strip, with support in various sections of the West Bank. In addition to Sheikh Ahmad Yassin and his father Hassan Yousef, Hamas scion-turned-defector Mosab Hassan Yousef also identifies Ayman Abu Taha, Jamil Hamami, Mahmud Muslih, Muhammed Jamal al-Natsah, and Jamal Mansour as founders of the organization,[1] which was created in 1987 as an offshoot of the Muslim Brotherhood with the aim of replacing the entire state of Israel with a Muslim state governed according to *sharia* law. *Jihad* and Islamist indoctrination are its two principal means of instituting this new state.

The U.S. State Department has estimated that Hamas has "tens of thousands of supporters and sympathizers,"[2] as well as many devoted members. Precise numbers are unknown, but more than 200,000 Palestinians—5.26 percent of the total population of the Palestinian Territories—attended the funeral procession for Sheikh Ahmed Yassin upon his death in 2004.[3]

In addition to its immediate goals, Hamas' founding charter also illustrates the organization's commitment to more universal Islamist principles. The slogan—"Allah is its goal [theocratic rule], the Prophet its model [importance of the Sunna], the Qur'an its Constitution [*sharia*], *Jihad* [terrorism] its path, and death [suicide-bombings] for the cause of Allah its most sublime belief"[4]—fully demonstrates the group's universal Islamist convictions. Though most Hamas members are Palestinian Sunni Arabs, the charter "welcomes all Muslims who share its beliefs and thinking, commit themselves to its course of action, keep its secrets and aspire to join its ranks in order to carry out their duty."[5]

The Hamas Charter echoes the sentiment of all Islamists in regard to the land of Palestine, all of which is believed to be "waqf land" that has belonged to Islam "since it was conquered by the Companion of the Prophet [c. 640]."[6] In accordance with Islamic law, Islamists stress that the land of Palestine belongs to Islam and must therefore be re-conquered by Islam, not specifically by the Palestinian people. Hamas clearly defines "Nationalism as part and parcel of the religious faith,"[7] thereby universalizing the notion of "nationalism" to include the entire Muslim *umma*, irrespective of actual "nationality." And like global *jihadists*, Hamas clerics have publicly expressed their support for re-establishing the Caliphate.[8]

To achieve its immediate goal of an Islamic Palestinian state, Hamas has steadfastly denounced the Oslo Accords, the Annapolis conference, and other diplomatic efforts to establish a lasting peace in the region as "contrary to the beliefs of the Islamic Resistance Movement."[9] However, when addressing Western audiences, Hamas leaders such as Ismail Haniyeh and Khaled Meshal have stated that they are willing to recognize Israel along pre-1967 borders[10] , even as the organization continues to reiterate, on a regular basis,its total rejection of Israel's existence.[11] Such doublespeak is a common Islamist tactic that finds its roots in Islam's doctrine of deception, known as *taqiyya*, which the various PA factions even implement against one another.[12]

In the style of Egypt's Muslim Brotherhood, Hamas has gained the support of the Palestinian people by providing social and welfare services and by presenting itself as Israel's implacable foe, as well as an opponent of the more corrupt, effete Fatah. Hamas is also steadily Islamicizing Palestinian society through indoctrination and propaganda. This method is a fundamental part of the organization's charter: "We must imprint on the minds of generations of Muslims that the Palestinian problem is a religious one," an "Islamic education based on the implementation of religious precepts [*sharia*]."[13] Hamas has gone to extreme lengths to indoctrinate young Palestinians into its beliefs, including the use of "*jihadi*" Mickey Mouse and Bugs Bunny lookalikes in its television programs.[14]

The organization's principal sources of funding traditionally include Iran (which, by 1995, had provided the organization more than $100 million[15] and in the latter half of 2008 pledged $150 million[16]); private charities, including those operating in the West (the most notorious being the Holy Land Foundation, now defunct, which channeled $12 million to Hamas[17]); and individual donors from the Gulf States.[18] In spite of funding from sympathizers, however, Hamas has suffered economic setbacks since attaining power. Hamas's refusal to recognize Israel has led to Western suspension of aid for Gaza development, hindering the organization's ability to govern.

Since 1993, the military wing of Hamas, the Izz ad-Din Qassam Brigades, is believed to have killed over five hundred people in more than 350 separate terrorist attacks, many of them suicide bombings.[19] As recently as July 30, 2010, Hamas continues to launch rocket attacks against towns in southern Israel[20] and is suspected of attempting to smuggle weapons from Egypt into Gaza.[21]

Palestinian Islamic Jihad (PIJ)

The Palestinian Islamic Jihad (literally, "the Islamic Jihad Movement in Palestine," i.e., *Harakat al-Jihād al-Islāmi fi Filastīn*) was founded sometime between 1979 and 1981[22] by several Muslim Brotherhood members who felt that the Brotherhood was too moderate and not fully committed to the principle of *jihad* and the establishment of a Palestinian state governed according to *sharia* law.[23] In addition, the founding members were also inspired by the 1979 Iranian Revolution.[24] Founders Fathi Shikaki and Abd al-Aziz Awda were schooled in Egypt, and—consistent with the teachings of the most extreme Egyptian Islamists—forged an organization whose ultimate aim was to destroy Israel by violent *jihad*. Unlike Hamas, which has at least proposed a tactical truce with Israel, the PIJ explicitly rejects any and all forms of recognition of Israel.

PIJ is small and highly secretive, and accurate estimates of membership are difficult to find. However, the organization is believed to have hundreds of active members and to operate largely underground.[25] The ethnic make-up of the group is overwhelmingly Palestinian Arab. PIJ relies on suicide-bombing operations, and was responsible for the April 2006 suicide bombing in Tel Aviv that killed eleven people.[26] The Israeli army has thinned the PIJ's ranks considerably through killings and arrests in recent years, including the arrest of a high-ranking PIJ official in December 2008[27] and two raids on June 30, 2010 that eliminated five PIJ members.[28]

According to the U.S. State Department, PIJ receives state sponsorship from Iran in the form of financial aid, and Syria provides a safe haven for PIJ by allowing it to maintain its headquarters in Damascus.[29] PIJ members (like former University of South Florida professor Sami al-Arian[30]) have also been operating on American soil, funneling money to PIJ. And since PIJ, unlike Hamas, does not seek the support of the Palestinian population by providing social services or taking part in the electoral process, the aid thereby collected is used exclusively for violence, terrorism, and suicide bombings.[31]

Jund Ansar Allah (JAA)

Jund Ansar Allah, or "Soldiers of the Companions of God," was first established in the Palestinian territory of Gaza in late 2008.[32] Like other Palestinian Islamist groups, JAA asserts that it will "fight *jihad*" for the sake of God "until the banner of unity is hoisted" and Islam's prophet Muhammad "is made victorious."[33] Made up of disgruntled former Hamas and PIJ members, it seeks to unify the Arab *mujahideen* under a new banner, and has criticized Hamas for insufficiently enforcing *sharia*.[34] JAA envisions implementing an Islamic emirate throughout the Middle East, and has declared "the soldiers of *tawhid* (unification) will not rest... until the entirety of Muslim lands are [sic] liberated and until our imprisoned Aqsa is purified from the desecration of the accursed Jews."[35]

Founded in the Gaza Strip city of Rafah, the group has spread rapidly throughout Gaza and claims to have some 500 members, most of them Palestinian Arabs, but including foreign fighters as well.[36] Hamas claims that the aim of JAA and other small Islamist groups is to "defame" Hamas. Furthermore, in an attempt to damage the reputation of JAA, which has often openly defied its authority in Gaza, Hamas has linked the organization with the notoriously corrupt Fatah, claiming that JAA has received weapons from former Fatah policemen and security officials in south Gaza.[37] Despite claims that JAA is linked to al-Qaeda, there is no direct evidence of such a connection, aside from a shared ideology.[38]

JAA's most brazen terrorist attempt involved ten of its members riding on horseback laden with explosives into the Karni border crossing, a passage point between Gaza and Israel that has been the site of considerable militant activity. Five JAA members were killed by Israeli troops as a result of the incident.[39] In August 2009, JAA clashed with Hamas forces, leading to the death of the group's leader, Abdel-Latif Moussa. Hamas has accused the group of bombing several Internet cafés and a wedding party attended by relatives of Muhammad Dahlan, a Fatah leader in the West-Bank.[40]

Jaysh Al-Islam (JI)

Jaysh al-Islam (JI), or "Army of Islam," is closely linked to the Dughmush clan of Gaza, a former ally of Hamas, and is believed to have several hundred members.[41] Similar to other Palestinian Islamist splinter groups, JI shares global *jihadist* objectives and is believed to be linked to al-Qaeda.[42] The group's most notable action was the March 2007 kidnapping of BBC journalist Alan Johnston in order to negotiate the release of al-Qaeda-affiliated Islamist militant Abu Qatada, then incarcerated in the UK.[43] The Johnston kidnapping, as well as an attack that killed five senior Hamas officials, led to a clash with Hamas in August 2008 that is said to have weakened the group.[44]

Jaljalat

In Arabic, the word *jaljalat* signifies something momentous. The group which adopted that name consists of two factions: 1) dissidents from Hamas' Izz ad-Din al-Qassam Brigades, who deserted the movement following a ceasefire with Israel in 2008; and 2) Hamas renegades released from the organization's prisons.[45] Jaljalat is led by Mahmoud Taleb, also known as Abu

Mutasem al-Madqisi, who was arrested by Hamas security forces in October 2009 for "violating national security."[46] The exact number of Jaljalat members is unknown, but one estimate places it at several thousand members.[47] Jaljalat has global *jihadist* aspirations and is allied with Jund Ansar Allah and other *jihadist* factions operating in the Palestinian Territories. It is openly critical of Hamas for being soft on Israel.[48] Like other Salafist groups in the PA, Jaljalat aims to establish an Islamic Emirate in Gaza.

The organization's most prominent attack was on June 27, 2009, against an Israeli Defense Forces detachment patrolling the Hoovers route, as a result of which one Israeli was killed and three were wounded.[49] In addition, the group has revealed its failed assassination plot against former U.S. President Jimmy Carter and former British Prime Minister Tony Blair, two "infidels," in September 2009.[50]

Jaysh Al-Ummah (JU)

Ideologically affiliated with al-Qaeda, Jaysh Al-Ummah (JU), or the "Army of the Nation," believes that "Muslims all over the world are obliged to fight the Israelis and the infidels until only Islam rules the earth."[51] The group was formed in January 2008 and is led by Abu Hafs al-Maqdisi. While the group's membership number is kept secret, it has claimed that it does not have the capability to strike targets outside of Gaza, suggesting it is a small organization.[52] JU, however, has been rather open in its criticism of Hamas since its inception. Most notably, it has criticized Hamas for arresting a JU field commander and other members as they were attempting to carry out terrorist operations.[53] At the same time, however, JU has said it would not try to escalate tensions with Hamas, but rather urge it to release its members who are in prison, asking Hamas "Whose side are you on?"[54] Such a comment underlies the general unhappiness of JU with Hamas, which it holds responsible for the influx of Iranian influence in Gaza.

Hizb-ut-Tahrir (HuT)

A pan-Islamist group, the "Party of Liberation" is active in at least 45 countries, with a minor presence in the PA despite its refusal to take part in PLC elections. The group's immediate aim is to establish a caliphate and implement *sharia* extending throughout the Muslim world; the long-term goal is to bring the entire world under Muslim rule.[55]

Despite HuT's well-documented support of the destruction of Israel, it does not directly engage in Islamist terrorism, nor do its branches maintain an armed wing. Rather, HuT seeks to "agitate and educate"[56] people in order to rally support for the idea of restoring the caliphate. While no reliable figures can be found regarding HuT's membership in the PNA, it is widely considered to be marginal.

To voice opposition to the 2007 Annapolis conference, HuT organized a demonstration with over 2,500 attendees in Hebron, culminating in the killing of one protestor by PA police. Soon after, over 10,000 gathered in Al-Bireh under the leadership of HuT in support of the slogan: "the caliphate is the rising force."[57] Most recently, in July 2010, PA security forces arrested thousands of HuT supporters rallying in Ramallah to lament the end of the caliphate, despite the rally being banned by the PA.[58]

Fatah

Though formally secular, the Palestinian Authority's ruling Fatah faction exhibits Islamist leanings. Its name, literally meaning "opening," is taken from the early Islamic conquests. The name of the military wing,[59] known as the al-Aqsa Martyrs' Brigade, is full of Islamic symbolism—from the importance of the al-Aqsa mosque, to the Islamist notion of "martyrdom," i.e., suicide bombings.

When he was alive, former Fatah leader Yasser Arafat at times "embraced Islamism and violence. At other times, he embraced secularism and talked of peace."[60] His contradictory statements are a byproduct of the Islamist doctrine of *taqiyya* (deceit, or doublespeak to be employed in times of weakness).[61] Soon after the Oslo Accords, Arafat also stated that "the *jihad* will continue and Jerusalem is not for the Palestinian people alone.... It is for the entire Muslim *umma*."[62] The sincerity of Arafat's rhetoric is unclear; it may just have been Fatah's attempt to win the support of an increasingly Islamist Palestinian population. Efforts to expand the organization's mass appeal might have been successful had it not been for its ruthless offensive in 2007 against Hamas, which led many Palestinians to fear Fatah and wonder "whether the Fatah-backed PA was any less brutal than Hamas in Gaza."[63]

Often seen as the only moderate faction in the PA, Fatah has traditionally received financial aid from foreign countries, including many Arab and Middle Eastern countries, the United States (which, in addition, has provided military training),[64] the EU, and even Israel on occasion in attempts to strengthen prospects for peace as well as to neutralize Hamas.[65]

ISLAMISM AND SOCIETY

Circumstantial evidence suggests that Hamas is more popular among Palestinians than its formally-secular rival Fatah. This was true even before Hamas' unexpected victory in the PA's 2006 legislative election, and the trendline has continued since the organization's abrupt seizure of power in Gaza in January 2007.

Some analysts stress that such support is attributable more to a rejection of Fatah's corruption than sincere support for Hamas' Islamism.[66] However, polls show conflicting data. According to one study carried out in June 2009, support for Hamas had declined sharply in the West Bank and Gaza following the Hamas-Israel conflict in late 2008, due primarily to discontent with slow-moving Palestinian unity talks and Israel's ban on Gaza reconstruction.[67] But this is not to suggest that Palestinians are embracing peace. Indeed, data collected in 2009 by the Pew Research Center for the People & Press suggest that there is strong support (68 percent) within the PA for suicide bombings and other terrorist operations in order to "defend Islam from its enemies."[68]

According to yet another poll, 58 percent of Gazans disapprove of Hamas' performance in governing, including its implementation of *sharia*.[69] Older data, however, found that 79.9 percent of Palestinians want the PA to follow *sharia* and 68.6 percent wanted *sharia* to be the exclusive code of law.[70] This may imply that there is more support for Islamism in theory rather than in practice. It should be noted that the reliability of most Middle-East polling data has been questioned by various analysts.[71]

Evidence also indicates that Christian minorities living under the PA suffer discrimination and persecution, including "entirely religiously motivated" attacks on churches, destruction of crosses and altars, and the kidnapping and forced conversion of Christian girls.[72] Because of this continued violence, Israeli scholar Justus Reid Weiner warned that "the very existence of the 2000 year-old Christian community is in doubt."[73] Even Christian participation in Palestinian intifadas may have been a product of "a frightened minority attempting to protect itself in a hostile and volatile environment," as American expert Jonathan Schanzer wrote in his book, *Hamas vs. Fatah*.[74]

The PA, whether under the leadership of Fatah or Hamas, constantly finds itself in a balancing act. When Fatah was in power, Hamas accused them of being too moderate and "selling the land [of the Palestinians to the Zionist enemy]."[75] Similarly, since Hamas has taken control it has been accused by various splinter groups of being too moderate and appeasing to the Israelis. Though the PA occasionally restricts Islamist activities within its jurisdiction, with praise from Israeli security officials,[76] it is more common for the PA to appease Islamist groups. For example, it cancelled a "Miss Palestine" beauty pageant in response to Islamist complaints[77] and willingly hosts Islamist rhetoric on its television station.[78]

ISLAMISM AND THE STATE

Since its inception in 1994, the PA has been struggling to achieve a lasting peace with Israel while at the same time being dogged by charges that it is abetting terrorists within its borders. Certainly Yasser Arafat's reputation as the Arab world's most famous terrorist (that is, until the rise of Osama bin

Laden) played a role in the criticism despite his sudden elevation to the position of a key partner in the peace process. The right of self-governance in the Gaza Strip and West Bank were predicated on Arafat's renunciation of violence which resulted in occasional joint Israeli-Palestinian patrols. According to a 2009 study by Israel's Security Agency, joint patrols have been a key factor in reducing the number of terrorist attacks emanating from the West Bank.[79]

Nevertheless, the threat of rising Islamism remains a concern, particularly in Gaza. Then, as now, radical Islamist groups such as Hamas and the Palestinian Islamic Jihad continued to conduct suicide operations against Israeli targets, albeit without the tacit blessing that they might have received prior to the establishment of the Palestinian Authority. Islamism within the PNA is simply too strong to suppress altogether.

The death of Yasser Arafat in November 2004 paved the way for a comparative moderate, Mahmoud Abbas, to assume the presidency of the PA. While Abbas continues to enjoy support, however limited at times, from Israeli and American policymakers, he is not above appeasing his more radical brethren and has even on occasion called into question Israel's right to exist[80] justifying the "resistance" against it by invoking international law.[81] Such statements, however, have done little to placate Palestinian extremists. Even Fatah's own armed wing, the al-Aqsa Martyr Brigades, which remained largely dormant during the Arafat years, has since joined forces with other terrorist groups in Gaza, suggesting that Abbas does not wield the same authority that Arafat possessed over the Palestinian people.

Arguably the most vitriolic anti-Abbas sentiment comes from Hamas, which emerged as the biggest winner of the 2006 legislative elections, leading to an uncomfortable unity government that quickly collapsed due to tensions between Fatah and Hamas. What followed, and is still being played out by the two factions, is a heated conflict known locally as *wakseh*. In December 2006, following already-heightened tensions and occasional clashes between supporters on both sides, Hamas alleged that the Palestinian Prime Minister and senior Hamas official Ismail Haniyah had been the target of a failed assassination plot by Fatah.[82] By June 2007, Hamas and Fatah were fighting for control over Gaza. Hamas obtained the upper hand, assuming all government duties and effectively running Fatah out of town. Shortly thereafter, Hamas reiterated its desire to turn the Palestinian Territories into an Islamist state, and even changed the name of one Gaza neighborhood from Tel al-Hawa to Tel al-Islam.[83] Fatah officials have since expressed concern over a potential coup in the West Bank by Hamas,[84] further hampering the PA's ability to achieve peace and stability within its borders. The war of words escalated once again in January 2009, upon the expiration of Abbas's term as president. Abbas unilaterally extended his rule, prompting a swift backlash from Hamas, which blasted his presidency as "illegitimate."[85]

A number of Arab states have waded in to Palestinian politics in an effort to end the *wakseh*, seeking to reconcile the two parties—albeit so far without without success.[86] To this day, the PA continues to operate in a diminished capacity, thereby hampering any real short-term prospects for peace with Israel and undermining the PA's ability to establish effective security mechanisms, particularly in Gaza.

ENDNOTES

[1] Mosab Hassan Yousef and Ron Brackin, *Son of Hamas: A Gripping Account of Terror, Betrayal, Political Intrigue, and Unthinkable Choices* (Carol Stream: Tyndale House, 2010), 253-255.

[2] U.S. Department of State, Office of the Coordinator of Counterterrorism, "Background Information on Foreign Terrorist Organizations," October 8, 1999, http://www.state.gov/s/ct/rls/rpt/fto/2801.htm.

[3] "Hamas Leader Killed In Israeli Air Strike," PBS *NewsHour*, March 22, 2004, http://www.pbs.org/newshour/updates/mideast_03-22-04.html.

[4] Hamas Charter (1988), Article Eight, http://www.thejerusalemfund.org/www.thejerusalemfund.org/carryover/documents/charter.html.

[5] Ibid., Article Four

[6] Ibidem, Introduction.

[7] Ibidem, Article Twelve.

[8] See instances documented by Palestinian Media Watch, http://www.pmw.org.il.

[9] *Hamas Charter*, Article Thirteen

[10] Amira Hass, "Haniyeh: Hamas Willing To Accept Palestinian State With 1967 Borders," *Ha'aretz* (Tel Aviv), September 11, 2008, http://www.haaretz.com/news/haniyeh-hamas-willing-to-accept-palestinian-state-with-1967-borders-1.256915.

[11] "While Shalit Negotiations Continue, Hamas Vows More Terror," Investigative Project on Terrorism, http://www.investigativeproject.org/blog/2009/11/while-shalit-negotiations-continue-hamas-vows. See also Intelligence and Terrorism Information Center, "Khaled Mashaal makes it clear that Hamas is determined to continue the path of 'resistance' (i.e., terrorism) and that 'other statements are political maneuvers.' He reveals that Hamas uses most of its financial resources in the Gaza Strip for military purposes rather than rebuilding," November 17, 2009, http://www.terrorism-info.org.il/malam_multimedia/English/eng_n/pdf/hamas_e089.pdf.

[12] Mindy Belz, "Lie To Me," *World*, July 18, 2009, http://www.worldmag.com/articles/15622.

[13] *Hamas Charter*, Article Fifteen.

[14] Gil Ronen, "Hamas' Mickey Mouse: Teaching Kids To Hate And Kill," Arutz Sheva, May 7, 2007, http://www.israelnationalnews.com/News/News.aspx/122365; Matthew Kalman, "Hamas Launches TV Bugs Bunny-Lookalike Who Declares 'I Will Eat The Jews,'" *Daily Mail* (London), February 12, 2008, http://www.dailymail.co.uk/news/article-513925/Hamas-launches-TV-Bugs-Bunny-lookalike-declares-I-eat-Jews.html.

[15] Sami Moubayed, "Iran's Hamas Patronage Almost Two Decades Old," *Gulf News*, January 10, 2009, http://gulfnews.com/news/region/palestinian-territories/iran-s-hamas-patronage-almost-two-decades-old-1.44494.

[16] "Iran Pledges To Continue Support Of Hamas," *Al-Sharq al-Awsat* (London), May 26, 2008, http://www.aawsat.com/english/news.asp?section=1&id=12877.

[17] "Holy Land Founders Get Life Sentences," JTA, May 28, 2009, http://jta.org/news/article/2009/05/28/1005480/holy-land-founders-get-life-sentences#When:10:32:00Z.

[18] "Hamas Funding," GlobalSecurity.org, n.d., http://www.globalsecurity.org/military/world/para/hamas-funds.htm.

[19] Council on Foreign Relations, "Backgrounder: Hamas," August 27, 2009, http://www.cfr.org/publication/8968/hamas.html.

[20] Israeli Ministry of Foreign Affairs, "Grad Rocket From Gaza Hits Ashkelon, Kassam in Sderot," July 30, 2010, http://www.mfa.gov.il/MFA/Terrorism-+Obstacle+to+Peace/Hamas+war+against+Israel/Grad_rocket_hits_Ashkelon_30-Jul-2010.htm.

[21] "Israeli Planes Bomb Gaza Tunnels," Reuters, August 10, 2009, http://www.irishtimes.com/newspaper/breaking/2009/0810/breaking42.htm.

[22] Meir Litvak, "Palestine Islamic Jihad – Background Information," Tel Aviv University *TAU Notes* no. 56, November 28, 2002, http://www.jewishvirtuallibrary.org/jsource/Terrorism/tau56.html. See also "Palestinian Islamic Jihad," Encyclopedia of the Middle East, n.d., http://www.mideastweb.org/Middle-East-Encyclopedia/palestinian_islamic_jihad.htm.

[23] "Islamic Jihad of Palestine," *The Oxford Dictionary of Islam*, n.d., http://www.oxfordislamicstudies.com/article/opr/t125/e1106.

[24] Jonathan Schanzer, *Hamas vs. Fatah: The Struggle for Palestine* (New York: Palgrave-MacMillan), 21.

[25] Parliament of Australia, Parliamentary Joint Committee on ASIO, ASIS, and DSD, "3. The Listing of Palestinian Islamic Jihad," 2004, http://www.aph.gov.au/house/committee/pjcaad/pij/report/chapter3.pdf.

[26] Alden Oreck, "Palestinian Islamic Jihad," Jewish Virtual Library, n.d., http://www.jewishvirtuallibrary.org/jsource/Terrorism/PIJ.html.

[27] "Border Police Arrests Top Islamic Jihad Operative In Bethlehem," *Jerusalem Post*, October 28, 2008, http://www.jpost.com/Home/Article.aspx?id=118527.

[28] Yaakov Katz, "IDF Kills Five Palestinians In Gaza Border Clashes," *Jerusalem Post*, June 2, 2010, http://www.jpost.com/Home/Article.aspx?id=177196.

[29] Council on Foreign Relations, "Backgrounder: Palestinian Islamic Jihad," April 10, 2008, http://www.cfr.org/publication/15984#p2.

[30] "Investigative Project on Terrorism, "Individual Terrorists: Sami al-Arian," July 9, 2008, http://www.investigativeproject.org/profile/100.

[31] "Islamic Jihad of Palestine."

[32] "Profile: Jund Ansar Allah," BBC, August 15, 2009, http://news.bbc.co.uk/2/hi/middle_east/8203239.stm.

[33] Ibid.

[34] "Five Facts About Jund Ansar Allah," Reuters, August 15, 2009, http://www.reuters.com/article/idUSTRE57E11A20090815.

[35] "Several Killed In Clashes Between Islamists And Hamas Police," France24, August 14, 2009, http://mobile.france24.com/en/20090814-fifteen-wounded-clashes-between-islamists-hamas-police-gaza-strip.

[36] "Profile: Jund Ansar Allah."

[37] Yaakov Katz, "Security And Defense: Smoke Screen?" Jerusalem Post, August 20, 2009, http://www.jpost.com/Home/Article.aspx?id=152475.

[38] Ibid.

[39] Intelligence and Terrorism Information Center, "News of Terrorism and the Israeli-Palestinian Conflict," June 2-9, 2009, http://www.terrorism-info.org.il/malam_multimedia/English/eng_n/html/ipc_e035.htm.

[40] "Blast Injures 50 At Wedding For Nephew Of Hamas Leader," CNN, July 21, 2009, http://www.cnn.com/2009/WORLD/meast/07/21/gaza.wedding.explosion/index.html.

[41] The Graduate Institute of International and Developmental Studies, "Army of Islam (Jaish al-Islam)," n.d., http://www.armed-groups.org/6/section.aspx/ViewGroup?id=7.

[42] Jonathan Dahoah Halevi, "Al Qaeda Affiliate Jaish al-Islam Receives Formal Sanctuary In Hamas-Ruled Gaza," Jerusalem Center for Public Affairs Jerusalem Issue Brief 8, no. 7, August 20, 2008, http://www.jcpa.org/JCPA/Templates/ShowPage.asp?DBID=1&LNGID=1&TMID=111&FID=442&PID=0&IID=2408.

[43] "BBC Reporter Alan Johnston Wearing Suicide Belt Appeals," LiveLeak, June 24, 2007, http://www.liveleak.com/view?i=b2c_1182727196.

[44] Dahoah Halevi, "Al Qaeda Affiliate Jaish al-Islam Receives Formal Sanctuary In Hamas-Ruled Gaza."

[45] Israel Security Agency, "The Jaljalat Phenomenon In The Gaza Strip," n.d., http://www.shabak.gov.il/English/EnTerrorData/Reviews/Pages/Jaljalat_en.aspx.

[46] "Hamas Captures Commander Of Pro-Al Qaida Militia," World Tribune, October 12, 2009, http://www.worldtribune.com/worldtribune/WTARC/2009/me_hamas0797_10_12.asp.

[47] Katz, "Security And Defense."

[48] Ibrahim Qannan, "Exclusive: New Gaza Faction Numbers 11,000,"

Ma'an (Ramallah), September 12, 2010, http://www.maannews.net/eng/ViewDetails.aspx?ID=277513.

[49] Ibid.

[50] "Hamas Foiled Carter-Blair Murder Plans," OneIndia, September 8, 2009, http://news.oneindia.in/2009/09/08/hamas-foiled-carter-blair-murder-pro-al-qaeda-body.html.

[51] As cited in Raymond Ibrahim, "War And Peace – And Deceit – In Islam," *Pajamas Media*, February 12, 2009, http://www.meforum.org/2066/war-and-peace-and-deceit-in-islam.

[52] "Jaish Al-Ummah Official: Expect Military Operation In South Lebanon Directed At Israel," NowLebanon, April 11, 2010, http://www.nowlebanon.com/NewsArchiveDetails.aspx?ID=159825.

[53] "Jaish Al Ummah To Hamas: 'Whose Side Are You On?'" CBS News *Internet Terror Monitor*, May 27, 2009 http://www.cbsnews.com/blogs/2009/05/27/monitor/entry5044608.shtml.

[54] Ibid.

[55] "About Us," Hizbuttahrir.org, n.d., http://www.hizbuttahrir.org/1-19-about-us.aspx.

[56] Jonathan Spyer, "Hizb ut-Tahrir: A Rising Force In Palestinian Territories," *Global Politician*, December 14, 2007, http://www.globalpolitician.com/23871-palestine.

[57] Jonathan Spyer, "A 'Rising Force,'" *Ha'aretz* (Tel Aviv), June 12, 2007, http://www.haaretz.com/hasen/spages/932087.html.

[58] "Hizb Ut-Tahrir: PA Attempts Arrest Of Member," *Ma'an* (Ramallah), December 17, 2009, http://www.maannews.net/eng/ViewDetails.aspx?ID=247723. See also "Hizb Ut-Tahrir: PA Arrests Thousands," Ma'an (Ramallah), July 17, 2010, http://www.maannews.net/eng/ViewDetails.aspx?ID=300222.

[59] "Palestinian Authority Funds Go To Militants," BBC, November 7, 2003, http://news.bbc.co.uk/2/hi/middle_east/3243071.stm.

[60] Schanzer, *Hamas vs. Fatah*, 63.

[61] Daniel Pipes, "Lessons From The Prophet Muhammad's Diplomacy," *Middle East Quarterly* 6, no. 3, September 1999, http://www.meforum.org/480/lessons-from-the-prophet-muhammads-diplomacy.

[62] Sami F. Musallam, "The Struggle For Jerusalem," *PASSIA*, May 1996, http://www.passia.org/jerusalem/publications/Struggle_for_jerusalem/SAMI_Struggle_for_jerusalem_txt1.htm.

[63] Schanzer, *Hamas vs. Fatah*, 125.

[64] David Bedein, *The Implications Of United States Military Training of Palestinian Security Forces* (Washington, DC: Center For Near East Policy Research, Ltd., 2009), http://www.scribd.com/doc/21587348/Assessment-of-US-Military-Aid-to-Fatah-US.

[65] "Europe, US And Israel Promise Aid To Fatah," *Der Spiegel* (Hamburg), June 18, 2007, http://www.spiegel.de/international/

world/0,1518,489139,00.html.

[66] Khaled Abu Toameh, "'Corruption Will Let Hamas Take W. Bank,'" *Jerusalem Post*, January 29, 2010, http://www.jpost.com/MiddleEast/Article.aspx?id=167194.

[67] Reuters and Avi Issacharoff, "Poll: Hamas Popularity Falls In Both West Bank And Gaza," *Ha'aretz* (Tel Aviv), June 29, 2009, http://www.haaretz.com/hasen/spages/1096472.html.

[68] Pew Global Attitudes Project, "Key Indicators Database: Support For Suicide Bombing," n.d., http://pewglobal.org/database/?indicator=19&country=168&response=Often/sometimes%20justified.

[69] Mark Silverberg, "As The Islamic Curtain Descends," International Analyst Network, November 30, 2009, http://www.analyst-network.com/article.php?art_id=3242.

[70] Andrew Bostom, *The Legacy of Islamic Anti-Semitism* (New York: Prometheus, 2008), 96.

[71] Adam Pechter, "Briefing: New Middle East Polling Data," Middle East Forum, August 13, 2009, http://www.meforum.org/2439/new-middle-east-polling-data.

[72] Schanzer, *Hamas vs. Fatah*, 110-111.

[73] Joseph Puder, "Christians Suffer Under The Palestinian Authority," *Pajamas Media*, November 15, 2009, http://pajamasmedia.com/blog/the-plight-of-christians-under-the-palestinian-authority/. See also David Raab, "The Beleaguered Christians Of The Palestinian-Controlled Areas," Jerusalem Center for Public Affairs *Jerusalem Letter/Viewpoints* no. 490, January 1-15, 2003, http://www.jcpa.org/jl/vp490.htm.

[74] Schanzer, *Hamas vs. Fatah*, 56.

[75] Jonathan Schanzer, "The Challenge Of Hamas To Fatah," *Middle East Quarterly* 10, no. 2, Spring 2003, http://www.meforum.org/516/the-challenge-of-hamas-to-fatah.

[76] Amos Harel and Avi Issacharoff, "Israeli Officials Laud PA Crackdown On Hamas," *Ha'aretz* (Tel Aviv), July 9, 2008, http://www.haaretz.com/hasen/spages/1018599.html.

[77] "Miss Palestine Pageant Cancelled," Jihad Watch, December 21, 2009, http://www.jihadwatch.org/2009/12/miss-palestine-pageant-canceled.html.

[78] "Palestinian Friday Sermon by Sheik Ibrahim Mudeiris: Muslims Will Rule America and Britain, Jews Are a Virus Resembling AIDS," The Middle East Media Research Institute *TV Monitor Project* no. 669, n.d., http://www.memritv.org/clip/en/669.htm.

[79] Israeli Ministry of Foreign Affairs, "ISA: Data And Trends In Palestinian Terrorism – 2009 Summary," January 15, 2010, http://www.mfa.gov.il/MFA/Terrorism-+Obstacle+to+Peace/Palestinian+terror+since+2000/ISA_summary_Palestinian_terrorism_2009.htm.

[80] "Mideast: Abbas Refuses To recognise Israel As Jewish State," AKI (Rome), April 27, 2010, http://www.adnkronos.com/AKI/English/Security/?id=3.0.3252928663.

[81] Jack Khoury, "Abbas: We Choose Peace, But Reserve Right To Resistance," Ha'aretz (Tel Aviv), April 8, 2009, http://www.haaretz.com/news/abbas-we-choose-peace-but-reserve-right-to-resistance-1.281370.

[82] "Hamas Accuses Fatah Over Attack," Al-Jazeera (Doha), December 15, 2006, http://english.aljazeera.net/news/middleeast/2006/12/200852513152100682.html.

[83] Ali Waked, "Hamas: We'll Execute Fatah Leaders," Yediot Ahronot (Tel Aviv), June 14, 2007, http://www.ynetnews.com/articles/0,7340,L-3412813,00.html.

[84] "Fatah: Hamas Preparing For West Bank Coup," Ma'an (Ramallah), May 6, 2009, http://www.maannews.net/eng/ViewDetails.aspx?ID=211033.

[85] Avi Issacharoff, "PLO Extends Abbas' Term As President; Hamas Denounces 'Illegitimate' Move," Ha'aretz (Tel Aviv), December 17, 2009, http://www.haaretz.com/print-edition/news/plo-extends-abbas-term-as-president-hamas-denounces-illegitimate-move-1.1977.

[86] "Fatah, Hamas Agree To Meet In Damascus Next Week," Xinhua (Beijing), November 2, 2010, http://news.xinhuanet.com/english2010/world/2010-11/02/c_13586093.htm.

JORDAN

In recent years, the Hashemite Kingdom of Jordan has faced a growing threat to its stability from extreme, violent and political Islamic groups. The wake-up call for the Jordanian government came in the form of a pair of events in 2005—rocket attacks on Aqaba in May of that year, and the simultaneous attacks on hotels in Amman that November—both of which were perpetrated by groups affiliated with the al-Qaeda organization in Iraq. Even prior to these attacks, however, the Jordanian regime had waged a wide-scale and determined ideological struggle against radical Islamic organizations on its soil. In this struggle, the Jordanian regime sought to de-legitimize jihadi Salafi ideology while disseminating a brand of moderate traditional Islam as a religious "vaccine" against it.

ISLAMIST ACTIVITY

Political Islam is not a new phenomenon in Jordan. Since the British created the Emirate of Transjordan in 1921 and placed King Abdallah I on its throne,

Islam has served as one of the cardinal building blocks of regime legitimacy. The genealogy of the Hashemite family as scions of the Prophet Muhammad's tribe was an important source of legitimacy for its rule in Syria, Iraq and Jordan, as it had been in the Hijaz. King Abdallah and his grandson Hussein took care to present themselves as believing Muslims, appearing at rituals and prayers, performing the pilgrimage to Mecca and embellishing their speeches with Islamic motifs. The Jordanian constitution of 1952 established Islam as the official religion of the kingdom and mandated that the king must be a Muslim born of Muslim parents. The constitution defines *sharia* as one of the pillars of legislation in the kingdom, while family law is in the exclusive hands of the *sharia* courts. However, in contrast to other Muslim countries where Islam plays a pivotal role, the Jordanian regime has hewed to a middle course. It never declared *sharia* to be the sole source of legislation, nor did it ever attempt to implement the *hudud* (Islamic penal law).[1]

The radical Islamic camp in Jordan is composed of two separate—but frequently overlapping—wings. The first is the main body of Jordanian Islamists, which identifies with the Muslim Brotherhood movement that originated in Egypt. The second is the radical *jihadi*-Salafi movement embodied by al-Qaeda and its ideological fellow travelers within Jordan.

The radical Islamic camp in Jordan writ large draws its strength from diverse and significant sources. Foremost among them are: its own organizational and ideological infrastructure inside the country; indirect influence and public sympathy from the wider Muslim Brotherhood movement, which has deep roots in the Jordanian public—both Trans-Jordanian and Palestinian—and the inflammatory influence of the war in Iraq and the ongoing Arab conflict with Israel. Confronting all of these factors is a weak official religious establishment that lacks popular support and is incapable of mobilizing those with religious authority to defend the regime's views.

The Muslim Brotherhood

The Muslim Brotherhood movement is deeply rooted in Jordan, manifested in the country's political arena through the Islamic Action Front (IAF) party and parliamentary faction, and in civil society (in mosques, labor and trade unions and universities). Since the birth of the Muslim Brotherhood movement in Jordan in the 1940s, internal struggles have occurred between a moderate stream that aspires to co-exist and maintain sound relations with the regime, and an extremist wing that draws its ideology from the *takfiri* doctrine of Egyptian Muslim Brotherhood leader Sayyid Qutb and as a result attempts to confront the regime both politically and ideologically. Throughout most of the movement's history in Jordan, the extremist wing has usually been identified with leaders of Palestinian origin, whose identification with the Hashemite regime was weaker than that of their Trans-Jordanian compatriots.[2]

In the past, this extremist wing was relatively marginal in the overall operations of the Muslim Brotherhood in Jordan. In the 1980s and 1990s, it devoted its main energies to the *jihad* in Afghanistan, and subsequently in Chechnya, Bosnia and other places. More recently, however, this stream has gained in strength and daring, as reflected by the results of the internal leadership elections carried out by the Brotherhood in early 2006, and manifested in particular in the composition of the IAF. The Muslim Brotherhood's religious rulings, or *fatwas*, express its identification with the Salafi worldview, identifying with the *jihads* in Iraq and Israel/Palestine, calling on Arab leaders to raise the flag of *jihad* and determining that any Muslim who provides support to the "occupying forces" commits an act of treachery (*khiyyana*) and war against Allah and his Prophet—an act tantamount to apostasy and abandonment of the nation of Islam.[3]

Developments in the Palestinian theater have exerted influence over Islamism in neighboring Jordan, and specifically in the behavior of the Muslim Brotherhood in its attempts to rally support within its constituency. These attempts, however, have inevitably drawn the movement into greater conflict with the Jordanian government and other political parties. For example, the movement leveraged protests by Hamas over the Egyptian fence, built to prevent smuggling of weapons to and from Gaza, into a domestic political issue, with the "*fatwa* committee" of the IAF issuing a religious decree prohibiting the construction of what it called the "Egyptian-Israeli-American wall."[4] Two key arguments served as the basis of the prohibition: 1) humanitarian arguments that the fence would strengthen the blockade of Gaza, undermine the lives of its inhabitants, damage their health, and halt Gaza's reconstruction; and 2) a political argument that the fence would undermine the *jihad* for the liberation of Palestine, because it would prevent the transfer of weapons to the *mujahideen* in Gaza. Therefore, the *fatwa* implies that by turning to the Americans and Israelis for its protection, Egypt becomes one of them, and hence the Egyptian government should be considered "apostate." This religious ruling by the IAF incorporates two central tenets of the Salafi *jihadist* ideology embraced by al-Qaeda. It accepts the approach that liberating all occupied Islamic territories, especially Palestine, is the "individual duty" of every Muslim, which must be carried out either by actively participating in the *jihad* or by providing the weapons and money needed for it. It also promulgates the view that a Muslim regime that works with the Jews and the Christians should be seen as "apostate."

In March 2006, the IAF's *Shura* Council elected Zaki Bani Irsheid as its Secretary General after receiving the approval to do so from the Muslim Brotherhood's *Shura* Council. Zaki Irsheid is an Irbid businessman, born in al-Zarqa' in 1957. Irsheid's election was anathema to the regime, due to his close ties with Hamas and his militant record. However, the Brotherhood leadership balanced Irsheid's election by elevating (in March 2006) two relatively-moderate leaders to senior leadership positions: Sheikh Salim al-Falahat as Inspector General and Hamza Mansour as head of the IAF's *Shura* Council.[5]

The regime's early concerns regarding Irsheid's political and militant approach, as well as his radical support of Hamas, were validated, as he quickly became a prominent oppositionist and a harsh, extremist critic of the regime's domestic and foreign policies.[6] Irsheid's radicalizing effect on the IAF's political doctrine was rapidly apparent: in July 2006, the party's Religious Sages Committee issued a religious ruling, stating that "it was obligatory to assist Hezbollah's *mujahideen* against Israel" in the Second Lebanon War.[7] At the same time, the Committee condemned Saudi religious sages, who characterized Hezbollah as heretical, and called for the group to be ostracized.

Irsheid similarly spearheaded the transformation of the IAF's platform for the country's November 2007 parliamentary elections. The new platform emphasized that the IAF's views and objectives stemmed from "Islamic religious law." On domestic issues, the new platform outlined a series of proposed constitutional reforms, including a new election law loosening regime control of mosques and restrictions on religious preaching. In foreign policy, the platform rejected Israel's existence and called on Jordan and Egypt to annul the peace treaties with Israel in favor of "active resistance" to any kind of normalization of relations. It also called for "providing comprehensive assistance, including military assistance, to the *Jihad* forces and the Resistance" that are acting against Israel in order to "fully liberate the land." At the same time, it attacked the United States, accusing it of "striving to gain control over the Arab countries and the Islamic world," and calling on Muslims to act to liberate countries "occupied" by the United States—specifically Iraq, Afghanistan, and Somalia.[8]

In the subsequent parliamentary elections, however, the IAF made a poor showing, with the number of its seats plummeting from 17 (out of 110) to a mere seven. The loss contributed directly to the dissolution of the Muslim Brotherhood's *Shura* Council later the same month.[9] In its statement regarding the dissolution, the Brotherhood blamed the Jordanian government and its agencies for rigging the elections and defaming the movement through biased state media.[10]

Subsequently, in February 2008, the Brotherhood held elections for a new *Shura* Council, choosing Abd al-Latif Arabiat, a moderate, as Council head. The internal power struggles associated with the election moderated the movement's drift toward radicalization, and eventually brought about a balanced division of power in the Muslim Brotherhood's institutions. The "hawkish" stream and the "Fourth Stream," which is affiliated with Hamas, gained control over the Council and won a combined 28 Council seats, while the "dovish" stream won 22 of the Council's 50 seats. Subsequently, the "hawks" accepted three seats in the Executive Bureau, which is in charge of conducting organizational policy, while the moderates won the remaining five.[11]

However, this balance proved only temporary. On April 30, 2008, the Brotherhood's new *Shura* Council elected a radical Islamist and longtime power broker, Dr. Hamam Sa'id, as the organization's fifth Inspector General. The election of Sa'id, a Jordanian of Palestinian origin, was the product of a coalition between hawkish factions within the organization.[12] With Sa'id's appointment, and the earlier appointment of Zaki Bani Irsheid as IAF Secretary General, the Brotherhood's internal issues and overall policy directions became dominated by charismatic, activist leaders with the most uncompromising views.

In the years that followed, the two leaders steered the organization onto a more confrontational course with the Jordanian regime. Sa'id, for example, supported a militant approach that advocates turning Jordan into "a country where military force is to be concentrated and a military outpost for the war against the heretics."[13] In other words, Sa'id not only advocates the central demand of his party and the Muslim Brotherhood that the regime abrogate the peace agreement with Israel, but goes as far as embracing the *Takfiri jihadist* approach that demands Jordan be transformed into a launchpad for military confrontation against nearby Israel. This opinion, voiced publicly on broadcast media, depicts the Palestinian issue as a Jordanian one.

On May 30, 2009 Zaki Irsheid was forced to resign his post as IAF's Secretary General. The 120 members of the IAF's *Shura* Council accepted his resignation, and those of eight members of the party's Executive Bureau (responsible for formulating party policies). Thereafter, they unanimously elected Dr. Ishak al-Farhan as the party's new Secretary General, and approved the list of eight new Executive Bureau members proposed by him.[14] Al-Farhan fulfilled the Brotherhood's pressing need for a transitional Secretary General; he was acceptable to many circles and on good terms with the government. Al-Farhan, in turn, promptly outlined a transitional plan to prepare the party for its next internal elections. He underscored the need for a pacific settlement of internal disputes, and vowed to take steps to harmonize relations with the government.[15] This more conciliatory line continues to be pursued by the party today.

Salafi jihadism

The institutional infrastructure of Salafi-*jihadi* Islamism in Jordan is diverse. It includes popular mosques not under the regime's supervision and bookstands that serve to propagate a radical, exclusionary religious worldview. The many websites of global *jihadist* groups provide a means for mass dissemination of this ideology. *Jihadist* activists arrested by authorities have been found to be indoctrinated via these outlets.[16] This indoctrination, in turn, has been facilitated by the presence of what anecdotal evidence suggests is a significant minority within Jordanian society that supports the Salafism and facilitates the recruitment of members by *jihadist* organizations—a proclivity illustrated in public opinion surveys conducted in recent years in Jordan.[17]

The Muslim Brotherhood movement in general, and its extremist wing in particular, plays a pivotal role in the dissemination and acceptance of the Salafi-*jihadi* message in Jordanian society, especially among the younger generation of citizens. Outbreaks of violence between Israel and the Palestinians, particularly in the Gaza Strip, and the wars in Iraq and Afghanistan, likewise have served to strengthen Salafi sentiment in Jordan. Extremist organizations, chief among them al-Qaeda in Iraq, appear to enjoy both support and admiration among a considerable percentage of the Jordanian public, which sees the group and its broader ideology as the principal standard-bearer in the war against the enemies of Islam.[18]

The ebb and flow of *jihadist* activity in Iraq profoundly affected Islamist organizations in Jordan. The 2006 killing of al-Qaeda in Iraq leader Abu Musab al-Zarqawi, Coalition successes against the group thereafter (as a result of the "surge" strategy adopted by the Bush administration), along with local Jordanian pressure, all served to create fissures in the Jordanian *jihadist* movement. The result was the emergence and rise of a more "pragmatic" wing of the movement, led by the prominent Salafi cleric Abu Muhammad al-Maqdisi. Since his release from Jordanian prison in 2008, al-Maqdisi has consistently criticized the school of thought epitomized by al-Zarqawi, which sanctioned intra-Muslim conflict due to ideological and political differences. Al-Maqdisi did not change the principles of *takfir*, the declaration of Muslims as heretics or apostates. However, he presented a case against *jihadist* attacks inside Jordan, thus revising his own views about the permissibility of collateral casualties among Muslims (or even their direct targeting) if necessary in order to kill "infidels."[19]

ISLAMISM AND SOCIETY

The Islamic movement in Jordan enjoys a broad popular base among both the country's Trans-Jordanian and Palestinian populace. In recent Pew polls, support in Jordan for the enactment of *sharia* law, including the *hudud* (stoning and amputation of limbs), measured at some 50 percent in support of segregation between men and women in work places, 58 percent in favor of stoning for the crime of adultery and 86 percent approval for capital punishment for apostates.[20] In recent years, Islamic dress—particularly for women—has become more and more ubiquitous. Islamic bookstores selling radical tracts now can be found near almost any mosque in Amman. Furthermore, at 34 percent, favorable attitudes toward al-Qaeda in Jordan are the highest in the Arab world.[21]

The Palestinian issue ranks high on the agenda of Jordan's Islamist groups, in particular the Brotherhood and IAF, for a number of reasons:

• The presence of a large number of citizens of Palestinian origin in the Brotherhood leadership.
• The Muslim Brotherhood's view of Jordan's large Palestinian population as its key constituency, not only for parliamentary elections, but for strengthening its positions in the trade unions and local authorities.
• The Palestinian issue is a perennial issue of interest in Jordan's politics and of major interest to the public.
• Traditional organizational ties with Hamas, stemming from the fact that the Muslim Brotherhood in Jordan and its Palestinian counterpart were part of same organization in the past.[22]

Moreover, the institutions and membership of the Muslim Brotherhood in Jordan and the Palestinian Hamas movement overlap considerably. One of the more obvious links is the existence of offices in the Gulf States that represent both organizations, staffed by officials of Palestinian origin. The bureaus are important to both organizations because they serve as means of raising funds from wealthy sources in the Gulf.[23]

This relationship, however, is in flux. In the second half of 2009, disputes, accompanied by a great deal of tension, broke out between the "hawks" and "doves" in the Muslim Brotherhood leadership regarding the ties between the movement in Jordan and Hamas. The moderate stream in the Brotherhood leadership in Jordan demanded the immediate severing of organizational ties between the Muslim Brotherhood and Hamas, claiming that this state of affairs goes against the Brotherhood's rules and regulations as well as against Jordan's constitution and the Political Parties Law.[24] The "hawks," on the other hand, supported a preservation of the *status quo*. The Brotherhood's Inspector General, Hamam Sa'id, ultimately took the position that the status quo should endure, but qualified his statement by describing the relationship as one between two independent organizations.[25]

The common denominator among the various Brotherhood factions is that the Palestinian issue is an integral part of their agenda in Jordan, and that ongoing consultations with Hamas are only natural. The Brotherhood, one official has explained, "has a religious and national obligation to support the

Palestinians and their problem."[26] The current Inspector General, Hamam Sa'id, has gone further, stating that the Brotherhood's involvement in the Palestinian arena serves to provide "the Palestinians [with] *jihadist* assistance and support."[27] Like the Palestinian issue generally, the Brotherhood's relationship with Hamas remains an important element of Islamist expression in Jordan.

ISLAMISM AND THE STATE

Salafi *jihadi* organizations in Jordan remain under intense pressure from the Jordanian government, which has succeeded in disrupting numerous attempted terrorist attacks inside the Kingdom in recent years. It has done so through the imprisonment of large numbers of *jihadist* activists and sympathizers, in the process wreaking havoc on their respective organizations and restricting their activities. A high point was the January 2009 trial of twelve members of a Salafi-*jihadi* group for attacks on a Christian church and cemetery, and for their involvement in the shooting of a group of Lebanese musicians performing in downtown Amman.[28]

Also notable was the December 2009, trial of twenty-four Islamists on criminal charges stemming from their management of the Islamic Centre Society (ICS), which had been dissolved three years prior. Before its dissolution, the ICS had served as the Muslim Brotherhood's financial arm, administering assets worth over a billion dollars, running scores of schools, health establishments and social centers. In 2006, at the height of internal tensions between the Muslim Brotherhood and the IAF, the government of former Prime Minister Marouf Bakhit dissolved the ICS. The government at that time charged ICS officials with corrupt practices, but Brotherhood leaders contended that the step was designed to deprive the Islamic Movement of the financial backing it had traditionally received. The move was widely believed to have been one of the key reasons behind the IAF's downturn in the November 2007 elections.[29]

Jordanian authorities, however, have also seen its fair share of defeats. On December 30, 2009, a suicide bomber killed seven CIA agents at Forward Operating Base Chapman in Khost Province of Afghanistan; an officer of Jordan's General Intelligence Directorate (GID) was also killed in the attack.

The real challenge facing the Brotherhood, moderates and radicals alike, appears to be the far-reaching reforms of the internal political system announced by King Abdallah in late November 2009. After the dissolution of the parliament, a new government headed by Samir al'Rifa'i was established for a transitional period, until the required parliamentary elections by the last quarter of 2010. The elections have a mixed effect on the Brotherhood. On the one hand, they now have the opportunity to regain their status in Parliament, following their crushing defeat at the November 2007 parliamentary elections. On the other hand, they have doubts about the regime's intention to implement the genuine political reform it had promised the political system and the public. From the Brotherhood's point of view, the implementation of a thorough political reform that would repeal the principle of "one person, one vote" and pledge to hold "honest and fair elections" are basic conditions for translating their potential electoral power into a significant quota of parliamentary seats and for subsequently making political and public gains.

The "Arab Spring" has not seriously undermined the Jordanian regime, at least so far. However, the fall of the Egyptian and Tunisian regimes and the unsettled situation in Yemen and Libya have encouraged the Jordanian Muslim Brotherhood to increase its pressure on the regime. This has been expressed in demonstrations under increasingly radicalized slogans, along with the classic demands for an end to corruption and abrogation of the peace treaty with Israel. These demonstrations escalated in March 2011, resulting in a number of casualties (though far less than in other Arab countries). The vanguard of the protests in Jordan appears to be more the Salafi *jihadi* movement than the Muslim Brotherhood itself. The violence has also exposed divisions between this contingent and the larger Salafi movement. The regime, however, accuses the protestors of receiving orders from the Muslim Brotherhood in Egypt and elsewhere. The threat to the regime has also undermined the normally quiescent attitude of the East-Jordanian political leadership. According to various reports, tribal leaders have warned the King that they will not tolerate a light hand in dealing with the threat, which they perceive as a Palestinian attempt to topple the Hashemite entity.[30]

ENDNOTES

[1] See Shmuel Bar, "The Muslim Brotherhood in Jordan," Moshe Dayan Center for Middle Eastern and African Studies *Data and Analysis*, June 1998, http://www.dayan.tau.ac.il/d&a-jordan-bar.pdf.

[2] Ibid., 50-52.

[3] Website of the Islamic Action Front, August 14, 2004, http://www.jabha.net. Nadwah al-Majali summarizes how the jihad stream, on one hand, and the Muslim Brotherhood, on the other hand, have a stranglehold on the state and seek to undermine its foundations: "One stream attacks the regime through violence, confrontation, takfir and bombing attacks, while the other stream gently tunnels below the regime's foundations, penetrates the society and its institutions, mobilizes the street against it and raises doubts about its direction. *Al-Rai* (Amman), June 27, 2006.

[4] Website of the Islamic Action Front, January 24, 2010, http://www.jabha.net.

[5] *Al Hayat* (London), March 19, 2006.

[6] *Al-Quds al-Arabi* (London), March 22, 2006.

[7] Al-Qods al-'Arabi, Al-Ra'I, Al-Ghad, 7 July 2006.

[8] Website of the Islamic Action Front, October 27, 2007, http://www.jabha.net.

[9] The *Shura* Council is the Movement's highest-ranking body, which outlines policies in cooperation with the IAF *Shura* Council.

[10] *IslamOnline*, November 30, 2007. The Brotherhood decided at the last minute not to participate in the local council elections held that year, out of concern that the elections would be biased in the regime's favour.

[11] *Al-Haqiqa al-Dawliya* (Amman), April 30, 2008; *Al-Hayat* (London), May 4, 2008.

[12] *Al-Haqiqa al-Dawliya* (Amman), April 30, 2008.

[13] As cited in *Al-Iman*, September 24, 2009.

[14] Al-Farhan had been the IAF's first Secretary General and had also been the Muslim Brotherhood's Shura Council head. Born in Jerusalem in the mid- 1930's, but of Palestinian origins, al-Farhan joined the Muslim Brotherhood while he was still in high school. He obtained an MA in literature from the University of Columbia in the United States and a Ph.D in Cultural Studies. In 1970, after working in the Ministry of Culture for about fifteen years, Wasfi al-Tal asked him to join his government as Minister of Culture, Education and Religious Affairs. Al-Farhan later held this office in the governments of Ahmad al-Lozi and Zeid al-Rifa'i. In 1989, he was elected to the Senate for four years and then headed the University of al-Zarqa. Throughout his career, al-Farhan held various political, public, and academic offices.

[15] *Mafkarat al-Islam*, May 31, 2009.

[16] A prominent example is Abed Shahadeh al-Tahawi, who is considered a source of religious law among extreme Islamic groups in Irbid. He preaches the takfir doctrine in mosques in the Irbid region. He was arrested and brought to trial. See *Al-Dustour* (Amman), May 23, 2005; *Al-Quds Al-Arabi* (London), June 6, 2005.

[17] According to a one survey conducted prior to the attacks in Amman on November 9, 2005, some 64 percent of the Jordanian public sympathized with the al-Qaeda organization in Iraq led by al-Zarqawi. *Al-Hayat* (London), December 15, 2005. However, this sympathy dropped sharply after the attacks in Amman. In a survey conducted immediately after these attacks, 72 percent of the sample believed that this organization is a terror organization, 20 percent believed that it is not a terror organization and 15.6 percent believed that it is a resistance organization. But after the killing of al-Zarqawi in June 2006, the percentage of those who regard the organization as a terror organization dropped to 54 percent, while 20 percent still believed it is not a terror organization. It should be noted that the data shows that 10 percent of those surveyed in 2004 believed that the al-Qaeda organization led by bin Laden is a terror organization, compared to 49 percent in 2005 and 41 percent in 2006. This indicates that there is greater sympathy for bin Laden's organization than for the al-Zarqawi organization. *Al-Quds Al-Arabi* (London), July 10, 2006.

[18] Pew Global Attitudes Project, "Muslim Publics Divided on Hamas and Hezbollah," December 2, 2010, http://pewglobal. org/2010/12/02/muslims-around-the-world-divided-on-hamas-and-hezbollah/; See also Pew Global Attitudes Project, "Osama bin Laden Largely Discredited Among Muslims in Recent Years," May 2, 2011, http://pewglobal.org/2011/05/02/osama-bin-laden-largely-discredited-among-muslim-publics-in-recent-years/.

[19] See al-Maqdisi's website, http://www.tawhed.ws/, and the subsequent debate with other Jihadi authorities such as Ma'asari. For a summary of these debates, see Joas Wagemakers, "Reflections on Maqdisi's Arrest," *Jihadica*, October 2, 2010, http://www.jihadica.com/reflections-on-al-maqdisis-arrest/.

[20] Pew Global Attitudes Project, "Muslim Publics Divided on Hamas and Hezbollah."

[21] Ibid.

[22] *Al-Haqiqa al-Dawliya* (Amman), December 29, 2009. According to a senior source in the Muslim Brotherhood, the Brotherhood's Inspector General, Hamam Sa'id, and two members of the Brotherhood's Executive Bureau are also members of the Hamas *Shura* Council and participate in its debates. See *Al-Sharq al-Awsat* (London), September 2, 2009.

[23] *Al-Siyasa* (Kuwait), October 23, 2009; *Al-Sharq al-Awsat* (London), September 2, 2009.

[24] *Al-Sharq al-Awsat* (London), September 2, 2009.

[25] *Al-Kifah al-Arabi* (Beirut), December 21, 2009.

[26] Ibid.

[27] Ibidem.

[28] *Dar al-Hayat* (London), January 28, 2009; *al-Ghad* (Amman), January 28, 2009.

[29] "Two Dozen Islamists Go on Trial on Corruption Charges," Deutsche Press-Agentur, December 24, 2009, http://monstersandcritics.com/news/middleeast/news/article_1521391.php/Two-dozen-Islamists-go-on-trial-on-corruption-charages.

[30] See, for example, Tim Lister, "Jordanian Tribal Figures Criticize Queen, Demand Reform," CNN, February 6, 2011, http://articles.cnn.com/2011-02-06/world/jordan.monarchy_1_jordanians-king-abdullah-ii-tribal-leaders?_s=PM:WORLD.

SAUDI ARABIA

QUICK FACTS

Population: 29,207,277

Area: 2,149,690 sq km

Ethnic Groups: Arab 90%, Afro-Asian 10%

Religions: Muslim 100%

Government Type: Monarchy

GDP (official exchange rate): $384 billion

Map and Quick Facts courtesy of the CIA World Factbook (last updated June 2010)

Since 1744, when the first Saudi emirate was established through a pact between tribal chief Muhammad ibn Saud and puritan preacher Muhammad ibn Abd al-Wahhab, the phenomenon which has come to be known as Wahhabism has been the official and dominant religious discourse in Saudi Arabia. In the 1960s, as the Saudis simultaneously tried to combat communism and the secular Arab nationalist tide sweeping across the Middle East, they adopted a policy allowing the immigration of Muslim Brotherhood members suppressed by other governments, such as that of Gamal Abd al-Nasser in Egypt. The Brothers, in turn, integrated into Saudi society and assumed influential roles in the government bureaucracy (especially in the education system).[1]

Although the influx of these Islamists achieved the main Saudi goal of reinforcing an Islamic society, the Brothers' interpretation of Islam posed the first major challenge to the Wahhabi establishment's uncontested legitimacy and discourse within the kingdom. That immigration policy coincided with the foreign policy of King Faisal, which centered on exporting Wahhabi doctrine through organizations like the Muslim World League, schools and literature, as well as supporting groups in Africa and Asia who were likewise opposed to more liberal forms of Islam, such as Sufism, and other "blasphe-

mous" religious practices.²

1979 proved to be another turning point in the evolution of Wahhabism, as the Soviet invasion of Afghanistan caused the Saudis to reactivate the long-dormant policy of jihad,³ while they concurrently funded a broad network of religious schools which eventually produced a new generation of sheikhs, professors, and students. And, just as Saudis were influenced domestically by the ideology of the Muslim Brotherhood, those who went to fight abroad were themselves influenced by other interpretations of Islam.

This is the context out of which the Islamist movements in Saudi Arabia emerged. Indeed, these movements are a reaction to, and a refutation of, the official religious and political discourse of the Saudi monarchy. On the one hand, the government promotes an extremely conservative social sphere, while at the same time conducting a secular foreign policy. That contradiction between government rhetoric and practice eventually boiled over, and the kingdom is still recovering from it.

ISLAMIST ACTIVITY

Islamism in Saudi Arabia is characterized by competing trends, which—while all conservative and fundamentalist—hold significantly different ideas about the relationship between political Islam and society.

One such trend can be termed "rejectionist." Its adherents oppose any role or voice in the nation's political discourse, and for that matter the Saudi state. They instead choose to focus solely on faith and ritual practice, rejecting all schools of Islamic jurisprudence (*fiqh*), and relying solely on the unmediated sayings of Prophet Muhammad (*hadith*). The "rejectionists" confine themselves to their own communities, where they educate their children and live a strict orthodox lifestyle. Like any other Islamist movement, the members of this trend are not monolithic, and some have formed socio-political protest movements.

The most well-known of these is the *al-Jama'a al-Salafiyya al-Muhtasiba* (JSM), which formed in the 1970s and was inspired by the Syrian religious scholar Nasr al-Din al-Albani.⁴ In 1979, JSM posed the first serious challenge in half a century to the Saudi regime when a group of its members, led by Juhayman al-Utaybi, seized the Grand Mosque in Mecca and announced over the loudspeaker that the messiah, or *mehdi*, had come in the form of Muhammad ibn Abdullah al-Qahtani, who was present inside the mosque.⁵ Eventually, after days of attempting to coax the zealots out of the mosque, the Saudis employed the help of French intelligence to end the siege; al-Qahtani was killed during the raid,⁶ and al-Utaybi and sixty-two other JSM members subsequently were publicly beheaded.⁷

After the Grand Mosque incident, the JSM fled to Kuwait, Yemen, and the northern Saudi desert, and returned to their preferred isolation. Despite being unsuccessful, the mosque takeover served as a tipping point for the Saudis. 1979 also saw the Islamic Revolution in Iran, Saudi Arabia's regional nemesis; Shi'a protests in Saudi Arabia's Eastern Province; and the Soviet invasion of Afghanistan. These events cumulatively drove the Saudis to undertake drastic measures to reclaim the banner of Islam and appease rising domestic extremism. They accomplished both objectives through the exportation of a politicized Wahhabism, which was directed as a foreign policy tool against the Soviets and competing strands of Islam alike.[8]

Another trend is the *Sahwa* (awakened) movement. *Sahwa* clerics trace their roots back to the 1960s and the rise to global prominence of the Muslim Brotherhood. As a natural result of their interaction with Brotherhood members who were their contemporaries, the ideology of *Sahwa* clerics has become a synthesis of Salafi-Wahhabi theological teachings and the political activism of the Brotherhood movement.[9] Far from being homogenous, the *Sahwa* are extremely diverse and include religious scholars, scientists, doctors, and academics. They are commonly divided into at least two main camps: those who follow Hassan al-Banna, the founder of the Brotherhood, and those who follow his more extreme ideological successor, Sayyid Qutb. Their ability to comment on a range of issues outside of religion, which the official Saudi religious establishment could not do, has garnered them broad public appeal.[10]

The *Sahwa* became widely recognized in 1990 for their virulent opposition to King Fahd's reliance on a non-Muslim military coalition, led by the United States, to defend the Arabian Peninsula from Saddam Hussein's Iraq. That royal decision, legitimized with a *fatwa* (religious edict) by Grand Mufti Sheikh Abd al-Aziz ibn Abdallah ibn Baz, stoked the ire of Salman al-Awdah and Saffar al-Hawali, two of the most famous firebrand clerics associated with the *Sahwa*. They, in turn, issued sermons denouncing the Saudi monarchy and the religious establishment.[11] In the eyes of these and other prominent *Sahwa* clerics, the legitimacy of the Al Saud leadership and the religious establishment was permanently destroyed.[12] Thereafter, the *Sahwa* called for greater Islamization of Saudi society and demanded a more prominent role in social and foreign affairs.[13] Between 1991 and 1992, they and other religious scholars directed two major critiques at the king. The first was the "Letter of Demands," signed by 400 scholars, calling for stricter rules in the public sphere. The second, signed by 107 scholars and entitled "Memorandum of Advice," was an extraordinarily blunt and wide-ranging call to the king to outlaw the teaching of Western law, create a half-million man army to fight the Jews and aid Muslims, and end foreign aid to atheistic regimes.[14]

In 1994, al-Awdah, al-Hawali, and nearly 1,300 *Sahwa* affiliates were arrested for their vehement opposition to the Saudi regime.[15] Their five years in prison cemented the clerics' standing as courageous men in the eyes of their followers, and granted them more popular legitimacy than the official *ulema*. However, upon being released in 1999, they were confronted with the choice of withdrawing from the public eye or acquiescing to the authority of the state. As a result, the *Sahwa* splintered; some of its members joined other Saudi Islamist movements, including the *jihadist* trend, or decided to abandon Islamism entirely. The tone of those that remained has since changed dramatically; they now rarely criticize the civilian government or religious establishment. In fact, they have come to defend the regime and condemn those who try to undermine stability in the kingdom.[16]

A distinct *jihadist* trend is also manifest in Saudi society, encapsulated most clearly (and notoriously) by the rise of Osama bin Laden's al-Qaeda network. Thought by many analysts to have been formally established in Peshawar, Pakistan by bin Laden and Palestinian *jihadist* theoretician Abdullah Azzam toward the end of the Soviet-Afghan war (1979-1989), al-Qaeda's services bureau (*makhtab al-khidamat*) supported the victorious Afghan *jihad* logistically and materially. Following the Soviet defeat, many *mujahideen* returned home as war heroes in the eyes of their Muslim brethren. The year 1990 proved to be pivotal in the evolution of al-Qaeda, after Saddam Hussein invaded Kuwait. A sense of invincibility pervaded the "Afghan Arabs," and bin Laden petitioned the Saudi monarch, King Fahd, to allow him and his men from the war in Afghanistan to defend the Arabian Peninsula, the birthplace of Islam. Unwilling to entrust the safety of the Peninsula to the *mujahideen*, the King declined bin Laden's offer and soon welcomed a U.S.-led Western coalition of nearly 500,000 troops for the mission. As bin Laden later said, by doing so Saudi Arabia "betrayed the *Ummah* [worldwide Muslim community] and joined the *Kufr* [infidels], assisting and helping them against Muslims."[17]

From 1999 through 2001, conflicts in the Muslim world (Chechnya, Kosovo, and the Palestinian Territories), and a powerful recruiting network in Saudi Arabia allowed bin Laden to attract a wave of Saudis to al-Qaeda's training camps in Afghanistan. Al-Qaeda's operations are known to be well-funded by Saudi individuals and organizations. In 2004, the 9/11 Commission reported that bin Laden used an informal financial network of charities, including the Al Haramain Islamic Foundation and other non-governmental organizations, which allowed Saudi and Gulf financiers to send funds to Arabs fighting in Afghanistan and then later to al-Qaeda.[18]

In early 2002, between 300 and 1,000 Saudi al-Qaeda members returned to Saudi Arabia after the network's base of operations in Afghanistan was compromised following the fall of the Taliban the previous year. Two independent networks were subsequently formed, and the organization's operatives began preparing for operations by stockpiling weapons, renting safe houses, setting up training camps, and recruiting other "Afghan Arabs."[19] Members of the organization were almost entirely male, with the exception of a small number of females who were involved in its logistics or media. Al-Qaeda militants were typically older than members of other Islamist groups, with an average age of 27, and most had only been educated to the high school level or below.[20] The organization consisted principally of Saudis, and maintained a small percentage of foreign nationals. Interestingly, the majority of al-Qaeda members were not from regions typically considered to be the most religiously conservative or impoverished rural areas. Rather, the overwhelming majority of the organization was formed of urbanites from Riyadh, most of whom had the shared experience of previously fighting in Afghanistan against the Soviets and later against the U.S.[21]

On February 14, 2003, bin Laden released a statement outlining his grievances against the Saudi regime and its Western allies. He lambasted the Saudi betrayal of the Ottoman Empire in favor of the British in World War I, leading to what he described as Crusader and Zionist domination of the Muslim world. The Saudis' greatest crime in his eyes, however, was forsaking the Palestinian cause in favor of "Jews and Americans," a transgression for which the monarchy should be overthrown. Bin Laden thus posited the struggle in Saudi Arabia in the context of pan-Islamism and unity of the greater Muslim nation, which served to justify al-Qaeda's "defensive *jihad*" as a religious duty to bring an end to Western oppression of Muslims throughout the world.

Over the next several years, al-Qaeda militants embarked on the longest-sustained violent campaign in the history of the modern Saudi state. They assassinated senior officers in the Ministry of Interior; killed nine people at the U.S. consulate in Jeddah on December 6, 2004;[22] and targeted the kingdom's largest oil processing facility at Abqaiq in February 2006. In total, between May 2003 and December 2004 AQS carried out more than 30 attacks, killing at least 91 foreign nationals and Saudi civilians, 41 security officers, and injuring nearly 730 people.[23]

According to Saudi officials, the campaign progressed through three phases: Momentum, Regrouping, and Fragmentation. From May 2003 to June 2004, the group planned and executed operations with a network of local and foreign individuals well-trained in document forgery, fundraising, publishing, weapons, and security. This initial "momentum" phase culminated with the May 29, 2004 attack on an office building and residential complex in Al-Khobar which killed 22, including one American and three Saudis.[24] (The phase is believed to have ended with the subsequent death of the organization's Saudi head, Abd al-Aziz al-Muqrin, in June 2004). During the subsequent "regrouping" phase, which spanned from June 2004 to April 2005, the organization split into smaller cells under new leadership in an effort to counter the initial counterterrorism successes of the Kingdom. That phase ended when Saudi forces killed al-Muqrin's successor, Saud al-Otaibi. In the final "fragmentation" phase, which is theoretically still in effect, the organization's cells in Saudi Arabia are far less organized, lack central leadership, and do not appear to retain the skills and training they previously demonstrated.[25]

The strength of Saudi counterterrorism efforts eventually caused al-Qaeda's Saudi branch to relocate to Yemen. In January 2009, the Saudi and Yemeni branches of al-Qaeda merged to become al-Qaeda on the Arabian Peninsula (AQAP), and a number of Saudis assumed leadership positions in the new franchise.[26] In its first year of joint operations, AQAP was nearly successful in assassinating Prince Muhammad bin Nayef, the Saudi Deputy Interior Minister in charge of counterterrorism.[27]

Cells of AQAP still operate in the Kingdom, though Saudi security forces have arrested hundreds of members over the past year. In November 2010, Saudi authorities announced that they had arrested more than 149 suspected members over the previous eight months and prevented attacks on government officials, media personalities, and civilian targets. The Interior Ministry reported that AQAP members had organized three networks that were unaware of each other, as well as smaller cells.[28] Many Saudis remain wanted outside of the Kingdom for their suspected links to the group, and on January 10, 2011 the Saudis released an updated "most wanted" list of 47 individuals between the ages of 17 and 39.[29] Interpol circulated a "red" list two days later to begin pursuing the men, and authorities suspected at the time that 16 were in Yemen, 27 in Afghanistan and Pakistan, and four in Iraq.

The final Islamist trend finds its home in the country's Shi'a minority. Regularly branded as unbelievers (*kuffar*) since the time of Muhammad ibn Abd al-Wahhab, Saudi Shi'a are still severely marginalized in the modern state.[30] And while Shi'a Islamists have never been nearly as organized as the *Sahwa*, or even the *jihadists* in Saudi Arabia, instances of Islamist activity have still taken place. One frequently-documented incident of Shi'a opposition took place in early 1980, in the wake of the Islamic Revolution in Iran. Radio Tehran's Arabic channel had been broadcasting propaganda against the Saudi regime to the Shi'a population, which is located primarily in the Kingdom's Eastern Province. That propaganda sparked a riot in Qatif, with citizens attacking the town's central market.[31] Since that time, the Saudi government has been extremely wary of any meddling in its affairs by Iran.

As Arab regimes across the Middle East face massive protests—dubbed the "Arab Spring" by many observers—Shi'a Islamists in Saudi Arabia have organized themselves through social media tools like Facebook and Twitter, issuing petitions for political and social reforms such as the transition to a constitutional monarchy and an end to sectarian discrimination. These protests, however, have not been able to mobilize significant numbers. The Saudi government has proven well prepared to suppress any potential for demonstrations, mobilizing its security forces and religious establishment.[32] Moreover, because Shi'a represent just 10 percent of the population, and the Sunni majority does not share the same grievances against the government, the purely Shi'a protests of the "Arab Spring" have served to alienate Sunnis, and transformed a potential cause for national unity into sectarian division.[33]

ISLAMISM AND SOCIETY

As a result of the conservative Islamic nature of Saudi Arabia, its vast oil wealth, and the Wahhabi mandate of allegiance to the ruler (*wali al-amr*), Islamist movements have failed to garner enough societal support to mount a sustained or serious challenge to the ruling House of Saud. The societal support that Islamists enjoy is difficult to quantify, but there are several telling cases which suggest that such support is substantial.

The *Sahwa* clerics became very influential when they contested the Islamic credentials of the ruling family and religious establishment between 1990 and 1994, and their imprisonment only increased their status and notoriety. A clear manifestation of their appeal was their ability to mobilize Saudis to fight in Iraq against Coalition forces. In an "Open Sermon to the Militant Iraqi People," issued on November 5, 2004, on the eve of the American siege of Fallujah,[34] twenty-six clerics signed on to a statement that legitimized participation in the Iraqi insurgency as part of a "defense jihad" against the "aggressor" Coalition. The number of Saudis who went to Iraq to fight against Western forces is believed to have peaked after the sermon was released.[35]

The bloody campaign waged by al-Qaeda against the Saudi state in 2003 and 2004 likewise was given a stamp of approval from radical clerics within the Kingdom, who utilized the Internet to propagate their messages. These clerics accused the Saudi ruling family of subservience to infidels, and insisted, using traditional Wahhabi discourse and authorities, that their aid to the infidels in Afghanistan against true believers justified them as targets for *jihad*.[36] Yet despite support from these clerics and substantial local manpower during those years, support for al-Qaeda remains weak in Saudi society as a whole. Generally, those of its members who returned from fighting in Afghanistan have been significantly more radicalized than Saudi society as a whole, and broad support for their effort to carry out *jihad* on the Arabian Peninsula is strikingly absent.[37] As a result, their attacks were denounced by the leading *Sahwa* clerics, who by that time became government-backers. Concurrently, the insurgency in Iraq was raging, gaining popular support and diverting attention and resources away from the organization. For many Saudis who would have been ideologically inclined to fight, the Iraqi cause was considered more legitimate as a defensive *jihad* against Western aggression.[38]

Since September 11, 2001, significant criticism has been directed toward Saudi Arabia and other Gulf countries, with allegations that both public and private funds from those countries contribute to financing terrorism abroad. In 2007, Former Under Secretary of the Treasury for Terrorism and Financial Intelligence Stuart Levey said that, "If I could somehow snap my fingers and cut off funding from one country, it would be Saudi Arabia."[39] The exact amount of financial support for terrorism from Saudi sources is extremely difficult to determine, though Islamic charities are commonly singled out as the primary source of illicit funds. Charitable contributions being one of the five pillars of Islam, they are often given anonymously and from all sectors of society. One former State Department official estimated in 2003 that Saudis donate between $3 billion and $4 billion annually, nearly $100 million of which is sent abroad.[40]

Saudis have been accused of funding numerous terrorist groups and activities during the past 30 years. The 9/11 Commission noted the "Golden Chain," a network of Saudi and other Gulf financiers used by Osama bin Laden to collect and channel funds to support the anti-Soviet *jihad* during the 1980s in Afghanistan. The financiers used charities and other NGOs as conduits for their donations to the *jihad* and this network later became influential in the establishment of al-Qaeda's base in Afghanistan in the late 1990s.[41]

In 2004, two civil lawsuits seeking $2 billion in damages were filed in the U.S. District Court of New York against Jordan's Arab Bank by families of victims killed or injured in terror attacks in Israel. The lawsuits claim that the Saudi Committee for the Support of the Al Quds Intifada, a government-sanctioned charity, funneled money through charities and individuals in the West Bank and Gaza Strip connected with Hamas, the Palestinian Islamic Jihad, and other terrorist groups. According to the lawsuits, the Committee used Arab Bank branches in the Palestinian Territories to provide "insurance benefits" to the families of suicide bombers and others who were casualties of conflict with Israel.[42] While the Arab Bank denied that it had prior knowledge of payments to the families of suicide bombers through its branches, executive manager of the Saudi Committee, Mubarak Al-Biker, said that, "We support the families of Palestinian martyrs, without differentiating between whether the Palestinian was a bomber or was killed by Israeli troops."[43]

On May 22, 2011, the Pakistani newspaper *Dawn* reported on a Wikileaks cable from 2008 which was sent by the former Principal Officer at the U.S. Consulate in Lahore to the State Department. The cable alleged that nearly $100 million in annual financial support to Deobandi and Ahl-i-Hadith clerics in southern Punjab was originating in the UAE and Saudi Arabia. Families with multiple children and severe financial difficulties would be targeted for recruitment, initially under the pretense of charity. Later a *maulana* from one of the two sects would offer to educate the children in his *madrassa* and "find them employment in the service of Islam." The children would undergo indoctrination suited to their ages, and teachers would assess their proclivity "to engage in violence and acceptance of *jihadi* culture." The parents of those who are chosen for martyrdom operations receive cash payments averaging $6,500 per child.[44]

These anecdotes of Saudi support for *jihad* and terrorist organizations are not necessarily indicative of broad approval from society. A late 2009 poll of Saudi attitudes found 75 percent of respondents to have an unfavorable view of al-Qaeda and its message, with just 20 percent "somewhat favorable" toward the organization. However, 36 percent of those polled said that they consider it an Islamic duty to provide "financial support for armed *mujahedin* fighting in various places around the world."[45] If these polling results are representative of Saudi society at large, they lend credence to the notion that Saudis indeed support *jihad*, but with strong consideration for the justifications of jihad in each locality and the methods by which the *mujahedin* attempt to reach their objectives.

ISLAMISM AND THE STATE

The ruling al-Saud family has a long history of suppressing Islamist challenges to maintain their hold on power. The al-Saud faced their first major Islamist uprising from a group known as the *Ikhwan* from 1914 through 1930. Several decades prior to that conflict, the *Ikhwan* had been considered idolatrous nomads whom the Wahhabi *ulema* converted to help enforce Saudi expansion. These nomads were gathered in communities called *hujara*, which were literally places of migration from the "abode of idolatry" to the "abode of Islam." This was an effective tool for the Saudis to depopulate areas of idolatry and unbelief in Arabia, as the tribesmen and clan leaders were trained in Wahhabi doctrine.[46] Gradually, they became zealous adherents to the Salafi notion of *al-wala' wa 'l-bara'* (association with Muslims and dissociation from infidels), a central principle of modern *jihadi* ideology. That put them in direct conflict with Ibn Saud, who accepted military subsidies from the British in order to conquer Arabia.[47]

Ibn Saud accepted some of the grievances of the *Ikhwan*, and subsequently imposed stricter regulations on Shi'a; Iraqi Shi'a were banned from entering Najd, and the Shi'a of al-Hasa were forcibly indoctrinated.[48] As the *Ikhwan* sought greater control over domestic affairs, however, Ibn Saud had to balance their demands with his duty as the Custodian of the Two Holy Mosques, a post that demanded he ensure religious pluralism and allow the Shi'a some leniency to practice freely and perform pilgrimage.[49] This strategy of internally consolidating their rule over a loyal population while accommodating deviations from the "true path" became a trademark of the Saudi regime. The *Ikhwan*, however, simply could not be reined in, and continued to conduct raids against tribes and towns in northern Arabia where Ibn Saud had no authority. The *Ikhwan* expected to participate as local governors and chiefs in newly conquered areas, rather than remaining Ibn Saud's agents for expansion. Ibn Saud would never allow them such a reward.[50] Finally, in December 1928, the *Ikhwan* raided a caravan of merchants in the Wahhabi stronghold of Burayda, which Ibn Saud considered an attack on his people. In response, between March 1929 and January 1930, Ibn Saud's troops battled the *Ikhwan*, eventually forcing them to surrender. Rather than punishing them harshly, however, he mixed their punishment with religious rehabilitation so as to mollify the zealous nature of the *Ikhwan*. That dual policy also became a staple of the Saudis in their subsequent struggle against *jihadis*.[51]

Throughout the 20th century, the official Wahhabi religious establishment used the tools of *hijra*, *takfir*, and *jihad* to consolidate the Saudi realm. *Hijra* (migration) requires an individual to physically migrate to the land of the pious state (Saudi Arabia) and abandon other lands of blasphemy and misguidance. *Takfir* (excommunication) was used to divide the pious Muslims from the non-believers, and was often directed against other secular Arab leaders like Gamal Abdel Nasser, Muammar Gadhafi, and Saddam Hussein. *Jihad* (struggle in the way of God) became defined as an armed struggle against Muslim oppression in Afghanistan.[52] The Saudis lent support to Islamists abroad in order to further their foreign policy objectives, while at home radicals were quelled.

Under King Faysal, the Saudis developed a policy of supporting Islamic institutions abroad in an effort to combat the spread of secularism and communism. In 1962, the World Muslim League (WML) was created to facilitate the spread of Wahhabi ideology, and the WML supported sects and organizations throughout the world that would challenge Sufi Islam and eliminate popular religious practices which are forbidden in the Wahhabi interpretation. In South Asia, the WML supported Deobandis, and groups like *Ahl-i Hadith* and *Jamaati Islami*. Missionaries who distributed religious literature were sent to West Africa, along with funding for schools in countries like Nigeria, Mali, Ghana, Ivory Coast, and Guinea.[53]

The WML was followed by a variety of other Saudi institutions, including the World Assembly of Muslim Youth (WAMY), the Al Haramain Foundation, and the International Islamic Relief Organization (IIRO), among others. From 1973-2002, Saudi government figures show that more than $80 billion was spent to build Islamic institutions and activities solely in the non-Muslim world. That largesse allowed for the construction of over 1,500 mosques, 150 Islamic centers, 202 Muslim colleges, and 2,000 Islamic schools.[54] With Saudi funding, there are now an estimated 10,000 Deobandi-run *madrassas* in India, Pakistan, and Bangladesh. The Balkan countries are also a major target for the Wahhabi mission, with large Muslim communities in Bosnia, Albania, and Kosovo. The Saudis have spent about $600 million alone in Bosnia.[55]

This unprecedented outreach campaign has brought nearly 80 percent of all Islamic institutions in the U.S. and Canada under its sponsorship, and Saudi-funded mosques and Islamic centers can be found in nearly every city in Western Europe. After 9/11, Saudi-sponsored institutions in the U.S. came under heavy scrutiny, and of nearly 50 that have been raided, shut down, or had their assets frozen because of suspected links to terrorism, most have been controlled or funded by Saudis. Among those institutions were the World Muslim League, the World Assembly of Muslim Youth, the Al Haramain Foundation, the SAAR Foundation, the International Institute of Islamic Thought, and the School of Islamic and Social Sciences.[56]

The Saudis have been largely successful at defeating the Islamist challenges inside their kingdom using a range of tools, from accommodation to repression to co-optation to lethal force. Against the JSM in 1979, they simply used force to retake the Grand Mosque from Juhayman al-Utaybi and his followers. To quiet the Sahwa, the Saudis repressed them and imprisoned their leaders until they agreed to fall in line with the government agenda. The same individuals who issued petitions to the government to enforce a more Islamic society in the 1990s are those who now align themselves closely with the regime and oblige the Saudi people to do the same.

To combat the *jihadist* threat posed by al-Qaeda, the Saudi approach has been more extensive, focusing on "men, money, and mindset." Between 2003 and 2008, Saudi security forces broke up al-Qaeda's cells in the Kingdom, arresting and killing thousands of militants and people suspected of planning attacks. Since then, officials from the Ministry of Islamic Affairs have continued to monitor tens of thousands of the country's nearly 70,000 mosques, in addition to schools and websites; reprimand those who express extreme or "deviant" ideologies; and to reeducate them. Saudi and U.S. officials have targeted individuals and organizations in Saudi Arabia and abroad that have been linked to financing terrorism, prosecuting, sanctioning or dissolving them.[57]

Lastly, the Saudi government is careful to leave the door open for extremists to be de-radicalized, and officially says that they hold "deviant" ideologies, rather than branding them as terrorists. There are two rehabilitation programs, one governmental, called the Counseling Program,[58] and one independent but government-supported, called *Al-Sakina* (Tranquility).[59] Both rely on clerics, some of them also former radicals, who engage the deviants in theological discussions in order to prove their faulty understanding of the religion. Prisoners who have not committed terrorist acts on Saudi soil, and can prove that they have renounced their extreme views, are released and assisted with jobs, government stipends for marriage and education, cars, and housing. Whereas the Saudis used to claim a 100 percent success rate for their government program, some estimates of the recidivism rate, that by which rehabilitated extremists return to militancy, place it at near 20 percent of all participants. Those numbers do not tell the entire story, however, as the only individuals released from the program are those who have not committed terrorist acts inside Saudi Arabia.

Saudi television regularly broadcasts interviews with repentant former militants who describe the errors in their previous ways. In 2003, following the initial al-Qaeda attacks in Riyadh, several high profile clerics espousing *takfir* (excommunication), appeared in public and renounced their views.[60] In recent months, former members of AQAP have similarly chosen—or were possibly forced to—relinquish their support for militancy. One of the men was Jabir al-Fifi, who reportedly tipped off Saudi authorities about the cargo bomb plot originating from Yemen in October 2010.[61] Another notable figure is Muhammad al-Awfi, who was a former field commander of AQAP and also an inmate at Guantanamo Bay. Al-Awfi surrendered to Yemeni authorities in February 2009, and appeared on television in November 2010 to discuss his experience and describe how the organization exploits Saudi youth to advance its own agenda.

With the outbreak of the "Arab Spring," the Saudis have moved swiftly to stave off potentially escalating demands for national reforms. Notably, the government recently approved an estimated $130 billion subsidy package for Saudi citizens, which includes 60,000 Ministry of Interior jobs, 500,000 new houses, and a minimum wage for the public-sector of 3,000 Saudi Rials ($800) per month. By contrast, in the private-sector, which provides nearly 8 million jobs and is dominated by foreign employees, the average wage is only 1,000 Saudi Rials per month.[62] Municipal elections have also been promised in September 2011, with voter registration currently underway, though women have predictably been forbidden from participating.[63]

ENDNOTES

[1] "Saudi Arabia Backgrounder: Who Are The Islamists?" International Crisis Group, September 21, 2004, 2, http://www.pbs.org/wgbh/pages/frontline/shows/saud/themes/backgrounder.pdf.

[2] David Commins, *The Wahhabi Mission and Saudi Arabia* (London: I.B. Tauris & Co Ltd., 2009), 152-3.

[3] David Commins, "The Jihadi Factor in Wahhabi Islam," UCLA Center for Near Eastern Studies, November 13, 2007, 8, http://www.international.ucla.edu/cms/files/davidcomminsrvsd.pdf.

[4] "Saudi Arabia Backgrounder: Who Are The Islamists?"

[5] See Commins, *The Wahhabi Mission and Saudi Arabia*.

[6] Rachel Bronson, *Thicker Than Oil America's Uneasy Partnership with Saudi Arabia* (New York: Oxford University Press, 2006), 147-8.

[7] "Mosque Has Violent Past," *The New York Times*, August 2, 1987, http://www.nytimes.com/1987/08/02/world/mosque-has-violent-past.html?src=pm

[8] Madawi al-Rasheed, *Contesting the Saudi State* (Cambridge: Cambridge University Press, 2007).

[9] Ondrej Beranek, "Divided We Survive: A Landscape of Fragmentation in Saudi Arabia," Brandeis University Crown Center for *Middle East Studies Middle East Brief* no. 28, January 2009, 3, http://www.brandeis.edu/crown/publications/meb/MEB33.pdf.

[10] Al-Rasheed, *Contesting the Saudi State.*

[11] Beranek, "The Sword and the Book."

[12] M. Ehsan Ahrari, "Saudi Arabia: A Simmering Cauldron of Instability?" *Brown Journal of World Affairs*, Summer/Fall 1999, 220, http://www.watsoninstitute.org/bjwa/archive/6.2/Essay/Ahrari.pdf.

[13] Rachel Bronson, "Rethinking Religion: the Legacy of the U.S.-Saudi Relationship," *The Washington Quarterly*, Autumn 2005, 127, http://www.twq.com/05autumn/docs/05autumn_bronson.pdf.

[14] Bronson, *Thicker Than Oil*, 212-3.

[15] Shmuel Bachar, Shmuel Bar, Rachel Machtiger and Yair Minzili, *Establishment Ulama and Radicalism in Egypt, Saudi Arabia, and Jordan* (Washington, DC: Hudson Institute, December 2006), 18, http://www.currenttrends.org/docLib/20061226_UlamaandRadicalismfinal.pdf

[16] When al-Qaeda on the Arabian Peninsula attacked three foreign housing complexes in Riyadh in May 2003, killing 34 and injuring 200, al-Awdah and al-Hawali issued a statement with nearly 50 other clerics, condemning the attacks and declaring the perpetrators ignorant, misguided young men. See "Saudi Bombing Deaths Rise," BBC (London), May 13, 2003, http://news.bbc.co.uk/2/hi/middle_east/3022473.stm; Then, in December 2004, al-Awdah, Aidh al-Qarni, and 33 other sheikhs signed a statement denouncing Lon-

don-based Saudi dissident Saad al-Faqih's attempts to organize demonstrations against the regime. See Toby Craig Jones, "The Clerics, the Sahwa and the Saudi State," Center for Contemporary Conflict Strategic Insights, March 2005, 4, http://www.nps.edu/Academics/centers/ccc/publications/OnlineJournal/2005/Mar/jonesMar05.pdf. Subsequently, in January 2005, in response to a failed attack on the Ministry of Interior in Riyadh the previous month, 41 clerics issued a statement on al-Awdah's website, *Islam Today*, warning against actions and discourse targeting the Saudi regime.

[17] For a detailed discussion, see the *World Almanac of Islamism's* chapter on "Al-Qaeda."

[18] National Commission on Terrorist Attacks Upon the United States, "The 9/11 Commission Report," July 22, 2004.

[19] Thomas Hegghammer, "Islamist Violence and Regime Stability in Saudi Arabia," *International Affairs* 84, no. 4 (2008), http://hegghammer.com/_files/Hegghammer_-Islamist_violence_and_regime_stability_in_Saudi_Arabia.pdf.

[20] Thomas Hegghammer, "Terrorist Recruitment and Radicalization in Saudi Arabia," *Middle East Policy*, Winter 2006, 42, http://chenry.webhost.utexas.edu/usme/2007/Saudi-Terrorist_Recruitmen_87543a.pdf.

[21] Ibid.

[22] Bruce Riedel and Bilal Y. Saab, "Al Qaeda's Third Front: Saudi Arabia," *The Washington Quarterly*, Spring 2008, http://www.twq.com/08spring/docs/08spring_riedel.pdf.

[23] Angel Rabasa et al., *Deradicalizing Islamist Extremists* (Santa Monica: RAND Corporation, 2008), http://www.rand.org/pubs/monographs/2010/RAND_MG1053.pdf.

[24] Anthony H. Cordesman, *Saudi Arabia: National Security in a Troubled Region* (Washington, DC: Center for Strategic and International Studies, 2009).

[25] Christopher M. Blanchard, "Saudi Arabia: Background and U.S. Relations," Congressional Research Service, June 14, 2010, http://www.fas.org/sgp/crs/mideast/RL33533.pdf.

[26] "Al-Qaeda in the Arabian Peninsula," *Al Jazeera* (Doha), December 29, 2009, http://english.aljazeera.net/news/middleeast/2009/12/2009122935812371810.html

[27] Scott Stewart, "AQAP: Paradigm Shifts and Lessons Learned," *Stratfor*, September 2, 2009, http://www.stratfor.com/weekly/20090902_aqap_paradigm_shifts_and_lessons_learned.

[28] "Saudi Arabia Arrests 149 Al Qaida Suspects," *Huffington Post*, November 26, 2010, http://www.huffingtonpost.com/2010/11/27/saudi-arabia-arrests-149-_n_788736.html

[29] http://ksa.daralhayat.com/ksaarticle/221869.

[30] Ahmad Moussalli, "Wahhabism, Salafism, and Islamism: Who is

the Enemy?" American University of Beirut, January 2009, 6, http://conflictsforum.org/briefings/Wahhabism-Salafism-and-Islamism.pdf.

[31] Bronson, *Thicker Than Oil*, 147.

[32] Madawi Al-Rasheed, "Preachers of Hate as Loyal Subjects," *New York Times*, March 14, 2011, http://www.nytimes.com/roomfordebate/2011/03/14/how-stable-is-saudi-arabia/preachers-of-hate-as-loyal-subjects.

[33] Bernard Haykel, "What Makes the Kingdom Different," *New York Times*, March 14, 2011, http://www.nytimes.com/roomfordebate/2011/03/14/how-stable-is-saudi-arabia/what-makes-the-kingdom-different.

[34] "The House of Saud: The Fatwa of the 26 Clerics: Open Sermon to the Militant Iraqi People," *PBS Frontline*, February 8, 2005, http://www.pbs.org/wgbh/pages/frontline/shows/saud/etc/fatwa.html.

[35] Thomas Hegghammer, "Saudis in Iraq: Patterns of Radicalization and Recruitment," *Revues.org*, June 12, 2008, http://conflits.revues.org/index10042.html.

[36] Commins, "The Jihadi Factor in Wahhabi Islam," 13.

[37] Hegghammer, "Terrorist Recruitment and Radicalization in Saudi Arabia."

[38] Hegghammer, "Islamist Violence and Regime Stability in Saudi Arabia."

[39] Brian Ross, "U.S.: Saudis Still Filling Al Qaeda's Coffers," *ABC News*, September 11,2007.

[40] Jonathan M. Winer, Testimony before the Senate Committee on Governmental Affairs, July 31, 2003.

[41] Christopher Blanchard and Alfred Prados, "Saudi Arabia: Terrorist Financing Issues," *Congressional Research Service*, September 14, 2007, 6, http://www.fas.org/sgp/crs/terror/RL32499.pdf

[42] Ibid., 8.

[43] Ra'id Qusti, "Saudi Telethon Funds Go Direct to Palestinian Victims," Arab News (Jedda), May 27, 2002. http://archive.arabnews.com/?page=1&section=0&article=15591&d=27&m=5&y=2002

[44] Qurat ul ain Siddiqui, "Saudi Arabia, UAE Financing Extremism in South Punjab," *Dawn*, May 22, 2011, http://www.dawn.com/2011/05/22/saudi-arabia-uae-financing-extremism-in-south-punjab.html

[45] David Pollock, "Polling Saudis and Egyptians: Iran, Jihad, and the Economy," *The Washington Institute for Near East Policy*, December 17, 2009, http://www.washingtoninstitute.org/templateC05.php?CID=3156

[46] Commins, *The Wahhabi Mission and Saudi Arabia*.

[47] Al-Rasheed, *Contesting the Saudi State*.

[48] Commins, *The Wahhabi Mission and Saudi Arabia*, 88.

[49] Ibid., 77.

[50] Madawi Al-Rasheed, *A History of Saudi Arabia*, (Cambridge: Cambridge University Press, 2002), 67.

[51] Commins, *The Wahhabi Mission and Saudi Arabia*.

[52] Al-Rasheed, *Contesting the Saudi State*.

[53] Commins, *The Wahhabi Mission and Saudi Arabia*, 152-3.

[54] Alexander Alexiev, *The Wages of Extremism: Radical Islam's Threat to the West and the Muslim World* (Washington, DC: Hudson Institute, March 2011), 44, http://www.hudson.org/files/publications/AAlexievWagesofExtremism032011.pdf

[55] Alexiev, "The End of an Alliance," *National Review*, October 28, 2002, http://old.nationalreview.com/flashback/flashback-alexiev112602.asp.

[56] Ibid.

[57] U.S. Government Accountability Office, "Combating Terrorism: U.S. Agencies Report Progress Countering Terrorism and Its Financing in Saudi Arabia, but Continued Focus on Counter Terrorism Financing Efforts Needed," September 2009, 13 http://www.gao.gov/new.items/d09883.pdf.

[58] Rabasa et al., *Deradicalizing Islamist Extremists*.

[59] Online at http://www.assakina.com/.

[60] Jones, "The Clerics, the Sahwa and the Saudi State," 4.

[61] Dan Murphy, "Who saved the day in Yemen bomb plot? Once again, a Muslim," *Christian Science Monitor*, November 2, 2010, http://www.csmonitor.com/World/Middle-East/2010/1102/Who-saved-the-day-in-Yemen-bomb-plot-Once-again-a-Muslim.

[62] Steffen Hertog, "The Costs of Counter-Revolution in the GCC," *Foreign Policy*, May 31, 2011, http://mideast.foreignpolicy.com/posts/2011/05/31/the_costs_of_counter_revolution_in_the_gcc.

[63]No Votes for Women in Saudi Municipal Elections," Reuters, March 28, 2011, http://www.reuters.com/article/2011/03/28/us-saudi-elections-idUSTRE72R65E20110328.

BAHRAIN

QUICK FACTS

Population: 738,004

Area: 741 sq km

Ethnic Groups: Bahraini 62.4%, non-Bahraini 37.6%

Religions: Muslim (Sunni and Shi'a) 81.2%, Christian 9%, other 9.8%

Government Type: Constitutional Monarchy

GDP (official exchange rate): $19.59 billion

Map and Quick Facts courtesy of the CIA World Factbook (Last Updated June 2010)

Bahrain is something of an anomaly among the Arab states of the Persian Gulf. While its ruling family and as much as 30 percent of its population are Sunni Muslims, the overwhelming majority of its citizens are Shi'ites. One of the first major oil exporters in the region, it was also the first of the Gulf "oil sheikhdoms" to face significant depletion of its petroleum reserves and the need to make the transition to a non-resource-based economy. Further, although it is far from qualifying as a free country, Bahrain also stands apart from other Gulf states in its relatively high degree of social and cultural openness: the sale and consumption of alcohol are permitted; movie theaters, discos and labor unions are allowed; freedom of worship is present; the press is somewhat free; the NGO sector is active (albeit regulated and constrained); and there is even a significant—albeit limited—degree of democracy.

While political parties are officially banned in Bahrain, an assortment of "political societies," most of them sectarian and Islamist, field slates of candidates for legislative elections, and in general function as political parties in all but name. The royal family has attempted to preserve Bahrain's stability (and their rule) by playing off Shi'ites against Sunnis and Islamists against secularists. Until recently, this strategy worked rather well. Although a few Bahrainis have traveled overseas to join in jihad, and others have been involved in pro-

viding financial or logistical support for al-Qaeda, Islamism in Bahrain has maintained an almost exclusively domestic focus, with recent Islamist efforts directed at confronting "morality" issues through political action rather than violence. While the presence of the U.S. Fifth Fleet in Bahrain would appear to make the country an attractive target for anti-American terrorism, neither Bahrain's government nor its Islamists appear ready to condone or facilitate such attacks.

ISLAMIST ACTIVITY

Bahrain's majority Shi'ite population is significantly poorer than its Sunni minority counterpart, and complains of discrimination in employment (particularly with regard to senior-level government and security-service jobs), housing, immigration policy, and government services. Accordingly, the Shi'ite opposition—which is almost entirely Islamist in character—has an agenda largely based around the attempt to redress these inequalities, in addition to more traditional Islamist goals such as imposing *sharia* law. The political and economic goals of the Shi'ite opposition include:

- Genuine democracy, in which the Shi'ite community, as the majority population, would have a much greater say in legislating and setting policy. This would necessitate the rewriting of Bahrain's constitution, as well as revising an electoral district system that favors Sunni candidates.[1]
- The dismantling, or at least a substantial weakening, of Bahrain's internal-security apparatus, and the release of political prisoners.
- Economic justice, including equality of opportunity in employment and equal provision of government services.
- Equal access to positions of authority in the government bureaucracy and the military/security services.
- An end to Bahrain's policy of facilitating Sunni immigration, which is perceived as a governmental effort to reduce or eliminate the Shi'ite demographic advantage. (Participants in the February 2011 demonstrations noted that many of the security personnel confronting them were immigrants from other Arab countries, and even Urdu-speaking Pakistanis, who had been granted Bahraini citizenship as an inducement to serve in the Bahraini security services.[2])
- Traditional Islamist moral and social issues, such as the elimination of alcohol, prostitution, and other "evils" from the kingdom, the application of *Sharia* law, etc.

It is worth noting that most Bahraini Shi'ites are adherents of the Akhbari school of Twelver Shi'ism, as opposed to Iranian Shi'ites (and most Iraqi Shi'ites), who are members of the more common Usuli Twelver faction.

Among other differences, Akhbaris believe that while clerics can and should advise political leaders, they should not seek or be given direct political power. As Akhbaris, Bahraini Shi'ites have traditionally claimed that they are loyal to the state and to its ruling family, seeking change within the system rather than wanting to overthrow it.[3] The Bahraini Shi'ite community does not have its own *marja* ("source of emulation") or any other religious figure of sufficient stature to constitute a Khomeini-style threat to the Bahraini establishment.

Despite the Shi'ite community's assertions of loyalty to Bahrain and its governing family (if not to its Constitution), many Bahraini Sunnis accuse the Shi'ites of being suspiciously close, culturally and politically, to Iran; the fact that Bahraini Shi'ite clerics are often trained in Iran adds some credibility to this accusation. Shi'ites respond by pointing out that many Bahraini Sunnis have just as much cultural connection to Iran, and that quite a few of these Sunnis in fact speak Farsi, rather than Arabic, at home.

The Bahraini government and others in the Sunni elite, as well as outside commentators concerned about Iranian influence in the region, have repeatedly claimed that Shi'ite unrest in Bahrain is the product of Iranian scheming, aided by allies and proxies such as Syria and Hezbollah. At first glance, such accusations are plausible: Iran is certainly not averse to meddling in other countries' affairs, and Iranian officials occasionally reassert their country's historical claim on Bahrain as Iranian territory.[4] However, no concrete, convincing evidence has ever been produced to back these claims, and neutral observers have pointed out that Shi'ite unrest can be quite adequately explained by the genuine grievances of Bahraini Shi'ites.[5] The recent unrest has not strengthened the case for an Iranian conspiracy to destabilize Bahrain; nothing in the protestors' goals or tactics is inconsistent with what would be expected from an entirely domestic movement.

Ultimately, as long as Bahrain's Shi'ites are kept relatively powerless, there is no way to validate their claims of loyalty to the country and its al-Khalifa rulers; and no matter how enthusiastically Shi'ite demonstrators wave Bahraini flags, many Bahraini Sunnis will continue to believe that the country's Shi'ites are, at best, a potential pro-Iranian fifth column. Even if Bahrain's Shi'ites are sincere in their expressions of patriotism, there is no question that, should they achieve significant political power, Iran will view Bahrain as "low-hanging fruit" and attempt to gain their allegiance.[6]

The most prominent Bahraini Shi'ite political "society" is the al-Wefaq National Islamic Society (*Jam'iyat al-Wifāq al-Watani al-Islāmiyah*, also known as the Islamic National Accord Association), led by Qom-educated cleric Sheikh Ali Salman, with some 1,500 active members.[7] (Salman himself is considered a "mid-level" cleric. Bahrain's most prominent Shi'a cleric, Ayatollah Isa Qassim, himself a disciple of Iraqi Grand Ayatollah Ali al-Sistani, does not openly take political positions but is considered an *al-Wefaq* supporter; in 2005 he publicly endorsed the group's decision to register as a "political society" and enter the Council of Representatives.[8]) After boycotting the 2002 elections to protest the new constitution's failure to provide a fully democratic constitutional monarchy, *al-Wefaq* decided to compete in the 2006 elections, and scored a resounding success: out of 17 candidates fielded by the group, 16 won their districts outright in the first round of voting (and the 17th candidate won his seat in a second-round run-off), making *al-Wefaq* by far the largest bloc in the Council of Representatives.[9] The group repeated this success in the 2010 elections, winning all 18 seats it contested; and were the Bahraini electoral system not gerrymandered to favor Sunni candidates, there is little question that, given the country's demographics, *al-Wefaq* would have easily won a commanding majority of the Council's 40 seats.[10]

Until the recent round of protests and the government's heavy-handed response to them, *al-Wefaq* had consistently positioned itself as a loyal opposition, working to achieve equality for Bahraini Shi'ites while maintaining allegiance to Bahrain and its monarchy, if not to the current Constitution and Cabinet. This stance has now been considerably shaken. All 18 *al-Wefaq* members of the Council of Representatives have resigned in protest, and the group's leaders have refused to enter a dialogue with the government until Prime Minister Khalifa al-Khalifa, perceived to be the driving force behind the marginalization of Bahraini Shi'ites, is replaced.[11] As the crisis has persisted, positions have hardened: there have even been calls among the demonstrators for the outright abolition of the Al Khalifa monarchy, and it will be difficult for *Al Wefaq's* leadership to maintain a conciliatory position if the group's Shi'ite supporters are no longer willing to work within the system.[12]

Al-Wefaq's main competition for the loyalty of Bahraini Shi'ites is the *Haq* Movement for Liberty and Democracy, founded in 2005 by a group consisting mostly of *al-Wefaq's* more radical leaders, who objected to *al-Wefaq's* decision to participate in the upcoming 2006 elections and thus grant an appearance of legitimacy to Bahrain's quasi-democratic constitution. *Haq's* agenda appears to be more specifically targeted at achieving full democracy, and the group is less identified with "morality" issues and Shi'ite sectarianism than its parent movement; in fact, one of *Haq's* leaders, Sheikh Isa Abdullah Al Jowder, is a Sunni cleric, and another founder (who recently left the movement[13]), Ali Qasim Rabea, is a secular leftist-nationalist.[14] Nonetheless, *Haq* is generally thought of as both Shi'a and Islamist, even though its leader, Hasan Mushaima, is a layman and the group is not endorsed by any senior Bahraini Shi'ite cleric.[15]

Haq has unquestionably benefited from the breakdown in the relationship between the Bahraini government and Bahraini Shi'ites, since—unlike *al-Wefaq*—*Haq* never invested its credibility in a political process that it perceived (and loudly denounced) as inherently unfair and dishonest. (In fact, *Haq* has consistently refused even to register as an official "political society,"[16] even though its rejectionist record is not absolute: Mushaima met with King Hamad in London in March, 2008.[17]) While *al-Wefaq* spent four years in the Council of Representatives ineffectually working for the Shi'ite community's interests, *Haq* (or, at least, groups of young Shi'ites apparently inspired by low-level *Haq* activists) was out on the streets throwing rocks at the police,[18] and *Haq* itself was submitting petitions to the United Nations and the United States calling for condemnation of the Bahraini government.[19] While the rocks and petitions accomplished no more at the time than did *al-Wefaq's* political maneuvering, they established *Haq* as a genuine "fighting opposition"—one respected by Shi'ites and feared (and persecuted) by the Bahraini government.

As part of the Bahraini government's efforts to confront *Haq*, officials have accused the organization's leaders of being in the pay of Iran, either directly or through Hezbollah intermediaries. While it is very difficult to prove that such a relationship does not exist, and many in the Sunni community take it as an article of faith that Bahraini Shi'ites are more loyal to Iran than to Bahrain, disinterested observers, including the U.S. Embassy in Bahrain, have pointed out that no convincing evidence has ever been produced to back these accusations.[20]

Haq Secretary General Hasan Mushaima returned to Bahrain from Great Britain in late February 2011 to a "rapturous" welcome; he had been charged and tried *in absentia* for conspiring against the government, but the charges against him were dropped as part of a package of government concessions aimed at establishing a dialogue with the Bahraini opposition.[21] Mushaima, one of the founders of *al-Wefaq*, who left that group to co-found *Haq*, is now attempting, with other opposition leaders, to formulate a unified platform of demands and expectations; *Haq's* participation in a united opposition will likely lend it credibility that *al-Wefaq* may have lost as Bahrain's Shi'ites have become more radicalized.[22]

A third Shi'ite opposition movement, *Wafa'* ("Loyalty"), was founded in early 2009 by Abdulwahab Hussain, a cleric who had been a leading Shi'a activist in the 1990s and a co-founder of *al-Wefaq*. Unlike *Haq*, *Wafa'* is "officially"

Shi'ite, and enjoys the open backing of senior cleric (and rival of Ayatollah Isa Qassim) Sheikh Abduljalil al-Maqdad. And unlike *al-Wefaq*, *Wafa'* has consistently and firmly opposed participation in Bahrain's quasi-democratic constitutional government.

The period when *Haq* leader Hasan Mushaima was in self-imposed exile presented something of an opportunity for *Wafa'* to attract support from Shi'a rejectionists However, despite the fact that *Wafa'* has the clerical backing *Haq* lacks and has credible, experienced leadership, it does not appear so far to have gained much traction among Bahraini Shi'ites. Now that Hasan Mushaima has returned to Bahrain and *al-Wefaq* has quit the Council of Representatives, *Wafa'* is likely to have a great deal of difficulty finding a meaningful niche for itself in Bahraini Shi'ite politics.[23]

Yet another rejectionist Shi'ite Islamist "political society" is *Amal* (the "Islamic Action Society," Jam'iyyat *al-Amal al-Islami*, also referred to by Bahrainis as "the Shirazi faction"). This group is "the non-violent heir to the defunct Islamic Front for the Liberation of Bahrain, which launched a failed uprising in 1981 inspired by Iran's Islamic revolution."[24] *Amal* refused to register before the 2002 election, did not win any seats in the 2006 election,[25] and decided not to participate in the 2010 election. The society's Secretary General, Sheikh Mohammed al-Mahfoodh, justified this decision by citing the usual objections to Bahrain's political system, claiming that "[W]e don't want to just be employees... the members of parliament are just employees who get a big salary."[26] It is not entirely clear, however, if Sheikh al-Mahfoodh's feelings would have been the same had there been a significant likelihood of his actually becoming one of these "employees."

The challenge for the "official" organized Shi'ite opposition, as well as for leaders of the young, self-organizing "Twitter generation" protestors and the leftist secular organizations that have joined the protests, is to agree on a set of demands that are ambitious enough to maintain the enthusiasm of the protestors (and, of course, to offer a realistic hope of solving the real problems facing Bahraini Shi'ites) but can also be palatable to Bahrain's ruling family and its Sunni allies.[27]

Unlike the majority Shi'ites, Bahrain's Sunni community is not uniformly Islamist in its beliefs; this means that Sunni "political societies" must compete with secular groups and independent candidates for voter support. Further, Sunni Islamist groups are constrained in their ambitions by Bahrain's demographic and economic situation: because Sunnis are a relatively wealthy, privileged minority, Sunni Islamists do not join their Shi'a colleagues in calling for genuine democratic reform (which would disempower them and their supporters), and—while they may aspire to "increase the standard of living for Bahrainis; strengthen political, social and economic stability; and enhance financial and administrative oversight of the government and industry"[28] —they quite understandably do not agitate for fully equal opportunity for Bahrain's Shi'ites. Because the American military presence contributes to Bahrain's economy and provides a bulwark against Iranian designs on their country, the mainstream Sunni Islamist groups do not oppose the infidel presence on Bahrain's territory. In short, Bahrain's organized Sunni Islamists are considered pro-government "societies," working at times for incremental modifications to the status quo but not advocating full democracy or other large-scale, disruptive changes.

There are two principal Sunni Islamist "political societies" in Bahrain. The first is the al-Menbar National Islamic Society (*al-Minbar al-Islami*), the political wing of the *al-Eslah* Society, Bahrain's branch of the Muslim Brotherhood. The second is the *al-Asala* Political Society, which in turn is the political wing of the Islamic Education Society (*al-Tarbiya al-Islamiya*), a conservative Salafist organization.

Al-Menbar is the more liberal of the two Sunni Islamist parties, and has, for example, taken positions in favor of women's rights.[29] However, this liberalism has its limits: in 2006 the group's Council of Representatives members formed part of a bloc that prevented Bahrain from ratifying the government's signature on the International Covenant on Civil and Political Rights, on the basis that the Covenant would mean "that Muslims could convert to another religion, something against the Islamic law, since those who do so should be beheaded."[30] *Al-Menbar* had promised to field several female candidates for the 2006 election, but as part of an electoral pact with *al-Asala*, which does not approve of women's standing for political office, this pledge was dropped. Further, *al-Menbar's* parent organization (with "support" from the Islamic Education Society) held a 2008 workshop opposing government efforts to promote gender equality.[31]

Its association with *al-Eslah,* which runs a network of mosques, gives *al-Menbar* a solid social support base among Bahraini Sunnis. Further, *al-Eslah* (and, by extension, *al-Menbar*) benefits from the official patronage of the Bahraini royal family (its President is Sheikh Isa bin Mohammed al-Khalifa), as well as from some of Bahrain's largest businesses.[32] While charitable contributions to *al-Eslah* do not necessarily provide direct support for *al-Menbar's* political activity, they unquestionably contribute to *al-Eslah's* standing in society, and thus to *al-Menbar's* credibility.

Al-Asala takes a harder line than *al-Menbar* on various issues. As noted above, *al-Asala* does not approve of fielding female candidates, and the group is, in general, opposed to Bahrain's comparatively modern, freewheeling character. It has also taken positions opposed to U.S. military action in Iraq. Despite their differences, however, *al-Menbar* and *al-Asala* have often cooperated, and, like *al-Menbar*, *al-Asala* cannot be accurately described as an opposition "society" even though it dissents from some Bahraini government policies.

In the 2006 elections, *al-Menbar* and *al-Asala* agreed to divide the Sunni electoral districts between them in order not to compete with each other and split the Sunni Islamist vote.[33] This strategy worked well, with the two groups winning seven seats each.[34] In 2010, however, they failed to come up with a similar arrangement. As a result, the two "societies" ran against each other in many districts, and the consequence was the loss of most of their seats: *al-Menbar* now has only two seats in the Council of Representatives, and *al-Asala* has just three.[35]

Unsurprisingly, Sunni Islamist organizations have not participated in the recent anti-government demonstrations in Bahrain; if anything, they may have been one of the forces behind several pro-government rallies that have taken place while Bahrain's Shi'ites were protesting against government policies.[36,37] While these were not openly acknowledged as *al-Menbar* or *al-Asala* events, there is no question that Bahrain's Sunnis consider Shi'ite protests to be a threat to their privileged situation, and Sunni "societies" need to be seen as promoting the interests of their constituents. Beyond any such cynical calculations, Sunni Islamists would be justifiably concerned that a Shi'ite-Islamist-governed Bahrain would be much less hospitable to Sunni practices and beliefs than a relatively liberal Sunni-dominated Bahrain—despite the latter's tolerance of various social vices. (It is also worth noting that these pro-government rallies may not have been quite the "spontaneous outpouring of affection" that they appeared to be: Bangladeshi expatriate workers claim that they were forced to participate.)[38]

ISLAMISM AND SOCIETY

In addition to political activities, many of the established Islamist groups in Bahrain engage in conventional charitable and "outreach" work: supporting widows and orphans (and other poor people), operating mosques and providing religious education, and proselytizing for their particular brand of Islam. *Al-Eslah*, in particular, appears to run a large charitable enterprise, supported by corporate *zakat* as well as private contributions. Notably, *al-Eslah* has also made a number of prominent humanitarian contributions to the Gaza Strip, including funding construction of a building at the Islamic University there in 2005 and sending five ambulances to Gaza in 2009.[39] The particular affinity of *al-Eslah* for aid to Gaza is explained by the fact that both *al-Eslah* and Hamas are offshoots of the Muslim Brotherhood; Hamas has ruled the Gaza Strip since 2007, and the Islamic University there has been associated with Hamas since its founding. (In fact, the university was founded by Sheikh Ahmed Yassin, ten years before he founded Hamas.)

As bitter rivals for political and economic power, Shi'ite and Sunni Islamists in Bahrain are not particularly comfortable cooperating, even when they agree. However, some issues are uncontroversial enough (at least within Islamist circles) that Shi'ite and Sunni leaders have joined forces to fight for their shared ideals, or at least have managed not to interfere with each others' efforts:

- While they have not been successful in completely banning the sale and consumption of alcohol in Bahrain, Islamists have done what they can to impose limits on drinking in the kingdom. Islamist organizations supported a government move to close bars in cheap hotels in 2009;[40] and a few years earlier, a mob of Islamist youths (of unspecified affiliation) stormed into a Manama restaurant and firebombed cars parked outside it, in a protest against its sale of alcohol.[41]
- Horrified by reports that Manama had been ranked as one of the top ten "vice cities" in the world, Islamists have attempted to eliminate prostitution—either by banning female entertainers in cheap hotels or by attempting to prevent the issuance of visas to women from Russia, Thailand, Ethiopia, and China. (The latter measure, proposed by the Salafist *al-Asala* "society," fell flat; even other Islamists in the Council of Representatives pointed out that it would cause diplomatic damage if passed, and probably not be very effective in any case.)[42]
- In 2007, Islamist parliamentarians condemned a performance by Lebanese composer/oudist Marcel Khalife and Bahraini poet Qassim Haddad that was presented as part of a government-sponsored culture festival, complaining that it included "sleazy dance moves" that would "encourage debauchery." It appears the show went ahead as planned.[43] A year later, the same Council members united again to attempt to ban a show by provocative Lebanese singer Haifa Wehbe; this show also went ahead, although Wehbe did tone down her act a bit in response.[44]

Traditionally, Bahraini Sunnis and Shi'ites have lived and worked together with minimal friction. However, the recent Shi'a protests and the Sunni government's response (including, in at least some cases, Sunni vigilante participation[45]) have done a great deal to damage the relationship between the two communities. Within a week of the February 14th onset of Shi'ite protests, Sunnis had begun to mount counter-demonstrations;[46] and as the crisis has continued, confrontations between Sunni and Shi'ite groups have become more frequent and more violent. Even assuming that a political settlement is reached between Bahrain's government and the organizations representing the Shi'ite majority, it is difficult to imagine that Bahrain's social atmosphere will quickly return to the comfortable *status quo* ante.

ISLAMISM AND THE STATE

After a turbulent period during the 1990s, the country's new king, Hamad bin Isa al-Khalifa, restored constitutional government in 2002. From then until January 2011, Bahrain's government was largely successful in channeling the energies of the country's Islamists into non-violent political activity rather than terrorism or major civil unrest. In accordance with the 2002 constitution, elections with universal suffrage are held every four years (most recently in October 2010) for the lower chamber of the National Assembly, the Council of Representatives (*Majlis an-nuwab*); all members of the upper chamber, the Consultative Council (*Majlis al-shura*), are appointed by the King. Both chambers must approve any legislation, giving each one effective veto power over proposed laws. As a result, since the one national body that is democratically elected has such limited ability to accomplish anything against the wishes of the ruling establishment, Bahrain's version of democracy has never been entirely satisfactory to the majority of the country's citizens. Still, even this limited form of democracy provided the people of Bahrain with a voice and hope for future improvement.

Nevertheless, Bahrain has retained most of the essential characteristics of traditional Gulf emirate governance. Real power is concentrated in the ruling al-Khalifa family, members of which occupy the most important governmental positions, including 20 of the country's 25 Cabinet seats.[47] The Prime Minister, Prince Khalifa ibn Sulman al-Khalifa, has held office since the country was granted independence in 1971, and is currently the world's longest-serving Prime Minister. He is the uncle of King Hamad, and is also thought to be one of the wealthiest people in Bahrain.[48] Even the Council of Representatives' ability to block legislation is not really much of a constraint on royal power; under the Constitution, the King retains the right to rule by Royal Decree, bypassing the legislature entirely.[49]

While the current Shi'ite unrest in Bahrain has eclipsed most other news about Bahraini Islamism, earlier news stories paint a more complex picture of a government quite willing to work with Islamists to achieve its goals, but equally willing to take strong measures to limit the actions and influence of such forces.

While the Bahraini government is generally perceived as working against Islamism (or at least working to limit Islamists to minor victories while preserving Bahrain's modern, open character), it is not above using Sunni Islamists as weapons against the Shi'ite community. In a 2006 report, the Gulf Centre for Democratic Development detailed a government effort led by Sheikh Ahmed bin Ateyatalla al-Khalifa to "manipulate the results of... elections, maintain sectarian distrust and division, and to ensure that Bahrain's Shi'as remain oppressed and disenfranchised." The initiative reportedly involved government payments to a number of individuals and NGOs, including both *al-Eslah/al-Menbar* and the Islamic Education Society/*al-Asala*. Among the tasks to be achieved by the various participants in this scheme were "running websites and Internet forums which foment sectarian hatred" and running "Sunni Conversion" and "Sectarian Switch" projects.[50]

The foreign-policy implications of Islamism can sometimes create problems for the Bahraini government. *Al-Eslah's* affinity for the Gaza Strip has already been mentioned, and is harmless enough when it involves sending ambulances and other forms of aid there. But when, in late 2009, *al-Eslah* leader Sheikh Fareed Hadi gave a sermon condemning the Egyptian government for building a steel barricade across the Egypt-Gaza Strip border, Bahrain's government, not wishing to ruffle feathers, stepped in and suspended him from delivering further sermons. The eloquently-named Bahraini Society to Resist Normalization with the Zionist Enemy promptly objected, reminding Bahrain's government and citizens of "the dangers of Zionism and its drive to infiltrate Arab and Islamic societies and influence them."[51]

Nevertheless, Bahrain is not known as a major source of *mujahideen*, terrorists, or financial/logistical support for overseas *jihad* in its various forms. Much of this is probably due to the fact that Bahrainis are neither especially impoverished nor exposed to the more radical forms of Wahhabi fundamentalism. Still, a small number of Bahrainis have traveled abroad to participate in *jihad*. One, Khalil Janahi, was arrested by Saudi authorities in the course of his religious studies in Riyadh, and was accused of being one of a group of 172 al-Qaeda militants planning "to storm Saudi prisons to free militants and attack oil refineries and public figures."[52] Another was royal family member Sheikh Salman Ebrahim Mohamed Ali al-Khalifa, who was captured near the Pakistan-Afghanistan border and held by the United States in Guantanamo Bay, Cuba as a Taliban/al-Qaeda supporter before eventually being released to return to Bahrain.[53]

Inside Bahrain itself, the government has acted against individuals providing funding or other support to al-Qaeda. For example, two men associated with a small Salafist movement known as "National Justice" were arrested in June

2008 for sending money to al-Qaeda; one was released shortly afterwards for lack of evidence,[54] and the other was among a group of prisoners officially pardoned in mid-2009.[55] Some other Bahrainis have been implicated in plots to support or engage in terrorism,[56] but the Bahraini government has far worse problems dealing with domestic Shi'ite popular unrest than it does with the global *jihad*.

In the months leading up to the 2010 elections, Bahrain's government instituted a crackdown on many political organizations and news outlets, and vigorously suppressed demonstrations and civil unrest.[57] The ostensible justification was that Shi'ite opposition leaders were planning to lead a revolt against the government. In February 2011, Bahrain experienced a new and significant round of demonstrations and rioting by Shi'ite citizens, triggered by this apparent rollback of democratic reforms and by the revolutions in Tunisia and Egypt. The beginning of the mass demonstrations also coincided with the February 14th anniversary of the restoration of constitutional government in 2002 and the referendum in 2001 that approved the new constitution.[58] The government's initial reaction to these demonstrations was an indecisive and unproductive vacillation between brutal suppression and attempts at conciliation. But after seven demonstrators had been killed and many more injured, Bahrain's rulers decided to back down from lethal confrontation, and on February 19th began a concerted effort, led by Crown Prince Salman bin Hamad al-Khalifa, to de-escalate the crisis and promote a "national dialogue" to iron out a solution.[59] At first, it appeared likely that such a dialogue would soon take place;[60] but Shi'ite leaders demanded substantial concessions before talks could begin, and, four months later, a starting date has yet to be set. Clearly, even once negotiations begin, they will be difficult; after four months of protests, repression, allegations of torture,[61] mass dismissal of Shi'ites from their jobs,[62] and demolition of Shi'ite mosques,[63] there is very little good will or mutual trust between Bahrain's Shi'ites and their government.

The Bahraini ruling establishment has a number of factors in its favor as it attempts to maintain the status quo:

- It appears to have solid support from almost all members of the country's Sunni minority, which holds most economic power and controls all of Bahrain's security forces.
- It enjoys substantial outside support from neighboring Sunni states— particularly Saudi Arabia, which is concerned about the possibility of unrest or even rebellion by its own large Shi'a minority and has a history of intervention to preserve Bahrain's Sunni regime. In mid-March, a 1,500-strong force of Gulf Cooperation Council troops and policemen

(which may in fact have been as large as 5000 or more men),[64] headed
by Saudi Arabia, entered Bahrain to assist government forces in restoring
order;[65] this force will apparently remain in place at least until the end of
2011,[66] and could indeed become a permanent feature of the Bahraini
landscape.[67]

- It is backed by the United States. Although the U.S. has been critical of
the Bahraini government's more extreme measures to confront the recent
unrest, and has called for more democratic rule and better protection
of human rights, Bahrain's importance as a naval base and the dangers
a regime collapse would pose to other Persian Gulf governments give
Washington little real maneuvering room.[68] In the words of one anonymous U.S. official, Bahrain is "just too important to fail."[69]

Nonetheless, it is clear that the Bahraini government has done tremendous
damage to its own perceived legitimacy, both at home and abroad. While it
would appear unlikely that the regime faces any real danger of being overthrown in the near future, it is equally true that unless it can find some way
to regain the trust of the country's Shi'ite community, Bahrain's ruling class
will have a difficult time maintaining stability in an era of increasing democratization and rising expectations.

ENDNOTES

[1] Mahjoob Zweiri and Mohammed Zahid, "The victory of Al Wefaq: The rise of Shiite politics in Bahrain," Research Institute for European and American Studies (RIEAS) *Research Paper* no. 108, 10-11, http://www.jcss.org/UploadPolling/224.pdf; Al Wefaq National Islamic Society, "Bahrain Split by Electoral Boundaries," June 9, 2010, http://alwefaq.net/~alwefaq/index.php?show=news&action=article&id=4723; "Bahrain Opposition Representation: Was it a Silent Majority or is it now a Loud Minority?" n.p., n.d., http://www.scribd.com/doc/49888133/Bahrain-Opposition-Representation.

[2] Robert Fisk, "Abolish Bahrain's Monarchy, Chant Shia Muslims," *New Zealand Herald,* February 21, 2011, http://www.nzherald.co.nz/democracy/news/article.cfm?c_id=171&objectid=10707688; "Several Hurt as Sunnis, Shiites Clash in Bahrain," Reuters, March 4, 2011, http://tribune.com.pk/story/127573/several-hurt-as-sunnis-shiites-clash-in-bahrain/.

[3] "Bahrain Shiites Eye Easing of Sunni Grip," Agence France Presse, October 23, 2010, http://www.arabtimesonline.com/NewsDetails/tabid/96/smid/414/ArticleID/161106/reftab/73/t/Bahrain-Shiites-eye-easing-of-Sunni-grip/Default.aspx.

[4] "Bahrain WikiLeaks Cables: Bahrain as 'Iran's Fourteenth Province,'" *Telegraph* (London), February 18, 2011, http://www.telegraph.co.uk/news/wikileaks-files/bahrain-wikileaks-cables/8334785/GENERAL-PETRAEUS-VISIT-TO-BAHRAIN.html.

[5] Christopher Hope, "WikiLeaks: Bahrain Opposition 'Received Training from Hezbollah,'" *Telegraph* (London), February 18, 2011, http://www.telegraph.co.uk/news/worldnews/wikileaks/8333686/WikiLeaks-Bahrain-opposition-received-training-from-Hizbollah.html; "US Embassy Cables: Bahrainis Trained by Hezbollah, Claims King Hamad," *Guardian* (London), February 15, 2011, http://www.guardian.co.uk/world/us-embassy-cables-documents/165861.

[6] Jonathan Spyer, "Gulf Regimes: The Real Game – Saudi Arabia," *Jerusalem Post,* March 11, 2011, http://www.jpost.com/Features/FrontLines/Article.aspx?id=211679; According to Spyer, "Iran... is adept, however, at turning political chaos into gain... If the Gulf regimes fail to effectively navigate the current unrest, Iran is fair set to begin to apply these practices in this area."

[7] Zweiri and Zahid, "The Victory of Al Wefaq," 9.

[8] "US Embassy Cables: Guide to Bahrain's Politics," *Guardian* (London), February 15, 2011, http://www.guardian.co.uk/world/us-embassy-cables-documents/168471; "Bahrain WikiLeaks Cables: Wafa': A New Shia Rejectionist Movement," *Telegraph* (London), February 18, 2011, http://www.telegraph.co.uk/news/wikileaks-files/bahrain-wikileaks-cables/8334607/WAFA-A-NEW-SHIA-REJEC-

TIONIST-MOVEMENT.html.

[9] Zweiri and Zahid, "The Victory of Al Wefaq," 11.

[10] Al Wefaq National Islamic Society, "Bahrain Split by Electoral Boundaries"; Note that in addition to having district lines that separate Sunni and Shi'a populations in order to create Sunni-majority districts, the population size of the districts drawn varies widely: some Sunni-majority districts have as few as 1,000 voters, while some Shi'ite-majority districts have as many as 15,000 voters.

[11] "MPs Urge Al Wefaq to Rethink Resignation," *Gulf Daily News,* March 9, 2011, http://www.gulf-daily-news.com/NewsDetails. aspx?storyid=301425; Adrian Bloomfield, "Bahrain King under Pressure to Sack Prime Minister Uncle," *Telegraph* (London), February 20, 2011, http://www.telegraph.co.uk/news/worldnews/middleeast/bahrain/8336934/Bahrain-king-under-pressure-to-sack-prime-minister-uncle.html.

[12] Robert Fisk, "Bahrain—An Uprising on the Verge of Revolution," *Independent* (London), February 21, 2011, http://www.independent.co.uk/news/world/middle-east/robert-fisk-in-manama-bahrain-ndash-an--uprising-on-the-verge-of-revolution-2220639.html.

[13] "Bahrain WikiLeaks Cables: Wafa': A New Shia Rejectionist Movement."

[14] "Shaikh Isa Al Jowder and the Haq Movement," *Chan'ad Bahraini* blog, May 31, 2006, http://chanad.weblogs.us/?p=487.

[15] "Bahrain WikiLeaks Cables: Wafa': A New Shia Rejectionist Movement."

[16] "US Embassy Cables: Guide to Bahrain's Politics."

[17] "Bahrain WikiLeaks Cables: Wafa': A New Shia Rejectionist Movement."

[18] "Bahrain – Political Parties," globalsecurity.org, n.d., http://www.globalsecurity.org/military/world/gulf/bahrain-politics-parties.htm.

[19] "US Embassy Cables: Guide to Bahrain's Politics."

[20] Ibid.

[21] "Bahrain Unrest: Shia Dissident Hassan Mushaima Returns," BBC, February 26, 2011, http://www.bbc.co.uk/news/world-middle-east-12587902.

[22] "Bahraini Shia Groups Seek to Unify Demands," *Financial Times,* February 27, 2011, http://www.ft.com/cms/s/0/a5766674-429e-11e0-8b34-00144feabdc0.html.

[23] "Bahrain WikiLeaks Cables: Wafa': A New Shia Rejectionist Movement"; "Wafa' ('loyalty')," globalsecurity.org, n.d., http://www.globalsecurity.org/military/world/gulf/bahrain-politics-parties-wafa.htm; "Wafa' ('loyalty')," globalsecurity.org, n.d., http://www.globalsecurity.org/military/world/gulf/bahrain-politics-parties-wafa.htm.

[24] "US Embassy Cables: Guide to Bahrain's Politics."

[25] Ibid.

[26] Zoi Constantine, "Opposition Party Votes against Bahrain Election," *The National* (UAE), August 26, 2010, http://www.thenational. ae/news/worldwide/middle-east/opposition-party-votes-against-bahrain-election.

[27] Joe Parkinson, "Bahrain is Roiled by Return of Shiite," *Wall Street Journal*, February 28, 2011, http://online.wsj.com/article/SB10001 424052748704430304576170661773277324.html; Joe Parkinson and Nour Malas, "Bahrain Opposition Steps Up Pressure," *Wall Street Journal*, March 7, 2011, http://online.wsj.com/article/SB100014240 52748704504404576183972416733938.html?mod=WSJEurope_ hpp_LEFTTopStories.

[28] "US Embassy Cables: Guide to Bahrain's Politics."

[29] Zweiri and Zahid, "The Victory of Al Wefaq," 7.

[30] Ibid.

[31] Suad Hamada, "Anti-Gender Equality Campaign Starts," womangateway.com, August 4, 2008, http://www.womengateway.com/NR/ exeres/7A81C4CA-5539-4C3D-9F97-38EB79F2A735.htm.

[32] National Bank of Bahrain, "Social Responsibility," n.d., http:// www.nbbonline.com/default.asp?action=category&id=6; "Sakana Contributes Zakat to Al Eslah Society," sakanaonline.com, October 7, 2010, http://www.sakanaonline.com/en/press-releases/sakana-zakat-al-eslah-society.html.

[33] "Bahrain: The Political Structure, Reform and Human Rights," *Eurasia Review*, February 28, 2011, http://www.eurasiareview.com/ analysis/bahrain-the-political-structure-reform-and-human-rights-28022011/.

[34] Ibid.

[35] Ibidem; Habib Toumi, "Al Asala, Islamic Menbar Join Forces in Bahrain," *Gulf News*, October 29, 2010, http://gulfnews.com/ news/gulf/bahrain/al-asala-islamic-menbar-join-forces-in-bahrain-1.703600.

[36] Michael Slackman and Nadim Audi, "Protests in Bahrain Become Test of Wills," *New York Times*, February 22, 2011, http://www. nytimes.com/2011/02/23/world/middleeast/23bahrain.html.

[37] Nancy A. Youssef, "Huge Bahraini Counter-Protest Reflects Rising Sectarian Strife," McClatchy, February 21, 2011, http://www. mcclatchydc.com/2011/02/21/109155/huge-bahraini-counter-protest.html.

[38] "Bangladeshis Say Being Forced to Take Part in Bahrain Pro Government Rally," ANI, March 18, 2011, http://www.sify.com/news/ bangladeshis-say-being-forced-to-take-part-in-bahrain-pro-government-rally-news-international-ldsrkjcfgba.html.

[39] Aniqa Haider, "Society Sends Five Ambulances," *Gulf Daily News*, January 15, 2009, http://www.gulf-daily-news.com/NewsDetails. aspx?storyid=240214; See also *Bahrain Tribune* (Manama), September

13, 2005.

[40] Habib Toumi, "Bahraini Islamist Societies Press for Closure of Bars, Discos," *Gulf News*, April 22, 2009, http://gulfnews.com/news/gulf/bahrain/bahrain-islamist-societies-press-for-closure-of-bars-discos-1.1880.

[41] "Islamists Threaten Bahrain Diners," BBC, March 18, 2004, http://news.bbc.co.uk/2/hi/middle_east/3525198.stm.

[42] Toumi, "Bahraini Islamist Societies Press for Closure of Bars, Discos"; Alexandra Sandels, "BAHRAIN: Islamists Seeking to Curb Prostitution Fail in Bid to Ban Women From 4 Countries," *Los Angeles Times Babylon & Beyond* blog, December 15, 2009, http://latimesblogs.latimes.com/babylonbeyond/2009/12/bahrain-conservatives-seeking-to-curb-prostitution-fail-in-bid-to-ban-visas-for-women-from-russia-thailand-ethiopia-and-china.html.

[43] "Marcel Khalife and Qassim Haddad Cause Fury in Bahrain's Parliament," FREEMUSE, March 27, 2007, http://www.freemuse.org/sw18500.asp.

[44] "Haifa Wehbe Sings in Bahrain," *Middle East Online*, May 2, 2008, http://www.middle-east-online.com/english/?id=25672.

[45] "Bahrain Protesters March on Palace as Gates Visits," Associated Press, March 12, 2011, http://www.washingtonpost.com/wp-dyn/content/article/2011/03/12/AR2011031201563.html.

[46] Youssef, "Huge Bahraini Counter-Protest Reflects Rising Sectarian Strife."

[47] Canadians for Justice and Peace in the Middle East, "Factsheet: Bahrain Protests Feb. 2011," *CJPME Factsheet Series* no. 114, February 22, 2011, http://www.cjpme.org/DisplayDocument.aspx?DocumentID=1474.

[48] Bloomfield, "Bahrain King under Pressure to Sack Prime Minister Uncle."

[49] "Bahrain Opposition Representation."

[50] http://www.bahrainrights.org/node/528.

[51] Habib Toumi, "Call to Reinstate Imam Who Criticised Egypt's Steel Fence," *Gulf News*, December 25, 2009, http://gulfnews.com/news/gulf/bahrain/call-to-reinstate-imam-who-criticised-egypt-s-steel-fence-1.557927.

[52] http://newsblaze.com/story/20090612184137sand.nb/topstory.html . .

[53] "The Guantanamo Docket: Sheikh Salman Ebrahim Mohamed Ali al Khalifa," *New York Times*, n.d., http://projects.nytimes.com/guantanamo/detainees/246-sheikh-salman-ebrahim-mohamed-ali-al-khalifa/documents/2/pages/1781.

[54] Bahrain Freedom Movement, "Two Men Accused of Funding al-Qaeda Groups," June 25, 2008, http://www.vob.org/en/index.php?show=news&action=article&id=324.

[55] http://newsblaze.com/story/20090612184137sand.nb/topstory. html.

[56] Ibid.

[57] See, for example, Jon Marks, "Bahrain returns to the bad old days," *Guardian* (London), September 13, 2010, http://www.guardian. co.uk/commentisfree/2010/sep/13/bahrain-opposition-protests.

[58] Canadians for Justice and Peace in the Middle East, "Factsheet: Bahrain Protests Feb. 2011"; Simeon Kerr, Robin Wigglesworth and Abigail Fielding-Smith, "Arab Regimes Brace for 'Days of Rage,'" *Financial Times*, February 3, 2011, http://www.ft.com/cms/s/0/ 63ce290c-2ef1-11e0-88ec-00144feabdc0.html#axzz1G7GakJjJ.

[59] "Bahrain King Orders Release of Political Prisoners," Associated Press, February 22, 2011, http://www.independent.co.uk/news/ world/middle-east/bahrain-king-orders-release-of-political-prisoners-2222371.html.

[60] "Bahrain's Shiite Opposition Set to Talk to Rulers," Associated Press, March 3, 2011, http://www.cbsnews.com/stories/2011/03/03/ ap/world/main20038661.shtml.

[61] Kristen Chick, "Bahrain Rights Activist's Wife Details Torture, Unfair Trial," *Christian Science Monitor*, May 16, 2011, http://www. csmonitor.com/World/Middle-East/2011/0516/Bahrain-rights-activ-ist-s-wife-details-torture-unfair-trial.

[62] Kristen Chick, "Amid Unrest, Bahrain Companies Fire Hundreds of Shiites," *Christian Science Monitor*, April 7, 2011, http://www. csmonitor.com/World/Middle-East/2011/0407/Amid-unrest-Bah-rain-companies-fire-hundreds-of-Shiites.

[63] "Shiite Mosque Demolished in Bahrain Crackdown," Associated Press, April 23, 2011, http://news.yahoo.com/s/ap/20110423/ap_on_ re_mi_ea/ml_bahrain.

[64] "Gulf States to Remain in Bahrain in 2011," *World Tribune*, May 13, 2011, http://www.worldtribune.com/worldtribune/WTARC/2011/ me_gulf0577_05_13.asp.

[65] "GCC Troops Dispatched to Bahrain to Maintain Order," *Al Arabiya* (Dubai), March 15, 2011, http://www.alarabiya.net/arti-cles/2011/03/14/141445.html.

[65] "Gulf States to Remain in Bahrain in 2011."

[66] "GCC Force may be Expanded," *Gulf Daily News*, May 20, 2011, http://www.gulf-daily-news.com/NewsDetails.aspx?storyid=306236; "Bahrain Moots Gulf Force Expansion," Khaleez Times, May 20, 2011, http://www.khaleejtimes.com/DisplayArticleNew.asp?col=& section=middleeast&xfile=data/middleeast/2011/May/middleeast_ May512.xml.

[67] Thomas Fuller, "Bahrainis Fear the U.S. Isn't Behind Their Fight for Democracy," *New York Times*, March 5, 2011, http://www.nytimes. com/2011/03/05/world/middleeast/05bahrain.html.

[68] Adam Entous and Julian E. Barnes, "U.S. Wavers on 'Regime Change,'" *Wall Street Journal*, March 5, 2011, http://online.wsj.com/article/SB10001424052748703580004576180522653787198.html?mod=WSJEUROPE_hpp_MIDDLETopNews.

QATAR

QUICK FACTS

Population: 840,926

Area: 11,586 sq km

Ethnic Groups: Arab 40%, Indian 18%, Pakistani 18%, Iranian 10%, other 14%

Religions: Muslim 77.5%, Christian 8.5%, other 14%

Government Type: Emirate

GDP (official exchange rate): $93.63 billion

Map and Quick Facts courtesy of the CIA World Factbook (Last Updated June 2010)

The tiny Gulf state of Qatar is a study in contradictions. Considerably more liberal than many of its neighbors, Qatar nevertheless is the only country other than Saudi Arabia to espouse Wahhabism as its official state religion. A traditionally conservative country whose authoritarian tribal rulers brook no opposition, Qatar is nevertheless host to the Al-Jazeera satellite television network, whose freewheeling reportage has occasionally led to diplomatic crises with neighboring countries. Moreover, Qatar is host the Al Udeid air base, regional home of the U.S. Central Command. The Qatari government has reportedly paid large sums of money to al-Qaeda to avoid being targeted by the organization in retaliation for its support for American operations in Iraq.

Domestically, Qatar has no active Islamist opposition, for the simple reason that the state has co-opted and involved Islamism in its governance from the very beginning. Wahhabi thought is especially influential among the Al Thani clan, which has ruled Qatar since the beginning of the nineteenth century. Its embrace of Wahhabism distinguishes Qatar religiously from its other neighbors, while promoting a close relationship—and occasional rivalry—with Saudi Arabia.

ISLAMIST ACTIVITY

Islamism is very much an "in house" phenomenon in Qatar. It has been pointed out that a necessary precondition for the rise of an Islamist opposition is a decline in government legitimacy and efficacy.[1] This, in a nutshell, explains the general lack of robust Islamic opposition to the governments of the Gulf States, and Qatar is no exception. A small, exceptionally wealthy country where the government subsidizes everything from petrol to education, Qatar so far has lacked serious challenges to the Islamic legitimacy of its government.

There likewise have been very few reported incidents of anti-Western terrorism in Qatar in recent years. In November 2001, two U.S. contractors were shot at the al-Udeid airbase, and an attempt was made to ram the base's gate in 2002.[2] These incidents, however, are believed to be the work of lone attackers.

In March 2005, Omar Ahmed Abdallah Ali, an expatriate Egyptian, blew himself up outside a theater in Doha. The attack, which killed a British school teacher, was the first suicide bombing in Qatar. Ali was believed to have ties to al-Qaeda in the Arabian Peninsula, whose leader had issued a communiqué two days before the attack calling on local citizens of a number of Gulf states to act against Western interests. Qatar was at the top of his list.[3] In the aftermath of this attack, allegations were made that Qatar's rulers had been paying protection money to al-Qaeda. A report in London's *Sunday Times* described an agreement made between the government of Qatar and al-Qaeda prior to the 2003 Iraq War, under which millions of dollars are paid annually to the terror network to keep Qatar off of its target list, despite the country's role as a U.S. ally.[4] This money is believed to be channeled via spiritual leaders sympathetic to al-Qaeda, and used to support the organization's activities in Iraq. After the attack in Doha, the agreement was renewed, according to the *Times*' source, "just to be on the safe side."[5] The *Times* report quoted an unnamed Qatari official as saying that Qatar is a "soft target" which prefers to pay to secure its national and economical interests, and that Qatar is not the only state doing so.[6]

The *Times* report highlights the fine line that Qatar treads in its relations with the U.S. and its neighbors. Because it hosts the Al Udeid airbase and Camp As Sayliyah, a pre-positioning facility for U.S. military equipment, Qatar is a more attractive target for terrorists than most neighboring countries, whose ties to the U.S. are less tangible. Qatar pays for the upkeep of the American military bases on its soil; the U.S. pays neither rent nor utilities on them.[7] Neither Qatar nor the U.S. makes any secret of these ties. It is thus surprising that Qatar has not been a more frequent target of al-Qaeda's attacks. The purported payment of "protection money" to al-Qaeda is one explanation for Qatar's relative safety; another reason may be that the absence of social and political discontents within the country's borders deprives al-Qaeda of willing local recruits. "Homegrown *jihadis*" are not as common in Qatar as they are in many neighboring countries.

Moreover, politics in the region are often played out on a very subtle level. While Qatar ostensibly enjoys a close relationship with Washington, these ties are balanced by a certain amount of independence when it comes to taking action in support of American interests. According to a State Department cable released by Wikileaks, Qatar was deemed "the "worst in the region" in counterterrorism efforts.[8] Qatar's security service was described as "hesitant to act against known terrorists out of concern for appearing to be aligned with the U.S. and provoking reprisals."[9]

Nor is it only in taking affirmative steps against known terrorists that Qatar is reluctant; the country has acquired a reputation as a financial backer of Islamist causes abroad, including terrorist organizations. Several charities based in Qatar have been accused of actively financing al-Qaeda and other terrorist organizations. One of these, the Qatar Charitable Society (QCS), was set up and operated by an employee of the Qatari government.[10] In April 2006, Qatar's government pledged $50 million to the new Hamas-led Palestinian government, after the U.S. and the EU withdrew their funding.[11] In April 2008, Ethiopia severed ties with Doha over alleged Qatari "support for armed opposition groups and their coordinators in neighboring countries."[12]

At times, this support has gone beyond financing. According to American intelligence officials, Abdallah bin Khalid al-Thani, a member of the Qatari royal family, helped wanted al-Qaeda chief Khaled Sheikh Mohammed elude capture in 1996. Abdallah bin Khalid, who was Qatar's Minister of Religious Affairs at the time, reportedly sheltered the wanted man on one of his own farms.[13] Mohammed is believed to have been employed for some years in Qatar's Department of Public Water Works, before slipping out of the country on a Qatari passport just ahead of an American attempt to capture him.[14]

Apparently, Abdallah bin Khalid was not alone in his sympathies to al-Qaeda. News reports have cited U.S. officials as saying there were others in the Qatari royal family who provided safe havens for al-Qaeda leaders.[15]

ISLAMISM AND SOCIETY

Wahhabism—the very strict interpretation of Islam espoused by 18th century preacher Muhammad ibn Abd al Wahhab—has shaped Qatar's history for more than a century. Among the tribes which adopted the Wahhabi interpretation in the late 19th century was the Al Thani—as contrasted with the ruling Al Khalifas of Bahrain, who rejected Wahhabism. When the Al Khalifas attempted to invade the peninsula of Qatar in 1867, the Al Thani and their followers, with the help of the British, repelled the invasion. This victory established the Al Thani family as Qatar's ruling clan. Thereafter, Qatar became the only country other than Saudi Arabia to espouse Hanbali-Wahhabism as the official state religion.[16] This set the stage for tensions between Qatar and its other neighbors.

Qatar's population is conservative, but overt religious discrimination has been rare. While non-citizens constitute a majority of Qatar's residents, most are from Southeast Asia or from other Muslim countries—a trend which has minimized the influence of Western culture.[17] Inter-Muslim friction is also minimized by the homogeneity of Qatar's citizenry. Sunni Muslims constitute the overwhelming majority of the population, while Shi'a Muslims account for less than five percent.[18] As a result, the main drivers for Islamist opposition are lacking in Qatar; the government espouses a distinctly Islamist ideology, while social inequities and cultural frictions have been kept to a minimum.

However, in contrast to Saudi Arabia, Wahhabi tenets are not officially enforced or strictly adhered to in most public settings in Qatar. Qatari society is generally moderate, and, among Arab countries, its civil liberties are ranked second only to Lebanon.[19] While instances of overt religious discrimination have been rare, anti-Semitic motifs are common in the mainstream media: Israel and world Jewry are frequently demonized in editorials and cartoons.[20]

The need to keep pace with global social and economic development has pushed Qatar gradually to shift its political structure from a traditional society based on consent and consensus to one based on more formal and democratic institutions. While Qatar's constitution institutionalized the hereditary rule of the Al Thani family, it also established an elected legislative body and made government ministers accountable to the legislature.[21] While formally accountable to no one, the Emir is still bound by the checks and balances of traditional Muslim Arab societies; all decisions must be in accordance with *sharia* and must not arouse the opposition of the country's leading families.[22]

ISLAMISM AND THE STATE

Qatar's government and ruling family have traditionally been strongly linked to Wahhabi-Hanbali Islam. Not only is Wahhabi Islam the official state religion, but Islamic jurisprudence is the basis of Qatar's legal system. Civil courts have jurisdiction only over commercial law.[23] Qatar's governmental structure, despite a written constitution, conforms closely to traditional Islamic constraints, with tribal and family allegiance remaining an influential factor in the country's politics. There is no provision in Qatar's constitutions for political parties, and hence there is no official political opposition.[24] Professional associations and societies, which in other Muslim countries play the role of unofficial political parties, are under severe constraints in Qatar, and are forbidden from engaging in political activities.[25]

The Qatari government has preferred to co-opt rather than oppose Islamism. Religious institutions are carefully monitored by the Ministry of Islamic affairs, which oversees mosque construction and Islamic education. The Ministry appoints religious leaders and previews mosque sermons for inflammatory language that might incite listeners to violence.[26]

Qatar has a longstanding tradition of granting asylum to exiled Islamists and radical preachers from other Muslim countries.[27] Following the 1979 attack on the Grand Mosque in Mecca by an extremist group, Qatar took in a number of radical exiles from Saudi Arabia, including Hanbali-Wahhabi scholar Sheikh Abdallah bin Zayd al-Mahmud, who subsequently was appointed Qatar's most senior cleric.[28]

Throughout the 1980s and 1990s, sympathy for Islamist causes ran high in Qatari society and among many members of the ruling clan. In fact, Sheikh Fahd bin Hamad al-Thani, the second-eldest son of the Emir, effectively eliminated himself from contention for the throne by surrounding himself with *jihadists* from the Afghan War.[29] A number of al-Qaeda leaders are believed to have travelled through Qatar during the 1990s under the protection of members of the ruling clan, including Abu Mus'ab al-Zarqawi and Osama bin Laden.[30] The Chechen leader Zelimkhan Yandarbiyev, who was killed in Doha in 2004, also found refuge for several years in Qatar.

During the 1980s, many Wahhabi exiles were appointed to senior and midlevel positions in Qatar's Interior Ministry, which controls both the civilian security force and the *Mubahathat* (secret police office). After 2003, Emir Hamad bin Khalifa began gradually weeding out the more extreme Islamist elements from government ministries, including the Interior Ministry; the Minister of the Interior, Sheikh Abdallah, a member of the Wahhabi clique, was removed from office in 2004. The Interior Ministry was then put under the *de facto* control of Sheikh Abdallah bin Nasser bin-Khalifa al-Thani, an Emir loyalist. However, a large number of Islamist appointees are believed to remain among mid-level Qatari security officials.[31]

In June 2003, the Emir created an independent State Security Agency, answerable directly to him. Additionally, all the most important police, military, and internal security services are headed by powerful members of the ruling family, who in turn answer to the Emir.[32] The creation of these parallel security agencies effectively bypassed the Interior Ministry's control of police and public security. These shakeups, however, have had more to do with political alliances than with government opposition to Islamists *per se*. Most Islamists, both domestic and immigrant, have become well integrated into the top echelons of Qatari society.[33]

Among the political exiles who sought refuge in Qatar are prominent figures of the Muslim Brotherhood, many of whom fled persecution at the hands of Nasser's Egyptian government during the 1950s. Some of these exiles reportedly laid the foundations for the Qatari Education Ministry, and taught at various levels there until the early 1980s.[34]

Given the great success of these elements, the country has no obvious need for an Islamist opposition. In 2007, Kuwaiti Islamist writer Abd Allah al-Nafisi called for the Egyptian Muslim Brotherhood to follow the lead of the Qatari branch and disband altogether. Al-Nafisi noted that from 1960 to 1980, Qatar went through a period of great Islamist intellectual activity and organization. In contrast to the experience of the Muslim Brotherhood in Egypt, the Qatari Muslim Brothers had no real conflict with the state.[35]

One of the most influential—not to mention controversial—voices in Islamist circles today is Egyptian Sheikh Yusuf al-Qaradawi, who has lived in Qatar since 1961. Qaradawi enjoys worldwide exposure via *Al Jazeera* television, through his weekly program "Sharia and Life" (*al-Shari'a wa-al-Hayat*). Until recently, he also oversaw the Islamist Web portal IslamOnline, established in 1997.[36] Many consider Sheikh al-Qaradawi to be the most influential Islamic scholar alive today; he is viewed as the spiritual leader of the Muslim Brotherhood, and "sets the tone for Arabic language Sunni sermons across the world."[37] Qaradawi has sparked considerable controversy in the West for his support for suicide bombings in Israel and the killing of American citizens in Iraq. Among Muslim audiences, however, his comparatively moderate views on the acceptability of Muslim participation in Western democracies have brought him both praise and condemnation.[38] This mixture of conservatism and reform informs Qaradawi's politics. He is one of the founders of the *wasatiyya* ("Middle Way") movement, which attempts to bridge the gap between the various interpretations of Islam.[39] Yet Qaradawi's political proclivities and involvement have led to some questionable connections: Qaradawi is listed as a founder of the Union of Good (*Itilaf al-Khayr*), a coalition of European Islamic charities now designated by the United States

Treasury as a channel for transferring funds to Hamas.[40]

Although the Qatari press is free from official censorship, self-censorship is the norm. Defense and national-security matters, as well as stories related to the royal family, are considered strictly out of bounds. The country's major radio and television stations, Qatar Radio and Qatar Television, are both state-owned.[41] And while newspapers in Qatar are all privately owned in principle, many board members and owners are either government officials or have close ties to the government. For example, the chairman of the influential daily *Al-Watan*, Hamad bin Sahim al Thani, is a member of the royal family.[42] Meanwhile, Qatar's Foreign Minister, Hamed bin Jasem bin Jaber al Thani, owns half of the newspaper.

Compared to the traditionally conservative and highly-censored Arab press, Qatar's *Al Jazeera* satellite network is a breath of fresh air. Formed in 1996 from the remnants of BBC Arabic TV, which had just been closed down, the station offers the kind of free and unfettered discussion of issues not usually broadcast in the Muslim world. *Al Jazeera* has established itself as a major international media player, and is increasingly being viewed as a political actor in its own right. Yet, although it does not seem very much like a traditional government-controlled propaganda outlet, *Al Jazeera* is in fact funded by the Qatari government, with its expenses reimbursed by the Ministry of Finance.[43] Sheikh Hamid bin Thamer, a member of the royal family, heads the station's board of directors.[44]

Since the September 11th attacks on New York and Washington, *Al Jazeera* has undergone a process of increasing "Islamization," with many of its more secular staff replaced by Islamists.[45] This process has been accompanied by subtle—and some not-so-subtle—changes in the station's reportage of happenings in the field. *Al Jazeera* is alleged to have moved away from its rather ideologically diverse origins to a more populist—and more Islamist— approach.[46] In addition, *Al Jazeera* is increasingly becoming a participant in the sectarian feud between Shi'as and Sunnis. Qatar itself is right in the middle of this battle; on the one hand, it hosts an American military base on its soil, where tanks and vehicles damaged in the fighting are serviced and sent back into battle to protect the Shi'ite-led government of Iraq. On the other, Qatar's Sunni majority sees Shi'ite Iran as the main threat in the region.

Al Jazeera rarely criticizes Qatar's ruling Al Thani family, although other Arab governments come in for severe censure.[47] This has not only infuriated those Arab governments on the receiving end of the station's critical coverage, but also raised the question of Qatari complicity in destabilizing its neighbors. Libya withdrew its ambassador from Qatar between 2000 and

2002 to protest *Al Jazeera's* less-than-complimentary coverage of the Qadhafi regime.[48] In 2002, Saudi Arabia likewise withdrew its ambassador to Doha, partly in response to *Al Jazeera* reportage. (Relations were restored six years later, and *Al Jazeera* has since toned down its Saudi coverage.) The Egyptian government also has repeatedly complained about the open forum given by *Al Jazeera* to representatives of the Egyptian Muslim Brotherhood.[49] Jordan and Lebanon have accused *Al Jazeera* of actively working to undermine their governments, while uncritically supporting their opposition Islamist movements.[50]

It is unclear how much of *Al Jazeera's* increasing Islamist slant is a matter of design and how much is evolution. Has the station been changing its approach in order to promote the interests of the Qatari ruling family, or is the shift a simple reflection of the growing popularity of Islamist causes in Arab society? Whichever is the true cause (and they are not mutually exclusive), *Al Jazeera* is more than a mirror of public opinion; it is increasingly taking the initiative in influencing events rather than just reporting on them.[51]

For some, there is no doubt that the network is subject to the political dictates of the Qatari government, which has become a significant player in many of the Middle East's disputes despite the country's small size. Government control over the channel's reporting appeared to U.S. diplomats to be so direct that the channel's output is said to have become a subject of bilateral discussions between Washington and Doha. An American diplomatic dispatch from July 2009 noted that the *Al Jazeera* could be used as a bargaining tool to repair Qatar's relationships with other countries, and called the station "one of Qatar's most valuable political and diplomatic tools".[52]

Al Jazeera's influence reflects the new reality of an increasingly media-driven Middle East. The station's rivalry with the newer Saudi *Al Arabiya* satellite channel is indicative of a deeper competition for regional influence. *Al Jazeera* may be seen an arm of Qatari foreign policy, a sort of electronic *Da'wah* (missionary activity). In effect, these governments use their control of the media to create a monopoly on reporting, making the reportage itself a tool in regional rivalries.

ENDNOTES

[1] Sheri Berman, "Islamism, Revolution, and Civil Society," *Perspectives on Politics* 1, no. 2, June 2003, 257-272.

[2] Oxford Analytica, "The Advent of Terrorism in Qatar," *Forbes*, March 25, 2005, http://www.forbes.com/2005/03/25/cz_0325oxan_qatarattack.html.

[3] Ibid.

[4] Uzi Mahnaimi, "Qatar buys off Al-Qaeda attacks with oil millions," *Sunday Times* (London), May 1, 2005, http://www.timesonline.co.uk/tol/news/world/article387163.ece.

[5] Ibid.

[6] Ibidem.

[7] Elizabeth Weingarten, "Qatar: 'Worst' on Counterterrorism in the Middle East?" *The Atlantic*, November 29, 2010, http://www.theatlantic.com/international/archive/2010/11/qatar-worst-on-counterterrorism-in-the-middle-east/67166/.

[8] Scott Shane and Andrew W. Lehren, "Leaked Cables Offer Raw Look at U.S. Diplomacy," *New York Times*, November 28, 2010, http://www.nytimes.com/2010/11/29/world/29cables.html?_r=1.

[9] Ibid.

[10] Steven Emerson, Testimony before the House of Representatives Committee on Financial Services, Subcommittee on Oversight and Investigations, February 12, 2002, 8-9.

[11] "Qatar Pledges $50M to Palestinian Government," Associated Press, April 17, 2006, http://toronto.ctv.ca/servlet/an/local/CTVNews/20060417/qatar_palestine_060417?hub=CalgaryHome.

[12] Panapress, "Ethiopia Accuses Qatar of Terrorist Funding and Severs Ties," *Afrik News*, April 21, 2008, http://www.afrik-news.com/article13306.html.

[13] Terry McDermott, Josh Meyer and Patrick J. McDonnell, "The Plots and Designs of Al Qaeda's Engineer," *Los Angeles Times*, December 22, 2002, http://articles.latimes.com/2002/dec/22/world/fg-ksm22.

[14] Brian Ross and David Scott, "Qatari Royal Family Linked to Al Qaeda," *ABC News*, February 7, 2003, January 12, 2010.

[15] Ibid.

[16] "Qatar: Wahhabi Islam and the Gulf," country-data.com, n.d., http://www.country-data.com/cgi-bin/query/r-11031.html.

[17] U.S. Department of State, Bureau of Near Eastern Affairs, "Background Note: Qatar," September 22, 2010.

[18] U.S. Department of State, Bureau of Democracy, Human Rights and Labor, *International Religious Freedom Report 2010* (Washington, DC: U.S. Department of State, November 17, 2010), http://www.state.gov/g/drl/rls/irf/2010/index.htm.

[19] "Qatar: Political Forces," *The Economist*, March 11, 2009, http://www.economist.com/node/13216406.

[20] U.S. Department of State, *International Religious Freedom Report 2010*.

[21] U.S. Department of State, "Background Note: Qatar."

[22] Ibid.

[23] Ibidem.

[24] "Qatar: Political Forces."

[25] U.S. Department of State, *International Religious Freedom Report 2010*.

[26] Ibid.

[27] Oxford Analytica, "The Advent of Terrorism in Qatar."

[28] Michael Knights and Anna Solomon-Schwartz, "The Broader Threat from Sunni Islamists in the Gulf," Washington Institute for Near East Policy *PolicyWatch* no. 883, July 25, 2004, http://www.washingtoninstitute.org/templateC05.php?CID=1761.

[29] Ibid.

[30] Barry Rubin, ed., *Guide to Islamist Movements* (London: M.E. Sharpe, 2009), 308-310.

[31] Oxford Analytica, "The Advent of Terrorism in Qatar."

[32] Ibid.

[33] "Qatar: Political Forces."

[34] Ehud Rosen, *Mapping the Organizational Sources of the Global Delegitimization Campaign Against Israel In the UK* (Jerusalem, Israel Jerusalem Center for Public Affairs, December 24, 2010), http://www.jcpa.org/text/Mapping_Delegitimization.pdf.

[35] Marc Lynch, "Muslim Brotherhood Debates," *Abu Aardvark* blog, February 28, 2007, http://abuaardvark.typepad.com/abuaardvark/2007/02/muslim_brotherh.html.

[36] Reuven Paz, "Qaradhawi and the World Association of Muslim Clerics: The New Platform of the Muslim Brotherhood," *PRISM Series on Global Jihad* no. 4/2, November 2004, 1-2, http://www.e-prism.org/images/PRISM_no_4_vol_2_-_Qaradhawi.pdf.

[37] Samuel Helfont, "Islam and Islamism Today: the Case of Yusuf al-Qaradawi," Foreign Policy Research Institute. January 2010. http://www.fpri.org/enotes/201001.helfonts.islammodernityqaradawi.html Retrieved 23 January 2011.

[38] Samuel Helfont, "Islam and Islamism Today: the Case of Yusuf al-Qaradawi". Foreign Policy Research Institute *E-Notes*, January 2010, http://www.fpri.org/enotes/201001.helfonts.islammodernityqaradawi.html.

[39] Ibid.

[40] U.S. Department of the Treasury, "PRESS RELEASE HP-1267: Treasury designates the Union of Good," November 12, 2008, http://www.treasury.gov/press-center/press-releases/Pages/hp1267.aspx.

[41] "Qatar: Political Forces."

[42] Jennifer Lambert, "Qatari Law Will Test Media Freedom," Carnegie Endowment for International Peace *Arab Reform Bulletin*, December 1, 2010, http://www.carnegieendowment.org/arb/?fa=downloadArticlePDF&article=42049.

[43] Kristen Gillespie, "The New Face of Al Jazeera," *The Nation*, November 9, 2007.

[44] Ibid.

[45] Ibidem.

[46] Ibidem.

[47] U.S. Department of State, "Background Note: Qatar."

[48] "Qatar: Political Forces."

[49] Zvi Bar'el, "Is Al Jazeera Trying to Bring Down the Palestinian Authority?" *Ha'aretz* (Tel Aviv), February 2, 2011, http://www.haaretz.com/print-edition/features/is-al-jazeera-trying-to-bring-down-the-palestinian-authority-1.340716.

[50] Gillespie, "The New Face of Al Jazeera."

[51] Zvi Bar'el, "Is Al Jazeera Trying to Bring Down the Palestinian Authority?"

[52] "Qatar Uses Al-Jazeera as Bargaining Chip: WikiLeaks," Agence France-Presse, December 5, 2010, http://www.google.com/hosted-news/afp/article/ALeqM5gqrdtYIc4k1ZzxfdOvlgFkyYXCwQ?docId=CNG.46b645b43dfaa2dc5d313fea1f79b408.121.

UNITED ARAB EMIRATES

QUICK FACTS

Population: 4,975,593

Area: 83,600 sq km

Ethnic Groups: Emirati 19%, other Arab and Iranian 23%, South Asian 50%, other expatriates (includes Westerners and East Asians) 8%

Religions: Muslim 96% (Shi'a 16%), other (includes Christian and Hindu) 4%

Government Type: federation with specified powers delegated to the UAE federal government and other powers reserved to member emirates

GDP (official exchange rate): $231.3 billion

Map and Quick Facts courtesy of the CIA World Factbook (Last Updated July 2010)

In the wake of the September 11, 2001 terrorist attacks on the United States, the United Arab Emirates has come to be identified as significantly, if indirectly, involved in Islamic terrorism. Two of the nineteen 9/11 hijackers were citizens of the UAE, while another resided there.[1] Nearly a decade after those attacks, much of the Arab world is in a state of upheaval, and the governments of two of the UAE's Arabian Peninsula neighbors, Bahrain and Yemen, are facing severe challenges to their authority. Yet the UAE, to all appearances, remains calm. This is due in large part to the cultural setting in which the interpretation and practice of Islam have evolved in the UAE, as well as to the nature of the country's leadership since its independence in 1971. The "father" of the UAE (and its president from the country's founding in 1971 until his death in 2004), Zayid bin Sultan Al Nahyan, promoted and personified a conservative but moderate interpretation of Islam, which helped to legitimate government efforts to check and contain Islamic extremism. Since 9/11, the UAE has devoted serious efforts to countering Islamic terrorism, the extreme forms of belief that promote it, and the financial support that facilitates it. Yet while these efforts have been overwhelmingly successful, international concerns remain that terrorist plots could be carried out from or through the UAE, and that some terrorist financing taking place within the country remains hidden or unacknowledged.

ISLAMIST ACTIVITY

The activity of Islamists in the UAE has been constrained by several factors, among them the generally moderate and non-political nature of the religion there, and the government's close monitoring of Muslim organizations, especially those with political agendas. Moreover, the largest cohort of Muslims in the country are South Asian expatriates, who have been drawn there for job opportunities and are subject to expulsion for any behavior deemed threatening to state security. Finally, astute government distribution of the country's vast hydrocarbon wealth has been effective in blunting the kind of discontent which might promote grassroots adherence to Islamism that challenges the writ of the state.

The Muslim Brotherhood

In the 1970s and 1980s, the Muslim Brotherhood, although never recruiting more than a relative handful of members, had a degree of influence in the UAE, principally in educational institutions, which were staffed in large part by Egyptians. By the 1990s, however, whatever influence the organization exercised had largely dissipated.[2] The 2008 defeat of the Brotherhood's candidates in the Kuwaiti parliamentary elections reflected a general setback for the group in its attempts to gain a foothold in the Gulf, even as it continued to be ineffectual in the UAE. An Islamist commentator lamenting negative developments for the Brotherhood recently observed that, in the UAE, "despite some interesting developments among the cadres and the youth of the MB, intense security obstacles prevented them from doing much by way of renewing their thought or engaging in popular actions."[3] Indeed, indications are that the UAE government views the Brotherhood as a political entity whose true aim is to establish a theocracy; thus, the organization is outlawed.[4] Given the stringent government controls imposed on it and the generally unpromising milieu in which it operates in the UAE, the Brotherhood is unlikely to exercise any considerable influence in the foreseeable future. As one analyst observed, "Islamist movements in the UAE, including those linked to the Muslim Brotherhood, are generally non-violent and perform social and relief work."[5] Nevertheless, there are several other Islamist movements that operate or seek to operate in the UAE, which are potentially menacing.

Al-Qaeda

The terrorist attacks of September 11, 2001 highlighted links between the UAE and the group responsible, al-Qaeda. Two of the operatives who carried out the attacks were Emiratis, another had resided there during the planning for the attacks, and the planners of the operation had frequently transited the UAE. A further connection stems from the UAE being one of only three countries to recognize the Taliban regime in Afghanistan (the others were Pakistan and Saudi Arabia).

Since 9/11, there have been no attacks carried out in the UAE or launched from its soil by al-Qaeda, but fairly numerous and credible threats have been discovered, although not always with a high level of certainty. The presence of al-Qaeda operatives has, however, been established. In November 2002, the suspected ringleader of the team that had attacked the *USS Cole* two years earlier in Aden, Yemen was captured in Dubai. In the same year, credible reports claimed that considerable numbers of al-Qaeda fighters captured in Afghanistan were UAE nationals and that welfare associations in Dubai and Fujairah had been encouraging young men to join terrorist groups. These associations were also accused of sending money to radical groups in Afghanistan and South Asia. Arrests occurring in 2004 suggested that Dubai continued to be a through point for al-Qaeda operatives.[6] In July 2005, a new group calling itself "The al-Qaeda Organization in the Emirates and Oman" issued a strong threat against the rulers in the UAE if U.S. military installations in the country were not dismantled immediately.[7]

Three years later, the British government issued warnings of the risk of terrorist attacks in the UAE, likely connected to threats from al-Qaeda. The warnings prompted discussions in *jihadi* internet forums, which speculated about a possible secret understanding between al-Qaeda and other terrorist organizations with the UAE, whereby the latter would turn a blind eye to those organizations maintaining contacts and raising money in the UAE.[8] American officials confirmed a report in 2009 that UAE authorities had broken up a major terrorist ring in Ras al-Khaimah that spring, which had been plotting to blow up targets in Dubai. In September of the same year, a Saudi tip led to interception in Dubai of explosives which operatives of al-Qaeda in the Arabian Peninsula (AQAP) claimed to have placed on UPS and FedEx flights.[9] Finally, in 2010, there were reports that a network of "semi-legal" mosques dominated by Salafi preachers posed a *jihadi* threat and suggested a threat from al-Qaeda. The reports, though coming from backers of Shaikh Khalid bin Saqr Al Qassimi, who is contesting the succession as ruler of Ras al-Khaimah, appeared credible, and fit a pattern of al-Qaeda linkage with the emirate initiated by Marwan al-Shehhi, the 9/11 hijacker and continued with the 2009 incitement noted above.

Despite these plots and threats, no terrorist group has succeeded in carrying out an operation in the UAE. Interestingly, some *jihadi* internet forum discussants have suggested that al-Qaeda's failure to strike the UAE reflects lack of support for the organization, owing in part to the non-militant nature of Emirati fundamentalists, which in turn constrains al-Qaeda's ability to recruit locals.[10]

The Taliban and Haqqani Network

Islamist activity involving South Asian residents in the UAE is significant, and reportedly has included support of terrorist groups operating in Afghanistan, Pakistan, and India. In October 2008, for example, a plot involving several individuals, including an Afghan, to provide funds to the Taliban was uncovered by national authorities. The U.S. government believes that the Taliban and the affiliated Haqqani Network are funded in part by donors in the UAE, drawing their support from the large Pashtun community there. The Taliban is also known to extort money from Afghan businessmen based in the UAE.[11] However, neither the size of voluntary contributions to the Taliban nor the scope of forced aid extorted by them is publicly known.

Lashkar-e-Taiba

The Pakistan-based Islamist terrorist group Lashkar-e-Taiba reportedly received large amounts of money from Gulf-based networks, including funders in the UAE.[12] There likewise appears to be a linkage between the UAE and terrorist activities carried out by the group against India; an investigation of the August 2003 bombings in Mumbai revealed a Dubai link, through which Lashkar-e-Taiba operatives in that emirate colluded with cells in India. Other urban terrorist attacks in India revealed a similar linkage. An important part of the equation is the set of operational ties between the Student Islamic Movement of India and militant student groups in the UAE, as well as elsewhere in the Gulf. Lashkar-e-Taiba developed out of the *Ahl-e-Hadith* movement, which has roots in both the Middle East and the Indian Subcontinent.[13]

ISLAMISM AND SOCIETY

Of the UAE's estimated population of just over 5 million, less than a fifth is made up of native Emiratis. Citizens are overwhelmingly Muslim, approximately 78 percent of them Sunni and 22 percent Shi'a, with a small Ahmadiyya Muslim community as well. About four percent of the total population is non-Muslim, made up of about 250,000 Christians and smaller numbers of Hindus, Buddhists, and others.[14] The country's constitution allows for freedom of religious practice "in accordance with established and accepted procedures, provided it does not disturb public peace or violate public morals."[15] The State Department has reported that "Non-Muslim religious leaders from within and outside the country regularly praised the country's governmental and societal attitudes toward allowing all persons to practice their religions freely."[16] Sunni Emiratis adhere to the Maliki school of Islamic law, which is officially recognized in Abu Dhabi and Dubai, and the Hanbali school that predominates elsewhere (except in Fujairah, where the Shafi'i school holds sway).[17]

Attitudes toward Islamic groups in the UAE are difficult to discern since there is no significant direct popular participation in government by these elements. While the constitution mandates freedom of speech, public assembly and association are still subject to government approval. Although the press is among the freest in the Arab world, it exercises self-censorship on sensitive issues, and the broadcast media are government-owned. Thus, attitudes concerning Islamic groups and their activities can be assessed mainly by inference rather than by consideration of explicit expressions of opinion.[18] (The first step toward representative government was taken in 2006, when elections were held for selection of some of the members of the Federal National Council. The FNC's powers are advisory and only a tiny percentage of UAE citizens, who themselves constitute under 20 percent of the total population, were eligible to vote.

Moreover, the identification of Islamist groups is itself somewhat problematic, because there is considerable overlap in the missions of organizations, notably in the areas of philanthropic and religious concern. Curiously, the government identifies fewer than three percent of associations in the UAE as religious.[19] Many of the groups placed under the headings "cultural," "folklore," and "human services" are to one degree or another Islamic in orientation. 16.5 percent of associations are defined as "foreign."

The sampling of Islamic groups examined below is broadly representative of those that are active in the UAE. This strata includes both organizations that are part of native Emirian society and those that belong to various expatriate Muslim communities. To the extent that UAE organizations are identified with the promotion of Islamic objectives, they generally reflect the conservative nature of Islam in the country. However, differences exist; organizations in Dubai tend to reflect the cosmopolitanism of that emirate, with its very large expatriate population, including more than 150,000 from Europe and the United States, while in Abu Dhabi they exhibit a generally more conservative nature in keeping with its character, and in Sharjah they reflect the ruler's commitment to upholding the strong Islamic norms of that emirate.

Emirati Islamic Groups
The Mohammed bin Rashid Al Maktoum Foundation was launched in 2007 by the prime minister and ruler of Dubai, who also serves as vice president of the UAE, with his personal donation of a $10 billion endow-

ment (one of the largest charitable donations in history). Also in keeping with Dubai's personality, the mission of the foundation is expansive—to be a knowledge hub in the Arab world with the ultimate aim of bridging the gap between the Arab region and the developed world, thereby promoting job creation and economic development. The Islamic component of the foundation's mission is not explicit, but it is nonetheless significant. In the speech that launched the foundation, Sheikh Mohammed called for governments, business leaders, educators and others to promote an understanding of Islam's tolerance and commitment to intellectual debate.[20] In addition, a central element of the foundation is the *Bayt ul-Hikma*, designed to disseminate knowledge in the Arab world and named for the House of Knowledge that represented the apogee of Islamic science and learning in the Abbasid Empire of the Middle Ages.[21]

In Abu Dhabi, the more modestly funded Sheikh Zayed bin Sultan Al Nahyan Charitable and Humanitarian Foundation was established in 1992 with a $100 million endowment, and has a 2011 budget of $31 million. Its mission is more overtly aimed at advancing Islamic goals than that of the Al Maktoum Foundation, including the support of mosques, educational and cultural institutions, and hospitals and clinics, both in the UAE and in Islamic countries and communities overseas.[22] (This foundation is not to be confused with the Zayed Center for Coordination and Follow-Up, created in 1999 as the think tank of the Arab League, and closed by Sheikh Zayed in 2003 after an international outcry over revelations that it had provided a platform for the expression of anti-Semitic and extreme anti-Israeli views.

The Tabah Foundation is a non-profit institution established in 2005 in Abu Dhabi that seeks to promote a more effective contemporary Islamic discourse to advance Islamic values and counter negative images of Islam. Funded by various institutions and individuals in the UAE, Tabah has recently entered into an agreement with the *Diwan* (Council of State) of the crown prince of Abu Dhabi, Sheikh Mohammed bin Zayed, to develop the Zayed House for Islamic Culture. Its most significant initiative would appear to be the work of its media department, comprising both a television and documentary film division.[23] It also provides advice and consultation to other organizations. In 2010, the foundation published "Beyond Flak Attack," a sophisticated essay directed at Muslim activists and scholars who seek to engage the mass media to try to balance its "predominantly negative" reporting on Islam and Muslims.[24]

In Sharjah, promotion of Islamic activities extends beyond the philanthropic to the commercial sector. Citing the importance of Islamic banking institutions, the chairman of the Sharjah Chamber of Commerce and Industry remarked that "It is important to reinforce Islamic trade all over the world and introduce diversified commercial products, Islamic funding and banking, and *halal* foodstuff. These all comply with *sharia*, which has gained greater global prominence.[25]

Islamic groups serving the Indian and Pakistani communities in the UAE
The very large Indian and Pakistani communities in the UAE are served by numerous organizations, each associated with varying degrees of Islamic activity. Estimates of the number of Indians in the UAE vary; the State Department has estimated as much as 1.75 million,[26] although this seems quite high. A recent report indicated that there are some 60 social and voluntary organizations serving the predominantly Muslim Indian community. Reflecting the challenge of securing funding for the support of Indian organizations, the UAE Indian Islamic Centre, founded in 1971, was unable to initiate construction of a building until 2008 (it was dedicated in 2011). Despite the center's name and predominantly Muslim membership, it involves all religious communities in its activities.[27] By contrast, the Dubai Indian Islamic Centre, located in the emirate with the greatest number of Indian residents, while committed to promoting a wide range of non-religious goals, is more narrowly focused on its Islamic mission. Its members are exclusively Indian Muslims, and an important part of its mission is to "promote and propagate the ideal teachings of Islam," apolitically and free of sectarian bias, through religious teaching centers, where modern subjects are included with religious education. Lacking an endowment, the center provides services through the financial support of sponsors who adopt specific projects.[28] Finally, the Indian Islahi Centre in the Emirate of Ajman, established in 1979, is still more explicitly dedicated to advancing the cause of Islam. It is an "Islamic *Da'wa* (Call)" organization, working particularly among Indians from Kerala, conducting a range of activities designed to spread the message of Islam among both Muslims and non-Muslims.

By contrast, there are few Islamic organizations in the Pakistani community in the UAE. Most Pakistani organizations in the country are business or financial associations or are devoted to providing aid to earthquake and flood victims in Pakistan. However, there is an Ismaili Centre in Dubai, dedicated in 2003 by the Aga Khan, spiritual leader of the Ismaili community, whose followers in the UAE are Pakistani and Indian expatriates. The site for the center was a gift of Sheikh Mohammed bin Rashid Al Maktoum, ruler of Dubai. The Ismaili Centre, which opened in 2008, is meant to serve, in the tradition of Muslim piety, by promoting enlightenment and mutual understanding among the various elements of the Muslim world community. To that end, it carries out a program of cultural and educational activities.[29]

As the above descriptions suggest, there is little if any political aspect to the missions and activities of the Islamic organizations in the UAE, both those serving the Emirati community and those serving the large expatriate Muslim communities. None could be characterized as extreme in any sense. All would appear to fit well within the mainstream of moderate Islamic activity.

Sporadic signs of extremist activity do exist, however. In April 2010, the Federal Supreme Court sentenced five UAE nationals and an Afghan on charges of funding the Taliban, and government officials indicated that those individuals had also planned to establish an al-Qaeda network in the UAE. At the end of the year, two Pakistanis were put on trial, charged with collecting money and recruiting individuals for al-Qaeda.[30] However, the scope of terrorist linkage with South Asia would appear to be limited, and the threat posed by al-Qaeda in the Arabia Peninsula, while it cannot be dismissed, has failed to manifest itself as a credible danger to the state.

ISLAMISM AND THE STATE

The government of the UAE funds or subsidizes nearly all Sunni mosques in the country, while about five percent are privately endowed. It employs all Sunni *imams*, and provides guidance to both Sunni and Shi'a clergy. Shi'a mosques are considered private, but may receive funds from the government upon request. The Shi'a community is largely concentrated in the emirates of Dubai and Sharjah, with the bulk of its members in the former.[31] A number of new mosques have been built, or are under construction throughout the country. Notable among them are mosques in Fujairah and Ajman. The Shaikh Zayed Mosque of Fujairah, although located in one of the smallest and poorest of the emirates in the UAE, will be the second largest in the country when it is completed in 2012. Funded by the Zayed bin Sultan Al Nahyan Charitable and Humanitarian Foundation of Abu Dhabi at a cost of $52.1 million, it follows in the mold of its namesake, the massive Shaikh Zayed Mosque in Abu Dhabi and the Grand Mosque in Dubai as an expression of local pride and the ruling family's commitment to Islam. By contrast, the much more modest mosque recently opened in Ajman (designed to hold 1,500 worshippers, as compared to the Fujairah mosque's 28,000) is being funded by a donation from Mr. Hamad Ghanem Al Shamsi, member of a distinguished and wealthy Ajman family.[32]

In December 2010, plans for four new Shi'a mosques were unveiled by the *Khoja Shia Ithna-Ashari Jamaat* (KSIMC) of Dubai, a private Shi'a religious philanthropy, with the sites for the structures given by the government of Dubai. The members of the Shi'a community, through a Shi'a endowment fund, the *Awqaf Al Jafferiah*, will raise the funds to construct the mosques.[33] There is no evidence that political or extremist motives play a role in promoting the creation of new mosques in the UAE.

From its birth in 1971, the UAE has been supportive of moderate, apolitical Islamic activities, while opposing those that might pose a threat to the government. Shaikh Zayed bin Sultan Al Nahyan, the father of the UAE and its president from inception until his death in 2004, embodied that philosophy both in his rule and in his personal life. He was generous in his support of religious leaders, thus arming himself and the state against attacks from secular or religious quarters.[34] (It should be recalled that the chief threat to the UAE in the first years of its independence was secular radicalism in the region, especially as given expression by the Marxist government of the People's Democratic Republic of Yemen (PRDY), or South Yemen, and the guerrilla movements supported by the PDRY in their efforts to overthrow the government of the Sultanate of Oman, the UAE's immediate neighbor. Because of Zayed's close and positive relations with the UAE religious leadership, and the lack of extremist Islamic activity in the UAE before the events of September 11, 2001, the UAE's connections with those events was shocking and deeply embarrassing to Zayed and the UAE government.

Post-September 11, the government reacted promptly (albeit cautiously) to the threat posed by al-Qaeda. While the generally moderate nature of Islamic belief and practice in the Gulf and the UAE precluded broad support for the ideology of al-Qaeda and other extremist groups, popular antipathy for some U.S. government actions in the Middle East has somewhat complicated the government's cooperation with the United States against Islamic terrorism.[35] In 2002, under Zayed's leadership, a contingent of UAE troops was deployed to Afghanistan to help in the struggle to unseat the Taliban, whose government the UAE had recognized before 9/11. Also in 2002, UAE authorities announced that they had arrested Abd al-Rahim al-Nashri, the apparent mastermind behind the October 12, 2000 attack on the *USS Cole* in Aden.[36]

Following these early actions, in the past few years the UAE has taken significant steps to counter Islamic terrorism, generally winning praise from the U.S. government for its efforts. The State Department noted that the UAE's preferred approach to the problem of Islamic extremism was to deny them a foothold rather than permit their participation in the political process.[37] Abu Dhabi Crown Prince Mohammed bin Zayed also cited a threat from Islamic extremism to the country's educational system, and sought to counter this by devoting considerable resources to modernizing curricula. Following the electoral victory of Hamas in 2006, the UAE informed the U.S. that it considered Hamas a terrorist organization and would not fund it unless Hamas renounced violence. However, it appears that funds continue to find their way from the UAE to Hamas to support housing projects, particularly the rebuilding of homes demolished by the Israeli army. A sense of the amount of financial support is conveyed by a March 2006 transfer of $20 million to Mahmoud Abbas to cover Palestinian Authority salaries and a commitment of $100 million for a Shaykh Khalifa housing complex, as part of humanitarian assistance promised in 2005. The UAE has long honored a commitment to provide financial assistance to the Palestinians on the West Bank and in Gaza.[38]

There is also concern that the UAE, while acting promptly when provided with evidence of a terrorist threat, does not have a proactive strategy for dealing with it.[39] The UAE likewise has exhibited considerable concern over the threat of Shi'a extremism, prompted largely by fears of infiltration by Iranian agents and Iran-linked sleeper cells that could sabotage critical UAE sectors, including energy and transportation. The existence of both was reportedly revealed in 2007 by a former Iranian consul in Dubai. Actions were taken in 2009, not against Iranians but against Lebanese accused of links to Hezbollah, Lebanon's powerful Iranian-supported militia. The UAE deported 44 Lebanese men, who had worked both in the public and private sectors, for sending small amounts of cash to groups affiliated with Hezbollah. The UAE government denied that the action reflected anti-Shi'a discrimination, noting that it was denying government jobs to anyone with "ties to any suspect Islamic group," including those with links to "ideologically strident Sunni groups such as the Muslim Brotherhood."[40]

The case of the Bank of Credit and Commerce International (BCCI), which was infiltrated and used for criminal money laundering and terrorist financing before its collapse in 1991, foreshadowed the complex and difficult problems that gained prominence after 9/11, when the UAE, with U.S. support and urging, tackled the problem of the financing of Islamic terrorism. Al-Qaeda was able to use a correspondent banking network to transfer funds from the Dubai Islamic bank to accounts in the United States for use by the 9/11 hijackers.[41] After 9/11, the UAE Central Bank took steps to counter money laundering. While refusing to ban the traditional *hawala* system of money exchange in wide use between South Asian expatriates in the UAE and their home countries, it imposed strict regulations on it and, in 2004, the bank hosted the Second International Hawala Conference to discuss with delegates from around the world more effective monitoring of informal money flows.[42] While the UAE's efforts against money laundering and terrorist financing have been significant, cause for worry remains. Particular attention focuses on Dubai and its large Free Trade Zone, because of its potential facilitation of a variety of criminal and terrorist activities, including the use of front companies, fraud, and smuggling, as well as exploitation of the *hawala* and banking systems. In 2011, the UAE reported that there had been a significant increase in the number of suspicious activity reports submitted by companies to the central bank for 2010 as compared to 2009. While this very likely reflects an improvement in the monitoring of money-laundering practices, the volume itself is cause for concern.[43]

ENDNOTES

[1] *The 9/11 Commission Report* (New York: W.W. Norton & Company, Inc., 2004), 162, 231, and 168.

[2] "The Muslim Brotherhood and the Salafis in the Gulf, July 2010," on Web site of Almesbar.

[3] Marc Lynch, "MB in the Gulf," *Abu Aardvark* blog, June 10, 2008, http://abuaardvark.typepad.com/abuaardvark/2008/06/mb-in-the-gulf.html.

[4] Samir Salama, "Muslim Brotherhood is Political and not Religious," *Gulf News*, September 22, 2008.

[5] Kenneth Katzman, *The United Arab Emirates (UAE): Issues for U.S. Policy* (Washington, DC: Congressional Research Service, 2010), 2.

[6] Christopher M. Davidson, "Dubai and the United Arab Emirates: Security Threats," *British Journal of MiddleEastern Studies*, 36, no. 3, December 2009, p. 444.

[7] Ibid., 446; reacting to the berthing of U.S. aircraft carriers in Dubai, after their planes had carried out missions to "bombard the Muslims in Iraq and Afghanistan," the organization stated that the UAE's ruling families would "endure the fist of the mujahideen in their faces" if their demand was not met.

[8] Abdul Hamied Bakier, "An al-Qaeda Threat in the United Arab Emirates?" Jamestown Foundation *Terrorism Focus* 5, iss. 25, July 1, 2008, http://www.jamestown.org/single/?no_cache=1&tx_ttnews[tt_news]=5025.

[9] "Terror Network Dismantled in U.A.E.," *Global Jihad*, September 17, 2009; "AQAP Unlikely Behind UPS Plane Crash - US Officials," Reuters, November 11, 2010, http://in.reuters.com/article/2010/11/11/idINIndia-52846520101111.

[10] Bakier, "An al-Qaeda Threat in the United Arab Emirates?"

[11] "US Embassy Cables: Afghan Taliban and Haqqani Network Using United Arab Emirates as Funding Base," *Guardian* (London), December 5, 2010, http://www.guardian.co.uk/world/us-embassy-cables-documents/242756.

[12] Animesh Roul, "Lashkar-e-Taiba's Financial Network Targets India from the Gulf States," Jamestown Foundation *Terrorism Monitor* 7, iss. 19, July 2, 2009, http://www.jamestown.org/single/?no_cache=1&tx_ttnews[tt_news]=35221.

[13] Ibid.

[14] The Muslim sectarian breakdown and population estimate is 5,148,664, based on extrapolation from the UAE's 2005 census. While estimates of the total population vary, most are close to this figure. See "United Arab Emirates," Central Intelligence Agency *World Factbook*, February 22, 2011, https://www.cia.gov/library/publications/the-world-factbook/geos/ae.html.

[15] The statement on religious tolerance in the UAE is from U.S. Department of State, Bureau of Democracy, Human Rights and Labor, 2010 Report on *International Religious Freedom* (Washington, DC: U.S. Department of State, November 17, 2010), http://www.state.gov/g/drl/rls/irf/2010/index.htm.

[16] Ibid.

[17] Malcolm C. Peck, *The United Arab Emirates: A Venture in Unity* (Boulder, CO: Westview Press, 1986), 60.

[18] This may soon change since, in the fall of 2010, through an agreement with the Crown Prince Court, the Gallup Organization opened a new research center in Abu Dhabi to conduct inquiries into attitudes of Muslims around the world. While the initial report which it issued looks broadly at the state of Muslim-West relations, the Abu Dhabi Gallup Center will also perform research specifically on attitudes in the UAE.

[19] In 1998, the country's Ministry of Labor and Social Affairs listed 103 associations, with only three described as "religious." See Munira A. Fakhro, "Civil Society and Democracy in the Gulf Region," 11th Mediterranean Dialogue Seminar: Security and Development in the Gulf Region, NATO Parliamentary Assembly, Doha, Qatar, November 26-28, 2005.

[20] Speech of Sheikh Mohammed bin Rashid Al Maktoum, May 19, 2007, http://www.sheikhmohammed.co.ae/vgn.

[21] Ibid.

[22] For a description of the foundation's activities and the budget and endowment figures, see http://goodgate.org/causes/view/the-zayed-bin-al-nahayan-charitable-and-humanitarian-foundation.

[23] See Tabah's newsletter, *Clarity*, iss. 1, Fall 2010, for a discussion of its programs.

[24] Nazim Baksh, "Beyond Flak Attack: A New Engagement with the Newsroom," *Tabah Foundation Tabah Essay Series* no. 2, 2010|.

[25] Quoted in Islamic Research and Information Center, "Sharjah to Host the Islamic Trade Exhibition and Islamic Countries' Private Sector Consortium," February 13, 2011, http://iric.org/newsdetail.asp?id=780.

[26] See U.S. Department of State, Bureau of Near Eastern Affairs, "Background Note: United Arab Emirates," March 16, 2011, http://www.state.gov/r/pa/ei/bgn/5444.htm.

[27] The number of organizations is given in "Indian Voluntary Organizations in UAE to Be Regularized," February 24, 2011, http://thaindian.com/newsportal/world-news/indian-voluntary-organizations-in-uae-to-be-regularized_100506770.html, and the Indian Centre opening is described in "Pratibha Patil Opens New Indian Islamic Centre Building in UAE," *Pravasi Today*, November 19, 2010, http://www.pravasittoday.com/new-Indian-Islamic-centre-building-in-use.

[28] "Dubai Indian Islamic Centre," n.d., http://diic.org/diic/content/about-us.

[29] Aga Khan, "Speech at the Foundation Laying of the Ismaili Centre in Dubai," by His Highness the Aga Khan, December 13, 2003, http://www.iis.ac.uk/view_article.asp?ContentID=101003.

[30] "UAE Sentences Six Convicted Taliban Agents," *World Tribune*, April 29, 2010, http://www.worldtribune.com/worldtribune/WTARC/2010/me_gulf0354_04_29.asp; See also "UAE Tries Two Pakistanis on Qaeda Links: Report," *Al Arabiya* (Baghdad), December 28, 2010, http://www.alarabiya.net/articles/2010/12/28/131278.html.

[31] "United Arab Emirates," in U.S. Department of State, *2010 Report on International Religious Freedom.*

[32] See "Large Mosque Rising in Fujairah," *Fulairah in Focus* blog, June 6, 2010, http://fujairahinfocus.blogspot.com/2010/06/large-mosque-rising-in-fujairah-uae.html; See also General Authority of Islamic Affairs & Endowments, "A New Mosque for 1500 Worshippers in Ajman," March 15, 2011, http://www.awqaf.gov.ae/Newsitem.aspx?Lang=EN&SectionID=16&RefID=1092.

[33] See KSIMC of Dubai, "Awqaf Al Jafferiah Launches Fund Raising for 4 New Mosque Projects in Dubai," December 14, 2010, http://dubaijamaat.com/latestnewsbloglayout/general-news/591-awqaf-al-jafferiah-launches-fund-raising-for-4-new.

[34] See Malcolm C. Peck, "Zayed bin Sultan Al Nuhayyan," in Bernard Reich, ed., *Political Leaders of the Middle East and North Africa* (New York, NY: Greenwood Press, 1990), 517-518.

[35] See Malcolm C. Peck, *Historical Dictionary of the Gulf Arab States,* 2nd ed. (Lanham, MD: The Scarecrow Press, Inc. 2008), 144.

[36] Sultan Al Qassemi, "The Sacrifice of Our Troops and a Need for Civil Society," *The National* (Abu Dhabi), February 28, 2010, http://www.thenational.ae/news/the-sacrifice-of-our-troops-and-a-need-for-civil-society; Mohammed Nasser, "Military Expert: Al Qaeda Present in the Gulf... but not Active," *Al-Sharq al-Awsat* (London), December 29, 2010, http://www.aawsat.com/english/news.asp?section=1&id=23598.

[37] "US Embassy Cables: Abu Dhabi Favours Action to Prevent a Nuclear Iran," *Guardian* (London), November 28, 2010, http://www.guardian.co.uk/world/us-embassy-cables-documents/59984.

[38] U.S. Embassy Abu Dhabi, "Scenesetter for Counterterrorism Coordinator," April 29, 2006, http://dazzlepod.com/cable/06ABUDHABI1725/2/.

[39] Ibid.

[40] Abdul Hameed Bakier, "Sleeper Cells and Shi'a Secessionists in Saudi Arabia: A Salafist Perspective," Jamestown Foundation *Terrorism Monitor* 7, iss. 18, June 25, 2009, http://www.jamestown.org/single/

?no_cache=1&tx_ttnews[tt_news]=35182.

[41] See Peck, *Historical Dictionary of the Gulf Arab States*, 297; Steve Barber, "The 'New Economy of Terror:' The Financing of Islamist Terrorism," *Global Security Issues* 2, iss. 1, winter 2011, 5, 9.

[42] Ibid.; "Middle East and North Africa Overview," in U.S. Department of State, Office of the Coordinator for Counterterrorism, *Country Reports on Terrorism 2005* (Washington, DC: U.S. Department of State, April 28, 2006), http://www.state.gov/s/ct/rls/crt/2005/64344.htm.

[43] "Huge Global Problem, Small UAE Improvement," *Money Jihad: The Blog Exposing Jihadist Financing*, February 10, 2011, http://moneyjihad.wordpress.com/2011/02/10/huge-global-problem-small-uae-improvement/.

KUWAIT

QUICK FACTS

Population: 2,789,132

Area: 17,818 sq km

Ethnic Groups: Kuwaiti 45%, other Arab 35%, South Asian 9%, Iranian 4%, other 7%

Religions: Muslim 85% (Sunni 70%, Shi'a 30%), other (includes Christian, Hindu, Parsi) 15%

Government Type: Constitutional Emirate

GDP (official exchange rate): $116.2 billion

Map and Quick Facts courtesy of the CIA World Factbook (Last Updated July 2010)

Kuwaiti soldiers and U.S. forces, as well as civilians in Kuwait, have been the targets of sporadic attacks by radical religious elements over the last few years. However, the phenomenon of the global jihad is less prevalent in Kuwait than in many of its Gulf neighbors. Rather, al-Qaeda and other terrorist groups use Kuwaiti soil for logistical activities such as the recruitment of fighters for jihad arenas (Iraq, Afghanistan and so on), and as a hub through which funds, operatives and equipment are transferred to other countries. While counterterrorism measures have been successful in preventing fatal attacks in the country, efforts against facilitation networks serving the global jihad have been lacking so far.

In the political arena, Kuwait preserves a delicate balance, allowing Islamists a presence in the nation's parliament yet vesting in the king power to dissolve parliament when Islamist ideas and criticism cross political red-lines. Kuwait's Islamists, for their part, have exhibited a subtle approach, working to gradually expand the role of sharia law within the day-to-day life of Kuwaitis while remaining loyal to the country's constitution.

ISLAMIST ACTIVITY

Kuwaiti security forces occasionally respond to terror attacks and expose plots inside the small Gulf country. While not a primary target for al-Qaeda and its allies, Kuwait does have a role within the global *jihadi* agenda, for two main reasons. First, its long-standing relationship with the United States, especially since the first Gulf War, symbolizes to a great extent the "imperialist presence" that Washington allegedly represents on the Arabian Peninsula. Kuwait currently hosts an extensive military presence (encompassing some 16 active and 6 inactive bases, and tens of thousands of soldiers) on its soil,[1] which serves as a natural target for al-Qaeda and individual extremists driven by Salafi *jihadist* ideology. The Kuwaiti regime is considered by Islamists to be a target as well, perceived to be pro-U.S. and to an extent "apostate" (not adhering completely to the Islamic, or *sharia*, law). Second, and perhaps more important, Kuwait serves as a transit country for money, equipment and operatives into countries in which "Holy War" is being waged—mainly Iraq, Pakistan and Afghanistan.

There is little known about the organized Islamist presence in Kuwait. However, terror attacks, arrests and interrogations in Iraq and Afghanistan have yielded indications that such a presence exists, though in small numbers. Core *jihadi* militants are estimated to be in the tens, with a few hundred indirect supporters in outer circles.[2]

Al-Qaeda is believed to be operating in Kuwait in a clandestine manner. Geographically, al-Qaeda's activity in Kuwait is supposedly subordinate to "al-Qaeda in the Arabian Peninsula" (AQAP), the official al-Qaeda franchise in the region. AQAP is mainly based in Saudi Arabia and Yemen, and there is little known regarding its actual operational control over *jihadist* activity in Kuwait. Nonetheless, AQAP's agenda strongly suggests that the organization's reach includes the entire Gulf region. Given the rise in attention garnered by AQAP during 2009, especially in Yemen, it is likely that the organization will be slower to expand its reach to the smaller countries under its supposed authority, including Kuwait.

AQAP's focus on Saudi Arabia and Yemen has opened the door for other actors to take part in attack planning against Western targets in Kuwait. Such players can be elements with historical ties to core al-Qaeda leaders in Afghanistan and Pakistan, who for years have been operating independently, carrying out sporadic attacks in the country. In this regard, one should remember that the most senior operational figures of al-Qaeda have Kuwaiti connections. "Bojinka plot" conspirators Abd al Karim Murad, Ramzi Yousef and above all Khalid Sheikh Mohamed (subsequently the September 11 attacks mastermind) were Kuwaiti residents and their large families still live in the country. In the years since September 11th, there have been few and relatively infrequent terror incidents in Kuwait, most of which have been attributed to al-Qaeda (though not always proven to be so).

- In October 2002, one U.S. Marine was killed and a second wounded after two Kuwaiti Muslim extremists opened fire at soldiers in Faylaka Island, about 10 miles off the coast of Kuwait City.[3] Both attackers, one of whom had allegedly pledged allegiance to Osama bin Laden, were killed during the altercation. In an audiotape that surfaced the next month, bin Laden praised the attack as the work of "zealous sons of Islam in defense of their religion."[4] Khalid Sheikh Mohamed, al-Qaeda's former chief of external operations, claimed full responsibility for the attack in his military court hearing.[5]
- In January 2003, two civilian contractors working for the U.S. military in Kuwait were attacked in an ambush a few miles from "Camp Doha," a U.S. military base. One was killed and the other injured.[6]
- In a series of raids conducted in early 2005, Kuwaiti authorities arrested about 30 operatives belonging to a global *jihadi* cell in the country. Amongst those arrested were many nationalities: Kuwaiti, Saudi, Jordanian, and Yemeni. While it is likely these activists were at least al-Qaeda affiliated, several other names were associated with the group, among them "The Brigades of the Two Shrines (i.e., Mecca and Medina) in Kuwait," "Sharia Falcons Squadrons" and "Peninsula Lion Brigades." The arrests followed other incidents during the same period in which Kuwaiti army officers plotted to attack American targets after they were allegedly inspired by anti-U.S. propaganda.[7]
- In a recent incident in August 2009, Kuwaiti authorities arrested members of a "terrorist network" linked to al-Qaeda, who were planning to attack the "Camp Arifjan" U.S. military base. The heavily-protected camp houses 15,000 U.S. soldiers and is used as a logistics base for troops serving in Iraq. The six arrested operatives were of Kuwaiti origin and had also planned to attack the headquarters of Kuwait's internal security agency.[8]

Aside from the aforementioned attacks directed against Western and government targets, the Kuwaiti arena is used for the benefit of other *jihadi* theaters.

First and foremost, Kuwait is an important transit point for the transfer funds, equipment and operatives from the Gulf countries to Pakistan and Afghanistan.[9] This route, only sparsely monitored by Kuwaiti authorities, is a significant pipeline that feeds insurgent and terror groups in the Afghan-Pakistan arenas. Through a network of smugglers and document forgers, Kuwait is used to support these organizations financially and militarily. Operatives of Kuwaiti origin consequently have grown into significant actors within the core al-Qaeda organization in Pakistan, playing both logistical and operational roles.[10]

Similarly, Kuwait has been a source of fighters and suicide bombers used by the al-Qaeda franchise in Iraq (al-Qaeda in Iraq or AQI).[11] Kuwaiti youth were and still are being recruited and sent to Iraq, usually through Syria, to perform their *"jihadi* duty" by fighting Coalition forces. According to one local AQI commander in Iraq, dozens of Kuwaiti nationals were operating in his area of command as of 2008.[12]

One of the greatest threats to Kuwait's national security stems from veteran *jihadists* of Kuwaiti nationality which have completed their "duty" in Afghanistan or Iraq, and wish to put the lessons they learned to use against targets in their homeland. These experienced fighters, who have widespread contacts with other militants and the necessary know-how in guerilla fighting and the construction of bombs, can significantly increase the threat to Western and Kuwait government targets in the country. According to some reports, there have been past attempts to use Kuwaiti veterans in attacks, and senior al-Qaeda officials in Pakistan are known to have entrusted Kuwaiti recruits with secret missions to be conducted in Kuwait.[13] However, so long as more attractive *jihad* arenas exist (such as Iraq, Afghanistan, Somalia, etc.), the phenomenon of experienced Kuwaiti *jihadists* launching attacks on Kuwaiti soil will remain limited.

Terrorism finance is another critical issue in Kuwait. While the source of the problem mainly lies in neighboring Saudi Arabia, there are also several terror supporters known to be operating in Kuwait and providing global *jihadists* in the Middle East and Asia with the funds necessary to carry out their terror activities. As official awareness to this phenomenon has grown, more effort has been put into interdicting and stopping illegal financial transfers. Similar initiatives have also been implemented by the UN Security Council's Sanctions Committee, designed to freeze financial assets and restrict the travel and arms trade of such operatives. The committee's effectiveness, however, is in question.[14]

The final element of Islamist activity in Kuwait lies in the role of fundamentalist religious scholars. The most famous among them is Hamid al-Ali, a Salafi cleric known for his considerable following. Al-Ali, previously a professor of Islamic studies at Kuwait University, has been officially designated by the U.S. government as a global terrorism financier and supporter. His views—at times radical and supportive of al-Qaeda (for instance, issuing *fat-*

was approving of crashing planes into buildings) and at others more aligned with the moderate approach imposed upon him by the regime—reach many young Muslims through the sermons and articles he publishes on the internet. Another important radical religious figure is Suleiman Abu Gheith, a former high school religion teacher in Kuwait City who became a leading figure within al-Qaeda. After joining the group in 2000, Abu Gheith was a member of the al-Qaeda legislation and consulting committee, or *Majles al Shura*. He was also the head of the organization's media committee responsible for propaganda and one of Osama bin Laden's top aides. Abu Gheith departed for Iran as part of a group of al-Qaeda senior leaders in 2003, and is reported to be there under some kind of protective custody.[15] Religious figures such as Hamid al-Ali and Suleiman Abu Gheith play a critical role in the education and indoctrination of Kuwaiti Salafis—especially those that join the armed *jihadist* struggle.[16]

ISLAMISM AND SOCIETY

Approximately 85 percent of Kuwait's total population of 3.4 million is Muslim, but Kuwaiti citizens (which comprise only 1 million of that total) are nearly all Muslims. While the national census does not distinguish between Sunni and Shi'ite adherents, approximately 70-75 percent of citizens, including the ruling family, belong to the Sunni branch of Islam. The remainder, with the exception of about 100-200 Christians and a few Baha'is, are Shi'ites.[17]

Tensions driven by religious differences between the Sunni and Shi'ite elements of Kuwaiti society do exist. However, despite the sectarian violence in neighboring Iraq, Kuwait maintains a relatively stable sectarian environment. The Shi'ites have sought to redress longstanding inequalities and expect an apology for accusations that they constitute a fifth column, allegations that surfaced during the 1980-1988 Iran-Iraq War. Those accusations abated as Shi'ites demonstrated their loyalty during the Iraqi invasion of Kuwait in August 1990. Generally speaking, Shi'ites in Kuwait are less organized politically than Sunnis.

Public support for Islamist activity and radicalism in general is hard to determine in Kuwait. Electoral preferences provide only limited insight, as over two-thirds of Kuwait's population consists of non-citizens who lack the right to vote. As in many other Arab countries, September 11th and the subsequent U.S. invasions of Iraq and Afghanistan ignited and exposed some of the inherent suspicion and hatred towards the West and the U.S. in particular, irrespective of the relatively fruitful cooperation at the governmental level.

Kuwait manages a delicate balance with regard to Islamic devotion. The society remains traditionally Muslim in many ways, although there are no *mutawwa* (religious police) as in Saudi Arabia, nor are the five daily prayer times strictly observed. The Kuwaiti public, however, generally supports Islamic traditions; alcohol, gambling, mixed dancing, and other such "Western symbols" are relatively rare. More extreme anti-Western voices are largely censored out of the country's otherwise fairly free press. They can still, however, easily be found on the Internet or in pan-Arabian media.

A 2007 Pew poll suggested that there is a significant fringe element inside Kuwait that actively supports or sympathizes with more extremist views and activities. According to the survey, 20 percent of Kuwaitis believe that suicide bombings "in defense of Islam" are sometimes justified, and 13 percent express "some confidence" in Osama bin Laden, al-Qaeda's founder and general chief.[18] Even though these views are a minority in Kuwait, they persist under the protective umbrella of some Islamist spokesmen, among them the aforementioned Sheikh Hamid al-Ali.

ISLAMISM AND THE STATE

Kuwait is a constitutional hereditary emirate.[19] The Emir Sabah al-Ahmad al-Jaber al-Sabah is the head of state, and has the power to appoint the prime minister, dissolve the parliament and even suspend certain parts of the constitution. Kuwait's constitution, which was approved in 1962, states that "the religion of the state is Islam and the *Shariah* shall be a main source of legislation." Though driven by Islamic belief, the government is less strict in the enforcement of Islamic law. *Sharia*, according to the constitution, is a "guideline" rather than the formal state law.

The ruling elite has put considerable effort into maintaining order, and is committed to achieving the right balance between recognizing the importance of Islam to its citizens and ensuring stability by blunting the rise of extremism. The Kuwaiti government exercises direct control over Sunni religious institutions and appoints Sunni *imams*, monitors their Friday sermons, and pays the salaries of mosque staff. It also finances the building of new Sunni mosques.[20]

The overall number of mosques in Kuwait exceeds 1,100. Only six of them are Shi'ite, with the rest Sunni.[21] There are no official reports delineating the number of mosques open to a radical interpretation of Islam, but several hints can be found on Kuwaiti Internet websites which suggest the number is derived from the external involvement and financial support of radical elements (mainly from Saudi Arabia).[22]

There are no formal political parties in Kuwait, as they were never regulated by law. Therefore, the 50 seats in the Kuwaiti parliament are occupied by quasi-political groups of Bedouins, merchants, moderate Sunni and Shi'ite activists, secular liberals, nationalists and independents. Instead of political parties, which are illegal, parliament members conform to unofficial national and religiously affiliated blocs.

The Islamist bloc, which functions as a *de facto* political party, is the most influential in the Kuwaiti Parliament. It consists mainly of Sunni Salafis and *Hadas* (Kuwaiti Islamic constitutional movement) members. Its principal long-term goal is to impose *sharia* law in Kuwait. However, the Islamist bloc operates conservatively in the short-term, attempting to wield influence within parliament in order to pass laws that conform to Islamic law. The bloc is composed of devoted Islamists, yet not necessarily extremists. To highlight that balance, they joined hands with Shi'ite Islamists and others to condemn both the September 11th attacks and the U.S. intervention in Afghanistan.

The Islamists have long called for an amendment to Article 2 of the constitution which states that *sharia* is "a main source of legislation," and to have the article rephrased to read that *sharia* is "*the* source of legislation." The amendment passed in parliament, only to be vetoed by the Emir.[23] A similar change requested by the Islamist bloc relates to Article 79, which states that: "No law may be promulgated unless it has been passed by the National Assembly and sanctioned by the Emir." To this the Islamists seek to add "and according to the *Shariah* [sic]."[24]

The Islamist bloc enjoys a changing number of parliament members, usually ranging from 15 to 24 members. Elections have become a common occurrence in recent years, as the parliament was dissolved by the Kuwaiti Emir four times in six years, most recently due to protests over election laws and allegations of fraud. In the 2009 elections, Sunni Islamists won only 13 seats (a sharp decrease compared to the last decade's rise in their power), while Shi'ite Islamists won six seats and Independents, mostly associated with the government, won 21—a significant portion of the total 50 seats of the parliament.[25]

A major development in the 2009 elections was the election of four women parliamentarians for the first time in the country's history.[26] Prior to that poll, men had filled the seats of Kuwait's parliament exclusively for nearly five decades, and it was only four years ago that the country granted women the right to vote and run for office.[27] This phenomenon, along with the loss of seats by Islamists, may signify a more moderate and liberal approach emerging in already relatively modernized Kuwait. To further exemplify the trend, Kuwait's highest court judged in 2009 that female MPs are not obliged to wear headscarves, striking yet another blow to Muslim fundamentalists.[28] Though the majority of Kuwaiti women do wear the *hijab*, it is not compulsory according to the country's law, as it is in the ultra-conservative neighboring Saudi Arabia.

The most prominent Islamic movement in Kuwait is called Al-Haraka al-Dostooriya al-Islamiya, or Hadas, also known as the Islamic Constitutional Movement (ICM).[29] The ICM was established in 1991, following the liberation of Kuwait from Iraqi control in the first Gulf War. The ICM serves as the political front of the Muslim Brotherhood in Kuwait, though in recent years the ICM has grown away from its parent organization. Neither the ICM nor the Muslim Brotherhood retains any legal status. The movement's main legally recognized manifestation is the Social Reform Society, a charitable nongovernmental organization.

ICM traditionally boasts between two and six MPs, yet their influence within the Islamist bloc is significant. It is also by far the best funded and most highly organized entity of the Islamist movements. The ICM, through the clandestine activity of the Kuwaiti Muslim Brotherhood and through the Social Reform Society, is involved in various social, charitable, educational and economic activities. ICM recruits its members via mosques as well as from university campuses, adding many doctors and other academics to its ranks.[30]

The ICM formally seeks the implementation of *sharia* law and the protection of a fairly conservative vision of Kuwaiti traditions and values. Other than leading and supporting the amendments mentioned above, the movement has occasionally introduced legislation in parliament that aims to implement various sharia provisions, such as a law that mandates payment of *zakat*, a religious tax. It is, however, interested in operating within the Kuwaiti constitutional order rather than overturning it.[31]

If able to unite with other Islamists, the ICM's electoral power could help the movement achieve its goal of expanding the role of Islamic law in the day-to-day life of Kuwaitis. Kuwaiti political history, however, suggests strong reasons for skepticism on that score, as the opposition has never been able to maintain a united front for very long, and the Kuwaiti government has tools at its disposal to disperse and even exclude dissenters.[32]

The ICM's gradual success is attributed largely to its discretion in picking its battles with the government and the ruling family. The ICM has strived to position itself simultaneously as an opposition movement and as a party accepting gradualism and the limitations of the Kuwaiti political system.[33] However, the Amir has dissolved the parliament on several occasions, many of which were precipitated by political disputes with the ICM.

It is worth mentioning that the ICM, regardless of its relative success, suffers criticism for being insufficiently dedicated to political opposition. A different line of criticism claims the ICM is masking its true, radical sentiments.[34]

Another factor in the Kuwaiti political system are the Salafis. Their main groups are the Islamic Salafi Grouping (*al-tajamu al-islami al-salafi*) and the Salafi Movement (*al-haraka al-salafiyya*), an offshoot of the former. Both signify a more extreme yet far less organized opposition to the regime. Many Salafi MPs are independent Islamists. A growth in their numbers, and especially the establishment of a wide and organized political movement for the Salafis to work from, might serve as a prelude for the country moving in a more fundamentalist path in the future.

In its fight against radicalization and as a part of the global effort against al-Qaeda, the Kuwaiti regime is implementing policies to control and prevent radical Islamists from engaging in terrorism—although not always doing so sufficiently. In addition to outright arrests and the targeting of Islamist financial flows, the Kuwaiti government has also initiated a number of other counterterrorism measures, including a wide-scale educational program aimed at countering the influence of unchecked radicalism. In addition, Kuwaiti imams are sporadically taken to court by the government, which accuses them of "activities contrary to the function of the Ministry of Islamic Affairs and the mosque."[35]

ENDNOTES

[1]See, for example, "Kuwait Facilities," globalsecurity.org, n.d., http://www.globalsecurity.org/military/facility/kuwait.htm.

[2] No comprehensive and reliable database for *jihadists* in Kuwait. The figures provided represent best assessments by the author, based on material relating to arrests and plots that has appeared in the open source.

[3] Andrew Buncombe, "American Marine On Maneuvers In Kuwait Is Killed By Terrorist Attack," *Independent* (London), October 9, 2002, http://www.independent.co.uk/news/world/middle-east/american-marine-on-manoeuvres-in-kuwait-is-killed-by-terrorist-attack-607899.html.

[4] "Al-Jazirah: Usama Bin Ladin Hails Recent Operations In Bali," *Al-Jazirah* (Doha), November 12, 2002. See full coverage of Bin Laden's statements, as transcribed by FBIS, at http://www.fas.org/irp/world/para/ubl-fbis.pdf.

[5] Verbatim transcript of combatant status review tribunal hearing for ISN 10024, March 10, 2007, 18, http://www.defense.gov/news/transcript_isn10024.pdf.

[6] "Camera May Have Recorded Kuwait Killing," CNN, January 21, 2003, http://edition.cnn.com/2003/WORLD/meast/01/21/kuwait.american/; Steven Gutkin, "Kuwait Terror Attack Kills 2 U.S. Soldiers," *The Battalion Online*, January 22, 2003, http://media.www.thebatt.com/media/storage/paper657/news/2003/01/22/FrontPage/Kuwait.Terror.Attack.Kills.2.U.s.Soldiers-515274.shtml.

[7] Stephen Ulph, "Terrorism Accelerates in Kuwait," Jamestown Foundation *Terrorism Focus* 2, iss. 3, February 2, 2005, http://www.jamestown.org/programs/gta/single/?tx_ttnews[tt_news]=27494&tx_ttnews[backPid]=238&no_cache=1.

[8] Kuwait 'Foils US Army Base Plot,'" BBC, August 11, 2009, http://news.bbc.co.uk/2/hi/middle_east/8195401.stm.

[9] "Walking the Talk: Forum Members Travel to Afghanistan and Iraq (Part 1)," Jihadica.org, June 30, 2008, http://www.jihadica.com/walking-the-talk-forum-members-travel-to-afghanistan-and-iraq-part-1/; "Walking the Talk: Forum Members Travel to Afghanistan and Iraq (Part 2)," Jihadica.org, July 2, 2008, http://www.jihadica.com/walking-the-talk-forum-members-travel-to-afghanistan-and-iraq-pt-2/; "Walking the Talk: Forum Members Travel to Afghanistan and Iraq (Part 3)," Jihadica.org, July 6, 2008, http://www.jihadica.com/walking-the-talk-forum-members-travel-to-afghanistan-and-iraq-pt-3/; "Walking the Talk: Forum Members Travel to Afghanistan and Iraq (Part 3)," Jihadica.org, July 8, 2008, http://www.jihadica.com/walking-the-talk-forum-members-travel-to-afghanistan-and-iraq-pt-4/.

[10] For example, Abu Obeida Tawari al-Obeidi and Abu Adel al-

Kuwaiti, who were killed in Waziristan in early 2009. "Terrorism: Three Al-Qaeda Leaders Killed in US Attack," AKI (Rome), February 5, 2009, http://www.adnkronos.com/AKI/English/Security/?id=1.0.1845929971.

[11] "Video Of Former Gitmo Detainee-Turned-Al-Qaida Suicide Bomber In Iraq," NEFA Foundation, January 2009, http://www.nefafoundation.org/multimedia-prop.html.

[12] "Abu Islam the Iraqi: Kuwaiti Young Men Are Being Manipulated, 25 Of Them Fought With Al-Qaeda in Diyala," *Al-Watan* (Kuwait), July 16, 2008, http://www.elaph.com/ElaphWeb/NewsPapers/2008/7/348810.htm.

[13] Walking the Talk: Forum Members Travel to Afghanistan and Iraq."

[14] David Pollock and Michael Jacobson, "Blacklisting Terrorism Supporters in Kuwait," Washington Institute for Near East Policy *Policywatch* 1333, January 25, 2008, http://www.washingtoninstitute.org/templateC05.php?CID=2709.

[15] "Al-Qaeda Spokesman 'In Iran,'" BBC, July 17, 2003, http://news.bbc.co.uk/2/hi/middle_east/3074785.stm.

[16] Chris Heffelfinger, "Kuwaiti Cleric Hamid al-Ali: The Bridge between Ideology and Action," Jamestown Foundation *Terrorism Monitor* 5, iss. 8, April 26, 2007, http://www.jamestown.org/single/?no_cache=1&tx_ttnews[tt_news]=4112.

[17] U.S. Department of State, Bureau of Public Affairs, "Background Notes: Kuwait," February 2009, http://www.state.gov/r/pa/ei/bgn/35876.htm.

[18] Pollock and Jacobson, "Blacklisting Terrorism Supporters in Kuwait."

[19] U.S. Department of State, Bureau of Public Affairs, "Background Notes: Kuwait."

[20] "Kuwait," in U.S. Department of State, Bureau of Democracy, Human Rights and Labor, *International Religious Freedom Report 2009*, October 26, 2009, http://www.state.gov/g/drl/rls/irf/2009/127351.htm.

[21] Ibid.

[22] See, for example, "Limadha al-Masajed? [Why The Multiplicity Of Mosques?]" *Al-Jarida* (Kuwait), March 15, 2009, http://www.aljarida.com/aljarida/Article.aspx?id=101363.

[23] Nathan J. Brown, "Pushing Toward Party Politics? Kuwait's Islamic Constitutional Movement," Carnegie Endowment *Carnegie Papers* no. 79, January 2007, 10.

[24] Wendy Kristianasen, "Kuwait's Islamists, Officially Unofficial," *Le Monde Diplomatique* (Paris), June 2002, http://mondediplo.com/2002/06/04kuwait.

[25] Michael Herb, "Kuwait Politics Database (in Arabic)," n.d., http://

www2.gsu.edu/~polmfh/database/database.htm; "Kuwait Parliamentary Election, 2009," Wikipedia.org, n.d., http://en.wikipedia.org/wiki/Kuwaiti_parliamentary_election,_2009.

[26] Robert F. Worth, "First Women Win Seats In Kuwait Parliament," *New York Times*, May 17, 2009, http://www.nytimes.com/2009/05/18/world/middleeast/18kuwait.html?_r=1&ref=middleeast.

[27] "Woman Elected In Kuwait Says Gender In Politics Is 'History,'" CNN, May 17, 2009, http://edition.cnn.com/2009/WORLD/meast/05/17/kuwait.women.elections/.

[28] "Kuwait: Headscarf Not A Must For Female Lawmakers," Associated Press, October 28, 2009, http://www.muslimmartyr.com/article/

YEMEN

Throughout its history, Yemen has played the role of safe haven to opposition and terror groups of varying political stripes. Prior to the unification of traditionalist North Yemen and Marxist South Yemen in 1990, the latter was used as a safe haven for a wide array of Palestinian and terror organizations with the support of local authorities. Since unification, this tradition of support for subversive groups and "freedom fighters" has continued, but with radical Palestinian and leftist organizations being replaced by radical and extremist Islamic organizations, especially those in opposition to the Saudi monarchy.[1]

Today, Yemen faces several complex and intertwined challenges: an economic crisis forced by declining oil reserves, severe and expanding water shortages, an ever-increasing population of internally displaced persons (IDPs), "the strain on political stability posed by the impending transition of power in 2013 and multiple internal threats to security"[2] posed by the "al Houthi rebellion in the north, the Southern Movement in the south, and al-Qaeda elements throughout the country".[3]

Widespread anti-government protests in Yemen following the fall of the regimes of Zine el-Abidine Ben Ali in Tunisia and Hosni Mubarak in Egypt have added a new dimension to the daunting economic, social and security challenges faced by the Saleh government. "The combined impact of these issues could collapse the central government or render its security apparatus ineffective,"[4] permitting al-Qaeda and other homegrown Islamist groups to operate freely within the country. The current situation has prompted fears, both at home and abroad, that protest movements could likewise push Yemen to the brink, with serious security implications well beyond the country's borders.

ISLAMIST ACTIVITY

The al Houthi Rebellion

Although the Yemeni military and security forces have been spread thin to deal with a variety of security issues throughout the country, the Saleh regime continues to devote a considerable amount of its resources to suppressing the al Houthi rebellion in the north, which is viewed as the most direct security threat to President Ali Abdallah Saleh's government. The Yemeni government accuses the Shi'a group of "trying to reinstate the clerical imamate" (Islamic government) that ruled northern Yemen for roughly 1,000 years to 1962,[5] while the al Houthis assert they are calling for "freedom of worship and social justice".[6]

The al Houthi rebels have engaged in a guerrilla war with the Yemeni government on and off since mid-2004, a conflict that has led to the death and displacement of thousands. Currently led by Abdul Malik al Houthi, the younger brother of the group's founder Sheikh Hussein Badreddin al Houthi, the group accuses the Yemeni government of "widespread corruption, aligning itself too closely with the United States, allowing too much Wahhabi (fundamentalist Sunni) influence in the country, and years of economic and social neglect in predominantly Shi'a parts of the country."[7]

The current conflict can to be traced back to 2003, when followers of the group 'Believing Youth' shouted anti-American and anti-Israeli slurs inside a Sa'ada mosque where President Saleh was attending service, at a time when he was trying to maintain strong relations with the West.[8] An uprising ensued after the Yemeni government responded by killing Hussein al Houthi in a firefight in September 2004.

The Saleh government, as well as Abdul Malik al Houthi, has expressed readiness for dialogue on a number of occasions, with several cease fire agreements being forged, but thus far all attempts at peace have ended in a resumption of violence. In mid-August 2009 the Yemeni military launched its sixth such operation against the group since 2004, dubbed Operation Scorched Earth, after al Houthi rebels had reportedly "taken control of large swaths of Sa'ada province, blockaded military installations in the north, arrested

Yemeni soldiers, taken control of sixty-three schools, kidnapped teachers and foreigners, and attacked numerous government buildings and mosques."[9] Throughout 2009, the conflict in the north between the Yemeni military and al Houthi rebels escalated; with the Saudi military joining the fight after an incursion onto Saudi soil by al Houthi rebels killed two Saudi border guards that November.[10]

The Saleh government has accused Iran of arming the Houthis. Western officials, however, say there is no firm evidence to support these accusations, and Tehran has vehemently denied them, while simultaneously condemning Saudi Arabia's involvement in the conflict. Meanwhile, the al Houthi rebels accuse Saudi Arabia of supporting Sana'a and aiding its offensives—something which the Saudi government has denied.[11]

Since February 2009, a fragile ceasefire agreement has held between al Houthi rebels, the Saleh government and allied tribes in the country's north. It is hard to say how long the current ceasefire will hold, however, especially as anti-government demonstrations spread and heavy-handed tactics by security forces against protestors increase. The situation could also change drastically if President Saleh were to step down without a plan for transition and a power struggle on political, tribal or religious grounds ensued.

Al-Qaeda

Al-Qaeda has a long-standing presence in Yemen. Elements sympathetic to Osama bin Laden's *jihad* predated the actual formation of al-Qaeda in late 1989, with Yemenis ranking second only to Saudis as members of the *mujahedeen* that fought the Soviet Union in Afghanistan in the 1980s. That war constituted a key milestone in the consolidation of radical Islam in Yemen.

From its inception until the late 1990s, al-Qaeda is known to have maintained training camps in various locations in Yemen.[12] In an October 2009 AEI report, analyst Christopher Harnisch cites examples of al-Qaeda's enduring interest in Yemen stating that, "in a November 1996 autobiography bin Laden provided to the Islamist journal *Nida'ul Islam*, the al-Qaeda chief boasted about supporting the *mujahedeen* fighting against the Communist party in South Yemen in the early 1980s and again in the early 1990s.[13] In 1997, bin Laden reportedly sent an envoy to Yemen to explore the possibility of setting up a base there in case the Taliban expelled him from Afghanistan.[14] The al-Qaeda leader in 2003 listed Yemen as one of six countries most in need of liberation."[15] Yemenites also "continued to train in Afghanistan under al-Qaeda's high command throughout the 1990s"and even up until the U.S. invasion of Afghanistan following the 9/11 terror attacks.[16]

In the immediate aftermath of 9/11, the Yemeni government implemented stiff counterterrorism measures, "including cooperating with the CIA to kill al-Qaeda leader Abu Ali al-Harithi in November 2002." By the end of 2003, however, Sana'a began to lag in its counterterrorism efforts; which "hit a low point in February 2006, when twenty-three al-Qaeda terrorists, including the mastermind of the 2000 *USS Cole* bombing, escaped from a Yemeni prison."[17] An October 2009 report by AEI asserts that "many Western intelligence analysts viewed elements of the Yemeni security apparatus as complicit in the prison break. The more relaxed security situation in Yemen stemmed both from complacency and the government's perceived need to reallocate security resources to address other domestic threats. Such circumstances made Yemen a favorable alternative location for al-Qaeda to plan, train for, and execute attacks against the regimes of Saudi Arabia and Yemen, both of which it views as hypocritical, apostate puppets of the West."[18]

Yemen has come to be viewed as a fragile state on the brink of failure. This potential opportunity has not been missed by al-Qaeda, which has long viewed Yemen as a potential base of operations. This view was a contributing factor in the formation of al-Qaeda in the Arabian Peninsula (AQAP), which represented a merger of Yemeni and Saudi branches of al-Qaeda. Yemen was a likely choice for the newly consolidated al-Qaeda movement to set up shop after the Saudi government imposed a crackdown inside its borders "following a string of deadly attacks throughout the Kingdom between May 2003 and December 2004" against oil company offices, foreign targets, Saudi government offices, and security targets.[19]

Since its establishment, AQAP has emerged as one of the most active branches of the bin Laden network. In 2009, AQAP was implicated in a number of terrorist operations, including: a suicide bombing against a group of South Korean tourists in Hadramawt and a South Korean diplomatic convoy to Sana'a; the attempted suicide bombing of Saudi Deputy Interior Minister Prince Mohammed bin Nayef; and the ambush and killing of seven Yemeni security officials near the Saudi border.[20] AQAP has also claimed responsibility for the attempted Christmas Day 2009 downing of Detroit-bound Flight 253 by Nigerian extremist Abdul Farouk Abumuttalab.[21] The number of Yemeni *mujahedeen* claiming allegiance to AQAP is unknown, although Foreign Minister Abu Bakr al-Qirbi claimed in late 2008 that Yemen was playing host to more than 1,000 *jihadist* fighters and al-Qaeda affiliates.[22]

More recently, AQAP claimed responsibility for the September 2010 downing of a UPS flight in Dubai, although U.S. officials have found no connection between the crash and terrorism, as well as for an attempted cargo plane bomb plot foiled in Dubai and the UK in October.[23]

Simultaneously, AQAP has worked to "establish links and put down roots with the tribes in the Marib, al-Jawaf and Shabwa governorates" of eastern Yemen.[24] The group has been largely successful in building alliances with tribes in the region, and currently feels little pressure from the Yemeni government. The result has been a new boldness on the part of AQAP, manifested through its reconstitution in Yemen and greater activism beyond its borders, in the Gulf region.[25]

The growing threat of AQAP has not been lost on Washington, with senior policymakers and analysts testifying before the House Homeland Security Committee in February 2011 that they "consider al-Qaeda in the Arabian Peninsula, with Awlaki as a leader within that organization, probably the most significant risk to the U.S. homeland".[26]

Al-Qaeda continues to use Yemen's domestic conflicts and demographics to its advantage; to maintain a safe haven while the Yemeni government is focused on the more direct threat posed by the al Houthi insurgency, and now popular protests throughout the country, as well as waiting to capitalize, if the possibility presents itself, on the potential of Yemen becoming a failed state. In the event of a Yemeni failed state, AQAP's capabilities could expand dramatically. Such a situation would enable AQAP to operate all the more freely, and in the absence of a central government, AQAP may attempt to fill the power vacuum. Many analysts view the failed state scenario as "perhaps the greatest appeal that Yemen holds for al-Qaeda" as it would provide the group "with the political and geographic space to operate unhindered; to plan and train for operations, set up training camps, establish safe houses, and shelter top leaders."[27]

The Southern Secessionist Movement

Aside from the al Houthi, the other indigenous threat to the Yemeni government is posed by the resurgent southern secessionist movement. Yemen's Southern Movement, or *al-harakat al-janubiyya*, is described by analyst Katherine Zimmerman of AEI as "an umbrella group for various southern anti-government factions that trace their roots back to the 1994 civil war between northern and southern Yemen."[28] The secessionists are not viewed as Islamist by nature and have not used Islamist rhetoric.

The Southern Movement poses less of a threat to state stability than the al Houthis and has not yet demonstrated that it can sustain a violent insurgency. Indeed, the greatest threat from this movement derives from the fact that the bulk of Yemen's already scarce oil reserves are located in the southern provinces as well as its history of providing a safe haven to foreign opposition and terrorist movements, including al-Qaeda.

The Southern Movement has held massive demonstrations and has clearly stated its grievances to the Saleh government. The grievances expressed by the secessionists include: "economic marginalization (much of the country's oil revenue is generated in the southern provinces but believed to be distributed throughout the country); forced early retirements and insufficient pensions for military officers from the south; and restrictions on press freedoms in the south for newspapers advocating secessionist agendas."[29]

The year 2009 witnessed a deteriorating security situation in Yemen with the Southern Movement's more militant factions increasingly being implicated in assassination attempts on government officials and ambushes on security checkpoints and military convoys, as well as anti-unity demonstrations held by supporters of the movement, which have turned violent on occasion. Despite the occasional violent clashes between demonstrators and the military, as well as the threat posed by the more militant factions to government and military officials, the conflict is still seen as manageable by the Saleh government and reconciliation is still viewed as a real and achievable option.[30] However, recent events have required Sana'a to reassess this view.

Emboldened by the success of popular uprisings throughout the region, the Southern Movement has tempered its calls for succession and joined the youth movements, along with the Houthi rebels and Joint Meeting's Party (JMP), in calling for President Saleh's resignation.[31] As demonstrations have increased in size and spread across major cities in Yemen, so to have violent tactics by security forces in an effort to put down protests. This is especially true in southern Yemen where the regime does not have the tribal support to maintain that it does in the north.

Although the southern movement is not motivated by Islamist ideology and extremism, it does present yet another security threat for the Saleh government, in addition to the al-Houthi rebels in the north and al-Qaeda elements that are using Yemen as a safe haven and base to launch their global jihad. AQAP has been able to manipulate the hydra of a security situation in Yemen and thus far has been kept relatively insulated due to the security priorities of the Saleh government, and a marriage of convenience with elements of the Southern Movement.

ISLAMISM AND SOCIETY

Historically, Yemeni society has been divided along two main religious identities, the Shi'a Zaydi sect primarily followed in the North and Northwest and the Salafi school of Sunni Islam mostly in the South and Southeast. Although no accurate and reliable statistics exist, Salafis are generally acknowledged to represent a majority among a population of 24 million in Yemen, while Zaydis claim around 35 percent of the population.[32] Zaydis are constituents of a Shi'a sect often described as moderate in its jurisprudence.[33]

In his studies Dr. Laurent Bonnefoy of the Institut Français du Proche-Orient, finds that "despite episodes of violent stigmatization orchestrated by certain radical groups, the vast majority of the population is at times indirectly (and most of the time passively) involved in the convergence of the once-distinct Sunni and Zaydi religious identities." He cites one such example of this as President Saleh, who himself is of Zaydi origin but never refers to his primary identity." Dr. Bonnefoy goes on to say that "at the grassroots level, many Sunnis do not mind praying in Zaydi mosques, and vice versa. Consequently, the religious divide only marginally structures political affiliations and adherence to specific Islamist groups."[34]

However, as anti-government protests have threatened his presidency, Saleh has drawn on his Zaydi identity "in an attempt to rally Zaydi tribal solidarity against what he also allegedly framed as a Shafei-led protest movement," even going so far as to suggest that he could be the "last Zaydi president."[35] Such actions have led to criticism that Saleh "is concentrating on solidifying tribal allegiances even at the cost of exacerbating sectarian divisions."[36]

In a November 2008 Chatham House report, journalist Ginny Hill describes Yemen as "an incomplete state where the majority of the population lives without regard to laws made in Sana'a. A corrupt, self-interested government that fails to provide the bare minimum of social services has little relevance and legitimacy outside, and even inside, the major urban areas. With a nascent civil society sector and a flimsy middle class, Yemen is unable to generate sustained momentum for political change. Low literacy rates, unreliable public data and the absence of grassroots democracy inhibit a genuine national debate that would create sustained internal pressure for accountability and reform."[37]

These are just some of the factors that contribute to the appeal of *jihadi* groups in relatively "isolated, underdeveloped regions (such as Marib, Shabwa, al-Jawf, and Abyan) and among peripheral and marginal tribal groups who do not benefit from state investments and infrastructure. It is these specific regions that international donors are targeting in order to undermine violence and support for radical groups through the establishment of development programs."[38]

Many Western observers have focused on the role of al Iman University in Sana'a. The institution has been portrayed by locals as one solely dedicated to Islamic higher learning. But this has not prevented outside observers from charging al Iman with "being akin to a terrorist ideological training camp". This view of al Iman University is primarily due to the fact that it is headed by Sheik Abdel Majid al-Zindani, "who is designated as a terrorist financier by the United Nation's 1267 committee and as a spiritual advisor to bin Laden by the U.S. Treasury Department."[39] It has also been supported by the history of some of its alumni, among them John Walker Lindh, the 'Orange County Taliban' who was captured in 2001 in Afghanistan and sentenced to 20 years in prison for his participation in the Taliban, and by the university's reluctance to open itself up to outside observers.[40] In a journal article for the Jamestown Foundation's *Terrorism Monitor*, Gregory Johnsen argues that the reality probably is somewhere in between the two arguments, with al Iman continuing "to straddle this divide as a legitimate religious institution and as a fundamentalist pipeline."[41]

Yemen's demography, social inequity, tribal societal structure, prolonged civil conflicts, and the absence of an effective central government has created the conditions for the development of homegrown terrorist groups like the al Houthi, as well as a safe haven for foreign fundamentalist and terror organizations. Yemen's education system, which utilizes textbooks containing some degree of anti-American and anti-Israeli ideology, coupled with an employment rate around 35 percent, are factors which play into the vulnerability of young men to be exploited by organizations such as al-Qaeda.[42]

In a statement to the *New York Times*, Princeton University's Gregory Johnsen summed up how uprisings in Yemen could swing in favor of Islamist groups like al-Qaeda. He contended that although a group like AQAP is "nowhere strong enough to make a play for control of the state," should Saleh leave office, raising hopes for rapid change and those expectations are not met, "in a year, that could open the way for al-Qaeda to say, 'You tried Saleh, you tried democracy now you have to try the way of the way of the prophet and the rule of Sharia law.'"[43] Such a situation would not bode well for Yemen's neighbor to the north, Saudi Arabia, and certainly not for U.S. counterterrorism efforts.

Further compounding the issue is the accessibility of weapons through Yemen's vast underground arms market; roughly three guns are said to exist for every one person in Yemen.[44] The Yemeni political and social landscape is replete with tribal leaders and Islamist groups that have the arms and power to deny the Yemeni government a monopoly on the use of violence.

Under these conditions, "piracy, smuggling and violent *jihad* can flourish, with implications for the security of shipping routes and the transit of oil"[45] through the Red Sea to the Suez Canal, further endangering security throughout the region and beyond.

ISLAMISM AND THE STATE

In a March 2009 journal article for The Middle East Review of International Studies (MERIA), Laurent Bonnefoy cites power-sharing as "one of the main features of Yemen's political system" which has also been a source of equilibrium in the country. He points to the "presence of a strong traditional 'civil society' in the form of tribal and religious groups, most of them armed or capable of opposing the state" as a source in "undermining the regime's capacity to monopolize all the levers of power and fulfilling any totalitarian dreams."[46] For years, the regime maintained such power-sharing arrangements out of self-interest (i.e. weakening its enemies, dividing political and religious groups, etc.).

More recently, shifting political alliances have put that system to the test, due in large part to the erosion of the legitimacy and power of the central government. Allegations of widespread corruption, an increasing view of the Saleh government as a U.S. and Saudi puppet by Islamist groups, and growing economic and resource inequity have all contributed to the government's domestic weakness and have also wrecked the equilibrium that the power-sharing model had helped to maintain. Many of these issues have their roots in the fallout from the Afghanistan *jihad* and the unification of North and South Yemen in 1990.

Unification was initially built upon a partnership between the two former ruling parties of North and South Yemen, within the framework of a power-sharing coalition. However, that partnership did not endure, with the Vice President of the coalition government, Ali Salim al-Baid, representing the south, fleeing to the city of Aden and accusing the government of marginalizing the south and attacking southerners in 1993. The conflict that ensued between leaders in the north and south paved the way for increased participation of Islamic groups in the government throughout the 1990s.

Sheik Abdel Majid al-Zindani was a key figure during the initial infiltration of radical Islam in Yemen as a senior Islamic religious leader and prominent Islamic political figure. Zindani was a central activist in recruiting Yemeni *mujahedeen* members for the *jihad* in Afghanistan, as well as himself being a combatant against the Soviets during the 1979-89 war. Upon his return to Yemen, Zindani established the Islah Islamic movement, which later became a political party now headed by Muhammed Abdallah al-Yadum.

Laurent Bonnefoy describes Islah as a "conservative religious movement that calls for social reform in accordance with Islamic principles and is generally described as the Yemeni branch of the Muslim Brotherhood. This party was created in September 1990, bringing together Islamist figures, tribal leaders, and businessmen. The party leadership claims to accept the current constitution, thus appearing to recognize the need to operate within Yemen's democratic framework, but Islah qualifies its support for the constitutional status quo by insisting that *sharia* law should form the basis of all legal rulings. Yemen's constitution already conforms to this position, but it is a very loose interpretation."[47]

After the first multiparty general elections in 1993, Abdel Majid al-Zindani became part of the five-man presidential council, while then head of al Islah,

Abdallah al-Ahmar, was elected as speaker of parliament.[48] As tensions rose with the socialist leaders in the coalition, President Ali Abdullah Saleh agreed to govern with al Islah. With the outbreak of war in May 1994 between the Saleh regime in the north and southern separatists, Zindani condemned the separatist movements in Yemen as a 'foreign conspiracy', and stressed the need both for the unity of Yemen and for allegiance to the regime. Al-Zindani, along with the al Islah party, was easily able to rally the returning veterans of the Afghan *jihad* behind the Saleh regime in the north, as a continuation of the *jihad* that had been waged in Afghanistan against the Marxist regime.

After the victory of Saleh's regime over the southern separatists in July 1994, and with the reunification of north and south Yemen, Saleh rewarded the Afghan veterans for their contribution by incorporating their leaders into the government.[49] One such example of this is Tariq al-Fadli, heir of the sultan of Abyan and former Afghan *mujahidin* leader, who later was appointed by the president to the Majlis al-Shura, the upper house of the parliament. Veteran *jihadists* were thus able to strike, what Bonnefoy describes as "a 'covenant of security' deal with the security services on their return home from Afghanistan;" where they would enjoy freedom of movement within Yemen in return for a promise of good behavior inside the country's borders. During this transition, greater participation by the Muslim Brotherhood could be seen in Yemeni politics, with al Islah members holding several important ministries, including justice, education, trade, and religious affairs.[50]

Throughout the 1990s, and into 2000, formal and informal integration of numerous Islamist groups into the state apparatus continued, with important posts in the army and security forces being held by individuals identifying with various sects of Islam. As a result of the diversity of the security and political body's repression of Islamist groups has been limited, and has also allowed easy access to political and tribal elites for Salafists, Sufis, Zaydi revivalists, Muslim Brothers, and some individuals sympathetic to *jihadist* doctrines.[51]

Al-Islah is well-entrenched Yemen's political landscape and in numerous regions of the country. One region where al-Islah seems to have considerable support is in the former Marxist South, where anti-socialist reaction is strong and which favors Islamist candidates and platforms. Nationally, the Islamist party has won an average of 18 percent of the vote during the 1993, 1997, and 2003 parliamentary elections. Although lack of transparency reduces the significance of these numbers', the influence of al-Islah in Yemen is still significant and should not be ignored.[52] Al-Islah, as one of two major parties in the JMP, a coalition of opposition parties (the other being the Yemeni Socialist Party), will have a significant role in negotiating and shaping any reforms, with or without President Saleh, as anti-government protests continue.

As anti-government protest become larger and more organized, and with security forces becoming more willing to use violence against demonstrators, alliances to Saleh's rule are being tested. Members of the ruling General People's Congress (GPC) have already begun to defect, once loyal tribal leaders have begun to speak out against the regime, and a longtime Saleh supporter added an 'Islamist element' to the turmoil taking grip when one of Yemen's most influential Salafi clerics, Abdel Majid al-Zindani, stood before protestors and pronounced that "an Islamic state is coming." Zindani went on to say that Mr. Saleh "came to power by force, and the only way to get rid of him is through the force of the people."[53]

But while Zindani has publicly backed anti-regime protesters, he seems far from cutting ties with Saleh. In fact, as head of the ulama council, Zindani is working with both the JMP and the regime on a compromise that would allow a peaceful transfer of power.[54] This is just one example of the balancing of alliances currently taking place as the Saleh's regime struggles to maintain its already loose grip on power.

The relationship of the Yemeni government with the United States is a double-edged sword for the Saleh regime. On the one hand, Yemen needs the financial, military and intelligence support to fight the Islamists living within its borders, whether AQAP or the al Houthi rebels. But on the other hand the support Yemen receives from the U.S. plays into the rhetoric of the al Houthi leadership and serves as a recruiting tool for both al Houthi and AQAP.

Saleh continues to walk a fine line with Washington; quietly receiving considerable political support and military aid from the U.S. while at the same time making statements accusing Washington of working to undermine Arab regimes in the region.[55] U.S. government officials, however, maintain that Saleh remains the best partner the U.S. has in its fight against AQAP.[56]

As the Saleh government's relationship with the United States has grown, the alliance between Islamists and the Yemeni government has become increasingly strained. This shift could be viewed in the context of the 1994 transition from the north-south coalition to the north-Islamist alliance that led the Republic of Yemen throughout the rest of the 1990s. In this context, the continued alienation of Islamist organizations may well lead to further deterioration of the Saleh regime's capabilities and intensified conflict between the government and Islamic militant groups like the al Houthi.

As the regime's response to anti-government demonstrations has grown more violent, Saleh's allies in the ruling GPC have begun to break ranks, and traditional tribal support has dwindled. However, as of this writing, the president still appears to have the backing of the more influential tribal confederations in the Yemen, including the Hashid and Bakil. Saleh will need all the friends he can get to weather the storm. This may mean distancing himself from Washington and its fight against al-Qaeda, in an effort to regain the support from al-Islah and other more Islamist supporters, who, along with the northern tribes, have historically been pillars of support for the Saleh government.

ENDNOTES

[1]Shaul Shay, *The Red Sea Terror Triangle* (R. Liberman, trans.) (New Brunswick: Transaction Publishers, 2005), 113-114.

[2] Laurent Bonnefoy, "Varieties Of Islamism In Yemen: The Logic Of Integration Under Pressure," Middle East Review of International Affairs (MEMRI) 13, no. 1, March 2009, http://www.gloria-center.org/meria/2009/03/bonnefoy.html.

[3] Katherine Zimmerman, "Yemen's Southern Challenge: Background on Rising Threat of Secessionism," American Enterprise Institute *AEI Critical Threats*, November 5, 2009, http://www.criticalthreats.org/yemen/yemens-southern-challenge-background-rising-threat-secessionism.

[4] Ibid.

[5] Hamida Ghafour, "Rebel Without A Clear Cause," *The National* (Abu Dhabi), August 21, 2009, http://www.thenational.ae/apps/pbcs.dll/article?AID=/20090822/WEEKENDER/708219838/1306; See also Christopher Harnisch, A Critical War in a Fragile Country: Yemen's Battle with the Shiite al Houthi Rebels," American Enterprise Institute *AEI Critical Threats*, August 31, 2009, http://www.criticalthreats.org/yemen/critical-war-fragile-country-yemens-battle-shiite-al-houthi-rebels#_edn3.

[6] Laurent Bonnefoy, "Varieties Of Islamism In Yemen."

[7] "Yemeni Government Steps Up Assault On Shiite Rebels," *Wall Street Journal*, August 12, 2009, http://online.wsj.com/article/SB125007847389825757.html?mod=googlenews_wsj.

[8] Ghafour, "Rebel Without a Clear Cause."

[9] Christopher Harnisch, "Denying Al-Qaeda a Safe Haven in Yemen," American Enterprise Institute *AEI Critical Threats*, October 30, 2009, http://www.criticalthreats.org/yemen/denying-al-qaeda-safe-haven-yemen#_edn2; See also Nasser Arrabyee, "Ending the Conflict," *Al-Ahram* (Cairo), August 22, 2009, http://weekly.ahram.org.eg/2009/961/re6.htm; See also "The Houthis Control 63 Schools Using them in Sabotage," Almotamar.net, August 12, 2009, http://www.almotamar.net/en/6545.htm.

[10] Abeer Allam, "Saudis tire of Yemen's failure to tame rebels," *Financial Times,* February 17, 2010. http://www.ft.com/cms/s/0/0e5b9944-1be9-11df-a5e1-00144feab49a.html.

[11] Ibid; Katherine Zimmerman and Steve Gonzalez, "Tracker: Saudi Arabia's Military Operations Along Yemeni Border," *AEI Critical Threats*, January 4, 2010, http://www.criticalthreats.org/yemen/tracker-saudi-arabia's-military-operations-along-yemeni-border; Ariel Farrar-Wellman, "Yemen-Iran Foreign Relations," *AEI Iran Tracker*, February 23, 2010, http://www.irantracker.org/foreign-relations/yemen-iran-foreign-relations.

[12] Lawrence E. Cline, "Yemen's Strategic Boxes," Small Wars Journal, Small Wars Foundation, January 2, 2010, http://smallwarsjournal.com/blog/journal/docs-temp/339-cline.pdf; Jonathan Schanzer, Testimony before the House Foreign Affairs Committee, February 3, 2010, http://www.pvtr.org/pdf/ICPVTRinNews/HouseForeignAffairsCommitteeHearing-YemenOnTheBrink-ImplicationsForU.S.Policy.pdf.

[13] Bruce Lawrence, ed., *Messages to the World: The Statements of Osama bin Laden* (London: Verso, 2005), 32.

[14] Jason Burke, *Al-Qaeda: The True Story of Radical Islam* (London: Penguin Books, 2004), 215.

[15] Harnisch, "Denying Al-Qaeda a Safe Haven in Yemen"; See also Lawrence, *Messages to the World*, 32;

[16] Ginny Hill, "Yemen: Fear of Failure," *Chatham House Briefing Paper*, November 2009, http://www.chathamhouse.org.uk/files/12576_bp1108yemen.pdf.

[17] Gregory Johnsen, "Waning Vigilance: Al-Qaeda's Resurgence in Yemen," Washington Institute for Near East Policy Policywatch 1551, July 14, 2009, http://www.washingtoninstitute.org/templateC05.php?CID=3088; "USS Cole Plotter Escapes Prison," CNN.com, February 5, 2006, http://www.cnn.com/2006/WORLD/meast/02/05/cole.escape/index.html; See also Harnisch, Denying Al-Qaeda a Safe Haven in Yemen.

[18] Harnisch, Denying Al-Qaeda a Safe Haven in Yemen.

[19] "Bombers Attempt Attack On Saudi Oil Facility," *New York Times*, February 24, 2006, http://www.nytimes.com/2006/02/24/world/africa/24iht-web.0224saudi.html; Chris Harnisch, "Christmas Day Attack: Manifestation of AQAP Shift Targeting America," *AEI Critical Threats*, December 29, 2009, http://www.criticalthreats.org/yemen/christmas-day-attack-manifestation-aqap-shift-targeting-america#_ednref5; P.K. Abdul Ghafour &Essam Al-Ghalib, "Kingdom Makes Remarkable Headway in Fight Against Terror: Naif," *Arab News*, November 11, 2004, http://archive.arabnews.com/?page=1&section=0&article=54339&d=11&m=11&y=2004

[20] Frederick Kagan and Chris Harnisch, "Yemen: Fighting al Qaeda in a Failed State," *AEI Critical Threats Project*, January 12, 2010, http://www.criticalthreats.org/sites/default/files/pdf_upload/analysis/CTP_Yemen_Fighting_al_Qaeda_in_a_Failing_State_Jan_12_2010.pdf.

[21] Ibid.

[22] Hill, "Yemen: Fear of Failure."

[23] "Al Qaeda Yemen Wing Claims Parcel Plot UPS Crash," Reuters, November 5, 2010, http://www.reuters.com/article/2010/11/05/us-usa-yemen-bomb-idUSTRE6A44PU20101105.

[24] Gregory D. Johnsen, "The Expansion Strategy of Al-Qa'ida in the Arabian Peninsula," Combating Terrorism Center at West Point *CTC Sentinel 2*, iss. 9, September 2009, 8-11, http://www.ctc.usma.edu/

sentinel/CTCSentinel-Vol2Iss9.pdf.

[25] Ibid.

[26] Michael Leiter, Statement before the U.S. House of Representatives Committee on Homeland Security, February 9, 2011, http://www.nctc.gov/press_room/speeches/Transcript-HHSC_Understanding-the-Homeland-Threat.pdf.

[27] Harnisch, "Denying Al-Qaeda a Safe Haven in Yemen"

[28] Zimmerman, "Yemen's Southern Challenge."

[29] Ibid.

[30] Bonnefoy, "Varieties Of Islamism In Yemen."

[31] "Popular Protests in North Africa and the Middle East (II): Yemen between Reform and Revolution," International Crisis Group *Middle East Report* no. 102, March 10, 2011, http://www.crisisgroup.org/~/media/Files/Middle%20East%20North%20Africa/Iran%20Gulf/Yemen/Popular%20Protest%20in%20North%20Africa%20and%20the%20Middle%20East%20_II_%20Yemen%20between%20Reform%20and%20Revolution.ashx.

[32] Bonnefoy, "Varieties Of Islamism In Yemen."

[33] Bernard Haykel, *Revival and Reform: The Legacy of Muhammad al-Shawkani* (Cambridge: Cambridge University Press, 2003), 151.

[34] Laurent Bonnefoy, "Les identités religieuses contemporaines au Yémen: convergence, résistances et instrumentalisations," *Revue des mondes musulmans et de la Méditerranée* 121-122, April 2008, 201-15; See also Bonnefoy, "Varieties Of Islamism In Yemen."

[35] "Popular Protests in North Africa and the Middle East (II)."

[36] Ibid.

[37] Hill, "Yemen: Fear of Failure."

[38] Laurent Bonnefoy and Renaud Detalle, "The Security Paradox and Development in Unified Yemen (1990-2005)," in Michael Lund and Necla Tschirgi, eds., *The Security/Development Nexus* (Boulder: Lynne Reiner, 2010); See also Bonnefoy, "Varieties Of Islamism In Yemen."

[39] Jane Novak, "Arabian Peninsula al Qaeda groups merge," *The Long War Journal*, January 26, 2009 , http://www.longwarjournal.org/archives/2009/01/arabian_peninsula_al.php ; See also Lawrence E. Cline, "Yemen's Strategic Boxes," Small Wars Journal, January 2, 2010, http://smallwarsjournal.com/blog/journal/docs-temp/339-cline.pdf.

[40] Lawrence E. Cline, "Yemen's Strategic Boxes."

[41] Gregory D. Johnsen, "Yemen's Al-Iman University: A Pipeline for Fundamentalists?", Terrorism Monitor 4/22, Jamestown Foundation, 16 November 2006.

[42] Harnisch, "Denying Al-Qaeda a Safe Haven in Yemen;" See also "Yemen Unemployment Rate," Index Mundi, n.d., http://www.index-mundi.com/yemen/unemployment_rate.html;

[43] Laura Kasinof and Scott Shane, "Radical Cleric Demands Ouster of Yemen Leader," *New York Times*, March 1, 2011, http://www.nytimes.

com/2011/03/02/world/middleeast/02yemen.html?_r=1.

[44] "Yemen Stems Weapons Trade," Saba Net, September 23, 2008, http://www.sabanews.net/en/news164686.htm; See also "Yemen Moves to Control Arms Trade," *Al-Motamar* (Sana'a), April 25, 2007, http://www.almotamar.net/en/2463.htm.

[45] Hill, "Yemen: Fear of Failure."

[46] Bonnefoy, "Varieties Of Islamism In Yemen."

[47] Ibid; And for a detailed examination of Islah's relations with the government, see also Amr Hamzawy, Between Government and Opposition: The Case of the Yemeni Congregation for Reform, Carnegie Papers, (Washington: Carnegie Endowment for International Peace, November 2009).

[48] Bonnefoy, "Varieties Of Islamism In Yemen."

[49] Peter Bergen, *Holy War Inc: Inside the Secret World of Osama Bin Laden* (London: Weidenfield & Nicolson, 2001), 190-191.

[50] Bonnefoy, "Varieties Of Islamism In Yemen."

[51] Ibid.

[52] Jillian Schwedler, "The Yemeni Islah Party: Political Opportunities and Coalition Building in a Transitional Polity," in Quintan Wiktorowicz, ed., *Islamist Activism: A Social Movement Theory Approach* (Bloomington: Indiana University Press, 2003), 205-29; See also *Faith in Moderation: Islamist Parties in Jordan and Yemen* (Cambridge: Cambridge University Press, 2007), 280.

[53] Kasinof and Shane, "Radical Cleric Demands Ouster of Yemen Leader."

[54] "Popular Protests in North Africa and the Middle East (II)."

[55] Ahmed al-Haj, "Yemeni President says U.S., Israel Behind Unrest," Associated Press, March 1, 2011, http://www.huffingtonpost.com/2011/03/01/yemen-protest-saleh_n_829594.html; Kasinof and Shane, "Radical Cleric Demands Ouster of Yemen Leader."

[56] Kasinof and Shane, "Radical Cleric Demands Ouster of Yemen Leader."

EGYPT

QUICK FACTS

Population: 80,471,869

Area: 1,001,450 sq km

Ethnic Groups: Egyptian 99.6%, other 0.4%

Religions: Muslim (mostly Sunni) 90%, Coptic 9%, other Christian 1%

Government Type: Republic

GDP (official exchange rate): $190.2 billion

Map and Quick Facts courtesy of the CIA World Factbook (Last Updated June 2010)

Egypt has played a central role in the history and the development of Islamism. In 1928, an Egyptian teacher named Hassan al-Banna founded the world's first modern organized Islamist movement. That group, named the Muslim Brotherhood, soon conceived an ideological framework that would go on to inspire most contemporary Islamists.

From the Nasser years to the recent overthrow of the Mubarak regime, the Muslim Brotherhood, although officially outlawed, constituted the major opposition group within Egypt's political system as well as the most influential force within society. A significant reorientation of the movement's ideology and action occurred in the 1990s, when the Muslim Brothers began distancing themselves from violence and their relationship to the Egyptian regime became comparatively more peaceful (albeit fragile). During that time, despite repeated crackdowns on its members, the movement was granted increasing space to expand its grip on civil society, while the state's concurrent repression of the country's democratic and secular opposition served to further reinforce the Brotherhood's outreach. The Brotherhood, for its part, long refrained from attacking the Mubarak regime, while the latter utilized this status quo to slow the pace of democratization and reforms, arguing that political liberalization would lead to the emergence of an Islamist state.

With certain nuances, many of the stages of development undergone by the Brotherhood occurred in other Egyptian Islamist groups as well. After a long period of confrontation with Cairo, the "Islamic Group" (Al-Gamaʿa al-Islamiyya) and "Islamic Jihad" (Al-Jihad) gradually renounced the use of violence, along a dynamic of "deradicalization" in their ranks.[1] However, the crackdowns and terrorist attacks of the last decade serve to remind us that there still exists a possibility for renewed violence in Egypt, especially now that Mubarak has left power. A group of radicals, Salafists in particular, continues to criticize the moderate course of Egyptian Islamism as at variance with the goal of establishing an Islamic state.[2]

After decades of repression of Islamists, the "Lotus Revolution" of February 2011 has opened a qualitatively new phase in Egypt's history. With the once-banned Brotherhood now finding itself propelled into prominence, an intense debate is underway over what role Islamists will play in Egyptian politics and whether they will ultimately attain power. The self-proclaimed "moderate" Muslim Brothers have recently expressed their readiness to serve as an alternative to Mubarak's "corrupt" era by bringing morality back into domestic politics and tackling poverty and unemployment. However, the Brotherhood's ascendance as a whole could also mean the affirmation of more radical narratives and worldviews—with potentially serious repercussions at the regional level.

ISLAMIST ACTIVITY

Egyptian Islamist movements have been active for decades, and reemerged in the public spotlight during the major wave of terrorist attacks that took place between 2003 and 2006 at several Red Sea seaside resorts, and in Cairo with the February 2009 bombing that killed several foreign tourists and locals.[3] These attacks marked an abrupt end to a period of relative moderation of Islamist groups, and served to highlight the fragility of the relationship between the now-defunct Mubarak regime and radical opposition forces.

Historically, three main Islamist movements have been present in Egypt. The first and most important is the *Muslim Brotherhood (Al-Ikhwan al-Muslimin)* founded in 1928 by Hassan al-Banna, the ideology of which states that a true "Islamic society" should be one in which all state institutions and the government obey strict Koranic principles.[4] Al-Banna, a teacher from a modest background, was heavily influenced by Syrian-Egyptian Salafist apologist Muhammad Rashid Rida, for whom a return to the ancestral foundations of Islam was the only solution to purge Muslim societies of Western influences and colonialism.[5] Initially, al-Banna's ambitions were moderate, and focused on moral and social reform within society. But his followers radicalized in the late 1940s as a result of the country's deepening political turmoil. Al-Banna's legacy was spread and developed by another key figure, Sayyid Qutb, who became the Brotherhood's chief leader in the 1950s and authored the famous Islamist manifesto *Milestones* (*Ma'alim fi-l-Tariq*) in which he calls Muslims to fight "paganism" (*jahiliyya*) through offensive *jihad* until the establishment of a united Islamic community worldwide.[6]

In the initial decades following its creation, the Muslim Brotherhood spread across the Islamic world. In the process, it provided many Islamists with inspiration in their attempts to establish Islamic states in their own countries, and to advocate for violent struggle as a means to achieve this goal. Due to its influence, the movement was officially outlawed in Egypt in 1954 and remained illegal until the February 2011 "Lotus Revolution", although it was largely tolerated by the former regime. Indeed, the primary strength of the group has been its ability to adapt with the times, and to the needs of its constituents; specifically, its leaders and members have succeeded in developing large social networks that offer basic services, jobs and healthcare to impoverished Egyptians. This impressive web of charities has allowed the Brotherhood to step in where the state had largely failed and to expand its grip over all levels of society, making it one of the most powerful grassroots Islamist movements in the region.

A second notable Islamist movement is the *Islamic Group (Al-Gama'a al-Islamiyya)*, which emerged in the late 1970s as a student offshoot of the Muslim Brotherhood. It was first active on university campuses and carried out further recruiting within Egyptian prisons, as well as in the country's poor urban and rural areas. Although loosely organized, the group was reportedly involved in the 1981 assassination of President Anwar Sadat, and in a series of attacks during the 1980s and 1990s aimed at deposing Egypt's secular, autocratic government and replacing it with an Islamic theocracy. These attacks included the 1997 killing of Western tourists in Luxor, the attempted assassination of President Hosni Mubarak in Ethiopia in 1995, the Cairo bombings of 1993, and several other armed operations against Egyptian intellectuals and Coptic Christians. The movement's spiritual leader, Umar Abd al-Rahman, was connected to Ramzi Yusuf, the perpetrator of the first World Trade Center bombing in 1993.[7] (Rahman and nine followers were subsequently arrested and convicted in New York of plotting to blow up the United Nations headquarters, the New York Fed, the George Washington Bridge, and the Holland and Lincoln Tunnels.) In 1999, the Islamic Group declared a unilateral ceasefire in its longstanding struggle against Cairo. This declaration marked a major ideological shift, and was accompanied by a steady drift away from the use of violence. While it has not dissolved, the Islamic Group's members have not claimed responsibility for any armed attack since.[8]

The third group of note is the *Islamic Jihad (Al-Jihad)*. Active since the 1970s, it was officially formed in 1980 as a result of the merger of two Islamist cells led by Karam Zuhdi and Muhammad Abd al-Salam Faraj. Faraj's famous manifesto, *The Absent Duty (Al-Farida al-Gha'iba)*, laid out the ideology of the new movement.[9] Like affiliates of the Islamic Group, members of the Islamic Jihad form a relative minority within Egypt's Islamist spectrum and are mostly former members of the Brotherhood. Some are believed to have fought alongside the Afghan *mujahideen* in the 1980s against the Soviet Union. The organization's stated objective was to overthrow the Egyptian "infidel" regime and establish an Islamic government in its place, but also to attack U.S. and Israeli interests in Egypt and abroad. The group is famous for having orchestrated the elimination of President Anwar al-Sadat in 1981, and for additional efforts to eliminate Egyptian government members in the early 1990s. It is also believed to have attacked Egypt's embassy in Pakistan in 1995 and to have been involved in planning bombings against U.S. embassies in Kenya and Tanzania in 1998. In June 2001, the group merged with al-Qaeda to form a new entity, called "*Gama'a Qa'idat al-Jihad*" and headed by Osama bin Laden's second-in-command, Ayman al-Zawahiri.[10]

Over time, this landscape has evolved considerably. One of the most significant changes has been a gradual "deradicalization" of Islamist movements and their ideological abandonment of violence. This process has primarily focused on the changing attitudes of many Islamists toward the use of terror; while the ideology of Egyptian Islamist groups might remain radical and anti-democratic in nature, there has been tangible movement away from violence as a vehicle by which to impose their political views.

In the late 1970s and early 1980s, the Muslim Brotherhood began undergoing broad deradicalization, and increasingly disavowed *jihad* in favor of political moderation. Hassan al-Hudaybi, the movement's supreme guide, released a book in 1969 entitled *Preachers not Judges*, in which he justified the decision to reject violence and developed a series of theological counterarguments to Qutb's radical views.[11] Under his influence and that of his successor Umar al-Tilmisani, the Brotherhood gradually distanced itself from armed action, gave an oath to Sadat not to use violence against his regime, and even named him a "martyr" after he was killed.[12] This ideological shift drew condemnation from other Islamist groups, most notably the Islamic Jihad and its commander Ayman al-Zawahiri, who severely condemned the Brotherhood's reorientation in a book entitled *The Bitter Harvest: The Muslim Brotherhood in Sixty Years (Al-Hasad al-Murr: Al-Ikhwan al-Muslimun fi Sittin 'Aman)*.[13]

A number of factors were necessary for this deradicalization to take root. Islamist ideas first had to be delegitimized through rational and theological arguments, with the process supported by charismatic and authentic former *jihadists*. One of the most prominent instances of this trend occurred within the Islamic Group. In July 1997, during a military tribunal, one of the group's activists, Muhammad al-Amin Abd al-Alim, read a statement signed by six other Islamist leaders that called on their affiliates to cease all armed operations in Egypt and abroad.[14] While it elicited considerable controversy within the Group, the statement heralded the beginning of its deradicalization. In March 1999, the group's leadership launched an "Initiative for Ceasing Violence" and declared a unilateral ceasefire. Ideologues and leaders— widely respected within the larger grassroots movement, and many still held in Egyptian prisons—were able to convince their base to renounce armed struggle and support their new course by authoring a series of texts to provide the ideological legitimation for their rejection of violence. Four books were issued in January 2002 under the title of *Correcting Conceptions (Silsilat Tashih al-Mafahim)*, addressing the reasons behind the Islamic Group's ideological reorientation and explaining why *jihad* in Egypt had failed. Twelve others followed, offering a critique of al-Qaeda's extreme ideology.[15]

A second factor that contributed to the deradicalization of Islamist movements was their interaction with external groups, among them "moderate" Islamists and non-Islamists. This, surprisingly, occurred within Egypt's prison facilities, where inmates discussed their beliefs and tactics, with such interactions resulting in the deradicalization of many prisoners. The Muslim Brothers were the first to undergo such a process following the execution of Sayyid Qutb in 1966. Members of the movement began questioning the relevance of *jihad* as a way to combat the government, and chose to reject violence. Another notable example of this positive dynamic—all the more significant since the trendline elsewhere has been toward greater radicalization within prisons—was the interaction between the Islamic Group and the smaller, more radical Islamic Jihad that began in the 1990s and culminated in 2007 when the former finally embraced moderation. Deradicalization efforts were led by the movement's former leader Sayyid Imam al-Sharif—also known as Abd al-Qadir Ibn Abd al-Aziz or "Dr. Fadl." His *Document for the Right Guidance of Jihad in Egypt and the World (Tarshid al-'Amal al-Jihadi fi Misr wa-l-'Alam)* had an enormous impact within prisons and led numerous inmates to renounce returning to *jihad*.[16]

Eventually, the state's use of repression coupled with inducements contributed as well to this broad deradicalization dynamic.[17] Following the September 11, 2001 terrorist attacks, the Egyptian regime—in an effort to appease Western anger—increasingly mobilized its resources to tame *jihadists*. In the case of the Islamic Group, it provided fighters with pensions, and the Interior Ministry offered other inducements such as business grants to redeemed

Islamists.[18] In addition, the success of Egyptian security forces in suppressing radical movements convinced the leadership of such groups that armed violence was no longer a favorable method to achieve their goals. Many came to believe that the plight of Islamists in prison was proof that God no longer supported their actions.

Yet, many of the Islamist groups that have undergone ideological and organizational deradicalization have faced difficulties in imposing the same on their membership. Attempting to convince low- and mid-level *jihadists* to renounce terrorism carries the risk of mutiny and internal factionalization. The case of the Islamic Jihad, where deradicalization has only been partially successful, is instructive in this respect. While the group's leaders have publicly abandoned violence, some affiliated factions have refused to renounce *jihad*, sometimes even leaving the movement (as one cell that is now openly allied with al-Qaeda did). The Islamic Group has faced similar difficulties. In a recent interview, Nagih Ibrahim, one of its leading ideologues, emphasized that although the group's formal rejection of violence had obviously helped limit the spread of violent Islamism in Egypt, such ideological revisions had had less impact on younger generations, especially on those sympathetic towards or active within hard-line *jihadist* groups such as al-Qaeda.[19] Also, he noted that de-radicalized fighters—many of whom generally have no education or skills—remained exposed to Islamist ideology (and open to a possible return to armed struggle) due to the state's failure to address their grievances.

Cases of re-radicalization within the Muslim Brotherhood have also been particularly troubling. Perhaps the most compelling evidence of this tendency has been the group's unprecedented affiliation with, and public support for, terrorist movements in recent years, such as Iranian-backed Hamas (itself a Brotherhood offshoot that always gave preference to violence) and the Hezbollah Shi'ite militia. In May 2009, following the dismantlement of a Hezbollah cell in the country, the Brotherhood took the unpopular position of supporting the group despite its repeated violations of Egypt's sovereignty. The group's former supreme guide, Muhammad Mahdi Akif, directly contradicted Cairo by declaring that Hezbollah "[did] not threaten Egyptian national security."[20] As well in 2009, during Israel's Operation Cast Lead in the Gaza Strip, the Brotherhood issued a communiqué demanding, among other things, the expulsion of the Israeli ambassador from Cairo, the opening of the Rafah crossing to Gaza, a cut-off of gas and oil supplies to Israel, and that all Arab governments "bolster the resistance and support [Hamas] by every possible means."[21] Akif's deputy, Ibrahim Munair, went one step further, condemning Egypt's relations with Washington, and telling *Al-Alam* television that the group "[wanted] to send a message to the Zionist entity, which supports [the Mubarak regime], and to the West, especially America."[22]

ISLAMISM AND SOCIETY

The terrorist attacks that hit Egypt between 2003 and 2009 led many to conclude that homegrown Islamism was on the rise again and that, quite paradoxically, the "deradicalization" of Islamist movements on a political level had brought about new and more radical discourses within Egyptian society. In particular, the quick rise and spread of Salafism in Egypt has been emblematic of the success of radical Islamists to rally the country's youth to their ideology.[23]

Besides, the complex combination of severe political repression and extremely tough economic conditions faced by most Egyptians has contributed to this reradicalization of the society at large. Inspired by Saudi Wahhabis, Salafists consider that the only true path is to abide by the practices of the first Muslims (*sahaba*) and that anything that deviates from the strictly literal interpretation of the Koran is innovation (*bidaa*) and therefore apostasy (*kufr*). Although few Egyptians openly identify themselves as Salafists, popular thinking has been critically influenced by this puritanical approach to faith in the last decade, which has reached into all sectors of society, as evidenced by the mounting number of women wearing the *niqab* (full veil) or men growing their beards. Beyond the traditional role of radical imams in mosques, television satellite channels with an overt Salafist tone—*Al-Naas* and *Al-Rahma* for instance—have also gained unprecedented audience.[24]

In recent years, Salafists have increasingly targeted Egyptian religious minorities. The January 1, 2011 blast at an Orthodox Coptic church in Alexandria which killed 23 and was allegedly carried out by al-Qaeda, has been particularly emblematic of the rise of anti-Christian sentiment in Egypt, and of the country's growing religious polarization.[25] This attack had been preceded in January 2010 by the killing of six Coptic Christians exiting a church in Naga Hammadi, Upper Egypt. Copts represent ten percent of Egypt's population. This community has been politically marginalized since Nasser's 1952 coup and has regularly accused the former regime of persecuting its members, a claim largely fueled by the absence of official responses to the Islamist violence against Christians. In the 1990s, dozens of Copts were killed by Islamists. These murders were accompanied by increasing attacks on Western tourists. By 1998, the situation had noticeably improved for the Copts and Pope Shenouda III himself declared that his community was no longer subject to coercion. Yet these events, and other similar incidents—anti-Coptic riots in Alexandria in 2005, and an attack on a Coptic Church in 2008—

combined with the rise of Islamists in the post-Mubarak era, could worsen sectarian violence.

Indeed, Islamists of Salafist sensibility appear to have grown increasingly intolerant towards Christians. In February 2009, for instance, a Salafist cleric called for the "Islamization" of Coptic women in order to destroy apostasy.[26] For Salafists, Copts are not citizens but *dhimmis*—a religious minority subjected to Muslim rule. They are commonly portrayed on Salafist television channels as infidels who conspire against Islam. Salafists also daily express their hatred on online forums and websites, often calling for violent attacks on them.[27]

It is interesting to note that Salafists have also targeted other sects such as Sufis, a mystical branch of Islam accused of "polytheism" for worshiping sheikhs and building mosques at their shrines.[28] A recent ban on *dhikr* (the Islamic devotional act of Sufi orders) was a victory for Salafists over moderate Sufism. Besides, Salafists regularly call for the banning of all Sufi ceremonies and succeeded in 2008 when the birthday celebration (*mawlid*) of the Prophet's granddaughter Zainab, was officially outlawed because of alleged risks of swine flu contagion as reported by Egyptian authorities. In addition to bashing Sufis as infidels, Salafists have also accused them of encouraging sin and debauchery by mixing the sexes at the shrines and during their rituals—which Salafists see as evil. They point to the mosque of Ahmad al-Badawi in Tanta—where the founder of the Sufi Ahmadiyya order is buried—which does not enforce segregation between men and women, except during prayers.

ISLAMISM AND THE STATE

From the 1960s until Mubarak's ouster in early 2011, the Egyptian state waged a continuous campaign against Islamists, detaining militants, jailing leaders, and cracking down on their finances. In particular, the official crackdowns on the Muslim Brotherhood were largely a response to its political gains and to the threat that its members posed to the ruling National Democratic Party (NDP). In 2005, the group won 88 seats in the country's national assembly—20 percent of the legislature—through "independent" candidates, thereby forming the largest political opposition bloc to Mubarak.

In 2007, in a clear attempt to curtail the Brotherhood's political participation, the Egyptian government engineered constitutional amendments and a restrictive new electoral law making it nearly impossible for Muslim Brothers to participate in either parliamentary or presidential polls. The electoral law outlawed all political activities and parties "based on any religious background or foundation," thereby targeting Islamist groups.[29] The year after, these restrictions resulted in the rejection of more than 800 Muslim Brothers as candidates for local council elections and the movement overall failing to participate in elections for professional lawyers and journalist syndicates. Additional constitutional changes also extended the "temporary" emergency law enforced after the assassination of Sadat in 1981 with the adoption of a new anti-terrorism law (article 179) that while pretending to protect democratic rights provided security forces with far-reaching powers to crack down on Islamists. The former regime also arrested many of the group's mid and high-level members, including the leader of its guidance council, Abd al-Muanim Abu al-Fatuh, in 2009.[30] This combination of preventive and repressive measures, along with the massive fraud that stained Egypt's December 2010 parliamentary polls, led the Brotherhood to temporarily withdraw from politics and forfeit all of its seats in the national assembly.[31]

Overall, the Brotherhood's ideological posture was significantly affected by these waves of repression. Over the last few years, the movement has undergone some sort of internal identity crisis, with growing ideological divergences within its ranks—particularly among the group's conservative old guard, its reformist branches, and a new generation of activists. These cleavages first emerged in June 2008 during the group's guidance council elections, when conservative elements conducted a campaign intended to remove reformers and marginalize their influence. In December 2009 and January 2010, during internal balloting aimed at selecting the 16 executive committee members of the "guidance council" (*shura*) and replace its leader Muhammad Mahdi Akif, the group bypassed several younger, more liberal incumbents who had gained prominence—including Akif's deputy, Muhammad Habib, a reformist strongly opposed to violence[32]—and empowered a conservative leadership instead.[33] The group's new and controversial supreme guide, Muhammad Badi, is known as a hardline Salafist devoted to the spirit and methods advocated by Qutb, with whom he was jailed in the 1960s.[34] For some, Badi's appointment and the renewed emphasis laid on religious matters constitute a regression for the movement that disengages from intellectual and political debate and have thus become less appealing to younger members.

While the apparent shift of Muslim Brothers towards a more conservative direction does not necessarily mean that the group intends to return to violence any time soon, such a scenario cannot be completely discarded. Even though the movement condemned most of the terror attacks that have hit Egypt in the past, some radical elements could very well choose to resume violence if their demands, both political and economic, are not heard by the future government.[35] Similarly, the threat of a reradicalization of Egypt's

Islamists remains. Several little-known violent offshoots of the Brotherhood, like the "Abdallah Azzam Brigades in Egypt" or the "Holy Warriors of Egypt," are believed to have been behind some of the terrorist attacks that hit the country since 2003.[36] In 2010, a Salafist group suspected of spreading *jihadist* ideology and accusing society and state institutions of apostasy was also arrested.[37]

ENDNOTES

[1]On the "deradicalization" of Egyptian Islamist movements, see Omar Ashour, *The Deradicalization of Jihadists: Transforming Armed Islamist Movements* (London: Routledge, 2009); Omar Ashour, "Lions Tamed? An Inquiry Into The Causes Of De-Radicalization Of The Egyptian Islamic Group," *Middle East Journal* 61, no. 4 (2007), 596-597; Rohan Gunaratna and Mohamed Bin Alia, "De-Radicalization Initiatives In Egypt: A Preliminary Insight," *Studies in Conflict & Terrorism* 32, no. 4 (2009), 277-291.

[2] On the Salafist trend in Egypt, see Chris Heffelfinger, "Trends in Egyptian Salafi Activism," Combating Terrorism Center (CTC) at West Point, December 2007, http://www.ctc.usma.edu/publications/pdf/Egyptian-Salafi-Activism.pdf.

[3] Jan Künzl, "Is Terror Coming Back To Egypt?" *Internationaler Terrorismus*, April 22, 2009, http://www.e-politik.de/lesen/artikel/2009/is-terror-coming-back-to-egypt

[4] For an overview of the Muslim Brotherhood's formative ideology, see Hassan al-Banna's writings and memoirs, among which the *Letter To A Muslim Student* posits the core principles of the movement. For the English translation, see http://www.jannah.org/articles/letter.html.

[5] For a detailed biography, see "Muhammad Rashid Rida," Encyclopedia Brittanica online, n.d., http://www.britannica.com/EBchecked/topic/491703/Rashid-Rida.

[6] Sayyid Qutb, *Milestones* (Kazi Publications, 2007).

[7] "The Trial Of Omar Abdel Rahman," *New York Times*, October 3, 1995.

[8] Holly Fletcher, "Jamaat al-Islamiyya," Council on Foreign Relations (CFR) *Backgrounder*, May 30, 2008, http://www.cfr.org/publication/9156/jamaat_alislamiyya.html.

[9] Youssef H. Aboul-Enein, "Al-Ikhwan Al-Muslimeen: the Muslim Brotherhood," *Military Review*, July-August 2003, 26-31, http://www.au.af.mil/au/awc/awcgate/milreview/abo.pdf.

[10] Another group, which has lost much of its influence for being too extreme, is the "Excommunication and Emigration" group (*Takfir wa-l-Hijra*) which emerged in Egypt in the 1960s as a splinter faction of the Muslim Brotherhood.

[11] Barbara Zollner, *The Muslim Brotherhood: Hasan al-Hudaybi and Ideology* (London: Routledge, 2008).

[12] See Umar al-Tilmisani, *Days with Sadat [Ayam Ma'a al-Sadat]* (Cairo: al-Itissam Publishing House, 1984).

[13] This book was first published in 1991 and attacks the Brotherhood for its "betrayal" after "recognizing the legitimacy of secular institutions" in Egypt and "helping the Tyrants [the government]" repress

jihadists. Ayman al-Zawahiri, *The Bitter Harvest: The Muslim Brother-hood in Sixty Years, trans. Nadia Masid,* (Egypt: 1991).

[14] Omar Ashour, "Lions Tamed? An Inquiry into the Causes of De-Radicalization of Armed Islamist Movements: the Case of the Egyptian Islamic Group," *Middle East Journal* 61, no. 4 (2007), 596-597; Rohan Gunaratna and Mohamed Bin Ali, "De-Radicalization Initiatives in Egypt: A Preliminary Insight," *Studies in Conflict & Terrorism* 32, no. 4 (2009), 277-291.

[15] Among these can be mentioned Karam Zuhdi, *The Strategy and the Bombings of Al-Qaeda: Mistakes and Dangers (Istratijiyyat wa Tajjirat al-Qa'ida: Al-Akhta' wa-l-Akhtar)* (Cairo: Al-Turath al-Islami, 2002); Nagih Ibrahim and Ali al-Sharif, *Banning Extremism in Religion and the Excommunication of Muslims (Hurmat al-Ghuluw fi-I-Din wa Takfir al-Muslimin)* (Cairo: Al-Turath al-Islami, 2002).

[16] On this interactional process, see Omar Ashour, "De-Radicalization of Jihad? The Impact of Egyptian Islamist Revisionists on Al-Qaeda," *Perspectives on Terrorism* II, no.5 (2008), http://www.terrorismanalysts.com/pt/index.php?option=com_rokzine&view=article&id=39&Itemid=54. See also Lawrence Wright, "The Rebellion Within: An Al Qaeda mastermind questions terrorism," *The New Yorker,* June 2, 2008, http://www.newyorker.com/reporting/2008/06/02/080602fa_fact_wright?currentPage=all.

[17] These various deradicalization factors are analyzed by Omar Ashour in *The Deradicalization of Jihadists: Transforming Armed Islamist Movements* (London: Routledge, 2009).

[18] Ashour, "Lions tamed?" 596-597.

[19] Mohammad Mahmoud, "Islamic Group theorist: al-Qaeda's ideology in a state of decline," *Al-Shorfa.com,* August 2, 2010, http://www.al-shorfa.com/cocoon/meii/xhtml/en_GB/features/meii/features/main/2010/08/02/feature-01.

[20] Myriam Benraad and Mohamed Abdelbaky, "Transition In Egypt: Radicals On The Rise?" Washington Institute for Near East Policy *Policywatch* 1588, September 24, 2009, http://www.washingtoninstitute.org/templateC05.php?CID=3126.

[21] "Akef Urges Arab , Muslim Rulers Take Joint Attitude Against Countries Blocking Gaza Ceasefire," *Ikhwanweb.com,* January 5, 2010, http://www.ikhwanweb.com/article.php?id=18989

[22] For more on these developments, see Benraad and Abdelbaky, "Transition in Egypt: Radicals On The Rise?"

[23] On the rise and spread of Salafism in Egyptian society, see Nathan Field and Ahmed Hamem, "Egypt: Salafism Making Inroads," Carnegie Endowment for International Peace *Arab Reform Bulletin,* March 9, 2009, http://www.carnegieendowment.org/arb/?fa=show&article=22823; Saif Nasrawi, "Egypt's Salafis: When My Enemy's Foe Isn't My Friend," *Al Masry al-Youm* (Cairo), April 27,

2010 http://www.almasryalyoum.com/en/news.

[24] On the media dimension, see Nathan Field and Ahmed Hamam, "Salafi Satellite TV In Egypt," *Arab Media & Society*, no. 8, Spring 2009, http://www.arabmediasociety.com/?article=712.

[25] Marwa Awad, "Egypt Church Bomb Hints at Al Qaeda Gaining Toehold," Reuters, January 5, 2011, http://www.reuters.com/article/2011/01/05/us-egypt-church-probe-idUSTRE7042TT20110105.

[26] *Bulletin of Christian Persecution*, February 2009, http://www.politicalislam.com/blog/bulletin-of-christian-persecution-feb-20/.

[27] Alaa Al Aswany (author of *The Yacoubian Building* novel and contributor to the Egyptian newspaper *Al-Shorouk*), "Who killed the Egyptians on their feast day?," *Globe and Mail* (Toronto), January 15, 2010.

[28] Baher Ibrahhim, "Salafi Intolerance Threatens Sufis," *Guardian* (London), May 10, 2010, http://www.guardian.co.uk/commentisfree/belief/2010/may/10/islam-sufi-salafi-egypt-religion.

[29] Nathan J. Brown, Michele Dunne, and Amr Hamzawy, "Egypt's Controversial Constitutional Amendments," Carnegie Endowment for International Peace, March 23, 2007, http://www.carnegieendowment.org/files/egypt_constitution_webcommentary01.pdf.

[30] See Peter Kenyon, "Opposition Crackdown In Egypt Heats Up Before Polls," *NPR*, February 25, 2010, http://www.npr.org/templates/story/story.php?storyId=124045764.

[31] See Kristen Chick, "Egypt Election Routs Popular Muslim Brotherhood From Parliament," *Christian Science Monitor*, December 1, 2010, http://www.csmonitor.com/World/Middle-East/2010/1201/Egypt-election-routs-popular-Muslim-Brotherhood-from-parliament.

[32] See Fawaz Gerges, "The Muslim Brotherhood: New Leadership, Old Politics," *Guardian* (London), January 20, 2010, http://www.guardian.co.uk/commentisfree/belief/2010/jan/20/muslim-brotherhood-egypt; Liam Stack, "Egypt's Muslim Brotherhood To Name New Conservative Leader Mohamed Badie," *Christian Science Monitor*, January 12, 2010, http://www.csmonitor.com/World/Middle-East/2010/0115/Egypt-s-Muslim-Brotherhood-to-name-new-conservative-leader-Mohamed-Badie.

[33] See Marwa Awad, "Egypt's Muslim Brotherhood Conservatives Win Vote," *Reuters*, December 21, 2009, http://www.reuters.com/article/idUSTRE5BK3CB20091221.

[34] See Hussam Tammam, "Egypt's Muslim Bothers hit turbulence," *Daily Star* (Beirut), March 5, 2010, http://www.dailystar.com.lb/article.asp?edition_id=10&categ_id=5&article_id=112382#axzz0vxks9MZx.

[35] See Sarah A. Topol, "Egypt's Muslim Brotherhood Fractures," *Newsweek*, February 23, 2010, http://www.newsweek.com/blogs/wealth-of-nations/2010/02/23/egypt-s-muslim-brotherhood-fractures.html.

[36] "Who are the Abdullah Azzam Brigades?" Reuters, August 4, 2010, http://uk.reuters.com/article/idUKTRE6733QJ20100804; Hugh Roberts, "Egypt's Sinai Problem," The Independent (London), April 26, 2006, http://www.crisisgroup.org/en/regions/middle-east-north-africa/north-africa/egypt/egypts-sinai-problem.aspx.

[37] See "Another Salafi-Jihadi Cell Arrested in Egypt," *MEMRI TV* no. 5017, January 4, 2010, http://www.memritv.org/report/en/4193.htm.

LIBYA

Islamism has found fertile ground in Libya, where economic woes and a dictatorial regime have fostered significant popular support for radical groups. Not least of these is the Muslim Brotherhood, whose founders were responsible for importing Islamist ideology from Egypt and whose members have faced prosecution at the hand of Libyan ruler Colonel Muammar al-Qadhafi.

Qadhafi, who came to power via military coup d'etat in 1969, possesses a secular militant radical ideology which justifies the use of violence and terrorism in order to promote Libyan interests and Qadhafi's personal ideology. Throughout the 1970s and 1980s, Libya provided funds, training facilities, safe haven and logistics for various Palestinian terror groups.[1] It also established and "hired" terror groups, using them to promote its own interests.[2] Libya's sponsorship of terrorist activity was revealed during the investigation of PA 103 bombing over Lockerby, Scotland – an investigation that was followed by the imposition of significant sanctions against Libya on the part of the United Nations.[3]

With the emergence of the Libyan Islamic Fighting Group (LIFG) in the late 1980s, Qadhafi faced his biggest radical Islamist threat. With a large amount of public support, the LIFG has plotted, albeit unsuccessfully, to overthrow the authoritarian regime in Tripoli. Recent reconciliation efforts between the LIFG and the regime created a tentative truce, although the real future of radical Islam in Libya remains uncertain.

ISLAMIST ACTIVITY

Libya won its independence from Italy by the end of World War II and declared itself a constitutional monarchy under King Idris. On September 1969, Colonel Muammar al-Qadhafi staged a military coup d'état in the country, establishing an Arab nationalist regime that adhered to an ideology of "Islamic socialism." Qadhafi has been the only leader of Libya since that time. It was not long before his regime began to generate resentment among Islamic circles in the country, which led to an Islamist revival beginning in the late 1970s. Today, this resistance continues, encapsulated in a number of Islamist movements:

The Muslim Brotherhood

The Muslim Brotherhood first appeared in Libya in the 1950s. The Libyan branch was founded by Egyptian cleric Ezadine Ibrahim Mustafa and several others, who were given refuge by former Libyan King Idris after fleeing political persecution in Egypt.[4] The king allowed them a relative degree of freedom to spread their ideology, and the movement soon attracted a number of local adherents. It gained further momentum through Egyptian teachers working in Libya.[5] Qadhafi, however, took a less accommodating stance, regarding the Brotherhood as a potential source of opposition.[6] Soon after coming to power, he arrested a number of the Brothers and repatriated them back to Egypt. In 1973, the security services arrested and tortured members of the Libyan Muslim Brotherhood, who, under pressure, agreed to dissolve the organization. As a result, the Brotherhood remained silent throughout the remainder of the 1970s.

However, in the early 1980s, the Brotherhood (which by then had renamed itself the "Libyan Islamic Group" or *Al-Jama'a al-Islamiya al-Libiia*) revived its aspirations to replace the existing secular regime with *sharia* law through peaceful means, and was once again beginning to gather popular support. The group was given a boost by a number of Libyan students who had returned from the United Kingdom and the U.S., and took an active role in helping to spread the Brotherhood ideology. The movement operated covertly in groups of interlinked cells active throughout the country. The group drew much of its popular appeal through the charitable and welfare work of its members. In particular, the movement attracted members of the middle classes and was especially strong in the eastern area of Benghazi, where the main tribes have traditionally opposed Qadhafi's rule.[7]

It was in the 1990s, however, that political Islam found strong popular support in Libya. Economic mismanagement, falling oil prices and the international sanctions (imposed in 1992 as a result of Qadhafi's refusal to hand over two suspects in the 1998 Lockerbie bombing) contributed to chronic socio-economic malaise. With no other political alternative under Qadhafi's tyranny, the population was ripe for the radical approach of political Islam. Not only did the Brotherhood garner greater support, but a number of new Islamic groups also emerged. These included the Islamic Gathering (*Harakat Atajamaa Alislami*), founded by Mustafa Ali Al-Jihani. Its support base was almost entirely in the east of the country, and its ideology was very similar to that of the Brotherhood. The global *Tablighi Jama'at* movement also succeeded in drawing popular support at this time, mainly in the western areas of the country. The *Tablighi Jama'at* choose, however, to distance themselves from politics, after a number of them had been arrested at the end of the 1980s, and subsequently became co-opted by the regime, with some being given posts as imams or speakers.[8] At any rate, it seems the number of *Tablighi* supporters in Libya currently is relatively small, since there is only one known *Tablighi* center in the country.[9]

By the end of the 1990s, the authoritarian regime had more or less wiped out organized Islamic opposition inside the country. However, Qadhafi has been unable to prevent the growing religiosity that has taken hold among the Libyan population, as it has across much of the Arab world. Increasing numbers of the population support Brotherhood-type ideologies and aspire to the kind of Islamic alternative promoted by the Brotherhood in what could be interpreted as a form of passive resistance to the regime.[10] The Brotherhood itself is able to continue its activities, conducting annual conferences and mainly preserving their political infrastructure and institutions as well as their social and charitable activities among the population.[11]

The Libyan Islamic Fighting Group (LIFG)

The dominant Islamist group challenging the Qadhafi regime currently is the Libyan Islamic Fighting Group (LIFG). LIFG did not officially announce its formation until 1995, but the roots of the group can be found in an underground jihadist movement formed in 1982 by Awatha al-Zuwawi. With no official name and under high security, the movement managed to spread and attract many followers throughout Libya over the span of more than a decade.[12] Unlike the Muslim Brotherhood, it advocated launching military operations against the regime in order to overthrow Qadhafi and plotted attacks against senior figures in his government. By 1989, authorities had discovered the insurgency and arrested many of the rebels, including Al-Zuwawi. Those who were not captured were forced to flee to Afghanistan.

The LIFG was engaged in long-term preparation for its military campaign, and to strengthen combat skills many of its members seized the opportunity to fight the Soviets in Afghanistan in the 1980s. There, they and other Libyans set up their own camp and underwent military training, at times instructed by al-Qaeda members.[13] While in exile in Pakistan and Afghanistan, the movement began to morph into an identifiable organization. Besides military training, the Libyan recruits were also indoctrinated in Afghanistan by influential *jihadist* clerics such as al-Qaeda founder Abdullah Azzam.[14] While the initial goal remained fighting the communist-led forces in Afghanistan, these recruits began to develop fighting skills in anticipation of the day they would return to Libya to fight Qadhafi's regime.

Like other Muslims who fought against the Soviet forces, many Libyans left Afghanistan between 1992 and 1993, following the Soviet withdrawal.[15] While some went on to aid militant groups in Algeria and Bosnia-Herzegovina, others, including LIFG members, became part of Osama bin Laden's Islamic Army Shura (consultative committee), a platform he created in Sudan in order to coordinate the international militant alliance he sought to form.[16] They delivered lectures in Khartoum and maintained regular contact with LIFG members in Libya. It was within this platform that LIFG members formed ties with operatives from various bin Laden affiliates, like the Algerian Armed Islamic Group (GIA) and the Egyptian terrorist group *Al-Gama`at al-Islamiyya.*[17]

Back in Libya, the LIFG, led by Commander Abu Abdullah al-Sadek, was establishing its structure and developing the leadership skills of those in charge of cells and units throughout the country.[18] Throughout the 1990s, the LIFG continued to conduct military operations against the Libyan regime, including several failed attempts to assassinate Qadhafi himself. The Libyan regime fought relentlessly against the LIFG, which suffered numerous losses, including that of Salah Fathi bin Suleiman (a.k.a. Abu Abdurrahman al-Khattab), one of its founding fathers, who was killed in a battle with Libyan soldiers near Darna in September 1997.[19]

Aggressive Libyan government operations throughout the country eventually crippled the LIFG's infrastructure within Libya and forced most of the remaining members to exit the country and resume their operations in exile. As a result, many LIFG members, such as al-Qaeda associate Abu Anas al-Libi, moved on to political activity in the United Kingdom, where the organization established a robust underground support network.[20] Others eventually fled to various Asian, Persian Gulf, African, and European countries, but ultimately Afghanistan became the preferred destination for LIFG members once again.[21]

Upon al-Qaeda's return to Afghanistan from Sudan, the LIFG ran at least two military training camps. One was the Shaheed Shaykh Abu Yahya Camp, located approximately 20 miles north of the capital, Kabul.[22] The camp included volunteers of several nationalities and was run by an LIFG commander known as Abu Mohammed al-Libi. Some of the training camps were shared by different terror groups and al-Qaeda affiliates, allowing the LIFG to form links with groups like the Moroccan Islamic Combatant Group (GICM). Past ties between the LIFG and al-Qaeda were strengthened during this time, as the two shared both human and material resources. Over time, those ties appear to have had an ideological effect on the LIFG as well, as its leaders embraced a more radical anti-Western approach affiliated with al-Qaeda.[23]

After the U.S.-led invasion of Afghanistan following the 9/11 attacks, some LIFG members were captured, while many fled the country, mainly to neighboring Pakistan.[24] Simultaneously, several prominent LIFG commanders stepped forward to take over prominent public positions within al-Qaeda's leadership and infrastructure in Afghanistan.

- Abu Faraj al-Libi became the overall chief of al-Qaeda's military committee (similar to "AQ chief of staff") until his arrest in the spring of 2005.[25]
- Abu Al-Laith al-Libi was one of the senior military commanders of al-Qaeda, fighting the coalition and Pakistani troops. He was responsible for the Khost, Paktia and Paktika provinces until he was killed by U.S. forces in the spring of 2008.[26]
- Abu Yahya al-Libi is the current head of al-Qaeda's religious committee.[27]
- During 2008-2009 Abdullah Sai'd been the head of internal regions (Afghanistan-Pakistan border zone) in al-Qaeda's military committee until he was killed by a U.S. drone attack.[28]
- Sheikh Atiya Allah is a prominent al-Qaeda senior leader who is considered to be very close to Ayman al-Zawahiri.[29]

In 2007, the LIFG was officially welcomed into al-Qaeda's fold in a statement released on the Internet by al-Qaeda's second in command, Ayman al-Zawahiri, and senior commander Abu Laith al-Libi.[30] Zawahiri called for the overthrow of the governments of Libya, Tunisia, Algeria and Morocco, while Abu Laith al Libi urged Libyans to join the fight against Qadhafi, the United States "and their brothers, the infidel of the West."[31]

ISLAMISM AND SOCIETY

Libya is a country of about 700,000 square kilometers and 5.8 million inhabitants, 1.5 million of whom are foreigners. Ninety-seven percent of the population is Sunni Muslim, with the rest belonging to different Christian churches.[32] The dominant school of Islamic thought among the Libyan population is the Malakite School.

Libya does not have a constitution, and hence there is no explicit legal provision for religion-society-state relations. However, a basis for some degree of legalizing these relations is provided in the Great Green Charter on Human Rights[33] of Libya that was adopted in 1988. According to the Charter, the government tolerates most minority religions but strongly opposes militant forms of Islam, which it views as a security threat. Religious practices that conflict with the government's interpretation of *sharia* are prohibited.

Islam is the equivalent of a state religion, as it is thoroughly integrated into everyday political and social life. As with all other aspects of individuals' lives in Libya, the government closely monitors and regulates Islam to ensure religious life includes no political dimension. Monitoring of mosques and a widespread culture of self-censorship generally ensure that both clerics and adherents stay within well-established lines of acceptable practice. Even mosques endowed by prominent families generally must conform to the government-approved interpretation of Islam. The government also maintains control over religious literature, including Islamic literature;[34] for example, the government denies public access to the Libyan Muslim Brotherhood Internet site.[35]

The World Islamic Call Society (WICS) is the official conduit for the state-approved form of Islam. With an emphasis on activities outside the country, it operates a state-run university for moderate Muslim clerics from outside the Arab world. To date, WICS has trained 5,000 students in Islamic thought, literature and history. Upon graduation, the government encourages students to return home and promote its interpretation of Islamic thought in their own countries.

A state-run religious endowments (*auqaf*) authority administers mosques, supervises clerics and has primary responsibility for ensuring that all religious practices within the country conform to the state-approved form of Islam.[36] Religious instruction in Islam is required in public schools, but the government does not issue information on the religious affiliation of children in public schools, and there were no reports of children transferring to private schools for alternative religious instruction.[37]

Despite all these measures taken by the state to control and monitor Islamic activity, Libya, like most countries in the region, experienced an Islamist revival from the late 1970s onward. Islamic ideologies continued to gain support among the Libyan population and many Libyan youth find their way abroad to participate in the global *jihad* wars in Afghanistan and Iraq. When tallied in 2005, Libyan fighters were estimated to constitute 18.8 percent of foreign fighters in Iraq, second only to Saudi Arabia's 41 percent.[38]

ISLAMISM AND THE STATE

During 2009, in a break from its past persecution of the LIFG, the Libyan regime launched a conciliatory policy toward the group and its members. Reports suggest that Saif al-Islam Qadhafi, the son and heir apparent of the current Libyan leader, held a clandestine series of negotiations in an attempt to achieve reconciliation between the Libyan state and the LIFG.[39] As a result of these efforts, on September 2009, LIFG leaders in Libya released a new "code" for *jihad* in the form of a 417-page religious document titled "Corrective Studies." The new code viewed the armed struggle against Qadhafi's regime as illegal under Islamic law and set down new guidelines for when and how *jihad* should be fought. It does, however, state that *jihad* is permissible if Muslim lands are invaded, citing Afghanistan, Iraq and Palestine as examples.[40]

Whether the LIFG still poses a major threat to Qadhafi is unclear. While the group may have shifted its policy regarding its internal military operations as a consequence of negotiations with the Qadhafi regime, it still maintains close ties with al-Qaeda, and some of its members hold senior positions within its ranks. This highlights a related threat posed by Libyan "veterans" of the wars currently taking place in Iraq and Afghanistan, who may one day use their experience to either bring the *jihad* back to their homeland or help other radical elements operating abroad.

The 2009 efforts at reconciliation possess an additional dangerous element. Even though above the surface, the Islamic radicals of the LIFG acknowledge the legitimacy of the Qadhafi regime, the "corrective studies code" legalized different aspects of Islamic (military) activity within the boundaries of the state. According to the code, *jihad* is allowed in Islamic countries that are invaded, and volunteering to fight in these areas is supported. By this definition, attempts by radical Islamist groups to attract Libyan youth to fight in *jihad* areas are allowed. In a few years, these activities may create a large infrastructure of radical Islamist elements within Libya that might eventually turn against the Qadhafi regime itself, despite their current tactical accommodation with it.

ENDNOTES

[1]Yonah Alexander et al., *Terrorism – The PLO connection* (New York: Taylor and Francis, 1989), 58.

[2] For Libyan involvement with the activity of NAYLP and ANO, see Ariel Merari and Shlomo Elad, *The International Dimension of Palestinian Terrorism* (Tel Aviv: Tel Aviv University Press), 1986, 61; See also Yossi Melman, *The Master Terrorist: The True Story Behind Abu Nidal* (New York: Adama Books, 1986), 93.

[3] Court opinion in Her Majesty's Advocate v. Abdelbaset Ali Mohmed Al Megrahi and Al Amin Khalifa Fhimah, Case No. 1475/99, Court of Edinburgh, Scotland, http://www.pixunlimited.co.uk/guardian/pdf/0131lockerbieverdict.pdf

[4] Allison Pargete, "Political Islam in Libya," Jamestown Foundation *Terrorism Monitor* 3, iss. 6, May 5, 2005, http://www.jamestown.org/single/?no_cache=1&tx_ttnews[tt_news]=306.

[5] Ibid.

[6] Ibidem.

[7] Ibidem.

[8] Ibidem.

[9] The facility is part of a comprehensive list of Tabligh facilities worldwide available here: http://adressmarkazjemaahtabligh.blogspot.com/

[10] Pargete, "Political Islam in Libya."

[11] Mohamed Ali, "Libyan MB Chairman: We seek Civil Society-Inspired Reform" *Ikhwanweb*, n.d., http://www.ikhwanweb.com/article.php?id=929.

[12] Pargete, "Political Islam in Libya."

[13] Evan F. Kohlmann, *Dossier: Libyan Islamic Fighting Group*, NEFA Foundation, October 2007, 3, www.nefafoundation.org/miscellaneous/nefalifg1007.pdf.

[14] Ibid. 4.

[15] "Interview with Neoman Bentoman," Jamestown foundation, March 15 2005. http://www.jamestown.org/news_details.php?news_id+101.

[16] Kohlmann, *Dossier: Libyan Islamic Fighting Group*, 5.

[17] Ibid. 6.

[18] Ibidem, 8.

[19] Ibidem, 8-11.

[20] Ibidem, 11

[21] Kohlmann, *Dossier: Libyan Islamic Fighting Group*, 12.

[22] Ibid., 13

[23] Ibidem, 12.

[24] Ibidem, 17.

[25] U.S. Department of Defense, Office for the Administrative Review of the Detention of Enemy Combatants at U.S. Naval Base Guan-

tanamo Bay, Cuba, "Summary of Evidence for Combatant Status Review Tribunal – Al Libi, Abu Faraj," February 8, 2007, http://www.defenselink.mil/news/ISN10017.pdf#1. From these allegations, one can conclude that he was at that time the military chief of al-Qaeda.

[26] Craig Whitlock and Munir Ladaa, "Al-Qaeda's New Leadership: Abu Laith al-Libi, Field Commander and Spokesman," Washington Post, 2006, http://www.washingtonpost.com/wp-srv/world/specials/terror/laith.html#profile and Claude Salhani, "Jihad Turning Point?" *Washington Times*, February 7, 2008, http://www.frontpagemag.com/readArticle.aspx?ARTID=29823.

[27] Yahya Al Libi has emerged as a public face for al-Qaeda, appearing in more than a dozen lengthy Internet videos since 2006. His claim to fame is his successful escape from a high-security U.S. military prison in Bagram, Afghanistan, in July 2005, along with three other al-Qaeda members. He styles himself as a theologian and has offered lengthy commentaries on a variety of political events and hence is probably the new head of the religious committee. See Whitlock and Ladaa, "Al-Qaeda's New Leadership."

[28] "Qaeda: Signs of Victory Looming Over Afghanistan," worldanalysis.net, May 12, 2009, http://worldanalysis.net/modules/news/article.php?storyid=629.

[29] Atiya Allah's position within al-Qaeda senior leadership was fully exposed through a series of correspondence he held with al-Qaeda Amir of Iraq Abu Mosab al Zarqawi on behalf of the al-Qaeda leadership. See West Point, Combating Terrorism Center, "Letter Exposes New Leader In Al-Qa'ida High Command," September 25, 2006, http://ctc.usma.edu/harmony/pdf/CTC-AtiyahLetter.pdf.

[30] Bill Roggio, "Libyan Islamic Fighting Group joins al Qaeda," *Long War Journal*, November 3, 2007, http://www.longwarjournal.org/archives/2007/11/libian_islamic_fight.php.

[31] Ibid.

[32] U.S. Department of State, Bureau of Democracy, Human Rights and Labor, *International Religious Freedom Report 2009*, October 26, 2009, http://www.state.gov/g/drl/rls/irf/2009/127353.htm.

[33] An online version of the Charter is available here: http://www.rcmlibya.org/English/Great_Green_Charter.htm.

[34] U.S. Department of State, Bureau of Democracy, Human Rights and Labor, *International Religious Freedom Report 2009*, October 26, 2009, http://www.state.gov/g/drl/rls/irf/2009/127353.htm.

[35] Ali, "Libyan MB Chairman: We seek Civil Society-Inspired Reform."

[36] U.S. Department of State, *International Religious Freedom Report 2009*.

[37] Ibid.

[38] Christopher Boucek, "Libyan State-Sponsored Terrorism: An His-

torical Perspective," Jamestown foundation *Terrorism Monitor* 3, iss. 6, May 5, 2005, http://www.jamestown.org/single/?no_cache=1&tx_ttnews[tt_news]=305.

[39] Nick Robertson and Paul Cruickshank, "New Jihad code threatens al Qaeda," CNN, November 10, 2009, http://edition.cnn.com/2009/WORLD/africa/11/09/libia.jihadi.code/.

[40] Ibid.

TUNISIA

QUICK FACTS

Population: 10,589,025

Area: 162,610 sq km

Ethnic Groups: Arab 98%, European 1%, Jewish and other 1%

Religions: Muslim 98%, Christian 1%, Jewish and other 1%

Government Type: Republic

GDP (official exchange rate): $40.04 billion

Map and Quick Facts courtesy of the CIA World Factbook (Last Updated July 2010)

The unprecedented social and political upheaval in Tunisia which began in December 2010, causing long-serving President Zine el-Abedine Ben Ali and his family to quit the country roughly a month later, continues to drive events and developments in the North African state. The so-called "Jasmine Revolution" was unexpected to Tunisian Islamists, as it was to all Tunisians and the international community at large. The revolt itself contained little overt involvement of Islamic groups, and very little Islamist rhetoric. It did, however, destroy the one-party structure that had defined political life since the country's independence in 1956, and prompted the re-emergence of thoroughly suppressed opposition movements, the return of politicians from exile, and the creation of many new political groupings.

Today, Islamists as well as other groups are preparing for the first stage of the creation of a new political order, the July 24th election of a National Constituent Assembly to draft a new constitution. How this election will be conducted, how the constituent council will be organized, and what powers it will exercise before parliamentary and presidential elections are scheduled remain open questions, however—the answers to which will determine the trajectory that political Islam will take in Tunisia. Notably, there has not been a surge in Islamist sentiment since the fall of the Ben Ali regime, and Tunisians remain generally supportive of the secular approach to social and political development.

ISLAMIST ACTIVITY

Al-Nahda

The Islamist movement in Tunisia was long embodied by *Hizb al-Nahda* (The Renaissance Party), which was thoroughly suppressed by the Ben Ali regime but became a legal party in early March 2011. Its leader, Rachid al-Ghannouchi, in exile in London since 1989, returned to Tunis shortly after Ben Ali's January 14th abdication of power to a tumultuous airport welcome, and the party has since been re-establishing its domestic organization. During the Ben Ali years, *al-Nahda* was estimated to have the support of 90 percent of Tunisian Islamists (although <u>not</u> 90 percent of Tunisians).[1] Whether its domination of the movement will continue in the new era, with the creation of other parties and greater political pluralism, remains to be seen, however.

The origin of Tunisia's modern Islamist movement was the Quranic Preservation Society, which was formed in 1970 with the government's approval. It was apolitical, dedicated primarily to encouraging faithfulness and piety. The Society was placed under the Ministry of Religious Affairs and supported by President Bourguiba as a counterweight to the country's political left.[2] The Islamists attracted to the Society were not necessarily anti-regime and, in fact, shared some of the regime's views, including its opposition to Communism.[3] They accordingly did not see the need to confront the government and did not see a role for themselves in social and political change, which was the province of the left.

Their approach began to change in the late 1970s, when growing social unrest in other sectors, especially organized labor, politicized the movement. Several Islamists broke from the Quranic Preservation Society—including Rachid al-Ghannouchi, who founded *al-Jamaat al-Islamiyya* (The Islamic Group) and explicitly called for the end of Bourguiba's one-party rule.[4] In 1978, a year that saw serious rioting across the country, the "Movement of Islamic Renewal" emerged as a loose coalition of Islamist groups; by the following year, Ghannouchi's group, then called the *Mouvement de la Tendence Islamique* (MTI), emerged as its backbone.[5]

MTI issued a political platform in 1981 that included calls for equitable economic reform, an end to one-party rule, and a return to the "fundamental principles of Islam."[6] These were sufficiently vague and appealing objectives to attract broad support from people across Tunisian society. The group requested recognition as a political party, but was denied such by the government, and most of its leaders were jailed until 1984, when they were released through a general amnesty.[7] During the course of the 1980s, MTI became younger and more populist in nature, and evolved into a well-organized social and political movement linked with the broader civil rights movement in the country.[8] It was considered pro-democracy and was the first Islamist group in the Arab world to explicitly adopt democratic principles; in his writings, Ghannouchi favored Islamist participation in pluralist politics.[9]

In November 1987, Zine el-Abedine Ben Ali, whom President Bourguiba had recently appointed Prime Minister, ousted him in a bloodless coup. The coup was greeted with relief by the public, as Bourguiba's age and poor health had seriously degraded his judgment and decision-making capabilities. Ben Ali promised reform and democratization, and Ghannouchi, who sought to openly participate in political life, undertook to cooperate with the new President. He signed Ben Ali's "National Pact," which was essentially a social contract between the government and civil and political groups, and then sought to run a list of candidates in the 1989 legislative elections.[10] But Ben Ali soon changed course and, among other measures, prohibited any party's name to contain the words "Islam" or "Islamic" (the prohibition of religiously-identified parties remains in place today.) The MTI duly renamed itself *Hizb al-Nahda*, the Renaissance Party. However, Ben Ali still refused to allow *Al-Nahda* to enter the elections as a recognized political party, although he did permit it to field "independent" candidates. Islamists subsequently received 15 percent of the nationwide vote (up to 30 percent in urban areas), but failed to win any seats in the legislature (by contrast, the five recognized secular opposition parties collectively received only 5 percent of the vote[11]). The ruling Constitutional Democratic Rally Party (RCD), the successor to Bourguiba's *Neo-Destour* (New Constitution) Party, received 80 percent of the vote—a function of both general voter satisfaction and effective regime vote-rigging and polling place intimidation. But the unexpectedly strong performance of the Islamists within the opposition, coupled with *Al-Nahda's* increasingly strident political rhetoric, caused the regime to deny *Al-Nahda's* second request for recognition. An escalating cycle of protest and repression ensued, and Ghannouchi fled to London in 1989.[12] By 1992, virtually all of *Al-Nahda's* leadership was imprisoned and its organizational capabilities within the country destroyed.

Although it was commonly understood that *al-Nahda* was effectively dismantled in the early 1990s, many Tunisians, including Ben Ali, believed it maintained a structure and presence in the country, albeit perhaps a "stand-by" or "sleeping" one. They pointed to the comparatively recent prosecution of several Islamists under a 1959 law prohibiting membership in an unauthorized association, and not under the country's 2003 counterterrorism law, as implying that the regime still believed the group to exist.[13]

Al-Nahda's ideology is thoroughly rooted in the ideology of its founder, Ghannouchi, who views the Koran and the *Hadith* as "an anchor for political thought and practice."[14] However, he appears to interpret Koranic texts in the context of Western political thinking and modern concepts of political freedoms: the dignity of human beings, human rights, and Koranic prohibitions against Muslim dictators.[15] Ghannouchi himself is a "literalist" and believes that it is the duty of Muslims to establish Islamic government where attainable; in practice, he has endorsed multi-party politics.[16] He does not advocate government by clerics, and has said that "[t]he state is not something from God but from the people... the state has to serve the benefit of the Muslims."[17] His idea of an Islamic political regime appears to be a strong presidential system with an elected president and elected parliament. In this structure, while *sharia* would dictate the constitution and laws, the *umma* (nation) should participate in legislating day-to-day activities of the state.[18] Notably, this structure represents an adaptation of the Islamic concept of *ijtihad* (scholarly interpretation of the Koran), infusing the parliament—rather than a council of scholars—with that power. Ghannouchi considers the elected parliamentary system a legitimate means of political participation.[19] The official ideology of *Al-Nahda*, therefore, appears to be compatible with the Tunisian political system as embodied in its constitution. Ghannouchi's public statements since his return, and those of other *Al-Nahda* figures, have been consistent with this pluralism. He has said that he will not run in the presidential elections, and that his party will accept the outcome of fair and democratic elections.[20]

Al-Nahda has had an ambiguous position on the use of political violence, and a mixed record of using and supporting violent unrest to further its aims. It is not associated with the few instances of recent violence in the country that have been attributed to *jihadist* elements or al-Qaeda in the Islamic Maghreb (AQIM). There is no evidence that *Al-Nahda* (or any Islamist movement, for that matter) played a significant role in the Jasmine Revolution. However, in 1978, organized labor and leftist groups fomented a wave of public violence against the regime that opened the Islamists (MTI) to the potential utility of violent confrontation, even though they did not participate in it. Similarly, the Islamists did not organize demonstrations in 1984 that resulted in bread riots, although they profited from associating with them because of the support the riots received from the public.[21] Moreover, Ghannouchi himself criticized the January 2007 clash between an Islamist band and security forces in the southern suburbs of Tunis (see below) as an obstacle to democracy.[22]

At present, *Al-Nahda* is re-establishing itself in order to compete in future elections, and reassuring the public that it is prepared to play by the rules. Nevertheless, there is concern among secular Tunisians that the party, simply by dint of its organization and the multiplicity of other parties, could score as much as 30 to 40 percent of the popular vote.[23]

Other Islamist movements

While *Al-Nahda* dominates Tunisian Islamism, other Islamist groups do exist, though they tend to be small in size and loosely organized. A potentially dangerous group is *Hizb al-Tahrir* (the Islamic Liberation Party), an international group founded in 1953 which seeks to re-establish the Caliphate by force. This group established a presence in Tunisia in 1973, but had only a few dozen members in the country.[24] It has now emerged publicly and stated its goal of competing in elections and offering its "alternative constitution" to the Constituent Council.[25] While the group claims to renounce violence, it does not rule out rebellion and civil disobedience to establish an Islamic state. It clearly believes in the re-establishment of the Muslim Caliphate and in *sharia* as the source of the constitution.[26] Its spokesman says that Hizb ut-Tahrir is preparing for an ideological and political struggle to save the nation.[27] Many Tunisians, including members of *Al-Nahda*, believe with good reason that *Hizb ut-Tahrir* would, if it won an election, ban other parties and implement "one man, one vote, one time."[28] Its request for a license to operate as a political party was denied by the Interior Minister on March 12th (as was that of the "Tunisian Sunni" party), and it will be interesting to observe what direction this organization will take.

Tabligh wa Da'wa ("transmission and preaching") is a group with origins in Pakistan focused on reinvigorating Islamic practices among the people of northern Africa. *Tabligh* is apolitical but, like virtually all civil associations in Tunisia, was illegal under the old regime.

There likewise is an inchoate Salafist movement which under the old regime devoted itself to religious studies and had no political component, but will apparently soon submit a request for a license to organize. It is not associated with violence, and one of its members described *jihadist*-style salafism as "destructive thought."[29]

The Tunisian Combatant Group (TCG) was formed in 2000 with the goal of establishing an Islamic regime in Tunisia. It reportedly established contacts with al-Qaeda shortly after its formation. Its membership derives from the Tunisian Diaspora and members have participated in violent operations in Europe, Iraq, and Afghanistan. The group has no evident capability to operate in Tunisia itself; in fact, observers disagree over whether the group still exists. While not on the State Department's formal list of foreign terrorist organizations, TCG is considered a terrorist entity and its assets are frozen under Executive Order 13224 and United Nations Security Council Resolution 1333.[30]

Although al-Qaeda in the Islamic Maghreb (AQIM) claimed responsibility for the February 2008 kidnapping of two Austrian tourists in southern Tunisia, it does not appear that AQIM has a significant presence or recruiting base in the country. In fact, from press reports, all of the perpetrators of that kidnapping infiltrated from outside, and none were Tunisian. That said, a January 2007 gunfight between a well-armed extremist group and authorities near Tunis shocked the country, especially since two members of the group were found to be security forces personnel. The group, which took the name "Assad Ibn Fourat's Army," consisted primarily of Tunisian nationals apparently led by an expatriate living in Italy who, with several companions and a few non-Tunisian Maghrebis, infiltrated from Algeria where they had been trained by the Salafist Group for Call and Combat (GSPC), AQIM's Algerian backbone.[31]

ISLAMISM AND SOCIETY

An increase in "fundamentalism" and outward expressions of personal piety are common to Muslim societies facing developments they cannot understand or control, such as globalization, foreign cultural inundation, economic recession, and uncontrolled political chaos. Tunisians have been spared much of this, but at the cost of their political freedoms. While Islamism has not, and most likely will not, take hold among Tunisians, pro-religious sentiment is growing, perhaps as a reaction to the country's socio-political situation. Youth are exposed to this phenomenon primarily at the university, especially when secular, modernist, and leftist movements are weak and marginalized. Beneath the modernism and sophisticated worldview exhibited by the population, which is far more substantial than the veneer of modernism seen elsewhere, Tunisia is a traditional society that values its religion and cultural heritage. The Ben Ali regime began to recognize this, and attempted to "Islamize" society and use religion to support government policies.[32] This "Official" or "Popular" Islam was designed to counter the extremist/terrorist threat by preaching the values of moderation and tolerance, and at the same time claiming Tunisians' Islamic identity, which was denied by past regimes.[33]

One manifestation of this is Radio Zeytouna, a religious radio station established in 2009 by the Ben Ali government as a counterweight to Islamist satellite networks. Zeytouna's content is popular with the public, and it has a good audience base. In the last several years, the government also opened Koranic schools in wealthy neighborhoods in Tunis and established Islamic banks.[34] The Ben Ali regime, during its tenure, tried to project an image that was both pro-Islam and anti-Islamist—"pro-religious, but modern at the same time."[35] This actually resonated with most Tunisians, who recognized that this "official Islam" was aimed at bolstering the state but preferred it to both the anti-Islam secularism of the Bourguiba era and the extremism of the radicals.

The course of Tunisian development since independence has not been characterized by social polarization or identity politics. Tunisians tend to be moderate in their views and behavior, a characteristic that inhibits the ability of

Islamists to exploit the socio-political situation. This moderation may be partially attributed to three factors of Tunisia's modern history:

First, Tunisia's colonial and liberation experiences were not marked by extensive violence. Bourguiba, supported by the public, set a moderate course at the very inception of the independence movement and followed through with it after the French left the region. Guerrilla warfare and terrorism did not characterize the struggle, and there were no violent purges and settling of accounts among the victors of the sort that led to continued crisis and near-civil war in neighboring Algeria. Tunisians viewed with horror the disaster that Algeria experienced in the 1990s, and the government is fond of pointing out that a similar catastrophe could befall Tunisia in the future should Islamists be granted political quarter. The prospect is sufficiently feared by a great many ordinary Tunisians, so much so that the regime does not need to expend much effort convincing the citizenry that Islamism must be constrained.

Second, sound economic decisions by the government and the creation of such rural development organizations as the Tunisian National Solidarity Fund have created a large middle class and a high percentage of home ownership. About four percent of Tunisia's population now lives below the poverty line (one-third that of Morocco and one-fifth that of Egypt). Unemployment is about 14 percent, which is high but in line with the rest of the Maghreb.[36] But relative prosperity as reflected in economic statistics was insufficient to prevent upheaval; the Jasmine Revolution was not about bread and jobs alone, but about dignity and the state's relationship with the people. A stroll along Avenue Habib Bourguiba in downtown Tunis is sufficient to reveal the extent of the unemployment or underemployment of young men. Without employment and the means to support a family, these young men cannot marry, start a family, and fully participate in society. Frustration is the result, and a portion of frustrated youth, albeit a very small one, is attracted to the fringes of society, including radical Islamism. This is not new, and there have been violent economic protests since the late 1970s spearheaded by the General Union of Tunisian Workers (UGTT), most recently by miners in the southern interior. Early on, the Islamists (MTI) realized that they could not offer the people any message that was not already provided by the government, which had moved to address the workers' concerns. Later, the MTI tried to attract labor support by talking about the "Islamic virtues" of trade unions, but even when *al-Nahda* tried to infiltrate the UGTT by putting up candidates for union elections, they attracted the support of no more than 10 percent of UGTT membership.[37]

The young men are still there on Avenue Habib Bourguiba, although their mood is different since January 14th. How long their mood remains positive will depend on how the new order will address their problems. However, it is clear from the past, and appears to remain so today, that Tunisians do not look to Islam or Islamists to solve their economic woes—rather, they see economic frustrations as a problem the government must fix.

Finally, a very efficient security apparatus made sure that the opportunities for collective protest and potential rebellion were strictly limited. In the mid-1970s, many felt that if popular unrest against the regime were to occur, it would first break out in soccer stadiums, the one place where Tunisians could gather in large numbers and express themselves. One could argue that the stadium can easily be replaced by the mosque as a forum for dissent; while this certainly has been true elsewhere, Tunisian mosques, at least under Ben Ali, were locked except for prayer times, Friday sermons were scripted and anodyne, and the clergy was tightly controlled.

Additionally, Tunisia is an unusually homogenous country for its neighborhood. Ninety-eight percent of the population is Sunni Muslim.[38] Shi'ites number perhaps in the thousands, mostly converts following the 1979 Iranian Revolution.[39] There is a small Jewish community concentrated on the island of Djerba, and there are virtually no indigenous Christians in the country. While there are differences between Arabs and Berbers, ethnicity is not a significant factor, and no "identity politics" exist to fuel conflict and instability. Nor is there a large socio-economic gulf between rich and poor to create tensions. As a result of some very sound economic decisions by the government, Tunisia has developed an expansive middle class, and a very large percentage of Tunisians have a stake in the system. There is a geographical "have/have not" gap in that the southern interior has not been a focus of development; most dissident movements, including the Islamists, have originated from this region, and it was obviously the cradle of the Jasmine Revolution. Equitable distribution of wealth to all regions remains an important issue, especially after the revelations of Ben Ali family corruption, and a number of Tunisians have advocated renationalizing businesses to ensure fairness.[40]

Although Islamists and *Al-Nahda* have failed over the years to gain the active support of the public, there is sympathy for the vision expressed by the movement—that is, political and economic reform and living by Islamic principles. Most Tunisians do not appear to consider Ghannouchi and other Islamists as leaders to be followed, but rather simply people who express an appealing vision.[41] Many of those who join the movement do not necessarily support the establishment of an Islamic regime.[42] Tunisians do not like violent transition, but they do believe in good governance, freedoms, and rule of law. They are very protective of their acquis (patrimony: the shared cultural, political, social, legal experiences) which they believe distinguishes them from their neighbors. Because of this, any political or religious movement that wants to play a role will have to preserve and improve these values, and not reject or destroy them. Therefore, a call for an "Islamic Republic" will have no standing in Tunisia. Most Islamists realize this, which is why *al-Nahda* moderated its discourse and its strategy to cope with the moderate nature and modern expectations of Tunisian society.[43] For *al-Nahda* to participate in political life, it must accept the framework of the national state, agree to safeguard the Tunisian tradition of modernization, and adopt progressive attitudes toward Tunisia's Arab and Islamic identities.[44] *Al-Nahda's* expressed rejection of the Ben Ali regime, and not its Islamic principles, gave the group what appeal it had. It, like other heretofore suppressed opposition groups, now must sell its message to a public suddenly faced with a plethora of alternatives.

Even if Islamism in Tunisia does not seriously threaten the state or the society, Tunisian Islamists are a threat to other countries and societies. Maghrebis, escaping from the frustration and social and economic despair they feel at home, are well-represented in the ranks of the *jihads* in Iraq and Afghanistan, for which AQIM has served as a recruiting office. Tunisian youths, however, tend to be recruited into *jihadist* groups in Europe, where they have migrated, legally or otherwise. Their radicalism and decision to act may be rooted in Tunisian socio-economic-political issues, but have been refined and given momentum by their often negative experiences as expatriates in Europe.[45] Cut off from their real community back home, many are attracted to the virtual community of *jihadist* websites and are drawn into extremist groups that promise to provide fulfillment in Iraq or Afghanistan. A number of Tunisians have been arrested in those countries, as well as in Syria and Europe, for their participation in terrorist plots or actual operations. Many have been extradited to Tunisia, where they are tried and imprisoned.

Even much of the extremist violence that occurs in Tunisia itself has an external dimension. Extremism began later in Tunisia than elsewhere in the Maghreb, and it appears that the extremism of recent years did not arise domestically, but rather was imported (or perhaps more accurately, repatriated) from Tunisian radicals residing in Europe.[46]

ISLAMISM AND THE STATE

Habib Bourguiba, the hero of the liberation and president between 1956 and 1987 (his popular title was *al-Mujahid al-Akbar*, "the greatest combatant") dominated the country through force of personality and an efficient political party structure organized down to the lowest grassroots. He made an early decision to devote the country's energies and limited resources to social modernization and economic growth and not to democracy and political development.

Bourguiba steadily consolidated government control over political life in order to avoid the chaos and serial *coups d'etat* that characterized much of the Arab and African post-colonial experience. The Tunisian people essentially shared this objective and acquiesced to extensive limitations on political participation. Bourguiba's politics were strictly secular, and he insisted that the country would be also. He ignored the country's Arab/Islamic history and connected modern Tunisia to a pre-Islamic past—its Carthaginian heritage—while simultaneously secularizing the state and weakening traditional Islamic institutions.[47] At the same time, his regime embarked upon an economic and social development program based on a socialist model. This model failed and the government changed course; the eventual result was impressive economic performance and very progressive social programs involving public education and literacy, economic mobility, and the position of women in society.

The process of tightening regime control accelerated after the 1987 "palace coup" by Ben Ali, who maintained that no accommodation with Islamists was possible, and considered Islamism to be a disease against which the public must be "inoculated." The country's 2003 anti-terrorism law allowed the jailing of those threatening national security. It was used almost exclusively against Islamists, primarily Islamist-leaning youths using the Internet "illegally" (i.e., blogging or visiting *jihadist* websites.)[48] The pre-January 14th state of affairs in Tunisia was one of comprehensive government domination of the public space and virtually all political activity—not just that of Islamists, but of all potential opposition groups. The Ministry of Interior and Local Development had full power and authority over civil associations and decided at will to register them or not. Without being officially registered, independent associations were not legal entities and could not establish offices, hire employees, raise funds, and conduct their activities.[49] North Africa scholar Kristina Kausch noted that "all truly independent organizations [in Tunisia] that work on issues related to human rights and democracy are denied legal recognition, operate under serious financial, organizational, and personal constraints, and are placed in constant confrontation with the regime."[50] The resulting lack of institutional experience will affect the ability of political groups to organize themselves to compete in elections. Under the current constitution, Islam is the state religion, but it has been a government-controlled version of the religion since independence. The state controlled mosque construction, sermon content, religious education, and appointment and remuneration of *imams*. While these constraints have been relaxed by the interim government, *imams* will not necessarily have *carte blanche* to speak out. When several *imams* delivered uncensored Friday sermons attacking politicians such as the outgoing interim Prime Minister Mohamed Ghannouchi, an official from the Ministry of Religious Affairs stated: "In the event of too many excesses, then measures will be taken. Mosques are not meant to be venues for defamation and personal attacks. An *imam* is not a judge, and the law is above all."[51]

More than 40 legal political parties now exist and are eligible to compete in elections, the first of which will occur on July 24th to elect the National Constituent Assembly, which in turn will draft a new constitution and guide the country to as yet unscheduled parliamentary and presidential elections. How this council will be elected and whether political parties will play a role in both the electoral process and the council's internal organization and processes remains unclear. A "higher court for the achievement of the objectives of the revolution, political reform and democratic transition," appointed by the interim government, has promulgated a new electoral procedures law governing the July 24th election. This group decided that the members of the Constituent Assembly will be elected under a one-ballot majority system as opposed to proportional representation based on party lists or a two-ballot majority (run-off) system.

This decision will have a major impact on the trajectory of Tunisian politics and of political Islam, as it favors strong parties but also encourages weaker parties to form electoral coalitions. If the new law permits successful parties to establish blocs within the Constituent Assembly, and if the assembly's decisions are majority or plurality-based, then a dominant party or coalition could essentially draft the new constitution (adoption of which, it should be said, will be put to a national referendum.) A new interim government will be drawn from the elected assembly, so a dominant party could also form the country's temporary executive. *Al-Nahda* is, at least hypothetically, in the best position to do well—as mentioned above, the party could score 30 to 40 percent of the votes. Tunisians are worried about this, and, as one expressed it, don't want the Islamists to "hijack the mood of the people."[52] Many, however, are equally worried about fringe parties on the left, and specifically single out the Communists.[53]

While the Jasmine Revolution has shaken off the old regime, Tunisians have not rejected the secular nature of the state and the society and in general are not predisposed to religious or political Islamism. A vigorous public debate on religion and politics—a taboo subject under the Ben Ali regime—is ongoing, and it is clear that it would not at all be easy for Islamists to hijack the revolution outside the electoral process, if they chose to try. *Al-Nahda's* electoral fortunes will rest in large measure on the ability of competing parties to offer the voters a compelling vision of Tunisia's future.

ENDNOTES

[1] Alaya Allani, "The Islamists in Tunisia between Confrontation and Participation, 1980-2008," *Journal of North African Studies* 14, no 2 (June 2009), 258.

[2] Christopher Alexander, "Opportunities, Organizations, and Ideas: Islamists and Workers in Tunisia and Algeria," *International Journal of Middle East Studies* 32 (2000), 465-490, 466.

[3] Jennifer Noyon, *Islam, Politics, and Pluralism: Theory and Practice in Turkey, Jordan, Tunisia, and Algeria* (London: The Royal Institute of International Affairs, 2003), 100.

[4] Alexander, "Opportunities, Organizations, and Ideas: Islamists and Workers in Tunisia and Algeria."

[5] Susan Walsh, "Islamist Appeal in Tunisia," Middle East Journal 40, no.4 (Autumn 1986), 652.

[6] Ibid., 653.

[7] Ibidem.

[8] Ibidem, 657.

[9] Noyon, *Islam, Politics, and Pluralism*, 99.

[10] Ibid., 101.

[11] Perkins, *A History of Modern Tunisia*, 190.

[12] Noyon, *Islam, Politics, and Pluralism*, 103.

[13] Author's correspondence with Tunisian academic and lawyer, September 2009.

[14] Noyon, *Islam, Politics, and Pluralism*, 99.

[15] Mohamed Elhachmi Hamdi, *The Politicisation of Islam: A Case Study of Tunisia* (Boulder, CO: Westview Press, 1998), 107.

[16] Noyon, *Islam, Politics, and Pluralism*, 101

[17] As cited in John L. Esposito and Francois Burgat, eds. *Modernizing Islam* (New Brunswick, NJ: Rutgers University Press, 2003), 78.

[18] Hamdi, *The Politicisation of Islam: A Case Study of Tunisia*, 109.

[19] Esposito and Burgat, *Modernizing Islam*, 79.

[20] Al-Munji Al-Suaydani, "Ennahda Movement Leader Talks to Asharq Al-Awsat," *Al-Sharq al-Awsat* (London), February 7, 2011, http://www.aawsat.com/english/news.asp?section=3&id=24070.

[21] Walsh, "Islamist Appeal in Tunisia," 656.

[22] Allani, "The Islamists in Tunisia between Confrontation and Participation, 1980-2008," 266.

[23] Author's discussions with civil society figures and officials in Tunis, March 10-12, 2011.

[24] Allani, "The Islamists in Tunisia between Confrontation and Participation, 1980-2008," 258.

[25] Interview with Tahrir spokesman Ridha Belhaj, *Assarih* (Tunis), March 11, 2011.

[26] Ibid.

[27] Belhaj interview with Al-Jazeera Television, March 10, 2011.

[28] Interview with an-Nahda official Abdelfattah Moro on Al-Jazeera Television, March 10, 2011.

[29] *Assabah* (Menzah) daily, February 28, 2011.

[30] U.S. Department of State, Office of the Coordinator for Counter-terrorism, "Appendix C: Background Information on Other Terrorist Groups," in *Country Reports on Terrorism 2007* (Washington, DC: U.S. Department of State, April 2008), http://www.state.gov/documents/organization/31947.pdf.

[31] "Chapter 2: Country Reports – Middle East and North Africa Overview," in *Country Reports on Terrorism*, http://www.state.gov/s/ct/rls/crt/2007/103708.htm.

[32] Kausch, "Tunisia: The Life of Others," 5.

[33] Author's correspondence with Tunisian academic and lawyer, September 2009.

[34] Kausch, "Tunisia: The Life of Others," 20.

[35] Ibid.

[36] "Tunisia," Central Intelligence Agency *World Factbook*, July 2010. Poverty line figure is 2005 est. Unemployment rate is 2009 est.

[37] Alexander, "Opportunities, Organizations, and Ideas: Islamists and Workers in Tunisia and Algeria," 467.

[38] This and other demographic statistics derived from the U.S. Central Intelligence Agency's *World Factbook*, https://www.cia.gov/library/publications/the-world-factbook/.

[39] "Tunisia Islamist Trends back to the Forefront," *Al-Arabiya* (Dubai), February 1, 2011, http://www.alarabiya.net/articles/2011/01/20/134294.html.

[40] Author's discussions with civil society figures and officials in Tunis, March 10-12, 2011.

[41] Author's correspondence with Tunisian academic and lawyer, September 2009.

[42] Lise Storm, "The Persistence of Authoritarianism as a source of Radicalization in North Africa," *International Affairs* 85, no. 5, September 2009, 1011.

[43] Author's correspondence with Tunisian academic and lawyer, September 2009.

[44] Allani, "The Islamists in Tunisia between Confrontation and Participation, 1980-2008," 258.

[45] Roberts, Address before the Center for Strategic & International Studies.

[46] Ibid.

[47] Noyon, *Islam, Politics, and Pluralism*, 96.

[48] Roberts, Address before the Center for Strategic & International Studies.

[49] Kausch, "Tunisia: The Life of Others," 9.

[50] Ibid., 5.

[51] Quoted in *Al-Musawwar* (Cairo), March 7, 2011.

[52] Author's discussions with civil society figures and officials in Tunis, March 10-12, 2011.

[53] Ibid.

ALGERIA

QUICK FACTS

Population: 34,596,184

Area: 2,381,741 sq km

Ethnic Groups: Arab-Berber 99%, European less than 1%

Religions: Sunni Muslim (state religion) 99%, Christian and Jewish 1%

Government Type: Republic

GDP (official exchange rate): $136.4 billion

Map and Quick Facts courtesy of the CIA World Factbook (Last Updated June 2010)

Since independence, Islamist parties and armed groups have made up the major opposition to successive Algerian regimes. The decade-long period of Islamist-related civil strife in Algeria (1988-1999), which pitted security forces against armed Islamist militants, claimed over 150,000 lives, most of them civilian. Such a level of brutality had not been witnessed there since Algeria's War of Independence from France (1954-62); however, the more recent decline of strife in Algeria should not be seen as synonymous with a diminution in the appeal and activities of Islamism in the country. The policy of national reconciliation initiated by the Algerian government in 1999 and again in 2005 has contributed to the decline of armed Islamism, but—perhaps unwittingly—serves to legitimate and empower political Islamism. Recent years have seen the rise of Islamism in the Algerian political sphere, with the growth of Islamist political parties and their entrenchment through the acquisition of parliamentary seats in national elections. While these parties have of late diminished in stature, the Islamist spirit nonetheless remains widespread in Algeria.

ISLAMIST ACTIVITY

GSPC/AQIM

Prior to its 2006 merger with the bin Laden network, the Salafist Group for Preaching and Combat, or GSPC, was—in the words of one member—"a military organization, following the Salafist creed and ideology, fighting in *jihad* against the Algerian regime, which has abandoned Islam and its masters among the Jews and Christians [in order] to restore the rightly guided Caliphate and to implement *Shari'ah* and remove the oppression and humiliation from the shoulders of our oppressed brothers."[1] Now retooled as al-Qaeda in the Islamic Maghreb (AQIM), the organization simultaneously follows this basic ideology and expands upon it. While maintaining a strong domestic and regional vision, it simultaneously seeks "to spread the fragrance of *jihad* in every country and region and ignite flames under the feet of the Jews, Christians, and apostates."[2]

GSPC/AQIM is concentrated mainly in the country's ethnically Kabylie region and in the Algerian south, along the Sahel, where it has conducted various operations. The state's relatively successful assaults on AQIM in the Kabylie region have compelled the group to move its activities to other areas. The group's membership includes a great number of Afghans and a multitude of smaller *jihadist* groups that the larger AQIM has absorbed over the past half-decade. Authorities estimate that AQIM now consists of fewer than 1,000 members, some of them Arab Afghans or other veterans of the war against the Soviets in Afghanistan.[3] As claimed by AQIM's leader, Abdelmalek Droukdel [a.k.a. Abou Moussab Abdel Wadoud], "the large proportion of our *mujahideen* comes from Algeria. And there is a considerable number of Mauritanians, Libyans, Moroccans, Tunisians, Mali's [sic] and Nigerians [sic] brothers."[4]

Knowledge of AQIM's organizational structure is incomplete; however, it is known that the group is divided into geographic zones, each constituting combatant units (*kata'ib*). The entire organization is presided over by a national leadership, which consists of the emir, religious scholars, a consultative committee, a political committee, a financial committee, and a media committee. The majority of the troops, about 700, are concentrated in the Kabylie region (the eastern part of Algeria), while some 200-300 are concentrated in the Sahara-Sahel area.[5]

Although there is no evidence that the GSPC received any financing from Osama bin Laden's organization, its conversion into AQIM in 2007 resulted in al-Qaeda extending at least rhetorical support to the newly-born regional franchise.[6] Though AQIM since has been weakened as a result of persistent counterterrorism operations carried out by Algerian security forces,[7] has virtually no support among the broader Algerian population and has suffered many defections, bin Laden's backing has been one of its sources of strength. The organization has refused to give up its *jihad* despite Algeria's Civil Concord (September 1999) and the Charter of Peace and National Reconciliation (September 2005), which basically grant amnesty to those militants who agree to lay down their arms. The group also imitates al-Qaeda's propaganda methods, videotaping attacks on ambushed soldiers.

AQIM claims that its methods differ from those of the Armed Islamic Group (GIA), from which it split in 1998. It alleges that it does not target civilians, but instead wages war against the *taghut* (the tyrannical "non-Islamic" state). The group has followed al-Qaeda's lead in suicide bombings, as evidenced by the spate of bombings carried out by the group in 2007. The most significant took place in Algiers in April, September, and December 2007 against government structures, including the seat of the government, the Constitutional Council, and security forces barracks, killing dozens of people. Subsequently, in March, June, August and October 2009, AQIM conducted suicide operations that also resulted in heavy casualties.[8] It has advertised for young recruits to conduct suicide bombings via the Internet.[9]

Evidence suggests these *istishhadyin* (martyrdom seekers) join AQIM not because of political grievances, but due to socioeconomic marginalization and for theological reasons. This new breed of *jihadi* is largely unknown to the country's security services, and is distinguished by its young age (generally 15-25).[10] Indeed, the core members of AQIM have now targeted vulnerable, unemployed, and/or delinquent young people, transforming them into nihilists to whom they promise entrance to heaven through martyrdom.

Nevertheless, in 2009, suicide attacks in Algeria declined;[11] four attacks, targeting the barracks of municipal guards and military barracks, were carried out, as opposed to five major ones in 2008[12] and six devastating attacks in 2007.[13] AQIM has also emulated al-Qaeda's attack methods by using lethal Vehicle Borne Improvised Explosive Devices (VBIED), which has led to numerous casualties among security forces since 2007.

AQIM has also internationalized its activities because of its links to al-Qaeda, thereby securing additional resources through kidnappings and illicit trafficking (drugs, small arms, cigarettes, and so forth). AQIM has also succeeded in attracting militants from neighboring countries. Although the breakdown in nationalities within the group is not known, security forces claim that many members come from Mauritania, Libya, and even Nigeria. The internationalization of AQIM and its association with al-Qaeda has allowed it to avoid the fate of the GIA, which was decimated following the killing of its leader Antar Zouabri by the security forces in February 2002.

Notably, this international shift in focus has created dissension within the Algerian Islamist movement. AQIM has lost support domestically for serving an alien organization and for importing methods abhorrent to Algerian society, such as suicide bombings.[14]

The income of AQIM comes mostly from smuggling, credit-card fraud, and car theft.[15] Kidnapping foreigners has also been used to finance AQIM's activities since many countries, such as Switzerland, Austria, Germany, and Canada, have paid ransoms in exchange for the release of their citizens. Conceivably, kidnapping foreigners furthers AQIM's political objectives by dissuading foreign investment and thus weakening the allegedly apostate regimes that the group is hoping to remove from power in the Maghreb-Sahel region. The combination of banditry, kidnappings, and armed actions have helped the group amass considerable resources for the pursuit of its activities. The most recent collection of funds came in the form of an 3.8 million Euro ransom for the summer 2010 release of two Spanish hostages.[16] And although the Canadian, Austrian, and French governments, each of whose citizens also had been kidnapped, deny having paid any ransoms to AQIM, reliable sources as well as media reports indicate that substantial amounts of money (estimated in tens of millions of Euros) have indeed been paid to secure their release.[17]

AQIM's kidnappings are not limited to foreigners; the group also resorts to kidnapping Algerian nationals, a fact rarely, if ever, reported in the Western media. In 2009 alone, more than 20 Algerians were kidnapped, mainly in the Kabylie region, where AQIM has a strong presence.[18] AQIM is also known to use phony roadblocks to extort money and belongings from citizens after reading them religious sermons. There is evidence that AQIM also receives money from drug trafficking. The United Nations has warned that "terrorists and anti-government forces in the Sahel extract resources from the drug trade to fund their operations, purchase equipment, and pay foot-soldiers."[19] This does not mean that AQIM has become simply a criminal group, however. To the contrary, it seems that the money it extorts is used to serve its ideological goals.

The Algerian state has recently instigated a relatively effective crackdown against AQIM. The state reacted to the deadly attacks that AQIM launched against security forces.[20] The losses within AQIM's ranks in 2009 are believed to have reached 200, including about 20 emirs.[21] The population has also helped thwart kidnappings, as in November in Tigzirt, when the Kabylie population forced the kidnappers to release an industrialist. Indeed, there has been an increase in the mobilization of villagers to resist AQIM's operations in that region. State security operations have continued to this day, with notable results. In the first eight months of 2010, 88 armed insurgents – including 15 emirs – were eliminated.[22]

Political Parties: FIS, MSP, Nahda, MRN

The emergence of Islamist political parties in Algeria is a comparatively recent phenomenon.[23] These parties gained legal status only after the political liberalization initiated by the regime following bloody riots in October 1988. Most of the Islamist parties born in the period between 1989 and 1991 emerged out of a heterogeneous Islamist movement that took root in the 1960s. The most powerful and radical of them was the FIS, which was banned in March 1992 following its overwhelming victory in the first round of the legislative elections the previous December. Notwithstanding its popularity (it won overwhelming victories in the 1990 municipal elections and in the 1991 legislative elections), its impressive organization, and its capacity to mobilize large segments of society, authorities banned the group because of its radical ideology and the threat it purportedly posed to the state and society. Although FIS is defunct today, its influence has not vanished. Some of its members joined the still-legal Islamist parties and/or voted for them during elections, while others joined the multitude of armed groups that have fought the state since the 1990s.

Today three legal Islamist parties remain active on the political scene: the Movement for Society and Peace (MSP), the Movement for Islamic Renaissance (Nahda), and its offshoot, the Movement for National Reform (MRN). All three endorse the eventual application of *sharia* law, but unlike the FIS, which wished to immediately implement it, these parties (the MSP in particular) seek a gradual implementation of Islamic principles.

MSP, the largest Islamist party in Algeria, was created in 1990 as the Movement for Islamic Society/HAMAS, but changed its name to conform to the 1996 constitution, which forbids the use of religion for political ends. The group belongs to the "presidential alliance," a conservative mixture of nationalist, Islamist, and technocratic parties. In 2007, the MSP secured 52 seats in the 389-member Popular National Assembly (APN) that serves as Algeria's Parliament.[24]

Nahda, meanwhile, split in 1999 when its charismatic founding leader, Abdallah Djaballah, created yet another party, the Movement for National Reform (MRN or Islah). MRN did very well in the 2002 local elections, coming in ahead of both the MSP and Nahda, after which it demanded a ban on the import of alcoholic beverages in 2004. However, Djaballah did quite poorly in the 2004 presidential election, receiving only 5 percent of the votes.[25] The party has undergone further crises and it is not clear what influence either Nahda or MSN have, for, like most Algerian political parties, the fate of the parties are often linked to the individual that founded them. In the 2007 legislative election, the two parties garnered only five and three parliamentary seats, respectively.

All three parties work in cooperation with the Algerian government, and abide by its constraints on political participation. In 2009, all three endorsed the candidacy of sitting president Abdelaziz Bouteflika for a third term in office.[26] This coexistence is a product of the comparative decline in popularity experienced by Islamist political parties in recent years, as well as their internal turmoil. For example, the MSP split into two factions in 2009 due to the loss of popularity of its president, Aboudjera Soltani, who served as a minister under various governments. Many members of the party did not

agree with Soltani's unconditional support for President Abdelaziz Bouteflika, and in June 2009 orchestrated a revolt inside the MSP.

However, the electoral decline of Algeria's Islamist political parties should
not be interpreted as a decline of Islamism in the country writ large.

ISLAMISM AND SOCIETY

Islam in Algeria is not simply the main religion of the population; it constitutes the primary foundation of identity and culture. Islamic beliefs and
practices regulate social behavior and, to a large extent, govern social relations. Neither Islam nor the Islamist phenomenon can be disconnected from
Algerian history. While the socioeconomic failure of the 1980s goes a long
way toward explaining the emergence of Islamism in Algerian society, its
doctrinal aspects derive at least in part from the crisis of identity generated by
132 years of colonial rule. France's often-brutal colonialism served to undermine the principal local religious institutions; mosques and religious schools
were closed and sometimes turned into churches or even bars, religious lands
were expropriated, and Islamic culture was openly held up to be inferior to
Christian/Western civilization. Because France resorted to coercion to establish its cultural hegemony, and because French colonialists treated the native
population and values with contempt, Algerians as a whole clung to Islam.
The country's nationalist movement used Arab-Islamic values as symbols for
popular mobilization against colonialism, and contemporary Islamists often
claim that they are the legitimate offspring of that effort, insisting that Sheikh
Abdelhamid bin Badis, head of the Association of *Ulama*, inspired the war
for independence through his famous motto, "Islam is our religion; Arabic is
our language; Algeria is our motherland."

In the 1980s, the FIS enjoyed considerable support among all segments of
society in Algeria because the party stood for Islamic ideals, such as social
justice and the elimination of corruption, that were widely viewed as benevo-
lent. Of added appeal was the group's promise to improve socioeconomic
conditions, which tapped into the population's feelings of betrayal by the
government's liberal policies of the 1980s and 1990s, which resulted in high
unemployment and the loss of social benefits Algerians had enjoyed under
the socialist welfare state. This popularity translated into overwhelming electoral victories on the part of the FIS in 1990 and 1991. However, the violence subsequently carried out by extremists in the 1990s gradually eroded
the popularity of Islamist groups.

Today, Islamism is still prevalent in Algeria; however, the majority of Algerians no longer support armed groups the way they did in the early and mid-
1990s. The brutal massacres the armed groups committed in 1996-1999

alienated large segments of the population, while authorities have progressively dismantled the small number of die-hard support groups. Currently, only a few marginalized youths are attracted by groups like AQIM. Rather, Islamism today has become a form of social conservativism with no institutional or partisan attachment.[27] As seen above, Islamist parties did rather poorly in the 2007 legislative elections. This decline was confirmed in the April 2009 presidential election during which the Islamist candidates were marginalized, with the Nahda candidate Djahid Younsi garnering a mere 1.3 percent of the votes and others even less. Based on this analysis, it is possible to conclude that Islamism, at least in its political form, is appealing to no more than two percent of the electorate.[28] Even if the relatively popular leader of the Movement for National Reform had not boycotted the election and participated, as he did in 2004 (when he obtained 5% of the votes), the Islamist vote would still be less than 10 percent.

Therefore, while it is hard to gauge the present popularity of Islamism as a social and political movement, what is certain is that the institutional parties as well as the armed groups have lost the appeal that they had throughout the 1990s and even in the early 2000s. One can advance four reasons for such decline: 1) the legacy of the civil strife which left more 150,000 dead, mostly innocent civilians; 2) the loss of legitimacy of the armed groups, which resorted to barbaric methods to impose their will upon the population; 3) the relative success of the 2005 National Reconciliation, which led to the surrender of thousands of armed militants and the extension of amnesty to numerous Islamists; and, 4) general disappointment with Islamist political parties, which are perceived as opportunistic and self-serving.

ISLAMISM AND THE STATE

In 1989, Algerian authorities, in violation of a constitution that forbade the existence of parties based on religion, legalized the newly-born radical Islamist party, the FIS. A front made up of a variety of forces, including Arab alumni of the Afghan *jihad*, the FIS eventually became one of the most potent armed groups against the state. In June 1990, the government organized nationwide municipal elections, the first pluralist elections in the country. In December 1991, the authorities went through with the first round of parliamentary elections despite the increasing intimidation wielded by Islamists against their opponents. The ultimate cancellation by the civilian-military authorities of the election results on grounds that the victory of the FIS would have put an end to the democratic process altogether, and the banning of the FIS shortly thereafter—along with the imprisonment of its leaders—resulted in a crisis of the state. The cancellation provided hardliners within the FIS with the ammunition to overrule more moderate elements favorable to peaceful electoral practices. By 1993, the rift within the FIS and the absence of clear leadership made possible the emergence of an armed insurrection carried out by various factions that until then had existed under the FIS umbrella. Some retained affiliation with the FIS under the banner of the Islamic Salvation Army (AIS). Other smaller and more obscure groups were led by self-proclaimed emirs who set up cells to conduct *jihad*. The civil strife that ensued not only pitted the security forces against armed groups but also spilled over to ravage the civilian population. The horrible collective massacres of 1997 and 1998 highlighted the Algerian tragedy and the limits of the *tout sécuritaire* option (an entirely security-related response to the insurrection) that so-called éradicateurs (eradicators) within the state had pursued throughout the conflict.

The intensity of the armed Islamist insurrection in the 1990s took Algeria's security forces by surprise. The authorities never envisioned the remarkable organization of the *jihadist* groups, or the significant resources available to them. The level of unrestrained destruction that the armed groups inflicted upon the state structures, personnel, intellectuals, journalists, moderate Islamists, and the various strata of society was such that some spoke of the demise of the Algerian state.[29] Out of fear of Islamist reprisals or other considerations, many foreign governments refused to assist Algerian authorities in the fight against terrorism. It was not until after the September 11, 2001 attacks that the international community mobilized to help the Algerian government in its fight against terrorism.

At the peak of the insurgency in 1994-95, Algerian authorities realized that unless they mobilized all the resources at their disposal, including the civilian population, they would fail to defeat armed Islamist groups. The police and *gendarmerie* services, though designed to defend a territory five times the size of France, were fewer in number than those in neighboring Morocco or tiny Tunisia. The public industrial sector and other state structures had little security.

Aware of the near-collapse of the state and its institutions, civilian and military authorities took measures to safeguard the state. The first action was to remove elected Islamist officials from the municipalities and replace them with state-appointed officials, because authorities feared they would provide logistical support for the insurgents. Armed Islamists eventually assassinated many of those replacements. The state also decided to arm thousands of people, many of them unemployed youths, throughout the country to serve as auxiliary forces for regular troops. These security agents, known as *gardes communaux*, played a critical role in fighting Islamist insurgents.

To protect public infrastructures, the authorities forced companies to create specially trained security services (known as the *services de sûreté interne d'établissements*) within those organizations. According to Algerian officials, within one year of their creation, the existence of such services reduced by 75 percent the number of acts of sabotage against social and economic structures.[30] The state also created the *détachements de protection et de sûreté*, brigades entrusted with the protection of industrial plants. Because *jihadists* targeted isolated villages and the suburbs of most cities, the authorities also set up the *groupes de légitime défense* [GLDs], which, though sometime deficient, did much to reduce terrorist attacks on innocent civilians.

Moreover, the government increased the size of the police force and provided new recruits with more efficient antiterrorist training, both in Algeria and abroad.[31] The police force acquired some adapted equipment imported from the former Soviet bloc, South Africa, and elsewhere. The state also took measures to thwart the financing of the insurgency; it incorporated a series of decisions, notably "*La lutte contre le blanchiment* (LAB) *et contre le financement du terrorisme* (CFT)," into the 2003 Finance Act (*Loi de Finance*)[32] to combat the funding of terrorist groups and money laundering. These laws allow authorities to trace the financial sources of the terrorist networks through numerous methods, from the freezing of suspicious assets and to the use of intelligence procedures to prevent suspicious financial operations.[33]

Although the government did not take adequate political measures by bringing the perpetrators to trial before they were pardoned, the Civil Concord, which garnered strong support in the September 1999 referendum, was rather successful since thousands of armed insurgents surrendered to the state authorities (although exact figures vary, depending on the source).[34] Subsequently, the 2005 Law on National Reconciliation offered clemency measures and/or pardon for those Islamist fighters who surrendered to the state. In October 2010, the authorities declared that 7,500 armed insurgents had done so.[35] Although relatively successful, the law elicited strong criticism as it did not seek justice against Islamists or members of security forces who committed crimes in the bloody decade of the 1990s; the fates of thousands of people reported missing remain unknown.

Since 9/11, Algeria has cooperated actively with the United States and European governments to fight terrorism. During the 1990s, these countries refrained from assisting Algeria, arguing that Islamist insurgency was a domestic matter triggered by bad governance.[36] However, merely a year after the September 11th attacks, the United States declared its willingness to supply Algeria with some of the weaponry needed to better combat terrorism.[37] Since then, Algeria has become a strategic partner in the U.S. counterterrorism effort against radical Islam.

The Algerian government likewise cooperates closely with the governments of countries in the Sahel, such as Mali and Niger. The most noteworthy pursuit is its participation in the U.S.-led Trans-Saharan Counter-Terrorism Partnership to fight terrorism in the Maghreb-Sahel region.[38]

ENDNOTES

[1]"An Interview with the Chief of the Media Wing from the Salafist Group for Prayer and Combat," *Al-Faath Magazine* 1; no. 1, December 2004, as cited in Evan F. Kohlmann, "Two Decades of Jihad in Algeria: the GIA, the GSPC, and Al-Qaida," The NEFA Foundation, May 2007, 12, http://www.nefafoundation.org/miscellaneous/nefag-spc0507.pdf

[2] Ibid.

[3] Julia Ficatier, Amine Kadi, and Aurore Lartigue, "Al-Qaida au Maghreb islamique, de l'Algérie au Sahel, " *La Croix* (Paris), July 26, 2010, http://www.la-croix.com/article/index.jsp?docId=2433608&rubId=4077#, accessed on 2 September 2010.

[4] "An Interview With Abdelmalek Droukdal," *New York Times*, July 1, 2008, http://www.nytimes.com/2008/07/01/world/africa/01transcriptdroukdal.html?scp=1&sq=droukdal&st=cse.

[5] Ibid; Author's interview with high-level Algerian national security official, Algiers, Algeria, September 2010.

[6] On the process of integration of the GSPC into al Qaeda, see Mathieu Guidère, *Al-Qaïda à la conquête du Maghreb— Le terrorisme aux portes de l'Europe* (Monaco: Editions du Rocher, 2007).

[7] In September 2010, it was reported that 88 terrorists had been killed from January to August 2010. See Neila B., "88 terroristes dont 13 'émirs' éliminés en 8 mois," *Liberté* (Algiers), September 5, 2010.

[8] See United States Department of State, Office of the Coordinator for Counterterrorism, *Country Reports on Terrorism 2009* (Washington, DC: U.S. Department of State, 2010), 115. Those attacks resulted in the deaths of two security guards in March, 18 officers in June, and seven security guards in October, while the attack in August injured 25 people, including 4 police officers. It should be noted that these attacks result in significant loss of life and injury among civilians as well.

[9] Ikram Ghioua, "Les salafistes, les cybers et l'endoctrinement, " *L'Expression* (Algiers), November 7, 2007.

[10] Madjid T. "Le groupe terroriste manipule les adolescents pour leur recrutement à 13 ans, dans les maquis du GSPC," *Liberté* (Algeirs), March 8, 2008, 3 ; See also Amel Boubekeur, "Salafism and Radical Politics in Post conflict Algeria," Carnegie Endowment for International Peace Carnegie Paper no. 11, September 2008, http://www.carnegieendowment.org/files/salafism_radical_politics_algeria.pdf.

[11] For a detailed account, see Madjid T. "Attentats terroristes: 2009 l'année la moins meurtrière," *Liberté* (Algeirs), December 29, 2009, http://www.liberte-algerie.com/edit.php?id=127655.

[12] United States Department of State, Office of the Coordinator for Counterterrorism, *Country Reports on Terrorism 2008* (Washington, DC: U.S. Department of State, 2009), 112.

[13] United States Department of State, Office of the Coordinator for Counterterrorism, *Country Reports on Terrorism 2007* (Washington, DC: U.S. Department of State, 2008), 104.

[14] B. Naila and Hakim Benyahia, "Le retrait de l'organisation d'Al Afghani ...un retrait tactique ou bien une fuite?" *Echorouk* (Algiers), August 16, 2009, http://www.echroukonline.com/fra/index.php?news=4801&print.

[15] Author's interviews with security officials, Algiers, Algeria, September, 2010.

[16] "Spanish Hostages Freed By Al Qaeda Return Home," *France 24*, August 24, 2010, http://www.france24.com/en/20100824-spanish-hostages-freed-al-qaeda-return-home-mali-mauritania-aqmi.

[17] See Diogo Noivo, "AQIM's Hostage Taking and the Ransom Dilemma," Institute of International Relations and Security *IPRIS Viewpoints* no. 21, October 2010.

[18] Madjid T. "Attentats terroristes: 2009 l'année la moins meurtrière," *Liberté* (Algiers), December 29, 2009, http://www.liberte-algerie.com/edit.php?id=127655.

[19] United Nations Office of Drugs and Crime, "Security Council debates 'devastating impact' of drug trafficking," December 9, 2009, http://www.unodc.org/unodc/en/frontpage/2009/December/security-council-debates-devastating-impact-of-drug-trafficking.html.

[20] In 2009, AQIM ambushes led to a death toll of 120 among security forces, who began carrying out major and effective counter-offensives against AQIM troops and support networks, leading to a reduction of AQIM attacks.

[21] Information has been compiled from various Algerian newspapers, in particular, T. Madjid, "Attentats terroristes 2009 l'année la moins meurtrière, " *Liberté* (Algiers), December 29, 2009, http://www.liberte-algerie.com/edit.php?id=127655&titre=2009; Djaffar Tamani, "Lutte antiterroriste: La résistance citoyenne s'impose de nouveau, " *El Watan* (Algiers), January 11, 2010, http://www.elwatan.com/Lutte-antiterroriste-La-resistance; and "Plus de 200 terroristes tués en 2009 : Al Qaida creuse sa tombe en Algérie, " *Réflexion* (Algeria), December 30, 2009, http://www.reflexiondz.net.

[22] See Neila B., "88 terroristes dont 13 "émirs' éliminés en 8 mois," *Liberté* (Algiers), September 5, 2010.

[23] Yahia H. Zoubir, "Islamist Political Parties in Contemporary Algeria," in Ibrahim M. Abu-Rabi', ed., *The Contemporary Arab Reader on Political Islam* (London: Pluto Press/University of Alberta Press, 2010).

[24] For an analysis of the 2007 election and the performance of the Islamist parties, see Louisa Dris-Aït-Hamadouche, "The 2007 Legislative Elections in Algeria: Political Reckonings," *Mediterranean Politics* 13, no. 1, March 2008, 87-94.

[25] For a detailed analysis, see Yahia H. Zoubir and Louisa Dris-Aït-Hamadouche, "L'islamisme en Algérie: institutionnalisation du politique et déclin du militaire," *Maghreb-Machrek* no. 188 (Summer 2006), 63-86.

[26] Louisa Aït-Hamadouche and Yahia H. Zoubir, "The Fate of Political Islam in Algeria," in Bruce Maddy-Weitzman and Daniel Zisenwine, eds., *The Maghrib in the New Century-Identity, Religion, and Politics* (Gainesville: University of Florida Press, 2007), 103-131.

[27] Rachid Tlemçani, "Les islamistes échappent aujourd'hui à tout contrôle institutionnel ou partisan," *El Watan* (Algiers), April, 23, 2009 , http://www.elwatan.com/Les-islamistes-echappent-aujourd.

[28] See Louisa Dris-Aït-Hamadouche, "Régime et islamistes en Algérie: un échange politique asymétrique?" *Maghreb-Machrek* (Paris) no. 200 (Summer 2009), 43.

[29] Graham Fuller, Algeria: The Next Fundamentalist State? (Santa Barbara: RAND, 1996).

[30] Yahia H. Zoubir and Louisa Aït-Hamadouche, "Penal Reform in Algeria," in Chris Ferguson and Jeffrey O. Isima, eds., *Providing Security for People: Enhancing Security through Police, Justice and Intelligence Reform in Africa* (London: Global Facilitation Network for Security Sector Reform, 2004), 75-84.

[31] Ibid.

[32] Abbas Aït-Hamlat, "Terrorisme au Maghreb-Al-Qaîda menace et l'UE resserre l'étau, " *L'Expression* (Algiers), September 24, 2008, http://www.lexpressiondz.com/article/2/2008-09-24/56544.html.

[33] See "Lutte contre le financement du terrorisme et le blanchiment d'argent. La fin du secret bancaire pour l'argent suspect," *Le Quotidien d'Oran*, January 8, 2003; See also Algeria's National Report, "Mise en œuvre de la Résolution 1373 (2001) Adoptée par le Conseil de Sécurité des Nations-Unies le 28 septembre 2001," which describes at length the actions taken by the Algerian government to implement UN Resolution 1373 on terrorism. See also Yazid F. "Algerie : Le Gouvernement durcit la législation sur les changes, " Ministère de l'Economie et des Finances, Cellule nationale du traitement des informations financières, September 13, 2010, http://www.centif.ci/news.php?id_news=67.

[34] See, for example, "Interview, Le général de corps d'armée Mohamed Lamari, Chef d'état-major de l'Armée nationale populaire (ANP) algérienne," *Le Point* (Paris) no. 1583, January 17, 2003, 44-45.

[35] Souhil B. "Bilan de la réconciliation nationale-7500 terroristes ont bénéficié des dispositions de la charte, " *El Watan* (Algiers), October 4, 2010, http://www.elwatan.com/actualite/7500-terroristes-ont-beneficie-des-dispositions-de-la-charte-04-10-2010-93047_109.php.

[36] Hakim Darbouche and Yahia H. Zoubir, "The Algerian Crisis in European and US Foreign Policies: A Hindsight Analysis," in Francesco Cavatorta and Vincent Durac, eds., *The Foreign Policies of the*

United States the European Union in the Middle East (New York: Routledge, 2009), 32-54.

[37] "The United States and Algeria: Hostility, Pragmatism, and Partnership," in Robert Looney, ed., *Handbook on US Middle East Relations* (London & New York: Routledge, 2009), 219-236.

[38] Yahia H. Zoubir, "The United States and Maghreb-Sahel Security," *International Affairs* 85, no. 5 (Fall 2009), 977-995.

MOROCCO

QUICK FACTS

Population: 31,627,428

Area: 446,550 sq km

Ethnic Groups: Arab-Berber 99.1%, other 0.7%, Jewish 0.2%

Religions: Muslim 98.7%, Christian 1.1%, Jewish 0.2%

Government Type: Constitutional monarchy

GDP (official exchange rate): $91.84 billion

Map and Quick Facts courtesy of the CIA World Factbook (Last Updated July 2010)

Unique among Muslim states, Morocco is a society that has enticed Islamist political movements to become full-fledged political parties, yet has been subjected to jihadist attacks and tolerates an Islamist movement that openly calls for the overthrow of the monarchy and creation of an Islamic state. Facing the dilemma of whether to co-opt Islamists or outlaw their activities, Moroccan ruler King Mohammed has pursued a two-track strategy of encouraging Islamists who oppose violence and support the monarchy to participate in politics, while arresting adherents to Salafist ideology. Whether this strategy will succeed in defusing the Islamist threat to the Moroccan state, however, is still an open question.

ISLAMIST ACTIVITY

A number of Islamist groups and movements, either indigenous or foreign, are currently active in Morocco. Unlike other Muslim nations, however, Islamism in Morocco is quite fragmented.

At-Tawhid
At-Tawhid was created in 1996 by the senior leaders of ash-Shabiba al-

Islamiya, which itself was a secretive militant Islamist movement started in the 1960s and subsequently implicated in several acts of violence including the assassination of Umar Bin Jallun, a famous Moroccan leftist leader.[1] Its goal was to ultimately gain legitimacy and become a political force in its own right. However, due to continued internal disagreement and refusal by the King to recognize its political legitimacy, between 1996 and 1997 At-Tawhid negotiated an arrangement with the Democratic Constitutional Movement (DCM) that ultimately integrated it into the DCM. The latter ultimately changed its name in 1998 to the Party for Justice and Development (PJD).[2] Today, the original leadership of At-Tawhid considers the PJD to represent its so-called "political wing."[3] (A full description of the PJD follows below)

Justice and Charity

Justice and Charity, formed in 1988, has been the most virulent Islamist political and religious movement in Morocco. Considered illegitimate and barely tolerated by the Moroccan government, JC has gained adherents though its role as the sole indigenous Islamist movement challenging the monarchy (including advocating its overthrow), and through its extensive social and charitable organizational network. The Moroccan government refuses to recognize JC as a political party.[4]

JC advocates a restoration of Islamic law (*sharia*), but asserts allegiance to democratic principles in order to differentiate itself as a political movement that opposes Morocco's autocratic political system. Since the 1970s, its leader and founder, Sheikh Abdessalam Yassine, has openly challenged the legitimacy of the Moroccan monarchy. For this, he was tried in 1984, and sentenced to house arrest—a sentence that remained in force until 1989.[5] The following year, JC was officially outlawed pursuant to a ban that would endure until modified by the current king, Mohammed VI, in 2004. Sheikh Yassine's daughter, Nadia Yassine, at present is the movement's chief political organizational leader.

JC is committed to the dissolution of Morocco's current constitutional system and the elimination of the monarchy. In its place, JC advocates the creation of an Islamic republic in Morocco. JC is openly critical of King Mohammed VI, and has placed itself in permanent conflict with Morocco's government. Nevertheless, JC opposes the use of violence and armed struggle, preferring to rely on civil disobedience to achieve its goals. The magnitude of support for JC is a closely guarded secret, both by the organization itself and by the Moroccan government, although most observers consider its support substantial given its extensive charitable and social network.[6]

Given the Moroccan government's intense opposition to JC internally, the group's leadership decided to "export" the JC movement to Europe, beginning roughly in 1996, through the creation of the Muslim Participation and Spirituality (MPS) Association.[7] MPS has established chapters in major capitals throughout Europe, headed by JC Islamist activists who have fled Morocco. The goal of MPS is to generate opposition to Morocco's king and government through political activities in order to win legal status for the JC inside Morocco.[8] The French and Belgian MPS branches regularly organize demonstrations against Morocco. Ms. Yassine also visits France regularly to denounce the repression of JC, and on June 17, 2006 she created the "New Europe-Morocco Friendship"—an association based in Belgium which convened a conference on the theme "Human Rights Flouted in Morocco."[9] In recent years, Ms. Yassine has undertaken several tours of Europe to strengthen the presence of MPS on the Continent.

The Party of Justice and Development (PJD)

In order to co-opt Islamist movements in Morocco, King Hassan II permitted the emergence of a new political movements that incorporated Islamist orientations – the most significant being Justice and Development Party (PJD), which draws on Islamic values and inspiration from Turkey's Justice and Development Party (although there is no official connection between the two parties).

Formed in 1967 and originally named the Constitutional and Democratic Popular Movement (MPDC), the PJD changed its name to the Justice and Development Party in 1998.[10] That year, the movement formally coalesced from a coalition of small, moderate Islamist organizations, including conservative Islamist pro-monarchial political figures. In contrast to JC, PJD is a political party that has competed in Morocco's parliamentary elections since 1997 (when it did so as the MPDC).

In 2002, PJD became the country's leading opposition party, having won 42 of 325 seats in Morocco's parliament, making it the third-largest group in the national legislature. In the legislative elections of 2007 (Morocco's last parliamentary elections), the PJD won the largest percentage of the popular vote (10.9 percent on local, and 13.4 percent on the national lists). As a result, the PJD gained 46 seats overall in the Chamber of Representatives, increasing its overall representation by four seats over the 2002 election.[11]

Unlike JC, PJD is non-revolutionary and pro-monarchist, and does not question Morocco's constitutional system. Nor does it advocate the creation of an Islamist state, or caliphate, in Morocco. Indeed, the PJD intentionally downplays any religious agenda. Nevertheless, it views itself as the guardian of Morocco's Muslim identity and conservative religious traditions, and opposes any effort that would compromise Morocco's Islamic character. Thus it opposes further westernization of Moroccan society, but it pragmatically recognizes the importance of Morocco's ties to the West. The PJD also regards itself as a bulwark against radical Islamic groups such as JC.

Contesting elections since 1997, PJD has gradually gained popular support throughout Morocco, and has become quite entrenched in Morocco's political process – balancing its participation in legislative affairs with its adherence to an Islamic political agenda. In recent years, PJD legislatures have focused their attention on ameliorating Morocco's significant social and economic challenges. Because it is in the opposition, however, the party's ability to influence actual policy is limited, with only marginal ability to translate its agenda into meaningful programs that would obtain greater popular support.

Moreover, the intentional ambiguity by which it approaches questions of Islam and religion has raised questions about whether the PJD's goal is to serve as a front for more extremist Islamic inclinations. Indeed, a 2006 report by the Congressional Research Service questioned PJD's agenda and asserted:

> ...like many Islamist groups across the globe, it is difficult to discern the PJD's true goals and objectives over the long run. Some believe that, although the party has agreed to work within the current political system, it remains committed to establishing an Islamic state in Morocco with Islamic law, or *Sharia*, as the basis for legislation.[12]

PJD's agenda in parliament has occasionally taken it into pure *sharia* territory—calling for prohibition against alcohol consumption and distribution, and challenging media that it views as defacing Islamic principles. On other occasions, however, the PJD has trended in the opposite direction. In 2005, for example, the party actively participated in the adoption of a new, more liberal version of the country's code regulating marriage and family life, known as the *Mudawana*.[13] The revision of the Mudawana greatly improved the social status of women in Morocco, and was ridiculed by more conservative Islamists. PJD's leader, Saad Eddine Othmani, defended the PJD's approval of the code's revision, asserting in 2006 that it had been approved by religious leaders, aided families, and was consistent with Islamic traditions.

Salafist Jihadism

Morocco has "numerous small 'grassroots' extremist groups"[14] that collectively adhere to Salafi-*jihadi* ideology. Indeed, Spanish anti-terror judge Baltazar Garzon has stated that "Morocco is the worst terrorist threat to Europe."[15] He estimated that al-Qaeda-linked cells in Morocco number more than 100 and that at least 1,000 terrorists are now being actively sought by Moroccan authorities.[16] Al-Qaeda's regional offshoot, al-Qaeda in the Islamic Maghreb (AQIM), has made recent efforts to bring these disparate groups (which number less than 50 members per grouping, on average) under its umbrella.

AQIM, likes its counterpart al-Qaeda in the Arabian Peninsula (AQAP), constitutes a potent regional terrorist threat not only to Morocco but to

Algeria, Mauritania, Mali and Tunisia. Formed when the Salafist Group for Preaching and Combat (GSPC) reconstituted itself into AQIM in early 2007, its goal has been to integrate all of the North African radical movements, including the Moroccan GICM (Moroccan Islamic Combatant Group).

Salafist *jihadis* as a whole remain a potent threat to Morocco and the West. Scores of young Moroccans traveled to Iraq and Afghanistan to fight Americans and there are continuing arrests of extremists.[17] Salafis also represent a challenge to the Moroccan state, as a number of recent incidents have underscored. On May 16, 2003, terrorists claiming to be members of the GICM launched a series of five coordinated suicide attacks in Casablanca, killing more than 40 people and wounding more than 100. In April 2007, a series of suicide bomb attacks occurred in central Casablanca, one taking place near the U.S. Consulate and one near the American Language Center. In February 2008, Moroccan authorities arrested nearly 40 members of an alleged terrorist network, led by Abdelkader Belliraj, a Belgian-Moroccan suspected of committing multiple assassinations in addition to arms smuggling and money laundering for al-Qaeda.[18] Press reports have at times asserted that more than 100 al-Qaeda-linked cells exist in Morocco, and that Moroccan police have either imprisoned or placed under house arrest/police surveillance over 1,000 Salafist *jihadists* either openly sympathetic to AQIM or part of other hard-core underground Islamist movements.[19]

In the past two years alone, Islamist activity has generated scores of arrests. In July 2008, Moroccan security services arrested 35 members of an alleged terrorist network specializing in the recruitment of volunteers for Iraq.[20] In August of the same year, another 15-person network calling itself "Fath al-Andalus" was reportedly disbanded in Layoune, the capital of the Western Sahara, for planning attacks on the UN peacekeeping force there.[21] There also have been reports of considerable numbers of Moroccans traveling to Mali and Algeria to receive training from AQIM elements.[22]

The impoverished slums in Morocco's inner cities and northern regions have produced many of these extremists, and many of the Moroccan extremist groupings are composed of family members and friends from the same towns and villages. Indeed, the north of Morocco has become especially fertile ground for Salafists who favored Saudi Wahhabism over Morocco's more tolerant version of Islam.

ISLAMISM AND SOCIETY

Under Moroccan law, the monarch is revered as the "Commander of the Faithful" and traces his lineage to the Prophet Mohammad. Consequently, the majority of Moroccans take great pride in their nation's embrace of moderate, tolerant Islam. But segments of the nation's rural regions are populated by adherents to Wahhabism. This is especially true in the northern parts of

Morocco, where the wearing of the *niqab*, or full face veil, is far more common than in Morocco's urban centers.

Social conditions also play a role in Islamist sentiment. Given Morocco's high unemployment rate, year after year thousands of Moroccans risk their lives attempting to illegally immigrate to Europe across the Straits of Gibraltar.[23] Many, however, are left behind, transforming cities like Tangier, Tetouan or Al Houcema into smuggling centers feeding criminal elements and opponents of the regime.

Despite the King's efforts to promote a legislative agenda to modernize Islamic laws governing civil society in Morocco (detailed below), the continued growth of political parties such as the PJD, and the continued political activities by the JC both inside Morocco and in Europe point to the fractures in Morocco's society between those who favor a more moderate, tolerant Islam and significant elements of Morocco's populace which prefer stronger Islamic control over the nation's society and its political system.

Morocco's urban slums and rural north continue to be fertile ground for extremism and its recruiters to AQIM. Indeed, scores, if not hundreds, of Moroccans have volunteered to fight in Iraq and Afghanistan against the United States.[24] Morocco's north, especially cities such as Tetouan and the surrounding Rif Mountain villages have become centers of *jihadist* agitation. It is in Morocco's north that Wahhabism has taken strongest root, as a result of institutional neglect. Following a Berber rebellion against his rule in the early 1980s, King Hassan II largely abandoned the northern tier of Morocco to its own devices. The King rarely visited the north during his reign, and consequently, government services were severely cut, and Islamists filled the void with a social and charitable network offering food and medical treatment to the population. While King Mohammed has reversed his father's policy of abandonment of the north (and even conducted an ancient traditional ceremony of mutual allegiance there[25]), the region is still severely impoverished and deeply dependent on Wahhabi and *jihadi* charitable networks for services not provided by the government.

ISLAMISM AND THE STATE

Following the 2003 Casablanca bombings, the Moroccan government focused increasing attention on modernizing Islamic teaching and Islamic infrastructure and adopted laws liberalizing civil marriage and the role of women in Morocco's society. The Ministry of Endowments and Islamic Affairs was provided new funding and authority to train more moderate Islamic clerics and to expand its educational programs in Morocco's educational system.

In 2005, partially as a retort to the Casablanca bombings, King Mohammed unveiled an unprecedented revision to the code regulating marriage and family life (the *Mudawana*).[26] The revision of the *Mudawana* greatly improved the social status of women, among other innovations. Although hailed by many as courageous effort, the revisions to the *Mudawana* provoked mass demonstrations before they were enacted.

One incident in particular points to Morocco's more aggressive stance against ultra-conservative Muslim clerics who oppose the government's efforts to modernize Morocco's Islamic infrastructure and its religious teachings. In September 2008, Sheikh Mohamed Ben Abderrahman Al Maghraoui issued a highly provocative *fatwa* legitimizing the marriage of underage women as young as nine years old.[27] The Moroccan government sought to discredit the *fatwa* and ordered the immediate closure of 60 Koranic schools under his control. The government also launched an inquiry into Sheikh Al Maghraoui's competence as an Islamic scholar, and the public prosecutor's office initiated a criminal case against him for encouraging pedophilia.[28]

Following the incident, King Mohammed unveiled his "proximity strategy," which represented a modernization program for Islamic institutions in Morocco. Under the program, 3,180 mosques were designated to be "modernized," (essentially a wholesale replacement of *imams* deemed by the regime to be opponents of moderate Islamic principles). Thirty-three thousand new *imams* were to be trained and the number of regional *ulama* councils (charged with overseeing Islamic teaching and the competency of *imams*) was increased from 30 to 70. Moreover, the King ordered the acceleration of a pioneering experiment of training and using women as spiritual guides in order to propagate religious tolerance.[29]

The aborted terrorist plot in 2007 and the continuing threat of *jihadi* sentiment in the country's north have had a negative effect on the pace of King Mohammed's reform agenda. In order to avoid antagonizing conservative Moroccans further, King Mohammed decided to slow the reforms governing the rights of women and the judiciary. Additionally, unlike his father, the King has refrained from playing an activist role in Middle East diplomacy.

For many years Morocco has permitted mainstream Islamic political parties that do not condone extremism and violence to exist and indeed, to participate in elections, although it continues to deny legal status to the JD. Since the Casablanca bombings in 2003, Moroccan authorities have maintained a vigilant and aggressive stance against any *jihadist* movement. Moroccan authorities currently have almost 1,000 prisoners considered to be Islamic radicals in jail.[30] And in July 2007, Moroccan authorities jailed six Islamist politicians who were accused of complicity in a major terrorist plot.[31] On the other hand, the Moroccan government has rewarded Islamic parties that have embraced more moderate Islamic principles, such as the PJD. Notwithstanding the ever-present scourge of *jihadi* operatives in Morocco, the Moroccan government has demonstrated ingenuity in its "divide and conquer" strategy against Islamists who challenge the state. In addition to adopting the above-referenced "proximity strategy" to replace recalcitrant *imams*, authorities have established a grassroots police operation to report on any suspicious activities by Islamists.[32]

The Moroccan government has also implemented a concerted social development program to combat the existence of Islamist-oriented charities that have nurtured radicalism. In the largest "bidonvilles" (shantytowns) in Morocco's cities, significant social welfare, health and education programs have been instituted and many families have been relocated to new affordable housing units.[33]

ENDNOTES

[1]Amr Hamzawy, "Party for Justice and Development in Morocco: Participation And Its Discontents," Carnegie Endowment for International Peace *Carnegie Paper* no. 93, July 2008, 7, http://www.carnegieendowment.org/publications/index.cfm?fa=view&id=20314.

[2] Ibid., 8.

[3] Ibidem, 16.

[4] Samir Amghar, "Political Islam in Morocco," Center for European Policy Studies *CEPS Working Document* No. 269, June 2007.

[5] Ibid.

[6] National Democratic Institute, *Final Report on the Moroccan Legislative Elections*, September 7, 2007.

[7] Amghar, "Political Islam in Morocco."

[8] Ibid.

[9] Ibidem.

[10] Mohammed Hirchi, "Political Islam in Morocco: The Case of the Party of Justice and Development (PJD)," *Concerned African Scholars*, August 2007.

[11] Daniel Williams, "Morocco Parliament May be Controlled by Islamic Party," Bloomberg, December 30, 2009, http://www.bloomberg.com/apps/news?pid=newsarchive&sid=aLXRR7EuJeEo.

[12] Jeremy M. Sharp, *U.S. Democracy Promotion Policy in the Middle East: The Islamist Dilemma* (Washington, DC: Congressional Research Service, June 15, 2006), 11, http://www.fas.org/sgp/crs/mideast/RL33486.pdf.

[13] Hamzawy, "Party for Justice and Development in Morocco: Participation And Its Discontents.".

[14] U.S. Department of State, Office of the Coordinator for Counterterrorism, *Country Reports on Terrorism 2008* (Washington, DC: U.S. Department of State, April 2009), 130, http://www.state.gov/documents/organization/122599.pdf.

[15] Olivier Guitta, "Morocco Under Fire," Weekly Standard, March 29, 2007, http://www.weeklystandard.com/Content/Public/Articles/000/000/013/470ucfqo.asp.

[16] Ibid.

[17] Mustapha Tossa, "Morocco's Fight Against Terrorism," Common Ground News Service, September 2, 2008, http://commongroundnews.org/article.php?id=23883&lan=en&sid=1&sp=0.

[18] U.S. Department of State, *Country Reports on Terrorism 2008*.

[19] Stephen Erlanger and Souad Mekhennet, "Islamic Radicalism Slows Moroccan Reforms," *New York Times*, August 26, 2009, http://www.nytimes.com/2009/08/27/world/africa/27morocco.html.

[20] U.S. Department of State, *Country Reports on Terrorism 2008*.

[21] Ibid.

[22] Ibidem.

[23] *See*, for example, Moha Ennaji, "Illegal Migration From Morocco To Europe," Paper presented before the 7th international Metropolis conference, Oslo, Norway, September 10, 2002, http://international.metropolis.net/events/Metromed/Ennaji_e.pdf.

[24] Andrea Elliott, "Where Boys Grow Up To Be Jihadis," *New York Times Magazine*, November 25, 2007, 16.

[25] Erlanger and Mekhennet, "Islamic Radicalism Slows Moroccan Reforms."

[26] Hamzawy, "Party for Justice and Development in Morocco."

[27] U.S. Department of State, *Country Reports on Terrorism 2008*.

[28] Ibid.

[29] Ibidem.

[30] Erlanger and Mekhennet, "Islamic Radicalism Slows Moroccan Reforms."

[31] Ibid.

[32] Tossa, "Morocco's Fight Against Terrorism."

[33] Ibid.

Sub-Saharan Africa

COUNTRIES

Mauritania
Mali
Sudan
Ethiopia
Somalia
South Africa

Regional Summary

Several countries in Sub-Saharan Africa face new and growing threats from Islamist movements. In West Africa, Mali and Mauritania have been directly affected by the rise of Al Qaeda in the Islamic Maghreb (AQIM), which has carved out a home in the Sahel, while another al Qaeda-affiliated group, al-Shabaab, is in the midst of a fierce insurgency against the weak Somali government. The Islamist threat there, while not new, has grown in potency over the past decade, with an Islamist umbrella group briefly seizing power in 2006, and a potent al Qaeda affiliate currently waging an insurgency against a weak transitional government. In Sudan, the government's own pro-Islamist tendencies have been tempered in recent years.

The impoverished and predominantly Muslim West African nation of Mali seems an inhospitable place for Islamist parties and ideas. It enjoyed a successful transition to democracy in the 1990s and has a history of religious tolerance and pluralism, while religiously-based political parties are explicitly banned by the constitution. Attempts by Iranian and Saudi agents to spread more fundamentalist interpretations of Islam have met with little success. Nevertheless, the ungoverned deserts of Mali now play host to one of al-Qaeda's newest and most dangerous affiliates, AQIM. The presence of AQIM has drawn attention and counterterrorism assistance from the United States, and forced Mali into regional security arrangements with its neighbors.

Like Mali, neighboring Mauritania is poor, predominantly Muslim, and grappling with the emergence of AQIM. However, unlike in Mali, Islamist parties are sanctioned by the government, which has oscillated between military dictators and democratic elections in recent years. Tawassoul constitutes the main Islamist opposition party, although it has hewed a moderate line and opposes acts of violence. AQIM, meanwhile, has proven capable of carrying out terrorist attacks inside Mauritania, including the country's first suicide bombing and the murder of an American aid worker in 2009. Yet there are few indications that the group's radical ideology has taken root among Mauritania's traditionally moderate population. The government has responded to AQIM's rise with an intense crackdown on Islamist suspects and sympathizers and, together with French forces, attacked AQIM encampments in the desert Sahel region in July 2010.

By contrast, few countries in the world are more unstable or more saturated with Islamist militancy than war-torn Somalia, which forms the figurative horn of Africa. Civil war, crushing poverty, and chronic instability have in recent years created space for the emergence of a myriad of Islamist groups, including a potent al-Qaeda affiliate, al-Shabaab, and an umbrella group of several violent Islamist movements known as Hizbul Islam. With little central authority to oppose them, in 2006 the radical Islamic Courts Union (ICU) seized power in Mogadishu. Ethiopian forces intervened shortly afterward in support of the weak Transitional Federal Government (TFG) and the Islamists were overthrown. However, the TFG—fractured and now ruled by the former head of the Islamic Courts Union—exerts limited authority throughout the country as it battles a fierce insurgency led by al-Shabaab, which now holds sway over vast parts of Somalia.

Ethiopia, though only one-third Muslim (and two-thirds Christian), is also home to a panoply of Islamist groups, including elements of al-Qaeda, Tablighi Jamaat, and the Wahhabi-inspired Takfir wal-Hijrah. However, Ethiopia's primary Islamist threats derive from its proximity to neighboring Somalia. Ethiopia was forced to intervene in Somalia in 1996 after cross-border terrorist attacks from the Somali-based AIAI. Again in 2006, Ethiopian forces entered Somalia to unseat from power the AIAI's successor, the Islamic Courts Union. Meanwhile, neighboring Eritrea, with which Ethiopia fought a war in 1998 over a still-unresolved border dispute, is known to support anti-Ethiopian Islamist movements across the region. Domestically, despite a sometimes tense relationship with the Christian-majority government, Ethiopia's Muslims have resisted radical Islamist ideologies and the country remains America's most important counterterrorism ally in the region.

Although Muslims constitute less than two percent of South Africa's population, the country experienced a bout of Islamist-inspired violence in the

1990s and is known to have been used by al-Qaeda's leadership as a safe haven and hub for financial activities. The country's most famous indigenous Islamist outfit, PAGAD, began in the 1980s as a social order movement but by the late 1990s was attacking public and Western targets with pipe bombs. Its leadership, however, was decimated in a crackdown in 2000 and the group has been dormant since. In general, South Africa's 1,000 mosques and educational centers have been unreceptive to radical forms of Islamism and South Africa's politics are dominated by the secular African National Congress, although an Islamist political group, Al-Jama-ah, emerged in 2007 to advocate for the imposition of sharia law.

Sudan, officially recognized by the U.S. as a state sponsor of international terrorism, has served as a hub for Islamist activity on the continent for decades. Islamist movements have been active in the country as early as 1881, when a jihad was launched against colonial British rule. Since the 1980s, a powerful offshoot of the Muslim Brotherhood led by Hassan al-Turabi has influenced Sudanese politics, with Turabi serving as speaker of the National Assembly during the 1990s. Under Turabi, Sudan opened its doors to a myriad of Islamist groups, including the Iranian Revolutionary Guard Corps and Egypt's Gamaa Islamiya. The country even welcomed Osama bin Laden in the 1990s, where the al-Qaeda leader set up training camps and built a financial empire. Turabi has since fallen out of favor with the country's longtime military dictator, Omar al-Bashir, who has curbed some of the Sudanese government's pro-Islamist policies in the years after 9/11.

MAURITANIA

QUICK FACTS

Population: 3,205,060

Area: 1,030,700 sq km

Ethnic Groups: mixed Moor/black 40%, Moor 30%, black 30%

Religions: Muslim 100%

Government Type: Military junta

GDP (official exchange rate): $3.279 billion

Map and Quick Facts courtesy of the CIA World Factbook (Last Updated July 2010)

Situated in northwest Africa on the fault line between the sub-Saharan portion of the continent and the Arab Maghreb along Africa's northern Mediterranean coast, Mauritania faces a host of political, economic and social challenges. Despite its official name, Mauritania has historically kept its distance from Islamist-oriented frameworks and policies. Indeed, the official name was adopted as part of an effort by a number of the country's rulers to consolidate some form of national identity that could be shared by Mauritania's diverse Arab and African populations. Islam, the one feature both groups had in common, served as a tool for securing some degree of national unity.

A military coup in 2005 helped pave the way for democratic elections in 2007, and subsequently by yet another military takeover in August 2008. Throughout, the country largely maintained its pro-Western foreign policy orientation and kept its distance from Islamist groups and ideas. Nevertheless, the emergence of a new, jihadi-oriented movement active in Mauritania in the form of al-Qaeda of the Islamic Maghreb (AQIM) has begun to alter the Mauritanian public and government's positions and attitudes toward Islamist activity. Indeed, in recent times Mauritania has witnessed an uptick in violence instigated by AQIM, followed by increased government repression.

ISLAMIST ACTIVITY

In Mauritania, Islamist activity oscillates between two extremes: a political arena where Islamist organizations compete as legitimate parties, and a violent (mostly foreign) *jihadist* presence that seeks the overthrow of the current regime and the installation of a "righteous" Islamic government in its stead.

The National Rally for Reform and Development (NRRD, or *Tawassoul*) – Both a moderate Islamist group and a political opposition party, the NRRD opposed the 2008 coup that overthrew former president Maouiyya Ould Taya and has cooperated with the opposition National Front for the Defense of Democracy (FNDD). In the past, it has publicly opposed violent acts of terrorism, such as the December 2009 kidnapping of three Spanish nationals and an Italian family.[1] This group is a relatively new actor in the country's politics, and does not differ at this stage from other new political parties in Mauritania. It has not been particularly vocal in its Islamist-oriented demands, and has not distanced itself from the prevailing status quo concerning the role of Islam in Mauritania. Observers have commented that the party is often seen as being more concerned about its own survival than promoting ideological tenets. Its long-term impact on Mauritanian society and Islam remain an open question.[2]

Al-Qaeda in the Islamic Maghreb (AQIM)—This group has been the most active in violent Islamist activity over the past year. It is not, however, a Mauritanian group per se. In fact, it is the new incarnation of Algeria's Salafist Group for Preaching and Combat (GSPC), which in September 2006 was recognized by al-Qaeda as its representative in North Africa. Most analysts contend that the group is deeply rooted in Algeria's Islamist violence. Although AQIM has shifted the focus of its activities from Algeria to the southern Sahel region (which includes Mauritania), taking advantage of the extensive desert region for its operations, security analysts contend that the group has become less ideologically inspired and motivated more by opportunistic factors. It has sought to raise funds by ransoming hostages and becoming involved in drug trafficking.[3] AQIM has been described as more of a criminal organization with a veneer of religious ideology, or in the words of one U.S. official, "a criminal organization with an attachment to al-Qaeda."[4] The group has proven its ability to carry out attacks in Mauritania, but its overall support among local Mauritanians (except those within its ranks) remains unclear. By most estimates, the involvement of Mauritanians in its activities is minimal, and cannot truly reflect any form of local endorsement. It has not yet left a lasting imprint on Mauritanian society, and its attacks have not been linked to domestic developments. AQIM's attacks have largely focused on foreign targets and nationals. Analysts note that the potential for greater local support for such a movement does exist, primarily among a

younger generation influenced and inspired by television images of the ongoing conflicts in Iraq, Afghanistan, and between Israel and the Palestinians.[5]

ISLAMISM AND SOCIETY

Mauritania's population (estimated at 3.1 million people in July 2009) confronts a host of socio-economic hardships, ranging from limited educational
opportunities, unemployment, poor health services and a very low quality of
life. The country's economic figures offer a glimpse of this reality: GDP per
capita is 2,100 U.S. dollars.[6] Life expectancy is low even by African standards, at 58 for men and 62 for women.[7] Its arid climate and desert landscape impede the possibility of developing a strong agricultural sector, which
could at least provide a framework for a sustainable economy. In addition,
the country suffers from periodic climatic calamities, such as severe droughts,
which further add to its economic woes. Although Mauritania started to produce oil in 2006 with the discovery of off-shore reserves of oil and natural
gas, there has been little positive impact to date on the country's economy,
which lacks any other natural resources.

Socially, the country's inhabitants, although entirely Muslim, are divided
between the Arab elite and black Africans, many of them referred to as *Haratines*, descendents of former African slaves. This ethnic group, the largest
among the country's ethnic composition, suffers from various forms of official and unofficial discrimination, and occupies the lowest rungs of Mauritanian society. Indeed, slavery altogether remains an ongoing issue in Mauritania. Although officially banned in 1981, many contend that slavery is
still practiced in various forms throughout the country, further exacerbating
existing tensions between the Arab elites and the "Black Mauritanians," as
they are commonly known.

Islam has served as the sole unifying element in this highly fractured society.
But despite this role, Islamism as a political force has remained limited and
restricted in Mauritania over the years. Islamist-oriented activity has had various manifestations, ranging from mostly charitable organizations to a loose
set of political groups inspired by Wahhabism, the Egyptian Muslim Brotherhood, and several Islamist figures (including the Sudanese activist Hassan
al-Turabi). The Mauritanian authorities' successful repression of Islamist
political activity over the years has further weakened any attempts to establish a strong Islamist political presence.

Nevertheless, observers point to the rising number of Islamist supporters and
sympathizers over the past decade as indicators that this tendency may be
changing.[8] These new adherents are largely residents of urban areas. They

include frustrated unemployed or under-employed educated young people, as well as those from the ranks of the Haratines. Urban poverty and criticism of the corrupt political class also has proven to be an effective strategy for Islamic groups to attract support for their organizations and ideologies. Observers have also asserted that many of these new supporters are also largely cut off from the West and its values, paving their way towards a movement that categorically rejects Western culture.[9] Finally, the support many of these groups are said to receive from Gulf-based Islamic charities is believed to expand their appeal among Mauritanians. As much of this funding is conducted through unofficial channels, it is difficult to estimate its volume and overall impact on the emergence of Islamist groups in Mauritania.[10]

Despite the rise in Islamist-oriented activity, the Mauritanian public has not displayed great sympathy or support toward these actions. The AQIM attack near the French embassy in August 2008, for example, was largely condemned by Mauritanians, including Tawassoul, whose spiritual leader, Mohamed Hassan Ould Dedew, deemed the attack "an act of barbarism" and "completely foreign" to Mauritanian Islam.[11] One observer has noted that Mauritanians view AQIM as serving a foreign ideology that is hostile to their traditional societal values.[12] Salafism is not viewed with high regard; it is seen as a fringe movement. Violent Islamism is also frowned upon and seen as a source of disorder and instability.[13]

As the year 2009 drew to a close, the specter of AQIM-inspired violence overshadowed political developments in Mauritania. Although the Mauritanian public appeared to be largely against such activities, the country's unstable political situation and its socio-economic problems could render it a new arena for radical Islamist violence. The aspirations of groups like AQIM also add to the potential for intensified activity of this sort. The Mauritanian military carried out attacks against AQIM targets in 2010, which were supported by local political parties. There was little to suggest that the Mauritanian public had become more involved in Islamist activities per se.

ISLAMISM AND THE STATE

One of the world's poorest countries, Mauritania received its independence from France in 1960 but faced pressure from its northern neighbor, Morocco, over parts of the former Spanish Sahara region, now known as the Western Sahara. Mauritania renounced its claims to the territory in 1979, but it remains prone to domestic political instability and periodic tensions with its neighbors over issues such as its position toward the country's black African population.

Seeking to entrench Islam into the country, Islamic law (*sharia*) was implemented in 1982 by Colonel Haidar, who had assumed power two years earlier. Upon taking control of the country in 1984, Maouiyya Ould Taya continued in this policy direction by imposing various restrictions that were sanctioned by Islam (including a ban on alcohol consumption). But Taya was careful not to allow Islamist-oriented political and social movements to gain traction in politics and society or become strong enough to threaten his rule. Nevertheless, the same dynamics that have generated support of Islamist movements in other Middle Eastern and North African countries—among them poverty, unemployment and a frustrated largely urban population seeking improved material conditions and an ideological sense of direction—have led to an increased Islamist political presence in Mauritania. By and large, these groups so far have steered clear of using violence, preferring instead to assert their presence within the country's political system.

While supportive of Islam, the Taya regime was an unequivocal opponent of Islamism. Under Taya, Islamist activists were pursued and persecuted by authorities. The formation of religion-based parties was formally banned in 1991. Taya contended that there was no place for Islamism in Mauritania, since the entire population was Muslim. Indeed, foreign observers asserted that Taya's regime had overblown the supposed "Islamist threat" in an effort to curry favor with the West and reduce international criticism of its dismal human rights record.[14]

Mauritania has experienced approximately a dozen coups or attempted coups since its independence. Many of these were underpinned by the efforts of the country's Arab elite to consolidate control over the rest of the population. The takeover led by Maaouiya Ould Taya in 1984 managed to install Taya in power until 2005. During Taya's rule, Mauritania sought to strengthen its ties with the U.S. (beginning in the mid-1990s) and ally itself with the West. It established full diplomatic relations with Israel in 1999, and participated in the U.S.-led War on Terror. The regime's unpopular policies, its repression of expression and violations of human rights and its corrupt nature ultimately led to its demise. The military government, which overthrew Taya in 2005, managed to steer the country toward democratic elections in March 2007, which led to the election of Sidi Ould Cheikh Abdallahi, a veteran Mauritanian political figure, who had received the endorsement of key social constituencies.

The alleged motive for the subsequent August 2008 coup was political tension over power between Abdallahi and the military. The coup's leader, General Mohamed Ould 'Abd al-Aziz, was elected president in elections conducted under an agreement with other Mauritanian political parties (July 2009).

Nevertheless, Mauritania's political future and the potential for greater political pluralism and democracy remain uncertain.[15]

The more open political climate that prevailed throughout the country following Taya's removal from power also affected Islamist groups. One such group, Tawassoul, was recognized and sanctioned by authorities, and in 2006 gained a seat in parliamentary elections representing Mauritania's capital, Nouakchott. Other manifestations of the regime's more tolerant approach toward Islam were the restoration of Friday as the country's day of rest, the construction of a mosque at the presidential palace, and frequent measures against commercial establishments selling alcohol in Nouakchott.[16]

The emergence of a new, *jihadi*-oriented movement active in Mauritania in the form of al-Qaeda of the Islamic Maghreb (AQIM) has in many ways altered the Mauritanian public and government's positions and attitudes toward Islamist activity. Indeed, throughout the early months of 2009, Mauritania witnessed an uptick in violence instigated by AQIM. In June, an American aid worker was murdered in Nouakchott, and in July, a suicide attack (the first of its kind in Mauritania) was carried out near the French embassy in the capital, wounding three people. AQIM claimed responsibility for both of these attacks.

This increase in violence brought with it intensified security measures on the part of Mauritanian authorities. The government aimed to decrease AQIM's presence and its ability to carry out attacks on Mauritanian soil. Scores of people, mostly suspected Islamist activists, were arrested as part of the government's counterterrorism measures. And many detainees, including those accused of belonging to AQIM, were kept incommunicado for prolonged periods. Some, especially alleged Islamist activists, reported that they had been tortured with electric shocks, a practice which has been reported in previous government crackdowns against Islamist activity.[17] Suspects accused of carrying out an attack on French tourists in December 2007 were put on trial in May 2010. Their lawyers stated that these individuals would plead not guilty, and that their confessions were obtained by torture.[18]

In early 2010, clashes between Mauritanian military forces and AQIM militants were reported in the northern provinces of Tinis and Zemmour. Some Mauritanian sources criticized the government for not taking the AQIM threat seriously enough, and for divorcing it from domestic partisan politics, despite the fact that there is little correlation between local politics and AQIM.[19] Mauritanian forces, along with French troops, initiated an attack on AQIM encampments in the desert Sahel region in July 2010. Malian officials claimed that the attack occurred in Northern Mali.[20] This attack was intended to secure the release of a French hostage held by AQIM. Although the French hostage was later reported to have been executed, the French defense ministry stated that Mauritania's action had "neutralized" the group. Mauritania's ruling party, the Union for the Republic (URP), declared after the attack that it would work with France against AQIM. Other political parties, such as the Alliance for Justice and Democracy/Movement for Renovation expressed support for the Mauritanian attack, noting that it was an act of self defense.[21] While the country's political establishment seemed determined to eradicate AQIM's presence, the group's overall impact on the country's public life remained questionable as of mid-2010.

ENDNOTES

[1] "Mauritania Bombing Update", *The Moor Next Door* blog, August 11, 2008, www.themoornextdoor.wordpress.com/2009/08/11/Mauritania-bombing-update/.

[2] "Addendum I on Mauritanian and Algerian Islamists", *The Moor Next Door* blog, November 25, 2009, www.themoornextdoor.wordpress.com/2009/11/25/addendum-i-on-mauritanian-and-algerian-islamists/.

[3] Laurent Prieur, "Mauritania Starts Trial of al-Qaeda Suspects", Reuters, May 16, 2010.

[4] Ambassador Vicki Huddleston, deputy assistant secretary of defense for Africa, as cited in " The Dynamics of North African Terrorism," Center for Strategic & International Studies Middle East Program *Conference Report*, March 2010, http://csis.org/files/attachments/100216_NorthAfricaConferenceReport.pdf.

[5] "La Mauritanie Entre Les Feux Des Prêches Des Oulémas Et Celles Des Fusils Des Disciplines," *Tahalil* (Nouachott), March 4, 2010, www.journaltahalil.com.

[6] "Mauritania," *CIA World Factbook*, July 22, 2010, https://www.cia.gov/library/publications/the-world-factbook/geos/mr.html.

[7] Ibid.

[8] Armelle Choplin, "Mauritania: Between Islamism and Terrorism", *Pambazuka* iss. 370, May 13, 2008, www.pambazuka.org/en/category/features/48058; Pierre Tristam, "Is Moderate Mauritania Radicalizing? Islamist and Terrorist Currents in Arab West Africa," About.com, n.d., www.middleeast.about.com/od/mauritania/a/me080216a.htm.

[9] Choplin, "Mauritania: Between Islamism and Terrorism"; Pierre Tristam, "Is Moderate Mauritania Radicalizing? Islamist and Terrorist Currents in Arab West Africa," About.com, n.d., www.middleeast.about.com/od/mauritania/a/me080216a.htm.

[10] Anouar Boukhars,"Mauritania's Vulnerability to al-Qaeda Influence," Jamestown Foundation *Terrorism Focus* 4, iss. 24, July 25, 2007, http://www.jamestown.org/single/?no_cache=1&tx_ttnews[tt_news]=4329.

[11] "Mauritania Bombing Update."

[12] Anouar Boukhars,"Mauritania's Vulnerability to al-Qaeda Influence," Jamestown Foundation *Terrorism Focus* 4, iss. 24, July 25, 2007, http://www.jamestown.org/single/?no_cache=1&tx_ttnews[tt_news]=4329.

[13] "Re: Recent Paucity," *The Moor Next Door* blog, March 22, 2010, www.themoornextdoor.wordpress.com/2010/03/22/re-recent-paucity/.

[14] "Islamist Terrorism in the Sahel: Fact or Fiction?" International Crisis Group *Africa Report* no. 92, March 31, 2005; "Islamism in North

Africa IV: The Islamist Challenge in Mauritania: Threat or Scapegoat," International Crisis Group *Middle East/North Africa Report* no. 41, May 11, 2005; Armelle Choplin, "La Mauritanie à L'épreuve De L'islamisme Et Des Menaces Terroristes," EchoGéo, Sur le vif 2008, http://echogeo.revues.org/index4363.html.

[15] Boubacar N'Diaye, "Mauritania, August 2005: Justice and Democracy, or Just Another Coup," *African Affairs* 105, no. 420, July 2006, 421-441; Boubacar N'Diaye, "To 'Midwife'-and Abort-A Democracy: Mauritania's Transition from Military Rule, 2005-2008," *Journal of Modern African Studies* 47, no. 1, March 2009, 129-152.

[16] Ibid.

[17] "Mauritania: Torture of Alleged Islamists Widespread," Amnesty International, June 12, 2008.

[18] Laurent Prieur, "Mauritania Starts Trial of al-Qaeda Suspects", Reuters, May 16, 2010.

[19] "Mauritania Update," *The Moor Next Door* blog, April 4, 2010, www.themoornextdoor.wordpress.com/2010/04/4/re-Mauritania-update/.

[20] John Irish, "France, Mauritania Strike on al Qaeda," Reuters, July 23, 2010; "France Targets 'al-Qaeda Militants' in Mauritania," BBC, July 23, 2010, www.bbc.co.uk/news/world-africa-10738467.

[21] "Mauritania Ruling Party Pledges Unity in Fight against AQIM," Maghrebia.com, July 28, 2010.

MALI

QUICK FACTS

Population: 13,796,354

Area: 1,240,192

Ethnic Groups: Mande 50% (Bambara, Malinke, Soninke), Peul 17%, Voltaic 12%, Songhai 6%, Tuareg and Moor 10%, other 5%

Religions: Muslim 90%, Christian 1%, indigenous beliefs 9%

Government Type: Republic

GDP (official exchange rate): $8.86 billion

Map and Quick Facts courtesy of the CIA World Factbook (Last Updated July 2010)

Although landlocked and impoverished, the West African nation of Mali has become a surprisingly successful democracy in the past two decades. Despite this progress, however, the country has not been immune from Islamism, or its attendant violence. Most conspicuously, the country's northern regions currently play host to al-Qaeda in the Islamic Maghreb (AQIM). Nevertheless, by most assessments, AQIM poses a security threat to the Malian state, rather than a political one. Politically, the influence of fundamental Islam has been limited by a state constitution that bans religious-based political parties. More significantly, the evolution of Islam in Mali, which has over time incorporated many animist traditions, has created a syncretic form of the religion that preaches tolerance and delegitimizes Islamist ideas.

ISLAMIST ACTIVITY

Mali's traditions of animist-infused Islam and tolerance have made it difficult for Islamist groups to gain a significant foothold in the country. By its nature, Mali's amalgamation of Islam operates in contrast to the strict interpretations of the religion espoused by Islamists. As a result, significant Malian-based

Islamist groups have not emerged in the country. The limited violent Islamist activity has primarily been from al-Qaeda's North Africa syndicate, al-Qaeda in the Islamic Maghreb (AQIM), which has used Mali largely as a staging ground for its regional activities.

Al-Qaeda in the Islamic Maghreb (AQIM)

Over time, AQIM has evolved from a localized Islamist terrorist group seeking to replace Algeria's government with an Islamic one to an al-Qaeda group preaching global *jihad* against the West. Formerly known as the Group Salafiste Pour la Predication et Combat (GSPC), AQIM has its roots in the Algerian civil war of the 1990s. In Mali, the group has taken advantage of the country's sparsely populated northern regions where the government has a limited reach. While accounting for two-thirds of the country's territory, Mali's three northern regions—Timbuktu, Gao and Kidal—contain only 10 percent of the population.[1] In the Sahara, AQIM appears to be a hybrid of sorts: part criminal network, part smuggling outfit and part Islamist insurgency.

An experienced operative, Abdelmalik Droukdel, became the leader of the GSPC in 2004. At the time, Droukdel aimed to transform the group into part of al-Qaeda's network. Droukdel used the Internet, propaganda and events like the American invasion of Iraq to gain the attention and respect of al-Qaeda's senior leadership.[2] Droukdel also took advantage of GSPC's access to smuggling routes in the Sahel to funnel fighters to Iraq, thereby making the group an appealing partner for al-Qaeda's leadership.[3] In September 2006, bin Laden's deputy, Ayman al-Zawahiri, formally announced GSPC's merger into al-Qaeda.[4] Highlighting the widened aims of the group, Zawahiri stated, "May this be a bone in the throat of American and French crusaders and their allies; and sow fear in the hearts of French traitors and sons of apostates."[5] A few months later, the group rebranded itself as al-Qaeda in the Islamic Maghreb. The evolution of GSPC into AQIM changed the group's focus from the near enemy (Algeria) to the far enemy (the West, particularly the United States and Israel) and the group increasingly targeted foreigners in its North African operations.

In solidifying its North Africa network, al-Qaeda ostensibly was looking for another way to push the *jihad* into Europe. However, AQIM has "instead placed increasing emphasis on its Saharan component."[6] AQIM's "southern zone" (the group's area of operation in southern Algeria, extending into the Sahara) was not initially viewed as an integral part of the group.[7] However, this arm gained increasing clout as a result of a number of factors including the decrease of *jihadist* activity in Algeria, AQIM leadership's increased need for financing, and the increased ability of the Southern Zone brigades to control and profit from the smuggling networks in the Sahel.[8] Additionally, the continued counterterrorism efforts of Algerian security forces have put the group on the defensive in Algeria, pushing them progressively further south.[9]

Prior to its merger with al-Qaeda, GSPC achieved international notoriety when it kidnapped 32 European tourists in Algeria in early 2003.[10] Seventeen members of the group were freed by Algerian forces in May 2010.[11] The remaining victims were forced by their captors to trek south across the desert into Mali.[12] In August, the rest of the hostages were released for a reported sum of Euro 5 million, save for one who died from heat stroke while in captivity.[13] The kidnapping was orchestrated by Ammari Saifi, who until his capture in May 2004 was one of the group's core leaders.[14] The incident illustrated GSPC's ability to operate freely in northern Mali's desert regions.[15]

In May 2007, AQIM kidnapped its first foreigner since the 2003 kidnapping. Between 2007 and now, there have been a number of high profile kidnappings that illustrate the group's continued ability to operate in northern Mali as several of these individuals were taken into the region after their capture. The kidnappings serve dual purposes for AQIM. The activity drives foreign investment away from the region and the ransom payments bring AQIM needed cash for weapons and supplies.[16]

In addition to kidnapping, AQIM also engages in profitable smuggling operations in the Sahel, with routes going through northern Mali. Prior to the group's merger with al-Qaeda, Droukdel used smuggling routes in the Sahel to funnel *jihadist* fighters to Iraq. One of Droukel's commanders, Mokhtar Belmokhtar, nicknamed "untouchable" by French intelligence, has become particularly adept at smuggling.[17] Belmokhtar was given command of GSPC's southern zone in 2000.[18] To enhance his smuggling activities, Belmokhtar forged relationships with some members of Mali's northern communities, first marrying into an Arab family in Timbuktu and subsequently taking "additional wives from Tuareg and Barbiche Arab tribes."[19] These relationships have given Belmokhtar the ability to operate in the region relatively untouched. He was able to develop the region as a safe haven for the group and its activities, which included establishing mobile training camps.[20] However, these relationships did not necessarily mean that AQIM and the Tuaregs shared a common goal or motivation. Rather than ideology, the Tuaregs are motivated by "cultural grievances" against the Malian government.[21] Over time, the Tuaregs have come to feel that their relationship with the Malian government was suffering as a result of their ties to AQIM.[22]

While AQIM remains a low-scale threat, its composition limits its reach. In the words of one expert, "AQIM cannot prove its commitment to 'Africanized' *jihad* without Africanizing at least some of its leadership."[23] Indeed, the group does not have any non-Algerian *jihadists* within the group's top echelon.[24] Additionally, there do not appear to be large numbers of Malians joining or training with the group.

AQIM remains a lower level threat in that the group is not launching attacks *en masse*. Rather, its activities appear to be geared primarily towards insuring its continued survival rather than focusing on offense. The group also appears to be limited in where it can conduct it operations; it has not been able to effectively attack targets or conduct operations beyond Algeria and some of the Saharan states.[25] However, the group's mobile commando units in Mali's northern reaches continue to be a security issue for the Malian government and its neighbors.

That AQIM's activities in Mali have been limited to relatively isolated incidents and low grade criminal activity highlights the group as a security threat, rather than a threat to the stability of the state.[26] The group has also failed to launch large scale attacks in Mali. It appears that the fruits of their labor go primarily to ensurimg their own survival rather than costly well-planned attacks. However, AQIM appears to be digging itself in for the long haul; the group is reportedly building fortified bunkers in the Malian-Algerian border region of the Sahara desert.[27] There are also indications that the group is having more success recruiting new members from Mali. However, those numbers are reported to be small.[29] In all likelihood, AQIM will continue to have a low-level presence in Mali for the foreseeable future. However, its efforts will remain hampered if the Malian government, and its counter-terrorism partners, exercise continued vigilance.

ISLAMISM AND SOCIETY

Like most African states, Mali is a diverse nation comprised of several ethnic groups speaking a variety of languages. However, while ethic competition has perpetuated conflict elsewhere, Mali remains generally peaceful. The majority of these groups share a common faith: Islam. The religion has a long history in Mali, first brought to the country in the eleventh century from the Mediterranean by Saharan nomads.[30] First settled in the twelfth century, Timbuktu became an epicenter for Islamic scholarship.[31] It is a reputation the city still holds today, with its extensive libraries of Islamic manuscripts.

In terms of composition, Mali is overwhelmingly Muslim, with some 90 percent of the population adhering to the Islamic faith.[32] Malian Islam is not typical of other Islamic states, however. In Mali, scholars have noted, "there is no uniform way of being Muslim."[33] The country's practice of the religion incorporates animist traditions of the region, including "absorbing mystical elements [and] ancestor veneration."[34] Mali's lengthy history figures prominently in the country's contemporary culture; Malians "regularly invoke Muslim rulers of various pre-colonial states and empires and past Muslim clerics, saints, and miracle-workers from the distant and more recent colonial and post-colonial past."[35] Islam and animism, in other words, have coexisted in Mali for centuries.[36]

Contributing to its relative stability, Malian culture boasts its own conflict resolution mechanisms, which aid the country's culture of tolerance. One such mechanism is called *cousinage*, which has been described as "so-called joking relationships between pairs of ethnic groups."[37] *Cousinage* "forbids conflict between ethnic groups or clans and encourages them to trade humorous insult with impunity."[38] These conflict resolution mechanisms serve not only to keep the peace among the population, but also perpetuate cultural diversity.

Nevertheless, Mali is susceptible to outside influences. Like it has in other countries, Saudi Arabia has attempted to influence Malian society using its wealth to build mosques and religious learning centers in the country.[39] In 2004, the *Chicago Tribune* reported that between 2001 and 2004, ultraconservative Wahhabis from Saudi Arabia "opened 16 mosques in Timbuktu, a development termed disturbing by the city's mayor, Aly Ould Sidi."[40] However, the Wahhabi influence upon Malian society and its Islam is by and large minimal. Former U.S. Ambassador to Mali Robert Pringle notes that the Wahhabis are typically "regarded by many Malians as the over privileged, conceited offspring of a wealthy, clannish merchant class, an image that the movement has never entirely shaken."[41] Iran has also attempted to peddle influence in Mali.[42] "Local observers believe that the Saudis and Iranians control only 3 to 5 percent of mosques in Mali."[43] Skeptical of the fundamentalists' ability to influence his country, President Toure commented, "Mali is a very old Islamic country where tolerance is part of our tradition."[44]

However, there are indications that al-Qaeda has some support among the Malian population. One report highlighted the "proliferation of Osama bin Laden photos in stalls at the Bamako market and the exponential increase of radio stations preaching radical Islam."[45] Still, given Mali's culture of tolerance and its relatively peaceful history, militancy is not inherent in the culture. Thus, while in the aftermath of the September 11th attacks reports surfaced noting that Malians appeared to be embracing bin Laden while criticizing their government for supporting the U.S. war on terror,[46] there do not appear to be large numbers of Malians willing to take up arms for bin Laden's cause.

ISLAMISM AND THE STATE

The end of the Cold War heralded the end of the strongman era in Africa, and Mali was no different. President Moussa Traoré had led Mali for 23 years under a military dictatorship. But in the early 1990s, opposition movements began to emerge, leading to confrontation with government forces. At a pro-democracy demonstration in March 1991, Malian troops opened fire, presumably on orders from President Traoré, killing several hundred protesters.[47] Within days, Malian army general Amadou Toumani Touré led a *coup d'etat* ending Traoré's reign. In his announcement of the coup to the nation on March 26, Touré stated that he would only hold power until elections took place.[48] A man of his word, Touré stepped aside once the nation's first multiparty elections occurred in April 1992, and Alpha Oumar Konaré became Mali's first democratically-elected president under its new constitution. Prior to his presidency, Konaré was a history and archaeology university professor.[49] Following the mandates in the constitution, Konaré stepped aside after two five-year terms, as Touré became president after winning the 2002 election.

Following the French tradition, religion in Mali "is understood as private and confessional."[50] The Malian constitution, adopted in 1992, maintains the country as a secular state. However, the 1990s saw a dramatic increase in the number of Islamic associations throughout the country, each with varying motivations and religious interpretations.[51] To oversee these groups, the High Islamic Council (Haut Conseil Islamique) was formed by the government in 2002.[52] While religious political parties are banned under the constitution, Mali's government supports the High Islamic Council as an "official and unique interlocutor of political authorities for all questions relative to the practice of Islam."[53]

As a Muslim majority state, issues such as marriage and inheritance have traditionally been overseen by *imams* or village elders.[54] However, the state has attempted to legislate in these areas. In 2001, the state announced a new set of family laws, referred to as the *Code de la Famille* (Family Code), to raise the minimum marriage age of girls, make both men and women equal in marriage and give them the same inheritance rights.[55] The marriage law was formally presented by President Konare in 2002.[56] However, it was "withdrawn in the face of considerable criticism."[57] At the time, leaders of Islamic associations stated that the government's legislative attempts contradicted Islamic law.[58] The current marriage law in Mali states that the husband is responsible for protecting the wife and in turn, the wife must obey the husband.[59]

Nearly ten years later, the government revisited the issue. The law was approved by the National Assembly in early August 2009.[60] However, it was met with widespread opposition spearheaded by Islamic groups, including the High Islamic Council. Instead of signing the law, President Touré sent it back to the Assembly for review, where it currently remains.[61]

While many Malian religious leaders stood in opposition to the legislation, not all Malian imams viewed the proposed law as a threat to Islam or Mali's cultural health. One *imam* from Kati was threatened after he wrote a letter to the High Islamic Council stating that the law in his view did not go against Mali's values or those of Islam.[62] Ultimately, he was relieved of his religious duties.[63]

The renewed opposition to the marriage law may be an indication that religious groups and conservative Islam are gaining influence in Mali. However, there is a difference between increased religious conservatism and Islamism. It does not appear that Islamist rhetoric is gaining significant momentum in Mali, nor does there appear to be a significant portion of the population willing to take up arms in the name of *jihad*.

AQIM's continued presence in the region has ensured that it remains on both the American and Malian security radar. After the 9/11 attacks, the United States placed a higher priority on the threats emerging from the region and attempted to combat the threat. The Bush administration added GSPC to the country's list of foreign terrorist organizations in March of 2002.[64] The United States subsequently began the Pan Sahel Initiative (PSI) in October 2002 to strengthen the Sahelian states' ability to fight terrorism and prevent the region from becoming a safe haven for terrorist organizations.[65] The first phase of the U.S. training program concluded in September 2004 involved roughly 1,200 troops from Mali, Niger, Chad and Mauritania.[66] In June 2005, the program expanded to include more countries from the region becoming the Trans-Saharan Counter-Terrorism Initiative (TSCTP).[67] The Initiative's Operation Flintlock provides anti-insurgency training to the armies of the seven participating states, including Mali.[68] Operation Flintlock has been reprised on several occasions between 2007 and 2010.[69]

In addition to the American efforts to bolster their military capabilities, Mali and its neighbors have made efforts to coordinate their counterterrorism activities. In July 2009, Algeria pledged to assist Mali in bolstering its security structures in the north.[70] Army commanders from Mali, Algeria, Mauritania and Niger met in August 2009 to further coordinate their counter-terrorism activities.[71] The transnational efforts continued into 2010. Algeria held a conference in March 2010 inviting leaders from Burkina Faso, Chad, Libya, Mali, Mauritania and Niger to build a joint security plan to tackle *jihadists*.[72] Subsequently, Algeria, Mauritania, Niger and Mali established a joint military base in Tamanrasset, southern Algeria in April 2010.[73] The partners aim to use the base to target AQIM's smuggling routes.[74] In the joint efforts, "Algeria will be in charge of air support, with Mali covering ground operations, Mauritania heading up communications, Niger handling logistics and Burkina Faso serving in an observation role."[75]

During the summer of 2010, Mali's counterterrorism cooperation with its neighbors increased in response to AQIM's continued activities. In July, AQIM forces attacked an Algerian security outpost near the Algerian-Mali border, killing eleven.[76] After the attack, Mali allowed Algerian forces to pursue the insurgents into Malian territory.[77]

France has also increased its counterterrorism operations in the region as its citizens have been targeted by AQIM. In an effort to free one of its citizens, who was kidnapped in April 2010, the French military launched a special forces attack in tandem with Mauritanian troops against an AQIM base camp in Mali in July 2010.[78] While the French hostage was not at the camp, security forces killed six AQIM militants in the raid.[79] The permission Mali gave to French forces—and has given to Algerian and Mauritanian troops—to perform operations within their borders illustrates the country's desire to quash the threat that AQIM poses, and its willingness to participate in multilateral actions to do so.

However, Mali's issues of poverty and underdevelopment present a significant challenge to the nation's overall health and, potentially, its susceptibility to fundamentalism. When the government formed the High Islamic Council in January 2002, a delegate to the convention commented, "Extremism here is a consequence of something, like a lack of jobs or development."[80] Mali's current human development ranking is among the lowest in the world; the nation ranks 178 out of 182 countries on the United Nations Development Programme's 2009 human development index.[81] An estimated 77.1 percent of the Malian population lives below the poverty line of $2 per day.[82] According to the CIA World Factbook, approximately 30 percent of Mali's population is unemployed.[83] In the long term, if left unaddressed, these factors may contribute to an increased risk of radicalism.

ENDNOTES

[1] William B. Farrell & Carla M. Komich, "USAID/DCHA/CMM Assessment: Northern Mali," *Management Systems International*, June 17, 2004.

[2] Jean-Pierre Filiu, "The Local and Global Jihad of al-Qa'ida in the Islamic Maghrib," *Middle East Journal*, Spring 2009, 221.

[3] Ibid., 222.

[4] Craig Whitlock, "Al-Qaeda's Far-Reaching New Partner," *Washington Post*, October 5, 2006, http://www.washingtonpost.com/wp-dyn/content/article/2006/10/04/AR2006100402006.html.

[5] Aron Lund, "Merger with Al Qaeda Deepens Threat from Algerian Radicals," *Christian Science Monitor*, October 3, 2006, http://www.csmonitor.com/2006/1003/p05s01-woaf.html.

[6] Jean-Pierre Filiu, "Al-Qa'ida in the Islamic Maghreb: A Case Study in the Opportunism of Global Jihad," *CTC Sentinel*, April 2010, 14.

[7] Ibid., 15.

[8] Ibidem.

[9] Lianne Kennedy-Boudali, Testimony before the United States Senate Committee on Foreign Relations, Subcommittee on African Affairs, November 17, 2009.

[10] Stephen Harmon, "From GSPC to AQIM: The Evolution of an Algerian Islamist Terrorist Group into an Al-Qa'ida Affiliate and its Implications for the Sahara-Sahel Region," *Concerned African Scholars Bulletin* no. 85, Spring 2010, 17, http://concernedafricascholars.org/docs/bulletin85harmon.pdf.

[11] Shaul Shay, "Al Qaeda in the Maghreb and the Terror Abductions," International Institute for Counter-Terrorism, May 6, 2010, http://www.ict.org.il/Articles/tabid/66/Articlsid/828/currentpage/1/Default.aspx.

[12] "Mali Gets Rid of Radicals," Agence France Presse, June 6, 2004, http://www.news24.com/Africa/News/Mali-gets-rid-of-radicals-20040609.

[13] Raffi Khatchadourian, "Pursuing Terrorists in the Great Desert," *Village Voice*, January 12, 2006, http://www.villagevoice.com/2006-01-17/news/pursuing-terrorists-in-the-great-desert/.

[14] Ibid.

[15] Harmon, "From GSPC to AQIM," 17.

[16] Michael Petrou, "Al-Qaeda in North Africa," *Maclean's*, May 11, 2009.

[17] Harmon, "From GSPC to AQIM," 19.

[18] Ibid.

[19] J. Peter Pham, "Al-Qaeda in the Islamic Maghreb: The Ongoing Evolution of Jihadist Terrorism in North Africa," *World Defense Review*, May 14, 2009, http://worlddefensereview.com/pham051409.

shtml.

[20] Anneli Botha, "Islamist Terrorism in the Maghreb: Recent Developments in Algeria," *Circunstancia*, January 2009, http://www.ortegaygasset.edu/contenidos.asp?id_d=802.

[21] "Mali (2010)," in *Freedom in the World 2010* (Washington, DC: Rowman & Littlefield/Freedom House, 2010), http://www.freedomhouse.org/template.cfm?page=22&year=2010&country=7871.

[22] Olivier Guitta, "Mali, a new haven for Al Qaeda," *Global Post*, February 20, 2010, http://www.globalpost.com/dispatch/worldview/100216/mali-al-qaeda.

[23] Jean-Pierre Filiu, "Could Al-Qaeda Turn African in the Sahel?" Carnegie Endowment for International Peace *Carnegie Papers*, June 2010, 1.

[24] Filiu, "Al-Qa'ida in the Islamic Maghreb," 14.

[25] Harmon, "From GSPC to AQIM," 29.

[26] Filiu, "Could Al-Qaeda Turn African in the Sahel?" 9.

[27] "Algeria, Mali: Militants Build Bunkers In Sahara," *Stratfor*, June 24, 2010. (http://www.stratfor.com/sitrep/20100624_algeria_mali_militants_build_bunkers_sahara)

[28] Filiu, "Al-Qa'ida in the Islamic Maghreb," 15.

[29] Ibid.

[30] John Hunwick, *West Africa, Islam and the Arab World* (Princeton: Markus Weiner Publishers, 2006), 25.

[31] Ibid., 26.

[32] "Mali," *CIA World Factbook*, August 3, 2010, https://www.cia.gov/library/publications/the-world-factbook/geos/ml.html.

[33] Benjamin F. Soares, "Islam in Mali in the Neoliberal Era," in Benjamin F. Soares and René Otayek, eds., *Islam and Muslim Politics in Africa* (New York: Palgrave Macmillan, 2007), 212.

[34] Lisa Anderson, "Democracy, Islam share a home in Mali," Chicago Tribune, December 15, 2004, http://articles.chicagotribune.com/2004-12-15/news/0412150328_1_mali-islamic-cinq.

[35] Soares, "Islam in Mali in the Neoliberal Era," 212.

[36] Robert Pringle, "Democratization in Mali: Putting History To Work," United States Institute of Peace Peaceworks no. 58, October 2006, 27, http://www.usip.org/resources/democratization-mali-putting-history-work.

[37] Ibid., 16.

[38] Ibidem.

[39] Anderson, "Democracy, Islam Share a Home in Mali."

[40] Ibid.

[41] Pringle, "Democratization in Mali," 28.

[42] Willy Stern, "Moderate Islam, African-Style," *Weekly Standard*, August 4, 2008, http://www.weeklystandard.com/Content/Public/Articles/000/000/015/369mhred.asp.

[43] Ibid.

[44] Anderson, "Democracy, Islam Share a Home in Mali."

[45] Guitta, "Mali, a New Haven for Al Qaeda."

[46] Joan Baxter, "Mali's Muslim Majority Enters Political Fray," BBC, April 22, 2002, http://news.bbc.co.uk/2/hi/africa/1939770.stm.

[47] Pringle, "Democratization in Mali," 19.

[48] Anderson, "Democracy, Islam Share a Home in Mali."

[49] Ofeibea Quist-Arcton, "Alpha Oumar Konare Elected New Chairperson of AU Commission," AllAfrica.com, July 11, 2003, http://allafrica.com/stories/200307110037.html.

[50] Soares, "Islam in Mali in the Neoliberal Era," 214.

[51] Nicolas Colombant, "Mali's Muslims Steer Back to Spiritual Roots," *Christian Science Monitor*, February 26, 2002, http://www.csmonitor.com/2002/0226/p08s02-woaf.html.

[52] Ibid.

[53] Soares, "Islam in Mali in the Neoliberal Era," 215.

[54] Carine Debrabandère, "Women's rights languish in Mali," *Deutche Welle*, March 8, 2010, http://www.dw-world.de/dw/article/0,,5323121,00.html.

[55] Soares, "Islam in Mali in the Neoliberal Era," 221.

[56] Ibid.

[57] Ibidem.

[58] Ibidem.

[59] Soumaila T. Diarra, "Muslim Conservatives Blocking New Family Law," *InterPress Service*, May 19, 2010, http://allafrica.com/stories/201005191339.html.

[60] Martin Vogl, "Mali Women's Rights Bill Blocked," BBC, August 27, 2009, http://news.bbc.co.uk/2/hi/8223736.stm.

[61] "Mali (2010)."

[62] "Mali Imam Living in Fear After Backing Women's Rights," BBC, May 10, 2010, http://news.bbc.co.uk/2/hi/africa/8672618.stm.

[63] Diarra, "Muslim Conservatives Blocking New Family Law."

[64] Audrey Kurth Cronin, Huda Aden, Adam Frost, and Benjamin Jones, *Foreign Terrorist Organizations* (Washington, DC: Congressional Research Service, February 6, 2004), 101.

[65] Harmon, "From GSPC to AQIM," 22.

[66] Lisa Anderson, "Democracy, Islam share a home in Mali," *Chicago Tribune*, December 15, 2004, http://articles.chicagotribune.com/2004-12-15/news/0412150328_1_mali-islamic-cinq.

[67] Harmon, "From GSPC to AQIM," 23.

[68] Ibid.

[69] Ibidem; See also "US Starts Anti-al-Qaeda Military Exercise in Sahara," BBC, May 3, 2010, http://news.bbc.co.uk/2/hi/africa/8658009.stm.

[70] Nazim Fethi, "Algeria Helps Mali Create Development Proj-

ects to Counter Terrorism," *Magharebia*, July 30, 2009, http://www.magharebia.com/cocoon/awi/xhtml1/cn_GB/features/awi/features/2009/07/30/feature-02?pollresult=yes&answer=no&id=awi-2010-05-03

[71] Hannah Armstrong, "Algeria hosts regional summit amid rise in terrorism," *Christian Science Monitor*, August 13, 2009, http://www.csmonitor.com/World/Middle-East/2009/0813/p06s10-wome.html.

[72] "Al-Qaida Digs in to Resist Region's Armies," United Press International, July 6, 2010, http://www.upi.com/Top_News/Special/2010/07/06/Al-Qaida-digs-in-to-resist-regions-armies/UPI-14121278441085/.

[73] "Brief: Saharan Countries' Cooperation Against AQIM," *Stratfor*, April 21, 2010, http://www.stratfor.com/node/160466/analysis/20100421_brief_saharan_countries_cooperation_against_aqim.

[74] Ibid.

[75] "AQIM: The Devolution of al Qaeda's North African Node," *Stratfor*, August 10, 2010, http://www.stratfor.com/analysis/20100808_aqim_devolution_al_qaedas_north_african_node.

[76] "Algeria: AQIM Attack Leaves 11 Police Officers Dead," *Stratfor*, July 1, 2010, http://www.stratfor.com/sitrep/20100701_algeria_aqim_attack_leaves_11_police_officers_dead.

[77] "Al-Qaida Digs in to Resist Region's Armies."

[78] "No News on Hostage After Mali Raid," Reuters, July 25, 2010, http://tvnz.co.nz/world-news/no-news-hostage-after-mali-raid-3672409.

[79] "French Hostage May Have Died Before Raid: PM," Agence France Presse, July 27, 2010, http://news.yahoo.com/s/afp/20100727/wl_africa_afp/malimauritaniafranceconflictqaedagovernment_20100727093128.

[80] "Islamic Militancy on the Rise in Mali," Voice of America, January 25, 2002, http://www1.voanews.com/english/news/a-13-a-2002-01-25-18-Islamic-67548272.html.

[81] United Nations Development Programme, "Human Development Report 2009," 2009, 146, http://hdr.undp.org/en/media/HDR_2009_EN_Indicators.pdf.

[82] Ibid.

[83] "Mali," *CIA World Factbook*, August 3, 2010, https://www.cia.gov/library/publications/the-world-factbook/geos/ml.html.

SUDAN

As the only country in the Horn of Africa included in the U.S. list of state sponsors of international terrorism, Sudan is key to understanding radical Islamism. It played a major role in the expansion of Islamism since the 1950s, serving as the first country to which the Muslim Brotherhood was exported from its neighbor, Egypt. For decades, Hassan al-Turabi, arguably Sudan's most prominent and recognizable political figure, led a largely-successful process of state Islamization. This openness led directly to Sudan's hosting of Osama bin Laden and his network during the early- to mid-1990s. Sudan's cooperation in the U.S.-led war on terror, by contrast, is comparatively recent. This role, coupled with the country's history as a defender of Islamism and terrorism, serves to create a muddled vision of Sudan's association with—and attitudes toward—radical Islam.

ISLAMIST ACTIVITY

The turn of the 20th century witnessed the politicization of religious movements in Sudan. In the country's first Islamic rebellion, which lasted from 1881 until 1885, Muhammad Ahmad Ibn Abdullah proclaimed himself the *mahdi* and declared *jihad* against local rule, which at the time was administered by the British Empire. After defeating the British ruler of Sudan, Major-General Charles Gordon, in the Battle of Khartoum, Abdullah's resulting *Mahdiyya* ruled the Sudan until 1898, when the British retook the country and set up the Anglo-Egyptian Condominium.

Islamism in Sudan was truly born, though, in the 1950s, when the ideas of Egypt's Muslim Brotherhood seeped through the shared border between the two countries. Sudan's Hassan al-Turabi, born in 1932, was especially inspired by the Brotherhood's Islamist rhetoric, and went on to become secretary general of the newly-created Islamic Charter Front, an offshoot of the Muslim Brotherhood, in 1964. Beginning as an Islamist student group, the organization worked for reform through politics with the same goals as its Egyptian progenitor—namely, to create an officially Islamic regime governed by *sharia* law. The group was later renamed the National Islamic Front, and has also been known as the Sudanese Muslim Brotherhood.[1]

To fully understand Islamism in Sudan, one must be acquainted with the country's political history, and Turabi's role in it. Turabi has been a key religious and political figure since the 1960s, his ideas influencing the evolution of Islamism both within and outside of Sudan. A politician, intellectual, religious cleric, and sponsor of terrorism, Turabi is today one of most famous Islamist leaders in the world. After studying in London and Paris in the 1950s, Turabi returned to Sudan and quickly decided to enter politics. He then married Wisal al-Mahdi, the sister of Sudanese politician Sadiq al-Mahdi, who led the *Umma* Party and served as prime minister. His first taste of politics took place during the October 1964 revolution against the military government of Ibrahim Abbud—a revolt which returned the country to civilian rule.[2]

Because of his academic training and familial ties, Turabi was able to rise to prominence in the realm of politics, becoming secretary general of the Islamic Charter Front.[3] Echoing the call of the Muslim Brotherhood in Egypt, Turabi unified disparate Islamic movements (mainly student organizations) in Sudan. The Islamic Charter Front's strategy was to throw its support behind nationalist leaders who also accepted Islamist principles. Because of this, in 1984, the organization allied itself with Gaafar Nimeiry, the military dictator who, during his second term, began to implement *sharia* under pressure from Islamists.[4] Five years later, the Front joined forces with Omar

Hassan Ahmad al-Bashir, a then-unknown brigadier in the Sudanese Army, who conducted a *coup d'état* on June 30, 1989 against the democratically-elected government of Sadiq al-Mahdi. Although related by marriage, Turabi and al-Mahdi had become political enemies by the mid-1980s.[5] The coup marked the birth of what one scholar has called "the First Islamist Republic" of Sudan.[6]

After Bashir came to power, Turabi renamed the ICF the National Islamic Front (*al-Jabha al-Islamiyya al-Qawmiyya*, or NIF), and in 1995 was elected speaker of the National Assembly. Turabi and the NIF were generally seen as the real leaders of the government.[7] After only four years, however, Turabi was dismissed from the government when tensions arose between him and Bashir, in part because of the former's ties to terrorist organizations. In 2004, Turabi was arrested on charges of having conspired to overthrow Bashir the year before. He was released on June 30, 2005, the regime's 16th anniversary. Since then, Turabi has been one of the most virulent opponents of Bashir's policies, especially in Darfur, where he supports autonomy.

Currently, Turabi's discourse and theory illustrate the evolution of Islamism in Sudan. Because Turabi participated in an attempt at an Islamic government and was frustrated in his efforts, he has a unique perspective. In 1983, he wrote that "[t]he ideological foundation of an Islamic state lies in the doctrine of *tawhid* – the unity of God and human life – as a comprehensive and exclusive program of worship."[8] In the mid-1990s, his views were markedly progressive for an Islamist from his time: he publicly supported women's rights and condemned the killing of apostates. Specifically, he denounced Ayatollah Khomeini's death sentence against the writer Salman Rushdie. He began advocating the gradual implementation of *sharia*, which he also believed should be binding only to Muslims.[9] Turabi's belief in the value of political consensus is apparent, given his concern over the crisis in Darfur, which has shattered Sudan's unity.

Over the last three decades, Sudan has experienced, on many occasions, terrorist attacks in the form of violence against resident foreigners. However, radical Islam was largely introduced into Sudan in 1991, when Turabi welcomed Osama bin Laden and his followers into the country, partly to help him build an Islamic republic and partly to support international *jihadists*. Bin Laden went on to establish a network of some 23 training camps in the country,[10] and create a business and financial empire there. The Iranian Revolutionary Guard Corps (IRGC) and Sudan's army, called the Popular Defense Forces, are known to have used these camps to train militants. The IRGC is also known to have built an additional 12 camps of its own in Sudan.[11] Bin Laden also started businesses, agricultural plants, and import-export activities. Some well-known places such as Port Sudan's airport and the 700-kilometer al-Tahaddi Road were built by the al-Qaeda leader, who also ran some Sudanese charities. During this period, the Sudanese government and Turabi repeatedly denied any knowledge of bin Laden's terrorist ties or violent goals. In 1996, however, bin Laden and his followers relocated from Sudan to Afghanistan. (It is rumored that offers from the Sudanese government to turn bin Laden over to the Clinton administration contributed to bin Laden's decision.)

Yet the association between al-Qaeda and Sudan did not end there. The ongoing links between Khartoum and the bin Laden network were exposed some five years later, following the fall of the Taliban in Afghanistan in the wake of the September 11th attacks on the U.S. Although many of bin Laden's supporters remained in the tribal areas of the Afghan-Pakistani border, many insurgents and leaders fled to more hospitable locations, including Yemen, Mauritania, and Sudan. Moreover, before Operation Enduring Freedom, large quantities of al-Qaeda's gold and gemstones were moved from Afghanistan to Sudan, where they are believed to be held in Khartoum's Islamic Banks.[12]

Within Sudan itself, a handful of other radical groups also exist, committing acts of violence against what they term to be "enemies of Islam." These elements believe that Turabi and the NIF are no longer the leaders of the Islamist movement. For example, members of the Ansar al-Sunna sect attacked mosques in 1994, 1997, and 2000 at Omdurman and Wed Medani. During the year 2000 incident, one man belonging to the group *Takfir wal-Hijra*, another extremist and violent organization, was discovered among the assailants. It is also highly probable that some members of *Takfir* attempted in the mid-1990s to kill bin Laden while he was in the country—a reflection of the group's sponsorship by Saudi Arabia, which by that time had turned on the bin Laden network and was seeking its destruction.[13]

Despite this domestic anti-establishment activism, Sudan as a whole serves as a notable exporter of Islamist ideology. Because Sudan hosted numerous training camps for *jihadists* before the attacks of September 11, 2001, it has become known globally as a refuge for radicals. For instance, many Hezbollah members or fighters from African countries, such as Mauritania, have spent time in Sudan learning guerilla warfare.[14] Following their training, these fighters are given false documents, money, and means of communication and are sent to fight in "lands of *jihad*" such as Saudi Arabia, Iraq or southern Sahara countries.[15]

The National Islamic Front and Turabi were also implicated in the Islamist attempt to assassinate Egyptian President Hosni Mubarak in 1995.[16] Backed by al-Qaeda's Ayman al-Zawahiri, the Egyptian group *Gamaa Islamiya* planned the attack, which was to take place during the summit of the Organization of African Unity in Addis Ababa. The group was able to send weapons to the Ethiopian capital from Khartoum on a Sudan Airways flight. When the assassination plan failed, some of the plotters fled to Sudan, where they successfully hid from authorities. Some historians point to this event as the beginning of the disintegration in Turabi and Bashir's relationship.[17]

ISLAMISM AND SOCIETY

Sudan is a nation of 597 tribes and subgroups, 175 major ethnic groupings, and more than 400 linguistic groups and various religious traditions.[18] A deep ethnic cleavage has divided Sudan's North and South for centuries, most obviously manifested by the enslavement of southern Arabs by northern Arabs. From a religious perspective, 30 percent of the 8 million people in the south are Christians, and 5 percent are Muslim. By comparison, 90 percent of northerners are Muslims. While religious diversity is not the key factor in the current conflict, the growing popularity and influence of political Islam has certainly aggravated tensions and given them a religious color.

The South resents any imposition of *sharia*; even moderate Muslims fear they ultimately will be forced into a second-class citizenship status.[19] Given the generally more pious nature of the population, acceptance of *sharia* in Northern Sudan has been more prevalent. Much of this trend is attributable to the fact that the North has historically been a more religiously and linguistically homogeneous area, compared to the more religiously-diverse South. This divide was widened after the 1989 coup, which initiated a deeper process of Islamization because of the influence of Hassan al-Turabi. For example, from 1986 to 2001, al-Bashir's government imposed strict Islamic legislation, but the Popular Defence Force (the Sudanese Army) tortured and raped southern inhabitants, who have also suffered from numerous forced evictions and displacements.

Another point of contention is oil. While most of Sudan's oil is located in the South, Khartoum and the North reap the benefits of the industry. Interestingly, the North has extensive interaction with Russia, China, and Iran, as well as their state-controlled companies, and through these associations receives weapons and support in its struggle against the South.[20]

It is difficult to quantify how much of a foothold radical Islam has in Sudan. While Turabi clearly is not the most radical Islamist among the national elites, he has never condemned the use of violence in the name of Islam.

However, while Sudan has supported Islamist causes all over the world, its political leaders generally do not see these causes as terrorist ones. Moreover, since September 2001, the Sudanese government has cooperated extensively with the U.S.-led War on Terror (see below).

ISLAMISM AND THE STATE

Since its birth in the 1950s, the Islamist current in Sudanese politics has taken a number of forms. The Sudanese branch of the Muslim Brotherhood was created in August of 1954, making Sudan one the first countries in Africa to adopt Hassan al-Banna's worldview. Thereafter, other Islamist organizations began to appear. The Islamic Charter Front was created in 1964, and has been deeply influenced by Brotherhood thought,[21] albeit with a more open, politically inclusive bent.[22] From 1964 to 1969, the ICF operated as a pressure group, agitating in favor of an Islamic Constitution for the country, even unsuccessfully putting forth a moderate draft of such a document prior to the 1969 coup.[23] Following the military takeover, Turabi decided to adopt a pragmatic policy toward the new regime, and to integrate the ICF into the Sudan Socialist Union, the only legal party at that time. This decision proved wise; by the late 1970s, the ICF had emerged as the only Islamist political party accepted as part of the Sudanese political landscape.[24] After military leader General Ja'afar Muhammad Numayri was deposed in April of 1985, Turabi renamed the ICF the National Islamic Front, subsequently garnering the third largest block of seats in parliament in legislative elections the following year. Turabi described the NIF at that time as "an advanced stage in the development of the Islamic movement... from a simple group to an integrated social organization and from a religious faction to a state institution."[25] After the subsequent 1989 *coup d'etat* (in which Hassan al-Bashir took power), the NIF dissolved of its own accord, reappearing in 1991 under the name National Congress, which was described by Turabi as a "national structure" rather than that of a political party.[26]

In August 1989, leaders of the international Muslim Brotherhood gathered in London and decided that Sudan should serve as a base and safe haven for Islamist movements from throughout the Muslim World.[27] After Bashir's coup, the NIF became the first agent for Islamization in Sudan. Turabi expanded and pluralized the ideological make-up of the *shura*, the regime's main religious institution, by facilitating the entry of new officials who had not been part of the Sudanese Muslim Brotherhood initially (having been religiously educated and indoctrinated by other groups). A new Islamic organization known as "the Special Entity" (*al Kayan al Khas*) was also created following the 1989 coup and eventually joined al-Bashir's National Congress Party.[28] (This organization would become a grouping of nationalists and

Islamists who remained faithful to the president following the 1999 Bashir-Turabi split.)

Turabi's efforts to enlarge Islamism in the Sudan, and connect it to other movements in the Muslim world, predominated throughout the early 1990s. In 1991, for example, the Sudanese government launched an effort to establish an inter-religious dialogue—an effort that culminated in April 1993 with the first inter-religious conference in Khartoum. A second such event took place in October 1994, and brought together hundreds of people from 30 countries and 50 churches and associations. Turabi's purpose was, in his own words, to make "Christians and Muslims [stand] against the irreligious in a common front."[29] On the other hand, however, Turabi sought to increase intra-Arab and Islamic solidarity. Following the Gulf War, he was active in the creation of the Popular Arab Islamic Congress (PAIC), an umbrella organization that sought to represent all major Islamic movements. By 1997, PAIC had branches in 55 Islamic and non-Islamic countries.[30] Its success has led some Western officials to conclude that the group carries out "Islamist activities" in the Middle East and Europe.[31]

September 11, 2001 served as a turning point for Sudan. Bashir began to collaborate with the U.S. government in its War on Terror. For instance, in 2002, the Sudanese government embraced the Intergovernmental Authority on Development's initiative to discuss how to deal with terrorism, and in 2004, it signed all 12 international conventions against terrorism (seven of which have been ratified by the Sudanese parliament). Regionally, Sudan has signed counterterrorism agreements with Algeria, Yemen and Ethiopia, and co-hosted (with the UN Office on Drugs and Crime) at least one workshop on regional terrorism and transnational crime. These efforts led the State Department in 2007 to compliment the Bashir regime, calling it a "strong partner in the War on Terror."[32]

Bashir's political opponents, by contrast, have aligned in opposition to counterterrorism cooperation with the West. Specifically, Turabi has bristled at American intervention in the area, and led the criticism of the Bashir regime's cooperation with the United States. He has additionally demanded that the United States, Britain, and France not meddle in the Darfur issue.[33]

ENDNOTES

[1] "Islamic Charter Front," Oxford Islamic Studies Online, April 26, 2010, http://www.oxfordislamicstudies.com/article/opr/t125/e1095?_hi=0&_pos=15.

[2] Abdullah A. Gallab, *The First Islamist Republic. Development and Disintegration of Islamism in the Sudan* (London: Ashgate, 2008), pp.62-63; "Profile: Sudan's Islamist leader," BBC, January 15, 2009, http://news.bbc.co.uk/2/hi/africa/3190770.stm.

[3] Gallab, *The First Islamist Republic*, 5.

[4] "Sudan," *Library of Congress Country Studies*, June 1991, http://lcweb2.loc.gov/cgi-bin/query/r?frd/cstdy:@field(DOCID+sd0137).

[5] Lee Smith, "Sudan's Osama," *Slate*, August 5, 2004, http://www.slate.com/id/2104814/.

[6] Gallab, *The First Islamist Republic*.

[7] Majid Jaber, "Iran and Sudan Behind Mubarak Assassination Plot?" *International Review* (1995).

[8] Ibid., 8; Hasan al-Turabi, "The Islamic State," in John Esposito, ed., *Voices of Resurgent Islam* (New York: Oxford University Press, 1996), 92.

[9] Graham E. Fuller, *The Future of Political Islam* (New York: Palgrave MacMillan, 2004); Hassan al-Tourabi (with Alain Chevalerias), *Islam. Avenir du monde [Islam, the World's Future]* (Paris: Broché, 1997).

[10] Ronald Sandee, "Islamism, Terrorism and Jihadism in the Sudan," remarks before the American Enterprise Institute, Washington, DC, August 6, 2004, 5, http://www.aei.org/docLib/20040809_SAND-EEremarks.pdf.

[11] Ibid.

[12] Ibidem, 9.

[13] Abdullah A. Gallab, *The First Islamist Republic*, 128.

[14] Ibid, 9.

[15] Ibidem.

[16] Jaber, "Iran and Sudan Behind Mubarak Assassination Plot?"

[17] Donald Petterson, *Inside Sudan. Political Islam, Conflict and Catastrophe* (Boulder, CO: Westview, 1999).

[18] Jok Madut Jok, *Sudan: Race, Religion and Violence* (London: Oneworld Publications, 2007), 158.

[19] Gérard Prunier, *Identity Crisis and the Weak State: The Making of the Sudanese Civil War* (London: WRITENET, 1996).

[20] Pieter Van Dijk Meine, ed., *The New Presence of China in Africa* (Amsterdam: Amsterdam University Press, 2009); See also Shireen T. Hunter, *Iran's Foreign Policy in the Post-Soviet Era: Resisting the New International Order* (Santa Barbara, Denver and Oxford: Praeger, 2010).

[21] Abdel Salam Sidahmed, *Politics and Islam in Contemporary Sudan*

(New York: St. Martins Press, 1996), 45; See also Claes-Johan Lampi Sorensen, *The Islamic Movement in Sudan: External Relations and Internal Power Struggle After 1989*, Master's Thesis, American University of Beirut, April 26, 2002, 33.

[22] Lampi Sorensen, T*he Islamic Movement in Sudan*, 33; See also Mohamed Elhachmi Hamdi, T*he Making of an Islamic Political Leader: Conversations with Hasan al-Turabi* (Colorado and Oxford: Westview Press, 1998).

[23] Lampi Sorensen, *The Islamic Movement in Sudan*, 34.

[24] Ibid.

[25] Hamdi, *The Making of an Islamic Political Leader*, 15-16.

[26] Lampi Sorensen, *The Islamic Movement in Sudan*, 35.

[27] Sandee, "Islamism, Terrorism and Jihadism in the Sudan."

[28] Robert I. Rotberg, ed., *Battling Terrorism in the Horn of Africa* (Virginia: Brookings Institution Press, 2005).

[29] Lampi Sorensen, *The Islamic Movement in Sudan*, 52; See also Muriel Mirak-Weissbach, "Khartoum Conference Seeks Solutions in Moral Realm," *Executive Intelligence Review,* November 11, 1994, http://aboutsudan.com/conferences/khartoum_conference.htm.

[30] Claes-Johan Lampi Sorensen, *The Islamic Movement in Sudan*, 52.

[31] Yossef Bodansky, *Offensive in the Balkans* (Washington: Sidney Kramer Books, Inc., 1995), 71-78, http://www.srpska-mreza.com/library/facts/bodansky2.html.

[32] Preeti Bhattacharji, "State Sponsors: Sudan," Council on Foreign Relations *Backgrounder,* April 2, 2008, http://www.cfr.org/sudan/state-sponsors-sudan/p9367#p6.

[33] Francis M.Deng, ed., *New Sudan in the Making? Essays on a Nation in Painful Search of Itself* (Trenton, NJ: The Red Sea Press, 2010).

ETHIOPIA

The U.S. Department of State describes Ethiopia as "a strategic partner in the Global War on Terrorism."[1] The title is more than merited, both for the Ethiopian government's actions abroad and for the challenges it faces at home. As the 2008 edition of the Department's Country Reports on Terrorism noted: "The Government of Ethiopia, facing a deteriorating security environment in Somalia that resulted in increased threats to its own security, and in support of the internationally recognized Transitional Federal Government of Somalia, battled insurgents and extremists that were formerly affiliated with the Council of Islamic Courts, including the al Qa'ida (AQ)-affiliated al-Shabaab factions. Until they announced their military withdrawal from Somalia in late 2008, Ethiopian forces provided critical support to the African Union Mission in Somalia (AMISOM) peacekeeping force, which was also targeted by extremist elements. In addition, Ethiopian forces countered individuals affiliated with organizations that attempted to conduct attacks inside Ethiopia."[2]

ISLAMIST ACTIVITY

For the moment, the primary Islamist threats to Ethiopia's security are external, coming from Somalia and Sudan, albeit less from the latter than was the case previously.

While a certain controversy surrounds the precise details of Islamism's introduction into Ethiopia, a bridgehead seems to have been established in and around the town of Harar fairly early on in the 20th century, perhaps during the Italian occupation (1936-1942), by pilgrims returning from the Muslim pilgrimage to Mecca, or *Hajj*. Later, in the 1960s and 1970s, a number of Oromo students returning from religious studies in Saudi Arabia further propagated the creed, not only in their native regions but also in Addis Ababa and Wollo. The May 1991 fall of the Derg dictatorship gave new impetus to these trends, as many returning Oromo exiles had been influenced by Wahhabi doctrines during their time abroad and the new government's policies facilitated contact with correligionists in other countries, who supported the establishment of mosques, schools, and associations.[3] Among the latter were two entities in Addis Ababa: the Ethiopian Muslim Youth Association, founded in the 1990s and linked to the Riyadh-based World Association of Muslim Youth (WAMY), and the Alawiyah School and Mission Center, owned since 1993 by the Saudi-controlled World Muslim League's International Islamic Relief Organization (IIRO).[4] IIRO has also donated food and medical relief to Ethiopia following natural disasters.[5] (In August 2006, the U.S. Treasury Department formally designated the Philippine and Indonesian branches of the IIRO for facilitating terrorism.[6])

Like their Wahhabi confrères elsewhere, Ethiopian Islamists have attacked what they regard as syncretism among other Muslims, as exemplified by certain Sufi-inspired practices like pilgrimages to various shrines and the celebration of *Mawlid* (the birthday of the prophet Muhammad). More recently, some zealots have pushed for a stricter observance of what they regard as compulsory practices such as the wearing of pants above the ankles and the use of face coverings by women. The tensions within the Muslim community were further aggravated when a branch of *Takfir wal-Hijrah* ("Excommunication and Exodus"), a radical group which originated in Egypt in the 1970s, was driven from Sudan and decamped first to Gondar and, subsequently, to a northern suburb of Addis Ababa.[7] The group labels most fellow Muslims, including other Wahhabis, as *kuffar* ("non-believers"). Although it has caused less of a sensation since the 2004 death of its leader in Ethiopia, Sheikh Muhammad Amin, the group continues to exist.[8] Details of the group's activities, capabilities and resources within Ethiopia, however, remain sketchy at best.

Al-Qaeda is also known to be active in Ethiopia. The organization has long viewed East Africa as a priority within its overall strategy. According to the Combating Terrorism Center at West Point, the nascent al-Qaeda, then based in Sudan, sought both to establish working relations with Islamist extremists in Somalia and create training camps in ethnic Somali areas of Ethiopia in the early 1990s.[9] More recently, the Ethiopian intervention in Somalia has given al-Qaeda reason to renew its interest both in the Horn of Africa in general and in targeting Ethiopia in particular. For example, in early 2007, Ayman al-Zawahiri called for attacks on Ethiopian forces in Somalia using "ambushes, mines, raids and martyrdom-seeking raids to devour them as the lions devour their prey," which analysts at the Combating Terrorism Center at West Point note "strongly suggests that al-Qa'ida desires to use the Horn as a theater of operations."[10] However, like with *Takfir wal-Hijrah* (above), accurate information on al-Qaeda's organizational make-up and capabilities in Ethiopia is far from complete, at least at the open-source level.

Another Islamist group active in Ethiopia is the world's largest *da'wa* (proselytizing) movement, *Tablighi Jamaat*. Founded in India in 1929, the group first came to Ethiopia from South Africa in the 1970s. Its activities, however, were very limited until after the fall of the Derg. Little is known about the group's activities other than that its center of operations seems to be the Kolfe district of Addis Ababa, where it is especially active within the Gurage community that has migrated to the city from their mountainous homeland southwest of there.

The principal Islamist threat to Ethiopia, however, comes from its regional neighbor, Somalia. Following the January 1991 collapse of the Muhammad Siyad Barre regime, the last effective central government of Somalia, the rise of *al-Itihaad al-Islamiya* (AIAI, "Islamic Union") posed serious challenges to Ethiopian security during the 1990s. While the AIAI's primary focus was on the establishment of an Islamist state in Somalia, it also encouraged subversive activities among ethnic Somalis in the Somali region of Ethiopia and carried out a series of terrorist attacks, including the bombing of two hotels and the 1995 attempted assassination of a cabinet minister in Addis Ababa, Abdul Majeed Hussein, an ethnic Somali Ethiopian whom the AIAI accused of being a traitor in claiming responsibility for the attack. AIAI's hostility to Ethiopia arises from its toxic mix of Islamism with Somali irredentism and the latter's designs on Ethiopian territory. The exasperated Ethiopian regime finally intervened in Somalia in August 1996, wiping out al-Itihaad bases in the Somali towns of Luuq and Buulo Haawa and killing hundreds of Somali extremists as well as scores of non-Somali Islamists who had flocked to the Horn under the banner of *jihad*.[11]

As it turns out, the defeat was only a temporary setback for the Somali Islamists, who regrouped under the banner of the Islamic Courts Union (ICU) with many of the same leaders as AIAI, including Sheikh Hassan Dahir Aweys, who had served as number two in AIAI and went on to chair the ICU's *shura* and later head the Asmara, Eritrea-based Alliance for the Re-Liberation of Somalia (ARS) after Ethiopian forces intervened in Somalia in December 2006 in support of the country's internationally-recognized, but weak "Transitional Federal Government." The presence of Ethiopian troops in Somalia, which lasted until early 2009, occasioned an Islamist insurgency spearheaded by the radical *Harakat al-Shabaab al-Mujahideen* ("Movement of Warrior Youth," al-Shabaab), a group that was designated a "specially designated global terrorist" by the U.S. Department of State in 2008[12] and "listed terrorist organization" by the Australian government the following year.[13] While the threat is external, it cannot be entirely separated from the internal threat to Ethiopian national security posed by dissidents within who align themselves with the country's foreign enemies.

Among the latter, Eritrea falls into a category all of its own given the bitter two-year war which the tiny state precipitated in May 1998, when it occupied a small sliver of territory that had up to then been peaceably administered by Ethiopia. While the regime of Eritrean President Isaias Afewerki is not known for its religiosity—in fact, the country was one of only eight countries placed on the list of "particular concern" by the George W. Bush administration and has been criticized by the Obama administration for its "very serious restrictions on free exercise of religion"[14]—that has not prevented it from supporting Islamist movements if they serve its overall strategic objective of undermining the Ethiopian government. To this end, it has lent support to, among other groups, the Islamist insurgency in Somalia[15] as well as the secessionist Ogaden National Liberation Front (ONLF) in Ethiopia, which has frequently partnered with its extremist ethnic kin in Somalia.[16]

ISLAMISM AND SOCIETY

Traditionally, the dominant ethnic group in Ethiopia has been the Amhara who, together with the Tigray, currently make up about 36.3 percent of the population, according to the last national census, conducted in 1994.[17] The Oromo, who live largely in the southern part of the country, constitute another 32 percent. Other important ethnic groups include the Somali (5.9 percent), Gurage (4.3 percent), Sidama (3.5 percent), and Welayta (2.4 percent). Religiously, about half of the population is Christian, mainly adherents of the Ethiopian Orthodox Tewahedo Church, an Oriental (Monophysite) Orthodox Christian body in communion with the Armenian, Coptic, and Syrian Churches. Another 40 percent or so is Muslim, drawn primarily from the Oromo and other southern peoples as well as the ethnic Somali. Given that the population of Ethiopia is estimated to be at least 85 million, the country has more Muslims than many Muslim states, including Afghanistan, Iraq, Saudi Arabia, and Sudan.[18]

Until the modern period, interactions between Christians and Muslims in Ethiopia have been relatively cordial. According to tradition, the prophet Muhammad even sent a group of his early followers to take refuge in Ethiopia, where they succeeded in obtaining the protection of the king of Aksum from the persecutions they were then being subjected to in Mecca.[19] The relationship became testier beginning in the fifteenth century, when Muslim raiders from the Somali port of Zeila began a series of incursions into the Ethiopian highlands. Although these forays were repulsed, the following century saw a full-scale *jihad* led by Ahmad ibn Ibrahim al-Ghazi, who aimed to end Christian power in Ethiopia. He succeeded in overrunning most of eastern and central Ethiopia, destroying numerous Christian churches and monasteries in the process before he was defeated and killed in 1543 by the Ethiopians with aid from the Portuguese.[20] In later centuries, the Ethiopians defeated several other Muslim attempts to overrun them, including invasions by the khedive of Egypt in 1875 and the forces of the Mahdi in the Sudan in 1888, although the latter were not repulsed until after they had sacked the former capital of Gondar, burning many of its churches.[21] Another milestone in Christian-Muslim relations in Ethiopia came when the Emperor Menelik II died in 1913 and was succeeded by his grandson Lij Iyasu. Three years later, Lij Iyasu announced his conversion to Islam, provoking a political firestorm among the ruling elite, who deposed him for abjuring the faith of his ancestors.[22]

Almost all Muslims in Ethiopia are Sunni, with a plurality, if not a majority, adhering to one or another Sufi *tarīqa* (order), the most widely-diffused being the Qadiriyya, although the Tijaniyya, Shaziriyya, and Semaniyya also have significant followings. Islam is most prevalent in eastern Ethiopia, particularly in the Somali and Afar regions, as well as in many parts of the Oromo region. While institutional Islam in Ethiopia tends to be decentralized, the Ethiopian Supreme Council for Islamic Affairs, formally established (although not accorded *de jure* recognition) in 1976, enjoys a certain prestige and its chairman is treated by the government as "representative of the Ethiopian Muslim community" and accorded the same courtesies as the heads of the Orthodox, Catholic, and Protestant Churches in state ceremonials.[23]

By and large, the Muslim community in Ethiopia has done well under the Ethiopian Peoples' Revolutionary Democratic Front (EPRDF) government, which lifted its predecessor's restrictions on the *Hajj*, ban on the importation of religious literature, and obstacles to the construction of mosques and religious schools.[24] The opening "produced a new consciousness among the Muslim population, generated new religious affiliations and paved the way for Islam in Ethiopia to become more visible."[25]

By and large, Ethiopian Muslims have resisted the attempts of radical co-religionists to promote political Islam. The main reasons for this failure of Islamism to gain traction include not only the deep roots of more traditional forms of Islam, especially those represented by the Sufi orders, and the strength of social ties that cross religious boundaries, but also the fact that the extremists have failed to offer concrete solutions to many of the problems faced by ordinary Ethiopians while the government, despite its limitations, has managed to deliver impressive rates of economic growth.[26] Nonetheless, the potential does exist for religion to be exploited to mobilize greater support by various separatist movements.

ISLAMISM AND THE STATE

Following the 1974 overthrow of the Emperor Haile Selassie, the communist Derg regime of Mengistu Hailemariam persecuted religious leaders and discouraged the practice of religion by Christians and Muslims alike. Since the defeat of the dictatorship, and the subsequent assumption of power of the current government led by the Ethiopian Peoples' Revolutionary Democratic Front (EPRDF) in 1991, the policy has shifted to one of religious tolerance, although the formation of political groups on the basis of religion is forbidden. According to the State Department's 2008 annual report on religious freedom, the Ethiopian constitution "provides for freedom of religion, and other laws and policies contributed to the generally free practice of religion" and "the law at all levels protects this right in full against abuse, either by governmental or private actors."[27]

Despite this tolerance, the Ethiopian government has taken a significant role in regional and international counterterrorism efforts. It served as host for the African Union's Center for Study and Research on Terrorism, and in 2008 ratified the Protocol to the OAU Convention on the Prevention and Combating of Terrorism.[28] From 2006 through late 2008, Ethiopia led the efforts in Somalia against extremists connected with the ICU, and provided "critical support" to the African Union Mission in Somalia (AMISOM) in their efforts against extremist groups.[29] The U.S. State Department currently considers Ethiopia to be an "important regional security partner."[30]

However, Ethiopia's counterterrorism efforts have drawn mixed reviews. Last summer, Ethiopia's Council of Ministers drafted an anti-terrorism law designed to discourage radical groups within Ethiopian borders, carrying penalties ranging up to life imprisonment and even the death penalty. Expressing support for terrorism was likewise criminalized: "Whosoever writes, edits, prints, publishes, publicises, disseminates, shows, makes to be heard any promotional statements encouraging... terrorist acts is punishable with rigorous imprisonment from 10 to 20 years."[31] The legislation, while recognized as an attempt to combat extremism, has drawn criticism from some human rights organizations who claim that the law's ambiguous language is an attempt by the EPRDF to cement its power and justify oppression of opposition groups.[32]

Other have pointed to the country's recent elections as further reason for concern. In the May 2010 vote, the EPRDF and its allies won 545 out of 547 seats in the country's parliament. While the lopsided results were partially attributable to divisions within the opposition, they nonetheless raised questions among some analysts about the future of democracy in the Ethiopia.[33] Not all experts see cause for concern, however. Rather, they emphasize the progress Ethiopia has made since ousting the Soviet regime in 1991—especially when placed into the context of its neighbors Eritrea, Somalia, and Kenya, who have all struggled with instability.[34] In fact, shortly after its victory was confirmed by the country's highest court, the Ethiopian government announced a peace deal with one faction of Ogadeni rebels.[35]

Nevertheless, the potential for conflict remains. After the fall of the communist Derg dictatorship, a constituent assembly convened by the EPRDF government adopted a constitution in 1994 that carried "a radical recognition of diversity and of a new kind of equality."[36] Each ethnic community is accorded the right and duty to manage its own affairs under the aegis of a federal government that serves as the center for state unity. While it is too early to declare the success or failure of this system of ethnic federalism, it does raise the specter of struggles for allegiance between religion and ethnicity as well as the distinct possibility that Islam in particular may be used by groups seeking to mobilize their ethnic kin to exercise the secession that the constitution affirms is an inherent part of the "unconditional right of self-determination" accorded to every "group of people who have or share a large measure of common culture or similar customs, mutual intelligibility of language, belief in a common or related identities, a common psychological make-up, and who inhabit an identifiable, predominantly contiguous territory."[37] Against this potential vulnerability, which external foes, both state and non-state will be eager to seize upon, the Ethiopian government will need to maintain constant vigilance.

ENDNOTES

[1]U.S. Department of State, Bureau of African Affairs, "Background Note: Ethiopia," June 2009, http://www.state.gov/r/pa/ei/bgn/2859.htm#relations.

[2] U.S. Department of State, Office of the Coordinator for Counterterrorism, "Country Reports: Africa Overview," in *Country Reports on Terrorism 2008*, April 30, 2009, http://www.state.gov/documents/organization/122599.pdf.

[3] See generally Haggai Erlich, *Saudi Arabia and Ethiopia: Islam, Christianity, and Politics Entwined* (Boulder, CO: Lynne Rienner, 2007).

[4] Terje Østebø, "The Question of Becoming: Islamic Reform Movements in Contemporary Ethiopia," *Journal of Religion in Africa* 38, no. 4 (2008), 421.

[5] David H. Shinn, "Ethiopia: Governance and Terrorism," in Robert I. Rotberg, ed., *Battling Terrorism in the Horn of Africa* (Cambridge, MA and Washington, DC: World Peace Foundation/Brookings Institution, 2005), 98.

[6] Press Release, "Treasury Designates Director, Branches of Charity Bankrolling Al Qaeda Network," U.S. Department of the Treasury, August 2, 2006, http://www.treas.gov/press/releases/hp45.htm.

[7] Timothy Carney, "The Sudan: Political Islam and Terrorism," in ibid., 122.

[8] Østebø, 422-423.

[9] Combating Terrorism Center at West Point, *Al –Qa'ida's (mis)Adventures in the Horn of Africa* (West Point, NY: U.S. Military Academy, Harmony Project, 2007), 38-40.

[10] Ibid., 1.

[11] Medhane Tadesse, *Al-Ittihad: Political Islam and Black Economy in Somalia. Religion, Money, Clan and the Struggle for Supremacy over Somalia* (Addis Ababa, 2002), 156-168.

[12] U.S. Department of State, Office of the Coordinator for Counterterrorism, "Designation of al-Shabaab as a Specially Designated Global Terrorist" (Public Notice 6137), February 26, 2008, http://www.state.gov/s/ct/rls/other/des/102448.htm.

[13] Commonwealth of Australia, Joint Media Release of Attorney-General Robert McClelland MP and Minister for Foreign Affairs Stephen Smith MP, "Listing of Al-Shabaab as a Terrorist Organisation," August 21, 2009, http://www.foreignminister.gov.au/releases/2009/fa-s090821.html.

[14] U.S. Department of State, Bureau of Democracy, Human Rights, and Labor, "Briefing by Assistant Secretary Michael H. Posner on Annual Report on International Religious Freedom," October 26, 2009, http://www.state.gov/g/drl/rls/rm/2009/130993.htm.

[15] J. Peter Pham, "Eritrea: Regional Spoiler Exacerbates Crisis in the

Horn of Africa and Beyond," *World Defense Review*, October 15, 2009, http://worlddefensereview.com/pham101509.shtml; See also Ahmed Mohamed Egal, "Eritrea's Repayment of its Fraternal Debt to the Somali People," *American Chronicle*, November 4, 2009, http://www.americanchronicle.com/articles/view/126773.

[16] J. Peter Pham, Testimony before the U.S. House of Representatives, Committee on Foreign Affairs, Subcommittee on Africa and Global Health, October 2, 2007, http://foreignaffairs.house.gov/110/pha100207.htm.

[17] "Ethiopia," *CIA World Factbook*, June 24, 2010, https://www.cia.gov/library/publications/the-world-factbook/geos/et.html.

[18] Ibid.

[19] Michael Cook, *Muhammad* (New York: Oxford University Press, 1983), 18.

[20] David H. Shinn and Thomas P. Ofcansky, *Historical Dictionary of Ethiopia, rev. ed.* (Lanham, MD: Scarecrow Press, 2004), lii.

[21] Ibid., 225.

[22] Richard Pankhurst, *The Ethiopians: A History* (Malden, MA: Blackwell, 2003), 201-208.

[23] Hussein Ahmed, "Coexistence and/or Confrontation?: Towards a Reappraisal of Christian-Muslim Encounter in Contemporary Ethiopia," *Journal of Religion in Africa* 36, no. 1 (2006), 11-12.

[24] Hussein Ahmed, "Islam and Islamic Discourse in Ethiopia (1973-1993)," in Harold G. Marcus, ed., *New Trends in Ethiopian Studies: Social Sciences* (Papers of the 12th International Conference of Ethiopian Studies, vol. 1 (Lawrenceville, NJ: Red Sea Press, 1995), 775-801.

[25] Østebø, "The Question of Becoming," 417.

[26] See Alex de Waal, ed., *Islamism and its Enemies in the Horn of Africa* (Addis Ababa: Shama Books, 2004).

[27] U.S. Department of State, Bureau of Democracy, Human Rights, and Labor, "Country Report: Ethiopia," in *International Religious Freedom Report 2009*, October 26, 2009, http://www.state.gov/g/drl/rls/irf/2009/127232.htm.

[28] U.S. Department of State, Bureau of African Affairs, "Background Note: Ethiopia."

[29] U.S. Department of State, Office of the Coordinator for Counterterrorism, "Country Reports: Africa Overview."

[30] U.S. Department of State, Bureau of African Affairs, "Background Note: Ethiopia."

[31] "Ethiopia Adopts Strict Anti-Terrorism Bill," Agence France Presse, July 7, 2009, http://www.google.com/hostednews/afp/article/ALeqM5hMqgOlskPvo1m_dSE35D1rFeICNw.

[32] Leslie Lefkow, Testimony before the House of Representatives, Committee on Foreign Affairs, Subcommittee on Africa and Global

Health, June 17, 2010.

[33] Barry Malone, "Ethiopia Court Rejects Final Poll Result Challenge," Reuters, July 20, 2010, http://af.reuters.com/article/topNews/idAFJOE66J0RW20100720.

[34] "Ethiopia's Ruling Party Set For Landslide Win," Reuters, May 24, 2010, http://af.reuters.com/article/ethiopiaNews/idAFL-DE64N1C220100524.

[35] William Davidson, "Ethiopian Government Plans to Sign Peace Deal With Ogaden Rebels Tomorrow," Bloomberg, July 28, 2010, http://www.bloomberg.com/news/2010-07-28/ethiopian-government-plans-to-sign-peace-deal-with-ogaden-rebels-tomorrow.html.

[36] Jon Abbink, "An Historical-Anthropological Approach to Islam in Ethiopia: Issues of Identity and Politics," *Journal of African Cultural Studies* 11, no. 2 (1998), 121-123.

[37] J. Peter Pham, "African Constitutionalism: Forging New Models for Multi-ethnic Governance and Self-Determination," in Jeremy I. Levitt, ed., *Africa: Mapping New Boundaries in International Law* (Oxford: Hart Publishing 2008), 188-190.

SOMALIA

QUICK FACTS

Population: 10,112,453

Area: 637,657 sq km

Ethnic Groups: Somali 85%, Bantu and other non-Somali 15% (including Arabs 30,000)

Religions: Sunni Muslim

Government Type: No permanent national government; transitional, parliamentary federal government

GDP (official exchange rate): $2.763 billion (2009 est.)

Map and Quick Facts courtesy of the CIA World Factbook (Last Updated July 2010)

The U.S. State Department's 2009 report on global terrorism trends summarized the threats emanating from Somalia by declaring that the failed state "remained highly unstable, and a permissive environment for terrorist transit and training," citing the fact that "the fragile hold on power of Somalia's Transitional Federal Government (TFG), a protracted state of violent instability, long unguarded coasts, porous borders, and proximity to the Arabian Peninsula, made Somalia an attractive location for international terrorists seeking a transit or launching point for operations there or elsewhere." Specifically, the report noted that "the terrorist and insurgent groups al-Shabaab and Hizbul Islam continued to exercise control over much of southern Somalia," while "the TFG and peacekeepers of the African Union Mission in Somalia (AMISOM) were confined to parts of Mogadishu."[1] Hampering the U.S. response to this threat is not only the absence of a viable partner government in the Somali capital of Mogadishu but also Washington's failure to creatively engage effective Somali authorities, including those in the unrecognized Republic of Somaliland.[2]

ISLAMIST ACTIVITY

The Islamist groups currently active in Somalia fall roughly into one of seven principal categories:

Harakat al-Shabaab al-Mujahideen ("Movement of Warrior Youth," al-Shabaab)

Known colloquially as al-Shabaab, this movement arose out of the militant wing of the Islamic Courts Union. Following the defeat of the latter by the Ethiopian intervention in early 2007, al-Shabaab broke with other Islamists who regrouped under the sponsorship of Eritrea to form the Alliance for the Re-Liberation of Somalia (ARS) to oppose the Transitional Federal Government (TFG) then installed in Mogadishu.

Founded in large part due to the efforts of Aden Hashi Ayro, a militant who had trained with al-Qaeda in Afghanistan prior to September 11, 2001, al-Shabaab's schism with other Islamists reflects Ayro's adherence to a more radical *jihadist* ideology that does not countenance cooperation with the non-Muslim Eritrean regime, even against a common enemy. Although divided into several factions even before Ayro was killed by a U.S. aerial strike in May 2008, al-Shabaab remains an effective fighting force overall. It has managed to seize control of large sections of southern and central Somalia, including parts of Mogadishu, where it has installed a strict Islamist regime that, to the horror of many Somalis, has carried out a number of harsh punishments—among them the stoning of a 13-year-old rape victim that it found "guilty" of alleged adultery.[3] The current senior leadership of al-Shabaab appears to be made up of veteran *jihadists* with experience on battlefields abroad, including in Afghanistan, Bosnia, and Kashmir.[4]

Over time, the group has shifted its emphasis from a purely local focus on driving out foreign forces to an increasingly international agenda—one evidenced by a twin bombing in Kampala, Uganda, in July 2010, during the FIFA World Cup final match, which left 74 people dead and scores injured, as well as by the organization's formal proclamations of its allegiance to al-Qaeda.

Hizbul Islam ("Islamic Party")

Led by Hassan Dahir 'Aweys, previously the military commander of Somali Muslim Brotherhood offshoot *al-Itihaad al-Islamiyya* (AIAI, the "Islamic Union") and subsequently chairman of the *shura* of the Islamic Courts Union, Hizbul Islam is the product of a merger of several groups. Its primary difference with al-Shabaab is that Hizbul Islam does not place as much emphasis on global *jihadist* objectives; rather, its two principal demands are the implementation of a strict version of *sharia* as the law in Somalia, and withdrawal of all foreign troops from the country. By and large, however, Hizbul Islam has cooperated with al-Shabaab, although the two groups have come into occasional conflict over the division of spoils. Hizbul Islam lost control of the strategic town of Beledweyne to al-Shabaab in June 2010, retaining only some territory in the southern and central Somali regions of Bay and Lower Shabelle. There have been reports of talks, allegedly mediated by foreign militants, between the two Islamist groups aimed at bringing about their merger.[5] Subsequently, during the Muslim holy month of Ramadan, the two groups cooperated on a joint offensive against TFG and AMISOM forces in Mogadishu.

Mu'askar Ras Kamboni ("Ras Kamboni Brigades")

Led by Hassan Abdullah Hersi ("al-Turki"), a former military commander for the Islamic Courts, and based in Middle and Lower Jubba Valley, where it gained control of several strategically located towns which control access to the Kenyan border, including Jilib Afmadoow, and Dhoobley, the Ras Kamboni Brigades were aligned with Hizbul Islam until the beginning of 2010, when it announced it was joining forces with al-Shabaab and the two groups proclaimed their adhesion to "the international *jihad* of al-Qaeda."[6]

Ahlu-Sunna wal-Jama'a (roughly, "[Followers of] the Traditions and Consensus [of the Prophet Muhammad]")

The original Ahlu Sunna wal-Jama'a was an umbrella group of traditional Somali Muslims organized by General Muhammad Farah 'Aideed as a counterweight to his Wahhabi-inspired opponents in AIAI.[7] In mid-2009, the excesses of al-Shabaab led to a revival of the movement to oppose the ideology which Shabaab and other Islamist insurgents have appropriated from some of their foreign sponsors. Loosely organized into armed militias on a clan basis and with roots in the Sufi brotherhoods, Ahlu Sunna wal-Jama'a fighters managed in a number of places to stop what, just a few months prior, had seemed to be the relentless surge of al-Shabaab forces. Trained and assisted by the defense forces of neighboring Ethiopia, which have allowed some of the movement's units the use of its territory, Ahlu Sunna wal-Jama'a is emerging as a force in southern and central Somalia. However, the group's opposition to al-Shabaab should not be confused for support of the TFG. In fact, the group's formal alliance with the TFG, brought about under tremendous pressure from regional and international actors, has largely fallen apart. In any event, while Ahlu Sunna wal-Jama'a has neither the international links nor global strategic vision of al-Shabaab, the group has an Islamist agenda of its own. For example, it has conducted operations against those who it felt were not properly observing the fast of Ramadan—a practice that may set it at odds with the more secular elements of Somali society.[8]

Transitional Federal Government (TFG) of Somalia

The current iteration of the TFG, the fifteenth interim authority since the fall of Muhammad Siyad Barre in 1991, must be classified as an Islamist entity given the presidency of Sheikh Sharif Sheikh Ahmed, former titular head of the Islamic Courts Union.[9] "Though professing moderation," *The Economist* has written of Ahmed, "he promotes a version of *sharia* whereby every citizen of Somalia is born a Muslim and anyone who converts to another religion is guilty of apostasy, which is punishable by death."[10] The International Crisis Group, which is usually not given to rhetorical excess, recently excoriated the TFG for "having squandered the support and goodwill it received and achieved little of significance," while "every effort to make the administration modestly functional has become unstuck."[11]

Al-Islah al-Islamiyya ("Islamic Movement")

Largely displaced during the period when the Islamic Courts Union was ascendant, al-Islah is undergoing something of a revival in Mogadishu since the return of Sharif Ahmed at the head of the TFG. Currently, its chief role is the administration of schools in the capitol which are supported by the group's foreign benefactors. It is not surprising, given how spectacularly state institutions have collapsed in Somalia, that "this naturally promoted fundamentalist trends (such as al-Islah) in local Islam, which had previously been largely Sufi in character, and these were encouraged by financial support from Saudi Arabia and other Middle Eastern centers."[12]

Al-Qaeda

While its earlier foray into Somalia did not prove particularly successful, al-Qaeda remains interested in Somalia both as a theater of operations in itself and as a jumping-off point for terrorist activities in the nearby Arabian Peninsula and elsewhere in Africa.[13] An audio statement released by Osama bin Laden in praise of the Islamist insurgency in Somalia and calling upon Muslims to support it underscored this reality.[14] Even analysts who previously discounted al-Qaeda's involvement in Somalia now acknowledge that since at least early 2008, al-Qaeda advisors have played a critical role in al-Shabaab operations,[15] a fact highlighted by the September 2009 strike inside Somalia by U.S. Special Operations Forces which killed Saleh Ali Saleh Nabhan, a Kenyan national wanted in connection with the 1998 bombings of the U.S. embassies in Dar es Salaam, Tanzania and Nairobi, Kenya. At the time of his death, Nabhan was running terrorist training camps and bringing in foreign trainers and fighters to support al-Shabaab, presumably at the behest of al-Qaeda.

ISLAMISM AND SOCIETY

Somali identity is historically rooted in patrilineal descent (*abtirsiinyo*, or the "reckoning of ancestors"), which determines each individual's exact place in society. At the apices of this structure are the five "clan-families": Darod, Dir, Hawiye, Isaq, and Digil/Rahanweyn (also known as Digil Mirifle). The first four are considered "noble clans," while the agro-pastoral Digil/Rahanweyn occupy a second tier in Somali society. A third tier also exists in Somali social hierarchy, consisting of minority clans whose members historically carried out occupations such as metalworking and tanning which, in the eyes of the nomadic "noble clans," rendered them ritually unclean.[16]

Traditionally, the Somali subscribe to Sunni Islam and follow the Shāfi'ī school (*mahdab*) of jurisprudence which, although conservative, is open to a variety of liberal views regarding practice.[17] Up until the time of Somalia's independence in 1960, although there were different movements within the Sunni Islam in Somalia, the most dominant were the Sufi brotherhoods (sing., *tarīqa*, pl. *turuq*), especially that of the Qadiriyya order (although the Ahmadiyya order, introduced into Somali lands in the 19th century, was also influential).[18] While traditional Islamic schools and scholars (*ulamā*) played a role as focal points for rudimentary political opposition to colonial rule in Italian Somalia, historically their role in the politics of the Somali clan structure was neither institutionalized nor particularly prominent. In part this is because *sharia* historically was not especially entrenched in Somalia. Being largely pastoralists, the Somali relied more on customary law (*xeer*) than on religious prescriptions.[19] Hence, Somali Islamism is largely a post-colonial movement which became active in the late 1980s and which was strengthened by the collapse of the state in 1991 and the ensuing civil war, international intervention, external meddling, and efforts by Somalis themselves at political reconstruction. Absent this chain of events, it is doubtful that militant Islamism would be much more than a marginal force in Somali politics.

Although its adherents often appeal to the early 20th century anti-colonial fight of the "Mad Mullah" Sayyid Muhammad 'Abdille Hassan,[20] Somali Islamism is, at its origins, an import dating back at most to the 1950s. The 1953 establishment in Mogadishu of an Institute of Islamic Studies run by Egyptian scholars from Cairo's al-Azhar University introduced both Arabic language curriculum and contact with the Egyptian Muslim Brotherhood (*al-Ikhwan al-Muslimoon*). As is well-known, unlike the Sufis who emphasize socialization, moral education, and spiritual preparation, the Muslim Brothers stress organization, activism, and the socio-political dimension of change directed toward the creation of a modern Islamic state. After Somalia's independence in 1960, Egyptians opened secondary schools in many of the country's towns. In the 1960s and 1970s, Saudi religious and educational institutions—especially the Islamic University of Medina, the Umm al-Qura University in Mecca, and the Imam Muhammad bin Saud Islamic University in Riyadh—joined al-Azhar in offering scholarships to the graduates of these institutions. This development has parallels with the entrenchment of radical Islam in nearby Sudan via the establishment of the Sudanese Muslim Brotherhood, the precursor to the currently-ruling National Congress Party (formerly the National Islamic Front).

By the 1970s, the nascent Somali Muslim Brotherhood was so visible that the dictatorial regime of Siyad Barre took measures to suppress it, driving its adherents underground. The Somali Muslim Brothers eventually coalesced into two groups: *al-Islah al-Islamiyya* ("Islamic Movement") founded in Saudi Arabia in 1978, and *al-Itihaad al-Islamiyya* (AIAI, the "Islamic Union"), established in the early 1980s. The memberships of the two and their leadership network overlapped considerably. The differences between them were, at least initially, largely a function of the circumstances of their clandestine origins. Both sought the creation of an expansive "Islamic Republic of Greater Somalia" and eventually a political union embracing all Muslims in the Horn of Africa.[21]

The collapse in January 1991 of the Siyad Barre regime led to internecine warfare that laid waste to Somalia. Ironically, AIAI found itself in conflict with Muhammad Farah 'Aideed, the warlord who would become America's Somali *bête noire*, and, after being defeated by him, was forced to withdraw after heavy fighting. This withdrawal, which coincided with the fall of the Derg in neighboring Ethiopia, allowed the Somali Islamists to regroup in the Somali region of Ethiopia where there were also large numbers of refugees from Somalia proper. After the evacuation of Mogadishu, AIAI tried to seize control of strategic assets like seaports and crossroads. Although it temporarily held the northern port of Bosaso and the eastern ports of Marka and Kismayo, the only area where it exercised long-term control was the economically vital intersection of Luuq, in southern Somalia, near the Ethiopian border, where it imposed harsh *sharia*-based rule from 1991 until 1996. From its base in Luuq, the Islamists of AIAI encouraged subversive activities among ethnic Somalis of Ethiopia and carried out a series of terrorist attacks, including the bombing of two hotels and the 1995 attempted assassination of an ethnic Somali Ethiopian cabinet minister, Abdul Majeed Hussein, in Addis Ababa. The exasperated Ethiopian regime finally intervened in Somalia in August 1996, wiping out AIAI bases in Luuq and Buulo Haawa and killing hundreds of Somali extremists as well as scores of non-Somalis who had flocked to the Horn of Africa under the banner of *jihad*. From this period emerged the cooperation between Somali Islamists and Ethiopian groups like the Ogaden National Liberation Front (ONLF), which continue to struggle against the newly-established government of Ethiopia.

Ironically, beginning in 1993, international interventions in Somalia unwittingly allowed the Islamists back into areas that from which they had been ejected by 'Aideed, where they proceeded to thrive politically and commercially. Following the departure of the second United Nations mission in Somalia (UNOSOM II), Islamic authorities cropped up in response to problems of crime, *sharia* being a common denominator around which different communities could organize.

From its inception, AIAI rejected the non-confessional nature of the Somali state and sought to establish an Islamic regime in the country based on a strict Wahhabi interpretation of the Muslim faith. When, in the aftermath of the collapse of the Siyad Barre dictatorship, it found the direct road to power blocked by Muhammad Farah 'Aideed, it adopted a more subtle and seductive approach based on the establishment of economic and other social programs together with Islamic courts.[22]

Islam has come to be seen by some Somalis as an alternative to both the traditional clan-based identities and the emergent criminal syndicates led by so-called "warlords." Religion's increased influence has been largely a phenomenon of small towns and urban centers, although increased adherence to its normative precepts is a wider phenomenon. Islamic religious leaders have helped organize security and other services and businessmen in particular were supportive of the establishment of *sharia*-based courts throughout the south, which was a precursor of the Islamic Courts Union established in Mogadishu in June 2006. The Islamists attempted to fill certain voids left by state collapse and otherwise unattended to by emergent forces like the warlords. In doing so, they also made a bid to supplant clan and other identities, offering a pan-Islamist identity in lieu of other allegiances.[23]

Given their previous experiences with Somali Islamism, especially in its AIAI incarnation, it was not surprising that after many of the same extremists emerged in positions of authority in the Islamic Courts Union, the Ethiopians intervened as they did in 2006 to support Somalia's internationally-recognized but weak "Transitional Federal Government" (TFG), the fourteenth such attempt at a secular national government since 1991.[24] Unfortunately, while the intervention ended the rule of the Islamic Courts Union, it also provoked an insurgency spearheaded by the even more radical *Harakat al-Shabaab al-Mujahideen* ("Movement of Warrior Youth," al-Shabaab), a group subsequently designated a "specially designated global terrorist" by the U.S. Department of State in 2008[25] and a "listed terrorist organization" by the Australian government the following year.[26] Even after Ethiopian troops withdrew in early 2009, the Shabaab-led insurgency against the TFG has continued, drawing the African Union Mission in Somalia (AMISOM), which was deployed to protect the transitional regime, deeper into the conflict and causing them to suffer increasing casualties with terrorist attacks like the suicide bombing of September 17, 2009, which killed seventeen peacekeepers and wounded more than forty others,[27] and that of December 3, 2009, which killed three TFG ministers as well as sixteen other people attending a graduation ceremony within the small enclave of Mogadishu thought to be still controlled by the beleaguered regime.[28]

ISLAMISM AND THE STATE

The Somali governmental policy toward Islamism is muddled, compromised by the complicity of the current TFG in Islamist thought and activity. As a result of the base of support which it enjoys by reason of the circumstances of its birth, while Somali Islamism was damaged by the military defeat dealt to the Islamic Courts Union following the Ethiopian military intervention in late 2006 and early 2007, the chaos into which the Somali territories (outside Somaliland) have subsequently sunk under the aegis of the TFG has served to revive their standing.[29] Consequently the Islamists will continue to be a competitive force among the Somalis. Indeed, as two seasoned observers have noted:

> Whatever the short-term future holds, the complex social forces behind the rise of the Islamic Courts will not go away. Indeed while warlords and secular governments have come and gone, the Islamic Courts have enjoyed relatively consistent support for over a decade. They have tended to garner support when the populace is fed up with insecurity and ineffectual and corrupt politicians. For these reasons alone, as well as the likely long-term failure of the Transitional Federal Government's reliance on foreign protection and unwillingness to reconcile with armed opponents, the forces behind the Islamic Courts—in one form or another—are likely to rise again.[30]

At the same time, two further topics require elucidation in the context of governmental response:

The Question of Somaliland
Although the sovereignty it reasserted has yet to be formally recognized by any other state, more than a decade and a half have passed since Somaliland (the north-western region of the former Somalia, bordering on Ethiopia and Djibouti) proclaimed the dissolution of its voluntary union with the central government. Perhaps most important, in the context of the rising tide of Islamist militancy in southern and central Somalia, is the fact that Somaliland's reliance on the older system of clan elders and the respect they

command "has served as something of a mediating force in managing prag-matic interaction between custom and tradition; Islam and the secular realm of modern nationalism," leading to a unique situation where "Islam may be pre-empting and/or containing Islamism."[31] The consequence of having an organic relationship between Somali culture and tradition and Islam appears to assure a stabilizing, rather than disruptive, role for religion in society in general and religion and politics in particular. In Somaliland, for example, the population is almost exclusively Sunni Muslim and the *shahada*, the Muslim profession of the oneness of God and the acceptance of Muham-mad as God's final prophet, is emblazoned on the flag; yet *sharia* is only one of the three sources of the jurisprudence in the region's courts alongside secular legislation and Somali traditional law. Unlike the rest of the Somali lands, the region is governed by a democratic constitution approved by 97 percent of the voters in a May 2001 referendum which provides for an execu-tive branch of government, consisting of a directly elected president and vice president and appointed ministers; a bicameral legislature consisting of an elected House of Representatives and an upper chamber of elders, the *guurti*; and an independent judiciary. Somaliland has held presidential elections in 2003 and 2010 and parliamentary elections in 2005, all three of which were judged "free and fair" by international observers.

Not surprisingly, the relative success of Somaliland has drawn the ire of the Islamists in southern and central Somalia. In 2008, on the same day that Shirwa Ahmed, a naturalized U.S. citizen from Minneapolis, Minnesota, blew himself up in an attack on the headquarters of the Puntland Intelligence Service in Bosaso, other suicide bombers from al-Shabaab hit the presidential palace, the UN Development Programme office, and the Ethiopian diplo-matic mission in the Somaliland capital of Hargeisa.[32]

Islamism and Piracy
While there is as yet no evidence of anything other than opportunistic instances of cooperation between Somalia's Islamists and pirates—the latter having played no small role in the ferrying of non-Somali *jihadists* into the country—the ongoing ascendancy of al-Shabaab and its allies does not bode well for efforts to stem the contemporaneous rise of the pirates.[33]

In this context, it might be useful to refute the canard that when the Islamic Courts Union briefly held power in Mogadishu in the second half of 2006, the Islamist regime actively fought piracy. There is only one instance where the Islamist forces did anything that could even remotely be character-ized as a counter-piracy operation. On November 8, 2006, Islamic Courts Union militia stormed the United Arab Emirates-registered cargo ship MV Veesham I, which had been hijacked off Adale, north of Mogadishu on the Somali coast, and arrested its captors. The operation, however, had less to do with any principled opposition to piracy and more to do with the fact that the owner of the Veesham was one of the key financial backers of the Islamist movement and that his contribution to its coffers would be affected if he lost his vessel and cargo to the pirates.

In early 2011, it was reported that al-Shabaab had reached a deal with one of the larger piracy syndicates for a 20 percent cut of all future ransoms from piracy and was even opening an office to specifically liaise with the pirates in the port of Xarardheere where the Islamist group would permit the hijackers to anchor seized ships while awaiting ransom payments.[34]

ENDNOTES

[1]U.S. Department of State, Office of the Coordinator for Counter-terrorism, "Country Reports: Africa Overview," in *Country Reports on Terrorism 2009*, August 5, 2010, http://www.state.gov/s/ct/rls/crt/2009/140883.htm.

[2] J. Peter Pham, "Peripheral Vision: A Model Solution for Somalia," *RUSI Journal* 154, no. 5 (October 2009), 84-90.

[3] Chris McNeal, "Rape Victim, 13, Stoned To Death In Somalia," *Guardian* (London), November 2, 2008, http://www.guardian.co.uk/world/2008/nov/02/somalia-gender.

[4] Roland Marchal, "A Tentative Assessment Of The Somali Harakat al-Shabaab," *Journal of Eastern African Studies* 3, no. 3 (2009), 389.

[5] 'Somalia's Top Islamist Leaders In Unity Talks," Agence France Presse, July 10, 2010, http://www.google.com/hostednews/afp/article/ALeqM5irS90-on69foc2Og6GR7484RocCA.

[6] Abdi Sheikh and Abdi Guled, "Somali Rebels Unite, Profess Loyalty To Al Qaeda," Reuters, February 1, 2010, http://www.reuters.com/article/idUSTRE6102Q720100201.

[7] Menkhaus, ""Somalia And Somaliland," 33.

[8] J. Peter Pham, "Somali Instability Still Poses Threat Even After Successful Strike against Nabhan," *World Defense Review,* September 17, 2009, http://worlddefensereview.com/pham091709.shtml.

[9] J. Peter Pham, "Somalia Stumbles Along With Sharif," *World Defense Review*, February 12, 2009, http://worlddefensereview.com/pham021209.shtml.

[10] "Somalia's Embattled Christians Almost Expunged," *The Economist,* October 24, 2009, 58.

[11] "Somalia: The Transitional Government on Life Support," International Crisis Group Africa Report 170, February 21, 2011, http://www.crisisgroup.org/~/media/Files/africa/horn-of-africa/somalia/Somalia%20The%20Transitional%20Government%20on%20Life%20Support.ashx.

[12] Ioan M. Lewis, *A Modern History of the Somali*, 4th rev. ed. (Oxford: James Currey, 2002), 299.

[13] Kinfe Abraham, *The Bin Laden Connection and the Terror Factor in Somalia* (Addis Ababa: Ethiopia International Institute for Peace and Development, 2006).

[14] J. Peter Pham, "Bin Laden's Somali Gambit," *World Defense Review*, March 26, 2009, http://worlddefensereview.com/pham032609.shtml.

[15] Ken Menkhaus, "Somalia: What Went Wrong?" *RUSI Journal* 154, no. 4 (August 2009), 12.

[16] Ioan M. Lewis, *A Pastoral Democracy* (London: Oxford University Press, 1961).

[17] Ioan M. Lewis, *Blood and Bone: The Call of Kinship in Somali Soci-*

ety (Princeton, NJ: Red Sea Press, 1994), 167.

[18] Ioan M. Lewis, *Saints and Somalis: Popular Islam in a Clan-Based Society* (Lawrenceville, NJ: Red Sea Press, 1998).

[19] Michael van Notten and Spencer Heath MacCallum, eds., *The Law of the Somalis: A Stable Foundation for Economic Development in the Horn of Africa* (Trenton, NJ: Red Sea Press, 2006).

[20] Robert L. Hess, "The 'Mad Mullah' And Northern Somalia," *Journal of African History* 5, no. 3 (1964), 415-433; see also Abdi Sheik-Abdi, *Divine Madness: Mohammed Abdulle Hassan* (1856-1920) (Atlantic Highlands, NJ: Zed, 1993).

[21] Medhane Tadesse, *Al-Ittihad: Political Islam and Black Economy in Somalia. Religion, Money, Clan and the Struggle for Supremacy over Somalia* (Addis Ababa, 2002), 16-24.

[22] Roland Marchal, "Islamic Political Dynamics In The Somali Civil War," in Alex de Waal, ed., *Islamism and its Enemies in the Horn of Africa* (Addis Ababa: Shama Books, 2004), 114-146.

[23] Shaul Shay, *Somalia between Jihad and Restoration* (New Brunswick, NJ: Transaction Publishers, 2007), 93-127; see also Kenneth J. Menkhaus, "Somalia and Somaliland: Terrorism, Political Islam, and State Collapse," in Robert I. Rotberg, ed., *Battling Terrorism in the Horn of Africa* (Washington, DC: Brookings Institution Press, 2005), 23-47; and "Risks and Opportunities in Somalia," *Survival* 49, no. 2 (Summer 2007), 5-20.

[24] Ken Menkhaus, "The Crisis In Somalia: Tragedy In Five Acts," *African Affairs* 106, no. 204 (2007), 357-390

[25] U.S. Department of State, Office of the Coordinator for Counterterrorism, "Designation of al-Shabaab as a Specially Designated Global Terrorist" (Public Notice 6137), February 26, 2008, http://www.state.gov/s/ct/rls/other/des/102448.htm.

[26] Commonwealth of Australia, Joint Media Release of Attorney-General Robert McClelland MP and Minister for Foreign Affairs Stephen Smith MP, "Listing of Al-Shabaab as a Terrorist Organisation," August 21, 2009, http://www.foreignminister.gov.au/releases/2009/fa-s090821.html.

[27] "21 Killed In Suicide Attack On African Union Base In Somalia," cnn.com, September 18, 2009, http://edition.cnn.com/2009/WORLD/africa/09/18/somalia.suicide.attack/index.html.

[28] Stephanie McCrummen, "Bombing Kills 19 In Somali Capital," Washington Post, December 4, 2009, A19.

[29] See J. Peter Pham, "Somalia: Insurgency and Legitimacy in the Context of State Collapse," in David Richards and Greg Mills, eds., *Victory Among People: Lessons from Countering Insurgency and Stabilising Fragile States* (London: RUSI, 2011), 277-294.

[30] Cedric Barnes and Harun Hassan, "The Rise And Fall Of Mogadishu's Islamic Courts," *Journal of East African Studies* 1, no. 2 (July

2007), 160.

[31] Iqbal Jhazbhay, "Islam And Stability In Somaliland And The Geopolitics Of The War on Terror," *Journal of Muslim Minority Affairs* 28, no. 2 (2008), 198.

[32] Andrew McGregor, "Somaliland Charges Al-Shabaab Extremists With Suicide Bombings," *Terrorism Monitor* 6, no. 23 (December 8, 2008), 7-9.

[33] See J. Peter Pham, "Putting Somali Piracy In Context," *Journal of Contemporary African Studies* 28, no. 3 (July 2010): 325-341."

[34] Mohamed Ahmed, "Somali Rebels Agree to Ransom Deal with Pirate Leaders," Reuters, February 22, 2011, http://af.reuters.com/article/worldNews/idAFTRE71L1GO20110222.

SOUTH AFRICA

QUICK FACTS

Population: 49,109,107

Area: 1,219,090 sq km

Ethnic Groups: black African 79%, white 9.6%, colored 8.9%, Indian/Asian 2.5%

Religions: Zion Christian 11.1%, Pentechostal/Charismatic 8.2%, Catholic 7.1%, Methodist 6.8%, Dutch Reformed 6.7%, Anglican 3.8%, Muslim 1.5%, other Christian 36%, other 2.3%, unspecified 1.4%, none 15.1%

Government Type: Republic

GDP (official exchange rate): $280.6 billion

Map and Quick Facts courtesy of the CIA World Factbook (Last Updated June 2010)

While South Africa has a small Muslim population, comprising just 1-2 percent of its population, Islamism has a distinct presence in the country. The country is generally considered peripheral to the global war on terror, given its distance from the traditional hotbeds of Islamism. But in recent years, both transnational and domestic Islamist groups have been active on South African soil. Given the nation's history of political violence, it faces a continued risk of Islamist-inspired violence. There were Islamist attacks in South Africa in the late 1990s and threats of attacks in recent years. Additionally, the country continues to confront significant obstacles that could raise its threat level, including considerable economic and social cleavages left over from the apartheid era, increasing crime rates, and high unemployment rates.[1] If not successfully tackled, these factors could contribute to a rise in radicalism and violence in the future. South Africa's liberal democratic government allows religious groups to be active in national politics. As a result, Islamist-inspired political parties and organizations that advocate for the imposition of sharia law are present in South African society today, although they do not enjoy mass support.

ISLAMIST ACTIVITY

While South Africa experienced Islamist-inspired violence in the 1990s, the country remains on the periphery of violent Islamist activity worldwide. Nevertheless, global Islamist groups have periodically used South Africa's territory as a staging ground, compounding the danger posed by native Islamist groups which have emerged within South Africa in recent years.

Al-Qaeda

Since the late 1990s, al-Qaeda has used South Africa as both a physical safe haven and a conduit of support. In 2004, a leaked U.S. Central Intelligence Agency report stated that "[a] new tier of al-Qaeda leaders is using South Africa as one of its bases," with as many as 30 of the organization's leaders "thought to be in and around Cape Town, Durban and the Eastern Cape."[2] It is unclear if those numbers remain the same today.

Al-Qaeda operatives have been apprehended in South Africa several times in recent years. Ahead of South Africa's 2004 presidential and parliamentary elections, for example, the country's police commissioner announced that authorities had arrested and deported several individuals linked to the bin Laden network. The actions led to subsequent raids and arrests in Jordan, Syria, and Great Britain.[3]

In addition to serving as a physical safe haven for al-Qaeda, South Africa has proven to be a conduit of financial support for the group. The country has a modern banking system that is loosely regulated. In January 2007, the U.S. Treasury designated two South African cousins, Farhad and Junaid Dockrat, for financing and facilitating al-Qaeda.[4] At the time, Farhad was a preacher at a mosque near Pretoria, and his cousin was a dentist.[5] In one instance, Farhad transferred approximately $62,900 to the Taliban's ambassador to Pakistan. The money was to be forwarded to an Afghanistan-based al-Qaeda charity, the Al Akhtar Trust, which had been previously designated by the U.S. Treasury.[6] In addition to acting as an al-Qaeda fundraiser, Junaid also helped send South Africans to Pakistan to train with al-Qaeda, communicating via phone and email with then al-Qaeda operations chief Hamza Rabi'a.[7]

In September 2009, the U.S. government closed its facilities across South Africa after it received credible threats against their safety.[8] The threats reportedly came from an al-Qaeda splinter group.[9] Different from al-Qaeda's typical *modus operandi* of no-warning attacks, the threat had been phoned in to the U.S. Embassy in Pretoria.[10] The U.S. State Department reopened its embassies and consulates a few days later. However, the incident shows that the risk for violent Islamist activity, particularly against Western targets by al-Qaeda, is present in South Africa.

People Against Gangsterism and Drugs (PAGAD)

An organization indigenous to South Africa, People Against Gangsterism and Drugs (PAGAD) formed in 1995 in reaction to the extraordinarily high crime rate in the Western Cape.[11] It was also heavily influenced by the Qibla Movement, also native to South Africa, which developed in the early 1980s "to promote the aims and ideals of the Iranian revolution in South Africa and in due course transform South Africa into an Islamic state."[12] Qibla is not directly linked to any violent Islamist activity in South Africa. However, its presence, desire to change South Africa into an Islamic state, and influence over other groups indicates that there is potential for the threat to grow. A number of Qibla veterans were known to be among PAGAD's ranks.[13]

PAGAD embraced an anti-Western and anti-government ideology. While the group's primary objective was ridding their communities of gang activity and drugs, its ideology and rhetoric was distinctly Islamist. The group held meetings in mosques and its spiritual advisor, Hafiz Abdulrazaq, was given the title *amir* (commander); the term, generally tied to Islamist groups, was until then unknown to South African clerics.[14] PAGAD's national coordinator, Abdus-Salaam Ebrahim, likewise legitimized violence in his speeches, calling on Muslims to "prepare themselves with steeds of war against the enemies of Allah… the enemy of the Muslims and the oppressed people."[15]

In its operations, PAGAD operated a dual strategy, acting as a community group while simultaneously operating covert military-style cells, known as the G-Force.[16] Through these methods, experts note, "Pagad roused Muslims into action and castigated those who questioned its methods."[17] The group initially targeted drug dealers and gang members and "spawned unprecedented levels of violence" in the Western Cape.[18]

Over time, however, the group's *modus operandi* changed. In 1998, it began targeting restaurants and public places as part of its Islamist objectives. During that year, there were a reported 80 pipe bomb explosions in the Western Cape, with the most notorious occurring at a Planet Hollywood restaurant.[19] The group subsequently was designated as a Foreign Terrorist Organization by the United States in 2001.[20]

PAGAD has not launched any violent attacks in recent years. In 2000, much of the group's leadership was arrested and prosecuted, grinding its activities to a halt. Even though the group is no longer active, however, its emergence in South Africa illustrates that such an organization can viably operate there. Additionally, experts say, "since the underlying reasons for its existence were never addressed, the possible re-emergence of PAGAD or similar organizations cannot be discounted." [21]

While active, PAGAD operated a series of offshoot and front groups including the People Against Prostitutes and Sodomites (PAPAS), Muslims Against Global Oppression (MAGO) and Muslims Against Illegitimate Leaders (MAIL). In early October 2001, MAIL initiated a campaign to recruit and send Muslim fighters to fight with the Taliban.[22] One MAIL operative subsequently claimed that "some 1000 South Africans" had arrived in Pakistan and Afghanistan to join Taliban ranks against the U.S.-led Coalition.[23]

ISLAMISM AND SOCIETY

Islam first arrived in South Africa in the 17th century, when the Dutch East India Company established the Cape as a halfway point for its trade ships traveling between the Netherlands and the East Indies. The first Muslims in South Africa came from what is now Indonesia. Today, Muslims constitute a minority in South Africa, with the majority of South Africans practicing Christianity. According to the nation's most recent census in 2002, there are 654,064 Muslims, comprising 1.46 percent of South Africa's total population of 44 million.[24] In 2009, the Pew Forum on Religion & Public Life estimated there to be approximately 731,000 Muslims in South Africa, comprising 1.5 percent of the total population.[25]

The majority of South Africa's Islamic population is comprised of Indians and "coloreds," those of Malay descent.[26] Apartheid and the isolation from the international community that it caused dramatically slowed the spread of Islam in South Africa.[27] But since the fall of apartheid, the Muslim population of South Africa has been changing. According to one study, "Africans constitute the fastest growing segment, having increased by 52.3 per cent since 1991, when they numbered 11,986. The proportion of Muslims who are African increased from 3.5 to 11.42 percent during this period [1991-2001]."[28]

Similar to other countries outside the Muslim world, Islam in South Africa has been influenced by international groups and events. South Africa's position as the economic powerhouse on the continent has made it a destination for immigrants from all over Africa seeking a new life. Reports indicate that immigrants from Central and West Africa have "brought with them a new 'Africanised Islam' more in line with black South Africans' identities than the religion practised by followers with closer links to Asia."[29]

Islamism in South Africa appears to have been more significantly influenced by the Iranian Revolution than by the Salafi movement, with the roots of South Africa's modern radicalism stemming largely from the Ayatollah Ruhollah Khomeini's brand of political Islam.[30] Qibla's formation in Cape Town followed on the heels of the Islamic Revolution,[31] and the movement was explicitly created to engender the ideals of the Iranian revolution in South Africa in an effort to one day transform the nation into an Islamic state.[32] As a testament to this fact, the group used the slogan, "One solution, Islamic Revolution."[33]

Qibla also formed the Islamic Unity Convention (IUC) in 1994, which serves as an umbrella organization to over 250 Muslim organizations in South Africa.[34] It is worth noting that Achmad Cassiem is both a leader in Qibla and head of the IUC.[35] The group has boycotted government elections in South Africa "under the pretext that leaders produced by democratic means, such as elections, are illegitimate."[36] To propagate its ideology, the group owns a radio station, Radio 786, through which it preaches its ideology.[37]

While Islamic states like Saudi Arabia and Iran have peddled their influence around the world, it appears that their influence in South Africa has been limited. Iqbal Jhazbhay, a senior lecturer at the University of South Africa, notes that nearly all of South Africa's mosques are controlled by the "mainstream" Muslim Judicial Council, and that "if a Taliban-inclined imam speaks at a mosque and says outrageous things, the worshippers there may ignore him."[38] By one count, there are over 600 mosques and over 400 educational centers in South Africa.[39] It is not sufficiently clear from where the majority of these mosques receive their funding. However, it has been noted that the Muslim Judicial Council is supported by Saudi Arabia.[40]

The legacy of apartheid has left deep cleavages within South African society. Within the Muslim community, reports indicate that there is a growing hostility between black Muslims and other Muslims. "The grievances of Black Muslims run the gamut, from racism and exploitation to the unfair distribution of zakat (alms)," experts say.[41] That divide presents a factor that could potentially be exploited by Islamists seeking greater influence and followers.

ISLAMISM AND THE STATE

Since the fall of apartheid and the introduction of a true multi-party electoral system, South African politics have been dominated by African National Congress (ANC). Competing with the ANC are a variety of smaller political parties representing geographic, ethnic and religious groups.

Notably, some advocate for the imposition of *sharia* law as the governing mechanism for the state. One such group is Al-Jama-ah, which was created in April 2007 as a political party for South Africa's Muslim youth.[42] Ahead of the 2009 elections, Al-Jama-ah aimed its campaign at sixteen- and seventeen-year-olds, noting that come 2009, they would be eligible to vote. The group advocates for the establishment of *sharia* law in South Africa.[43] Ahead of the elections, the group posted a statement on their website to that effect, writing:

"Voters must choose. There is a new space for fresh ideas to be heard in politics. Is it going to be ideas from the shariah or will it continue to be the unruly mix of corrupt crony capitalists including some of the Muslim elite (Islam is bad for business types), conservative patriarchs, liberals, social democrats or Stalinists and die hard communists. The shariah [sic] was suppressed in Parliament under the eyes of Muslim lawmakers and their deliberate cooperation. Aljama will change this. We will be proud of our Shariah [sic] and not apologists, prejudiced against our own values."[44]

South Africa's history of apartheid and resistance movements has put it in a unique position in today's war on terrorism. Embracing its new democracy and pluralistic society, South Africa "is obsessed with protecting basic rights—a preoccupation which could be exploited by international terrorists working in tandem with local militants."[45] This may also be compounded by the widespread corruption plaguing South Africa.[46] Additionally, the state has porous borders and large immigrant communities that have the ability to harbor *jihadists*.[47] South Africa also suffers from a high crime rate.[48] However, "what distinguishes the crime in South Africa from elsewhere is the level of gratuitous violence associated with these crimes, as criminals are not hesitant to use lethal weapons in the course of carrying out their activities."[49] This propensity towards violence, if coupled with a rise in Islamist activity, may increase South Africa's risk for Islamist-inspired attacks against targets within the country.

However, the state appears to have been making efforts to reach out to the religious communities in South Africa to "manage the expression of Islam."[50] The ANC's Commission for Religious Affairs was developed in 1995.[51] The group meets with the President several times per year to discuss relevant issues.

The South African government has generally hoped that its neutrality in the war on terror, coupled with its pro-Palestinian stance, would spare the nation from being targeted by Islamists.[52] Indeed, one of the greatest threats to South African security may come from the state's reluctance to admit that there is, in fact, a potential threat posed by militant Islam.[53]

ENDNOTES

[1] According to the CIA *World Factbook*, South Africa has an unemployment rate of 24 percent and ranks 173 out of 200 countries in terms of its unemployment rate. "South Africa," CIA *World Factbook,* August 3, 2010, https://www.cia.gov/library/publications/the-world-factbook/geos/sf.html.

[2] Neil Mackay, "After Egypt, Where Will al-Qaeda Strike Next? The Deadly Tentacles," *Sunday Herald,* October 10, 2004., http://findarticles.com/p/articles/mi_qn4156/is_20041010/ai_n12591815/.

[3] "Transcript: SAF/AL-QAIDA," *Voice of America,* May 27, 2004, http://www.globalsecurity.org/security/library/news/2004/05/sec-040527-3f9dbb85.htm.

[4] U.S. Department of the Treasury, "Treasury Targets Al Qaida Facilitators in South Africa," January 26, 2007, http://www.ustreas.gov/press/releases/hp230.htm.

[5] Michael Georgy, "Al-Qaeda Inroads into Sleepy SA Town?" *Mail & Guardian* (South Africa), January 29, 2007, http://www.mg.co.za/article/2007-01-29-alqaeda-inroads-into-sleepy-sa-town.
U.S. Department of the Treasury, "Treasury Targets Al Qaida Facilitators in South Africa."

[6] Ibid.

[7] "South Africa: Security Threat Closes U.S. Diplomatic Offices," AllAfrica.com, September 23, 2009, http://allafrica.com/stories/200909230863.html.

[8] "South Africa: Al-Qaeda Threatened U.S. Offices – Report," AllAfrica.com, September 24, 2009, http://allafrica.com/stories/200909240664.html.

[9] "South Africa: A Deeper Look at a Telephonic Threat," *Stratfor,* September 24, 2009, http://www.stratfor.com/sitrep/20090924_south_africa_al_qaeda_behind_u_s_embassy_closure.

[10] Anneli Botha, "PAGAD: A Case Study of Radical Islam in South Africa," Jamestown Foundation *Terrorism Monitor* 3, iss. 17, September 14, 2005, http://www.jamestown.org/single/?no_cache=1&tx_ttnews%5Btt_news%5D=561.

[11] Ibid.

[12] Goolam Vahed and Shamil Jeppie, "Muslim Communities: Muslims in Post-Apartheid South Africa," in John Daniel, Roger Southall and Jessica Lutchman, eds., *State of the Nation: South Africa 2004 – 2005* (Cape Town, South Africa: Human Sciences Research Council Press: 2005), 257.

[13] Heinrich Matthée, *Muslim Identities and Political Strategies: A Case Study of Muslims in the Greater Cape Town Area of South Africa, 1994-2000* (Kassel, Germany: Kassel University Press GmbH, 2008), 157.

[14] Ibid., 159.

[15] Botha, "PAGAD: A Case Study of Radical Islam in South Africa."

[16] Vahed and Jeppie, "Muslim Communities: Muslims in Post-Apartheid South Africa," 256.

[17] Ibid., 258.

[18] Ibidem.

[19] Holt, "South Africa in the War on Terror."

[20] Botha, "PAGAD: A Case Study of Radical Islam in South Africa."

[21] Moshe Terdman, "Factors Facilitating the Rise of Radical Islamism and Terrorism in Sub-Saharan Africa," The Project for the Research of Islamist Movements African *Occasional Papers*, March 2007, http://www.terrorism-info.org.il/malam_multimedia/English/eng_n/html/prism0307.htm.

[22] Ibid.

[23] Vahed and Jeppie, "Muslim Communities: Muslims in Post-Apartheid South Africa," 252.

[24] "Mapping the Global Muslim Population," Pew Forum on Religion & Public Life, October 2009, 31, http://pewforum.org/newassets/images/reports/Muslimpopulation/Muslimpopulation.pdf.

[25] Ibid., 253-254.

[26] Nicole Itano, "In South Africa, Many Blacks Convert to Islam," *Christian Science Monitor*, January 10, 2002, http://www.csmonitor.com/2002/0110/p13s1-woaf.html.

[27] Vahed and Jeppie, "Muslim Communities: Muslims in Post-Apartheid South Africa," 253.

[28] Gordon Bell, "Islam is Spreading Among Black South Africans," Reuters, November 14, 2004, http://www.iol.co.za/index.php?set_id=1&click_id=139&art_id=qw1100423885802B264.

[29] Schmidt, "Islamic Terror Is Not a Problem for SA."

[30] Terdman, "Factors Facilitating the Rise of Radical Islamism and Terrorism in Sub-Saharan Africa."

[31] Ibid.

[32] Ibidem.

[33] Botha, "PAGAD: A Case Study of Radical Islam in South Africa."

[34] Ibid.

[35] M. A. Mohamed Salih, "Islamic Political Parties in Secular South Africa," in M. A. Mohammed Salih, ed., *Interpreting Islamic Political Parties* (New York, New York: Palgrave Macmillan, 2009), 199.

[36] Ibid.

[37] Schmidt, "Islamic Terror Is Not a Problem for SA."

[38] Moulana Ebrahim I Bham, "Muslims in South Africa," *Prepared for The Challenges and Opportunities of Islam in the West: The Case of Australiia Conference*, Griffith Univeristy, Brisbane, Australia, March 3-5, 2008, http://www.griffith.edu.au/__data/assets/pdf_file/0006/58308/Bham.pdf.

[39] *Jane's Islamic Affairs Analyst*, December 1, 2006, http://www.ever-

fasternews.com/index.php?php_action=read_article&article_id=299.

[40] Reuven Paz and Moshe Terdman, "Islam's Inroads," *The Journal of International Security Affairs* no. 13, Fall 2007, http://www.securityaffairs.org/issues/2007/13/paz&terdman.php.

[41] Salih, "Islamic Political Parties in Secular South Africa," 195.

[42] "Al Jama-ah Targets Young Voters," *The Voice of the Cape* (South Africa), October 12, 2007.

[43] "Choose: The Shariah or Unruly Mix," Al-Jama-ah Website, November 20, 2008, (http://aljama.co.za/2008/11/choose-the-shariah-or-unruly-mix/.

[44] Paz and Terdman, "Islam's Inroads."

[45] Ibid.

[46] Ibidem.

[47] Overseas Security Advisory Council (OSAC), "South Africa 2010 Crime & Safety Report," June 9, 2010.

[48] Ibid.

[49] Schmidt, "Islamic Terror Is Not a Problem for SA."

[50] "The ANC and Religion," ANC Website, n.d., http://www.anc.org.za/ancdocs/misc/anc_and_religion.html.

[51] Terdman, "Factors Facilitating the Rise of Radical Islamism and Terrorism in Sub-Saharan Africa."

[52] *Jane's Islamic Affairs Analyst*, December 1, 2006.

EUROPE

Regional Summary

Buoyed by steady immigration from the Middle East and North Africa, as well as negative native demographics among continental states, the Muslim communities in Europe are becoming larger, more complex and more vocal. Within these communities, the past year saw Islamism continue to grow in strength as a political phenomenon.

The dominant mode of Islamist activism in Europe remains to operated within the parameters of existing political systems. Some groups, such as the Union of the Islamic Communities and Organizations of Italy, confine themselves to expanding the participation of Muslims in national politics, while others, like the Muslim Association of Britain, work to promote Islamist political thought, as well as the message and appeal of foreign Islamist groups such as the Muslim Brotherhood. Only a small minority—exemplified by England's al-Muhajiroon, among other fringe elements—has advocated violence against, and the overthrow of, European governments. Those elements are closely monitored and proscribed by the authorities in question.

Perhaps as a result of Islamism's mostly-political expression in Europe, local governments generally have been slow to address or confront the phenomenon, and the national debate on the topic remains relatively unsophisticated in places such as Italy and Spain. Further east, in the Balkans, the relative corruption and/or weakness of the Kosovar, Macedonian and Albanian governments similarly has allowed Islamist groups and more extreme interpretations of the Muslim religion to proliferate and gather strength.

Elsewhere on the Continent, however, signs of pushback against the encroachment of Islamist forces and values are increasingly visible. In France, after years of laissez faire attitudes toward the growth of political Islam, certain segments of the body politic are now demonstrating newfound emphasis on national identity and secularism as a reaction to Islamist influence. Denmark also has seen growing awareness of—and a hardening of attitudes toward—Islamist groups and individuals since the 2005 controversy surrounding publications of cartoons of the Prophet Muhammad by the newspaper Jyllands-Posten. Likewise, in The Netherlands, there is growing attention to the "values gap" between the country's indigenous population and its small, mostly immigrant, Muslim minority. Since the 2004 murder of controversial filmmaker Theo Van Gogh, there has also been a noticeable hardening of response to instances of Islamic radicalism throughout Denmark.

Beyond the general sphere of lawful Islamist activity in Europe, however, is the more ominous (albeit informal) one embodied by radical jihadist elements. Today, both Sunni and Shi'a terrorist groups, among them Lebanon's Hezbollah militia and the Palestinian Hamas movement, boast a sizeable presence on the Continent (particularly in Germany and the United Kingdom). By and large, however, these organizations appear to prefer to use Europe as an area for staging, fundraising and recruitment, rather than seeing it as a target for operations.

Although European governments to date have been slow to address the political aspects of Islamism, there is considerable activism in the sphere of counterterrorism. A number of high-profile terrorist attacks in the past decade—for example, the March 11, 2004 Madrid train attacks and the subsequent July 7, 2005 London train bombing—resulted in a major focus on counterterrorism throughout the Eurozone. As a result, in recent years, authorities in multiple Europe countries have successfully apprehended and dismantled Islamist terrorist cells operating on their soil or against targets within their borders. Many of these groups and individuals have been connected to global terrorist groups such as al-Qaeda. Some, however, have proven to be "home grown" or autonomous in nature.

This, in turn, has led to growing recognition of an alarming phenomenon associated with Islamism in Europe: the rise of spontaneous Islamist terrorism by individual radicals. During the mid-2000s, the U.S.-led war in Iraq served as a major catalyst for this tendency among European Muslims, a sizeable number of whom traveled abroad to seek training for the purpose of fighting the Coalition in Iraq or targeting it in Europe and elsewhere. More recently, while the relative abatement of hostilities in Iraq has lessened its appeal as a destination for European jihadists, the ongoing conflict in Afghanistan remains a call to arms for the small minority of radicalized European Muslims who decide to take up arms against the West.

UNITED KINGDOM

The United Kingdom is arguably the European hub for numerous forms of Islamist activity, ranging from violent jihadist terrorist cells to "soft power" Islamists.[1] Although the threat from jihadist terrorists is widely recognized and accepted by both government and civil society in Britain, there remains relatively little interest in the wide variety of ostensibly non-violent Islamists who wield significant power and influence. Senior politicians from across the mainstream political spectrum are largely in agreement about the threat faced by terrorism, but they are far from reaching any consensus on how to deal with Islamists and what role, if any, they should play in countering extremism and terrorism.

Particularly since the July 7, 2005 London bombings, Islamist groups in Britain have tried to position themselves as the gatekeepers of British Muslims, claiming to represent everything from their political opinions to their views on halal meat products. These organizations also assert that they alone have the credibility to convince young British Muslims to turn their backs on violence, and to instead involve themselves in the political process. They argue that Islamist terrorism is a natural response to government policy, both foreign and domestic, and that the threat will only diminish once a number of their demands are met.

ISLAMIST ACTIVITY

British Islamists fall into four fluid and often overlapping categories. The groups from these different categories agree on many issues, particularly on the need to withdraw foreign troops from what they describe as "Muslim lands" and the central role that *sharia* law should play in the lives of all Muslims. The major differences often surround issues such as participation in the democratic process and the legitimacy and necessity of violent *jihad*.

The Muslim Brotherhood/Jamaat-e-Islami nexus

Although these are two separate movements that originate from different countries, the British manifestations of Egypt's Muslim Brotherhood and South Asia's *Jamaat-e-Islami* are closely aligned in both ideological and strategic terms. While they represent only a small minority of British Muslims, these movements are among the best organized and funded of any other British Islamic groups.

French Muslim Brotherhood specialist Brigitte Marechal has described how the Muslim Brotherhood in Europe continues to promote Islam as an all-encompassing framework which "suggests that Islam should be understood as a complete system that concerns state and nation, beliefs and legislation, cult and behaviour, and the social, political and historical."[2] This all-encompassing ideology, which Muslim Brotherhood founder Hasan al-Banna referred to as *shumuliyyat al-Islam*, is one of the driving forces for *jihadist* terrorists who are currently trying to enforce *sharia* in Afghanistan, Iraq, Somalia, Indonesia, Malaysia and numerous other fronts.

The intention of the Muslim Brotherhood in Britain is not to recruit suicide bombers, but rather to peacefully promote the *shumuliyyat al-Islam* in the hope that it will gradually initiate a reform of society along Islamist lines. Using front groups such as those described below, the organization disseminates its ideology among British Muslims by organizing events and lectures, and has seen some success in creating culturally and nationally transcendent, "*ummah*-centric" mindsets, whereby young Muslims feel a greater affinity with fellow Muslims around the globe than with their non-Muslim fellow citizens. Similarly, the British *Jamaat*, which was established in the country before the Muslim Brotherhood, are followers of the group's founder, Sayyid Abul A'ala Maududi, and propagate their form of comprehensive Islamic identity through their own set of organizations. Due to their close ideological affinity, the two have effectively joined forces, forming a partnership: the *Jamaat*, with its roots in Pakistan and Bangladesh, has more appeal to British South Asian Muslims, while the Arab origins of the Muslim Brotherhood give it more traction with British Arabs and North Africans. The main method through which the soft Islamist mission is carried out in Europe is *dawa* (prosletyzing), whereby Islamist objectives are pursued through missionary and ideological programs.

The main British Muslim Brotherhood institutions and organizations include:

- <u>The Muslim Welfare House (MWH)</u>. Founded as a charity in 1970 with the original aim of assisting foreign Muslim students in Britain, the MWH gradually became one of the central Muslim Brotherhood bodies in the country. It now acts as both a mosque and a community center, and despite its relatively low public profile wields significant influence over the national direction of the movement. The Muslim Brotherhood's connections with the MWH are extensive: until 2007, of the five registered owners and trustees of the MWH, three were also directors of the Muslim Association of Britain (MAB), the Brotherhood's other, more publically active, representative in the United Kingdom.[3] Among the owners were Mohammed Sawalha, (see below), and Abdel Shaheed el-Ashaal, who is referred to by the Muslim Brotherhood magazine *Islamism Digest* as a "senior member of the Muslim Brotherhood"[4] and who until 2000 was the company secretary for the Hassan al-Banna Foundation, one of the stated aims of which was "to give a correct image of the thoughts, ideology and life of Imam Shaheed Hassan el-Banna."[5] In 2007, all five trustees were replaced, and at least two of their successors--Wanis al-Mabrouk[6] and Hany Eldeeb[7]--also hold positions within the Federation of Islamic Organizations in Europe (FIOE) or one of its affiliates. The FIOE is the Muslim Brotherhood's European umbrella organization which loosely connects all of the group's European front organizations.[8]

- <u>The Muslim Association of Britain (MAB)</u>. The MAB is the main British representative of the Muslim Brotherhood global network. It was set up in 1997[9] by Kemal el-Helbawy, then the Muslim Brotherhood's official spokesman in Europe.[10] It has been described by scholars Peter Bergen and Paul Cruickshank as "a Muslim Brotherhood group."[11] It is also the official British representative of the FIOE.[12] The MAB is primarily a political activist organization, which promotes Islamist political thought among British Muslims. According to its website, the MAB "attempts to fill in the gap in terms of Islamic Dawah work in Britain where the call for a comprehensive Islam that encompasses all aspects of life is lacking."[13] This comprehensive Islam is precisely the vision set out in the above mentioned *shumuliyyat al-Islam* as envisioned by Hasan al-Banna.

- <u>The British Muslim Initiative (BMI)</u>. Founded as a limited company in

2006, the BMI is an offshoot of the MAB, and was founded by known Islamist Mohammed Sawalha,[14] who also serves as the organization's president. Its main spokesman is former MAB director Anas al-Tikriti, who appears to run much of the group's day-to-day operations. Since its inception, it has taken on much of the MAB's political activism and is one of the main organizers of large anti-Israel and pro-Hamas marches through London. Like the MAB, it also has a close alliance with the Stop the War Coalition.[15]

- The Cordoba Foundation (TCF). TCF was founded as a limited company in 2005 by Anas al-Tikriti, who is also the group's CEO.[16] In 2008, the then-head of the Conservative Party (and current British Prime Minister) David Cameron, identified TCF as a "front for the Muslim Brotherhood" and claimed that "even the most basic research would reveal that the Cordoba Foundation has close connections to people with extremist views, including Azzam Tamimi, the UK representative of Hamas."[17] The role of TCF differs slightly from that of other British Muslim Brotherhood groups in that it describes itself as an "independent research and Public Relations organization."[18] Although it also takes part in political Islamist activism, TCF styles itself as an Islamist think-tank which, among other things, publishes a quarterly journal, *Arches Quarterly*, featuring a mix of prominent Islamist thinkers and non-Muslim academics sympathetic to their cause. Through its academic and research based approach, TCF seeks to further sanitize and mainstream the Islamist ideology.

- The North London Central Mosque (NLCM). Also known as the Finsbury Park Mosque, the NLCM was founded in 1988 as a charity. After 9/11, it became notorious as the pulpit of the *jihadist* preacher Abu Hamza al-Masri, whose followers included "shoe bomber" Richard Reid and the twentieth 9/11 hijacker, Zacarias Moussaoui. In early 2005, Abu Hamza was removed from the NLCM, and it was taken over by a new management committee made up of senior members of the British Muslim Brotherhood.[19] Indeed, its five trustees--Mohamed Kozbar, Mohamed Sawalha, Ahmed Sheikh Mohammed (Treasurer), Abdel Shaheed El-Ashaal (Chairman) and Hafez al-Karmi[20]--were, until 2007, the registered owners of the MWH. In addition, all of the NLCM trustees apart from al-Karmi were also former directors of the MAB. After the takeover, MAB founder Kemal el-Helbawy acted as the mosque's spokesman for a brief period.[21] In 2007, the NLCM received £20,000 from the government's Preventing Violent Extremism fund, a grassroots initiative designed to fund moderate Muslim organizations to help prevent young British Muslims from falling prey to extremism.[22]

The main *Jamaat-e-Islami* organizations and institutes in Britain include:

- The UK Islamic Mission (UKIM). The UKIM was established in 1962 as an official offshoot of the *Jamaat-e-Islami*, with the express goal of establishing the party and its ideology as a major political and social force.[23] With around forty branches, over thirty-five mosques and numerous Islamic schools all across the country, it is the biggest single Islamist organizaiton in Britain.[24] Since its inception, the UKIM has used its considerable financial resources to promote Islam in Britain as "a comprehensive way of life which must be translated into action in all spheres of human life" with the eventual aim of "moulding the entire human life in accordance with Allah's will" and creating an "Islamic social order in the United Kingdom in order to seek the pleasure of Allah."[25] In recent years, and particularly since 9/11, the UKIM has softened its hard-line Islamist rhetoric but does not seem to have altered its core ideology. It continues to disseminate the works of Maududi as well as those of senior Muslim Brotherhood figures such as Jamal Badawi.[26]

- The Islamic Foundation (IF). Founded in 1973, the Islamic Foundation (IF) was set up as the official research institute of the burgeoning *Jamaat* network in Britain and is the main publisher and translator of Maududi's works in the country. It is based on a ten-acre campus in Leicester and runs classes and research projects focused on spreading Islamist ideology. In 2000, the IF established the Markfield Institute of Higher Education, which offers postgraduate degrees in Islamic studies and is a crucial center through which IF develops the *Jamaat's* political ideas.[27] Islam scholar Gilles Kepel has referred to the IF as "one of the most important centres for the propagation of militant Sunni Islamist thinking in the world," also noting that much of its work is in English, which reflects their attempts to "challenge Western cultural hegemony (whether 'secular' or 'Christian') on its own linguistic territory."[28] The IF is also known to be a key facilitator of the close relationship between the British *Jamaat* and Muslim Brotherhood.

- The East London Mosque (ELM). Founded in 1985, the ELM is, according to a 2009 British government report, "the key institution for the Bangladeshi wing of JI [Jamaat-e-Islami] in the UK."[29] The Mosque has been at the centre of numerous controversies ranging from their regular hosting of extremist speakers, to their attempts to manipulate the British political system in order to advance their Islamist agenda. In 2003-2004, the Mosque claims to have received £2.4 million in public funds,[30] and in the years 2007-2009 the ELM has received nearly £35,000 from the government's Preventing Violent Extremism fund.[31] The ELM has twice (in 2003[32] and again in 2009[33]) played host to al-Qaeda's Anwar al-Awlaki, spiritual mentor of failed Christmas Day bomber Umar Farouk Abdulmuttalab and one of al-Qaeda's emerging intellectual heavy-

weights.
- The Islamic Forum of Europe (IFE). The IFE is a subsidiary organization of the ELM, based within the Mosque's sprawling complex. In keeping with the *Jamaat's* mission of promoting the all-encompassing Islamist identity, its mission statement proclaims that "Islam offers a comprehensive system and the challenge to us all is to learn and embody the teachings of Islam and convey them to others in a wise, sensible and beautiful manner," and that the group "helps to enable individuals to learn and apply the basic tools required to achieve this within a collective framework helping to develop the Muslim community and benefit the wider society."[34] The primary mission of the IFE is to train young Muslims in *da'wa*, so that future generations can continue to propagate the movement's message. A six-month investigation by Channel 4 and the *Daily Telegraph* into the IFE and ELM, which culminated in a 2010 documentary, uncovered a detailed Islamist indoctrination program based on the teachings of Maududi. Among the revelations was the transcript of IFE's 2009 recruit training course which told new members that its goal was "to create the True Believer, to then mobilise those believers into an organised force for change who will carry out *dawah*, *hisbah* [enforcement of Islamic law] and *jihad*. This will lead to social change and *iqamatud-Deen* [Islamic social, economic and political order]."[35]

Muslim political organizations

Campaigning and lobbying is an important element of the British soft Islamist strategy. Presenting themselves as representatives of the rights of downtrodden Muslims, Islamists have acquired significant support and large media profiles, often appearing as the voice of British Muslims on television and in newspapers. They are often criticized by mainstream, secular Muslims for pushing extremist agendas and fostering inflammatory notions about a war against Islam and Muslims waged by western governments.

- The Muslim Council of Britain (MCB). In the years following the *Satanic Verses* affair,[36] the British government saw the need for a single umbrella body that could represent the political and social views of British Muslims. This lead to the creation of the MCB in 1997, headed by Iqbal Sacranie, one of the most vocal critics of the novelist Salman Rushdie and his book.[37] The MCB expanded rapidly, and eventually claimed to have around 400 Muslim and community groups under its aegis, including the MAB, IFE and ELM. Despite a seemingly wide range of voices within the MCB, the leadership was, and remains, almost exclusively Islamist, taking its ideological cue from Maududi's teachings in particular.[38] After the 7/7 London bombings, the MCB took center stage as the government's main advisors on extremism and radicalization and used this influential position as an opportunity to attempt to effect real change in the government's foreign policy. Following the attacks, the MCB issued an open letter to the then-Prime Minister Tony Blair, imploring him to change government policy so as to prevent any future attacks.[39] Their approach to domestic policy is centered on the belief that soft Islamists such as themselves are the strongest bulwark against al-Qaeda as they can use their supposed credibility among vulnerable British Muslims to prevent them from turning to violence. As part of this approach, the MCB remain among the staunchest defenders and supporters of Yusuf al-Qaradawi, the global advocate of this bulwark theory. In 2008, when he was denied a visa to enter Britain on national security grounds, the MCB, along with the BMI, were openly critical of the government's decision.[40]

- The Federation of Student Islamic Societies (FOSIS). Based in North London, FOSIS was established in 1962 as a joint venture of the Muslim Brotherhood and *Jamaat-e-Islami*, acting as the student wing of both of these groups. A 2009 government report on influential Islamic organizations notes that "the Jamaat-e Islami (JI) along with the Muslim Brotherhood were pioneers in developing student activism through the Federation of Student Islamic Societies (FOSIS)."[41] To this day, FOSIS remains a vehicle for Islamist activism, and coordinates the ideological direction of dozens of British university Islamic societies. It claims to represent over 90,000 students and its events have featured leading British as well as international Muslim Brotherhood and Jamaat-e-Islami figures including Anas al-Tikriti,[42] Rashid El Ghannouchi,[43] Azzam Tamimi,[44] Dr. Muhammed Abdul Bari[45] and Jamal Badawi.[46] Much of its activism is concerned with Gaza, and this has become an even more central concern for FOSIS since Israel's Operation Cast Lead in 2008-2009.

- The Islamic Human Rights Commission (IHRC). The IHRC is a Khomeinist Islamist organization founded in London in 1997. According to its mission statement, the organization aims to "promote a new social and international order, based on truth, justice, righteousness and generosity, rather than selfish interest."[47] Its definition of human rights is couched in Islamist terminology and IHRC co-founder and current chair, Massoud Shadjareh, has described how a lack of Islamic human rights is why "the enemies of Islam are able to plunder, kill and rape Muslims, and deny the most basic rights of Muslims even in Britain today." His suggested solution is "to promote Islam and the justice of Islam as a means of salvation for the whole world."[48] Shadjareh, the co-founder of the IHRC, is also a vocal supporter of Lebanese Shi'ite terrorist group Hezbollah.[49] Under Shadjareh, the IHRC holds the annual "al-Quds day," an event which was originally instituted by Ayatollah Khomeini. During the march through central London, protesters wave Hezbollah flags and chant anti-Israel slogans.[50] Many of the IHRC's campaigns are in support of convicted *jihadists*, who are often presented as victims of anti-Muslim government legislation. In 2006, for example, the IHRC campaigned for *jihadist* recruiter Abu Hamza al-Masri, who was convicted of inciting murder.[51]

- Cageprisoners (CP). CP was founded as a limited company in 2003 by former Guantanamo Bay inmate Moazzam Begg to "raise awareness of the plight of the prisoners at Guantanamo Bay and other detainees held as part of the War on Terror."[52] In a similar vein to the IHRC, CP presents all terrorist prisoners as victims rather than aggressors and campaigns for leading *jihadists*. Since 2006, one of CP's main *causes célèbres* has been pro-al-Qaeda preacher Anwar al-Awlaki, whose work they continue to promote on their website.[53] "Defensive *jihad*" is for CP a central and undeniable tenet of Islam. Indeed, CP founder Moazzam Begg is a supporter of Abdullah Azzam, who has written that, "By consensus of the Islamic schools of thought, *jihad* becomes an individual obligation, like prayer and fasting, on Muslim men and women when their land is occupied by foreign enemies." He continues by arguing that the obligation to take part in *jihad* "extends to neighbouring lands until the enemy has been expelled."[54]

- Muslim Public Affairs Committee UK (MPACUK). MPACUK was founded in 2002, in the aftermath of Israel's invasion of the West Bank. As a political lobbyist group, it urges Muslims to become politically active along purely sectarian, Islamist lines, and organizes campaigns against what they perceive as pro-Israel politicians. Referring to themselves as *mujahids* (holy warriors), MPACUK members see their actions as a form of *jihad* against a supposedly Jewish-led anti-Muslim conspiracy in Britain intent on marginalizing and disenfranchising Muslims.[55] During the 2010 British General Election, the group organized the "Operation Muslim Vote" campaign, which involved MPACUK activists mobilizing Muslims to vote against "several pro-Zionist war mongering MPs."[56]

Democratic Rejectionists

Unlike the groups profiled above, which have developed a utilitarian approach to democracy, this category of British Islamists rejects any form of participation in the political process. While they acknowledge that other Islamists are gaining influence through their successful manipulation of the system, democracy is still seen as an unacceptable concession. For these organizations, taking part in the current secular democratic system is a form of *shirk* (polytheism) that acknowledges laws that are above those of God. Although they differ from Salafi *jihadists* on issues such as when and where violence is legitimate in order to establish an Islamic state, their stance on secular democracy is almost indistinguishable from that of al-Qaeda.

- Hizb ut-Tahrir (HuT). HuT is a worldwide revolutionary Islamist political party with a political interpretation of Islam inspired by the Muslim Brotherhood that works toward the re-creation of the Caliphate in the Middle East as an aggressive, expansionist entity that will eventually encompass the entire globe, thus uniting the global *umma* (community of Muslim faithful).[57] The fundamental differences between the British wings of HuT and the Muslim Brotherhood and *Jamaat* are tactical, not strategic—they share the same goal of creating an Islamic super-state but disagree on what is the most effective way to do so. HuT also claims to be non-violent, and the party currently pursues a grassroots strategy which recruits a core of loyal members who work to implant Islamist ideology within British Muslims, preparing them for the country's eventual annexation by the Caliphate after they have succeeded in its re-establishment in the Middle East.[58] HuT's recruitment and indoctrination program is often pursued through numerous front organizations based in the heart of major British Muslim communities as well as universities, which organize discussions and other events featuring leading members of the group presenting their ideology as the only true form of Islam. HuT's support for overseas terrorism in the "defensive *jihads*" in Iraq, Israel and Afghanistan and their views on Jews and homosexuals have led them to be banned from appearing on British campuses by the National Union of Students.[59] In addition, senior politicians from both major British political parties, including former Prime Minister Tony Blair and current Prime Minister David Cameron, have in the past pledged to ban the group under anti-terrorism legislation, but this has yet to materialize.[60]

- Al-Muhajiroun (AM). AM was founded in 1996 as a direct offshoot of HuT by the former leader of HuT in Britain, Omar Bakri Mohammed.[61] Mohammed split from HuT due to a dispute with the party's hierarchy: Bakri wanted the party to change tactics and concentrate on establishing an Islamic state in Britain rather than re-creating the Caliphate in the Middle East. He therefore formed AM with the aim of creating a cadre of activist Muslims who campaigned for the immediate creation of an Islamic state in Britain. Since its creation, AM has also supported "defensive *jihad*" in Israel, Kashmir, Afghanistan and Iraq.[62] The group has campaigned and organized marches on various issues, including a number of anti-voting initiatives, and was one of the main driving forces behind the mass protests in London against the Danish Mohammed cartoons in 2004.[63] The group was officially disbanded in 2004 to avoid proscription, though it continued to hold meetings in Islamic centers around the country. After the 7/7 London bombings, Bakri fled the country, handing over the leadership to his deputy, Anjem Choudhary.

In 2005, AM regrouped under the banner of *Ahlus Sunnah wal Jamaah*, and later formed two more offshoots, *al-Ghuraaba* and Saved Sect, both of which were banned in 2006 for glorifying acts of terrorism.[64] Despite the bans, Choudhary and his followers were still able to operate as *Ahlus Sunnah wal Jamaah*, which was never banned, and in 2008 they began working under the name of Islam4UK. A year later, they announced the re-launch of al-Muhajiroun.[65] The entire movement was ultimately banned by the government in January 2010.[66]

"Homegrown" jihadist terrorists
Since the 7/7 attacks, the specter of British "homegrown" terrorism has remained a central concern for the country's security services. Although there has not been a successful attack since, numerous plots, many in the final stages of planning, have either failed or been prevented. The majority of those convicted on terrorism charges are British citizens of Pakistani origin. Indeed, between 1999 and 2009, they represented over a quarter of all Islamist-related offences in Britain.[67]

ISLAMISM AND SOCIETY

According to the last official estimates, taken from the country's 2001 Census, Britain has a Muslim population of 1.6 million (2.8 percent of the overall population), making them the second largest religious group in the country, after Christians. The same Census also found that three-quarters of Muslims (74 percent) were from an Asian ethnic background, of which 43 percent were Pakistani, sixteen percent were Bangladeshi, eight percent were Indian, and six were "other Asian." Eleven percent of Muslims in Britain were found to be from a White ethnic group, and four percent classified themselves as White British. Seven percent were classified as "White other" and six percent were of Black African origin.[68]

It is difficult to gauge the exact level of support for Islamist groups among Muslims in Britain, though a number of polls have tried to assess the level of support British Muslims have, both for specific British Islamist groups as well as certain aspects of Islamism, such the establishment of *sharia* law and violence in the name of Islam. In 2005, the polling company Populus asked British Muslims about their views on a number of British Islamist organizations. Twenty-five percent of respondents in that survey claimed that the Muslim Brotherhood/*Jamaat e-Islami*-aligned Muslim Council of Britain "absolutely" or "broadly" represented their views, and nineteen percent made the same claim about the Muslim Association of Britain, one of the Muslim Brotherhood's main representatives in the country.[69] However, it should be noted here that it is unlikely many of those polled were aware of these organizations' Islamist roots, and would have heard of them primarily through the many political campaigns and other events they hold around the country.

On British Muslim views regarding certain aspects of Islamism, the most extensive poll was taken in 2007. Commissioned by the think tank Policy Exchange and carried out by Populus, the poll found that thirty-six percent of 16-to-24-year-old British Muslims believed the death penalty should apply to Muslims who change their religion, compared to 19 percent of Muslims over 55. It also found that 59 percent of British Muslims were happy to live under British law, with 28 percent preferring some form of *sharia* law.[70] Of the 16-to-24-year-olds, 37 percent preferred *sharia*, whereas among the over 55s this number was only 17 percent. On the specific issue of support for al-Qaeda, the poll found that seven percent of British Muslims "admire" the group and others like it, and that 13 percent of 16-to-24-year-olds agreed with the statement that al-Qaeda and its affiliates are worthy of admiration because they fight the West. This was compared with only three percent of those surveyed over 55 who shared the same view. These, and other figures like them, indicate that the younger generation of British Muslims have stronger sympathies for elements of radical Islam than their parents, and this is consistent with similar assessments that have been made by many analysts.[71]

British Islamist groups are regularly discussed in the mainstream media, often in controversial circumstances. For example, after the deputy secretary of the Muslim Council of Britain, Daud Abdullah, signed a statement in support of violent *jihad* against Israel (see below section for more), it was covered across a range of different newspapers and media outlets.[72] In addition, Hazel Blears MP, the government secretary who liaised with the Council, and Daud Abdullah both published articles stating their respective positions.[73] There is a significant element of Islamist influence in important areas of civic life. The head of the Muslim Council of Britain and Chairman of the East London Mosque (which, as mentioned earlier, twice hosted al-Qaeda ideologue Anwar al-Awlaki), Dr. Muhammed Abdul Bari, recently sat on the panel for a University College London inquiry into the radicalization of their student, Umar Farouk Abdulmutallab,[74] who on Christmas Day 2009 attempted to detonate explosives hidden in his underwear on a plane over Detroit. Considering that Anwar al-Awlaki is widely regarded as a major inspiration for Abdulmutallab's actions, Dr. Bari's involvement in the inquiry was seen by some as inappropriate.[75]

ISLAMISM AND THE STATE

Since the July 2005 London terror attacks, the relationship between the British state and national Islamist groups has been characterized by inconsistency. The government's current counterterrorism strategy, dubbed CONTEST, is split into four parts: Pursue, Protect, Prepare and Prevent. The first three of these priorities are straightforward, hard power methods to be implemented by the security services. However the fourth—Prevent, also known as Preventing Violent Extremism (PVE) —is a new and unique approach, which is implemented through the Department for Communities and Local Government (DCLG). Designed with the intention of applying measures which could mitigate the influence and effect of "violent extremists," its primary function was to act as a fund for local community organizations that pledged to tackle radicalization on a grassroots level. Between 2006 and 2009, the Prevent fund distributed around £12 million to hundreds of organizations around the country, and quickly began to court controversy.[76] Soon after the fund began, there were revelations that a number of Islamist organizations were in receipt of Prevent funds despite their involvement in extremist activity. In 2008, for example, it was reported that the aforementioned Cordoba Foundation, while in receipt of Prevent funds, organized an event entitled "Has Political Participation Failed British Muslims?" which included on its panel Abdul Wahid, the Chairman of the British wing of Hizb ut-Tahrir. Indeed, Wahid's arguments were persuasive, as the predominantly Muslim audience voted against political participation at the end of the debate.[77]

The issue of the previous Labour government's dealings with Islamist groups came to a head in early 2009, when the Deputy Secretary General of the Muslim Council of Britain, Daud Abdullah, was a signatory (along with Mohammed Sawalha of the Muslim Association of Britain) to what became known as the "Istanbul Statement," a conference document of unequivocal support for violent *jihad* against Israel.[78] At the time, the MCB was a governmental partner on Prevent, and the then-Secretary for the DCLG, Hazel Blears, warned the MCB that Abdullah must either resign or the government would sever all ties with them. It should be noted here that in her implementation of Prevent, Blears believed that preventing terrorism was more than just an issue for the security services—it was also a societal concern. She identified that one of the roots of terrorism lay in ideological inspiration, and recognized that the Islamist ideology which inspired terrorists went against all the most basic values of British society. Thus, she pursued a values based approach, whereby Prevent would only engage with organizations with so called "shared values." It is this attitude which led to Blears' demand, to which the MCB responded in typical fashion, portraying Blears' request as an attempt to exercise control over an independent Muslim body, and refused to back down. Blears followed through with her threat, and cut ties with the MCB. Months later, however, Blears was replaced by John Denham, a minister with a more sympathetic view toward the MCB, and they were brought back into the fold shortly thereafter.[79]

Since the Labour party lost power to a Liberal Democrat/Conservative Party coalition in May 2010, the new government's position on the MCB is not yet clear, though before he became Prime Minister David Cameron stated that under his government, there would be no formal ties with the MCB until it had distanced itself from Abdullah.[80] Furthermore, at the Conservative Party Conference in October 2010, the new Home Secretary, Theresa May, made a number of statements which suggested a shift back to the Blears approach to dealing with Islamists.[81]

ENDNOTES

[1] The term "soft Islamist" will be used throughout this entry to refer to Islamist groups that use "soft power" in pursuit of their goals, in particular the two main revivalist organizations: the Muslim Brotherhood and the *Jamaat-e-Islami.*

[2] Brigitte Maréchal, "Universal Aspirations: The Muslim Brotherhood In Europe," International Institute for the Study of the Muslim World *ISIM Review* no.22, Autumn 2008, 36-37.

[3] *UK Land Registry,* Title Number: NGL700045.

[4] "Six Decades of Repression: An Interview With Adbel Shaheed al-Ashaal," St. Andrews University Centre for the Study of Terrorism and Political Violence Islamism Digest, February 2007.

[5] *Hassan al-Banna Foundation Certificate of Incorporation as a Limited Company,* Companies House, February 11, 1997.

[6] Federation of Islamic Organizations in Europe, "President Of The Federation And Head Of The Assembly Of Islamic Imams Meet President Of The Commission And European Parliament President," n.d., http://www.euro-muslim.com/En_u_news_Details.aspx?News_ID=214.

[7] "EU Muslim Converts Sharing Experiences," *IslamOnline,* April 12, 2009, http://www.islamonline.net/servlet/Satellite?c=Article_C&cid=1237706102893&pagename=Zone-English-Euro_Muslims%2FEMELayout.

[8] Maréchal, "Universal Aspirations."

[9] It is unclear if it was originally set up as a limited company. Official company records for the MAB only date back to 1999.

[10] "Kemal El-Helbawy CV," n.d., http://www.khelbawy.com/about.html.

[11] Peter Bergen and Paul Cruickshank, "The Unraveling: The Jihadist Revolt Against Al-Qaeda," *The New Republic,* June 11, 2008.

[12] Federation of Islamic Organizations in Europe, "FIOE Organisations," n.d., http://www.euromuslim.com/En_u_Foundation_Details.aspx?News_ID=211

[13] Cited on the official website of the MAB, www.mabonline.net.

[14] Mohammed Sawalha is the central figure of all Muslim Brotherhood activity in Britain, and in 2006 was described by the BBC's *Panorama* program as a "fugitive Hamas commander" and "the most influential Muslim Brother in Britain today." See "Faith, Hate And Charity," BBC *Panorama,* July 28, 2006.

[15] Richard Phillips, "Standing Together: The Muslim Association Of Britain And The Anti-War Movement," Institute of Race Relations *Race and Class* 50, no. 2 (2008), 101–113.

[16] *2008 Appointments Report for The Cordoba Foundation LTD,* Companies House.

[17] David Cameron speech delivered at the Community Security Trust in London, 4 March 2008

[18] The Cordoba Foundation, "About us," n.d., http://www.thecordobafoundation.com/about_us.php.

[19] "The Battle For The Mosque," BBC News, February 7, 2006.

[20] NLCM press release, "New Era For North London Central Mosque," February 5, 2005.

[21] Bergen and Cruickshank, "The Unraveling."

[22] Taxpayers' Alliance, "Council Spending Uncovered II, No.5: The Prevent Strategy," September 8, 2009.

[23] Michael Whine, "The Penetration of Islamist Ideology in Britain," Hudson Institute *Current Trends in Islamist Ideology* 1, May 2005.

[24] According to the official website of UKIM, www.ukim.org.

[25] UKIM, "Introduction," n.d., as cited in Giles Kepel, *Allah in the West: Islamic Movements in America and Europe* (Oxford: Polity Press, 1997).

[26] UKIM, "UK Islamic Mission Dawah: Resource To Online Islamic Books & Articles," n.d., http://www.ukim.org/webpages/Dawah.aspx.

[27] Sayyed Vali Resa Nasr, *The Vanguard Of The Islamic Revolution: Jamaat-e-Islami of Pakistan* (Berkeley: University of California Press, 1994).

[28] Kepel, *Allah in the West*.

[29] Department for Communities and Local Government, "The Pakistani Muslim Community In England," March 2009; For more on ELM connections with the *Jamaat-e-Islami*, also see Delwar Hussain, "Bangladeshis In East London: From Secular Politics To Islam," *Open Democracy*, July 6, 2006, http://www.opendemocracy.net/democracy-protest/bangladeshi_3715.jsp.

[30] ELM press release, "Exposing Dispatches," n.d., http://www.eastlondonmosque.org.uk/uploadedImage/pdf/2010_03_15_17_14_22_ELM_dispatches_response.pdf.

[31] Tax Payers' Alliance, "Council Spending Uncovered II, No.5: The Prevent Strategy," September 8, 2009.

[32] Audio of Awlaki's speech at the ELM is available at http://www.youtube.com/watch?v=GyCf25XujkM&feature=youtube_gdata.

[33] Gordon Rayner, "Muslim Groups 'Linked To September 11 Hijackers Spark Fury Over Conference,'" *Daily Telegraph* (London), December 27, 2008, http://www.telegraph.co.uk/news/uknews/3966501/Muslim-groups-linked-to-September-11-hijackers-spark-fury-over-conference.html; "Councillor Slams Muslim Lecture 'New York In flames' Poster," *East London Advertiser*, December 31, 2008.

[34] IFE, "Islamic Forum Of Europe: Responding To The Call," n.d., http://www.islamicforumeurope.com/live/ife.php?doc=intro.

[35] Andrew Gilligan, "IFE: Not Harmless Democrats," *Guardian* (London), March 4, 2010.

[36] After novelist Salman Rushdie published *The Satanic Verses* in 1988, there were widespread protests and riots by Muslims in Europe, the Middle East and South Asia who considered the content of the book blasphemous and insulting to the Prophet Mohammed. This culminated in the issuing of a *fatwa* by the Iranian Supreme Leader, Ayatollah Ruhollah Khomeini, in February 1989, which called on Muslims to kill the author in the name of Islam and Mohammed. This saga is widely seen as a watershed moment in the political "awakening" of Western Muslims, and is probably best recounted by Kenan Malik in *From Fatwa to Jihad: The Rushdie Affair and Its Legacy* (London: Atlantic Books, 2009).

[37] Sacranie famously said of the novelist: "death, perhaps, is a bit too easy for him? His mind must be tormented for the rest of his life unless he asks for forgiveness to Almighty Allah." See "Rushdie In Hiding After Ayatollah's Death Threat," *Guardian* (London), February 18, 1989.

[38] Martin Bright, *When Progressives Treat With Reactionaries: The British State's Flirtation With Radical Islamism* (London: Policy Exchange, 2006).

[39] "Full Text: Muslim Groups' Letter," BBC News, August 12, 2005, http://news.bbc.co.uk/1/hi/4786159.stm.

[40] "Muslim Outrage As Yusuf al-Qaradawi Refused UK Visa," *Times of London*, February 7, 2008.

[41] Department for Communities and Local Government, "The Pakistani Muslim Community In England," March 2009.

[42] "FOSIS Annual Conference 2005," http://oldsite.fosis.org.uk/FAC/conference05/poster.jpg.

[43] "FOSIS Annual Conference 2007," http://oldsite.fosis.org.uk/FAC/FAC2007/programme.html.

[44] "FOSIS Annual Conference 2003," http://web.archive.org/web/20030801182249/http:/www.fosis.org.uk/events/articles/annualconf_jun2003.htm.

[45] Ibid.

[46] FOSIS, "Muslim Contribution To Civilisation, Dr. Jamal Badawi, February 2010," n.d., http://fosis.org.uk/sc/calendar/details/94-jamal-badawi-speakers-tour/145%7C139.

[47] IHRC, "Aims and Objectives," n.d., http://www.ihrc.org.uk/about-ihrc/aims-a-objectives.

[48] Massoud Shadjareh, "Human Rights, Justice & Muslims In The Modern World," n.d., http://www.ihrc.org.uk/show.php?id=10.

[49] In July 2006, it was reported that in a speech he gave in London, Shadjareh called upon his audience to provide Hezbollah with "financial, logistical and informational support." See Harry Macadam, "Fanatic's Cash Aid Call," *The Sun* (London), July 6, 2006.

[50] IHRC, "The Annual al-Quds Day 2009," August 30, 2009, http://

www.ihrc.org.uk/events/9048-the-annual-al-quds-day-demonstra-tion-2009-in-support-of-palestine.

[51] "Britain Convicts Muslim Cleric Of Inciting Murder," Associated Press, February 7, 2006, http://www.ctv.ca/servlet/ArticleNews/story/CTVNews/20060207/jury_almasri_060207/20060207?hub=World.

[52] CP, "About Us," n.d., http://www.cageprisoners.com/page.php?id=2.

[53] CP, "Book Reviews From Behind Bars: Anwar al-Awlaki," n.d., http://www.cageprisoners.com/articles.php?id=24871.

[54] Moazzam Begg, "Jihad And Terrorism: A War Of Words," Cordoba Foundation *Arches Quarterly* 2, iss. 1, Summer 2008.

[55] MPACUK, "Watford Campaign Starts With A Bang!," April 18, 2010, http://www.mpacuk.org/story/180410/watford-campaign-starts-bang.html.

[56] MPACUK, "Operation Muslim Vote," May 5, 2010, http://www.mpacuk.org/story/020709/operation-muslim-vote.html.

[57] Hizb ut-Tahrir, *Hizb ut-Tahrir* (London: Al-Khilafah Publications, 2000).

[58] For more on HT in Britain, see Houriya Ahmed and Hannah Stuart, *Hizb ut-Tahrir: Ideology and Strategy*, (London: Centre for Social Cohesion, 2009).

[59] "'Stealth' Islamists Recruit Students," *Times of London*, October 16, 2005.

[60] "Blair Announces Summary Deportation For Extremists," *Times of London*, August 5, 2005; David Cameron, speech delivered at the Community Security Trust in London, March 4, 2008.

[61] "Jews Fear Rise Of The Muslim 'Underground,'" *Guardian* (London), February 18, 1996.

[62] Suha Taji-Farouki, "Islamists And The Threat Of *Jihad*: Hizb al-Tahrir And al-Muhajiroun On Israel And The Jews," *Middle Eastern Studies* 36, no. 4, October 2000, 21-46.

[63] "Reaction Around The World To Cartoon Row," BBC News, February 4, 2006, http://news.bbc.co.uk/2/hi/europe/4676930.stm

[64] "Reid Bans Two Radical Muslim Groups," *Guardian* (London), July 7, 2006.

[65] "Islamist Al-Muhajiroun Relaunch Ends In Chaos Over Segregation Attempt," *Guardian* (London), June 18, 2009.

[66] "Islam4UK To Be Banned, Says Alan Johnson," *Guardian* (London), January 12, 2010.

[67] These include offenses contrary to anti-terror legislation (namely the Terrorism Act 2000 and the Terrorism Act 2006) and those which include a clear threat designed to intimidate the public, in particular other religious groups.

[68] Office for National Statistics, *Census 2001*, April 2001, http://www.statistics.gov.uk/census2001/census2001.asp.

[69] Poll prepared by Populus on behalf of *Times* newspaper, December 2005.

[70] The results of this poll were used in Munira Mirza, Abi Senthilkumaran, and Zein Ja'far, *Living Apart Together: British Muslims and the Paradox of Multiculturalism*, (London: Policy Exchange, 2007).

[71] See for example Phillip Lewis, *Young, British and Muslim* (London: Continuum, 2007); See also Parveen Akhtar, "Return To Religion And Radical Islam," in *Muslim Britain: Communities Under Pressure*, (London: Zed Books, 2005); Mark Huband, "Radicalisation And Recruitment In Europe: The UK Case," in Magnus Ranstorp, ed., *Understanding Violent Radicalization* (New York: Routledge, 2010).

[72] "British Muslim Leader Urged To Quit Over Gaza," *Guardian* (London), March 8, 2009; "Hazel Blears' Standoff With Muslim Council Overshadows New Anti-Terror Launch," *Guardian* (London), March 25, 2009; "Government Ties With MCB Restored But Not For Deputy," *Daily Telegraph* (London), January 15, 2010.

[73] Daud Abdullah, "My Reply To Hazel Blears," *Guardian* (London), March 26, 2009; Hazel Blears, "Our Shunning Of The MCB Is Not Grandstanding," *Guardian* (London), March 26, 2009.

[74] *Umar Farouk Abdulmutallab: Report to UCL Council of independent inquiry panel*, University College London, September 2010.

[75] See for example, Paul Goodman, "Why The Conservative Party Should Have Nothing To Do With The East London Mosque," *Conservative Home*, October 12, 2010. Until May 2010, Mr. Goodman was a Member of Parliament and Shadow Communities Secretary for the Conservative Party.

[76] For a comprehensive breakdown of all Prevent funded groups, see Tax Payers' Alliance, "Council Spending Uncovered II, No.5: The Prevent Strategy," September 8, 2009.

[77] "Muslim Pressure Group Wins Anti-Democracy Debate," *East London Advertiser*, February 27, 2008.

[78] "British Muslim Leader Urged To Quit Over Gaza," *Guardian* (London), March 8, 2009.

[79] "Government Seeks To Recast Relations With British Muslims," *Guardian* (London), August 10, 2009.

[80] "Conservatives Would Cut Ties With Muslim Council Of Britain Over Daud Abdullah," *Times of London*, March 26, 2010.

[81] Theresa May, speech to Conservative Party Conference, Birmingham, England, October 5, 2010.

FRANCE

QUICK FACTS

Population: 64,057,792

Area: 643,427 sq km

Ethnic Groups: Celtic and Latin with Teutonic, Slavic, North African, Indochinese, Basque minorities

Religions: Roman Catholic 83-88%, Protestant 2%, Jewish 1%, Muslim 5-10%, unaffiliated 4%

Government Types: Republic

GDP (official exchange rate): $2.666 trillion

Map and Quick Facts courtesy of the CIA World Factbook (Last Updated June 2010)

France houses a large Muslim minority, primarily of North African provenance. While many immigrants are non-observant (in line with a general French tendency toward secularism and a de-emphasis of religious affiliation), Islamist organizations actively promote a resurgence of a politicized and ideological Muslim identity. Target groups include youth, especially in the ethnic ghettos of cities where immigrant populations are concentrated. There is considerable tension within the Muslim leadership between advocates of secular French identity and proponents of the Islamist goal of a communitarian cultural separatism. In addition, the trans-Mediterranean immigration patterns and historical French colonial ties to North Africa contribute to a spill-over of Islamist terrorist activity from Algeria into France. Jihadist activists with links to al-Qaeda move between Algeria and France, as well as other European countries. French Islamism, in turn, has become part of global jihadist networks.

The response of the French state has evolved from earlier efforts to portray itself as the bridge between the Arab world and Europe to a more recent insistence on the value of French identity and the importance of secularism, exem-

plified in regulations such as the 2004 prohibition on the wearing of headscarves in public schools. Furthermore, in contrast to the weak French response to terrorism in the 1980s, France more recently has developed an effective and robust set of counter-terrorism practices.

ISLAMIST ACTIVITY

Union des organizations islamiques de France (UOIF)

Founded in 1983 as a small circle of foreign student activists with Islamist leanings, the Union of Islamic Organizations in France has grown into an umbrella organization claiming to represent between one to two hundred Muslim groupings in France. It plays a role in coordinating activities among its member associations, and is the owner of some mosques in the major cities of France.[1] The UOIF is the French member of the London-based Federation of Islamic Organizations in Europe, active in promoting the study of Islam through its European Institute for the Human Sciences, dedicated to Islamic theology and related studies, with two campuses in France.[2] The UOIF has also established several specialized organizations, including the Young Muslims of France (JMF), the Muslim Students of France (EMF), and the French League of the Muslim Woman (LFFM).[3] These organizations contribute to the dissemination of Islamist positions and the construction of separatist communitarian identity politics. While the UOIF presents itself simply as an advocate of Muslim interests, critics point out that it engages in a "double discourse," paying lip service in public to the priority of tolerance for secular French values, while at the same time promoting Islamist content (replete with intolerance, misogyny, homophobia and anti-Semitism) to its target populations.[4]

The UOIF has attained considerable public and political resonance through a disproportionate role within the French Council of the Muslim Religion (CFCM) which was established in 2003 by then-Minister of the Interior Nicolas Sarkozy as the official representation of Muslims in France.[5] The CFCM's responsibilities pertain to interactions between the French state and the Muslim community, e.g., the construction of mosques, oversight of *halal* food, provision of Muslim spiritual services in the military and in prisons, etc. In contrast to the CFCM's administrative and technical functions, the UOIF has wider cultural and political ambitions. "In France, the extremist UOIF has become the predominant organization within the government's Islamic Council" where it can eclipse moderate or secular Muslim voices, experts have noted.[6] While the inclusion of the UOIF in the CFCM may have been intended as a strategy of cooptation to move it toward the center, it has allowed the relatively small UOIF to appear as an influential representative of the much more diverse and generally less ideological Muslim population in France.[7]

While the UOIF's explicit goals include the religious, cultural, educational, social and humanitarian needs of the Muslim population of France, with priority given to facilitating religious practice, critics allege that it is close to the Egyptian branch of the Muslim Brotherhood and pursues a goal of communitarian separatism.[8] This agenda involves two aspects: transforming France into a safe haven for radicals engaged in militant Islamist politics in North Africa or elsewhere, especially in the Arab world, while also exercising political identity pressure on the Muslims in France to conform to increasingly repressive interpretations of Islam: a sort of "reactionary and paternalist populism."[9] "The UOIF tries to rein in the Muslims of France. Some associations affiliated with the movement claim the right to say who is a good Muslim and who is, therefore, an apostate," observes Islam expert Fiametta Venner. "This is all the more alarming since these people are not theologians—almost none of the directors of the UOIF pursued studies in this area—and they have a very narrow vision of Islam. They are satisfied with instrumentalizing the religion to pursue a reactionary political project of separatism."[10]

Front islamique francais armé (FIFA)

The Armed French Islamic Front is a violent organization that claimed responsibility for the October 2004 bombing of the Indonesian embassy in Paris. In that incident, it demanded the release of two members of the Armed Islamic Group (GIA), a terrorist organization considered close to al-Qaeda which has as its goal an Islamist transformation of Algeria.[11] The FIFA also called for French support for the admission of Turkey into the European Union and a rollback of France's stance on secularization.[12] In addition, it demanded the censorship of all anti-Muslim publications, singling out in particular the novel *Platform* by the French author Michel Houllebecq, which addresses questions of immigration and global terrorism.[13] (In 2002 Houllebecq was brought to court for statements critical of Islam, but he was acquitted of the hate speech charge.) There is no up-to-date information readily available on FIFA, however, and the organization appears to be dormant and/or inactive.

Al-Qaeda au pays du Maghreb Islamique (AQIM)

Al-Qaeda in the Islamic Maghreb is a terrorist group based primarily in Algeria. Over time, however, it has transformed from an organization committed to a local Islamist insurgency into a wider network pursuing a program of global *jihad*. As a result, AQIM has begun to be recognized as a threat in Europe, especially (but not exclusively) in France. As the State Department's *2008 Country Reports on Terrorism* noted, "France remained a target for al-Qaeda in the Islamic Maghreb (AQIM), which posed a considerable threat to French interests, underscored in statements made by al-

Qaeda (AQ) senior leadership or AQIM itself."[14] Similarly, Europol's *EU Terrorism Situation and Trend Report* for that year asserts that "France, Italy, Spain and Portugal consider that the increasing activities of al-Qaeda in the Islamic Maghreb (AQIM) aiming at international targets have an impact on the threat level in their member states."[15]

Given the long history of French colonialism in Algeria, the large North African population in France, and trans-Mediterranean cultural contacts, politics in Algeria have often spilled over into France. Yet the recent emergence of AQIM as a threat in Europe derives from important shifts in the character of Islamist radicalism in Algeria itself. In 1992, the Algerian military government cancelled elections in which an Islamist coalition, the Islamic Salvation Front, was likely to come to power. A violent civil war erupted, during which the Armed Islamic Group (GIA) became notorious for its brutality against civilians in Algeria. However, the GIA also carried out attacks in France, most notoriously a 1995 bombing in Paris at the Saint-Michel underground station, causing eight deaths and wounding more than 100.[16]

Fearing that the GIA strategy was undermining the Islamist cause, a splinter group known as the Salafist Group for Preaching and Combat (GSPC) was formed. The GSPC was similarly dedicated to Islamist militancy, but embraced alternative tactics that would not endanger civilians. While this tactical moderation led initially to a surge in popular support and a growth in the GSPC's membership (peaking at around 28,000 in the late 1990s), a successful counter-terrorism campaign by Algerian forces eroded the group's numbers significantly.[17] However, in 2004, GSPC leader Abdelmalek Droukdal reached out to al-Qaeda in Mesopotamia leader Abu Musaf al-Zarqawi, and the GSPC, with its Algeria focus, was reinvented as AQIM. Just as Al-Qaeda in Mesopotamia was compelled to relocate into marginal territories (in their case, the mountainous tribal areas between Pakistan and Afghanistan), so too did AQIM develop operational skills in desert regions, especially Chad, as well as the Algerian hills outside of Algiers. Its aspirations grew from local insurgency to a pan-Maghreb transformation and finally to global *jihadism*, leading to a series of attacks, kidnappings and murder, targeting Europeans in North Africa and international organizations, including a UN site in Algiers.

AQIM has also turned its sights on Europe. In September 2005, Droukdal designated France as "our No. 1 enemy, the enemy of our religion and of our community."[18] While the threat has not yet resulted in major attacks in France on the scale of Madrid (2004) or London (2005), this may be due to the success of French counterterrorism efforts; over the years since, a number of Algerians and French-Algerians plotting terrorist attacks have been arrested in France.[19] AQIM, meanwhile, remains active outside of Europe. In the words of EUROPOL, "In 2007, AQIM further adapted its tactics and propaganda to the model of al-Qaeda in Mesopotamia, Iraq. It committed several suicide attacks with high numbers of causalities. AQIM demonstrated the threat it poses to Europe by specifically targeting European citizens and international bodies in Algeria. In April 2007, AQIM claimed an attack, which ... targeted the Interpol office in Algiers."[20] While the preponderance of AQIM activity remains in North Africa, its victims increasingly include Europeans, as well as North Africans, and there are strong indications that it is trying to develop the capacity to carry out attacks in France and possibly other European countries as well.

ISLAMISM AND SOCIETY

The French tradition of secularism derives from the eighteenth-century Enlightenment, the revolution of 1789, and the firm establishment of the separation of religion and state through the conflicts between the French state and the Catholic Church in the late nineteenth century. A core value of the French republic is *laïcité*, meaning a commitment to the non-confessional character of public life. Historically, the French population was, in terms of religious affiliation, extensively Catholic, with small Protestant and Jewish minorities. During the nineteenth and twentieth centuries, the processes of secularization took root in earnest, contributing to a widespread decline in the importance of religious affiliation as a feature of cultural modernity.

Since 1872, French law has prohibited any census of religious affiliation. According to one recent poll, 64 percent of French citizens described themselves as Catholic in 2009 (in contrast to 81 percent in 1965). However only 4.5 percent of those same respondents reported attending Mass on a weekly basis.[21] In contrast, the 2003 *CIA World Factbook* counts 88 percent of the French as Catholic, 2 percent as Protestant, and 1 percent as Jewish.

Islam, barely present in France before 1945, arrived along with a wave of immigrant labor, primarily from North Africa, and has become the second largest religious affiliation in France. It now claims 5-10 percent of the population, and is the religion of two-thirds of all immigrants. According to an Interior Ministry report in the year 2000, there are approximately four million Muslims in France, of which 1,550,000 have an Algerian background and 1,000,000 are Moroccan. The report likewise estimates that 40,000 French citizens have become converts to Islam.[22]

Of the French Muslim population, about a third describes itself as "observant." An extensive secularization of the Muslim population is consistent with the decline of observant practices in other religious traditions. The rise of a minority Islamism within the Muslim community can therefore be viewed in part as a reaction against the modernization of lifestyles within immigrant communities. The mobilization of Islamist identity frequently involves younger generations rebelling against the aspirations for integration harbored by older generations of immigrants.[23]

Islamist recruitment in France has multiple dimensions. Of the estimated 1,500 mosques or prayer halls in France, about 80 are considered to be at risk of radicalization and 20 are under close government surveillance.[24] In some cases, the mosque imam provides the radical ideology, but in others *jihadist* recruiters may be active without the knowledge of the imam. Significant recruitment, including proselytization, likewise takes place in prisons; French prison populations are often more than 50 percent Muslim, at times reaching 80 percent in certain areas.[25] Activists reach out both to non-observant Muslim inmates, as well as to non-Muslims who are prospects for conversion. A third avenue of recruitment involves contact with French *jihadis*, i.e., veterans of the conflicts in Afghanistan, Bosnia, Chechnya and Iraq, who have returned to France and who may form *ad hoc* groups to support or carry out terrorist attacks.[26]

The conflict between modernizing pressure and Muslim identity underlies the controversy regarding the headscarf, or *hijab*. Islamist pressure to establish separatist communitarian identity focuses on symbols and practices to separate Muslims from secular French society. In 2004, facing a growing Muslim population in public schools with increasing numbers of women wearing the headscarf, the French government promulgated a law banning ostentatious religious symbols in the schools, in the spirit of *laicité*.[27] While the law also pertains to Christian and Jewish symbols, the key issue was the Muslim headscarf or veil. The controversy underscored the gap between French norms of secular modernity and the neo-traditionalism of Islamist behavior. (It should be noted, as a point of comparison, that until recently headscarves were similarly banned in Turkish universities, a legacy of the secularist foundations of the modern Turkish state.[28]) A primary goal of Islamism involves the assertion of patriarchal norms and the resistance to the spread of equal rights to Muslim women.[29]

Muslim immigrant populations are frequently concentrated in the ethnic ghettos of the *banlieues*, the working-class suburbs surrounding French urban centers, where they remain marginalized, facing discrimination and weathering high unemployment rates. This concentration of social problems has led repeatedly to outbreaks of mass violence. In 2005, in response to the deaths of two teenagers in Clichy-sous-Bois, near Paris, local rioting erupted, spreading rapidly across the country. A state of emergency was declared, resulting in three thousand arrests. Damage to property totaled 200 million Euros.[30] Another series of riots broke out in 2009.[31] Such unrest has contributed to a profound social anxiety about *sécurité*, a term which has implications stretching from crime-in-the-streets to terrorism.

Youth in the ghettos are viewed as susceptible to the radical ideologies purveyed by Islamist organizations. Particular violence has erupted toward Jewish communities—the French Jewish community is the largest in Europe, and includes significant numbers of immigrants from North Africa. However, some Muslim leaders (among them the *imam* of the Mosque of Drancy) have been vocal critics of anti-Semitic words and deeds, in turn facing attacks themselves.[32] An especially grisly crime involved the kidnapping of Ilan Halimi, the son of Moroccan Jewish immigrants, in Bagneux, a suburb south of Paris, by a group of Muslim delinquents that dubbed itself the "gang of barbarians." The group held Halimi for ransom because he was Jewish, subjecting him to torture before abandoning him outdoors in the winter; he succumbed to his wounds.[33] The ensuing 2009 trial attracted widespread attention. While the perpetrators were not directly involved in political Islamist ideological movements, they operated in a milieu in which Islamist predispositions, including a cult of violence and anti-Semitism, were commonplace. However, within the larger Muslim population in France—including the two-thirds which is not observant—such radicalism is rare. There are vocal criticisms of Islamism articulated by Muslims who advocate the ideal of the modern, tolerant republic.[34] However, the alienated fringe of the ghettoes provides fertile ground for the spread of Islamist beliefs and organizations.

The circulation of Islamist ideas in parts of the Muslim community in France results from multiple sources: the connection to foreign organs of global *jihadism* (such as AQIM), the domestic advocacy of proponents of Islamist identity (like UOIF) as well as certain aspects of the larger context of French politics. In the wake of the U.S. response to the 9/11 attacks, including the invasion of Afghanistan and Iraq, then-President of France Jacques Chirac became a vocal opponent of U.S. foreign policy. The resulting trans-Atlantic tension between France and the United States amplified some long-standing differences, and contributed to a wave of anti-Americanism. Suspicion toward American culture and foreign policy became widespread in the French public, and that milieu in turn contributed to the incubation of anti-modern and anti-American Islamist sentiments in the Muslim subculture. For example, Thierry Meyssan's 2002 book *9/11-The Big Lie*—with its fringe allegation that the terrorist attacks in New York and Washington were the result of a U.S. government conspiracy—became quite popular. Meyssan himself is hardly mainstream, and his positions have been denounced in the country's centrist press, yet his volume won wide distribution—a telling indicator of the anti-American currents in French culture. Islamist radicalization in France, therefore, can represent simultaneously a rejection of French secular modernism and an imitation of some widely held French animosities toward the U.S. The anti-Americanism of the Chirac presidency has subsided only comparatively recently, with the election of Nicolas Sarkozy in France in 2007 and Barack Obama in the U.S. in 2008.[35]

ISLAMISM AND THE STATE

A modern liberal democracy with a tradition of secularism dating back to the eighteenth century, France is also a key ally of the United States, despite occasional foreign policy differences. French troops have played an important role in the war in Afghanistan, while the French state opposes Islamist developments and is actively engaged in resisting Islamism, both domestically and internationally.

Nonetheless, some policies of the French state have contributed to the growth of Islamism in France—most notably the official encouragement of Muslim immigration, especially from North Africa, into France. As noted earlier, Islamists represent only a small minority within the French Muslim population; yet it is also the case that Islamism in France is inseparable from the history of immigration and the associated policies that have failed to integrate the immigrant communities into French society. Pro-immigration policies to attract low-wage labor without effective integration have created the social problems of the *banlieues*, where Islamism has been able to fester.

Building on its history of colonialism, France, especially under Charles de Gaulle, aspired to become the European gateway to the Arab world through a systematic courting of the post-colonial regimes of North Africa. Public discourse in France, therefore, tended to be more pro-Arab than elsewhere in the West. However the rise of an emphatically religious Islamism ran counter to French commitments to *laïcité*, generating policy shifts under Sarkozy, in particular an open promotion of French national identity. In October 2009, Eric Besson, the Minister of Immigration, called for public debate over "the theme of what it is to be French, what are the values we share, what are the relations that make us French and of which we should be proud." He insisted on a particular valorization of Frenchness: "We must reaffirm the values of French national identity and the pride in being French."[36] This effort by the state to mobilize a focus on nationality was intended as an effort to overcome immigrant (and especially Islamist) separatism, and in the years since, this discussion has shifted increasingly toward secularism. To question the role of religion in the public sphere in France is, above all, a vehicle to inquire about the status of politicized Islam.

Yet the conflict between the republican secularism of the state and the politicization of religion inherent in Islamism continues. In 2009, a new debate began over prospective legislation to ban full-length cloaks, the *burqa* and the *niqab* (the latter leaves the eyes uncovered). Taking the longer view, however, it is clear that there has been a profound shift in France from the era of emphatic trans-Mediterranean cooperation to the current state promotion of French national identity and integration over multicultural separatism. The traditional French value of secularism serves as the basis for public criticism and legislative action against symbols of Islamist allegiance.

This cultural-ideological resistance to Islamism on the part of the state accompanies a muscular set of policing and counterterrorism practices that distinguish the current French response to Islamist violence. French counterterrorism has matured over the past three decades. During the 1980s, Middle Eastern terrorist organizations carried out repeated attacks in France, exposing the inadequacy of French intelligence services. France gained the unenviable reputation as a terrorist haven, in part as a corollary to its pro-Arab foreign policy. Nonetheless, counterterrorist capacities grew during the 1990s, and French forces successfully interrupted plots to carry out attacks at the World Cup (1998), the Strasbourg Cathedral (2000) and the American Embassy (2001).[37]

In 1986, legislation centralized the French counter-terrorism strategy by locating all judicial proceedings in the Trial Court of Paris. This organizational strategy has allowed the development of specialized expertise relevant to terrorism cases. Rather than leaving the sophisticated and security-sensitive cases in the hands of potentially inexperienced provincial magistrates, the 1986 law mandates the priority of the Parisian venue to maximize the utilization of specialist expertise. These judges, the *juges d'instruction*, combine judicial and police functions, insofar as they are charged with conducting inquiries, authorizing searches and overseeing wiretaps and other related matters—all of which in the U.S. would be dependent on independent judicial control. The *juges d'instruction* regularly collaborate with the *Direction de la Surveillance du Territoire* (DST), the domestic security service that is part of the Ministry of the Interior. This sort of cooperation between judicial and executive powers is less controversial within French political culture than it would be in the U.S.

Nevertheless, French counterterrorism practices have faced criticism on civil rights and human rights grounds. The promulgation of laws criminalizing terrorist conspiracies (rather than simply terrorist attacks themselves) has elicited denunciations on the grounds that it represents an ominous expansion of state power. However, this pursuit of conspiracies has been defended as the only way to prevent catastrophic attacks, such as the successful disruption of the plans for terrorist violence at the World Cup at the *Stade de France*.[38] Still, Amnesty International and other watchdogs continue to criticize France for its prosecution of conspiracy charges as a "criminal association in relation to a terrorist undertaking."[39]

For civil rights activists, the situation was exacerbated by 2008 legislation that authorized preventive detention in certain cases. After the completion of a sentence, an individual whom a judge deems to be dangerous may face an extended sentence for renewable periods of one year. In addition, the police were granted the authority to develop intelligence files on all individuals over the age of thirteen who are deemed to represent a threat to public order. While criticisms of this counterterrorism regime continue, to date France has been successful in thwarting domestic attacks; there has as yet been no return to the violence of the 1980s, when terrorists seemed able to act in France with impunity and little fear of sanctions.

ENDNOTES

[1] Fiametta Venner, *OPA sur l'Islam de France: Les Ambitions de l'UOIF* [OPA within French Islam: the Ambitions of the UOIF] (Paris: Calman-Lévy, 2005).

[2] The online home of the Institute is http://www.ieshdeparis.fr/.

[3] Venner, *OPA sur l'Islam de France*, 133-153; Michèle Vianès, Silence, on Manipule: les Islamistes en Manoeuvre [Exploiting the Silence: Islamists in Action] (Paris: Editions Hors Commerce, 2004), 58.

[4] Venner, *OPA sur l'Islam de France*, 158.

[5] Representation in the CFCM depends on the size of mosque space controlled by an organization. See Vianès, *Silence, on Manipule*, 18-19.

[6] Lorenzo Vidino, "The Muslim Brotherhood's Conquest of Europe," *Middle East Quarterly* 12, no. 1 (Winter 2005), 25-34.

[7] Stéphanie Le Bars, "'Pour la Majorité des Musulmans, la Séperation du Religieux et du Politique est Acquise'" [For the Majority of Muslims, the Seperation of Religion and Politics is Artificial], *Le Monde* (Paris), April 4, 2011, http://www.lemonde.fr/societe/chat/2011/04/04/l-islam-est-il-soluble-dans-la-laicite_1502963_3224.html#ens_id=1460876.

[8] For the objectives of the UOIF, see its official website at http://www.uoif-online.com/v3/spip.php?article20; On the radicalism of UOIF, see the interview with Fiametta Venner, "La Face Cachée de l'UOIF et des Frères Musulmans en France," [The Hidden Side of the UOIF and the Muslim Brothers in France], *Le Post*, March 12, 2009, http://www.lepost.fr/article/2009/12/03/1822346_la-face-cachee-de-l-uoif-et-des-freres-musulmans-en-france.html; on the influence of the Muslim Brothers, see Brigitte Maréchal, *The Muslim Brothers in Europe: Roots and Discourse* (Leiden: Brill, 2008).

[9] Xavier Raufer, ed., *Atlas de l'Islam Radical* [Atlas of Radical Islam] (Paris: CNRS Editions, 2007), 13.

[10] "La Face Cachée de l'UOIF et des Frères Musulmans en France."

[11] Lauren Vriens, "Armed Islamic Group (Algeria, Islamists)," Council on Foreign Relations, n.d., http://www.cfr.org/algeria/armed-islamic-group-algeria-islamists/p9154.

[12] "Front Islamique Francais Arme," Wikipedia.fr, n.d., http://fr.wikipedia.org/wiki/Front_islamique_français_armé.

[13] Raufer, *Atlas de l'Islam Radical*, 71.

[14] U.S. Department of State, Office of the Coordinator for Counterterrorism, *Country Reports on Terrorism 2008* (Washington, DC: U.S. Department of State, April 2009), 71, http://www.state.gov/documents/organization/122599.pdf.

[15] EUROPOL, *TE-SAT 2008: EU Terrorism Situation and Trend Report* (Brussels: European Police Office, 2008), 19, http://www.

europol.europa.eu/publications/EU_Terrorism_Situation_and_
Trend_Report_TE-SAT/TESAT2008.pdf.

[16] Raufer, *Atlas de l'Islam Radical*, 55-58.

[17] Andrew Hansen and Lauren Vriens, "Al-Qaeda in the Islamic Maghreb (AQIM)", Council on Foreign Relations, n.d., http://www. cfr.org/north-africa/al-qaeda-islamic-maghreb-aqim/p12717.

[18] Souad Mekhennet et al., "Ragtag Insurgency Gains a Lifeline from Al Qaeda," *New York Times*, July 1, 2008, http://www.nytimes. com/2008/07/01/world/africa/01algeria.html?pagewanted=1&_r=2 &sq=ragtag&st=cse&scp=1; Raufer, Atlas de l'Islam Radical, 73.

[19] EUROPOL, TE-SAT 2008, 22.

[20] Ibid., 26.

[21] "The Collapse of the Church in France," Rorate Caeli blog, January 2011, http://rorate-caeli.blogspot.com/2010/01/collapse-of-church-in-france.html.

[22] *L'Islam dans la République* [Islam in the Republic] (Paris: Haut Conseil à l'intégration, 2000), 26.

[23] Valérie Amiraux, "From Empire to Republic: the French Muslim Dilemma," in Anna Triandafyllidou, *Muslims in 21st Century Europe: Structural and Cultural Perspectives* (London: Routledge, 2010), 137-159.

[24] Raufer, *Atlas de l'Islam Radical*, 45.

[25] Ibid.

[26] Ibidem, 48-53.

[27] Alain Houziaux, *Le Voile, que Cache-t-Il?* [The Veil: What Does it Hide?] (Paris: Editions ouvrières, 2004).

[28] Ibid.

[29] Vianès, *Silence, on Manipule*, 51-73.

[30] Centre d'Analyse Stratégique, *Enquêtes sur les Violences Urbaines: Comprendre les Émeutes de November 2005* [Investigations into Urban Violence: Understanding the Riots of November 2005] (Paris: La Documentation Française, 2006).

[31] Angelique Chrisalfis, "Three Nights of Riots in French Town After 21-Year-Old Dies in Police Custody," *Guardian* (London), July 10, 2009, http://www.guardian.co.uk/world/2009/jul/10/french-police-fight-rioting-youths.

[32] "L'Imam Français Agressé par les Frères Musulmans et le Hamas!" [French Imam Attacked by the Muslim Brothers and Hamas!], JSS-news.com, January 26, 2010, http://jssnews.com/2010/01/26/limam-modere-agresse-par-mes-freres-musulmans-et-le-hamas-en-france/

[33] Ruth Halimi and Emilie Frèche, *24 Jours: La Vérité sur la mort d'Ilan Halimi* [Twenty-four Days: The Truth Behind the Death of Ilan Halimi] (Paris: Seuil, 2009); Alexandre Lévy, Le Gang des Barbares: L'Affaire Ilan Halimi [Gang of Barbarians: The Ilan Halimi Affair] (Paris: Hachette, 2009).

[34] Vianès, *Silence, on Manipule*, 47.

[35] Russell A. Berman, *Anti-Americanism in Europe: A Cultural Problem* (Stanford: Hoover Press, 2008).

[36] "Besson Relance le Débat sur l'Identité Nationale" [Besson Relaunches the Debate over National Identity], *Le Monde* (Paris), October 25, 2009.

[37] Jeremy Shapiro and Bénédicte Suzan, "The French Experience of Counter-terrorism," *Survival* 45, iss. 1 (Spring 2003), 68.

[38] Ibid., 85-86.

[39] See, for example, Human Rights Watch, "In the Name of Prevention: Insufficient Safeguards in National Security Removals," June 5, 2007, http://www.hrw.org/en/reports/2007/06/05/name-prevention-0; Human Rights Watch, *Preempting Justice: Counterterrorism Laws and Procedures in France* (New York: HRW, 2008), http://www.hrw.org/en/reports/2008/07/01/preempting-justice; "France," in *Amnesty International Report 2009: State of the World's Human Rights* (London: Amnesty International, 2010), http://report2009.amnesty.org/en/regions/europe-central-asia/france.

Spain

QUICK FACTS

Population: 40,548,753

Area: 505,370 sq km

Ethnic Groups: Composite of Mediterranean and Nordic types

Religions: Roman Catholic 94%, other 6%

Government Type: Parliamentary monarchy

GDP (official exchange rate): $1.466 trillion

Map and Quick Facts courtesy of the CIA World Factbook (Last Updated June 2010)

Not only is Islam in Spain steadily growing, it is also on a clear path to radicalization. Social integration of the country's rapidly expanding Muslim community is proving more and more difficult, while insular religious radicalism and the spread of intolerant ideas among Spanish Muslims is on the rise. This has coincided with the targeting of Spain by foreign jihadist elements. Today al-Andalus—the territory lost by Islam in the fifteenth century, which includes the Iberian Peninsula (Spain and Portugal) and part of southern France—is no longer simply an abstract cause, but has become a concrete jihadist objective.[1]

The Spanish government's response to this rising Islamism has been lackluster. Although the Zapatero administration has maintained law enforcement pressure on terrorist cells plotting to carry out terrorist attacks inside the country or financing and giving support to jihadist groups abroad, its tendency toward multiculturalism has at times undermined its efforts to influence the discourse about, and among, Muslims in Spain. Indeed, the Spanish government appears to have abdicated the "battle of ideas" between moderate and extreme interpretations of Islam altogether. For the country's main political parties, meanwhile, the issue of Islamic radicalism remains largely taboo.

Nonetheless, grassroots sentiment regarding the need to place limits around what Muslim immigrants can and should do regarding customs, norms, and respect for national laws is increasingly palpable—if still without coherent voice or direction.

ISLAMIST ACTIVITY

Today's Islamist activism in Spain can be defined along two lines: its overt political and legal dimension, and its more clandestine presence in the country. While radicalization may be minimal within the well-rooted Spanish Muslim community, which numbers more than one million individuals, it nonetheless represents a threat to its integrity—and thus to Spanish society as a whole. Spain's Interior, Justice and Labor Ministries recently published a definitive report on the topic, which concluded that despite the comparatively small percentage of radicals among Spain's Muslims, there are reasons for serious concern regarding both the intensity of their radicalism and their adeptness in nourishing and promoting it.[2]

Aside from Ceuta and Melilla, the two Spanish cities along the Mediterranean coast of North Africa, across the Strait of Gibraltar, it is Catalonia that has the highest concentration of Muslims on Spanish soil, followed closely by Andalusia. In the main, Muslims in Spain tend to belong to the following associations: the *Federación Española de Entidades Religiosas Islámicas* (FEERI), the *Unión de Comunidades Islámicas de España* (UCIDE), and, more marginally, the *Junta Islámica de España*. FEERI has a significant Moroccan composition, and the Islamist group *Al Adl wal Ihsan* (Justice and Charity)—illegal but tolerated in Morocco—has attempted to infiltrate it in the past. UCIDE, by contrast, involves Muslim laity and clergy of Syrian and Saudi origin. FEERI and UCIDE are, together, the key members of the Islamic Commission of Spain, the official Islamic partner of the Spanish government. By contrast, the smaller *Junta Islámica* is more overtly political, involving converts to Islam and so-called "progressives" and promoting a distinctive version of Islam that is occasionally at variance with the state.[3] None of the three provide figures concerning their membership or organizational structures, however.

Out of the more than 1,000 mosques throughout Spain, experts deem around ten percent to be radical.[4] Out of that tally, 50 mosques are classified as Salafist and around 30 preach the *Tabligh* doctrine.[5] Tablighi Jama'at's leader in Spain is Laarbi al-Lal Maateis and, in Ceuta, he competes with *imams* proposed or appointed by neighboring Morocco's Directorate of Religious Affairs.

The main efforts of Islamic radicals to impose their vision are currently concentrated in Catalonia and Murcia and their surrounding areas. The debate about the prohibition of the *burka* and the *niqab* in public buildings began in Catalonia, where the wearing of these garments in localities of high Muslim concentration has begun to unsettle locals. Eleven mosques and prayer rooms, run by Salafist preachers and located in smaller municipalities of Lleida, Barcelona, and Tarragona, decided to challenge the proposed ban in court in July 2010.[6] Cases of coercion against Muslims by Salafist leaders are more and more frequent; however, they are usually difficult to prove in court due to the control that these leaders exert over the faithful.[7] In short, the advance of Salafism has been chronicled in numerous studies and investigations, including those commissioned by several city councils or conducted by the *Mossos d'Esquadra*, the autonomous regional civilian police of Catalonia.[8]

In the Mediterranean region of Murcia, where there are an estimated 120 mosques and prayer rooms, Islamist activism within the Muslim community has largely been a staple of the followers of *Al Adl wal Ihsan*. Founded in 1983 by Moroccan preacher Sheikh Abdesalam Yassine, the organization is today well established in poor districts as well as Moroccan university circles. The group does not recognize the religious legitimacy of the Moroccan Crown. Mounir Benjelloun, vice president of Murcia's Islamic Federation (FIRM), had his Spanish naturalization application rejected in 2010 due to his ties to *Al Adl wal Ihsan,* on the grounds that Spanish authorities consider the latter to be a radical group that hampers the integration of Muslims into the state.

The pro-government UCIDE competes here for influence with FIRM, as it does with other local federations throughout Spain. FIRM is reported to be in control of 45 out of the 120 existing mosques and prayer rooms in the region and, through them, *Al Adl wal Ihsan* can disseminate its fundamentalist message throughout Alicante and Almería, Murcia's bordering provinces, each with a significant Muslim presence.[9]

The issue of radical Islamism on Spanish soil is difficult to define despite the significant number of well-known Salafist *jihadist* commanders in prison (among them the cell of Imad Eddin Barakat Yarkas, alias Abu Dahdah, which has been directly linked to al-Qaeda and the 9/11 attacks, and groups, cells and individuals connected with the 2004 Madrid bombings, some of which are elements of the Moroccan Islamic Combatant Group, or GICM). Traditionally, the most radicalized groups on Spanish soil have ties with different groups working in Northern Africa, which are progressively converging into the framework of al-Qaeda in the Islamic Maghreb (AQIM).[10] The footprint of Salafist *jihadism* in Spain itself is complex. The country has served as an important nucleus for the Algerian Armed Islamic Group (GIA) and the Salafist Group for Preaching and Combat (GSPC), whose members enjoy extensive interaction with the GICM as well as with radicals in Catalonia, which boasts the second largest community of Pakistanis on European soil after the United Kingdom.[11]

The recent trial and sentencing of elements of the Algerian *Comando Dixan* cell—broken up by France and Spain in 2002—and the legal processes against militants captured during *Operación Tigris*, which broke up a *jihadist* network in the Catalan city of Santa Coloma de Gramenet, proved definitively the existence of organized, transnational terrorist groups on Spanish soil and the importance of Spain in global *jihadist* strategy.[12] Other trials, however, have highlighted the legal difficulties associated with state efforts to prosecute *jihadist* networks. These include:

- The May 18, 2010 acquittal by Spain's National Court (*Audiencia Nacional*) of two *jihadists* accused of trying to make dirty bombs with, among other components, red mercury.[13]
- The arrest by Guardia Civil officers of ten Algerians with alleged ties to the GSPC and al-Qaeda in Alicante, Granada, and Murcia on November 23, 2005. They had turned to credit card forgery to raise funds and finance the GSPC. Five of these men ended up being tried in the National Court in May 2010, only to be acquitted of terrorism charges; however, three of them have been sentenced to prison for forgery.[14]
- The sentencing of eleven Pakistanis arrested in Barcelona in January 2008 and accused of plotting terrorist suicide attacks against the Barcelona metro system under the instructions of Taliban leader Baitullah Mehsud. On December 14, 2009, the eleven detainees were sentenced to prison on different grounds, but found not to be complicit in the commission of a terrorist crime, since the plot had not reached the level necessary to be a terrorist conspiracy.[15]

In brief, the radical Islamist cells operating in Spain have traditionally involved immigrants from the Maghreb (mainly Algerians and Moroccans) and Pakistanis due to the Spanish involvement with northern Africa and the historical presence of a huge Pakistani immigrant community in Catalonia, in northeast Spain. Moroccans usually belong to those terrorist groups and cells that operate in their home country (the GICM and the *Jihadia Salafiya*), as do Algerians (the Islamic Armed Group in the 1990s and the Islamic Group for Preaching and Combat and AQIM more recently). Cells and networks have traditionally been small and autonomous, rather than interconnected. However, investigations by security forces and legal prosecutions have detected increasing links connecting these radicals with those outside of the nation's borders. Pakistanis, by contrast, are influenced by the TTP (the

Pakistani Taliban Movement) agenda, which is very much connected with the Afghan battlefield—where Spain is fully involved in political, cooperation and on the military battlefield.

ISLAMISM AND SOCIETY

As of the end of 2009, Spain's Muslim population constituted approximately 1.5 million people, or 3.26 percent of the country's total 46 million inhabitants.[16] The percentage is lower than Europe's overall five percent average of Muslim inhabitants, and significantly lower than that of some of Spain's neighboring countries, including France (where Muslims make up between five and ten percent of the population).[17]

Nevertheless, it would be erroneous to conclude—based solely on these numbers—that Islam is a fringe phenomenon in Spain. To the contrary, the rapidity with which Islam has grown and expanded in Spain makes it both notable and potentially problematic. According to the United Nations, in the year 2000, Spain had around 400,000 Muslims—accounting for about one percent of the population.[18] Ten years later, that number practically quadrupled. Indeed, if not for the constant flow of Latin American immigration to Spain in recent years, the current percentage of the population made up by Muslims would undoubtedly be much higher.

Unlike other immigrant communities in Spain, the Muslim community is not evenly distributed throughout the country. Rather, Spanish Muslims are concentrated mainly in three regions: Catalonia (368,000), Andalusia (240,000), and Madrid (234,000).[19] Catalonia counts for the majority of Muslim immigrants, in part because the region's official antagonism to the Spanish language has led regional authorities to give priority to non-Spanish speaking people, convinced that it would be easier to immerse the newcomers into a Catalanist environment. Andalusia, due to its geographic proximity to North Africa and need for extensive manpower for agriculture, has likewise attracted comparatively high levels of Muslim immigrants. So has Madrid, which serves as Spain's biggest magnet of economic growth and thereby provides greater opportunities for employment for immigrants.[20]

Spain's Muslim population, unlike that of its European partners, is heavily shaped by the predominance of Moroccans among Muslim immigrants—who, according to sources within the Islamic community itself, may represent as much as 50 percent of the total Muslim population.[21] This population is also relatively young, and exhibits extensive adherence to religious practices and a determination to preserve its Muslim identity. Finally, Muslims dominate migration patterns in Spain; as of early 2010, Muslims accounted for 21 percent of the total number of immigrants to the country.[22]

The comparatively recent, explosive growth of the Muslim population in Spain has been mirrored by a growth of Islamic institutions. While the number of legal, officially-approved mosques in the country remains low (no more than two dozen), a large number of cultural associations have sprung up in recent years, filling the need for new venues for worship and prayer. The 2007 census conducted by the Ministry of Justice's Office of Religious Affairs identified around such 450 associations.[23] However, UCIDE has admitted to the existence of more than 700 such facilities, and law enforcement authorities estimate that there are actually over 1,000 illegal mosques in existence in Spain today.[24]

As the statistics above suggest, Spain's Muslim community is religious—and increasingly so. In its April 2010 survey of national religious attitudes, the Spanish government found a marked increase in piousness among the country's Muslims (with religious adherence rising from 41 percent in 2006 to 52 percent in 2009). Simultaneously, the number of non-practicing Muslims declined from 18 percent in 2006 to 12 percent in 2009.[25] These statistics stand in stark contrast to the prevailing trend of widespread secularism among the country's native population that has evolved in recent decades. For example, less than 20 percent of Spaniards today define themselves as practicing Catholics, compared to 50 percent in 1976. As such, it is not an exaggeration to say that in Spain there are more people praying at mosques on Fridays than at churches on Sundays.

According to the same study, around four percent of Muslims in Spain do not condemn the use of violence in pursuit of political objectives. In other words, around 50,000 to 60,000 Muslims in Spain can be considered potentially radical and at least somewhat susceptible to the call of *jihad*. The larger Muslim community, meanwhile, is riven by divisions—and by a comparatively large percentage of the country's Muslims that fall outside official religious institutions. FEERI and UCIDE, the two main Muslim organizations in Spain, together account for just 70 percent of all Muslim groups in Spain.[26] Additionally, disagreements concerning religious authority and interpretation abound between groups led by Spanish converts and those whose leaders are immigrants. Finally, there is a struggle underway between the competing interpretations of Islam and Islamic law practiced by Morocco and Saudi Arabia. Both versions of Islam are conservative (although the Saudi is considerably more so), while the Moroccan is additionally nationalistic, claiming sovereignty over Spanish territories in North Africa—namely, the cities of Ceuta and Melilla, two smaller territories (Peñón de Vélez de la Gomera and Peñón de Alhucemas), and the Chafarinas archipelago.

ISLAMISM AND THE STATE

The current government of President Luis Rodríguez Zapatero has announced its intention to pass a new, more progressive and secular Religious Freedom Law to replaced the existing version (which was created in 1980). The draft of the law already being circulated suggests the Zapatero administration hopes to redefine Spain as secular and neutral to all forms of religious expression.[27] The impact is likely to be profound, involving the banning of Christian symbols in public places and schools as well as religious services and state funerals, among other things, while certain religious expressions on the part of the Muslim minority (such as the wearing of the veil in schools) will be accepted and not questioned.

While the federal government is trending toward official religious neutrality, local and state governments are moving in the opposite direction. Over the past couple of years, local city councils and organizations in Spain's various regions have floated initiatives to outlaw the wearing of the *burka* and *niqab* in public buildings. The issue has since risen to national prominence, with the Spanish Senate's June 2010 passage of a motion urging the government to introduce the necessary legal reforms to ban both garments in public places and in the street.[28] Yet the Zapatero administration rejected the proposal, and blocked the passing of that same motion in Congress days later.[29]

Simultaneously, the Zapatero government has continued its pursuit of *jihadist* cells on Spanish soil, perpetuating the aggressive counterterrorism policy established following the 2004 Madrid bombings. Fears of a new terrorist attack in Spain have led the government to adopt quick intervention policies in cases of suspected terrorism—in many instances, doing so without having the necessary evidence to guarantee a conviction. Whereas in 2001 a total of four Islamists were known to be imprisoned (and 18 detained) in Spain, by 2005 the numbers had jumped to 117 and 108 respectively.[30] However, while there are currently a greater number of radicals detained by the Spanish state, this has not translated into a higher rate of formal trials and convictions; on numerous occasions, judges have released the defendants for lack of evidence. Therefore, in 2010, only 65 Islamists were arrested; 43 have been found guilty and were imprisoned while 22 are still awaiting trial.[31]

ENDNOTES

[1] For more, see Rafael L. Bardaji and Ignacio Cosidó, "Spain: from 9/11 to 3/11 and Beyond," in Gary J. Schmitt, ed., *Safety, Liberty, and Islamist Terrorism: American and European Approaches to Domestic Counterterrorism* (Washington, DC: AEI Press, 2010).

[2] In the study, radical views were found in five percent of the 2,000 adult respondents. See Ministerios de Interior, Justicia y Trabajo, *La Comunidad Emigrante En España De Origen Musulmán* (Madrid: Demoscopia, April 2010); Comments on this report can be found in Olga R. Sanmartin, "Rubalcaba Dice Que El Gobierno 'Observa' Las Mezquitas Radicales [Rubalcaba Says the Government 'Observes' Radical Mosques']," *El Mundo* (Madrid), April 8, 2010, 14.

[3] The websites of FEERI, UCIDE and the Junta are, respectively, www.feeri.eu, es.ucide.org, and www.juntaislamica.org. They provide some details as to the organization's ideologies and their program of activities.

[4] See, for example, Soeren Kern, "Spain Goes On Mosque—Building Spree: Churches Forced to Close," Grupo de Estudios Estratégicos *GEES Analysis*, January 10, 2010, http://www.gees.org/articulos/ spain_goes_on_mosque_building_spree_churches_forced_to_close_ 8379.

[5] C. Echeverría Jesús, "*Aproximación al Terrorismo Yihadista Salafista En y Desde Marruecos* [Approach to the Jihadi-Salafist Terrorism In and From Morocco]," Grupo de Estudios Estratégicos *GEES Analysis*, February 20, 2009, www.gees.org.

[6] Jesús Garcia and Ferrán Balsells, "Rebelión Salafista Por El 'Burka' [Salafist Rebellion by Burqa]," *El País* (Madrid), July 9, 2010, 36.

[7] Ferrán Balsells, "*La Policía No Haya Pruebas Del Supuesto Juicio Islámico De Tarragona* [Spanish Police does not Find Evidence of the Supposed Islamic Trial]," *El País* (Madrid), June 20, 2010, 27.

[8] Ferrán Balsells, "El Salafismo Se Hace Con El Control De Cinco Mezquitas En Tarragona [Salafism Takes Control Of Five Mosques In Tarragona]," *El País* (Madrid), June 21, 2010, 31.

[9] A. Negre, "Justicia Vincula A La Federación Islámica De La Región Con Una Organización Radical [Justice Ties The Islamic Federation Of The Region To A Radical Organization]," *La Verdad* (Murcia), May 6, 2010, 1-3; "UCIDE Dice Que La Federación Islámica Controla Siete Mezquitas Radicales [UCIDE Says That The Islamic Federation Controls Seven Radical Mosques]," *La Verdad* (Murcia), May 7, 2010, 13

[10] See "Marruecos Desarticula Un Grupo Terrorista Vinculado Al 11-M [Morocco Arrests a Terrorist Cell Connected with the March 11, 2004 Attacks]," *La Vanguardia* (Barcelona), March 3, 2010, 17.

[11] C. Echeverría Jesús, "La Conexión Paquistaní se Consolida Tam-

bién en España [The Pakistani Connection Is Also Acting in Spain],"
Grupo de Estudios Estratégicos *GEES Analysis*, January 23, 2008,
www.gees.org.

[12] For a fact-based, detailed account, see Judge Javier Gomez Bermu-
dez, *No Destruirán Nuestra Libertad* [They Will Not Destroy Our Free-
dom] (Madrid: Temas de Hoy, 2010).

[13] Manuel Marraco, "Una 'Leyenda Urbana' al Banquillo Islamista
[An 'Urban Legend' to the Islamist Bench]," *El Mundo* (Madrid), May
19, 2010, 11.

[14] Al Goodman, "5 Terror Suspects On Trial In Madrid," CNN, May
23, 2010, http://edition.cnn.com/2010/WORLD/europe/03/23/
spain.terror.trial/index.html.

[15] See "Recent Highlights in Terrorist Activity," Combating Terrorism
Center at West Point *CTC Sentinel* 3, iss. 1, January 2010, 27.

[16] Kern, "Spain Goes On Mosque—Building Spree: Churches Forced
to Close."

[17] "France," Central Intelligence Agency *World Factbook*, March 22,
2011, https://www.cia.gov/library/publications/the-world-factbook/
geos/fr.html.

[18] See ,for example, Hossein Kettani, "Muslim Population in Europe:
1950-2020," *International Journal of Environmental Science and Development* 1, no. 2. June 2010, http://www.ijesd.org/papers/29-D438.
pdf.

[19] See "Poblacion Musulmana En España [Muslim Population Of
Spain]," *El País* (Madrid), June 10, 2010.

[20] Ibid.

[21] *Unión De Comunidades Islámicas De España: Estudio Demográ-
fico De La Población Musulmana* [Union Of Islamic Communities
Of Spain: Demographic study Of The Muslim Population] (Madrid:
UCIDE, December 2009).

[22] Pew Forum, "The Future of the Global Muslim Population," January 27, 2011, http://pewforum.org/future-of-the-global-muslim-pop-
ulation-regional-europe.aspx#4.

[23] See Escobar Stemman and Juan José, "Activismo Islámico En
España [Islamic Activism In Spain]," *Política Exterior* 124, July/August
2008.

[24] Kern, "Spain Goes On Mosque—Building Spree: Churches Forced
to Close."

[25] Authors' collection.

[26] Patricia Bezunartea, Jose Manuel Lopez, and Laura Tedesco, "Muslims in Spain and Islamic Religious Radicalism." *Microcon*, May 2009,
http://www.microconflict.eu/publications/PWP8_PB_JML_LT.pdf.

[27] "Ni Crucifijos Ni Funerales Católicos [Neither Catholic Crucifixes
Nor Funerals]," *El Pais* (Madrid), June 13, 2006.

[28] "Spanish Senate Calls for Nationwide Burqa Ban," Deutsche Press-

Agentur, June 23, 2010, http://www.monstersandcritics.com/news/
europe/news/article_1565614.php/Spanish-Senate-calls-for-nation-
wide-burqa-ban.

[29] Alan Clendenning and Harold Heckle, "Spain Rejects Burqa Ban
– For Now," Associated Press, July 20, 2010, http://www.huffington-
post.com/2010/07/20/spain-rejects-burqa-ban_n_653254.html.

[30] See, for example, Kathryn Haahr, "Catalonia: Europe's New Center of Global Jihad." Jamestown Foundation *Terrorism Monitor* 5, iss.
11, July 6, 2007, http://www.jamestown.org/programs/gta/single/?tx_
ttnews[tt_news]=4210&tx_ttnews[backPid]=182&no_cache=1.

[31] "Al Qaeda En El Magreb Podría Pedir La Liberación De Alguno
De Los 65 Islamistas Presos En España [Al-Qaeda In The Maghreb
Could Request The Release Of Some Of The 65 Imprisoned Islamists
In Spain]," *El Confidencial* (Madrid), December 10, 2009.

GERMANY

QUICK FACTS

Population: 82,282,988

Area: 357,022 sq km

Ethnic Groups: German 91.5%, Turkish 2.4%, other 6.1% (made up largely of Greek, Italian, Polish, Russian, Serbo-Croatian, Spanish)

Religions: Protestant 34%, Roman Catholic 34%, Muslim 3.7%, unaffiliated or other 28.3%

Government Type: Federal Republic

GDP (official exchange rate): $3.273 trillion

Map and Quick Facts courtesy of the CIA World Factbook (Last Updated July 2010)

Germany has the highest number of Muslim citizens in Western Europe, as well as in the member states of the European Union as a whole. It is also a hotbed of Islamist activity. Most notably, the attacks of 9/11 were organized in part in Germany by the "Hamburg cell" headed by Mohammed Atta.[1] Today, Islamists from Germany, including homegrown terrorists, pose a real threat to the security of the German state—as well as to that of the United States and other countries, such as Afghanistan, Pakistan, and Iraq.

Islamism in Germany has deep roots, stretching back to a symbiosis between the German state and radical religious elements during the First World War. These ties endured during the Second World War, fueled by the Third Reich's close ties to the Grand-Mufti of Jerusalem, Haj Amin al-Hussaini, and throughout the decades of the Cold War against the Soviet Union, before emerging to challenge the stability of the Federal Republic in the post-Cold War era.

ISLAMIST ACTIVITY

There exists considerable ideological and operational difference between lawful Islamism, which seeks the gradual imposition of *sharia* (Islamic law), and violent *jihad*, which is aimed at the overthrow of the established state. In Germany, Islamism of the lawful variant predominates, although instances of *jihadi* activity have been documented as well. As of 2009, Germany's internal security service, the Federal Office for the Protection of the Constitution (*Verfassungsschutzbericht*), estimated that some 29 Islamist organizations with a total of 36,270 members were active within the country.[2] These include:

Milli Görüs

With some 29,000 members, the Turkish *Milli Görüs* is by far the largest Islamist group in Germany.[3] Its funding derives from donations and membership fees.[4] Founded in the early 1970s by former Turkish Prime Minister Necmettin Erbakan, *Milli Görüs* now runs 323 mosques and associated centers in Germany.[5] Since January 23, 1995, its umbrella organization has been known as the Islamic Community *Milli Görüs* (IGMG).[6]

For years, the organization has spread anti-Semitic ideology through a range of media. It promotes radical television broadcasts, such as the Iranian TV series "Zehra's Blue Eyes" (which revolves around a fictional Israeli candidate for Prime Minister who kidnaps Palestinian children in order to harvest their organs for Jewish use—and glorifies suicide bombing in response).[7] It also has disseminated written anti-Semitic works, such as Turkish translations of Henry Ford's *The International Jew*.[8] Notably, the dissemination of such literature is contrary to German law. At least some portion of the group also has endorsed and promoted *jihadist* activities abroad.[9]

Hezbollah

The Lebanese Shi'ite militia Hezbollah is also active in Germany, where it has had a presence since the 1980s.[10] While it has no official representatives, the organization is known to have some 900 members/supporters inside the country, and to actively recruit there through a network of some 30 cultural centers and mosques.[11] The militia likewise is known to maintain active fundraising in Germany through a wide network of charities, nonprofits and ostensibly humanitarian groups. A 2009 investigation by the European Foundation for Democracy, for example, found that the group "directly channels financial donations from Germany to the Lebanese Al-Shahid Association, a known part of Hezbollah's fundraising network, via an organization known as the Orphans Project Lebanon based in Goettingen, Germany."[12] The amount of money thus funneled to the organization is unknown, but experts estimate that Germany is the group's "main fund raising center in Europe."[13]

Hamas

Hamas is estimated to have approximately 300 members in Germany. These activists raise funds for the Palestinian terror group in collaboration with the Palestinian Return Center (PRC) in London.[14] While Hamas does not have any official representatives in the country, it has been known to work through like-minded organizations to raise funds and promote its political objectives there. In July 2010, for example, Germany banned the Humanitarian Relief Foundation, or IHH, because its close ties to Hamas.[15] The IHH was noteworthy as the organization behind the controversial Gaza Flotilla of May 2010, and is accused of transmitting 6.6 million Euros from Germany to Hamas in the Gaza Strip.[16]

Muslim Brotherhood

The Muslim Brotherhood (MB) is estimated to have some 1,300 members in Germany.[17] While it has no formal representation in the country, the organization is known to run Islamic centers in Nuremberg, Stuttgart, Frankfurt, Cologne, Marburg, Braunschweig, and Munich.[18]

The Brotherhood has a long history in the Federal Republic, beginning with a 1958 initiative to build a mosque in Munich—an effort which resulted in the creation of the "Islamische Gemeinschaft in Deutschland e.V." (IGD), the "Islamic Community in Germany." Today, the IGD is headquartered in Cologne and serves as the unofficial representative of the group in national affairs. From 2002 to 2010, it was headed by one Ibrahim el-Zayat; since 2010, Samir Fallah is its head.[19] El-Zayat was general secretary of the World Assembly of Muslim Youth (WAMY), a Saudi organization active in the spread of Wahhabi ideology abroad.[20] The IGD was a founding member of the London-based "Federation of Islamic Organisations in Europe" (FIOE). According to journalist Ian Johnson, FIOE "is headquartered in a small village in northern England" and has established a series of institutions to "push the Muslim Brotherhood worldview."[21] The IGD tries to create a political climate positive to political Islam, and promote a more pious way of life in Germany. It also collects money for Islamist causes abroad, including raising funds for Hamas during the 2009 Gaza War.[22]

Homegrown terrorism

Homegrown terrorism, including domestic groups with connections to international *jihadist* organizations, constitutes a real threat to German security. The country faces potential threats from *jihadists* now resident in Germany, as well as *jihadists* of German origin operating abroad who may eventually return to target the Federal Republic. Both groups can be defined as "third generation" *jihadists*, i.e., those not necessarily under the auspices of al-Qaeda, but who share their Islamist ideology and terrorist approach.[23] Such elements have been implicated in plots to carry out terror attacks in

Germany,[24] as well as receiving training from *jihadist* elements abroad.[25] "Several dozen" German *jihadists*—including members of the IJU, the Uzbek Islamic Movement (IBU), the Islamic Movement of Uzbekistan (IMU), and the German Taliban Mujahedin ("Deutsche Taliban-Mudschahidin," or DTM)—are currently believed to be active in Pakistan's Waziristan region.[26]

Iranian influence

The influence of the Shi'a variant of Islamism propounded by the Islamic Republic of Iran can be found in Germany as well. The Islamic Center Hamburg (IZH), founded in 1962, is a pro-Iranian institution closely linked to the Islamic Republic. Its head, the Ayatollah Reza Ramezani,[27] was appointed to his post by the Iranian Foreign Ministry.[28] The IZH, in turn, tries to spread the idea of the "Iranian Revolution" via brochures, events, prayers, rallies, and other activities, and exerts an influence over a number of Islamic organizations within Germany. These include:

- The Islamic Center Salman Farsi Maschee Langenhagen e.V. in Hannover
- The Academy Baghiatallah e.V. in Bremen
- The Iranian Islamic Cultural Community Berlin e.V. in Berlin
- The Islamic Association Bavaria e.V. in Munich; and
- The Ehli-Beyt-Alevit Religious Community Ehli Beyt Alevi Federasyonu e.V. in Frankfurt a.M.[29]

Furthermore, the IZH is actively involved in the following institutions:

- The Council of Islamic Communities in Hamburg
- The Central Council of Muslims in Germany
- The Islamic Community of Shi'a Communities in Germany; and
- The Islamic-European Union of Shi'a scholars and Theologians.[30]

The Gülen Movement

The Turkish Gülen Movement has become increasingly influential in Germany. Founded by Turkish Islamist Fethullah Gülen (born 1938), it is based on the ideas of Faid Nursi (1876-1960).[31] The Gülen movement runs high schools in Germany[32] and does not publicly advocate violence. Rather, it has taken pains to distance itself from bin Laden and al-Qaeda. This stance, however, appears to stem from Gülen's 2004 declaration that non-state actors (such as al-Qaeda) are not permitted to wage war,[33] rather than from an aversion to armed *jihad* writ large. Gülen's Turkish branch of political Islam espouses the idea of the gradual imposition a *sharia*-based democracy.[34] The Gülen Movement runs at least 20-25 schools in Germany, not including some 200 groups for the coaching of pupils after school.[35] There are no official membership numbers available the Gülen Movement, but the group is believed to be increasingly popular as a result of its educational activities.[36]

ISLAMISM AND SOCIETY

At 4.1 million people, Germany's Muslim population is the highest[37] among the 27 states that make up the European Union.[38] Of this number, the majority (2.56 million) is from Turkey, while roughly half a million (536,000) is from the former Yugoslavia. Iran (70,000), Afghanistan (89,000), Morocco (163,000), Pakistan (67,000), Egypt (37,000), Iraq (97,000), Lebanon (127,000) and Syria (35,000) make up the other significant countries of origin.[39]

For decades, however, the former Federal Republic of Germany did not consider these immigrants to be true citizens, instead terming them *Gastarbeiter*, or guest workers. Over time, such a fiction has become increasingly hard to sustain; Turkish workers, in particular, stayed in Germany, and their families followed them. Racism was and remains a widespread phenomenon in Germany, due to the specific German national concept of citizenship, which until recently was defined along blood, rather than territorial, lines. Thus, being born in Germany did not necessarily mean that you were German in the popular conception. This began to change in 1999 with the passage of a new law granting children of non-German residents citizenship by birth.[40]

Since 9/11, and particularly over the past several years, political Islam has become a major topic of public debate in Germany. The wearing of the headscarf, honor killings, forced marriages, and support for terrorism and anti-Zionist activity are among the main topics of discussion surrounding both Islam and Islamism. Yet many newspapers, researchers, and politicians, as well as the general public at large, remain reluctant to deal with these issues. Those political groups or parties which express their opposition to political Islam do so out of ideological and/or racist grounds, rather than as a result of careful analysis of specific elements of political Islam. Likewise, many groups opposed to Islam are also against other foreigners (as well as those considered to be not "German" enough).

Nevertheless, a tiny but growing number of public intellectuals, scholars, activists, authors, and journalists have emerged publicly as critics of Islamism in recent years. These individuals have faced resistance on the public policy front. Some institutions, like the Berlin Center for Research on Antisemitism (ZfA),[41] have equated any meaningful criticism of Islam with anti-Semitism, often framed as "Islamophobia."[42] Many journalists and mainstream scholars even compare or equate Islamist preachers of hate with pro-Western scholars, writers or activists,[43] and reject any military response to Islamism or Islamic *jihad*.[44] Most instead portray Islam as harmless or interesting, and look uncritically upon figures like leading Sunni Islamist Yusuf al-Qaradawi.[45]

Considerable grassroots support for Islamism and even violent jihad is visible at the grassroots level in Germany, as evidenced through sporadic rallies in German cities in support of various radical causes.

ISLAMISM AND THE STATE

Germany has a close and complex relationship with Islamism. From the First World War through the Nazi era and the post-war period, the idea of *jihad* was intimately interwoven with the German state. The scholar Wolfgang G. Schwanitz has written:

> The *jihad* was the idea of Max von Oppenheim, the German "Abu Jihad." (…) he designed a master plan at the end of October 1914: "fomenting rebellion in the Islamic territories of our enemies." The emperor confirmed Oppenheim's suggestion to incite Muslims to *jihad* under the leadership of the Ottoman sultan-caliph. This was the plan: the sultan proclaims the *jihad* against the British, the French, and the Russians. Berlin delivers money, experts, and material.[46]

Although that *jihad* did not materialize, German efforts to support Islamism re-emerged during the Third Reich. The grand *mufti* of Jerusalem, Haj Amin al-Hussaini, was welcomed by Adolf Hitler, financially supported by the Nazi regime, and used Germany as a base from which to communicate anti-Jewish propaganda into the Middle East.[47] After 1945, Islam was used both by the Federal Republic of Germany and the U.S. (via the CIA) as a tool against the Soviet Union and its allies during the Cold War.[48] As part of this effort, Gerhard von Mende, a former Nazi in the "Ostministerium" (department of Eastern affairs), engaged the services of Muslims like Nurredin Nakibhodscha Namangani, a former imam for the Nazi Schutzstaffel (SS). In 1958, Namangani began a "Mosque Construction Commission" in Munich, which became the starting point for political Islam in post-war Germany (if not the whole of Europe). From the start, however, it was clear—given the ideologies and past histories of those Islamists and their German allies—that anti-Semitism and anti-Western thought would become staples of the ideology thereby promoted.

Nevertheless, both the government of the Federal Republic and the U.S.

intelligence community embraced the use of Islamism as a tool against enemies (like the Soviet Union) during the decades of the Cold War. "If you want to understand the structure of political Islam, you have to look at what happened in Munich," says historian Stefan Meining. "Munich is the origin of a network that now reaches around the world."[49] Soon, Said Ramadan, the representative of the Muslim Brotherhood in Europe, became part of that mosque project. The Muslim Brotherhood has remained a fixture, albeit an informal one, in German society since.[50]

Other Islamist groups have fared less well in Germany, however. *Hizb ut-Tahrir*, for example, was formally banned on January 10, 2003, a decision that was affirmed at the federal level in January 2006.[51] Hezbollah's dedicated television channel, *al-Manar*, was proscribed in hotels and coffee shops in Germany on October 29, 2008.[52] (However, private households in Germany can still watch it via Saudi and Egyptian satellites). More recently, in August 2010, the al-Quds mosque in Hamburg—a Salafi religious center known to be a significant source of Islamist indoctrination[53] —was belatedly shuttered.[54]

The German government, for its part, has also attempted to participate in—and to influence—the dialogue over Islam taking place inside the country. In 2006, it established an official "Islam Conference," which continues to convene several times a year. At this venue, leading Muslim congregations, along with independent activists, authors, and scholars, discuss the relationship of Muslims and German society with German politicians, headed by the Federal Minister of the Interior. This approach has garnered disapproval from critics, who say that the conference itself has been co-opted by its inclusion of Islamists and suspicious groups. These include the German Islam Council ("*Islamrat für die Bundesrepublik Deutschland e. V.*," or IRD), which was excluded from the Islam Conference in 2010 due to criminal investigations against some of its members over their ties to Islamism.[55]

Additionally, the German government has maintained a permissive policy toward the Islamic Republic of Iran. In 2009, Germany was Iran's second biggest trade partner and its most important Western trade partner, racking up exports of some $5.3 billion.[56] German politicians frequently visit Iran and support the Islamist regime in Tehran.[57] Iran still has an embassy in Germany, which proudly proclaims that Iran and Germany share a history of close relations dating back to 1941.[58] German officials likewise have failed to ban Hezbollah. Despite considerable pressure from foreign governments (such as that of Israel) and private actors, "Hezbollah remains a legal entity in Germany and its 900 members are active in promoting Iran's revolutionary Islam," investigative reporter Benjamin Weinthal has noted.[59]

This schizophrenic approach has led leading critics to contend that Germany, despite its role in international counterterrorism efforts (including Coalition operations in Afghanistan), still lacks a real anti-terror strategy.[60]

Still, there are signs of a growing awareness of Islamic radicalism among government officials. On November 17, 2010, for example, former German Interior Minister Thomas de Maiziére warned publicly that Islamic *jihadists* were on their way to the country with the intent of committing a terrorist attack.[61] His successor, Hans-Peter Friedrich, has gone further, announcing in March 2011 that he intends to hold a "prevention conference" dealing with Islamism and Islamic Jihad in Berlin in 2011.[62] This marks the first time that the German government has engaged the country's Muslim community in a joint effort to combat Islamism. The prospects for such a union, however, are far from certain, as most of the Muslim organizations participating in the state's official "Islam conference" have rejected the outreach.[63]

ENDNOTES

[1] The *9/11 Commission Report: Final Report of the National Commission on Terrorist Attacks Upon the United States* (New York: WW Norton & Co., 2004).

[2] German Interior Ministry, *Verfassungsschutzbericht 2009 [Constitutional Protection Report 2009]*, June 2010, http://www.verfassungsschutz.de/download/SHOW/vsbericht_2009.pdf.

[3] Ibid.

[4] North Rhine Westfalia Interior Ministry, *Verfassungsschutzbericht 2005* [Constituional Protection Report 2005, of North Rhine Westfalia], March 20, 2006, http://www.im.nrw.de/imshop/shopdocs/verfassungsschutzbericht_2005.pdf.

[5] German Interior Ministry, *Verfassungsschutzbericht 2009*.

[6] Thomas Lemmen, *Islamische Vereine und Verbände in Deutschland* [Islamic Associations and Federations in Germany] (Bonn: Friedrich Ebert Stiftung, 2002), 40. The German name of the group is Islamische Gemeinschaft Milli Görüs e.V.

[7] "Antisemitische Hetzvideos bei der 'Islamischen Gemeinschaft Milli Görüs' [Antisemitic hate videos of the Islamic Community Milli Görüs]," hamburg.de, July 13, 2006, http://www.hamburg.de/archiv/232516/hetzvideos-igmg-artikel.html.

[8] Ibid.

[9] "Report München," ARD, February 8, 2010, http://www.youtube.com/watch?v=-Ka6mV0-99M .

[10] Mark Dubowitz and Alexander Ritzmann, "Hezbollah's German Helpers," *Wall Street Journal*, April 16, 2007, http://www.defenddemocracy.org/index.php?option=com_content&task=view&id=11779494&Itemid=0.

[11] Ibid.

[12] Alexander Ritzmann, "Hezbollah Fundraising in Germany Tax-Deductible," European Foundation for Democracy *EFD Report*, July 10, 2009, http://www.europeandemocracy.org/publications/other-publications/efd-report-hezbollah-fundraising-in-germany-tax-deductible.html.

[13] "Hezbollah's International Reach," Anti-Defamation League, December 7, 2004, http://www.adl.org/terror/hezbollah_print.asp.

[14] German Interior Ministry, *Verfassungsschutzbericht 2009*.

[15] Benjamin Weinthal, "Germany Bans IHH for Hamas Links," *Jerusalem Post*, July 12, 2010, http://www.jpost.com/SpecialSection/Article.aspx?ID=181187.

[16] "Milli Görüs und die Hamas. 'Einfluss auf 60.000 Muslime' [Milli Görüs and Hamas. 'Influence on some 60.000 Muslims']," *Tageszeitung* (Berlin), July 14, 2010, http://www.taz.de/1/politik/deutschland/artikel/1/direkter-einfluss-auf-60-000-muslime/ (12.11.2010).

[17] German Interior Ministry, *Verfassungsschutzbericht* 2009.

[18] Ibid.

[19] Ibidem.

[20] Ibidem; For possible ties of WAMY to al-Qaeda, see "Al Qaeda linked World Assembly of Muslim Youth (WAMY) Jihad through Da'wa group working with Novib/Oxfam on Somali 'educational' initiatives," *Militant Islam Monitor*, October 16, 2006, http://www.militantislammonitor.org/article/id/2473.

[21] Ian Johnson, Statement before the Human Rights Caucus of the U.S. House of Representatives, February 9, 2006, http://www.aifdemocracy.org/policy-issues.php?id=1727; See also Lorenzo Vidino, "The Muslim Brotherhood's Conquest of Europe," Middle East Quarterly, Winter 2005, 25-34.

[22] German Interior Ministry, *Verfassungsschutzbericht* 2009.

[23] Kai Hirschmann, "Der Jihadismus: Ideologie, Organisation und Bekämpfungsmöglichkeiten [The Jihadists: Ideology, organization and fighting capabilities]," in Kurt Graulich and Dieter Simon, eds., *Terrorismus und Rechtsstaatlichkeit. Analysen, Handlungsoptionen, Perspektiven* [Terrorism and rule of law. Analyses, action options, perspectives] (Berlin: Akademie Verlag, 2007), 99-121, 114.

[24] For a more detailed analysis of the group members, see Rolf Clement and Paul Elmar Jöris, *Die Terroristen von nebenan. Gotteskrieger aus Deutschland* [The terrorists from next door: Holy warriors from Germany] (Munich/Zurich: Piper, 2010); *Radio Deutschlandfunk*, May 12, 2009, http://www.dradio.de/download/104169/.

[25] Yassin Musharbash and Matthias Gebauer, "De Maizière warnt vor Anschlag in Deutschland [De Maizière warns of attack in Germany]," *Der Spiegel* (Hamburg), November 17, 2010, http://www.spiegel.de/politik/deutschland/0,1518,729603,00.html.

[26] Ibid.

[27] German Interior Ministry, *Verfassungsschutzbericht* 2009.

[28] Ibid.

[29] Ibidem.

[30] Ibidem.

[31] Ralph Ghadban, lecture, Aalen, Germany, May 5, 2010.

[32] Author's correspondence with Ralph Ghadban, November 2010.

[33] Ralph Ghadban, lecture.

[34] Ibid.

[35] Author's correspondence with German Islamism expert Claudia Dantschke, Berlin, Germany, April 2011.

[36] Claudia Dantschke, *Muslime – Ihre Einrichtungen und Vereine im Berliner Bezirk Neukölln. Überblick über die Strukturen und ihre religiösen sowie politischen Ausrichtungen. Eine Handreichung für die Jugendarbeit* [Muslims - mechanisms and associations in the Berlin district of Neukölln. Overview of the structures and their religious as

well as political adjustments.] (Berlin: Zentrum Demokratische Kultur, 2009), 44. For an overview about the Gülen Movement and its ideology see ibid, 42-45.

[37] France is a possible exception in this regard. However, French laws outlawing formal surveys of citizens by confession make an authoritative determination currently impossible.

[38] Pew Research Center, *Muslim Networks and Movements in Western Europe*, September 15, 2010, http://features.pewforum.org/muslim/number-of-muslims-in-western-europe.html.

[39] Sonja Haug, Stephanie Müssig and Anja Stichs, *Muslim Life in Germany. A study conducted on behalf of the German Conference on Islam* (Nuremberg: Federal Office for Migration and Refugees, 2009), 76, http://www.bamf.de/SharedDocs/Anlagen/EN/Migration/Publikationen/Forschung/Forschungsberichte/fb6-muslimisches-leben,templateId=raw,property=publicationFile.pdf/fb6-muslimisches-leben.pdf.

[40] „Staatsbürgerschaftsrecht. Reform verabschiedet [New law on citizenship passed]," *Der Spiegel* (Hamburg), May 7, 1999, http://www.spiegel.de/politik/deutschland/a-21229.html.

[41] Conference of the Center for Research on Antisemitism, Technical University Berlin, Berlin, Germany, December 8, 2008, http://zfa.kgw.tu-berlin.de/feindbild_muslim_feindbild_islam.pdf.

[42] The Berlin Center for Research on Antisemitism (ZfA) equated the situation of Jews in the late 19th century with the situation of Muslims today in Germany at a conference dedicated to that topic on December 8, 2008 (see footnote above). See Clemens Heni, "Antisemitism is not the same as Islamophobia," *Jerusalem Post*, December 3, 2008, http://www.jpost.com/Opinion/Op-EdContributors/Article.aspx?id=122938 .

[43] A leading voice in equating critics of Islamism with Islamists is historian Wolfgang Benz (head of the above mentioned Berlin Center for Research on Antisemitism (ZfA) from 1990-2011), see his article "Hetzer mit Parallelen. Antisemiten des 19. Jahrhunderts und manche "Islamkritiker" des 21. Jahrhunderts arbeiten mit ähnlichen Mitteln an ihrem Feindbild. [Agitators with Parallels. Anti-Semitism in the 19th Century and some „critics of Islam" in the 21st century use similar tools in portraying their concepts of enemies]," *Süddeutsche Zeitung* (Munich), January 4, 2010, http://www.sueddeutsche.de/politik/antisemiten-und-islamfeinde-hetzer-mit-parallelen-1.59486

[44] See the German role in the debate about Islam and the West, David Blankenhorn et al., *The Islam/West Debate: Documents from a Global Debate on Terrorism, U.S. Policy, and the Middle East* (Lanham, MD: Rowman & Littlefield Publishers, 2005).

[45] Qaradawi has been portrayed as "moderate" in the German political discourse because he rejects suicide bombing as long as it is not aimed at Jews and Israel. Clemens Heni, "'Global Mufti' Qaradawi

and German Middle Eastern Studies," *Human Rights Service* (Norway), September 14, 2010, http://www.rights.no/publisher/publisher. asp?id=56&tekstid=4116 . For an overview on German Islamic Studies after 9/11 see Clemens Heni, Schadenfreude. Islamforschung und Antisemitismus in Deutschland nach 9/11 [Schadenfreude. Islamic Studies and antisemitism in Germany after 9/11] (published by The Berlin International Center for the Study of Antisemitism (BICSA), June 2011, 370 pages).

[46] Wolfgang G. Schwanitz, *The German Middle Eastern Policy, 1871-1945* (Berlin: Trafoberlin, 2004), http://www.trafoberlin.de/pdf-dateien/German%20Middle%20Eastern%20Policy.pdf

[47] Jeffrey Herf, *Nazi Propaganda for the Arab World* (New Haven: Yale University Press, 2009), 259-286.

[48] Ian Johnson, *The Beachhead: How a Mosque for Ex-Nazis Became Center of Radical Islam.*

"Documents Reveal Triumph by Muslim Brotherhood in Postwar Munich," *Wall Street Journal*, July 12, 2005.

[49] Ibid.

[50] Ibid; See also Ian Johnson, *A Mosque in Munich: Nazis, the CIA, and the Rise of the Muslim Brotherhood in the West* (Boston and New York: Houghton Mifflin Harcourt, 2010); see also the new monograph of Stefan Meining, *Eine Moschee in Deutschland. Nazis, Geheimdienste und der Aufstieg des politischen Islam im Westen* [Nazis, Secret Sevices, and the rise of political Islam in the West] (Munich: C.H. Beck 2011).

[51] See *Decision by German Federal Administrative Court*, January 25, 2006, http://lexetius.com/2006,604?version=drucken.

[52] John Rosenthal, "Germany Does Not Ban Hezbollah TV," *Pajamas Media*, November 26, 2008, http://pajamasmedia.com/blog/germany-does-not-ban-hezbollah-tv/?singlepage=true.

[53] "Salafistisches Islamseminar in der Taiba - Moschee (ehemals Al-Quds-Moschee) vom 09.-11.04.2010 [Salafist Islam seminar in Taliba mosque (former al-Quds-mosque) in Hamburg, April 9-11, 2010]," hamburg.de, April 28, 2010, http://www.hamburg.de/schlag-zeilen/2231544/salafismusseminar-fhh-hamburg.html.

[54] "Die 9/11-Moschee ist dicht [9/11 mosque in Hamburg has been shut down]," *Tageszeitung* (Berlin), August 9, 2010, http://www.taz.de/1/leben/alltag/artikel/1/beruehmte-moschee-ist-dicht/.

[55] Statement by the Organizers of the German Islam Conference, May 15, 2010, http://www.deutsche-islam-konferenz.de/cln_117/nn_1319098/SubSites/DIK/DE/DieDIK/NeueTeilnehmer/neue-teil-nehmer-node.html?__nnn=true.

[56] StopTheBomb, "Deutsch-iranische Wirtschaftsbeziehungen [German-Iranian Trade Relations]," March 2010, http://de.stopthebomb.net/d-iran.html.

[57] See, for example, Matthias Küntzel, "Vom 'kritischen' zum

kriecherischen Dialog. Deutsche Kulturpolitiker in Teheran [From criticism to critical dialogue: German culture politicians in Tehran]," November 5, 2010, http://www.matthiaskuentzel.de/contents/vom-kritischen-zum-kriecherischen-dialog.

[58] See the Homepage of the Iranian Embassy in Germany, Überblick über die bilateralen Beziehungen zwischen der Islamischen Republik Iran und der Bundesrepublik Deutschland, [Overview on the bilateral relations of the Islamic Republic of Iran and th Federal Republic of Germany] http://www.iranembassy.de/ger/political_relations.htm (accessed April 13, 2011).

[59] Benjamin Weinthal, "Why is Germany Playing Down Radical Islam?" *Weekly Standard*, October 13, 2010, http://www.weeklystandard.com/blogs/why-germany-playing-down-radical-islam_508630.html

[60] Guido Steinberg, *Im Visier von al-Qaida: Deutschland braucht eine Anti-Terror-Strategie* [In the Sights of Al-Qaeda: Germany Needs an Anti-Terror Strategy] (Hamburg: edition Körber Stiftung, n.d.), http://www.koerber-stiftung.de/fileadmin/user_upload/edition/pdf/leseproben/978-3-89684-139-1_001-012_01.pdf.

[61] "Bundesregierung warnt vor Anschlägen in Deutschland [Federal Government Warns before Attack in Germany]," Reuters, November 17, 2010, http://de.reuters.com/article/topNews/idDEBEE-6AG0CT20101117 [62] "Friedrich plant 'Präventionsgipfel' [Friedrich intends a "prevention conference"]," *Stern* (Berlin), March 29, 2011, http://www.stern.de/news2/aktuell/kampf-gegen-islamistischen-extremismus-friedrich-plant-praeventionsgipfel-1668747.html.

[63] "Friedrich provoziert Eklat [New German Minister of Interior provokes a scandal]," N-TV (Frankfurt), March 29, 2011, http://www.n-tv.de/politik/Friedrich-provoziert-Eklat-article2965396.html.

ITALY

While Italy only recently began to experience Muslim immigration on a large scale, Islam in both its moderate and radical forms is already a significant presence in the country. The Union of Islamic Communities and Organizations of Italy (UCOII) has been at the forefront of the debate for the representation of the highly fragmented Italian Muslim community. With regard to jihadist activities, Italy remained simply a logistical base until October 2009, when an attempted bombing by a Libyan radical in Milan shattered popular illusions that Italy was safe from extremist attacks. The event sparked a lively public debate, but the Italian government so far has failed to respond effectively to Islamism as a political and societal force.

ISLAMIST ACTIVITY

Italy's Muslim community is extremely diverse and fragmented. Those characteristics, combined with Sunni Islam's intrinsic lack of clerical hierarchy, cause it to suffer from weak internal cohesion and a poor level of organization. This is reflected in the community's chronic inability to produce a unified leadership. Twenty years after the first significant wave of Muslim immigration, Italy's Muslim community is characterized by the presence of many organizations, none of which can legitimately claim to represent more than a fraction of it. Moreover, the relationships among these organizations are often characterized by sharp disagreements and even personal hatreds, leaving the country's Muslims deprived of a unified leadership.

The Italian Islamist panorama, while not as sophisticated as that of many northern European countries, is quite heterogeneous. The one group that has repeatedly made a claim to the leadership of the country's Muslim community is the Union of the Islamic Communities and Organizations of Italy, or UCOII. The union traces its origins to the Union of Muslim Students in Italy (USMI), a small organization of Muslim students that was created in Perugia and other university cities at the end of the 1960s.[1] Comprised mostly of Jordanian, Syrian and Palestinian students, the USMI's ideology was close to the positions of the Muslim Brotherhood.[2] By the second half of the 1980s, when the first notable wave of North African immigrants arrived in Italy, a student organization such as the USMI could no longer satisfy the needs of the new, large Muslim population. In January 1990, representatives of USMI, six mosques from six Italian cities, and 32 individuals formed the UCOII.

Since its founding, the UCOII has been extremely active on the political scene, attempting to become the main, if not the only, interlocutor of the Italian state. The UCOII has managed to achieve an important position within the Muslim community, thanks to the significant degree of control it exercises over Italian mosques. While its claim to control 85 percent of Italy's mosques is difficult to verify independently, it is undeniable that the UCOII plays a predominant role in the life of Italy's practicing Muslim community and that a large number of mosques are, to varying degrees, linked to it.[3]

While today the organization has no formal ties to the Muslim Brotherhood or any affiliated outfit in the Middle East, its worldview is still inspired by the group's ideology.[4] Like most other Brotherhood-inspired organizations throughout Europe, the UCOII aims at swaying the Muslim population of Italy to its interpretation of Islam through the activities of its capillary network of mosques. Given the lack of other social structures on Italian territory, many Muslim immigrants seeking the comfort of familiar faces, languages and smells congregate in its mosques, which are often seen more as community centers than simply places of worship. The UCOII seeks to use its virtual monopoly over mosques to spread its ideology and exercise what Italian expert on Islam Renzo Guolo has defined as a "diffuse cultural hegemony" over the country's Muslim community.[5] Taking advantage of the community's considerable fragmentation, the UCOII has become the most visible, vocal and organized voice of Italy's Muslims. In terms of representation to the outside world, it can be said that control of the Italian Muslim community has been conquered by an active minority, which has prevailed easily over an unorganized silent majority.[6]

Aside from the UCOII, other Islamist outfits operating in the country, albeit only marginally, are Hizb ut-Tahrir, the transnational pan-Islamist Sunni movement, and Tablighi Jamaat, the peaceful Islamic missionary movement that intelligence agencies worldwide suspect of having been infiltrated by radicals.[7] The Moroccan movement Justice and Charity also has a significant influence on several mosques in northern Italy.[8] Finally, two Shi'a organizations, Naples-based Ahl al-Bayt and its Rome-based spin-off Imam Mahdi, have attracted the attention of authorities because of their radical positions and because many of their members are Italian converts with a past association to militant right wing groups.[9] All of these groups and movements operate with various degrees of sophistication and success, competing amongst themselves and with non-Islamist organizations for influence in the virgin territory that is Islam in Italy. The battle that takes place on a daily basis for the control of Islamic places of worship and, more generally, for influence over Italian Muslims, is something that Italian authorities can only watch from afar.

In addition, *jihadist* networks have existed in Italy since the late 1980s, though they seldom have they targeted the country. Italy historically has been used by various *jihadist* outfits as a logistical base ideal for acquiring false documents, obtaining weapons, and raising funds. This traditional use of Italian territory appeared to change on October 12, 2009, when Mohammad Game, a legal immigrant from Libya, detonated an explosive device hidden on his person at the gates of the Santa Barbara military base in Milan. The attack seriously injured him and lightly injured the *carabiniere* who tried to stop him. The ensuing investigation revealed that Game had recently become more religious and political. Acquaintances described how he had frequently stated that Italian troops should have left Afghanistan, framing his diatribes in increasingly religious terms. Game reportedly made similar remarks to the ambulance personnel that transported him to the hospital after the attack. Within a few days, authorities arrested two men, an Egyptian and a Libyan, who reportedly helped Game in his plan. Forty kilograms of the same chemical substances used by Game in the attack were also retrieved in a basement to which the men had access.

Prior to October 12th, Game and his accomplices began to attend services at Milan's Islamic Cultural Institute (Viale Jenner mosque), a place that has been at the center of terrorism investigations for almost 20 years. Yet they did not appear to have acted under the direction of, or even in remote cooperation with, any established group. To the contrary, their characteristics, from their sudden radicalization to the lack of sophistication of their *modus operandi*, resemble that of the homegrown networks that have become common in most European countries but that had not yet appeared in Italy.

ISLAMISM AND SOCIETY

Traditionally a country of emigration rather than immigration, only by the 1970s did Italy begin to attract small numbers of immigrants, coming mostly from the Philippines and Latin America. The Muslim presence was limited to the diplomatic personnel from Muslim countries, a few businessmen and some students. Those numbers increased significantly in the 1980s, when immigrants from North and Sub-Saharan Africa began to choose Italy as their initial or final destination in their migration to Europe. Immigration has peaked since the mid-1990s, and, according to Italy's official census bureau (ISTAT), as of December 2006, there were 2,670,514 foreign citizens residing in Italy.[10] While no exact data on the number of Muslims living in Italy exist, most estimates put their number at around one million, corresponding to almost two percent of the population.[11]

Various features characterize Italy's Muslim community, starting with its significant ethnic diversity. The two countries that have contributed the largest number of Muslim immigrants to Italy are Morocco (28.5 percent) and Albania (20.5 percent).[12] Most other Muslims living in Italy come from Tunisia, Senegal, Egypt, Bangladesh, Pakistan, Algeria, Bosnia and Nigeria, contributing to the ethnically diverse community. Only in the sectarian aspect is Italy's Muslim community quite homogeneous—98 percent of Italy's Muslims are Sunni.[13] Other distinctive characteristics of Italy's Muslim population when compared to other European Muslim communities are its higher number of non-citizens and illegal immigrants, higher percentage of males, and higher level of geographic dispersion.[14]

Most Italian Muslims seem to adopt a moderate interpretation of Islam. According to polls, only five to 10 percent of Muslims living in Italy regularly attend Friday prayers at a mosque.[15] Even though the percentage would probably be higher if there were more mosques throughout the territory, the data square with the analysis of most sociologists, who believe that the majority of Muslims living in Italy are not practicing ones. Most of them fast for Ramadan and celebrate Eid al-Fitr but are not significantly more practicing than Italian Catholics.[16] On the other hand, Italy's lack of mature debate over Islamism and scarcity of integration policies represent conditions that could allow Islamist groups to increase their influence over the country's burgeoning Muslim population.

If there is one certainty about the future of Islam in Italy, it is that its presence will only grow. The influx of immigrants from North and Sub-Saharan African seems to be virtually unstoppable, given migration patterns and socio-economic conditions in Africa. Moreover, in the next few years, Italy will start to see second generation Muslim immigrants, like most other European countries already have. Many of them will hold Italian citizenship and, furthermore, the number of Muslims carrying an Italian passport will also increase through marriages and conversions. It seems clear that Islam is destined to have a more visible and stable presence in the country and this is already evident in the impressive increase of mosques throughout Italy. According to a report of the security services, Italy had 351 mosques in 2000, 696 in 2006 and 735 in the first semester of 2007. The same report also indicates that 39 new mosques and Islamic organizations were set up just between January and May 2007, an average of one every four days.[17]

The predominance of the UCOII at the organizational level has strong repercussions on the relationship between the Italian state and the Muslim community and the legal recognition of Islam, a source of major political controversies. The Italian Constitution (Article 19) gives all citizens the right to freely practice and proselytize for any religion (unless its rites are deemed to be against morality). All religions are free to organize themselves and, according to Article 8, their relationship with the state is regulated by law, based on agreements signed by the state with the representatives of each religious community. The Catholic religion enjoys a separate and privileged treatment, which was negotiated by the Vatican and the Italian state in 1929 and then incorporated in the republican Constitution of 1948. In order to be recognized and receive legal and financial benefits similar to those of the Catholic religion, all other religions have to sign an agreement (known in Italian as *intesa*) with the government, which regulates mutual rights and obligations.

Over the last 25 years various religious communities have done so. Islam, which is *de facto* the country's second largest religion, has not yet been recognized by the Italian state as a religion. While the opposition of some political forces to the recognition of Islam has in some cases interfered with the process, the main reason for this seemingly paradoxical situation is to be found in the lack of a unified leadership in the Italian Muslim community. In order to sign the *intesa* the Italian government needs to find a representative of the Muslim community, something the Italian Muslim community so far has been unable to produce. *Intesa* proposals submitted over the years by various groups that entertain cordial relationships with the Italian state have been turned down, as none of the applicants were deemed able to legitimately claim to represent the majority of Italian Muslims.[18]

Conversely, the Italian state has experienced the opposite problems when dealing with the proposals of intesa submitted by the UCOII since 1990. The UCOII seems to be, *prima facie,* the Muslim organization with the largest following and with characteristics that make it the closest of all Italian Muslim organizations to the notion of representation that Italian authorities are looking for. Yet its *intesa* drafts have been turned down because authorities are skeptical of the UCOII's nature. Given these dynamics, Islam is not recognized as an official religion, a situation that creates practical difficulties and generates the perception among many Italian Muslims that authorities discriminate against Islam.

ISLAMISM AND THE STATE

Even though small clusters of *jihadist* groups made plans for attacks against targets in Milan, Cremona, Bologna and Rome in the past, Italian authorities were clear in stating, as of early 2009, that the primary use of Italian soil for radical Islamists has been logistical in nature and that there were no indications of networks planning attacks in Italy or from Italy against other countries.[19] An intelligence report submitted to the Italian Parliament in February 2009 cautioned that the threat in Italy was "multifaceted, volatile, and prone to sudden shifts," but the homegrown threat was not yet apparent in the country.[20]

Mohammad Game's homegrown terrorist attack in Milan changed that view. The episode came as a shock to Italian authorities, who for the first time dealt with a case of homegrown terrorism of Islamist inspiration. On November 6th, Interior Minister Roberto Maroni publicly stated the Italian government's reassessment of the role of *jihadist* cells operating in the country. "Until the action in Milan," said the minister, "the cells identified in Italy were involved in fundraising and recruitment. We now believe that there are cells that form, fundraise and train to carry out attacks in Italy. We are not yet at the 'homegrown terrorism' we have seen in the United Kingdom and Spain, but we are very close to it."[21]

The Milan attack, while providing the blueprint for possible future terrorism scenarios, also brought to the fore a more general debate over radical Islam in the country. Unlike most other European countries, which, since 9/11, have engaged in a more or less sustained debate about Islam and Islamism, Italy has followed a different trajectory. As disparate international (terrorist attacks in other countries, global crises) and domestic (the occasional arrest of *jihadist* militants or "honor killing") events appear on the radar, they generate a heated domestic debate that often becomes highly politicized and lacks nuance. Yet, as the dust from these events inevitably settles, the debate is not followed by any systematic governmental initiative seeking to address the many issues, whether related strictly to the security aspect or, more broadly, to integration and social cohesion, that arise from Islamism. Despite some notable exceptions, official attention to Islamism has tended to be sporadic, uninformed, and not conducive to the development of concrete policy.

To be fair, the violent aspects of Islamism in Italy by and large have been extensively and effectively monitored by Italian authorities since the early 1990s. Over the last 15 years, dozens of complex investigations have brought to light *jihadist* networks throughout the peninsula.[22] The combination of experienced security services and law enforcement agencies, proactive investigative magistrates, and adequate legal framework have allowed Italian authorities to be among the most aggressive and successful in Europe in dismantling *jihadist* networks, uncovering extensive links spanning throughout Europe and the Middle East. While these successes have not always been followed by convictions and long sentences once the cases went to trial, it is fair to say that Italian authorities have been quite efficient in keeping in check violent Islamist networks.

Things are quite different, however, when the focus shifts from traditional counterterrorism measures to a broader frame of analysis. While many European countries have been implementing or at least discussing plans to stem radicalization among their Muslim communities, Italy is severely lagging behind in even rationally approaching the issue. Moreover, the Italian debate over forms of non-violent Islamism has often shifted, with some notable exceptions, between schizophrenic overreaction, naïve whitewashing, and, most commonly, utter lack of interest. In most other Western European countries, excesses on both sides of the debate, from conflating Islamism with Islam to labeling as racist any question raised over aspects of Islamism, have slowly been replaced by more nuanced and balanced positions. Italy's public debate on the issue, on the other hand, seems to be only occasional and far less mature.

ENDNOTES

[1] UCOII, "History of UCOII," n.d., http://www.islam-ucoii.it/artcomuni.htm.

[2] Stefano Allievi, "I musulmani in Italia: chi sono e come ci vedono [Muslims In Italy: Who They Are And How They See Us]," *Limes*, iss 3 (2004), 100.

[3] UCOII, "History of UCOII."

[4] Renzo Guolo, *Xenofobi e Xenofili: Gli Italiani e l'Islam* [Xenophobes And Xenophiles: Italians and Islam] (Bari: Laterza, 2003), 10.

[5] Ibid., 11.

[6] Guolo, *Xenofobi e Xenofili: Gli Italiani e l'Islam*, 5-6.

[7] *59th Report of CESIS (Executive Committee for the Intelligence and Security Services) to Parliament*, January-May 2007, 71.

[8] Author's interviews with Italian government officials and Muslim community leaders, Rome, Italy, February and July 2007.

[9] "Pulsioni antimondialiste e vecchio antisemitismo [Anti-globalist Trends And Old Anti-Semitism]," SISDE *GNOSIS* Iss. 4 (2005).

[10] ISTAT population findings for the year 2006.

[11] Allievi, "I musulmani in Italia: chi sono e come ci vedono," 97. The 2007 annual report by Caritas/Migrantes puts the number at 1,202,052.

[12] Federico Di Leo, "Il nostro Islam in cifre [Our Islam In Numbers]," *Limes*, Iss. 3 (2004), 123.

[13] Stefano Allievi, "Islam in Italy," in Shireen T. Hunter, ed., *Islam, Europe's Second Religion*, (Westport, CT: Praeger Publisher, 2002), 82.

[14] Ibid., 79-80.

[15] Maurizio Stefanini, "Le forme degli Islam nostrani [The Forms Of Our Islam]," *Limes*, Iss. 3 (2004), 116.

[16] A local survey conducted by the Veneto Region revealed that 38 percent of Muslims polled considered themselves practicing, while 36 percent considered themselves believing but not practicing. Eighty-one percent of those surveyed said they fasted during Ramadan, and 84.5 percent celebrated Eid al Fitr. As detailed in Andrea Spreafico, "La Presenza islamica in Italia [The Islamic Presence in Italy]," *Instrumenta* 25 (January-April 2005), http://ssai.interno.it/pubblicazioni/instrumenta/25/09%20-%20spreafico.pdf.

[17] *59th Report of CESIS (Executive Committee for the Intelligence and Security Services) to Parliament*, 71.

[18] Elena Dusi, "Il fantasma della Consulta," *Limes*, Iss. 4 (2007), 155.

[19] Bi-annual report of the security services to the Italian Senate, February 28, 2009. Pp. 56-7.

[20] Ibid., 58.

[21] "Maroni: In Italia cellule affiliate ad Al Qaeda [Maroni: In Italy Cells Linked To Al Qaeda]," *Apcom*, November 6, 2009.

[22] For an extensive analysis of *jihadist* networks in Italy, see Lorenzo Vidino, "Islam, Islamism and Jihadism in Italy," *Current Trends in Islamist Ideology* 7 (2008).

NETHERLANDS

QUICK FACTS

Population: 16,783,092

Area: 41,543 sq km

Ethnic Groups: Dutch 80.7%, EU 5%, Indonesian 2.4%, Turkish 2.2%, Surinamese 2%, Moroccan 2%, Netherlands Antilles and Aruba 0.8%, other 4.8%

Religions: Roman Catholic 30%, Dutch Reformed 11%, Calvinist 6%, other Protestant 3%, Muslim 5.8%, other 2.2, none 42%

Government Type: Constitutional Monarchy

GDP (official exchange rate): $783.3 billion

Map and Quick Facts courtesy of the CIA World Factbook (Last Updated July 2010)

The story of Islamism in the Netherlands revolves around migration and integration. Historically, the Netherlands was known for its religious tolerance. In the 17th and 18th centuries, the Republic of the United Provinces was a free haven for Jews and Protestants from across Europe. The Golden Age of the Republic has long since passed, however; in the early 19th century, the Republic turned into a monarchy, and in the 21st century religious tolerance is on the wane. The reasons are manifold, but at their core is a growing gap between political elites and the masses, and increasing atomization within society. This social transformation has allowed Islamists to push the political envelope and expose the value gap between the Dutch majority and its immigrant population.

ISLAMIST ACTIVITY

The General Intelligence and Security Service of the Netherlands (AIVD) began its reporting on domestic recruitment for *jihad* after it became clear that two young Moroccans linked to the al-Fourkaan mosque in Eindhoven were killed by Indian troops in Kashmir in January 2002. That December, the AIVD published a memo entitled *Recruitment for the Jihad in the Netherlands: From Incident to Trend.*[1] In it, the Service concluded that "the phenomenon of recruitments in the west for the violent Islamic war forms an intrinsic part of a globally spreading radical Islamic movement."[2] Based on their investigation, the AIVD deduced that Islamist recruitment in the Netherlands represents the "first tangible illustrations of a tendency, closely related to a stealthy entrance of a violent radical Islamic movement in Dutch society."[3] Finally, the Service concluded that "the Islamists involved are indeed aware of the 'favorable' polarizing effect of Islamist-inspired violent activities. Such violent activities promote the prejudices of the Dutch population about all Muslims. As a result thereof Muslims also increasingly get the idea that they are alienated from the Dutch society and the chance that they become susceptible to radical ideas becomes bigger."[4]

When Dutch politician Pim Fortuyn was murdered in 2003, the Dutch elite were relieved that the murderer was discovered to be a radical animal rights activist rather than an extremist Muslim. A year on, however, the November 2004 murder of filmmaker, politician and activist Theo Van Gogh revived the specter of Islamist militancy in the Netherlands. However, it was not al-Qaeda or another international Islamist terrorist movement that killed Van Gogh. Rather, the assailant, Mohammed Bouyeri, was a highly educated young man who grew up in the Netherlands and was radicalized there; a true homegrown terrorist. (Bouyeri was given a life sentence, and is now held in a maximum security prison.[5])

In the days after the murder of van Gogh, the situation in the Netherlands became tense. At least twelve mosques and two Islamic schools were torched; Molotov cocktails were thrown at a mosque and an explosion hit two Islamic schools linked to the radical Fourkaan Mosque in Eindhoven. In response, at least seven churches and six schools were torched.[6] These disturbances prompted the Dutch government to begin dealing in a new and more serious way with radical Islam in its permutations among the various Muslim communities within the country.

Turks

Turks make up the largest group of Muslims in the Netherlands. The majority are believed to be Sunni Muslims, although recent research suggests that about 40 percent of Turks in the Netherlands may in fact be Shi'ites of the Alevi school.[7] The main Muslim organizations within the Turkish community are Diyanet, which is run by the Turkish Ministry of Religious Affairs, and the non-governmental Milli Görüs movement, which has its headquarters in Cologne, Germany.[8] When surveyed in 2000, Diyanet controlled 130 mosques, and the Milli Görüs 43.[9]

The Turkish government was for decades hostile to the Islamist and German-based Milli Görüs. The group was never under the control of the secular Turkish government, which historically was suspicious of its Islamist tendencies. Milli Görüs was never explicitly active in Dutch politics but retains a power base within the closed Turkish community, and their influence continues to grow. More recently, Milli Görüs has become more politically active and is participating in pro-Gaza and anti-Israel demonstrations.

In recent years, and especially since the Justice and Development Party (AKP) came to power in Turkey in 2002, the differences between government-controlled Diyanet and the Milli Görüs have begun to evaporate. Both groups have now been likened to the Turkish version of the Muslim Brotherhood. In the Netherlands, both Diyanet and the Milli Görüs are cooperating in umbrella organizations like the Council for Mosques (Raad voor Moskeeën) or the Contact Body Muslims (with the) Government (Contactorgaan Moslims Overheid).[10] The German leadership of Milli Görüs is now under investigation by German authorities for embezzlement of funds and other criminal charges, and also for support of terrorist organizations.[11] This case likely will have spillover implications for the Dutch Milli Görüs organization.

The Kaplan or *Teblig* movement is an offshoot of Milli Görüs. In the Netherlands, it controls three mosques and is headquartered in the southeastern town of Oss. The movement is also called the *Kalifat* movement—a reflection of its aim to restore the old Ottoman Caliphate. Its tone is far more radical than that of Milli Görüs. The group is known to have received money from Middle Eastern sources, specifically from radical Egyptian cleric Yusuf Qaradawi, who has long been connected to the Muslim Brotherhood.[12] *Teblig's* leader, Metin Kaplan, was convicted by a German court for incitement to murder in November 2002, and served a four year sentence. He was subsequently extradited to Turkey, where he was sentenced to life in prison for planning to violently overthrow the Turkish government.[13] The *Teblig* movement historically has not been strong in the Netherlands, however, and since the imprisonment of its leader the organization has experienced difficulty obtaining financing.

The radical pan-Islamist organization Hizb ut-Tahrir (HuT) has its main following among highly educated young Turkish men. The group is especially strong in the Rotterdam area, but its number of followers is assessed to be in the low hundreds. In mid-2009, the country's National Coordinator for Counter Terrorism reported that the HuT was trying to extend its influence in the Netherlands and that their main vehicle was the Amsterdam Islamic student organization Al Furqan.[14]

Moroccans

A number of dynamics may be having a negative effect on the integration of the Moroccan community into Dutch society. In its 2001 annual report, the Dutch National Security Service outlined that "a key question is whether the Moroccan representatives and interest organizations... actually represent the group they claim to represent and whether they are using hidden agendas. Such a hidden agenda might be dictated by the Moroccan government or by certain political, religious or other interests."[15] "[F]or nationalist and mainly financial reasons," the report concluded, "the Moroccan government still does not want to loosen its grip on the Moroccans abroad."[16]

After 9/11, it was determined that a small number of Dutch citizens were willing to actively support or carry out violent terrorist activities, and that most of them were Moroccans. On the surface, this group appeared to have integrated in Dutch society, but "some turn[ed] out to have such radical, anti-Dutch and anti-western ideas that they are willing to participate in violent terrorist activities," the AIVD wrote in its 2002 Annual Report.[17] The radicalization within the Moroccan community is said to develop not only within mosques but also in homes.

The Moroccan Arrahmane mosque in Amsterdam has become the headquarters of the Tablighi Jamaat in the Netherlands. The Tablighis normally urge others to convert to their ultra-orthodox version of the Islamic faith, and are in principle an apolitical movement. The AIVD saw reasons for concern, however, "because the Jamaat Al-Tabligh Wal-Dawa may further the social isolation and radicalisation of segments of the Moroccan community."[18] Within the Arrahmane mosque a power struggle is being fought today between the mosque's executive committee and a group of "moderate Muslims" who object to the Tabigh preaching at their mosque. The executive committee defends the organization's weekly use of the mosque by arguing that it was bought with money from donors from Saudi-Arabia, Qatar and the United Arab Emirates who support the Tabligh.[19] In recent years, the Tabligh has been seen more and more as an incubator for aspirant terrorists. Recruits are rumored to have used the Tabligh to get from European countries into Pakistan, where they were then picked up and disappeared into the Federal Administered Tribal Areas to be trained in *jihadi* training camps.[20]

Salafis

From the mid-1980s until 2001, Salafism was able to build its infrastructure in the Netherlands largely without hindrance.[21] Forty percent of Dutch mosques are Moroccan, and Salafis are estimated to have access to around 30 percent of those—or around 15 percent of all Dutch mosques.[22] Salafi lectures at these institutions generally draw around 100 people apiece.[23] Salafi centers are the main places of radicalization in the Netherlands and the main centers of Salafism are the el-Tawheed mosque in Amsterdam, al-Waqf al-Islami (al-Fourkaan mosque) in Eindhoven, the as-Sunnah mosque in The Hague and the Islamic Foundation for Education and Transmission of Knowledge (ISOOK) in Tilburg.[24] *Imams* at these mosques preach a radical Islamist creed aimed at young Muslims, according to the AIVD, and "create a climate of intolerance within which these young people may become susceptible to radicalization and even to recruitment for the *jihad.*"[25]

The al-Fourkaan mosque in Eindhoven is the oldest Salafi institution in the Netherlands and many prominent orthodox Muslim leaders have emerged from it. Ahmad Salam, the most influential Salafi preacher in the Netherlands (who likewise has a following in Germany) was an *imam* and trustee of the al-Fourkaan mosque before he founded his own mosque (ISOOK) in Tilburg. Mohammed Cheppih, the founder of the Poldermosque in Amsterdam and chairman of the Dutch chapter of the Muslim World League, also has a connection to the al-Fourkaan mosque, with his father serving as a trustee. Yahia Bouyafa, the leader of the Muslim Brotherhood in the Netherlands, was once a trustee of the Foundation for Islamic Elementary Schools in Eindhoven which is linked to *al-Waqf al-Islami*. One of the influential young Salafi preachers in the Fourkaan mosque is the Dutch convert Abdul-Jabbar van de Ven, who was an inspiration to Jason Walters, one of the members of the Hofstad group, the primary homegrown *jihadi* group in the Netherlands.

The leaders of the mosques in The Hague, Amsterdam, and Tilburg together form the board of the Foundation for the Islamic Committee for Ahl-Sunnah in Europe. This foundation is part of a European network of political Salafis which is run from Saudi Arabia by the Syrian Salafi leader Adnan al-Arour.[26] Arour spoke a few times during "Islamic conferences" at the ISOOK mosque in Tilburg and in the al-Fourkaan mosque in Eindhoven. The conferences at the al-Fourkaan mosque were attended in 1999 by half-a-dozen members of the so-called September 11th "Hamburg cell" and their inner circle.[27] Another mosque rumored to have been visited by at least three of the 9/11 hijackers—Ramzi Binalshib, Mohammed Atta and Marwan al-Shehhi—in mid-1999 is the El-Tawheed mosque in Amsterdam.[28] Two young men who were attending services in the al-Fourkaan mosque were killed in Kashmir in 2002. One was a son of one of board members of the mosque.[29] One of the board members of *al-Waqf al-Islami* which controls the Fourkaan mosque is Adil Hamad Abderrahman al-Husayni, mentioned in the "Golden Chain" document of possible funders to al-Qaeda.[30]

Salafis appear to have made a strategic decision not to undermine their standing in the Netherlands by insisting that potential *jihadists* not conduct their activities within Europe. Interestingly, the Salafi mosques have a multinational membership base, in contrast to many of the regular Moroccan or Turkish mosques. Muslims from Pakistan, Afghanistan, Turkey, the Middle East, North Africa, the Horn of Africa and Dutch converts all visit the Salafi centers.[31]

In the face of government pressure, a change in tactics is taking place among Salafists in the Netherlands. There is evidence that a new generation of Salafi preachers is being trained, with a clear goal: they emphasize *dawa* (proselytization) and want to expand the faith among non-practicing Muslims. These young "traveling" Salafi preachers hold frequent lectures in 30-40 mosques and youth centers.[32] And their audience is growing. According to the U.S. intelligence community, "[t]he number of locations, lectures and active preaching at least doubled between 2005 and the first half of 2007."[33] Salafists also have been known to take over more moderate and loosely organized Moroccan mosques. They are willing to sow discord within the mosque, drive out *imams* and eventually take over when they are strong enough.[34] This new generation of preachers is often born and raised in the Netherlands and preach in Dutch, giving them a large advantage in reaching Dutch converts.

The Muslim Brotherhood

Although not a grassroots movement in the Netherlands, the Muslim Brotherhood is growing in power. Most of this growth can be attributed to its chairman in the Netherlands, Yahia Bouyafa.[35] Around 2006, Bouyafa was able to convince authorities in the Slotervaart quarter in Amsterdam to allow him build a mosque.[36] This is the first mosque of the Federation of Islamic Organizations in the Netherlands (FION), the umbrella organization of the Muslim Brotherhood in the Netherlands.[37]

The Muslim Brotherhood in the Netherlands is growing in influence, supported by the organization's European umbrella, the Federation of Islamic Organizations in Europe (FIOE). The personal ambitions of chairman Bouyafa appear to be to gain more political influence and take over the representation of the Muslim community in the Netherlands. With the help of the Europe Trust (the European financial vehicle of the Muslim Brotherhood based in Birmingham, England), its Dutch spin-off, the Europe Trust Netherlands, was able to buy its own real estate in The Hague and begin the construction of a mosque in Amsterdam.[38] In both cases, the sources of funding for these projects, over two million Euros, went undisclosed.

As part of his political ambitions, Bouyafa has worked to become chairman of one of the two government-approved organizations that represent Muslims in a dialogue with the government. Bouyafa is currently the chairman of the heterogeneous Contact Group Islam (CGI). This group was created as a counterweight to the Sunni-dominated Contact Body Muslims Government (CMO). The CGI was to represent Shi'a Muslims, Alawites, Ahmadiyya and Sufi groups, but after the Bouyafa took over it too came under Sunni control. The CMO is highly influenced by the Turkish Milli Görüs. Now both organizations that represent Muslims in a dialogue with the Dutch government are Sunni-dominated and highly influenced by Muslim Brotherhood ideology.

ISLAMISM AND SOCIETY

According to one assessment of Islam in the Netherlands, "Whereas today many of the Dutch majority population support the idea of migrants adopting Dutch norms and values, the migrants themselves aspire to a combination of independent cultural development."[39] But it has become increasingly evident that the value gap between the Dutch majority and the migrant minority is significantly greater than in other countries. While "[t]he majority have developed remarkably uniform, progressive ideals," a significant conservative Muslim immigrant minority has not—placing it in conflict with broader Dutch society. As a result, the country as a whole "is losing its ability to cope with cultural differences."[40]

In 2004, the country's official statistics bureau estimated that there were nearly one million Muslims residing in the Netherlands, accounting for 5.8 percent of the total population.[41] In 2007, these estimates were revised downward, to 857,000 Muslims or 5 percent of the total population.[42] These numbers, however, account only for those Muslims legally in the Netherlands; the illegal population is much harder to quantify, but is believed to be in the thousands.[43]

The two largest groups of Muslims in the Netherlands are Turks (nearly 325,000, or 38 percent) and Moroccans (over 260,000, or 31 percent). Other large groups of Muslims come from Suriname (34,000), Afghanistan (31,000), Iraq (27,000), Somalia (20,000), Pakistan (18,000), Iran (12,000), and Egypt (12,000). Lastly, the number of native Dutch that are Muslim stands at around 12,000. This group consists of converts and children belonging to second-generation Muslims with a foreign background.[44]

The number of mosques in the Netherlands is estimated to be around 550.[45] The mosques are identified by nation. The Turkish mosques number 211, followed by the Moroccan mosques with a total of 150. Smaller numbers of mosques are associated with Suriname (35), Pakistan (10), Somalia and Sudan (10), Afghanistan (5), Bosnia (5), the Moluccan islands and Indonesia (5), Egypt (3) and Tunisia (1).[46] Notably, most Dutch mosques and Islamic organizations are organized by ethnicity, which raises questions about whether there is an organized "Muslim community" in the Netherlands, or in fact several.[47]

ISLAMISM AND THE STATE

After the murder of film director and activist Theo van Gogh in 2004, the Dutch government increased its pressure on Salafi centers in the Netherlands. Public prosecutors didn't find enough evidence to close these centers outright, so the Dutch government launched a program to disrupt them as much as possible.[48] Three *imams* of the al-Fourkaan mosque were declared *personae non grata* and deported from the country. The government strategy remains to isolate dangerous radicals, disrupt radicalization and identify radical activities at an early stage and address them. Another goal of the government is to strengthen the voice of moderate Muslims that resist radicalization, and to strengthen the bonds between Muslim immigrants and Dutch society, particularly its democratic political system.[49]

The attacks on the Madrid mass transit system in 2004, and the disorganized European approach that followed, were the primary reasons for the Dutch government to jumpstart its policies against terrorism. A new body, the National Coordinator for Counter Terrorism (NCTb), was created, tasked with a clear mission: "to minimize the risk of terrorist attacks in the Netherlands and to take prior measures to limit the potential impact of terrorist acts. The NCTb is responsible for the central coordination of counterterrorism efforts and ensures that cooperation between the parties involved is and remains of a high standard."[50] The main focus of the NCTb became de-radicalization, and one of its first major projects became an operation in which the different government and law enforcement agencies began to "disrupt" the work of the main Salafi centers in the Netherlands.[51]

This effort was part of the larger project of de-radicalization applied domestically by the Dutch government.[52] De-radicalization is also being promoted through the use of law enforcement officials and social workers familiar with local conditions in various towns and villages. Such an approach, however, has proved to have limited utility; most of the radicalization in the Netherlands is known to happen in small study groups at home and through the Internet.[53]

According to the latest, December 2009, report of the AIVD, there have been some successes in the fight against Islamism in the Netherlands, but de-radicalization efforts can boast far less progress. A core of motivated potential *jihadis* in the Netherlands remains, and could become active at any time.[54] The AIVD also sees signs of a recent stagnation of the Salafist movement in the Netherlands, but it is as yet too early to report a real, sustained change in the trend.[55]

ENDNOTES

[1]AIVD, *Recruitment for the Jihad in the Netherlands*. From Incident to Trend, Leidschendam, December 3, 2002, https://www.aivd.nl//english/publications/aivd-publications/@6264/recruitment-for-the

[2]Ibid.

[3]Ibidem.

[4] Ibidem.

[5] "Van Gogh Killer Jailed For Life," BBC (London), July 26, 2005, http://news.bbc.co.uk/2/hi/europe/4716909.stm.

[6] Ministry of the Interior and Kingdom Relations, National Crisis Centrum, *Situation Report* NCC2004/81492/nr.1, November 10, 2004; NCC2004/81492/nr.2, November 11, 2004; NCC2004/81759/nr.3; November 12, 2004; November 13, 2004; NCC2004/81759/nr.4, November 15, 2004; NCC2004/81759/nr.6, November 16, 2004; NCC2004/82039/nr.7, November 23, 2004; NCC2004/82663/nr.11, November 26, 2004; NCC2004/83053/nr.12, November 30, 2004; "Golf van aanslagen sinds dood Van Gogh," *Brabants Dagblad*, November 2004, http://www.brabantsdagblad.nl/algemeen/bdbinnenland/terreur//article28503.ece.

[7] Anja van Heelsum, Meindert Fennema and Jean Tillie, "Moslim in Nederland: Islamitische organisaties in Nederland," Sociaal Cultureel Planbureau (SCP) *werkdocument* 106, July 2004, 11-12.

[8] Nico Landman, *Van mat tot minaret: De institutionalisering van de islam in Nederland* (Amsterdam 1992), 80-82.

[9] Toine Heijmans, "Minaretten in de polder," *De Volkskrant*, April 29, 2000.

[10] Heelsum, Fennema and Tillie, *Moslim in Nederland*, 16.

[11] "Kölner Islam-Funktionär unter Verdacht," WDR, March 20, 2009, http://www.wdr.de/themen/panorama/26/koeln_ermittlungen_islamfunktionaer/index.jhtml; Helmut Frangenberg, „Ermittlungen gegen Islam- Funktionäre," *Kölner Stadt-Anzeiger*, March 20, 2009, http://www.ksta.de/html/artikel/1233584156089.shtml.

[12] Personal communication from senior European Intelligence official, early 2007.

[13] "Profile: The Caliph of Cologne," BBC (London), May 27, 2004; http://news.bbc.co.uk/2/hi/europe/1705886.stm.

[14] NCTb, Tenth Counterterrorism progress report, 5602436/09, June 19, 2009, 3-4.

[15] National Security Service (BVD), Annual Report 2001, 17; Landman, *Van mat tot minaret*, 160-161.

[16] National Security Service (BVD), Annual Report 2001, 17.

[17] General Intelligence and Security Service (AIVD), Annual Report 2002, 27.

[18] Ibid., 25.

[19] Jaco Alberts, "Marokkanen willen 'hun' moskee terug," *NRC Handelsblad*, September 20, 2003.

[20] See, for example, Omar Nasiri, *Inside the Jihad: My life with Al Qaeda* (Cambridge: Basic Books, 2006), 109-115.

[21] National Coordinator for Counterterrorism (NCTb), *Salafism in the Netherlands. A passing phenomenan or a persistent factor of significance?* (The Hague, March 2008), 25-26.

[22] Ibid.

[23] NCTb, 7e voortgangsrapportage terrorismebestrijding, November 26, 2007, 5516003/07/NCTb, p. 5

[24] National Coordinator for Counterterrorism, *Salafism in the Netherlands.*

[25] General Intelligence and Security Service (AIVD), Annual Report 2003, 24.

[26] Chamber of Commerce, dossier number 34153259; National Coordinator for Counterterrorism (NCTb), *Salafism in the Netherlands*, 31.

[27] Ian Johnson and Crawford, "A Saudi Group Spreads Extremism in 'Law' seminars, Taught in Dutch," *Wall Street Journal*, April 16, 2003.

[28] "Official: Terrorists Met in Amsterdam," Associated Press, September 13, 2002.

[29] AIVD, *Saudi influences in the Netherlands. Links between the Salafist mission, radicalisation processes and Islamic terrorism*, 2004; Chamber of Commerce, Foundation Waqf, dossier number 41091392.

[30] Chamber of Commerce, dossier number 41091392; Tareek Osama, file number 41 (Golden Chain document).

[31] National Coordinator for Counterterrorism (NCTb), *Salafism in the Netherlands*, 29.

[32] Ibid., 32, 37.

[33] Ibidem, 40.

[34] Ibidem.

[35] Janny Groen and Annieke Kranenberg, "Bouyafa met argusogen bekeken," *De Volkskrant*, December 21, 2009, http://www.volkskrant.nl/binnenland/article1329605.ece/Bouyafa_met_argusogen_bekeken

[36] Moskee Moslim Broederschap in Slotervaart vormt geen gevaar, April 21, 2009, http://allochtonen.web-log.nl/allochtonen/2009/04/moskee-moslim-b.html; "FION announces building of Mosque in Slotervaart (in Arabic)," March 2008, http://www.islamonline.net/arabic/arts/2008/03/01.pdf; "SP wil opheldering ove FION moskee in Slotervaart," February 16, 2009; http://allochtonen.web-log.nl/allochtonen/2009/02/sp-wil-ophelder.html.

[37] Ronald Sandee, *The Influence of the Muslim Brotherhood in the Netherlands*, NEFA Foundation, December 2007, http://www1.nefafoundation.org/miscellaneous/nefambnetherlands1207.pdf

[38] Joost de Haas, "MOSLIMBROEDERS RUKKEN OP; Peper-

duur pand aangekocht voor nieuw 'hoofdkwartier' in Den Haag? 'Achterliggend doel is invoering van sharia' 'Ze zien er niet uit als extremisten,'" *De Telegraaf* (Amsterdam), May 31, 2008; See also *Answers of the mayor of Amsterdam to questions of the Amsterdam city council*, February 19, 2009, http://biodata.asp4all.nl/andreas/2009/09012f978057b028/09012f978057b028.pdf.

[39] Jan Willem Duyvendak, Trees Pels and Rally Rijkschroeff, "A Multicultural paradise? The cultural factor in Dutch integration policy," Paper presented at the 3rd ECPR Conference, Budapest, Hungary, September 8-10, 2005, 7.

[40] Ibid.

[41] "Nearly one million Muslims in the Netherlands," CBS Statistics Netherlands *Web Magazine*, September 20, 2004 http://www.cbs.nl/en-GB/menu/themas/bevolking/publicaties/artikelen/archief/2004/2004-1543-wm.htm.

[42] "More than 850 thousand Muslims in the Netherlands," CBS Statistics Netherlands *Web Magazine*, October 25, 2007, http://www.cbs.nl/en-GB/menu/themas/bevolking/publicaties/artikelen/archief/2007/2007-2278-wm.htm; Marieke van Herten and Freddy Otten, "Naar een nieuwe schatting van het aantal islamieten in Nederland," CBS, Bevolkingstrends, 3e Kwartaal 2007.

[43] Sheila Kamerman, "Illegal Aliens like Helen can't hack it in the Netherlands," *NRC Handelsblad*, February 11, 2010, http://www.nrc.nl/international/Features/article2481118.ece/Illegal_aliens_like_Helen_cant_hack_it_in_the_Netherlands

[44] "More than 850 thousand Muslims in the Netherlands."

[45] NCTb, 7e voortgangsrapportage terrorismebestrijding, November 26, 2007, 5516003/07/NCTb, 5.

[46] Heijmans, "Minaretten in de polder."

[47] Heelsum, Fennema, Tillie, "Moslim in Nederland," 3.

[48] NCTb, Derde Voortgangsrapportage terrorismebestrijding, December 5, 2005, 5388583/05/NCTb.

[49] Ibid.; Minstry of Justice, Nota radicalisme en radicalisering, August 19, 2005; 5358374/05/AJS.

[50] National Coordinator for Counter Terrorism of the Netherlands, "About the NCTb," n.d., http://english.nctb.nl/organisation/about_the_NCTb/.

[51] NCTb, Derde Voortgangsrapportage terrorismebestrijding, December 5, 2005, 5388583/05/NCTb; Minstry of Justice, Nota radicalisme en radicalisering, August 19, 2005; 5358374/05/AJS.

[52] Ministry of Justice and Ministry of Interior, Operationeel Actieplan Polarisatie en radicalisering 2007-2011, August 27, 2007, http://www.tweedekamer.nl/images/297540141bijlage01_118-182859.pdf.

[53] Ministry of Justice of The Netherlands, "Court has ruled in case of Hofstad group suspects," March 10, 2006, http://www.rechtspraak.

nl/Gerechten/Rechtbanken/s-Gravenhage/Actualiteiten/Rechtbank
+heeft+uitspraak+gedaan+in+zaken+verdachten+Hofstadgroep.htm;
Janny Groen and Annieke Kranenberg, *Strijdsters van Allah, Radicale moslima's en het Hofstadnetwerk* (Amsterdam: J.M. Meulenhoff, 2006) 69-99, 127-137.

[54] AIVD, *Lokale jihadistische netwerken in Nederland. Veranderingen in het dreigingsbeeld*, December 2009, https://www.aivd.nl/actueel/nieuw-op-de-site/dreiging-lokale.

[55] AIVD, *Actuele trends en ontwikkelingen van het Salafisme in Nederland. Weerstand en Tegenkracht*, December 2009, https://www.aivd.nl/@124762/rapport-'weerstand.

DENMARK

QUICK FACTS

Population: 5,515,575

Area: 43,094 sq km

Ethnic Groups: Scandinavian, Inuit, Faroese, German, Turkish, Iranian, Somali

Religions: Evangelical Lutheran 95%, other Christian (includes Protestant and Roman Catholic) 3%, Muslim 2%

Government Type: Constitutional monarchy

GDP (official exchange rate): $311.9 billion

Map and Quick Facts courtesy of the CIA World Factbook (Last Updated July 2010)

Since the September 2005 publication in the Danish daily Jyllands-Posten of 12 cartoons that were widely perceived as depictions of the Prophet Mohammad, Denmark has become a prime target of al-Qaeda and like-minded groups. From 2009 through 2010, three separate plots against the Jyllands-Posten, and another against one of its cartoonists, were successfully thwarted. In June 2008, the Danish embassy in Islamabad was attacked with a car bomb.

The history of militant Islamism in Denmark, however, dates back to the 1990s, when veterans of the Afghan jihad against the Soviet Union found safe haven there. Today, violent Islamism in Denmark remains far from a well-organized domestic phenomenon, although there have been notable instances of homegrown extremism among Danish Muslims, with individuals connecting to—and even joining—foreign militant movements such as al-Qaeda. In the main, however, violent Islamists are few in number, and vastly outnumbered by non-violent Islamist groups which themselves are increasingly disconnected from international organizations.

ISLAMIST ACTIVITY

Militant Islamism in Denmark dates back to the 1990s, when several former *mujahideen* from the Soviet-Afghan war (1980-89) found safe haven there. One of the most prominent personalities in this group was an Egyptian, Talaat Fouad Qassem aka Abu Talal (1957-1995), who was a high ranking member of the militant Egyptian group *al-Gamaat al-Islamiyya*.[1] In 1982, Abu Talal was sentenced to seven years imprisonment in Egypt for his alleged role in the assassination of Egyptian President Anwar Sadat. He escaped during a prison transfer in 1989, and in 1992 an Egyptian court sentenced him to death *in absentia*.[2] In 1989, he had gone to Afghanistan, where he joined the anti-Soviet *mujahideen* and his personal acquaintance, Ayman al-Zawahiri. In 1992, he migrated to Denmark, where he was granted political asylum in three years later.[3]

Abu Talal was extremely well-connected to international *jihadists*. He had close ties to Egyptian cleric Omar Abdel Rahman, the "blind sheikh" who was an unindicted co-conspirator in the 1993 bombing of the World Trade Center, who visited Denmark twice in 1990 and 1991 respectively.[4] Investigations of the WTC attack revealed that three other Egyptians residing in Denmark—and part of the same group as Abu Talal—were directly related to the perpetrators of this attack.[5] Abu Talal was also well connected to Anwar Shabaan,[6] head of Milan's controversial Islamic Cultural Institute, which has been the subject of terrorist investigations since the 1990s. Abu Talal is believed to have been the victim of an early form of "rendition" when he was intercepted in 1995 in Croatia by U.S. intelligence while on his way to Bosnia. He was apparently sent back to Egypt, where he subsequently disappeared.[7]

Another prominent member of this first generation of *jihadists* was Danish-Moroccan Said Mansour (b. 1960). Mansour hosted Omar Abdel Rahman during one of his visits to Denmark. As an ardent supporter of the Algerian terrorist group GIA, and involved in the distribution of their newsletter *Al Ansar*, Mansour was also affiliated with the notorious London-based terrorist Abu Qatada. Mansour ran a publishing house, Al Nur Islamic Information, through which he disseminated material inciting Muslims to violence. (Materials from Al Nur was subsequently found worldwide at locations related to terrorist investigations in Germany, Italy, Spain, Belgium and the U.S.).[8] In 2007, Mansour was convicted by a Danish court of "incitement to violence," and imprisoned for two years. He was released in 2009.

After 9/11, a new iteration of militant Islamism appeared in Denmark. In contrast to the first generation embodied by Abu Talal and Mansour, this second generation is primarily "internal" in nature, and often includes first-generation Danes. For some years now, the Taiba mosque in the northwestern part of Copenhagen has been the center of a subculture of young men supportive of militant Islamism. Some of these individuals were acquainted with Said Mansour, who used to attend the mosque. Young men from this group have been involved in two cases leading to convictions under the Danish anti-terrorism legislation: the Glostrup case, with linkages to al-Muhajiroun in London, and the Glasvej case, tied to al-Qaeda in Pakistan.

The Glostrup case—also known as the Sarajevo case—started in October 2005 when a Bosnian-Swede and a Danish-Turk, both part of the Taiba mosque group, were arrested in Bosnia in possession of explosives. They were later convicted, along with two others, of planning a terrorist attack at an undisclosed location. Some of their associates in Copenhagen were arrested a week later. Three Danish citizens of Arabic backgrounds, and a Bosnian who had grown up in Denmark, were subsequently put on trial; one was convicted, while the others were acquitted. Notably, the group was well connected internationally. In 2005, some of the young men had visited Omar Bakri Muhammed, the leader of *al-Muhajiroun* in London. In the UK, the young Danes also had online contacts to Younis Tsoulis AKA "Irhabi007" (al-Qaeda's "web-master" in London), Tariq al-Daour (Abu Dudjana), and Wasim Ahmad Mughal, all of whom were later convicted for terrorism.[9] Furthermore, members of the Glostrup group had online contacts to two individuals subsequently convicted of terrorism in the U.S.: Ehsamul Islam Sadequee and Said Harris Ahmed.[10]

The Glasvej case, on the other hand, had direct links to al-Qaeda in Pakistan.[11] In 2007, a Danish-Pakistani traveled to Pakistan, where he linked up with people from the Red Mosque (*Lal Masjid*) in Islamabad. There, he reportedly met up with a high-ranking "al Qaeda facilitator" who helped him gain access to a terrorist training camp in North Waziristan.[12] Upon his return to Denmark, he and an Afghan friend began to produce explosives. In September 2007, the two men (along with some of their friends) were arrested by Danish authorities, and in October 2008 were convicted for producing explosives and conspiring to commit an act of terrorism at an undisclosed location.

Another locus of Islamist militancy is Aarhus, the second largest city in Denmark.[13] The only Danish detainee at Guantánamo Bay—Danish-Algerian Slimane Abderrahmane—lived there. In the wake of the so-called "cartoon crisis," Aarhus has been the site of several plots against the *Jyllands-Posten* newspaper, which is published there. Moreover, the most controversial of the cartoonists involved in the scandal resided there at one time. In February 2008, in an incident soon to be known as the "Tunisian case," two Tunisians were arrested and detained under suspicion of preparing an attack against the cartoonist in question, Kurt Vestergaard. The Tunisians were administratively expelled from the country on "secret evidence" presented to the court by the Danish intelligence service. However, due to human rights concerns, they were not repatriated back to Tunisia; one left Denmark for an undisclosed Middle Eastern country, while the other was acquitted in 2010 following a closed trial. Since the case was not carried out in open court, little is known of their links to Islamists abroad.

Subsequently, on January 1, 2010, a Danish-Somali forced his way into the residence of cartoonist Kurt Vestergaard with an axe. The man was arrested on location, and in February 2011 was convicted for the attack under Danish terrorism legislation. Beforehand, the plaintiff had been to Somalia where, according to the Danish security and intelligence service, he had close connections to Somalia's *al-Shabaab* and al-Qaeda elements in East Africa.[14] He had subsequently returned to Denmark in 2008, where he recruited and raised money for *al-Shabaab* in both Denmark and Sweden.[15] In 2009, he was preventatively detained in Kenya prior to a visit there of U.S. Secretary of State Hillary Clinton. Nothing, however, indicates that he was directly related to a specific plot against Mrs. Clinton.

A final locus of internal Islamist militancy is the city of Odense. In 2007, three men—a Danish-Syrian, an Iraqi Kurd and a Danish-born convert to Islam—were convicted in the Vollsmose case for conspiring to commit an act of terrorism at an unspecified location. A bottle of explosives as well as metal splinters and ammonium nitrate had been discovered at various locations. There was no clear evidence, however, that the group had acquired militant experience abroad or had established connections to any Islamist organization.

Ever since the outbreak of the cartoon crisis in 2005, and the subsequent republication of the cartoons by several Danish newspapers in 2008, Denmark has become a prime target of foreign militant organizations, including of al-Qaeda and like-minded groups (*Lashkar-e Taiba*, AQIM, AQAP, and *al-Shabaab*), as well as of autonomous cells operating in Europe.

- David Coleman Headley, a U.S. citizen of Pakistani origin involved in planning the 2008 Mumbai attack, pleaded guilty in March 2010 to planning an attack against employees at the *Jyllands-Posten*. Headley had been befriended by both Hafiz Muhammad Saeed—the titular head of the Pakistani terrorist group *Lashkar-e Taiba*—and Ilyas Kashmiri, a member of the al-Qaeda-linked Pakistani group *Harkat al-Jihad ul-Islami*. In the U.S., Headley cooperated with Tahawwur Hussain Rana, a

Canadian citizen of Pakistani decent who financed Headley and provided him with false identification. Headley traveled twice to Copenhagen, where he took photographs of his intended target, the *Jyllands-Posten*. His plot included the beheading of employees at the paper. Headley was arrested in October 2009 in Chicago before he was able to carry out his plan.

- In September 2010, a Chechen-born Belgian citizen traveled to Denmark, carrying a bomb that inadvertently went off in his hotel. The Belgian was arrested and later charged for terrorism because, the prosecution has charged, the bomb was intended for the *Jyllands-Posten*. No connection to an organized militant group has so far been revealed; the trial was slated to begin in May 2011.

- In December 2010, a Tunisian living in Sweden and two Swedish citizens of Arabic extraction were arrested on the outskirts of Copenhagen. Yet another Swedish citizen of Tunisian decent was subsequently arrested in Sweden. According to Danish authorities, the suspects plotted to access *Jyllands-Posten's* office in Copenhagen and subsequently kill as many employees as possible. The Swedish group was well connected internationally. One of the suspects previously had been arrested in Pakistan; another had been arrested in Pakistan and Kenya on prior occasions.[16] Danish security officials will not rule out the possibility that the group had contact with David Headley, who himself had visited Sweden in 2008.[17]

Nevertheless, the number of Muslims in Denmark who actively support violent Islamism is limited. As of this writing, nine Danes or Danish residents have been convicted for terrorism related to Islamism since September 11, 2001. Militant Islamists are far outnumbered by Muslims involved in non-violent political groups. Some of these organizations, organized around a common Muslim identity, are very vocal and visible in public sphere.

Among the most controversial is *Hizb ut-Tahrir* (HuT). *Hizb ut-Tahrir* put down roots in Denmark in the mid-1980s,[18] although the Danish branch of the organization was not formally established until the mid-1990s.[19] British HuT members were instrumental in the establishment of the group's Danish contingent,[20] and the movement's Copenhagen leadership committee was subsequently elevated to head the group's regional affairs, as reflected in its current title "Hizb ut-Tahrir Scandinavia."[21] The organization has an estimated 150 active members, but attracts around 1,000-1,200 people at public meetings.[22]

Ideologically, it aims to reestablish a Caliphate in the Muslim world and therefore, unlike the classical Muslim Brotherhood, are against the modern notion of the "state." HuT considers democracy an un-Islamic invention, and urges Danish Muslims not to engage in politics or take part in elections. It does, however, seek to engage in debates with select intellectuals. The organization as a whole does not engage in violent activities, but supports "defensive *jihad*" in places such as Iraq or Afghanistan. The group's public meeting in January 2011 caused considerable controversy, as it endorsed continued resistance in Afghanistan, which was interpreted by many as encouragement to kill Danish soldiers serving there.[23] Former HuT spokesperson Fadi Abdullatif has been convicted twice for "threats, flagrant insults and incitement to murder" against Jews and former Danish prime minister (and current NATO Secretary General) Anders Fogh Rasmussen.[24] Various political parties have argued that HuT should be banned, however, in 2004, the Danish Attorney General ruled that there were no legal foundations for such a ban.[25]

Aside from Hizb ut-Tahrir, The Islamic Society (*Wakfl Islamisk Trossamfund*) is one of the most visible and vocal Islamic organizations in Denmark. In contrast to HuT, it was established by first generation immigrants as one of the various ethnic-religious organizations that manage and administer Muslim places of worship in Denmark. It has a broad constituency all over Denmark, and is active in the public sphere as well as on the political scene. Unlike Hizb ut-Tahrir, it has adopted a strategy of dialogue and participation in Danish society, formally cooperating with the Danish intelligence service on de-radicalization efforts. The Islamic Society has no formal ties to the Muslim Brotherhood in Egypt, but its worldview is somewhat infused by the group's ideology, albeit not in the classical form as it was articulated by Hassan al-Banna or Sayyid Qutb.[26] In April 2011, the youth organization of the Islamic society—*Munida*—caused a great stir by inviting the controversial Canadian Muslim preacher, Bilal Philips, to give a public speech in Copenhagen.

Yet another cluster of "domestic" Islamic groups is represented by The Muslim Council *(Muslimernes Fællesråd)*, an umbrella organization that unites 13 separate Muslim organizations. A group very active in the public debate is the Muslims in Dialogue (MID) that was established in 2003. Another organization that actively takes part in debates about identity politics, *sharia*, etc. is Critical Muslims. Like MID, Critical Muslims was established by the second generation of Muslims in Denmark and can—as the Muslim Council—be considered as a Muslim lobby-group. Hence, they intervene in public debates whenever sensitive issues related to Islam reach the top of the public agenda or proactively try to set the agenda on issues concerning the establishment of mosques, graveyards, Muslim eldercare, etc.

ISLAMISM AND SOCIETY

Muslim immigration to Denmark began in the 1960s, and proceeded in essentially two waves. During the 1960s and 1970s, immigrants from Turkey, Pakistan, North Africa and the former Yugoslavia came to Denmark to work. After the mid-1970s, a second wave of newcomers to the country was made up primarily of refugees, as well as the families of earlier immigrants who had stayed in Denmark. Conflicts in the Arab and Muslim world (including the Iran-Iraq war, as well as the civil wars in Lebanon, the former Yugoslavia, and Somalia) also prompted Muslim immigration to Denmark, as have the more recent wars in Afghanistan and Iraq.

While no official census of Muslims in Denmark exists, some preliminary data is available. Between 1999 and 2006, the proportion of Muslims in the total population grew from 2.9 percent to 3.8 percent (207,000[27]), as a result of a growing number of refugees from Iraq and Somalia, as well as family reunifications among Turkish and Pakistani immigrants.[28] Denmark's Muslim community is ethnically very diverse. The largest group are Turks (24.7 percent), followed by Iraqis, Lebanese and Pakistanis (11.7 percent, 10.7 percent and 8.3 percent, respectively).[29]

A precise estimate of the level of support for violent Islamist groups among Danish Muslims is difficult to obtain since—in contrast to the Swedish security service *Säpo*—the Danish intelligence service does not make such estimations public. Similarly, it is difficult to identify the reasons some Danish Muslims are attracted to violent Islamism; a general climate of Islamophobia in Denmark is often cited as one such cause, yet concrete evidence of such a surge in anti-Muslim sentiment is lacking.

It is, however, beyond doubt that since September 11, 2001, public debates on Islamism have become increasingly incendiary, culminating with the publication of 12 cartoons in the newspaper *Jyllands-Posten* in 2005. The year 2001 also coincided with the rise to power of a conservative government that—for the first time in Danish history—depended on parliamentary support from the country's anti-immigration and Islam-critical nationalist party, the Danish Peoples Party (DPP). The DPP has been instrumental in articulating a "struggle of values" against Islam, which it considers necessary in order to defend Christianity and "Danishness."[30] In public debates, Islamism has increasingly come to be framed as a security issue.[31] Successive ministers of foreign affairs have repeatedly maintained that Islamism constitutes "the most important totalitarian threat today."[32] Similarly, Muslim politicians who have tried to run for Parliament were, notwithstanding their protestations, accused of supporting *sharia* law, if not constituting a threat to Danish democracy outright. Most recently, no less than the newly-appointed

Minister for Integration declared that he had always been lukewarm towards the idea, since what was needed was, in fact, "assimilation."[33]

ISLAMISM AND THE STATE

Since the September 11, 2001 terrorist attacks, the Danish parliament has passed two Anti-Terrorism Acts (I and II), in 2002 and 2006 respectively.[34] The first Act *de facto* amended the Danish penal code by introducing a separate terrorism provision (Chapter 13, §114) that increased the punishment for a variety of previously-proscribed acts if carried out with the *intention* of "frightening a population," "unduly forc[ing] Danish or foreign authorities to act or abstain from acting," or destabilizing "the fundamental political, constitutional, economic or social structures of a country or an international organization."[35] The maximum sentence for committing an offense under the new terrorism provision was raised to life in prison.

The Anti-Terrorism Act also penalizes the act of providing financial services to terrorist groups. The fact that a group is included on the UN or the EU list of terrorist groups is not, in principle, enough to have it considered as such in a Danish trial, however; specific evidence must be produced in court. To date, there has been one conviction related to the financing of terrorism, albeit not in relation to an Islamist group (rather, support to Colombia's FARC). While a trial concerning financing for Hamas did take place, it did not lead to a conviction.[36] The Anti-Terrorism Act similarly equipped authorities with new tools to fight terrorism, including secret searches; the logging of telephone and Internet communications; easier access to computer-surveillance; expanded ability to refuse or withdraw residence permits, and so forth.

Following the July 7, 2005 subway bombings in London, Danish perceptions of the threat from militant Islamism changed, and the greatest danger is now seen as "homegrown." State antiterrorism policies soon focused on preventing the "radicalization" of Danish Muslims, leading to the establishment of a government "office for democratic community and the prevention of radicalization" under the country's Ministry of Integration. A working group, which included the aforementioned office, subsequently prepared a report—entitled *A Common and Safe Future: an Action-Plan for the Prevention of Extremist Attitudes and Radicalization*[37] —which was published in June 2008. It suggested a whole range of softer initiatives to deal *preventively* with the phenomenon of radicalization, including: courses on democracy and citizenship; role-model and mentor initiatives; focus on radicalization in the cooperation between schools, social authorities and police (SSP-cooperation); preventive talks with selected individuals; dialogue forums between the Danish Intelligence Service and selected *imams*; and formalized accreditation procedures for *imams* in Danish prisons. All of these initiatives are currently being implemented.

ENDNOTES

[1] Michael Taarnby, "Jihad in Denmark," Danish Institute for International Studies *DIIS Working Paper* 35, November 2006, p. 9. http://www.diis.dk/sw30537.asp.

[2] Ibid.

[3] Tribunale de Milano, "Ruling of Judge Presiding Over Preliminary Investigations," n.d., 44, http://www.washingtonpost.com/wp-srv/world/documents/milan_warrants.pdf.

[4] Taarnby, "Jihad in Denmark," 17; Uwe Max Jensen, "Aros a Terrorist Target?" *Nordjyske* (Aalborg), September 9, 2010, http://www.nordjyske.dk/ditnordjyske/forside.aspx?ctrl=10&data=53,3660259,2 825,3.

[5] See Manni Crone and Mona Sheikh, "Muslims as Danish Security Issues," in Jørgen S. Nielsen, ed., *Islam in Denmark* (London: Ashgate, forthcoming).

[6] Taarnby, "Jihad in Denmark," 17.

[7] Human Rights Watch, *Black Hole: The Fate of Islamists Rendered to Egypt,* May 9, 2005, http://www.hrw.org/en/node/11757/section/6; Claus Blok Thomsen, "CIA's første bortførte fange kom fra Danmark" [CIA's First Abducted Catch Came from Denmark], *Dagbladet Politiken* (Copenhagen), October 20, 2007, http://politiken.dk/indland/article399819.ece

[8] Søren Astrup, "Said Mansour Accepterer Dom" [Said Mansour Accepts Ruling], *Dagbladet Politiken* (Copenhagen), April 24, 2007, http://politiken.dk/indland/ECE290271/said-mansour-accepterer-dom; Taarnby, "Jihad in Denmark," 22.

[9] Author's personal notes from the 2008 trial of EIH at the Eastern High Court; See also Morten Skjoldager, *Truslen indefra: De danske terrorister* [The Threat Within: Danish Terrorists] (Copenhagen: Lindhardt & Ringhof, 2009).

[10] Author's personal notes from the 2008 trial of EIH at the Eastern High Court.

[11] At a press conference following the arrests, Danish security and intelligence service head Jakob Scharff maintained that the plot had "direct links to al Qaeda." See "BAGGRUND: Hvad handler Glasvej-sagen om?" [Background: What's the Glasvej Case About?], *Daglabet Politiken* (Copenhagen), August 11, 2008, http://politiken.dk/indland/fakta_indland/ECE550307/baggrund-hvad-handler-glasvej-sagen-om.

[12] Author's personal notes from the Glostrup trial.

[13] Lene Kühle and Lasse Lindekilde, "Radicalization among Young Muslims in Aarhus," Aarhus University Centre for Studies on Islamism and Radicalization, January 2010, http://ps.au.dk/fileadmin/site_files/filer_statskundskab/subsites/cir/radicalization_aarhus_FINAL.pdf.

[14] Claus Blok Thomsen, Bo Maltesen and Jesper Strudsholm, "Drabssigtet var indblandet i terrorsag i Kenya" [Murder Aim was Implicated in Terrorist Case in Kenya], *Dagbladet Politiken* (Copenhagen), January 2, 2010, http://politiken.dk/indland/ECE871906/drabssigtet-var-indblandet-i-terrorsag-i-kenya.

[15] Elisabeth Arnsdorf Haslund, "Rollemodel og islamistisk øksemand" [Role model and Islamist Hatchet Man], *Berlingske* (Copenhagen), January 18, 2011, http://www.b.dk/danmark/rollemodel-og-islamistisk-oeksemand.

[16] "Svenske terrorsigtede er gamle kendinge" [Swedish Terror Accused is old Acquaintances], *Berlingske* (Copenhagen), http://www.b.dk/danmark/svenske-terrorsigtede-er-gamle-kendinge.

[17] "Terrorsag trækker tråde til Headley-sag" [Terrorist Case Pulls Threads for Headley Case], TV2, December 20, 2010, http://nyhederne-dyn.tv2.dk/article.php/id-36155559:terrorsag-tr%C3%A6kker-tr%C3%A5de-til-headleysag.html.

[18] Jean-Francois Mayer, "Hizb ut-Tahrir: l'évolution d'un parti islamiste transnational en Occident," in Samir Amghar, ed., *Islamismes d'Occident* (Paris: Éditions lignes de repères, 2006).

[19] Kirstine Sinclair, "The Caliphate as Homeland: Hizb ut-Tahrir in Denmark and Britain," doctoral dissertation, University of Southern Denmark, 2010, 12.

[20] Ed Husain, *The Islamist* (London: Penguin, 2008).

[21] Sinclair, "The Caliphate as Homeland," 12.

[22] Ulla Abildtrup, "Forsker: Hizb ut-Tahrir stagnerer" [Researcher: Hizb ut-Tahrir Stagnates], *DR*, November 16, 2010, http://www.dr.dk/Nyheder/Indland/2010/11/10/113614.htm.

[23] "Hizb ut-Tahrir opfordrer til væbnet kamp" [Hizb ut-Tahrir Calls for Armed Struggle], *Information* (Copenhagen), December 28, 2010, http://www.information.dk/telegram/254933.

[24] Rigsadvokaten (The Attorney General), *Supplerende redegørelse om eventuel opløsning af Hizb ut-Tahrir i henhold til Grundlovens § 78* [Supplementary statement on the potential closure of Hizb ut-Tahrir in accordance with Basic Law § 78], June 2008, http://www.rigsadvokaten.dk/default.aspx?id=58&recordid58=1190, 13, 18.

[25] Ibid., 43.

[26] One of the more visible links has been established through references to contemporary Brotherhood ideologues such as Yusuf al-Qaradawi as a primary source of inspiration. See Jesper Termansen, "Omstridt islamist er forbillede for ny stærk imam" [Disputed Islamist is an Example for Strong New Imam], Islamic Faith Society in Denmark, March 31, 2007, http://www.wakf.com/wakfweb/news.nsf/0/C9C8B0F8CCBDF89FC12572AF00749622?OpenDocument.

[27] Brian Jacobsen, "Muslimer i Danmark", in Margit Warburg and Brian Jacobsen, eds. *Tørre tal om troen* [Mere Figures of Faith] (Højb-

jerg: Forlaget Univers, 2007), 158.

[28] Ibid.

[29] Ibidem.

[30] Søren Krarup, *Systemskiftet.* I kulturkampens tegn [Systemic Shift: Characters in the Cultural Battles](Copenhagen: Gyldendal, 2006).

[31] See Crone and Sheikh, "Muslims as Danish Security Issues."

[32] For example, Per Stig Møller, "'Jeg savner de intellektuelle'" ['I Miss the Intellectuals'] *Dagbladet Politiken* (Copenhagen), December 11, 2010, http://politiken.dk/debat/ECE1139648/jeg-savner-de-intellek-tuelle/.

[33] "The 'assimilation' minister speaks out," *The Copenhagen Post,* March 17, 2011, http://www.cphpost.dk/culture/culture/51215. html?task=view.

[34] Jørn Vestergaard, "Dansk lovgivning om bekæmpelse af terrorisme" [Danish Legislation on Terrorism], in Lars Plum and Andreas Laursen, eds. *Enhver stats pligt... International strafferet og dansk ret* [Duty of Every State... International Criminal Law and Danish Law] (Copenhagen: DJØF Forlag, 2007), 391-424.

[35] Ibid.

[36] Michael Jonsson and Christian Nils Larson, "Scandinavian Trials Demonstrate Difficulties of Obtaining Terrorist Financing Convictions," Jamestown Foundation *Terrorism Monitor* 7, iss. 5, March 13, 2009, http://www.jamestown.org/single/?no_cache=1&tx_ttnews%5Btt_news%5D=34698.

[37] Ministry of Flytgninge, Immigration and Integration, *A Common and Safe Future: an Action-Plan for the Prevention of Extremist Attitudes and Radicalization,* June 2008, http://www.nyidanmark.dk/NR/rdon-lyres/A797F73E-33E0-431A-9224-EE8BC39C932B/0/en_faelles_fremtid.pdf.

[38] Lasse Lindekilde, "Forebyggelse af radikalisering, miskendelse og muslimsk minoritetsidentitet" [Preventing Radicalization, Misrepresentation and Muslim Minority Identity], *Tidsskrift for Islamforskning* no. 2, 2010, http://www.islamforskning.dk/Tidsskrift_2_2010/fore-byggelse_af_radikalisering.pdf.

ALBANIA

QUICK FACTS

Population: 3,659,616

Area: 28,748 sq km

Ethnic Groups: Albanian 95%, Greek 3%, other 2% (Vlach, Roma (Gypsy), Serb, Macedonian, Bulgarian)

Religions: Muslim 70%, Albanian Orthodox 20%, Roman Catholic 10%

Government Type: Republic

GDP (official exchange rate): $11.86 billion

Map and Quick Facts courtesy of the CIA World Factbook (Last Updated June 2010)

While Albania's most severe terrorist-related activities appear to be consigned to history (specifically, the chaotic, post-communist 1990s), a new Islamist challenge is emerging there today. This phenomenon is essentially a social and cultural one, playing out—for the moment—chiefly within the country's Muslim community. This rhetorical (and occasionally physical) confrontation is being supported by external Islamic states and organizations, some of which have established or allied with like-minded local Islamist groups.

Today's Islamist stirrings in Albania parallel similar developments in other Balkan countries. Such states are characterized by their indigenous Muslim populations, their transition from former autocratic socialist or communist governments, and by their recent experience of foreign Islamist forces attempting to educate local Muslims, build mosques, provide public services, make investments and so on. Albania does support a small population of fundamentalist Wahhabi Muslims, though it is more modest than those found in Macedonia, Kosovo, Bosnia, or the Sandzak region that straddles Serbia and Montenegro. Nevertheless, Albania's extremist Muslims, who tend to be young and educated in the Arab or wider Muslim world, are tightly connected with fellow ideologues in the region, and will continue to threaten the authority of the mainstream Muslim community in the country while also taking part in Islamist activities outside of Albania itself.

ISLAMIST ACTIVITY

Almost 80 percent of Albania's 3.6 million citizens are Muslims.[1] The Muslim Community of Albania is the major body representing the country's Sunni Muslims, and Albanian Muslims in general, and is deemed to be the "legitimate" one by the state and by the international community.[2] In addition, the World Bektashi Center in Tirana is the official representative of the Shi'ite Bektashi Sufi order, which has a longstanding presence in Albania and some similarities with Turkey's Alevi Muslims.[3] However, the Bektashi order, compromising around 20 percent of Albania's Muslim population, is considered heretical by many Muslims for its more relaxed, liberal practices and differing theology. The Bektashi are particularly despised by the third and most dangerous Islamic group present in Albania—the puritanical Wahhabi minority attracted to the extreme forms of Islam prevalent in the Arab world and specifically to Wahhabism, the state religion of Saudi Arabia.

It is difficult to quantify the number of Wahhabis in Albania, as they operate largely outside of official structures. Although they continue to make determined efforts, as elsewhere in the region, to usurp power from the country's legitimate Islamic representatives, Wahhabis have also established parallel institutions, ranging from mosques to schools and charities.

A growing trend in Islamist activities in Albania, and the Balkans in general, is the manipulation of the concept of "civil society." As part of this process, Islamist groups employ the liberal rhetoric of human rights and religious freedom in pursuit of an Islamic supremacist agenda. This is chiefly done through the public discourse of non-governmental organizations (NGOs)—entities that are tacitly beyond reproach, having been devised by Western liberals in the 1990s as tools in the broader democratization movement in post-Communist Eastern Europe. NGOs and charities are also attractive for money laundering purposes, as their financial records can easily be manipulated, and can achieve disproportionate influence in poor, rural areas.[4]

One of the more conspicuous non-governmental organizations is the Muslim Forum of Albania (MFA), a prominent NGO that has been accused of creating "parallel structures" from those of the official Muslim Community.[5] The organization was created in 2005, during a heated feud between moderates and radicals over the official Muslim Community's bylaws, leading some seasoned foreign and local observers to conclude that the MFA was created to compete with official Islamic bodies.[6] However, the MFA claims merely to be interested in protecting human rights and oppose discrimination against Muslims. Nevertheless, its public statements have revealed a more single-minded agenda, including: attacking Pope Benedict XVI for his comments on violence in Islam; condemning Christian groups and all church-building initiatives; speaking out against the Danish cartoonist who famously drew the Prophet Mohammed; petitioning the government to accept Chinese Uighur prisoners being released from Guantanamo Bay; and insinuating that Albania's foreign Islamist residents are oppressed.[7]

While the degree of influence such organizations currently wield in shaping the public discourse remains limited, it is clear from their deliberate use of the English language and attempts to petition international organizations to their cause that they are interested not only in the internal, local audience, but in becoming part of a broader, globalist Islamic movement. For Albania's national security and social cohesion, the biggest concern here are attempts by Islamists to create divisions within the nation on religious grounds; Albanians have historically taken pride in their ability to maintain ethnic cohesion, despite being cumulatively composed of differing Christian and Muslim groups.

Most significantly, Islamic organizations (and informally organized groups) have been used to challenge the legitimate Muslim leadership in the country, in order to implement a more radical policy and to overthrow the leadership. Notably, this type of activity has undergone a natural progression in the past decade. While Islamic extremism in Albania once was solely funded and fomented from abroad, in recent years it has found a foothold within the country itself. (The current activities of foreign Islamist charities and groups are discussed in greater detail below.)

As part of this evolution, extremists of Albanian background have been trained abroad, and some have returned and taken up active roles in Albania (operating independently or as part of Islamist groups). Following the September 11, 2001 terrorist attacks, the Bush administration asked Albania to shutter several such charities; one, al Haramain, was suspected of organizing the murder of a moderate Muslim Community leader, Salih Tivari, in January 2002.[8] Tivari had pledged to remove foreign Islamist elements from the country. In fact, it is believed that local Albanian extremists trained in Islamic states actually carried out the murder itself.[9] In 2006, other Muslim Community leaders received death threats after an extremist group tried, but failed, to change one of the Community's official statutes.[10]

Leadership challenges and internal conflicts within the Albanian Muslim community are allowing radicalism to flourish, as moderates become increasingly intimidated and mired in controversy. The Muslim Community is Albania's second-largest landowner, and some of the "scandals" frequently invoked by critics of the Community's leadership have to do with alleged profiteering from land sales. At present, this state of affairs has caused a division within the Community's General Council, between supporters of head *mufti* Selim Muca and his opponents. The former seem currently to hold the upper hand: on September 21, 2010, following an attempt by Muca's opponents to prosecute him for corruption, a special session of the General Council reconfirmed Muca's authority, and sacked four prominent opponents among the Islamic leadership.[11]

This sort of political jockeying, however, has been deeply injurious. Not only has it created internal frictions within Albania's Muslim community, it has also taken the attention of its leadership away from attempts by religious extremists to strengthen their foothold there. Muca, for example, has been criticized for not stopping the formation of a union of *imams* with reported Wahhabi leanings in the large town of Kavaja, located between Tirana and the Adriatic coast. In opposition to Muca, the above-mentioned Muslim Forum of Albania held an event in Kavaja in February 2008, attracting Islamists from Kosovo, Macedonia and elsewhere.[12] A new group, the Union of Islamic Youth, is registered here and believed to be associated with Wahhabi elements (although information regarding it is sparse). In any case, local and foreign observers agree that the mosque and its worshippers here are increasingly wary of outsiders and seem to have more fundamentalist views.[13]

Such loose associations have been greatly expedited by the Internet, and tend to operate across borders, with like-minded brethren coming and going to spread the word in Wahhabi-controlled mosques throughout the region. One advantage of this method of operations is that its activities, funding and directives remain completely unregulated and unrestricted by any law or official body. This is not to say, however, that Islamists do not wish to take over the Muslim community of Albania. That is, in fact, their ultimate goal—one that, if achieved, will confer control over vast amounts of money, properties and, crucially, legitimacy by default in the eyes of the state and the international community.

ISLAMISM AND SOCIETY

A 2009 survey carried out by a Tirana newspaper, and citing Muslim Community officials, reveals that at present Albania has 568 Sunni mosques, as well as 70 Bektashi *tekkes* (lodges) and mausoleums.[14] The number constructed solely since the end of the Cold War, however, was not delineated.

Despite its clear Muslim majority, Albania also has notable Catholic and Orthodox Christian populations (the latter located chiefly in the southern part of the country, bordering Greece), and the same survey indicated that there are over 1,100 Catholic and Orthodox churches. Nevertheless, secularism prevails, especially in rapidly-modernizing Tirana, and Albanian Muslims are much less devout in their practice than are ethnic Albanians in neighboring Kosovo and (especially) the Republic of Macedonia. As in these countries and throughout the Balkan region, however, the Islamist creed that is most aggressively expanding is the Wahhabi fundamentalist one. This new generation of Islamists is aggressively seeking to "convert" other Muslims (and non-Muslims) by providing access to funds, travel, education and jobs, all with the sponsorship of outside Islamic states and interests.

While most Albanians are relatively secular-minded, an important trend for the future will be the relationship between the country's different religious groups. The government has been criticized by secularists for its plan to introduce the category of religious affiliation to the national census planned for 2011; this will no doubt exacerbate the politicking between different faiths in advance of the count, and especially the politico-religious rhetoric about it afterwards.

The internal struggles of a nation questioning its religious values vis-à-vis broader personal and national aspirations have occasionally resulted in fireworks. For example, in October 2003, the outspoken author Kastriot Myftari was arrested for "inciting religious hatred" after writing that Albanian Muslims should convert to Catholicism. (Myftari was ultimately acquitted).[15] More controversially, in November 2005 Islamists reacted sharply when then-President Alfred Moisiu, speaking before the Oxford Union in England, stated that Albanians followed a "shallow" sort of Islam, as the country's Christian heritage has much deeper roots.[16] The MFA and other Islamist groups accused Moisiu of "insulting Islam."

Inter-religious strife likewise has registered in more tangible ways. The northern, majority-Catholic city of Shkoder, bordering Montenegro, has provided visible examples. After a cross was put up there, it was vandalized (in January 2006), presumably by Islamists, who have been very active in competing with the city's Christian population. When local leaders announced that national hero Mother Teresa would be commemorated with a statue, three Muslim NGOs—the MFA, the Association of Islamic Intellectuals and the Association of Islamic Charities—condemned the initiative as a "provocation" against Islam.[17] (While the MFA is the most visible of the three organizations, the Association of Muslim Intellectuals is older, dating from the early 1990s, paralleling the creation of other, similar Islamist intellectual organizations in Bosnia and elsewhere.[18] In 1991, it was led by Bashkim Gazidede, whose tacit assistance to foreign terrorist-linked entities while serving as director of Albania's national intelligence agency is discussed in detail below.)

Another local Islamist organization, the Albanian Institute of Islamic Thought and Civilization, also has kept a fairly low profile, despite having existed since 1994. According to the organization, it is active chiefly in educational areas, such as teaching and the translation of Islamic texts from Turkish, Arabic and Persian. It also aims to preserve Islamic culture, and has links with likeminded organizations both inside the country and abroad.[19] Notably, some of the AIITC's foreign partners are on record as having extremist ties. For example, in October 2010 the AIITC announced a plan to cooperate on translation projects with the Libyan World Islamic Call Society (also known as the World Association for the Islamic Call); this Libyan umbrella group of 250 charities, established by Libyan strongman Muammar Ghaddafi himself, has been linked by American investigators to spreading radical Islam and funding Hamas.[20]

Foreign Islamic charities still operating in the country have moved beyond the initial phase of relief and infrastructure projects, and are now becoming more involved with social issues. For example, one of Albania's intractable problems—the practice of clan vendettas in the mountainous northeast, which continues to restrict the movement and social life of entire families— is being exploited by foreign Islamists. Dedicated efforts have been made to increase Islamist teaching in these areas, which are historically associated with smuggling, paramilitary activities and isolationism. Hundreds of students are reportedly undertaking Islamic education in rural towns like Koplik, with some going on to study in Turkey or the Middle East.[21] Support of orphans, and therefore, raising them according to Islamist ways, is another main area of work for such charities. Taking the lead in developing programs to solve vendettas and poverty via Islamic means is the UK-registered (but globally active) charity Islamic Relief.[22] The charity has operated in Albania since 1991.[23]

Finally, Turkey's presence in Albania is evolving. The Islamist-leaning government of Prime Minister Recep Tayyip Erdogan in Ankara has repeatedly indicated its interest in expanding its sphere of influence throughout former Ottoman lands, including Albania. Turks have justifiable concern about the state of Ottoman mosques and other monuments, in light of the massive efforts to co-opt them that have been made by Saudi Arabia and other Islamic states with no historic legacy in the region. Thus, since the end of Communism, a key component of Turkey's relationship with its former province has been in the area of cultural preservation. Nevertheless, there is increasingly a fine line between restoration and education work and the fundamentalist proselytizing of Turkish Islamist groups such as the *Insani Yardim Vakfi* (the Foundation for Human Rights and Freedoms and Humanitarian Relief, commonly referred to as the IHH). Known for its humanitarian work, the IHH has long been suspected by Israel of broader terrorist links (the charge was investigated, though not fully, by the U.S. government following the controversial "aid flotilla" it sent to Gaza on May 31, 2010).[24]

The final aspect of note in Turkey's relationship with Albanian Muslims is the Bektashi order, a more liberal and mystical variety of Islam with strong ties between the two countries, which is being targeted by Wahhabi elements as heretical. With different factions tolerating and opposing the Bektashi, the degree of Turkish support for them will help determine whether they survive in the face of extremist challenges. The Bektashi themselves, who do not engage in proselytizing, are aware that they are vulnerable. However, while Iran has offered funding to help ensure their future, the Bektashi leadership claims that it has not and will not accept funds from Iran.[25]

ISLAMISM AND THE STATE

Historically, the Albanian state's relationship with Islam has been critical in the evolution and practice of Islam in the country. Under Ottoman rule (from the 14th to the early 20th centuries), large numbers of Albanians converted to Islam in order to capitalize on better opportunities for state employment and career advancement. Sunni Islam became most popular in central and northern Albania, while the Shi'ite Bektashi Dervish order became established, from the 18th century onwards, primarily in southern Albania. The latter, more liberal form of Islam in 1923 dropped Ottoman-enforced practices such as polygamy and the forced wearing of the *hijab* (veil) by women. The same post-WWI Albanian government took in 25,000 members of the Bektashi order expelled from Turkey in 1926 during Mustafa Kemal Ataturk's secularization campaign; the World Bektashi Center remains based in Tirana to this day.

Later, under the Communist dictatorship of Enver Hoxha, religion itself was banned (in 1967) and all religious groups were persecuted by the state. Nevertheless, two years after democracy arrived in 1990, the Albanian leadership approved making Albania Europe's first (and to date, only) member of the Organization of Islamic Conference (OIC), and welcomed large-scale investment and proselytizing from Islamic states—including allowing senior al-Qaeda figures to establish an operational base on Albanian territory.

While that specific terrorist network was dismantled in the 1990s, the state has recently sought to use its connections with Islamic governments abroad for political ends (for example, to lobby for them to recognize the independence of their ethnic brethren in Kosovo), with reciprocal obligations as yet unknown. Finally, fundamentalist Islamists, operating via non-governmental organizations and with the assistance of foreign Islamist organizations and states, are increasingly seeking to influence political and social life.

The most pivotal moment in the modern Albanian state's relationship with Islam came when the first post-Communist government opened its arms to outside Islamist governments and interests. Then-president (and current prime minister) Sali Berisha himself was not religious, but merely sought out foreign investment of any kind. His election in 1992 was therefore followed by visits from Kuwaitis offering an "ambitious" investment plan in exchange for building mosques. Soon thereafter, the Islamic Development Bank (IDB) offered substantial investment and opportunities for Albanians to learn Arabic and study in Islamic states.[26] President Berisha also made Albania the first European member of the Organization of the Islamic Conference; one momentous consequence of this decision was the "unilateral abolition" of visa requirements for citizens of Muslim countries, making Albania an easy way for internationally-wanted terrorists to disappear into Europe.[27]

By 1994, private Saudi investors in the telecom, textile, banking and transport sectors, often through the IDB, were extending multi-million-dollar lines of credit to Albania. In the same year, and ahead of similar investments from the West, the Arab-Albanian Islamic Bank was established in Tirana.[28] Osama bin Laden was reportedly the majority stockholder and founder of this bank.[29] The bank built hundreds of mosques, sent Albanians to Islamic universities abroad, and paid poor Albanians on condition that their women wear the chador (veiled outer garment).[30] Hundreds of young Albanians went to study in Islamic countries, or undertook the *Hajj*—in 1993 alone, more than 1,000 Albanians made the pilgrimage to Mecca.[31] The "true agenda" of the foreign investors was to over time transform Albania into an Islamic state, through economic aid, proselytization, and finally the establishment of Islamic governance.[32]

Most sinister, however, was the Albanian state's relationship with the world's most dangerous Islamist terror networks. While President Berisha was not ideologically motivated, other high-level figures were in fact devoted Islamists, such as the late Bashkim Gazidede, then director of the national intelligence agency (SHIK). By 1994, the increasing presence of foreign *jihadists* in Islamic charities had made Western security officials "deeply suspicious."[33] Osama bin Laden, then based in Sudan, visited Tirana that year, presenting himself as a wealthy Saudi businessman offering humanitarian aid.[34] However, bin Laden was actually sponsoring the charity Al Haramain, later classified as a terrorist entity by the United States government.[35]

The Albanian government welcomed other dangerous charities like the Revival of Islamic Heritage Society, *Muwafaq* ("Blessed Relief") Foundation, the bin Laden-linked World Assembly of Muslim Youth, Taibah International and Iran's Ayatollah Khomeini Society. Another terror-linked charity, the International Islamic Relief Organization (IIRO), employed Mohammed al-Zawahiri, younger brother of future al-Qaeda second-in-command Ayman al-Zawahiri. He had reportedly been tasked by bin Laden himself with finding "legitimate cover" for Egyptian Islamic Jihad members involved with assassinations or attempted assassinations of Egyptian leaders.[36] The arrival of an Egyptian foreign ministry delegation in 1995 prompted the CIA to reach out to the by-now highly-compromised SHIK. One detained Islamist became an informant, marking a temporary breakthrough on the intelligence front. This informant in turn revealed the embarrassing truth that Albania had come to be known among *jihadists* as a "safe hotel" where they could hide out, with the tacit approval of the state.[37]

Indeed, despite the assistance provided by the SHIK on this occasion, the Islamist penetration continued and assistance provided by the agency to the U.S. suffered a corresponding decline. The SHIK would only be truly reformed once the Berisha government was ousted; in January 1997, the collapse of an investment pyramid scheme left ordinary Albanians penniless, leading to total anarchy and the looting of state arsenals. In April 1997, the SHIK was suspended by the caretaker government. June elections saw the ascent of an Orthodox Christian prime minister, Fatos Nano, who had previously been jailed by Berisha. Ex-SHIK director and *jihad* sympathizer Bashkim Gazidede reportedly escaped to the Middle East, and several arrest warrants were later issued for him by the new government.

The Nano government cooled relations with the Islamic world, irritating Islamist "investors" when it failed to send a delegate to the 1998 OIC conference. A CIA re-training course for the SHIK, and the removal of pro-Islamist SHIK officials and Islamic Community leaders, came at a time when the result of a merger of Ayman al-Zawahiri's Egyptian Islamic Jihad and al-Qaeda was being assessed by the CIA as among Europe's most dangerous terrorist entities.[38] Local experts in Albania noted that the EIJ's Tirana cell was among its most important, as it was expert in falsifying documents to facilitate the transit of suspected terrorists.[39]

In mid-1998, a renewed round of CIA-ordered SHIK kidnappings of *jihadis* in Tirana led to the rendition of several men to Egypt; unfortunately, covert American involvement was leaked by "euphoric" SHIK agents, enraging the *jihadist internationale*.[40] A letter released by a London-based al-Qaeda newsletter on August 5, 1998 promised a violent response: just two days later, terrorists bombed the U.S. embassy in Nairobi, Kenya, killing 213 people and injuring more than 4,000. A second embassy attack, in Dar es Salaam, Tanzania, killed 11 and injured 85. These incidents revealed that counter-terrorist operations in Albania could trigger Islamist attacks globally, putting the Balkan country into the new and nebulous category of dangerous ally. The U.S. State Department temporarily closed diplomatic facilities in Albania and Americans were warned to avoid the country altogether.

Nevertheless, Albania was also a key ally for the Clinton administration's determined efforts to arm and train Muslim Albanian separatists in the neighboring Yugoslav province of Kosovo.[41] (Ironically, at the same time American officials were also stating openly that Albania was hosting Iranian, Chechen, Afghan, Algerian and Egyptian *mujahideen* who were offering their services for a Kosovo *jihad*.[42]) Yet U.S. support for Kosovar Muslims (and Bosnian Muslims in their own previous war against the Serbs) failed to make America beloved throughout the Muslim world. However, during the brief Kosovo refugee crisis in the spring of 1999, the U.S. government allowed massive humanitarian activity to be carried out by some of the very same foreign organizations and individuals that it had identified as dangerous.[43] (The connection between such charities and Albanian extremists active in the Balkans was noted over a decade later, when a radical *imam* was expelled from Kosovo).[44]

It was thus little surprise that adverse security conditions persisted in Albania during the following months; for example, then-Defense Secretary William Cohen had to cancel a celebratory visit to the country in mid-July 1999, as he had been targeted by remaining al-Qaeda operatives in Tirana.[45] Several months earlier, the police had detained a Saudi-trained Albanian national accused of surveilling U.S. facilities, as well as two well-armed terrorist cell members in Tirana.[46]

Soon after the September 11, 2001 terrorist attacks, U.S. government officials, speaking off the record, disclosed a connection between the al-Qaeda plotters and Albania-based Islamic terrorists.[47] In Tirana, attention turned to Yassin al-Qadi, founder and chief investor in the Muwafaq Foundation. Although he denied all charges, al-Qadi subsequently was designated a terrorist sponsor by the U.S. Treasury Department in October 2001.[48] The multi-millionaire Saudi investor was accused of laundering $10 million for Osama bin Laden through his business interests and charities. In 2002, the Albanian government seized a 15-story business center owned by al-Qadi in Tirana and expelled his business partner, Abdul Latif Saleh; the latter had been associated with the Tirana charities created by al-Qaeda, and was accused by U.S. investigators of cooperating with al-Qaeda while in Albania.[49]

The current status of Albania's state relations with radical Islamist groups is more opaque. In July 2005 elections, the Nano government was defeated and Sali Berisha reclaimed power; ex-SHIK chief Gazidede, the charges against him having been dropped since 2003, returned from exile and took up a different function in Berisha's new government (he has since died of natural causes). Although many of the charities and terrorist-linked entities that plagued Albania during Berisha's first stint in power have been uprooted, a new and multifaceted dynamic is visible today in the activities of the Albanian state concerning Islamism.

Albania's membership in the Organization of Islamic Conference—ignored, but not abrogated during the Nanos government—has been restored, in recognition of the OIC's growing influence in the United Nations and as a means of lobbying Muslim countries to recognize Kosovar independence.[50] Through this, the Albanian government is also seeking to show the world that it has some degree of influence in world affairs. At the same time, while it is constitutionally prevented from funding religious facilities, the government has approved the Muslim Community's plan to create an Islamic university in Tirana—an initiative being presented as a proactive effort to counter extremism by affording students the opportunity to study at home (rather than in the broader Arab world).[51] Nevertheless, Albania's courtship with foreign Islamic funders, begun in the early 1990s, appears to be continuing, with the Islamic Development Bank (IDB) in October 2010 offering millions of dollars for infrastructure and other projects.[52] The announcement came only three months after Prime Minister Berisha hosted a high-level IDB delegation, and thanked them for their assistance (past and present) in developing Albania.[53]

The Albanian state's strengthened cooperation with the pro-Islamist government in Turkey, which has its own Balkan aspirations, is another sign of current relations with outside Islamist forces. In June 2010, the official headquarters of the Muslim Community of Albania was renovated by the Turkish International Cooperation and Development Agency (TIKA), at a cost of roughly $350,000 REF.[54] At the time, TIKA officials together with Albanian government and Islamic officials disclosed that Turkey plans to reconstruct other Islamic facilities (as it has done since the end of Communism).[55] The Albanian government is also allowing large-scale proselytizing and relief works led by the previously-mentioned Turkish IHH, among other charities and organizations that could reasonably be considered to have extremist ties. Yet on even the level of basic social discourse, Turkey looms large in the current re-thinking of Albanian identity, given its Ottoman past and Albania's place within it.[56]

While Wahhabi groups remain very much a minority among Albanians today, it is clear that they do have supporters within the government and the "mainstream" Islamic community. Of concern is the likely future need of any Albanian government to interact with such groups, as they continue to seek a more prominent role in the religious and political life of the country. This will invariably have the side-effect of legitimizing them and their demands, something that will add to the increasing prominence of Islamism in public discourse. Thus, while Albania can no longer be said to pose the terrorist threat it did during the 1990s, its fortunes are of pivotal interest as part of the broader social phenomenon of growing Islamism in the Balkans.

ENDNOTES

[1]See Tracy Miller, ed., *Mapping the Global Muslim Population: A Report on the Size and Distribution of the World's Muslim Population* (Washington, DC: Pew Research Center, October 2009), http://pewforum.org/newassets/images/reports/Muslimpopulation/Muslimpopulation.pdf.

[2] The community's website is www.kmsh.al.

[3] The official Bektashi order website can be found at www.bektashi.net.

[4] Thus, while arguing that Albania's generally tolerant and pro-Western outlook prevents it from becoming radicalized, analyst Arben Kullolli notes that "foreign supporters of Islamic organizations have started to work more intelligently, operating through think-tanks and continuing to convert Albanian Muslims into Wahhabism, especially in poor rural regions." Arben Kullolli, *Proselytization in Albania by Middle Eastern Islamic Organizations*, (Monterey, CA: Master's Thesis Naval Postgraduate School, March 2009)

[5] Risto Karajkov, "The Young And The Old: Radical Islam Takes Root In The Balkans," *Transitions Online*, May 3, 2006, www.tol.cz.

[6] See Miranda Vickers, "Islam In Albania," Advanced Research and Assessment Group, Defence Academy of the United Kingdom, March 2008, www.da.mod.uk.

[7] The MFA's official website is www.forumimusliman.org.

[8] U.S. Treasury Department, "Press Release JS-1703: Additional Al-Haramain Branches, Former Leader Designated By Treasury As Al Qaida Supporters," June 2, 2004, www.ustreas.gov.

[9] Vickers, "Islam In Albania."

[10] Karajkov, "The Young And The Old."

[11] "Selim Muca Reconfirmed As Head Of Albanian Muslim Community," *Alsat Television* (Skopje), September 20, 2010.

[12] Although it was created in the northern city of Shkodra, the MFA has long had a power base in Kavaja.

[13] Vickers, "Islam In Albania."

[14] Entela Resuli, "Ne Shqiperi 638 Xhami Me 1.119 Kisha (In Albania There Are 638 Mosques And 1,119 Churches)," Tirana Observer, December 23, 2009.

[15] "Albania," in U.S. Department of State, Bureau of Democracy, Human Rights, and Labor, *International Religious Freedom Report 2004* (Washington, DC: U.S. Department of State, 2005), www.state.gov.

[16] The comments that incensed Islamists were perhaps taken out of context; the president was speaking about religious tolerance among the Albanians. Nevertheless he caused a sensation by stating "that part of the Albanians which did not convert into Islam has in its tradition not simply fifteen centuries of Christianity, but two thousand years of Christianity... The Islamism in Albania is an Islam with a Euro-

pean face. As a rule it is a shallow Islamism. If you dig a little in every Albanian you can discover his Christian core." The original text of the speech was published on the official website of the President of Albania, www.president.al.

[17] Llazar Semini, "Mother Teresa Statue Causes Friction," Associated Press, March 20, 2006

[18] Mentioned in Xavier Bougarel, "Islam And Politics In The Post-Communist Balkans," Harvard University Kokkalis Program on Southeastern and East-central Europe, 6, http://www.hks.harvard.edu/kokkalis/GSW1/GSW1/13%20Bougarel.pdf.

[19] The group keeps an informative official website, www.aiitc.org.

[20] Matthew Levitt, *Hamas: Politics, Charity and Terrorism in the Service of Jihad* (New Haven: Yale University Press, 2007), 187. The announcements about book production and translation cooperation between the World Islamic Call Society and the AIITC were posted in October 2010 on the Society's group's official website, www.islamic-call.net, as well as in other Islamic media.

[21] This testimony is recorded in an online summary of a recent trip to Albania by young Islamists from the Turkish IHH (Humanitarian Relief Foundation, or Insani Yardim Vakfi in Turkish), and available at the organization's website, www.ihh.org.tr. The unusually significant proselytizing efforts going on in Koplik in the 1990s were noted long ago, for example in Miranda Vickers and James Pettifer, *Albania: From Anarchy to a Balkan Identity* (New York: New York University Press, 1997), 100.

[22] On its main website, www.islamic-relief.com, Islamic Relief describes itself as "an international relief and development charity which envisages a caring world where people unite to respond to the suffering of others, empowering them to fulfill their potential."

[23] The charity's efforts to combat clan vendettas and develop rural places like Koplik can be seen on their website, www.islamicreliefalbania.com.

[24] *CRS Report for Congress: Israel's Blockade of Gaza, the Mavi Marmara Incident, and Its Aftermath* (Washington, DC: Congressional Research Service, June 23, 2010).

[25] Vickers, "Islam In Albania."

[26] Vickers and Pettifer, *Albania: From Anarchy to a Balkan Identity*, 102-105.

[27] Remzi Lani and Fabian Schmidt, "Albanian Foreign Policy Between Geography And History," *The International Spectator XXXIII*, no. 2 (April-June 1998).

[28] Grace Halsell, "Special Report: Albania And The Muslim World," *Washington Report on Middle East Affairs*, June 1994, http://www.washington-report.org/backissues/0694/94006020.htm.

[29] J. Milton Burr and Robert O. Collins, *Alms for Jihad: Charity and*

Terrorism in the Islamic World (Cambridge: Cambridge University Press, 2006), 147-149.

[30] Franz Gustincich, "From Lenin To Bin Laden," *Gnosis: Online Italian Intelligence Magazine* (March 2005), www.sisde.it.

[31] Damian Gjiknuri, "Albania's Counter-Terrorism Policy Options: Finding A Strategy Of Common Sense," U.S. Naval Postgraduate School Thesis, 2004, 12.

[32] Ibid., 15.

[33] Vickers and Pettifer, *Albania: From Anarchy to a Balkan Identity*, 105.

[34] Chris Stephens, "Bin Laden Opens European Terror Base In Albania," *Sunday Times*, November, 29 1998.

[35] US Treasury Press Release, "JS-1703: Additional Al-Haramain Branches, Former Leader Designated By Treasury As Al Qaida Supporters," June 2, 2004, www.ustreas.gov.

[36] Burr and Collins, *Alms for Jihad: Charity and Terrorism in the Islamic World*, Ibid, 146.

[37] John Crewdson and Tom Huntley, "Abducted Imam Aided CIA Ally," *Chicago Tribune*, July 3, 2005.

[38] Andrew Higgins and Christopher Cooper, "CIA-Backed Team Used Brutal Means To Break Up Terrorist Cell In Albania," *Wall Street Journal*, November 20, 2001.

[39] Kullolli, *Proselytization in Albania by Middle Eastern Islamic Organizations*, 58.

[40] R. Jeffrey Smith, "US Probes Blasts' Possible Mideast Ties," *Washington Post*, August 12, 1998.

[41] Wayne Madsen, "Mercenaries In Kosovo: The U.S. Connection To The KLA," *The Progressive*, August, 1999.

[42] See "Kosovo Seen As New Islamic Bastion," *Jerusalem Post*, September 14, 1998, and Barry Schweid, "NATO Braces For Wider Kosovo Fight," Associated Press, June 17, 1998.

[43] For example, see the following exquisitely-detailed summary of Saudi-led refugee efforts, with financial totals, activities carried out, and organizations and individuals involved. Hussein Saud Qusti, "Unsung Heroes", *Saudi Aramco World* 50, no. 4, April 1999, http://www.saudiaramcoworld.com/issue/199904/unsung.heroes.htm.

[44] Kastriot Duka, an *imam* originally from Elbasan in Albania, told journalists that he had been assisted in his efforts to build mosques, teach orphans and preach in a Kosovo village during the 1999 relief efforts by a member of an Islamic charity based in Britain. See Paola Casoli, "Terror And Gratitude: Albanian Imam's Kosovo Mission," www.serbianna.com, December 29, 2007. Duka, who continued to rely on funding from UK-based "charities," would be deported from Kosovo back to Albania by Kosovar authorities in March 2010 for allegedly preaching radical Islam. See Linda Karadaku, "Kosovo

Deports Self-Proclaimed Imam, Closes Mosque," *Southeast Europe Times*, March 11, 2010, http://www.setimes.com/cocoon/setimes/xhtml/en_GB/features/setimes/features/2010/03/11/feature-03.

[45] "Pentagon Chief Cancels Albania Visit Over Terror Threat," CNN, July 15, 1999.

[46] The incidents were widely reported, for example see "Albanian Police Arrest More Islamists," *RFE/RL Newsline* 3, no. 33, February 17, 1999.

[47] Bill Gertz, "Hijackers Connected To Albanian Terrorist Cell," *Washington Times*, September 18, 2001.

[48] US Treasury Press Release, "JS-2727: Treasury Designates Bin Laden, Qadi Associate," September 19, 2005, www.ustreas.gov.

[49] Ibid.

[50] Author's correspondence with OIC official, October 2010.

[51] Kullolli, *Proselytization in Albania by Middle Eastern Islamic Organizations,* 62.

[52] As part of this outreach, Albania—along with other IDB member states such as Pakistan, Sudan, Indonesia and Uzbekistan—is slated to receive a portion of a new $772 million tranche for development projects. See "IDB Approves $772m For New Projects," *Arab News*, October 6, 2010, http://www.gulfbase.com/site/interface/NewsArchiveDetails.aspx?n=153337.

[53] See "Islamic Development Bank Expresses Interest In Albania For Increase Of Bank's Presence Through Private Sector," Balkans.com, July 6, 2010.

[54] The event was covered by various local media outlets, as well as foreign Islamist ones. See, for example, "Turkey Rebuilds Albanian Muslim Community's Headquarters," worldbulletin.net, June 30, 2010; See also the official TIKA Web site, www.tika.gov.tr.

[55] Ibid.

[56] For example, see the following interview, which tacitly implies that the Ottoman period represented the high point of Albania's development, and that Islam is thus a "normal" part of the country's future path. Vahide Ulusoy, "Interview With Ervan Hatibi On Albanian Muslims," Worldbulletin.net, July 22, 2008.

Kosovo

QUICK FACTS

Population: 1,815,048

Area: 10,887 sq km

Ethnic Groups: Albanians 92%, other (Serb, Bosniak, Gorani, Roma, Turk, Ashkali, Egyptian) 8%

Religions: Muslim, Serbian Orthodox, Roman Catholic

Government Type: Republic

GDP (official exchange rate): $3.237 billion

Map and Quick Facts courtesy of the CIA World Factbook (last updated July 2010)

Although Islam has been present in Kosovo for the past seven centuries, the most significant developments have occurred since the 1999 NATO intervention, which enabled numerous Islamic states and fundamentalist-oriented charities to enter the country, then under the jurisdiction of the United Nations Mission in Kosovo (UNMIK). For the first time, Islamic governments, donors and proselytizers had open access to this economically underdeveloped, war-ravaged corner of Europe.

Today, Kosovo is an independent state (though still not recognized as such by many countries), and the domestic discussion of Islam—and Islamism—has entered a new phase. Although foreign Islamists left behind numerous new mosques and religious schools, they have, at least so far, failed to re-orient the majority of Kosovo's Muslims toward a strict Wahhabi interpretation of the religion. At the same time, efforts by Catholic and Protestant missionaries from abroad have generated a countervailing pressure. Yet a number of violent incidents within Kosovo, and terrorist attacks abroad involving Kosovar Muslims, showcase the potential for a growth in Islamic radicalism—and its spillover into the international arena.

ISLAMIST ACTIVITY

Ethnic Albanians comprise 90 percent of Kosovo's population of two million. The vast majority is Muslim, although the lack of recent census data makes accurate figures hard to ascertain.[1] Approximately three percent of Kosovo's Albanians are Catholic, though this population seems to be increasing, while various foreign Protestant denominations have tried (so far, with lesser success) to convert Kosovo's Muslims to their faith. The beleaguered Serbian minority of 120,000 persons, largely concentrated around a few scattered central enclaves and in more compact northern municipalities around the ethnically-divided city of Mitrovica, is Orthodox Christian. However, there is also a small Serbian-speaking Slavic Muslim minority, the Gorani, who primarily inhabit the mountainous southwestern area around Dragas, nestled between Macedonia and Albania. The small Roma (Gypsy) minority is mainly Muslim as well, but less active, limited by having an idiosyncratic lifestyle on the margins of society.

In Kosovo, Islam has played an important role in shaping national identity. The country is often referred to as the "cradle" of the medieval Serbian empire, which left abundant reminders of its presence in scores of Orthodox Christian churches and monasteries. However, Kosovo was captured by the Ottoman Turks in the late 14th century. Islam thereafter became the dominant religion, with considerable privileges conferred on those who converted (such as the gradually increasing ethnic Albanian population). During Communist Yugoslav rule, all religions were strictly controlled, while the Kosovo Albanian population increased further and several thousand ethnic Turks and Albanians emigrated to Turkey.

Today's Islamist activity in Kosovo (in terms of an organized and foreign-influenced version of Islam) began around the time of the NATO intervention that ended Yugoslav rule over the province in summer 1999. The Kosovo crisis sparked considerable sympathy among foreign Islamic donors (and also brought some additional fighters to the region), though the nationalist character of the uprising meant that the Albanian rebels sought to downplay any religious element in their protest. Indeed, the majority of funding for the resistance, the Kosovo Liberation Army (KLA), came from other means— from the personal donations of patriotic Diaspora Albanians, as well as from the proceeds of narcotics trafficking conducted by tight-knit Albanian mafia structures involved with heroin distribution in Europe.[2]

Any detailed discussion of Islamist activity in Kosovo must begin with an acknowledgement of the complexity and singularity of the prevailing local conditions, which cumulatively have created a friendly environment for a certain kind of Islamism to take root. Powerful clan structures and pervasive organized crime have long fueled allegations of crime and corruption against local and international leaders alike. Frustration among the general public after 1999 was also fueled by the perceived lack of political and economic change in the post-Yugoslav "transition" period. The unaccountable and uninvolved nature of an international UN mission that changed staff frequently and had no long-term responsibilities for Kosovo's well-being also hindered prospects of real change. And, most visibly, there has been the continuing political impasse with Serbia, which refuses to concede Kosovo's independence—a policy in which it is still supported by a majority of the world's nations. All of these local realities have created in Kosovo a situation in which Islamism can be presented both as a long-term social solution and in the short-term manipulated for violence in otherwise ethnic-based incidents.

The first foreign Islamist actors in Kosovo came via an assortment of Islamic charities, the most important being an umbrella organization of the Saudi government, the Saudi Joint Commission for the Relief of Kosovo and Chechnya (SJCRKC), and its official Kuwaiti counterpart, the Kuwaiti Joint Relief Committee (KJRC). Along with waves of returning Albanian refugees, representatives of these groups (and the Islamic charities organized within them), entered the country from neighboring Albania, where Albanian and U.S. authorities had been monitoring, and working to control, suspected international terrorist suspects. The Saudis initially allocated over $22.5 million for the rebuilding (or construction of new) mosques and schools, and also for supporting orphans in Kosovo.[3]

Aside from charities, a major opportunity for foreign Islamic development, recruitment and intelligence activity came as a result of the broad participation of many nations (including major Muslim states) in the interim UN Mission in Kosovo (UNMIK), and the Kosovo Force (KFOR) peacekeeping units authorized by UN Security Council Resolution 1244. Muslim states like Saudi Arabia, Malaysia, Pakistan, Egypt and Turkey used this rare "official cover" in a previously closed part of Europe to develop their own interests in Kosovo. For example, in October 1999 alone, Saudi sponsors donated 200,000 copies of the Koran in Albanian/Arabic translation as part of efforts to promulgate the Kingdom's official brand of Islamism in the Balkans.[4]

Although the volume of such personnel would gradually diminish over time, and in some cases disappear completely with the progressive downsizing of the UN mission, there is little doubt that Kosovo was vulnerable to foreign Islamist penetration in the early years of post-Yugoslav rule. The legal limbo of Kosovo's international status also meant a no-visa policy, which opened up the borders and made Kosovo Europe's primary "safe zone" for foreign radicals.

From early on, Western experts raised concerns regarding the arrival of Wahhabism—the Saudi state's ultra-conservative version of Islam—and what it could portend for Kosovo's future. However, Kosovar Islamic leaders maintained (then as now) that the appeal of such worldviews was limited and represented no threat to the traditional fabric of Islamic society.[5] Indeed, overly aggressive Wahhabi sponsors angered local Albanian Muslims on a number of occasions, such as when they desecrated tombs and demolished parts of shrines belonging to the traditional Bektashi order of Islam—a more relaxed, Shi'ite-influenced hold-over from Ottoman times that was and is considered heretical by many Sunnis (including the Wahhabis).[6] This aggressive strategy caused a backlash among local Muslims, leading Wahhabi groups to cease destroying "heretical" structures and simply concentrate on building new mosques in the distinctive Arab style.

The dynamic of Islamist activity in Kosovo has changed gradually, along with the political and social situation. In the early years, a key target was the country's non-Muslim population. Chronically antagonistic relations between Albanians and Serbs have largely been ethnic in character but, as a 2010 U.S. Department of State report noted, "the close link between ethnicity and religion [have] made it difficult to determine if events were motivated by ethnic or religious animosity."[7]

These animosities and related attacks are indeed difficult to ascertain, though there has undeniably been a religious aspect to violence on both sides. According to Albanian sources, 216 of the 513 mosques that existed in Kosovo in the year 2000 had been damaged in fighting during the 1990s, while over 80 Christian churches and mosques were attacked by Albanians (*after*, not before, the arrival of 40,000 NATO peacekeepers in July 1999).[8] And there is no question that the major post-war conflagration—the country's March 2004 riots, in which 50,000 Albanians targeted Serbs and foreign nationals across Kosovo—had an Islamic aspect. For example, after over 30 Serbian Orthodox churches were attacked, DVDs of the destruction were soon being circulated in radical Western European mosques; further, a confidential NATO document subsequently indicated that the alleged masterminds of these pre-planned riots had had ties to Hezbollah and al-Qaeda.[9]

Whereas traditional antagonisms were ethnic in nature (albeit with religious overtones), recent years have seen an emergence of intra-ethnic tensions within the Albanian Muslim community, as well as hostility from Albanian Muslims toward Albanian Catholics, and finally toward local and foreign members of the Catholic and Protestant denominations. This is due to two factors: first, the steady decline of the Serbian minority and Kosovo's 2008 declaration of independence, both of which minimized the Serbs' traditional status as the primary oppressive force restricting the freedom of Albanians; and second, the internal struggles for control between rival Muslim factions, as a young generation trained abroad or exposed to foreign versions of Islam openly contests the worship practices of their elders.

This phenomenon is similar to that currently seen in neighboring Albania and Macedonia, where ethnic Albanians also comprise the vast majority of local Muslim populations. Internet websites, social media, book printing and distribution, and use of non-governmental organizations (NGOs) have been the main vehicles for "networking Islam" within Kosovo (and its neighboring countries). As in these and other parts of the Balkans, it is commonly believed that the sect members are paid by foreign Islamic groups for men to grow long beards and to cover women. (Evidence of such a connection, however, is limited to the anecdotal testimony of local Muslims.) It is significant to note that these younger, foreign-oriented Muslims do not call themselves Wahhabis (now a pejorative term in the Balkans) but rather see themselves as "brothers" or simply "believers."

Tensions within the wider Islamic community in Kosovo over control of mosques or other religious institutions likewise have been witnessed. For example, an elderly *imam* in the Drenica region of Kosovo was attacked in January 2009 by numerous bearded Wahhabis from the area in an act of intimidation believed to be associated with a desire to "take over" the mosque.[10] Attacks of this type have been witnessed throughout the Balkans in recent years.

A common facet of Islamist activity has been the use of charities and NGOs, and appropriation of public facilities such as sports halls for fundamentalist preaching. This is something authorities and international watchdogs have noted and tried to counter when possible. For example, the State Department's 2009 *Country Reports on Terrorism* noted that Kosovo police and the UN Mission in Kosovo "continued to monitor suspected terrorist activity," believing that several NGOs were involved in "suspicious activities." These authorities were also trying "to prevent extremists from using non-governmental organizations to gain a foothold in Kosovo," and "to prevent misuse of facilities for events that had no consent from the relevant religious community."[11] Such events, some of which are also held in private residences or apartments, have been recorded by Islamists and circulated on DVD or Internet websites.

Islamist activity has also targeted foreign Christian groups attempting to establish themselves in Kosovo. Unsurprisingly, Evangelical Christian attempts to convert local Muslims, particularly in more violence-prone provincial areas, have yielded a severe response. In recent years, Protestants have increasingly reported threats and intimidation from local Islamists; in one high-profile case, personal data on members of the Protestant community was reproduced by up to 100 Islamic websites. Subsequently, in May 2010, a missionary reported being physically attacked by Islamists in the southern town of Prizren, a long-acknowledged center of Islamism in Kosovo.[12]

The most dangerous, and unpredictable, aspect of Islamist activity related to Kosovo often occurs outside of its borders. Over the past few years, Kosovar Albanians in the Diaspora have been found involved in both terrorist cells and organized crime.[13] In the United States, these extremists were implicated in the foiled 2008 attack on Fort Dix in New Jersey,[14] and in a more recent but similar foiled plot against the U.S. Marine Corps base in Quantico, Virginia.[15] However, an organized al-Qaeda terrorist cell is not believed to exist in Kosovo currently. In recent years U.S. and other intelligence services have estimated that there may well be loose connections on the individual level between local Muslims and radicals abroad.

ISLAMISM AND SOCIETY

Kosovo has one of the youngest populations in Europe, and is plagued by high unemployment, pervasive organized crime and limited socio-economic opportunity—factors known to contribute to violent extremism. As such, the situation in Kosovo bears careful monitoring.

The officially recognized Muslim organization in the country is the Islamic Community of Kosovo (in Albanian, *Bashkësia Islame e Kosovës*, or BIK), led by Chief Mufti Naim Trnava.[16] It is intended to represent the totality of Islam in the country, though there are traditional Bektashi Sufi communities, particularly in western Kosovo, that have certain differences in doctrine and practice. Nevertheless, both the Bektashi and Hanafi Sunni Muslims generally get along and are united by a strong sense of ethnic Albanian nationalism. There are, however, foreign-oriented Wahhabi Muslims who fall outside the cracks of the BIK and its control. Their numbers are notoriously difficult to calculate, as there is no strict doctrine or separate institutions governing them; they simple consider themselves "better," more committed Muslims than the rest.

As discussed, in the aftermath of the NATO intervention, Muslim charities made extensive efforts in the areas of proselytization, orphan care, Islamic education, banking and loans, and so on. However, while their more aggressive efforts met with resistance from Albanians determined to preserve their own traditions and local control, foreign states have succeeded in some respects. With unemployment remaining high and the social needs of the country's poorest and neediest still often neglected, Islamic groups have sought to style themselves as alternative service providers. Saudi Arabia, Kuwait and other countries thus have built numerous mosques and educational facilities, with a clear strategic goal: in the words of one Kosovar commentator, "to create a new generation of loyal Muslims – not (loyal) to Kosovo but to the Islamic international."[17]

While these efforts have failed to make notable inroads among the majority of Kosovo's Muslim population, they have succeeded in building a tangible and ideological infrastructure in terms of new, Saudi-style mosques and young *imams* and students educated in Islamic states. Their subtle but increasingly vocal influence has manifested itself in occasional protests over issues such as bans of the head scarf in public institutions, and protests against construction of churches by their Catholic ethnic kin. In post-Serbian Kosovo, these examples of discord may mark new cleavages to come between secular and religious Albanians, and among Albanians of different faiths.

Islamists have typically used Islamic NGOs and youth groups to foment protests and shape common policies on these controversial issues. For example, in May and June 2010, Islamist groups organized street protests after a high school student in the town of Ferizaj was expelled for wearing a headscarf. While the Kosovo government has sought to implement strictly secular laws in this regard, a local court had given Islamists room for hope in overturning another, similar ban on a schoolgirl from Vitina who wished to wear a headscarf. Veiled Muslim women have also complained that employers will not hire them.[18]

Emerging discord between Albanian Muslims and Catholics became apparent in September 2010, when the new Catholic Cathedral of the Blessed Mother Teresa—the famed nun of Calcutta is an ethnic Albanian national hero—was opened in the capital, Pristina. The building drew the ire of Muslim groups, who chafed at the apparent preferential treatment from the government received by Catholics (who comprise only about three percent of the population), and for good reason; a 2004 Muslim demand for a grand mosque had been turned down by authorities. This refusal was deemed "unacceptable" by Ferid Agani, chairman of the pro-Islamic Justice Party of Kosovo (a small but vocal conservative party which holds two out of Kosovo's 120 parliamentary seats) and as a "political decision" by *imams* in media testimony.[19] Soon after the Pristina cathedral was opened, threatening graffiti began to appear throughout the city proclaiming that Islamist worship would be conducted in it.[20] Other pro-Islamist figures at the time argued that "fairness" required a mosque to be built if a church was—an argument identical to the one that their co-religionists continue to make throughout the region.

Although the Catholic population of Kosovo is a mere 60,000 persons, it has a disproportionate significance, for both historical and contemporary reasons. Before the arrival of the Turks in the late-14th century, Albanians were Catholic. However, they subsequently converted to Islam for the social benefits it conferred. Therefore, the idea of "returning" to an "original religion" is an argument sometimes encountered in Kosovo. Further, the idea that becoming Christian will give one a better chance of acceptance in Western Europe is also widely held.[21] In 2005, former Albanian president Alfred Moisiu provoked an uproar from Islamist groups following a speech in England in which he stated that Albanians follow a "shallow" sort of Islam, and have deeper Christian roots.[22]

Further, with the erection of the Pristina cathedral, the Catholic Church there has been upgraded to the status of diocese by the Vatican. It is clear from recent events that the Roman Catholic Church is taking a greater interest in spreading Catholicism in Kosovo. Significantly, on February 10, 2011, the Vatican commissioned its first apostolic delegate to Kosovo, Papal Nuncio in Slovenia Juliusz Janusz. While the Vatican has made clear that it does not recognize Kosovo's independence, and takes pains to not "offend" the Serbian Orthodox Church on this issue, it clearly seems to believe that the time has come to promote Catholicism more strongly against Islamic expansionism.[23]

Islamic assistance to Kosovar society has come over the years from a variety of organizations, starting with the Saudi Joint Committee and continuing with numerous foreign-based charities which have sought to develop local offshoots and self-sustaining entities. Their social impact is still not clear, in part because they have concentrated on Islamic education for the young and very young (orphan sponsorship and care has been a main project of numerous charities). While a number of "suspicious" charities were closed in the aftermath of 9/11, major global organizations like Islamic Relief Worldwide (IRW) continue to operate. Aside from typical charity activities, such groups offer loans and "micro-credit" schemes in a bid to extend Islamic influence over small businessmen and rural communities. By 2004 alone, the IRW had handed out over 500 loans "based on Islamic principles" to Kosovar businesses.[24] The organization remains very active in Kosovo today, as well as in other Balkan states.[25]

The issue of Islam in social assistance has led to some difficult choices for average Kosovars. A prominent example was the case of Kastriot Duka, a former *imam* in the village of Marina, near Mitrovica. Although the locals were grateful for the financial and other assistance he had provided through contacts with a British-based charity, Rahma Mercy, the religious conservatism he promoted in the mosque—such as veiling four-year-old girls—was widely seen as excessive. By order of the local mayor, Duka was sent back to his native Albania (officially, on charges of visa violation). Duka's expulsion came after a petition against him was signed by 6,000 locals.[26] This kind of difficult decision between social care and fundamentalism will continue as the weak state struggles to care for its citizens, and as international disagreements over Kosovo's legal status continue to hamper the country from full participation in all international institutions.

ISLAMISM AND THE STATE

Long before becoming an independent state in 2008, Kosovo's relationship with Islam had been heavily influenced by external considerations. After the spectacle of thousands of "Afghan-Arab" *mujahideen* joining the Muslim side during the Bosnian war (1992-1995), the KLA considered it wise to ignore offers for help from foreign fighters in the subsequent conflict in Kosovo, in order to win political support from the United States. Although numerous Muslim charities and state actors were welcomed into Kosovo in the immediate aftermath of the 1999 NATO intervention, the 9/11 attacks had a sobering effect, and the Kosovar administration, then heavily controlled by the UN Mission, attempted to purge those NGOs and charities seen as linked to terrorism. At the same time, partisan critics of Kosovo Albanian separatism increasingly tried to draw connections between Kosovo and Islamic terrorism, making Islam a highly political (and opaque) issue.

The subsequent U.S. wars in Afghanistan and Iraq led American diplomats to search the globe for examples of "success stories" in "pro-American" Muslim states. Kosovo was an obvious choice in this regard. The drive toward Kosovo independence, a goal supported by powerful countries such as the U.S., UK and Germany, led to the depiction of Kosovo's brand of Islam as harmless, a sort of "Islam-lite."[27] However, the Kosovar state also was trying to woo the Arab world—which had poured billions into the country's development and anticipated Islamic re-direction, to little apparent effect—and reverse Serbia's initial successes in preventing the major Islamic states from recognizing Kosovo. Although powerful states such as Saudi Arabia have since recognized Kosovo, Belgrade pledges to continue to slow the recognition process as much as it can, while Pristina seeks to win further recognition.[28]

The ongoing political impasse with Serbia, as well as highly combustible issues impairing Kosovar-EU relations—such as alleged involvement of Kosovo's top leaders in wartime organ trafficking and drug smuggling—have left one country as the clear beneficiary: Turkey. The current Islamist-leaning government in Ankara seeks to expand its influence in formerly Ottoman lands, and in Kosovo it has done so through development work, investment and political engagement. Moreover, many Kosovars have relatives in Turkey, as a 1950s-era resettlement program by former Yugoslav leader Josip Broz Tito sent thousands of Kosovar Albanians there. These ties, and the Western desire for Islam to remain "moderate" in the Balkans, feed naturally into the idea of a Turkish expansion in Kosovo and neighboring states.

In this regard, the relative strength of Kosovar state institutions is of paramount importance. A major test of this came with the above-mentioned terrorist plot against the Marine base in Quantico, Virginia in 2009. When the FBI sought to extradite a chief supporting suspect, Bajram Asllani, a judge with the European Union Rule of Law Mission in Kosovo (EULEX) ruled that he could not be rendered for lack of a valid bilateral agreement, and insufficient evidence.[29] Although it is not known whether fears of an Islamist backlash played a role in the judge's strange decision, this dysfunctional trans-Atlantic security cooperation is clearly benefiting the increasingly confident and assertive Islamist groups of Kosovo.

ENDNOTES

[1] At time of writing, Kosovo was planning its first post-independence national census for fall 2011. In noting these tentative religious group calculations, a 2010 US State Department mentions that the last reliable census was held in the 1980s (during the former Yugoslavia). See United States Department of State, Bureau of Democracy, Human Rights, and Labor, *International Religious Freedom Report 2010*, November 17, 2010.

[2] For the first, see Dutch filmmaker Klaartje Quirijns's 2005 documentary *The Brooklyn Connection* (www.thebrooklynconnection.net), which details how Albanian-American Diaspora leaders were able to raise $30 million for weaponry which they then smuggled to the KLA. There is a vast literature on the second aspect; for example, read the very detailed contemporary testimony of then-Interpol Assistant Director Ralph Mutschke, who gives an impressive assessment of the range of activities, geographical scope, profits and international crime partners of the major Albanian syndicates, as well as comments on links between such organized crime proceeds and terrorism. See Ralf Mutschke, Testimony before the House of Representatives Judiciary Committee, October 24, 2006.

[3] A detailed contemporaneous description of the specific Kosovar refugee relief operations undertaken by Arab groups in Albania, and their subsequent entrance from there into Kosovo, is found in Hussein Saud Qusti, "Unsung Heroes," *Saudi Aramco World*, July/August 1999. Regarding the role of U.S. and Albanian authorities targeting Islamist groups in Albania during the mid-1990s, see the *World Almanac of Islamism* chapter on Albania.

[4] Frank Brown, "Islam Builds a Future in Kosovo, One Mosque at a Time," Religious News Service, September 12, 2000.

[5] Ibid.

[6] Examples include United Arab Emirates soldiers forcing Albanian villagers in Vushtrri to destroy two historic graveyards in October 1999, and the Saudi bulldozing of a 16th-century Koranic school and Ottoman library in Djakovica in August 2000. See Jolyon Naegele, "Yugoslavia: Saudi Wahhabi Aid Workers Bulldoze Balkan Monuments," *Radio Free Europe/Radio Liberty*, August 4, 2000.

[7] See United States Department of State, *International Religious Freedom Report 2010*.

[8] Brown, "Islam Builds a Future in Kosovo, One Mosque at a Time."

[9] See Christopher Deliso, *The Coming Balkan Caliphate: The Threat of Radical Islam to Europe and the West* (Santa Barbara: Praeger, 2007), 65-67.

[10] The story appeared in numerous local media, including on *Radio Television Kosova*, January 12, 2009.

[11] "Chapter 2 Country Reports: Europe and Eurasia Overview," in United States Department of State, Office of the Coordinator for Counterterrorism, *Country Reports on Terrorism 2008* (Washington, DC: U.S. Department of State, April 30, 2009).

[12] Cases cited in United States Department of State, *International Religious Freedom Report 2010*. (Protestant community members have also reported independently to the author of having been physically assaulted by Islamists in Kosovo). This report also notes the official Kosovo Islamic Community's "concerns about radical Islamic groups they alleged were operating from private homes and led by persons from outside of the country."

[13] The full story of this interaction is reported only partially, and in various sources. See "Kosovo Drug Baron among Terrorists," *Blic* (Belgrade), September 27, 2006. See also Genc Morina, "Radical Islam: Wahhabism a Danger to Kosovo's Independence!" *Express* (Pristina), October 15, 2006. For official reactions to the acquittal, see Nina Berglund, "Reaction Mixed to Terror Acquittal," *Aftenposten* (Oslo), June 4, 2008

[14] Geoff Mulvihill, "Man pleads guilty in Fort Dix plot case," Associated Press, October 31, 2007.

[15] See Gerry J. Gilmore, "FBI, Navy Foil Alleged Terror Plot on Quantico," American Forces Press Service, September 25, 2009. See also U.S. Department of Justice, "Kosovar National Charged with Terrorism Violations," June 17, 2010.

[16] The official web site of the BIK is www.bislame.net.

[17] See Genc Morina, "Radical Islam: Wahhabism a Danger to Kosovo's Independence!"

[18] United States Department of State, *International Religious Freedom Report 2010*.

[19] Gjergj Erebara, "Kosovo's New Cathedral Stirs Muslim Resentment," BalkanInsight, October 4, 2010

[20] Ibid.

[21] See Christopher Deliso, "Lost in Conversion?" www.balkanalysis.com, October 23, 2008.

[22] The original text of the speech was published on the official website of the President of Albania, www.president.al.

[23] See Matteo Albertini, "The Vatican's Growing Prominence in Kosovo," www.balkanalysis.com, April 14, 2011

[24] Deliso, *The Coming Balkan Caliphate*, 65-67, 120-121. Islamic Relief still has extensive activities in Kosovo and helps maintain the UK-Kosovo axis of Islamist activity.

[25] A list of the charity's projects in Kosovo is available on its official website, www.islamic-relief.com.

[26] Linda Karadaku, "Kosovo Deports Self-Proclaimed Imam," *SETimes*, March 11, 2010.

[27] This could be seen in media pieces printed immediately after the independence declaration, such as "Kosovo Touts 'Islam-lite,'" Associated Press, February 21, 2008.

[28] At the time of writing, a total of 76 countries have recognized Kosovo's independence. The major Muslim countries that immediately or eventually recognized Kosovo include Afghanistan, Turkey, United Arab Emirates, Saudi Arabia, Jordan, Somalia, Qatar and Oman. However, powerful nations such as Russia, China, Brazil, India, Israel, South Africa and Iran, still do not. A number of other countries are said to be deciding soon, such as Kuwait, but diplomatic pressure from both Pristina and Belgrade continues to play a role.

[29] For background, see Fatos Bytyci, "Alleged Jihadist Wanted by FBI Lives Openly in Kosovo," Reuters, November 24, 2010. The suspect remains on the Bureau's most-wanted list.

MACEDONIA

QUICK FACTS

Population: 2,072,086

Area: 25,713 sq km

Ethnic Groups: Macedonian 64.2%, Albanian 25.2%, Turkish 3.9%, Roma (Gypsy) 2.7%, Serb 1.8%, other 2.2% (2002 census)

Religions: Macedonian Orthodox 64.7%, Muslim 33.3%, other Christian 0.37%, other and unspecified 1.63% (2002 census)

Government Type: Parliamentary democracy

GDP (official exchange rate): $9.371 billion (2009 est.)

Map and Quick Facts courtesy of the CIA World Factbook (Last Updated July 2010)

Although largely ignored by international observers, the rapid growth of Islamism in the Republic of Macedonia is of greater importance as a social phenomenon than anywhere else in Southeastern Europe, on a par with similar developments in Bosnia-Hercegovina and the Sandzak region overlapping Serbia and Montenegro. Since the demise of Yugoslavia and Macedonia's independence in late 1991, foreign Islamists have found fertile soil in this small and economically-underdeveloped country. Yet other issues of greater urgency have forced successive governments and observers, foreign and local alike, to overlook the Islamist threat, and thereby have afforded Islamists the opportunity to expand their activities in Macedonia relatively undisturbed. They have done so via a formidable infrastructure of official and semi-official NGOs, charities, and educational groups, as well as through the construction of hundreds of mosques over the past decade with funds from Saudi Arabia and other Arab states. The concurrent Islamist strategy of radicalizing or intimidating the mainstream Muslim population, while taking over control of the legitimate organs of organized Islam in the country, has created a serious challenge to the country's historic, tolerant Hanafi and Bektashi tradi-

---

tions.

ISLAMIST ACTIVITY

Islamist activity in Macedonia is most widespread in those areas where the Muslim population—the vast majority of whom are ethnic Albanians—is concentrated. This includes parts of the capital, Skopje, and the towns and villages between Kumanovo and Tetovo (near the border with Kosovo), as well as Gostivar, Debar and Struga (along the western border, near Albania). However, ethnically-mixed areas exist elsewhere, as in the central mountain massif south of Skopje, and Islamist activity also occurs in such areas.

Islamist groups are also beginning to concentrate on areas where few Muslims live, in the south and east of the country, with an eye to expanding their influence and territorial control nationwide. Since Muslims in the latter areas are mainly ethnic Turks and Roma (Gypsies), the Turkish government and various charities also see an opportunity here for development.[1] Turkey is also very active through schools, NGOs and its international development agency (TIKA) in reaffirming the tangible signs of its Ottoman legacy in the country.[2] Under the current, pro-Islamist AKP government in Ankara, Turkey's initiatives in Macedonia extend beyond simple cultural heritage preservation; Turkey also seeks to bring the country into the orbit of powerful international Islamic institutions to help fulfill its neo-Ottoman foreign policy of "strategic depth."[3]

The organization that officially represents Macedonia's Muslim population of 675,000 is the Islamic Community of Macedonia (ICM).[4] The ICM's leading cleric, known as the *reis-ul-ulema*, is presently Sulejman Rexhepi.[5] In July 2010, following a fight and near-riot in a Skopje mosque under Wahhabi control, Rexhepi admitted publicly that the ICM had lost its authority over several mosques in the capital.[6] And in September 2010 (following a fruitless private pleading with the United States ambassador four months earlier), he publicly called upon the U.S. and EU representatives in Skopje to help the ICM counter the growing influence of radical Islam in Macedonia.[7]

However, this plea has generally fallen on deaf ears; while international diplomats have for years been warned about fundamentalist threats to Macedonia's stability, most tend to take a cynical view, considering Islamic infighting to be little more than internal politicking between rival ethnic Albanian parties over property proceeds and other financial interests, and not as an issue of genuine religious extremism. Nevertheless, in Macedonia today, fundamentalist Islam (in the form of veiled women, men in baggy trousers and long beards, and increased public challenges to secularism) is unmistakably becoming more visible in daily life.[8]

While there is certainly some truth to the skeptics' charge of Islamism as mere "business," the violence involved in internal disputes is indisputable. A young and aggressive generation of foreign-trained Islamists continues to make serious attempts to take over ICM property and its leadership; this is logical, given that official positions also come with control over funds and assets, while providing access to both money-making and ideological opportunities. As a result, several violent confrontations have occurred since 2003, sparked by armed extremists seeking to install their candidates in Macedonia's mosques, especially in the capital of Skopje.[9]

Thus, rather than destroying existing Islamic institutions, today's extremist faction simply wishes to take over authority nation-wide, and to redirect activities in a more fundamentalist direction. To accomplish this strategy, they are tactically manipulating the Western-based concept of "civil society" to conceal their true motives. Using the "legitimate cover" of various NGOs, charities and publishing entities, they thus participate in domestic and international conferences, political events, "human-rights" activities and various demonstrations.[10] At the same time, these radicals have expedited the goals of Saudi Arabia and other Islamic states by overseeing the construction of hundreds of foreign-funded mosques.[11]

The ICM has existed since former Yugoslav times as an official religious body, and as a result has specific rights and responsibilities. Pinpointing the activities of Macedonia's Islamic extremists, on the other hand, is usually difficult. Those elements tend to converge under the auspices of a variety of Islamic NGOs, charities, educational organizations and other entities deliberately kept out of the light of public scrutiny. Further, they also possess tacit sympathizers within Macedonian society, including businessmen, media bodies, security companies, and public institutions (generally, in areas with a large concentration of Muslims). Thus, certain individuals or groups that may not immediately seem to be associated with Islamism may actually be intimately involved with its expansion. (Examples of such activities are numerous, and include the donation of funds by local businessmen for the construction of mosques, the printing of Islamist literature by local publishing houses, and so forth.)

Islamist funding streams are similarly opaque. The official wealth of the ICM itself, in terms of funds, real estate and other assets, is neither publicly known nor discussed. Even less well-known is the total level of funding available to radical groups, and the ways in which it is transmitted. Part of this has to do with established tradition, such as the custom of communal payments seen in the construction of village mosques; locals can simply donate anonymously, drop cash in a box, and so on. Even when police have managed to trace some funds to extremist groups abroad, authoritative figures have never been publicly disclosed. Nor do Islamists, despite their frequent calls for officials to show greater transparency, detail the provenance or amounts of their own funding.[12] As a result, investigators have had to work deductively, and to some extent rely on anecdotal or comparative information.

In general, officials believe that Islamists in Macedonia (as elsewhere in the region) employ a creative combination of methods to move money. The use of Islamic students returning from the Gulf as cash "mules" is sometimes mentioned by police. Other financial sources include money from narcotics proceeds, or money raised from the sale of items ranging from plastic chairs to silver and gold. To escape attention from the authorities, Islamists sometimes attempt to eschew large bank transactions, instead breaking up payments into smaller amounts. Finally, donations from ideologically-minded businessmen, officials and Diaspora Muslims for religious projects such as mosques, schools and publications are also in evidence. Indeed, the donating country or organization is often prominently displayed on the entrance of the structure in question, or in the beginning of the book.

It is also widely believed, though difficult to prove, that poor Muslims are being paid to adhere to fundamentalist mores and dress the part.[13] Considering that monthly stipends are said to exceed the average monthly wage ($300-400) it is not difficult to see how even non-extremist Muslims can be drawn into this lifestyle. The destitute and vulnerable Roma (Gypsy) Muslim population in particular is now being eyed as a "growth market" by Islamists.

Islamist activity in Macedonia over the past decade-and-a-half has been guided largely by outside interests, such as Saudi and other Gulf state charities, and proselytizers from Pakistani groups like the Tablighi Jama'at or countries like Turkey and Malaysia.[14] Often global Islamist NGOs registered locally or via Western Europe (the UK is a major hub) are used as intermediaries. However, since the 1990s, relatively fewer suspicious charities have been allowed to register in the country, in comparison to Albania, Kosovo and Bosnia, due to a measure of resistance from Macedonian security officials.[15]

Specific Islamist activity has taken different forms. One key area is the strategic construction of mosques along major highways, high ridgelines, near pre-existing churches or in close proximity to other mosques. According to a detailed Macedonian newspaper investigation in 2010, over 300 mosques have been built in the last decade – 88 alone between Skopje and Tetovo, the main ethnic Albanian-majority city, in northwestern Macedonia.[16] At a cost estimated by the newspaper to reach $1.5-$2.5 million per mosque, the sum expended is staggering. According to the same report, Saudi Arabia alone has committed over $1.2 billion over the past ten years to building mosques, providing education, and sending local Muslims on the *Hajj*.[17]

Aside from mosque construction, Islamists in and related to Macedonia continue to take part in extremist activities around the world. The infamous "Fort Dix Six" plot to attack the U.S. Army base in Ft. Dix, New Jersey involved three ethnic Albanian émigrés from Macedonia, and another from Kosovo.[18] And in Switzerland, the popular referendum banning minaret construction began after an Islamist group led by another Albanian originally from Macedonia agitated in favor of such building.[19] During ethnic Albanian paramilitary uprisings in Kosovo and Macedonia in 1999 and 2001, respectively, Albanian Islamists openly sought to raise funds for the cause in Great Britain, Germany and elsewhere in Europe.[20] Although these revolts were generally secular, small numbers of foreign *mujahideen* are known to have fought in both wars.

At the same time, Muslims from Macedonia, some of whom have studied in radical *madrassas* in Pakistan, have gone on to join al-Qaeda's *jihad* against the United States and the Coalition in Afghanistan (an estimate published in the British media in 2010 put the number at approximately 50).[21] While the Macedonian government has been reticent to raise the issue publicly, lest it damage the country's international reputation, other governments have been less so; Israeli Foreign Minister Avigdor Liberman, for example, did state for the record that radical Islam in Macedonia and the Balkans is a major concern during a joint press conference with Macedonian prime minister Nikola Gruevski in January 2010.[22] Ironically enough, this comment came only four months before three Muslims from Macedonia participated in the controversial "humanitarian flotilla" to break the Israeli blockade of Gaza, organized by the Turkey-based Islamic charity, Humanitarian Relief Foundation (IHH).[23]

For years, security experts have warned about rising Islamism in Macedonia—albeit without arousing much attention. In late 2004, for example, French counterterrorism expert Claude Moniquet estimated publicly that up to 100 individuals linked to terrorist organizations were present in Macedonia, and that the country was effectively being used as a terrorist safe haven.[24] A year later, Macedonian intelligence officials disclosed that Malaysian proselytizers were regularly arriving to carry out missionary activities in Muslim towns and villages. The influx was a product of necessity; apparently, some of the visiting Islamists had either been expelled or feared being expelled from

EU countries, due to political or extremist activities there.[25]

Since the 1990s, hundreds of young Muslims from Macedonia have also gone to study in Islamic states, such as Egypt, Syria, Saudi Arabia and Malaysia, while others have come into contact with radical Islam while working in Europe. Pakistan's Tablighi Jama'at movement has also sent large numbers of missionaries to Macedonia, and has brought hundreds of Muslims to study in radical *madrassas* in Pakistan. In turn, small groups of "believers" are said to be spending 3-4 months of the year in Afghanistan and Pakistan, with their families enjoying financial support in their absence.[26]

An unfortunate long-term result of this trend has been the development of a "next-generation" of local Islamists who have built their own networks. Not only are these cadres in constant contact via Internet message boards and direct electronic means, they also frequently travel throughout the region to spread, and to reconfirm, a message of religious conservatism and hatred of the U.S. and Israel. Occasionally these activities are publicly reported, but since much takes place in an informal setting (makeshift mosques or private residences), a great deal is by necessity missed. At the same time, Balkan Muslims ensnared by radical Islam while working abroad have developed these networks further upon their return back home. For example, a two-year investigation of radicals in northern Italy by the DIGOS special police resulted in the detention of 29 Balkan Muslims, some of whom were believed to be linked to al-Qaeda.[27]

ISLAMISM AND SOCIETY

The greatest defining—and most complicating—factor relating to Islamism in Macedonia is its intimate linkage with ethnic identification and ethnic-based politics. Local attitudes toward Islamic groups, and Islam in general, are not rigidly defined and remain in a perpetual state of flux, as does the general sense of ethnic identification among different groups, Christian and Muslim alike. This unique situation arguably makes a true understanding of Islam and society more difficult in Macedonia than in any other country in Europe.

Nearly 70 percent of the national population of two million is composed of ethnic Macedonians, a Slavic people who speak a language similar to Bulgarian and Serbian. While most are Orthodox Christian, a small number are Muslim—holdovers from Ottoman times, when those who converted enjoyed special benefits. Ethnic Albanians, who comprise 25 percent of the population, are almost entirely Muslim, and predominantly from the Gheg sub-group common to northern Albania and Kosovo. Other Muslim populations include Turks (four percent of the total population), Roma (around three percent), and about 17,000 Bosniaks.[28]

The chronic polarization between ethnic Macedonians and Albanians intensified during the 2001 conflict, when Kosovo-led Albanians took up arms, allegedly for more rights and civic employment opportunities, in the so-called National Liberation Army (NLA). Under international pressure, a peace treaty—the Ohrid Framework Agreement—was signed shortly thereafter by leaders of the four major political parties existing at the time. The agreement stipulated a quota system for things like public sector hiring, flag and language use, and so on. Thus followed a territorial decentralization that amounted to political horse-trading between the then-ruling coalition of the Socialist SDSM and the DUI, an ethnic Albanian party formed by the leadership of the former rebel group, the NLA.

The decentralization has institutionalized the ascendancy of Islam over large and territorially contiguous swathes of the population, particularly in northern and western Macedonia, where the majority of the country's Albanian Muslims live. The artfully-designed new municipalities of 2005 ensured that Albanian mayors would be elected for the first time in ethnically-mixed towns like Struga, in the southwest, and that historically Turkish municipalities would also fall into Albanian hands. The Turks were rewarded, however, when two ethnically-Macedonian Muslim municipalities, Plasnica and Centar Zhupa, were declared "Turkish." However, this new situation also caused resentment within the larger Muslim community as Albanian nationalism was employed to change whole demographics. To win votes, Macedonian Muslim populations were (and are) told that they were "really" Albanian, since they were Muslim; at the same time, savvy Albanians were telling outside observers that they themselves were not particularly religiously observant, in order to avoid being perceived as radicals.

One result of this political tug-of-war has been the rise of a new identity: that of the "Torbeshi." Once used in a demeaning fashion, the name derives from the Macedonian word for bag (*torba*); historically, it insinuated that those thus classified would change their religion for whatever riches were given to them (by the previous Ottoman authorities). The ethnically-Macedonian Muslims thus classified are typically the odd ones out in society: while they speak the Macedonian language of their Christian kin, they are Muslims, like the Albanians. Fitting in with neither side, they are now turning to their religion as a defining factor, or else starting to identify themselves as Muslim Albanians. In this respect, the 2011 census will have serious implications for Macedonia's future, as ethnic Albanian parties will continue exerting pressure on the Macedonian Muslims of the western Mavrovo-Rostuse and

Struga-area villages to declare themselves Albanians. This process of ethnic "conversion" directly expedites the dreams of Albanian ultra-nationalists who seek the federalization or territorial division of Macedonia along ethnic and religious lines.

One victim of the growth of fundamentalist Islam has been the country's more peaceful Bektashi Order—a minority within a minority. Comprised primarily of ethnic Albanians, this more liberal branch of Islam is considered heretical by many Muslims worldwide; in Macedonia, they are particularly despised by Salafis, who condemn them as being even worse than Christians and Jews.[29] During and after the brief 2001 war, the country's main Bektashi shrine, the historic Harabati Baba Tekke in Tetovo, was vandalized and partially occupied by Islamic radicals associated with the NLA. Members of the order who have spoken out against the extremists have been threatened and, despite entreaties to successive Macedonian governments, the Bektashis still cannot register themselves as a distinct religious group.

In October 2010, the ICM controversially authorized a rival, so-called "Bektashi" order from the southwestern village of Zajas as the only legitimate such community in Macedonia.[30] However, the "real" Bektashis, led by the elderly Baba Mundi in Tetovo, are acknowledged by outside Bektashi organizations (and their worldwide leader, Haxhi Dede Reshat Bardhi); they have thus denounced the Zajas group as imposters hastily assembled to solve Macedonia's "Bektashi problem," and to thereby give the ICM future control over any properties claimed from the state under the denationalization process.[31]

On a broader level, the major social issue within the Muslim community is the apparently insurmountable gap between the younger and older generations of Muslims. Young Islamists, confident in their own studies in Arab states, tend to depict older leaders of Macedonia's Islamic Community as "communists" who do not understand Islam correctly, due to their different experience growing up in the former Yugoslavia.[32] Yet the perceived discrepancy is rarely put to the test (say, a televised theological debate); rather, it is generally carried out through violence and intimidation. And since intimidation is often carried out subtly and occurs within tight-knit communities, it is seldom reported.[33] For the time being, therefore, the primary victims of Islamist activity in Macedonia remain the country's Muslims themselves.

ISLAMISM AND THE STATE

While none of the several Macedonian governments elected since the country's 1991 independence have ever directly aided Islamism, neither have any of them done anything to stop it. This is largely due to the need to confront larger issues, such as the poor economy and infrastructure, the Macedonia name dispute with Greece, and chronic nationalist demands from the ethnic Albanian side. But the state's non-confrontational policy is also due to a lack of confidence, present and former officials attest.[34]

Islamists in Macedonia have, since the 1990s, cleverly disguised their true agenda under the rhetoric of human rights and "religious freedom," and American and European diplomats have responded sympathetically, pressing authorities to act on the complaints. In particular, since the Clinton administration and its intervention in Bosnia, successive American administrations have sought to present its engagement with Balkan Muslims as a positive example to the wider Muslim world. This policy has only been reinforced by the conflicts in Afghanistan and Iraq, which have stoked feelings of greater anti-Americanism abroad. At the same time, Macedonian authorities are hesitant to act against Islamist groups, out of fear of upsetting ethnic Albanian sensitivities.[35] And Western diplomats, conscious of Macedonia's latent ethnic tensions, have never publicly called for a crackdown on Islamic extremists—a fact that has led successive Macedonian governments to fear that they will not receive political support from the international community should they take a more active stance.

Without a doubt, the masterstroke of Macedonia's Islamists has been their strategy of manipulating potent Albanian nationalism for their own ends. Well before the country's brief ethnic war in 2001, international diplomacy in Macedonia has been fundamentally driven, and conditioned, by the "Albanian issue." Islamist leaders are well aware that because of the diplomatic dependence on political correctness, any religious initiative will be beyond reproach, if it can be cloaked in the guise of ethnic grievances.

This has allowed both the ICM and Islamist elements to press ever more aggressively to develop Islam in historically non-Muslim areas. For example, near the southern border with Greece, the ICM has demanded that a mosque be built in the tiny village of Lazhec, south of the city of Bitola. In response, members of the local Orthodox Christian community have publicly aired fears that the ultimate goal of Islamists is to drive the non-Muslim population out, questioning why the desired mosque was planned for the Christian part of the village, far from the homes of the few Muslim Albanians there.[36] At the same time, ICM leader Rexhepi sought to bolster his image by assailing leaders in Bitola (like Prilep, one of the towns most important to ethnic Macedonian Christian identity): apparently, an "offense against Islam" was being perpetrated in the city's Ottoman mosque-turned art gallery in Bitola, because a painting in it displayed the naked female form.[37]

By and large, the state's efforts to confront Islamist threats have been disastrous. During the (pre-9/11) 2001 war, the government failed to get Western media interested in the participation of foreign *mujahideen* in the NLA. The following year, a police shooting of several Pakistanis was denounced by Western diplomats as a blatantly staged execution. Finally, in 2003, alleged Macedonian government assistance in "rendering" a foreign Muslim (a German citizen of Arab background) to the CIA resulted in a firestorm of criticism from European officials, with warnings that such cooperation could endanger Macedonia's EU aspirations, along with condemnations from groups like the American Civil Liberties Union.[38] In October 2010, the European Court of Human Rights endorsed a lawsuit against the Macedonian government presented by George Soros.[39] The liberal financier's Open Society Institute is the most powerful and pervasive funder of the "civil society" sector in Macedonia, with close ties to the major opposition party, SDSM.

More dangerous still, certain political appointees and elected officials on the local and national levels are known to be directly expediting Islamist causes. This support, driven by a variety of motives, runs the gamut from granting permission for NGOs to operate and mosques to be built locally, to high-level diplomatic assistance with Islamic donor countries and potential investors in Macedonia's developing economy. Since being elected in 2006 (and re-elected in 2008), the country's current center-right government has made attracting foreign investment its number one priority. With the opposition harping on its perceived failure to do so, the government is hardly in a position to exclude potential investors—including those from the prosperous Persian Gulf and elsewhere in the Muslim world—because of security issues. (In fact, the Middle East and Turkey are being depicted as especially promising trade partners for local businessmen). And, in order to maintain a positive image of the country and its stability, the government is also reticent to bring up the topic of Islamism publicly—although some political and security officials are believed to be frustrated with this ineffective situation. In the long run, a confrontation is inevitable.

ENDNOTES

[1] For example, in the year 2010 alone, some 80 Islamic students from Turkey were known to be studying at the *madrassa* in the eastern town of Stip—with an announced plan for increasing this number in coming years to 500, and eventually to 1,500. "Turski Studenti Go Sardisaa Stip (Turkish Students Occupy Stip)," *Dnevnik* (Skopje), December 28, 2010.

[2] For one example, Turkish State Minister Faruk Celik visited Skopje in December 2010 to mark the TIKA's renovation of the magnificent 15th-century mosque of Mustafa Pasha. He also met with top leaders of the country's Islamic community. See "Turkey Says To Continue Repairing Ottoman Arts In Macedonia," www.worldbulletin.net, December 21, 2010.

[3] For more on the doctrine of "strategic depth," developed by influential Turkish Foreign Minister Ahmed Davutoglu, see Ioannis N. Grigoriadis, "The Davutoglu Doctrine and Turkish Foreign Policy," Hellenic Foundation for European and Foreign Policy (ELIAMEP), April 2010.

[4] The ICM's official website is www.bim.org.mk. This acronym comes from the Albanian-language version of the name, Bashkesia Fetare Islame. Note that the institution is often referred to by its Macedonian name and acronym, Islamska Verska Zaednica (IVZ). International sources also refer to it as the Islamic Religious Community (IRC). All of these acronyms refer to the same official body.

[5] As in many other instances of local language spellings, this name has other variants; the more phonetic one, "Suleiman Redzepi," is often encountered in media accounts.

[6] Svetlana Jovanovska and Branko Gjorgeski, "Radical Islam In Macedonia Worries Western Observers," *WAZ/EU* Observer, July 8, 2010.

[7] "Macedonia: Moderate Muslims Seek Help Against Sect," Associated Press, September 20, 2010.

[8] The most comprehensive analysis of the developing Islamist trend in Macedonia, which includes the testimony of Western and local intelligence officers and the local Muslims themselves, is provided in Christopher Deliso, *The Coming Balkan Caliphate: the Threat of Radical Islam to Europe and the West* (Santa Barbara: Praeger Security International, 2007).

[9] The most infamous examples of Salafi violence date from the turbulent reign of former Skopje mufti Zenun Berisha, who used a sort of Islamist private guard to take over several mosques, impose preferred candidates for jobs, and generally assert his authority. Accounts of intimidation, beatings and attacks against moderates such as former Reis Arif Emini and former Skopje mufti Taxhedin Bislimi were widely reported in the local media. A comprehensive account of these events,

citing some of the leaders involved, is given in Deliso, *The Coming Balkan Caliphate*, 82-86.

[10] Islamic NGOs in Macedonia include both international franchises such as El Hilal and local entities such as Merhamet and Bamerisija. Some belong to umbrella organizations such as the Union of NGOs of the Islamic World (www.theunity.org), which allows them to participate in a variety of events internationally, and thereby network with likeminded ideologues from Islamic states such as Yemen, Iran, Pakistan, Malaysia and Saudi Arabia.

[11] Bojan Pancevski, "Saudis Fund Balkan Muslims Spreading Hate Of The West," *The Sunday Times* (London), March 28, 2010. Further factual details are cited in "Milijarda Evra Investirani Co Radikalniot Islam (Billion-euro Investment In Radical Islam)," *Nova Makedonija*, July 6, 2010.

[12] For an example of this prevailing hostile attitude, note the comments of Islamic NGO leader Bekir Halimi to a journalist: "We are fully entitled to receive funding from both governmental and nongovernmental sources from Saudi Arabia." Pancevski, "Saudis Fund Balkan Muslims Spreading Hate Of The West." In the article, it is also noted that Halimi "refuses to name the sources of his funding."

[13] Ibid.

[14] Deliso, *The Coming Balkan Caliphate*, 73-78.

[15] For example, a former Macedonian counterintelligence chief, Zoran Mitevski, recounted that in 1996 U.S. diplomats accused him of being "undemocratic" when he blocked several terror-linked Saudi charities from registering in the country. Deliso, *The Coming Balkan Caliphate*, 81.

[16] "Milijarda Evra Investirani Co Radikalniot Islam (Billion-Euro Investment In Radical Islam)."

[17] Ibid. These figures roughly correspond with those given in Pancevski, "Saudis Fund Balkan Muslims Spreading Hate Of The West," as well as with figures given to the author by Macedonian security officials.

[18] Three of the men involved in the plot, brothers born in the Albanian-majority town of Debar, were arrested for their role in the failed attacks on U.S. soldiers at Ft. Dix. Garentina Kraja and William J. Kole, "Brothers Behind Fort Dix Plot Were From Pro-U.S. Enclave," Associated Press, May 10, 2007. When the AP journalists visited Debar, distant relatives of the accused men expressed their disbelief at the arrests. The large, Saudi-style mosque currently under construction in Debar had apparently not been begun at the time.

[19] Devorah Lauter, "Swiss Voters OK Ban On Minarets," *Los Angeles Times*, November 30, 2009.

[20] Organizations such as the former "Albanian Islamic Society" in London, located near the notorious Finsbury Park Mosque, raised

money for fighters in 1999 and 2001. British media also reported that mosques in Britain frequented by Albanians were also being solicited for war donations. See David Bamber and Chris Hastings, "KLA Raises Money in Britain for Arms," April 23, 2000. When ethnic Albanians in Macedonia rebelled in 2001, Jakup Hasipi, a nationalist imam from the remote village of Slupcane in northeastern Macedonia, was dispatched to preach and solicit funds in Albanian Diaspora mosques, in European cities like Leverkusen and Hamburg. As with other leading Islamists, videos of this now-deceased *imam* delivering his sermons in such places are widely available on the Internet.

[21] Pancevski, "Saudis Fund Balkan Muslims Spreading Hate Of The West;" See also "Vahabisti Vrvuvaat Borci Za Dzihad Bo Makedonija (Wahhabis Recruit Fighters For Jihad In Macedonia)," Vecer (Skopje), March 29, 2010. These claims correspond with testimony made by different Macedonian security officials and local Muslims to the author since 2004.

[22] A summary of the foreign minister's statements are available on the website of the Israeli Ministry of Foreign Affairs (www.mfa.gov.il).

[23] Goce Mihajloski, "Makedonskite Humanitarsi Se Vratija Od Israel (Macedonian Humanitarians Returned From Israel)," *A1 Televizija* (Skopje), June 5, 2010.

[24] Christopher Deliso, "Fissures In Balkan Islam," *Christian Science Monitor*, February 14, 2006.

[25] "Malaysian, EU-Rejected Islamists Penetrate Macedonia," www.balkanalysis.com, September 28, 2005.

[26] Deliso, "Fissures in Balkan Islam."

[27] "Wahhabis In Labunista Antagonize Locals, As New Details Emerge About Italian Arrests," www.balkanalysis.com, January 5, 2007. Two ethnically Macedonian Muslims were later expelled from Italy; classified DIGOS wiretap transcripts seen by the author indicate that they were in touch with Bosnian radical groups and were aiding the movement of Bosnian and Arab extremists into Macedonia.

[28] These numbers derive from the 2002 national census. The data is available in several PDF files on the official website of the State Statistical Office of Republic of Macedonia, www.stat.gov.mk. With another census due in spring 2011, highly politicized showdowns over ethnic and religious affiliation are sure to increase in the months ahead.

[29] Author's interviews with Islamist Muslims, Gostivar, Macedonia, May-June 2010.

[30] "IVZ Prizna Bekteska Verska Grupa Bo Makedonija (The IVZ Recognized A Bektashi Religious Group In Macedonia)," *Kanal 5 Televizija* (Skopje), October 21, 2010.

[31] "Koj Se Vistinskite Bektasi Vo Makedonija? (Who Are The Real Bektashi In Macedonia?)," *Deutsche Welle-Macedonian*, November 14, 2010.

[32] "Opasnost Od Radikalizam I U Macedonikija (Danger From Radicalism In Macedonia Too)," RFE/RL, September 11, 2010. In the author's personal experience, the meme of "old Communists" (older, traditionalist Muslims) as being allegedly ignorant is a very pervasive one, and invoked frequently by Islamists in the country.

[33] Some examples include: physical attacks against clerics deemed to be in the way of Islamists and their goals; pressure for females to wear conservative religious dress; orders for moderate Muslims not to associate with Christians; injunctions against shopkeepers against selling alcohol; perpetuation of the archaic custom of arranged marriages for teenage girls; threats against young Muslims seen to be engaging in Western "hedonism;" violence against Muslim journalists seeking to report on any such issues, and so on.

[34] "Dali Radikalniot Islam E Sakana Po Bezbednost Ha Makedonija (Is Radical Islam A Threat To Macedonian Security)," *AI Televizija* (Skopje), March 29, 2010.

[35] Ethnic Albanian political parties are of course included in every governing coalition, but they too must tread carefully when dealing with Islamists, since Islam is so basic a part of their own social and economic fabric.

[36] "Vo Lazhec, Ne Se Velat Nitu Dobar Den (In Lazec, People Are Not Even Saying Good Day To Each Other)," *Utrinski Vesnik* (Skopje), September 22, 2010.

[37] "Rezhepi: Bitolskata Jeni Dzamija Namesto Za Molitva, Cuva Zhenski Aktovi (Rexhepi: Bitola's Jeni Mosque, Instead Of Being A Place For Praying, Displays Female Nudes," *Kanal 5 Televizija* (Skopje), October 14, 2010.

[38] "Statement: Khaled El-Masri," American Civil Liberties Union, December 6, 2005.

[39] Richard Norton-Taylor, "Macedonia Called To Account Over Extraordinary Rendition Case," *Guardian* (London), October 14, 2010.

EURASIA

COUNTRIES
Turkey
Azerbaijan
Kazakhstan
Turkmenistan
Uzbekistan
Kyrgyzstan
Tajikistan
Russia

Regional Summary

Situated at the intersection of Europe and Asia, the countries of Eurasia have long grappled with the competing pulls of secularism and Islamism. Today, regional states find themselves under new pressure from resurgent grassroots Islamist sentiment, which has exploited the failings of the area's largely-authoritarian governments—and flourished in spite of heavy-handed official responses.

In the west, Turkey is in the throes of significant geo-political transition. Since its founding as a largely-secular republic by Mustafa Kemal Ataturk in 1919, historically-religious Turkey often has struggled to reconcile the facets of its national persona. With the rise to power of the Justice and Develop-ment Party (AKP) in 2003, however, the country has hewed a more overtly religious—and Islamist—direction. Nevertheless, Turkish Islam remains sig-nificantly more moderate and less insular than the variants of the religion practiced elsewhere in the Muslim world (such as Saudi Arabia). This, in turn, has made the country a sporadic target of jihadist groups such as al-Qaeda, notwithstanding the AKP's active support of Islamist ideas and prac-tices.

Comparatively, however, the authoritarian regimes that populate the so-called "post-Soviet space" of the Caucasus and Central Asia face a far greater challenge from Islamism. The collapse of the Soviet Union in 1991 was followed by the emergence of six new majority-Muslim countries in Central Asia and the Caucasus. It also saw the rise of newfound religiosity among the previously-captive Muslim populations of the Soviet Union. Ever since, regional regimes have struggled to contain, and to control, the Islamist currents present in their respective societies, often resorting to violence in order to do so.

The geo-strategic location of Azerbaijan, located on the shores of the Caspian Sea and flanked by Iran and Turkey, has made it an attractive target for Islamist elements. In particular Iran, which itself has a sizeable Azeri minority, has been implicated in fomenting instability there, either directly or operating through proxies such as Hezbollah. Also notable is Azerbaijan's proximity to Russia's restive North Caucasus republics, which made it a hub for extremists operating in Chechnya, Dagestan and Ingushetia. Gulf states likewise have exerted their influence over Islam and political discourse and Azerbaijan, with Saudi Arabia in particular operating through charities as well as civic and religious institutions to promote its puritanical Wahhabi creed. These drivers have led to an increasing radicalization of religion in Azerbaijan in recent years, even as the government of President Ilham Aliyev has succeeded in charting some notable counterterrorism successes.

Uzbekistan and Kyrgyzstan suffer from similar problems posed by spreading Islamist sentiment. In particular, Hizb-ut Tahrir and other grassroots Islamist organizations have come to pose a considerable ideological challenge to regional regimes (most directly in Uzbekistan and Kyrgyzstan). Violent jihadism, too, is in evidence, with al-Qaeda and the affiliated Islamic Movement of Uzbekistan (IMU) now active in the region. Both (and especially Uzbekistan) have responded to these trends in heavy-handed fashion, which has contributed to alienation among international partners and served to aggravate the local grievances that feed instability. Yet both have also demonstrated surprising flexibility and innovation in devising "soft power" strategies for countering the appeal of Islamist ideas.

Tajikistan, which waged a protracted civil war against Islamists during the 1990s, continues to struggle with religious extremism. A recent uptick in Islamist violence has shed light upon the Islamic re-awakening now taking place in the country—and on its potentially violent manifestations. Both Hizb-ut Tahrir and the al-Qaeda-affiliated IMU are active in Tajikistan, and their message and militancy have been amplified by growing religious sentiment and expression within Tajik society. Observers have cautioned that these ingredients could make Tajikistan a "hotbed" of religious militancy that could spread throughout the region.

Islamism in Kazakhstan, by contrast, is far less pervasive, in both its violent and nonviolent forms. Islamist ideas and practices have found purchase in the country via three distinct routes: as an import from neighboring China, from the Ferghana Valley, a regional extremist hotbed, and as a result of the teachings of Hizb-ut Tahrir. Terrorist activities, however, are few and far between, and as a result the Kazakh government has tended to toe a softer line toward Islamist movements at large, although the country boasts an elaborate counterterrorism infrastructure.

Comparatively, Turkmenistan has been untouched by the Islamic extremism endemic to its neighbors, in large part because of the strange, authoritarian cult of personality of president Saparmurat Niyazov, or "Turkmenbashi," which prevailed from the republic's independence in 1991 until his death in 2006. The practice of "folk" Islam, a Sufi-related variant of the religion, is widespread in Turkmenistan, and—coupled with state efforts to coopt religious discourse, both during the Soviet era and under Niyazov—has helped dilute the appeal and reach of Islamism.

It is Russia, however, that can be said to have been hardest hit by Islamist militancy. After two decades, and despite considerable efforts, the Kremlin has failed to neutralize the violent Islamism that permeates its restive South Caucasus republics. Rather, fueled by assistance from foreign mujahideen and by the Russian government's own heavy-handed tactics, Islamist militancy in the republics of Chechnya, Dagestan and Ingushetia remains both resilient and dangerous. This radicalism, moreover, has increasingly spread eastward into the Russian heartland, where the country's traditional, moderate strain of Tatar Islam now increasingly finds itself in competition with extreme Salafi interpretations of the religion. Innovative grassroots responses to this trend on the part of Russian authorities, however, are not yet in evidence.

TURKEY

QUICK FACTS

Population: 77,804,122

Area: 783,562 sq km

Ethnic Groups: Turkish 70-75%, Kurdish 18%, other minorities 7-12%

Religions: Muslim 99.8% (mostly Sunni), other 0.2% (mostly Christians and Jews)

Government Type: Republican parliamentary democracy

GDP (official exchange rate): $608 billion

Map and Quick Facts courtesy of the CIA World Factbook (last updated June 2010)

While Turkey has sporadically experienced Islamist terrorism since the Iranian revolution of 1979, the level of terrorist activity has been largely nonexistent since the 2003 Istanbul bombings carried out by al-Qaeda. By contrast, political Islamism has consistently gained in strength since the 1980s, peaking with the electoral victory of the Islamist-rooted AKP in November 2002. Islamism is increasingly visible in local communities as the AKP government continues to solidify its hold on political power, placing Islamists and those sympathetic to it in key posts in all three branches of the Turkish government and state bureaucracies, while using state power to help its cronies build business empires.[1]

The secular traditions of the Turkish Republic limit the appeal of radical Islamism among the Turkish society, in spite of the fact that religiosity is important to a large majority of Turks.[2] Nevertheless, while the Turkish government is by and large effective in combatting Islamist terrorism,[3] the deficiencies of Turkish democracy[4] make it possible for Islamists to exploit religiosity and surreptitiously extend their reach in politics. And, with the rise of the AKP, Islamist brotherhoods and organizations increasingly are becoming the dominant political forces steering the Turkish ship of state, and working to broaden Islamism's appeal for ordinary Turks.

ISLAMIST ACTIVITY

Islamist activity in Turkey generally takes place via one of the three channels: (1) through Islamist terrorist groups; (2) through the activities of charities and business organizations; and, most important, (3) through the activities of the Islamist brotherhoods—*tariqats*, communities and lodges—where political influence leads to cronyism and, ultimately, to corruption.

Terrorist Organizations

The *Islamic Great Eastern Raider Front (IBDA-C)* is a Sunni Salafist group that supports full Islamic rule in Turkey. The group's members organize independently, without any defined hierarchy or central authority, and both its legal and illegal actions are carried out via local "front" groups which cooperate with other opposition elements in Turkey when necessary.[5] The group supports the establishment of a "pure Islamic" state, to replace the present "corrupt" Turkish regime that is cooperating with the West.[6] IBDA-C was founded in 1985 as a breakaway faction of the National Salvation Party, at the time headed by Islamic fundamentalist (and future prime minister) Necmettin Erbakan. The organization borrows its core ideology from Turkish poet and historian Necip Fazil Kisakurek (1905-1983), who advocated a return to "pure Islamic values" and the restoration of a universal Islamic caliphate in the Muslim world. Kisakurek also argued that the secular nature of Turkey was responsible for the state's inability to ward off what he saw as Western Imperialism.[7] The organization is highly decentralized, and consists of independent cells united by common goals and ideology, yet operating either autonomously or in concert depending on the circumstances. IBDA-C joined al-Qaeda in claiming responsibility for the November 2003 bombings in Istanbul.[8] The group has not been involved in any activity since, and its leader Salih Izzet Erdis, also known as Salih Mirzabeyoglu, who was captured in late 1998 and subsequently sentenced to life in prison in June 2008.[9] The current status of IBDA-C is unknown.

Turkish Hizbullah is a Kurdish Islamic (Sunni) extremist organization founded in the 1980s by Huseyin Velioglu, an ethnic Kurd and former student activist, in the southeastern city of Diyarbakır. The purpose of the organization, which is unrelated to the Lebanese Shi'ite militia of the same name, is the establishment of an Islamic state. It seeks the establishment of an Islamic state through three distinct phases: (1) a period of propaganda and indoctrination, known as *tebliğ*, or "communication"; (2) the consolidation of a popular base, known as *cemaat*, or "community"; and (3) a *jihad* to overthrow the secular order and establish an Islamic state.[10] Beginning in the mid-1990s, Turkish Hizbullah expanded its activities from killing

Kurdistan Workers' Party (PKK) militants to conducting low-level bombings against liquor stores, bordellos, and other establishments that the organization considered "anti-Islamic."[11] The Turkish government initially largely ignored Hizbullah, even hoping that its Islamism might provide an ideological bulwark against the PKK's atheistic Marxism. By the late 1990s, however, Turkish authorities finally acknowledged that Hizbullah had become a major threat in its own right, and moved against the group.[12] Huseyin Velioglu was killed in a shootout with Turkish forces at a safehouse in Istanbul in January 2000. The incident touched off a series of counterterrorism operations against the group that resulted in the detention of some 2,000 individuals and the arrests of several hundred on criminal charges. Turkish Hizbullah has not conducted a major operation since it assassinated the popular Diyarbakir police chief in 2001.[13] In January 2010, five members of the group were freed in accordance with a new national law restricting the amount of time suspects can be held while awaiting the final verdict in their cases.[14]

The Caliphate State, also known as the Kaplan group and ICB-AFID, is a Turkish fundamentalist terrorist group that operates in Germany and seeks to overthrow the secular Turkish government and establish an Islamic state modeled after Iran. The group was founded by Cemalettin Kaplan, following his parting with the National View political movement in Turkey. Its immediate purpose is to gather the Muslim masses living in Europe under an Islamic banner to reject democracy and Western culture. Its ultimate goal is to establish a federative Islamic state on Anatolian soil based on *sharia* by overthrowing the Constitutional state and the secular order. Since Cemalettin Kaplan self-appointed himself "the caliph" in 1994, the organization has been referred to as the Caliphate State. After Kaplan's death in 1995, his son Metin Kaplan was elected the new caliph, causing divisions within the organization. Following his declaration of *jihad* against Turkey, the new self-styled caliph, Metin, was arrested by the German authorities and served a four-year prison sentence in Germany for inciting members of his group to murder a rival Islamic leader. He was then extradited to Turkey, where he was sentenced to life in prison for treason. His followers have reportedly become even more devoted to Kaplan, who is believed to have a fortune worth millions, considering him a martyr for the cause of Allah.[15] The group, organized as *Verband der Islamischen Vereine und Gemeinden e.V.* (Islami Cemaat ve Cemiyetler Birligi/ ICCB) with 1,200 members in Germany and an estimated membership of 5,000 around Europe, was outlawed by the German authorities in 2002.[16]

The Army of Jerusalem (Kudüs Ordusu or Tevhid-Selam) is an illegal organization which emerged in 1985. Using the publication of several magazines, including *Tevhid* and *Selam*, as cover, the group often collaborated with other organizations and received its inspiration from the "Qods (Jerusalem) Force" paramilitary unit of Iran's Islamic Revolutionary Guard Corps.[17] In the year

2000, twenty-four members were indicted for attempting to overthrow the country's secular regime and establish a state based upon religious law, and for their involvement in the assassinations of several pro-secular journalists and academics during the 1990s. Fifteen of them were subsequently convicted in 2002, with three receiving a death sentence.[18]

Al-Qaeda is also active in Turkey. In 2003, a Turkish chapter of the Bin Laden network surfaced, possibly in collaboration with IBDA-C members, to conduct terrorist attacks against two synagogues, an HSBC bank and the British consulate.[19] According to Richard Barrett, the head of the UN's al-Qaeda and Taliban monitoring group, there are over 100 Turkish-speaking al-Qaeda members along the Pakistan-Afghanistan border.[20] Since the Istanbul bombings, Turkish authorities have cracked down on the members running the group's operations in Turkey, sentencing many of them to life in prison.[21]

Finally, there is *Hizb ut-Tahrir*. Founded in 1953, the group made its way to Turkey in 1978, espousing its aims of establishing an Islamic caliphate and introducing *sharia* law. The group was outlawed by a Turkish court in 2004.[22] The Turkish police have often detained members of the organization. The latest raid came in 2009 with the authorities detaining 165 suspected Hizb ut-Tahrir members.[23] Though the exact size and breadth of the group's Turkish branch is not known, documents and maps confiscated during the 2009 raids have exposed the organization's plans to establish a caliphate spanning from Ukraine to Spain in Europe, from Kazakhstan to India in Asia, from Morocco to Gabon and from Egypt to Mozambique in Africa and from Madagascar to Indonesia in the Indian Ocean.[24] Hizb ut-Tahrir is active in Turkey, despite having been formally banned by the Turkish courts, and boasts an organizational office in the capital city of Ankara, as well as a dedicated website under the name of *Türkiye Vilayeti*, or Turkish province.[25]

Charities/Organizations

In their efforts to better organize and expand their reach, Turkish Islamists have expanded their activity from terrorist groups to NGOs. Nearly every *tariqat*, lodge or brotherhood has formed its own organization, be it charity or business.

The *IHH (The Foundation for Human Rights and Freedoms and Humanitarian Relief)*, which organized the May 2010 humanitarian aid flotilla to the Gaza Strip that resulted in a raid by the Israeli forces, leaving nine dead, is not considered a terrorist group. The group operates as a humanitarian relief organization and has close ties to Turkey's ruling Justice and Development Party (AKP).[26] Formed to provide aid to Bosnian Muslims in the mid-1990s,[27] it has held "Special Consultative Status" with the United Nations Economic and Social Council since 2004.[28] However, French counterterrorism magistrate Jean-Louis Bruguiere has accused the group of helping *muja-*

hideen to infiltrate the Balkans in the mid-1990s, and alleges that the IHH is affiliated with al-Qaeda.[29] For its part, the Intelligence and Terrorism Information Center, an Israeli NGO with close ties to the country's military, does not dispute the IHH's legitimate philanthropic activities, but says that the organization is an overt supporter of Hamas and has helped provide weapons and funds for Hamas and other Islamic terrorist groups in the Middle East.[30]

Established in 1990, the vision of *MUSIAD (the Independent Industrialists and Businessmen's Association)* is "[t]o become the number one business association in Turkey which is trusted and valued by the majority of our people, which represents its country in the best way both domestically and internationally and whose members are sincerely loyal to their faith, by blending with the thousand year old values of its people."[31] While MUSIAD claims that its name is an acronym for "Independent" ("*Müstakil*"), most Turks suspect that it stands for "Muslim (*Müslüman*) Industrialists and Businessmen's Association." Indeed, the organization appears to have originally been formed as a more religious counterpoint to the country's predominant business group, the Turkish Industry and Business Association (TUSIAD).[32] The group does not appear to engage in illegal activity, but operates to extend the reach of Islamist capital—what is called *yeşil sermaye*, "green money," in Turkey. Green money is basically money from wealthy Islamist businessmen and Middle Eastern countries that, through careful investment, is funneled into legitimate businesses that end up serving as an engine for Islamist parties.[33]

Brotherhoods

One cannot present an accurate picture of Turkey without highlighting the social activities and political influence of Islamist brotherhoods—namely, the *tariqats*, the *cemaats*, the *tekke* and their varying extensions. The problem with the brotherhoods does not lie in their political involvement, however corrupt it may be, but rather in the unconditionally submissive tribal nature of the group to a sheik or a *hoca*, i.e., to the wishes of a single gang leader.

While numerous *tariqats* exist, three groups in particular—the *Kadiris*, the Nakshibendis and the *Nurcus*—founded the *Milli Nizam Partisi* (National Order Party) in 1970, and then the *Milli Selamet Partisi* (National Salvation Party) a couple years later. In doing so, they sowed the seeds for the modern political Islamist movement in Turkey. The Nakshibendis and the *Nurcus* have increasingly become the dominant forces in Turkey in the last decade.

The most deeply-rooted *tariqat*, originating in Middle Asia centuries ago, <u>Nakshibendis</u> in Turkey are comprised of the Suleyman, Iskenderpasha, Erenkoy, Ismailaga, Işıkçılar, Menzilci and Haznevi groups (communities and lodges) among others.[34] The Nakshibendis have a long track record of supporting conservative parties on the right, including Islamist parties like Refah and its modern iteration, the AKP. The Suleymancis have dominated the state-controlled Directorate of Religious Affairs since the 1940s.[35] The Ismailaga lodge has focused on spreading its influence among poor voters,[36] while the Erenkoy and Iskenderpasha lodges have appealed to middle- to upper-class voters. Turkish political leadersIslamist leader Necmettin Erbakan, prime ministers Turgut Ozal and Tayyip Erdogan—have all been a part of or close to the Iskenderpasha community.[37,38]

The *Nur cemaat* emerged some time in the first quarter of the 20th century (no exact date can be found anywhere, including the movement's own websites) as a Sunni movement based on the teachings of its founder—a Muslim Kurd named Said-i Kurdi (also known as Said-i Nursi), who, in a 1922 letter to Ataturk demanded that the new republic base itself on Islamic principles.[39] The group was often subjected to pressure by successive Turkish governments until Nursi's death in 1960. Thereafter, the movement has split into different groups, the most active of which is the Fethullah Gulen *cemaat*, which has schools not only in all regions of Turkey, but also internationally from Africa to the Far East Asia,[40] including the United States. In addition to schools, the movement includes the Journalists and Writers Foundation, various businesses, and media outlets such as *Zaman* and its English-language edition, *Today's Zaman, Samanyolu TV*, and *Aksiyon Weekly*. According to a detailed 2009 study, the movement seeks to fundamentally transform Turkish society via its extensive network of media, bureaucratic, academic and economic connections.[41] Concerns over the political agenda of the group has been raised by U.S. government officials as well. The Gulenists have supported the AKP (Justice and Development Party) since 2002.

ISLAMISM AND SOCIETY

Turkey's population of nearly 79 million is 99.8 percent Muslim, most of them Sunni, the remainder Christian and Jewish.[42] During the reign of the Ottoman Empire, religious communities were allowed to govern themselves under their own system (*millet*)—*sharia* for Muslims, Canon Law for Christians and Halakha for Jews. In the *millet* system, people were defined by their religious affiliations, rather than their ethnic origins. The head of a *millet*—most often a religious hierarch, such as the Greek Orthodox Patriarch of Constantinople—reported directly to the Ottoman Sultan.[43]

After the demise of the Ottoman Empire following the First World War, the Republic of Turkey was founded upon the ideals of modernism and secularism.[44] The founders of the modern Republic considered the separation of religion and politics an essential step to adopting Western values and secularism, and as mandatory condition for its accomplishment in a Muslim nation.[45] The new regime therefore abolished the Ottoman sultanate in 1922 and the caliphate in 1924, replacing laws based on *sharia* with European legal codes.[46] Additionally, they switched from the Arabic alphabet to the Latin and from the Islamic calendar to the Gregorian while restricting public attire associated with atavistic Ottoman and religious affiliations (outlawing the fez and discouraging women from wearing the veil).

With the abolition of the caliphate, Islam no longer constituted the basis for the Turkish legal system. However, vestiges remained; despite the abolishment of *Şeyhülislam*, the superior authority in the matters of Islam, and the Ministry of Religious Affairs and Pious Foundations,[47] Islam was still preserved as the state religion by the Constitution of 1924,[48] and the Directorate for Religious Affairs, *Diyanet*, was established to oversee the organization and administration of religious affairs. The Unification of Instruction, *Tevhid-i Tedrisat*, brought all educational establishments under the control of the state.[49] Hence, the transformation from a tribal entity to a national entity – from an *ummah* to a modern nation-state – was initiated.

Since the start of the multi-party democracy in 1946 and the ensuing victory of the Democratic Party, *Demokrat Parti*, four years later, the Islamist groups consisting of Sufi brotherhoods - *tariqats*, communities and lodges - and have managed to take advantage of the appeasement strategies of political parties in competition for votes and have increasingly become powerful players in Turkish politics, often exploiting the deficiencies of the nation's young democratic system. Islamist terrorism has also become a factor since the 1980s, gaining momentum after the 1990s.

In today's Turkey, indigenous Islamist groups imitate the strategies of foreign Islamists. Political sociologists and commentators have long warned of this phenomenon. For example, in a 1999 letter to then-Prime Minister Bulent Ecevit, political scientist Gurbuz Evren warned about the importation of ideas and strategy from the Muslim Brotherhood:

> The political Islamist segment is currently trying to establish the Egypt-originated 'Muslim Brotherhood' model in Turkey. This model aims to create an "alternative society within a society." According to the model, the fundamental needs of the poverty-stricken masses and the low-income segments are designated. Then, hospitals and medical centers that provide free medical services are established, scholarships are increasingly provided for students, religious educational institutions are disseminated, the number of soup kitchens and charities that hand out clothes and financial aid are increased. On days like wedding days, holidays and child births, people are paid visits to make them feel they are not alone and are given gifts. In short, a society comprised of peo-

ple who are made to believe that their problems can be solved not by the current order, but via the religion of Islam that embraces them... a society comprised of people who are dressed differently with totally different lifestyles... a society comprised of people who will eventually toil to influence and pressure the rest of the society will be created.[50]

Evren had even warned that a new party based on this model was most likely to be founded out of a cadre of the Islamist *Refah Partisi* (Welfare Party) and *Fazilet Partisi* (Virtue Party). As predicted, the AKP—which contains former members of both *Refah* and *Fazilet*—was founded on August 14, 2001, and went on to win the country's November 2002 parliamentary elections.

Grassroots Islamism in Turkey is also strengthened by the infusion of "green money" from other Middle Eastern states. These vast financial flows, estimated by government officials and Turkish economists at between $6 billion and $12 billion from 2002 to 2005,[51] have given both imported and domestic interpretations of Islamism considerable voice in Turkish society. Moreover, terrorist groups active in Turkey appear to be financed not only through domestic methods (including donations, theft, extortion, and other illicit activity), but also via funds from abroad as well as training and logistics. The amount and origin of such funding is not fully known, but are understood to be substantial. For example, documents recovered in the January 2000 raid against Hizbullah in Istanbul helped to expose the significant financial and logistical support Iran has been providing for the group. Foreign contributions such as this go a long way toward defining the effectiveness of these groups. Since such raids by the security forces often disrupt group activity, foreign support serves as a much-needed lifeline in terms of sanctuary, training, arms, ammunition, food and clothing.[52]

Turkish society in general does not appear as susceptible to Islamism as that of other Muslim nations, or the Muslim communities in Europe. When it comes to religious conservatism, 42 percent of Turks consider themselves irreligious or slightly religious, 37 percent are somewhat religious while just half that number, 21 percent, identify themselves as very religious or extremely religious (with only 1.6 percent falling into the latter category).[53] However, Islamist groups in the form of "Islamic holdings" have been known to prey on the religious communities in Anatolian Turkey and the religious Turkish population in Germany, borrowing directly from lenders without using any financial intermediaries and accumulating large sums of capital.[54] The support for Islamist terror groups by the Turkish society, on the other hand, has been negligible and is restricted to the extreme minority.

ISLAMISM AND THE STATE

Since the founding of the Turkish Republic, the Turkish state has made an effort to separate Islam from Islamism. In its attempt to erect a tradition of "state Islam," the government has regulated religious affairs via the *Diyanet* (the Directorate of Religious Affairs established in 1924). The *Diyanet*, directly tied to the office of the Prime Minister, coordinates the building of mosques, trains and appoints *imams* and determines the topics for weekly Friday sermons by *imams*. Thus, in contrast with other regional states (where governments finance, certify, and supervise mosques but underground radical mosques, *Koranic* schools, and *imams* successfully compete with government establishments, more or less unchecked) state Islam in Turkey has enjoyed a near-monopoly on legitimate expression of the Muslim faith.[55]

Over the years, the formally secular nature of the Turkish state has led to constraints on political participation as well. Article 2 of the Turkish Constitution, which codifies that "The Republic of Turkey is a democratic, secular and social state governed by the rule of law,"[56] has served as the basis for the closure of four political parties—the *Millet Partisi* (the Nation Party), *Milli Nizam Partisi, Refah Partisi* and *Fazilet Partisi*—each of which was charged with violating the secular nature of the Republic. Twenty-two other parties have been banned for other reasons.[57]

While the Turkish military has been involved in several interventions (commonly termed as "coups") over the years, only one—the 1997 warning from the country's National Security Council that led to the resignation of Necmettin Erbakan's ruling Islamist coalition—was related to a violation of secularism. Turkey's transition to a multi-party system and the evolution of the Turkish democracy has since been marked by friction between the competing pulls of modernization and traditional societal mores. Successful collective political action by tribal leaders, in combination with the appeasement policies of political leaders, has given tribal entities a disproportionate voice in Turkish politics, allowing the more traditional minority to dominate the country's political scene.[58] As a result, even the *Diyanet*, established to control the religious exploitation common in an earlier age, has ended up being dominated by one of the Islamist bodies it was intended to control, namely the Suleymancis of the Nakshibendi *tariqat*. The outcome has been further "Sunni-ization" of Turkey over the years, despite the supposed neutrality of the state toward all religions and their branches. In keeping with this trend, the U.S. State Department's 2010 *Report on International Religious Freedom* notes that the Turkish state "provided training for Sunni Muslim clerics" while "religious communities outside the Sunni Muslim mainstream have not found a suitable system to train leadership inside the country within the current legal framework."[59] The report goes on to detail that "Alevi children received the same compulsory religious education as all Muslim students, and many Alevis alleged discrimination in the government's failure to include any of their doctrines or beliefs in religious instruction classes in public schools."[60]

The nature of the game is the power struggle to dominate the political system that does not take into account the true voice of the people, as it does not allow the voters to elect their own parliamentary representatives. The party leaders handpick the members of the parliament and practically dictate which decisions they make, just as the sheiks and the hocas do. It is usually one political elite against another, who even collude when necessary, playing the same "Islam game" to squeeze out an advantage while tribalism resists modernity and keeps feeding off the Turkish people.

The counterterrorism efforts of the current Turkish government continue to be largely successful with regard to Islamism; Turkey has not been afflicted by Islamist terrorism since the al-Qaeda bombings in late 2003. By contrast, the Turkish government has not fared as well against the Kurdish terrorist group PKK, which continues to carry out subversive activities and acts of violence against the Turkish state.[61]

ENDNOTES

[1] Richard C. Morais and Denet C. Tezel, "Turkey's Double Edge," *Forbes*, February 11, 2008, http://www.forbes.com/forbes/2008/0211/080.html.

[2] "KONDA Research: Religion, Secularism and the Veil in Daily Life Survey September 2007," *Milliyet* (Istanbul), December 2007.

[3] "Istanbul Bombacisi 6 El Kaideci Yakalandi," [Six Al-Qaeda Hand Istanbul Bombers Arrested] *Aksam* (Istanbul), September 16, 2009, http://aksam.medyator.com/2009/09/16/haber/guncel/6772/istanbul_bombacisi_6_el_kaideci_yakalandi.html.

[4] Okan Altiparmak, "Turkey's Uncertain Future: A Symposium," *The American*, April 30, 2008, http://www.american.com/archive/2008/april-04-08/turkey2019s-uncertain-future-a-symposium.

[5] Yoni Fighel, "Great East Islamic Raiders Front (IBDA-C) – A Profile," International Institute for Counter-Terrorism, January 12, 2003, http://www.ict.org.il/Articles/tabid/66/Articlsid/565/currentpage/19/Default.aspx

[6] U.S. Department of State, Office of the Coordinator for Counterterrorism, "Appendix C: Background Information on Other Terrorist Groups,"n.d., http://www.state.gov/documents/organization/31947.pdf.

[7] Center for Defense Information, "In the Spotlight: The Great East Islamic Raiders Front (IBDA-C)," October 8, 2004, http://www.cdi.org/program/issue/document.cfm?DocumentID=2535&IssueID=56&StartRow=1&ListRows=10&appendURL=&Orderby=DateLastUpdated&ProgramID=39&issueID=56.

[8] "Turkey Buries Latest Bomb Victims," CNN, November 21, 2003, http://articles.cnn.com/2003-11-21/world/turkey.blast_1_attacks-on-british-interests-bomb-attacks-qaeda?_s=PM:WORLD.

[9] "IBDA-C lideri Salih Mirzabeyoglu'na müebbet hapis," [IBDA-C Leader Salih Mirzabeyoglu Gets Life Imprisonment,] Ihlas Haber, June 13, 2008, http://www.iha.com.tr/haber/detay.aspx?nid=25163&cid=13.

[10] Gareth Jenkins, "Back with a Vengeance: Turkish Hezbollah," Jamestown Foundation *Terrorism Monitor* 6, iss. 2, January 25, 2008, http://www.jamestown.org/programs/gta/single/?tx_ttnews%5Btt_news%5D=4684&tx_ttnews%5BbackPid%5D=167&no_cache=1.

[11] Department of State, "Appendix C: Background Information on Other Terrorist Groups."

[12] Jenkins, "Back with a Vengeance."

[13] Department of State, "Appendix C: Background Information on Other Terrorist Groups."

[14] İzgi Güngör, "Release of Turkish Hizbullah members sparks controversy over its future strategy," *Hurriyet* (Istanbul), January 9, 2010,

http://www.hurriyetdailynews.com/n.php?n=release-of-turkish-hiz-bullah-members-sparks-controversy-over-its-future-strategy-2011-01-09.

[15] "Profile: The Caliph of Cologne," BBC, May 27, 2004, http://news.bbc.co.uk/2/hi/europe/1705886.stm.

[16] "Kaplancilar'ın itirazi kabul edilmedi," [Kaplan Objection was not Accepted] *Mynet Haber*, November 28, 2002, http://haber.mynet.com/detay/dunya/kaplancilarin-itirazi-kabul-edilmedi/32157.

[17] Keles: Mumcu cinayeti cozuldu," [Keles: Mumcu's Murder Solved] NTVMSNBC, July 11, 2000, http://arsiv.ntvmsnbc.com/news/16885.asp.

[18] "Ugur Mumcu aniliyor," [Ugur Mumcu Remembered] *Hurriyet* (Istanbul), January 24, 2002, http://webarsiv.hurriyet.com.tr/2002/01/24/79593.asp.

[19] Emrullah Uslu, "Was Alleged al-Qaeda Attack a Failed Attempt to Occupy the U.S. Consulate in Istanbul?" Jamestown Foundation *Terrorism Monitor* 5, iss. 27, July 23, 2008, http://www.jamestown.org/programs/gta/single/?tx_ttnews[tt_news]=5073&tx_ttnews[backPid]=246&no_cache=1.

[20] Tolga Tanis, "En az 100 Turk El Kaideci," [More than 100 Turkish al-Qaeda Hands] *Hurriyet* (Istanbul), October 10, 2010, http://www.hurriyet.com.tr/dunya/16004291.asp.

[21] Aysegul Usta, "El Kaide'ye 7 muebbet hapis," [7 al-Qaeda get Life in Prison] *Hurriyet* (Istanbul), February 17, 2007, http://hurarsiv.hurriyet.com.tr/goster/haber.aspx?id=5969387&p=2.

[22] Patrick Wrigley, "Turkey Hems in its Islamist Fringe," *Asia Times*, August 7, 2009, http://www.atimes.com/atimes/Middle_East/KH07Ak02.html

[23] "Turkey Detains 165 Suspected Members of Radical Islamist Group Hizb ut-Tahrir," *Fox News*, July 27, 2009, http://www.foxnews.com/story/0,2933,534927,00.html

[24] "Hizb-ut Tahrir'in "Hilafet Devletinin topraklari," [Hizb-ut Tahrir's "Caliphate State Lands"] *Radikal* (Istanbul), July 27, 2009, http://www.radikal.com.tr/Radikal.aspx?aType=RadikalDetayV3&ArticleID=946898&Date=28.07.2009&CategoryID=77

[25] "Hizb-ut Tahrir Turkiye Vilayeti," n.d., http://turkiyevilayeti.org/html/iltsm/iltsm.html.

[26] Damien McElroy et al., "Gaza flotilla: Turkey Accused of Behaving like Iran by Israel," *Telegraph* (London), June 3, 2010, http://www.telegraph.co.uk/news/worldnews/europe/turkey/7801641/Gaza-flotilla-Turkey-accused-of-behaving-like-Iran-by-Israel.html.

[27] Factbox: Turkish Charity Group Behind Gaza-Bound Convoy," Reuters, May 31, 2010, http://www.reuters.com/article/2010/06/01/us-palestinians-israel-turkey-group-fact-idUSTRE64U4SO20100601.

[28] The list of non-governmental organizations in consultative status with the Economic and Social Council as of September 2009 is available at United Nations Economic and Social Council, E/2009/INF/4, September 1, 2009, http://esango.un.org/paperless/content/E2009INF4.pdf.

[29] "Turkey's Radical Drift," *Wall Street Journal*, June 3, 2010, http://online.wsj.com/article/SB10001424052748703561604575282423181610814.html.

[30] Alexander Christie-Miller & James Hider, "Turkish Charity that Sent Aid Convoy to Gaza 'has Links to Terrorism,'" *Sunday Times* (London), June 3, 2010, http://www.timesonline.co.uk/tol/news/world/middle_east/article7142977.ece.

[31] Vision, MUSIAD website, http://www.musiad.org.tr/en/Musiad-Hakkinda.aspx?id=2

[32] Eylem Turk, "Omer Cihad Vardan, Son dönemin yükselen muhafazakar dernekleri," [The rising conservative associations of the recent era] *Ekonomi, Milliyet*, August 1, 2009, http://www.milliyet.com.tr/Ekonomi/HaberDetay.aspx?aType=HaberDetay&ArticleID=1123854&Date=20.03.2011&Kategori=ekonomi&b=Son%20donemin%20yukseleni%20muhafazak%C3%A2r%20dernekler; TUSIAD US, "Mission Statement," n.d., http://www.tusiad.us/about.cfm?TEMPLATE=1.

[33] Michael Rubin, "Green Money, Islamist Politics in Turkey," *Middle East Quarterly*, Winter 2005, 13-23, http://www.meforum.org/684/green-money-islamist-politics-in-turkey.

[34] Okan Konuralp, "Turkiye'nin tarikat ve cemaat haritasi," [Turkey's Religious Order, and Community Map] *Hurriyet* (Istanbul), September 17, 2006, http://www.hurriyet.com.tr/pazar/5097892.asp?m=1&gid=112&srid=3432&oid=4.

[35] "Suleymancilar: Gizlilik Yemini," [Suleymancilar: A Privacy Oath] *Sabah* (Istanbul), September 20, 2006, http://arsiv.sabah.com.tr/2006/09/20/cp/gnc113-20060917-102.html.

[36] "Yakin plan tarikat rehberi," [Close-up Sect] *Sabah* (Istanbul), September 20, 2006, http://arsiv.sabah.com.tr/2006/09/20/cp/gnc111-20060917-102.html.

[37] Timur Soykan, "Naksibendi seyhi oldu," [Naqshibandi Sheikh is Dead] *Radikal* (Istanbul), February 5, 2001, http://www.radikal.com.tr/2001/02/05/turkiye/01nak.shtml

[38] Sefa Kaplan, *Recep Tayyip Erdogan: Gelecegi Etkileyecek Siyasi Liderler*, Istanbul: Dogan Kitap, 2007). ISBN 9752935563

[39] "Said-i Nursi'nin Ataturk'e 88 yillik mektubu," [Said-i Nursi's Ataturk 88-Year Letter," *Gazetevatan*, January 4, 2011, http://haber.gazetevatan.com/saidi-nursinin-ataturke-88-yillik-mektubu/350685/1/Haber.

[40] Konuralp, "Turkiye'nin tarikat ve cemaat haritasi" [Turkey's reli-

gious order, and community map].

[41] Rachel Sharon-Krespin, "Fethullah Gulen's Grand Ambition," *Middle East Quarterly*, Winter 2009, 55-66, http://www.meforum. org/2045/fethullah-gulens-grand-ambition.

[42] "Turkey," Central Intelligence Agency *World Factbook*, May 26, 2011, https://www.cia.gov/library/publications/the-world-factbook/ geos/tu.html

[43] Ortaylı, Ilber. "*Son Imparatorluk Osmanli (The Last Empire: Ottoman Empire)*", Istanbul, Timas Yayinlari, 2006, pp. 87–89, ISBN 975-263-490-7.

[44] Kemal Karpat, "Modern Turkey," in P.M. Holt et al., eds. *The Cambridge History of Islam*, 1970, vol I, 528; Yael Navaro-Yashin, *Faces of the State: Secularism and Public life in Turkey* (Princeton: Princeton University Press, 2002).

[45] Stanford J. Shaw and Ezel K. Shaw, *History of the Ottoman Empire and Modern Turkey: Reform, Revolution and Republic* vol. 2 (Cambridge: Cambridge University Press, 1977), 384.

[46] M. Winter, "The Modernization of Education in Modern Turkey," in Jacob M. Landau, ed., *Atatürk and the Modernization of Turkey* (Leiden: Brill, 1984), 186.

[47] Karpat, op cit, p. 533-4.

[48] Shaw and Shaw, *History of the Ottoman Empire and Modern Turkey*, 385.

[49] Republic of Turkey Presidency of Religious Affairs, "The State and Religion in Modern Turkey," n.d., http://www.diyanet.gov.tr/english/ weboku.asp?id=795&yid=31&sayfa=10.

[50] Author interview with Gurbuz Evren, Ankara, Turkey, August 2007.

[51] Rubin, "Green Money, Islamist Politics in Turkey," 13-23.

[52] Turkish National Police, "Teror Orgutlerinin Finans Kaynaklari," n.d., http://www.egm.gov.tr/temuh/terorizm10_makale5.htm.

[53] "KONDA Research: Religion, Secularism and the Veil in Daily Life Survey September 2007."

[54] Gul Berna Ozcan & Murat Cokgezen, "Trusted Markets: The Exchanges of Islamic Companies," *Comparative Economic Studies* (2006), http://pure.rhul.ac.uk/portal/files/778768/Trust%20and%20 Islamic%20companies.pdf.

[55] Soner Cagaptay, Duden Yegenoglu, and Ekim Alptekin, "Turkey and Europe's Problem with Radical Islam," Washington Institute for Near East Policy *PolicyWatch* 1043, November 2, 2005, http://www. washingtoninstitute.org/templateC05.php?CID=2391.

[56] Constitution of the Republic of Turkey, Article 2, http://www. anayasa.gov.tr/images/loaded/pdf_dosyalari/THE_CONSTITU-TION_OF_THE_REPUBLIC_OF_TURKEY.pdf.

[57] "Fazilet, kapatılan 25. Parti," [Virtue, 25 Party Closed] *Hur-*

riyet (Istanbul), June 22 2001, http://dosyalar.hurriyet.com.tr/hur/turk/01/06/22/turkiye/85tur.htm.

[58] Mancur Olson, *The Logic of Collective Action: Public Goods and the Theory of Groups* revised edition (Boston: Harvard University Press, 1971).

[59] U.S. Department of State, Bureau of Democracy, Human Rights, and Labor, *International Religious Freedom Report 2010*, November 17, 2010, http://www.state.gov/g/drl/rls/irf/2010/148991.htm.

[60] Ibid.

[61] Claire Berlinski, "Two Galling Hypocrisies," *Ricochet*, May 17, 2011, http://ricochet.com/main-feed/Two-Galling-Hypocrisies.

AZERBAIJAN

Azerbaijan's strategic location in Eurasia makes it an attractive target for radical Islamic organizations seeking to destabilize the North and South Caucasus. Since its independence in 1991, Azerbaijan has been targeted by several organizations inspired or directed by Iran, utilized by groups involved in terrorism in teh Russian republics of Chechnya, Dagestan, and Ingushetia, and exploited by transnational organizations as a base for external jihadist activities, including the movement of people, money, and contraband through the Caucasus. Azerbaijan's government has actively opposed these elements, charting some notable successes in recent years.[1]

ISLAMIST ACTIVITY

Contemporary Islamist activity in Azerbaijan has taken three dominant forms over the past decade-and-a-half.

The "Iranian hand" and Hezbollah
    Azerbaijan's relations with Iran are complex. Azerbaijan has strong com-

mercial relations with the Islamic Republic, and a quarter of Iran's population – including Supreme Leader Ayatollah Ali Khamenei himself – is ethnically Azeri. Iran resents seeing oil- and gas-rich Azerbaijan prosper, and simultaneously fears that a strong Azerbaijan could prompt the empowerment of ethnic separatist movements inside Iran.[2] Thus Tehran has employed Shi'a Islam as a tool to destabilize its northern neighbor. In that task, Iran had to overcome Azerbaijan's religious traditions, which are more tolerant than those in Iran and have been further diluted by more than seven decades of Soviet rule, leaving the country vulnerable to the influence of aggressive Iranian Shi'a proselytizers.

Baku has repeatedly accused Tehran of interfering in its internal affairs, with some merit. According to Azeri officials, Iran was behind protests that took place in mid-2002 in the suburbs of Baku, and has financed separatist movements on Azeri soil, among them the Islamic Party of Azerbaijan, which was banned by authorities in Baku in 2003. These attempts at subversion led then-President Heydar Aliyev to publicly allude in mid-2002 to "outside forces" that were seeking to transform Azerbaijan into an "Islamic state."[3]

That effort has evolved in two stages. The first took place after the fall of the Soviet Union, when Iranian clerics flocked to Azerbaijan as part of an effort to promote the Islamic Republic's political and religious ideology. Their goal was to subordinate Azerbaijan's brand of Shi'a Islam to the political (*velayat-e-faqih*, or "rule of the jurisprudent") and spiritual (*marja-al-taqlid*, or "source of emulation") leadership of Iran's Supreme Leader. This bold strategy meant reopening the Shi'a-Sunni rift in Azeri society – a tactic that provoked considerable resentment among Azeris.[4]

Tehran's current strategy is more refined. After a period of relative political inactivity during the 1990s, Iran has once again commenced a political/religious campaign inside Azerbaijan. While efforts at ideological subversion still persist,[5] the current focus is on the promotion of the viewpoints of sympathetic Shi'a figures, such as the late Grand Ayatollah Fazil Lenkerani. This has aided in a "renaissance" of Shi'ism in Azerbaijan, with growing adherence among Azeris, particularly Azeri youth.[6]

A major terrorist plot on Azerbaijani soil involving Iranian operatives was uncovered in 2006, when 15 Azeris who had received training from Iranian security forces were charged with plotting violence against Israelis and Westerners.[7] Surveillance initiated as a result of that case contributed to the discovery in 2008 of a plot to bomb the Israeli Embassy in Baku. The plot was uncovered following the assassination in Damascus, Syria of Imad Mughniyeh, the chief operations officer of the Hezbollah terrorist organization. Hezbollah blamed Israel for the death, and in response to the killing – working in tandem with Iran's intelligence service – reportedly mobilized a secret cell.[8] In May 2008, several weeks prior to the planned attacks, police in Baku captured two Hezbollah militants from Lebanon in a car containing explosives, binoculars, cameras, pistols with silencers and reconnaissance photos. A number of Lebanese, Iranian and Azerbaijani suspects, however, escaped by car into Iran.[9]

Currently two Lebanese citizens who held false Iranian passports at the time of arrest are charged with espionage, preparation of terrorist acts, drug trafficking and arms smuggling, while four citizens of Azerbaijan involved in this conspiracy are accused of state treason, as well as preparation of terrorist acts.[10] On July 8, 2009, one of them gave evidence to authorities revealing his contacts with Hezbollah and Iran's Islamic Revolutionary Guard Corps (IRGC).[11] In early October 2009, the court sentenced two Hezbollah militants to fifteen years imprisonment.[12]

Khawarij ("expelled") Members of the Abu Bakr community and the Forest Brothers

The Abu Bakr mosque in Baku is the focal point for the country's Salafi community, and has been seen as a hotbed of Muslim radicalism, terrorism and extremism. The majority of the members of this community, however, are not considered violent, and the mosque's discourse is concentrated mainly on religious values and morality. However, there are the extremist ("expelled") members (*khawarij* in Arabic) who have undertaken violent action to demonstrate their opposition to the current leaders of the Muslim community. The *khawarij* minority believes that it is permissible to rebel against the government and regard as infidels those Muslims who do not share their views.[13]

The imam of the Abu Bakr mosque, G. Suleymanov, is reportedly loyal to the Azeri government and actively opposes "armed jihad against the infidels."[14] On August 17, 2008, a grenade explosion inside the mosque killed two people and left 18 wounded, including the Imam – effectively shuttering the house of worship.[15] (A Baku court subsequently ordered the mosque to reopen, but thereafter reversed its decision.[16])

The following month, Azerbaijan's Ministry of National Security released a public statement on the attack. In it, authorities alleged that Ilgar Mollachiyev, an Azeri citizen associated with extremist activities in the Russian region of Dagestan, together with his brother-in-law Samir Mehtiyev, had masterminded the attack. Mollachiyev, Mehdiyev, and their accomplices had illegally crossed from Dagestan into Azerbaijan and settled in the capital, Baku, and in the city of Sumgayit. There, they plotted to revive the defunct Forest Brothers armed group, which had been disbanded by authorities in 2007. Their aim was the disruption of socio-political stability in Azerbaijan.

Another leader of this ring is a Saudi citizen, Nail Abdul Karim al-Bedevi. He, together with 17 other individuals charged with setting up an illegal armed group linked to al-Qaeda, was issued a jail sentence in July 2008.[17] Subsequently, the case against the new, reconstituted "Forest Brothers" group has been taken up by Azerbaijan's Court of Grave Crimes, where it is now underway.[18]

The "Forest Brothers" case is instructive, insofar as it demonstrates the extent of foreign influence in the growth of Salafi Islam in Azerbaijan. Construction of the Abu Bakr mosque was financed by the Azerbaijani branch of a Kuwaiti society called The Revival of Islamic Heritage. Imam Sulemanov, meanwhile, is a graduate of the World Islamic University of Medina.[19] This is a typical pattern throughout the former Soviet Union, where the lack of local higher religious education and funds allows Arab organizations engaged in *da'wa* (proselytization) to put down roots and expand their influence. The impact, however, should not be underestimated; eight thousand people – most under 35 years old – regularly attended Friday prayer at the Abu Bakr mosque. The total number of the Salafi Muslims, including those in Northern Azerbaijan, bordering Dagestan and Chechnya, is estimated at around fifteen thousand.[20] In other words, around one-third of Salafi Muslims in Azerbaijan attend this one mosque.

Gulf States and the Wahhabi connection

The Wahhabi sect of Islam is considered one of the most anti-status quo movements in Azerbaijan. A subset of the broader Salafi fundamentalist movement, Wahhabism is hostile toward Shi'a Muslims, toward the West, and toward secularism generally. It is pervasive in the north of Azerbaijan. Wahhabi activities are usually financially and organizationally linked to the Saudi government or Saudi Islamic charities, to some Kuwaitis, or other natives of Gulf States.[21]

A number of Saudi charities have been implicated in the support of radical Islamic activities in Azerbaijan. The Saudi charity Al-Haramain, which has supported extremist religious groups in Chechnya and Dagestan, was shut down by Azerbaijani authorities in the early 2000s.[22] Similarly, the Jeddah-headquartered International Islamic Relief Organization (IIRO) is active in Azerbaijan, involved in the distribution of food and provision of medical care through a network of camps and clinics.[23] In the early 2000s, IIRO is known to have provided the Palestinian terror group Hamas with some $280,000 – money which observers say can be traced back to members of the Saudi royal family.[24] Recent events in Azerbaijan suggest that Gulf State support for Sunni radicals in the former Soviet republic remains strong – among them attempted attacks targeting the U.S. and British embassies, as well as the Baku offices of several major oil companies, which have been traced back to Wahhabi organizations sustained by foreign support.[25]

ISLAMISM AND SOCIETY

The majority of the Azerbaijan's 7.5 million person population considers itself Muslim. Of that number, some 70 percent are Shi'a, and the rest Sunni.

Sunni Islam is dominant in the northern and western parts of Azerbaijan, bordering the Russian Caucasus, while central, eastern and southern parts of Azerbaijan, which borders Iran, as well as the capital city of Baku, are traditionally Shi'ite.

The number of devout followers of Islam has increased significantly since the country's independence in 1991. This trend, however, has tended to follow nationalistic lines. During Soviet times, the USSR's official atheism prompted a large segment of Azerbaijan's population to perceive Islam as a part of national identity, rather than a religious belief.[26] With independence, this sentiment has reemerged with a vengeance, utilizing the comparatively newfound freedom to publicly express one's faith.

In recent years, however, both internal and external drivers have led to a radicalization of the Muslim religion in Azerbaijan. The Islamic Republic of Iran and Persian Gulf states such as Saudi Arabia and Kuwait alike have used the growth in Islamic fundamentalism there to influence the domestic and foreign policy of Azerbaijan, and have contributed to the expansion of radical Islam in the former Soviet republic.

Here, Azerbaijan follows a pattern familiar in post-Soviet authoritarian countries: domestic problems, such as corruption, poverty, and official repression, coupled with a general disillusionment with the West,[27] elevate radical Islam as a channel for expressing opposition to the government. So, paradoxically, has the promotion of human rights by Western nations, which has allowed radical Islamic ideas to proliferate under the guise of freedom of religion.

ISLAMISM AND THE STATE

Preserving the separation of state and religion and defeating the threat posed by terrorism are vital national priorities for the Azeri government. The speedy growth of religious activity by Muslim/Arab, Iranian, and Turkish missionaries in the early 1990s generated concern from authorities in Baku. In response, Azerbaijan's parliament in 1996 adopted an amendment to the Law on Freedom of Religious Belief which banned the activities of "foreigners and persons without citizenship" from conducting "religious propaganda."[28]

The following year, the government also required all religious communities to renew their registration. The establishment of the State Committee for Work with Religious Associations in 2001 was another step by which the government sought to control the activities of foreign missionaries.[29] These measures were intended to help contain the spread of radical Islam in the country, though some Islamic communities voiced concerns that such actions had the effect of curtailing religious freedoms. There is some merit to these claims; the threat of Iranian-style Islamic revolution is used to justify state registration of religious organizations, control the import of religious literature, and keeping religious leaders away from political life.[30]

Azerbaijan has taken steps to identify and counter terrorist financing flows by distributing lists of suspected terrorist groups and individuals to local banks. These efforts, however, thus far have fallen short of meeting international standards. At the end of 2008, the government was working on a draft law on money laundering, aimed at creating an anti-money laundering and counter-terrorist finance regime, a Financial Intelligence Unit, and other measures, which will make Azerbaijan compliant with international standards.[31]

Combating organized crime, in particular illegal arms and drug trafficking, is an integral part of the war on terrorism being waged by Baku. Azerbaijan focuses on implementation of the United Nations *Convention against Transnational Organized Crime* and its associated *Protocol on The Illegal Production and Turnover of Firearms*. Azerbaijan likewise is a party to the international Chemical and Biological Conventions.[32] In recent years, Azerbaijan has intensified its fight against illegal drug trafficking, which flows through Iran, the contested region of Nagorno-Karabakh, Armenia, Georgia, Russia and Europe. In 2007 alone, the activity of five transnational and 18 national organized criminal groups was foiled. As a result, 496,857 kilograms of narcotics, 328,154 kilograms of hashish, as well as submachine guns and cartridges, were seized. These seizures led to the initiation of 22 separate criminal cases, involving a total of 82 persons, including 11 foreigners.[33]

The United States and Azerbaijan have cooperated closely in the realm of counterterrorism. Azerbaijan has supported U.S. and Coalition military operations in Afghanistan by granting overflight rights and approving numerous landings and refueling operations at the Baku airport. The two sides additionally have been involved in information-sharing and law-enforcement cooperation. Azeri soldiers have served in Afghanistan since November 2002, and Azerbaijan recently augmented this contingent, bringing the total number of personnel to 90.[34] Azeri cooperation with the United States through the framework of export control and related border security and Cooperative Threat Reduction programs is aimed at fostering its capacity to secure its borders against terrorist infiltration for the trafficking of people and materiel.[35]

ENDNOTES

[1]United States Department of State, Office of the Coordinator for Counterterrorism, *Country Reports on Terrorism 2008* (Washington, DC: U.S. Department of State, April 2009), 60, http://www.state.gov/documents/organization/122599.pdf.

[2] Ilan Berman, *Tehran Rising: Iran's Challenge to the United States* (Lanham, MD: Rowman & Littlefield Publishers, 2005), 94-95.

[3] Ibid., 95.

[4] Altay Goyushov, "Islamic Revival in Azerbaijan," *Current Trends in Islamist Ideology 7* (2008), 73-74, http://www.futureofmuslimworld.com/docLib/20081117_CT7final%28lowres%29.pdf.

[5] Berman, *Tehran Rising: Iran's Challenge to the United States*, 94-95.

[6] Altay Goyushov, "Islamic Revival in Azerbaijan," *Current Trends in Islamist Ideology 7* (2008), 78, http://www.futureofmuslimworld.com/docLib/20081117_CT7final%28lowres%29.pdf.

[7] Sebastian Rotella, "Azerbaijan Seen as a New Front in Mideast Conflict," *Los Angeles Times*, May 30, 2009, http://articles.latimes.com/2009/may/30/world/fg-shadow30.

[8] Ibid.

[9] Ibidem.

[10] Anar Valiyev, "Alleged Iranian and Hezbollah Agents on Trial for Targeting Russian-Operated Radar Station in Azerbaijan," Jamestown Foundation *Terrorism Monitor 7*, Iss. (July 9, 2009), http://www.jamestown.org/single/?no_cache=1&tx_ttnews%5Btt_news%5D=35246.

[11] "Cell Sent By Hezbollah To Attack Israeli Embassy", Ynet.com, July 7, 2009, http://www.ynetnews.com/articles/0,7340,L-3743694,00.html.

[12] Michael J. Totten, "Hezbollah Isn't A Model For Afghanistan," *Commentary*, October 14, 2009, http://www.aijac.org.au/?id=articles&_action=showArticleDetails&articleID=6673

[13] Anar Valiyev, "Salafi Muslims in Azerbaijan: How Much of a Threat?" *Azerbaijan in the World* I, no. 13 (August 1, 2008), http://ada.edu.az/biweekly/issues/153/20090327035841498.html.

[14] Elmir Guliev, *Central Asia 2008 Analytical Annual* (Sweden: Institute for Central Asian, Caucasian Studies & Institute of Strategic Studies of the Caucasus, 2009), 95, http://www.ca-c.org/annual/2008-eng/14.shtml.

[15] Ibid., 94.

[16] K. Zarbaliyeva "Azerbaijani Supreme Court Not Resumes Abu Bakr Mosque's Activity," *Journal of Turkish Weekly*, May 27, 2009, http://www.turkishweekly.net/news/78375/-azerbaijani-supreme-court-not-resumes-abu-bakr-mosque-s-activity.html.

[17] "Ring Leader Who Staged Mosque Blast Killed In Russia," Assa-Irada (Baku), September 8, 2008, http://www.un-az.org/undp/bul-

news63/ds1.php.

[18] Ramil Mammadil, "'Forest Brothers' Group Gives Testimony In The Court," APA (Baku), August 3, 2009, http://en.apa.az/news.php?id=105785.

[19] Sofie Bedford, "Islamic Activism in Azerbaijan: Repression and Mobilization in a Post-Soviet Context," Doctoral thesis before the Stockholm University Department of Political Science, 2009, 104, http://su.diva-portal.org/smash/record.jsf?pid=diva2:200259.

[20] Ibid.

[21] Geybullayeva, "Is Azerbaijan Becoming a Hub of Radical Islam?" 5.

[22] Dore Gold, *Hatred's Kingdom* (Washington, DC: Regnery Publishing Inc., 2003), 154.

[23] NGO Directory, "International Islamic Relief Organization (IIRO)," n.d., http://www.azerweb.com/en/ngo.php?id=227

[24] Dore Gold, "Saudi Arabia's Dubious Denials of Involvement in International Terrorism", Jerusalem Center for Public Affairs *Jerusalem Viewpoints* no. 504 (October 1, 2003), http://www.jcpa.org/jl/vp504.htm.

[25] Fariz Ismailzade, "Azerbaijan's Leaders Fear Spread of Radical Islam, Especially in Military," Jamestown Foundation *Eurasia Daily Monitor* 4, iss. 207 (November 6, 2007), http://www.jamestown.org/single/?no_cache=1&tx_ttnews%5Btt_news%5D=33146.

[26] Bedford, "Islamic Activism in Azerbaijan," 90-91.

[27] Arzu Geybullayeva, "Is Azerbaijan Becoming a Hub of Radical Islam?" *Turkish Policy Quarterly,* Spring 2007, http://www.turkishpolicy.com/images/stories/2007-03-caucasus/TPQ2007-3-geybullayeva.pdf.

[28] State Committee of the Azerbaijani Republic for the work with Religious Organizations, *The Law of the Republic of Azerbaijan "On Freedom of Religious Belief,"* August 20, 1992 (Contains changes and additions of 1996 and 1997), http://www.dqdk.gov.az/eng/zakon_svoboda_e.html.

[29] Bedford, "Islamic Activism in Azerbaijan," 142.

[30] Ibid., 168.

[31] *Country Reports on Terrorism 2008.*

[32] Ministry of National Security of the Republic Of Azerbaijan, "Combating Transnational Organized Crime: Struggle Against Illegal Traffic In Arms", n.d., http://www.mns.gov.az/qanunsuzsilah_en.html.

[33] Ministry of National Security of the Republic Of Azerbaijan, "Combating Transnational Organized Crime: Struggle Against Illegal Drug Trafficking and Smuggling," n.d., http://www.mns.gov.az/narkovas_en.html

[34] United States Department of State, Bureau of European and Eurasian Affairs, "Background Note: Azerbaijan," October 2009, http://

www.state.gov/r/pa/ei/bgn/2909.htm.
[35] *Country Reports on Terrorism 2008.*

KAZAKHSTAN

QUICK FACTS

Population: 15,460,484

Area: 2.724,900 sq km

Ethnic Groups: Kazakh (Qazag) 53.4%, Russian 30%, Ukrainian 3.7%, Uzbek 2.5%, German 2.4%, Tatar 1.7%, Uyghur 1.4%, other 4.9%

Religion: Muslim 47%, Russian Orthodox 44%, Protestant 2%, other 7%

Government Type: Republic; authoritarian presidential rule, with little power outside the executive branch

GDP (official exchange rate): $108.3 billion

Map and Quick Facts courtesy of the CIA World Factbook (Last Updated June 2010)

Historically, the government of Kazakhstan has argued that there were few terrorists on its soil. This position, however, began to change in the early 2000s, driven by a growing appreciation of the asymmetric threat posed by terrorism and religious extremism to the security and stability of the Kazakh state. While there are numerous reports of terrorism in Russia and throughout most of the Commonwealth of Independent States (CIS), it is hard to come across similar news from Kazakhstan. The casual observer could easily get the impression that Kazakhstan is "an oasis of security" in the former USSR, devoid of extremists or terrorists. But this first impression is misleading, as Kazakhstan is not immune from internal threats, nor does it have a guarantee against regional extremist spillovers[1], as evidenced by ongoing volatility in the Fergana Valley and beyond. Kazakhstan's national leadership and government, however, have combined multi-ethnic and multi-confessional tolerance with the tough pursuit of extremism.

ISLAMIST ACTIVITY

In the two decades since its independence from the USSR, Islamism has been imported into the Republic of Kazakhstan along three principal routes. The first is from neighboring China, and the long-running Uighur separatist campaign in the autonomous Xinjiang region. The second is from the notoriously unstable Fergana Valley to Kazakhstan's south, stretching between Uzbekistan, Kyrgyzstan, and Tajikistan. And the third is driven by the global Islamist movement and its vanguard in Central Asia, Hizb ut-Tahrir al-Islami (Islamic Party of Liberation).

The most recent terrorist attack in Kazakhstan happened as long ago as 2000, when two police officers were shot dead in Almaty. The Uighur Liberation Organization (currently known as the East Turkistan Liberation Organization), which advocates an independent Turkistan, is suspected of having perpetrated the incident.[2] The attack, though comparatively minor in terms of lethality, was symbolically significant; while Kazakhstan has mostly been used as a transit territory for radical organizations acting against the governments of Uzbekistan, China, and Russia, the incident indicated that Kazakhstan had shifted from being a mere waypoint for Islamist activity to an actual target for extremists.[3]

According to Kazakhstan's Ministry of the Interior, a number of foreign religious organizations, among them Tablighi Jamaat, Sulaymaniyah, and Nurshyla now operate in Kazakhstan, and some of their missionaries spread "destructive ideas among the masses."[4] Of these, arguably the most prominent is Hizb ut-Tahrir al-Islami (HuT), a clandestine, cadre-based radical Islamist political organization that operates in 40 countries. With headquarters currently believed to be in London, HuT's goals are *jihad* against America and the replacement of existing political regimes with a caliphate (*Khilafah* in Arabic), a theocratic dictatorship based on *sharia* (Islamic religious law). The model for HuT is the "righteous" caliphate, the militaristic Islamic state of the 7th and 8th centuries ruled by Prophet Muhammad and his four successors.[5] A number of Western experts believe HuT to be first and foremost a political organization, and secondarily a religious one.[6] Its goal is to work covertly with opposition elements in various countries, and ultimately to eliminate the ruling secular government and establish the caliphate there.[7]

In Kazakhstan, HuT was first detected in 1998 in the country's south. At that time, an illegal distribution of leaflets and brochures calling for change in the constitutional system and the establishment of the caliphate was intercepted by local authorities. HuT was not formally banned in Kazakhstan until March 2005.[8]

In late 2006, Kazakh and Kyrgyz authorities launched a joint operation to eliminate the HuT "analytical center" in Central Asia, dismantling routes that were used to deliver propaganda materials with extremist content and financing from abroad.[9] As a result of the operation two key HuT leaders were arrested. Uzbek resident Otabek Muminov, the leader of the HuT information-analytical center, was detained and extradited to Uzbekistan. Mahamat-Yusuf Mamasadykov, the head of the organization's headquarters for Central Asia, was arrested in Jalalabad, Kyrgyzstan. Investigations revealed that he had been a key figure in forming the underground structure of HuT in Kazakhstan in 2002-2004.[10] HuT's existing network of cells was thereby dismantled in Kazakhstan and neighboring countries. The synchronized operation is known to have confiscated computers, over 25,000 pamphlets, dozens of religious extremist books and advanced printing equipment during the operation.[11]

Thereafter, in August 2007, five activists of the organization were arrested in the town of Janaozen, where the party had set up a cell in 2006. In the raid, law enforcement confiscated computers, CDs, magazines and brochures and over 400 leaflets. Also that year, 30 HuT leaders and activists were put on trial in Karaganda.[12]

In 2008, the majority of the 41 criminal cases on extremism and terrorism in Kazakhstan were connected to the dissemination of literature and propaganda by HuT. Police were able to find and confiscate large quantities of literature, CDs, DVDs and other materials, in addition to detaining 21 HuT members in June 2008 in Almaty and in the Southern Kazakhstan.[13] In 2009, Kazakh authorities arrested and prosecuted two other radical Sunni cells, encompassing a total of eight people.[14] No further authoritative detailed arrest statistics were available for 2009 or 2010. Nevertheless, the organization is believed to remain active in the former Soviet Republic, exploiting a fertile environment for extremist ideas among the impoverished population.[15]

In addition, in 2008, nine members of a global radical organization called Jamaat Takfir were detained in Kazakhstan's western region, and subsequently prosecuted.[16] The little-known group, like other Salafist organizations active in the region, appears to advocate mandatory participation in *jihad*, with the objective of establishing a global Islamic state. Unlike others, however, Jamaat is said to advocate the punishment of *takfir*—unbelief or departure from Islam. That concept emerged in Kazakhstan in the mid-1990s, following the mass return of Kazakh citizens studying at religious educational institutions in Bashkortostan and Tatarstan, but the exclusionary idea has created a considerable fissure among Kazakh Muslims.[17]

Likewise, al-Jihad al-Islami, an offshoot of the al-Qaeda-affiliated Islamic

Movement of Uzbekistan (IMU), is known to be active in Kazakhstan. It preaches anti-Western ideology and, like the IMU, opposes secular rule in Uzbekistan and aims at establishing a government there based upon Islamic law.[18] Kazakhstan's National Security Committee (KNSC), an internal security service, has alleged that the group—like its parent organization—has ties to al-Qaeda, has cells in Kyrgyzstan, Uzbekistan and Russia, and has been involved in attacks in Uzbekistan. Little is known about al-Jihad's structure and size at the current time.

ISLAMISM AND SOCIETY

Kazakhstan is a multiethnic country, with a long tradition of tolerance and secularism. The government does not permit religious education in public schools.[20] According to the country's 2009 national census, approximately 65 percent (or 10.5 million) of Kazakhstan's 16.4 million person population identify themselves as Muslim.[21] The overall majority of the Muslim population is Sunni, of the Hanafi school. Less than one percent of the population professes to be Shafi'i Sunni, or Shi'a, Sufi, and Ahmadi Muslim.[22] The highest concentration of practicing Muslims is located in Kazakhstan's southern region, bordering Uzbekistan. As in neighboring states, the number of mosques, churches, and synagogues has grown since the independence. However, the population is somewhat concerned with minority ("non-traditional") religious groups and groups that proselytize.

In 2009, there were 2,308 registered mosques affiliated with the Spiritual Association of Muslims of Kazakhstan (SAMK), and around 70 independent mosques.[23] SAMK is a national organization with close ties to the government, which sometimes pressures unaffiliated *imams* and congregations to affiliate and make their practices more mainstream. It has powerful influence over the practice of Islam in the former Soviet republic, including but not limited to licensing construction of mosques, carrying out background checks on *imams* and the coordination of *Hajj* travels, which involves authorization of travel agencies to provide travel services to Muslim pilgrims bound for Saudi Arabia.[24]

ISLAMISM AND THE STATE

Kazakhstan's leadership does not take the Islamist threat lightly. To tackle the terror threat the Kazakh National Security Committee (KNSC, or KNB according to its Russian acronym) established Anti-Terrorist Center in late 2003. A year later, the center disclosed the arrests of over a dozen members of the Islamic Jihad Group/Union of Uzbekistan, shocking many Kazakhs.

In the first half of 2007, Kazakh newspapers reported that HuT members were turning themselves in *en masse,* suggesting massive penetration of the organization by security services. All told, one hundred and forty HuT members deserted the party in six *oblasts* (regions): Almaty, Jambyl, Kyzylorda, Pavlodar, Karaganda, and South Kazakhstan. The surrendering HuT members brought with them more than 3,000 copies of printed materials with extremist content. According to the KNSC press service, 15 former members of the party assisted in the investigation.[25]

Subsequently, that December, 30 alleged HuT members were sentenced for 18 months to seven years in prison by a district court in Karaganda. They were convicted of participating in "an illegal extremist organization and inciting ethnic and religious enmity."[26] The closed door trials raised protests from human rights activists, who voiced concerns about due process and questionable evidence. They claimed that the government was punishing the defendants for their religious devotion and independence from the state-controlled SAMK.[27]

In reality, the situation is more complex. While Kazakhstan's Constitution formally provides for freedom of religion, it also defines the country as a secular state and provides the right to decline religious affiliation. Islamists do not believe in a secular state and do all they can to overthrow it. Activities aimed at overturning the existing constitutional order, especially when violence is used or preached, is subject to law enforcement in all democracies around the world. The question is whether or not these efforts are perceived as legitimate.

The KNSC has characterized the fight against "religious extremism" as a top priority of the country's internal intelligence service. A 2005 extremism law, which applies to religious groups and other organizations, gives the government broad powers in identifying and designating a group as an extremist organization, banning a designated group's activities, and criminalizing membership in a banned organization. HuT is prohibited under this law. In 2008, the Islamic Party of Turkistan was added to this list of banned terrorist and extremist organizations by the government of Kazakhstan.[28] This list is released by the office of the Prosecutor General and approved by the Supreme Court.[29] It is periodically updated and includes, among others: Hizb ut-Tahrir; the Islamic Movement of Uzbekistan; al-Qaeda; the Taliban; the Muslim Brotherhood; Kongra-Gel, a Kurdish separatist group; Boz Kurt (Gray Wolves), a Turkish right-wing group; Pakistan's Lashkar-e Taiba; Kuwait's Social Reforms Society; Lebanon's Asbat al-Ansar; and Uighur separatist groups.[30]

The past two years has seen the leadership of Kazakhstan expand its anti-terrorism activities still further. In September 2009, President Nursultan Nazarbaev signed the law "On Counteracting Legalization (Laundering) of Ill-gotten Proceeds and Terrorist Financing."[31] This law enhances Kazakhstan's anti-money laundering/combating terrorism financing (AML/CTF) functions, and brings Kazakhstan into compliance with the international Financial Action Task Force on Money Laundering (FATF) "40+9" Recommendations.[32] The 1999 Law on Countering Terrorism is still used as the legal basis for combating terrorism in Kazakhstan today.[33] In 2008 the Kazakh parliament considered, but did not pass, a new, stricter counterterrorism law.[34]

This legal framework has paved the way for growing counterterrorism activity at home, and greater Kazakh cooperation with international organizations. In addition to the cases mentioned in the above, counterterrorism actions have included a series of detentions and court prosecutions in 2008-2010, including:

- The February 2008 sentencing of two members of an Islamic extremist group to 12 years in prison, and six others to nine years imprisonment, for plotting terrorist attacks during the autumn of 2006;[35]
- The March 2008 sentencing of 15 members of a terrorist group to prison terms ranging from 11 to 19 years by a court in Shymkent. The prisoners were detained in April 2007 on charges of organizing terrorist acts against the local office of the KNSC.[36]
- The November 2008 detention of an Uzbek citizen wanted for membership in religious-extremist, separatist, and fundamentalist organizations in the southern Zhambyl District of Almaty. His extradition to Uzbekistan is currently pending.[37]
- The April 2009 sentencing of five HuT members "inflaming social, ethnic, racial, and religious hostility" and for creating and participating in "illegal public and other unions."[38] The closed door trials took place in Almaty and Taldykorgan.
- The September 2009 charging of six members of a radical Islamist group with terrorism, illegal acquisition of weapons and ammunition, the involvement of minors in criminal activity, violence and distribution of propaganda materials by a court in the city of Kandyahash in Aktyubinska oblast. The sentences varied from ten to seventeen year terms.[39]
- The November 2009 conviction of two suspects of propagating terrorism, inciting public to commit acts of terrorism and creating and directing a terrorist group called "Al Farabi" by a court in Astana. The two men, who happen to be cousins, were eached sentenced to eight years in prison. Their appeal was denied on February 12, 2010.[40]

In 2008, Kazakhstan also passed five interagency laws regulating the counterterrorism efforts of public bodies, and carried on 148 interagency counterter-rorism training programs.[41] According to the KNSC, the level of activity was not atypical; there were 63 anti-terrorism trainings in the first half of 2009 alone.[42]

On the international level, Kazakhstan in 2008 approved treaties expanding counterterrorism cooperation with Slovakia and the United Arab Emirates.[43] Kazakhstan and China have likewise reached an understanding, encapsulated in a joint communiqué issued in October 2008, to strengthen exchange of information and coordinate actions to counteract terrorism, religious extrem-ism, separatism, smuggling, illegal drug trafficking, transnational crime, and illegal migration.[44] At the head of states meeting of the Shanghai Coopera-tion Organization (SCO) in August 2008, the Kazakh representative signed on to a series of agreements dealing with logistical cooperation, joint coun-terterrorism exercises by member states of the SCO, and joint efforts to com-bat the illegal circulation of weapons, ammunition and explosives.[45] As the result of these framework documents, Kazakhstan will host the anti-terror drills known as "Peace Mission 2010," which involve anti-terrorist command and staff exercises of the SCO member-states, in September 2010.[46]

Given Kazakhstan's role as a location for the production of Soviet nuclear weapons during the Cold War, the government has also been a proponent of nuclear non-proliferation, and experts in this area are concerned about the threat posed by nuclear terrorism. To this end, in June 2008 Kazakhstan hosted the training exercise "Anti-Atom Terror," which was attended by more than 15 partner nations from the Global Initiative to Combat Nuclear Ter-rorism.[47] More than 900 military, intelligence, law enforcement, and secu-rity personnel from Kazakhstan were involved in this field exercise, which took place at the Institute of Nuclear Physics in Ala-Tau.[48]

The government has also advanced interfaith dialogue, outlining a Program for Ensuring Religious Freedom and Improvement of Relations between the Government and Religions between 2007 and 2009.[49] The program delin-eates plans for "increasing the stability of the religious situation" and prevent-ing religious extremism through education and government-sponsored media inserts. In addition, the program criticizes increasingly active "nontraditional religious groups," for causing interfaith tension and ignoring existing tradi-tions.[50] In 2008, Kazakh law enforcement bodies held conferences, round tables and seminars with the participation of authoritative state officials and religious leaders for students and pupils on preventing religious extremism.[51] The program likewise calls for new legislation to augment control over mis-sionaries and the distribution of religious information.[52]

ENDNOTES

[1]S. Sakhiev, "Kazakhstan i Rossiya: Vmeste protiv terrorisma i za bezopasnoste v Tsentralnoy Azii [Kazakhstan and Russia: Together Against Terrorism and for Security in Central Asia]," *Asia and Africa Today* no. 2, February 2008, 40.

[2] "Kazakh Police Suspect Uighur "Separatists" Of Murdering Two Policemen," BBC Monitoring Central Asia Unit, September 2000, http://www.start.umd.edu/gtd/search/IncidentSummary.aspx?gtdid=200009240004 .

[3] Dosym Satpayev, "Uzbekistan Is Subject To The Worst Risk Of Terrorism In The Central Asian Region," fergana.ru, September 2009, http://enews.ferghana.ru/article.php?id=599&print=1 .

[4] Ministry of Internal Affairs of the Republic of Kazakhstan, "Activity Of MIA In Counteraction To Extremism In The Territory Of The Republic Of Kazakhstan," n.d., http://www.mvd.kz/eng/index.php?p=razdel&id1=71 .

[5] Ariel Cohen, "Hizb ut-Tahrir: An Emerging Threat to U.S. Interests in Central Asia," Heritage Foundation *Backgrounder* no. 1656, May 30, 2003, http://www.heritage.org/research/russiaandeurasia/bg1656.cfm .

[6] See Bruce Pannier, "Ten Years After Terror's Arrival In Central Asia," *Radio Free Europe/Radio Liberty*, February 16, 2009, http://www.rferl.org/content/Ten_Years_After_Terrors_Arrival_In_Central_Asia/1494081.html , and Zeyno Baran, Hizb Ut-Tahrir: Islam's Political Insurgency (Washington, DC: the Nixon Center, December 2004), 17, http://www.nixoncenter.org/Monographs/HizbutahrirIslamsPoliticalInsurgency.pdf .

[7] Ibid.

[8] Gulnoza Saidazimova, "Kazakhstan: Government Moves To Add Hizb Ut-Tahrir To List Of Terror Groups," *Radio Free Europe/Radio Liberty*, March 18, 2005, http://www.rferl.org/content/article/1058033.html .

[9] Ibid.

[10] Ibidem.

[11] "Hizb ut-Tahrir Network Dismantled In Kazakhstan," Interfax (Moscow), December 22, 2006, http://www.interfax-religion.com/?act=news&div=2412.

[12] Roger McDermott, "Kazakhstan Cracking Down on Hizb-Ut-Tahrir," *Jamestown Foundation Eurasia Daily Monitor* 4, iss. 162, September 4, 2007, http://www.jamestown.org/single/?no_cache=1&tx_ttnews%5Btt_news%5D=32966.

[13] Ibid.

[14] Manshuk Asautaj, "The History Of Kazakh 'Terrorism'" No Attacks, But One Dead 'Terrorist,'" RadioAzattyk.org, April 2, 2010,

http://rus.azattyq.org/content/kazakhstan_terrorism_azamat_karim-baev/2000401.html; See also Juslan Kugekov, "The Court in Astana Declined an Appeal of the Convicted on Charges of Terrorism Muslim Bothers," RadioAzattyk.org, February 12, 2010.

[15] Center for Strategic and Social Studies, Moscow, "Hizb-ut-Tahrir's Activity in Central Asia," August 2008, http://www.iraq-war.ru/article/173544 .

[16] McDermott, "Kazakhstan Cracking Down on Hizb-Ut-Tahrir."

[17] Rouben Azizian, "Islamic Radicalism in Kazakhstan and Kyrgyzstan: Implications for the Global War on Terrorism," Defence Academy of the United Kingdom, September 2005, 9, http://www.da.mod.uk/colleges/arag/document-listings/special/csrc_mpf-2005-10-17/05(56).pdf .

[18] "Islamic Jihad Union (IJU)," Counterterrorism Calendar 2009, United States National Counterterrorism Center, http://www.nctc.gov/site/groups/iju.html .

[19] Jim Nichol, *Kazakhstan: Recent Developments and U.S. Interests* (Washington, DC: Congressional Research Service, August 2009), 3.

[20] "Kazakhstan" in United States Department of State, International Religious Freedom Report 2009 (Washington, DC: United States Department of State, 2009), http://www.state.gov/g/drl/rls/irf/2009/127366.htm .

[21] Ibid.

[22] Ibidem.

[23] Ibidem.

[24] Ibidem.

[25] Farid Yumashev, "Giving Themselves Up," *Kazakhstanskaya Pravda*, May 2007, http://www.knb.kz/page.php?page_id=59&lang=2&article_id=3129&fontsize=12&fontfamily=Times%20New%20Roman&page=1 .

[26] "Kazakhstan" in United States Department of State, *International Religious Freedom Report 2009.*

[27] Ibid.

[28] United States Department of State, Office of the Coordinator for Counterterrorism, *Country Reports on Terrorism 2008* (Washington, DC: United States Department of State, April 2009), 147, http://www.state.gov/documents/organization/122599.pdf.

[29] "Kazakhstan Updates List of Banned Terrorist Groups," *Radio Free Europe/Radio Liberty*, October 12, 2006, http://www.rferl.org/content/article/1071987.html.

[30] Ibid.

[31] President of the Republic of Kazakhstan, "Law of the Republic of Kazakhstan on Counteracting Legalization (Laundering) of Ill-gotten Proceeds and Terrorist Financing," effective March 9, 2010, http://www.eurasiangroup.org/files/documents/Kazakhstan%20laws/

Kazakh_AML_CFT_Law_Aug_2009_eng.doc
[32] "Kazakhstan Adopts AML/CFT Legislation," The Eurasian Group on Combating Money Laundering and Financing of Terrorism, September 1, 2009, http://www.eurasiangroup.org/en/news_59.html.
[33] On Counteracting Terrorism, Law #416-1 of the Republic of Kazakhstan, July 13, 1999, as obtained from the Soyuz-PravoInform database, http://www.base.spinform.ru/show_doc.fwx?Regnom=1372.
[34] *Country Reports on Terrorism 2008.*
[35] Ibid.
[36] Ibidem.
[37] Ibidem.
[38] "Kazakhstan" in *International Religious Freedom Report 2009.*
[39] Alima Abdirova, "The Trial of Six "Terrorists" in Kandyahash Lasted Only 3 Days," RadioAzattyk.org, September 28, 2009, http://rus.azattyq.org/content/Kandyagash_court_terrorists/1837791.html.
[40] Juslan Kugekov, "The Court in Astana declined an Appeal of the Convicted on Charges of Terrorism Muslim Bothers," RadioAzattyk.org, February 12, 2010, http://rus.azattyq.org/content/Zhasulan_Suleimenov_Kuat_Zhobolaev/1956423.html.
[41] *Country Reports on Terrorism 2008.*
[42] Press Release, "Terrorism and Extremism Counteraction," Kazakh National Security Committee, August 21, 2009, http://www.knb.kz/page.php?page_id=42&lang=1&article_id=4104&fontsize=12&fontfamily=Times%20New%20Roman&page=1.
[43] Ibid.
[44] "Kazakhstan And China Have Expressed Their Intention To Pursue A Tough Fight Against Terrorism, Extremism And Organized Crime – Prime Minister PRC," Central Asian News Service, October 2008, http://www.ca-news.org/news/41691.
[45] Shanghai Cooperation Organization, "Chronicle of main events at SCO in 2008," December 31, 2008, http://www.sectsco.org/EN/show.asp?id=66.
[46] "SCO-Led Anti-Terror Drills In Kazakhstan Will Benefit Security – Chinese Minister," Interfax (Moscow), December 25, 2009, http://www.interfax.com/newsinf.asp?id=138208.
[47] *Country Reports on Terrorism 2008.*
[48] Conrad Olson and James Martin, "The Global Initiative to Combat Nuclear Terrorism: Progress to Date," *Nuclear Threat Initiative*, August 5, 2009, http://www.nti.org/e_research/e3_global_initiatives.html
[49] "Kazakhstan" in *International Religious Freedom Report 2008.*
[50] Ibid.
[51] "Activity Of MIA In Counteraction To Extremism In The Territory Of The Republic Of Kazakhstan."
[52] "Kazakhstan" in *International Religious Freedom Report 2008.*

TURKMENISTAN

QUICK FACTS

Population: 4,940,916

Area: 488,100 sq km

Ethnic Groups: Turkmen 85%, Uzbek 5%, Russian 4%, other 6%

Religions: Muslim 89%, Eastern Orthodox 9%, unknown 2%

Government Type: Defines itself as a secular democracy and presidential republic; in actuality displays authoritarian presidential rule, with power concentrated within the executive branch

GDP (official exchange rate): $16.24 billion

Map and Quick Facts courtesy of the CIA World Factbook (Last Updated June 2010)

Over a period of centuries, Islam in Turkmenistan has become an unusual blend of Sufi mysticism, orthodox (Sunni) Islam, and shamanistic and Zoroastrian practices. The cult of ancestors is still observed, and reverence for members of the four holy tribes (the owlat) is still strong. Popular or 'folk' Islam is centered around practices and beliefs related to Sufism, the mystical dimension of Islam that originated in Central Asia. The veneration of holy places, which are generally tombs connected with Sufi saints, mythical personages, or tribal ancestors, continues to play an active role in the preservation of religious feeling among the population.

The pervasive nature of folk Islam, together with the Soviet-era repression of religion and the authoritarian nature of the country's political system, have acted as barriers to the growth of Islamist ideology in Turkmenistan. Thus, the leadership has sought to capitalize on the popularity of Sufism in order to encourage religion to conform to local popular practices as well as to combat the emergence of Islamism. As in other parts of Central Asia, the distinction between religious and 'national' rituals is blurred in Turkmenistan; since the perestroika period of the late 1980s, the leadership has attempted to co-opt

Islam as a fundamental component of its overarching nation-building campaign.

ISLAMIST ACTIVITY

In much of Central Asia, the broad process of re-Islamization that took place in the late 1980s and early 1990s was accompanied by the emergence of political movements that espoused a greater adherence to Islamic tenets. In Turkmenistan, however, there has been no movement to introduce elements of *sharia* or to establish parties based on Islamic principles. The vast majority of the population appears to prefer to disassociate religion from politics altogether, and would be unlikely to lend support to any attempt to replace secular with religious rule, especially if it were to involve a political struggle.

Perhaps more than any other factor, the desire to perpetuate religious beliefs and practices that are widely regarded as 'national' traditions in Turkmenistan has disempowered Islamism—an ideology calling for change—as a potent force for social mobilization. Turkmenis generally view Islam as a crucial part of national culture, encompassing a set of local customs that sets them apart from outsiders. As such, Islam has a significant secular component that has made it relatively immune to politicization and the penetration of Islamist ideologies. 'Folk' Islam (*Islam-i halq*) rather than orthodox Islam (*Islam-i kitab*) is dominant, and is primarily concerned with the celebration of life cycle rituals, the observation of the principle of sacrifice and the preservation of mystical beliefs. The practice of shrine pilgrimage (*ziyarat*) is at the heart of Islam in Turkmenistan.

To be sure, some of the most widespread practices among Turkmen believers are considered heretical by purist Muslims, such as warding off the evil eye through the use of plants and amulets or performing pilgrimages to the graves of local Sufi saints. As Central Asia expert Ahmed Rashid pointed out, fundamentalists have criticized Sufi followers to little avail for diverging from the commands of the Koran and tolerating non-Islamic influences.[1] The inherent tension between folk Islam and an Islamist ideology that calls for greater orthodoxy has served to stymie any potential popular support for the latter.

Despite the apparent dearth of Islamist activity, the closed nature of polity and society in Turkmenistan has made it difficult to definitively ascertain the presence or absence of Islamist groups, and has also given rise to speculation that Islamist activity may exist within the former Soviet republic. For example, official reports on an unexpectedly fierce two-day battle that broke out in a northern suburb of Ashgabat in September 2008 provided little information, prompting Russian media and some Western wire services to make unconfirmed assertions that the violence was instigated by Islamist extremists.[2] Similarly, despite reports that the Islamist group Hizb-ut-Tahrir has won converts in Turkmenistan's labor camps and prisons, a significance presence in the country has yet to be established.[3]

ISLAMISM AND SOCIETY

In addition to the popular nature of Islam, the durable changes to religious practice experienced by the population during the Soviet period provides a second explanation for the limited appeal of Islamist groups in Turkmenistan. Some analysts have argued that the Soviet legacy is the key factor hindering the present-day development of Islamism in Central Asia, given that the region was isolated from the rest of the Muslim world—including its intellectual centers—for more than seventy years.[4] During Soviet rule, Islam in particular was rejected as contrary to modernization, with the consequence that all but a handful of mosques were either closed or turned into museums of atheism. The clergy was persecuted and religious literature was destroyed, all Islamic courts of law, *waqf* holdings (Muslim religious endowments that formed the basis of clerical economic power) and Muslim primary and secondary schools were liquidated. Local shrines acted as the real centers of religious life in the absence of functioning mosques during the Soviet period, thereby ensuring that they have remained an important part of worship in Turkmenistan.

However, while it is undeniable that the aggressive anti-religious campaign launched by the Soviet authorities placed even greater distance between Central Asian Islam and the Islam practiced in "mainstream" Muslim countries in the Middle East, South and Southeast Asia or Africa, Islamic doctrine had never taken as firm root in Turkmenistan as it had in other Muslim areas, including the older, sedentary territories of Central Asia. Well before the Bolshevik Revolution, the Turkmen, like other nomadic peoples, preferred to pray in private rather than visit a mosque.[5] A mobile lifestyle necessarily favored a non-scriptural, popular version of Islam while naturally curtailing the presence of professional clergy. As the expert Adrienne Edgar noted, any man who could read and recite prayers was given the title of *mullah*, or cleric.[6] Particularly in the nomadic regions, teachers of Sufi orders, or *ishans*, played a more influential role than the *ulema* (Muslim scholars). The independent Turkmen tribes lacked Muslim *kadis* who judged in accordance with Islamic law, with the result that *sharia* only held sway in the sphere of family law, and was implemented by mullahs at birth, circumcision, marriage and funeral ceremonies.[7]

In the twenty-first century, Turkmenis continue to be governed less by Islamic law than by tribal customary law, or *adat*, which has been passed down for many centuries. As the majority of Turkmenis do not practice their religion in a formal or institutional way, mosques remain conspicuously empty, including Central Asia's largest and grandest mosque, the Turkmenbashi Ruhy Mosque in former President Niyazov's hometown of Gypjak, which is only visited by a significant number of male worshippers on Fridays.

ISLAMISM AND THE STATE

The strict state control of religion is a third, albeit less important, reason why Islamism has thus far failed to attract a significant following in Turkmenistan. Were Islamist groups to appear in Turkmenistan, state security forces would most certainly act swiftly and firmly to repress any and all manifestations of activity.

In order to prevent the emergence of Islam as a locus of oppositional activity, the Turkmenistani leadership has acted to thoroughly co-opt the official religious establishment. Beginning in the late 1980s, Turkmenistan's iron-fisted ruler, Saparmurat Niyazov, who was first secretary of the Communist Party of the Turkmen SSR from 1985-1991 and the country's first president from 1991 until his death in 2006, sanctioned the revival of Muslim practices while simultaneously striving to keep religion within official structures. Thus, Niyazov endorsed the construction of mosques, the teaching of basic Islamic principles in state schools, the refurbishment of holy places and the restoration of Islamic holidays. Whereas in 1987 there were only four functioning mosques in the Turkmen SSR, by 1992 that number had risen to eighty-three, with another sixty-four mosques under construction.[8] In 1991, Turkmenistan's first *madrassah* (Islamic seminary) was founded in Dashhowuz to help alleviate the country's acute shortage of trained religious clergy. Shrine pilgrimage was acknowledged by Niyazov as a fundamental component of Turkmen identity and even as an expression of patriotism. Seeking to improve their Islamic credentials, both Niyazov and his successor, Gurbanguly Berdimuhammedov, have made pilgrimages to Mecca and Medina, thereby adding the title of *hajji* to their already long lists of distinctions.

Yet, even while taking limited measures to promote Islam, the Turkmenistani leadership required all religious communities to obtain legal registration and banned all religious parties. In April 1994, Niyazov set up a Council for Religious Affairs, the *Gengesh*, within the presidential apparatus "to ensure the observance of the law." In July 2000, a long-serving official in the *Gengesh* acknowledged that his organization controls the selection, promotion and dismissal of all clergy in Turkmenistan, thereby allowing the state to exert control on religious matters right down to the village level.[9]

In 1997, the leadership initiated a crackdown on Islamic activity by closing many of the mosques that had been opened just a few years earlier (mostly in Mary Oblast), shutting down virtually all institutions of Islamic learning, halting the importation of foreign religious literature, and tightening restrictions on the legal registration of religious communities. These restrictions endure to this day. Congregations that are not registered with the Ministry of Fairness (formerly the Ministry of Justice) are prohibited from gathering publicly and disseminating religious materials, with violators subject to penalties under the country's administrative code. The Dashowuz *madrassah* was closed in 2001, and in 2005 cutbacks were made at the Faculty of Muslim Theology at Magtymguly Turkmen State University, which remained the only official institution for training imams.

To an even greater degree than other Central Asian Muslims, Turkmenis have been unable to travel and receive an education in *madrassahs* abroad. The government has aimed to restrict the population's contact with fellow believers abroad by limiting the number of Turkmen Muslims—including secret police and state officials—performing the *hajj* to Mecca each year to 188 pilgrims, which represents less than five percent of the quota allocated by the Saudi authorities.[10]

As in other Central Asian states, Turkmenistani authorities have sought to limit unwanted Islamist trends by promoting a vision of Islam that is concerned with the preservation of tradition. In similar fashion to neighboring Uzbekistan, the leadership has attempted to capitalize on the popularity of Sufism in order to encourage religion to conform to local popular practices as well as to combat the emergence of Islamism. In so far as orthodox Islamic doctrine rejects and condemns as idolatrous some Sufist practices, such as the veneration of local saints and local shrine pilgrimages,[11] it is held that the promotion of Sufism will serve to dampen any inclination among Turkmeni believers to support the more purist—and potentially Islamist—forms of ideology.[12]

Consequently, the Turkmenistani leadership has taken some steps to foster the Sufi tradition and incorporate it into the regime's larger nation-building project. Thus, the Niyazov leadership provided the mosque and mausoleum complex of the twelfth-century Sufi scholar, Hoja Yusup Hamadani, with a modern-day reconstruction. Located in the Mary Region, this holy site is one of the most important places of shrine pilgrimage in Turkmenistan, even remaining open during the Soviet period, albeit under strict control. Likewise, rather than seeking to prohibit local pilgrimages to sacred places, both the Niyazov and Berdimuhamedov governments have encouraged it, even providing free accommodation for pilgrims in some instances.[13] In 2009, citing fears concerning the spread of swine flu, Turkmenistani authorities barred aspiring Muslim pilgrims from making the *hajj* to Saudi Arabia altogether, urging them instead to sojourn to 38 sacred sites across the country, although most of the sites had historical or cultural rather than religious significance.[14]

Under Niyazov, the state-sponsored form of Islam in Turkmenistan underwent an unusual twist when the president made his extensive cult of personality a centerpiece of religious practice by configuring himself as a prophet with his own sacred book, the *Ruhnama* (Book of the Soul). Niyazov regularly urged his country's citizens to study and memorize passages from it, and knowledge of the *Ruhnama* was made a requirement for university entrance and for work in the public sector, which remained the main source of employment. Imams were obliged to display the *Ruhnama* inside mosques and to quote from it in sermons or face possible removal or even arrest. In direct violation of *sharia*, Niyazov even ordered that passages from the *Ruhnama* be inscribed alongside passages from the Koran on the walls of the cathedral mosque in Gypjak; an inscription above the main arch reads: "*Ruhnama* is a holy book, the Koran is Allah's book."

In 2003, the country's long-serving senior Muslim cleric and deputy chairman of the Gengesh, Nasrullah ibn Ibadullah, was replaced for expressing dissent by repeatedly objecting to the *de facto* status of the *Ruhnama* as a sacred book on a par with the Koran, and to its extensive use in mosques. In 2004, he was sentenced to 22 years in prison on treason charges, but was amnestied in August 2007. Upon his release Ibadullah thanked the president and accepted a post as an adviser at the president's State Council for Religious Affairs, thus remaining under the close supervision of administration officials. Since coming to power in 2007, President Berdimuhamedov has gradually phased out the cult of Niyazov's quasi-spiritual guidebook for the nation, although its study remains part of the education curriculum.[15]

ENDNOTES

[1] Ahmed Rashid, *The Resurgence of Central Asia: Islam or Nationalism?* (Karachi: Oxford University Press, 1994), 246-247.

[2] Annette Bohr, "Turkmenistan," in *Nations in Transit. Democratization from Central Europe to Eurasia 2009* (New York: Freedom House, 2009), 522, http://www.freedomhouse.org/uploads/nit/2009/Turkmenistan-final.pdf. For an excellent, detailed analysis of both the international and domestic media reports on the September clashes, see Vitaliy Ponomarev, *Sobytiia v Ashkhabade 10–13 Sentiabria 2000g* [Events in Ashkhabad September 10–13, 2008] (Moscow: Memorial Human Rights Center, November 5, 2008).

[3] *Cracks in the Marble: Turkmenistan's Failing Dictatorship*, International Crisis Group, January 2003, 25, http://www.crisisgroup.org/~/media/Files/asia/central-asia/turkmenistan/Cracks%20in%20the%20Marble%20Turkmenistan%20Failing%20Dictatorship.ashx.

[4] Krzysztof Strachota and Maciej Falkowski, *Jihad vs. The Great New Game: Paradoxes Of Militant Islamic threats In Central Asia* (Warsaw: Centre for Eastern Studies, January 2010), 48-49.

[5] Carole Blackwell, *Tradition and Society in Turkmenistan: Gender, Oral Culture and Song* (Richmond: Curzon Press, 2001), 35.

[6] Adrienne Lynn Edgar, *Tribal Nation. The Making Of Soviet Turkmenistan* (Princeton: Princeton University Press, 2004), 26.

[7] W. Konig, *Die Achal-Teke. Zur Wirtschaft und Gesellschaft einer Turkmenen-Gruppe im XIX Jahrhundert,* 74, as cited in Paul Georg Geiss, *Pre-Tsarist and Tsarist Central Asia: Communal Commitment And Political Order In Change* (London: RoutledgeCurzon, 2003), 38.

[8] Alexander Verkhovsky, ed., *Islam i politicheskaya bor'ba v stranakh SNG* [Islam and political struggle in the ⬛IS (⬛ommonwealth of Independent States)] (Moscow: Panorama, 1992), 27.

[9] S. Demidov, "Religioznie protsessy v postsovetskom Turkmenistane," [Religious protests in post-Soviet Turkmenistan," *Tsentral'naia Aziia i Kavkaz* no. 5 (2001).

[10] Felix Corley, "Turkmenistan Religious Freedom Survey, August 2008," Forum 18 News Service, August 5, 2008, http://www.forum18.org/Archive.php?article_id=1167.

[11] See Maria Elisabeth Louw, *Everyday Islam in Post-Soviet Central Asia* (London: Routledge, 2007), 50.

[12] However, as some have noted, the relationship between folk Islam, orthodox Islam and Sufism is complex. While some folk customs might contradict the precepts of *sharia*, Sufi brotherhoods often successfully used the *murid* organization to spread orthodox Islam. Geiss, *Pre-Tsarist and Tsarist Central Asia*, 94n3.

[13] *Cracks in the Marble*, 25.

[14] Felix Corley, 'Turkmenistan: Exit Bans, Haj Ban, Visa Denials Part

Of State Religious Isolation Policy," Forum 18 News Service, February 2010, http://www.forum18.org/Archive.php?article_id=1403; Bruce Pannier, "Turkmen Pilgrims Make A Homegrown Hajj," *Radio Free Europe/Radio Liberty*, November 25, 2009, http://www.rferl.org/content/Turkmen_Pilgrims_Make_A-Homegrown_Hajj/1887880.html.
[15] Bohr, "Turkmenistan," in *Nations in Transit. Democratization from Central Europe to Eurasia 2010* (New York: Freedom House, 2010), 544, http://www.freedomhouse.hu/images/nit2010/NIT-2010-Turkmenistan-final.pdf.

UZBEKISTAN

Recent political developments in Uzbekistan confirm the thesis that, in the process of violent interaction with authorities, religious political organizations undergo a transformation into extremist ones. Already a decade ago, largely as a result of repressive measures on the part of Uzbek law enforcement agencies, various religio-political groups banded together under the banner of the Islamic Movement of Uzbekistan (IMU). In turn, the IMU became part of the global network of international terrorism spearheaded by al-Qaeda. While today the IMU is in retreat in Uzbekistan, battered by effective Uzbek and Coalition counterterrorism action, the organization still holds the potential to become a serious and real threat to the security of the Central Asian states. So do other Islamist groups, such as Akramiyya, now active on Uzbek soil, which advocate the removal of Uzbekistan's authoritarian government and its replacement with a "just" Islamic one.

ISLAMIST ACTIVITY

Uzbekistan has been the site of activity for a range of Islamist groups for most of the two decades since its independence from the USSR. These groups range in their ideology, objectives and methods. All, however, share the broad goal of transforming Uzbekistan from a secular authoritarian regime into a state based upon – and governed by – *sharia* law.

Islamic Movement of Uzbekistan (IMU)

The IMU traces its origins back to 1988-1989, when the group's leaders, Tahir Yuldashev and Jumabai Hodgiev (Juma Namangani), became members of the extremist organization *Tablykh*, which was aimed at overthrowing the existing political system of Uzbekistan.[1] In January 1991, in the city of Namangan, the two established another radical religious/political group, known as *Adolat* (Justice), with the aim of building an Islamic state in Uzbekistan.[2] This was followed by the creation of multiple, disparate religious groups in Uzbekistan, including the *Markazi Islam* (Islamic Center) in the city of Namangan, which became a hub for *jihadi* activity. On December 8, 1991, it organized an unauthorized rally and they captured the office building of the Namangan regional committee of the Communist Party of Uzbekistan, levying an ultimatum to Uzbek authorities and demanding President Islam Karimov swear on the Koran and proclaim the establishment of an Islamic state.[3] The resulting state clampdown led to thousands of arrests, prompting an exodus of Islamic radicals from Uzbekistan to Tajikistan.[4]

During this early period, Yuldashev and others are known to have traveled to Afghanistan, where they made contact with alumni of the Afghan *jihad* and established training camps for Uzbek militants.[5] These contacts created a conveyor for radicalization, and the following years saw a number of Uzbek militants pass through Afghan training camps before returning to Uzbekistan to destabilize the situation in the Ferghana Valley and elsewhere in the former Soviet republic.

In 1995, the "Islamic Center" became the foundation for the Islamic Revival Movement of Uzbekistan (IRMU), which officially became known as the Islamic Movement of Uzbekistan (IMU) the following year. The organization's headquarters, headed by its leader (*amir*), Tahir Yuldashev, was set up in Peshawar, and later relocated to Kabul. Given the difficulty in creating such a militia, and in supporting, clothing, equipping, and arming between 500 to several thousand fighters in another country, significant foreign funding is presumed.[6]

Beginning in 1997, the IMU commenced an organized insurgent campaign against the Uzbek state. Its strategy was not to conduct large-scale violence against Uzbekistan and Kyrgyzstan, but to seize power by way of destabilizing terror, sabotage and banditry. It was only after the Taliban and al-Qaeda suffered defeat as a result of U.S. counterterrorist operations in Afghanistan in October 2001 that the IMU – which also suffered heavy losses, including the death of its head, Juma Namangani, near Mazar i-Sharif in November 2001 – ceased its armed incursions in the region.

The organization survived by rebranding itself the *Hizb Islami Turkestan*, or Islamic Party of Turkestan. This organization, still led by Tahir Yuldashev, maintains the same outlook and ambitions as its precursor, the IMU. Estimates of its strength vary; according to Pakistani officials, Yuldashev could command as many as 4,800 Uzbek militants, as well as "groups of Chechens, the Libyan Islamic Fighting Group, [and] Uighur militants of the East Turkestan Islamic Movement."[7] The organization is currently believed to be most active in Afghanistan and parts of Pakistan. Yuldashev himself was reportedly killed in August 2009 in South Waziristan as a result of a U.S. Predator drone strike.[8]

The group remains active in Central Asia, and the past year-and-a-half has seen an upsurge in terrorist activity in that theater, including:

- Bombings in Khanabad and Andijan in May 2009 claimed by the Union of Islamic Jihad, an offshoot of the IMU;[9]
- Attacks by IMU fighters in the Jalabad region of Kyrgyzstan in June 2009;[10]
- CLashes between suspected IMU militants and security forces in the Gorno-Badakhshan autonomous region of Tajikistan in July 2009;[11] and
- An August 2009 shootout between Islamic militants and police in Tashkent that killed three people.[12]

Akramiyya

The founder of Akramiyya, Akram Yuldashev, was born in 1963 in Andijan, Uzbekistan.[13] A teacher by profession, his 1992 treatise "Lymonga Yul" emphasizes that the ultimate goal of his organization is the assumption of power and the creation of an Islamic state.[14] Members of Akramiyya called themselves *birodarami*, or brothers, but the people of Central Asia know them as *akramists*. There are now said to be tens of thousands of such "brothers."[15] They first appeared in the Ferghana Valley in 1998, where – motivated by the ideology of Hizb ut-Tahrir – they espoused a selective reading of the Quran, arguing in favor of *sharia* as the answer to the modern, "unfavorable" period for Muslims in Central Asia.

Yuldashev is said to have structured the activities of his group in five phases, beginning with the indoctrination of new members, extending to the accumulation of wealth for charitable Islamic works, and concluding with the gradual, "natural transition" to Islamic rule in Uzbek society.[16] Ideologically, Akramiyya is an outgrowth of the "Ahl al-Quran" movement, which existed in the 1940s in Uzbekistan. Members of this movement categorically refused to recognize the teachings of other Sunni schools (*mazh'hab*). They adhered to very austere views, rejected the "Soviet way of life" and did not recognize official clergy. Members of Akramiyya believe only in Allah, and do not worship the Prophet Mohammed. Nor do they recognize any nation in the world. They ignore state laws, renounce their parents, and subject themselves exclusively to the direction of the group's leaders.[17]

Most Akramiyya members are of Uzbek nationality. Its members are mostly businessmen with small agricultural enterprises, funds and industrial warehouses. The organization is known to control dozens of commercial firms, which do business under a unified leadership.[18]

Akramiyya has been targeted by authorities in Tashkent for some time. Its leader, Akram Yuldashev, was sentenced in the spring of 1998 to two-and-a-half years in prison for violating Article 276 (drug possession) of the Uzbek Criminal Code.[19] In late December of the same year, he was amnestied, only to be rearrested the day after a bombing in Tashkent in February 1999. In May 1999, Yuldashev was sentenced to 17 years in prison under several articles of the Uzbek Criminal Code: 155 (terrorism), 156 (incitement of religious hatred), 159 (encroachment on constitutional system), 161 (sabotage), 216 (unlawful association), 216-1 (luring into an illegal organization), 242 (organization of a criminal association), 244-1 (dissemination of materials against public safety), 276 (drug possession) and 248 (possession of weapons, ammunition and explosives).[20] As of this writing, Yuldashev remains jailed in Tashkent.

During the same period (1998-1999), 22 other young members of Akramiyya were given various terms in prison. They were accused of the following articles of the Criminal Code of the Republic of Uzbekistan: 159-4 (anti-constitutional activity), 242-1 (the organization of a criminal association), 244-1, (distribution of materials containing a threat to public safety) and 244-2 (establishing, managing participation in religious extremist, separatist, fundamentalist or other banned organizations). Two of the arrested members – Jurakhon Asimov (aged 34) and Hamdamzhon Bobojonov (29 years old) – died from torture while in prison. Others are still at large.[21]

The organization continued to exist until the Andijan massacre of 2005, when some of its members were shot by state security forces for participating in riots. In its aftermath, many members of fled from Uzbekistan through Kyrgyzstan to the West, leading to the gradual dissolution of the group.

Hizb ut-Tahrir (HuT)

Unlike the IMU, Hizb-ut-Tahrir is a truly transnational movement, which enjoys considerable support among young Muslims in Western Europe and has a broad organizational base in London. HuT originated in the Middle East in 1950, and is aimed at creating a worldwide Caliphate. The dissemination of its ideas in Central Asia began in early 1990.[22] The party acquired adherents first in Uzbekistan, where it had (and still has) the greatest number of followers, and then migrated to neighboring Kyrgyzstan, Tajikistan and Kazakhstan. In these states, the party first recruited its followers among ethnic Uzbeks, but gradually young ethnic Kyrgyz, Tajiks and Kazakhs became involved in HuT, causing a rapid expansion of the group during the late 1990s.

The ideology of Hizb ut-Tahrir was "imported" to Uzbekistan by a Jordanian, Atif Salahuddin, in 1995. The same year, the organization was officially founded in the city of Tashkent, and subsequently in the Andijan, Samarkand, Tashkent and Fergana provinces of Uzbekistan. HuT cells were mostly composed of local youth. Party members condemned the "godless government" in Uzbekistan, "the enemies of Islam" – the United States and Israel – and called for the creation of a worldwide Islamic state. Members of Hizb ut-Tahrir, distinguished not so much by their desire for strict adherence to Islamic norms, but by their religious and political activities. Young people enjoyed the opposition position of the party and open discussion of political issues inside the party.

The activities of HuT did not attract the attention of Uzbek authorities until May 1998, when party members began to distribute leaflets in public places. The response was rapid; between August and November of 1998, at least 15 members of the Tashkent branch of the party were arrested. Mass arrests of members of Hizb ut-Tahrir throughout Uzbekistan began the following year.[23]

Following the events of September 11, 2001, many members of Hizb ut-Tahrir in Uzbekistan went underground, fearing large-scale retaliation. The group has largely remained there to this day, as a result of unprecedented violent measures on the part of Uzbek authorities. In 2008, the group exhibited only nominal activity within Uzbekistan, although experts caution that this lull may only be temporary.[24]

Elsewhere in the region, however, HuT has expanded its activities. As authorities in Uzbekistan ratcheted up their counterterrorism activities, party activists were forced to seek refuge among Uzbek communities in neighboring countries, primarily in Kyrgistan, to where the headquarters of the party has moved.

ISLAMISM AND SOCIETY

Although the majority of the Uzbekistan's population of 27.6 million is Sunni Muslim (88 percent), this group by and large does not support the idea of the establishment of the Caliphate in their country and prefer a secular state system. Muslim leaders in Uzbekistan have demonstrated themselves to be very critical of Hizb ut-Tahrir, and have argued that the movement is essentially a political rather than religious organization, and that Muslims should not be engaged in politics. However, some *imams* do not want to alienate members of Hizb ut-Tahrir from their mosques, because the number of parishioners determines the level of donations (*Sadaka-Fitr* and *zakat*) that flow into their coffers.[25]

While most moderate Muslims in Uzbekistan reject the goals and ideology of the movement, they tend to sympathize with its members because of the repression the latter face at the hands of local authorities, and as a result of the movement's efforts to draw attention to official corruption. HuT leaflets highlighting corruption, inequality and oppression tend to find a receptive ear among the Uzbek population, and especially among its more disadvantaged segments. The organization's call for social justice, meanwhile, appears to resonate at a grassroots level among a population that routinely experiences hardship and privation.

Nevertheless, neither the IMU nor Hizb ut-Tahrir can boast widespread support anywhere in Central Asia. both organizations appeal only to a small fraction of the regional population – and then this support is localized, strongest in parts of the Fergana Valley, possibly in south Uzbekistan, and in some areas of Tajikistan. While it is impossible to accurately determine the level of this support, Uzbek observers place the current number of active supporters of these groups at less than 10 percent of the regional population.[26]

Most ordinary Muslims in Uzbekistan do not support political activities in mosques, and do not share radical Islamist ideas. Nevertheless, the scale of support received by radical groups may expand if dissatisfaction with the current political and economic system increases. It is understood that support for Hizb ut-Tahrir and other extremists in Uzbekistan is fed more by disappointment with the state of contemporary politics than by a conscious commitment to extremist ideology. After years of government enforced repression, many have been discouraged from trying to use the available ways to protest against the government and in general against the injustices of modern society, and therefore they were attracts by a more idealized vision. The fact that people are often recruited by their friends and acquaintances contributes to a less critical view of Hizb ut-Tahrir among Uzbek Muslims.

ISLAMISM AND THE STATE

In early 1990, the newly independent Uzbek government launched a series of measures to eliminate all secular opposition groups, and therafter directed its attention toward Islamic associations, fearful that any form of religious expression not controlled by the state could serve as a vehicle for popular discontent. This pattern has continued uninterrupted for the past two decades; state intelligence agencies work to eleminate and marginalize those Islamic leaders who do not share the official vision of religion as an instrument of a state policy. Uzbek security forces, meanwhile, routinely utilize the most repressive methods against Islamic organizations, often failing to differentiate between radical groups like the IMU and more grassroots oriented ones like Akramiyya. Adherents to all of these organizations are subject to arbitrary arrest and torture, based upon suspicions of extremism.[27]

Today, the Uzbek government continues to prosecute any activity which is regarded as the uncontrolled expression of the Muslim faith. This state repression, however, has been coupled with a subtle and surprisingly sophisticated "soft power" approach to combating Islamist ideology. This approach finds its roots in the nature of Central Asian Islam itself, where the dominant branch of Sunni Islam is the Khanafi school – one of the most tolerant and liberal in that religion. Its pluralistic and largely apolitical disposition is one of the main reasons that Khanafi believers survived and avoided mass repression during the Communist era, when Soviet ideologues sought to eliminate doctrinal competition with Marxism-Leninism.

This approach leverages an asset shared by the Central Asian states: a strong knowledge base with which to fight radical Islamists. Since gaining independence, the countries of the region have managed to educate considerable numbers of knowledgeable experts in Islam. Moreover, in these countries, the Koran and *Hadith* have been translated into local languages, and many academics and *imams* are applying their knowledge on a practical level.

By necessity, Central Asian governments, especially those in Uzbekistan and Kyrgyzstan, have created and developed an extensive educational system – spanning from kindergarten to university – that inculcates the moral norms and social principles of tolerant Islam, and which respects the value of human life (be it Muslim, Christian, Jewish, or other). The system provides textbooks for schools, cartoons for children, education for *imams* of local mosques, a network of counselors in Islamic affairs for central and local administrations, and television and radio talk shows that challenge the intolerant Wahhabi interpretation of the Koran and *Hadith* and provide listeners with a religious alternative.[28]

These realities have bred a cadre of Central Asian scholars and religious authorities that are ready and able to confront radical Islam. Dr. Abdujabar Abduvakhitov, the rector of the Westminster International University in Tashkent, Uzbekistan, is one such official. According to him, the mission of state educational establishments should be to erode the base of "supporters" of radical Islam, and to educate young Muslims in the spirit of tolerant, traditional Central Asian Islam. Other experts have echoed these prescriptions. Dr. Zukhriddin Khusnidinov, rector of the Islamic University of Uzbekistan, believes that university activities – as well as radio and TV broadcasting – are necessary in order to provide young people with a proper understanding of Islamic principles.[29]

ENDNOTES

[1]Pravda *Vostoka* (Tashkent), October 21, 2000.

[2] Igor Rotar, "The Islamic Movement of Uzbekistan: A Resurgent IMU?" Jamestown Foundation *Terrorism Monitor* 1, iss. 8, December 17, 2003, http://www.jamestown.org/single/?no_cache=1&tx_ttnews[tt_news]=26187.

[3] Orozbek Moldaliyev, *Islam i Politika: Politizatsiya Islama ili Islamizatsiya Politiki? (Islam and Politics: The Politicization of Islam of the Islamization of Politics?)* (Bishkek: n.p., 2008), 269; See also A. Starkovsky, "Armia Izgnanikov, Chast I" (Army of Outcasts, Part I) freas. org, January 18, 2004, http://freeas.org/?nid=2367; Vitaly Ponomarev, *Ugroza "Islamskovo Ekstremisma" v Uzbekistane: Mifui i Realnosti (The "Islamic Extremist" Threat in Uzbekistan: Myth and Reality)* (Moscow: Memorial, 1999).

[4] Ibid; See also *Res Publica*, September 15-21, 1998.

[5] Moldaliyev, *Islam i Politika*, 271.

[6] Author's interview with former IMU member, Osh, Kyrgyzstan, August 11, 2004; See also Alex Alexiev, "Oil Dollars to Jihad: Saudi Arabia Finances Global Islamism," *Internationale Politik* 1 (2004), 31.

[7] Author's interview with Pakistani researcher, Almaty, Kazakhstan, July 24, 2009.

[8] Bill Roggio, "Tahir Yuldashev Confirmed Killed In U.S. Strike In South Waziristan," *Long War Journal*, October 4, 2009, http://www.longwarjournal.org/archives/2009/10/tahir_yuldashev_conf.php.

[9] Farangis Najibullah, "Uzbek Attacks Trip Alarm Bells In Ferghana," *Radio Free Europe/Radio Liberty*, May 27, 2009, http://www.rferl.org/content/Uzbek_Attacks_Trip_Alarm_In_Ferghana/1740949.html.

[10] Roman Muzalevsky, "Kyrgyz Operation Against IMU Reveals Growing Terrorist Threat," Johns Hopkins University Central Asia-Caucasus Institute *CACI Analyst*, July 1, 2009, http://www.cacianalyst.org/?q=node/5144.

[11] Talk of the author with an official from the Center for Strategic Research of Republic of Tagikistan.

[12] Confidential materials provided by Uzbek human rights activist. (author's collection)

[13] Bakhtiyar Babadjanov, "Akramia: A Brief Summary," Carnegie Endowment for International Peace, May 2006, http://www.carnegieendowment.org/files/Akramiya.pdf.

[14] Ibid.

[15] Author's interview with Uzbek expert on Islam B. Babadzhanov, Tashkent, Uzbekistan, September 14, 2009.

[16] Ibid.

[17] Author's interview with Uzbek expert on Islam I. Mirsaidov, Tashkent, Uzbekistan, September 16, 2009.

[18] Author's interview with B. Babadzhanov.

[19] Moldaliyev, *Islam i Politika*, 286.

[20] Ibid., 286-287.

[21] Ibidem.

[22] Ibidem, 283.

[23] Ibidem.

[24] Author's interview with Uzbek expert on Islam Ⓧ.P., Tashkent, Uzbekistan, September 11, 2009.

[25] Author's interview with I. Mirsaidov.

[26] Timur Kozukulov, *Problemy Borby s Religioznim Ekstremismom v Usloviakh Globalizatsiyii v Ferganskoy Doline (Problems of Combating Religious Extremism in the Ferghana Valley under Globalized Conditions)* (Osh, Kyrgyzstan: Oshskii Gosudarstviniy Universitet, 2008), 72.

[27] See, for example, United Nations Human Rights Committee, "Human Rights Committee Concludes Consideration of Uzbekistan's Third Report," March 12, 2010, http://www.un.org/News/Press/docs/2010/hrct719.doc.htm.

[28] For a detailed analysis of the "soft power" counterterrorism approaches of Central Asian states, see Evgueni K. Novikov, *Central Asian Responses to Radical Islam* (Washington, DC: American Foreign Policy Council, 2006).

[29] Author's interview, Tashkent, Uzbekistan, July 2004.

KYRGYZSTAN

After seventy-four years of official atheism, during which the Soviet ideological and political system pushed the Islamic faith out of the social and political life, the past two decades have seen a religious revival of sorts in the Republic of Kyrgyzstan. The collapse of the Soviet Union ushered in a "return to Islam" among the country's population, complete with a renaissance of religio-cultural values and traditions. These religion freedoms are protected by national Constitution, but have come under fire from Kyrgyz political leaders, who fear the political challenge posed by Islam and by Muslim religious leaders. This has entailed a reestablishment of governmental control over religious organizations, and progressively more restrictive regulations on religious practices.

Official concerns are not without merit. The opening of Kyrgyzstan to the world resulted in an influx of foreign influence in the form of funds (used for the construction and reconstruction of mosques and religious schools), and an upsurge in missionaries from Muslim countries and the publication or importation of religious literature. And while this activity has been by and large benign, there are nonetheless troubling signs of Islamist elements

– most prominently the radical grassroots movement Hizb-ut Tahrir – have expanded their influence in the former Soviet republic, capitalizing upon the religious renaissance now underway there.

ISLAMIST ACTIVITY

Radical Islam boasts a long and checkered history in post-Soviet Kyrgyzstan. Its roots stretch back to the days after the fall of USSR, when a number of former communist leaders (including former president Askar Akayev and current head-of-state Kurmanbek Bakiyev) gravitated to Muslim theology and Islamic discourse. Their ideological about-face was by and large tactical; these former Marxists were hardly true believers. Rather, most opted to abandon Soviet dogma and embrace Islamic revivalism as a pragmatic way of staying in power.

The results were profound. To burnish their credentials as champions of Islam, local leaders opened their doors to Saudi-sponsored Wahhabi Islam. Riyadh, for its part, took advantage of the invitation, expanding its financial and political foothold in the "post-Soviet space." Thus, in the early 1990s, Saudi influence came to the newly independent states of Central Asia in the form of new mosques and religious education.[1]

The scope of this outreach was staggering. Shamshibek Shakirovich Zakirov, a veteran Kyrgyz expert on religious affairs, estimates that after 1990, ten new mosques were constructed with the help of Saudi Arabia in the Kyrgyz city of Osh alone.[2] The Saudi effort, Zakirov says, also included the provision of Wahhabi literature in local languages for these new mosques.[3] This entrenchment of influence was replicated many times over in other corners of the former Soviet Union.

Though initially appreciative of Saudi largesse, Kyrgyz leaders quickly felt its destabilizing potential. Saudi money and educational materials were intended to promote the Kingdom's intolerant, puritan strain of Islam, which encouraged opposition forces to support the creation of an Islamic Caliphate, rather than reinforcing the rule of local post-Soviet governments. By the early 1990s, according to an official Kyrgyz government assessment, the "numbers of illegal private religious schools [had] increased... and their contacts with foreign (Saudi) Muslim organizations expanded. As a result of such contacts not only the functioning character of these centers, but also their ideology, changed. Those schools of traditional Islamic education turned into independent radical religious centers, the programs of which, except for training, included the propagation of their own social and political views."[4]

The impact on civil society in Kyrgyzstan was profound. As experts have noted, the question was not one of "a trivial reshuffling of power, but rather a truly radical revolution" in which Wahhabi ideology confronted national secular elites. "National intelligentsia would undoubtedly fall prey to radical Islamization of public life. Secular, atheistic and 'Europeanized' elite would be unable to fit into an Islamic model of development. Iranian and Afghan examples leave no room for illusions."[5]

These fears were made all the more acute by the strategy employed by Kyrgyz Islamic radicals. At home, these elements challenged the new "Islamic" ideology of local ruling elites and threatened their positions of power by encouraging Muslim clergy and members of fundamentalist groups to assume state power. Even more ominously, regional experts say that these forces also became active recruitment organs, seducing hundreds of young Kyrgyzs to venture abroad to study at Islamic educational institutions in nations throughout the Muslim world, often with the active support of radicals in those countries.[6]

The destabilizing potential of these activities goes a long way toward explaining why, time and again, Kyrgyz scholars, intellectuals and activists have tended to support local leaders, "whenever fundamentalist Islam reared its head."[7]   At the same time, they have formulated a remarkably complex response to the inroads made by Islamic radicals, harnessing religious texts, state education, and public diplomacy in an effort to offer an alternative to the Wahhabi worldview.

Today, the most popular Islamist group in Kyrgyzstan is Hizb-ut-Tahrir (HuT), a broad fundamentalist movement that seeks as a central component of its ideology the "unity of Muslims all over the world." In Kyrgyzstan, HuT has evolved into a political opposition movement, styling itself as the Islamic alternative to regime corruption. Ideologically, however, the movement looks beyond the Kyrgyz state; the declared goal of its programs is "the restoration of Islamic way of life and dissemination of the call (da'vat) to Islam in the world."[8]   Officially, HuT renounces the use of violence to achieve this objective. However, there is a broad consensus among experts that the organization serves as an incubator of sorts for Islamic radicalism, priming adherents to subsequently take up arms against opponents.

Details about HuT's origins in Central Asia are sketchy. The organization's first cells in Kyrgyzstan, however, are known to have appeared in Jalal-Abad and Osh in 1997–1998. By 1999, the movement had evolved into well-developed structural units, and the number of adherents increased dramatically—driven in part by the repressive measures employed against the group across the border in neighboring Uzbekistan. Since then, HuT's ideas have found fertile ground among the socially disadvantaged Kyrgyz populations of the Kara-Suu, Bazar-Korgon, Suzak, Aravan, Uzgen districts, and within the cities of Osh and Jalal-Abad. In fact, the organization's second largest base of support can be found in Kyrgyzstan—a figure estimated at some 3000 citizens.[9] The organization's regional headquarters is now located in Kyrgyzstan, where it serves as a communications hub for HuT activities throughout Central Asia.[10]

Since its inception, HuT has boasted a vertical, tightly organized hierarchy. Local branches of the movement depend on the organization's central committee for financial support. The Chairman of the group, as well as its regional leaders (*mutamad*) and local leaders (*naqib*) have appointed treasurers to collect donations. According to official estimates, approximately 5,000 of the organization's followers live in Kyrgyzstan, and more than 80 percent of them live in the south of the republic, where there are 93 district and regional cells. In the north of the republic, the majority of cells are located in the city of Bishkek and in the Chui region, as well as in the Issyk-Kul region.[11] Most recently, Hizb ut-Tahrir has begun to attract new members in the Naryn and Talas oblasts (regions).

Hizb ut-Tahrir has adapted its tactics in Kyrgyzstan in recent years in order to more adequately mold them to the country's current political situation. In doing so, the movement has developed unique strategies for each one of Kyrgyzstan's seven geographic regions. It has paid special attention to social projects and outreach, including the provision of assistance to poor families, the distribution of food, and aid to the families of those who have been imprisoned by Kyrgyz authorities. Such charitable activities are aimed at expanding HuT's popularity among the Kyrgyz population. It has also stepped up its proselytization among prison inmates, with some success. Official estimates indicate that the number of HuT supporters in local Kyrgyz jails has increased.[12] Those thereby converted later become the organization's adherents and foot-soldiers. Another innovation is the organization's efforts to place its own people in government agencies, including law enforcement units, even though such involvement ostensibly contradicts HuT principles.

Between January 2008 and July 2009, an expert group of the Kyrgyz State Agency for Religious Affairs undertook a comprehensive analysis of hundreds of seized items of HuT religious literature, leaflets, DVD and CDs, magazines, calendars and newspapers. Their conclusion was that HuT activities were commonplace throughout the former Soviet State.[13] And while instances of dissemination of HuT literature have decreased in recent years, the organization has intensified its public activities—such as public protests against local authorities.

ISLAMISM AND SOCIETY

The establishment of Kyrgyzstan as an independent state in 1991, and the creation of a new constitution enshrining religious freedoms within it, led to a new focus upon Islam in Kyrgyz society. In the years that followed, the construction of mosques and religious schools (*madrassas*) mushroomed, fueled by aid from Turkey, Egypt, Saudi Arabia and other countries in the Muslim world. The number of Kyrgyz students in Islamic schools surged. National religious traditions and holidays were reinstated after being abolished during the Soviet era.

Kyrgyzstan's religious revival attracted international attention. Missionaries from Muslim countries became involved in local religious activities, and a great deal of religious Islamic literature was published and imported. Clergy and internationally known theologians began to educate local communities on religious matters, taking into account the historical traditions and mentality of local people.

This revival, however, has by and large not been radical. The majority of Kyrgyz Muslims do not support the activities of religious extremist organizations, including HuT. Many citizens understand the organization's origins, its foreign links, and its ultimate goal of creating a global Islamic caliphate, and reject it for those reasons. Rather, Hizb ut-Tahrir's support comes mainly from the disadvantaged sectors of the population.

Most mosques are located in southern Kyrgyzstan, where religious traditions run deeper. There are a total of 1338 mosques currently operating in Kyrgyzstan, including 601 in the Osh region, 450 in Jalal-Abad region, and 247 in the Batken region. Forty-nine mosques currently exist in the city of Osh. In the north of the republic there are 587 mosques. Construction of new mosques in Kyrgyzstan is mainly carried out by foreign sponsors, who generally provide some 70 percent of project costs. Foreign financial support of state-sanctioned Muslim activities is almost negligible, and is mainly provided by Turkey.[14]

ISLAMISM AND THE STATE

Even after the Cold War ended, Central Asia's Soviet-trained political leaders preferred to keep the Soviet model of secularism, fearful of the potential political challenge from Islamic religious leaders. Kyrgyzstan was no different; in the 1990s Kyrgyz authorities re-established state control over religious organizations, and invited former employees of the country's Soviet-era Council for Religious Affairs to serve in its newly-founded State Commission on Religious Affairs.

In 1993, the religious institutions of Islam in Kyrgyzstan underwent significant structural changes. The government established the country's highest spiritual governing body—known as the Spiritual Administration of Muslims of Kyrgyzstan (SAMK)—which united the Kyrgyz Muslims, Islamic religious organizations, societies, religious educational institutions, mosques and other groups under its umbrella. The activities of these organizations are based on the Koran and the religious tenets of Islam, as well as the works of prominent Muslim leaders and internationally recognized experts.

The growing influx of religious literature into Kyrgyzstan has heightened interest in Islam among the local population. In response, in recent years SAMK has initiated the publication of many religious brochures that explain Muslim prayers and ceremonial sites and tell people about the peculiarities of fasting and Muslim holidays. It also published collections of religious scriptures and brief biographies of the Prophet Muhammad. Supplementing this education effort, foreign Muslim countries have sent a substantial number of editions of the Koran and other religious literature to the Republic.

The Kyrgyz government has established a national religious newspaper, *Islam Madaniyaty*, which is today published in the city of Bishkek in both Russian and Kyrgyz. Regional religious papers also exist in the Jalal-Abad and Osh regions.

SAMK continues to operate as the governing religious body of Kyrgyzstan. It is comprised of seven regional offices, one Islamic university, eight institutes, and sixty-five *madrassas* and classes to study the Koran. Its job is to fulfill the religious and spiritual needs of the republic's Muslims and to train clergy in the Qur'an and *hadiths* of the Prophet Muhammad, akyyda sciences, and Fiqh. It also maintains liaisons with various foreign religious organizations and centers, participates in international conferences on theological issues and participation in the construction of Islamic religious sites, and organizes and holds festive prayers during the holidays of Ramadan and Eid. In addition, the SAMK organizes and coordinates the activities of mosques and *madrassas*, and is engaged in charity.

Between 2000 and 2001, signs of a stricter governmental policy toward Hizb ut-Tahrir began to emerge. Authorities were concerned about the ability of the state to counteract the spread of religious extremism, especially given its limited material, technological, and ideological resources. This was the motivation behind the Kyrgyz Attorney General's Office and the Supreme Court of Kyrgyzstan's 2003 determination to outlaw four organizations: Hizb ut-Tahrir, the Turkistan Liberation Organization, the East Turkistan Islamic Party and the Islamic Party of Turkestan. All were recognized as sponsors or perpetrators of terrorism.

Measures taken since by law enforcement agencies to combat religious extremism in the region have had little effect, however. After serving short sentences under Article 299 of the Penal Code of the Kyrgyz Republic ("Incitement to racial, ethnic and religious enmity") for insulting other religions and nationalities, members of Hizb ut-Tahrir simply continue their extremist activities. Moreover, in the country's prisons they have the opportunity to recruit hundreds of new activists. As a result, despite these steps, Hizb ut-Tahrir's membership base is growing, fueled by popular discontent with regime repression.

ENDNOTES

[1]Zeyno Baran, *Hizb ut-Tahrir: Islam's Political Insurgency* (Washington, DC: The Nixon Center, 2004), 71.

[2] Author's interview with Shamshibek Shakirovich Zakirov, Osh, Kyrgyzstan, August 2004.

[3] Ibid.

[4] *Islam in Kyrgyzstan: Tendencies of Development*, Official Report of the State Commission on Religious Affairs (Bishkek, Kyrgyzstan: Government of the Kyrgyz Republic, 2004), 35.

[5] Roald Sagdeev and Susan Eisenhower, eds., *Central Asia: Conflict, Resolution, and Change* (Washington, DC: The Eisenhower Institute, 1995), 175.

[6] Author's interview with Shamshibek Shakirovich Zakirov.

[7] Sagdeev and Eisenhower, *Central Asia: Conflict, Resolution, and Change*, 175.

[8] http://www.hizb-ut-tahrir.org.

[9] Author's interview with police officers, Osh, Kyrgyzstand, June 21, 2009.

[10] Author's interview with Kyrgyz State Commission on Religious Affairs official, Bishkek, Kyrgyzstan August 10, 2009.

[11] Author's interview with Ministry of Internal Affairs official, August 12, 2009.

[12] Ibid.

[13] Ibidem.

[14] Author's interview with Kyrgyz State Commission on Religious Affairs Deputy Chairman, Bishkek, Kyrgyzstan, August 27, 2009.

TAJIKISTAN

QUICK FACTS

Population: 7,487,489

Area: 143,100 sq km

Ethnic Groups: Tajik 79.9%, Uzbek 15.3%, Russian 1.1%, Kyrgyz 1.1%, other 2.6%

Religions: Sunni Muslim 85%, Shi'a Muslim 5%, other 10%

Government Type: Republic

GDP (official exchange rate): $4.741 billion

Map and Quick Facts courtesy of the CIA World Factbook (Last Updated June 2010)

The former Soviet republic of Tajikistan, a nation of nearly 7.5 million people made up of nearly 80 percent Tajiks and 15 percent Uzbeks, is struggling to undermine its Islamic roots and establish itself as a modern, secular state.[1] But a rash of recent violence in Tajikistan provides clear evidence of an Islamic re-awakening taking place in the former Soviet republic, as extremists aggressively respond to years of successive mismanagement by a Tajik central government turned increasingly unresponsive and authoritarian since the collapse of the USSR and the aftermath of the Tajik civil war. This Islamic re-awakening is being supported and sustained by changes taking place within Tajik society itself, as families increasingly turn to Islamic leaders and doctrine for aid and advice and Tajik youth embrace the Muslim faith in greater numbers. Today, there are real fears among observers that the recent attacks and bombings in Tajikistan may be merely a foretaste of greater instability to come, and that the growing Islamic militancy there "could become a hotbed of Islamic insurgency capable of destabilizing Tajikistan and Central Asia as a whole."[2]

ISLAMIST ACTIVITY

The end of the Soviet Union brought independence as well as instability to Tajikistan, as regional clans who "enjoyed privileged economic status during the Soviet era" sought to maintain their grip on the levers of state power.[3] Former Communist political elites from the Kulyab region in southeast Tajikistan seized control of Dushanbe and elected Emomali Rakhmonov as President.[4] An opposition group, the United Tajik Opposition (UTO)—comprised of Islamists from the Islamic Renaissance Party of Tajikistan (IRPT) and secularists, including democratic, nationalist, and separatist movements—coalesced to oppose the new government, provoking the Tajik civil war.[5] That conflict raged until 1997, when the Tajik government and the UTO agreed to a ceasefire and a UN-brokered peace deal. The peace deal gave the UTO, mostly the IRPT, a 30 percent stake in the central government.[6]

But in spite of the power-sharing agreement, the Islamists suffered a blow to their prestige and credibility; the Tajik people recognized the motivations of the IRPT and their betrayal of Islamic principles in favor of a union with secularists through which to fight for power.[7] And although the IRPT survived as an Islamic political party, the only one of its kind in Central Asia, it effectively has been marginalized. This was evident from Tajikistan's February 2000 parliamentary elections, in which the IRPT only managed to win 7.5 percent of the votes and secure only two seats in the lower house of the country's Supreme Assembly.[8]

As the IRPT has resorted to political maneuvering to stay in power and remain relevant, Hizb ut-Tahrir al-Islami (HuT, the Islamic Party of Liberation), has gradually grown to become Tajikistan's most prominent Islamist group. According to experts, HuT's ability to "frame the social and economic problems in Tajikistan as a result of secularism, widespread corruption in the government, Western cultural influence and the absence of a strong universal Islamic state" has given the group "ideological superiority" and put it in a favorable position to recruit disillusioned Tajiks.[9] HuT's radical but non-violent approach has also succeeded in attracting extremists to its ranks, and opened the door for more radical and violent Islamist groups, like the Islamic Movement of Uzbekistan (IMU), to re-emerge.

Hizb ut-Tahrir

Hizb ut-Tahrir arrived in Tajikistan in the late 1990s and rose to prominence as its sometime competitors for influence among the country's Muslims, most directly the Islamic Renaissance Party of Tajikistan and the Islamic Movement of Uzbekistan, declined in popularity. The former lost its religious cachet as it developed into a political party and migrated into the political mainstream, while the latter joined the Taliban against U.S.-led forces in Afghanistan and was almost completely routed as a result.

Like the IMU, HuT has called for the overthrow of the Tajik government, albeit through peaceful means, in order to establish an Islamic state. Over time, it became popular among ethnic Uzbeks and Tajiks alike through the widespread promulgation of radical Islamic literature. The two groups, however, gravitated to HuT for different reasons; Uzbeks in Tajikistan joined on account of the group's promotion of Muslim solidarity, while Tajiks joined to rally against the rampant social and economic problems in Tajik society.[10] Recognizing the threat, the Tajik government moved swiftly to declare HuT an illegal political party in 1999, and subsequently arrested and prosecuted HuT members under Article 187 (arousing religious and ethnic dissension) and Article 307 (calling for the overthrow of the government) of the Tajik criminal code.[11] Between 2000 and 2005, about 500 alleged members of HuT were arrested;[12] yet only about 150–200 of those HuT members were prosecuted and are serving sentences currently in Tajik prisons.[13]

Because of the intense crackdown on HuT, Tajik authorities suspect that the group has gone underground, making it more difficult to fully eradicate. Tajik security officials have admitted that the state "will continue to have problems with Hizb ut-Tahrir, no matter how hard they try to undermine them."[14]

Islamic Movement of Uzbekistan

During the late summer and early fall of 2010, the Islamic Movement of Uzbekistan (IMU) demonstrated a rejuvenated ability and eagerness to carry out violence in Central Asia, and has even ventured to establish ties with European-based terrorist operations. The IMU's renewed sense of radicalism has in large part resulted from the death of long-time leader Tohir Yuldashev, who was killed in an August 27, 2009 drone strike by Coalition forces in Afghanistan.[15]

Yuldashev had been "quite content operating as an armed wing for the Taliban in Pakistan, working as a supporting group."[16] From the group's inception, Yuldashev had served as the IMU's ideological leader, touring the Middle East establishing contacts with other terrorist organizations—including al-Qaeda. His counterpart, Juma Namangani, served as the group's tactical commander. Namagani, who had fought with the Soviets in Afghanistan and with the IRPT in Tajikistan's civil war, commanded the IMU's narcotics-trafficking and insurgent campaign to overthrow the government of Uzbekistan. It was Namangani that led the IMU into combat against U.S. forces and the Northern Alliance in Afghanistan following the U.S. invasion in October 2001, resulting in the group's near-annihilation and his own death the following month. By 2004, the group's main military wing had been decimated while smaller factions broke away, leading experts to speculate as to whether the group had survived.

The IMU subsequently regrouped in the mountains along the Afghanistan-Pakistan border, and supported the Taliban on cross-border raids and helped revitalize the insurgency in Northern Afghanistan. But Yuldashev's death has apparently energized the group to return to its founding cause: overthrowing the Uzbek government and destabilizing Central Asia.[17] Experts agree that the socio-economic "conditions in Central Asia are presently ripe for an IMU comeback" and recent events chronicle the IMU's resurgence in Tajikistan.[18]

These include the August 2010 jailbreak of 25 inmates with Islamic militant ties from the State Committee for National Security's high-security prison in Dushanbe,[19] as well as the September 2010 suicide car bomb attack on a police station in the Northern Tajikistan city of Khujand—an attack the IMU has been accused of masterminding.[20] Also in September 2010, the IMU conducted a brazen ambush of a Tajik military convoy in the Rasht Valley, killing 25 soldiers.[21] Abdufattoh Ahmadi, a spokesman for the IMU, issued a statement claiming responsibility and demanding that the Tajik government cease its crackdown on Islamic society.[22] This series of recent violent events has sparked a government campaign to capture the escaped inmates and counter the growing insurgency in the Rasht Valley of Tajikistan.

ISLAMISM AND SOCIETY

The Islamic Movement of Uzbekistan's call for Tajikistan to cease its crackdown on Islamic society is a reflection of a broader trend in Tajik society. *Radio Free Europe/Radio Liberty* reports that "Islamic names are the new fashion"[23] and families are increasingly turning to *sharia* law to resolve disputes."[24] In fact, a Gallup poll conducted in August 2010 revealed that "85 percent of Tajiks said religion was an important part of their lives, with only 12 percent saying it was not, making Tajikistan first among Central Asian states in terms of religiosity."[25] Indeed, so rapidly has Islam and Islamism increased in popularity that the Tajik government now fears that it could undermine the influence of the state.[26]

Islamism was not always so prominent in Tajikistan. Following the end of the Tajik civil war in 1997, ordinary Tajiks grew so disillusioned by the ambitions of the warring-Islamist factions that many turned their backs on the rhetoric of religious radicals. In her book *Muslim Youth: Tensions and Transitions in Tajikistan*, scholar Collette Harris comments that "in Dushanbe, on the surface at least, modernization appeared to be a far stronger force than religion. Almost none of the locals I saw dressed in a conspicuously Islamic fashion. In fact, there seems to be little support for any kind of Islamization among Dushanbe's population."[27]

Unfortunately, modernization in Tajikistan has barely limped along, with the corrupt and authoritarian elites hoarding power and refusing to invest in the country's troubled economy and civil society. In a 2009 study, the International Crisis Group judged that Tajikistan is "far from being a bulwark against the spread of extremism and violence from Afghanistan;" rather, it said, the country looks "increasingly like its southern neighbour – a weak state that is suffering from a failure of leadership."[28] The ICG goes on to explain that Tajikistan is on the road to failure as the government will be "confronted with serious economic problems" as the poor get poorer.[29]

Signs of disenchantment with the government and a preference for Islamic reforms began with the winter crises of 2008 and 2009, when the Tajik people shivered through harsh winters as a result of Tajikistan's dilapidated energy infrastructure. Despite government assurances of available gas and electric power, people put their trust in collecting combustible fuel for heating and cooking. In a clear expression of dissatisfaction, some Tajiks even exclaimed, "Even in the civil war we had electricity!"[30] Outrage peaked during the economic slowdown of 2009 because the Tajik economy, fueled by remittances from Tajik migrant laborers and devastated by the lack of jobs at home and abroad, nearly failed. As a result, according to one NGO study, approximately 30 percent of migrant workers returned home, while 60 percent of Tajiks at home "who say they need medical care are forced to treat themselves" and "roughly 40 percent [of Tajiks] say they cannot afford enough food, while 70 percent report they rarely eat meat."[31] As a result of these conditions, Tajiks are said to be living in "survival mode."[32]

According to experts, the lack of competent leadership in Tajikistan has served to exacerbate the country's economic crisis.[33] The government's failures and the public's outrage illustrate the vacuum created by the lack of social order—a vacuum that Islamism has recently begun to fill. And while remittances have gradually picked up once again, the effects of the global economic crisis and governmental neglect can still be felt. Gross unemployment remains the norm, and unemployed and defiant young men, who have not migrated abroad for work, are particularly vulnerable for Islamist recruitment and increasing radicalization.

ISLAMISM AND THE STATE

Fears of an impending Islamic re-awakening—and the attendant threat of anti-state terror—has led the Tajik government to launch a major effort to make the practice of religion in Tajikistan more restrictive. Even before it passed new legislation in March 2009 hindering the practice of religion, the

Tajik government had a history of banning religious expression deemed foreign and religious movements deemed threatening. Thus Hizb ut-Tahrir was declared illegal soon after its emergence in Tajikistan in 1999, and its members arrested and thrown in jail. In March 2006, Tajikistan similarly banned the Islamic revivalist movement Tablighi Jama'at, claiming that members of the movement were perpetrating subversion of Tajikistan's constitutional order.[34] In April 2007, the government of Tajikistan imposed a dress code on university students by banning the *hijab*, the Islamic headscarf. Miniskirts and skimpy tops were also banned, with these articles of clothing declared foreign and inappropriate.

Subsequently, in January 2009, the Tajik government formally banned Salafism as an ideological movement, claiming it to be a potential threat to national security.[35] And then, in March 2009, the Tajik parliament passed the new, groundbreaking religion law, artfully named the "Law on the Freedom of Consciousness," which "imposes censorship on religious literature and restricts performing rituals to state-approved venues."[36] The law "makes it harder for new religious communities to get registration."[37] Furthermore, it requires religious groups to report funding sources and any foreign contacts, restricts construction of new mosques and requires parental consent for young people under the age of 18 seeking religious education.[38] While Tajik officials claim that the new law is "fully in line with the constitution, and is a well-designed set of ground-rules that seeks principally to prevent the growth of radical religious groups," it has been roundly criticized by international bodies such as the United Nations, the European Union, the Organization for Security and Cooperation in Europe and the United States Commission on International Religious Freedom.[39] The latter has charged that the new religion law essentially legalizes "harsh policies already adopted by the Tajik government against its majority Muslim population."[40]

In tandem with the passage of repressive religious policies, Tajik government authorities have intensified their monitoring of religious expression and regularly break up unauthorized religious practices. In early July 2010, authorities raided seven unregistered religious schools, or *madrassas*, in the Isfara, Istaravshan, Panjakent and Ghafurov districts.[41] The following month, Tajik police raided a separate unregistered *madrassa* in the Rudaki district south of Dushanbe and detained the founder, Mavlavi Abduqahor, and 70 of his students.[42] President Emomali Rakhmon has continued his campaign against Islamic dress in schools by urging Tajik women not to don the *hijab*. Authorities are now extending the *hijab* ban beyond the universities and into public places like the bazaar.[43] Education officials are now also pressuring parents of Islamic students studying abroad. In August 2010, President Rakhmon reportedly "asked parents to recall their sons and daughters from foreign madrasahs and universities lest they join extremist or even terrorist groups."[44]

But mounting state pressure against prevailing socio-religious attitudes is frustrating and alienating many ordinary Tajiks and moderate Muslims. Religious imams at registered mosques, like Muhammad-jon Ortiqov of the grand mosque in Ghafurov district, have expressed concerns about the authorities' apparent fear and suspicion of religious expression, and say such an approach is bound to alienate moderate Muslims.[45] Further intervention in the name of suppressing extremism will likely create the opposite effect by "driving disgruntled Muslims into the hands of covert extremist groups."[46] And extremist groups like the IMU will likely continue to raise the banner of violent resistance against the authoritarian and corrupt government of Tajikistan. Indeed, there are fears that the recent attacks and bombings in Tajikistan may be merely a foretaste of greater instability to come, and that the growing Islamic militancy there "could become a hotbed of Islamic insurgency capable of destabilizing Tajikistan and Central Asia as a whole."[47]

ENDNOTES

[1]"Tajikistan," CIA *World Factbook*, November 9, 2010, https://www.cia.gov/library/publications/the-world-factbook/geos/ti.html.

[2] Farangis Najibullah, "Some Fear Tajik Opposition Stronghold Could Become Hotbed For Islamic Insurgency," Eurasianet.org, September 28, 2010, http://www.eurasianet.org/print/62035.

[3] Emmanuel Karagiannis, "The Challenge Of Radical Islam In Tajikistan: Hizb ut-Tahrir al-Islami," *Nationalities Papers* 34, no. 1, March 2006.

[4] In early April 2007, President Emomali Rakhmonov officially de-Russified his name and became Emomali Rakhmon, he also called on all Tajiks to follow suit.

[5] Notably, the Tajik civil war was driven first and foremost by religious, rather than ethnic, interests and tensions. Shirin Akiner, a prominent Central Asia scholar, points out that the civil war was not "primarily 'driven' by deep-rooted animosities between regional or ethnic groups. Instead the conflict in Tajikistan had the classic dynamics of a civil war in which different interest groups mobilized to contest control of the state and its resources." Shirin Akiner and Catherine Barnes, "The Tajik Civil War: Causes And Dynamics," *Conciliation Resources*, March 2001, http://www.c-r.org/our-work/accord/tajikistan/causes-dynamics.php.

[6] Karagiannis, "The Challenge Of Radical Islam In Tajikistan: Hizb ut-Tahrir al-Islami," 3.

[7] Ibid.

[8] Ibidem.

[9] Ibid., 10.

[10] Ibid., 6-7.

[11] Ibid., 4.

[12] Ibidem.

[13] Aleskender Ramazanov, "Tajikistan: Islamic Radicals Lying Low," Institute for War & Peace Reporting, February 21, 2005, http://iwpr.net/print/report-news/tajikistan-islamic-radicals-lying-low.

[14] Ibid.

[15] Bill Roggio, "Islamic Movement Of Uzbekistan Confirms Leader Tahir Yuldashev Killed," The Long War Journal, August 16, 2010, http://www.longwarjournal.org/archives/2010/08/islamic_movement_of_1.php.

[16] Anonymous, "Central Asia: The Islamic Movement Of Uzbekistan Undergoing Dangerous Transformation," Eurasianet.org, October 19, 2009, http://www.eurasianet.org/departments/insightb/articles/eav102009b.shtml.

[17] Ibid.

[18] Ibidem.

[19] Lola Olimova, "Mass Jailbreak Causes Ripples In Tajikistan," Institute for War & Peace Reporting, September 6, 2010, http://iwpr.net/print/report-news/mass-jailbreak-causes-ripples-tajikistan.

[20] Farangis Najibullah, "Suicide Car Bomber Hits Tajik Police Station," Radio Free Europe/Radio Liberty, September 3, 2010, http://www.rferl.org/articleprintview/2147120.html.

[21] Roman Kozhevnikov, "Al Qaeda Ally Claims Tajik Attack, Threatens More," Reuters, September 23, 2010, http://www.reuters.com/article/idUSTRE68M28M20100923.

[22] Ibid.

[23] Farangis Najibullah, "In Tajikistan, Islamic Names Are The New Fashion," Radio Free Europe/Radio Liberty, October 7, 2010, http://www.rferl.org/articleprintview/2182689.html.

[24] Kayumars Ato, "Tajiks Increasingly Turning To Shari'a To Resolve Disputes, Family Affairs," Radio Free Europe/Radio Liberty, September 7, 2010, http://www.rferl.org/articleprintview/2150615.html.

[25] Ibid.

[26] Ibidem.

[27] Collette Harris, *Muslim Youth: Tensions and Transitions in Tajikistan* (Oxford: Westview Press, 2006), 16.

[28] *Tajikistan: On the Road to Failure* (International Crisis Group, February 2009), i, http://www.crisisgroup.org/~/media/Files/asia/central-asia/tajikistan/162_tajikistan___on_the_road_to_failure.ashx.

[29] Ibid.

[30] Ibid., 11.

[31] David Trilling, "More Horrifying Economic Stats for Tajikistan - New Report," Eurasianet.org, May 7, 2010, http://www.eurasianet.org/node/61009.

[32] Ibid.

[33] "Tajikistan: Rahmon Admits Extent Of Domestic Financial Crisis," Eurasianet.org, April 14, 2009, http://www.eurasianet.org/departments/news/articles/eav041509.shtml.

[34] Andrew McGregor, "Counterterrorism Operations Continue In Tajikistan," Jamestown Foundation *Terrorism Monitor* 7, iss. 25, August 13, 2009, http://www.jamestown.org/single/?no_cache=1&tx_ttnews[tt_news]=35410.

[35] Farangis Najibullah, "Salafi Ban Reflects Tajik Officials' Growing Fear," Radio Free Europe/Radio Liberty, January 9, 2009, http://www.rferl.org/articleprintview/1368347.html.

[36] "Tajikistan Criticized Over Restrictive Religion Law," Radio Free Europe/Radio Liberty, March 26, 2009, http://www.rferl.org/articleprintview/1562436.html.

[37] Ibid.

[38] "Tajikistan: Campaign To Soften Religion Law," Institute for War & Peace Reporting, July 15, 2009, http://iwpr.net/print/report-news/

tajikistan-campaign-soften-religion-law.

[39] Ibid.

[40] "Tajikistan Criticized Over Restrictive Religion Law."

[41] Farangis Najibullah, "Tajik Officials Keep Sharp Eye On Islamic Teaching," Radio Free Europe/Radio Liberty, August 7, 2010, http://www.eurasianet.org/print/61682.

[42] Alexander Sodiqov, "Tajik Police Detain Islamic School Leader And Students," Jamestown Foundation *Eurasia Daily Monitor* 7, iss. 154, August 10, 2010, http://www.jamestown.org/single/?no_cache=1&tx_ttnews[tt_news]=36732.

[43] "Tajik Pressure Said To Be Growing Over Islamic Dress," Radio Free Europe/Radio Liberty, September 17, 2010, http://www.rferl.org/articleprintview/2160501.html.

[44] "Tajikistan Wants Students At Islamic Schools Abroad To Return," Radio Free Europe/Radio Liberty, October 12, 2010, http://www.rferl.org/articleprintview/2188047.html.

[45] "Tajik Officials Keep Sharp Eye On Islamic Teaching."

[46] "Tajikistan: Campaign To Soften Religion Law."

[47] "Some Fear Tajik Opposition Stronghold Could Become Hotbed For Islamic Insurgency," Eurasianet.org, September 28, 2010.

RUSSIA

QUICK FACTS

Population: 139,390,205

Area: 17,098,242 sq km

Ethnic Groups: Russian 79.8%, Tatar 3.8%, Ukrainian 2%, Bashkir 1.2%, Chuvash 1.1%, other or unspecified 12.1%

Religions: Russian Orthodox 15-20%, Muslim 10-15%, other Christian 2%

Government Type: Federation

GDP (official exchange rate): $1.232 trillion

Map and Quick Facts courtesy of the CIA World Factbook (last updated July 2010)

Muslims comprise the Russian Federation's second largest confessional group, numbering some 15 million (10 percent of the overall population), and are divided by geography, history, ethnicity and confessional differences.[1] Although Islamic institutions were largely destroyed and believers forced underground under Soviet rule, Islam has experienced a quick, vibrant, variegated but still ill-defined revival since the collapse of the USSR, with various tendencies competing for the support of society and state. Since the late Soviet era of Mikhail Gorbachev's reformist restructuring, or perestroika, the number of Islamic communities in Russia has grown exponentially. Among Russia's Muslims, the explosion of ethno-nationalism sparked by the USSR's implosion in the late 1980s and early 1990s has been replaced to a considerable degree by religious identification. However, only a small portion of Russia's Muslims have Islamist tendencies, and a fraction of those have been drawn to a violent Islamism or jihadism since the period between the first and second post-Soviet Russian-Chechen wars.

ISLAMIST ACTIVITY

The Caucasus Emirate

The main *jihadist* group, a network of *jihadist* cells (or *jamaats*) spread across the North Caucasus called the "Imarat Kavkaz" or "Caucasus Emirate" (CE), evolved through the radicalization of the Chechen national separatist movement community.

The CE and its predecessor organization evolved from the Chechen separatist movement that emerged as the Soviet Union began to collapse in the early 1990s. Although there were some radical political Islamic elements within Chechen society and first Chechen president Dzhokar Dudaev did implement elements of *sharia* law, the Chechen movement was a predominantly nationalist movement through the first post-Soviet Russo-Chechen war in 1994-1996. However, following the 1996 Khasavyurt peace agreement signed between Russian President Boris Yeltsin and Dudaev's successor, Aslan Maskhadov, the quasi-independent Chechen Republic of Ichkeria (ChRI) devolved into a state of permanent chaos, criminality, and civil strife. The political vacuum was used by a small number of internal Islamist-oriented wartime field commanders and foreign *jihadist* elements, including al-Qaeda, to establish a *jihadi* bridgehead in the form of indoctrination and terrorist training camps.

As early as 1996, Osama bin Laden's chief deputy, Ayman al-Zawahiri, attempted to visit incognito and establish a presence in Russia, but he was discovered and deported. In a subsequently published book, he targeted Russia for *jihad* and the establishment of an expansive southern Eurasian caliphate.[2] At about the same time, Shamil Basaev, then a Chechen field commander, visited Afghanistan and received training there in 1994 and 2001.[3] Thereafter, al-Qaeda operative Abu Ibn al-Khattab arrived in Chechnya, and amid the inter-war lawlessness established camps where perhaps several hundred foreign *jihadi* fighters as well as locals trained in terrorist tactics. These units spearheaded the August 1999 invasion of Dagestan organized by Basaev and Khattab and aimed at creating an Islamist enclave there—an offensive which set off the second post-Soviet Chechen war.[4]

As during the first Chechen war, Russia deployed a brutal offensive, and by 2002 had defeated the militants in conventional war, driving the bulk of the ChRI government and parliament into foreign exile; many finding refuge in places like Washington, London, Istanbul, Baku, the United Arab Emirates, and Qatar. The more die-hard extremist elements retreated into the mountain forests in southern Chechnya and Georgia, where the ChRI began a classic guerilla insurgency campaign punctuated by occasional large-scale attacks. With the national separatists isolated abroad, the *jihadists* gradually consolidated power over the movement over the next five years.

In summer 2002, an expanded emergency meeting of the underground remnants of the ChRI government and armed forces convened in the mountains of Chechnya. The meeting was attended by President Maskhadov, internationally-wanted terrorist Shamil Basaev, the ChRI's leading field commanders, and several foreign *jihadists* and al-Qaeda operatives. The meeting was a *coup d'etat* of sorts; as a result, a *sharia*-based order was adopted, with the goal of expanding the insurgency across the North Caucasus.[5]

Thereafter, Basaev began to travel across the Caucasus seeking out young radicals and establishing a network of combat *jamaats* in Ingushetia, Dagestan, Kabardino-Balkaria, and Karachaevo-Cherkessia.[6] The results of Basaev's organizational activity soon produced a series of terrorist incidents. The most prominent was the Dubrovka theatre hostage-taking in October 2002, which ended in 130 deaths when Russian forces stormed the theater. In 2003, there was a series of suicide attacks in Moscow that killed and wounded over 100.[7] 2004 saw a summer of terror, included the June 2004 attack on Nazran's MVD building, the bombing of an outdoor concert, and suicide bombings, including the simultaneous mid-air explosions of two airliners. This terror offensive concluded with the seizure of School No. 1 in Beslan in early September – a terrorist incident in which 333, including 186 children, were killed. Since then, however, *jihadi* terrorist activity has been confined to the North Caucasus's Muslim republics, in particular Ingushetia, Chechnya, Dagestan, and Kabardino-Balkaria, where *mujahideen* have carried out 200-400 attacks per year on civilian, police, security and military officials and servicemen.[8]

In March 2005, Russian forces apprehended ChRI president Maskhadov, and his bodyguards reportedly killed him so he would not fall into enemy hands. He was succeeded by Sadulaev, who quickly institutionalized the broader Caucasus *jihad*, creating Caucasus and Dagestan Fronts that encompassed Ingushetia, Kabardino-Balkaria, and Karachaevo-Cherkessia as well. The following months included an upsurge in *jihadist* violence, most prominently an October 2005 attack by approximately two hundred *mujahideen* in Kabardino-Balkaria's capitol, Nalchik, that killed 47 and wounded more than one hundred.[9] Then, in early 2006, Basaev called for the establishment of a council of Islamic scholars (*ulema*) who would be charged with selecting the emir of the Caucasus. In May 2006 ChRI president/amir Sadulaev declared the formation of Urals and Volga Fronts, institutionalizing his occasional calls for the liberation of all "Muslim lands" on Russian territory. Sadulaev in turn was killed by Russian forces in June 2006, and was succeeded by Doka Umarov, who appointed Basaev to the posts of premier and vice president, making him Umarov's *de facto* top deputy and designated successor. But with Basaev's subsequent death, and because of some Russian successes and policy adjustments (among them a broad amnesty from September 2006 to January 2007, and the creation of a national and regional antiterrorism committees), the ChRI *mujahideen* witnessed a major downturn in their fortunes.[10] However, in Spring 2007, the ChRI rebounded thanks to a number of internal changes, from the retargeting of its operations from Chechnya to Ingushetia to a fundraising campaign conducted on Arab language sites.[11] Since summer 2007, Ingushetia has been the center of the Caucasus *jihad*, with more terrorist attacks occurring in that republic than in any other in summer and fall 2007, in 2008 (372 attacks total, 138 in Ingushetia), and 2009 (511 attacks, 175 in Ingushetia).[12]

The CE functions as a decentralized network, consisting of local combat *jamaats* loosely tied together and subordinate to sectors, which are in turn subordinated to the CE's virtual 'provinces,' referred to by the *mujahideen* in the Arabic as veliyats, and fronts. Subordination is indicated by the taking of the Islamic loyalty oath (*bayat*). The CE includes six known *veliyats*: Veliyat Nokchicho (Chechnya); Veliyat Gyalgyaiche (Ingushetia and Ossetia); Veliyat Dagestan; the United Veliyat of Kabardia, Balkaria, and Karachai (the KBR, the KChR, and probably Adygeya); and Veliyat of the Nogai Steppe (Krasnodar Krai and Stavropol Krai). The CE's new structure and organization included Umarov's abolition of the ChRI government and parliament in exile and is thereby a complete break with the nationalist separatism of the past.[13] An emir who has taken the Islamic loyalty oath or *bayat* to the CE cheif heads each veliyat. The CE's military structure includes: Caucasus, Dagestan, Volga, and Urals Fronts. Combat *jamaats* are allowed to design and undertake small-scale operations independently, but larger operations in theory require approval from a higher-ranking *emir*.[14]

The size of the CE's network is extremely difficult to estimate. *Jihadi* sources are silent on the subject, except to refute the accuracy of official Russian estimates. The most reliable, recent, official estimates from the security and law enforcement bodies put the number of active fighters in a range from 400-1,500.[15] Politicians put the numbers much lower and absurdly so, with Chechen President Ramzan Kadyrov having claimed victory over the *jihadists* several times over, and putting their numbers in Chechnya at just 50-60.[16] The CE's operational capacity, reflected in the number of attacks and other indicators, suggest membership may be closer to the higher end of law enforcement's estimates. It is reasonable to assume that there may be more than 1,000 CE fighters, and thousands of additional facilitators.[17]

The CE retains the late ChRI's goals of establishing a *sharia*-based Islamist state across the Caucasus and eventually liberating all Muslim lands in Russia. The CE has retained the Urals and Volga Fronts, which target Tatarstan, Bashkortostan, and perhaps other regions where Muslim khanates existed in the past and Muslim populations survive into the present in the Urals and Volga areas. In late 2004, then-field commander and ChRI security council chairman Umarov called for the liberation of Siberia, where a Tatar khanate once existed, and the Far East, and outlined a plan for the creation of three new, large sectors, mega-sectors or zones – Western, Siberian, and Far Eastern – in order to extend war and terror to Russia's "economic heart."[18]

In a February 2010 interview, Umarov vowed to liberate once-Muslim lands in Krasnodar Krai, Astrakhan and the Volga.[19] Ultimately, the CE's conceptualization of "Muslim lands" in Russia is indefinite. Thus, a map of the future "Caucasus Emirate" that CE-affiliated websites circulate shows the entire North Caucasus region from the Black to the Caspian Seas, including non-Muslim republics like Krasnodar and Stavropol krais and North Ossetia, to be CE territory. Moreover, Russian territory 'proper' to the north of the North Caucasus as well as the Transcaucasus (Georgia, Armenia, and Azerbaijan) to the south are labeled as "Muslim lands occupied by infidels and apostates."[20]

In his declaration of the CE's creation, its *emir*, Doku Umarov, also declared *jihad* against all those fighting against *mujahideen* in Iraq, Afghanistan, Palestine, or anywhere in the world – a statement tantamount to a declaration of war against the U.S., Great Britain, Israel, and their allies.[21] The CE's ideology finds its inspiration in the same ideological and theological works that permeate the global *jihadi* movement.[22] In short, the CE has ideologically and politically allied itself with the most virulent elements of the global *jihadist* movement, including al-Qaeda, the Taliban, Islamic Jihad, Hezbollah, and others, and repeatedly posts articles in support of their respective *jihads*.

The CE is composed of members from each of the Muslim ethnic groups in Russia, as well as members of non-Muslim ethnic groups. Chechens, Ingush and various Dagestani (Avars, Dargins, Kumyks, Nogais, Tabasarans, etc.) predominate, but the Muslim Alans (Karachais and Balkars) and Circassians (Kabards, Cherkess, and Adygs) are also well represented. In short, the CE puts into practice the *jihadi* principle that Islam is universal; the 'lifting of Allah's word above all others' countenances no ethnic or national boundaries.

During the first Russo-Chechen war and in the period thereafter, the ChRI received funding from elements of the Chechen mafia, narcotics trafficking, illicit oil exports, and the lucrative hostage-taking industry run by Chechen field commander and Moscow mafia chief, Khozh-Akhmed Nukhaev.[23] For the most part, these sources were cut off with the onset of the second war, the displacement of the ChRI leadership abroad, and a more aggressive international and Russian effort to combat money-laundering as a source of terrorist financing.

There is little original source material regarding the CE's current sources of financing. It remains likely that Arab and other foreign Islamic governments, businesses, and philanthropists still provide funds, despite the Russian authorities' efforts to put an end to such activity. It is believed that elements in local government and criminal circles, including narcotics traffickers, provide budget and illicit funds, respectively, to the CE by way of money laundering and other activities.[24] According to both the Russian authorities and the *mujahideen* themselves, the local population provides limited financial support and considerable logistical and other material support, such as weapons, safe houses, and food provisions.[25]

The declaration of the CE has coincided with an upsurge in *mujahideen* operations. In 2008, the first full year of the CE's existence, its *mujahideen* executed 372 attacks/incidents, 370 of them in the North Caucasus.[26] In 2009, the CE's capacity strengthened significantly in potency if not in reach, with 511 attacks/incidents. Moreover, the CE revived the late Basaev's unit for suicide martyrdom operations, the 'Riyadus Salikhin' Martyrs Battalion, and carried out 17 successful suicide bombing attacks in 2009.[27]

Other Jihadist Groups

In the past, likely al-Qaeda operatives such as Khattab, Abu Walid, Abu Havs and now Abu Seif and Muhannad have joined the ChRI/CE, but there is no open source evidence that al-Qaeda or other foreign *jihadist* groups operate in Russia independently from the CE. Russian law enforcement occasionally claims that al-Qaeda operatives number among killed and captured CE *mujahideen*, but such claims are never documented. The only other *jihadist* organization recently reported to be active in Russia is the Uighur-Bulgar Jamaat (UBJ), members of which went on trial in April 2009 pursuant to their arrest the previous August after a shootout with Bashkir police in Salavat, Bashkortostan. According to Bashkir authorities, the Uighur-Bulgar Jamaat operates along the Afghanistan-Pakistan border and was founded by Pavel Dorokhov, a native of Bashkiria's Baimak district, who was trained in al-Qaeda and Taliban camps.[28] The UBJ may or may not be one and the same organization as the apparently ethnic Tatar 'Bulgar Jamaat' currently fighting in Afghanistan.[29]

Other domestic groups

Several small Tatar groups have Islamist tendencies but are at least equally or predominantly national separatist in nature, confining their activity to Tatarstan and, to a lesser degree, Bashkortostan. They include: Ittifak, Mille Mejlis, and elements within the All-Tatar Public Center.[30] In the past year, these organizations continued to confine themselves to occasional declarations, conferences, and small demonstrations. Some of their official statements and documents are sent to the North Caucasus *mujahideen* websites, but unlike a few years ago it is unclear whether these documents were sent by Tatars to the *mujahideen* sites.[31]

ISLAMISM AND SOCIETY

Since the collapse of the Soviet Union, Islam has undergone a revival among its traditionally Muslim ethnic groups. According to Russia's leading mufti,

Chairman of the Council of Muftis of Russia (CMR) Ravil Gainutdin, the number of mosques in Russia grew from 150 in 1991 to some six thousand by October 2005.[32]

Russia's Muslims are divided by geography, history, ethnicity, and divergent confessional movements (Sufis, Sunnis, and Shi'ites) and legal schools (*maskhabs*). The overwhelming majority of Russia's Muslims are Sunni. Shi'a are predominantly located in the southern North Caucasus, particularly among Dagestan's rather small ethnic Lezgin population. Sufism predominates in the North Caucasus, consisting mostly of Naqshbandi and Qadiri *tariqats* (brotherhoods or orders). There are some 15 such brotherhoods in the Republic of Dagestan alone. Brotherhoods tend to be mono-ethnic, or nearly so. Each Islamic school of jurisprudence, or *maskhab*, is represented in Russia, but almost all of Russia's Muslims adhere to the Hanafi interpretation. There is, however, a significant Shafi presence in the North Caucasus. Tatarstan's Muslims and the Tatar internal diaspora, meanwhile, are experiencing a revival of the Islamic reformist or 'jadidist' school of Islamic thought.

Although Muslim communities can be found all across the length and breadth of the vast federation, the largest concentrations of ethnic Muslims (ethnic groups that traditionally have adhered in overwhelming numbers to the Islamic faith) are found in the North Caucasus's Muslim republics—Chechnya, Ingushetia, Dagestan, Adygeya, Kabardino-Balkaria (KBR), and Karachaevo-Cherkessia (KChR)—and in the Volga and Urals republics of Tatarstan and Bashkortostan. There are also large Muslim populations in Moscow and St. Petersburg, but these are more Russified, urbanized, and secularized than those in other regions, especially the North Caucasus. The Muslims of the North Caucasus remain largely rural, traditionally religious, and indigenously ethnic or clan-oriented.

The North Caucasus's Muslims are divided into three linguistic groups (Turkic, Persian, and Ibero-Caucasian) and some 40 traditionally Muslim ethnic groups. The ethnic groups are themselves divided by various administrative-territorial borders and strong sub-ethnic clan allegiances.

Russia's other main ethnic Muslim groups, Tatars and Bashkirs, are concentrated to a great extent in the Tatarstan and Bashkortostan Republics. Tatars make up a slim majority in Tatarstan, while ethnic Russians outnumber Bashkirs in Baskortostan (Bashkiria). Both Tatars and Bashkirs are better integrated into Russian life than are the North Caucasians. In recent years, some historically non-Muslim ethnic groups are seeing some of their members convert to Islam, including ethnic Russians.[33] Ethnic Russian Muslims have organized their own socio-political organization, the National Organization of Russia's Muslims (NORM), which purports to have 2,500-3,000 members.[34]

Russia's Muslims are not strongly self-organized. Rather, they are well-organized "from above" by the Islamic clergy and the Russian state. Muslim communities must be registered with the government, and each is then incorporated into a regional Muslim Spiritual Administration (MSA), every one of which is included under one of the three main Muslim umbrella organizations: the Council of Muslims of Russia (CMR), the Central Muslim Spiritual Administration (CMSA), and the Coordinating Council of the Muslims of the North Caucasus (CCMNC). The CMR at present is the most influential of the umbrella organizations, with its leader, the ethnic Tatar mufti Ravil Gainutdin, on good terms with the Kremlin. Two smaller umbrella organizations – the MSA of the European part of Russia and the MSA of the Asian part of Russia – are subordinated to two of the abovementioned. In all, there are known to be approximately 60 regional MSAs, all of which are included under one or another of the umbrella organizations.[35] These various structures help organize Muslims' *hajj* travel and study abroad, support Islamic universities and *madrassas* in Russia, and recruit and train Islamic clergy. The various Muslim spiritual councils (*Dukhovnyie Upravlenii Musulman* or DUM in Russian) receive state funding for mufti's salaries, university and *madrassa* development, and the building of mosques. Independent Muslim communities and mosques persist but are illegal and are usually discovered by the authorities and incorporated into the official administrations. Typically, these have manifested Islamist tendencies, and some have produced *jihadist* terrorist organizations, leaders, and cadres.[36]

With regard to political ideology, Russia's Muslims are divided among democrats, conservatives, Eurasianist and Islamist reactionaries, much as ethnic Russians are divided among democrats, conservatives, Eurasianist and Russian nationalist reactionaries. However, since under Russian law political parties based on any communal identification are forbidden from participating in elections, it is difficult to attain a detailed picture of Muslims' distribution on Russia's political spectrum.

Political Islam is in evidence at both the official and unofficial levels. Media controlled by official Islamic structures carry numerous articles on introducing elements of *sharia* law in Russia, including the introduction of Islamic banking and insurance.[37] Also, there are strong anti-American, anti-Western, anti-Israeli, and even anti-Semitic tendencies not just among Russia's Islamists but among Russia's traditional Muslims as well.[38]

Generally, however, there is very limited support for Islamism in both Russia's Muslim and non-Muslim populations. The country's Islamic clergy feels threatened and virulently opposes manifestations of political Islam, and Islamists have found limited support in the Muslim community. That said, many young Muslims are increasingly fascinated by – and sympathetic toward – radical trends, including Islamism as represented by charismatic *mujahjideen* like Caucasus Emirate rising star Said abu Saad Buryatskii. Perhaps because of this lack of support, Muslim communities in the North Caucasus have tended to radicalize quickly, evolving into *jihadist* groups.[39]

ISLAMISM AND THE STATE

The Russian state, federal and/or local, depending on the region, pays some part of official muftis' salaries and finances the building of mosques, *madrassas*, and Islamic universities and centers. The Russian state's alliance with the official Islamic clergy is complicated by generational and demographic factors, however. Many official muftis and imams hail from the Soviet era and may be tainted by cooperation with the atheist regime and poor knowledge of Islam. These factors and corruption, both real and perceived, among officials and allied official clergy serve to discredit both, especially in the eyes of younger Muslims. High fertility rates in places like the North Caucasus relative to the rest of the country make this a demographic critical for overall Russian political stability, and containment of the *jihad* that has characterized politics in the North Caucasus for two decades.[40]

Both the Russian state and official Islamic clergy are strongly opposed to and greatly fear any manifestation of Islamism. As a result, the state has banned political parties based on religion (as well as on ethnicity and gender), and the Islamic clergy cooperates closely with the state apparatus in combating independent Islamic or Islamist groups and supporting reformist, Euro-Islamic, and other more secularized Islamic trends as an antidote to Islamism. The leading mufti Gainutdin, as well as the leadership of the Republic of Tatarstan, has led in this effort.[41]

Past experience has taught Russian authorities to treat Islamists severely, and they move quickly and often illegally to put them away for long terms. Arrests of Islamists in non-violent but illegal organizations such as HuT and Tablighi Jamaat are often accompanied by official charges of conspiracy to commit terrorist attacks and claims that searches produced not only extremist literature but also weapons and explosives.[42]

The extent to which these policies and practices lead to significant violations of Muslims' civil, political, and human rights, creates a tendency of Muslim youth to leave for the forest, mountains, and *jihad*. Putin-era amendments to Russia's laws "On Extremism" and "On Combating Terrorism" give the Federal Security Service (FSB), the Ministry of Internal Affairs (MVD), Justice Ministry, and General Prosecutor's Office broad leeway in holding suspects and determining what constitutes "extremist literature." Searches are conducted on shaky pretexts, detention can often result in beating, and some convictions are based on trumped up charges. These practices are more prevalent in the North Caucasus, especially in Chechnya under President Ramzan Kadyrov, where authorities have even carried out extra-judicial retribution against the families of suspected and actual terrorists, including the abductions of relatives and the burning of homes. It needs to be stressed that some of this extra-legal law enforcement activity is carried out by special battalions comprised of former separatist fighters and is driven by local Caucasus customs of blood revenge.

ENDNOTES

[1]Calculated in Gordon M. Hahn, Russia's Islamic Threat (New Haven and London: Yale University Press, 2007), 9, from data produced by Russia's 2002 census on the number of Russian citizens belonging to ethnic groups that are traditionally Muslim.

[2] Faisal Devji, *Landscapes of Jihad: Militancy, Morality, and Modernity* (Ithaca, NY: Cornell University Press, 2005), 130-131; Dore Gold, *Hatred's Kingdom: How Saudi Arabia Supports the New Global Terrorism* (Washington, D.C.: Regnery, 2003), 137; and Hahn, *Russia's Islamic Threat*, 36-37.

[3] Michael Reynolds, "False Comfort on Afghanistan," *Middle East Strategy at Harvard*, August 31, 2009; Mike Bowker, "Western Views Of The Chechen Conflict," in Richard Sakwa, ed., *Chechnya: From Past to Future* (London: Anthem Press, 2005), 235.

[4] Hahn, *Russia's Islamic Threat*, 37-39 and 104-110.

[5] "Aslan Maskhadov: 'My sozdadim polnotsennoe Islamskoe Gosudarstvo," *Kavkaz-Tsentr*, March 8. 2010, www.kavkazcenter.com/russ/content/2010/03/08/71101.shtml; See also "Prezident ChRI Sheik Abdul-Khalim. Kto On?" Kavkaz-Tsentr, March 12, 2005, www.kavkazcenter.com/russ/content/2005/03/12/31285.shtml; "Abdallakh Shamil Abu-Idris: 'My oderzhali strategicheskuyu pobedu,'" *Kavkaz-Tsentr*, January 9, 2006, www.kavkazcenter.net/russ/content/2006/01/09/40869.shtml; and Paul Murphy, *The Wolves of Islam: Russia and the Faces of Chechen Terrorism* (Dulles, VA: Brassey's Inc., 2004), 171-75.

[6] Hahn, *Russia's Islamic Threat*, 43, 158; Vadim Rechkalov, "'Pochemu spetssluzhby ne mogut poimat' Shamilya Basaeva," *Izvestiya* (Moscow), December 6-10, 2004; "Shamil Basaev: 'Segodnya voyuet ves chechenskii narod'," *Kavkaz-Tsentr,* August 17, 2005, www.kavkazcenter.net/russ/content/2005/08/17/36759.shtml; Aleksandra Larintseva, Timur Samedov, and Olga Allenova, "Koltso kavkazskoi natsionalnosti," *Kommersant-Vlast* (Moscow), September 29—October 5 2003, 20; Valerii Khatazhukov, "Kabardino-Balkariya Crackdown on Islamists," IWPR'S Caucasus Reporting Service no. 199, August 2003; Mayrbek Vachagaev, "Evolution of the Chechen Jamaat," Jamestown Foundation *Chechnya Weekly* VI, iss. 14 (April 6, 2005); and Timur Samedov, "Podozrevaemyie iz 'Yarmuka'," Kommersant Daily (Moscow), December 15, 2004, 4. On Basaev's role in Yarmuk's recommitment to the ChRI after Maskhadov's death and Sadulaev's formation of the Caucasus Front, see "Amir Seifulla o protsesse podgotovki k provoglasheniyu Kavkazskogo Ekirata," *Kavkaz-Tsentr*, November 20, 2007, www.kavkazcenter.com/russ/content/2007/11/20/54479.shtml.

[7] A detailed discussion of the 2003 suicide bombing campaign can be found in Yossef Bodansky, *Chechen Jihad: Al Qaeda's Training Ground*

and the Next Wave of Terror (New York: Harper, 2007).

[8] Hahn, *Russia's Islamic Threat*, 49-53.

[9] "Godovshchina myatezha v Nal'chike: versii proizoshedshego sil'no raznyatsya," *Kavkaz uzel*, October 13, 2006, www.kavkaz.memo.ru/ newstext/news/id/1078940.html.

[10] Ibid.

[11] The rise of the Ingush *jihadists* is reflected in Umarov's appointment of an ethnic Ingush, Akhmed Yevloev or "Magas," as the ChRI's military amir. Ibidem. On Muhannad's fundraising see "Militants Target Arabs in Massive Fundraising Campaign for Chechen Insurgents," Defense Department Center for International Issues Research *Transnational Security Issues Report*, December 13, 2007.

[12] See Gordon M. Hahn, "Russia's Counter-Terrorism Operation in Chechnya Ends – the Jihadi Insurgency Continues," *Russia – Other Points of View*, May 11, 2009, www.russiaotherpointsofview. com/2009/05/russias-counterterrorism-operation-in-chechnya.html; See also Gordon M. Hahn, "The Caucasus Emirate's 'Year of the Offensive' in Figures: Data and Analysis on the Caucasus Emirate's Terrorist Activity in 2009," *Islam, Islamism, and Politics in Eurasia* Report 7, January 18, 2010, www.miis.edu/media/view/19071/original/iiper_7.doc; Gordon M. Hahn, "Comparing the Level of Caucasus Emirate Terrorist Activity in 2008 and 2009," *Islam, Islamism, and Politics in Eurasia Report* 8, February 5, 2010.

[13] "Dokka Umarov podpisal Omra o sozdanii Shury IK i uprazdnenii Vilaiyata Iriston," *Kavkaz-Tsentr*, May 11, 2009, www.kavkazcenter.com/russ/content/2009/05/11/65571.shtml; "Amir Imarat Kavkaz uprazdnil Kabinet Ministrov i Parlament byvshei ChRI," *Kavkaz-Tsentr*, December 10, 2007, www.kavkazcenter.com/russ/content/2007/12/10/54917.shtml.

[14] Hahn, *Russia's Islamic Threat*, 63-64.

[15] "MVD RF: na Severnom Kavkaze deistvuyut okolo 500 boevikov," *Kavkaz uzel*, March 26, 2010, www.kavkaz-uzel.ru/articles/167037/; "Yedelev: v Chechnye deistvuyut do 500 boevikov," *Kavkaz uzel*, January 21, 2009, www.kavkaz-uzel.ru/articles/148344; "MVD: v Chechnye deistvuyut ne menee 400 boevikov," *Kavkaz uzel*, February 6, 2008, www.kavkaz-uzel.ru; and "IMARAT KAVKAZ. Moskva pereschitala modzhakhedov. Ikh okazyvaetsya 1500 boitsov," *Kavkaz-Tsentr*, May 20, 2009, www.kavkazcenter.com/russ/content/2009/05/20/65749. shtml.

[16] "Tsyganok: dannye prezidentov Chechni i Ingushetii o boevikakh otlichayutsya ot dannykh MVD i FSB," *Kavkaz uzel*, May 26, 2009, www.kavkaz-uzel.ru/articles/154588.

[17] Hahn, *Russia's Islamic Threat*, 67-68.

[18] Paul Tumelty, "Chechnya: A Strategy for Independence," Jamestown Foundation *North Caucasus Analysis* 6, iss. 30, August 3, 2005,

http://www.jamestown.org/single/?no_cache=1&tx_ttnews[tt_news]=2989.

[19] "Amir Imarata Kavkaz Dokku Abu Usman: 'My osvobodim Krasnodarskii krai, Astrakhan i Povolzhskii zemli...", *Kavkaz-Tsentr*, March 8, 2010, www.kavkazcenter.com/russ/content/2010/03/08/71087.shtml.

[20] The map can be seen at "Zaglyadyvaya vpered," *Hunafa.com*, March 4, 2010, http://hunafa.com/?p=3187.

[21] "Ofitsial'nyi reliz zayavleniya Amira Dokki Umarova o provozglashenii Kavkazskogo Emirata" and "Komu vygodna provokatsiya pod nazvaniem 'Kavkazskii Emirat'."

[22] See, for example, "Ibn Taymiya: Glava o dzhukhade," *Kavkaz-Tsentr*, August 5, 2009, www.kavkazcenter.com/russ/content/2009/08/05/67191.shtml; See also *Islamdin.com*, July 7, 2009, www.islamdin.com/index.php?option=com_content&view=artic le&id=489:2009-07-07-13-40-34&catid=4:2009-02-04-14-07-09&Itemid=28 and *Islamdin.com*, July 8, 2009, www.islamdin.com/index.php?option=com_content&view=article&id=490:2009-07-08-14-28-51&catid=4:2009-02-04-14-07-09&Itemid=28.

[23] Pavel Khlebnikov, *Razgovor s Varvarom: Besedy s chechenskim polevym komandirom Khozh-Akhmedom Nukhaevym o banditizme i islame* (Moscow: Detektiv-Press, 2004); Paul Klebnikov, *Godfather of the Kremlin: The Decline of Russia in the Age of Gangster Capitalism* (Orlando, FL: Harcourt, 2001); A. Khinshtein, *Berezovskii i Abramovich: Oligarkhi s bol'shoi dorogi* (Moscow: Lora, 2007).

[24] OECD Financial Action Task Force, *Second Mutual Evaluation Report – Anti-Money Laundering and Combating the Financing of Terrorism – Russian Federation*, June 20, 2008, 17-19, www.fatf-gafi.org/dataoecd/31/6/41415981.pdf.

[25] "Khazbiev: chinovniki Ingushetii soderzhat boevikov," *Kavkaz uzel*, July 24, 2009, www.kavkaz-uzel.ru/articles/157053; Alexei Malashenko, "The Kremlin's Violent Underbelly," *Moscow Times*, July 29, 2009.

[26] Hahn, "The Caucasus Emirate's 'Year of the Offensive' in Figures: Data and Analysis on the Caucasus Emirate's Terrorist Activity in 2009" and Hahn, "Comparing the Level of Caucasus Emirate Terrorist Activity in 2008 and 2009."

[27] Gordon M. Hahn, "The Caucasus Emirate's Return to Suicide Bombing and Mass Terrorism," *Islam, Islamism, and Politics in Eurasia Report 3*, November 30, 2009, www.miis.edu/media/view/19031/original/iiper_3.doc; Hahn, "The Caucasus Emirate's 'Year of the Offensive' in Figures: Data and Analysis on the Caucasus Emirate's Terrorist Activity in 2009".

[28] "V Bashkirii 'shyut' delo 'Uiguro-Bulgarskogo dzhamaata,'" Islam.ru, April 29, 2009, www.islam.ru/rus/2009-04-29/.

[29] For the Bulgar Jamaat's Russian-language website, see http://tawba. info or http://jamaatbulgar.narod.ru.

[30] Hahn, *Russia's Islamic Threat*, 213-214.

[31] For such contacts before 2005, see Hahn, *Russia's Islamic Threat*, 205-206.

[32] Neil Buckley, "Russia's Islamic Rebirth Adds Tension," *Financial Times*, October 28, 2005.

[33] Although there are no exact figures on the number of converts, it is clear that a Russian/Slavic Islamic community is emerging. According to one report, almost 50 thousand people, mostly ethnic Russians and young women, converted to Islam in the city of Moscow alone from January 2002 to October 2004. This figure comes from a posting on a Qatar-based website IslamOnLine citing an anonymous source from the Council of Muftis of Russia cited in "S 2002 Islam v Moskve prinyali pochti 50 tys. chelovek," *Islam.ru*, October 7, 2004, www.islam. ru/press/rus/2004/10/07/. An ethnic Russian Muslim community emerged in Omsk in 2004. Aleksei Malashenko, "Shadow of Islam over Europe," *International Affairs* (Moscow) 50, no. 5 (September-October 2004), 70.

[34] Aleksandr Ignatenko, "Krovavaya doroga v rai," *Nezavisimaya gazeta-religiya* 12, July 16, 2003, 1, and Dmitrii Sokolov-Mitrich, "Russkii Ben Laden," *Izvestiya* (Moscow), January 21, 2005, www. izvestia.ru/conflict/1043323_print. Another organization, 'Direct Path,' is headed by Muslim journalist and ex-Orthodox priest Ali Polosin. Daghestan has set up a committee for converts to Islam. Just as the Afghan war produced Soviet converts to Islam, there are cases of Russian soldiers who fought in Chechnya converting to Islam. Malashenko, "Shadow of Islam over Europe," 70.

[35] Shireen Hunter, *Islam in Russia: The Politics of Identity and Security* (Armonk, NY: M.E. Sharpe, 2002), 54-55.

[36] A. Zhukov, "Kabardino-Balkariya: Na puti k katastrofe," *Kavkaz-uzel*, n.d., www.kavkaz-uzel.ru/analyticstext/analytics/id/1231255. html.

[37] See, for example, Rinat Bekkin, "Esly by ne krizis... R. Bekkin o roste interesa k islamskim finansam v Rossii," Islam.ru, n.d., www. islam.ru/pressclub/gost/esbikaznu/. Islam.ru is affiliated with the MSA of Dagestan and frequently carries articles and interviews on the subject, in particular those of a key lobbyist for the introduction of Islamic financing in Russia, Rinat Bekkin.

[38] Gordon M. Hahn, "Anti-Americanism, Anti-Westernism, and Anti-Semitism Among Russia's Muslims," *Demokratizatsiya* 16, no. 1 (Winter 2008), 49-60.

[39] Zhukov, *Kabardino-Balkariya: Na puti k katastrofe.*

[40] Hahn, *Russia's Islamic Threat*, 8-12.

[41] Ravil Gainutdin, *Islam v sovremennoi Rossii* (Moscow: Fair Press,

2004), 264-297; Hahn, *Russia's Islamic Threat*, 183-186.

[42] "Rodnym obvinyaemykh v chlenstve v 'Khizb ut-takhrir' prishlos' proryvat'sya v zal suda," Islam.ru, February 27, 2009, www.islam.ru/rus/2009-02-27/; "V Chelyabinskoi oblasti predstanut pered sudom 5 'khizb ut-takhrirovtsev,'" Islam.ru, August 17, 2009, www.islam.ru/rus/2009-08-17/#27984.

SOUTH ASIA

Regional Summary

With over one fifth of the world's population, South Asia is home to as many Muslims (350 million) as the entire Arab world. Of the four countries that have suffered most at the hands of Islamist terrorism over the past decade, three are in South Asia: Pakistan, Afghanistan, and India.

India, the largest country in the region with 1.2 billion people, contains a sizable Muslim minority (13.4 percent), and has been a frequent target of Islamist terrorism. Despite local grievances among its indigenous Muslim population, however, the majority of Islamist-driven violence in India is conducted not by Indian Muslims, but by Islamists based in Pakistan.

India is host to the longest-running Islamist insurgency in the region, in the disputed territory of Kashmir, where Pakistani-backed insurgents have been waging a terrorist campaign since 1989, resulting in over 42,000 fatalities. Since 2001, however, improved Indian security measures and intermittent dialogue between New Delhi and Islamabad have contributed to a relative diminution of violence.

But as the Kashmir insurgency has calmed, India has fallen victim to sensational attacks by Islamist insurgents in the Indian heartland, most notably the November 2008 Mumbai attack, in which Islamist militants trained in Pakistan and affiliated with Lashkar-e Taiba killed 164 people. India has been spared violence on such a grand sale since, but continues to face smaller-scale terrorist plots.

Pakistan, the world's only Muslim-majority nuclear power, is both one of the greatest victims of Islamist violence and, by many counts, one of its greatest supporters. In the decade since the September 11, 2001 attacks, Pakistan has formally supported the U.S.-led Coalition's campaign in Afghanistan, providing logistics and intelligence support, assisting the CIA predator drone campaign and periodically arresting or killing Islamist militants based in Pakistan. Nearly 3,000 Pakistani soldiers and 22,000 civilians have been killed in recent years battling extremists.

However, Pakistan faces persistent accusations that its military-intelligence agency, the ISI, provides direct support to Islamist militant groups. These include the Afghan Taliban and allies like the Haqqani network, as well anti-India *jihadist* outfits like Lashkar-e Taiba. The CIA has uncovered evidence of the ISI's direct involvement in terrorist plots, including the bombing of the Indian Embassy in Kabul in 2008. Together with the discovery of Osama bin Laden residing in a wealthy Pakistani suburb, and the country's refusal to root out militants from their stronghold in North Waziristan, U.S.-Pakistani relations have reached a nadir. Domestically, meanwhile, polling and anecdotal data suggest considerable sympathy for Islamists, and their ideology continues to permeate Pakistani society, with liberal politicians, journalists, and public officials increasingly silenced by conservative Islamist forces.

In Afghanistan, the U.S.-led coalition's early victories in the swift overthrow of the Taliban regime have been dealt a serious blow by a resurgent Taliban, which has been waging an effective campaign from their safe havens in Pakistan to retake parts of the country since 2006. The temporary "surge" of military forces authorized by the Obama administration in December 2009 appears to have blunted Taliban advances, at least for the time being. However, the planned U.S. drawdown of military personnel could soon provide the ousted Islamist movement with far greater freedom of action in its campaign to retake the country and re-impose its strict, puritanical brand of Islamic law there.

Farther afield, Bangladesh—formerly East Pakistan—has a tradition of moderate, culturally-focused strains of Islam, but political Islamist groups such as Jama'at-i-Islami operate legally and enjoy some societal support, despite faring poorly in national elections. The country is also host to two large but nonviolent Islamist revivalist movements, the Tablighi Jamaat and the Ahl-e Hadith. The groups claim tens of millions of followers and seek to organize society around Islamic principles, but are strictly apolitical. Al-Qaeda and other radical Islamist groups, such as Harakat ul Jihad al-Islam, have also made a home in Bangladesh.

The island chain that constitutes the Maldives has a similar history of religious moderation and tolerance, but under the reign of longtime president Maumoon Abdul Gayoom (1978-2008), experienced an Islamic revival. The proliferation of conservative mosques and religious education on his watch is evident in increasingly conservative cultural norms that are prevalent today. A new constitution, drafted in 1997, declared Islam the state religion and forbade non-Muslims from proselytizing or conducting public worship. No known Islamist terrorist groups operate in or out of the Maldives, but groups such as Lashkar-e Taiba and al-Qaeda have converted Maldivian youth and several hundred have been recruited by Pakistani *jihadists*. Moreover, radical Islamist charities were able to gain a foothold in the country after the 2004 Indian Ocean tsunami. In 2008, the country made a successful transition to multi-party democracy, and since has reestablished diplomatic relations with Israel, is attempting to draft a new counterterrorism bill, and has worked to combat the activities of transnational Islamist organizations.

AFGHANISTAN

Since October of 2001, the United States has been deeply involved in Afghanistan as part of its ongoing effort to confront radical Islam abroad, and to prevent its various manifestations from reasserting their domination in that country. The past year in Afghanistan was characterized by a renewed focus upon the conflict after a number of years of holding operations on the part of the International Security Assistance Force (ISAF), and some local successes on the part of the Taliban. In general, ISAF's operations have focused upon breaking the control that the Taliban had established over the southern part of the country, especially in the regions close to the Pakistan border. Sometimes in tandem, sometimes in opposition, ISAF forces and Pakistani forces have succeeded in putting the Taliban on both sides of the border on the defensive. Concurrent with this military offensive, there has been a political offensive (focused mainly at the Hizb-e-Islami of Gulbuddin Hekmatyar) to detach some radical Muslims from the Taliban and bring them into the political process.

ISLAMIST ACTIVITY

Violent Islamist activity in Afghanistan can be attributed to several militant groups: the Taliban and their affiliates, including the Haqqani network, foreign elements (mostly associated with al-Qaeda, but also encompassing other radicals from all over the Muslim world and Europe), and the Hizb-e-Islami. Although there is a substantial Shi`ite population in Afghanistan, there is no evidence of radical activity associated with it. The Taliban, the primary locus of opposition, can be viewed in purely religious or in tribal terms. If the conflict is described in religious terms, then the Taliban portray themselves as recreating the events of the 1970s and 1980s, where a minority of Afghans collaborated with an invading foreign non-Muslim force attempting to impose an alien way of life upon Afghans. If the conflict is portrayed in tribal terms, then the Pashtuns, who comprise most of the Taliban's rank-and-file, have traditionally been locked out of power by the country's ethnic Tajiks, who, together with the Uzbeks and others, have tended to dominate the region.

Between 2001 and 2005, the Taliban were largely in disarray. This period of the conflict was characterized by raids upon ISAF forces and sporadic operations in major centers in the country's south (notably Kandahar). In general, the Taliban controlled the countryside but were unsuccessful in attacking ISAF forces directly. Any time pressure was applied to one of their strongholds, elements of the Taliban would take refuge across the border in Pakistan. During this period, the northern section of Afghanistan was largely free from Taliban activity (although Kabul was frequently a target of Taliban attacks).

However, during the period between 2005 and 2008, there was a marked upswing in Taliban operations, and their success. The use of suicide attacks already had become more common in 2004-05, but this trend multiplied exponentially during 2005-08, to the point where there were approximately 100-130 suicide attacks in the country each year.[1] Much of this activity was associated with the charismatic leadership of Mullah Dadullah (killed in 2007).[2] During this period, the Taliban also benefited immensely from a consolidation of their position in Pakistan; a Pakistani offshoot of the Afghan Taliban, the Tehrik-e-Taliban-e-Pakistan, gained control over parts of Pakistan's Northwest Frontier Province and Federally Administered Tribal Areas and plunged that country into a low-grade civil war. Taliban operations during this period expanded into the north (most notably into the area of Nuristan and Kunduz), and west (around Herat), while the region around Kandahar came to be virtually controlled by the Taliban.[3]

With world attention focused upon Iraq during this period, the Taliban began to utilize Iraqi tactics (namely suicide attacks) in Afghanistan, albeit with mixed results. While Iraqi radicals used indiscriminate suicide attacks, killing large numbers of civilians, the Taliban, rooted in the traditional Pashtun honor code, did not target Afghan civilians during 2005-08, viewing such killings as dishonorable and anti-Islamic. Furthermore, most of the large number of suicide attacks that were directed against ISAF soldiers proved unsuccessful.[4] Targeting foreign nationals, usually aid workers, was much more successful as a tactic, and caused the breakdown of most foreign aid programs designed to reconstruct Afghanistan during this period. Occasionally other Iraqi tactics, such as kidnapping, were utilized as well (although beheadings were generally avoided).

By the inauguration of the Obama administration, however, conditions on the ground had deteriorated further, and ISAF forces were on the defensive. President Obama responded with a "surge" in U.S. forces and a marked shift in counterinsurgency tactics under a newly-installed commander, Gen. Stanley McChrystal. According to his major policy speech of December 1, 2009, President Obama detailed that the purpose of this surge would be to strategically defeat the Taliban during the course of the next four years, and then to withdraw U.S. troops in their entirety by the beginning of 2013. Characteristic of this new policy has been the attempt to go on the offensive against Taliban strongholds in the south and east of the country (which effectively had been under Taliban rule), and to increase the use of drone attacks against the bases of the Taliban in Pakistan. Gen. McChrystal was replaced in June 2010 by Gen. David Petraeus, who had previously commanded the "surge" offensive in Iraq (2007-9). By and large, however, the main thrust of U.S. policy remains the same as of this writing.

A second major component of Islamist activity in Afghanistan is al-Qaeda and the foreign *jihadis* that support it. Although the core of al-Qaeda is Arab, its ranks also include fighters from Chechnya,[5] Uzbekistan,[6] and Muslims of European descent[7] as well as other nationalities[8] These affiliated radicals cannot be easily distinguished from their counterparts in Pakistan (nor are all of them necessarily members of al-Qaeda "central"), and regularly utilize bases scattered throughout Pakistan's Northwest Frontier Province to carry out raids into Afghanistan. While the Taliban have tried to minimize civilian casualties from suicide attacks, al-Qaeda and its allies are not known for such restraint, and are presumed to be responsible for the bloodier mass-casualty, Iraq-style suicide attacks that have occurred in the country since 2005.[9] In addition, the organization carried out one of the most successful penetration suicide attacks against the CIA in Khost on December 30, 2009.[10] However, while al-Qaeda and its allies might supply shock-troops and suicide bombers to the Taliban, their overall role in the fighting is minimal. Rather, al-Qaeda's primary aid to the Taliban is in the form of sophisticated Internet and media propaganda.[11]

The third Islamist component is the Hizb-e-Islami of Gulbuddin Hekmatyar. Hekmatyar was an important commander in the anti-Soviet *jihad*, but during the 1992 civil war contributed significantly to the destruction of Afghanistan (especially Kabul), and fled to Iran in order to escape the Taliban in 1996. His base of support within Afghanistan collapsed, and although he returned in 2002 he has not been able to mobilize mass support since.[12] Most of the fighters that belong to Hizb (there do not appear to be any authoritative numbers in this regard) operate in the eastern section of the country, close to the Pakistan border, and are ethnically Pashtuns.[13] The principal division between Hizb and the larger Taliban resistance appears to be personal; as Hekmatyar was one of the major warlords against whom the Taliban fought in 1992-6, and, as an old-style Afghani leader, he is not viewed as being very aggressive in his operations against the ISAF. However, Hizb does appear to be responsible for several assassination attempts against President Hamid Karzai in 2007 and again in 2008,[14] as well as a number of rocket attacks. As of March 2010, Hekmatyar appeared to be conducting negotiations with the Karzai government.[15]

ISLAMISM AND SOCIETY

Located at the crossroads of the Middle East, Central Asia and South Asia, Afghanistan is divided by geography and ethnicity. The northern section of the country is bisected by the Hindu Kush mountains (impassable except through the Salang Pass), while the southern section is divided from Pakistan by the mountainous region of the Northwest Frontier Province, and consists of semi-mountainous and arid regions tapering into full desert along the Iranian border.

Ethnically, the Pashtuns comprise about 40-42 percent of the population (speaking Pashtu), located in the south and east along the Pakistani border, while Tajiks make up an additional 30-35 percent (speaking Dari, a dialect of Farsi) and are located in the region around Kabul and along the Iranian border to the west. Significant other minorities include the Uzbeks (approximately 9 percent) located along the border with Uzbekistan to the north, and Hazaras (approximately 9 percent) located in the central mountainous region. A number of other minorities including Turkmen, Aimaks and Balochis, comprise the rest of the population.[16]

In general Sufism has had a central place in Afghani Muslim society. There are three major Sufi orders: the Naqshbandiyya (which tends to be closer to mainstream Sunnism), the Chishtiyya (associated with India) and the Qadiriyya (which is pan-Islamic). The Tajik population has traditionally had a close cultural relationship with the Sufi heritage of Persia (but not with its Shi`ite aspect), while the Pashtuns have been more influenced by the reformist Deobandi movements originating in India and Pakistan. For the most part Afghani cities had a semi-secular elite that was either pro-western in its orientation or pro-communist during the period prior to the rise of the Taliban in 1996.

Afghanistan generally has been characterized by a weak central government more adept at playing off foreign attempts at domination than actually ruling it. The efforts of reformist rulers such as King Amanullah (1919-29), who sought to establish a strong, liberal regime, were overwhelmingly unsuccessful.[17] Starting in the 1950s, the USSR established close relations with Afghanistan and gradually built up both its interests as well as the local Communist party, culminating in the overthrow of the monarch in 1973 and the establishment of a Communist-dominated regime there five years later. This regime based its power upon the Pashtun Durrani tribe (in opposition to the traditional cultural domination of the Tajiks), but was quickly beset by popular opposition. The USSR came to the aid of the regime, and invaded the country in 1979. The Soviets remained, and became embroiled in a bloody, protracted fight against the largely Islamist opposition (based out of Peshawar, Pakistan), until ultimately withdrawing in 1989.

Although the conflict ended in defeat for the USSR, Afghanistan's Islamists were unable to adequately exploit the Soviet Union's withdrawal and instead fell to fighting among themselves. The resulting civil war persisted until 1992, when Kabul was finally captured by Northern Alliance chief Ahmad Shah Massoud after a number of the prominent communist supporters switched sides.[18]

The period between 1992 and the rise of the Taliban in 1994-96 was characterized by the balkanization of Afghanistan. Tribal and local Islamist leaders carved out separate fiefdoms throughout the country, and bombarded Kabul whenever they could. During this period, the country's dependence upon the drug trade grew immensely. The Taliban ("the students" in Farsi) first appeared in 1994, portraying themselves as a movement of youth dedicated to eliminating anarchy and chaos.[19] Until 1997, they appeared invincible, capturing Kabul in 1996, and pushing government supporters (led by the charismatic Ahmad Shah Massoud) into the far northeast corner of the country. While the Taliban suffered reverses in 1997 and 1998 (and responded with massacres), by 2001 they were in control of approximately 95 percent of the territory of Afghanistan.

Especially after 1998, the Taliban under their leader Mullah `Umar, lacking allies or outside support, began to rely upon foreign radical Muslims, mainly (but not exclusively) those associated with Osama bin Laden's al-Qaeda organization. Many radicals gravitated to Afghanistan because of the Taliban's strict imposition of *sharia* law, and their influence was indicated by the March 2001 destruction of the Buddhas of Bamiyan.[20] The Taliban, however, were reluctant to anger the United States overtly, and apparently opposed the September 11, 2001 attacks that were orchestrated and carried out by al-Qaeda.[21] When the U.S. invaded Afghanistan in response during October of 2001, the Taliban and al-Qaeda banded together to oppose it.

In general, since 2002, there has been a much closer ideological relationship between the Taliban and al-Qaeda than there was previously. While the pre-September 11 Taliban had elements in their leadership that strongly opposed globalist attacks—even according to some accounts sought to warn of the coming al-Qaeda attacks[22]—after losing power the two ideologies converged more closely. There still is some tension between the Taliban, whose roots are in the Deobandi reformist school of north India and its ramifications in Pakistan, and globalist radical Muslims, whose roots are Arab-centered and purely Salafi. Traditionally Deobandis have not cultivated the same abhorrence of Sufism that is characteristic of Salafism, and thus were able to win support among the Pashtuns (themselves largely influenced by Sufism) and other Afghanis. However, currently Taliban commanders regularly comment favorably concerning al-Qaeda; a good example is that of Mullah Dadullah (killed 2007), who stated: "We like the al-Qaeda organization. We consider it a friendly and brotherly organization, which shares our ideology and concepts. We have close ties and constant contacts with it. Our cooperation is ideal."[23]

A major factor in the success of the Taliban has been to portray themselves as the representatives and guardians of Islam in Afghanistan. Because their primary opponent, the ISAF, is separated from the Afghan people by language, culture and religion, and has frequently employed air-strikes that kill inordinate numbers of civilians, the Taliban have been able to mobilize popular support effectively. As guerillas they have sought to create chaos and disrupt public order in order to highlight another major selling point for Afghans: that they imposed order during the period of 1994-2001, and removed the corrupt and violent warlords that had dominated the country in the wake of the Soviet departure. Although most of the Afghan *ulema* at present decry the tactics of the Taliban, there is surprisingly little opposition to the movement on religious grounds. Interviews with Afghan religious elders reveal a view of the Taliban as good but "misguided" Muslims.[24]

Perhaps the most contentious issue from both a socio-economic and a religious point of view is that of opium cultivation. Opium serves as the mainstay of the Afghan economy in the southern section of the country.[25] Once harvested, it is taken either northward over the mountain passes through Central Asia to Russia, eastwards to Pakistan or, less commonly, westwards to Iran. After the collapse of the Taliban regime in 2001, opium cultivation regained prominence in the south, and although ISAF and a network of NGOs have tried to either eradicate it or offer more constructive alternatives to the farmers, opium production continues to be an economic mainstay in southern Afghanistan. There is ample evidence that the Taliban and other radical Muslim organizations protect the cultivation of opium and benefit financially from it.[26] Annual intake from the cultivation of opium poppies is estimated to be approximately $4 billion.[27] According to some sources, the Taliban earn between $100 and $300 million each year from this trade.[28] One of the primary goals of ISAF's "surge" has been to break this economic support for the Taliban.

ISLAMISM AND THE STATE

The central government of Afghanistan is weak and relies upon the support of both local elites (meaning traditional tribal elders and city-based elites) and foreign aid (both governmental and from NGOs) in order to survive.[29] Traditional tribal support is reflected in the institution of the *loya jirga*, a tribally appointed body that ratified the Afghani constitution in December 2003. Members, numbering a total of 502, were drawn from all over the country, and were elected with reserved seats for women and religious minorities. The institution of the *loya jirga* is one that is rejected by radical Muslims because of its tribal character, and some Afghanis resent the presence in it of former warlords and those who are guilty of crimes during the period 1992-96.

The government's support for political Islam is reflected in Chapter 1, Article 2 of the Constitution, where it states "The religion of the state of the Islamic Republic of Afghanistan is the sacred religion of Islam."[30] In general, the Islamists have sought to portray the Karzai government as one that is subservient to the wishes of the United States, and is corrupt and un-Islamic as a whole.[31] Although the Taliban have not been as dogmatic in their opposition to democratic elections (in 2005 and 2009) as have other radical Muslims, they have frequently threatened voters with violence.[32] These tactics, however, have not been successful (although Afghans are far from satisfied with their elected officials). Because of the violent opposition towards the Sufi practices of most Afghans, the Taliban and al-Qaeda also suffer from a public relations problem.

There are, however several Islamic parties that are allied with the government or participate in the political process. The Jami`at-i Islami, led by Dr. Abdullah Abdullah (who served as foreign minister in the Karzai regime) consistently either supports the government or participates in the elections. Other Islamists maintain an antagonistic relationship with the state, hoping in the near future to supplant it, and return the country to *sharia* rule. The Karzai regime, in its turn, attempts to do everything that it can to maintain its Islamic legitimacy and give the radicals no opening for accusations of being non-Muslim. Occasionally, Karzai himself has even spoken of the possibility of a reconciliation with the Taliban or even of himself joining their movement.[33]

ENDNOTES

[1] Figures are drawn from both the official United Nations report on suicide attacks in Afghanistan (listing 123 for 2006, and 77 for 2007 [until June 30]), and the *Afghanistan Conflict Monitor*, listing approximately 150 for 2010. See United Nations Assistance Mission in Afghanistan, "Suicide Attacks in Afghanistan (2001-2007)," September 9, 2007, http://www.reliefweb.int/rw/RWFiles2007.nsf/Files-ByRWDocUnidFilename/EKOI-76W52H-Full_Report.pdf/$File/Full_Report.pdf; and "Security Incidents," Human Security Report Project *Afghanistan Conflict Monitor*, September 2010, http://www.afghanconflictmonitor.org/incidents.html.

[2] Matthias Gebauer, "The Star Of Afghanistan's Jihad," *Der Spiegel* (Hamburg), March 1, 2007, http://www.spiegel.de/international/0,1518,469172,00.html; on suicide attacks, see Brian Glyn Williams, "Mullah Omar's Missiles: A Field Report on Suicide Bombers in Afghanistan, *Middle East Policy* 15, no. 4 (2008), 1-21, http://74.125.47.132/search?q=cache:Kx0tc1iiKBoJ:www.carlisle.army.mil/ietcop/documents/MEP%2520-%2520Mullah%2520Omars%2520Missiles%2520-%2520A%2520Field%2520Report%2520on%2520Suicide%2520Bombers%2520in%2520Afghanistan%2520-%2520Winter%252008.pdf+Mullah+Omar%27s+Missiles&hl=en&ct=clnk&cd=2&gl=us&client=firefox-a; Ahmad Muwaffaq Zaydan, *Su`ud Taliban: al-imara al-thaniyya* (Beirut: al-Ahliyya, 2007), 172-79.

[3] "Taliban Control Half of Afghanistan, Report Says," *Telegraph* (London), November 22, 2007, http://www.telegraph.co.uk/news/worldnews/1570232/Taliban-control-half-of-Afghanistan-says-report.html.

[4] Williams, "Mullah Omar's Missiles"; For a general overview of the Afghan conflict, see Brian Glyn Williams, *Afghanistan: The Longest War* (Pittsburgh, PA; University of Pennsylvania Press, 2011).

[5] As cited in Tom Vanden Brook, "Marines Fighting Taliban Strive to Win Afghan Locals' Trust," *USA Today*, August 3, 2009, http://www.cnas.org/node/3065.

[6] "Full President Obama Speech Text on Afghanistan," *Los Angeles Times*, December 1, 2009, http://latimesblogs.latimes.com/washington/2009/12/obama-speech-text-afghanistan.html.

[7] Brian Glyn Williams, "The CIA's Covert Drone Campaign in Pakistan, 2004-2010: The History of an Assassination Campaign," *Studies in Terrorism and Conflict* no. 33, Winter 2010.

[8] Peter Bergen and Katherine Tiedemann, "The Year of the Drone," New America Foundation, n.d., http://counterterrorism.newamerica.net/drones.

[9] Williams, "The CIA's Drone War in Pakistan, 2004-2010."

[10] Bryan Glyn Williams, *Afghanistan Declassified: A Guide to America's Longest War* (Pittsburgh; University of Pennsylvania Press, 2011), esp. the chapter entitled "Obama's War."

[11] Ahmed Rashid, *Jihad: The Rise of Militant Islam in Central Asia* (New Haven: Yale University Press, 2002), esp. chapter 7.

[12] Brian Glyn Williams, "On the Trail of the Lions of Islam: A History of Foreign Fighters in Afghanistan and Pakistan, 1980 to 2010," *Orbis* 55, iss. 2, (2011).

[13] See, for example, Nicola Smith, "Irishman Wants To Kill For Islam," *Sunday Times* (London), November 15, 2009, http://www.timesonline.co.uk/tol/news/world/ireland/article6917485.ece; Stefan Nicola, "Analysis: German Suspects In Afghanistan," UPI, May 1, 2008, http://www.spacewar.com/reports/Analysis_German_suspects_in_Afghanistan_999.html; "Dozens of Westerners Attending Terror Camps," MSNBC, October 19, 2009, http://www.millennium-ark.net/NEWS/09_Terror/091020.Westerners.terror.camps.html.

[14] Such as Uighur radicals; See B. Raman, "Suspected Death of Yuldashev: Good News for Uzbekistan, China, Germany," South Asia Analysis *Group Paper* no. 3442, October 3, 2009, http://www.southasiaanalysis.org/%5Cpapers35%5Cpaper3442.html.

[15] Williams, "Mullah Omar's Missiles"; see also "'I Agreed to Become a Suicide Bomber,'" BBC (London), November 12, 2009, http://news.bbc.co.uk/2/hi/south_asia/8357011.stm.

[16] Robert Baer, "A Dagger to the CIA," GQ, April 2010, http://www.gq.com/news-politics/politics/201004/dagger-to-the-cia; for the suicide video, see http://www.youtube.com/watch?v=HB1NJ8zOOso.

[17] See, for example, its online journal, *Tala'i` Khurasan*, at http://www.e-prism.org/images/kurasan_No.11-_121428_-_28-12-07.pdf.

[18] Zaydan, *Su`ud Taliban*, 157-70.

[19] "Hizb-i-Islami (Islamic Party)," Globalsecurity.org, n.d., http://www.globalsecurity.org/military/world/para/hizbi-islami.htm.

[20] Responsibility for these assassination attempts has been disputed, and the Taliban also claimed the 2008 attempt.

[21] "Hekmatyar Gives Karzai 15 Demands for Possible Peace Pact with Govt," ANI, March 23, 2010, http://www.thaindian.com/newsportal/world-news/hekmatyar-gives-karzai-15-demands-for-possible-peace-pact-with-govt_100338249.html.

[22] "Afghanistan," Central Intelligence Agency *World Factbook,* June 24, 2010, https://www.cia.gov/library/publications/the-world-factbook/geos/af.html.

[23] Stephen Tanner, *Afghanistan: A Military History from Alexander the Great to the war against the Taliban* (Cambridge, MA.: Da Capo Press, 2009).

[24] Ahmed Rashid, *Taliban: Militant Islam, Oil and Fundamentalism in Central Asia* (New Haven: Yale Note Bene Books, 2001), esp. chapters 1-3.

[25] Fahmi Huwaydi, *Taliban: jundallah fi al-ma`raka al-ghalat* (Beirut: Dar al-Shuruq, 2001), 9-31; for official statements, see http://www.alemarah.info/english/.

[26] Barry Bearak, "Afghan Says Destruction of Buddhas is Complete," *New York Times*, March 12, 2001, http://www.nytimes.com/2001/03/12/world/afghan-says-destruction-of-buddhas-is-complete.html.

[27] Kate Clark, "The Taliban Minister, The U.S. Envoy and the Warning of September 11 That Was Ignored," Centre for Research on Globalization, September 7, 2002, http://globalresearch.ca/articles/CLA209A.html.

[28] Kate Clark, "Taliban 'Warned US of Huge Attack,'" BBC (London), September 7, 2002, http://news.bbc.co.uk/2/hi/south_asia/2242594.stm.

[29] Brian Glyn Williams, "Suicide Bombings in Afghanistan," Jane's Islamic Affairs Analyst, September 2007, 5, http://www.brianglynwilliams.com/IAA%20suicide.pdf.

[30] United Nations Office of Drugs and Crime, *Afghanistan Opium Survey 2007: Executive Summary*, August 2007, http://www.unodc.org/pdf/research/AFG07_ExSum_web.pdf.

[31] Jon Lee Anderson, "The Taliban's Opium War," *New Yorker*, July 9, 2007, http://www.newyorker.com/reporting/2007/07/09/070709fa_fact_anderson; Gretchen Peters, "How Opium Profits The Taliban," United States Institute of Peace *Peaceworks* no. 62, August 2009, http://www.usip.org/files/resources/taliban_opium_1.pdf.

[32] United Nations Office of Drugs and Crime, *Afghanistan Opium Survey 2008: Executive Summary*, August 2008, http://www.unodc.org/documents/publications/Afghanistan_Opium_Survey_2008.pdf.

[33] "Poppy Cultivation: Arms Funding for Taliban," MERINews, June 25, 2008, http://www.merinews.com/article/poppy-cultivation-arms-funding-for-taliban/136344.shtml; "Afghan Surge Aims to Break Poppy Trade," UPI, April 29, 2009, http://www.upi.com/Top_News/2009/04/29/Afghan-surge-aims-to-break-poppy-trade/UPI-40031241008160/.

[34] *The Constitution of Afghanistan*, n.d., http://www.afghan-web.com/politics/current_constitution.html.

[35] "Taliban: Winning the War of Words?" International Crisis Group *Asia Report* no. 158, July 24, 2008, http://www.crisisgroup.org/home/index.cfm?id=5589&l=1.

[36] See "Afghanistan's Election Challenges," International Crisis Group

Asia Report no. 171, June 24, 2009, http://www.crisisgroup.org/
home/index.cfm?id=6176&l=1.

[37] "Karzai To Lawmakers: 'I Might Join the Taliban,'" Associated
Press, April 5, 2010, http://www.msnbc.msn.com/id/36178710/.

PAKISTAN

QUICK FACTS

Population: 177,276,594

Area: 796,095 sq km

Ethnic Groups: Punjabi 44.68%, Pashtun (Pathan) 15.42%, Sindhi 14.1%, Sariaki 8.38%, Muhajirs 7.57%, Balochi 3.57%, other 6.28%

Religions: Muslim 95% (Sunni 75%, Shia 20%), other (includes Christian and Hindu) 5%

Government Type: Federal republic

GDP (official exchange rate): $168.5 billion

Map and Quick Facts courtesy of the CIA World Factbook (last updated June 2010)

Pakistan was established in 1947 as a homeland for South Asia's Muslims following the end of British colonial rule on the Indian Subcontinent. The majority of Pakistanis practice a moderate form of Sufi Islam, but Islamist political parties exercise significant influence within society and through the courts and help shape the political debate, foreign policy, and the development of legislation. Moreover, throughout Pakistan's history, its military and intelligence services have created and cultivated ties with violent Islamist groups to achieve regional strategic objectives. The U.S. war in Afghanistan following the September 11, 2001 terrorist attacks, and Pakistan's role in fighting terrorism in recent years, has severely complicated the Islamist militant landscape in Pakistan. The emergence of a violent indigenous Taliban movement in Pakistan's tribal border areas which seeks to overturn the Pakistani state and which retains links both to the Afghan Taliban and al-Qaeda poses questions about the future stability of the Pakistani state.

Pakistan will continue to grapple with its status as a Muslim constitutional democracy, and with developing ways to channel Islamist ideologies that have played a significant role in its identity since 1947. While Islamist political parties are unlikely to take power in the near future, they will continue to influence the country's legal framework and political discourse in ways that restrict personal freedoms, subordinate women and minorities, and enhance the role of clergy within the country's democratic institutions. While societal attitudes will also shape Islamist trends in Pakistan, it can be argued that the military's posture and attitude toward violent Islamists will be the single most important factor determining the future direction of the country, i.e., whether it remains positively engaged with Western countries or takes a decisively Islamist turn that severs its traditionally strong relations with the U.S.

ISLAMIST ACTIVITY

Pakistan's Federally Administered Tribal Areas (FATA), which consist of seven semi-autonomous tribal agencies along the border with Afghanistan, constitute one of the most dangerous terrorist safe havens in the world today. In 2002, al-Qaeda's leadership moved from Afghanistan into Pakistan's North and South Waziristan sections of the tribal border areas, where they established networks with like-minded Pakistani groups such as the Jaish-e-Muhammed and the Lashkar-e-Taiba.[1] There are currently some 150,000 Pakistani troops in the FATA fighting al-Qaeda, the Taliban, and related militant groups.

Pakistan has long relied on violent Islamist groups to accomplish its strategic objectives in both Afghanistan and India. In recent years, however, as Pakistan has stepped up its military operations in the tribal border areas, some of these militants have turned their guns on the Pakistani state.

The Afghan Taliban

Pakistan's military and intelligence services (particularly the Inter-Services Intelligence Directorate, or ISI) historically have had close ties with the Afghan Taliban, which ruled Afghanistan from 1996–2001. Before the terrorist attacks of September 11, 2001, the Pakistani government openly supported and recognized Taliban rule in Afghanistan. Although Pakistani officials largely disagreed with the Taliban's harsh interpretation of Islam, they viewed the Taliban as their best chance to achieve their own strategic objectives in the region. Pakistan continued to support the Taliban into the late 1990s, long after Osama bin Laden took refuge there in 1996 and despite the growing problems that it created in Islamabad's relations with Washington. Pakistan's high-stakes policy vis-à-vis the Taliban derived from its aims of denying India, as well as Iran and the Central Asian countries, a strong foothold in Afghanistan and ensuring a friendly regime in Kabul that would refrain from making territorial claims on Pakistan's Pashtun areas along the

Pakistan-Afghanistan border.

Despite pledging to break ties with the Taliban after the U.S. invasion of Afghanistan in 2001, Islamabad failed to crack down forcefully on Afghan Taliban leaders or to actively disrupt their activities in Pakistan. Indeed U.S. officials have acknowledged that officials within Pakistan's Inter-Services Intelli¬gence (ISI) directorate maintain relationships with Afghan Taliban leaders and see benefits in keeping good ties with the Taliban in the expectation that the Taliban will again play a role in Afghan politics.

Tehreek-e-Taliban Pakistan (TTP)

The Tehreek-e-Taliban Pakistan (TTP), an amalgamation of Pakistani militant groups loosely affiliated with al-Qaeda and the Afghan Taliban, was formed in 2007 and has conducted numerous suicide attacks against Pakistani security forces and civilians throughout 2008-10. Indeed the number of terrorist attacks in Pakistan increased from 254 in 2005 to 2,148 in 2008. In 2009 alone, around 3,000 Pakistanis lost their lives to terrorist attacks.[2] U.S. officials have sought to convince Pakistan that its dual policies of supporting some terrorists while fighting others are counterproductive in ensuring Pakistan's own security and stability and in pursuing broader efforts to rein in international terrorism.

The Haqqani network

Jalaluddin Haqqani is a powerful independent militant leader whose followers operate in the border areas between Khost in Afghanistan and North Waziristan in FATA. He has been allied with the Afghan Taliban for nearly 15 years, having served as tribal affairs minister in the Taliban regime in the late 1990s. Jalaluddin's son, Sirajuddin, is reportedly increasingly taking operational control of the militant network.

The Haqqani network has been a major facilitator of the Taliban insurgency in Afghanistan, and responsible for some of the fiercest attacks against U.S. and coalition forces. Haqqani forces were responsible for a truck bombing that killed two U.S. soldiers in Afghanistan's Khost province in March 2008, the storming of the Serena Hotel in Kabul during a high-level visit by Norwegian officials in January 2008, and an attack on the U.S. Bagram Air Base in mid-May 2010.[3]

The source of the Haqqanis' power lies primarily in their ability to forge relations with a variety of different terrorist groups (al-Qaeda, the Afghan Taliban, the Pakistani Taliban, and India-focused groups like the Jaish-e-Muhammed), while also maintaining links to Pakistani intelligence. Pakistani military strategists apparently view the Haqqani network as their most effective tool for blunting Indian influence in Afghanistan. Credible U.S. media reports indicate that the Haqqani network, in cooperation with Pakistani intelligence, was responsible for the bombing of the Indian embassy in Kabul in July 2008, killing more than 50 people, including two senior Indian officials.[4] U.S. officials have appealed to Pakistani leaders to crack down on the Haqqani network, but have been rebuffed with declarations that the Pakistani military is over-stretched and incapable of taking on too many militant groups at once.

Lashkar-e-Taiba and Jaish-e-Mohammed

Groups like the Lashkar-e-Taiba (LeT) and Jaish-e-Mohammed (JeM – formerly the Harakat-ul-Ansar) focused their attacks throughout the 1990s on Indian security forces in Jammu and Kashmir but now conduct attacks throughout India and target both Indian and Western civilians. The Pakistan Government's failure to shut down groups like JeM and LeT, responsible for the November 2008 attacks in Mumbai, is creating instability in the region and increasing the likelihood of additional international attacks, particularly against India, but also involving citizens of other nations. Indeed, recent investigations of David Headley, the terrorist suspect arrested in Chicago in early October 2009 for plotting with the LeT to attack targets in India and a Danish newspaper, have raised questions about whether there was official Pakistani involvement in the Mumbai attacks. Headley's "handler" was a retired Pakistani Army major.[5]

Following the Mumbai attacks, Islamabad responded to U.S. and Indian pressure by arresting seven LeT operatives, including those that India had fingered as the ring leaders of the attacks--Zaki ur Rehman Lakhvi and Zarar Shah. The Pakistani government also reportedly shut down some LeT offices throughout the country. Despite these actions, there are indications that the LeT continues to operate relatively freely in the country. Pakistan released from detention LeT founder Hafez Muhammed Sayeed in June 2009, when the Lahore High Court determined there was insufficient evidence to continue his detainment.

The LeT has put down roots in Pakistani society, especially in central and southern Punjab, through its social welfare wing, the Jamaat-ud-Dawa (JuD), which runs schools and medical clinics. The headquarters of the LeT/JuD is a 200-acre site outside Lahore in the town of Muridke. The JuD increased its popularity through its rapid response in helping victims of the October 2005 earthquake in Pakistani Kashmir. The U.S. government views the JuD as a surrogate or front organization of the LeT. The U.S. State Department designated the LeT as a Foreign Terrorist Organization in December 2001, and later included the JuD on the Specially Designated Global Terrorist Designation list as an alias of the LeT.[6] On December 11, 2008, the United Nations Security Council imposed sanctions on JuD, declaring it a global terrorist group.[7]

There are well-known links between both the LeT and JeM to international terrorism. Shoe bomber Richard Reid apparently trained at an LeT camp in Pakistan; one of the London subway bombers spent time at the LeT complex in Muridke; and al-Qaeda leader Abu Zubaydah was captured from an LeT safe house in Faisalabad, Pakistan. The LeT signed Osama bin Laden's 1998 *fatwa* for Muslims to kill Americans and Israelis.

Reports indicate that one of the prime suspects in the 2006 London airliner bomb plot had family ties to Maulana Masood Azhar, the leader of JeM. The JeM has also been linked to the kidnapping and brutal murder of *Wall Street Journal* reporter Daniel Pearl in January 2002. Pakistan officially banned the JeM in 2002, but Azhar has never been formally charged with a crime. Omar Sheikh confessed to Pakistani authorities that he masterminded Pearl's kidnapping and in July 2002 was sentenced to death by an anti-terrorism court in Pakistan.

LeT involvement in Afghanistan has picked up since 2006. LeT members apparently trained at camps in Kunar and Nuristan provinces in the 1990s but did not fight alongside the Taliban at that time.[8] In the last four years, however, as the Taliban has regained influence in Afghanistan, the LeT has supported the insurgents by recruiting, training, and housing fighters and facilitating their infiltration into Afghanistan from the tribal areas of Pakistan. LeT fighters were also likely part of the group that attacked a U.S. outpost in Wanat, Afghanistan in 2008 that killed nine U.S. soldiers.

ISLAMISM AND SOCIETY

The strategic environment in South Asia over the last 30 years and the Pakistani response to these regional challenges has influenced Islamist trends in society and heightened religious-inspired violence. The war against the Soviets in Afghanistan in the 1980s and the Islamization policies of Pakistani president General Zia ul-Haq during the same period strengthened Islamist political forces and puritanical sects like the Deobandis, over the more moderate Barelvis.[9] Pakistani society today is in a state of transition, as people face regular terrorist strikes throughout the country and economic instability that has led to power shortages and skyrocketing food prices. According to South Asia scholar Moeed Yusuf, Pakistani society is inherently conservative but this religious conservatism should not be interpreted as extremism.[10] The influence of Sufism, dating back to the eighth and ninth century in South Asia, also has had a moderating influence on how most Pakistanis practice and interpret the Islamic faith.

Muslim revivalist movements developed late in the nineteenth century in South Asia in response to the decline in Muslim power in the region and as a reaction to British colonial rule. The first attempt to mobilize pan-Islamic sentiment on the Subcontinent was in 1919 through the launching of the Khilafat movement, which agitated against the abolition of the Ottoman caliphate.[11] Although the movement dissolved after the Turkish government abrogated the Muslim caliphate in 1924, it roused Muslim political consciousness and catalyzed a sense of communal identity.[12]

The Jamaat-e-Islami was founded by Islamic scholar Maulana Abul Ala Maududi in 1941. Maududi came of age as British colonial rule was ending on the Subcontinent and an Indian national identity was developing. Witness to Hindu-Muslim communal tensions, Maududi believed the only way Muslims could safeguard their political interests was to return to a pure and unadulterated Islam that would not accommodate Hindus. He denounced nationalism and secular politics and held that the Islamic state was a panacea for all the problems facing Muslims. He further held that for Muslims to mobilize their resources against the Hindus, they had to break free of any Western influences.[13] Reflecting Maududi's early linking of the Muslim struggle with both Indian Hindus and western forces, modern Islamist extremist literature in Pakistan draws parallels between British colonial rule in the nineteenth century and U.S. ascendancy since the middle of the twentieth.[14]

In contrast with Maududi, Pakistan's founding father and leader of the Muslim League, Muhammed Ali Jinnah, supported the idea of Islam serving as a unifying force, but envisioned the country functioning largely as a secular and multiethnic democratic state. Thus, although the argument to establish a separate Pakistani state was based on religious exclusivity, Jinnah's ultimate goal was not to establish Pakistan as a theocratic state.[15] However, soon after the creation of Pakistan, debate about the role of religion in the country's constitutional and legal systems was increasingly influenced by the idea that Islamic principles should inform the conduct of the state.[16]

Maududi's contrasting vision for Pakistan created problems for him and the JI during the early years after partition. The Pakistani authorities questioned JI members' allegiance to the state and even incarcerated Maududi for his controversial positions on the Indo-Pakistani dispute over Kashmir.[17] After spending time in jail, Maududi eventually stopped questioning the legitimacy of the Pakistani state and focused on encouraging Islamization of the government and the adoption of an Islamic constitution.

Today's Jamaat-I-Islami (JI) political party in Pakistan, led by Qazi Hussain Ahmed, draws most of its support from middle class urban Pakistanis. It has generally performed only marginally at the polls, capturing about five percent of the vote in most elections held during the last two decades. The party's influence on Pakistani politics and society outweighs its electoral performance, though, primarily because of its effectiveness in mobilizing street power, its ability to influence court cases, and its adeptness at using Pakistan's Islamic identity to bring pressure on military and democratic governments alike to adopt aspects of its Islamist agenda.[18] In the 2002 elections, the JI formed an alliance with five other religious political parties, and the coalition garnered over 11 percent of the national vote. The resulting coalition of Islamist parties grabbed enough votes in the North West Frontier Province (NWFP) to form the government, marking the first time the Islamists were charged with running a provincial government (see below).

The other major Islamist movement in South Asia is the Deobandi movement. This movement originated in 1866 in the city of Deoband in the Indian state of Uttar Pradesh with the establishment of the Dur ul-Ulum *madrassa*, still the largest operating Deobandi *madrassa*. Deobandism was a reformist movement that developed in reaction to British colonialism and from the belief among Muslim theologians that British influence on the Indian subcontinent was corrupting the religion of Islam. The Deobandis solidified a puritanical perspective toward Islam for South Asian Muslims, much as the Wahhabis have done in present-day Saudi Arabia.[19]

Although Deobandi clerics were initially concerned with strengthening the Islamic character of individuals and society, several of them later became politically focused and joined the Jamiat Ulema-e-Hind (JUH), a political party established in pre-partition India in 1919.[20] In the lead-up to partition, the Deobandis split between those who supported Gandhi's Indian National Congress and those who supported the creation of a separate state of Pakistan as proposed by Muslim League leader Muhammed Ali Jinnah. The pro-Muslim League faction became the Jamiat Ulema-e-Islam (JUI), while the JUH maintained links with the Indian National Congress, arguing that the creation of Pakistan would divide and weaken the Muslims of the Subcontinent.[21]

The Deobandis gained considerable strength during the war against the Soviets in Afghanistan in the 1980s when *madrassas* (religious-based schools) mushroomed in Pakistan, partially to accommodate the three million Afghan refugees that fled there. The Taliban leaders who made their debut in Kandahar, Afghanistan in 1994 came mostly from these Deobandi *madrassas*.[22] As a political party, JUI draws support from rural voters, mostly among Pashtuns in the northwest.

Three wars and several military crises with India have also bolstered the influence of religious extremists, with the backing of the Pakistani state. During the 1990s, the JI focused its agenda on supporting Kashmiri militants, while the JUI turned most of its attention to supporting the Taliban in Afghanistan. More recently, both the JUI and JI have rallied their political supporters against U.S. policies in the region, taking advantage of high levels of anti-American sentiment fueled by the post 9/11 American and NATO military presence in Afghanistan and U.S. pressure on Pakistan to tackle terrorists on its own soil. Most Pakistanis blame their country's counterterrorism cooperation with the U.S.—not past support for religious extremists—for the incessant suicide bombings and attacks across the nation that claimed more than 3,000 Pakistani lives in 2009 alone.[23]

The erosion of respect for religious pluralism in Pakistan has also been facilitated by exclusionary laws and the proliferation of minority-hate material in public and private school curriculums. Several studies have also documented a broad-based connection between *madrassa* education and the propensity toward gender, religious, and sectarian intolerance and militant violence in Pakistan.[24] *Madaris* (the plural of *madrassas*) are spread throughout Pakistan, but most analysts believe that only about 5–10 percent of Pakistani school children attend these Islamic seminaries. A number of these schools are financed and operated by Pakistani Islamist parties, such as the Jamaat-e-Ulema Islam (JUI), and by Pakistani expatriates and other foreign entities, including many in Saudi Arabia. In a seminal study entitled "Islamic Education in Pakistan," South Asia scholar Christine Fair notes that while there is little evidence that *madaris* contribute substantially to direct recruitment of terrorists, they do help create conditions that are conducive to supporting militancy.[25] While mainstreaming and expanding the curriculums of *madaris* is part of reversing extremist trends, it is equally important for Pakistan to improve and modernize its public education sector and to revise textbooks that encourage an intolerant and militant culture.

Discrimination against religious minorities–including Christians, Hindus, Sikhs, Ahmadis, and Shi'a–has led to a threefold increase in religious and sectarian violence in the country over the last 30 years. The rising violence against the Shi'ite community (which make up about 25 percent of Pakistan's total population) has been part of the upward trend in sectarian attacks. For example, in December 2008, at least 20 people were killed by a bombing near a Shi'ite mosque in Peshawar,[26] while a funeral procession for a murdered Shi'ite cleric was attacked in February 2009, resulting in more than 25 dead.[27] The difference between Sunnis and Shi'a is one of interpretation and the right to lead the Muslim community.

The minority Ahmadi community also is suffering severely from the growing culture of religious intolerance in Pakistan. The Ahmadiyya Jamaat has approximately 10 million followers in the world, including approximately 3 to 4 million in Pakistan. Toward the end of the 19th century, Mirza Ghulam

Ahmad (1835-1908), founder of the Ahmadiyya Jamaat, broke with centuries-old Islamic dogma by claiming to be an Islamic prophet. (Mainstream Muslims believe that the Prophet Mohammad was the last prophet.) Six years after Pakistan's independence, Islamists led by Anjuman-i-ahrar-i-Islam (Society of Free Muslims) started a mass movement to declare the Ahmadi sect as non-Muslim, arguing that Ahmadiyya was an entirely new religion that should not be associated with Islam. In late May of 2010, militants armed with hand grenades, suicide vests, and assault rifles attacked two Ahmadi mosques, killing nearly 100 worshippers.[28] Human rights groups in Pakistan criticized local authorities for their weak response to the May attacks and for failure to condemn the growing number of kidnappings and murders of members of the Ahmadi community. The U.S. State Department's 2010 Human Rights Report noted that according to the Ahmadiyya Foreign Mission, 11 Ahmadis were killed in Pakistan the preceding year because of their religious beliefs.[29]

Even mainstream Muslim religious sites in Pakistan have fallen prey to the culture of intolerance and hate. In an apparent effort to push their hard line Islamist beliefs and to intimidate the more tolerant Muslim communities in Pakistan, militants conducted suicide bombings on Pakistan's most revered Sufi shrine in Lahore in July 2010, killing more than 40 and wounding nearly 200.[30] The shrine--a burial site of a respected Persian Sufi saint who lived in the 11th century--represented the heart of Muslim culture in the city. In orthodox interpretations of Islam, the veneration of Sufi mystics is considered heresy.

The rash of suicide bombings, like those on the Sufi shrine in Lahore, are leading average Pakistanis to disassociate themselves with the goals of the Taliban and al-Qaeda. Polls show that Pakistani opinion has turned sharply against the Taliban and al-Qaeda over the past two years. A public opinion poll carried out in Pakistan in 2009 by the Pew Global Attitudes Project found that 70 percent of Pakistanis rated the Taliban unfavorably, compared to only 33 percent just one year prior. Similarly the percentage of Pakistanis with an unfavorable view of al-Qaeda jumped from 34 percent to 61 percent between 2008 and 2009.[31] Still, high levels of anti-Americanism persist in Pakistan. A recent Pew Global Attitudes Project survey revealed that six in ten Pakistanis consider the U.S. an enemy of their country.[32]

The London-based think tank, Quilliam, warns in its August 2009 report that Pakistani youth are a prime target for Islamist recruitment.[33] With the size of Pakistan's population between ages 15-24 estimated to be around 36 million and below the age of 15 to be an additional 58 million,[34] the need for specific policies to counter the Islamists' agenda is apparent. The Quilliam report argues that without the development of a compelling Pakistani identity, pan-Islamism is starting to fill the void.[35] A World Public Opinion Poll released in January 2008 revealed that a majority of Pakistanis support a moderate, democratic state, but they also want Islam to play a larger role in society.[36]

The 2007 Red Mosque siege and the events that followed have played a significant role in Pakistani society's current perception of Islamist movements. Early in 2007, students of the notorious Red Mosque in the heart of Islamabad and an adjacent *madrassa* for women launched a vigilante-like campaign to force their view of Islam on the Pakistani people. They burned CD and video shops, took over a local children's library, and kidnapped women who they accused of running a brothel, as well as several Pakistani policemen.

On July 5, 2007, Pakistani troops started a clearing operation to force the students to vacate the mosque and *madrassa*. While 1,200 students surrendered and the government sought to negotiate a peaceful resolution, over one hundred armed militants hunkered down in the mosque and *madrassa* and vowed to fight until death. On July 10, military troops stormed the buildings. After two days of fierce fighting, the military gained control of the premises but only after 19 troops and 62 militants were killed.

The Pakistani general public reacted negatively to the military operation, with Islamist circles questioning the use of force against the country's own citizens and mosques, and more liberal commentators faulting the government for allowing the situation to get out of hand in the first place, noting the past strong ties of Pakistani intelligence to the mosque. The Islamist political parties faced a dilemma in that they largely agreed with the policies the Red Mosque leaders were pursuing but did not support the idea of engaging in violent confrontation with the government to achieve these goals.[37] Following the military operation that ended the siege, JI leader Qazi Hussain held the state "wholly responsible" for the confrontation. In addition, the two Islamist parties hailed the Red Mosque militants as "*mujahideen* who fought for enforcing Islam in its true spirit."[38]

However, in April 2009 when pro-Taliban militants moved from the Swat Valley into neighboring districts following a peace deal with the government, most observers believe the militants overplayed their hand and revealed their long-term intentions of expanding influence throughout the NWFP. Pakistanis living outside of the northwest province had previously believed the Taliban's activities could be contained within the tribal areas and Swat Valley. A video that circulated in the Pakistani national media in early April 2009 showing Taliban leaders whipping a young girl also helped turn Pakistani public opinion against the militants.

In early 2009 the Pakistan military, with backing from the central government, pursued a peace deal with the pro-Taliban militant group, the Tehreek-e-Nafaz-e-Shariat-e-Mohammadi (TNSM – Movement for the Enforcement of Islamic Law), whose objective is to enforce *sharia* throughout the country. In 2007, the movement succeeded in taking over much of the Swat Valley in the settled areas of the Northwest Frontier Province (NWFP). The Pakistan military deployed some 12,000 troops to the area for 18 months in 2007-2008 before ceding the territory to the militants. The surrender of Swat occurred despite the overwhelming vote in favor of the secular Pashtun Awami National Party in the February 2008 elections, demonstrating the people of the region did not support the extremists' agenda but were merely acquiescing in the absence of support from the government to counter the militants.

Tensions came to a head in mid-April 2009, when the pro-Taliban forces moved from the Swat Valley into the neighboring district of Buner. On April 24, 2009, under both Pakistani public and U.S. pressure, the Pakistan Army deployed paramilitary troops to the region and Chief of Army Staff (COAS) General Ashfaq Kayani sent a warning to the militants that the Army would not allow them to "impose their way of life on the civil society of Pakistan."[39] The statement was a positive first step in clarifying Pakistani policy toward the militants and was followed by aggressive military operations.[40] By midsummer, the Pakistan military cleared Swat Valley of the militants and normalcy began to return to the region.

Demonstrating further resolve against militants challenging the Pakistani state, the Pakistani Army launched extensive operations in South Waziristan in the tribal areas beginning in mid-October, 2009. While the Army's resolve in fighting militants in Swat and South Waziristan signals greater clarity within the military establishment about the threat to the state from the Pakistani Taliban, there are few signs the Pakistani Army leadership is ready to accommodate U.S. requests to crack down on other groups that target U.S. and coalition forces in Afghanistan, like the Jalaluddin Haqqani network that operates out of North Waziristan and Afghan Taliban leaders that reportedly operate mainly from Quetta, Baluchistan.

ISLAMISM AND THE STATE

Following the 9/11 attacks, former Pakistani President Pervez Musharraf broke off official ties with the Taliban, supported the U.S. invasion of Afghanistan, granted over-flight and landing rights for U.S. military and intelligence units, facilitated logistical supply to military forces in Afghanistan, and contributed substantially to breaking up the al-Qaeda network in the region. Pakistan helped captured scores of senior al-Qaeda leaders, most notably 9/11 mastermind Khalid Sheikh Mohammed.

However, the government's various relationships with Islamist groups were not entirely severed and progress has been mixed. In addition to sporadic military operations, the Pakistani government in the past pursued several peace deals with the militants, which contributed to destabilizing the Pakistani state and facilitating insurgent attacks against coalition forces in Afghanistan.

The first peace deal in March 2004, referred to as the Shakai agreement, was interpreted by the locals as a military surrender.[41] A February 2005 peace agreement with now-deceased TTP leader Baitullah Mehsud also backfired, emboldening Mehsud to form the Tehrik-e-Taliban Pakistan. Baitullah Mehsud directed a string of suicide attacks against both Pakistani security forces and civilians in 2008 - 2009. Mehsud was killed by a U.S. drone strike in August 2009 and was replaced by Hakimullah Mehsud.

There are indications the Pakistani military has learned from its past mistakes in conducting counterinsurgency operations and is beginning to have more success in countering the insurgent/militant threat in the border areas. In the past, the Pakistan military employed heavy-handed tactics to crack down on Pakistani Taliban militants in the border areas, which alienated the local population. Pakistani operations were not sustained over time nor did they involve a "rebuild" phase to help locals in the aftermath of the fighting. Furthermore, while fighting some local Taliban elements, Pakistan's intelligence services simultaneously supported Taliban activities in Afghanistan.[42]

The Pakistan military remains the most powerful institution in the country, despite the establishment of a democratic government following elections in February 2008. Thus the country's success in countering violent Islamist movements will largely be determined by both the military's capabilities in beating back Islamist insurgencies in the northwest part of the country, as well as its policies toward violent extremist groups it previously nurtured.

Throughout Pakistan's troubled political history, both military leaders and democratic politicians have contributed to the Islamization of society and political discourse. Pakistan has endured military rule for about half its existence (during the periods 1958 – 1971; 1979 – 1988; and 1999 – 2008). Even when democratic governments have been in power, the Pakistani Army continued to wield tremendous influence, particularly on matters related to foreign policy and the nuclear program. The Army leadership has proved itself adept at using religion and the Islamist political parties to stifle political opposition.[43] During the 2002 elections, then-President Musharraf pursued steps, such as campaign restrictions and candidate selection policies, which favored the Islamist parties over the democratic opposition, thus helping religious parties garner their greatest percentage of votes ever and catapulting the Islamist coalition to power in the NWFP.

In contrast to their showing in the 2002 elections, Pakistan's Islamist political parties performed poorly in the country's February 2008 elections. They garnered only two percent of the national vote and 11 seats in the NWFP provincial elections, losing to a secular Pashtun party, the Awami National Party (ANP), which took 30 seats. The ANP now leads a coalition government with the PPP in the province and supports the PPP government at the center. The ANP's election victory was initially hailed as a sign that the people of the region were more interested in pursuing democratic than Islamist politics. However, militant attacks and creeping Talibanization in the province persisted after the landmark elections. Provincial officials complained that the central government was ignoring the escalating violence and instability.

The democratic parties, during their tenures, have also sought to co-opt the religious parties in various ways and use religion to consolidate their power base. Pakistan's first elected Prime Minister, Zulfiqar Ali Butto, passed a resolution in 1974 declaring Ahmadis to be non-Muslims. The legislation barred Ahmadis from calling themselves Muslims, calling their places of worship mosques, performing the Muslim call to prayer, and using the traditional Islamic greeting in public. In 1998, when he was serving his second stint as Prime Minister, Nawaz Sharif proposed a law to introduce *sharia* as the law of the land. If passed, it would have nullified the existing civil code and made Sharif the *Amir-ul-Momineen* (Commander of the Faithful) with absolute power. Fortunately, the motion failed.

What has been most damaging to the democratic character of Pakistan—and contributed significantly to the country's current instability—has been the Pakistan military's reliance on religious militants to achieve strategic objectives vis-à-vis Afghanistan and India.[44] The Pakistan Army's support for militancy as an instrument of foreign policy has eroded religious tolerance and created strong links between the Islamist political parties and militant groups.[45]

The Pakistani security establishment's unwillingness to crack down on the Afghan Taliban and related groups threatens the entire U.S. and coalition mission in Afghanistan. After months of mounting frustration in Washington over Pakistan's refusal to clamp down on Afghan Taliban leaders, Pakistan has recently engaged in cooperation that could reflect a recalibration of its strategy toward Afghanistan. Pakistani and U.S. authorities confirmed that they captured the number two Taliban leader, Mullah Baradar, in early February. Additional reports indicate that at least four other senior Taliban leaders also may have been captured in Pakistan, including Mullah Abdul Kabir, a deputy prime minister in the former Taliban regime and a member of the Taliban Shura; former Taliban finance minister Agha Jan Mohtasim; and two "shadow governors" of Afghan provinces. Pakistan's Lahore High Court has ruled that Baradar and four other unnamed Taliban leaders could not be extradited to any other country.

It is unclear why Pakistan is now cracking down on some leaders of the Afghan Taliban. Most U.S. observers believe that Islamabad may be seeking to ensure that it will have a role in determining any potential settlement of the conflict in Afghanistan. Afghan leaders, along with the former United Nations senior representative in Afghanistan Kai Eide, claim the Pakistani arrests were merely aimed at disrupting peace talks between the Afghan government and the Taliban. Given Pakistan's long track record of support for militant groups fighting in Afghanistan and India, it is too early to determine whether these most recent arrests signal a reversal of past policies, or merely a tactical shift to demonstrate leverage in the region.

The Obama Administration has recently begun to challenge the Pakistanis on their lack of consistency in countering terrorist groups in the region. The Kerry-Lugar bill passed by the Senate last September (the Enhanced Partnership with Pakistan Act of 2009) authorizes $7.5 billion in civilian aid to Pakistan over the next five years but also conditions military assistance on Pakistani measures to address terrorist threats. Former U.S. Defense Secretary Robert Gates hinted that Pakistan could be doing more to fight terrorism when he noted in a recent op-ed in the Pakistani daily *The News* that seeking to distinguish between different terrorist groups is counterproductive.[46] Then-U.S. Director of National Intelligence Admiral Dennis Blair elaborated on this point when he testified before Congress on February 2, 2010, that "Pakistan's conviction that militant groups are strategically useful to counter India are hampering the fight against terrorism and helping al-Qaeda sustain its safe haven."[47] U.S. Secretary of State Hillary Clinton stated bluntly on at least two occasions that she believed Pakistani government officials likely had information on the whereabouts of Osama bin Laden that they withheld from the U.S. government.[48]

The siege of the Red Mosque demonstrated that in certain situations the Pakistan military is prepared to confront extremists, even those with whom it previously had an intelligence relationship. The army links to religious militants revolve more around regional strategic calculations than deep sympathies with the Islamists' ideology. Thus, while it may take time to fully sever ties between elements of the military/ISI establishment and Islamist militant groups, it is certainly possible. Indications that the Red Mosque confrontation caused some dissension within the Army ranks demonstrate the challenges of convincing the Pakistan military to confront its former proxies, without causing major discord within the only Pakistani institution capable of taking on the militants. Any such process will take time and circumspection in order to anticipate and minimize the chances of revolt inside the military ranks.

While Pakistan faces enormous challenges with its economy and from extremists seeking to overturn the government, the strength and professionalism of its Army combined with the democratic impulse of middle class Pakistanis who are familiar with a tradition of practicing moderate Islam should act as bulwarks against a potential Islamist revolution similar to the one in Iran in 1979.

ENDNOTES

[1] Haider A.H. Mullick, "Pakistan's Security Paradox: Countering and Fomenting Insurgencies," *Joint Special Operations University Report 09-9* (Hurlburt Field: JSOU Press, 2009), 50.

[2] The Pakistan Institute for Peace Studies, at http://san-pips.com/index.php?action=ra&id=psr_list_1.

[3] Jane Perlez, Eric Schmitt and Carlotta Gall, "Pakistan Is Said to Pursue Foothold in Afghanistan," *New York Times*, June 24, 2010 at http://www.nytimes.com/2010/06/25/world/asia/25islamabad.html.

[4] Mark Manzetti and Eric Schmitt, "Pakistanis Aided Attack in Kabul, U.S. Officials Say," *New York Times*, August 1, 2008, http://www.nytimes.com/2008/08/01/world/asia/01pstan.html.

[5] "Pak Major Key Link Between Headley, Terrorist Leaders," indianexpress.com, December 8, 2009, http://www.indianexpress.com/news/pak-major-key-link-between-headley-terrorist-leaders/551463/.

[6] U.S. Department of State, Office of the Coordinator for Counterterrorism, *Country Reports on Terrorism 2008* (Washington, DC: U.S. Department of State, April 30, 2009), http://www.state.gov/s/ct/rls/crt/2008/122434.htm.

[7] Zahid Hussain and Eric Bellman, "Pakistan Says It May Outlaw Islamic Group," *Wall Street Journal*, December 11, 2008 at http://online.wsj.com/article/SB122889700300394357.html.

[8] Stephen Tankel, "Lashkar-e-Taiba in Perspective: An Evolving Threat," New America Foundation *Counterterrorism Strategy Initiative Policy Paper*, February 2010, 2.

[9] For a discussion of the Barelvi school of Islamic thought, see Haider A.H. Mullick and Lisa Curtis, "Reviving Pakistan's Pluralist Traditions to Fight Extremism," Heritage Foundation *Backgrounder* no. 2268 (May 4, 2009), http://www.heritage.org/Research/AsiaandthePacific/bg2268.cfm.

[10] Moeed Yusuf, "Prospects of Youth Radicalization in Pakistan: Implications for U.S. Policy," Brookings Institution *Analysis* Paper no. 14, October 2008.

[11] Joshua T. White, *Pakistan's Islamist Frontier: Islamic Politics and U.S. Policy in Pakistan's North-West Frontier Province* (Arlington, VA: Center on Faith and International Affairs, 2008), 25.

[12] Seyyed Vali Reza Nasr, *The Vanguard of the Islamic Revolution: The Jamaat-I-Islami of Pakistan* (Berkeley, CA: University of California Press, 1994), 11.

[13] Ibid, 4-8.

[14] Husain Haqqani, "The Ideologies of South Asian Jihadi Groups," *Current Trends in Islamist Ideology* 1 (2005), 12.

[15] Stephen Philip Cohen, *The Idea of Pakistan*, (Washington, DC: The Brookings Institution, 2004), 161.

[16] Fatima Mullick and Mehrunnisa Yusuf, *Pakistan: Identity, Ideology, and Beyond* (London: Quilliam, August 2009), 11.

[17] Nasr, *The Vanguard of the Islamic Revolution*, 121.

[18] White, *Pakistan's Islamist Frontier*, 38.

[19] Mullick and Curtis, "Reviving Pakistan's Pluralist Traditions to Fight Extremism."

[20] White, Pakistan's Islamist Frontier, 25.

[21] Ibid., 26.

[22] Haqqani, "The Ideologies of South Asian Jihadi Groups," 21.

[23] Declan Walsh, "Pakistan Suffers Record Number Of Deaths Due To Militant Violence," *Guardian* (London), January 11, 2010, http://www.guardian.co.uk/world/2010/jan/11/pakistan-militant-violence-death-toll.

[24] Mullick and Curtis, "Reviving Pakistan's Pluralist Traditions to Fight Extremism."

[25] C. Christine Fair, "Islamic Education In Pakistan," United States Institute of Peace, March 26, 20 06, http://home.comcast.net/~christine_fair/index.html.

[26] "Bomb Rips Through Peshawar Market," *Al-Jazeera* (Doha), December 6, 2008, http://english.aljazeera.net/news/asia/2008/12/20 0812515535698747.html.

[27] "32 Killed At DI Khan Funeral Blast," *Daily Times* (Lahore), February 21, 2009, http://www.dailytimes.com.pk/default. asp?page=2009\02\21\story_21-2-2009_pg1_4.

[28] Rizwan Mohammed and Karin Brulliard, "Militants Attack Two Ahmadi Mosques In Pakistan; 80 Killed," *Washington Post*, May 29, 2010, http://www.washingtonpost.com/wp-dyn/content/article/2010/05/28/AR2010052800686.html.

[29] United States Department of State, Bureau of Democracy, Human Rights and Labor, "2009 Human Rights Report: Pakistan," March 2010, http://www.state.gov/g/drl/rls/hrrpt/2009/sca/136092.htm.

[30] Declan Walsh, "Suicide Bombers Kill Dozens At Pakistan Shrine," BBC, July 2, 2010, http://www.guardian.co.uk/world/2010/jul/02/suicide-bombers-kill-dozens-pakistan-shrine.

[31] The Pew Global Attitudes Project, "Pakistani Public Opinion: Growing Concern about Extremism, Continued Discontent with the U.S.," August 13, 2009, http://pewglobal.org/reports/pdf/265.pdf.

[32] Pew Research Center Global Attitudes Project, "Concern About Extremist Threat Slips in Pakistan: America's Image Remains Poor," July 29, 2010, 15.

[33] Mullick and Yusuf, *Pakistan: Identity, Ideology, and Beyond*, 9.

[34] Ibid., 2.

[35] Ibidem, 9.

[36] C. Christine Fair, Clay Ramsay, and Steven Kull, "Pakistani Public Opinion on Democracy, Islamist Militancy, and Relations with

the U.S." WorldPublicOpinion.org and the United States Institute of Peace, January 7, 2008.

[37] Joshua T. White, "Vigilante Islamism in Pakistan," *Current Trends in Islamist Ideology* 7 (2008), 56.

[38] Ibid, 59.

[39] "Pakistani Taliban Withdraw from Key Northwestern District," Voice of America, April 24, 2009.

[40] Lisa Curtis, Testimony before the U.S. Senate Committee on Homeland Security and Governmental Affairs, Subcommittee on Federal Financial Management, Government Information, Federal Services, and International Security, July 7, 2009.

[41] C. Christine Fair and Seth G. Jones, "Pakistan's War Within," *Survival* 51, no. 6 (December 2009–January 2010), 171.

[42] Mullick, "Pakistan's Security Paradox: Countering and Fomenting Insurgencies," 53.

[43] Yusuf, "Prospects of Youth Radicalization in Pakistan: Implications for U.S. Policy," 10; Frederic Grare, *Reforming the Intelligence Agencies in Pakistan's Transitional Democracy* (Washington, DC: Carnegie Endowment for International Peace, 2009), 23.

[44] Yusuf, "Prospects of Youth Radicalization in Pakistan: Implications for U.S. Policy," 19-20.

[45] Haqqani, "The Ideologies of South Asian Jihadi Groups," 14.

[46] As cited in "Pakistan Army: No New Offensives For 6 Months," Associated Press, January 21, 2010, http://www.msnbc.msn.com/id/34970909/ns/world_news-south_and_central_asia/.

[47] Dennis C. Blair, "Annual Threat Assessment of the US Intelligence Community for the Senate Select Committee on Intelligence," February 2, 2010, http://intelligence.senate.gov/100202/blair.pdf.

[48] "Clinton Accuses Pakistani Officials Of Holding Back On Bin Laden Intelligence," foxnews.com, May 10, 2010, http://www.foxnews.com/politics/2010/05/10/clinton-accuses-pakistani-officials-holding-bin-laden-intelligence/; Richard Sisk, "Hillary Clinton Says Pakistan Should Give U.S. Intel On Al Qaeda, Bin Laden Whereabouts," *New York Daily News*, July 19, 2010, http://www.nydailynews.com/news/politics/2010/07/19/2010-07-19_hillary_clinton_says_pakistan_should_release_intel_on_al_qaeda_bin_laden_whereab.html.

INDIA

QUICK FACTS

Population: 1,173,108,018

Area: 3,287,263 sq km

Ethnic Groups: Indo-Aryan 72%, Dravidian 25%, Mongoloid and other 3%

Religions: Hindu 80.5%, Muslim 13.4%, Christian 2.3%, Sikh 1.9%, other 1.8%, unspecified 0.1%

Government Type: Federal republic

GDP (official exchange rate): $1.095 trillion

Map and Quick Facts courtesy of the CIA World Factbook (Last Updated July 2010)

A peculiar urgency attaches itself to the question of radical Islam in India today, as Islamist terrorist attacks occur with frequency across wide areas of the country. The crisis is deepened by the rising instability of the South Asian region and the location of what has now become the fountainhead of international Islamist terrorism—Pakistan—in India's immediate neighborhood. Beyond Pakistan, there is a multiplicity of centers of Islamist militancy that have affected India, including, on one hand, Iran, Afghanistan and the Arab world, and on the other, Bangladesh, where radical interpretations of Islam influence millions, including significant proportions of expatriate Indian workers and their families.

In an age of an enveloping threat of global Islamist terrorism and reflexive Islamophobia, however, the Indian Muslim has refused to yield to stereotypes. A community of nearly 161 million Muslims[1] —the third largest in the world, after Indonesia and Pakistan—lives in relative harmony within India's multicultural, multi-religious, secular democracy. Such coexistence is not, of course, without its frictions; communal clashes with other religious fraternities have a long history since (and, indeed, long before) the carnage of partition in 1947, when the British Indian Empire was cleaved in two, with nearly half a million people killed in mutual slaughter. There are also sectar-

ian clashes within Islam. Islamist terrorism has, moreover, certainly had significant impact in India—a separatist movement inspired by Sunni extremism and sustained by Pakistani support has plagued the north Indian State of Jammu & Kashmir for two decades now,[2] and Islamist terrorist attacks by both foreign and indigenous groups, in each case supported by Pakistan, have been witnessed in virtually every part of the country.

ISLAMIST ACTIVITY

Islamist terrorism in India, overwhelmingly spawned and supported by Pakistan, has long found its principal concentration in the north Indian state of Jammu & Kashmir (J&K)—where it was sustained at the level of a high intensity conflict (over 1,000 fatalities per annum) for 17 years, before the dramatic transformation of the post 9/11 world and growing internal instability in Pakistan created the conditions for a relative diminution in violence. Even at these diminished levels, however, J&K saw 377 fatalities in 2009 in Islamist terrorism-related violence.[3]

India has been confronted with Pakistan-backed Islamist subversion virtually since the moment of the twin birth of these nations,[4] but experienced an asymmetric escalation after 1988, when then-Pakistani dictator General Zia-ul-Haq, flush from the successful *jihad* against the Soviets in Afghanistan, decided to extend his strategy to J&K. Successive governments in Islamabad, both military and "democratic," have actively sustained this policy. The result has been unrelenting terrorism in J&K for two decades, inflicting—as of 2009—a total of 42,657 fatalities in the state.[5] Gradually, as international pressure to wind down the *jihad* in J&K mounted on Pakistan, and as domestic circumstances in that country worsened, terrorist groups substantially controlled by the Inter-Services Intelligence Directorate (ISI),[6] Pakistan's notorious spy agency, have found it necessary to base their cadres increasingly into areas outside J&K, within a wider pan-Islamist ideological framework that dovetails more seamlessly into the psyche of extremist groups and the logic of the "global *jihad*." A steady stream of Islamist terrorism and subversion has been sustained in widening theaters across India over the past years,[7] culminating in the Mumbai attacks of November 26, 2008.[8]

The networks and support structures of the multiplicity of Islamist terrorist organizations operating in India have been painstakingly constructed by the ISI, backed by enormous flows of financial support from West Asia and from affluent expatriate Muslim communities in the West, as part of a sustained strategy of "erosion, encirclement and penetration" that has been substantially documented elsewhere.[9]

Lashkar e-Taiba (LeT)

The LeT was created in 1990 by the ISI under the command of Hafiz Mohammad Saeed in the Kunar province of Afghanistan. Initially, it trained with—and participated in—the Taliban/al-Qaeda campaigns in that country. It is part of the "al-Qaeda compact"[10] and is a member of the "International Islamic Front for the struggle against the Jews and the Crusaders" (*Al-Jabhah al-Islamiyyah al-'Alamiyyah li-Qital al-Yahud wal-Salibiyyin*) established by Osama bin Laden. In 1993, its forces were diverted to the Pakistan-backed *jihad* in Indian J&K, where it has operated continuously since. At the same time, it has extended its networks and strikes across the rest of India, crystallizing the strategy that Saeed first articulated publicly on February 18, 1996, in an address at the Lahore Press Club: "The *jihad* in Kashmir would soon spread to entire India. Our *mujahideen* would create three Pakistans in India."[11]

The organization is headquartered at Muridke on a large plot of land widely acknowledged to have been gifted to it by the Pakistan government,[12] and is known to have run terrorist camps in Muzaffarabad and Gilgit (in Pakistan-occupied Kashmir), Lahore, Peshawar, Islamabad, Rawalpindi, Karachi, Multan, Quetta, Gujranwala and Sialkot. The group runs at least 16 Islamic centers, 135 "secondary schools," 2,200 offices and a vast network of *madrassas* (religious seminaries), orphanages, medical centers and charities across Pakistan.[13] The U.S. State Department's 2008 *Report on International Religious Freedom* noted that "schools run by Jamat-ud-Dawa continued… teaching and recruitment for Lashkar-e-Tayyiba, a designated foreign terrorist organization."[14]

Until its designation as a terrorist group by the UN Security Council in December 2008, the LeT published a number of journals, papers and websites.[15] Crucially, it remains a "loyal" group, and unlike many others created by the ISI which have since turned against Islamabad or whose loyalties are now suspect, continues to coordinate its activities with Pakistani state agencies. Finances for the group—as for all Pakistan-backed Islamist terrorist groupings—are provided via tacit state support, including the transfer of large quantities of fake Indian currency that Indian Intelligence sources contend, on the basis of interrogations of arrested terrorists and couriers, is printed at Pakistani Security Presses at the Mlair Cantonment in Karachi, and at Lahore, Quetta and Peshawar, and which Pakistan uses to finance its *jihad* against India. Significant in this regard is the Indian government's August 2009 announcement that it intends to take up the issue of the importation of currency standard ink and paper by Pakistan from the UK, Sweden and Switzerland, with various international agencies, including Interpol.[16] In addition to very substantial seizures of fake Indian currency notes (FICN) from Pakistan-linked couriers, there have been instances of such currency also being recovered from Pakistan Embassy staff.[17] India's Ministry of

Home Affairs has reportedly found that "the ISI has managed to get access to the configuration, specifications and other secret codes of the genuine Indian currency notes from six European companies that supply Indian currency papers fitted with security features, and another company in Switzerland that supplies the security ink used in printing these currency notes in India."[18] LeT financial sources also include "charitable" contributions that support both its vast social network across Pakistan and its terrorist activities; and a range of external contributions from diaspora communities and various international Islamist charities, including several prominent ones from Saudi Arabia. The Pakistani state channeled a large proportion of international aid received in the wake of the earthquake in Kashmir in 2005 through the LeT, withholding state relief operations in order to facilitate the LeT's further consolidation in the affected areas.[19]

There is now no doubt that the Mumbai carnage of November 26-29, 2008 was engineered by the LeT, which is permitted to operate openly in Pakistan under a different name, *Jamaat-ud-Dawa* (JuD), since its supposed official ban (imposed as a result of U.S. pressure) in 2002. American involvement and pressure on Pakistan in the aftermath of that attack forced some apparent action against visible leaders of the LeT/JuD, though a long process of denial and obfuscation by Pakistan's top leadership and authorities suggests that the group will be allowed simply to reinvent itself under a new identity, as it has done previously.

While the LeT was not, as a result of tremendous international focus and pressure, able to execute any significant incidents of terrorist violence in India outside J&K through 2009 and the first nine months of 2010, the group's involvement was confirmed in at least 154 incidents in J&K during 2009, and another 101 incidents in 2010 (through early October). Of these, at least 15 were major incidents (involving three or more fatalities) in 2009, and another nine in 2010.[20]

The "Harkat Triad"

In addition to the LeT, the most significant terrorist groups created by the ISI which operate in India include what can be termed the "Harkat Triad," comprising the *Harkat-ul-Jihad-Islami (HuJI)*, the *Harkat-ul-Mujahideen (HuM)* and the *Jaish-e-Mohammad (JeM)*, each of which is also linked to the Afghan *jihad*, the Taliban and al-Qaeda.

Harkat-ul-Jihad Islami (HuJI) came into existence in 1980 and had a long history of fighting in Afghanistan. After the end of the Afghan war against the Soviet occupation, HuJI turned its attention to Kashmir. HuJI cadres have also fought in Islamist campaigns in a number of other countries, including Bosnia, Myanmar and Tajikistan. HuJI was one of the major organizations that sent hundreds of its *mujahideen* into Afghanistan during the campaigns against the Northern Alliance and the U.S.-led Coalition's

Operation Enduring Freedom. It is also a member organization of bin Laden's "International Islamic Front." HuJI's greatest surviving strength is in Bangladesh, since the organization has been marginalized in Pakistan by the emergence and consolidation of more effective organizations in that country. HuJI Bangladesh (BD) was established as a distinct organization with direct aid from Osama bin Laden in 1992 and seeks to establish Islamic *hukumat* (rule) there. Since 2005, HuJI-BD has been involved in a number of major Islamist terrorist operations in India, executing joint operations with a number of Pakistani terrorist groups, including the LeT, the JeM and HuM, and coordinates closely with the ISI.

The Harkat-ul-Mujahiddeen was set up in 1985 at Raiwind in Pakistani Punjab by Maulana Samiul Haq and Maulana Fazlur Rehman, leaders of factions of the *Jamiat-ul-Ulema-e-Islam* (JUI), to participate in the *jihad* against Soviet forces in Afghanistan. Samiul Haq's *madrassa*, the Dar-ul-Uloom Haqqania at Akora Khattak near Peshawar, later emerged as a primary training ground for the Taliban, and also came to dominate the HuM's terrorist mobilization and training projects. Within months of its creation, the HuM was exporting recruits, initially from Pakistan and Pakistan-occupied Kashmir, but subsequently from a welter of other countries, including Algeria, Egypt, Tunisia, Jordan, Saudi Arabia, Bangladesh, Myanmar and the Philippines. HuM is one of the original members of bin Laden's "International Islamic Front." The primary area of HuM's activities, after the Afghan campaigns, was J&K, though it has suffered a continuous erosion of its stature as a leading player, as the Lashkar-e-Taiba and HuM's breakaway, Jaish-e-Mohammed, consolidated their role through a succession of dramatic attacks, both within and outside the State.

Jaish-e-Muhammad (JeM) is one of the most virulent Pakistani groups operating in India. It was set up in early 2000, following Azhar Masood's triumphant return to Pakistan upon his release from India as part of a hostage exchange. Masood split with his parent HuM as a result of differences over matters of "finance and influence." Bin Laden is believed to have extended generous funding to the JeM.[21] The JeM has also been extraordinarily successful in motivating second-generation South Asian Muslims in the West to join the *jihad*. These include Ahmed Sayeed Omar Sheikh, one of the conspirators in the 9/11 attacks in the U.S., and Daniel Pearl's killer; as well as "Abdullahbhai," a Birmingham (UK) resident, the suicide bomber in the Badami Bagh incident of December 2000 in Jammu & Kashmir.

Hizb-ul-Mujahideen (HM) is numerically the largest terrorist formation operating in J&K, with a cadre base drawn from both indigenous and foreign sources. It was, at one time, the most important in terms of its effectiveness in perpetrating terrorist violence, but has been progressively marginalized by the LeT and JeM, as those groups became more central to Pakistan's strategic objectives in India. More recently, with the LeT and JeM bases and networks in Pakistan coming under increasing international scrutiny, there has been some effort to restore HM's operational ascendancy in J&K, though with limited success, since the group's operational leadership has been systematically decimated over the past years.[22] HM is a proscribed terrorist group in India, the United States and the European Union. It continues, however, to operate openly from its headquarters at Muzzafarabad in Pakistan-occupied Kashmir, under the leadership of Yusuf Shah (a.k.a. Syed Salahuddin), who also serves as the chairman of the United Jihad Council—a multi-group conglomerate of India-directed *jihadi* organizations supported by the Pakistani state and also headquartered at Muzzafarabad. The HM came into being in the Kashmir Valley in September 1989 as the militant wing of the Jamaat-e-Islami Jammu & Kashmir (JeI-JK), with Master Ahsan Dar as its chief. Dar was arrested by Indian security forces in mid-December 1993. The JeI-JK was tasked with setting up the Hizb by Pakistan's ISI, to counter the Jammu and Kashmir Liberation Front (JKLF), which had advocated complete independence of the State. The Hizb, by contrast, advocates the integration of J&K with Pakistan. Since its inception, the HM has also campaigned for the Islamization of Kashmir. Overseas, HM is allegedly backed by Ghulam Nabi Fai's Kashmir American Council and Ayub Thakur's World Kashmir Freedom Movement in the U.S. Early in its history, the Hizb established contacts with Afghan *mujahideen* groups such as Hizb-e-Islami, as part of which some of its cadres allegedly received arms training. The proscribed Students Islamic Movement of India is also believed to have links with the Hizb-ul-Mujahideen.[23]

There are a number of other Pakistan-based groups operating in India, playing roles of varying significance in the machinery of Islamist terror that has been assembled over the years, including some that boast substantial Indian membership.[24] The most important among them in recent years has been the Student's Islamic Movement of India (SIMI). SIMI has been involved in terrorist activities, principally as a facilitator to various Pakistan-based groups, since the 1990s, providing a range of services, such as couriers, safe havens and communication posts, for specific terrorist operations or terrorist cells. Since 9/11, however, SIMI's significance in Pakistan's strategic projections has grown, as Islamabad came under increasing international pressure to dismantle the terrorist networks it had constructed and deployed. Pakistan has sought, consequently, to project an increasing proportion of its operations in India as "indigenous terrorism" purportedly sparked by "discontented Muslims" in "Hindu India," and the role of "indigenous terrorists" has seen an abrupt spike. SIMI's role in these operations has gradually increased. Initially, its cadres joined with the various Pakistani groups to participate in collaborative operations, and eventually, in the Ahmedabad and Delhi bombings of July and September 2008, respectively, operating "independently" under the identity of the "Indian Mujahideen." Crucially, however, the top leadership and cadres of SIMI receive safe haven and training in, and resources from, Pakistan, and it is there that they locate their operational command centers.[25]

ISLAMISM AND SOCIETY

Islamism in Indian society occupies a continuous ideological spectrum. Indeed, many of the root ideologies that have fed terrorism in South Asia find their sources on Indian soil—though, as already stated, at least some of these "sources" have sought to distance themselves from the interpretations and activities of terrorists.

Four broad sources can be identified on the landscape of revivalist, fundamentalist and extremist Islamism in South Asia: the Deobandi school; the Barelvi school; the modernist-revivalist streams, such as the influential Jamaat-e-Islami; and the Ahl-e Hadith, which finds its inspiration in Wahhabi doctrines and support and funding from Saudi Arabia.

The Deobandis, the earliest of these four groups, date back to 1867 and the establishment of the Dar-ul-Uloom seminary at Deoband, a small town in western Uttar Pradesh in India. Founded by Maulana Muhammad Qasim Nanautawi and Maulana Rashid Ahmed Gangohi, the seminary developed a structured curriculum, with an overwhelming emphasis on religious education based on original Arabic texts, rather than on later and "corrupted" interpretations. The impetus for these developments was the marginalization of the Muslim community in British India, and increasing concerns regarding Westernizing and other non-Islamic influences. The Deobandis formally subscribe to the Hanafi School of Islamic jurisprudence, and emphasize a puritanical interpretation of the faith. In 1919, Deobandi leaders created a political front, the Jamiat Ulema-e-Hind (JUH). The issue of the demand for a separate state of Pakistan split the JUH, and the Jamiat Ulema-e-Islam (JUI) came into being in 1945, uniting the votaries of Partition, who lent their support to the dominant political formation favoring the communal division of British India, the Muslim League (ML). The JUI and a variety of Deobandi formations have been immensely influential, both socially and politically, in Pakistan, even as they have directly contributed to and shaped the course of sectarianism, extremism and militancy in, and exported from, Pakistan. The Taliban in Afghanistan, and the Harkat Triad in India, claim Deobandi affiliation. Significantly, however, the *ulema* of the Dar-ul-Uloom Deoband have repeatedly and explicitly condemned all aspects of terrorism, stating, "there is no place for terrorism in Islam" and declaring it an "unpardonable sin."[26] In February 2008, for instance, the Deoband Ulema organized an anti-terrorism conference at the Dar-ul-Uloom, which was attended by "tens of thousands of clerics and students from around India."[27]

The Barelvi order, established by Ahmed Raza Khan toward the end of the 19th century in Uttar Pradesh state, also adhered to an interpretation of the Hanafi School, but at wide variance with the Deobandi reading of it. The Barelvi School, in fact, sought to emphasize the very syncretic elements of South Asian Islam that were explicitly rejected by the Deobandis. Deeply influenced by mystical Sufi practices and beliefs, they attributed extraordinary, indeed, many divine qualities to the Prophet, conceiving of him more as holy presence than mortal man. They likewise believed strongly in the power of the intercession of holy personages and saints, and gave greater import to the personal rather than social and political aspects of religion. Unsurprisingly, the Barelvi philosophy is anathema to the puritan reformist movements and schools of Islam, which condemn the Barelvis as shrine- and grave-worshipping deviationists. The Barelvis have not been significantly associated with terrorism in India, and have been systematically targeted by Deobandi terrorist groups in Pakistan.

The Ahl-e Hadith is a relatively small movement that has benefited enormously from Saudi support in recent times, and represents one of the most radicalized elements within Sunni fundamentalist factions in South Asia. Inspired by Sayyed Ahmed 'Shaheed' (The Martyr) of Rae Bareilly (in the present Indian State of Uttar Pradesh), who fought the Sikh Maharaja Ranjit Singh in 1826-31 in the Peshawar region. The Ahl-e Hadith sought to restore Islam to the purity of the original Faith, as articulated in the Koran and the *Hadith.* They formally claimed to be distinct from the Wahhabis, but their beliefs and practices have much in common with the dominant creed of Saudi Arabia. While the Ahl-e Hadith insist that they do not follow any one of the four schools of Islamic jurisprudence, they have moved progressively closer to the Hambali interpretation that is also the basis of Wahhabi practices. Their interpretation of Islam is puritanical and legalistic, and they reject all manner of perceived deviations and "idolatrous" practices that they claim have crept into the other major traditions. While their numbers are believed to be small, and the movement no longer has more than a trace presence in India, it has remained vibrant in Pakistan, from where it has exercised disproportionate influence and demonstrated a great capacity for violence in recent years. Lashkar-e-Taiba proclaims adherence to the Ahl-e Hadith ideology.

The *Jamaat-e-Islami* is one of the most influential revivalist movements in South Asia, and has had tremendous political influence, both in pre-Partition India and, subsequent to its creation, in the history of Pakistan. It is the most explicitly political of the various movements, and categorically denies the very possibility of a distinction between the religious and the political, indeed, even further, between the religious and the personal, within a genuinely Islamic order. Abu Ala Maududi, the ideologue and founder of the Jamaat-e-Islami, declared that, in an Islamic state—the ideal and objective of the organization—"no one can regard his affairs as personal and private... An Islamic state is a totalitarian state."[28] Maududi sought to "enunciate an all-inclusive school of Islamic thought," and one that was "not bound by any school of law."[29] To a large extent, Jamaat practice follows upon interpretations of Maududi's vision.

Hizb-ul-Mujahideen and the Students' Islamic Movement of India trace their roots to Jamaat ideology. Nevertheless, the Jamaat-e-Islami Hind rejects all linkages with these groups, including SIMI—which it created as its student wing in 1977, but which was "expelled" in 1981 due to its increasing radicalization. The Hizb remains intimately connected with the Jamaat-e-Islami Jammu & Kashmir.

Tablighi Jamaat (TJ) is a radical Muslim revivalist movement, founded by Muhammad Ilyas in 1926 in Mewat (in the present Indian State of Haryana), which reaches out to Muslims in all social and economic classes and seeks to purify the Islamic faith of all "idolatrous deviations." One of the most rapidly growing Islamist organizations, TJ primarily operates in India, Pakistan and Bangladesh, but has extended its network in other parts of the world as well. It is "a loosely controlled mass movement, not a rigidly controlled organization" and "has no fixed membership and the leaders of the movement do not exercise a total control on its activists."[30] TJ's founder, Mohammad Illyas, emphasized the *jihad-bin-nafs*, or the internal *jihad* of the spirit, over the *jihad-bin-saif, jihad* by the sword, and the organization has long been criticized by other Islamists for its apolitical orientation. In recent years, however, linkages between TJ followers and Islamist terrorism have surfaced with increasing frequency.[31]

Today, some of the Indian Muslim community's disadvantages are structural, and relate to accidents of history and of geography. The partition divested the community of its leadership and its elites across North India, and Muslims have remained largely directionless and mired in backwardness over the intervening decades. On virtually all social indicators, Muslims are worse off than other major religious communities in India. Higher poverty and illiteracy levels in the community (38.4 percent of Muslims below the poverty line in urban areas and 26.9 percent in rural areas, as against an Indian average of 22.8 and 22.7 percent, respectively; 59 percent literacy among Muslims, as against a national average of 65 percent)[32] limit capacities for productive employment, especially at higher levels. The distribution of Muslim populations has crucial impact on these factors: The community is disproportionately located in some of the poorest, most backward and ill-governed States of India. In 2001, for instance, just four of India's 28 States and seven Union Territories—Uttar Pradesh (31.8 million), Bihar (17.5 million), West Bengal (20.2 million), and Assam (8.3 million)—with some of the poorest human-development profiles in the country, accounted for 56.3 percent of India's Muslim population.[33] Relatively higher Muslim population growth, disproportionately concentrated in the most backward regions and among the most disadvantaged population segments, exacerbate existing ills. Higher poverty and illiteracy levels are directly related to higher reproduction rates among the Muslims, though rates have declined proportionately among segments of the Muslim population that have escaped these blights. Significantly, in many of the better administered and more prosperous States, the gap between the general population profile and the Muslim population profile tends to diminish on a number of variables. In Kerala, for instance, Muslim literacy in 2001 stood at 89.4 percent, compared to a State average of 90.9 percent.[34] Nevertheless, Muslim poverty remains higher than the average in most States in the country.

In terms of Muslim education, it is crucial to understand that the Indian *madrassa* has little in common with the "*jihad* factories" that have been established in a large proportion of Islamic educational institutions in Pakistan and, to some extent, in Bangladesh as well. There are no authoritative estimates of the number of *madrassas* in India, but current approximations put the figure at between 30,000 and 45,000.[35] Divergent estimates put the proportion of Muslim children going to *madrassas* variously at 2.3 and 4 percent of the 7-19 years age group. The proportion is higher in rural areas and among males.[36] The government runs programs supporting modern curricula in *madrassas*, and a significant number of such institutions have accepted such curricula.[37] Crucially, *madrassas* are often found to be providing the only option for schooling in areas where the state's education system has failed.

Nevertheless, a fraction of *madrassas* have been found to have some linkages with the Islamist extremist enterprise, and there has been a particular growth of such institutions—obviously funded from the outside—along the most porous stretches of India's borders. In February and March 2006, for instance, officers of a border security agency disclosed that 2,365 mosques and *madrassas* had sprung up on the Indian side of the Indo-Nepal border, and some 700 on the Nepal side, over the preceding decade, of which some 50 or 60 were considered "sensitive."[38] A significant rise in the number of *madrassas* along the Indo-Bangladesh border also has been reported.[39] At least some terrorist incidents have been linked backward to networks established among elements within the mosque-*madrassa* complex in the country.[40]

ISLAMISM AND THE STATE

"India's secular democratic constitution," scholar and diplomat Husain Haqqani observes, "empowers the country's Muslims more than their co-religionists in Muslim majority states."[41] India's constitutional and legal order is rigorously secular[42] and goes out of its way to protect minorities or to accommodate them through "reverse discrimination" provisions.

Nevertheless, Muslims—along with other disadvantaged groups—do endure significant discrimination in a deeply inequitable and iniquitous social, economic and political order. Weak governance and a crumbling justice system across vast areas of the country have meant that injustice, neglect and injury are often disregarded, and their victims have little practical recourse, despite the elaborate framework of statutory provisions. While the broad trajectory of trends in "communal violence" is not discouraging,[43] periodic bloodbaths—the most recent of these in Gujarat in 2002, where some 2000 persons were killed, primarily Muslims—continue to poison relationships between communities, and undermine the confidence of the minorities in the institutions of the state. Crucially, such violence often "bears the imprimatur of the state,"[44] as parties in power abandon constitutional values and subvert the agencies of the state.

Among the most visible indicators of systemic discrimination against Muslims in India is their share in government employment, which recently stood nationwide at 4.9 percent of the total number of such employees, when Muslims constituted 13.4 percent of the country's population. When tallied in 2006, Muslims made up just 3 percent of the Indian Administrative Service, 1.8 percent of the Indian Foreign Service and 4 percent of the Indian Police Service.[45] Much of this is, however, a consequence of poor education and the relatively paucity of qualified aspirants to these posts. Thus, "the success rate of Muslims is about the same as other candidates," though "the small number of Muslim candidates appearing in the written examination of the Civil Services is a cause of concern."[46]

Despite the popular narrative, however, the successes of Islamist radicalism demonstrate no coherent correlation to specific grievances, atrocities or deprivations among the Muslim community.[47] Islamist extremism is, in fact, rooted in a powerful, sustained process of ideological mobilization that has its roots in Pakistan. Indian Muslims have overwhelmingly resisted these efforts at subversion and radicalization. Nevertheless, fringe elements within the community remain vulnerable to radicalization and recruitment by terrorist and anti-state forces. Clearly, areas with heavy Muslim concentrations would have greater vulnerabilities to such extremist mobilization, and these vulnerabilities are compounded where these areas lie along borders with hostile neighbors, particularly Pakistan and, at least until recently, Bangladesh. The growth of *madrassas*, particularly where these are substantially foreign-funded, along and on both sides of India's borders, is, in this context, a matter of deep concern, though only a small minority of all *madrassas* in the country have proven to be susceptible to radicalization.

The critical element of India's abiding success against radical Islamist mobilization, within this dismal picture of responses, is the constitutional and civilizational underpinnings of secularism within the country. It is, of course, the case that Indian society and politics is yet to become "socially and emotionally secular,"[48] despite Constitutional secularism and long histories of co-existence—and the periodic recurrence of communal conflagrations and manifestations of religious extremism are evidence of this. Nevertheless, structural and cultural factors constrain even radical players from their greatest excesses. Thus, for instance, electoral considerations have repeatedly forced the Hindu right to accommodate Muslim concerns. Similarly, even where some state agencies have colluded with extremist elements—as, for instance, in the Gujarat riots—constitutional checks and balances have, eventually, reasserted themselves to bring offenders to some measure of justice.

While the threat of Islamist radicalization and terrorism has endured for decades, and Pakistan gives every sign of being intent upon an asymmetric war of attrition, Indian responses have remained largely fitful, event-led and *ad hoc*. Indeed, India has no clearly articulated counterterrorism policy.[49] This deficiency is compounded by endemic deficits of capacity in the security, intelligence and justice systems,[50] which make any planned and comprehensive response impossible. As noted elsewhere,

> The absence of strategy and the incoherence of tactics have long afflicted India, as the country finds itself responding continuously and insufficiently to provocations by its neighbours, and to a rising tide of subversion and terrorism. Worse, the pattern of responses has, with rare exception, reflected a quality of desperation and directionless-ness that, after decades of contending with these problems, is impossible to fathom. With over 25 years of Pakistan sponsored Islamist terrorist activity on Indian soil, the country is still to correctly define the problem that confronts it, or to craft an appropriate 'strategic architecture' and to derive policies and practices that are in conformity with such an overarching design.[51]

If Islamist terrorism, nevertheless, gains little traction, and if the state is still able to achieve significant successes against both terrorists and against extremist ideologies, the credit must go to small handfuls of exceptionally dedicated individuals in the intelligence and security community, on the one hand, and an enveloping culture that rejects terrorism on the other. India's democracy, which has gone great lengths to accommodate minority sentiments, is part of this culture, and it is through the instruments and dynamics of democracy that extremism is constrained.

ENDNOTES

[1] The current population of Muslims in India is 160,945,000 according to the *Pew Forum on Religion and Public Life*, October 2009, http://pewforum.org/docs/?DocID=451.

[2] Indeed, low grade *jihadi* subversion and Pakistani incursions commenced almost from the moment of Partition. See Praveen Swami, *India, Pakistan and the Secret Jihad: The Covert War in Kashmir 1947-2004* (New Delhi: Routledge, 2007).

[3] Violence in J&K peaked in 2001, with 4,507 fatalities in that year, and remained continuously at the high intensity conflict level between 1990 and 2006. All data from the *South Asia Terrorism Portal* database, "J&K: Annual Fatalities in Terrorist Violence, 1988-2009," http://www.satp.org/satporgtp/countries/india/states/jandk/data_sheets/annual_casualties.htm.

[4] Swami, *India, Pakistan and the Secret Jihad.*

[5] "J&K: Annual Fatalities in Terrorist Violence, 1988-2009."

[6] See, for instance, Ashley Tellis, Testimony before the House of Representatives, Committee on Foreign Affairs, Subcommittee on the Middle East and South Asia, March 11, 2010, http://www.carnegieendowment.org/files/0311_testimony_tellis.pdf.

[7] See Institute for Conflict Management, South Asia Terrorism Portal, "Major Islamist Terrorist Attacks outside Jammu & Kashmir and Northeast since 2000," n.d., http://satp.org/satporgtp/countries/india/database/OR_9-11_majorterroristattacks.htm; and "ISI related modules Neutralised outside J&K and Northeast, 2004-09", http://satp.org/satporgtp/countries/india/database/ISImodules.htm.

[8] On November 26, 2008, a group of ten terrorists from Pakistan, affiliated with the Lashkar-e-Taiba, with demonstrated connections with the ISI-Army-State structure in Pakistan, attacked multiple targets in the coastal city and India's financial capital, Mumbai. 166 persons were killed in this terrorist outrage. The attack was covered live virtually throughout the 62 hours of its execution by India's many television channels. Conversations between the terrorists and their handlers in Pakistan were fully recorded by Indian and American intelligence agencies, and subsequent investigations have established linkages not only to the LeT in Pakistan, but to a number of serving and retired Army officers there. See, *Ministry of Home Affairs, Annual Report 2008-09*, Government of India, p. 20; *Mumbai Terrorist Attack: Dossier of Evidence*, http://www.hindu.com/nic/dossier.htm; Rajeev Deshpande, "26/11 Probe: US may ask for Pak major's extradition", *Times of India*, December 9, 2009; "Five army officers held for link with Chicago suspects," *Daily Times*, November 25, 2009; "Headley Link: 5 Pak Army officers held," *Hindustan Times*, December 23, 2009.

[9] Ajai Sahni, "South Asia: Extremist Islamist Terror and Subversion",

in K.P.S. Gill and Ajai Sahni, eds., *The Global Threat of Terror: Ideological, Material and Political Linkages* (New Delhi: ICM-Bulwark Books, 2002), esp. 212-229; Tellis, Testimony before the House of Representatives, Committee on Foreign Affairs, Subcommittee on the Middle East and South Asia; Swami, *India, Pakistan and the Secret Jihad.*

[10] The expression was used by the then-Indian National Security Advisor, M.K. Narayanan, to describe the global network of al-Qaeda-linked organizations. See Bruce Tefft, "LeT is part of al Qaeda Compact," *The Hindu*, August 14, 2006.

[11] See, Ajai Sahni, "Offensive from Pakistan," *Wars within Borders*, n.d., http://www.satp.org/satporgtp/ajaisahni/09fablime04.htm.

[12] See, for instance, Aarish Ullah Khan, "The Terrorist Threat and the Policy Response in Pakistan," Stockholm International Peace Research Institute *Policy Paper* no. 11, September 2005, 22. Khan notes, "The land for building the complex was given by the government of President Zia ul-Haq, with a huge investment from Abdul Rehman Sherahi, as a gift to Markaz al Dawa wal Irshad during the *jihad* years..."; See Mariam Abou Zahab and Olivier Roy, *Islamist Networks: The Afghan–Pakistan Connection* (Hurst: London, 2004), 32; and Amir Rana, "Jamaatud Dawa splits," *Daily Times* (Lahore), 18 July 2004.

[13] Wilson John, "Lashkar-e-Toiba: New Threats Posed by an Old Organization," Jamestown Foundation *Terrorism Monitor* 3, iss. 4, May 5, 2005, http://www.jamestown.org/single/?no_cache=1&tx_ttnews%5Btt_news%5D=314.

[14] "Pakistan," in U.S. Department of State, Bureau of Democracy, Human Rights and Labor, *International Religious Freedom Report 2008* (Washington, DC: U.S. Department of State, 2009), http://www.state.gov/g/drl/rls/irf/2008/108505.htm.

[15] These include www.jamatuddawa.org; an Urdu weekly called Gazwa; an English monthly, *Voice of Islam*; an Urdu monthly, *Al Dawa*; an Arabic monthly, *Al Rabat*; an Urdu youth magazine, *Mujala-e-Tulba*; and an Urdu weekly, *Jihad Times*.

[16] Vishwa Mohan, "India to take up fake currency note issue at global fora," *Times of India*, August 4, 2009.

[17] Ajit Kumar Singh, "Subversion sans Borders," *Outlook India*, November 20, 2006, http://www.outlookindia.com/article.aspx?233169; Tara Shankar Sahay, "Hijackers with Pak military intelligence, says ISI ex-chief," rediff.com, January 3, 2000.

[18] Aman Sharma, "Economic Terror no Fake Threat," *India Today*, August 5, 2009, http://indiatoday.intoday.in/site/Story/55177/LATEST%20HEADLINES/Economic+terror+no+fake+threat.html. See also, for further details, Ajai Sahni, "Blood Money," *Defence & Security of India*, April 2009, http://www.satp.org/satporgtp/ajaisahni/09ASdsivw.htm.

[19] See, for instance, Jan McGirk, "Kashmir: The Politics Of An Earth-

quake," Open India, October 18, 2005, http://www.opendemocracy. net/conflict-india_pakistan/jihadi_2941.jsp.

[20] Numbers compiled from the *South Asia Terrorism Portal's* "Timelines," www.satp.org.

[21] See, for instance, Jamal Afridi, "Kashmir Militant Extremists," Council on Foreign Relations *Backgrounder*, July 9, 2009, http://www. cfr.org/publication/9135/.

[22] See Kanchan Lakshman, "J&K: Dying Embers of Terror," *South Asia Terrorism Review* 7, no. 29, January 7, 2009; Praveen Swami, "A homecoming for yesterday's jihadists?" *The Hindu* (Chennai), August 21, 2009.

[23] "Hizb-ul-Mujahideen," *South Asia Terrorism Portal*, n.d., http:// www.satp.org/satporgtp/countries/india/states/jandk/terrorist_outfits/hizbul_mujahideen.htm.

[24] A detailed listing and profile of principal groups can be found at "India: Terrorist, insurgent and extremist groups," South Asia Terrorism Portal, n.d., http://www.satp.org/satporgtp/countries/india/terroristoutfits/index.html.

[25] See, for instance, Praveen Swami, "Islamism, modernity and Indian Mujahiddeen," *The Hindu* (Chennai), March 23, 2010; "The Lashkar-e-Taiba's Army in India," *The Hindu* (Chennai), January 17, 2009; "Lashkar trained Indian terrorists pose growing threat," *The Hindu* (Chennai), December 19, 2008.

[26] "Darool-Uloom Deoband says terrorism is anti-Islam," Reuters, February 26, 2008.

[27] Ibid.

[28] Abu A'la Maududi, "Political Theory of Islam," as cited in K.K. Aziz, *Pakistan's Political Culture* (Lahore: Vanguard, 2001), 265.

[29] Seyyed Vali Reza Nasr, *Mawdudi & the Making of Islamic Revivalism* (New York: Oxford University Press, 1996), 114.

[30] Yoginder Sikand, "Plane 'Plot': Media Targets Tablighi Jamaat," *The Milli Gazette*, August 19, 2006, http://tablighijamaat.wordpress. com/2008/06/16/plane-plot-media-targets-tablighi-jamaat/#more-19; See also Yoginder Sikand, *The Origins and Development of the Tablighi Jama'at* (1920-2000): A Cross-Country Comparative Study (Hyderabad: Orient Longman, 2001).

[31] Praveen Swami, "Shattered certitudes and new realities emerge in terror link investigation," *The Hindu* (Chennai), July 8, 2007.

[32] *A Report on the Muslim Community of India: High Level Committee Report on Social, Economic and Educational Status of the Muslim Community of India* (Sachar Committee Report), November 2006, (New Delhi: Akalank Publications, January 2007), 159-160.

[33] Ibid., 265.

[34] Ibid., 287.

[35] Manzoor Ahmed, in his study of Indian Muslim education, esti-

mated the number of *madrassas* at around thirty thousand. Manzoor Ahmed, *Islamic Education: Redefinitions of Aims and Methodology* (New Delhi: Genuine Publications, 2002), 32. Yoginder Sikand puts the number at about 30,000. Yoginder Sikand, *Bastion of the Believers: Madrassas and Islamic Education in India* (New Delhi, Penguin India, 2005), 95. Shabeeb Rizvi's estimate goes as high as 45,000. Shabeeb Rizvi, "The rise and rise of Wahabism," *Telegraph* (New Delhi), May 10, 2009, www.telegraphindia.com/1090510/jsp/7days/story_10942907.jsp#.

[36] Sachar Committee Report, 77.

[37] See Yoginder Sikand, "Voices for Reform in the Indian Madrasas," in Farish A. Noor and Yoginder Sikand, eds., *The Madrasa in Asia* (Amsterdam: Amsterdam University Press, 2008), 31-65, esp. 59-64.

[38] Vishwa Mohan, "A New Terror Trail Leads to Nepal," *The Times of India*, February 12, 2006; "1900 madrassas mushrooming along Indo-Nepal border," rediff.com, March 24, 2006, http://www.rediff.com/news/2006/mar/24border.htm.

[39] Union Minister of Home in the Ministry of Home Affairs Vidyasagar Rao, Rajya Sabha (Upper House of Indian Parliament), Unstarred Question no. 700, March 6, 2002.

[40] See, for instance, Praveen Swami, "Fortresses of Faith," *Frontline* 23, iss. 20, October 7-20, 2006; K.P.S. Gill, "Gujarat: New Theatre of Islamist Terror," *South Asia Intelligence Review* 1, no. 11, September 30, 2002, http://www.satp.org/satporgtp/sair/Archives/1_11.htm.

[41] Husain Haqqani, "India's Islamist Groups," in Hudson Institute *Current Trends in Islamist Ideology* 3, 2006, 22.

[42] Justiciable "fundamental rights" under the Constitution, for instance, guarantee equality before law and equal protection by the law; prohibit discrimination on the grounds of religion, race, caste, sex and place of birth; freedom of conscience and right to freely profess, practice and propagate religion; right to manage religious institutions and affairs; protection of minorities right to conserve language, script or culture; right to establish and administer educational institutions of their (minorities') choice, etc.

[43]

Year	2002*	2003	2004	2005	2006	2007	2008
Incidents	722	711	677	779	698	761	943
Fatalities	1130	193	134	124	133	99	167
Injured	4375	2261	2132	2066	2170	2227	2534

*The spike in year 2002 principally reflects incidents in Gujarat.

2002-2007 Data is drawn from Ministry of Home Affairs, Government of India, *Status Paper on Internal Security Situation*, September 1, 2008, 41. 2008 data is drawn from Ministry of Home Affairs, Government of India, *Annual Report 2008-09*, 2009, 48.

[44] Neera Chandoke, "The new tribalism," *The Hindu* (Chennai), April 4, 2002.

[45] *High Level Committee Report on Social, Economic and Educational Status of the Muslim Community of India* (New Delhi: Akalank Publications, January 2007), p. 165.

[46] Ibid., 166-67.

[47] See, for example, Praveen Swami, *India, Pakistan and the Secret Jihad: The Covert War in Kashmir, 1947-2004* (London: Routeledge, 2007), 2.

[48] Partha S. Ghosh, "Demographic Trends of Muslim Population in India: Implications for National Security," Demographic Dynamics in South Asia And their Implications on Indian Security (New Delhi: Institute for Conflict Management, unpublished 2006), 29.

[49] For a detailed assessment, see Ajai Sahni, "Counter-terrorism and the 'Flailing State,'" *Eternal India* 1, no. 5, February 2009, http://www.satp.org/satporgtp/ajaisahni/09AS-7EtInd.htm.

[50] For details, see Ajai Sahni, "Strategic *Vastu Shastra*," *South Asia Intelligence Review* 7, no. 24, December 22, 2009; Ajai Sahni, "The Peacock and the Ostrich," South Asia Intelligence Review 8, no. 7, August 24, 2009.

[51] Ajai Sahni, "Counter-terrorism and the 'Flailing State.'"

BANGLADESH

The nature of Islam in Bangladesh exerts a profound influence on the country's society and politics. Islamist activity in Bangladesh, viewed generally, takes three broad forms: the traditional revivalism of grassroots movements such as the Ahl-i-Hadith and Tablighi Jama'at; the incremental political Islam of Islamic political parties (most prominently the Bangladesh Jama'at-i-Islami; and the more radical, subversive activism of jihadist organizations such as the Harkatul Jihad al-Islam (HUJIB) and Jagrato Muslim Janata Bangladesh (JMB), which seek to capture state power through unconstitutional or violent means. Bangladesh has emerged as a moderate Muslim country through the accommodation made by successive governments between Islamic and secular values, in large part because of Islam's preeminence in as a source of religio-cultural identity.

ISLAMIST ACTIVITY

Islamist activity in Bangladesh, viewed generally, takes three broad forms: the traditional revivalism of grassroots movements, the incremental political Islam of the country's Islamic political parties, and the more radical, subversive activism of *jihadist* organizations.

Islamic revivalism

Islamic revivalism in Bangladesh is typified by two main movements. The first, the Ahl-i-Hadith Bangladesh, was founded in British India in the 1830s, and matured significantly in Bengal. Siddiq Hasan and Syed Nazir Hossain were the original founders of this traditional Islamist group.[1] In 1946, All Bengal and Assam Jamat-i-Ahl-i-Hadith was formed and headquartered in Calcutta. Following the independence of Pakistan from India, the East Pakistan Jamiat-i-Ahle Hadith was founded in Pabna in 1953 by Maulana Abdulla Hil Baki.[2] Still later, the organization was renamed the Bangladesh Jamiat-e-Ahle Hadith. This group is known to be Wahhabi in outlook, following the exclusionary teachings of Saudi Arabia's Islamic *ulema* (clergy). As part of this worldview, the Ahl-i-Hadith does not recognize any single school of law, and relies only on the Koran and *Hadith*.[3] For this reason, they are called la-Mazhabi, meaning that they do not believe in any of the four Mazhabs or school of law.[4] It claims to be the only group in the Muslim community that follows the Koran and *Hadith* correctly and exactly. Apart from donations and charity from its members, the group reportedly receives considerable foreign donations, especially from Saudi Arabia and other Arab countries.[5] The group exists in about 40 districts, and claims more than 25 million people as followers.[6] It aims to disseminate the knowledge of the Koran and the *Hadith*, and does not openly involve itself in political controversy. Instead, it seeks to reorganize the Muslim community and implement the principle of the *Kalemai Tayeba* (faith) in all walks of life.[7]

The second is the Tablighi Jama'at, founded in the 1920s by Mohammad Ilyas Shah with the objective of educating non-practicing Muslims on the subcontinent how to perform daily prayer (*salat*) and lead a Muslim life in accordance with the teaching of Prophet Muhammad.[8] Devotion to Allah as a means of self purification, respect to others and missionary works constitute the organization's three most important tenets. The famous Kakrail mosque in Dhaka serves as the group's headquarters in Bangladesh. The missionary movement is organized by the voluntary input of dedicated religious individuals of all classes, but the middle class is dominant.[9] The goal of the Tablighi Jama'at is to infuse Islamic ideals and culture among the Muslims who have deviated from the practice of Islam for material gain.[10] The movement depends on the endeavor, dedication and labor of its members. It organizes meetings, seminars and symposia, as well as an annual *Istema* (assembly) attended by millions of people worldwide—the second largest congregation of Muslims in the world, after Mecca, held annually in the industrial town of Tongi on the banks of the Turag River. Although it does not have links with any political party, Tablighi Jama'at receives support from the Bangladeshi government in logistics, maintenance of law and order, traffic, health and sanitation services.[11] Millions of followers are active throughout Bangladesh, and the movement has significant impact on social life within the country.

Political Islam

The Jama'at-i-Islami (JI) was founded in the early 1940s in British India by Islamic ideologue Syed Abul Ala Moududi. It began operating in Bangladesh in 1979 under its acting *Amir* (head) Abbas Ali Khan. He was succeeded in 1991 by Professor Golam Azam, who oversaw the group's activities before voluntarily resigning in 2002.[12] Maulana Motiur Rahman Nijami was then elected as *amir*, a post he continues to occupy to this day. The main goal of JI is to establish an Islamic state through democratic elections and the constitutional process. The JI believes in both Bangladeshi nationalism and the idea of "Islamic democracy."[13]

The party is organized, disciplined and enjoys a modicum of popular support. It is the largest functioning Islamic party in Bangladesh, and is popular among students, the academic intelligentsia, civil servants, the military and other important sectors of Bangladeshi society.[14] However, its overall political impact remains limited; in the country's 2008 election, JI received just 4.5 percent of the popular vote.[15]

The party boasts a broad financial network. It indirectly operates many financial institutions, including Islamic banks and Islamic insurance companies, as well as private universities, medical colleges and private schools. These businesses generate huge profits, which in turn go to fund party operations. (The amount of yearly income of the JI has never been disclosed publicly.) The party also has large numbers of supporters and sympathizers in Middle Eastern countries, Europe and North America, who contribute regularly to the party fund.[16] Despite its fundamentalist Islamic ideology, however, JI has managed to successfully attract western-educated elites,[17] and is now considered to be the premier mainstream Islamic modernist party in the country.

Apart from JI, several other minor Islamic parties exist in Bangladesh. They include the Bangladesh Muslim League, Nizam-I Islam, Bangladesh Khilafat Andolon, Bangladesh Khilafat Majlis, Islamic Andolon, Jamat-i Ulema Islam, and the Islamic Oikko Jote.[18] All operate legally under the country's constitution, but their organizations are weak and support bases slim. Like JI, each advocates the imposition of Islamic law in Bangladesh.

Radical Islam

Against the backdrop of September 11th and the ensuing War on Terror, the bin Laden network has gravitated to Bangladesh, attracted by the country's fragile economy and weak capacity to combat terrorism. Since the 1990s, al-Qaeda has boasted a considerable presence in Bangladesh, represented by underground organizations such as Harkatul Jihad al-Islam (HUJIB) and Jagrato Muslim Janata Bangladesh (JMB).

Harkatul Jihad al-Islam was founded in Bangladesh in 1992. The goal of the HUJIB is to establish Islamic *hukumat* (rule) in Bangladesh via *jihad*.[19] Comprised of veterans of the Afghan *jihad*, HUJIB is reported to have received initial funding from bin Laden's International Islamic Front.[20] In 2008, the U.S. listed HUJIB as a terrorist organization,[21] and the government of Bangladesh has formally banned the organization as well.[22] HUJIB's principal areas of activities are limited to the area between Cox's Bazaar, Bangladesh and the border with Myanmar.[23] The HUJIB reportedly maintains six camps in the hilly Chittagong Hill Tract region where its cadres are provided arms training. While there is no authoritative information on the actual size of the group, it is estimated to have around 15,000 members.[24] Since 2005, frequent raids on HUJIB centers by Bangladeshi Rapid Action Battalion (RAB) police and army—and the continuous monitoring of their activities by law enforcement agencies—have significantly weakened the group's capabilities.[25] HUJIB reportedly receives financial assistance from Pakistan, Saudi Arabia and Afghanistan via Muslim non-governmental organizations active in Bangladesh.[26] Its operational commander, Mufti Hannan, was arrested in 2007 and is currently facing trial under Bangladeshi law.

The *Jammatul Mujahideen Bangladesh* (JMB) came into existence in 1998 with the aim of establishing *sharia* law in Bangladesh through armed revolution. Its supreme leader was Shaikh Abdur Rahman, and second in command was Siddiqur Rahman (a.k.a. Bangla Bhai), who also led its military wing, the Jagroto Muslim Janata Bangladesh (JMJB). In 2004, Bangla Bhai unleashed a reign of terror in the northern part of Bangladesh as part of an ostensible war on outlawed Marxist extremists. But the proximate targets of the JMB onslaught were judges and lawyers, who were targeted in a bid by the group to establish an Islamic legal system.[27] The group's last large-scale attack was a series of bombings in August 2005. The organization reportedly receives funding from various sources, including individual donors from Kuwait, Saudi Arabia, the UAE, Bahrain, Pakistan, and Libya.[28] Funding for the group also flows through NGOs, which—in spite of their ostensibly-humanitarian activism—have aided the activities of the JMB.[29] Several international NGOs—among them the Kuwait-based Revival of Islamic Heritage and Doulatul Kuwait, the UAE-based Al Fuzaira, the Bahrain-based Doulatul Bahrain and the Saudi Arabia-based Al Haramain Islamic Institute—reportedly have provided funding to the group.[30] The JMB reportedly has approximately 10,000 fulltime and 100,000 part-time members, including teachers, students and ordinary citizens.[31] JMB was banned in 2005 by the government of Prime Minister Khaleda Zia. Its principal leader, Abdur Rahman, its second-in-command, Bangla Bhai, and four other members of the *Majlish-e-sura* (the group's top decision making body) were tried and executed in Bangladesh in 2007.[32]

ISLAMISM AND SOCIETY

Bangladesh, widely regarded as a moderate Muslim democracy, is 89.7 percent Muslim and 9.2 percent Hindu, 0.7 percent Buddhists, 0.3 percent Christian. Animist and believers in tribal faith constitute 0.1 percent of the population.[33] Islam serves as the religio-cultural identity of the predominantly Muslim country. More than 98 percent of the population is ethnic Bengali. Non-Bengalis include a minute number of Urdu-speaking Biharis. Among the country's Muslims, more than 99 percent are Sunni and follow the Hanafi school of thought. Several Shi'a and Ahmadiya sects are also represented, albeit only nominally.[34]

Mosques in Bangladesh serve as active centers of religious activity. In the country's 65,000 villages, there are an estimated 133,197 mosques, which act as focal points for daily and weekly prayers and assembly.[35] Local donations, as well as donations from West Asian and African Muslim countries, provide for the construction and maintenance of these religious centers.[36] A parallel structure of some 58,126 *maqtabs* (informal Islamic schools) imparts basic Islamic knowledge to young children (including how to read the Koran, pray, etc.) Mosque *imams* act as influential elders in the country's rural power structure. On the whole, therefore, society in Bangladesh can be termed "mosque-centric."

Most Bangladeshis follow an orthodox, traditional version of Islam—one which includes the traditional teachings of their forefathers. Their beliefs are centered on the five pillars of Islam: 1) faith in Allah, 2) the performance of *salat* (formal prayer), 3) the observance of fasting, 4) the performance of the *Hajj* (journey to Mecca), and 5) the payment of *zakat* (alms). *Madrassas* (Islamic schools) have long been considered to be the center of traditional Islamic studies and the guardians of the orthodox Islam in Bangladesh.[37] Of these, there are two types: *Qomi madrassas* are private in nature, receive no financial support from the government, and subsist on religious endowments or *zakat* and donations from the faithful. *Alia madrassas*, by contrast, are controlled by the government, which pays 80 percent of the salaries of their teachers and staff, as well as considerable portion of their development budget. One estimate shows that the total number of *madrassas* (both *Qomi* and *Alia*) is 13,406, with 230,732 teachers and 3,340,800 students.[38] These schools constitute the main current of traditional Islam in Bangladeshi society.

ISLAMISM AND THE STATE

The forty-year political history of Bangladesh is typified by an official embrace of—and accommodation with—Islam by a succession of ruling governments.

At the time of the country's independence in December 1971, the government of Sheikh Mujibur Rahman introduced a secular democracy and later, one-party authoritarianism. But the government did not exile Islam from public life. Prime Minister Rahman (commonly known as "Mujib") established Islamic foundations in Bangladesh under public patronage for the research and analysis of Islamic culture and society. Under his direction, Bangladesh also joined the Organization of the Islamic Conference (OIC). Beyond that, however, the practice of Islam in political form was severely circumscribed.

This balance was shattered in 1975 by a *coup d'etat* that unseated Mujib and installed a military regime. Bangladesh's new rulers wasted no time dropping secularism from the constitution and inserting a proviso emphasizing "absolute trust and faith in Almighty *Allah*" as part of its efforts to satisfy religious constituents in society and the Islamic World. Simultaneously, the new government allowed Islamic parties, through constitutional amendment, to return to politics, and included a constitutional addendum compelling Bangladesh to maintain fraternal relations among the Islamic countries based on Islamic solidarity.[39] After the assassination of President Ziaur Rahman in May 1981, power was assumed by another General, Hossein Mohammad Ershad, who established Islam as the state religion, ushering a period of relative religio-political stability.

In 1990, however, the Ershad regime was ousted as a result of a massive political revolt and purge, and power was assumed by Rahman's widow, Khaleda Zia, who became the first female prime minister in the new parliamentary democracy. Like her late husband, Zia pursued a pro-Islamic policy both domestically and abroad. In 1996, Sheikh Hasina, one of Mujib's surviving daughters, rose to power as part of the opposition Awami League political party, only to be subsequently ousted by a coalition government with Khaleda Zia at its helm. In 2008, however, Sheikh Hasina returned to power, buoyed by her pledge "not to harm Islam." However, her government has unmistakably trended toward secularism, highlighting the contradiction between her election pledges and her actual performance.

Indeed, Islam is so intimately tied to Bangladeshi society that current Prime Minister Sheikh Hasina and former Prime Minister Khaleda Zia were obliged to cover their heads for public appearances.[40] Although Khaleda Zia accommodated moderate Islamic forces in her ruling coalition, she did not compromise with *jihadists*. The country's present Prime Minister, Sheikh Hasina, has reinforced secularism and generally sought to combat Islamist forces. In February 2009, her government passed two key pieces of legislation in this regard: the Money Laundering Prevention Act (MLPA) and the Anti-terrorism Act (ATA).[41] The former empowered the Bangladesh Bank to freeze the accounts of suspected terrorist financiers, and directed it to take preventive measures against monetary transactions that might be used for financing terror acts. Together with the ATA, it also instituted the death penalty for terror financing and politically-motivated acts of violence.[42] Under the statutes of the ATA, "Anyone resorting to murder, kidnapping or damaging property to create panic among the people and jeopardize the country's security by using explosives, arms and chemicals, will be charged with committing terrorist offence."[43] In tandem, the Hasina government's prosecution of "war criminals"—namely, those Bangladeshis who actively sided with Pakistan in attempting to prevent Bangladesh's independence—has effectively weakened Islamic forces, especially the JI.[44]

Troublingly, however, Sheikh Hasina has demonstrated willingness to make common cause with religious radicals for political gain, signing an agreement with Khilafat Majlis—a group considered by some to be a pro-Taliban style Islamist group—as a strategy to win the country's January 2007 election.[45]

ENDNOTES

[1] Sufia M. Uddin, *Constructing Bangladesh: Religion, Ethnicity and language in an Islamic Nation*, (Chapel Hill: The University of North Carolina Press, 2006), 56.

[2] K.M Mohsin, "The Ahl-i-Hadis Movement in Bangladesh," in Rafiuddin Ahmed, ed. *Religion, Nationalism and Politics in Bangladesh* (New Delhi: South Asian Publishers, 1990), 181.

[3] Sufia M. Uddin, *Constructing Bangladesh*, 56.

[4] Muin-ud Diin Ahmad Khan, "Muslim Renaissance in Bangladesh : Pan Islamic and Khilafat Movement," in Ak. M Ayub Ali, M.A. Aziz & Shahed Ali eds., *Islam in Bangladesh Through Ages* (Dhaka: Islamic Foundation Bangladesh, 1995), 189.

[5] The Kuwait based NGO Saudi Revival of Islamic Heritage (RIHS) is the main source of funding to the Ahle Hadith Bangladesh. See PROBE 9, iss. 14, September 24-30, 2010, http://www.probenews-magazine.com.

[6] Ibid.

[7] Mohsin, "The Ahl-I Hadis movement in Bangladesh," 179-182.

[8] Uddin, *Constructing Bangladesh*, 161-62.

[9] M. Rashiduzzaman, "Islam, Muslim Identity and Nationalism in Bangladesh," *Journal of South Asian and Middle Eastern studies* 18, no. 1 (1994), 54.

[10] Ahmed Shafiqul Huque and Muhammad Yehia Akhter, "The Ubiquity of Islam: Religion and Society in Bangladesh" *Pacific Affairs* 60, no.2 (1987), 217.

[11] Rashiduzzaman, "Islam, Muslim Identity and Nationalism in Bangladesh," 54.

[12] Ishtiaq Hossain and Noore Alam Siddiquee, "Islam in Bangladesh: the role of the Ghulam Azam of Jamaat-i-Islami," *Inter Asia Cultural Studies* 5, no. 3 (2004), 384.

[13] As opposed to secular Bengali nationalism, the JI prefers Bangladeshi nationalism which recognizes the importance of Islam in national life. The JI, which claims to be a modern democratic Islamic political party, has been working to establish a liberal parliamentary system of democracy. See Zaglul Haider, "Role of Military in the Politics of Bangladesh: Mujib, Zia and Ershad Regimes (1972-1990)," *Journal of South Asian and Middle Eastern Studies* 22, no. 3 (1999), 74; Muhammad Ghulam Kabir, *Changing Face of Nationalism: The Case of Bangladesh* (Dhaka: The University Press Limited, 1995), 685; Bangladesh Jamaat-I Islami, Election Manifesto 2008, n.d., http://www. Jamaat-i-Islami.org/index.php?option.com_archieve8.

[14] Hossain and Siddiquee, "Islam in Bangladesh," 384.

[15] Zaglul Haider, "The Ninth General Election in Bangladesh: The Fall of the Bangladesh Nationalist Party and the Rise of the Bangla-

desh Awami league" (unpublished research paper).

[16] The party supporters, workers and well-wishers working abroad regularly contribute to the party fund, whether monthly, annually or occasionally as part of their political and moral responsibilities. Author's interviews with JI leaders and activists, Bangladesh, August 2006.

[17] Talukder Maniruzzaman, "Bangladesh Politics: Secular and Islamic Trends," in Rafiuddin Ahmed, ed., *Religion, Nationalism and Politics in Bangladesh* (New Delhi: South Asian Publishers, 1990), 84.

[18] Emajuddin Ahmad and D.R.J.A. Nazneen, "Islam in Bangladesh: Revivalism or Power politics?" *Asian Survey* 30, no.8 1990, 802.

[19] Summit Ganguly, "The Rise of Islamist Militancy in Bangladesh" United States Institute of Peace *Special Report*, August 2006, http://www.usip.org/files/resources/SRaug06_2.pdf.

[20] Bruce Vaughn, *Islamist Extremism in Bangladesh* (Washington, DC: Congressional Research Service, January 31, 2007), http://www.fas.org/sgp/crs/row/RS22591.pdf.

[21] Ibid.

[22] On October 17, 2005, Bangladesh's government banned the activities of the HUJIB.See *Harkatul Jihad banned at last.* See , *The Daily Star* October 18,2005 .Online: <http://www.thedailystar.net/2005/10/18/d5101801033.htm>

[23] "Harkat-ul-Jihad-al Islami Bangladesh (HuJI-B)," South Asia Terrorism Portal, n.d., http://www.satp.org/satporgtp/countries/bangladesh/terroristoutfits/Huj.htm.

[24] Ibid.

[25] Ibidem.

[26] Ibidem.

[27] "Jama'atul Mujahideen Bangladesh," South Asia Terrorism Portal, n.d., http://www.satp.org/satporgtp/countries/bangladesh/terroristoutfits/JMB.htm.

[28] Ibid.

[29] Joyeeta Bhattacharjee, "Understanding 12 extremist groups of Bangladesh," *Observer India*, June 7, 2009, http://www.observerindia.com/cms/export/orfonline/modules/analysis/attachments/Bangladesh-Militant-Groups_1246945884723.pdf .

[30] "Jama'atul Mujahideen Bangladesh," South Asia Terrorism Portal.

[31] Ibid.

[32] Abdul Kalam Azad, "Six Militant Linchpins Hanged," *New Age* (Dhaka), March 31, 2007, http://www.newagebd.com/2007/mar/31/front.html.

[33] BANBEIS, Bangladesh Bureau of educational, Information, And Statistics .Online: <http://www.banbeis.gov.bd/bd_pro.htm>

[34] For example, the international Sunni organization Khatma Nabuat continuously puts pressure on the government to declare the Ahama-

dya sect as non-Muslim.

[35] Rashidduzzaman, "Islam, Muslim Identity and Nationalism in Bangladesh," 36-60.

[36] Ahamed and Nazneen, "Islam In Bangladesh: Revivalism or Power politics?" 798.

[37] Mumtaz Ahmad, " Madrasa Education in Pakistan and Bangladesh," in Satu P. Limaye, Mohan Malik and Robert G. Wirsing, eds., *Religious Radicalism and Security in South Asia* (Honolulu, Hawaii: Asia Pacific Centre for Security Studies, 2004), 101.

[38] Ibid., 105.

[39] Zaglul Haider, *The Changing Pattern of Bangladesh Foreign policy: A Comparative study of the Mujib and Zia regimes*, (Dhaka: The University Press Limited, 2006), 204.

[40] Farah Deeba Chowdhury, "Problems of Women's Participation in Bangladesh Politics," *The Round Table* 98, iss. 404, 2009), 557.

[41] "10 Bills Sail Through Opposition Protest," *New Age* (Dhaka), February 25, 2009, http://www.newagebd.com/2009/feb/25/front.html#1.

[42] "Bangladesh Enacts Tough Anti-Terrorism Law," *Hindustan Times*, June 13, 2008, http://www.hindustantimes.com/Bangladesh-enacts-tough-anti-terrorism-law/Article1-317131.aspx.

[43] Ibid.

[44] United States Commission on International Religious Freedom, USCIRF Annual Report 2010 - *Additional Countries Closely Monitored: Bangladesh*, 29 April 2010, Online, http://www.unhcr.org/refworld/docid/4be28407d.html.

[45] Bruce Vaughn, *Bangladesh: Background and U.S. Relations* (Washington, DC: Congressional Research Service, August 2, 2007), 4, http://www.fas.org/sgp/crs/row/RL33646.pdf.

MALDIVES

QUICK FACTS

Population: 395,650

Area: 298 sq km

Ethnic Groups: South Indians, Sinhalese, Arabs

Religions: Sunni Muslim 80%, Shi'a Muslim 19%, other 1%

Government Type: Islamic Republic

GDP (official exchange rate): $13.47 billion

Map and Quick Facts courtesy of the CIA World Factbook (Last Updated July 2010)

Although the population of the Maldives is one hundred percent Muslim, mostly Sunni, and the government prohibits the practice of other religions, Maldivian society was largely moderate and tolerant until comparatively recently.[1] Today, however, Islamic clerics and lay preachers disseminate a radical strain of Islam across the country, mostly in impoverished and secluded locales such as Ukulhas (in North Ari atoll). Islamist organizations, including Jamiyyatul Salaf (JS) and the Islamic Foundation of Maldives (IFM), have proliferated as well, growing to dominate the socio-cultural landscape and dictate the way of life. Even mainstream political parties in the Maldives, such as Adhaalath (Justice), now support the strict implementation of Islamic law in all walks of life.

ISLAMIST ACTIVITY

The process of grassroots radicalization in the Maldives is comparatively recent, and can be traced back to 2003, when posters of al-Qaeda leader Osama bin Laden began to appear on walls in Edhyafushi Island, the capital city of Baa Atoll. Then, in 2005, Islamists attacked a shop in the national capital, Male, for displaying an image of Santa Claus in its window.[2] Subsequently, in the early months of 2007, a religious faction in Himandhoo began issuing death threats to locals who refused to collaborate with them. The same year, Islamists warned people in Himandhoo not to send their children to local schools because of the impure influence of "foreign" teachers, the English language and non-Islamic subjects. In reaction, Islamists established competing Islamic schools that teach the *Koran* and *Hadith*.[3]

This growth in grassroots activism has been mirrored by the establishment of several notable Islamist outposts. One is the Dar-ul Khair mosque on the island of Himandhoo, which has served as a major source for the propagation of conservative Islam. After ignoring the Dar-ul-Khair mosque for years, authorities in Male ordered its demolition in October 2006. The ensuing government action met considerable local resistance, resulting in the arrest of at least 16 people.[4] Soon thereafter, the Himandhoo residents rebuilt the mosque and it resumed disseminating Islamist ideology. The Ukulhas Island in North Ari atoll also harbors extremists; many inhabitants there have been influenced by self-proclaimed Islamic scholars, and further radicalized through access to extremist literature and CDs.[5]

The first Islamist terrorist attack in the Maldives occurred in Male in September 2007, when a crude bomb wounded 12 foreigners, including British, Japanese and Chinese tourists in Male's Sultan Park. The attack was obviously aimed at the country's thriving tourism industry and the so-called "alien influence" of tourism on local culture. Following the bombing, security agencies rounded up over 50 suspects, including two Bangladeshi nationals. Many more suspects fled to Pakistan and Sri Lanka. Three terrorists, all in their early 20s, were ultimately sentenced to 15 years in jail in connection with the attack, after confessing to their roles in the incident during the trial. All three have reportedly admitted their goal, was to "target, attack and injure non-Muslims to fulfill jihad."[6]

The bombing prompted authorities to crack down on extremist elements holed up in the illegal Dar-ul-Khair mosque in October 2007. The situation erupted into a violent confrontation between members of the Dar-ul-Khair mosque and security forces when the latter attempted to carry out a search and sweep operation. Both Maldivian police and the Maldives National Defense Force (MNDF) successfully put down the violent uprising, arresting more than 50.[7] The incident at Dar-ul-Khair was subsequently mentioned in an al-Qaeda video.[8]

Taliban-style public flogging is also emerging in the Maldives. A 2009 investigation found that Muslim courts in the country had sentenced almost 150 women to public flogging for adultery.[9] The prevalent thinking appears to be that public flogging will deter immoral practices in society.

Radical political parties, such as *Adhaalath* (Justice), which is now part of the government's ruling coalition, have long clamored for the strict implementation of sharia in all parts of the Maldives. *Adhalaath*, which is sympathetic to the Taliban, also controls the nation's Ministry of Islamic Affairs. *Adhaalath* favors the Islamization of the Maldives, and holds conservative views on gender issues—opposing, for instance, the eligibility of women to contest Presidential elections. Under its influence, the Ministry of Islamic Affairs has regularly invited foreign scholars and preachers with extreme religious views to the Maldives to address large and small groups on religious matters. The party has also proscribed visits to Sufi tombs and shrines because its leadership deemed praying and making wishes there to be un-Islamic. The *Adhaalath* Party also supports reinstating a ban on public visits to the *Medhu Ziyaaraiy*, the tomb of Abu Barakat Berberi, who is credited with introducing Islam to the Maldives, citing religious justifications.[10] (The country's Islamic Ministry, however, has ordered the shrine to remain open on the condition that no flags would be hoisted in and around it.) The current government in Mali has one representative of *Adhaalath* as the minister for religious affairs, and the party exerts considerable pressure on the administration of current President Mohamed Nasheed (on account of its support for Nasheed in the last election in his successful bid against sitting President Maumoon Abdul Gayoom).

Maldivian society also boasts a number of Islamist organizations. The most prominent among them is the *Jamiyyatul Salaf* (JS), a non-governmental religious group which propagates an ultra-conservative strain of Islam. JS boasts Wahhabi/Salafi lineage, and a strong anti-secular ideology. It supports Islamizing education in the country and promotes intolerance towards other religions, especially Christianity. Many of its members are known to have been educated in Saudi Arabia and Pakistan. As part of its campaign to raise Islamic awareness and promote the values of Islam, the group regularly invites Islamic preachers and scholars to the Maldives in conjunction with the Ministry of Islamic Affairs. The JS is also actively engaged in moral policing; in 2008, it declared music to be *haram* (forbidden) and forced a school library in Male to close because it contained Christian books.[11]

The Islamic Foundation of the Maldives is a relatively new non-profit organization, similar to JS, that was registered in April 2009. It was founded by Ibrahim Fauzee, an Islamist previously arrested in Karachi, Pakistan and detained at Guantanamo Bay for his links to al-Qaeda. According to its website, the IFM aims to "promote and protect Islamic tenets and ethics, create religious awareness, and to uphold social events within the boundary of

Islamic principles and [the] Religious Unity Act in the Maldives."[12] After Mohamed Nazim declared himself a Maldivian and not a Muslim, the IFM implored the state both to revoke Nazim's citizenship and execute him if he did not repent.[13]

While there are no known organized *jihadi* groups operating in or out of the Maldives, the country has proven a fertile ground for *jihadist* recruitment. *Lashkar e-Taiba* (LeT) and al-Qaeda have both successfully recruited youth already radicalized in Islamic schools there.[14]

The December 2004 tsunami in the Indian Ocean provided an opening in this regard. In the aftermath of the disaster, radical Islamists gained a foothold in the country in the guise of humanitarian charities. The most significant of these was the *Idara Khidmat-e-Khalq* (IKK), which is affiliated with the Pakistan-based *Jammat ud Dawa/Lashkar-e-Taiba*. The IKK is linked to the *Jamaat Ahl-e-Hadith* sect active in the Maldives, Afghanistan and Pakistan. Many *Ahl-e-Hadith* groups are known to be involved in the *jihadi* struggle in South Asia, and most are affiliated with Kashmir-centric terrorist groups such as *Lashkar-e Taiba* and *Harkat-ul Mujahideen*. Its followers prefer to call themselves Salafis, in order to stress their closeness to the Saudis. Intelligence sources confirm that the IKK has spearheaded LeT's activities in the Maldives, which prioritizes youth recruitment.[15] The IKK claims to have spent 17.2 million Pakistani Rupees (roughly $282,000) on tsunami relief in the Maldives, Sri Lanka and Indonesia during 2005 as post-tsunami relief although the Maldivian government denies that the organization provided any relief.[16] Ostensibly as part of that aid, the IKK reportedly facilitated trips for many Maldivian youth to Pakistan, enrolling them in various radical *madrassas* (Islamic seminaries) there.

Sporadic incidents of *jihadi* activity within the Maldives have also occurred. In April 2005, for example, Indian police arrested Maldivian national Asif Ibrahim who allegedly frequented the Indian state of Kerala to procure arms and ammunition for the LeT's Maldives operation. Ibrahim confessed to planning to blow up a government-run mosque and assassinate then-President Maumoon Abdul Gayoom. An official release from the Maldivian government indicated that Asif Ibrahim had become a member of the UK-based extremist Islamic group *Jama'ah-tul-Muslimeen* in 2001.[17] More recently, in the early weeks of February 2010, nine alleged Maldivian terrorists arrested in Pakistan's troubled South Waziristan tribal region in March 2009 were repatriated to the Maldives.[18] According to national police, the nine have ties to the bombing that took place in Male's Sultan Park in September 2007, and may have left the country for Pakistan via Sri Lanka for further training and indoctrination.[19]

The current Maldivian government admits that Pakistan-based terrorist groups have successfully recruited hundreds of Maldivian Muslims to fight against government forces in Pakistan.[20] The bin Laden network has done so as well; an al-Qaeda video circulated in November 2009 featured Ali Jaleel, a Maldivian national who fought alongside pro-Taliban forces in Pakistan.[21] Soon thereafter, another recruitment video featured a previously unknown al-Qaeda cell operating in the Maldives, and exhorted *jihadists* to travel to the country, stating "Your brothers in the Maldives are calling you."[22]

International concerns over the growth of Islamic extremism in the Maldives have risen since the May 2002 arrest of Ibrahim Fauzee. Fauzee, a Muslim cleric (now heading the Islamic Foundation of Maldives), was arrested in a suspected al-Qaeda safe house in Karachi, Pakistan and subsequently held in the Guantanamo Bay detention camp until his release and repatriation to the Maldives in March 2005.[23] The incident sparked concerns about the spread of radical Islam and the penetration of international terror groups like al-Qaeda and *Lashkar-e-Taiba* into the social fabric of this Indian Ocean archipelago.

The Fauzee case was not an isolated event, however. There is growing evidence of Maldivian youths frequenting Pakistan for reasons unknown or suspicious in nature, though enrollment in various *madrassas* (Islamic seminaries) is usually cited as the prime reason for their travel.[24] Intelligence agencies of the United States and India have noted this development with concern, and believe that growing religious extremism in the Maldives is a Pakistani import.[25] Additionally, the Maldives' Controller of Immigration and Emigration, Sheikh Ilyas Hussain Ibrahim, believes that expatriates from Bangladesh now under surveillance have been instrumental in spreading religious extremism in the country.[26]

ISLAMISM AND SOCIETY

Persian travelers and Islamic preachers brought Islam to the Maldives in the 12th century.[27] It was then that Sheikh Yusuf Samsuddin of Tavrezh (now Tabriz, Iran) converted King Darumavanta Rasgefanu and his subjects to Islam. Another account by the Persian traveler Ibn Batuta indicates that Abu Barakat Berberi, a Sufi saint, converted the Maldives' then-Hindu (Buddhist) King and his subjects.[28] After this phase, known as the Spiritual Revolution in the annals of the Maldives, Islam was embraced and widely disseminated by successive Sultans. Under their direct patronage, Islamic laws were enforced and mosques and *madrassas* were built across the country. Islam became the foundation of the state and the fount of its laws, customs and traditions. This trend was more formally institutionalized in the 20th century, with the constitution of 1932, adopted during the rule of Sultan Muhammed Samusuddin Iskandar III, which made *sharia* the basis of all administrative and political governance.

Islam in the Maldives has traditionally been very moderate, as evidenced by the freedoms enjoyed by women and their comparatively high status in Maldivian society. The country is completely Muslim, with citizenship strictly confined to practitioners of the Islamic faith. Of these, most belong to the Shafi school of Sunni Islam.

However, the culture of the Maldives has undergone a sea of change in recent years, and is progressively being Arabized (or Wahhabized). Today, the influence of external, and more extreme, Islamic ideology can be seen in changing dress codes for women, the increasing frequency with which men sport beards, and in the name changes adopted by foreign-funded mosques around the country. And although the full veil is illegal in the Maldives and even headscarves are banned for female television anchors, many women on Himandhoo Island have begun to cover themselves completely.[29] Full headscarf and Arabic-style robes, meanwhile, have become the dress code for women in general.

Spanish scholar Xavier Romero-Frias observed at the end of the 20th century that, "[t] he changes brought about have been of such magnitude and in such a short time, that there is now a whole young generation who, having not known how things were previously, take for granted that their home nation has always been so orthodox and impersonal."[30] He further noted that Maldivian religious practices have changed "significantly and irreversibly since the beginning of the 1980's."[31]

This radical undercurrent has at times broken into the open, as it did in December 1998 when the country's Supreme Council for Islamic Affairs (which later became Ministry of Islamic Affairs) appealed to the national Police Service to impose a ban on night clubs and discotheques on the eve of New Year celebrations.[32] That same year, the Supreme Council for Islamic Affairs barred Maldivians from listening to Christian missionary radio.[33] Other incidents of state-backed religious intolerance and discrimination came to light when Christians were imprisoned in June 1998 on religious grounds and held captive at the notorious prison on Dhoonidhoo Island.[34] The arrests followed government-sanctioned search and sweep operations of homes of Christians living in the country (some, but not all, have subsequently been released). The government reportedly expelled nearly 20 foreigners as part of that crackdown.

In July 2000, then-President Maumoon Abdul Gayoom, reportedly under pressure from radicals, declared in a public address that the Maldives have no room for any religion but Islam. He subsequently reiterated his stance on numerous occasions, and went on to accuse foreigners of destroying religious unity by introducing other faiths.[35] Gayoom claimed that the Maldives achieved and sustained its sovereignty by adhering only to Islamic principles.

ISLAMISM AND THE STATE

With the adoption of the country's 1997 constitution, Islam became the state religion and the chain of nearly 1,200 coral islands was declared 100-percent Islamic.[36] Non-Muslims are forbidden from proselytizing and conducting public worship in the Maldives. Any Muslim who converts to another faith is breaking *sharia* law and can lose his or her citizenship. Migrant workers of other faiths are denied the ability to practice their faith. The government also prevents the importation of non-Muslim books and other religious items. However, people from other religions are given permanent resident permits to live and work, mostly in the country's thriving hospitality industry, which serves as the economic lifeline of the Maldives. Notably, despite its economic benefits, many radical Islamic groups active in the Maldives have denounced what they view as tourism's negative influence on local Islamic culture.

During the reign of Maumoon Abdul Gayoom, himself an alumnus of Cairo's famed Al Azhar University, where he was a student of Islamic jurisprudence, the country experienced a new Islamic revival. In the 1980s and early 1990s, intense indoctrination was undertaken and mosques were built en masse. During that time period, Koranic schools also emerged as major educational institutions. In November 1984, the president of the Maldives laid the foundation of a major Friday Mosque complex; the estimated $7 million cost of the project was funded in large part by the Persian Gulf states, Pakistan, Brunei, and Malaysia.[37] Today, the golden-domed mosque, named *Masjid-al Sultan Mohamed Thakurufaanu-al-A'z'am*, is a testament to the growing Arabian influence over Maldivian society.

Gayoom has been accused of having brought Islamic fundamentalism into the country, and of using "Islam as a tool of governance,"[38] Under the Gayoom regime, Islamic preachers and *madrassas* received unconditional political and financial support, paving the way for the rise of Islamism, which has obstructed movement toward democratization.[39] After almost three decades of authoritarian rule, the Maldives became a multi-party democracy in 2008 with the election of the liberal Mohamed Nasheed as President. Although Nasheed's party, the Maldivian Democratic Party (MDP), has progressive views on religion, its main ally, the *Adhalaath* Party, holds conservative views on religious and cultural matters. Gayoom's right-wing party, the *Dhivehi Rayyithunge* Party (DRP), often accuses the ruling government of being too liberal in cultural and religious matters. The DRP's leader, Ahmed Thasmeen Ali, once alleged that the current government intended "to wipe out Islam in the Maldives."[40]

Since 2009, the Maldivian government has been working on a counterterrorism bill with the help of the United Nations Office on Drugs and Crime (UNODC) and Interpol. The drafting committee includes officials from the Maldives Police, National Defence Force, Attorney General's Office, Prosecutor General's Office and Maldives Monetary Authority. This bill, which will replace or supplement the existing Prevention of Terrorism Act,[41] would provide adequate legal standing against growing radicalism in the country and empower security agencies to "act preemptively on matters of national security, including terrorism." The proposed bill has been vehemently criticized by the IFM for its potential use against religious activities in the name of preserving national security. The IFM fears that the law would target Muslim religious scholars, enabling their extradition and obstructing the preaching of Islam in public.[42]

Many in the Maldivian political establishment feared that renewing diplomatic ties with Israel would expose the Maldives to terrorist attacks. Nevertheless, the Maldives reestablished diplomatic relations with Israel in 2009, and allowed a team of Israeli eye doctors to perform free surgery in the country during a visit in early December 2010. This development, however, was condemned by the Islamic Foundation, which urged the government to "shun all medical aid from the Zionist regime." It also accused Israeli doctors for illegally harvesting organs from non-Jews around the world.[43]

Increasingly, the Maldives has been grappling with Salafi *jihadi* ideology, which is gaining currency among the population at large and among the nation's youth in particular. In January 2011, an investigative report, citing Maldivian intelligence officials, concluded that Maldivian youths are increasingly attracted to the idea of transnational *jihad*. According to one official quoted in the report, there were at least seven radicals running in the 2008 elections, though all of them lost the electoral battle.[44]

The Ministry of Islamic Affairs claims to have developed de-radicalization methods and has been taking measures to curb the activities of the various transnational Islamic organizations that have arrived in the Maldives in recent years.[45] However, radical interpretations of the religion and calls for *jihad* against non-believers have many more supporters in the Maldives now than in the past, and threaten to continue inducing Muslim youth in that country to join global *jihadi* groups.

ENDNOTES

[1] Devin Hagerty, *South Asia in World Politics* (Lanham: Rowman & Littlefield, 2005), 104.

[2] John Lancaster, "Islamism Comes to Paradise: Looking for Osama in the Maldives," *Slate*, May 28, 2007.

[3] "Himandhoo Situation: Breakaway Religious Group Keeping their Children out of School Due to Foreign Teachers," *Haveeru Online*, October 10, 2007, http://www.haveeru.com.mv/english/?page=details&id=18770.

[4] "Maldives Police Demolish Unauthorized Prayer House, Arrest 16," *Haveeru Online*, October 25, 2006.

[5] "Ukulhas on Verge of Becoming Another Extremist Den," *Haveeru Online*, October 20, 2007.

[6] "Sultan Park Suspects on Run in Pakistan," *Minivan News*, November 7, 2007, http://minivannews.org/news_detail.php?id=3814.

[7] "50 Held in Maldives Mosque Siege," *Guardian* (London), October 9, 2007, http://www.guardian.co.uk/world/2007/oct/09/randeepramesh.

[8] "Five Jailed For Ten Years Over Himandhoo 'Terrorism,'" *Minivan News*, May 15, 2008, http://minivannews.org/news_detail.php?id=4476.

[9] Andrew Buncombe, "150 Women Face Adultery Flogging on Maldives," *Independent* (London), July 22, 2009, http://www.independent.co.uk/news/world/asia/150-women-face-adultery-flogging-on-maldives-1757150.html.

[10] "Sacred Shrine Opened to Public," *Dhivhei Observer*, March 29, 2009.

[11] Sudha Ramachandran, "Maldives Faces Up to Extremism," *Asia Times*, Nov 11, 2009, http://www.atimes.com/atimes/South_Asia/KK11Df02.html.

[12] Islamic Foundation of the Maldives, "About Us," n.d., http://www.islamicfoundationofthemaldives.org/node/1.

[13] Islamic Foundation of the Maldives, "Islamic Foundation's views about the apostate," May 29, 2010, http://islamicfoundationofthemaldives.org/sites/default/files/Press%20release%202.pdf

[14] Policy Research Group, "Storm of Protests in Maldives Over Settling 2 Guantanamo Bay terrorists," June 15, 2010, http://policyresearchgroup.com/maldives/770.html.

[15] "US Concerns on Maldives Valid: IB," Rediff.com, September 10, 2009.

[16] "India Links Emerge in Maldives Terror Probe," *The Hindu*, November 14, 2007, http://www.hindu.com/2007/11/14/stories/2007111461541700.htm.

[17] "Gayyoom's Dirty Conspiracies is Baseless and Hold No Ground,"

Dhivehi Observer, May 6, 2005. See also "Leaked Cable from 2008 Reveals US Concerns about Maldivian National's 'Unspecified Links to al-Qaida,'" *Minivan News*, December 7, 2010, http://minivannews.com/politics/leaked-cable-from-2008-reveals-us-concerns-about-maldivians-unspecified-links-to-al-qaida-14132.

[18] "9 Armed Maldivians Arrested in Waziristan," *Miadhu News*, April 2, 2009; "Maldivian Detainees Repatriated from Pakistan," Minivan News, February 8, 2010, http://minivannews.com/politics/maldivian-detainees-repatriated-from-pakistan-3296.

[19] "Aim was to Perform Jihad by Targeting Non Muslims – Police," Miadhu News, November 8, 2007.

[20] "Radicals in Pak Recruiting our Youth: Maldives," CNN-IBN (New Delhi), October 25, 2009, http://ibnlive.in.com/news/radicals-in-pak-recruiting-our-youth-maldives/103903-2.html.

[21] "Video Interview of Maldivian Jihadist Available on Internet," *Haveeru Online*, November 8, 2009; "Man Appearing in Terrorist Video is my Brother – Jalla," *Miadhu News*, November 10, 2009.

[22] "First Video of al-Qaeda in Maldives Released," Adnkronos International, November 20, 2009.

[23] See details of Fauzee's arrest, detention and release, "Guantanamo Docket: Ibrahim Fauzee," *New York Times*, n.d., http://projects.nytimes.com/guantanamo/detainees/730-ibrahim-fauzee; See also "Timeline: Guantanamo Bay Prison," *Al-Jazeera* (Doha), October 7, 2009, http://english.aljazeera.net/focus/2009/07/20097221092685420.html.

[24] "Radicals in Pak recruiting our youth: Maldives"; "Maldivians in Pakistan rejects President's comment," *Merinews*, October 27, 2009.

[25] The Pakistan links was refuted by Dr. Jamal, then second secretary of Pakistan High Commission in Maldives. See "Religious extremism is not a Paki import –Dr. Jamal," *Miadhu News*, November 12, 2007.

[26] "Controller Warns Maldives Should Fear Rising Expatriate Population," Haveeru Online, January 18, 2011; "Maldives Worried over Increasing Expats," *Asian Tribune*, January 28, 2011, http://www.asiantribune.com/news/2011/01/27/maldives-worried-over-increasing-expats.

[27] John L. Esposito, *The Oxford Dictionary of Islam* (New York: Oxford University Press, 2004), 137.

[28] Hasan Ahmed Maniku, *The Maldives Islands: A Profile* (Male: Novelty Publishers, 1977), 2; See also Zafar Ahmad, *Future of Islam in South Asia* (Leiden: Authors Press, 2003), 221.

[29] "Maldives Moves against Veiled Women, Jihadis," *Daily Times* (Lahore), November 15, 2007, http://www.dailytimes.com.pk/default.asp?page=2007/11/15/story_15-11-2007_pg4_21.

[30] Romero-Frias Xavier, *The Maldives Islanders, A Study of the Popular Culture of an Ancient Ocean Kingdom* (Barcelona: Nova Ethnographia

Indica, 1999).

[31] Ibid.

[32] "Ministry Asks Police to Ban Discos," *Minivan News*, December 31, 2008.

[33] "Maldives Fast Acquiring a Radical Islamic Colour: Report," *Hindustan Times*, October 5, 2006, http://www.hindustantimes.com/Maldives-fast-acquiring-a-radical-Islamic-colour-Report/Article1-157773.aspx.

[34] "Christians Expelled from Maldives," *Christianity Today*, September 7, 1998, http://www.ctlibrary.com/ct/1998/september7/8ta27d.html.

[35] Gayoom said while addressing a 4,000 strong crowd that "We want to bring reform to the Maldives, reform that leaves no room for other religions." See "Asia's Longest-Serving Leader in Maldives Run-Off," Associated Press, October 27, 2008, http://www.usatoday.com/news/nation/2008-10-27-2185416197_x.htm.

[36] Article 10 of the Maldivian Constitution states the religion of the Maldives is Islam and Islam shall be the basis for all laws in the land. The constitution granted right to freedom of expression in the Article 27, however, it stipulates that the right only exists as long as it is "not contrary to any tenet of Islam."

[37] The estimated cost was mentioned in Abdul Rauf, *Illustrated History of Islam* (Lahore: Ferozsons, 1994).

[38] Maldivian Democratic Party leader Mohamed Latheef once said that Gayoom is the person who brought Islamic fundamentalism. See "Radical Islam Shows up in Maldives," CNN-IBN (New Delhi), June 21, 2007, http://ibnlive.in.com/news/maldives-turns-to-islamic-extremism/27821-2.html.

[39] "Maumoon Abdul Gayoom - the Father of Maldivian Extremism," *Dhivehi Observer*, October 10, 2007; "Allegations Repeated That Gayoom's Abuse of Islam Introduced Extremism in Maldives," *Dhivehi Observer*, October 5, 2007.

[40] "Maldives Grants Full Freedom to Islamic Scholars, says President," Minivan News, January 16, 2011, http://minivannews.com/politics/maldives-grants-full-freedom-to-islamic-scholars-says-president-15107.

[41] Prevention Of Terrorism Act (Act No. 10/1990), http://www.agoffice.gov.mv/pdf/sublawe/Terrorism.pdf.

[42] "Islamic Foundation Condemns Reports of "Pre-emptive" Anti-Terrorism Bill," *Minivan News*, January 23, 2011, http://minivannews.com/politics/islamic-foundation-condemns-reports-of-pre-emptive-anti-terrorism-bill-15394.

[43] "Islamic Foundation Calls on Government to Sever Diplomatic Ties with Israel," *Minivan News*, November 25, 2010, http://minivannews.com/society/islamic-foundation-calls-on-government-to-sever-

diplomatic-ties-with-israel-13703; See also "Israeli Eye Surgeons Visiting Maldives to 'illegally harvest organs,' claims Islamic Foundation," *Minivan News*, November 29, 2010, http://minivannews.com/politics/israeli-eye-surgeons-visiting-maldives-to-illegally-harvest-organs-claims-islamic-foundation-13872.

[44] "A Malevolent Link," *The Week*, January 16, 2011.

[45] "Islamic Ministry Proposes Extremist Rehabilitation Centre," *Minivan News*, March 18, 2010, http://minivannews.com/society/islamic-ministry-proposes-extremist-rehabilitation-centre-4640.

EAST ASIA

Regional Summary

East Asia faces a growing problem with Islamist extremism, which has taken different forms and seen varying degrees of success across the region. In Thailand, the Philippines, and China, Islamist activism has largely paralleled ethno-religious separatism, while Indonesia and Malaysia, the only two countries with majority-Muslim populations, have grappled with powerful domestic Islamist political groups seeking the implementation of *sharia* law as well as violent *jihadist* groups with ties to Islamic terror organizations.

The region's southeast has a history of religious moderation and tolerance, with literalist forms of Islam largely rejected by its inhabitants. However, from the 1970s onward, pan-Islamist influences from Salafists and the Muslim Brotherhood have been making inroads in Indonesia. By the 1990s, Islamist parties operating within the Indonesian political system were successfully challenging country's commitment to secularism, expanding the authority of religious courts, and abolishing bans on the headscarf in school. In the Indonesian province of Aceh, Islamists won a federal exception in 2002 to implement *sharia* as the official legal system for Muslims and in districts of West Java, *sharia* serves as the de facto law of the land. The most active and deadly radical Islamist group in Indonesia—indeed, in the region—remains Jemaah Islamiyah (JI). The group conducted a string of sensational terrorist attacks on civilian targets in Indonesia throughout the 2000s, prompting a fierce crackdown by Indonesian security forces and, as a consequence, a significant diminution of their leadership and capabilities.

Malaysia, with the second largest Muslim population in the region, has also experienced a slide toward religious conservatism in recent decades. After taking power in 1981, longtime ruler Mahathir Mohammad and his nominally secular UMNO party implemented wide-ranging efforts to elevate Islam's prominence in Malay society, restructuring education and banking to better conform with Islamic practices. The country's active Islamist opposition party, the PAS, has pushed for the expansion of *sharia* law, but recently abandoned efforts to convert Malaysia into an Islamic state. Two radical Salafist groups, the KMM and Al Maunah, remain active in Malaysia. The former has designs on creating an Islamic state in Malaysia; however, neither has engaged successfully in violent terrorist attacks, and each appears committed to a domestic religio-political agenda. They remain under close scrutiny by Malaysian security forces.

In the majority-Christian Philippines, radical Islamism has taken root in the form of violent secessionist insurgencies, focused in the country's southern islands. Three violent Islamist groups, the MNLF, MILF, and Abu Sayyaf, have been battling the Filipino state for decades, with some assistance from external Islamist groups such as JI. However, today the three groups remain divided and suffer from weak or fractured leadership. Their popularity among the Filipino Muslim population appears to have waned, while government security forces—aided by U.S. training and supplies as well as some 500 Special Forces personnel—have significantly diminished their capabilities. No broad-based Islamist movements, either societal or political, have taken hold in the Philippines, although Islam remains the fastest-growing religion in the country and Islamic NGOs remain small but active.

Much like the Philippines, Thailand's experience with violent Islamic groups has been in the context of a separatist insurgency, albeit one characterized by a stark ethnic-religious divide. This overwhelmingly-Buddhist country has been grappling with Muslim separatists in the country's three Muslim-majority, southernmost provinces since its borders were drawn in 1902. The insurgency is not an exclusively Islamist phenomenon, involving communists and secular ethno-nationalists. However, it is dominated by the BRN-C, a primarily-Islamist group fighting to establish an independent Islamic state for Malay Muslims. No Islamist party exists on the Thai political scene and no political parties endorse the insurgency or its goals. However, funds from Arab countries have supported Islamic educational institutions and NGOs in the country since the 1990s, and the Tablighi Jamaat, which is growing in stature in the Muslim south, constructed the largest mosque in Thailand in 2008.

The most populous country in the world, China, has a relatively small Muslim population (just 1.6 percent), but an Islamist movement that carries disproportionate strategic and political significance. Beijing officially recognizes Muslims as one of China's "five peoples" and recognizes ten Muslim nationalities. Yet China suffers from a tumultuous relationship with its Muslim population. The country's westernmost province of Xinjiang, where most Chinese Muslims reside, is ethnically and religiously distinct from the Han majority which rule the country. Active in Xinjiang since the 1940s, a handful of Islamist separatist groups re-emerged with radical agendas in the 1990s, promoting separatism and/or greater autonomy for the region's predominant Uighur ethnic group. However, while some are known to have links to the Taliban, al-Qaeda, and other transnational *jihadi* groups, terrorist activity against the Chinese state has been limited. Beijing has combated this perceived threat with strict controls on religious practice and education in Xinjiang, as well as the liberal use of state security forces in suppressing dissent and demonstrations.

As in China, Muslims constitute less than two percent of the Australian population. Unlike China, however, Australia has had relatively few problems with its Muslim population and Islamist groups have found Australia inhospitable for planning or conducting terrorist attacks, although they have made attempts at recruiting and fundraising on the island continent. Some Islamist civil society and charity groups, most notably Hizb ut Tahrir, remain active in Australia, but the population at large has expressed determined opposition to the most basic Islamist ideas and ideologies.

CHINA

QUICK FACTS

Population: 1,330,141,295

Area: 9,596,961 sq km

Ethnic Groups: Han Chinese 91.5%, Zhuang, Manchu, Hui, Miao, Uyghur, Tujia, Yi, Mongol, Tibetan, Buyi, Dong, Yao, Korean, and other nationalities 8.5%

Religions: Daoist (Taoist), Buddhist, Christian 3-4%, Muslim 1-2%; officially atheist

Government Type: Communist State

GDP (official exchange rate): $4.814 trillion

Map and Quick Facts courtesy of the CIA World Factbook (Last Updated July 2010)

Prior to 1949, China's Nationalist government recognized Muslims as one of the "five peoples" constituting the Chinese nation—along with Manchus, Mongols, Tibetans and Han. The Communist Party of China (CPC) has maintained this recognition and continued to push Muslims toward integration. China, in the words of one official, "allows the practice of religion, but not at the expense of the state."[1] In all, Beijing recognizes ten separate Muslim nationalities, with the largest being Uighurs, Hui and Kazakhs.

China has a total of 21,667,000 Muslims, representing 1.6 percent of the Chinese population and 1.4 percent of the world's Muslims.[2] The spread of Islam in China, particularly in the Xinjiang Uighur Autonomous Region (Xinjiang)—a sprawling Western region of inhospitable deserts and mountains—has long been a source of official concern, resulting in numerous laws restricting religious practices and teaching. Put succinctly, "to be a practicing Muslim in Xinjiang is to live under an intricate series of laws and regulations intended to control the spread and practice of Islam."[3] Nevertheless, signs from the last two years suggest Islam's popularity continues to grow, along with Muslim dissatisfaction with official policies, particularly in the region of Xinjiang.

ISLAMIST ACTIVITY

Chinese authorities divide their struggle against the "three forces" of separatism, extremism and terrorism into five phases between 1990 and 2007.[4] During this period, religious radicalism within China underwent a significant metamorphosis:

- 1990-1995: Four terrorist organizations emerged-*East Turkestan Islamic Movement (ETIM) [aka al-Hizb al-Islami al-Turkistani* (Turkistan Islamic Party -TIP)], the East Turkestan Islamic Reform Party, the East Turkestan Democratic Reform Party, and the East Turkestan Justice Party - and low grade violence and civil disobedience increased. (Of these, only ETIM/TIP is still active.)
- 1996-1997: Emerging Islamist movements pushed for the politicization of religion to boost recruitment.
- 1997-1999: Islamist expanded their extremist activities and links to foreign actors and began attacks beyond Xinjiang.
- 2000-2002: Terrorist activities were rolled back as regional law enforcement officials cracked down on Islamists.
- 2003-2007: Islamist radicals became more involved in criminal conduct such as weapons and drug smuggling.

The Xinjiang Autonomous Region is the epicenter of these concerns, and the focal point of China's long-running anti-terror campaign. There, China currently contends with a small but notable challenge from two organizations: ETIM/TIP and the World Uyghur Congress (WUC).

ETIM/TIP

Effectively shut out of official politics for over five decades, "a very small minority within the [Uighur] minority"[5] have become politically active through illegal Islamist groups established to promote Uighur rights and/or separatism. ETIM/TIP is generally accepted as the most active Uighur separatist organization seeking an independent Islamic state in Xinjiang, yet there remains substantial disagreement regarding the extent and sources of its foreign funding as well as its size, location, and ideological influences.

The evolution of the militant Uighur separatist movement—particularly Islamist-based separatism—began in the 1940s, when *Hizbul Islam Li-Turkistan* emerged in Xinjiang to oppose local warlords and later the CPC. After numerous failed uprisings, the movement faded from view for over two decades until reemerging during the relative freedom of the 1980s. In this period, Abdul Hakeen, a founder of *Hizbul Islam Li-Turkistan*, was released and established a series of underground religious schools in Xinjiang to expand the reach of Islam and Uighur nationalist ideologies; among his students was ETIM's founder, Hasan Mahsum.[6]

In April 1990, after Uighur Islamists in Xinjiang were discovered plotting an uprising, Beijing launched a series of what it called "strike hard" campaigns to suppress the nascent Islamist rebellion. The clampdown, however, did not have its intended effect; while in prison, Uighur separatists arrested in these crackdowns honed and spread their Islamist-separatist ideologies. The result was the development and dissemination of increasingly extreme Islamist ideologies and the expansion of interpersonal networks among Uighur radicals. According to the global intelligence firm Stratfor, during the 1990s ETIM's efforts to gain support from the Uighur Diaspora in Saudi Arabia, Pakistan and Turkey failed, forcing them to turn to more radical elements in the Taliban, al-Qaeda and the Islamic Movement of Uzbekistan (IMU) for support.[7] Between 1998 and the U.S. invasion of Afghanistan in 2001, Stratfor reports that ETIM was based in Kabul and "recruiting and training Uighur militants while expanding ties with the emerging *jihadist* movement in the region."[8] In a 2009 interview, ETIM's current leader, Amir Abdul Haq, also claimed to have attended training camps in Afghanistan with his ETIM colleagues in the late 1990s.[9]

For at least a decade, Beijing has stridently declared that ETIM/TIP received substantial funding as well as weapons, transportation, and safe haven for wanted Uighurs, from the Taliban and al-Qaeda.[10] After September 11, 2001, Beijing pressed Washington to name the group a terrorist organization and freeze all of its U.S. assets—something Washington agreed to do in August 2002. Indeed, both U.S. and Chinese intelligence agencies believe that ETIM/TIP has received "training and funding" from the al-Qaeda terror network.[11]

But there is disagreement within the U.S. government on this score. On June 20, 2008, for instance, in the case of *Parhat v. Gates*, the U.S. Court of Appeals for the District of Columbia Circuit rejected the government's evidence of an al-Qaeda-ETIM link, noting that "The grounds for the charges that ETIM was 'associated' with al Qaida [sic] and the Taliban, and that it is engaged in hostilities against the United States or its coalition partners, were statements in classified documents that do not state (or, in most instances, even describe) the sources or rationales for those statements."[12] Similarly, in June 2008 Congressional testimony, former Deputy Assistant Secretary of State for East Asia Randall G. Schriver explained that "the information provided by the Chinese government about suspected terrorists groups was unreliable, and very likely tied to ulterior political motives."[13] He said that U.S. officials resisted Chinese pressure to designate other Uighur groups as terrorists, but agreed in the case of ETIM/TIP.[14]

Contemporary ETIM/TIP ideology seeks to weave Uighur political objectives with the oppression of Muslims and the suppression of Islam in Xinjiang. Between 2007 and 2009, ETIM/TIP disseminated numerous online videos, narratives, and messages glorifying the Uighur people's history and calling for continued struggle against China. Yet there is disagreement regarding the current source of ETIM/TIP's funding and ideology. Some analysts say that Uighur publications lately have shown a trend toward rhetoric preferred by al-Qaeda and affiliated groups – a sign that "either the Turkistan Islamic Party is trying to associate itself with al-Qaeda and allied Salafi-Jihadi groups or al-Qaeda is aiming to attract 'Turkistanis' to their global *jihadi* movement."[15] Others, however, suggest that al-Qaeda's ideology has not had as much influence over the evolution of ETIM/TIP as that of Hizb ut-Tahrir; a nonviolent pan-Islamic Sunni movement whose objective is the creation of "an Islamic society such that all of life's affairs in society are administered according to the *Shari'ah* [sic] rules."[16] Yet, as Uighur resentment and frustration with Chinese rule mounted in 2008-09, violent Hizb ut-Tahrir splinter groups appear to have exerted greater influence over ETIM/TIP's ideology and tactics.[17] Meanwhile, Haq himself has acknowledged that ETIM/TIP was part of the military wing of IMU, which is reported to have trained the group's militants after U.S and Chinese forces forced them from Afghanistan and Xinjiang, respectively.[18]

Whatever the source of its funding and ideological influence, in 2008-9 ETIM/TIP's growing radicalism was reflected in both its increasingly Islamist rhetoric and an uptick in attacks against Chinese targets. One Uighur separatist publication, *Turkistan al-Muslimah* (Muslim Turkistan), regularly links Islam and separatism by claiming ETIM/TIP is "seeking freedom and independence and to be ruled by God's *Shari'a*."[19]

World Uyghur Congress

WUC is the most well known international Uighur political organization. It is an umbrella group of smaller Uighur nationalist organizations formed after the East Turkestan National Congress and the World Uyghur Youth Congress merged in April 2004.[20] Participants elect the WUC leadership and General Assembly to serve three-year terms. WUC claims to "peacefully promote the human rights, religious freedom, and democracy for the Uyghur people in East Turkestan."[21] By contrast, Beijing believes that Western nations have used the WUC to clandestinely channel funds and weapons into Xinjiang.[22]

These fears have been fanned by the leadership of the WUC itself. At the organization's third General Assembly in Washington, DC on May 21-25, 2009, delegates and observers unanimously reelected Rebiya Kadeer as president.[23] Ms. Kadeer is a controversial figure; she served as a member of the Chinese People's Political Consultative Conference (CPPCC) in 1992, and a member of China's delegation to the UN's Fourth World Conference on Women in 1995, but after criticizing China's treatment of Uighurs at the 1997 CPPCC session she was stripped of her party membership and forbidden to travel abroad. In 1999, while on her way to meet a U.S. Congressional delegation, Ms. Kadeer was arrested and sentenced to eight years in prison for allegedly "stealing state secrets."[24] The mother of eleven children, she spent six years in a Chinese prison before being released to the United States in 2005. Before her arrest she was also a well-known businesswoman and at one time the seventh wealthiest person in China.[25] China's state-run media has vilified Kadeer,[26] and Chinese officials have accused her of "carrying out reactionary propaganda and deceptive agitation" with the help of "the anti-China forces in the West."[27]

ISLAMISM AND SOCIETY

China has a total of 21,667,000 Muslims (about 2-3 million less than Saudi Arabia), representing 1.6 percent of the Chinese population and 1.4 percent of the world's Muslims.[28] Prior to 1949, China's nationalist government recognized Muslims as one of the "five peoples" constituting the Chinese nation—along with Manchus, Mongols, Tibetans and Han. The CPC expanded this recognition to ten separate Muslim nationalities—with the largest being Uighurs, Hui and Kazakhs—and continues to push Muslims toward integration.

The Uighurs, a Turkic Muslim minority that historically has had tense relations with the Han ethnic group, populates the rugged, mineral-rich territory of Xinjiang. Uighurs are the largest ethnic group in Xinjiang, accounting for 46 percent of the region's total population of roughly 21 million.[29] Many Uighurs favor independence or greater autonomy for Xinjiang, which makes up one-sixth of China's land mass and borders eight Central Asian countries. Uighur activists often refer to Xinjiang as East Turkistan—a onetime-independent republic that existed intermittently since before the Common Era, most recently from 1933 to 1934 and again from 1944 to 1949, before Communist troops took control.[30]

The Uighurs began adopting Sunni Islam in the 10th century. Although patterns of belief vary, Islam has enjoyed a surge in popularity after the harshest decades of Communist rule. There are now roughly 24,000 mosques and 29,000 religious leaders in Xinjiang, and Muslim piety is especially strong in Kashgar, Yarkand, and Khotan.[31] Han Chinese discriminate against Uighurs, who have long complained about officially encouraged Han emigration to Xinjiang and government restrictions on Uighur religion, language and culture. China's authorities largely reject such claims, saying Uighurs should be grateful for Xinjiang's rapid economic development and government targeted investment over the last decade. In 2008-09, these tensions fueled protests against state policies that control the spread the Islam. Beginning in March 2008, a series of Uighur attacks against the authorities and their Han neighbors precipitated a range of increasingly restrictive measures culminating in the mob violence of July 2009.

With a population of about 10 million, the Hui, who make up about half of China's Muslims, are scattered throughout China. They are most numerous in the Ningxia Hui Autonomous Region, Gansu, Qinghai, Henan, Hebei, Shandong, and Xinjiang. Although anthropologists and historians debate their origin, the Hui people are generally accepted as mixed race. Their ancestors include Central Asians, Persians, Han Chinese, and Mongols. During the Tang and Yuan Dynasty, peoples from Central Asian and Persia migrated to China along the fabled Silk Road. Over centuries they intermarried with Mongols and Han Chinese, giving rise to the Hui people. Over time, the Hui have lost their proficiency in Arabic and/or Central Asian languages and become Chinese speakers. Today's Hui are best understood as sinicised Muslims that (unlike other official Muslim groups) look Han and speak Mandarin and/or local dialects. Unlike the Uighurs—whose claim to Xinjiang predates that of the Han—the Hui moved to settle in areas dominated by ethnic Hans.[32]

Hui and Han Chinese generally coexist peacefully, but in October and November 2004 violent clashes broke out in Nanren, Henan. Fierce fighting between the two communities raged for hours and left more than a hundred dead and more than 400 injured.[33] Authorities moved quickly to quell the violence, even deploying paramilitary troops. Yet despite this and other sporadic frictions, the Hui today enjoy far more religious freedom than they did in the first decades of Communist rule, when all religion was repressed. Yet, more religious freedom has also led to an increase in mosque attendance among Hui—a tendency that makes them appear clannish to many Han.[34]

Approximately one million Kazakh Muslims are located in the north of Xinjiang, on the border with Kazakhstan. Unlike the Hui, Kazakhs speak their native language and feel a close connection to clans in neighboring Kazakhstan. In Kazakh society rituals are generally performed in accordance with Islamic tradition, and include prayers, fasting, observance of the *Hajj* (pilgrimage to Mecca), and adherence to Islamic burial rites. Similarly, Kazakhs supplement their legal marriages with traditional ceremonies. Generally speaking, Kazakhs have maintained a better relationship with the Han than have the Uighurs.[35]

The tight controls on information within China, and in Xinjiang in particular, coupled with the severe penalties associated with either financial or rhetorical support for unrecognized Islamic organizations, makes it impossible to determine who gives to Islamist groups and how much. It appears, however, that the Uighur community (rather than the Hui or Kazakhs) is the primary domestic constituency and support base for Islamist movements calling for Xinjiang's independence. *Turkistan al-Muslimah*, for instance, publishes articles on government persecution of Uighurs, but does not mention the plight of Hui or Kazakh Muslims in Xinjiang.[36] The magazine publishes only the names of "martyred" Uighurs and in its first issue the journal stated its aim was exposing "the real situation of our Muslim nation in East Turkistan, which is living under the occupation of the Communist Chinese."[37] Publications of this ilk do not appear to exist within either the Hui or Kazakh communities.

ISLAMISM AND THE STATE

China maintains an intricate system of control over its Muslim minorities. China's Islamic educational institutions, which span grades 1 through 12, are closely monitored by the region's Commission on Religious and Ethnic Affairs (CREA), and its teachers and clergy are thoroughly vetted by the parallel Islamic Association to ensure they do not harbor extremist ideas or tendencies. As a practical matter, this has meant the creation of a series of state sponsored and tightly-controlled religious schools for Chinese Muslims.[38]

Despite policies that give Uighurs preferential admission to China's secular universities, there remains a lack of university-level Islamic education. China currently possesses no Islamic universities or upper level curricula in Islamic affairs.[39] Those Muslims interested in becoming *imams* or religious leaders, therefore, must travel to established Islamic universities in the Middle East, such as Egypt's al-Azhar University, to complete their theological instruction. These educational institutions, however, have historically served as breeding grounds for Islamic extremism (al-Azhar was the birthplace of the Muslim Brotherhood in the early 20th century) thus creating the potential for the radicalization of China's Muslims in the last stage of their theological training.[40]

Foreign funds flowing to Islamic schools—historically a source of radicalization among Muslim communities in other parts of the world—are tightly controlled in China. Foreign funds for education in Muslim communities are channeled through CREA and the official Islamic Association, and the independent construction of mosques and religious schools is strictly prohibited.[41] At the same time, the CPC supplies students' textbooks, thereby controlling the content of what is taught in Muslim educational institutions.

Like all students in China, in order to advance Muslims must reproduce answers that reflect history as described within officially approved texts.

Limits on religious activity likewise abound. Until the unrest of 2008-09 (described below), propaganda and education controls coupled with ample security appeared to have sufficiently mitigated Islamist activity within China's Muslim communities. After widespread unrest in Xinjiang began, however, authorities sought to rigidly enforce laws and provisions that severely restrict the practice and teaching of Islam. These regulations, which had been on the books for years, were now publicly posted online and on banners throughout Xinjiang.[42] Examples of policies that limit Islamic activity include:

- Half-hour limits on sermons
- Prohibition on prayer in public areas
- Prohibitions on the teaching of the Koran in private
- Restrictions on worship, with Muslims only permitted to attend their hometown mosques
- Restrictions on the studying of Arabic to special government schools
- Prohibitions on government workers and CPC members from attending mosque

Two of Islam's five pillars—the sacred fasting month of Ramadan and the *Hajj*—are also carefully controlled in China. To reduce exposure to Islamist teachings, authorities use propaganda and control of passports to compel Muslims to join government-run *Hajj* tours rather than travel illegally to Mecca.[43] Yet, policies that compel students and government workers to eat during the holy month of Ramadan have faced the most pushback. In 2007, one university in Kashgar forced students to eat during the day by locking its gates and putting glass shards atop the campus walls to prevent them from returning home after dark to break the daily fast.[44]

Similarly, China's Muslims are systematically shut out of national (although not regional) politics. One major reason is that Han Chinese—even those with progressive tendencies toward constitutional democracy—often cannot see the difference between a politically active Uighur and a separatist.[45]

Until quite recently, China did not have a terrorism problem, at least not one as commonly understood in the West. Although low-grade insurgent activity did unquestionably exist, regional law enforcement agencies appeared to have effectively neutralized Islamist radicals until 2008-9. While there was, and remains, no indication that radicals in Xinjiang enjoy widespread popularity in other parts of the country, the state's increasingly tight controls on the practice of Islam and limits on speech and movement have engendered widespread frustration and anger among Muslims, Uighurs in particular. Building resentment of heavy-handed state intervention in religious life—not the insidious intervention of foreign influences, as Beijing claims—has solidified the separatist movement, given it grassroots support, and catalyzed a campaign of Uighur aggression against the state in 2008-9.

Although the details remain unclear, it appears that state repression of Islam was the catalyst for a wave of Uighur unrest including a variety of attacks against the Chinese authorities, military, and the Han citizenry that took place in the spring and summer of 2008. Between May and August 2008, Uighur separatists reportedly attacked police in Wenzhou using an explosive-laden tractor,[46] bombed a Guangzhou plastic factory,[47] and coordinated a series of deadly bus bombings in Shanghai and Kunming.[48] These attacks culminated with two deadly terrorist attacks in early August 2008—the first involving an assault on police officers in Kashgar,[49] and the second involving a series of 12 homemade pipe bombs that simultaneously hit a public security station, the industrial and commercial administrative office, a local department store, a post and telecommunications office and a hotel in the city of Kuqa.[50]

In response, Chinese authorities launched a series of countermeasures. In August 2008, hundreds of Uighurs were detained and thousands of paramilitary forces were deployed throughout Xinjiang. Police patrolled Kashgar's Uighur neighborhoods, entering houses to check occupants' names against a government list.[51] By the end of that month, approximately 200,000 police had been mobilized to "check and register" the transient Uighur population. Police swept hotel rooms, rental apartments, and remote villages for separatists and set up checkpoints between townships and villages.[52] These enhanced security efforts reportedly uncovered 12 cells operating in Kashgar, resulting in 66 arrests; five cells in Urumqi, resulting in 82 arrests, and; the destruction of "41 training camps that had been engaged in illegal proselytizing and the training of *jihadists*."[53] The crackdown culminated in the reinstatement of the "10-household mutually insured system" in Kashgar and Khotan. Under that policy, if one person is found guilty of anti-state activities, the 10 neighboring families will also be held responsible.[54]

The state's campaign targeting the "three evil forces" also led to greater emphasis on regulations restricting Islam by local governments within Xinjiang.[55] The strict enforcement of laws designed to inhibit the practice and spread of Islam appears to have significantly eroded public support for the state and galvanized public anger and resentment into a force that extremists can manipulate. In this way, increased security measures have served to confirm Islamist claims about state repression. Indeed, almost 1,300 state security-related arrests were carried out in Xinjiang between January-November 2008, and about one-half of all trials in China related to the crime of endangering state security take place in Xinjiang.[56]

Beijing has long had a policy of encouraging Uighur migration to other parts of China in the hope that economic opportunities and intermarriage will gradually integrate Muslim Uighurs into secular Chinese society. Although the incidents that sparked the large-scale ethnic violence in July 2009 took place thousands of miles away in Shaoguan, Guangdong,[57] the massive scale of the Uighur response in Urumqi reflected widespread public hostility towards the state's tightened restrictions on Islamic activity. Thousands took to the streets on July 5th in an initially peaceful protest that turned violent against the state and ethnic Hans. The Han responded with their own wave of anti-Uighur violence and when the smoke cleared nearly 200 were dead and at least 1,680 injured, most of them Han.[58]

Soon after state security suppressed the Urumqi riots, authorities in Yining "smashed two violence gangs, and arrested more than 70 suspects," according to Jiao Baohua, secretary of the Yining city CPC committee.[59] In all, the Chinese state has implemented a series of new measures designed to prevent further violence. These steps entailed:

- *Increased security*, including the deployment of thousands of armed police, special police, and public security personnel to patrol the Uighur sections of Xinjiang's capital city, Urumqi, and carry out numerous raids;[60] new city government ordinances calling on all local businesses and residents to register guests with the authorities;[61] new traffic restrictions and a city-wide after dark curfew;[62] harsh sentences for those involved in the riots;[63] and manhunts for suspected Islamists.[64]

- *Expanded propaganda*, including the initiation of "face-to-face interactions to explain the truth and expose the lies and sinister intentions of the hostile forces both at home and abroad, and preach the importance of nationality solidarity and stability";[65] the creation of Uighur working groups "to conduct intensive propaganda and educational work and to safeguard social stability";[66] and the deployment of some 2,100 more officials and police to communities in Urumqi "to explain government policies and solve disputes."[67]

- *Improved information and financial controls*, including the suspension of text-messaging and Internet services in Xinjiang between July 2009 and January 2010;[68] and a region-wide effort by law enforcement agencies throughout 2009 to target the finances and properties of extremists and groups agitating for Uighur independence.[69]

- *Legal controls*, including new restrictions on—and warnings to— lawyers,[70] as well as death sentences for some rioters and harsh prison sentences for others.[71]
- *Investment*: Investment injected from the central government and state-owned enterprises will help Xinjiang "realize fast-paced economic development." The central government has also paired up Chinese municipalities and provinces with different areas of Xinjiang to provide large amounts of capital, technology and talent. (The term "talent" may be a euphemism for "Han Chinese labor immigration," a major source of irritation within the Uighur minority.)[72]
- *A reshuffle of governmental personnel*, including the ouster of Urumqi's Communist Party Secretary, Li Zhi, and Xinjiang's regional police chief. Wang Lequan, the hard-line secretary of the CPC Committee of Xinjiang for 15 years and an ally of President Hu Jintao, came under unprecedented pressure but managed to retain his post until April 2010.[73] He was finally transferred to Beijing and replaced with Zhang Chunxian, who as Party chief of Hunan province gained the reputation as a soft-liner.

Today Xinjiang remains a difficult place to practice Islam. A vicious cycle of repression and rebellion now exists whereby the state's suppression of Islam continues to broaden the appeal of extremist Islamist ideologies among Uighurs.

ENDNOTES

[1]Interviews by American Foreign Policy Council scholars, Xinjiang, China, June 2008.

[2] "Mapping the Global Muslim Population: A Report on the Size and Distribution of the World's Muslim Population," *The Pew Forum on Religion and Public Life*, October 2009. http://pewforum. org/docs/?DocID=458 [3] Edward Wong, "Wary Of Islam, China Tightens A Vise Of Rules," New York Times, October 18, 2008, http://www.nytimes.com/2008/10/19/world/asia/19xinjiang.html?_ r=3&hp&oref=slogin

[4] Interviews by American Foreign Policy Council scholars, Xinjiang, China, June 2008.

[5] Randal G. Schriver, Testimony before the U.S. House of Representatives Committee on Foreign Affairs, Subcommittee on International Organizations, Human Rights and Oversight, June 16, 2009, http:// www.internationalrelations.house.gov/hearing_notice.asp?id=1083.

[6] Rodger Baker, "China and the Enduring Uighurs," *Stratfor Terrorism Intelligence Report*, August 6, 2008, http://www.stratfor.com/weekly/ china_and_enduring_uighurs.

[7] Ibid.

[8] Ibidem.

[9] Murad Batal Al-Shishani, "Journal of the Turkistan Islamic Party Urges Jihad in China," Jamestown Foundation *Terrorism Monitor 7*, iss.9, April 10, 2009, http://www.jamestown.org/programs/gta/single/ ?tx_ttnews[tt_news]=34838&tx_ttnews[backPid]=412&no_cache=1.

[10] Sean L. Yom, "Uighurs Flex Their Muscles," *Asia Times*, January 23, 2002, http://www.atimes.com/china/DA23Ad01.html.

[11] Holly Fletcher and Jayshree Bajoria, "Backgrounder: The East Turkestan Islamic Movement (ETIM)," Council on Foreign Relations, July 31, 2008, http://www.cfr.org/publication/9179/east_turkestan_ islamic_movement_etim.html#p1.

[12] "On Petition for Review of an Order of a Combatant Status Review Tribunal," *Huzaifa Parhat v. Robert M. Gates, Secretary of Defense et. al.*, United States Court of Appeals for the District of Columbia Circuit, June 20, 2008, 7, www.fas.org/sgp/jud/parhat.pdf.

[13] Schriver, Testimony before the U.S. House of Representatives Committee on Foreign Affairs, Subcommittee on International Organizations, Human Rights and Oversight.

[14] Ibid.

[15] Al-Shishani, "Journal of the Turkistan Islamic Party Urges Jihad in China."

[16] "About Hizb ut-Tahrir," Official website of Hizb ut-Tahrir, n.d., http://web.archive.org/web/20070927200032/www.hizb-ut-tahrir. info/english/about.htm.

[17] Baker, "China and the Enduring Uighurs."

[18] Al-Shishani, "Journal of the Turkistan Islamic Party Urges Jihad in China."

[19] Ibid.

[20] "Introducing the World Uyghur Congress," Official Website of the World Uyghur Congress, n.d., http://www.uyghurcongress.org/en/?cat=149.

[21] Ibid.

[22] "Jiangdu, gai kongxi cilue," (Uighur separatists changed terrorism strategy) *Ta Kung Pao* (Hong Kong), August 11, 2008. http://www.takungpao.com/news/08/08/11/BJ-945008.htm.

[23] "Introducing the World Uyghur Congress."

[24] Erik Eckholm, "Exile in the U.S. Becomes Face of Uighurs," *New York Times*, July 8, 2009, http://www.nytimes.com/2009/07/09/world/asia/09kadeer.html.

[25] "Biographical sketch of Rebiya Kadeer," Official Website of the Uyghur American Association, October 12, 2006, http://www.uyghuramerican.org/articles/595/1/Biographical-sketch-of-Rebiya-Kadeer/Biographical-sketch-of-Rebiya-Kadeer.html.

[26] "Rebiya Kadeer Lies Again," Xinhua (Beijing), August 12, 2009, http://www.china.org.cn/china/xinjiang_unrest/2009-08/12/content_18319555.htm.

[27] "Rebiya shi Xinjiang kongximu hou yuan xiong," (Rebiya accused of being behind Uighur terrorist attack) Ta Kung Pao (Hong Kong), September 12, 2008, http://www.takungpao.com/news/08/09/12/ZM-59848.htm.

[28] "Mapping the Global Muslim Population."

[29] Chris Buckley, "Heavy security in China's Xinjiang, stability urged," Reuters, July 12, 2009, http://www.reuters.com/article/idUS-TRE56907020090712.

[30] "East Turkistan: A Crossroads of Civilizations," undated online posting. http://www.eastturkestan.net/china03.html.

[31] Wong, "Wary of Islam, China Tightens a Vise of Rules."

[32] Richard Baum, *China Watcher: Confessions of a Peking Tom* (Seattle: University of Washington Press, 2010) 204.

[33] Jehangir S. Pocha, "Violent ethnic clashes plague China: Growing divide after deadly riots," *Boston Globe*, December 19, 2004, http://www.boston.com/news/world/articles/2004/12/19/violent_ethnic_clashes_plague_china/?page=2

[34] Ibid.

[35] Iraj Bashiri, "The Kazakhs of China," Personal website hosted by Angelfire, 2002, http://www.angelfire.com/rnb/bashiri/kazakhschina/kazakhschina.html.

[36] Al-Shishani, "Journal of the Turkistan Islamic Party Urges Jihad in China."

[37] Ibid.

[38] Interviews by American Foreign Policy Council scholars, Xinjiang, China, June 2008.

[39] Ibid.

[40] Ibidem.

[41] Ibidem.

[42] Wong, "Wary of Islam, China Tightens a Vise of Rules."

[43] Ibid.

[44] Ibidem.

[45] Louisa Greve, Testimony before the Congressional-Executive Commission on China, February 13, 2009, http://frwebgate.access.gpo.gov/cgi-bin/getdoc.cgi?dbname=111_house_hearings&docid=f:48222.wais.

[46] "Uighur Group Claims China Bus Blasts, Threatens Olympics," Agence France Presse, July 26, 2008, http://www.channelnewsasia.com/stories/afp_asiapacific/view/362893/1/.html.

[47] Ibid.

[48] "Chinese Police Deny 'Terrorist Attacks' Behind Recent Explosions," The People's Daily (Beijing), July 27, 2008, http://english.peopledaily.com.cn/90001/90776/90882/6459960.html.

[49] Edmond Wong, "2 Uighurs Sentenced to Death for West China Police Assault," The New York Times, December 17, 2008. http://www.nytimes.com/2008/12/18/world/asia/18kashgar.html

[50] "Xinjiang Kuche jingbao Beijing jingjie shenggao," [Explosion in Kuqa, Xinjiang, Beijing raised security alarm.] Apple Daily (Hong Kong), August 11, 2008. http://tw.nextmedia.com/applenews/article/art_id/30842646/IssueID/20080811.

[51] Jill Drew, "China's Uighurs Wary, Worried After Attack," Washington Post, August 6, 2008, http://www.washingtonpost.com/wp-dyn/content/article/2008/08/05/AR2008080502383.html?nav=rss_world/asia.

[52] Chi-yuk Choi, "Security Stepped Up In Xinjiang For National Day," South China Morning Post (Hong Kong), August 28, 2008.

[53] "Keshi wujing yuxi shiliu si zhuanjia zhi jiangdufenzi suowei jingao: zuohao yiqie zhunbei duidang gezhong weixie," [Chinese experts link Xinjiang terror attacks to international backgrounds] Wen Wei Po (Hong Kong), August 5, 2008, A01.

[54] "200,000 Military Police Conduct Carpet Search for Terrorist Suspects To Prevent Terrorist Strikes During the 1 October Period," Hong Kong Information Centre for Human Rights and Democracy, August 27, 2008, http://www.hkhkhk.com/engpro/messages/2457.html.

[55] Wong, "Wary of Islam, China Tightens a Vise of Rules."

[56] Greve, Testimony before the Congressional-Executive Commission on China.

[57] After rumors circulated that Uighur employees a toy factory had

---

raped a Han woman a Han mob beat two (of their nearly 800) Uighur coworkers to death with iron bars and prevented medics from treating their injuries. The rape rumors were false and when word reached Xinjiang the lynching pushed simmering Uighur anger over the boiling point. See "Death Penalty Upheld For Man In South China Factory Brawl," Xinhua (Beijing), October 28, 2009, http://www.highbeam.com/doc/1P2-20946078.html; See also Kathleen E. McLaughlin, "Fear Grips Shaoguan's Uighurs," *Far Eastern Economic Review*," July 17, 2009, http://www.feer.com/politics/2009/july58/Fear-Grips-Shaoguans-Uighurs.

[58] Kristine Kwok, "Campaign To 'Strike hard' At Xinjiang Rioters," *South China Morning Post* (Hong Kong), November 4, 2009, http://eng.chinamil.com.cn/news-channels/2009-11/03/content_4073113.htm.

[59] Zhu Jingzhao, "Xinjiang yining dadiao liangbaoli fanzui tuanhuo, zhuabu shean qishiyuren," (Yining, Xinjiang wiped out two groups of violent crime suspects, arrested more than 70 people) *Zhongguo Xinwen She* [Beijing], July 13, 2009. http://news.qq.com/a/20090713/001079.htm

[60] "Jiehou Wulumuqi jianwen: wending yadao yiqie," (Life in Urumqi after the festival: Stability is everything), *Ta Kung Pao* [Hong Kong], July 18, 2009, http://www.takungpao.com/news/09/07/18/xjsl_xgbd-1113938.htm

[61] "Riot-Hit Urumqi To Tighten Migrant Population Administration," Government of the People's Republic of China, August 9, 2009, [62] http://www.gov.cn/english/2009-08/09/content_1387239.htm.

[63] "China Imposes Curfew In Capital Of Xinjiang ," *Kyodo News Agency* (Japan), September 7, 2009, http://home.kyodo.co.jp/modules/fstStory/index.php?storyid=458736.

[64] "Times Topics: Uighurs," *New York Times,* November 10, 2009, http://topics.nytimes.com/top/reference/timestopics/subjects/u/uighurs_chinese_ethnic_group/index.html?inline=nyt-classifier.

[65] Kwok, "Campaign To 'Strike hard' At Xinjiang Rioters."

[66] "Jiehou Wulumuqi jianwen," (Life in Urumqi after the festival).

[67] "Wulumuqi jixu zengjia jinli weihu shehui wending," (Urumqi keeps sending in police to maintain social stability) *Zhongguo Xingwen She* [Beijing] July 31, 2009. http://www.xj.chinanews.com/html/V69/2010/02/20/8304634919.htm

[68] "2,100 Officials Sent To Appease Uygur, Han People," *China Daily* (Beijing), September 6, 2009, http://www.chinadaily.com.cn/china/2009-09/06/content_8660271.htm.

[69] Andrew Jacobs, "China Restores Text Messaging in Xinjiang," *New York Times*, January 17, 2010, http://www.nytimes.com/2010/01/18/world/asia/18china.html.

[70] "Xinjiang Police Launches Anti-Crime Campaign To Safeguard

Stability," *China Military Online*, November 3, 2009, http://eng.chinamil.com.cn/news-channels/2009-11/03/content_4073113.htm.

[71] Human Rights Watch, "China: Xinjiang Trials Deny Justice, Proceedings Failed Minimum Fair Trial Standards," October 15, 2009, http://www.hrw.org/en/news/2009/10/15/china-xinjiang-trials-deny-justice

[72] Cui Jia, "Murderers in Urumqi riots will not appeal," *China Daily* (Beijing), October 27, 2009. http://www.chinadaily.com.cn/cndy/2009-10/27/content_8852664.htm.

[73] Cui Jia, "Xinjiang to receive massive input," *China Daily* (Beijing), March 15, 2010.

[74] Christopher Bodeen, "China Xinjiang Chief Survives Political Firestorm," Associated Press, September 6, 2009, http://abcnews.go.com/International/wireStory?id=8502607.

THAILAND

QUICK FACTS

Population: 66,404,688

Area: 513,120 sq km

Ethnic Groups: Thai 75%, Chinese 14%, other 11%

Religions: Buddhist 94.6%, Muslim 4.6%, Christian 0.7%, other 0.1%

Government Type: Constitutional Monarchy

GDP (official exchange rate): $269.6 billion

Map and Quick Facts courtesy of the CIA World Factbook (Last Updated June 2010)

Since January 2004, the three southernmost provinces of Thailand have been in the throes of an ethno-religious insurgency. Malay-Muslim rebellion is not new in the overwhelmingly Buddhist kingdom, and has erupted sporadically since the 1902 Sino-British demarcation of the border that left a Malay majority in the provinces of Yala, Pattani, Narathiwat, Saitun and parts of Songkhla. Since then, official Thai government policy has been based on assimilation of the 1.3 million Muslims there (of the total 1.8 million population in the south), which has further alienated the local population. All-out insurgency raged from the 1960s to the 1990s. However, the insurgents themselves were riddled with factional and ideological differences. They included Islamists, more-secular ethno-nationalists, and groups affiliated with the Malayan Communist Party. Some favored independence, others union with Malaysia, and others simply greater autonomy. The Thai government, though fairly brutal in its counterinsurgency operations at first, was able to defeat these groups one by one, and began to implement general amnesties and pour development funds into the region. By the mid-1990s, the last major insurgent group, the Pattani United Liberation Organization (PULO), accepted the government's amnesty, and by 2002 the government declared victory, dismantling the key agencies that brought the insurgency to an end. Yet local

---

grievances remained deep-seated, and a small cadre of Islamists and veterans of the Afghan jihad went underground, organizing amongst the youth in madrassas, private Islamic schools and mosques. After a decade-long incubation, the insurgency re-ignited in 2004.

Though it began on a small scale, Thai government missteps and egregious human rights violations, compounded by political posturing, have led to an increase in the scope of violence and degree of support for the current insurgency. Now in its eighth year, and fifth government, no end is in sight, with more than 4,500 people dead, and nearly 10,000 wounded. While violence declined dramatically in 2008 (with the death toll falling by 40 percent from 2007), the level of violence increased anew in 2009-2010.[1] In the process, the social fabric of southern Thailand has been irreparably harmed, with little hope of reconciliation among its various communities. Counterinsurgency operations, meanwhile, have been hampered by weak intelligence, human rights abuses and a lack of political concern at the national level.

ISLAMIST ACTIVITY

The current insurgency is being led primarily by two groups: most directly, the *Barisan Revolusin Nasional Coordinasi* (BRN-C) and, to a lesser extent, the *Gerakan Mujiheddin Islamiya Pattani* (GMIP). In addition, former members of New PULO and other now-defunct insurgent groups are also active. These groups tend to be loose-knit in nature, and organized horizontally.

The BRN-C has evolved significantly since the 1970s, when its precursor, the BRN, was more closely allied with the Malayan Communist Party. The BRN subsequently splintered and the BRN-C—one of three offshoots—became increasingly Islamized. The BRN-C operated and recruited through a large network of mosques and private Islamic schools that were beyond the reach of the Thai state. Its top leaders, such as Sapaeng Basoe, Masae Useng, and Doromae Kuteh, were masters at several key Islamic schools in the region. In 1992, they established a quasi-overt youth organization known as *Pemuda*.[2] The BRN-C operates through a network of some 300 schools.[3]

The BRN-C's averred goal is to establish an independent Islamic state for the Malay Muslims who inhabit southern Thailand. The organization has a clear social agenda: the Islamization of society in the southern provinces. While the local community—which is adjacent to, and closely intertwined with, the Malaysian Islamist political opposition's heartland in Northeastern Malaysia—is pious and culturally very conservative, the BRN-C is imposing what amounts to the total Islamization of institutions and values. The group has targeted secular institutions—schools in particular, but also hospitals and courts—in order to force the community into parallel Islamist institutions.

It has forced the separation (*purdah*) of men and women, and increased pressure for the full veiling (beyond the traditional *hijab*) of women. While much of the group's campaign of violence has been oriented at driving Thai Buddhists from the region, the BRN-C also has espoused a policy of isolation and non-contact with Buddhists, forbidding people to work or do business with Thais of that religion. Muslim women have increasingly forgone treatment at public hospitals, which are largely staffed by Buddhists from the north. Home births, coupled with the lack of registration of newborns so conceived, are putting a generation of Thai Muslims outside the purview of state institutions. As such, infant mortality in the south is now three times the national average.[4] Diseases such as polio likewise are spreading, due to a decline in vaccinations.[5]

The handful of BRN-C documents captured by authorities to date suggests a strategy of protracted (30-40 year) struggle, with the ultimate goal of establishing an independent Islamic state. The short-term goals of the group are more achievable: driving out "Siamese *kaffirs*" (unbelievers), the inculcation of Islamic values, the establishment of Islamic institutions to supplant all secular institutions, and the elimination of political rivals, in particular moderate Muslims who either collaborate with or support reconciliation with the Thai state. Indeed, well over half of the victims of the insurgents to date have been their co-religionists.

The BRN-C appears to be horizontally-organized, but that is in part a reflection of how little is known about the group. While Thai security officials have identified a top cadre of leaders, they know very little about the organization's middle-managers. Moreover, the group is highly atomized; the arrest of thousands of low-level operatives has garnered very little by way of understanding of the organization as a whole. There is a regional structure (*ayoh*) that is comprised of cells at the district and village levels. Most are localized in nature, bound to their villages, but some cells have a regional mandate.

The size of the BRN-C likewise is uncertain. Thai security forces have asserted that it is in the tens of thousands, but the number of actual cadres involved in the group's management and operations is much smaller—probably in the low thousands. The number of activists and supporters, however, is closer to the Thai government's estimate. *Pemuda* itself is believed to have several thousand members.

The second group widely involved in the insurgency is the *Gerakan Mujiheddin Islamiya Pattani* (GMIP). The GMIP was originally a criminal gang closely linked to GAM, the Acehnese resistance movement in Indonesia for whom it ran guns. The GMIP was implicated in contract killings and affiliated with criminal syndicates until two veterans of the Afghan *mujahideen* took over the organization. Though much smaller than the BRN-C and lacking the latter's broad-based social network of *madrassas* and mosques, the GMIP is a very violent organization with significant operational capabilities. It had close working ties with cells of *Jemaah Islamiya*h in Malaysia.[6] The leadership of the GMIP includes: Nasae Saning, Mahma Maeroh, and Wae Ali Copter Waeji.

Unlike in the period from the 1960s-1990s, when disparate insurgent groups were riddled with factionalism, the BRN-C and GMIP today appear to work together closely. They have shared goals and ideology, and do not operate at cross-purposes or try to discredit one another. Indeed there is a significant degree of operational cooperation between the two organizations.

Funding for the insurgency is broad-based and thus not vulnerable to Thai government attempts at interdiction. At the local level, insurgents rely on extortion of local businesses and often leave letters with exact demands at businesses and homes. They have applied the concept of *dhimmitude* (second class citizenship for non-Muslims) to Buddhists.[7] They also rely on voluntary contributions by the local Muslim community, as well as funds from like-minded sources throughout the region and Middle East. As of 2005/2006, an estimated 6 million ($183,000) in Ramadan donations was believed to have been received by Thai insurgents from Muslims in Egypt, Libya, Sweden, Indonesia, and Malaysia.[8] The Thai government has consistently alleged that insurgents fund themselves through their involvement in the drug trade. However, there has been only mixed evidence to support this. Though there is a sizeable amount of drug smuggling into Malaysia, it is widely controlled by criminal syndicates. Moreover, the Malaysian government's zero tolerance policy towards drugs makes the narcotic trade an unattractive one for Thai insurgents, exposing them to greater risk of government action.

Significant money from the Middle East, in particular from Saudi Arabia, came into the region during the 1990s and early 2000s to support *madrassas* and Islamic education. Such funding has come from the Muslim World League (MWL), the Al Haramain Foundation, the International Islamic Relief Organization (IIRO), and from the *Al-Auqaf* (Welfare Department) and Islamic Call Society in Kuwait.[9] In 2004, the Thai Minister of Defense accused the IIRO of donating more than Bt100 million ($2 million) to Thai organizations.[10] Ismail Lutfi Japagiya, the rector of the Yala Islamic College, a school with deep ties to the insurgency, has admitted publicly to accepting $13 million from the IIRO, and some U.S. $7.8 million from Kuwait.[11] Not coincidentally, Lutfi serves as one of the few non-Arab directors of the MWL.[12] The Saudi Om al-Qura Foundation also had close ties to a cell of the al-Qaeda-linked terrorist organization Jemaah Islamiyah active in southern Thailand. Much of the Gulf money came through a Thai-registered charity, the Pusaka Foundation, which has since been shut down. Thai security officials, however, are convinced that the Pusaka Foundation continues to operate and distribute funds through Islamic banks in neighboring Malaysia.[13] The imposition of Salafi values such as veils and the closing of shops on Fridays, rather than violence, appears to have been the key to winning financial support from the Gulf.

It should be noted that Thailand's is a low-level insurgency and does not require significant funding. Most weapons are acquired through theft or after battles with government forces or local village defense volunteers. Most materials for bomb-making are readily available via purchases and/or theft. Mosques and *madrassas* controlled or supportive of insurgents are self-supporting. While some operatives who have been captured have confessed to being paid for operations, the amounts thus received are trifling.

Violence is down from its peak in 2007. In July of that year, the Thai army authorized its own "surge" of forces, and there are currently more than 60,000 troops deployed in the south. In 2008, in part as a result of this expansion of military power, violence dropped precipitously. By January 2008, the average daily rate of killing was down to three, while the average number of weekly acts of violence had fallen by half, from 40 to 20. In 2008, the death toll fell by 40 percent from its 2007 peak. But since the current government of Abhisit Vejjajiva assumed power in mid-December 2008, violence has escalated steadily and the death toll has risen by 11 percent. Over 830 people have been killed, and nearly 1,500 people have been wounded, since the Democrats took over in mid-December 2008. In that time, there have been over 300 bombings, including five car bombings, nine beheadings, and 29 incidents of the burning or desecration of corpses. There have been over 50 arson attacks, including 12 schools. The government has spent 145 billion baht (close to $5 million) during the past seven years to support military operations in the South but is unable to quell the violence. Undoubtedly, Thailand is the single most lethal such conflict in the region.[14]

ISLAMISM AND SOCIETY

Popular support for Islamist groups in Thailand is hard to gauge. Whereas public opinion polling has demonstrated high levels of distrust towards the state on the part of Malay Muslims, the degree of popular support for the BRN-C and GMIP is unknown. Like at the onset of any insurgency, these organizations are widely viewed as a fringe group of extremists. But government crackdowns, abuses and extra-judicial killings have increased their appeal dramatically, allowing insurgents to convince the local population that the Thai state is repressive and patently anti-Muslim. As a result, Thai officials estimate that 30 percent of the country's Muslim community supports the insurgents.[15]

The Thai state has lost much of its legitimacy, and its constant reliance on death squads has alienated the population.[16] The 2005 Emergency Decree that governs southern Thailand has also infuriated the local population. The decree allows for detention without trial for up to 28 days. Due to police incompetence and a lack of public assistance, the charges against most suspects are dropped, and nearly 90 percent of those captured on charges of participating in the insurgency are released. This again further legitimizes the latter while discrediting the state.

For example, by November 2007 some 1,930 insurgent suspects had been detained. Nonetheless, only 300 had been linked to acts of violence, and according to a March 2007 Human Rights Watch report, only 15 of some 350 people arrested had been charged.[17] The Army ignited a firestorm of protest when, in mid-2007, it initiated a program that forced suspected detainees into an army-run vocational training program upon their release after the 28-day detention expired. In all, more than 300 individuals were forcibly detained, until the courts shut down the program and allowed all suspects to be released.[18] Of the 7,860 people detained since January 2004, the government has only charged 1,500 of them (19 percent), and the acquittal rate of those charged has been 43 percent.[19]

But how much real support there is for the insurgency is unknown. As mentioned above, the militants have killed more of their co-religionists than they have Buddhist civilians or security officials. Yet sadly, even Muslim victims tend to attribute the violence to government forces. In much of the countryside, which has only a limited and static security force, the insurgents have free reign to impose their will and social mores on society. The Thai government has over 80,000 security forces deployed in the south, but most are confined to large bases and if they are deployed, remain in fixed positions. Villagers have little sense of security, and those perceived as being collaborators are killed or threatened.

There is not currently an official Thai Islamist political party, and no political party publicly endorses the insurgency or its goals. Indeed, southern Thailand is the bastion of the Democrat Party, which currently leads the government. Though political support has waned considerably in the past few six years, it remains the largest single political party in the region. Before the start of Thailand's political turmoil in 2006, there was a bloc of Muslim politicians, including several avowedly Islamist ones, who were co-opted and brought into the party of former prime minister Thaksin Shinawatra, *Thai Rak Thai* (TRT). Buoyed by Thaksin and TRT's enormous popularity, the *Wadah* faction, as it was known, became the first political challenge to the Democrat Party in the region. But the party fell out of favor, and took issue with Thaksin's heavy-handed approach to the insurgency. There have been allegations that senior members of the *Wadah* faction have some personal ties to the insurgency[20], though the party as a whole has distanced itself from the unrest. The legal and political dismantling of the TRT party since the September 2006 coup, meanwhile, has moved *Wadah* into its own orbit, and it merits further scrutiny in the future. There are some *Wadah* members in the *Pueh Thai* Party, the latest re-incarnation of the TRT, but they do not possess the cohesion and clout they did under Thaksin. The leading voice of the *Wadah* faction is Waemahadi Waedaoh, who has gained prominence for his calls for autonomy for the Muslim south.[21]

The insurgents finance their operations through a wide variety of means, both legal and illegal, and donations undoubtedly play a role. However, the extent to which members of the insurgency divert funds from local mosques and charities into the insurgency's coffers with the knowledge or support of the local community is unclear.

Gauging the popularity of the insurgency is all but impossible. It clearly has more grassroots support than it did when it began in January 2004. Much of that comes as public dissatisfaction and moral outrage toward the government's handling of the insurgency has soared.[22] Government security forces get little in the way of public support. Tellingly, nearly no senior leaders of the insurgency have been killed or captured. Even at the local level, people are unwilling to provide intelligence or evidence to assist official investigations. How much of this is due to intimidation on the part of the insurgents is impossible to guess. The public often attributes killings to the government, even when the evidence often points to insurgents.

For their part, the insurgents seem to have calibrated the degree of violence necessary to achieve their short-term goals. There is no reason why the daily death tolls could not be significantly higher. Insurgents regularly use improvised explosive devices (IEDs), but most of the casualties come from drive-by shootings carried out by pillion motorcycle riders. There are few frontal assaults on police or army posts, despite the absence of physical or resource constraints on escalating the violence. The overwhelming consideration appears to be a potential loss of popular support if insurgents choose to drastically escalate the violence.

Public opinion and commitment towards Islamism generally has improved and deepened. The influence of Malaysia's neighboring Kelantan state, which the fundamentalist Pan-Malaysian Islamic Party (or PAS) has dominated since 1999, is strong. The Muslim public in southern Thailand tends to see PAS' rule as being far better than anything the Thai government has provided. As importantly, they credit PAS for ridding the province of the corrupting influences of the non-Muslim community.

There has been a flurry of both mosque and *madrassa* construction since the mid-1990s, and the tempo has not subsided in the past few years. While much of the funding through 2004-05 was foreign, little has come through legal Thai channels. Thai officials are concerned that the funding is coming in via Malaysia, though the latter has not been forthcoming in providing assistance to stem the flow.

Perhaps the fastest growing Islamist organization in Southern Thailand is the Tablighi Jamaat. While nominally apolitical, there is considerable concern that this organization's stringent and intolerant form of Islam is fueling the conflict. In 2008, the group finished construction of the largest mosque in Thailand, in a remote area of the border town of Sungai Golok, and since has stepped up their construction of a network of *madrassas*.[23]

ISLAMISM AND THE STATE

Since annexation in 1902, Thai policies towards the Malay Muslim community have been based on assimilation. Malayu has been banned as an official language or language of instruction. Malayan style dress was at times proscribed. Despite these attempts to Siamize the Malayan population, there was never any wholesale effort to repress the Muslim community or to inhibit the spread of the religion through limits on mosque and *madrassa* construction, *da'wa* (proselytization) activities or participation in the *haj*. There was considerable freedom of religion, though many other ethno-linguistic and cultural aspects were repressed. The overly centralized nature of the Thai state ensured that until the 1997 Constitution provincial leaders were chosen by the government in Bangkok, and not through local-level elections.

With the insurgency's onset, the Thai state has tried to work with moderate Muslim leaders in the various provincial Islamic committees, though without much success. Insurgents have targeted these Islamic committee leaders and others deemed to be collaborators. In general, Thai leaders have been blasé about the religious nature of the conflict and have gone out of their way to deny that religion played any role in the insurgency. During his tenure, for example, former Prime Minister Thaksin Shinawatra saw the conflict as something that could be resolved largely through development funds. The National Reconciliation Commission established in 2005 similarly was in total denial about the Islamist nature of the conflict. Its final report, issued in 2006, denied both that the conflict was religious in nature and that the insurgents were secessionists. Instead, it simply argued that the root cause of the conflict was corruption and the lack of social justice.[24]

The Thai government has spent considerable diplomatic resources lobbying the Organization of the Islamic Conference (OIC), which it feared would take a forceful stance against the Thai government's handling of the insurgency. In 2006, Malaysia, which then held the rotating presidency of the OIC, issued a number of reports and statements that whitewashed the Thai government's actions, to the point that an OIC delegation was targeted by insurgents.

Following the September 2006 coup that ousted Thaksin, the interim government headed by a former Royal Thai Army commander with long experience in the South, Surayud Chultanont, dedicated significant efforts to resolving the insurgency. In addition to very public apologies for the previous government's human rights violations and missteps, Surayud's government made numerous promises to the Muslim community, including a willingness to implement *sharia* law.[25] To this end, the government offered to increase education funds to Thai Muslim communities, and announced the hiring of 900 more Islamic teachers.[26] Interestingly, there was for the first time explicit acknowledgement by the government of the insurgents' Islamist agenda and demands.[27] The government also said that it would allow Malayu as the language of instruction in classrooms in the south and pledged a large budget increase for the region, which Thaksin had starved of funds.[28] By early 2011, few of these initiatives had been implemented, however, and many of the pledges to hold security forces more accountable have been scrapped—a state of affairs that has infuriated Thailand's Muslim community

ENDNOTES

[1]Thomas Fuller, "Muslim Insurgents Confound Military in Thailand," *New York Times*, September 1, 2009, http://www.nytimes.com/2009/09/01/world/asia/01iht-thai.html?_r=1&ref=world.

[2] "Southern Thailand: Insurgency, Not Jihad," International Crisis Group *Asia Report* no. 18 (2005); Author's interview, Bangkok, Thailand, January 12, 2006.

[3] "Fugitive Headmaster May Be Top Insurgent," *The Nation* (Bangkok), December 17, 2004.

[4] For more on the public health crisis in the south, see Sanitsuda Ekchai, "Silent Deaths in Restive South," *Bangkok Post*, February 17, 2011, http://www.bangkokpost.com/opinion/opinion/222013/silent-deaths-in-restive-south.

[5] "Childbirth Deaths At Crisis Level In South," *The Nation* (Bangkok), December 20, 2006, http://www.nationmultimedia.com/2006/12/20/national/national_30022022.php; "Southern Provinces A Hotbed For Polio," *The Nation* (Bangkok), December 7, 2006, http://www.nationmultimedia.com/search/read.php?newsid=30021027&keyword=Southern+violence; "Health Problems Rife In Narathiwat," *The Nation* (Bangkok), February 9, 2007, http://www.nationmultimedia.com/search/read.php?newsid=30026379&keyword=Southern+violence.

[6] Andrew Perrin, "Thailand's Terror," *Time–Asian Edition*, November 25, 2002, http://www.time.com/time/asia/covers/1101021125/thailand.html.

[7] "Extremists Kill 2, Warn Buddhists," *Bangkok Post*, December 13, 2006.

[8] "Separatists Divided On Peace Offer," *Bangkok Post*, November 20, 2006; Author's interview, Kuala Lumpur, Malaysia, April 19, 2005.

[9] Wan Kadir Che Man, *Muslim Separatism: The Moros of the Southern Philippines and the Malays of Southern Thailand* (Singapore: Oxford University Press, 1990), 104–105.

[10] John R. Bradley, "Waking Up To The Terror Threat In Southern Thailand," *Straits Times* (Singapore), May 27, 2004.

[11] Author's interview, Bangkok, Thailand, June 24, 2005.

[12] "Interview with Ismail Lutfi Japagiya," *Krungthep Thurakit (Business Bangkok)*, n.d.

[13] Quoted in "Thailand Fears More Attacks As Muslim Separatists Blamed For Violence," Agence France Press, April 30, 2004.

[14] My figures are conservative for two main reasons: First, they are based on open source reporting and not official government statistics and there is inconsistent media coverage. Second, many of those reported as wounded later die, which goes unreported.

[15] Vasana Chinvarakorn, "Tak Bai Sits Heavy on the Conscience," *Bangkok Post*, October 27, 2007.

---

[16] For more on extrajudicial killings see, Human Rights Watch, "It Was Like Suddenly My Son No Longer Existed: Enforced Disappearances in Thailand's Southern Border Provinces," March 19, 2007, http://www.hrw.org/en/reports/2007/03/19/it-was-suddenly-my-son-no-longer-existed-0.

[17] "Villagers' Arrest Creating Resentment: Lawyers," *The Nation* (Bangkok), July 24, 2007, http://www.nationmultimedia.com/search/read.php?newsid=30042141&keyword=Southern+Unrest.

[18] "31 Held in Fresh Sweeps," *The Nation* (Bangkok), August 8, 2007, http://www.nationmultimedia.com/2007/08/08/national/national_30044197.php; Rachel O'Brien, "Detainees' Families Suffer in Thai South," Agence France Presse, September 1, 2008,

[19] Author's interview with representatives of the Muslim Lawyers Association, Bangkok, Thailand, July 10, 2010; "Seven Years Afterward - An Achievement of Failure," Isara News Service, January 3, 2011; Sanitsuda Ekchai, "Silent Deaths in Restive South," *Bangkok Post*, February 17, 2011, http://www.bangkokpost.com/opinion/opinion/222013/silent-deaths-in-restive-south.

[20] Author's interview, Bangkok, Thailand, March 16, 2005.

[21] "PM: No Autonomy for South," *Bangkok Post*, November 3, 2009, http://www.bangkokpost.com/breakingnews/159213/pm-not-support-autonomous-areas-plan.

[22] Robert B. Albritton, "The Muslim South in the Context of the Thai Nation," unpublished manuscript, November 2007, 13.

[23] Author's interview, Sungai Golok, Thailand, June 16, 2008.

[24] *Final Report of the National Reconciliation Council,* June 5, 2006. (author's collection)

[25] Charlotte McDonald-Gibson, "Thai PM Supports Islamic Law in Restive South, Rules Out Separation," Agence France Presse, November 8, 2006; "No More Blacklist: Surayud," *The Nation* (Bangkok), November 8, 2006, http://www.nationmultimedia.com/breakingnews/read.php?newsid=30018420.

[26] Sirikul Bunnag, "A New Face for Islamic Teaching: Interview with Prasert Kaewphet," *Bangkok Post*, July 12, 2007.

[27] Ibid.

[28] "Budget Distribution in South is to be Completed," Thai News Agency, May 19, 2007.

INDONESIA

Indonesia is one of the most pluralistic societies in the world in terms of the ethnic, linguistic, cultural, and religious affiliations of its population. Much of this diversity is attributable to the country's topography and geography. The Indonesian archipelago consists of more than 17,800 islands and islets. Indonesia is the most populous Muslim country in the world, where approximately 87 percent of its population are Muslims of different doctrinal and eschatological persuasions, and it is the largest Muslim-majority democracy. The Indonesian government officially recognizes only five religions— Islam, Protestantism, Catholicism, Buddhism, and Confucianism. While the pluralism of the archipelago has meant that for much of history, Indonesia has been given to conflict and pogroms, since 1966 much of this was contained by the repressive authoritarian regime of former Indonesian President Suharto. The end of Suharto's thirty-two year rule in 1998 was accompanied by intense jockeying on the part of various social and political groups and organizations—including Muslims—for newfound political space in Indonesia.

In Indonesia, Islamism is not a monolithic phenomenon.[1] While the vir-

ulent brand of Islamist activism epitomized by the ideology and agenda of both jihadi and paramilitary groups is undoubtedly a feature of the broader social-political terrain in post-Suharto Indonesia, they form but a small faction of the wider Muslim community. And while trends of religious conservatism are clearly evident in the social and cultural sphere in recent years, this has not translated to significant support for the Islamist agenda of the implementation of Islamic state and Islamic law.

ISLAMIST ACTIVITY

Since Indonesia's struggle for sovereignty and its consequent independence from the Dutch in 1945, Muslim leaders, Islamic political parties, and Muslim groups have been divided over the legal status of Islam in the multi-ethnic and multi-religious state. While the issues of adopting sharia into the Indonesian Constitution and the establishment of an Islamic state are still hotly contested, Islamic political parties have begun to adopt a more inclusive political agenda, promoting pluralistic ideology and focusing on the implementation of universal Islamic values. Following the collapse of Suharto's New Order regime in May 1998, new electoral laws were passed, spawning the creation of additional political parties. The sole principle policy of *Pancasila* was lifted and many organizations claimed Islam as their ideology.

Political parties
PKS - Partai Keadilan Sejahtera (Prosperous Justice Party)
    PKS, originally named *Partai Keadilan, PK* (Justice Party), was founded in July 1998. It was a new party that emerged from the *Lembaga Da'wah Kampus* (LDK, or University Students' Body for Islamic Predication) of the early 1980s.[2] The suppression of student movements in 1977-1978 had resulted in the proliferation of Muslim student activists inspired by the Muslim Brotherhood in Egypt, who carried out their *dawah* (proselytization) activities in mosques. The movement is linked to the educational system developed by the Brotherhood. By the early 1980s, LDK had expanded into a large organization and its alumni subsequently entered the political arena by establishing the Justice Party.[3]

    In the 2004 elections, PKS secured 7.3 percent of votes, and 45 out of 550 seats, in the country's parliament, making it the only Islamic party to improve its position since the previous election. It managed to essentially retain this level of popular support in the 2009 elections. PKS's success has in part been due to a political agenda that emphasized, not the implementation of *sharia* or the creation of an Islamic state, but the broadly popular theme of "clean and caring government" in opposition to incumbent parties—both Islamist and secularist—that were widely perceived by voters to be corrupt and elitist.[4] Nonetheless, PKS is still considered a religious party, with its primary focus the promotion of Islamic values.

PKS is also the most organized of all Indonesian parties, with some 400,000 carefully selected and well-trained cadres, and has cultivated an image of collective decision-making in which no individual leader stands out. Additionally, PKS has been able to contain its internal differences and prevent internal schisms. The party is popular with the modernist Islamic constituency, especially among students and educated middle class Muslims. Apart from representing its members' aspirations in parliament and engaging in tarbiyah (educational) activities, PKS provides public services. For example, PKS set up a *Pos Keadilan* ("Justice Post") from which its members could provide assistance to affected communities in recent crises such as ethnic/religious conflicts or natural disasters. In December 1999, this was institutionalized into the *Pos Keadilan Peduli Umat* (Justice Post Concerning Muslim Society), and expanded to include assistance to farmers in selling their underpriced crops.[5]

PKS is rooted in the powerful tarbiyah movement found in secular state universities.[6] Campus activism is one of the main conduits of Islamic political communication in Indonesia. That activism is also in line with the party's advocacy of a transformation of society. The *tarbiyah* movement engages its members through hundreds, if not thousands, of regular gatherings. These meetings are not only attended by party elites but also by ordinary members. Such regular contact allows the party easy access to thousands of its followers. These meetings do not necessarily focus on substantive political issues; often, they are geared more towards the advancement of religious understanding. Furthermore, these meetings also become catalysts for member interaction, establishing party discipline and new recruitment. Given this extensive political machinery, the PKS is well placed to mobilize members quickly during election times.

PBB – Partai Bulan Bintang (Crescent Star Party)

The PBB, which claims to be the descendant of the largest Islamic party of the 1950s, Masyumi, was founded in July 1998. Masyumi was banned in the 1960s by President Sukarno and its leaders were jailed. After they were released, former Masyumi leaders decided to establish the DDII (*Dewan Da'wah Islamiyah Indonesia*) to maintain its members and leadership networks as well to insulate themselves from further political gridlock and turbulence. The DDII is a modernist Islamic organization and has close relations with other similar bodies such as the Muhammadiyah and Persis.[7] The PBB was eventually formed from this corpus.

The PBB is an Islamist party with a party ideology based on Islamic principles and practice. As heir to the Masyumi legacy, PBB espouses a classic Islamist political agenda—the adoption of *sharia* into the constitution. Both the PBB and PPP (elaborated below) advocated the formal adoption of *sharia* into the constitution in the 2002 annual session of the People's Consultative Assembly. In the 2004 elections, the party garnered 2.6 percent of votes, a slight increase from its previous performance in the 1999 elections. Although PBB sees itself as the descendant of Masyumi, its 2.6 percent of votes is far below the support Masyumi received in its day.

PPP – Partai Persatuan Pembangunan (United Development Party)

The PPP emerged from a merger of four Islamic parties that was compelled by Suharto's regime in 1973, and was one of the three legal parties during the New Order. From 1973-1998, the PPP was politically neutered, but remained the medium for the expression of Islamic concerns within the regime. While the PPP never posed a serious threat to the then-incumbent Golkar party, it defeated Golkar in strongly Islamic provinces such as Aceh and occasionally posed a serious challenge to Golkar's electoral dominance in West Sumatra, South Sumatra, East Java and South Kalimantan. The PPP's status as the main opposition party ended when Abdurrahman Wahid withdrew his 30 million-strong Nahdlatul Ulama (NU) from the party in 1984, resulting in the resignation of most NU leaders.

The party's share of votes has declined drastically over the years, with its popularity dropping by more than two percent (to 8.2 percent of votes) in 2004, as compared to its performance in the 1999 elections.[8] Nevertheless, the PPP has managed to endure the transition from a regime-sponsored party to a democratic party after 1998 because it retained some standing as a voice of Islamic interests and because of the continued involvement of a range of both modernist and traditionalist Islamic leaders who had participated in the party during the Suharto era.[9]

Like the PKS and PBB, the PPP officially states that its ideological basis is Islam. The most significant example of this ideological position was when the party advocated the formal adoption of *sharia* into the constitution in the 2002 annual session of the People's Consultative Assembly. The PBB, PPP, and PKS share similar perspectives on *sharia*, but differ on the means by which to promote them. While the PKS does not focus on the formal adoption of *sharia*, the PBB and PPP advocate the incorporation of principles of Islamic jurisprudence through constitutional amendment.

Radical Salafi-Islamist Groups
FPI - Front Pembela Islam (Front of the Defenders of Islam)

The FPI was founded by Muhammad Rizieq Syihab (b. 1965), a young man of Hadrami descent born into a family of *sayyids* (reputed descendants of the Prophet Muhammad).[10] Before establishing FPI, Syihab was a prominent religious preacher in addition to his daily tasks as a religious teacher in an Islamic school of the Jamiatul Khair Hadrami organization in Tanah Abang, Central Jakarta.[11] Tanah Abang has been known to be an important center of sayyid influence in the Indonesian capital to which powerful figures associated with the New Order have affiliated themselves.[12]

Laskar Pembela Islam, the paramilitary division of Front Pembela Islam, was a loosely organized entity with an open membership.[13] The majority of its members were from mosque youth associations and a number of Islamic schools (*madrassas*) in Jakarta. Other members, particularly among the rank and file, were simply unemployed youths, including those from the notorious *preman* (thug) groups, whose motivation in joining was economic reward for carrying out militant actions. Members were indoctrinated by Syihab, who taught that they should "live nobly, or better, die in holy war as a martyr."[14] Laskar Pembela Islam eventually succeeded in expanding its network to cities outside Jakarta; it claims to have established eighteen provincial and more than fifty district branches with tens of thousands of sympathizers throughout the country.[15]

Laskar Pembela Islam first made its presence felt in a mass demonstration on August 17, 1998, where it decried Megawati Soekarnoputri's presidential candidacy. In line with its puritanical ideological beliefs, it became "the most active group in conducting what it called *razia maksiat* (raids on vice)" to assert its political demands more visibly.[16] Moreover, the group demanded that the government abrogate the policy of *asas tunggal* ("sole foundation") which required all political and social organizations to accept the longstanding ideology of the state, Pancasila.[17] In addition, the group rallied support for the instatement of the Jakarta Charter, which would have given Islamic law constitutional status. On one occasion, the group also reportedly ransacked the offices of the National Human Rights Commission, which it felt "had not been objective in its investigation of the Tanjung Priok massacre (where the army had shot hundreds of Muslim demonstrators)."[18] In addition, the FPI also threatened Americans in Indonesia, apparently in retaliation for the United States' attack on the Taliban in Afghanistan.[19]

Laskar Jihad (Holy War Force)

Laskar Jihad first captured the attention of the public in early-2000, when it mobilized in response to purported Christian violence against Muslims in the Moluccas, and the apparent inability of the Indonesian central government to protect local Muslims. The *Laskar Jihad* was a paramilitary group established by Ja'far Umar Thalib (b. 1961) and leading Salafi personalities such as Muhammad Umar As-Sewed, Ayip Syafruddin and Ma'ruf Bahrun. According to reports, Ja'far was born into a Hadrami family active in al-Irsyad, which was known to be a modernist Muslim organization made up of predominantly Indonesian Hadramis.[20]

Before its militant turn in 2000, Laskar Jihad had mostly been an apolitical and quietist movement that was however influenced by puritanical Wahhabi Salafism.[21] Many of its members had the experience of tertiary level education. Many too, were at some point part of campus Islamic student movements, or had been in surreptitious contact with the Darul Islam. They had come under the charismatic influence of Thalib, who had spent years studying in conservative and radical circles in Saudi Arabia and Yemen, following which he had been dispatched to Afghanistan to take part in *jihad*.[22] Is it widely known that from 1994 to 1999, the cadres of Laskar contented themselves with teaching and preaching Wahhabi Islam. However, it was the conflict in the Moluccas, alluded to earlier, that propelled them into radical activism and violence. Shortly after the conflict started, the group established a training camp in West Java and was dispatching thousands of its members to the Moluccas, both as relief workers as well as fighters.[23]

Modeled after a military organization, *Laskar Jihad* consisted of "one brigade divided into battalions, companies, platoons, teams and one intelligence section."[24] As its symbol, the group adopted the image of two crossed sabres under the words of their creed: "La ilaha illa Allah, Muhammad Rasul Allah" (there is no God but Allah and Muhammad is His messenger).[25]

In terms of its doctrinal positions, *Laskar Jihad* dismisses man-made laws in favor of its own interpretation of *sharia*. It rejects notions of democracy and popular sovereignty, maintaining that they fundamentally contradict the teachings of Islam. In the Indonesian context, the group was also outspoken in its condemnation of Megawati's presidency on the grounds that the president was from the female gender. Although the organization claims that it is not interested in politics – and specifically, in replacing the current regime with an Islamic state, Thalib was known to have frequent meetings with military commanders and other power brokers, thereby indicating the existence of ties between the group and other political actors. During the height of its activism, *Laskar Jihad* repeatedly instigated violent street riots, often for proclaimed reasons of the implementation of *sharia*. Other acts of violence included attacks on cafes, brothels, gambling dens and other places which they considered representations of "vice."

In the aftermath of the Bali bombings of October 2002, however, public opinion swung decidedly away from these local paramilitary groups as Indonesian Muslims expressed outrage at the targeting of co-religionists. At the same time, their patrons from the security services withdrew support and endorsement because of international attention concerned for the evident emergence of Islamist terrorism and violence in Indonesia. Both *FPI* and *Laskar Jihad* were quickly disbanded.

Radical Non-Salafi-Islamist Groups
MMI – Majelis Mujahidin Indonesia (Jihad Fighter Group of Indonesia)

The MMI "places a different emphasis on sharia discourse than does LJ and FPI, associating it with the Jakarta Charter and the historical struggle of the Darul Islam movement (described below)."[26] It appears to be a front for various groups that have some relation with the Darul Islam. The group's key organizer is Irfan S. Awwas; its chief religious authority is Abu Bakar Ba'asyir.

Of the militant organizations that have become active during the post-New Order era in Indonesia, the MMI is arguably one of the oldest. According to observers, "it is a loose alliance of a dozen minor Muslim paramilitary organizations that had been scattered among cities such as Solo, Yogyakarta, Kebumen, Purwokerto, Tasikmalaya and Makassar. Notable member groups are *Laskar Santri* (Muslim Student Paramilitary Force), *Laskar Jundullah* (God's Army Paramilitary Force), *Kompi Badar* (Badr Company), *Brigade Taliban* (Taliban Brigade), *Corps Hizbullah Divisi Sunan Bonang* (God's Party Corps of the Sunan Bonang Division), *Front Pembela Islam Surakarta* (Front of the Defenders of Islam of Surakarta/FPIS) and *Pasukan Komando Mujahidin* (Holy Warrior Command Force)."[27]

MMI members continue to lobby for the incorporation of *sharia* into the constitution. At the local and regional level (particularly former Darul islam strongholds), MMI has also been actively pressing the issue of the enactment of *sharia*. Additionally, one of the MMI's main objectives is to establish an Islamic *khilafah* (caliphate). MMI has also been active in making calls for *jihad*, particularly in the Moluccas and other troubled spots. In contrast to the large scale mobilization of *Laskar Jihad* however, MMI has preferred to operate in small units that are well trained and armed.

HuT — Hizb-ut-Tahrir (Party of Liberation)

HuT is a political organization founded in 1952 in Lebanon by Taqi al-Din al-Nabhani.[28] It is unclear when HuT came to Indonesia, but some scholars trace the organization's presence as far back as the 1970s.

Before the fall of Suharto's regime, HuT remained underground, moving from one mosque to another. It avoided any documentation or public coverage that might reveal its existence and activities. Therefore, HuT's presence was largely unknown until Suharto stepped down. During the subsequent era of *Reformasi* (political reform), however, the group made its appearance through several public rallies. But, for fear of prosecution, HuT has never revealed the identity of the leader of its Indonesian branch. Its public representative, Ismail Yusanto, claims that he is just the group's spokesperson. It may be that the experiences of HuT leaders in other countries, where they have been repressed, tortured, and jailed, has influenced this decision.

HuT advocates the implementation of the *sharia* in daily life, viewing Islam as not just a religion but a political system and a way of life.[29] Like the MMI, its most important objective is to establish an Islamic *khilafah*.[30] Aligned with this dogma is the promulgation of one global government for all Muslims. It is not surprising, therefore, that this group rejects the idea of nationalism or the nation-state.

Darul Islam and Jemaah Islamiyah

The Darul Islam movement, led by S. M. Kartosoewirjo, first emerged in the mid-1940s in West Java as part of the broader armed anti-colonial movement against Dutch reoccupation after the Second World War. Kartosoewirjo declared the formation of an Indonesian Islamic State (Negara Islam Indonesia, NII) based on *sharia* in 1949. At the same time, armed elements from the Darul Islam movement launched insurgency operations against the newly formed Indonesian Republic, which Kartosoewirjo viewed as a betrayal of the anti-colonial enterprise. By 1954, the movement had spread to Central Java, Aceh, South Sulawesi, and South Kalimantan, posing a serious internal security threat. A combination of military campaigns and offers of amnesty to Darul Islam members, however, gradually eroded the influence of the movement.[31]

The collapse of the Darul Islam Movement did not signal the end of extremist Islam. Rather, it forced those extremist forces to evolve and take on a different, more clandestine form. In 1993, a new and more lethal extremist movement known as al-Jama'ah al-Islamiyyah – commonly referred to as *Jemaah Islamiyah*, or JI – was founded by two former Darul Islam leaders, Abdullah Sungkar and Abu Bakar Ba'asyir. JI saw itself as the heir of Darul Islam, although it sought to achieve the goal of an Islamic state through more militant means, including the deliberate targeting of civilians. Many prominent members of JI were veterans of the *jihad* against the Soviet Union in Afghanistan during the 1980s, and had been recruited through Darul Islam channels.[32] The Bali bombings of October 2002, however, proved to be a watershed for JI, sparking an internal debate over the issue of the killing of Muslims and whether the organization should focus its immediate attention on proselytization rather than bombings in order to advance its goals.

Together with a crackdown by Indonesian security forces, this schism eventually forced a split in JI, with a hardline faction led by two key Malaysian leaders – Noordin Top and Azahari Husin – breaking away from the main organization and continuing a reign of terror with the Australian Embassy bombing (September 2004), the JW Marriott Hotel in Jakarta (August 2003), and the Marriott and Ritz-Carlton hotels in Jakarta (July 2009). While security operations have since led to the deaths of both men, the spring 2010 emergence of a heretofore unknown group in Aceh, called al-Qaeda in Indonesia, underscores the fact that while on the run from increasingly effective security operations, *jihadi* groups and individuals may be active and evolving.

ISLAMISM AND SOCIETY

Like most of the Muslim world, Indonesia was not immune from the global

Islamic resurgence that began in the late 1960s and early 1970s as a consequence of the failure of Arab nationalism. During this period, numerous students made their way to the great Islamic learning centers of the Arab world. Many were also sent to secular schools and universities in Europe on government scholarships, where Islamic civil society movements were active among Muslim communities. Locally, an Islamic *dawah* (proselytization) movement began in Bandung around the campus-based Salman mosque and soon spread across the country to other tertiary education institutions. This movement was organized around study groups modelled after the Egypt Muslim Brotherhood. The related *tarbiyah* (education) movement began in the early 1980s at various university campuses.[33] The legacy of this Islamization process remains evident today in the increased social activism of the country's various Muslim communities.

A driving force for the development of the *dawah* movement was the socio-political dislocation of Islamist intellectuals. The Suharto administration had placed substantial restrictions on the expression of religiously-referenced political aspirations on the part of the Muslim majority, to the extent that socially active Muslim groups like the NU and Muhammadiyah were effectively de-politicized. In addition, more conservative Muslims were also concerned for the increasing assertiveness of what was thought to be "liberal" Islamic ideas in Indonesian society. Moreover, in the words of one scholar, "the general mass media, as another manifestation of the public sphere, tended to serve as the state ideological apparatus in championing modernization. The media was thus preconditioned to be sympathetic to the renewal movement. Realizing that the public sphere was hostile to their ideo-political aspirations, the Islamist intellectuals created a subtle and fluid social movement, which was relatively impervious to state control, as a new foundation for constructing collective solidarity and identity."[34]

Salafi influences can largely be traced to the late 1950s, when a small number of modernist Muslim intellectuals were attracted to the ideas of the Muslim Brotherhood.[35] However, it was not until the late 1970s and early 1980s that these ideas and organizational techniques began to win a sizeable following. The main group that was influenced by these ideas was known as the *Tarbiyah* group. Unlike in Malaysia, where Islamists leaders had direct relationships with *Ikhwan* and *Jamaat* leaders, Indonesian Islamist leaders learned these ideas mainly through Indonesian translations of books written by *Ikhwan* activists. It should be born in mind that during this period, Indonesia was still ruled by the authoritarian New Order regime which was extremely suspicious of Islamic parties and groups. It was Natsir and his organization, the DDII, that was chiefly responsible for encouraging Islamic student activism in Indonesian universities.[36] While it is difficult to establish the extent of

Natsir's relationship with *Ikhwan* and *Jamaat* leaders, it is clear that he played a major role in facilitating the travel of Indonesian students to *Ikhwan* and *Jamaat*-dominated universities in the Middle East and Pakistan. He was also responsible for introducing the *Ikhwan's* religio-political ideas and methods of organization to Muslim students on various campuses. It was these students who established the *Lembaga Dakwah Kampus*, LDK (Campus Proselytising Network). *Ikhwan*-inspired students subsequently formed a separate organization, the *Kesatuan Aksi Mahasiswa Muslim Indonesia*, KAMMI (Indonesian Muslim Undergraduate Action Association). With the collapse of the New Order regime, activists of KAMMI formed the *Partai Keadilan, PK* (Justice Party), since renamed as the *Partai Keadilan Sejahtera, PKS* (Prosperity Justice Party). PKS maintains strong links with the broader transnational Salafi network, often attending international Islamist gatherings organized by the *Ikhwan* and *Jamaat*.

While conservative forces aligned themselves behind the Salafi movement and the various social and, eventually, political organizations that drew on it for support during the New Order period, alternative patterns of thinking were also emerging elsewhere within the Indonesian Muslim community during the late 1970s and early 1980s—particularly among younger intellectuals who sought to recalibrate Islam's role in Indonesian society. This phenomenon, initially called the "reform movement" (*gerakan pembaruan*) and more recently "cultural Islam" (*Islam kultural*), consciously rejected the political agenda and aspirations of Islamist parties since independence and sought to redefine Islam's relations with—and role in—the state from a purely apolitical, cultural perspective. Among the chief proponents of this movement were former president Abdurrahman Wahid and the well-known intellectual, the late Nurcholish Madjid.[37]

Cultural Islam was particularly critical of political Islam (or Islamist activism) on several counts. Islamist parties had experienced very limited success in achieving their goals. Moreover, they had not been able to unite Muslims politically, nor managed to garner a majority of votes at general elections, nor succeeded in getting Islamic laws implemented in local and national government. What was required instead, proponents of cultural Islam believed, were alternative ways of achieving the aspirations of Indonesian Muslims to live pious lives—aspirations that had in fact been hampered by the preoccupation of Islamist leaders with politics. The movement's position on the formal role of the sharia in the state was highly controversial. Many younger intellectuals repudiated the concept of an Islamic state, arguing that the Koran contains no prescription for the structure of the state. Instead, they supported the religiously neutral Pancasila as the basis of the Indonesian state, asserting that the pluralism and religious equality inherent in this were consistent with

Islamic principles. In addition, the assumption that good Muslims should only support Islamic parties was strongly disputed. The stance was that pluralist, "deconfessionalized" parties were not less virtuous for Muslims to belong to than exclusively Islamic ones.[38]

ISLAMISM AND THE STATE

The relationship between Islamism and the state in Indonesia can be traced to debates among nationalists regarding the place of Islam as an organizing factor of post-colonial Indonesia. While Indonesia is often considered a secular state, it is officially a state based on religion as premised in the first principle of the Pancasila, which enshrines "belief in Almighty God" (*Ke Tuhanan yang Maha Esa*). This was, in effect, a compromise between those wanting a secular state and those favoring an Islamic state. While there is no official state religion or formal acknowledgment of the authority of religious law in the constitution, the use of the term "Almighty God" implies monotheism, a concession to Muslim sentiment.

Indonesia's political and constitutional history would reveal that among the most divisive debates is the issue of the formal role of Islam in the state and the question of the position of *sharia* in the constitution. Much of this debate focused on the Jakarta Charter, an agreement struck between Muslim and nationalist leaders on June 22, 1945 as part of the preparations for Indonesia's independence. The most controversial part of the charter was a seven-word clause: "with the obligation for adherents of Islam to practice Islamic law" (*dengan kewajiban menjalankan syari'at Islam bagi pemeluk-pemeluknya*). Although often portrayed as an attempt to make Indonesia an Islamic state, the inclusion of these seven words in the constitution would not, by itself, have had this effect. Rather, it remained to be seen whether Islamic parties would have the will and numbers in parliament to push through *sharia*-based legislation needed for the state to enforce Islamic law.[39] Islamic leaders also succeeded in having a stipulation inserted into the draft constitution that the president be a Muslim.

On August 18, 1945, the day after the proclamation of independence, pro-charter Muslim leaders came under strong pressure from 'secular' Muslims, nationalists, and religious minorities to drop the seven words regarding the practice of Islamic law, despite the initial agreement of the committee responsible for finalising the constitution. Those opposing the clause were concerned that the embryonic Indonesian nation would break up as pressure from Islamists caused the non-Muslim dominated outer islands to secede. Eventually, Muslim leaders were persuaded, in the interest of national unity, to exclude the charter. In addition to that, a clause requiring the president of the country to be Muslim was also dropped.

Thereafter, it was not until the 1970s that Islam experienced a resurgence in Indonesia. That period witnessed a surge in mosque attendance, enrolment in religious classes, adoption of Islamic dress (including the veil, worn by women), and expansion of Muslim education and social organizations. Although there were a small number of extremists at its fringe, the Islamic resurgence was never politically radical. Its primary social impulse was pietistic and ethical, aimed at heightening the role of Islam in social life.[40]

The resurgence put greater pressure on the government to make concessions in favor of Indonesia's Muslims. In response, Suharto began to extend greater aid to the country's Muslim community in the late 1980s. He also lifted an earlier ban on the veil in state schools, and imposed tighter restrictions on the activities of Christian missionaries. Suharto likewise increased state subsidies for mosque building, Islamic education, Muslim television programming, the celebration of religious holidays, and preferential treatment for Muslim entrepreneurs in state contracts. The president even went as far as to sponsor an Islamic faction in the armed forces, previously a bastion of conservative secular nationalism, with the assistance of his son-in-law, Prabowo Subianto.[41]

While major Muslim organizations agreed to cooperate with the New Order regime in facilitating and implementing its social and educational initiatives, they also subtly pressed for democratic reforms. This challenge from moderate Muslims led Suharto to change his political strategy in the mid-1990s, and to reach out to hardline groups like Dewan Dakwah Islamiyah Indonesia (DDII - Indonesian Council for Islamic Predication) and Komite Indonesia Untuk Solidaritas dengan Dunia Islam (KISDI – the Indonesian Committee for Solidarity of the Islamic World), which had developed reputations for being strongly anti-Western and anti-Christian. Suharto's efforts had a backlash effect, however. "With the onset of the Asian economic crisis in late 1997, support for the Suharto regime waned, and the President was forced from power in May 1998. Sadly, the months leading up to his resignation were marked by anti-Chinese and anti-Christian riots, some of which showed the tell-tale signs of regime provocation."[42]

Nevertheless, the end of Suharto's rule did not spell the end of efforts to exploit religious tensions for political advantage in Indonesian politics. After May 1998, and in the wake of the upheaval of post-Suharto democratisation in Indonesia, more than a few politicians and leaders appealed to ethno-religious sentiments in order to enhance their credentials. The tactic had an especially bloody consequence in Maluku, Central Kalimantan, and

Sulawesi, upsetting a delicate demographic balance between Christians and Muslims with the rise of sectarian paramilitaries and bloody campaigns of ethnic cleansing.

The slew of legislative and institutional concessions to the Muslim community was a strong indicator of the New Order's new stance towards Islam beginning from the late 1980s. Prominent among them were "the expansion of the authority of religious courts in 1989, the establishment of the Indonesian Muslim Intellectuals association (ICMI) in 1990, lifting of the ban on female state school students wearing headdresses (*jilbab*) in 1991, the upgrading of government involvement in alms collection and distribution, the founding of an Islamic bank (BMI) in 1992, and the abolition of the state lottery (SDSB) in 1993."[43]

Despite the lack of official support for the implementation of *sharia*, the issue appears to be gaining some traction at the regional level. One such case would be the north Sumatran province of Aceh, where *sharia* was promulgated under special autonomy laws in early 2002, though there is intense debate within the local Islamic community over the scope of the laws and the details of their implementation. The *sharia* issue has also attracted strong support from Muslim groups in South Sulawesi, West Sumatra and Banten, but is still well short of receiving majority support. In a number of districts in West Java, *sharia* has been implemented in a de facto fashion by local Muslim groups, often in concert with district government officials and *ulama*.[44]

ENDNOTES

[1] Greg Fealy, "Divided Majority: Limits of Indonesian Political Islam," in Shahram Akbarzadeh and Abdullah Saeed, eds., *Islam and Political Legitimacy* (London: RoutledgeCurzon, 2003), 151.

[2] Anies Rasyid Baswedan, "Political Islam in Indonesia: Present and Future Trajectory," *Asian Survey* 44, no. 5 (October 2004), 675.

[3] Bambang Sulistiyo and Alfian, "Voices of Democracy from Within the Tarbiyah," in Asrori S. Karni, ed., *A Celebration of Democracy* (Jakarta: PT. Era Media Informasi, 2006), 200.

[4] R. William Liddle and Saiful Mujani, "Indonesia in 2004: The Rise of Susilo Bambang Yudhoyono," *Asian Survey* 45, no. 1 (January 2005), 123.

[5] Baswedan, "Political Islam in Indonesia," 677.

[6] Liddle and Mujani, "Indonesia in 2004," 121.

[7] The NU was a non-political Islamic organization that was founded in 1926, became a political party in 1952, and participated in the 1955 and 1971 elections. In 1973, the NU was merged into the PPP. In 1984, the NU declared itself *kembali ke khittah* (return to origin) as a non-political religious movement, and officially retreated from partisan politics. The NU remained neutral until it made a return to partisan politics by establishing the PKB (National Awakening Party) in July 1998.

[8] Stephen Sherlock, *The 2004 Indonesian Elections: How the System Works and What the Parties Stand For* (Canberra: Centre for Democratic Institutions, Research School of Social Sciences, Australian National University, 2004), 17.

[9] Stephen Sherlock, The 2004 Indonesian Elections: How the System Works and What the Parties Stand For (Canberra: Centre for Democratic Institutions, Australian National University, 2004) 32.

[10] See http://igitur-archive.library.uu.nl/dissertations/2006-0705-200332/c1.pdf, 3.

[11] Ibid.

[12] "Sayyid" is an honorific given to male descendants of the Prophet. In Southeast Asia, the Sayyids often trace their ancestry through the Arab andHadrami traders who have been trading with maritime Southeast Asia's coastal kingdoms since the ninth century A.D.

[13] Sherlock, *The 2004 Indonesian Elections*, 17.

[14] See http://igitur-archive.library.uu.nl/dissertations/2006-0705-200332/c1.pdf, 6.

[15] For more details, see Edward Aspinall, "Indonesia," in Bogdan Szajkowski, ed., *Revolutionary and Dissident Movements of the World* (London: John Harper Publishing, 2004).

[16] http://igitur-archive.library.uu.nl/dissertations/2006-0705-200332/c1.pdf, 4.

[17] M. Rizieq Syihab, *Kyai Kampung: Ujung Tombak Perjuangan Umat Islam* (Ciputat: Sekretariat FPI, 1999).

[18] "Police Question Rights Body Over FPI Attack," *Jakarta Post*, May 26, 2010.

[19] "Indonesia's Muslim militants," BBC (London), August 8, 2003, http://news.bbc.co.uk/2/hi/asia-pacific/2333085.stm.

[20] Ibid.

[21] Salafis are those who attempt to reform Islam by taking it away from its traditional association with syncretism and re-orienting it towards scripturalism.

[22] Syihab, *Kyai Kampung: Ujung Tombak Perjuangan Umat Islam.*

[23] See Kirsten E. Schulze, "Laskar Jihad and the Conflict in Ambon," *The Brown Journal of World Affairs* 9, iss.1 (Spring 2002).

[24]http://igitur-archive.library.uu.nl/dissertations/2006-0705-200332/c1.pdf, 6.

[25] Ibid.

[26] See Martin van Bruinessen, "Genealogies of Islamic Radicalism in Post-Suharto Indonesia," in Joseph Chinyong Liow and Nadirsyah Hosen (eds.), Islam in Southeast Asia. Vol.IV (London: Routledge, 2009) 52-53. In the 1950s, the Darul Islam (DI, the Islamic State) movement, spread to South Sulawesi and Aceh under the leadership of Kahar Muzakkar and Daud Beureu'eh respectively. At its core, DI is a political movement which was dissatisfied with the policies of the central government under President Sukarno. However, they used Islam to legitimize their existence and at the same time to denounce the nation-state of Indonesia.

[27]http://igitur-archive.library.uu.nl/dissertations/2006-0705-200332/c1.pdf, 7.

[28] Saiful Umam, "Radical Muslims in Indonesia: The Case of Ja'Far Umar Thalib and The Laskar Jihad," *Explorations in Southeast Asian Studies* 6, no. 1 (Spring 2006), 11.

[29] Ibid.

[30] Ibidem.

[31] Greg Fealy, Virginia Hooker and Sally White, "Indonesia," in Greg Fealy and Virginia Hooker, eds., *Voices of Islam in Southeast Asia: A Contemporary Sourcebook* (Singapore: Institute of Southeast Asian Studies, 2006), 49.

[32] Ibid.

[33] Andreas Ufen, "Mobilising Political Islam: Indonesia and Malaysia Compared," *Commonwealth & Comparative Politics* 47, no. 3 (2009), 316. For further reading on the *dakwah* movements and *tarbiyah* movements, see Yudi Latif, "The Rupture of Young Muslim Intelligentsia in the Modernization of Indonesia," *Studia Islamika* 12, no. 3 (2005), 373-420, and Salman, "The Tarbiyah Movement: Why People Join This Indonesian Contemporary Islamic Movement," *Studia*

Islamika 13, no. 2 (2006), 171-240.

[34] Latif, "The Rupture of Young Muslim Intelligentsia in the Modernization of Indonesia," 391. Some scholars refer to the renewal movement (*gerakan pembaharuan*) as reform movement (*gerakan pembaruan*).

[35] Muhammad Natsir was the former Prime Minister and Information Minister of Indonesia. He was leader of the Masyumi party which was banned under the New Order regime in 1965. For more on Natsir, see Luth Thohir, *M. Natsir: Dakwah dan Pemikirannya*, (Jakarta: Gema Insani, 1999).

[36] Any Muhammad Furkon, *Partai Keadilan Sejahtera: Ideologi dan Praksis Kaum Muda Muslim Indonesia Kontemporer* (Jakarta: Penerbit Terajau, 2004), 124.

[37] Greg Fealy, "Divided Majority: Limits of Indonesian Political Islam," in Shahram Akbarzadeh and Abdullah Saeed, eds., *Islam and Political Legitimacy* (London: RoutledgeCurzon, 2003), 161.

[38] Ibid., 162.

[39] Ibidem, 155.

[40] Robert W. Hefner, "State, Society, and Secularity in Contemporary Indonesia," in Theodore Friend, ed., *Religion and Religiosity in the Philippines and Indonesia* (Washington: Southeast Asia Studies Program, 2006), 42.

[41] Ibid.

[42] Ibidem.

[43] Fealy, "Divided Majority: Limits of Indonesian Political Islam," 163.

[44] Ibid., 164-165.

MALAYSIA

QUICK FACTS

Population: 26,160,256

Area: 329,847 sq km

Ethnic Groups: Malay 50.4%, Chinese 23.7%, Indigenous 11%, Indian 7.1%, other 7.8%

Religions: Muslim 60.4%, Buddhist 19.2%, Christian 9.1%, Hindu 6.3%, Confucianism , Taoism, other traditional Chinese religions 2.6%, other or unknown 1.5%, none 0.8%

Government Type: Constitutional monarchy

GDP (official exchange rate): $209.8 billion

Map and Quick Facts courtesy of the CIA World Factbook (Last Updated July 2010)

Malaysia has long been viewed as a developed, pro-Western, and moderate Muslim-majority country. In recent decades, however, the country as a whole has been experiencing a swing toward Islamic conservatism. This shift appears to be gaining momentum, as evidenced by the increasing popularity of sharia law in public discourse, the state-sanctioned suppression of civil rights and liberties in the name of Islam, the inability of civil courts to stand up against controversial sharia court decisions, increasing cases of moral policing by Islamic religious authorities (including policing of non-Muslims in some instances), and more frequent references to the "Islamic state."[1] This increasing visibility of Islam in Malaysian society and politics is driven not only by the Islamist opposition party Parti Islam Se-Malaysia (Islamic Party of Malaysia, or PAS), but also by the United Malays National Organization (UMNO), whose members were apparently the architects of Malaysia's brand of progressive, moderate Islam.[2] Alternative actors such as nongovernmental organizations (NGOs) and civil society groups likewise are increasingly participating in the politicization of Islam in Malaysia today, at times even eclipsing mainstream political parties in terms of intensity.

Islam in Malaysia is arguably fragmented and variegated in both sub-stance and expression, with religious vocabulary and idioms being mobilized by the state, opposition forces, and a wide array of civil society groups. While Malaysian Islamists nominally operate within the boundaries of mainstream political processes in Malaysia, they also work to define those boundaries. Moreover, even as the Muslim opposition attempts to shed its doctrinaire image in pursuit of an agenda of reform, the "moderate" UMNO-led gov-ernment has pursued an agenda that has resulted in the constriction of the country's cultural and religious space.

ISLAMIST ACTIVITY

PAS - Parti Se-Islam Malaysia (Pan Malaysian Islamic Party)

PAS was established as the Pan Malaysian Islamic Party in 1951 by dis-sidents from UMNO's Bureau of Religious Affairs, and has participated in every Malaysian parliamentary election since 1955.[3] Since its inception, PAS has advocated for the promotion of Malay interest and protection of Mus-lim rights. In its early days, PAS maintained a more rural constituency, par-ticularly among Arabic and religiously educated Malays.[4] By 1982, however, PAS's political stance was infused with Islamist aspirations. During this time, old-guard ethno-nationalists were voted out via party elections and replaced by *ulama* (religious scholars) leadership. This transformation coincided with burgeoning sentiments among Malay-Muslims that Islam is *addin* (a way of life), and had to be accorded greater prominence not only in their per-sonal lives, but in the public sphere as well.[5] The global resurgence of Islamic consciousness during the 1970s and early 1980s, coupled with the religious leadership epitomized by the likes of Fadzil Noor, Abdul Hadi Awang and Nakhaie Ahmad, contributed to the party's pronounced Islamic agenda.[6] The resulting public battle between PAS and UMNO that has taken place since hinges on the discourse of morality, with PAS admonishing UMNO for mar-ginalizing the position of Islamic laws in the Federation of Malaya and the political leadership's failure to observe Islamic ethics and morals. From the outset, the party's goal was a *sharia*-based state in which economic, political and social systems conformed to Islamic values.

A steady expansion of PAS's support base in states such as Terengganu, Kedah and Perlis and in the universities throughout the country in the 1990s indicated the party's rising popularity and the appeal of *sharia*-centered pol-itics. In fact, PAS's commitment to its religious agenda has prevented the party from fruitful cooperation with secular opposition allies.[7] The party's outlook is buttressed by its unyielding belief that the Islamic state is both a viable and necessary alternative to the UMNO-dominated secular state. Since 1990, when it was returned to power in the state of Kelantan, PAS has presented draft proposals to the parliament for the introduction of *hudud* criminal law in Kelantan.[8] Similar efforts were made after the PAS electoral triumph in Terengganu in 1999. However, as criminal law falls under the jurisdiction of the federal and not the *sharia* courts, the motions have been withdrawn on both occasions.

A turning point in the party's Islamic-state agenda came in the run-up to the March 2008 elections. Given the party's subsequent dismal showing in the 2004 elections, PAS leaders promised to soften the party's stance on the Islamic-state issue.[9] This shift has been echoed by ex-deputy prime minister of Malaysia and current PKR adviser, Anwar Ibrahim, who claimed that "PAS's intention to establish an Islamic state is no longer an issue."[10] In the 2008 election, PAS distanced itself from the Islamic-state objective and attempted to leverage the consternation of Malaysia's ethnic minorities in the wake of UMNO's rallying call of Malay primacy.[11]

In an obvious effort to woo non-Muslim votes, PAS leaders have made clear that their election campaign at the national level will focus on a manifesto that holds out the promise of a welfare state system, known as "*negara kebajikan*," accessible to all Malaysians.[12] Components of this agenda include populist initiatives such as free education, free water utilities throughout the country, cheaper fuel and health subsidies.[13] Furthermore, wealth and income distribution will be pursued through a taxation policy that focuses on large businesses in order to offset subsidies earmarked for the poor.[14] Not only will the welfare-state concept dull the edges of its Islamist agenda, it can in the larger picture enhance the appeal of the party across the electorate, particularly since specific reference has also been made to issues of meritocracy and the importance of the presence of non-Malay ministers.[15] Indeed, these were important developments in ensuring non-Muslim support for PAS in the 2008 elections.

Radical Salafi groups

Malaysia is home to a pair of notable radical Islamist groups who adhere broadly to the exclusionary Salafi strain of political Islam:

The *KMM (Kumpulan Mujahidin Malaysia/Kumpulan Militan Malaysia, or Malaysian Mujahidin Group/Malaysian Militant Group)*, an alleged underground militant group, was uncovered through an attempted bombing of a shopping mall in Jakarta in August 2001. The group is reported to favor the overthrow of the Mahathir government and the creation of a regional Islamic state.[16]

Subsequent investigations revealed that the KMM was apparently formed on October 12, 1995 by Zainon Ismail, and had its roots in *Halaqah Pakindo*, a clandestine movement formed in 1986 as an alumni association for Malaysian graduates from religious institutions in Pakistan, India, and

Indonesia.[17] It was later made known by the government that eight of the ten KMM detainees were PAS members.[18] The Malaysian government has alleged that, although Nik Adli Abdul Aziz is allegedly the elected leader of the KMM, real leadership for the group flows through Abu Bakar Bashir and Hambali (Riduan Isamuddin), the spiritual and operational leaders of the Indonesia-based regional terrorist network *Jemaah Islamiyah*.[19] No evidence is publicly available to corroborate these conclusions, however.

KMM has differed from other militant organizations in Malaysia in terms of its reach. Though established in Malaysia, several sources have indicated that KMM enjoys close links with *Jemaah Islamiyah* in Indonesia.[20] Nevertheless, the exact nature of this relationship remains murky. Despite inconclusive evidence, Malaysian intelligence sources also revealed that KMM allegedly participated in religiously inspired riots in Maluku and Ambon in 2000, and supplied arms to radical Muslims involved in those incidents.[21] Subsequent arrests found leaders having in their possession "documents on guerrilla warfare and map reading, along with studies of militant groups in the Philippines, Chechnya, Afghanistan and Indonesia."[22] In response, Malaysian security forces launched a nationwide operation to detain remaining KMM members. Eventually, up to seventy KMM members were detained without trial under the ISA (Internal Security Act) for allegedly trying to overthrow the government through violent means in the name of *jihad*.[23]

Al-Maunah (Brotherhood of Inner Power) was a non-governmental organization involved in the teaching of martial arts, particularly the development of one's inner powers and the practice of Islamic traditional medicine. At its most prolific, it is said to have more than 1,000 members in Malaysia and overseas, particularly in Tripoli, Libya.[24]

In June 2000, the *Al-Maunah* movement managed to successfully carry out an arms heist from two Malaysian Armed Forces military camps in Perak. The heist served as a major source of embarrassment for the government given the manner in which members of the group managed to penetrate the camp's security infrastructure by dressing up in military fatigues and driving jeeps painted in camouflage green, indicating the likelihood that the heist was an inside job.[25] According to police reports, the group had at least several hundred members led by a former army corporal, Mohammad Amin Razali. Several other sources revealed that civil servants, security services personnel, and even some UMNO members numbered among its ranks.[26] Upon ascertaining *Al-Maunah's* responsibility for the arms heist, Malaysian security forces embarked on a high-profile operation against the organization's camp in Sauk, Perak in July 2000 where nineteen members were eventually captured. Apprehended members of *Al-Maunah* were subsequently charged with treason and plotting to overthrow the government, with the intention of establishing an Islamic state.

It is important to note that both KMM and *Al Maunah* cite local issues as primary causes of grievances, pursuing a predominantly domestic political agenda. For example, the *Al-Maunah* perpetrators demanded for the resignation of Prime Minister Mahathir and his Cabinet while in the case of the KMM, its three key objectives - "to seek religious purity among Malay-Muslims", "to ensure that PAS' political struggle was maintained and encouraged", and "to implement *shari'a* within Malaysia", all pertained to domestic political concerns, despite efforts on the part of the government to link them to a transnational terrorist agenda.[27]

Additionally, evidence linking these militant movements with external organizations remains nebulous and inconclusive. Although these domestic movements share some degree of ideological affinity as well as rudimentary contacts with external organizations, they are purportedly not under the control of external organizations.[28] Therefore, despite attempts to associate KMM with external groups and regional objectives such as the grandiose vision of a *Darul Islam Nusantara* in the region, no mention was made about links with either *Jemaah Islamiyah* or al-Qaeda in the formal charges against the organization. KMM was charged under the ISA solely for its attempt to overthrow the government.[29]

ISLAMISM AND SOCIETY

With the changing complexion of PAS, and the UMNO-led government's systematic Islamization of the bureaucracy, social consciousness and political discourse in Malaysia has been catapulted to a new, more religious dimension. An immediate outcome of this process was the intensification of the UMNO–PAS competition where the focus was on linking credibility and legitimacy to Islam. However a concurrent Islamic discourse rooted in an increasingly vibrant civil society sphere that encompassed NGOs as well as alternative expressions of Islamic consciousness, namely alternative media sources beyond the mainstream government-controlled channels, and the Internet, also emerged to add to the dynamics of Malaysian politics. Even as the heavily contested politics of UMNO and PAS began to converge, a parallel form of civic activism was emerging, which banded together not just political parties but also professional organizations, civil society organizations, educational institutions, and religious institutions.

It appears that NGO activism in Malaysia usually peaks during periods of major social upheaval that occurs on an otherwise comparatively peaceful sociocultural environment. For instance, the dakwah phenomenon that emerged in the early 1970s spawned a number of Islamist NGOs such as ABIM and *Al Arqam*, the *Reformasi* movement of the late 1990s launched a new generation of civil society groups and rejuvenated more established groups. Lately, the issues of apostasy, religious freedom, and the sanctity of the *shari'a* have spurred another round of NGO political and discursive activism that has challenged the hegemony of the state along with the policies of the opposition PAS. Muslim and non-Muslim groups that extend across the political spectrum have in their own way, spoken to, for, and against the positions and policies of UMNO as well as PAS, at times compelling these mainstream political parties to negotiate their politics and recalibrate their narratives.

Islamic NGOs and civil society organizations are not the sole challengers of the religiopolitical agenda of both UMNO and PAS. Considering the demographic realities of Malaysia, any debate on Islamism would certainly elicit responses from the non-Muslim community as well. This has certainly been the case in recent times, where non-Muslims' have accelerated concerns for their place in Malaysian society especially with the intensification of Islamist discourse and its increasingly hegemonic nature. The Malaysian Consultative Council for Buddhism, Christianity, Hinduism, and Sikhism (MCCBCHS) is an example of a non-Muslim interfaith organization that seeks to enhance dialogue and cooperation not only among Buddhists, Christians, Hindus, and Sikhs, but also between these communities and the Muslims in Malaysia. Since 2001, MCCBCHS has been leading an effort driven by the non-Muslim community to establish an Inter-Religious Council (IRC) that would encourage dialogue across religious boundaries. In particular, MCCBCHS felt that the "proper procedures" regarding marriage, divorce, and child custody issues relating to converts to Islam required clarification from Islamic clerics.[30] The group believed that there were "several gray areas in this matter, which has caused much emotional suffering and confusion for family members of converts," aside from the tension it has placed on intercommunal relations.[31]

In Malaysia, civil society groups are basically popular discourse in its more organized and mobilized form. Conversely, cyberspace and various alternative media sources are the new outlets and pathways of political expression that take Islamist debates deeper into Malaysian society.[32] Controversies related to various judicial rulings on the matter of apostasy, declarations by Malay-Muslim political leaders that Malaysia is an Islamic state, and the government's apparent intolerance of open discussions on the "sensitive" issue of Malay-Muslim rights and primacy, have been the primary driving factors behind the increasingly vital role these new avenues play in the Malaysian political scene by providing a forum for contrarian views, or for supporting the government's policies couched as a defence of the faith. Weblogs (henceforth referred to as blogs), chat rooms, and listserves have interestingly been shown to socially (re)construct agendas and offer interpretive frames as a focal point, thus contributing to the shaping and constraining of larger political debate.[33]

It can be argued that in general one would find, within the increasingly intense discursive arena of cyberspace, a noticeable schism between the opinions and perspectives that can be found on Malay-language blogs and English-language blogs, with regards to recent Islamic state declarations and high-profile *murtad* (apostasy) cases. While individuals from a variety of ethnic and religious backgrounds comfortably delve in English-language blogs, Malay-language blogs seem largely monopolized by Malay-Muslims.[34] Another discernible trend is that regardless of ethnicity and religion, there is a general consensus on English-language blogs in relation to the status of Malaysia as an Islamic state. However, a comparison of English and Malay blogs would show a clear disjuncture of perspectives on the issue. In the same vein, reactions to the high-profile apostasy cases that have emerged in recent years also show that sentiments are divided along religious lines, regardless of the language. Nevertheless, Malay and English blogs show an acute contrast in opinions, with the former expressing decidedly more conservative and exclusionary views and the latter purveying more openness to the idea of conversion out of Islam and religious freedom rights.

These trends, evident in virtual social networks, appear to emulate face-to-face patterns of physical interaction, wherein there is an inclination to communicate and associate (by virtue of participants leaving comments and linking one's blog to another) with like-minded individuals that hold generally compatible sentiments on any given set of issues. For instance, the majority of Malay bloggers who show more accommodative tendencies also tend to express their opinions on English blogs, whereas champions of Malay-Muslim primacy usually confine their activities to Malay blogs. Comments in response to a blog post are also more often conciliatory rather than critical. Although virtual space allows for honest, open, anonymous exchange (that at times border on temerity), the impermeability of ideas between the English and Malay language blogs point to a possible latent desire in Malaysia to avoid dialogue, engagement, and bridging of opinions between conflicting mindsets as well as ideas.

These trends speak to larger shifts in the sentiments on the ground. Malaysian society on the whole has been experiencing a swing toward Islamic conservatism. This swing seems to be gaining momentum, as demonstrated by the increasing popularity of *sharia* in public discourse, state-sanctioned curtailment of civil rights and liberties in the name of Islam, the incapacity of civil courts to challenge controversial *sharia* court decisions, increasing incidences of moral policing by Islamic religious authorities (including policing of non-Muslims in some instances), and the alarming regularity of references to the "Islamic state." For example, a 2006 survey of 1000 Muslim respondents revealed that 7.7 percent wanted stricter Islamic laws in place, and 44 percent supported a more active role for state religious authorities to police morality.[35]

In spite of the vast array of channels for political expression, two trends are worth highlighting. First, while the number of avenues for expression may have expanded, given the prevalence of entrenched views on the primacy of Islam among most Malay-Muslim civil society groups, NGOs, and bloggers, it is evident that the parameters of discourse have not changed significantly. Arguably too, there have been instances when Malay-Muslim popular opinion were more "fundamentalist" than either UMNO or PAS on matters such as moral policing, sanctity of the *sharia*, defense of the faith, and Malaysia's courting of the Islamic state ideal. Second, it is important to note that some of the most intense national debates spanning a range of issues at the heart of the rise of Islamism in Malaysia—namely apostasy, Islamic governance and government, and the sanctity of the constitution and of *sharia* law—are taking place not in the sphere of mainstream partisan politics but in cyberspace among ordinary citizens. This situation points to how Malaysian society is polarized over the question of Islam's salience as an ordering principle for law and politics; the discourse regarding apostasy legislation, where the gradual division of Malaysian society along ethnic and creedal lines becomes apparent, is a case in point.

ISLAMISM AND THE STATE

Islamization in Malaysia is essentially a social change phenomenon with significant political implications. It has been accelerated by the UMNO and PAS's search for an Islamic ideal that would translate into legitimacy, popularity, and electoral support. By placing greater significance on Islamic laws, values, and practices, the early 1980s saw UMNO and PAS enter a "race" to determine which of the two parties' vision of Islam was most successful in Malaysia.

When Mahathir Mohammad assumed office in July 1981, the global Islamic resurgence was at its peak. In an effort to build on this trend, Mahathir set out to Islamize the Malaysian government, enacting a number of policies to achieve these ends. This Islamization campaign was made public during the UMNO general assembly in 1982, when Mahathir announced that the party would embark on a new strategy aimed "to change the attitude of the Malays in line with the requirements of Islam in this modern age."[36]

One of the most important initial steps in Mahathir's Islamization program was the winning over of Anwar Ibrahim, a popular and charismatic Islamist activist, and his followers, and their integration into the UMNO. Mahathir's overall Islamization strategy was linked to the creation of think tanks that would in turn churn out intellectual and ideological impetus for policy. Armed with the necessary knowledge and expertise to ensure that the state was "pro-Islam" while still modernizing the country – especially segments within the Malay community – without sacrificing Islamic values, the Mahathir administration was able to design and implement Islamization policies that would undercut and outbid PAS. Several institutions were either created or improved to serve in the Islamization of the bureaucracy. This strategy resulted in the creation of the ideological machinery that the state has since used to manage and harness Islamic discourse in Malaysia, disseminating an "official" position on intellectual, cultural, educational, and legal matters with regards to Islam.

The UMNO government not only ordered the restructuring (both in scale and in scope) of a range of Islamic institutions, it expanded the state bureaucracy to accommodate the return of a growing number of Malaysian students sent abroad on government scholarships during the Mahathir administration for degrees in Islamic studies, along with the graduates of local Islamic institutions as well. The government also transformed the operations of *sharia* courts and mosques, and reorganized banking structures, foundation and charity work, *zakat* collection, as well as educational institutions. Making religious knowledge an examinable subject in the mainstream school curriculum was one of the Mahathir administration's most significant and controversial endeavors. The Islamic Teachers Training College was established in 1982 to accommodate this change in syllabus. Another notable high point of Mahathir's enterprise of creating and restructuring Islamic institutions was the introduction to Islamic banking.[37] With the creation of an Islamic bank the larger objective of the Islamization of the economy was achieved; it was also an important expression of Mahathir's interpretation of Islamic values (*Nilai-nilai Islam*), whereby Malays can "seek wealth in a moral and legal way" and "obtain prosperity in this world and hereafter."[38]

At the same time, Mahathir worked actively to suppress other interpretations of political Islam at variance his own. Events like 1987's Operation Lallang, the banning of *Al Arqam* in 1994, and the arrests of several prominent political figures, particularly from PAS, demonstrate the Mahathir administration's use of the ISA to remove all perceived obstacles standing in the way of Mahathir's Islamization policies and broader political agenda, even when the threat of some of these obstacles were suspect.

In the process of Islamization, the question of sharia is bound to arise. The controversies linked to *hudud* law in Terengganu and apostasy law in Perlis bring into sharp focus unresolved structural tensions that exist in Malaysia related to the question of jurisdiction and enforcement powers over alleged wrongdoings that have a religious aspect. These tensions are apparent at two stages. In the first level, confusion is caused by the legal governance system, at times hybridized and at times parallel, revolving around the Malaysian constitution and reinforced by the system of federalism that brings about a dispersal of power on the issue of the formulation of Islamic law. Essentially, states may have the power to formulate religious laws, but these formulations require ratification by the federal Parliament for it to be codified as legally binding and enforced. The second equally confounding instance is the dynamic that defines the relationship between civil and Islamic law. In a 1988 constitutional amendment, Article 121 1(A) stipulated that federal high courts "shall have no jurisdiction in respect of any matter within the jurisdiction of the *sharia* courts." Criminal law falls into federal jurisdiction, however the constitution is ambiguous in such a way that it assigns power to create and punish offenses against the laws of Islam through Schedule 9 List 11 Item 1, which has allowed many state religious authorities to interpret their jurisdiction expansively.

The boundaries of Muslim politics in Malaysia may seem straightforward, with PAS the Islamist opposition on one end, demanding that Malaysia's public spaces be governed by *sharia*, and UMNO at the other end, the "secularist" Muslim government that is apparently set on restricting Islamism and keeping religion within the private sphere. However this is but an illusion. As recent controversies over apostasy and the right of non-Muslims to use the word "Allah" go to show, differences between UMNO and PAS are not the least bit cast in stone, and PAS has begun taking inclusivist positions on issues relating to Islam even as UMNO has become discernibly strident and "fundamentalist" in its defence of the primacy and exclusive rights of Muslims. In other words, the track record of PAS is considerably more inconsistent than its strident and unwavering rhetoric of exclusivist Islamism of the early 1980s would admit. On the other hand, the "secularist" UMNO party harbors many Islamist tendencies as well. This trend was especially noticeable since the Mahathir administration, with many elements of a conservative and orthodox Islamic government put in place even as PAS wavered on its own visions of models of governance.

There are many questions left unanswered with regards to the lengths the state and federal governments are prepared to push the possibilities for Islamic governance in Malaysia's multicultural social landscape, especially when neither state nor federal authorities, nor civil or religious authorities, have been able to resolve the blatantly contradictory policies and the obvious discrimination that riddle both UMNO and PAS's vision of Islamic governance in Malaysia.

ENDNOTES

[1]For example, a recent survey of 1,000 respondents revealed that 77 percent wanted stricter Islamic laws in place, and 44 percent supported a more active role for state religious authorities to police morality. See Patricia Martinez, "Islam, Pluralism, and Conflict Resolution in Malaysia: The Case of Interfaith Dialogue," paper presented at the Association of Asian Studies Annual Conference, San Francisco, California, April 6-9, 2006.

[2] Consider, for example, how former UMNO president and Malaysian prime minister Abdullah Badawi regularly made references to Islam in his public speeches, or how *Mingguan Malaysia* [Malaysia Weekly], a best-selling government-linked daily, has weekend columns offering advice on various matters pertaining to religion in everyday life. Malaysia has also regularly hit the country-level limit set by the Saudi government for Haj pilgrims, and there is now a three-year waiting list for Malaysians wanting to make the pilgrimage.

[3] Angel M. Rabasa, *Political Islam in Southeast Asia: Moderates, Radicals and Terrorist* (New York: Oxford University Press Inc., 2003), 39.

[4] Saliha Hassan, "Islamic non-governmental organizations." in Meridith L. Weiss and Saliha Hassan, eds., *Social Movements in Malaysia* (New York: Routledge, 2003), 98.

[5] Joseph Chinyong Liow, "Political Islam in Malaysia: Problematising Discourse and Practice in the Umno-PAS 'Islamisation Race,'" *Commonwealth and Comparative Politics* 42, no. 2 (July, 2004), 186.

[6] Ibid.

[7] Ibidem.

[8] See Joseph Chinyong Liow, *Piety and Politics: The Shifting Contours of Islamism in Contemporary Malaysia* (New York: Oxford University Press, 2008), 58-64.

[9] Beh Lih Yi, "PAS to 'soften' stance on Islamic state", *Malaysiakini*, January 20, 2005, http://www.malaysiakini.com/news/33013.

[10] Ibid.

[11] Azamin Amin, "*Hindraf: PAS kesal hak asasi rakyat dicabuli*" ("HINDRAF: PAS regrets human rights abuses"), *Harakah Daily*, November 25, 2007, http://www.harakahdaily.net/bm/index.php/utama/hindraf-pas-kesal-hak-asasi-rakyat-dicabuli.html. PAS was careful to warn, however, that it did not agree with all of Hindraf's demands either. See Dato' Seri Tuan Guru Abdul Hadi Awang, "*Hak berhimpun diakui, tetapi sebahagian tuntutan Hindraf melampau*" ("HINDRAF's right to assemble must be respected but some of its demands are unacceptable"), *Harakah Daily*, December 3, 2007, http://www.harakahdaily.net/bm/index.php/arkib-utama/hak-berhimpun-diakui-tetapi-sebahagian-tuntutan-hindraf-melampau.html.

[12] Basiron Abdul Wahab, "*Pilihan raya umum: Negara kebajikan,*

tabung biasiswa antara tawaran PAS" ("General elections: PAS offers a welfare state and bursary fund"), *Harakah Daily*, August 28, 2007, http://www.harakahdaily.net/bm/index.php/arkib-pahang-darul-makmur/pilihan-raya-umum-negara-kebajikan-tabung-biasiswa-antara-tawaran-pas.html.

[13] *"PAS mampu lahirkan negara kebajikan bila diberi peluang tadbir pusat"* ("PAS can establish welfare state if allowed to administer at the federal level"), *Harakah Daily*, January 22, 2008, www.harakahdaily.net/bm/index.php/arkib-kelantan-darul-naim/pas-mampu-lahir-kan-negara-kebajikan-bila-diberi-peluang-tadbir-pusat.html; See also Basiron Abdul Wahab, *"Pilihan raya umum: Negara kebajikan, tabung biasiswa antara tawaran PAS"* ("General elections: General elections: PAS offers a welfare state and bursary fund"), *Harakah Daily*, August 28, 2007, http://www.harakahdaily.net/bm/index.php/arkib-pah-ang-darul-makmur/pilihan-raya-umum-negara-kebajikan-tabung-biasiswa-antara-tawaran-pas.html.

[14] Muda Mohd Noor, *"PAS akan lantik orang Cina jadi menteri"* ("PAS will appoint Chinese minister"), *Malaysiakini*, February 6, 2008, http://www.malaysiakini.com/news/77875.

[15] Ibid.

[16] "Terrorist Group Profiles. Kumpulan Mujahidin Malaysia (KMM)." Terrorism Research Center, n.d., http://www.terrorism.com.

[17] It is not clear from reports how many members Halaqah Pakindo had, or how regular were its meetings. See Joseph Chinyong Liow, *Piety and Politics: The Shifting Contours of Islamism in Contemporary Malaysia* (New York: Oxford University Press, 2008), 9.

[18] Ibid.

[19] Ibidem.

[20] See Kamarulnizam Abdullah, "Islamic Militancy Problems in Malaysia," *SEACSN Bulletin*, January-March 2003.

[21] Ibid.

[22] "Asian Militants With Alleged Al Qaeda Ties Are Accused Of Plotting Against Embassies," *Asian Wall Street Journal*, January 2, 2002.

[23] Ibid.

[24] "Religious Cults And Sects, Doctrines And Practices: Al-Ma'unah," apologeticsindex.org, n.d..

[25] *Liow, Piety and Politics*, 7.

[26] "Two Policemen And Nine More Soldiers Identified As Belonging To The Movement," *New Straits Times*, July 13, 2000.

[27] Kamarulnizam Abdullah, "Islamic Militancy Problems in Malaysia," *SEACSN Bulletin*, January-March 2003, 7.

[28] *Liow, Piety and Politics*, 16.

[29] Ibid.

[30] "Suhakam to Consider Proposal to Set Up Interreligious Council," *New Straits Times*, August 27, 2002.

---

[31] Ibid.

[32] See, for example, Marc Lynch, *Voices of a New Arab Republic: Iraq, Al Jazeera, and Middle East Politics Today* (New York: Columbia University Press, 2006).

[33] A weblog is a regularly updated Web page that provides unedited commentary and hyperlinks to other Web sites and weblogs. Weblogs focus on a variety of topics, ranging from hobbies and celebrity gossip to personal diaries and politics.

[34] Needless to say, this general remark is made based on bloggers who actually sign their names to their posts.

[35] Martinez, "Islam, Pluralism, and Conflict Resolution in Malaysia: The Case of Interfaith Dialogue."

[36] See Mahathir's speech at the 33rd Annual UMNO General Assembly, Kuala Lumpur, Malaysia, September 10, 1982.

[37] See Norhashimah Mohd. Yasin, *Islamisation/Malaynisation: A Study on the Role of Islamic Law in the Economic Development of Malaysia: 1969–1993* (Kuala Lumpur, Malaysia: A. S. Noordeen, 1996), 261–64. The bank did not offer any interest on deposits it received. Instead, it would share the profits earned from investing the deposits with the bank's customers. The bank was also not charging interest on credit that it extended.

[38] Hajrudin Somun, *Mahathir: The Secret of the Malaysian Success* (Kuala Lumpur, Malaysia: Pelanduk Publications, 2004), 164.

PHILIPPINES

QUICK FACTS

Population: 99,900,177

Area: 300,000 sq km

Ethnic Groups: Tagalog 28.1%, Cebuano 13.1%, Ilocano 9%, Bisaya/Binisaya 7.6%, Hiligaynon Illongo 7.5%, Bikol 6%, Waray 3.4%, other 25.3%

Religions: Roman Catholic 80.9%, Muslim 5%, Evangelical 2.8%, Iglesia ni Kristo 2.3%, Aglipayan 2%, other Christian 4.5%, other 1.8%, unspecified 0.6%, none 0.1%

Government Type: Republic

GDP (official exchange rate): $160.6 billion

Map and Quick Facts courtesy of the CIA World Factbook (Last Updated July 2010)

Since 1972, the overwhelmingly Catholic Philippines has experienced long-running Muslim secessionist insurgencies in the Southern islands of Mindanao and in the Sulu archipelago. Government abuses, crippling poverty and low levels of human development have fueled Muslim demands for an independent homeland. Yet the three primary insurgent groups currently active there are woefully divided along tribal and ideological lines. Since 2002, the United States has stepped up military assistance to the Philippine government, and since 2004 it has deployed some 500 Special Forces personnel to the southern Philippines to provide intelligence support and training. Nonetheless, the Armed Forces of the Philippines (AFP) are hobbled by corruption and stretched thin—preoccupied with confronting a low-level communist insurgency in the rest of the country.

ISLAMIST ACTIVITY

There are three main organizations fighting—to various degrees—in the southern Philippines: The Moro National Liberation Front (MNLF), the Moro Islamic Liberation Front (MILF), and the Abu Sayyaf Group (ASG). They are riddled with factionalism, leadership contests and disputes over tactics.

Moro National Liberation Front

Nur Misuari, a Manila-based Muslim academic, founded the MNLF in the early 1970s, and for the next decade it served as the sole revolutionary organization for the indigenous Muslim population, known as the Moros. The MNLF was an ethno-nationalist movement, and predominantly secular, although it included Islamist elements. The group received considerable material and financial support from Libyan leader Col. Muammar Qadhafi, who's *Green Book* espoused leftist Muslim anti-colonialism.[1] The MNLF was also aided by the senior minister of the neighboring Malaysian state of Sabah, Tun Mustapha, who was angered by Philippine President Ferdinand Marcos's claims to the territory, once part of the Sultanate of Sulu.[2] The MNLF was closely allied with the communist New People's Army, which launched its own insurgency at the same time, prompting a declaration of martial law and the country's subsequent deterioration.

In 1976, Qadhafi attempted to broker a peace agreement, but the government showed little interest in implementing the proposed autonomy deal. After the failed talks, the MNLF became internally divided and suffered significant battlefield losses. They were never a serious military threat to the Republic of the Philippines again. In 1996, the MNLF and the government signed the Tripoli Accords, which established the Autonomous Region of Muslim Mindanao (ARMM).[3] Nur Misuari became the governor of the region, which included only five provinces; the other eligible provinces having failed to pass plebiscites. Some two thousand MNLF combatants were integrated into the AFP and the national police.[4] The ARMM agreement was never fully implemented and the ARMM region never achieved the promised political and economic autonomy. Rampant corruption and inept leadership also hobbled the ARMM, and remain prevalent to this day.

In 2001, the MNLF executive committee voted to replace Misuari, who in turn staged a short-lived rebellion against the government. The rebellion was quickly put down and Misuari captured, thereafter living under house arrest until 2007 (though he was never formally charged). The MNLF lost control of the ARMM government in the 2006 elections, and the organization has fallen apart since. Though Muslimin Semma formally heads the Executive Council, Misuari and his loyalists do not recognize his authority. In 2007, certain MNLF units picked up arms again, joining forces with the Abu Sayyaf.[5] The organization has shed its secular image, now espousing a "light" version of Islamism.[6] Yet, the MNLF remains deeply factionalized and unable to accept the fact that they are no longer the vanguard of Moro aspirations. That mantle has fallen to the 11-12,000-strong Moro Islamic Liberation Front (MILF).

Moro Islamic Liberation Front

Salamat Hashim, a Muslim scholar educated at Egypt's Al Azhar university, broke away from the MNLF in 1978 and formally founded the MILF in 1984, basing its headquarters in the *Jamaat-I Islamiya's* compound in Lahore, Pakistan. The MILF saw itself as part of the global *jihad*, inspired by the influence of the *mujahideen* in Afghanistan.[7] From the start, the MILF was far more Islamist than the secular ethno-nationalist MNLF; and its avowed goal was to establish an Islamic homeland for the Moros.[8] The MILF began as a small group, whose growth and popularity caught Philippine forces by surprise. The MILF rejected the 1996 MNLF-Government peace pact that established the ARMM and benefited by mass defections from MNLF ranks.[9] By 1999, the MILF had over 11,000 men under arms and controlled vast swaths of central Mindanao. Yet it was never able to broaden that base of support throughout the Sulu archipelago, where the ethnic Tausig-dominated MNLF remained strong.

Starting in 1996, members of the nascent terrorist organization and regional al-Qaeda affiliate, *Jemaah Islamiyah*, began to conduct training for their members and MILF combatants in MILF camps.[10] Al-Qaeda dispatched a handful of senior trainers, such as Omar Al-Faruq, to MILF camps to increase the group's military capacity. Nonetheless, in 1997 the MILF and Philippine government under President Fidel Ramos, who had just concluded an autonomy agreement with the MNLF the previous year, began formal peace talks. The year 2000 election of President Joseph Estrada, however, led the government to revert to a hard-line stance. Estrada ordered the country's military to resume operations against the group, culminating in the capture of the MILF's main base camp. Peace talks resumed in 2001, following Estrada's ouster via a popular uprising. His successor, President Gloria Macapagal Arroyo, resumed peace talks with the MILF in 2002. Nonetheless, in 2003 peace talks broke down and wide-scale fighting erupted, with Philippine military personnel seizing several large MILF camps.

Following the mid-2003 death of Salamat Hashim, the MILF has been led by Chairman Ebrahim Murad and Vice Chairman Aleem Abdulaziz Mimbintas. Murad has *de facto* accepted a broader autonomy agreement, cognizant that the MILF could not win an independent homeland on the battlefield. Formal talks over autonomy began in 2003, and in November 2007, a draft autonomy agreement over the MILF's "ancestral domain" was finally concluded.[11] Nonetheless, Christian lawmakers in Mindanao, the Armed Forces of the Philippines (AFP) and hard-line members of the cabinet rejected the agreement in December 2007. The country's Supreme Court found it to be unconstitutional in August 2008.[12] As a result, widespread fighting resumed. Although President Arroyo pledged to restart talks, formal talks never resumed before her term ended in May 2010. The breakdown of talks led to renewed fighting by the MILF and attacks on Christian villages in 2008-09, which left 400 dead and thousands displaced. The stalled peace process also saw the withdrawal of the small Malaysian-led contingent of peace monitors at the end of 2009. Formal talks faltered in 2010, as President Arroyo completed her lame-duck term in office.

The MILF remains the largest Muslim group, strongly represented amongst the Maguindanao and Maranao ethnic groups, though it has little following among Tausigs. The MILF is a much weaker organization than it was at its peak in 1999-2000, and there are signs of increasing factionalism as negotiations for autonomy have floundered (detailed below). In February 2011, as the administration of President Benignoy Aquino, Jr. prepared to resume formal negotiations with the MILF, a hard line commander quit the MILF and vowed to resume offensive military operations.[13] The MILF previously was known to receive funding from Saudi Arabia and other Gulf sources, although the scope of this aid is not publicly known. Of late, however, it is said that money for the MILF from these sources is said to have dried up, with the group forced to increase its self reliance. The MILF engages in criminality, such as extortion and a limited amount of kidnapping. The MILF has, in the past three years, also been increasingly linked to marijuana cultivation. The MILF remains a somewhat cohesive guerilla-based resistance movement, but the resignation of a senior commander, Ustadz Ameril Umbra Kato, in mid-2010 and his subsequent charges that the current MILF leadership is revisionist portends greater sectarian conflicts. The MILF's hardliners have always been wary of Murad's peace negotiations with the government, and contend that the protracted nature of the talks is indicative of the government's lack of good will. More importantly, the peace process has dissipated the military preparedness and combat capability of the MILF. There are reasonable concerns that other field commanders will join Kato and quit the peace process.

Abu Sayyaf

The third Islamist organization active in the Philippines is the Abu Sayyaf Group (ASG), an organization which vacillates from terrorism to criminality. The ASG was founded in 1991 by a veteran of the Afghan *mujahideen*, Abdurrajak Janjalani, apparently with seed money from al-Qaeda.[14] Osama bin Laden's brother-in-law, Muhmmed Jamal Khalifah, moved from Quetta, Pakistan where he ran a branch of the Rabitat (Muslim World League) that was funneling aid to the *mujahideen*, to the Philippines.[15] From 1991 to late-1994, he ran branches of two Saudi charities, the Muslim World League and the Islamic International Relief Organization, in Mindanao and Sulu—organizations that Philippine security forces saw as conduits of aid for the various

Moro secessionist organizations.

From 1991-1995, the Abu Sayyaf, which was mainly comprised of ethnic Tausig defectors from the larger and more secular Moro National Liberation Front (MNLF), began a spate of bombings, assassinations and kidnappings against non-secular targets, including churches and Christian missionaries in Sulu province. Following the loss of support from al-Qaeda in 1995, the group degenerated and became synonymous with bold kidnapping attacks, such as the April 2000 raid on the Malaysian island of Sipidan and the May 2001 assault on the Philippine resort island of Palawan. Together, these attacks netted the group some 50 foreigners, which it proceeded to hold for ransom.

Between 2000 and 2001, the ASG took some 140 hostages including school children, teachers, priests and western tourists, and was responsible for the death of 16. Starting in 2003, the ASG all but ceased kidnapping and—in conjunction with members of the Indonesian-based terrorist organization *Jemaah Islamiyah*—resumed a campaign of terrorist attacks, including the bombing of a ferry in February 2004 that killed 116. Between 2004 and 2007, the few kidnappings that the group did perpetrate resulted in executions, not ransoms. The shift had much to do with the consolidation of power carried out in 2003 by Khadaffy Janjalani, the younger brother of the organization's founder, who sought to return the group to its secessionist roots, as well as with the neutralization of several other leaders following the onset of U.S. training and assistance to the Philippine military in early 2002.

By early 2005, several top JI leaders were known to be in Jolo, protected by the ASG. An August 2006 campaign by the Armed Forces of the Philippines, supported by a contingent of U.S. Special Forces troops who provided training and intelligence, led to a sustained offensive against the ASG through mid-2007. In September 2006 and March 2007, two top ASG leaders, Khadaffy Janjalani and Abu Solaiman, were killed. The ASG quickly degenerated with a spike in kidnappings from 2007-2010.

The current leadership of the ASG is somewhat unclear. Isnilon Totoni Hapilon, the group's 43-year old hardline commander on Basilan, and Radullan Sahiron, a 72-year old former MNLF commander based in Jolo, Albadar Parad and Umbra Abu Jundail (aka Gafur Jumdail and Dr. Abu) remain the best known figures in the group's hierarchy. But the organization boasts no single identified leader. The size of the ASG is estimated to be between 300-400 at any given time. However, it is often supported and bolstered by disaffected MNLF combatants, such as Habier Malik, whose leaders negotiated a peace pact with the government in 1996, but which has come under strain in recent years.[16] The ASG has increased kidnapping since 2007, and has frequently beheaded individuals for whom ransom is not paid. Nonetheless, the ASG targets U.S. forces when possible, such as the October 2009 IED attack in Jolo that killed two U.S. Special Forces soldiers.[17]

The Philippines lacks any truly broad-based Islamic movements. The Muslim Brotherhood is not strongly represented in the country, nor do the Philippines have any large mass-based Muslim civil society organizations, such as Indonesia's *Nadhalatul Ulama* or *Mohammidiyah*. The MILF does have significant control of or support from the Islamic clergy. There is no shortage of Muslim-based NGOs—indicative of Philippine society at large—but these remain small, under-resourced and often operating along ethnic lines. Muslim civilians have proven to be every bit as factionalized as their armed counterparts. The MILF has tried to establish an umbrella organization for these Muslim and Islamist NGOs, known as the Meredeka coalition, but with limited success. Moreover, there is no Muslim or Islamist political party at the national level. Although the MNLF ostensibly acts like a political party, and will contest elections in the ARMM region, it is weak and factionalized. Since 2006, it has not governed the ARMM.

ISLAMISM AND SOCIETY

Islam came to the Philippines via Yemeni traders who spread the religion throughout the Malay and Indonesian archipelagos. Spanish colonization led to brutal clashes, and the Muslims—known as Moros, a derivation of the Spanish word Moors—took great pride in their resistance to colonial domination. When the Philippines became an American colony, the Moros continued their fight for independence, and only after U.S. military intervention was the southern Philippines pacified.

At the end of WWII, when the U.S. was preparing Philippine independence, Moro leaders requested that the United States give them their own independent homeland. The U.S., however, never acknowledged this request, and the Muslim region was incorporated into the Republic of the Philippines. Decades of Christian migration fundamentally altered the ethnic balance, and in vast swaths of the region, Muslims became the minority. By most every measure of human development, however, the Muslim region lags behind the rest of the country.

With these shortcomings has come a measure of support for radical interpretations of the Islamic faith. There is some support in Philippine society for all three of the organizations mentioned above, although it is not as strong as those leaders appear to believe. Each organization, over time, has alienated sections of the Muslim population.

For example, on the Sulu archipelago, and in particular Jolo Island, there is support for the Abu Sayyaf—albeit for no other reason than that it is a closely-knit society based on clan and kinship. The group is not popular, nor does it have a positive message or social agenda. The ASG simply has a vehemently anti-Christian, anti-state, and anti-American identity. It relies on kidnappings for much of its funding. Almost all kidnapping victims are Christians. On the few occasions that the ASG has kidnapped Muslims, it has tended to execute them, because they were working on U.S.-funded projects. When the ASG does receive foreign funds, kidnapping ceases and bombings resume. This cyclical pattern makes the group of limited appeal, attractive to only a small segment of ethnic Tausig society. By and large, the ASG is rejected by both Muslims and Christians because of its conduct, but clan-based loyalties and kinship ties sustain them. To date no authoritative polling has been done to quantify the level of support the ASG enjoys, either in the Sulu archipelago or in the Philippines at large.

The Moro National Liberation Front (MNLF) likewise has become more marginal and internally divided, and no longer can be said to serve as the vanguard of the interests of the Moro people. The MNLF no longer has broad representation among all the major Moro tribes and ethnic groups, and has become a predominantly Tausig organization. Most MNLF members and supporters in Mindanao joined with the MILF, something that the MNLF has simply not accepted.

Politically, the MNLF is divided between the followers of Nur Misuari, who was released from house arrest in late 2007, and the supporters of the MNLF's Executive Council, under the leadership of Muslimin Semma.[18] These divisions are real; in 2007, some MNLF field commanders unilaterally quit the peace process and joined up with the Abu Sayyaf. Though the MNLF leaders were able to contain that dissension, there is widespread dissatisfaction towards the government, and a general belief that authorities have failed to fully implement the accord. This is a strong theme of MNLF statements and political rhetoric. Interestingly, the MNLF was traditionally a secular organization, though nearly all of its members were Muslim. That is less true today, when the MNLF has much more of a Muslim identity and Islamic consciousness. The MNLF appears not to have extensive funding (authoritative estimates are unavailable), though individual members are often quite wealthy. The MNLF is fundamentally a weaker organization than it was in the 1970s and 1980s and institutionally the party has been gutted.

The Moro Islamic Liberation Front (MILF) is the largest armed Islamist organization in the country. It was treated by the government as a fringe element in the early 1990s, when Manila was engaged in talks with the MNLF. The government never imagined a) that there would be mass defections from the MNLF, doubling the MILF's ranks; and b) that the MILF would use the region's mosques and religious leaders to effectively recruit and garner popular support. The MILF works very closely with the Islamic clergy across Mindanao, and has deputized many clergy to serve as Islamic judges in the shadow government that the MILF runs in the territory under its control. The MILF is the leading voice for the Maranao and Maguindanao tribes, as well as a handful of smaller tribes such as the Yaccans on Basilan Island. The MILF has very little support amongst the Tausigs in Sulu or Tawi Tawi. It controls significant territory in Lanaao del Sur, Cotabato, Maguindanao, Sultan Kudarat, Sharif Kabungsan and Sarangani provinces, as well as territory in provinces in other parts of the southern Philippines. It has lost large chunks of territory since 2000, some at the hands of government operations, and others simply by the spread of roads and other aspects of economic integration.

Despite all this, the MILF should be in a much stronger position than it is currently. In the areas it controls, the group provides little in the way of social services. It has some *madrassas* and a small medical corps, but is not able to match—or compete with—the resources marshaled by the Philippine state. In some ways, the MILF actually alienates the very community it seeks to represent. The MILF is a largely horizontal organization, and individual base commanders often compete over turf; i.e., what villages they can tax. There is also growing concern about the peace process; while most Muslims in the region do blame the government for the breakdown of the peace process in late 2007, that the MILF has been unable to deliver on its promises is also disheartening. There are hard-core elements of the MILF who have picked up arms since November 2007 and resumed fighting, and who are, at the same time, trying to discredit the moderate leadership of MILF chairman Ebrahim el Haj Murad. In July 2010, one of the most conservative religious commanders, Ustadz Ameril Umbra Kato, quit the organization, and has subsequently attracted the organization's more radical youth, unhappy with the stalled peace process, away from the fold.[19] In short, the longer the peace process drags on, the more the hardliners are vindicated. The MILF claims to be 12,000 to 15,000 members in size,[20] although circumstantial evidence suggests the organization is significantly smaller and weaker today. The protracted peace process similarly has weakened the MILF's battlefield preparedness.

Islam is growing at a grassroots level as well. There is constant construction of new mosques occurring in the southern Philippines. However, most of these structures are today very small and built at the village level. In contrast with the 1990s, when a large portion of new mosque and *madrassa* construction was known to be funded by Saudi and Gulf charities, today it is difficult to discern from where funds for such new construction is coming.

Since 9/11, there has been significantly more scrutiny on the flow of foreign funds into the Muslim South. A number of financiers and middlemen have been arrested in the past few years. Philippine authorities have also arrested a number of foreign nationals suspected of supporting terrorism. In one infamous case, Philippine intelligence officials arrested a Saudi national, but he was quickly released before he could be interrogated after the Saudi Arabian embassy appealed to President Arroyo.

With the crackdown on JI in Indonesia and Malaysia, as well as stepped up maritime border patrols, the Philippines is less important as a training center. The maritime border region between Indonesia, Malaysia and the Philippines is much less lawless than in the past. Malaysia has increased maritime patrols off of Sabah state, while Australia provided the Philippines with six coastal patrol craft. Regional and U.S. intelligence officials now see the Southern Philippines as being a much less hospitable place for terrorist training.

One of the most interesting trends in the Philippines is the spread of "*Balik* Islam"—literally, "return to Islam." *Balik* Islam is a movement of Christian converts to Islam. Islam is the fastest growing religion in the Philippines. Conversion takes place through two general processes. One is the conversion of workers while overseas in the Middle East,[21] often for financial reasons (since being a Muslim can lead to better job opportunities). The other, which takes place in the Philippines, is via the network of *Balik* Islam centers scattered throughout the archipelago, primarily in slum areas of cities. For instance, of the 1,890 *madrassas* in the Philippines, only 1,000 or so are in Mindanao; the remainder spread across the rest of the country. The center of Balik Islam is in the northern city of Baguio, on Luzon island. Much of the funding for Balik Islam's *da'wa* work comes from the Gulf.[22] *Balik* islam preaches a Salafi interpretation of Islam, and encourages its members to live in exclusive parallel communities.[23] A radical fringe of *Balik* Islam, the Rajah Solaiman Movement, has worked closely with the ASG and been implicated in a number of terrorist acts.

There are two major organizations that lead the *Balik* Islam movement, the Islamic Studies Call and Guidance (ISCAG) and Islamic Wisdom Worldwide Mission (IWWM). Both have been substantially funded from Middle East and Gulf sources. The IWWM is the successor organization of a front foundation used by Osama bin Laden's brother-in-law, Mohammed Jamal Khalifa, who was forced out of the Philippines in late 2004, which was thought to have been used in the planned terrorist operations of Ramzi Yousef and his uncle Khalid Sheikh Mohammed. ISCAG was established in the mid-1990s in Saudi Arabia by a group of primarily *Balik* Islam converts. ISCAG is a rapidly growing NGO and has been featured in the press, due to its rapid expansion of operations and sponsorship of mosque and madrassa construction. The organization has come under more scrutiny by state authorities after its original head, Humoud Mohammad Abdulaziz al-Lahim, was forced out of the Philippines in April 2002 on allegations of sponsoring terrorism. He is currently based in Saudi Arabia, where he continues to fundraise for ISCAG.[24]

ISLAMISM AND THE STATE

The Philippine government has never had policies that discriminated against Islam and the spread of Islamist institutions. Indeed, Islamic courts for family law are active in the country's south. Mosque and *madrassa* construction generally proceed unhindered. Overall, Islam is the fastest growing religion in the country, and as mentioned above, the Balik Islam movement is robust.

This has led to extensive contacts between the Philippines and the broader Muslim world. The country has observer status in the Organization of the Islamic Conference, or OIC; has increased the number of *hajj* pilgrims; and has allowed foreign aid organizations, *da'wa* organizations and Islamist charities to have access to the country. There is no shortage of civil society organizations in the Philippines, including Islamic NGOs. The presidential administration in Manila likewise has an office of Muslim affairs, and Muslims are viable candidates in political elections.

Muslims in Mindanao and Sulu have been angered at the loss of ancestral domain to Christian migration, heavy-handed government responses to Muslim secessionist movements, and a lack of political will or commitment to the peace process. There is concern that the government's extensive counterterrorism cooperation with the United States since 9/11 has led to a hardening of its official positions in the peace process, even as it has sought a military solution against the Abu Sayyaf. The United States has pledged continued military assistance to, and cooperation with, the Philippines for the foreseeable future. The government's failure, and one which the United States has played into, is that it maintains a "divide and conquer" approach to the three different Muslim groups and has never come up with a holistic solution to the Muslim south. And the country's Muslims themselves are divided and unable to present a common negotiating platform. President Aquino seems unwilling to push through a bold peace deal that would give Muslims meaningful autonomy, and there is little support for such a deal in the Philippine Congress. As such, low-level violence and insecurity can be expected to continue to pervade the southern Philippines.

ENDNOTES

[1]On October 7, 1971, Libyan leader Muammar Qadhafi stated that if "the genocide still went on against the Muslims in the Philippines," he would assume responsibility" for protecting them. That year he established the Islamic Call Society (ICS) to support Islamic revolutions around the world. The ICS became a major force in Libyan foreign policy-making and had offices not just in Africa, but also in Thailand, Malaysia, the Philippines, and Indonesia. Khadhafi, through the ICS, became the major patron of the MNLF. See Saleh Jubair, *Bangsamoro: A Nation Under Endless Tyranny*, 3rd ed. (Kuala Lumpur: IQ Marin SON BHD, 1999), 150.

[2] The Philippines has never legally renounced its claim to Sabah, though it has de facto done so through its diplomatic ties with Malaysia.

[3] The ARMM was established on November 6, 1990 by *Republic Act 6734*. It was legally possible to do so because of the promulgation of a new constitution in 1987 that allowed for the establishment of autonomous regions.

[4] Deidre Sheehan, "Swords into Ploughshares," *Far Eastern Economic Review*, September 20, 2001, 30-31. This USAID program is known as the Livelihood Enhancement and Peace Project. For more on this project, see Dan Murphy, "Filipinos Swap Guns for Rakes," *Christian Science Monitor*, March 5, 2002.

[5] Veronica Uy, "Duereza to MNLF: Deal with Malik," *Philippine Daily Inquirer*, April 16, 2007.

[6] Author interviews with MNLF leaders, Sulu, Zamboanga and Cotabatao, June 2007.

[7] Salamat Hashim, *The Bangsamoro Mujahid: His Objectives and Responsibilities* (Mindanao, Bangsamoro: Bangsamoro Publications, 1985), 18-19.

[8] Derived from the MILF's old webpage, http://morojihad.stcom. net/milf.html.

[9] Rasmia Alonto, "Interview: We Assert our Legitimate Rights to Self-Determination, That Is, Independence," in Salamat Hashim, *Referendum: Peaceful Civilized, Diplomatic and Democratic Means of Solving the Mindanao Conflict* (Camp Abu Bakre As-Siddique: MILF Agency for Youth Affairs, 2002), 45; Rigoberto Tiglao, "Hidden Strength: Muslim Insurgents Shun Publicity and Grow in Power," *Far Eastern Economic Review*, February 23, 1995.

[10] Indonesian National Police (INP), "Interrogation of Mohammad Nasir bin Abbas," Jakarta, Indonesia, April 18, 2003.

[11] In addition to the five provinces of the ARMM, the MILF demanded an addition 1,478 villages, while the government contended that only 618 villages were majority-Muslim. Ultimately

the two sides agreed on 712 villages. See "Philippines in 'Separatist Deal, '" BBC, November 15, 2007, http://news.bbc.co.uk/2/hi/asia-pacific/7096069.stm.

[12] Manny Mogato, "MILF: Peace Talks now in 'Purgatory,'" Reuters, August 31, 2008.

[13] MILF Admits Major Split Ahead of Talks," Agence France Presse, February 5, 2011.

[14] For the history of the Abu Sayyaf, see the author's *Balik Terrorism: The Return of the Abu Sayyaf* (Carlisle, PA: Strategic Studies Institute, Army War College, September 2005).

[15] National Intelligence Coordinating Agency, "Mohammad Khalifa's Network in the Philippines," n.d., 2.

[16] Veronica Uy, "Duereza to MNLF: Deal with Malik," *Philippine Daily Inquirer*, April 16, 2007.

[17] "2 U.S. Soldiers Killed In Philippines Bomb Blast," CNN, October 2, 2009.

[18] "Special Report: Nur Misuari, Muslimin Sema and the Future of the MNLF," *The Mindanao Examiner*, April 28, 2008.

[19] MILF Admits Major Split Ahead of Talks," Agence France Presse, February 5, 2011.

[20] Rigoberto Tiglao, "MILF Boasts Bigger, Better Army," *Philippine Daily Inquirer*, June 9, 2000.

[21] Overseas foreign workers are the backbone of the Philippine economy. Although, they only comprise six percent of the population, their share of the country's GDP is 11 percent. There are over one million OFWs from the Philippines in the Middle East.

[22] Though dated, the best study of the Balik Islam phenomenon is Luis Q. Lacar, "Balik Islam: Christian Converts to Islam in the Philippines, c. 1970-98," *Islam and Christian-Muslim Relations* 12, no. 1 (January 2001), 39-60, esp. n4, 57.

[23] Simon Montlake, "In Philippines, A Watchful Eye on Converts," *Christian Science Monitor*, November 28, 2005.

[24] For more, see Marites Dañguilan Vitug, "The New Believers," *Newsbreak*, May 27, 2002; Philippine Center for Investigative Journalism, "Troubled Return of the Faithful," *imagazine* IX, no. 2 (April-June 2003); Johnna Villaviray, "Muslims Identify With 'Terrorist' Ideals," *Manila Times*, November 19 2003; and ISCAG's website, available at http://www.islamicfinder. org/surf.php?ht=http://www.angislam.org.

AUSTRALIA

QUICK FACTS

Population: 21,515,754

Area: 7,741,220 sq km

Ethnic Groups: white 92%, Asian 7%, Aboriginal and other 1%

Religions: Catholic 25.8%, Anglican 18.7%, Uniting Church 5.7%, Presbyterian and Reformed 3%, Eastern Orthdox 2.7%, other Christian 7.9%, Buddhist 2.1%, Muslim 1.7%, other 2.4%, unspecified 11.3%, none 18.7%

Government Type: Federal parliamentary democracy and Commonwealth realm

GDP (official exchange rate): $930.8 billion

Map and Quick Facts courtesy of the CIA World Factbook (Last Updated June 2010)

The shallow presence and short history of Islamism in Australia is very much a function of Australia's comparatively small Muslim population (just 1.7 percent of the country's total of 21.5 million, or approximately 366,000 people).[1] By world standards, the threat of Islamist violence in Australia is relatively low. While recent years have seen several Islamists convicted of terrorism-related offenses, none of these trials have provided evidence of any specific, well-developed terror plots that were nearing execution. Generally, Australia has not proven fertile ground for global terrorist organizations, despite some attempts by such groups to recruit and fundraise there. The overwhelming majority of those convicted under the country's anti-terrorism laws seem to have belonged to small, independent, self-starting groups with no clear connection to any well-established global terrorist organization. Similarly, the very few individuals to have been in contact with such organizations have long since left them, and have shown little, if any, intention of undertaking terrorist acts in Australia. Accordingly, violent Islamism in Australia fits a decentralized model of political behavior, rather than a more traditional, structured, organizational one.

ISLAMIST ACTIVITY

The Benbrika group

In November 2005, Australian federal and state intelligence and law enforcement agencies carried out the largest counterterrorism raids in the country's history as part of a long-running investigation known as "Operation Pendennis." Seventeen people were arrested and charged across Sydney and Melbourne at that time, with another charged a week later and an additional three charged in late March 2006.[2] The senior figure in the affair was Abdul Nacer Benbrika, also known as Abu Bakr, an immigrant from Algeria who, at the time of his arrest, was variously reported as being 45 or 46. The rest of those charged were considerably younger, mostly between 18 and 28. All except one came from immigrant families, with the dominant ethnicity among them Lebanese. A majority of the Melbourne group was Australian-born, and one of the accused was an Anglo-Australian convert to Islam. Neither the Melbourne nor Sydney groups seem to have been highly educated or wealthy. Most were tradesmen or laborers, and only one participant had a tertiary degree. Moreover, several had minor criminal records for fraud, theft and firearms charges.[3]

Members of the Melbourne cluster were all charged with being members of a terrorist organization involved in the fostering or preparation of a terrorist act (a legal designation under Australian law). Some were also charged with providing resources or making funds available to a terrorist organization, as well as possessing materiel connected to terrorism. Benbrika himself was also charged with intentionally directing the activities of a terrorist organization.[4] The Sydney cluster faced more serious charges of conspiring to plan a terrorist attack.

The Melbourne trial commenced first, resulting in seven convictions, four acquittals, and one retrial. In February 2009, Benbrika was sentenced to 15 years in prison with a non-parole period of 12 years—considerably less than the maximum 25-year sentence available under the relevant legislation.[5] It is possible this was due to the relatively embryonic nature of the group. For example, the court found that the group had not reached the stage of plotting to blow up specific targets.

By contrast, the Sydney cluster was more advanced, with considerable stockpiles of weapons and chemicals.[6] In October 2009, following the longest-running criminal trial in Australian legal history, five of its members were convicted (in addition to four others who had pled guilty) and subsequently sentenced to prison terms ranging from 21 to 28 years.[7]

Links between the Benbrika group and global terrorist organizations seem to have been sparse. Of the Melbourne cluster, Anglo-Australian Shane Kent was the only one to have attended a training camp overseas in Afghanistan where he reportedly pledged allegiance, and may have been introduced, to Osama bin Laden.[8] Nevertheless, prosecutors dropped charges alleging

Kent provided support to al-Qaeda.[9] The Sydney cluster seems to have had some deeper international experience, with up to three of them having visited Lashkar-e-Taiba (LeT) training camps in Pakistan.[10] Benbrika himself, however, appears to have had no sustained contact with global terrorist organizations. The only encounter on the public record was in 1994, when the British-based al-Qaeda sheikh Abu Qatadah visited Australia as a guest of the Melbourne-based Salafi imam Mohamed Omran. News reports suggest Benbrika's radicalization can be traced to his exposure to Abu Qatadah's speeches during that tour.[11]

Abu Qatadah's host, Mohamed Omran, is one of Australia's highest-profile Wahhabi-Salafi imams, the head of the Ahlus Sunnah Wa-l-Jamaah Association, and a central figure in any consideration of radical Islamism in Australia. To date, no public evidence has emerged connecting Omran to terrorism directly, and the suspicion that surrounds him is by association. In addition to his connections with Abu Qatadah, he has been named in Spanish court documents as an associate of al-Qaeda's Abu Dada (a charge which he has denied).[12] At the time of Abu Qatadah's speaking tour of Australia, and for several years thereafter, Benbrika was one of Omran's followers. Their relationship seems to have ended some years before Benbrika's arrest, when he left Omran's organization because he found it insufficiently radical.[13] Benbrika's own followers in the Melbourne cluster appear to have continued attending Omran's center, but there is no doubt that Benbrika was their most important influence at this time.[14]

Ideologically, the Benbrika group clearly held to a Wahhabi-Salafi ideology. First, the group believed in a bifurcated view of the world in which there was to be hostility between those who adhered to their version of Islam and everyone else. Second, it believed that Islam was under attack from the Western world, particularly the United States, but also Australia. Third, the group held that the perceived campaigns against Islam waged by the West in Afghanistan and Iraq imposed on the group's members an obligation as devout Muslims to act in defense of Islam and Muslims. Fourth, that obligation took the form of an individual religious obligation to embark upon violence in Australia.[15] Thus, the group's views of their militancy were larger defensive, rather than imperial; they saw themselves as acting in the defense of Islam and Muslims, rather than proceeding from an explicit desire to Islamize Australia or the world.

Consistent with its independent, self-starting nature, the Benbrika group was informally and independently funded. Some members would contribute to a sanduq, or central fund, mainly through minor crimes such as car theft and credit card fraud.[16] By all accounts, it received no external funding from well-established terrorist organizations.

Operation Neath

August 2009 saw the culmination of Australia's second-largest counter-terrorism operation, in which five men were ultimately arrested and charged with conspiring to plan a terrorist attack on Holsworthy Barracks, an Australian Army training base.[17] The apparent plan was for members of the group to kill as many Australian soldiers as they could with automatic weapons before they themselves were killed.[18] The matter is currently before the courts.

The five men, all Australian citizens from Melbourne, were of Lebanese and Somali extraction. Authorities believe they were part of a broader group of 18 men, also ethnically Lebanese and Somali.[19] The group seems to have similar professional and educational backgrounds to the Benbrika group discussed above. None were believed to have tertiary education, and most were either laborers or taxi drivers.[20] Likewise, there appears to have been an absence of a well-formulated overarching ideology; although the group was definitively Wahhabi/Salafi in orientation, its political narrative appears to have been reactive and defensive. Members regularly expressed anger at the presence of Australian troops in Muslim countries, possibly Iraq and Afghanistan, although they did not mention these places by name.[21]

Unlike the Benbrika group, however, there appears to be no clear religious authority figure in this case. All of those charged are young, and while the contours of the group will emerge more fully as evidence is presented in court, publicly available information suggests the group to be horizontal in structure.

The other key development in this case is the group's Somali connection—the first alleged involvement of Somali Australians in radical Islamist activity. Indeed, a 2007 investigation by the Australian Federal Police of extremism within the Australian Muslim Somali community found no evidence of any illegal activity.[22] However, authorities believe that the group apprehended in Operation Neath possessed links with Somalia's Al-Shabaab, an al-Qaeda affiliate banned in the United States, and which American authorities allege has been actively recruiting Somali-American Muslims.[23] News reports suggest several members of the group had attempted to travel to Somalia to train with al-Shabaab.[24] A spokesman for al-Shabaab, however, has denied the allegations, claiming it has "no involvement at all" with the group and no people based in Australia.[25]

Individuals connected to terrorism

While the abovementioned events are certainly the most important in the history of Islamist militancy in Australia, several other individual Islamists have been convicted of terrorism-related offenses. Some of these have been Australian citizens who have made connections with Islamist terrorist groups overseas. Others are foreign nationals who attempted unsuccessfully to infiltrate Australia. None are presently active members of radical Islamist organizations. They are:

- **David Hicks**, an Anglo-Australian convert to Islam who travelled to Albania and joined the Kosovo Liberation Army (KLA).[26] Hicks undertook four weeks of training with the KLA and enlisted with NATO, but the conflict ended before he could do any fighting, and he was sent home under NATO orders.[27] Upon returning to Australia he attempted to join the Australian Army, but was rejected.[28] In November 1999, he flew to Pakistan, where he spent three months in a Lashkar e-Taiba training camp. From there, he traveled on to Afghanistan where he spent eight months in 2001 in an al-Qaeda training camp. He saw Osama bin Laden approximately eight times during this time, and spoke to him once.[29] Following the U.S.-led invasion of Afghanistan, Hicks was sent to the front line to fight with the Taliban. He insists he saw no action, and never fired his weapon. Indeed, the front to which he was sent collapsed only hours after he arrived. Two weeks later, Hicks attempted to leave the country, but was captured by the Northern Alliance, which transferred him to U.S. Special Forces for $1,000.[30] Hicks subsequently was detained in the Guantànamo Bay detention facility for just under five-and-a-half years. He was first charged by a Military Commission in August 2004, but that commission was abolished in 2006, after the Supreme Court ruled it illegal in *Hamdan v. Rumsfeld*. Subsequently, in March 2007, Hicks was formally charged with providing material support for terrorism and tried before a Special Military Commission. He pleaded guilty and became the first person convicted by the Guantànamo Military Tribunal. He was sentenced to seven years' imprisonment, all but nine months of which was suspended.[31]

  Hicks has since served his sentence and been released into the community. Initially, he was placed under a control order that required him to report to a police station three times weekly. The control order expired in December 2008, however, and the Australian Federal Police did not seek to renew it—indicating Hicks was no longer considered a threat.[32] Moazzam Begg, a former Guantànamo Bay detainee who met Hicks in detention, has said that Hicks is no longer a Muslim, and ceased being one some time early in his detention.[33]
- **Joseph Thomas**, who in early 2001 travelled to Afghanistan to join the Taliban's fight against the Northern Alliance. There, Thomas received training in al-Qaeda's Camp Faruq, spent time with David Hicks, and met Osama bin Laden at least once.[34] Thomas spent a week on the front line in Afghanistan after his training, but did not participate in any combat. Over the four months that followed, he was in contact with senior al-Qaeda figures such as Ayman al-Zawahiri, Mohammed Atef, and Saif el Adel, seeking help with income and accommodation. He claims he

did not know who these people were at the time.[35] With the commencement of the U.S.-led invasion of Afghanistan, Thomas remained to fight American forces. At that time, he shared a guesthouse with 9/11 planner Ramzi bin al-Shibh, and was asked by al-Qaeda's Abu Zubaida to "do some work."[36] Thomas' time with Abu Zubaida took him to Pakistan, where he met the alleged mastermind of the *USS Cole* bombing, Khalid bin Attash. Bin Attash asked Thomas to undertake an attack in Australia.[37] Thomas was given $3,500 and a plane ticket to Australia for this purpose. However, he has maintained at all times that he had no intention of executing such an attack, and that the money he received was merely compensation for his time and maintenance, rather than for terrorism.[38] Yet, before he could board his flight, Thomas was arrested by Pakistan's ISI, and subsequently was tortured.

Around this time, the Australian Federal Police and the Australian Security and Intelligence Organization questioned Thomas, who provided a detailed statement. In June 2003, Pakistani authorities released Thomas and flew him to Australia, where he remained free for around 17 months until finally arrested. Thomas was charged with receiving funds and resources from a terrorist organization that would assist in a terrorist attack, as well as with travelling on a falsified passport.[39] Following a high-profile trial, Thomas was acquitted of the most serious offenses—largely because most of the evidence on which they were based was tainted by his torture at the hands of the ISI. At the end of the appeal process, Thomas was finally convicted on the falsified passport charge, as well as for receiving funds from a terrorist organization. He was sentenced to nine months in prison, and upon his release, was made subject to a control order that, among other restrictions, prohibits him from contacting certain figures involved in terrorism and imposes a curfew.[40]

- **Faheem Lodhi**, an Australian citizen, immigrated to Australia from Pakistan in 1996. In June 2006, he was convicted of acting in preparation for a terrorist attack and sentenced to 20 years' imprisonment. Key elements of the prosecution's case included that Lodhi had sought information about chemicals capable of making explosives, possessed a terrorism manual, and had maps of the electricity grid.[41] It is suspected that he was targeting the national electricity supply, as well as various Army barracks and training areas. During the trial, it emerged that Lodhi had trained with LeT in Pakistan, where he met al-Qaeda operative Willie Brigitte. Lodhi was also Brigitte's main contact when Brigitte visited Australia.[42] Brigitte himself was deported from Australia for visa violations, before finally being convicted in a French court and sentenced to nine years in prison for planning a terrorist attack in Australia.[43]
- **Jack Roche**, a British immigrant to Australia who converted to Islam

in his late 30s. Soon after his conversion, Roche had contact with twin brothers Abdulrahman and Abdulrahim Ayub, who are suspected of being Australia's representatives of the Indonesian terrorist group Jamaah Islamiah (JI). The Ayub twins sent Roche to Malaysia and JI leader Hambali. From there, Roche was sent to Pakistan, where he trained in explosives in an al-Qaeda camp and met Osama bin Laden.[44] Al-Qaeda subsequently asked Roche to return to Australia to gather information about the Israeli embassy in Canberra, as well as on Joseph Gutnick, a wealthy Jewish-Australian businessman. In June 2000, Roche set to work, filming the outside of the embassy. However, he could not go through with the attack and went to the Australian Intelligence and Security Organization to tell them of these events. Yet, in Roche's words, "no one seemed to be particularly interested in what was going on."[45]

It was only after the Bali bombings in October 2002 that Australian law enforcement and security agencies took a fresh look at domestic militancy, which resulted ultimately in Roche's arrest and conviction for the embassy plot.[46] He was sentenced to nine years in prison with a parole period of half that time, and was released in May 2007.[47]

Non-violent Islamist groups

The fact that Australia is a liberal democracy means Islamist groups can form freely and remain in existence provided they remain within the law. Accordingly, a number of Islamist organizations remain.

The most worrisome, from a security perspective, is Mohamed Omran's Ahlus Sunnah wa-l-Jamaah Association. Nothing on the public record links the Association to violence directly, and its representatives have consistently denied their support for terrorism.[48] But public concerns surround Omran because of his connections with the al-Qaeda figures discussed above, and for his statements in support of Osama bin Laden (whom he insists did not have any involvement with the 9/11 attacks).[49]

The other prominent Wahhabi-Salafi organization of note is the Islamic Information and Services Network of Australasia headed by Samir Mohtadi. This organization is more politically moderate than other Wahhabi-Salafi groups, and broke from Omran's group many years before domestic terrorism became a public issue. Mohtadi testified during the trial of the Benbrika group, saying that he warned Benbrika he would notify the authorities if he intended to do "anything stupid," and that Australia was a "peaceful country".[50]

A range of other Wahhabi-Salafi organizations with similar attitudes exist, most notably Sydney's Global Islamic Youth Centre, led by Sheikh Feiz Mohamed,[51] though it appears to lack the connections of Omran's group. None of these groups publicly advocate the forceful Islamization of Australia. To the extent they are radical, they tend to articulate their activism in defensive terms, rather than offensive ones. Mohtadi's group is focused on *dawah*, or preaching, rather than the forceful transformation of society.

The most overtly Islamist organization in Australia is undoubtedly Hizb ut-Tahrir. The group attracted a slew of media attention following the 2005 London bombings, when banning the group became a public discussion in Australia, mirroring Britain's public calls for a ban on the group.[52] However, while HuT is a major presence in many countries, its members in Australia are very small in number and confined mostly to Sydney.[53]

ISLAMISM AND SOCIETY

As a nation with a British political inheritance, a very small Muslim population and a strong enduring alliance with the United States, Australia is a hostile environment for Islamist movements, particularly violent ones. Islamism has no discernible public or governmental support as an ideology. Anyone who calls publicly for the incorporation of some part of Islamic law (typically family law) into the Australian legal system faces swift denunciation, to say nothing of those who openly support more radical Islamist ideas.[54]

Accordingly, none of the aforementioned Islamist organizations receive government patronage, and there is little if any evidence that their popularity and level of support in the Australian community extends significantly beyond their own memberships. Debate continues in Australia as to whether or not HuT, for instance, should be banned.[55]

As the Muslim population of Australia continues to grow, both through procreation and immigration, Muslim organizations can be expected to expand in size and number. However, while an increase in the number of mosques is inevitable as a result, there is no evidence of a surge in mosque construction, and there is nothing in the public domain to suggest an impending rise in terrorist activity beyond what has been seen since 2005. It is probably true that HuT's voice is gradually becoming louder (facilitated by media attention) but it remains closely monitored and of marginal influence.[56]

Funding arrangements for Islamic organizations are more difficult to discern. The record to date suggests that would-be terrorist groups in Australia are not reliant on overseas funding for their plots, and indeed, as discussed above in relation to the Benbrika group, have attempted their own fundraising, often through fraudulent means.

More mainstream Islamic organizations have long been recipients of funding from both Australian and overseas governments. Among the most active has been the Saudi government, which is thought to have spent around AU$120 million in Australia since the 1970s.[57] It is reasonable to assume that this financial support played an important role in the emergence of Wahhabi Salafism in Australia over the decades that followed. In this regard, there have been periods of consternation in the Australian press over funding from the Saudi government, particularly of esteemed institutions such as Australian universities.[58] There is little to suggest, however, that funding flows from abroad have increased in the past decade, while the associated media coverage indicates that such funding arrangements would be heavily scrutinized once publicly known. The Australian government, too, has actively funded Islamic studies in Australian universities—most directly through the establishment of a National Centre of Excellence in Islamic Studies across three universities in three states at a cost of AU$8 million.[59] The center was conceived as part of the government's social cohesion, harmony and security strategy, and aims at teaching Islam in an Australian context.[60]

ISLAMISM AND THE STATE

The Australian government responded to the 9/11 terrorist attacks and the subsequent 2002 Bali bombings with a flurry of legislative activity. The suite of anti-terrorism laws introduced since that time have created new terrorism-related offenses and greatly expanded the powers of police and intelligence agencies.[61] These laws have certainly been controversial for their impact on civil liberties, and there has been much criticism of the legislative process that produced them,[62] as well as the occasionally improper use of these powers and instances of improper conduct by police and intelligence agencies.[63] These new regulations, however, have netted concrete results; the terrorism-related convictions of the Benbrika group, Joseph Thomas, Faheem Lodhi and Jack Roche were all secured under the new, post-9/11 legal regime in Australia.

Some controversy has also attached to the manner in which counterterrorism raids have been conducted, particularly where excessive force has been used, or where it appears media organizations have known of them in advance. This was most clear in the case of "Operation Neath," and has prompted an Australian Federal Police investigation.[64]

Australian authorities have also taken some steps towards a social approach to counterterrorism. In September 2005, the Howard government established a Muslim Community Reference Group to look into areas of social need in Muslim communities, including those elements thought to contribute to radicalization—such as education, employment and social cohesion.[65] Similarly, some police forces around the country, including the Australian Federal Police, have expanded their community engagement programs.[66]

Not all of these measures have been well received among Australian Muslims. The introduction of anti-terrorism laws caused significant Muslim protest, and these measures have been regularly criticized by Muslim groups for contributing to further alienation and facilitating coercive and intimidating behavior from authorities.[67] While there is some evidence suggesting that the impact of harsh legislation and the negative tone of public discourse are having a radicalizing effect in Australia,[68] this is impossible to quantify. Similarly, the Muslim Community Reference Group has faced criticism for being a forum for lecturing to the Muslim community and encouraging Muslims to identify radicals for the government under the guise of community engagement, as well as for perpetuating the connection between Muslims and terrorism.[69]

Whatever the impact of these government responses has been, it remains true that the threat from Islamism in Australia, while real and continuing, is small by global standards. To date, in spite of the occasional overuse of force, attempts at law enforcement have been successful in monitoring and prosecuting the main threats stemming from Islamic radicalism. No global terrorist organization of any note has established deep links in Australia, and the threat seems to be confined to largely disconnected, home-grown and independently-organized groups. Whatever connections exist with major global organizations are typically shallow, or confined to individuals that have already been convicted of terrorism offenses.

ENDNOTES

[1]Figures derived from "Australia," CIA *World Factbook*, November 9, 2010, https://www.cia.gov/library/publications/the-world-factbook/geos/as.html.

[2] "Tip Off Led To Intense 16-Month Investigation," *The Age* (Melbourne), September 17, 2008, http://www.theage.com.au/national/tipoff-led-to-intense-16month-investigation-20080916-4hxp.html?page=-1.

[3] Mitchell D. Silber and Arvin Bhatt, *Radicalization In The West: The Homegrown Threat* (New York: New York City Police Department, 2007), 27-28

[4] "Benbrika Guilty Of Terrorism Charges," *The World Today*, ABC Radio *The World Today*, September 15, 2008, http://www.abc.net.au/worldtoday/content/2008/s2364860.htm.

[5] "Benbrika Jailed For 15 years," *The Age* (Melbourne), February 3, 2009, http://www.theage.com.au/national/benbrika-jailed-for-15-years-20090203-7w7y.html.

[6] "Five Guilty Of 'Mass' Terror Plot In Sydney," *Daily Telegraph* (Surry Hills), October 16, 2006, http://www.news.com.au/national/five-guilty-of-mass-terror-plot-in-sydney/story-e6frfkvr-1225787524969.

[7] "Long Sentences For Sydney Terror Plotters," ABC Radio PM, February 15, 2010, http://www.abc.net.au/pm/content/2010/s2820249.htm.

[8] "Terror Suspect 'Met Osama,'" Australian Associated Press, December 20, 2005, http://www.smh.com.au/articles/2005/12/20/1135032012529.html.

[9] "Shane Kent Pleads Guilty On Eve Of Terror Trial, But Al-Qa`ida Charge Dropped," *The Australian*, July 28. 2009.

[10] Silber and Bhatt, *Radicalization In The West: The Homegrown Threat*, 51.

[11] "Suspect Linked To radical UK Cleric," *Times of London*, November 13, 2005, http://www.timesonline.co.uk/tol/news/world/article589625.ece.

[12] Sally Neighbour, "How They Spotted Terror Suspects," *The Australian*, November 4, 2005, 2.

[13] "Terror Links To Radical Sheikhs," *The Australian*, November 10, 2005, 1.

[14] Ibid.

[15] "Long Sentences For Sydney Terror Plotters."

[16] 'Tip-Off Led To Intense 16-month Investigation," *The Age* (Melbourne), September 17, 2008, http://www.theage.com.au/national/tipoff-led-to-intense-16month-investigation-20080916-4hxp.html; Silber and Bhatt, *Radicalization In The West: The Homegrown Threat*, 52.

[17] "Army Base Terror Plot Foiled," *The Australian*, August 4, 2009, 1; Milanda Rout, "Terror Suspect Saney Aweys Says He's 'Victimised' In Prison," *The Australian*, November 7, 2009, http://www.theaustralian. com.au/news/nation/terror-suspect-saney-aweys-says-hes-victimised-in-prison/story-e6frg6nf-1225795202644.

[18] Cameron Stewart, "Phone Call Sparked Operation Neath," *The Australian*, August 4, 2009, 1, 4.

[19] Ibid.

[20] Ibidem.

[21] "Army Base Terror Plot Foiled."

[22] Ibid.

[23] Spencer S. Hsu, "U.S. Says Men Ran Terror Network," *Washington Post*, November 24, 2009, http://www.washingtonpost.com/wp-dyn/content/article/2009/11/23/AR2009112303999.html.

[24] "Phone Call Sparked Operation Neath."

[25] "Militant Somali Group Denies Australia Link," *ABC News*, August 7, 2009, http://www.abc.net.au/news/stories/2009/08/07/2648501.htm.

[26] Raymond Bonner, "Australian Terrorism Detainee Leaves Prison," *New York Times*, December 29, 2007, http://www.nytimes.com/2007/12/29/world/asia/29hicks.html?_r=1.

[27] "The Case Of David Hicks," ABC Television *4 Corners*, October 31, 2005, http://www.abc.net.au/4corners/content/2005/s1494795.htm.

[28] Ibid; "Australian Terrorism Detainee Leaves Prison."

[29] "The Case of David Hicks."

[30] Ibid.

[31] Michael Melia, "Australian Gitmo Detainee Gets 9 Months," *Washington Post*, March 31, 2007, http://www.washingtonpost.com/wp-dyn/content/article/2007/03/31/AR2007033100279.html.

[32] Australian Federal Police National Media Release, "David Hicks' Control Order Not To Be Renewed," November 20, 2008, http://www.afp.gov.au/media_releases/national/2008/david_hicks_control_order_not_to_be_renewed.

[33] Penelope Debelle, "Hicks No Longer A Muslim: Ex-Detainee," *The Age* (Melbourne), June 24, 2006, http://www.theage.com.au/news/national/hicks-no-longer-a-muslim-exdetainee/2006/06/23/1150845378125.html.

[34] "The Convert," ABC Television *4 Corners*, February 27, 2006, http://www.abc.net.au/4corners/content/2006/s1580223.htm.

[35] Ibid.

[36] Ibidem.

[37] Ibidem.

[38] Ibidem.

[39] Ibidem.

[40] "Government Places Curfew On Jack Thomas," ABC Television *Lateline*, August 28, 2006, http://www.abc.net.au/lateline/content/2006/s1726436.htm.

[41] Leonie Lamont, "Lodhi 'Deserves' 20 Years," *The Age* (Melbourne), August 23, 2006, http://www.theage.com.au/news/national/lodhi-gets-20-years/2006/08/23/1156012586528.html.

[42] "Bomb Plotter 'Guilty By Association' With Brigitte," *The Australian*, November 6, 2007, 9.

[43] "Brigitte Jailed For Planning Aust Terrorist Attacks," *ABC News Online*, March 16, 2007, http://www.abc.net.au/news/newsitems/200703/s1873090.htm.

[44] Sally Neighbour, "My Life As A Terrorist," *The Australian*, December 4, 2007, http://www.theaustralian.com.au/national-affairs/defence/my-life-as-a-terrorist/story-e6frg8yx-1111115023061.

[45] Ibid.

[46] "Jack Roche: The Naive Militant," BBC, June 1, 2004, http://news.bbc.co.uk/2/hi/asia-pacific/3757017.stm.

[47] "Terrorist Roche Released From Jail," ABC News *Online*, May 17, 2007, http://www.abc.net.au/news/newsitems/200705/s1925403.htm.

[48] "Militant Networks," *The Australian*, November 18, 2006, http://www.theaustralian.com.au/news/features/militant-networks/story-e6frg6z6-1111112542554.

[49] "Sheikh Moves To Clarify Bin Laden Comments," ABC Television *Lateline*, July 25, 2005, http://www.abc.net.au/lateline/content/2005/s1422054.htm.

[50] "Moderate Cleric Claims Benbrika Described Australia As A Land Of War," ABC Radio *PM*, August 2, 2006, http://www.abc.net.au/pm/content/2006/s1704344.htm.

[51] Richard Kerbaj, "Radical Phones Home For Sermons," *The Australian*, July 26, 2007, 1.

[52] See, for example, Janet Albrechtsen, "It Is Time We Banned Hizb ut-Tahrir," *The Australian*, July 8, 2007, http://blogs.theaustralian.news.com.au/janetalbrechtsen/index.php/theaustralian/comments/it_is_time_we_banned_hizb_ut_tahrir/P50/.

[53] Barney Zwartz, "Working On The Margins," *The Age* (Melbourne), January 13, 2007, http://www.theage.com.au/news/in-depth/working-on-the-margins/2007/01/12/1168105181403.html.

[54] See, for example, the reflections of *Age* journalist Barney Zwartz after he reported on a call for an Islamic family law tribunal. Barney Zwartz, "Sharia In Australia: Sanity Or Shocking," *Sydney Morning Herald*, October 18, 2009, http://www.smh.com.au/opinion/blogs/the-religious-write/sharia-in-australia-sanity-or-shocking/20091018-h32b.html.

[55] See for example, Sally Neighbour, "Hardliners Teach How To

Get Islamic State In Sydney," *The Australian*, July 8, 2010, http://www.theaustralian.com.au/news/nation/hardliners-teach-how-to-get-islamic-state-in-sydney/story-e6frg6nf-1225889152531; Carl Ungerer and Anthony Bergin, "Cry Halt When Islamists Take Liberties," *The Australian*, July 9, 2010, http://www.theaustralian.com.au/news/opinion/cry-halt-when-islamists-take-liberties/story-e6frg6zo-1225889557751.

[56] Sally Neighbour, "Extremists With Caliphate On Their Minds, Not Bombs In Their Belts," *The Australian*, July 2, 2010, http://www.theaustralian.com.au/news/world/extremists-with-caliphate-on-their-minds-not-bombs-in-their-belts/story-e6frg6ux-1225887074605.

[57] Richard Kerbaj and Stuart Rintoul, "Saudis' Secret Agenda," *The Australian*, May 3, 2008, http://www.theaustralian.com.au/news/features/saudis-secret-agenda/story-e6frg6z6-1111116230270.

[58] "Saudi Money; Australian Universities and Islam – where is the line in the sand?" ABC Radio National *The Religion Report*, April 30, 2008, http://www.abc.net.au/rn/religionreport/stories/2008/2231183.htm.

[59] Minister for Education Science and Training, "$8m For Centre Of Excellence For Islamic Education National Action Plan," July 16, 2006, http://www.dest.gov.au/Ministers/Media/Bishop/2006/07/B002160706.asp.

[60] Ibid.

[61] See, for example, the *Security Legislation Amendment (Terrorism) Act 2002* (Cth) and the *Australian Security and Intelligence Organisation Legislation Amendment (Terrorism) Act 2003* (Cth).

[62] See, for example, Andrew Lynch, "Legislating With Urgency—The Enactment Of The *Anti-Terrorism Act* [No 1] 2005," MULR 30, iss. 3 (2007), 747-781.

[63] See, for example, the legal judgments in *R v Ul-Haque*, NSWSC 1251 (2007); *R v Mallah*, NSWSC 358 (2005); *R v Thomas*, VSCA 165 (2006).

[64] AFP National Media Release, "AFP Investigation Into Media Leak—Operation Neath," August 5, 2009, http://www.afp.gov.au/media_releases/national/2009/afp_investigation_into_media_leak_-_operation_neath.html.

[65] Janet Phillips, "Muslim Australians: E-Brief," *Parliamentary Library of Australia*, March 6, 2007, http://www.aph.gov.au/library/INTGUIDE/SP/Muslim_Australians.htm.

[66] See, for example, "Building A Relationship With Melbourne's Islamic community," *Platypus Magazine* 97, December 2007, 28-29, http://www.afp.gov.au/__data/assets/pdf_file/64549/28_29_Building_a_relationship.pdf.

[67] See, for example, Australian Muslim Civil Rights Advocacy Network, submission no 88, Parliamentary Joint Committee on ASIO, ASIS and DSD Review of Division 3 Part III of the ASIO Act 1979:

ASIO's Questioning and Detention Powers, https://www.aph.gov.au/HOUSE/committee/pjcaad/asio_ques_detention/subs/sub88.pdf.

[68] Sharon Pickering, David Wright-Neville, Jude McCulloch and Peter Lentini, *Counter-Terrorism Policing and Culturally Diverse Communities: Final Report 2007* (Clayton: Monash University, 2007)

[69] See for instance Basia Spalek and Alia Imtoual, "Muslim Communities And Counter-Terror Responses: 'Hard' Approaches To Community Engagement In The UK And Australia," *Journal of Muslim Minority Affairs* 27, iss. 2, August 2007, 185-202, 193-196.

GLOBAL MOVEMENTS

MOVEMENTS

Al-Qaeda
Hezbollah
Lashkar-e Taiba
Taliban
Muslim Brotherhood
Hizb ut-Tahrir
Tablighi Jamaat

AL-QAEDA

QUICK FACTS

Geographical Areas of Operation: East Asia, Eurasia, Europe, Latin America, Middle East and North Africa, North America, South Asia, Sub-Saharan Africa

Numerical Strength (Members): Exact numbers unknown

Leadership: In May 2011, Osama Bin Laden was killed in Abbotabad, Pakistan during a raid by U.S. commandos. Al-Qaeda's second-in-command, Ayman al-Zawahiri, was formally appointed as Bin Laden's successor in June 2011.

Religious Identification: Sunni Islam

(Quick Facts courtesy of the U.S. State Department's Country Reports on Terrorism)

Al-Qaeda is the most notorious Islamic terrorist group in existence today. In the years since it orchestrated the devastating September 11, 2001 attacks on the World Trade Center and the Pentagon, its leaders, Osama bin Laden and his second-in-command, Ayman al-Zawahiri, have become internationally recognized figures and heroes to Islamists and aspiring jihadists the world over. Indeed, al-Qaeda has taken on a global reach in recent years to the point that groups that are actually affiliated with it are blurred with those that are simply inspired by it.

HISTORY AND IDEOLOGY

Though the attacks of September 11, 2001 are perhaps the most profound symbols of al-Qaeda's notoriety, the group's violent history stretches back well over two decades and finds its roots in another, more conventional, war.

Al-Qaeda is believed to have been formally created toward the later years of the Soviet-Afghan war (1979-1989), sometime around 1988-1989. Various theories have been offered as to the etymology of "al-Qaeda"—which in Arabic literally means "the base"—including that it refers to a "database" of names of Arab-Afghan *mujahideen*, compiled by Osama bin Laden, and later mobilized for terrorist missions.[1] However, there is no reason to doubt bin Laden's own explanation, that *al-Qaeda* was originally used as a generic phrase to denote the *mujahideen's* base of combat or operations.[2] This is borne out by the fact that al-Qaeda sometimes refers to itself as *qaedat al-jihad*, "base of *jihad*."[3]

Coming on the heels of the Islamic Revolution of Iran, when Islamist fervor reached a fever pitch internationally, the Soviet-Afghan theater lured many *mujahideen*, or *jihadists*, from around the Arab world. Among these was multi-millionaire Osama bin Laden, who, in conjunction with Palestinian *jihadist* theoretician Abdullah Yusuf Azzam, opened a "services bureau" (*maktabat al-khadamat*) in Peshawar, Pakistan, supporting the Afghan *jihad* logistically and materially.[4] Ayman al-Zawahiri, an Egyptian physician who would become al-Qaeda's second-in-command, also made periodic stops in Peshawar, lending his physician skills to wounded *mujahideen*.[5] Bin Laden himself reportedly entered into the field of combat against the Soviets and often recounts his spiritual, near-death experiences and feelings of spiritual tranquility in the midst of furious shelling.[6]

The victory of the *mujahideen* over the Soviets, and the subsequent collapse of the USSR, led to a sense of invincibility across the Muslim world; it was viewed as a harbinger of even greater Muslim glory to come.[7] Ascribing their win to divine intervention, Islamists and *jihadists* around the world became more confident of their strength against better-equipped and technologically advanced foes. In short, it made Islamists more ambitious. It was in this atmosphere that al-Qaeda was born.

After returning to his homeland of Saudi Arabia, where he was hailed as a hero, Osama bin Laden found another opportunity to test the mettle of his cadre of seasoned *mujahideen*, the "Afghan Arabs:" Iraqi president Saddam Hussein's 1990 invasion of Kuwait. This, along with neighboring Saudi Arabia's fears that it was next on Saddam's list of targets, furnished bin Laden with an ideal opportunity to muster the unemployed fighters, this time to defend not just a peripheral Muslim nation but also the sanctity of Arabia, home of Islam and its *haramin* (the Two Holy Mosques, or "sanctities," in Mecca and Medina). He petitioned Saudi Arabia's monarch at the time, King Fahd, to allow the Afghan Arabs to defend the country, only to be rebuffed; Fahd opted to take up the offers of the U.S. and other so-called "infidel" forces to deploy their troops on Arabian soil, which bin Laden would later refer to in his 1996 *fatwa* as the "latest and greatest aggression" from the West.[8] Meanwhile, the Saudi regime, according to bin Laden, "betrayed the *Ummah* and joined the *Kufr* [infidels], assisting and helping them against the

Muslims."[9]

Because of bin Laden's opposition to the Saudi monarchy, the former Afghan war hero was ostracized and exiled from the Kingdom, fleeing to Sudan. Khartoum had just experienced its own Islamist *coup d'état* and was welcoming co-religionists from around the world—particularly millionaire investors such as bin Laden. During this time (1992-1996), Ayman al Zawahiri and his organization, the Egyptian Islamic Jihad, also used Sudan as a base to launch operations against the Egyptian government. Inspired by Muslim Brotherhood ideologue Sayyid Qutb and, like others, radicalized by the outcome of the Six Day War, Zawahiri was transformed from a pious Muslim to an ardent *jihadist*. He was arrested in the aftermath of the assassination of President Anwar Sadat, but soon thereafter left for Pakistan to join the *jihad* against the Soviets in Afghanistan. By 1991, Zawahiri rose to the leadership of the Egyptian Islamic Jihad, eventually merging it with al-Qaeda and expanding the scope of its *jihad* well beyond Egypt's borders.[10]

Bin Laden's continuing criticisms of the Saudi king, along with Zawahiri's botched terrorist missions against the Mubarak regime (including failed assassination attempts on the Egyptian Prime Minister and President Mubarak himself),[11] created significant international pressure on the Sudanese government to evict al-Qaeda. (Interestingly, offers were made to the Clinton administration to hand over bin Laden, but President Clinton declined the offers. In one interview given after 9/11, Clinton argued that at the time, the U.S. did not have sufficient proof to hold bin Laden. A second proposal to the Clinton Administration was rebuffed allegedly because the President was distracted by the Monica Lewinsky scandal.[12]

In 1996, al-Qaeda's leadership returned to Afghanistan and found refuge with another Islamist regime, the Taliban. The Islamist militant faction made up of former students indoctrinated in the *madrassas* of Pakistan had risen out of the chaos that followed the Soviet withdrawal from Afghanistan. The Pakistani-backed Taliban government in Kabul welcomed bin Laden and his Afghan Arabs and allowed them to set up militant bases and training camps. It is at this juncture that al-Qaeda began to crystallize into the organization it is known as today.

In 1998 Zawahiri, bin Laden, and others joined forces under the umbrella of *al-Jibha al-Islamiyya al-'Alamiyya* ("World Islamic Front"), and began their terrorist campaign against the West in earnest. In contrast to bin Laden's lengthy 1996 *fatwa*, in which he declared a vague global *jihad*, the group's 1998 *fatwa* succinctly and unequivocally called on all Muslims "to kill the Americans and their allies—civilians and military... to kill the Americans and seize their money wherever and whenever they [Muslims] find them."[13]

Al-Qaeda is described best as a Salafist organization. Salafism denotes the literal emulation of Muhammad and the early generations of Muslims, *al-salaf al-salah* (righteous forbears). The ultimate goal of Salafists the world over is to resurrect, and make supreme, a global Caliphate that enforces *sharia* law, in an attempt to recreate the perceived "golden age" of Islam (c. 632-656).

The Salafist worldview is not unique to al-Qaeda, however. Rather, it is the form of Islamism increasingly subscribed to by other Islamist activists, both militant and non-violent (e.g., the non-violent Hizb ut-Tahrir, which seeks to revive the Caliphate).[14] It should also be noted that, whereas the Salafist approach ignores centuries of *sharia* development according to Islam's *madhahib* (four mainstream schools of thought) and *ijtihad* reasoning (wherein more contemporary issues unaddressed either by the Koran or the Sunnah are resolved and applied according to experts in *sharia* law), certain aspects of it most associated with al-Qaeda—such as the military component of *jihad* and the requirement to make *sharia* the supreme law of the land—do find consensus among Islam's mainstream *madhahib*.

Even the particularly ruthless character of al-Qaeda is rationalized by its adherents, such as Zawahiri, through *qiyas*, or the analogical interpretation of various Muslim doctrines. For instance, because infidel armies were on Muslim territory, defensive *jihad*, as stressed in the 1998 fatwa, is deemed obligatory (*fard ayn*) in Islam.[15] Based on this, and because of the unbalanced power relationship between the West and the Muslim world, several *rukhsa* (relaxations of religious law) based on the *sharia* principle that "the forbidden becomes permissible when necessary" are used to rationalize al-Qaeda's ostensibly nihilistic brand of terrorism.[16]

Al-Qaeda defends the attacks of September 11, 2001, during which nearly 3,000 civilians were killed, with the *sunna* (examples or acts from the Prophet Muhammad's life) which tells of Muhammad employing catapults during the siege of the town of Ta'if.[17] Similarly, al-Qaeda excuses the otherwise Koranically forbidden act of killing women and children by referring to reported permission to do so granted by the Prophet himself.[18] Al-Qaeda continues by quoting the early jurisprudent Al Awza'i (d. 774), who claimed that "it is compulsory that this [the possibility of hitting women, children, and Muslims] not dissuade the launching of an incursion against them [infidels], firing arrows and utilizing other [weapons]—even if one dreads hitting a Muslim."[19]

Al-Qaeda also supports "martyrdom operations," or suicide bombings, the number of which has risen noticeably in recent years. The group again refers to early Islamic history and Muhammad's assertions to uphold its views on suicide bombings.[20] For example, one verse calls on believers to "kill and be killed" (Surah 9:111). Others simply call for violence, such as the famous "sword verse:" "fight and slay the Pagans wherever ye find them, and seize them, beleaguer them, and lie in wait for them in every stratagem (of war)."[21] Such warfare methods also receive justification from influential Muslim scholars, including Muslim Brotherhood ideologue Yusif al Qaradawi.[22]

Another *rukhsa* regularly used by al-Qaeda and other Islamist groups is the practice of *taqiyya*,[23] a doctrine that espouses deceit in the face of the enemy when the latter is in a dominant position or during war, two conditions that al-Qaeda believes apply today. In his lengthy treatise, "Loyalty and Enmity," Zawahiri dedicates an entire section to *taqiyya*, quoting various classical *ulema* (clerics) who believed that Muslims under the authority of non-Muslims should behave loyally while actually harboring feelings of hatred toward them.[24] In another treatise, Zawahiri quotes Muhammad's famous assertion that "war is deceit."[25]

While violence and terror are emblematic of al-Qaeda's strategy, the group has also mastered the use of propaganda and doublespeak, particularly when addressing its Western rivals. Primarily, it has and continues to send communiqués citing any number of grievances—Israel often topping the list, followed by objections to the stationing of so-called infidel troops on the Holy Land of Saudi Arabia, as well as the perceived U.S. policy of fragmenting Arab states, and crippling sanctions against Iraq following the Gulf War[26] —in order to justify terrorism, which is portrayed as "reciprocal treatment." By 2007, the organization was estimated to be producing and delivering such messages nearly every 72 hours.[27]

Bin Laden even posits the strikes of 9/11 as reciprocal responses to American-Israeli aggression against Muslims in Lebanon: "With Allah as my witness, I say to you that we had never considered striking the towers; however, after things became unbearable, and we witnessed the oppression and atrocities perpetrated against our people in Palestine and Lebanon by the American-Israeli coalition—it was then that I got the idea."[28] Following the July 2004 London bombings, Zawahiri said, "I speak to you today about the blessed raid on London that... made it take a sip from the same glass from which it had long made the Muslims drink.... So taste some of what you have made us taste."[29]

When addressing Muslims in the Arabic tracts it disseminates, al-Qaeda makes perfectly clear that its animus to the West is first and foremost based on religious doctrine, which is one of the reasons that it has been well-received by many young and devout Muslims. One of Zawahiri's ultimate stated goals is making "Islam supreme in its [own] land and then spreading it around the world."[30] Bin Laden claims that the relationship between Muslims and non-Muslims should be one of "enmity, evidenced by fierce hostility, and an internal hate from the heart" based on his reading of Koranic verse 60:40.[31]

Al-Qaeda's propaganda largely has been successful including among Muslims long since frustrated by their governments which they view as either inattentive to society's needs, insufficiently Islamic, or simply corrupt. Westerners are not immune to the al-Qaeda vision, as demonstrated by mainstream Western acceptance that al-Qaeda's war is entirely fueled by grievances against the West—even when bin Laden himself asserts that the animosity between the West and the Muslim world is inherent. Even former CIA analysts such as Michael Scheuer[32] and Bruce Riedel[33] have accepted the al-Qaeda narrative of grievances and similarly cite the Arab-Israeli conflict as the source of all woes, despite al-Qaeda's broader position that Muslims should be intrinsically hostile to the West.

GLOBAL REACH

The organization's core leadership, including bin Laden and Zawahiri, is believed to be based in the badlands between Pakistan and Afghanistan, the same area where bin Laden first opened a services bureau some 25 years earlier. Elsewhere, al-Qaeda has affiliate branches in Saudi Arabia and Yemen, where al-Qaeda in the Arabian Peninsula is based. Al-Qaeda maintains a strong presence in other Muslim countries as well, either by merging or allying with existing Islamist groups. Thus, while the U.S. was once focused primarily on "al-Qaeda" proper, it must now also monitor and disrupt al-Qaeda affiliates, including al-Qaeda in the Maghreb (Algeria), al-Qaeda in Bilad al-Sham (Syria), and the al-Qaeda Organization in the Levant-Umar Brigade (Lebanon).

In order to expand the potential for *jihadist* operations, bin Laden's al-Qaeda, with its Afghan Arab veterans, formally merged in 1998 with a number of other *jihadist* groups including the Egyptian Islamic Jihad, Jamiat-ul-Ulema-e-Pakistan, the Egyptian Islamic Group, and the Jihad Movement of Bangladesh.[34] Before that formal merger, a nascent al-Qaeda may have been involved in various attacks, beginning with the 1992 hotel bombings in Aden, Yemen. Bin Laden has asserted that al-Qaeda was responsible for the ambush of American forces in Mogadishu in 1993, the National Guard Training Center in Riyadh in 1995, and the Khobar Towers bombing in 1996, but experts emphasize that "there is no evidence to substantiate these claims."[35] It is reasonable to assume, however, that bin Laden at least contributed financial support to those attacks. As opposed to later al-Qaeda targets, the aforementioned attacks were aimed at military targets, not civilian ones, and therefore are not deemed "terrorist attacks" by some Western analysts.[36]

After the formation of the World Islamic Front, al-Qaeda was clearly linked to spectacular terrorist strikes, increasingly against civilians. These include the 1998 U.S. Embassy bombings in Kenya and Tanzania, where some 300 people were killed; the 2000 bombing of the *USS Cole* in Yemen, where 17 American servicemen were killed; and, most notoriously, the 9/11 attacks, where 2,669 American civilians were killed. In addition, in 2004, the Madrid train bombings killed 190 commuters. While certain aspects of the attack— including the fact that it occurred exactly 911 days after 9/11—allude to direct al-Qaeda involvement, official investigations determined that it was carried out by a cell inspired by al-Qaeda.[37] Similarly, there is dispute as to whether the London train bombings of 2005, which killed 52 people, are directly linked to al-Qaeda.[38] In late 2009, the Islamic State of Iraq, which evolved from the late Abu Musab al-Zarqawi's al-Qaeda wing, killed some 300 people in two separate attacks.[39] The organization has since claimed responsibility for additional attacks in Baghdad in April, June, and August 2010, suggesting the group is experiencing a resurgence.

These terrorist strikes connote the truly global reach possessed by al-Qaeda.[40] In today's shifting global environment, it is unclear whether such attacks are linked directly to al-Qaeda, or carried out by like-minded groups or individuals merely inspired by al-Qaeda and seeking public association with it. Even the various al-Qaeda wings, or "franchises," around the world are at their core Salafist groups that were often formed years before they became affiliated with the bin Laden network. For example, al-Qaeda's branch in North Africa, known as al-Qaeda in the Islamic Maghreb, or AQIM, was originally called the Salafist Group for Preaching and Combat and only became an al-Qaeda franchise relatively recently, in 2006.[41]

Other al-Qaeda franchises—including in Libya, Turkey, and the Levant—are similarly in their adolescent phases. Al-Qaeda also appears to have meaningful connections among Palestinian groups operating within the Palestinian Authority; Hamas reportedly assisted an al-Qaeda cell in carrying out attacks on Western targets in Taba and Sharm Al Sheikh resorts,[42] and has otherwise been conflated with al-Qaeda.[43]

RECENT ACTIVITY

With the invasion of Taliban-ruled Afghanistan and the start of the U.S.

War on Terror in late 2001, al-Qaeda's infrastructure and training camps in that country were destroyed or disrupted. Since then, the organization has claimed credit for other terrorist attacks, but these have tended to be smaller in scale, and it remains unclear whether or not the group is actually or directly responsible. Perhaps al-Qaeda's largest source of influence today is the power to inspire other Islamist groups to follow in its footsteps.

Those attacks have been frequent and numerous. In 2007, the Maghrebi wing of al-Qaeda claimed responsibility for a bombing in the Algerian capital of Algiers that killed 30 people.[44] And al-Qaeda may have been responsible for the 2008 explosion outside of the Danish Embassy in Pakistan, which killed six people, following the republication of Danish cartoons originally printed in 2005 that were seen as insulting of the Muslim prophet Muhammad.[45] Most recently, al-Qaeda's Yemeni wing—known as al-Qaeda in the Arabian Peninsula—was behind the botched 2009 Christmas Day terrorist attempt on the U.S., having trained the young Nigerian Muslim, Abdul Farouk Abdulmutallab, who attempted to detonate a bomb aboard a passenger plane en route to Detroit.[46]

In many ways, the attempted Christmas Day attack is indicative of al-Qaeda's contemporary status and the natural culmination of its role. Abdulmutallab was radicalized before coming into direct contact with al-Qaeda, and, unlike the Afghan Arabs, is certainly not a product of the Afghan-Soviet war.[47] Rather, he, as well as virtually every other Islamist group, accepted the narrative espoused by al-Qaeda that the West is out to subdue the Islamic world and that it is up to individual Muslims to respond through *jihad*. In fact, while Operation Enduring Freedom may have disrupted al-Qaeda's ability to operate in the open, the organization manages to stay relevant and connected to its sympathizers thanks to its Internet presence. Exploiting a general lack of Internet security, the world's most hunted terrorist organization can still reach out to potential recruits and even offer remote training using chat rooms, various websites, and social media tools such as YouTube.[48]

Through the Internet, Abdulmutallab discovered an outlet for his Islamist convictions in Yemen, and moved there for a month to be trained by al-Qaeda operatives.[49] Yet it remains unclear whether these operatives are closely linked to the group's core leadership or whether they are simply like-minded Salafists. The matter is further clouded by the fact that bin Laden may exaggerate al-Qaeda's links to terror strikes in order to appear in charge of the wider global *jihad*; at least one senior U.S. official has opined that, despite bin Laden's attempts to claim responsibility for the Christmas Day bombing, he may not even have known about the plot.[50]

This phenomenon of independent Islamists taking up the mantle of al-Qaeda, making the group's name almost synonymous with "radical Islam," was likewise evinced in the massacre in Fort Hood, Texas in October 2009, when an American Muslim soldier, Nidal Malik Hasan, opened fire on fellow soldiers, killing 13 people. Based on his actions and behavior, there is little doubt of Hasan's Islamist convictions—many of which have been stressed or rearticulated by al-Qaeda in their treatises.[51] In turn al-Qaeda, through its American propagandist, Adam Gadahn, made a point to profusely praise his actions and stress that Muslims should emulate Hasan.[52] Yet, even if Hasan was inspired by al-Qaeda's words and deeds, there is no evidence of a formal linkage between him and the terrorist organization.[53]

Still, al-Qaeda continues to pose both an intrinsic and instrumental threat to the West, as evidenced by an uptick in chatter regarding the group's future plots in the aftermath of Abdulmutallab's arrest. In and of itself, the organization has the experience, skills, and reach to terrorize foreign nations, probably more so than any other Islamic terrorist organization. The group consists of seasoned *jihadists* with decades of experience in plotting, executing, and inciting terrorism, and they are viewed by Islamists the world over as the natural leaders of the global *jihad*.[54] It is this symbiotic relationship between al-Qaeda and sympathetic Salafists around the world that has magnified both its scope and reach. Perhaps al-Qaeda's greatest achievement to date is having spawned a network of radical Islamists who can function independently and can continue to thrive even without direction from the organization or its original leadership.

In May 2011, Osama bin Laden was killed in Abbotabad, Pakistan during a raid by U.S. commandos. Al-Qaeda's second-in-command, Ayman al-Zawahiri, was formally appointed as bin Laden's successor in June 2011.

ENDNOTES

[1]Robin Cook, "The Struggle Against Terrorism Cannot Be Won By Military Means," *Guardian* (London), July 8, 2005, http://www.guardian.co.uk/uk/2005/jul/08/july7.development.

[2] "Transcript Of Bin Laden's October Interview," CNN, February 5, 2002, http://archives.cnn.com/2002/WORLD/asiapcf/south/02/05/binladen.transcript/index.html.

[3] "Al-Qaeda Deputy Ayman Al-Zawahiri Claims Responsibility For The London Bombings, Discusses Elections In Afghanistan, And Declares: 'Reform Can Only Take Place Through Jihad,'" Middle East Media Research Institute *Special Dispatch* no 989, September 20, 2005, http://www.memri.org/report/en/0/0/0/0/0/0/1480.htm.

[4] Lawrence Wright, *The Looming Tower: Al-Qaeda and the Road to 9/11* (New York: Random House, 2007), 119.

[5] Lawrence Wright, "The Man Behind Bin Laden," *New Yorker*, September 16, 2002, http://www.lawrencewright.com/art-zawahiri.html.

[6] Mark Long, "Ribat, Al-Qa'ida, And The Challenge For US Foreign Policy," *Middle East Journal* 63, no. 1, Winter 2009, http://www.britannica.com/bps/additionalcontent/18/36183756/Ribat-alQaida-and-the-Challenge-for-US-Foreign-Policy.

[7] Rohan Gunaratna, "Al Qaeda's Ideology," Hudson Institute *Current Trends in Islamist Ideology* vol. 1, May 19, 2005, http://www.current-trends.org/research/detail/al-qaedas-ideology.

[8] Douglas Jehl, "A NATION CHALLENGED: SAUDI ARABIA; Holy War Lured Saudis As Leaders Looked Away," *New York Times*, December 27, 2001, http://www.nytimes.com/2001/12/27/world/a-nation-challenged-saudi-arabia-holy-war-lured-saudis-as-rulers-looked-away.html.

[9] NewsHour With Jim Lehrer, "TRANSCRIPT: Bin Laden's Fatwa," PBS, n.d., http://www.pbs.org/newshour/terrorism/international/fatwa_1996.html.

[10] Wright, "The Man Behind Bin Laden."

[11] "Egyptian Islamic Jihad," Encyclopedia of the Middle East, n.d., http://www.mideastweb.org/Middle-East-Encyclopedia/egyptian_islamic_jihad.htm.

[12] Caspar Weinberger, "Bill Clinton's Failure On Terrorism," *Washington Times,* September 1, 2003, http://www.washingtontimes.com/news/2003/sep/1/20030901-102359-9067r/.

[13] World Islamic Front for Jihad Against Jews and Crusaders, "Initial 'Fatwa' Statement," February 23, 1998, http://www.library.cornell.edu/colldev/mideast/fatw2.htm.

[14] http://www.hizb.org.uk/hizb/who-is-ht.html

[15] Majid Khadduri, *War and Peace in the Law of Islam* (Baltimore: Johns Hopkins Press, 1955), 60.

[16] http://www.islam-qa.com/en/pda/ref/130815

[17] http://islam.pakistanway.com/showtopic.aspx?topicid=259&typeid=25

[18] Raymond Ibrahim, *The Al Qaeda Reader* (New York: Doubleday Publishers, 2007), 165.

[19] Ibid.

[20] Ibidem, 152-157.

[21] At Taubah, *Surah 9: Repentance*, http://www.muslimaccess.com/quraan/arabic/009.asp#5.

[22] "The Qaradawi Fatwas," *Middle East Quarterly* XI, no. 3, Summer 2004, http://www.meforum.org/646/the-qaradawi-fatwas.

[23] For a detailed discussion, see Raymond Ibrahim, "How Taqiyya Alters Islam's Rules Of War," *Middle East Quarterly* XVII, no. 1, Winter 2010, http://www.meforum.org/2538/taqiyya-islam-rules-of-war.

[24] Ibrahim, *The Al Qaeda Reader*, 73-74.

[25] Ibid., 142.

[26] World Islamic Front for Jihad Against Jews and Crusaders, "Initial 'Fatwa' Statement."

[27] Bruce Riedel, T*he Search for Al Qaeda: Its Leadership, Ideology, and Future* (Washington DC: Brookings Institution, 2010), 123.

[28] Ibid., 215.

[29] Ibidem, 238.

[30] Ibidem, 113.

[31] Ibidem, 43.

[32] Raymond Ibrahim, "Osama Bin Laden: Man Of Love?" *Middle East Strategy at Harvard*, September 10, 2008, http://blogs.law.harvard.edu/mesh/2008/09/osama_bin_laden_man_of_love/.

[33] John McCormack, "An Obama Adviser's Not-So-Bright Idea For Winning In Afghanistan," weeklystandard.com, February 20, 2009, http://www.weeklystandard.com/weblogs/TWSFP/2009/02/an_obama_advisers_notsobright.asp.

[34] Rohan Gunaratna, *Inside Al Qaeda: Global Network of Terror* (New York: Columbia University Press, 2002), 60-61.

[35] Lawrence Wright, *The Looming Tower: Al-Qaeda and the Road to 9/11* (New York: Albert A. Knopf, 2007), 246.

[36] Audrey Kurth Cronin, "Terrorist Attacks By Al Qaeda," Memorandum to the House Government Reform Committee, March 31, 2004, http://www.fas.org/irp/crs/033104.pdf.

[37] Paul Hamilos, "The Worst Islamist Attack In European History," *Guardian* (London), October 31, 2007, http://www.guardian.co.uk/world/2007/oct/31/spain.

[38] Riedel, *The Search for Al Qaeda*, 130

[39] "Baghdad Bomb Fatalities Pass 150," BBC (London), October 26, 2009, http://news.bbc.co.uk/2/hi/middle_east/8325600.stm; "Baghdad Car Bomb Cause Damage," BBC (London), December 8. 2009,

http://news.bbc.co.uk/2/hi/middle_east/8400865.stm.

[40] Jason Burke, *Al Qaeda: The True Story of Radical Islam* (London: I.B. Tauris, 2004), 1-22.

[41] Andrew Hansen and Lauren Vriens, "Al-Qaeda In The Islamic Maghreb (AQIM)," Council on Foreign Relations *Backgrounder*, July 21, 2009, http://www.cfr.org/publication/12717/alqaeda_in_the_islamic_maghreb_aqim_or_lorganisation_alqada_au_maghreb_islamique_formerly_salafist_group_for_preaching_and_combat_or_groupe_salafiste_pour_la_prdication_et_le_combat.html.

[42] Riedel, The Search for Al Qaeda, 125-127.

[43] "PA Detains 6 Al-Qaeda Men," *Yediot Ahronot* (Tel Aviv), February 10, 2010, http://www.ynetnews.com/articles/0,7340,L-3847352,00.html.

[44] "Al Qaeda Claims Responsibility For Algiers Bombing," ABC News Australia, April 12, 2007, http://www.abc.net.au/news/stories/2007/04/12/1894940.htm.

[45] "Al Qaeda Linked To Danish Embassy Attack," CNN, June 3, 2008, http://www.cnn.com/2008/WORLD/asiapcf/06/03/pakistan.blast/index.html.

[46] Richard Esposito and Brian Ross, "Investigators: Northwest Bomb Plot Planned By Al Qaeda In Yemen," ABC News *The Blotter*, December 26, 2009, http://abcnews.go.com/Blotter/al-qaeda-yemen-planned-northwest-flight-253-bomb-plot/story?id=9426085.

[47] Andrew Johnson and Emily Dugan, "Wealthy, Quiet, Unassuming: The Christmas Day Bomb Suspect," *Independent* (London), December 27, 2009, http://www.independent.co.uk/news/world/americas/wealthy-quiet-unassuming-the-christmas-day-bomb-suspect-1851090.html.

[48] See, for example, Giuseppe Valiante, "Glossy Al-Qaida Magazine Focuses On How-To Tips, Politics," Vancouver Sun, July 18, 2010, http://www.vancouversun.com/news/Glossy+Qaida+magazine+focuses+tips+politics/3293466/story.html.

[49] Esposito and Ross, "Investigators: Northwest Bomb Plot Planned By Al Qaeda In Yemen."

[50] "Bin Laden Claims Responsibility For Christmas Bomb Attempt," FoxNews.com, January 24, 2010, http://www.foxnews.com/story/0,2933,583758,00.html.

[51] Raymond Ibrahim, "Nidal Hasan And Fort Hood," *Pajamas Media*, November 18, 2009, http://www.meforum.org/2512/nidal-hasan-fort-hood-muslim-doctrine.

[52] "Adam Gadahn Praises Nidal Hasan, Calls For More Lone Wolf Attacks," Middle East Media Research Institute *Special Dispatch* no. 2847, March 8, 2010, http://www.memri.org/report/en/0/0/0/0/0/0/4020.htm.

[53] Richard Esposito, Matthew Cole and Brian Ross, "Officials: U.S.

Army Told Of Hasan's Contacts With Al Qaeda," ABC News *The Blotter*, November 9, 2009, http://abcnews.go.com/Blotter/fort-hood-shooter-contact-al-qaeda-terrorists-officials/story?id=9030873.
[54] Timothy Furnish, *Holiest Wars; Islamic Mahdis, Their Jihads, and Osama bin Laden* (Westport: Praeger, 2005), 156-158

HEZBOLLAH

Hezbollah (the Party of God) is not only a major political party and pro-vider of social services in Lebanon, it is also a militant organization that fields both a well-armed and well-trained militia in Lebanon and a terrorist wing integrated with elements of Iranian intelligence services operating abroad. Even as the movement has undergone a process of "Lebanonization," through which it has successfully integrated itself into the Lebanese parliamentary political system, it remains committed not only to its Lebanese identity but to its revolutionary pan-Shi'a and pro-Iran identities as well.

HISTORY AND IDEOLOGY

Founded in the wake of the Israeli invasion of Lebanon in 1982, Hezbollah was the product of a Shi'a awakening in Lebanon that followed the disappearance of Sayyid Musa al-Sadr in 1978 and the Islamic Revolution in Shi'ite Iran the following year. Long neglected by the Lebanese government and underrepresented in the country's social and political institutions, Lebanese Shi'a leaders organized to empower their disenfranchised community. Already eager to follow in the footsteps of the Iranian revolution, young Lebanese Shi'a were driven to break with established parties like Shi'a Amal and gravitated to Hezbollah as a result of the Israeli invasion and subsequent occupation of southern Lebanon. Iran was more than willing to help, eager as it was to export its Islamic revolution to other Shi'a communities throughout the Middle East. Iranian assistance included financial backing and training at the hands of the Islamic Revolutionary Guard Corps (IRGC) and was facilitated by a Syrian regime pleased with the prospect of developing a proxy in Lebanon capable of preventing Israel and its allies in Lebanon from controlling the country. It was the IRGC, however, that shaped Hezbollah's ideological foundations and informed its operational policies.

Hezbollah is simultaneously a Lebanese party, a pan-Shi'a movement and an Iranian proxy group. These multiple identities form the foundation and context for the group's ideology of Shi'a radicalism. Though it has since been downplayed, the establishment of an Islamic republic in Lebanon was a central component of Hezbollah's original political platform, released in 1985.[1] The fight against "Western Imperialism" and the continued conflict with Israel also feature prominently in that document. Hezbollah is ideologically committed to the Ayatollah Ruhollah Khomeini's revolutionary doctrine of *Velayat-e faqih* (Guardianship of the Jurist), creating tension between its commitment to the decrees of Iranian clerics, its commitment to the Lebanese state, and its commitment to the sectarian Shi'a community in Lebanon and its fellow Shi'ites abroad. As a result, its objectives include the sometimes competing goals of establishing an Islamic republic in Lebanon; promoting the standing of Shi'a communities worldwide; undermining Arab states with Shi'a minorities in an effort to export the Iranian Shi'a revolution; eliminating the State of Israel; challenging "Western imperialism;" and serving as the long arm of Iran in coordination with the Qods Force of Iran's Islamic Revolutionary Guard Corps. The consequences of these competing ideological drivers was clear after Hezbollah dragged both Israel and Lebanon into a war neither wanted by crossing the UN-demarcated Israel-Lebanon border and killing three Israeli soldiers while kidnapping two more in July 2006.

Hezbollah receives significant financial support from the contributions of Hezbollah supporters living abroad, particularly from Lebanese nationals living in Africa, South America and other places with large Lebanese Shi'a expatriate communities. Over time, these communities developed into a global support network available not only to raise funds but to provide logistical and operational support for Hezbollah operations. Such support networks, sometimes comprising a few individuals and in other cases developed cells, have developed in Latin America, North America, Europe, Africa and in Middle Eastern countries with minority Shi'a populations such as Saudi Arabia.

GLOBAL REACH

Hezbollah is well known for several international terrorist attacks, most notably the 1992 and 1994 bombings of the Israeli embassy and Jewish community center (AMIA), respectively, in Argentina, and the 1995 Khobar Towers attack in Saudi Arabia. Hezbollah's global footprint, however, is broader still, with support networks in regions as far afield as Africa, Southeast Asia, North and South America and Europe.

For example, Hezbollah has leveraged its support networks in Europe to help operatives use the Continent as a launching pad for entering Israel to conduct attacks or collect intelligence there. Hussein Makdad, a Lebanese national, entered Israel from Switzerland under a forged British passport in 1996. He was critically injured when a bomb he was assembling exploded in his Jerusalem hotel room.[2] In 1997, a German convert to Islam, Stefan Smirnak, flew to Israel from Amsterdam using his own passport.[3] Fawzi Ayoub, a Canadian of Lebanese decent, infiltrated Israel on a boat traveling from Europe in 2000. Discarding his Canadian passport in Europe, he used a forged American passport to enter Israel in order to plot attacks there. He was later arrested in Hebron.[4] In 2001, Jihad Shuman, a British citizen of Lebanese decent, flew to Israel from the UK. He flew from Lebanon to Europe on his Lebanese passport, and then on to Israel using his British passport.[5]

Throughout the 1990s, Hezbollah maintained an active support network in Southeast Asia as well. Hezbollah infiltrated at least one Malaysian operative, Zinal Bin-Talib, into Israel to collect intelligence.[6] Hezbollah has conducted significant fundraising in Southeast Asia, nearly succeeded in bombing the Israeli embassy in Bangkok in 1994[7], and collected intelligence on synagogues in Manila and Singapore.[8] Hezbollah members are known to have procured and cached weapons in Thailand and the Philippines.[9] They collected intelligence on El-Al's Bangkok office and on U.S. Navy and Israeli commercial ships in the Singapore Straits.[10] The network additionally recruited local Sunni Muslims and sent several to Lebanon for training.[11]

In Africa, Hezbollah operatives have long helped finance the group's activities by dealing in conflict diamonds in places like Sierra Leone and Liberia. According to David Crane, the prosecutor for the Special Court in Sierra Leone, "Diamonds fuel the war on terrorism. Charles Taylor is harboring terrorists from the Middle East, including al-Qaeda and Hezbollah, and has been for years."[12] Hezbollah also raises funds in Africa from the local Shi'a expatriate community. In some cases, Shi'a donors are unwittingly conned into funding Hezbollah, while in others they are knowing and willing participants in Hezbollah's financing efforts.[13] In 2002, Ugandan officials disrupted a cell of Shi'a students who were recruited by Iranian intelligence agents and sent on scholarships to study at the Rizavi University in Mashhad, Iran. Upon their return, one student recruit, Shafri Ibrahim, was caught, while another, Sharif Wadulu, is believed to have escaped to one of the Gulf States. The two were trained by the MOIS, together with new Lebanese Hezbollah recruits, and sent home with fictitious covers to establish an operational infrastructure in Uganda.[14]

Hezbollah activity in South America has been well documented, including its frenetic activity in the Tri-Border region. The group's activities received special attention in the wake of the 1992 bombing of the Israeli embassy in Buenos Aires, Argentina and the 1994 bombing of the AMIA Jewish community center there. What is less well known, however, is that Hezbollah is also active in Chile, Venezuela, Cuba, Panama and Ecuador. Of particular concern to law enforcement officials throughout South America is Hezbollah's increased activity in free trade zones, especially under the cover of import-export companies.[15]

Finally, Hezbollah maintains a sizeable presence of supporters and operatives in North America. The U.S. Treasury Department has designated Hezbollah charities in the Detroit area, while individuals and cells have been prosecuted across the U.S. and Canada for raising funds and procuring weapons and dual use technologies like night vision goggles. The most prominent case to date occurred in Charlotte, North Carolina, where Hezbollah operatives engaged in a cigarette smuggling enterprise raised significant sums for Hezbollah while maintaining direct contact with Sheikh Abbas Haraki, a senior Hezbollah military commander in South Beirut.[16] Members of the Charlotte cell received receipts back from Hezbollah for their donations, including receipts from the office of then-Hezbollah spiritual leader Sheikh Mohammad Fadlallah. The Charlotte cell was closely tied to a sister network in Canada that was primarily engaged in procuring dual-use technologies such as night vision goggles and laser range finders for Hezbollah operational squads. The Canadian network was under the direct command of Hajj Hassan Hilu Lakis, Hezbollah's chief military procurement officer, who is also known to procure material for Iran.[17]

RECENT ACTIVITY

The period of 2008-2010 has been one of major gains and significant setbacks for Hezbollah. Even as the Shi'a militia has consolidated its power and improved its political position at home, it has confronted unprecedented international scrutiny of its global activities.

Hezbollah in Lebanon
    May 2008 represented a turning point of sorts for Hezbollah in Leba-

non. With the position of the country's President vacant since the previous November, an ongoing presidential crisis presented the backdrop for what would prove to be the most violent intrastate fighting in Lebanon since the fifteen-year civil war ended in 1991. In early May of that year, the Lebanese government reported discovering a Hezbollah surveillance camera situated at the Beirut airport. In response, the camera was removed and the army commander in charge of airport security, Brig. Gen. Wafiq Choucair, a suspected Hezbollah sympathizer, was rotated to a new position.[18] At a cabinet meeting that week, the government announced it would no longer tolerate Hezbollah's "illegal" fiber optic communications network and described such activities on the part of Hezbollah as an "attack on the sovereignty of the state."[19] In response, Hezbollah revealed its strategic priorities, putting the maintenance of its independent weapons, communications and intelligence infrastructure ahead of the greater interests of Lebanon. In the words of Hezbollah leader Hassan Nasrallah, "Those who try to arrest us, we will arrest them. Those who shoot at us, we will shoot at them. The hand raised against us, we will cut it off."[20]

Over the next few days, Hezbollah took to the streets, shutting down the Beirut airport road and temporarily taking control of much of the city by force.[21] In the course of the fighting, nearly one hundred Lebanese were killed and 250 wounded.[22] While the Lebanese Armed Forces (LAF) ultimately deployed and stopped the fighting, Hezbollah successfully leveraged its military strength for political advantage over the already-weakened Lebanese government. The result, after five days of Qatari mediation, was the Doha Agreement under which Hezbollah secured a "blocking third" in a new national unity government, among other concessions. Controlling just over a third of the cabinet, Hezbollah could henceforth block any government initiative. At the negotiating table in Doha, then-Principal Deputy Director of National Intelligence Donald Kerr explained a few days later, participants "were faced with the implicit threat of further violence if opposition demands were not met. March 14 Coalition leaders cited their awareness of public fears about continued violence as a motivation for making the compromises necessary to reach an agreement at Doha."[23]

Hezbollah also successfully tabled addressing the fact that it remained the only militia in Lebanon to maintain a private arsenal of weapons. The Doha Agreement left the issue of Hezbollah's weapons—maintained in blatant violation of UN Security Council resolutions 1559 and 1701—unresolved. UNSCR 1559, for example, calls for the dismantling of "all Lebanese and non-Lebanese armed groups."[24] This was particularly significant for Hezbollah, which had promised that its "weapons of resistance" maintained to fight Israel and defend Lebanon would not be used against fellow Lebanese. Preventing serious discussion of this issue at the talks in Doha was a public relations coup for Hezbollah, which was left politically exposed after turning its guns on fellow Lebanese. As Kerr commented just days later, "Events in Lebanon since May 7 demonstrate that Hizballah—with the full support of Syria and Iran—will in fact turn its weapons against the Lebanese people for political purposes."[25]

Despite the insertion of a more robust United Nations presence in southern Lebanon in the wake of the July 2006 war, Hezbollah has successfully restocked its arsenal of missiles. Indeed, Hezbollah is now believed to have more rockets, with longer ranges and larger payloads, than it did prior to the 2006 war. According to Israeli estimates, in the years since the war Hezbollah has stockpiled tens of thousands of rockets both in south Lebanon and in the area north of the Litani River, just beyond the jurisdictional reach of UNIFIL forces. These reportedly include dozens of C-802 land-to-sea missiles, several hundred Faajr 5 missiles with a range of 75 kilometers, at least 20,000 40-kilometer rockets, and Zilzal rockets with a range of 250 kilometers and capable of penetrating deep into Israel even from above the Litani River.[26] Most disturbingly, on April 13, 2010 Israeli President Shimon Peres accused Hezbollah of acquiring Scud missiles with the capability to strike any location within Israel, including the nuclear reactor at Dimona.[27]

Twice, in July and October of 2009, explosions at Hezbollah arms depots in southern Lebanon exposed Hezbollah's hidden arms caches. In the first incident, a two story building in the village of Khirbet Slem, 12 miles from the Israeli border, exploded. When UN troops attempted to go to the site of the explosion they were stopped by Hezbollah forces.[28] Surveillance footage showed Hezbollah fighters removing unexploded rockets and munitions from the site. According to Alain Le Roy, the head of UN peacekeeping operations in Lebanon, "a number of indications suggest that the [arms] depot belonged to Hezbollah and, in contrast to previous discoveries by UNIFIL and the Lebanese Armed Forces of weapons and ammunition, that it was not abandoned but, rather, actively maintained."[29] Three months later, another Hezbollah arms cache exploded at the home of a Hezbollah member in Tayr Filsay, near Tyre. An Israeli aircraft reportedly filmed several men carrying what appear to be rockets from the home and delivering them to a different home in another village a few kilometers away.[30]

In May 2009, the German weekly *Der Spiegel* revealed that the UN special tribunal investigating former Lebanese Prime Minister Rafiq Hariri's assassination had implicated Hezbollah. The revelation was momentous; for most of the Tribunal's existence, Syria had been the main suspect in Hariri's murder. Accusing the Shi'ite Hezbollah of killing the leader of Lebanon's Sunni community, by contrast, threatened the stability of the country. According to the report, which cites Lebanese security sources, investigators identified cell phones linked to the plot and found that "all of the numbers involved apparently belonged to the 'operational arm' of Hezbollah." The report identified Abdulmajid Ghamlush as one of the main suspects and described him as "a Hezbollah member who completed training courses in Iran." The investigation of Ghamlush, who reportedly purchased the mobile phones, led officials to Hajj Salim, the alleged mastermind of the assassination plot and commander of a "special operational unit" reporting directly to Hezbollah secretary-general Hassan Nasrallah.[31] Later reports would also identify Mustapha Badreddine, the brother-in-law of slain external operations chief Imad Mughniyah and allegedly one of Hezbollah's top military commanders, as a key player in the plot.[32]

With its domestic standing under threat by the Tribunal's accusations, Hezbollah moved to deflect criticism through an aggressive media campaign portraying the Tribunal as a Zionist-American plot. In a speech following the *Der Spiegel* report, Hezbollah leader Hassan Nasrallah accused Israel of being behind "the attempt to accuse Hezbollah of assassinating martyr Rafiq Hariri in order to foment a sectarian sedition in Lebanon.[33] The discovery of an alleged Israeli spy network in the Lebanese main telecommunications provider and the release of aerial footage from Israeli spy planes which appeared to follow Hariri's known travel routes through Beirut and other parts of the country, were used as evidence of Israeli involvement.[34] Hezbollah leaders concurrently accused the Tribunal of relying on the testimony of "false witnesses," claiming that recanted testimonies from early witnesses proved the politicization of the investigation.[35]

In early January 2011, it became evident that the Tribunal's chief prosecutor, Daniel Bellamere, would submit a draft indictment to the pre-trial judge for review. While the actual contents of the indictment would continue to be under seal for several months, Hezbollah pre-empted the indictment's release and withdrew its support for Saad Hariri's government, forcing its collapse.[36] Subsequently, aided by sympathetic leaders of Lebanon's Christian and Druze communities, Hezbollah was able to raise billionaire Najib Mitaki to the premiership, cementing Hezbollah's control over the Lebanese state.[37]

Hezbollah abroad

In the spring of 2009, as the Hezbollah-led "March 8" coalition campaigned ahead of Lebanon's June 7th elections, the group was suddenly forced to contend with the unexpected exposure of its covert terrorist activities both at home and abroad. At home, Hezbollah now stands accused of playing a role in the assassination of former Lebanese Prime Minister Rafiq Hariri. Abroad, law enforcement officials have taken action against Hezbollah support networks operating across the globe, including in Egypt, Yemen, Sierra Leone, Cote d'Ivoire, Azerbaijan, Belgium, and Colombia. Together, these activities pose what Hezbollah leader Hassan Nasrallah described as "the largest and most important and serious challenge" facing Hezbollah today.[38]

Hezbollah's fortunes began to take a turn for the worse in April 2009, when Egyptian authorities publicized the November 2008 arrest of dozens of Hezbollah operatives accused of funneling arms to Hamas and targeting Israeli tourists and Suez Canal shipping. According to Egyptian prosecutors, the operatives were instructed to collect intelligence from villages along the Egypt-Gaza border, at tourist sites, and at the Suez Canal. Nasrallah himself confirmed to the *Financial Times* that one of the men arrested was Sami Shihab, a Hezbollah member who was on "a logistical job to help Palestinians get [military] equipment."[39] The cells reportedly established commercial businesses as fronts for their operational activities, purchased apartments in al-Arish and the Egyptian side of Rafah for use as safe houses, and contacted criminal elements in Egypt to procure forged Egyptian passports so they could leave Egypt as needed and purchase or rent apartments. Some of the cell members reportedly worked for the Egyptian bureau of al-Manar, Hezbollah's satellite television station, as cover for their activities in Egypt. While Shihab and his co-conspirators were eventually convicted in April 2010, the cell escaped from Egyptian prison during the pro-democracy uprising in early 2011.[40]

Following the exposure of the Hezbollah cells operating in Egypt, UN special envoy Terje Roed-Larsen commented that there has recently been "a growing concern that Hezbollah has engaged in clandestine and illegal militant activities beyond Lebanese territory."[41] Indeed, in March of 2009, Yemeni president Ali Abdullah Salih publicly accused Hezbollah of training Shi'ite rebels in Yemen.[42]

Hezbollah operatives were under stress in the far corners of Africa as well. There, two local Hezbollah supporters, Kassim Tajideen and Abdulmenhem Qubaisi, were exposed when the U.S. Treasury Department added them to its list of designated terrorists.[43] According to information released by Treasury, Tajideen has contributed tens of millions of dollars to Hezbollah and has funneled money to the group through his brother, a Hezbollah commander in Lebanon. Tajideen, a dual Lebanese-Sierra Leonean citizen, and his brothers also run cover companies for Hezbollah in Africa, according to Treasury. In 2003, following a four-month international investigation by Belgium's Economic Crimes Unit, Tajideen was arrested in Belgium in connection with fraud, money laundering, and diamond smuggling. Judicial police raided the Antwerp offices of Soafrimex, a company managed by Tajideen, arrested several of its officials, and froze its bank accounts on charges of "large-scale tax fraud, money laundering, and trade in diamonds of doubtful origin, to the value of tens of millions of Euros."[44] According to Treasury, Qubaisi is a Hezbollah supporter and fundraiser who functions as Nasrallah's "personal representative" in the country and also "helped establish an official Hezbollah foundation in Cote d'Ivoire, which has been used to recruit new members for Hezbollah's military ranks in Lebanon."[45]

In December 2010, Treasury built upon their earlier action by designating Kassim Tajideen's two brothers, Ali and Husayn, along with their businesses in Gambia, Lebanon, Sierra Leone, the Democratic Republic of Congo, Angola, and the British Virgin Islands.[46] These designations were particularly timely, coming just a month after Israeli officials issued warnings to Israeli businesspersons traveling to Europe in response to what was described as "pinpoint" intelligence of a specific threat. In August 2008, Israel issued similar warnings of a pending Hezbollah attack targeting Israelis in Africa. A few weeks later, senior Israeli officials confirmed that two attempts by Hezbollah operatives to kidnap Israeli citizens abroad had been thwarted.

On the other side of the globe, reports began to leak out of a Hezbollah and IRGC plot to bomb the building housing the Israeli, Thai, and Japanese embassies, as well as a radar tower in Baku, Azerbaijan. According to Israeli officials, the operatives also planned to kidnap the Israeli ambassador to Azerbaijan.[47] The plot was foiled in the weeks following the February 2008 assassination of Imad Mughniyeh, Hezbollah's chief of external operations. Azeri prosecutors subsequently tried two Lebanese Hezbollah operatives, Ali Karaki, described as "a veteran of Hezbollah's external operations unit," and Ali Najem Aladine, a "lower-ranking explosives expert." The two men reportedly traveled to Iran several times, using Iranian passports. When they were arrested, police had found explosives, binoculars, cameras, pistols with silencers and surveillance photographs in their vehicles. Though the two men subsequently were convicted in October 2009 and sentenced to 15 years in prison, Iran managed to secure their release in August 2010 in a prisoner swap with the Azerbaijani government.[48]

Just a week prior to the exposure of the Baku plot, Argentine prosecutor Alberto Nisman announced that an international arrest warrant had been issued for Samuel Salman al-Reda, a Colombian of Lebanese descent and suspected Hezbollah operative who previously lived in Buenos Aires and is charged with playing a key role in the 1994 bombing of the AMIA Jewish charities headquarters that killed 85 people and wounded approximately 300.[49] According to the original AMIA indictment, a government witness identified al-Reda as a Hezbollah member who fought in southern Lebanon. The indictment says al-Reda coordinated the activities of "dormant" cells in the Tri-border area where Argentina, Brazil and Paraguay meet and provided "all the necessary support" to carry out the attack.[50] According to information provided by the Argentine intelligence service, SIDE, and cited in the AMIA indictment, al-Reda is also suspected of being a senior operative involved in the 1992 bombing of the Israeli embassy in Buenos Aires. An FBI report on the AMIA bombing notes that "additional information has identified Samuel Reda as an active member of Hezbollah who was in Buenos Aires during the attack after having moved from the city of Iguacu Falls, Brazil. It is alleged [that] Reda was the contact for members of Hezbollah, of Iran, and of Lebanon."[51]

Feeling the heat from these international setbacks, and worried about the possible impact they would have on Hezbollah's political standing at home, Hezbollah leader Hassan Nasrallah gave his final major address before the June elections on May 29, 2009. The speech was broadcast live on Hezbollah's al-Manar satellite television station and projected on a giant screen at a Resistance and Liberation Day rally in the Beka'a Valley celebrating the ninth anniversary of the Israeli withdrawal from southern Lebanon. In it, Nasrallah bemoaned what he described as an Israeli effort to "return to the strategy of introducing Hezbollah as a terrorist organization that attacks countries and peoples and threatens world security."[52]

Despite the increased attention directed towards the group's international presence, Hezbollah is still willing to carry out attacks abroad. According to leaked diplomatic cables cited by Israel's Ha'aretz newspaper, Hezbollah was also responsible for the January 2010 bombing an Israeli diplomatic convoy in Jordan. During a meeting just after the attack, Israeli Defense Forces Chief of Staff Gabi Ashkenazi revealed to the United Nations envoy to Lebanon that Israel had obtained information linking Hezbollah to the bombing. The attack was reportedly conducted as a response to the 2008 assassination of Imad Mughniyeh in Damascus.[53] This is in addition to six other attempted attacks, all thwarted by Israel.[54] While the Israeli diplomats were unhurt, Hezbollah continued to threaten revenge, with Hezbollah second in command Naim Qassem stating in February 2010 that the "commitment exists," but "the (attack) period and specifications, however, will be come in due time."[55]

ENDNOTES

[1]Rafid Fadhil Ali, "New Hezbollah Manifesto Emphasizes Political Role in a United Lebanon," Jamestown Foundation *Terrorism Monitor* 7, iss. 38, December 15, 2009, http://www.jamestown.org/single/?no_cache=1&tx_ttnews[tt_news]=35830&tx_ttnews[backPid]=13&cHash=42a34967d2.

[2] Joel Greenberg, "Israel Says Lebanese Bomber Caused Blast in Jerusalem Hotel," *New York Times,* May 17, 1996, http://www.nytimes.com/1996/05/17/world/israel-says-lebanese-bomber-caused-blast-in-jerusalem-hotel.html.

[3] Margot Dudkevitch, "Charges Pressed Against German Suspected Of Planning Suicide Attack," *Jerusalem Post*, December 26, 1997.

[4] Mitch Potter, "Canadian Appears in Israeli Court," *Toronto Star*, November 1, 2002; Stewart Bell, "Canadian a Suspect in Plot to Kill Israeli PM," *National Post*, April 5, 2003; "Army Announces Arrest of Hezbollah Operative in Israel," Agence France Presse, October 31, 2002.

[5] Israel Ministry of Foreign Affairs, "Details of Arrest of Jihad Shuman, Communicated by the Prime Minister's Media Advisor," February 27, 2001, http://www.mfa.gov.il/MFA/Templates/Hasava.aspx?NRMODE=Published&NRNODEGUID={69C5A658-DDBA-4B5D-91C0-4AF61D30ABCA}&NRORIGINALURL=%2FMFA%2FGovernment%2FCommuniques%2F2001%2FDetails%2Bof%2BArrest%2Bof%2BJihad%2BShuman%2B-%2B21-Feb-2001.htm%3FWBCMODE%3DPr%3FDisplayMode%3Dprint&NRCACHEHINT=Guest&DisplayMode=print&WBCMODE=Pr.

[6] Zachary Abuza, "Bad Neighbours: Hezbollah in Southeast Asia," *Australia/Israel Review*, November 2006, http://www.aijac.org.au/review/2006/31-11/abuza31-11.htm

[7] Ely Karmon, "Fight on All Fronts: Hizballah, the War on Terror, and the War in Iraq," Washington Institute for Near East Policy Research Memorandum no. 45, December 2003, http://www.washingtoninstitute.org/templateC04.php?CID=18.

[8] Zachary Abuza, "Bad Neighbours."

[9] John T. Hanley, Kongdan Oh Hassig, and Caroline F. Ziemke, "Proceedings of the International Symposium on the Dynamics and Structures of Terrorist Threats in Southeast Asia, Held at Kuala Lumpur, Malaysia," Institute for Defense Analyses, September 2005.

[10] "Hizbollah Recruited Singaporeans: The Muslims Were Recruited Through religious Classes in Singapore to Aid a Plot to Blow Up US and Israeli Ships," *Straits Times* (Singapore), June 9, 2002; "Indonesian Government Expect Escalation in Terrorist Bombings; Hizballah Ops Out of Singapore Also Noted," *Defense & Foreign Affairs Daily* 20, no. 104 (2002); Hanley, Hassig and Ziemke, "Proceedings of the

International Symposium on the Dynamics and Structures of Terrorist Threats in Southeast Asia, Held at Kuala Lumpur, Malaysia."

[11] Maria A. Ressa, *Seeds of Terror: An Eyewitness Account of Al-Qaeda's Newest Center of Operations in Southeast Asia* (New York: Free Press, 2003); Hanley, Hassig and Ziemke, "Proceedings of the International Symposium on the Dynamics and Structures of Terrorist Threats in Southeast Asia, Held at Kuala Lumpur, Malaysia."

[12] "U.N. Prosecutor Accuses Taylor of Al Qaeda Links; More," United Nations Foundation *U.N. Wire*, May 15, 2003, http://www.unwire. org/unwire/20030515/33747_story.asp.

[13] Douglas Farah, "Hezbollah's External Support Network in West Africa and Latin America," International Assessment and Strategy Center, April 15, 2009, http://www.strategycenter.net/research/ pubID.118/pub_detail.asp.

[14] Matthew Levitt, "Hizbullah's African Activities Remain Undisrupted," *RUSI/Jane's Homeland Security and Resilience Monitor*, March 1, 2004.

[15] Matthew Levitt, "Hezbollah Finances: Funding the Party of God," in Jeanne K. Giraldo and Harold A. Trinkunas, eds., *Terrorism Financing and State Responses: a Comparative Perspective* (Palo Alto: Stanford University Press, 2007) .

[16] *United States v. Mohamad Youssef Hammoud, et al.* United States Court of Appeals for the Fourth District; U.S. Department of the Treasury, "Twin Treasury Actions Take Aim at Hizballah's Support Network," July 24, 2007, http://www.treasury.gov/press-center/press-releases/Pages/200772410294613432.aspx.

[17] *United States v. Mohamad Youssef Hammoud, et al;* "Twin Treasury Actions Take Aim at Hizballah's Support Network."

[18] "Hezbollah's Power Play," *Washington Times,* May 18, 2008, http:// www.washingtontimes.com/news/2008/may/18/hezbollahs-power-play/.

[19] Tom Perry, "Beirut Cabinet Challenges Hezbollah, Tension Rises," Reuters, May 6, 2008, http://www.alertnet.org/thenews/newsdesk/ L06877939.htm.

[20] Nicholas Blanford, "Hezbollah Phone Network Spat Sparks Beirut Street War," *Christian Science Monitor*, May 9, 2008, http://www. csmonitor.com/World/Middle-East/2008/0509/p05s01-wome.html.

[21] Hugh Macleod, "Hizbullah Capture of Mountain Village Seen as Threat to Israel," *Guardian* (London), May 13, 2008, http://www. guardian.co.uk/world/2008/may/13/lebanon.israelandthepalestinians.

[22] Nadim Ladki, "Lebanese Forces Pledge Crackdown; Force To Be Used to Quell Fighting That Has Killed 81," *Montreal Gazette*, May 13, 2008.

[23] Donald Kerr, Speech before the 2008 Soref Symposium of the

Washington Institute for Near East Policy, Washington, DC, May 29, 2008, http://www.washingtoninstitute.org/templateC07. php?CID=397.

[24] United Nations Security Council Resolution 1559, September 2, 2004, http://daccess-dds-ny.un.org/doc/UNDOC/GEN/ N04/498/92/PDF/N0449892.pdf?OpenElement.

[25] Kerr, Speech before the 2008 Soref Symposium.

[26] Israel Defense Forces, Strategic Division, Military-Strategic Information Section, "The Second Lebanon War: Three Years Later," July 12, 2009, http://www.mfa.gov.il/MFA/About+the+Ministry/ Behind+the+Headlines/The-Second-Lebanon-War-Three-years-later-12-Jul-2009.

[27] Richard Spencer, "Israel Accuses Syria of Providing Scud Missiles to Hezbollah," *Telegraph* (London), April 13, 2010, http://www. telegraph.co.uk/news/worldnews/middleeast/israel/7586789/Israel-accuses-Syria-of-providing-Scud-missiles-to-Hizbollah.html

[28] Ethan Bronner, "Israel Sees Evidence Of Hezbollah's Rearming In An Explosion In Southern Lebanon," *New York Times*, July 16, 2009, http://www.nytimes.com/2009/07/16/world/middleeast/16mideast. html.

[29] "Hezbollah Threat To Rain Rockets On Tel Aviv As It Rearms For Fresh War; Lebanon," *Times of London*, August 5, 2009.

[30] Yaakov Katz and E.B. Solomont, "Hizbullah Has Hidden Arms Caches In Dozens Of Villages In Southern Lebanon, Defense Officials Say," *Jerusalem Post,* October 14, 2009.

[31] Erich Follath, "New Evidence Points to Hezbollah in Hariri Murder," *Der Spiegel* (Hamburg), May 23, 2009, http://www.spiegel.de/ international/world/0,1518,626412,00.html.

[32] "Report: Mughniyeh's brother-in-law suspect in Hariri killing," *YNET* (Tel Aviv), July 7, 2010. http://www.ynetnews.com/articles/ 0,7340,L-3927186,00.html.

[33] "Hezbollah Leader Says Iran Ready to Arm Lebanon, New Challenges to Be Faced," BBC, May 31, 2009.

[34] "Hezbollah Says Israel Controls Telecom Network," Reuters, June 30, 2010; Maha Barada, "Nasrallah Reveals Hariri Murder 'Evidence,'" BBC, August 9, 2010, http://www.bbc.co.uk/news/world-middle-east-10922045.

[35] Zeina Karam, "Hezbollah, Syria Seek to Discredit Hariri Tribunal," Associated Press, October 5, 2010, http://abcnews.go.com/International/wireStory?id=11803607&page=1.

[36] Laila Bassam, "Hezbollah and Allies Resign, Toppling Lebanon Government," Reuters, January 12, 2011, http://www.reuters. com/article/2011/01/12/us-lebanon-hariri-resignation-idUS-TRE70B26A20110112.

[37] "Hezbollah-Backed Najib Mikati Appointed Lebanese PM," BBC,

January 25, 2011, http://www.bbc.co.uk/news/world-middle-east-12273178.

[38] Transcript of speech by Hassan Nasrallah, *NOW Lebanon*, May 30, 2009, http://nowlebanon.com/NewsArchiveDetails.aspx?ID=96217.

[39] "Hezbollah Denies Egypt Accusations," *Al Jazeera* (Doha), April 11, 2009, http://english.aljazeera.net/news/middleeast/2009/04/200941019538502350.html.

[40] Patrick Galey, "Hezbollah man Escapes Egypt Jail," *Daily Star* (Beirut), February 4, 2011, http://www.dailystar.com.lb/article.asp?edition_id=1&categ_id=2&article_id=124532#axzz1DVJ6ZRlF.

[41] Barak Ravid, "Hezbollah: UN Envoy Biased in Favor of Israel," *Ha'aretz* (Tel Aviv), May 9, 2009, http://www.haaretz.com/hasen/spages/1084219.html.

[42] Hakim Almasmari, "President Saleh: Houthis Were Trained by Hezbollah Experts," *Yemen Post*, March 29, 2009, http://yemenpost.net/Detail123456789.aspx?ID=3&SubID=456&MainCat=3.

[43] U.S. Department of the Treasury, "Treasury Targets Hizballah Network in Africa," May 27, 2009, http://www.treasury.gov/press-center/press-releases/Pages/tg149.aspx.

[44] "Con in the Congo—The Moral Bankruptcy of the World Bank's Industrial Logging Model," Greenpeace report, April 11, 2007, http://www.greenpeace.org/raw/content/eu-unit/press-centre/reports/carving-up-congo-part-3.pdf.

[45] U.S. Department of the Treasury, "Treasury Targets Hizballah Network in Africa," May 27, 2009, http://www.treasury.gov/press-center/press-releases/Pages/tg149.aspx.

[46] U.S. Department of the Treasury, "Treasury Targets Hizballah Financial Network," December 9, 2010, http://www.treasury.gov/press-center/press-releases/Pages/tg997.aspx.

[47] Yossi Melman, "Hezbollah, Iran, Plotted Bombing of Israel Embassy in Azerbaijan," *Ha'aretz* (Tel Aviv), May 31, 2009, http://www.haaretz.com/hasen/spages/1089204.html.

[48] "Two Lebanese Jailed for Baku Plot," BBC, October 5, 2009, http://news.bbc.co.uk/2/hi/middle_east/8291378.stm; Jack Khoury, "Report, Azerbaijan Releases Men Jailed for Israel Embassy Plot," *Ha'aretz* (Tel Aviv), August 15, 2010, http://www.haaretz.com/print-edition/news/report-azerbaijan-releases-men-jailed-for-israel-embassy-bomb-plot-1.308051

[49] "Condemning the Attack on the AMIA Jewish Community Center in Buenos Aires, Argentina," U.S. House of Representatives Resolution No. 156, July 17, 2009, http://frwebgate.access.gpo.gov/cgi-bin/getpage.cgi?dbname=2009_record&page=H8340&position=all.

[50] AMIA Indictment, Federal Judge Juan José Galeano, Judicial Branch of the Nation, Case No. 1156, court file pages 106,265 - 106,467, José F. M. Pereyra, Federal Court Clerk, Court Office No. 17

of the National Federal Court on Criminal and Correctional Matters No. 9, Buenos Aires, Argentina, March 5, 2003.

[51] "The Attack on AMIA," Report of the task force of the Federal Bureau of Investigations Analysis of the attack on the seat of the Mutual Israeli Argentinean Association (AMIA) 18th of July, 1994 Buenos Aires, Argentina, August 1998, 25.

[52] "Hezbollah Leader Says Iran Ready to Arm Lebanon, New Challenges to Be Faced," BBC, May 31, 2009.

[53] Barak Ravid, "IDF Chief Reported: Hezbollah was Involved in Attack on Israeli Convoy in Jordan," *Ha'aretz* (Tel Aviv), December 8, 2010, http://www.haaretz.com/news/diplomacy-defense/idf-chief-reported-hezbollah-was-involved-in-attack-on-israeli-convoy-in-jordan-1.329486.

[54] "Israelis Brace for Hezbollah's Revenge," UPI, January 25, 2010, http://www.upi.com/Top_News/Special/2010/01/25/Israelis-brace-for-Hezbollahs-revenge/UPI-96931264452942/.

[55] "Qassem: Hizbullah Still Seeking Revenge for Mughniyeh's Assassination" *Naharnet*, February 14, 2010, http://www.naharnet.com/domino/tn/Newsdesk.nsf/Lebanon/AB2CBB67B98570ACC22576C A0026FD40?OpenDocument.

LASHKAR-E TAIBA

Of all the terrorist groups present in South Asia—and there are many—it is Lashkar-e Taiba that represents a threat to regional and global security second only to al-Qaeda. Founded in Pakistan in 1987, LeT over time has expanded its ambitions and reach far beyond Southeast Asia, and now boasts a presence in some twenty-one countries, and its activities continue to be tacitly supported by the Pakistani state. However, it was not until the November 2008 massacre in Mumbai, India—a terrorist attack which claimed the lives of close to 200 people, including 26 foreigners of 15 nationalities—that the international community recognized that LeT's ambitions transcend India and are part of a larger war with the West and with liberal democracies more generally.

HISTORY AND IDEOLOGY

Although Lashkar-e Taiba (LeT) is linked in popular perceptions mainly to terrorism in the disputed regions of Jammu and Kashmir, the operations and ideology of this group transcend the violence directed at the Indian state. An adherent of Sunni Wahhabism, LeT seeks to establish a universal Islamic Caliphate with a special emphasis on gradually recovering all lands once under Muslim rule. That strategic objective has made LeT a strong ideological ally of al-Qaeda, while the emphasis on recovering "lost Muslim lands" in Asia and Europe has taken LeT to diverse places such as the Palestinian Territories, Spain, Chechnya, Kosovo and Eritrea.

That LeT is a constituent member of Osama bin Laden's International Islamic Front should not be surprising given that one of its three founders, Abdullah Azzam of the International Islamic University in Islamabad, was reputedly associated with Hamas and has been widely described as one of bin Laden's religious mentors.[1] Together with Hafiz Saeed, LeT's current *amir*, and Zafar Iqbal of the Engineering University, Lahore, Azzam formed LeT in 1987 as the armed wing of the Markaz Dawat-ul Irshad (MDI), the Center for Proselytization and Preaching, which sought to actualize the universal Islamic state through *tableegh* (preaching) and *jihad* (armed struggle).[2] The group's founding occurred at a time when Pakistan was in the throes of Islamic ferment. General Zia ul-Haq's decade-long program (1977-88) of Islamizing Pakistan had by then grown strong domestic roots, providing a plethora of armed groups such as LeT with a steady supply of volunteers, funding and, most important of all, concerted state support.

In the fervid atmosphere of the 1980s, when numerous extremist groups were emerging in Pakistan under the patronage of the country's principal intelligence agency, the Inter-Services Intelligence (ISI), LeT's militant attitude to political change, and its commitment to exploiting modern science and technology in support of its ideological ends, quickly made it an ISI favorite because its uncompromising commitment to *jihad* could be manipulated to advance Pakistan's own strategic goals. As Saeed noted in a January 1998 interview with *Herald*, a Pakistani news magazine, "many Muslim organizations are preaching and working on the missionary level inside and outside Pakistan... but they have given up the path of *jihad* altogether. The need for *jihad* has always existed and the present conditions demand it more than ever."[3]

LeT's earliest operations were focused on the Kunar and Paktia provinces in Afghanistan, where LeT had set up several training camps in support of the *jihad* against the Soviet occupation. LeT's initial focus on Afghanistan is significant because it refutes the common misapprehension—assiduously fostered since the early 1990s—that the group has always been a part of the indigenous Kashmiri insurgency. Nothing could be further from the truth. LeT is composed primarily of Pakistani Punjabis and has been so from its inception. In fact, its Punjabi composition, along with its inflexible ideology, is precisely what made it so attractive to the ISI to begin with, because it could be controlled and directed far more effectively by its Punjabi-dominated sponsor, the Pakistani Army, than could any local Kashmiri resistance group. Because of LeT's founding ties to al-Qaeda, however, its Punjabi core has over the years been episodically supplemented by Libyans, Central Asians, and Sudanese—although these non-Pakistani elements have generally been marginal to the group's numerical strength.

LeT's early contribution to the anti-Soviet campaign was consistent with its mission of armed struggle against the infidels. In its earliest official supporters, General Akhtar Abdur Rahman and Lieutenant General Hamid Gul, the ISI's Director Generals during the late 1980s, the group found kindred spirits who were also tantalized by the lure of an international *jihad*. The *mujahideen's* defeat of the Soviet Union in Afghanistan empowered both the ISI and various *jihadi* groups within Pakistan, which came to see state-sponsored insurgency as the key to advancing Islamabad's myriad strategic interests. *Jihad* undertaken by sub-national groups with state support would thus become the instrument that allowed Pakistan to punch above its geopolitical weight: its campaign in Afghanistan had already contributed to the fall of a superpower and Pakistani military and intelligence officials were nothing if not ambitious during the 1980s and the 1990s, when they sought to replicate the same outcome against India.

The indigenous uprising which broke out in 1989 in Jammu and Kashmir provided this opportunity. Just as Pakistan had supported the Sikh insurgency against New Delhi earlier in the decade, Islamabad now threw its weight behind the Kashmiri resistance—a development that was in many ways inevitable, given Pakistan's longstanding claims to the disputed state. Unfortunately for Pakistan, its strategy of defeating India through armed insurgencies failed in Kashmir, just as it did in the Punjab. By 1993, the native Kashmiri uprising spearheaded by the Jammu and Kashmir Liberation Front (JKLF), a secular organization composed largely of Kashmiris, was defeated by the Indian military, just as the Khalistan movement in the Punjab, also supported by Pakistan, was slowly being beaten back at about the same time.

These twin defeats, first in the Punjab and then in Jammu and Kashmir, demonstrated that Pakistan's national strategy of supporting domestic insurgencies in order to checkmate Indian power had failed conclusively. But the larger objective of keeping India "off-balance" and weakening it through persistent attacks had not disappeared, rooted as it was in a dangerous medley of deep geopolitical dissatisfactions, the ambitions of a self-serving military that rules even when it does not govern, and the possession of nuclear weapons.

By 1993, when it became clear that the strategy of sustaining domestic insurgencies against India was simply not paying off in the manner expected,

Islamabad responded with an alternative strategy. Using the instruments engendered by the *jihad* in Afghanistan, the ISI focused on injecting combat-hardened aliens into India in order to sustain a large-scale campaign of murder and mayhem intended to bring New Delhi to its knees.

Consistent with this strategy, the earliest LeT presence in India was detected in 1993, when a cohort of the group's Punjabi cadres crossed the Line of Control into Jammu and Kashmir.[4] The group's presence, however, was not publicly recognized until early 1996—a full six years after the local Kashmiri resistance burst forth—when a group of LeT terrorists massacred sixteen Hindus at Barshalla in Kashmir's Doda district. Since then, hundreds of terrorist attacks involving LeT militants have occurred throughout India. LeT has been implicated in terrorist attacks in New Delhi in October 2005; in Bangalore in December 2005; in Varanasi in March 2006; in Nagpur in June 2006; and in the July 2007 train bombings in Bombay. It took, however, the devastating attacks of November 2008 in Bombay—a bloodbath that claimed the lives of close to 200 people, including 26 foreigners of 15 nationalities—for the international community to recognize that LeT's ambitions, transcending India, were actually part of a larger war with the West and with liberal democracies more generally.

Today, LeT's close ties with al-Qaeda in Pakistan, its support for the Afghan Taliban's military operations (despite the ideological divide between the two groups' interpretations of Islam), and its close collaboration with Jamiat al-Dawa al-Quran wal-Sunna, a Salafist group based in the Kunar province of Afghanistan, in operations against American troops in Afghanistan's Korengal Valley, remain only the latest in a long line of hostile activities—most of which have remained *sub rosa*—affecting U.S. citizens, soldiers or interests.[5]

As LeT grew over the years, in part by siphoning resources from its charities run under the rubric of Jamaat-ud-Dawa, the group's autonomy from the ISI has gradually increased. LeT's ability to raise funds independently from mosques in Pakistan and business and charities in the Middle East and Europe has allowed it greater freedom of action than existed during the 1990s. Today, LeT relies on the ISI primarily for safe haven and political protection for its leadership, intelligence on selected targets and threats, campaign guidance when necessary, and infiltration assistance, particularly with long distance operations involving transits through third countries. Most LeT operations against India today do not require the other forms of assistance witnessed during the organization's early years. They also do not require formal sanction or exchanges of information from the ISI; operating within the bounds of the extant strategy of striking India by any means, LeT operations are undertaken with minimal reference to its state guardians, with sufficient care taken to ensure that these attacks cannot be readily attributable to the ISI, the Pakistani Army, or formally to the Pakistani state.[6] Because the requirement of plausible deniability lies at the heart of ISI's relationship with LeT operations against India, the Pakistani intelligence services has always preferred directional, rather than detailed, control.

Pakistan's desire to control Afghanistan—an objective that dominated Islamabad's strategic policies during the 1980s and 1990s—and its commitment to religious renewal through participation in armed struggle has made the LeT one of the key beneficiaries of ISI support. For over two decades, and currently, the ISI has maintained strong institutional, albeit subterranean, links with LeT and has supported its operations through generous financing and combat training. At many points in the past, this support has included the provision of sophisticated weapons and explosives, specialized communications gear, and various kinds of operational assistance—aid which helped expand the lethality of the group as it conducted its missions in Afghanistan and against India.[7] Since the inauguration of the global war on terror, ISI assistance to LeT has become even more hidden, but it has by no means ended—even though the organization was formally banned by then-Pakistani President Pervez Musharraf on January 12, 2002.

GLOBAL REACH

That LeT pursues goals that go beyond India, even if it has focused on the latter disproportionately, is now acknowledged even by those who were initially skeptical of the group's larger ambitions. While India has occupied the lion's share of LeT attention in recent years, the organization has not by any means restricted itself to keeping only India in its sights. Like many other radical Islamist groups, the LeT leadership has on numerous occasions singled out the Jewish community and the United States as being among the natural enemies of Islam. Saeed warned, for example, that although his outfit was consumed at the moment by the conflict with India, "let's see when the time comes. Our struggle with the Jews is always there."[8] This enmity with the Jewish people is supposedly eternal and ordained by God himself. When Saeed was asked in the aftermath of the tragic 2005 earthquake in Pakistan whether then-President Musharraf's solicitation of aid from Israel was appropriate, he had no hesitation in declaring forthrightly that Pakistan "should not solicit help from Israel. It is the question of Muslim honor and self-respect. The Jews can never be our friends. This is stated by Allah."[9] This twisted worldview found grotesque expression during the November 2008 LeT atrocities in Bombay when the group deliberately targeted the Jewish Chabad center at Nariman House. Justifying this attack as reprisal for Israeli security cooperation with India, the Jewish hostages at Nariman House were not simply murdered but humiliated and brutally tortured before finally being killed during the three-day siege.[10]

Since Israel and India are viewed as part of the detestable "Zionist-Hindu-Crusader" axis that includes the United States, it is not surprising that LeT has long engaged in a variety of subversive activities aimed at attacking American interests. Although the ideological denunciation of the United States as an immoral, decadent, and implacable enemy of Islam was part of the group's worldview from its founding, its war against the United States took a decidedly deadly turn after the Clinton administration launched missile attacks against several al-Qaeda camps in Afghanistan in August 1998. Although these attacks did not kill Osama bin Laden, their intended target, they did kill many LeT operatives and trainers who had been bivouacked in these facilities. Shortly thereafter, the LeT formally declared a *jihad* against the United States, and began a variety of operations globally aimed at targeting U.S. interests. Asserting unequivocally that LeT intends to "plant the flag of Islam in Washington, Tel Aviv, and New Delhi,"[11] the group intensified its collaboration with al-Qaeda, supporting bin Laden's efforts as a junior partner wherever necessary, while operating independently wherever possible. In South Asia today, and especially in Pakistan's tribal belt, along its northwestern frontier, and in Afghanistan, LeT cooperates with al-Qaeda and other militant groups, such as the Taliban, in the areas of recruiting, training, tactical planning, financing, and operations.[12] Senior al-Qaeda operative Abu Zubaydah, for example, was captured in a LeT safe house in Faisalabad, Pakistan, indicating the close ties existing between both terrorist organizations.[13]

LeT's universal ambitions do not permit the group to confine itself only to South Asia. After declaring that it would provide free training to any Muslim desirous of joining the global *jihad*—a promise upon which the LeT has since delivered—the group's operatives have been identified as engaging in:

- liason and networking with numerous terrorist groups abroad, particularly in Central and Southeast Easia and the Middle East;
- the facilitation of terrorist acts, including in, but not restricted to, Chechnya and Iraq;
- fundraising in the Middle East, Europe, Austrlia, and the United States;
- the procurement of weapons, explosives, and communications equipment for terrorist operations from both the international arms markets and Pakistani state organizations such as the ISI;
- the recruitment of volunteers for suicidal missions in South Asia as well as the Middle East;
- the creation of sleeper cells for executing or supporting future terrorist acts in Europe, Australia, and likely the United States; and

- actual armed combat at least in India, Afghanistan, Pakistan, and Iraq.[14]

Indian intelligence currently estimates that LeT maintains some kind of terrorist presence in twenty-one countries worldwide with the intention of either supporting or participating in what Saeed has called the perpetual *"jihad* against the infidels."[15] Viewed in this perspective, LeT's murder of the six American citizens during the November 2008 attacks in Bombay is actually part of a larger war with the West and with liberal democracies more generally.

LeT is a terrorist organization of genuinely global reach. Although the nature of its presence and activities vary considerably by location, LeT has demonstrated the ability to grow roots and sustain operations in countries far removed from South Asia, which remains its primary theater of activity. As significantly, it exhibits all the ideological animus, financial and material capabilities, motivation and ruthlessness required to attack those it believes are its enemies because of their adherence to different faiths or their residence in secular, liberal democratic states. Furthermore, like al-Qaeda, LeT has demonstrated a remarkable ability to forge coalitions with like-minded terrorist groups. These alliances are most clearly on display within Southern Asia. In India, for example, LeT has developed ties with Islamic extremists across the country including in states distant from Pakistan such as Karnataka, Andhra Pradesh, and Tamil Nadu; in Pakistan, LeT cooperates actively with the Pakistani and Afghan Taliban and coordinates operations with al-Qaeda and the Haqqani network against Afghanistan; in Central Asia, LeT has cooperated with both the Islamic Movement of Uzkekistan and local Islamist rebels in the Caucasus; and, in Europe, LeT was actively involved in supporting the Muslim resistance in Bosnia while raising funds and building sleeper cells in countries such as Spain and Germany.[16]

When viewed from the perspective of the United States, it is safe to say that LeT has long undermined U.S. interests in the global war on terror. It threatens U.S. soldiers and civilians in Afghanistan and has now killed U.S. citizens in Bombay. Thus far, however, it has not mounted any direct attacks on the American homeland, but that is not for want of motivation. Rather, U.S. targets and allies in Southern Asia present more immediate and vulnerable—and therefore more inviting—targets. The effectiveness of U.S. law enforcement after September 11, 2001, and the deterrent power of U.S. military capabilities have had much to do with reinforcing this calculus. Consequently, LeT operations in the United States thus far have focused mainly on recruitment, fundraising and procurement rather than on lethal operations. Yet, with the deliberate killing of American citizens in Bombay, a new line may have been crossed in terms of LeT activities.

RECENT ACTIVITY

Unlike many of the other indigenous terrorist groups in South Asia whose command and control structures are casual and often disorganized, LeT's organizational structure is hierarchic and precise, reflecting its purposefulness. Modeled on a military system, LeT is led by a core leadership centered on its amir, Hafiz Mohammed Saeed, and his deputies, who oversee different aspects of the group's functional and charitable operations. These activities are implemented through various branch offices throughout Pakistan, which are responsible for recruitment and fundraising as well as for the delivery of social services such as education, healthcare, emergency services, and religious instruction. LeT's military arm is led by a "supreme commander" and a "deputy supreme commander" who report to Saeed directly. Under them are several "divisional commanders" and their deputies. Within the South Asian region, the divisional commanders oversee specific geographic "theaters" of operation, which are then subdivided in certain defined districts. These are controlled by "district commanders," each of whom is ultimately responsible for various battalions and their subordinate formations.[17]

The entire command edifice thus reflects a crude model of "detailed control," with orders being executed at the lowest level after they are approved by a chain of command that reaches to the top echelons of the group. This hierarchic command and control structure, although susceptible to decapitation in principle, nonetheless became institutionalized because LeT owed its origins primarily to the charismatic leadership of three individuals—of which Hafiz Saeed quickly became the *primus inter pares*. A hierarchic structure was also particularly appropriate, given the covert activities carried out by its military wing both autonomously and for the ISI—with the latter in particular insisting on a combination of high effectiveness, unremitting brutality, durable control, and plausible deniability as the price for its continued support. Because LeT was from the very beginning a preferred ward of the ISI, enjoying all the protection offered by the Pakistani state, the vulnerability that traditionally afflicts all hierarchic terrorist groups was believed to be minimal in this case.

This judgment, turned out to be accurate; even when Pakistan, under considerable U.S. pressure, formally banned LeT as a terrorist organization in 2002, the LeT leadership remained impregnable and impervious to all international political pressure. Not only did it continue to receive succor from the ISI, but its continued close links with the Pakistani state raised the understandable question of whether the 2008 terrorist strikes in Bombay were in fact authorized either tacitly or explicitly by the Pakistani secret services, as other attacks on India have been in the past. The interrogation of David Headley, the American citizen connected with the November 2008 terrorist attacks conducted by Lashkar-e-Taiba in Bombay, has now established that there were concrete ISI connections with the Bombay attacks.[18] In addition, Pakistan's management of the LeT detainees connected with those attacks and the halting progress of their trial demonstrates that the ISI has no intention of eviscerating LeT (or any other anti-Indian *jihadi* groups) because of their perceived utility to Pakistan's national strategy vis-à-vis India. Whether the strategy ultimately succeeds or fails in destroying the Indian polity has become quite irrelevant; rather, attacking India appears to be an end in and of itself.

The threat posed by LeT to India today is not a danger posed by "a stateless sponsor of terrorism," as it was unfortunately described by President George W. Bush on December 21, 2001.[19] Rather, LeT represents a specific state-supported and state-protected instrument of terrorism that operates from the territory of a particular country—Pakistan—and exemplifies the subterranean war that Islamabad, or more specifically Rawalpindi—where the headquarters of the Pakistan Army is located—has been waging against India since at least the early 1980s. This war no longer relies on "fomenting insurgencies"[20] —that is, exploiting the grievances of a dissatisfied section of the Indian populace against its state. Instead, it is a war that is centered on "fomenting terrorism" by unleashing large scale, indiscriminate attacks by groups with little or no connection to any existing internal grievances within India. In other words, LeT is one of the faces of the Pakistani Army's ongoing war with India. Yet, because of what LeT is—a terrorist organization that also counts Israel and the United States as its enemies solely for ideological reasons—it also represents the war that extremist forces in Pakistan, including some in its own government, are waging against many liberal states in the international community.

The 2008 attacks in Bombay reflect the LeT's classic *modus operandi*: since 1999, the group has utilized small but heavily armed and highly motivated two- to four-man squads operating independently or in combination with each other on suicidal—but not suicide—missions intended to inflict the largest numbers of casualties during attacks on politically significant or strategically symbolic sites. These missions invariably are complex and entail detailed tactical planning; historically, they have taken the form of surprise raids aimed at heavily guarded facilities such as Indian military installations, command headquarters, political institutions, or iconic buildings—all intended to inflict the highest level of pain, underscore the vulnerability of the Indian state, and embarrass the Indian government. (In Afghanistan, by contrast, LeT operations have focused principally on targeting Coalition forces, disrupting reconstruction efforts, and supporting other terrorist groups in their efforts to undermine the Karzai regime.) In any event, the

LeT personnel involved in the majority of these attacks seek to escape the scene whenever possible—in fact, they come carefully prepared to endure yet exfiltrate—but appear quite willing to sacrifice themselves if necessary, if in the process they can take down a larger number of bystanders, hostages, and security forces.

The targets attacked in Bombay are consistent with this pattern. They included the symbols of Indian success (luxury hotels), reflections of Indian history and state presence (a historic railway station) and emblems of India's international relationships (a restaurant frequented by tourists and a Jewish community center). The targeted killing of the Jewish residents at Nariman House, and possibly the murder of the Western tourists at the Leopold Café (if indeed they were deliberately targeted), would also be consistent with LeT's past record, which has included the focused slaughter of non-Muslims such as Hindus and Sikhs. Although the use of small arms—to include pistols, automatic rifles, grenades, plastic explosives, and occasionally mortars—has been the norm in most past LeT attacks, the group has also undertaken true suicide missions, including car bombings. Operations in Afghanistan, where recruitment for suicide bombings appears to be a specialty, have seen the use of larger crew-served weapons, mines, mortars, rocket-propelled grenades, and even primitive air defense systems.

ENDNOTES

[1] John L. Esposito, *Unholy War: Terror in the Name of Islam*, (Oxford: Oxford University Press, 2002), 7.

[2] Wilson John, "Lashkar-e-Toiba: New Threats Posed By An Old Organization," Jamestown Foundation *Terrorism Monitor* 3, no. 4 (May 5, 2005), http://www.jamestown.org/single/?no_cache=1&tx_ttnews[tt_news]=314.

[3] Zaigham Khan, "Allah's Army Waging Jihad In Kashmir," *Herald* (Karachi), January 1998.

[4] South Asia Terrorism Portal, "Lashkar-e-Toiba: Army Of The Pure," n.d., http://www.satp.org/satporgtp/countries/india/states/jandk/terrorist_outfits/lashkar_e_toiba.htm.

[5] Stephen Tankel, "Lashkar-e-Taiba In Perspective: An Evolving Threat," New America Foundation *Counterterrorism Strategy Initiative Policy Paper*, February 2010, 2.

[6] Ashley J. Tellis, testimony before the House Committee on Foreign Affairs, Subcommittee on the Middle East and South Asia, March 11, 2010.

[7] Ibid.

[8] Patrick French, "Why The Terrorists Hate Europe," *New York Times*, December 8, 2008, http://www.nytimes.com/2008/12/08/opinion/08iht-edfrench.1.18490114.html.

[9] "Exclusive Interview with Jamatud Dawa Founder," *Rediff India Abroad*, October 24, 2005, http://www.rediff.com/news/2005/oct/24inter1.htm.

[10] Alastair Gee, "Mumbai Terror Attacks: And Then They Came For The Jews," *Times of London*, November 1, 2009, http://www.timesonline.co.uk/tol/news/world/asia/article6896107.ece.

[11] Ashley J. Tellis, Testimony before the Senate Committee on Homeland Security and Governmental Affairs, January 28, 2009, http://www.carnegieendowment.org/publications/index.cfm?fa=view&id=22676.

[12] Ibid.

[13] Arun Kumar, "US Imposes Sanctions On Four Lashkar-e-Toiba Leaders," *Hindustan Times*, May 28, 2008.

[14] Tellis, Testimony before the Senate Committee on Homeland Security and Governmental Affairs.

[15] Amir Mir, "In the Name of God," *The News*, December 7, 2008, http://jang.com.pk/thenews/dec2008-weekly/nos-07-12-2008/dia.htm#4.

[16] Tellis, Testimony before the Senate Committee on Homeland Security and Governmental Affairs.

[17] South Asia Terrorism Portal, "Lashkar-e-Toiba."

[18] Jason Burke, "Pakistan Intelligence Services 'Aided Mumbai Terror Attacks,'" *Guardian* (London), October 18, 2010, http://www.guard-

ian.co.uk/world/2010/oct/18/pakistan-isi-mumbai-terror-attacks.

[19] White House, Office Of The Press Secretary, "President's Statement on Pakistan Extremist Groups," December 21, 2001, http://georgewbush-whitehouse.archives.gov/news/releases/2001/12/20011221-12.html.

[20] Haider A. H. Mullick, *Pakistan's Security Paradox: Countering and Fomenting Insurgencies* (Hurlburt Field, Florida: The JSOU Press, 2009).

TALIBAN

QUICK FACTS

Geographical Areas of Operation: South Asia

Numerical Strength (Members): Estimated in the tens of thousands

Leadership: Muhammed Omar, Abdul Ghani Baradar, Obaidullah Akhund

Religious Identification: Sunni Islam

(Quick Facts courtesy of the U.S. State Department's Country Reports on Terrorism)

After decades of intra-state conflict, social and economic crisis, and external meddling, Afghanistan resembled a broken skeleton of its former self by the early 1990s. The societal shifts occurring in Afghan society during the Soviet occupation of Afghanistan in the 1980s led to the militarization of Afghan society, promoting both self-styled resistance leaders and galvanizing the role of the mullah, or Islamic teacher, to statuses traditionally reserved for tribal leaders and wealthy land owners. The bloody conduct of the Soviet-Afghan war led to widespread destruction of Afghanistan's social and physical infrastructure: more than one-third of all Afghans became refugees in neighboring Pakistan or Iran and civil war quickly erupted following the violent end of the Soviet-backed Najibullah regime in 1992-93.[1] The ensuing chaos and banditry led to public demand for law and order. In response, a little known former resistance fighter named Mullah Mohammad Omar, and his Taliban (religious students) led a brief but well received campaign to rid southern Afghanistan's Kandahar region of its predatory commanders and bandits in the spring of 1994.

News quickly spread throughout southern Afghanistan of Mullah Omar and his band of puritanical justice-seeking vigilantes. With logistical and financial help from Pakistan's Inter-Services Intelligence (ISI) and manpower provided by religiously indoctrinated Afghan refugees living in Pakistan's tribal areas, the Taliban movement spread through Afghanistan like wildfire.

Following the Taliban's seizure of Kabul in 1996, the Taliban began to host a number of outlawed Islamist terrorist networks, including Osama bin Laden's al-Qaeda and a number of Kashmiri Islamist movements. Their influence shaped the Taliban's internal and external policies, which ultimately created rifts and divisions among the Taliban's clerical leadership. By 2000, the Taliban regime was largely at war with itself. Refusing to give in to U.S. demands to hand over Osama bin Laden following the September 11, 2001 terrorist attacks, Mullah Omar's reign of power ended shortly after the U.S.-led coalition attacked Afghanistan and toppled the Taliban regime.

Many of the Taliban's top leadership including Mullah Omar, Mullah Abdul Ghani Berader, Mullah Dadullah and Mullah Obaidullah slipped over the border into Pakistan and reestablished an ad hoc command-and-control center in the Pashtunabad neighborhood of Quetta, earning the moniker "the Quetta Shura" from U.S. and Afghan intelligence agencies. The Taliban slowly manifested itself into a more organized, centralized, and capable organization, and by 2006 launched a protracted campaign of violence and intimidation throughout Afghanistan's southern and eastern provinces. Similarly, a Pakistani off-shoot of the Taliban emerged as several tribal shuras supportive of the Afghan Taliban pledged bayat (allegiance) to Mullah Omar and began cross-border attacks providing manpower, weapons and logistical support to insurgent fronts in eastern Afghanistan and beyond. The tempo of the insurgency has continued to increase on both sides of the border, prompting U.S. and NATO forces in Afghanistan to conduct a "surge" of additional manpower and weaponry into the region beginning in 2009 and completed by September 2010.

HISTORY AND IDEOLOGY

Rising from the ashes of Afghanistan's devastating three-year civil war (1992-1994), the puritanical Islamist Taliban movement emerged in Afghanistan in 1994 and, following a ruthlessly effective military campaign, came to dominate the country from 1996 to 2001. Their victory led to the draconian implementation of *sharia* (Islamic Law) and the transformation of Afghanistan into a safe haven for international terrorist organizations such as Harakat ul-Mujahideen (HUM) and al-Qaeda. The original organization can be best described as a reactionary security force inspired by the breakdown in social order and stability, the main objectives of which were to disarm unruly commanders and their predatory militias and to impose order based on Islamic doctrine. The core of the original Taliban movement originated from a clerical *andiwal* (war comrades) network of Islamic conservatives, made up of *madrassa*-educated Pashtun men from poor or lower class backgrounds.

During its formation in the 1990s, the Taliban successfully transcended tribal and cultural norms, representing a strict form of Sunni Islam based on Deobandi doctrine, a dogmatic form of Islam originating in northern India that reinforces the Islamic ethical code.[2] Although the Taliban was predominantly Pashtun, due to its origin in the predominantly Pashtun Kandahar region, tribal lineage overall had very little to do with its formation; its members have come from both Duranni and Ghilzai tribes, which have been known to clash. Additionally, the movement initially tried to appeal to all of Afghanistan's ethnicities, and at least one Tajik sat on its *majlis-shura* (leadership council).[3] Uzbeks and northern Badakhshi Afghans were reportedly in charge of local Taliban missions in Paktia province.[4]

The most prominent characteristic of the Taliban, aside from its Deobandi interpretation of Islam, is its class make-up. Early manifestations of the Taliban were comprised of local religious clerics who typically grew up Afghanistan's rural and poor environs.[5] With little education and few literate commanders, the Taliban was responsible for gross mismanagement and a misunderstanding of how to govern once the movement began to gobble up territory across the country. Although the Taliban movement represented a socio-religious military organization, the Taliban consisted of several additional overlapping components and sponsors.

Within six months of Mullah Omar's liberation of much of Kandahar province, the government of Pakistan, whose economic interests in Afghanistan revolved around securing trade routes to the newly independent Central Asian states, sought Taliban security for a military convoy of goods destined for Turkmenistan as it traversed through the Spin Boldak-Chaman border crossing in Kandahar province. As Mullah Omar and his vigilante militia began to spread their influence throughout Afghanistan, Pakistan's Inter-Services Intelligence (ISI), the Pakistani military, and the Pashtun "trucking mafia" located in Quetta offered the Taliban logistical and financial aid to help secure the roadways following the success of the rescued Pakistani convoy at Kandahar's airfield. The Taliban also began to incorporate some former communist regime elements, particularly those loyal to former Defense Minister Shahnawaz Tanai, who remained under ISI protection in Peshawar. Through the ISI's help, Tanai allegedly mobilized his network of former military subordinates; whose technical and combat skills supported the Taliban's thrust toward Kabul.[6] Some government functionaries were kept in place at the local level while a Taliban representative oversaw and managed the day-to-day operations to ensure that the government acted within the boundaries of *sharia*.

Most of the original Taliban leadership came from the same three southern provinces—Kandahar, Uruzgan and Helmand—and nearly all of them fought under one of the two main clerical resistance parties during the war against the Soviets: Hezb-i-Islami (Khalis) and Mohammad Nabi Moham-madi's Harakat-I Ineqelab-ye Islami. Most of the Taliban *ulema* (religious scholars and clerics) had completed their studies at Deobandi *maddrassas* in Pakistan's Northwestern Frontier Province, one of the most famous being the Dar-ul-Uloom Haqqania located in Akora Khattak. Experts estimate that almost all of the Taliban leaders and cadres, as well as over 70 percent of the leaders and cadres of the Sunni Islamist movements Harakat ul-Muja-hideen (HUM), Jaish-i-Mohammad (JEM), Lashkar-e-Taiba (LET), Lash-kar-i-Jhangvi (LEJ), and Sipah-e-Saheba Pakistan (SSP), are products of the *madrassas.*[7]

The original Taliban has accurately been described as a "caravan to which different people attached themselves for various reasons."[8] This description remains largely accurate today. During an interview in 2006, Afghanistan's former Interior Minister, Ali A. Jalali, offered one of the most poignant descriptions of the post-2001 Taliban movement, calling it "an assortment of ideologically motivated Afghan and foreign militants, disillusioned tribal communities, foreign intelligence operatives, drug traffickers, opportunist militia commanders, disenchanted and unemployed youth and self-inter-ested spoilers… more of a political alliance of convenience than an ideolog-ical front."[9] The Taliban's former ambassador to Pakistan, Mullah Salaam Zaeef, now under house arrest in Kabul, stated the group does not refer to its forces as Taliban, but as *mujahedeen*, because only one in ten fighters is a true Taliban, while the rest are "ordinary Afghans."[10]

Indeed, the question of just who the Taliban is continues to baffle analysts and pundits alike. Some experts interpret the movement as a loose network of militants based along tribal lineage, some describe the Taliban as a Paki-stani-created and funded proxy army, while others suggest the Taliban are an umbrella organization of various militant networks, marginalized tribes and clans, criminal gangs, some of whom pledge allegiance to the core element of the former Taliban government, Mullah Mohammad Omar and the so-called *Quetta Shura*. The organizational construct of the Taliban movement in Afghanistan, its offshoots, and its Pakistani extension, the *Tehrik-i-Taliban Pakistan*, are presented below.

Quetta Shura Taliban (QST): The remnants of the former Taliban government manifested itself as the Quetta Shura in 2002, named after the Pakistani city where Mullah Omar sought refuge following his ouster from Afghanistan. Initially, the movement consisted of a ten man *Rahbari Shura* (Leadership Council) consisting of eight old guard Taliban military commanders from southern Afghanistan and one from Paktika and another from Paktia.[11] In

March 2003, Mullah Omar expanded the *Rabhari Shura* to include a total of 33 commanders and later, in October 2006, announced the creation of the *majlis al-shura* (consultative council) consisting of 13 members and some additional "advisers."[12]

Since that time, the Quetta Shura has become far more complex. As the Taliban began to spread its influence and gain *de facto* control of some rural areas in southern Afghanistan, the Quetta Shura began assigning shadow government positions to various areas and regions with heavy Taliban support. The Quetta Shura ballooned in size, likely because of its effort to manage and bring some organizational efficiency to what was and essentially is a franchise of tribal and communal networks with loose ideological and physical relations. According to several documents published by the Taliban between April 2008 and May 2009, the Taliban has created additional councils to perform specific tasks; these are managed under the Supreme Leadership of Mullah Omar. The Taliban outlined the structure of its organization in an official statement published in the insurgent magazine *Al Samood* in the spring of 2008.[13] While some view the manifesto is nothing more than an attempt by the Taliban to portray itself as a unified organization capable of running the state, it nevertheless outlines the nine councils that make up the Quetta Shura Taliban: the Military Commander's Council, Ulema Council, Military Council, Financial Council, Political Council, Cultural Council, Invitation (Recruitment) Council, Training and Education Council, and the Council of Affairs of the Prisoner's and Martyr's Families. The latter two are thought to exist in theory only.

The Taliban organization is centered on its Supreme Leadership head, Mullah Mohammad Omar, and his military and political deputy Mullah Abdul Ghani, best known under his *nom de guerre* Mullah Berader Akhund, and a series of military councils, which in turn help facilitate the functioning of the Taliban's four regional zones. Mullah Berader, the Taliban's most competent and respected military commander, was captured in a covert ISI-CIA sting operation in Karachi Pakistan sometime in early February 2010.[14] The Taliban's operational command over daily events is nowled by a seasoned field commander from Helmand province: Mullah Ghulam Rasoul, better known as Mullah Abdul Zakir; and his deputy, Mullah Abdul Rauf Alizai. Both Zakir and Abdul Rauf were detained by U.S. forces operating in Afghanistan in late 2001 and sent to the military detention center at Guantanamo Bay, Cuba. Following tribunal hearings, both Zakir and Rauf were repatriated to Afghanistan on December 12, 2007 before corrupt officials facilitated their release from custody in early 2008.[15] Maluvi Abdul Kabir, a senior Taliban leader from Nangarhar and close confident of Mullah Mohammad Omar, is head of the Peshawar Shura and acts as a liaison to the Taliban-affiliated

Haqqani Network.

Each of the Taliban's zones is broken down geographically as follows: the Quetta Shura is responsible for insurgent activities in Kandahar, Uruzgan, Farah, Zabul, Nimroz and parts of Helmand. The Peshawar Shura, led by Maluvi Abdul Kabir, is thought to influence operations in Nangarhar, Laghman, Kunar, Nuristan, Logar, Kabul, Wardak, and possibly areas in the northeast. The Miram Shah Shura is run out of North Waziristan and its military head is Siraj "Khalifa" Haqqani; its area of responsibility includes Paktia, Paktika, Khost, parts of Nangarhar, Logar, Wardak, Ghazni and Kabul. The Girdi Jungle Shura, named after the large refugee camp located in Pakistani Baluchistan, is responsible for activities in Helmand province. Although the Taliban may have distinct networks operating throughout the country—for example, the Haqqani Network, which enjoys a great deal of tactical autonomy—it is clear most of these groups share many political and ideological objectives.

Tehrik-i-Taliban Pakistan: Tehrik-i-Taliban Pakistan is an umbrella front bringing together rogue resistance organizations like Lashkar-e Jhavangi, Jaish-e Muhammad, Sipah-e Sahaba Pakistan and possibly some of the banned Kashmiri groups like Harakat ul-Mujahedin.[16] Though the group was officially formed in 2007, its seeds were sown as early as 2001 as a result of Afghan-Pakistani militant communication and collaboration.

Following the U.S.-led invasion of Afghanistan in October 2001, Taliban supporters and sympathizers in Pakistan's western tribal areas quickly pledged support and provided additional manpower and resources to help the Afghan Taliban resistance. The Pashtun tribes who dominate the western tribal agencies of Pakistan share ancestral lineages with many of Afghanistan's Pashtun tribesman and both have long resisted colonial attempts of occupation. Even in a modern context, the core of the Afghan resistance movement against the Soviet occupation of Afghanistan was based in these same areas, using Peshawar as a *de facto* capital and the tribal agency's of North and South Waziristan as training areas and key junctions for transiting personnel and weapons into Afghanistan.

The initial flow of Taliban fighters into Pakistan's Federally Administered Tribal Areas (FATA) became a tidal wave following the collapse of the Taliban regime in Kandahar and after the monumental battle of Tora Bora in December 2001 and the subsequent spring 2002 battle of the Shah-i-khot Valley (Operation Anaconda). Along with the Taliban came hundreds of fleeing Arab and foreign fighters linked to al-Qaeda, many of whom settled among their Pashtun supporters and sympathizers in North and South Waziristan.

Many of these supporters had voluntarily fought against the Soviet army during the 1980s under the clerical-led *mujahedeen* factions Hezb-i-Islami (Khalis) and Mohammad Nabi Mohammadi's Harakat-i Ineqelab-ye Islami. Following the Soviet withdrawal and subsequent collapse of the Afghan communist regime in 1992, many of the Pakistani volunteers returned to their villages following the start of the civil war.

One of the earliest networks in place to support the Taliban and al-Qaeda's exodus from Afghanistan was the Tehrik-e Nafaz-e Shariat-e Muhammadi (Movement for the Enforcement of Muhammadan *Sharia* Law or TSNM). Founded in 1992 in the Malakand tribal agency, the TSNM has fought for the implementation of *sharia* throughout the FATA and North Western Frontier Province and has shared ideological tenants with the Afghan Taliban. The TSNM has taken root in Bajur Agency, sheltering al-Qaeda fugitives and sponsoring a new generation of militants throughout the Salafi *madrassa* network under their charismatic leader Maulana Faqir Mohammad. The second most important bastion for Taliban fighters, supporters and sympathizers is North and South Waziristan. Home of the legendary *mujahedeen* commander Jalaluddin Haqqani, North Waziristan is also the operational space of many al-Qaeda leaders and the network of Hafiz Gul Bahadur.

These networks were largely disorganized although supportive of the Afghan Taliban from 2001-2004. The U.S. successfully killed one of the main militant commanders in the region in 2004 when missiles launched from a Predator drone slammed into a compound housing Nek Mohammad Wazir. Similar to the Afghan Taliban's approach, tribal leaders and influential khans were systematically targeted and killed by militants, replacing the traditional power systems with those of mullahs and militia commanders.

Baitullah Mehsud soon emerged as a charismatic Pakistani version of Mullah Omar. Young, radical but oddly unschooled in Islamic *madrassas*, Baitullah hailed from the Mehsud tribe and gained prominence in February 2005 when he signed a "peace accord" with the Pakistani government.[17] As part of that deal, Baitullah pledged not to support al-Qaeda and restrained his forces from attacking Pakistani state targets and military targets in exchange for the end of Pakistani military operations in South Waziristan. The deal disintegrated in 2006, leaving South Waziristan a largely independent militarized zone where Taliban officials and al-Qaeda leaders found sanctuary. Baitullah Mehsud commanded a core of 5,000 hardened loyalists, mostly tribally affiliated Mehsud kinship, launching spectacular raids and ambushes against the superior Pakistani military forces.[18]

On December 14, 2007, a militant spokesman announced the formation of the Tehrik-i-Taliban Pakistan (TTP). Baitullah Mehsud was appointed the *amir* of the TTP's forty-man *shura*; Hafiz Gul Bahadur was appointed as the *naib amir* (deputy); and Maulana Faqir Mohammad of the Bajaur Agency was appointed third in command.[19] The group quickly entrenched its supporters throughout all of FATA's seven tribal agencies as well as the settled Northwest Frontier Province (NWFP) districts of Swat, Bannu, Tank, Lakki Marwat, Dera Ismail Khan, Khohistan, Buner and Malakand.[20] The TTP consolidated their objectives to enforcing *sharia* throughout the FATA, uniting against NATO forces in Afghanistan by supporting Mullah Omar's Afghan Taliban, seeking to remove Pakistani military checkpoints from the FATA, and vowing to protect the Swat district and Waziristan from future Pakistani military operations. Following the Pakistani government's siege of the Red Mosque in Islamabad in July 2007, Baitullah Mehsud and the TTP turned their guns on the Pakistani government. The following month, forces loyal to Mehsud humiliated the Pakistani military when they ambushed and captured 200 government soldiers.[21] Subsequently, the assassination of presidential candidate Benazir Bhutto in December 2007 reverberated around the world and drew considerable attention to the deteriorating security situation in Pakistan.

The Pakistani government quickly blamed Baitullah Mehsud and the TTP for orchestrating the assassination of Bhutto, offering transcripts of alleged phone conversations with Mehsud and his operatives discussing the attack, a claim Mehsud and the TTP strongly denied.[22] Rifts between rival commanders under the TTP banner impacted the organization's unity throughout 2008, eventually leading to major disputes between Hafiz Gul Bahadur, Baitullah Mehsud and Maulavi Nazir. The situation worsened after nine tribal elders allied with Maulavi Nazir were gunned down by TTP militiamen linked to Baitullah Mehsud and Uzbek forces loyal to the Islamic Movement of Uzbekistan *amir* Tahir Yuldashev. An increase in U.S. unmanned aerial vehicles striking targets in North and South Waziristan strained the TTP as top and mid-level leaders were liquidated throughout 2008 and 2009 and scores more arrested and dispersed in 2010. The Pakistani military moved on the TTP and the TSNM in Bajur and Swat, prompting a closer cooperation among militants who renewed their vows of union in February 2009 when they formed the *Shura-Ittehad-al-Mujahedeen* (United Mujahedeen Council) which again brought Hafiz Gul Bahadur, Baitullah Mehsud, Maulavi Nazir and Siraj Haqqani together.

Major Pakistani military ground operations (Operation Rah-e Nijat) targeted the TTP in South Waziristan in October 2009 and concluded by April 2010. Beginning in October 2009, the Pakistani military launched a major offensive against Taliban strongholds in South Waziristan. The symbolic village of Makeen, the hometown of Baitullah Mehsud, as well as Ladha, Kotkai, Kaniguram, and Sararogha were primary targets of the operation.[23] Three weeks into the operation, Pakistani military officials claimed to have killed 300 militants while losing 45 soldiers.[24] Pakistani Prime Minister Yousuf Raza Gilani announced the completion of the ground offensive on December 19, 2009. He claimed that 589 Taliban fighters and their supporters were killed in the offensive and that 79 Pakistani soldiers also died from combat.[25] Nearly 35,000 Pakistani troops remained in South Waziristan during the late winter of 2010 to help guard roads, provide security for development projects and towns, and prepare for the return of about 41,000 displaced families, according to media reports.[26]

Just prior to the South Waziristan operation, an American UAV strike killed Baitullah Mehsud, his second wife, and several of his bodyguards on August 5, 2009. A chaotic rebuttal from TTP spokesmen denied his death but within two weeks, and following an alleged power struggle within the TTP for the top leadership position, the TTP acknowledged Mehsud's death and announced Hakimullah Mehsud as his replacement, the new second-in-command Waliur Rehman, and other top positions to Maulana Faqir Mohammad and Qari Hussein Mehsud, the TTP's top suicide-bomber facilitator. Hakeemullah was reportedly killed in or as a result of a drone strike in South Waziristan Agency in January 2010.[27] The TTP released a series of audio messages from Hakeemullah and before March, Hakeemullah appeared in a 43-minute videotaped interview submitted to a global media outlet proving he survived the attack.[28]

In the wake of the operation, much of the TTP leadership and foot soldiers dispersed throughout the region, mostly into Orakzai Agency, North Waziristan, and to a lesser degree, Kurram Agency. To date, no major Pakistani military operation has occurred in North Waziristan, a focal point the United States continues to push with Pakistani officials. According to Pakistani Foreign Office spokesman Abdul Basit, "any decision regarding the launch of an operation in North Waziristan will be determined by Pakistan alone, and will depend on the security situation in the area."[29]

The Haqqani Network: Once a key recipient of U.S. funding and arms during the Soviet-Afghan war of the 1980s, Jalaluddin Haqqani has maintained his status as a prominent *mujahideen* commander who holds sway in several southeastern provinces in Afghanistan. His preservation of power and prestige has largely surpassed that of the Taliban's elusive supreme leader Mullah Mohammad Omar, especially among Haqqani's Karlanri Pashtuns of eastern Afghanistan. However, it is Jalaluddin's oldest son, Sirajuddin, who may have gained the most prominence. Siraj, also known as "Khalifa," has been described by U.S. military officials as "one of the most influential insurgent commanders in eastern Afghanistan," who has "eclipsed his father in power and influence and is said to rival Mullah Omar for the Taliban leadership."[30]

The Haqqani Network is based out of a Taliban bastion in neighboring Pakistan. The village of Dande Darpa Khel near Miramshah (North Waziristan) is its main headquarters, while Zambar village in the northern Sabari district in Khost province serves as the group's major operations hub.[31] The group also maintains a major presence in the Zadran dominated districts between Paktia and Paktika provinces, which also serve as a major transit point for insurgents piercing into Logar Province and southern Kabul. The Haqqani family owned and operated an extremist *madrassa* in the Dande Darpa Khel village just north of Miram Shah before the Pakistani military launched a raid and shut it down in September 2005 and subsequent U.S. drone strikes destroyed its two main compounds and killed scores of Haqqani relatives and fighters in September 2008.

The Haqqanis belong to the eastern Zadran tribe (Mezi sub-tribe), as does the commander of the Taliban's "eastern zone," Maulavi Abdul Kabir, a veteran Taliban official and military commander closely associated with Mullah Omar. The Haqqanis hold clout on both sides of the border and through Siraj's leadership, the group provides a critical bridge to Pakistani Taliban groups and al-Qaeda linked foreign fighters.

The elder Haqqani's past relationship with the Pakistani intelligence apparatus, the Inter-Service Intelligence or ISI, has virtually guaranteed Jalaluddin's freedom of movement on the Pakistan side of the border as several failed operations against him have proven. Electronic signal intercepts by U.S. and Indian intelligence agencies reportedly confirm a link between ISI officers and Haqqani operatives who are said to have jointly planned and executed the deadly suicide car bomb attack against India's embassy in Kabul on July 7, 2008.[32]

Jalaluddin Haqqani, never part of the original Kandahari Taliban, was franchised into the Taliban in 1996 as the religious militia neared his stronghold of Paktia. Since then, Jalaluddin Haqqani (and later Siraj Haqqani) has pledged *bayat* (allegiance) to Mullah Mohammad Omar, becoming the Minister of Tribal and Border Affairs, the Governor of Paktia and eventually the Taliban's overall military commander. In 2003, Jalaluddin led the Taliban's strategy for the eastern zone. Suspected of suffering from lupus for some time, the elderly Haqqani handed the reins of his terror network over to his son Siraj in 2007 after coming down with serious health concerns. Afghanistan's intelligence service began to circulate rumors of Jalaluddin's death in the summer of 2007. Taliban spokesmen rebuffed several journalists' queries at the time, neither confirming nor denying the rumors. At this point, Siraj became the Taliban's overlord for three provinces, Paktia, Paktika and Khost, although each province now has separate Taliban shadow provincial shadow governors, with Siraj serving as "regional governor" for the tri-province area known locally as Loya Paktia. U.S. Special Operations against the Taliban and the Haqqani Network increased substantially in 2010, resulting in 900 low and mid-level commanders being arrested or killed, according to U.S. military officials.[33] Additionally, Pakistani officials reportedly arrested Naisruddin Haqqani, a top financier and son of Jalaluddin Haqqani, in late December 2010 as he traveled from Peshawar to Miram Shah, North Waziristan.[34] Mullah Muhammad Jan, a top Haqqani Network military commander, and two associates were also reported to be traveling with Naisruddin during the time of his arrest. The Haqqanis have been making inroads toward Kabul since 2007. Ghazni, Logar, Wardak, Nangarhar and Kabul are now areas with known Haqqani Network presence, while reports in early 2009 suggest Haqqani associates and bomb experts may be operating in southern Kandahar Province, a traditional Quetta-Taliban stronghold.[35]

A series of complex assaults against Afghan government and economic institutions in Kabul, Jalalabad, and Khost City have been attributed to the Haqqani Network and its "Kabul Strike Group," a shadowy guerrilla front that plans and conducts sophisticated attacks usually including a commando style raid with suicide-bombers against urban targets in Kabul City. The brazen day-light attack which involved gunmen and suicide bombers dressed as border police against Jalalabad's main bank on February 19, 2011 killed least 42 people and wounded more than 70 is one of the most deadly attacks attributed to the Haqqani Network this year.[36]

Past attacks attributed to the Haqqani Network include the multi-pronged assault on two Afghan ministries and a prison headquarters in the Kabul that left 19 people dead and more than 50 wounded, the 11-man commando-style suicide bombing raid against several government facilities in Khost City, and the July 4, 2009 assault against a remote U.S. outpost in Paktika's Zerok district that killed two U.S. soldiers and injured four others. On July 21, 2009 suicide bombers armed with rocket-propelled grenades and assault rifles attacked government installations and a U.S. base in the cities of Gardez and Jalalabad. However, one of the most brazen attacks attributed to the Haqqani Network occurred in Kabul on October 4, 2009 when terrorists dressed in police uniforms assassinated the security guard protecting the UN's Bahktar guest house and stormed the facility, eventually detonating several suicide vests and killing at least six foreign UN personnel and six others. The deadly suicide bombing of an American CIA forward operating base in Khost on

December 30, 2009 that killed seven senior CIA operatives and a Jordanian intelligence offer has been speculatively attributed to the Haqqani Network, the TTP and al-Qaeda in Afghanistan.

Tora Bora Nizami Mahaz (Tora Bora Military Front) – Following the death of Younis Khalis, a legendary *mujahedeen* commander and the leader of his own Hizb-e-Islami faction, Khalis' son Anwur-ul Haq Mujahid created his own resistance front called the *Tora Bora Nizami Mahaz*. After announcing the group's formation in early 2007, Mujahid claimed responsibility for a rash of attacks against Afghan and coalition forces in the eastern province of Nangarhar, an area more prone to narco-cartels and smuggling mafias than Taliban groups. The Tora Bora Front has been blamed for the deadly car-bombing of a U.S. Marine convoy in the Shinwar district—an attack that prompted a heavy-handed response from the fleeing U.S. convoy which left over three dozen civilians injured and 12 killed.[37] The group publishes its own propaganda magazine, *Tora Bora*, and maintains its own website, Al Emarah, separate from the Taliban's main propaganda components. In October 2007, the Taliban announced a reshuffling of its "eastern zone" and appointed Maulavi Abdul Kabir as the new *amir de zon* (zonal chief), a decision allegedly fully supported by Mujahid.[38] Several large scale attacks and suicide bombings in Nangarhar have been attributed to the Tora Bora group. In June 2009, Pakistani media reports indicated Mujahid was arrested during a sting operation in Peshawar, a claim denied by Mujahid's network and his relatives.[39] Speculation regarding his detention subsided after credible reports indicated Mujahid delivered a sermon at the funeral of Awal Gul, a senior Taliban leader who died while in detention at Guantanamo Bay, and whose body was subsequently returned to Nangarhar province for burial in February 2011.[40] The Tora Bora Front continues to function in some capacity, intermittently maintaining and updating its website, producing its quarterly Tora Bora magazine, and launching occasional attacks in Nangarhar province. The group's support base remains strongest in Khalis' native district of Khogyani and the volatile areas of Pachir Agam and Shinwar.

Taliban Jamiat Jaish-e Moslemim (Muslim Army of the Taliban Society): Saber Momen, a senior Taliban commander operating in southern Afghanistan, announced the creation of Taliban Jamiat Jaish-e Moslemim (Muslim Army of the Taliban Society) in August 2004. Internal rifts and criticism over weak leadership prompted Mullah Sayeed Muhammad Akbar Agha to split from the Quetta Shura and create the new faction. The Taliban quickly dismissed the offshoot organization, stressing that all "Taliban commanders are united under the leadership of Mullah Omar.[41]

Jaish-e Moslemim is credited with the high-profile abduction of three foreign

UN election officials from Kabul in October 2004. Pakistani authorities later arrested Akbar Agha and 17 of his associates in December 2004, effectively leading to the demise of the group in June 2005 when the remaining 750 Jaish operatives folded back into the Taliban movement.[42]

Jaish al-Mahdi (the Army of the Mahdi): During the summer of 2007, a militant Afghan and Arab organization Jaish al-Mahdi (Army of the Mahdi) announced its creation. Led by Abu Haris, a Syrian commander who fought against the Soviets in Afghanistan during the 1980s, Jaish al-Mahdi claimed to have 250 fighters and maintained close links with both al-Qaeda and the Taliban.[43] The group sought refuge in Pakistan's North Waziristan tribal area and enjoyed a strategic relationship with the Haqqani Network also based in North Waziristan. On September 8, 2008, a U.S. airstrike killed Abu Haris, three other al-Qaeda fighters and a number of Jalaluddin Haqqani's relatives near the town of Miram Shah.[44] It is unclear how much operational capability Jaish al-Mahdi retains, but reports in 2007 suggested a large number of foreign fighters linked to al-Qaeda and the Taliban were fighting in Helmand province, scores of whom were reportedly killed in clashes with coalition forces. In 2008, a coalition operation against the Taliban in Helmand's Garmsir district killed 150 fighters in one week's time, many of them foreigners. The total number of fighters in the district at the time was estimated to be 500, again, most of them foreigners.[45]

Khaddam al-Furqan (Servants of the Koran)[46] : Shortly after the collapse of the Taliban government in December 2001, a cadre of Taliban "moderates" regrouped in Pakistan and announced the creation of Khaddam al-Furqan (Servants of the Koran). The Taliban's former minister of foreign affairs, Wakil Ahmad Mutawakkil, the former education minister, Mawlawi Arsala Rahmani, the Taliban's UN envoy, Abdul Hakim Mujahed, and the former deputy minister for information and culture, Abdul Rahman Hotak, make up the group's core. Mohamad Amim Mojadeedi, an Islamic cleric and the son of Maulavi Mohammad Nabi Mohammadi, the former leader of the highly influential Harakat-e Enqalab party that resisted the Soviet occupation in the 1980s, serves as the head of Khaddam al-Furqan.[47] The group distanced itself from the policies of Omar's Taliban regime and made overtures to Hamid Karzai's feeble Pashtun coalition, who allowed the group to participate in the Emergency *Loya Jirga* held in June 2002.

In 2004, only Mohammad Amin Mojadeedi traveled to Kabul in an attempt to register the group to run in the Parliamentary elections, an indication that *Khaddam* suffered from a fractured structure and shaky constituency. By 2005, *Khaddam al-Furqan* continued to exist, albeit shrouded in mystery, but publicly identified itself when four high-ranking former Taliban officials entered into negotiations with the government. In 2008, *Khaddam al-Furqan* continued to promote reconciliation between the Afghan government and the Taliban, offering up a seven-point strategy to help facilitate a political resolution to the current conflict.[48]

Hezb-i-Islam (Party of Islam): A young Islamist named Gulbuddin Hekmatyar, a Kharoti Pashtun from the northern Afghan province of Kunduz, formed the Hezb-i-Islami political faction in Pakistan in 1976 in response to the growing influence of leftist movements in the Afghan government and university campuses. During the 1980s, Hekmatyar, along with guidance from Pakistan's ISI and financial assistance from American and Saudi intelligence services, propelled Hezb-i-Islami into the biggest mujahedeen organization fighting against the Soviet occupation. Hekmatyar is infamous for his brutal battlefield tactics and backstabbing political deals, including the assassination of many of his political rivals.[49]

His reign of terror also included the shelling of Kabul during the 1992-1994 civil war, one of the only known instances when an acting prime minister bombarded his own capital. During the rise of the Taliban, Hekmatyar lost several of his key strongholds and weapons dumps, including the Spin Boldak armory in Kandahar in 1994 and Charasayab, a region south of Kabul, before being exiled to Iran following the Taliban's capture of Kabul in 1996. Many of Hekmatyar's loyalists sought refuge in Pakistan during Taliban period, although some commanders and militiamen folded into the Taliban government. Post-2001, Hekmatyar clandestinely left his sanctuary in Mashhad, Iran, and has remained a fugitive ever since, floating between Pakistan and Afghanistan and orchestrating attacks against the Afghan government and international forces. Hekmatyar has reactivated some of his loyal cadres in northern and eastern Afghanistan, namely in the provinces of Takhar, Badakshan, Baghlan, Nangarhar, Kabul, Logar, Laghman, Kunar, Nuristan, Wardak and parts of Paktia, Paktika and Khost. The U.S. military has estimated Hekmatyar's forces to number around 400-600, although experts suggest the number is more likely to total around 1,500 full-time fighters.[50] Hezb-i-Islami cadres have fallen out of favor with many Taliban fronts at the local level, with violent clashes and killings attributed to both sides occurring throughout 2010.[51] Unlike the Taliban, Hezb-i-Islami leaders have participated in clandestine and overt talks with the Afghan government since 2009, both abroad and in Afghanistan an indicator the group is militarily weakened and biding its time for a political rebirth and to bolster its rank-and-file.

GLOBAL REACH

The Afghan Taliban movement has restricted its efforts to attacks within the borders of Afghanistan, although violent clashes on the frontier areas with Iran and Tajikistan have been occasionally reported. These clashes are likely smuggling operations gone awry as Afghanistan's frontier regions with Iran and Tajikistan are well established narcotics and weapons smuggling routes. Occasionally, Afghan Taliban leaders have threatened attacks against NATO countries whose soldiers are operating in Afghanistan, namely Germany, Spain and the UK; although none of the terrorist attacks in any of these countries have ever been attributed to the Taliban.[52] In the fall of 2009, the Taliban made an effort to promote a new "foreign policy" by releasing several statements on their website declaring the movement poses no regional or international security threat. Mullah Omar, the Supreme Commander of the Taliban, repeated this rhetoric in one of his two annual Eid statements to the Afghan people, which appeared in mid-November 2010.[53] The public outreach came at a time of increasing prospects for negotiations and a possible political accommodation between the Afghan government and Taliban fronts which NATO, the U.S., the UN and Pakistan have all endorsed in various capacities.

The TTP, especially following the Baitullah Mehsud's reign of terror between 2007 and 2009, have shown interest in not only attacking Afghan government and security targets but also Pakistani state institutions and security targets. On several occasions in 2008 and 2009, Baitullah Mehusd threatened to launch attacks against international targets including the White House.[54] Others in the TTP are believed to be prepared to act on it; on January 19, 2009, Spanish authorities seized 14 suspected associates of Mehsud in Barcelona on suspicion of plotting a series of suicide-bomb attacks which were to coincide with the run-up to the March 9 parliamentary elections and the March 11 anniversary of the Madrid commuter train bombings.[55] Similarly, Mehsud claimed credit for the April 4, 2009 shooting attack at an immigration center in Binghamton, New York where 13 people lost their lives to a lone gunman.[56] However, investigators quickly identified the gunman as a deranged Vietnamese immigrant with no ties to international terrorist groups or radical Islamist movements.

Mehsud's close association with Arab al-Qaeda leaders and Uzbek militants in South Waziristan partially explains his global-*jihadist* rhetoric. Following his death in August 2009, the TTP's *shura* struggled to nominate a new leader that pleased both the Pashtun tribal constituency and the more global minded *jihadists* of al-Qaeda. Al-Qaeda's influence won out, and Hakeemullah Mehsud, the radical TTP commander of the Orakzai Agency, became the new *amir* for the TTP. Hakeemullah ordered a number of deadly attacks against Pakistani and U.S. military targets in the region with some reports indicating he helped facilitate the suicide bombing attack against a U.S.

intelligence base in eastern Afghanistan's Khost province.[57] The deadly attack killed eight CIA officers and left six others severely injured on December 28, 2009.

RECENT ACTIVITY

Since the Taliban movement's formation in 1994, their capture of Kabul two years later, and their eviction by international forces in late 2001, the group has significantly altered and redefined its organizational, political and ideological constructs. The Taliban has reconstituted itself partly based on criminal activities such as extortion, kidnapping for ransom and participating in Afghanistan's burgeoning narcotics industry. Although there is little evidence to suggest the Taliban is directly involved in the cultivation, processing and distributing of narcotics, it is clear the Taliban benefits from taxing the industry through religious taxes like *ushr* and "voluntary donations" such as *zakat*. In May of 2010, the Taliban also issued a third edition of their *layeha*, or "code of conduct," in an effort to strengthen unity among the rank-and-file, low level commanders, and the provincial military councils that are active throughout the country. Out of the 85 rules in the 2010 *layeha*, 47 were repeated from the 2009 version, 14 were modified/altered, and 24 were new (18 of which are new additions, six additional articles replace the omissions from the 2009 layeha).[58] Most of the new regulations were organizational directives seeking to establish provincial and district level commissions that oversee the political and military conduct of Taliban fighters, and offer directions on establishing "complaint" councils that allow local residents to communicate any grievances or allegations of abuse committed in the name of the Taliban to an authoritative council that would subsequently launch an investigation into the matter.

In late 2009, U.S. and NATO military officials estimated there were approximately 25,000 full-time Taliban fighters now operating in Afghanistan, up from 7,000 in 2006.[59] Outside observers estimate the size of the Taliban to be around 20,000 members, although some reach higher estimates of 32,000 to 40,000.[60] Deteriorating security conditions, seasonal fighters and so-called "blue-collar insurgents" (those who engage in insurgent activities for supplemental income) inflate the number of supplemental insurgents that fight alongside "full-time" fighters at any given point.

In terms of aggressive tactics, like the *mujahedeen* who fought against the Soviets between 1979 and 1989, the Taliban and other insurgent groups prefer asymmetrical attacks and guerilla warfare like hit-and-run ambushes, assassinations, rocket attacks and land-mine and improvised-explosive (IED) attacks. The number of IEDs against coalition forces in Afghanistan has spiked considerably over the past several years, jumping from 100 per month in 2006 to over 800 a month during the summer of 2009, peaking in August 2009 with over 1,000 recorded IED incidents.[61] Similarly, 41 U.S. and NATO soldiers were killed by IEDs in Afghanistan in 2006, 172 troops died from an astounding 3,276 IEDs in 2008, and 250 U.S. and NATO soldiers were killed by IEDs in Afghanistan by mid-December 2009.[62] In 2010, 372 U.S. and coalition forces died in combat from IED blasts in Afghanistan, making it the deadliest year for IED fatalities since the conflict began.[63]

Suicide bombings, a new phenomenon in Afghanistan, appeared in low numbers following the Taliban's defeat in 2001. Taliban leaders Mullah Dadullah "Lang" and Jalaluddin Haqqani facilitated cadres of suicide bombers in the tribal areas of Pakistan during the incubation phase of the current insurgency (2002-03) and by 2006-07, suicide bombings became a common battlefield tactic among three leading insurgent groups in Afghanistan; the Taliban, *Hezb-i-Islami*, and *Tora Bora Nizami Mahaz* (Tora Bora Military Front). Aside from suicide attacks, tactics imported from connections with radical militants in Chechnya and Iraq appeared in Afghanistan by 2005 and 2006, including videotaped beheadings, sniper attacks, and larger truck bombs.[64] Suicide bombers are now used in conjunction with armed assaults against fortified structures and compounds, usually coalition bases or Afghan government buildings. Such complex attacks have occurred in Kandahar, Kunduz, Baghlan, Farah, Nangarhar, Kunar, Nuristan, Helmand, Nimroz, Kabul, Khost, Paktia and Pakitka since 2008.

In 2008 and 2009, 98 percent of Afghanistan's opium was produced in seven provinces in southwestern Afghanistan, all of which are areas under contested control or under the influence of the Taliban.[65] UN, U.S., NATO and Afghan officials differ on how relevant income derived from drug trafficking is for the Taliban. The U.S. and NATO suspect the Taliban earns between $60 million and $100 million a year from the drug industry, the UN estimates the number to be $125 million, and Afghan observers have put the number as high as $500 million a year.[66] Richard Holbrooke, the former U.S. special representative for Afghanistan and Pakistan, declared that the Taliban makes more money from donations from wealthy supporters in the Arab Gulf than they do from the drug trade.[67]

Nevertheless, the Taliban and other insurgents' participation in the narcotics trade is widespread on the battlefields of southern Afghanistan. Drug traffickers provide the Taliban motorcycles, cellular phones, SIM cards, weapons and explosives in exchange for protection of their processing workshops, refinement labs, opium markets and trafficking routes.[68] A growing phenomenon since 2008 is the advent of "narco-suicide terrorism"; drug traffickers are outsourcing the technical skills of the Taliban and other groups to conduct suicide attacks against counter-narcotics personnel and their headquarters. In 2008, the UN tallied 78 fatalities caused by mine explosions, gun attacks, and suicide bombings against eradication teams and counter-narcotics personnel; an increase of about 75 percent over 2007 tallies.[69] The trend of narco-criminals in conjunction with the Taliban supporting or facilitating attacks against eradication personnel and government targets has continued in 2009; prior to the 2009 opium harvesting, four suicide attacks targeting counternarcotics personnel and their headquarters in Helmand and Nimroz provinces left 16 people dead and 55 wounded, according to local media reports.[70] Although the coalition no longer actively conducts poppy eradication campaigns, Afghanistan's Government Led Eradication (GLE) initiative, a coalition-financed anti-narcotics strategy that tasks provincial counterdrug forces with destroying poppy crops, has had mixed results and remains vulnerable to insurgent and anti-government attacks. During the 2010 GLE campaign, insurgents and angry farmers attacked GLE forces in Helmand province at least eight times during eradication operations, and there have also been attacks in Nangarhar.[71] A total of 24 police and three farmers were killed in these attacks, with 21 police, six farmers and five tractor drivers were injured.

Often billed as "the stable and secure" northern areas, Afghanistan's northern provinces have been the target of a burgeoning Taliban insurgency since 2004. The Taliban have implemented a two-pronged approach that includes establishing a stronghold in the northwest province of Badghis to sever the supply routes through the Herat-Badghis Sabzak Pass, the sole entry into northwestern Afghanistan, while creating a northeastern jump-off point in northern Baghlan and Kunduz Provinces. Afghan authorities are increasingly concerned about what they view as the Taliban's expansion into non-traditional conflict zones such as Sar-i-Pul, Samangan and Balkh provinces, although the Governor of Balkh attributes more of the instability to Hezb-i-Islami.[72]

The northern province of Kunduz has borne much of the brunt of insurgent activity, including a protracted suicide and roadside bomb campaign initiated by Taliban and foreign fighters. On October 8, 2010, the long-standing provincial governor of Kunduz was killed along with 19 others in a blast as throngs of worshippers gathered at a mosque in neighboring Takhar province.[73] Abdul Wahid Omerkhail, the long-time governor of Kunduz's Chardara district, died after a suicide bomber detonated himself at the governor's office on February 10, 2011.[74] Two weeks later, another suicide bombing in the Imam Sahib district killed 31 civilians as residents lined up at the local government census office. Residents and security officials claimed the

Mohammed Ayoub Haqyar, the district governor, was the intended target of the blast.[75]

The Taliban's northern offensive, orchestrated since 2007 under the leadership of the Quetta Shura's Mullah Shah Mansoor Dadullah, Mullah Berader and, to an extent, Mullah Mohammad Omar, has recently proved successful in targeting NATO's unity and its mission in Afghanistan. Since major hostilities peaked in Kunduz during the summer of 2009, ramped up efforts by NATO, Afghan forces, and Pakistan's security services to restore stability in Kunduz resulted in several Taliban leaders in Kunduz being killed and captured as well as the high-profile arrest of Mullah Berader, the mastermind behind the Taliban's nationwide military strategy.[76]

Operations against the Taliban in Kunduz continued in 2010, and at least three formerly Taliban controlled areas, the Imam Sahib, Dasht-i-Archi and Chaharra Darra districts, are once again under nominal government authority after Operation Khorshid cleared many insurgents from the area.[77]

The Taliban has also ramped up its efforts against "soft-targets" in urban centers such as Kabul, Kandahar, Jalalabad, and Kunduz City in an attempt to shatter the secure and stable image of Afghanistan's population centers. This trend is an alarming parallel to previous campaigns unleashed by the Taliban, the Haqqani Network and Hezb-i-Islami that steadily saw an increase in urban guerilla warfare.

In 2009, the Taliban launched major suicide attacks against NATO convoys in Kabul, conducted a deadly suicide-bomber assault against UN guesthouse complexes in the Shar-e-Naw neighborhood and detonated a massive truck bomb targeting senior Afghan officials and Western personnel in the fortified Wazir Akhbar Khan neighborhood. These high-profile attacks and others like it throughout the country highlight the perception that the Taliban can "strike anywhere at any time." Similar attacks in 2008 and early 2009 rocked Kabul as well, including the deadly suicide-bombing assault on the Justice and Education Ministries as well as on an office of the Prisons Department.[78]

ENDNOTES

[1] Although the Kabul based regime of Najibullah fell to the resistance in March 1992, areas in southern Afghanistan, particularly Helmand province, were still in control of Communist militias allied with Najibullah until 1993.

[2] Gilles Dorronsoro, *Revolution Unending: Afghanistan, 1979 to the Present* (New York: Columbia University, 2005), 50-51.

[3] Ahmed Rashid, *Taliban: Militant Islam, Oil and Fundamentalism in Central Asia* (New Haven: Yale University Press, 2001).

[4] Sippi Azerbaijani Moghaddam, "Northern Exposure for the Taliban," in Antonio Giustozzi, ed., *Decoding the New Taliban* (New York: Columbia University Press, 2009), 251.

[5] Gilles Dorronsoro, *Revolution Unending: Afghanistan, 1979 to the Present* (New York: Columbia University, 2005), 272.

[6] Michael Griffin, *Reaping the Whirlwind: Afghanistan, Al Qa'ida and the Holy War, revised edition* (London: Pluto press, 2000), 68.

[7] Moghaddam, "Northern Exposure for the Taliban," 259.

[8] Robert D. Crews and Amin Tarzi, eds. *The Taliban and the Crisis of Afghanistan*, (Cambridge: Harvard University Press, 2008), 242.

[9] Personal communication with author, August 3, 2007.

[10] Jason Straziuso, "The Kabul Quagmire," Associated Press, October 17, 2009.

[11] Tarzi and Crews, eds. *Taliban Crisis in Afghanistan*, 295.

[12] Antonio Giustozzi, *Koran, Kalashnikov, and Laptop: the Neo-Taliban Insurgency in Afghanistan* (New York: Columbia University Press, 2008), 46-47, 83, 90.

[13] See Ahmad Mukhtar, "Administrative Structures of the Taliban Islamic Movement," *Al Samood*, March 2008.

[14] Mark Mazzetti and Dexter Filkins, "Secret Joint Raid Captures Taliban's Top Commander," *New York Times*, February 16, 2010.

[15] United States Department of Defense, "Consolidated Chronological Listing of GTMO Detainees Released, Transferred or Deceased," November 25, 2008 (date declassified), http://www.dod.mil/pubs/foi/detainees/09-F-0031_doc1.pdf; See also Kathy Gannon, "Former Gitmo Detainee Said Running Afghan Battles," Associated Press, March 3, 2010.

[16] Thomas Ruttig, "The Other Side: Dimensions of the Afghan Insurgency: Causes, Actors and Approaches to 'Talks,'" *Afghanistan Analysts Network*, July 2009, 24.

[17] Amir Mir, "War and Peace in Waziristan," *Asia Times,* May 4, 2005.

[18] Amir Mir, "The Most Wanted Pakistani Talib," *Pakistan Post*, December 10, 2007.

[19] Ibid.

[20] Hassan Abbas, "A Profile of Tehrik-i-Taliban Pakistan," Combating Terrorism Center at West Point *CTC Sentinel* 1, Iss. 2, January 2008.

[21] Christina Lamb, "High-Profile Victories in the Battle Against Terror," *Times of London*, August 9, 2009.

[22] "Fighters Deny Bhutto Killing Link," *Al Jazeera* (Doha), December 30, 2007.

[23] Kotkai is the home village of TTP leader Hakeemullah Mehsud and Kaniguram is a village where Uzbek militants established a headquarters and training area.

[24] Zahid Hussein, "Pakistan's South Waziristan Offensive Reaches Crucial Stage in Ladha," *The Times* (Lahore), November 5, 2009.

[25] "South Waziristan Offensive Over: Pakistani PM," *CBC News,* December 12, 2009, http://www.cbc.ca/world/story/2009/12/12/south-waziristan-offensive-ends.html.

[26] Karin Brulliard and Haq Nawaz Khan, "After Major South Waziristan Offensive, Pakistan Still Faces Serious Obstacles," *Washington Post*, November 19, 2010, http://www.washingtonpost.com/wp-dyn/content/article/2010/11/19/AR2010111902617.html.

[27] Kristen Chick, "Pakistani Taliban Leader Hakeemullah Mehsud is Dead, say Officials," *Christian Science Monitor*, February 10, 2010, http://www.csmonitor.com/World/terrorism-security/2010/0210/Pakistani-Taliban-leader-Hakeemullah-Mehsud-is-dead-say-officials.

[28] Bill Roggio, "Taliban Release Videotape of Hakeemullah Mehsud," *Long War Journal*, February 28, 2010, http://www.longwarjournal.org/archives/2010/02/taliban_release_vide.php.

[29] "'Pakistan Alone will Determine Necessity of N Waziristan Operation,'" *The Express Tribune* (Karachi), January 13, 2011, http://tribune.com.pk/story/103264/pakistan-alone-will-determine-necessity-of-n-warisitan-operation/.

[30] Bill Roggio, "Targeting Taliban Commander Siraj Haqqani," *Long War Journal*, October 20, 2007, http://www.longwarjournal.org/archives/2007/10/targeting_taliban_co.php.

[31] Matthew DuPee, "The Haqqani Networks: Reign of Terror," *Long War Journal*, August 2, 2008.

[32] Mark Mazzetti and Erich Schmitt, "Pakistanis Aided Attack in Kabul, US officials Say," *New York Times*, August 1, 2008, http://www.nytimes.com/2008/08/01/world/asia/01pstan.html.

[33] Tom Vanden Brook, "U.S.: Raids have Taken Out 900 Taliban Leaders," *USA Today*, March 7, 2011, http://www.usatoday.com/news/world/afghanistan/2011-03-08-taliban08_ST_N.htm.

[34] Sami Yousafzai and Ron Moreau, "Pakistan Arrests Key Taliban Leader," *Newsweek*, December 23, 2010.

[35] Murray Brewster, "Deadlier Taliban Network Surfaces," Canadian Press, February 9, 2009, http://www.thestar.com/SpecialSections/article/584508.

[36] Rafiq Sherzad, "Afghan Attack Toll Rises, Making it Worst in 8 Months," Reuters, February 20, 2011; Bill Roggio, "Afghan Intel Links Jalalabad Bank Attack, Other Suicide Attacks to Pakistan," *Long War Journal*, February 27, 2011, http://www.longwarjournal.org/archives/2011/02/afghan_intel_links_j.php#ixzz1FOQFf0x2.

[37] Arthur Bright, "Pentagon Inquiry Finds US Marine Unit Killed Afghan Civilians," *Christian Science Monitor*, April 16, 2007, http://www.csmonitor.com/2007/0416/p99s01-duts.html.

[38] Janullah Hashemzada, "Taliban Appoint Maulvi Kabir as new Zonal Chief," *Pajhwok Afghan News*, October 20, 2007.

[39] Abdul Rauf Lewal, "Tora Bora Group Leader Arrested in Peshawar," *Pajhwok Afghan News*, June 6, 2009; Javed Hamim, "Mujahid's Arrest Denied," Pajhwok Afghan News, June 7, 2009.

[40] Rod Nordland, "Karzai Calls on the U.S. to Free a Taliban Official," *New York Times*, February 8, 2011; Thomas Joscelyn and Bill Roggio, "Tora Bora Military Front Commander Speaks at Funeral of Former Gitmo Detainee," *Long War Journal*, February 8, 2011.

[41] Tarzi and Crews, Taliban Crisis in Afghanistan, 301.

[42] Giustozzi, *Koran, Kalashnikov, and Laptop*, 82.

[43] Waliullah Rahmani, "Al-Qaeda Uses Jasish al-Mahdi to Gain Control over Helmand Province," Jamestown Foundation *Terrorism Focus* 4, iss. 34, October 24, 2007.

[44] "Guard: Al Qaeda chief in Pakistan killed," *CNN*, September 8, 2008.

[45] Jefferey A. Dressler, "Securing Helmand: Understanding and Responding to the Enemy," Institute for the Study of War *Afghanistan Report* no. 2, September 2009, 10.

[46] Tarzi and Crews, *Taliban Crisis in Afghanistan*, 268-269, 303.

[47] Giustozzi, *Koran, Kalashnikov, and Laptop*, 82.

[48] Thomas Ruttig, "The Other Side: Dimensions of the Afghan Insurgency: Causes, Actors and Approaches to 'Talks,'" *Afghanistan Analysts Network*, July 2009.

[49] The most notorious attack against political rivals in known as the "Farkhar massacre" when a Hekmatyar sub-commander named Sayed Jamal killed 30 of Ahmed Shah Massoud's *Shura-e Nezar* commanders after a joint-meeting on July 9, 1989. Ishtiaq Ahmad, *Gulbuddin Hekmatyar: An Afghan Trail from Jihad to Terrorism* (Islamabad: Pan Graphics, 2004), 24.

[50] Giustozzi, *Koran Kalashnikov and Laptop*, 132.

[51] Matthew DuPee and Anand Gopal, "Tensions Rise Between Hizb-i-Islami and the Taliban in Afghanistan," Combating Terrorism Center at West Point *CTC Sentinel*, August 2010.

[52] David Montero, "Taliban to Germany: Leave Afghanistan or lose Oktoberfest," *Christian Science Monitor*, September 28, 2009; "Taliban Threatens Attacks on West: Spanish Radio," Agence France

Presse, November 26, 2008; "Dead Taliban Leader was Training U.S. Recruits," ABC News *The Blotter*, May 14, 2007.

[53] "Taliban Leader Mullah Omar Issues Statement on Eid Al-Adha, Rejects Media Reports of Peace Talks as 'Baseless Propaganda' Aimed at 'Wrongfully Raising Hollow Hopes in the Hearts of… People,'" Middle East Media Research Institute *Special Dispatch* no. 3380, November 15, 2010, http://www.memri.org/report/en/0/0/0/0/0/0/4769.htm.

[54] Sara A. Carter and Eli Lake, "Taliban Threatens Attack in D.C.," *Washington Times*, April 1, 2009, http://www.washingtontimes.com/news/2009/apr/01/fbi-issues-alert-on-taliban-threat/.

[55] Kathryn Haahr, "Spanish Police Arrest Jamaat al-Tabligh Members in Bomb Threat," Jamestown Foundation *Terrorism Focus* 5, iss. 6, February 13, 2008, http://www.jamestown.org/single/?no_cache=1&tx_ttnews%5Btt_news%5D=4722.

[56] Tina Moore, "Pakistani Taliban Leader Claims Responsibility for Binghamton Shooting; Authorities Quickly Refute," *New York Daily News*, April 4, 2009, http://www.nydailynews.com/news/national/2009/04/04/2009-04-04_pakistani_taliban_leader_claims_responsi.html#ixzz0fMx6DAQX.

[57] M. Ilyas Khan, "'CIA Bomber' Video Indicates Taliban's Reach," BBC, January 9, 2010.

[58] Thomas H. Johnson and Matthew C. DuPee, "Analyzing the New Taliban Code of Conduct (Layeha): An Assessment of Changing Perspectives and Strategies of the Afghan Taliban," *Central Asian Survey* (forthcoming).

[59] Adam Entous, "Taliban Numbers have Quadrupled," Reuters, October 10, 2009.

[60] David Killcullen, *The Accidental Guerrilla: Fighting Small Wars in the Midst of a Big One* (Oxford: Oxford University Press, 2009), 48-9.

[61] Greg Grant, "Afghan IEDs Hammered Soviets," *DoD BUZZ*, December 15, 2009.

[62] Jason Motlagh, "Roadside Bombs: An Iraqi Tactic on the Upsurge in Afghanistan," *Time*, June 9, 2009, http://www.time.com/time/world/article/0,8599,1903583,00.html#ixzz0c9hARmK8; Greg Grant, "Afghan IEDs Hammered Soviets," *DoD BUZZ*, December 15, 2009. In comparison, the Soviets lost 1,995 soldiers killed and 1,191 vehicles to mines during the conflict in Afghanistan.

[63] Ian S. Livingston, Heather L. Messera, and Michael O'Hanlon, *Brookings Afghanistan Index: Tracking Variables of Reconstruction & Security in Post-9/11 Afghanistan* (Washington, DC: The Brookings Institution, December 31, 2010), 12.

[64] Tom Coghlan, "Taliban Train Snipers on British Forces," *Daily Telegraph* (London), July 23, 2006.

[65] UNODC, "Afghanistan's Opium Survey 2008," November 2008.

[66] "Afghanistan's Narco War: Breaking the Link Between Drug trafficking and Insurgents," Hearing of the Senate Foreign Relations Committee, 111th Congress, 1st Session, August 10, 2009; Gretchen Peters, *Seeds of Terror: How Heroin Bankrolls the Taliban and al Qaeda* (New York: Thomas Dunne Books, 2009).

[67] Slobodan Lekic, "US Envoy: Most Taliban Funds Come From Overseas," Associated Press, July 28, 2009.

[68] Joanna Wright, "The Changing Structure of the Afghan Opium Trade," *Jane's Intelligence Review*, September 2006; Joanna Wright and Jerome Starkey, "Drugs for Guns: How the Afghan Heroin Trade is Fuelling the Taliban Insurgency," *Independent* (London), April 29, 2008; "Blood Flowers Afghanistan's Opium Industry Remains Robust," *Jane's Intelligence Review*, December 2008; Gretchen Peters, "How Opium Profits the Taliban," United States Institute of Peace Peaceworks, August 2009, 19.

[69] UNODC, *Afghanistan Opium Poppy Survey 2008: Executive Summary*, 19-20.

[70] Matthew DuPee, "Opium Den," *Himal Southasian Magazine*, July 2009.

[71] U.S. Department of Defense, *Report on Progress Toward Security and Stability in Afghanistan*, November 2010, 84.

[72] "Hezb-e-Islami Involved in Violence in North: Balkh Governor," *Tolo TV News*, September 20, 2011, http://www.tolonews.com/en/component/content/article/567-hezb-e-islami-involved-in-violence-in-north-balkh-governor.

[73] Joshua Partlow and Javed Hamdard, "Governor of Afghanistan's Kunduz Province, 19 Others Killed in Bombing at Mosque," *Washington Post*, October 10, 2010, http://www.washingtonpost.com/wp-dyn/content/article/2010/10/08/AR2010100804196.html.

[74] "Suicide Blast Kills Afghan District Governor: Police," Agence France Presse, February 10, 2011.

[75] Alissa Rubin, "31 Killed in Suicide Attack on Afghan Census Office," *New York Times*, February 21, 2011.

[76] Giles Whittell, "US Hails Capture of Taleban Commander Mullah Abdul Ghani Baradar," *Times of London*, February 18, 2010.

[77] "2 Districts in Kunduz Cleared of Insurgents," Sada-e-Azadi, January 31, 2011; "Afghan, Nato Forces Clear 5 Villages in Kunduz," *Tolo TV News,* December 29, 2010.

[78] Alan Cullison and Habib Zahori, "Taliban Strike Heart of Afghan Capital," *Wall Street Journal*, January 18, 2010.

MUSLIM BROTHERHOOD

Founded in 1928 in Egypt, the Muslim Brotherhood is one of the world's oldest, largest and most influential Sunni Islamist groups—and an inspiration for the ideology and actions of a majority of contemporary Islamist movements. In the first decades of its existence, the movement advocated armed struggle (jihad) as a means to impose Islamic law (sharia) at home, while seeking to fight Western colonialism and the State of Israel in the Middle East. Following Gamal Abdel Nasser's assumption of power in Egypt in 1952, the Brotherhood was formally outlawed and moved into the political opposition, alternatively demonized, repressed or silently tolerated during the decades that followed. Throughout this period, the movement developed a wide network of social and religious charities and programs, expanding its influence across the entire Muslim world, and beyond it. Simultaneously, however, it has gone through key ideological transformations, in particular a de-radicalization embodied in the renunciation of one of the key tenets of its doctrine: violent jihad. This move, however, has prompted deep cleavages within the Brotherhood itself, making it difficult to characterize the Brotherhood as a coherent and homogenous organization. Today, the "Lotus Revolution" and the end of the Mubarak regime have raised fundamental questions about the Brotherhood's future role in Egypt, and its place in Arab politics writ large.

HISTORY AND IDEOLOGY

The "Society of the Muslim Brothers" (*Jama'at al-Ikhwan al-Muslimin*) was founded in 1928 by Hassan al-Banna, a young primary school teacher from the city of Isma'iliyya in southern Egypt.[1] In its pristine form, the Brotherhood was a religious, youth and educational group which advocated moral reform and a revival of Islam in Egypt and the Middle East, and did so at a time when secular nationalism had gained momentum across the region. Inspired by the thinking of Muslim scholars Muhammad Abdu (1849-1905), Rashid Rida (1865-1935) and Jamal al-Din al-Afghani (1839-1897), al-Banna had become convinced that Muslims had been corrupted by a process of "Westernization" and that secular sentiments were among the first reasons for the decline of Islam. He felt that the weaknesses of the Muslim world could only be cured by a return to the original form of faith, its literal prescriptions, derived from the Koran and the prophetic tradition and applicable to all aspects of life, including the political arena. Islam was for him the only solution to the afflictions which had been plaguing Muslim societies, and the only way toward their regeneration. Al-Banna spelled out the pillars of this revolutionary ideology in his manifesto *On Jihad*,[2] in which he explained how Islam had deserted its roots and become dominated by Western influences, and how social revolution and anti-colonial struggle—against the British occupation in Egypt, the corrupt monarchy, and against Jewish presence in Palestinian lands—were the prerequisites of a genuine Islamic revival.

To achieve these goals, al-Banna was the first to promote *jihad* (the struggle against infidels, in word and in action) as a legitimate tool to fight Western decadence and its impact on the contemporary Muslim world.[3] According to him, *jihad* was, however, not restricted to the struggle against "apostates" (*kuffar*), but a more comprehensive awakening of Muslim hearts and minds. In the 1930s, Al-Banna's animosity towards colonialism found expression in an organization that began to recruit numerous followers, who saw appeal in its ideology on issues ranging from poverty, education, nationalism to the nascent Israeli-Palestinian conflict. By using support networks of mosques, welfare associations, neighborhood groups, and professional syndicates, the Muslim Brotherhood was able to indoctrinate Egyptians—in particular those from the deprived lower class in search of salvation, and among the middle class, whose aspirations had been largely ignored. The movement's popularity grew as scores of its leaders came under government repression and were jailed and tortured. As a result, they were increasingly viewed as heroes fighting against British colonial rule. Consequently, the Brotherhood moved beyond charitable and educational activities to become an openly political movement, extending its membership from a thousand members in 1936 to nearly two million in 1948.[4] It was after al-Banna's assassination in 1949 by the secret police of King Faruk (who blamed the Brotherhood for anti-government acts such as the murder of Prime minister al-Nuqrashi in 1948) that the movement's second ideologue—Sayyid Qutb—emerged and reinforced its doctrine and creed.

Through his passionate writings, still cited by Islamists today, Qutb declared that Egyptians had deviated from Islam and that Muslims had the obligation to use *jihad* as a means to combat Western powers, regarded as morally decadent, idolatrous and intrinsically hostile to the Islamic faith. In his influential manifesto *Milestones (Ma'alim fi-l-tariq)*,[5] published in 1964, Qutb expressed his belief that Islam, understood as a complete sociopolitical system, a "way of life," was the remedy to all problems of contemporary Arab and Muslim societies. In fact, the decline of the Muslim world stemmed from ills directly imported from the West—immorality, secularism, corruption— that had taken Muslims back to a pre-Islamic state (*jahiliyya* in Arabic). As an antidote, Qutb called for absolute submission to the principles of Islam. In this view, anything non-Islamic was evil by essence, including a political authority said to be "democratic" that ran contrary to a genuine government based on the rule of Islamic law.

Qutb understood early on that he would have to use pragmatic methods to carry out his vision, which led him to ally himself with the Brotherhood to promote his ideas and assert his leadership. Indeed, at that time the movement provided an organizational structure able to stage active *jihad* and already held great political and intellectual influence in Egypt. It thus constituted the ideal vehicle for establishing an Islamic state, a notion that Qutb had in common with his predecessor, Hassan al-Banna.[6] Following this alliance, Qutb began to openly endorse violence and advocate *jihad*, recommending that all pious Muslims isolate themselves from society to fight all manifestations of apostasy and all forms of oppression. In 1954, he was arrested along with other members of the Brotherhood and remained in prison for most of the rest of his life. It was during his incarceration that Qutb endured degrading treatments, like torture, which led him to further radicalize. It is also at that period that he completed his most influential writings,[7] before finally being executed in 1966 on charges of conspiring against the Egyptian regime.

Throughout the decades, the Muslim Brotherhood's ideology has not varied much from al-Banna and Qutb's primary arguments. However, like a majority of other social movements, the Brotherhood has undergone a number of fundamental transformations. Of all, the most striking has been the continued ideological "de-radicalization" of its leadership and its subsequent abandonment of armed *jihad*. This dynamic was initiated in the late 1970s and early 1980s, when leaders started to increasingly disavow violence in favor of moderation and political participation. Hassan al-Hudaybi, al-Banna's successor as the Supreme Guide of the Brotherhood,[8] published a book in 1969, *Preachers not Judges*, in which he justified this rejection of violence and provided a series of theological arguments to counter Qutb's radical views.[9] It was under his influence and under that of his successor, Umar al-Tilmisani, that the group distanced itself from the *jihadist* approach and even went so far as to name Sadat a "martyr" after he was assassinated in 1981.[10] A number of factors were necessary for this de-radicalization to occur, in particular the sustained de-legitimization of Islamist ideas through the use of rational arguments, supported by charismatic former *jihadists* and the state's use of repression.[11] This process contributed to the increasingly popular characterization of the group as a "moderate" movement, especially in the West.[12] And to be sure, the Brotherhood is considerably less radical than it was in the days of Qutb.

However, the Muslim Brotherhood's efforts to rebrand itself as a moderate group that has renounced *jihad* has prompted fierce criticism among other Islamist groups. Prominent al-Qaeda leaders, such as Ayman al-Zawahiri, have called the movement's shift and its participation in Egypt's political debate and elections—a posture contrary to God's sovereignty (*hakimiyya*)—a "betrayal."[13] Moreover, the Brotherhood's deradicalization has been tempered by the continued influence of its core beliefs; while many Muslim Brothers now claim to have embraced democracy, the ideology that was initially developed by al-Banna and Qutb, in which Islam must govern all matters, still carries significant resonance. Recent years also have witnessed a relative reversal of this benign trend towards the reaffirmation of more radical discourses within the organization. This is exemplified in the stance of some of the Brotherhood's offshoots, which still back armed struggle under the banner of "resistance" against "occupation." For example, the Islamist group Hamas, originally formed by the Palestinian Muslim Brothers, condemned the choice made by the Egyptian Brotherhood to renounce violence and continues to see *jihad* as the only viable way to rid Muslim lands of infidel presence. Criticism of the Brotherhood's ideological and political shifts has also emanated from Syria, where the group's leadership has openly supported attacks against Israel and the U.S. in Iraq and voiced full support for Hamas and the Iranian-backed Shi'ite militia Hezbollah.[14]

Even more significant are the endogenous divides that the Muslim Brotherhood's steps toward moderation have prompted, structured around a growing conflict between the movement's conservative old guard, longtime reformists, and a younger generation of militants, themselves divided between democrats and a minority of radicals tempted by the resumption of *jihad* in Egypt.[15] As of 1996, several prominent members of the Brotherhood broke away to form new political factions such as the "Center Party" (*Hizb al-Wasat*) or the "Movement for Change," also known as *Kefaya*—"enough" in Egyptian Arabic. In 2007, the movement released a platform that laid out fairly clearly the inflexible principles that its old guard continues to follow, including the rejection of the civil nature of the state and a call to establish a theocratic government and exclude non-Muslim minorities (Copts) from domestic politics.[16] The debate over this platform has served to highlight the growing schism underway within the movement between moderates and conservatives who have regained influence and been more vocal since the election of their new Supreme Guide, Muhammad Badi, in January 2010.[17] Since then, the Brotherhood seems to have adopted a more radical discourse towards the U.S., which is described as an "infidel" nation that "does not champion moral and human values and cannot lead humanity." Badi has also stated that America and Israel were "the Muslims' real enemies," and that "*jihad* against both is a commandment of God which cannot be disregarded."[18]

In many ways, these evolutions are reminiscent of an early episode in the Brotherhood's history: by the late 1930s, there had already been great friction between a wing of the organization that wished to pursue armed *jihad* against the British, and its leadership which was fearful that such a strategy would ultimately damage the Brotherhood's future. Today, "re-radicalization" of segments of the movement is particularly conspicuous among the youth, influenced by a Salafist doctrine which considers the only true path to be a return to the practices of the first Muslims (*sahaba*) and rejects as apostasy (*kufr*) anything deviating from a strict interpretation of the Koran.[19] Although only a few Brothers publicly identify themselves as Salafists, their thinking has been increasingly marked by this puritanical approach to faith. This trend, moreover, is poised to gain currency within the movement itself, since the Brotherhood's Supreme Guide, Muhammad Badi, is known to be a hard-line Salafist devoted to the spirit and methods advocated by Qutb, with whom he was jailed in the 1960s.[20]

GLOBAL REACH

Although banned and clandestine, the Muslim Brotherhood has managed to grow over the years and set up branches throughout the Muslim world, especially in Egypt's neighboring countries—Lebanon, Syria, Iraq, Sudan, Jordan, the Palestinian territories—as well as in the Arabian Peninsula (Saudi Arabia, Kuwait, Yemen, Oman, Bahrain). The movement has also achieved global status by expanding well beyond its traditional Middle Eastern borders and establishing branches in the West. Although these different offshoots maintain close symbolic and ideological ties with the Egyptian base, they remain largely independent.

In the 1930s, the Brotherhood began to spread its ideology in the Middle East as a response to colonial presence. In Palestine, the movement was established in 1935 by the brother of al-Banna himself, Abd al-Rahman, along with other figures such as Izz al-Din al-Qassam, one of the leaders of the armed resistance against the British.[21] The Brotherhood's activities were, at that time, primarily of a social and religious nature, and included the creation of associations, schools and the establishment of mosques intended to "bring an Islamic generation up."[22] It was in 1987, in the context of the first *Intifada* (Palestinian uprising), that the Brotherhood politicized by founding the Islamic Resistance Movement (Hamas),[23] which in turn took on a further military bent. By way of contrast, such politicization occurred earlier in countries like Syria and Jordan, where the Brotherhood became an opposition force to the regime in the first years after national independence.[24] A group like the Islamic Action Front (IAF),[25] the Jordanian Brotherhood's political wing, is, for instance, the country's only established opposition party and has positioned itself as a leading player in the 2011 anti-government protests by denouncing public corruption and poverty.[26]

As in Egypt, most of the Brotherhood's offshoots have also been banned and repressed. In Syria, after the 1963 Ba'athist coup, the group became the main (Sunni) opposition force to the (Shi'ite Alawite) Assad clan. The conflict developed into an open armed struggle which culminated in the Hama uprising of 1982, which was famously crushed by the military.[27] Since that time, the movement ceased to be politically active inside the country, but has managed to maintain a support network there. Syrian Brothers have renounced violence and adopted a more reformist approach calling for the establishment of a pluralistic and democratic political system.[28] A similar transformation has characterized the Jordanian Brotherhood, which now seeks reform and no longer aspires to revolution.[29] In Iraq, where the group's history remains relatively unknown, the Iraqi Islamic Party, its main manifestation, was banned during the 1960s and forced underground by Saddam Hussein. It reemerged in 2003, and has since displayed an ambiguous posture, voicing harsh criticism against the U.S. while at the same time taking part in the transitional process.[30]

In the Gulf, the Brotherhood possesses branches in several countries, most of which were established by militants driven out of Egypt in the 1950s. Many found shelter in Saudi Arabia, but were seen as a challenge to that country's official Wahhabi creed. The movement was never allowed to deal with religious issues, and therefore invested its energies in the educational field as a way of disseminating its ideology. This led to the emergence of movements like the "Awakening" (*Sahwa*), known for its support of rebellion against the

Sauds.[31] But Wahhabism, in turn, influenced the Brotherhood and drew many of its members toward the more conservative Islamic trend. Elsewhere, such as in the United Arab Emirates and Qatar, the Brotherhood relied on a strong intellectual and media presence to influence local populations.[32] With the exception of Oman, where the Brotherhood has faced severe crackdowns, the movement also managed to gain seats in parliaments throughout the region; in Kuwait via the *Hadas* movement;[33] in Yemen through *Islah* or the "Congregation for Reform;"[34] or in Bahrain, where the *Al-Minbar* Islamic Society has been, since 2002, the largest elected party.[35]

In North Africa, the Brotherhood's expansion was also a result of colonial rule. In Algeria, its members took part in the uprising against the French during that country's war for independence, before being marginalized by the secular FLN party. In the 1990s, the Algerian Brotherhood did not join *jihadist* factions in their fight against the state; instead, the group favored a peaceful conflict resolution and a return to democracy, even taking part in the coalition backing current president Abdelaziz Bouteflika in the early 2000s.[36] In Tunisia, the Brotherhood influenced Islamists, in particular *Al-Nahda* (the Renaissance Party) founded in 1989, whose leaders advocate democracy and pluralism "within an Islamist framework."[37] Outlawed by the Ben Ali regime, *Al-Nahda* has made a historic return in the wake of the 2011 "Jasmine Revolution"[38] and is now a legalized party likely to benefit from considerable popular support in the upcoming elections.[39] In Libya, the Brotherhood has been present since the 1940s when King Idris I offered Egyptian Brothers refuge. However, following his seizure of power via coup, Muammar al-Qadhafi considered the Muslim Brothers a menace, and worked to eliminate them. Despite this repression, the Brotherhood has maintained a vast network of sympathizers in Libya, and notably supports the current anti-Qadhafi insurgency taking place in the North African state.[40] Finally, in Sudan, the Brotherhood enjoys a significant, though informal, presence, and has launched mass Islamization campaigns which allowed its representatives to infiltrate virtually all state institutions.[41]

In addition to its traditional geography, the Brotherhood has gained significant ground in Europe through regional forums such as the Federation of Islamic Organizations in Europe, the Forum of European Muslim Youth and Student Organizations, the European Council for Fatwa and Research and others.[42] Since the 1960s, members and sympathizers of the group moved to Europe and set up a vast and sophisticated network of mosques and Islamic charities and schools, such as in England (Muslim Association of Britain), France (Union des Organisations Islamiques de France), Germany (Islamische Gemeinschaft Deutschland), the Netherlands and Italy (Unione delle Comunita' ed Organizzazioni Islamiche in Italia).[43] With considerable foreign funding and the relative tolerance of European governments seeking to engage in a dialogue with Muslim minorities,[44] Brotherhood-related organizations have gained prominent positions on the sociopolitical scene—presenting themselves as the legitimate representatives of Muslim communities in Europe and "moderate" interlocutors for governments and the media.

In addition to its presence in Europe, the Brotherhood has also reached out to Muslims in the United States, where its members have been present since the 1960s. The movement launched its first long-term strategy there in 1975, focusing on proselytizing efforts and the creation of specific structures for youth and freshly-arrived Muslim immigrants. Seeking to exert political influence at the state and federal levels, Muslim Brothers have been represented within multiple organizations such as the Muslim Students' Association (MSA), the Islamic Society of North America (ISNA), the Islamic Circle of North America (ICNA), the Muslim American Society (MAS) and a variety of other activist groups. On May 22, 1991, the Brotherhood issued a programmatic memorandum titled "The General Strategic Objective for the [Brotherhood] in North America,"[45] which highlighted its goal to penetrate American society at its heart. The memorandum stated that all Muslims had to "understand that their work in America [was] a grand *jihad* in eliminating and destroying Western civilization from within and sabotaging its miserable house by their hands so that God's religion [Islam] is victorious over all religions."[46] Over time, the Brotherhood would work to impose Islamic values and traditions from within American society.[47]

RECENT ACTIVITY

In 2005, for the first time in its history and to the surprise of most experts, the Brotherhood won 20 percent of the seats in Egypt's legislature. This victory was made possible by a more open political climate, and the Mubarak regime's decision to grant the movement unprecedented freedom to campaign through "independent" candidates.[48] Nonetheless, thousands of Brothers were arrested and imprisoned for urging political reform and liberalization in opposition to Mubarak's ruling National Democratic Party (NDP). As a result of further constitutional amendments passed in 2007, it became even more difficult for the group to run in either legislative or presidential polls.[49] In the face of restrictive electoral laws which only allowed registered parties to run and banned all religious forces, the Brotherhood subsequently boycotted the country's December 2010 polls.[50]

Today, however, Egypt's historic "Lotus Revolution" has emboldened the movement, and propelled it into political prominence. The Brotherhood has already expressed its readiness to provide a remedy to Mubarak's "corrupt" era by bringing morality back into politics and tackling poverty and unemployment, two promises that have long guaranteed its popularity. In mid-February, Muslim Brothers also announced their willingness to form a party and participate in upcoming elections.[51] With a solid base and recognition for its social achievements and commitment to reform, the Brotherhood will certainly come to play a significant role in the current transition, even though it kept a low profile during the anti-regime demonstrations. The question is more whether the movement will contribute to a true democratic opening in Egypt, or exploit it to further a radical agenda?[52]

The ideological fissures and apparent internal fragmentation of opinion within the group only serve to reinforce these concerns. While a number of reformist Brothers have stated that they would not seek to establish an Islamic state if they take control of the next government, the movement as a whole has not publicly renounced its central ideal of setting up an Islamic regime in Egypt. Additionally, the Brotherhood's new hard-line leadership has called into question the 1981 Egyptian-Israeli peace treaty, and has not ruled out a future embrace of violent *jihad*.[53] Many observers are also divided over what the movement's rise to power would mean for the protection of religious minorities, human rights and women's rights in the country.[54]

On the one hand, the Brotherhood remains regarded as the country's best-organized opposition force, and enjoys an image of integrity and piety which fundamentally differs from that of the Mubarak regime. In the eyes of its sympathizers, the defense of Islamic principles and values make it more capable of running a government by effectively implementing long-awaited economic reforms and ensuring greater social justice.[55] On the other hand, however, many accuse the movement of opportunism and of exploiting the revolution to ultimately seize power.[56] At this juncture, it is clear that the Brotherhood today confronts the challenge of operating in an open political climate, and that while it has long been the only opposition in Egypt and other countries of the region, it is not the unique political alternative. The prospect of a takeover by the movement is far from a foregone conclusion, in other words, but such an eventuality should not downplayed.[57]

ENDNOTES

[1] For an overview of the Muslim Brotherhood's core ideology, see Hassan al-Banna's writings and memoirs, in particular the *Letter To A Muslim Student*, which develops the main principles of the movement. For the English translation, see http://www.jannah.org/articles/letter. html; see also Brynjar Lia, *The Society of the Muslim Brothers in Egypt: The Rise of an Islamic Mass Movement, 1928-1942* (New York; Ithaca Press, 1998) and Richard Paul Mitchell, *The Society of the Muslim Brothers* (London & New York: Oxford University Press, 1969).

[2] "The Way of Jihad: Complete Text by Hassan Al Banna founder of the Muslim Brotherhood," *Militant Islam Monitor*, January 16, 2005, http://www.militantislammonitor.org/article/id/379; See also *Five Tracts of Hasan al-Banna (1906-1949): A Selection from the Majmu'at Rasa'il al-Imam al-Shahid, Charles Wendell*, trans. (Berkeley: University of California Press, 1978).

[3] Hassan al-Banna, "On Jihad,"n.d., http://www.youngmuslims.ca/online_library/books/jihad.

[4] According to Robin H. Hallett in *Africa Since 1875: A Modern History* (Ann Arbor: University of Michigan Press, 1974), p. 138.

[5] Sayyid Qutb, *Milestones* (Kazi Publications, 2007).

[6] One of his first manuscripts, *Dirasat islamiyya*, a collection of articles written from 1951 to 1953, contains clear references to Qutb's commitment to the Muslim Brotherhood.

[7] In addition to Milestones, one can cite Qutb's other important volume In the *Shade of the Qur'an*, which he began in 1952.

[8] Barbara H. E. Zollner, *The Muslim Brotherhood: Hassan al-Hudaybi and Ideology* (London: Routledge, 2008).

[9] Ibid.

[10] Umar al-Tilmisani, *Days with Sadat [Ayam Ma'a al-Sadat]* (Cairo: al-Itissam Publishing House, 1984).

[11] See the Egypt chapter of the American Foreign Policy Council's *World Almanac of Islamism*.

[12] Robert S. Leiken and Steven Brooke, "The Moderate Muslim Brotherhood," *Foreign Affairs*, March/April 2007, http://www.foreignaffairs.com/articles/62453/robert-s-leiken-and-steven-brooke/the-moderate-muslim-brotherhood.

[13] Ayman al-Zawahiri's videotape, released on January 6, 2006; see also Lydia Khalil, "Al-Qaeda & the Muslim Brotherhood: United by Strategy, Divided by Tactics," *Terrorism Monitor* 4, no 6, Jamestown Foundation, March 23, 2006, http://www.jamestown.org/programs/gta/single/?tx_ttnews[tt_news]=714&tx_ttnews[backPid]=181&no_cache=1; Jean-Pierre Filiu, "The Brotherhood vs. Al-Qaeda: A Moment Of Truth?," *Current Trends in Islamist Ideology* 9, November 12, 2009, http://www.currenttrends.org/research/detail/the-brotherhood-vs-al-

qaeda-a-moment-of-truth.

[14] A recent poll also shows that nearly half of the Egyptians support Hamas, and call for a strong Islamic government in Egypt. See Richard Auxier, "Egypt, Democracy and Islam," Pew Research Center, January 31, 2011, http://pewresearch.org/pubs/1874/egypt-protests-democracy-islam-influence-politics-islamic-extremism; See also "Syria: Muslim Brotherhood Chief Urges Assad to Learn From Egypt and Tunisia," AKI (Rome), February 14, 2011, http://www.adnkronos.com/IGN/Aki/English/Politics/Syria-Muslim-Brotherhood-chief-urges-Assad-to-learn-from-Egypt-and-Tunisia_311681506741.html.

[15] Sarah A. Topol, "Egypt's Muslim Brotherhood Fractures," *Newsweek*, February 23, 2010, http://www.newsweek.com/blogs/wealth-of-nations/2010/02/23/egypt-s-muslim-brotherhood-fractures.html.

[16] Amr Hamzawy, "Regression in the Muslim Brotherhood's platform?" *Daily Star* (Beirut), November 1, 2007, http://www.carnegieendowment.org/publications/index.cfm?fa=view&id=19686.

[17] On the Muslim Brotherhood's internal factionalism, see the excellent analysis by Carrie Rosefsky Wickham, "The Muslim Brotherhood After Mubarak," *Foreign Affairs*, February 3, 2011, http://www.foreignaffairs.com/articles/67348/carrie-rosefsky-wickham/the-muslim-brotherhood-after-mubarak.

[18] "Muslim Brotherhood Supreme Guide: 'The U.S. Is Now Experiencing the Beginning of Its End'; Improvement and Change in the Muslim World 'Can Only Be Attained Through Jihad and Sacrifice,'" Middle East Media Research Institute *Special Dispatch* no. 3274, October 6, 2010, http://www.memri.org/report/en/0/0/0/0/0/0/4650.htm.

[19] On the Salafist trend in Egypt, see Chris Heffelfinger, "Trends in Egyptian Salafi Activism," Combating Terrorism Center at West Point *CTC Report*, December 2007, http://www.ctc.usma.edu/publications/pdf/Egyptian-Salafi-Activism.pdf.

[20] Fawaz Gerges, "The Muslim Brotherhood: New Leadership, Old Politics," *Guardian* (London), January 20, 2010, http://www.guardian.co.uk/commentisfree/belief/2010/jan/20/muslim-brotherhood-egypt; Liam Stack, "Egypt's Muslim Brotherhood To Name New Conservative Leader Mohamed Badie," *Christian Science Monitor*, January 12, 2010, http://www.csmonitor.com/World/Middle-East/2010/0115/Egypt-s-Muslim-Brotherhood-to-name-new-conservative-leader-Mohamed-Badie; Myriam Benraad and Mohamed Abdelbaky, "Transition In Egypt: Radicals On The Rise?" Washington Institute for Near East Policy *Policywatch* 1588, September 24, 2009, http://www.washingtoninstitute.org/templateC05.php?CID=3126.

[21] Amnon Cohen, *Political Parties in the West Bank under the Jordanian Regime, 1949–1967* (Ithaca, NY: Cornell University Press, 1982).

[22] Ziad Abu-Amr, "Hamas: A Historical and Political Background,"

Journal of Palestine Studies 22, no 4, Summer 1993, 5-19.

[23] See the Palestinian Authority chapter of the American Foreign Policy Council's *World Almanac of Islamism.*

[24] Robin Wright, *Dreams and Shadows: the Future of the Middle East* (New York: Penguin Press, 2008); Olivier Carré and Gérard Michaud, *Les Frères musulmans: Egypte et Syrie (1928–1982)* [The Muslim Brothers: Egypt and Syria (1928-1982)] (Paris: Gallimard, 1983).

[25] Jillian Schwedler, *Faith in Moderation: Islamist Parties in Jordan and Yemen* (Cambridge: Cambridge University Press, 2006).

[26] Heather Murdock, "Muslim Brotherhood Sees Opportunity in Jordan," *Washington Times*, March 1, 2011, http://www.washingtontimes.com/news/2011/mar/1/muslim-brotherhood-sees-opportunity-in-jordan/.

[27] See the Syria chapter of the American Foreign Policy Council's *World Almanac of Islamism.*

[28] Radwan Ziadeh, "The Muslim Brotherhood in Syria and the Concept of Democracy," Paper presented at CSID's 9th Annual Conference, May 14, 2008, https://www.csidonline.org/9th_annual_conf/Radwan_Ziadeh_CSID_paper.pdf.

[29] Curtis R. Ryan, "Islamist Political Activism in Jordan: Moderation, Militancy and Democracy," *Middle East Review of International Affairs* 12, no 2, June 2008, 1-13, http://www.meriajournal.com/en/asp/journal/2008/june/ryan/1.pdf.

[30] See the Iraq chapter of the American Foreign Policy Council's *World Almanac of Islamism*; for further details, see "Iraqi Islamic Party," globalsecurity.org, n.d., http://www.globalsecurity.org/military/world/iraq/iip.htm.

[31] Toby Craig Jones, "The Clerics, the Sahwa and the Saudi State," Center for Contemporary Conflict *Strategic Insights* 4, no 3, March 2005, http://kms1.isn.ethz.ch/serviceengine/Files/ISN/34006/ichaptersection_singledocument/90678113-7f09-49dc-8c77-e546acacb75a/en/jonesmar05.pdf.

[32] See the United Arab Emirates and Qatar chapters of the American Foreign Policy Council's *World Almanac of Islamism.*

[33] See the Kuwait chapter of the American Foreign Policy Council's *World Almanac of Islamism.*

[34] See the Yemen chapter of the American Foreign Policy Council's *World Almanac of Islamism*; Amr Hamzawy, "Between Government and Opposition: The Case of the Yemeni Congregation for Reform," Carnegie Endowment for International Peace *Carnegie Papers* no. 18, November 2009, http://www.carnegieendowment.org/files/yemeni_congragation_reform.pdf.

[35] "MB in Bahrain Urges Bahrainis to Engage in Dialogue," *IkhwanWeb*, March 17, 2011, http://ikhwanweb.com/article.php?id=28237.

[36] "Islamism, Violence and Reform in Algeria: Turning the Page," International Crisis Group *Middle East Report* no. 29, July 30, 2004, http://www.crisisgroup.org/en/regions/middle-east-north-africa/ north-africa/algeria/029-islamism-violence-and-reform-in-algeria-turning-the-page.aspx.

[37] See the Tunisia chapter of the American Foreign Policy Council's *World Almanac of Islamism*; Rajaa Basly, "The Future of al-Nahda in Tunisia," Carnegie Endowment for International Peace *Arab Reform Bulletin*, April 20, 2011, http://www.carnegieendowment.org/arb/ ?fa=show&article=43675.

[38] "As Tunisians Cheer Egypt, Islamist Leader Returns," *NPR*, January 30, 2011, http://www.gpb.org/news/2011/01/30/ as-tunisians-cheer-egypt-islamist-leader-returns?utm_ source=feedburner&utm_medium=feed&utm_campaign=Feed%3A+ GPBNewsFeed+%28GPB+News%29.

[39] "Tunisia's Islamists to Form Party," *Al-Jazeera* (Doha), March 1, 2011, http://english.aljazeera.net/news/middlee-ast/2011/03/201131132812266381.html; David Kirkpatrick and Kareem Fahim, "More Officials Quit in Tunisia Amid Protests," *New York Times*, January 18, 2011, http://www.nytimes.com/2011/01/19/ world/africa/19tunis.html?_r=1&scp=1&sq=More%20officials%20q uit%20in%20tunisia&st=cse.

[40] Paul Cruickshank and Tim Lister, "Energized Muslim Brotherhood in Libya Eyes a Prize," *CNN*, March 25, 2011, http://articles.cnn. com/2011-03-25/world/libya.islamists_1_moammar-gadhafi-libyan-regime-benghazi?_s=PM:WORLD.

[41] Gabriel R. Warburg, "The Muslim Brotherhood in Sudan: From Reforms to Radicalism," Project for the Research of Islamist Movements (PRISM), Global Research in International Affairs (GLORIA) Center, August 2006, http://www.e-prism.org/images/Muslim_ BROTHERS.PRISM.pdf.

[42] Lorenzo Vidino, "The Muslim Brotherhood's Conquest of Europe," *Middle East Quarterly XII*, no. 1 (Winter 2005), 25-34, http://www. meforum.org/687/the-muslim-brotherhoods-conquest-of-europe.

[43] Ibid.

[44] Ibidem.

[45] Douglas Farah, Ron Sandee and Josh Lefkowitz, "The Muslim Brotherhood in the United States: A Brief History," NEFA Foundation, October 26, 2007, http://www1.nefafoundation.org/miscella-neous/nefaikhwan1007.pdf.

[46] Ibid.

[47] For additional details, see the United States chapter of the American Foreign Policy Council's World Almanac of Islamism.

[48] "Egypt's Muslim Brothers: Confrontation or Integration?" International Crisis Group *Middle East/North Africa Report* no. 76, June 18,

2008, http://www.crisisgroup.org/~/media/Files/Middle%20East%20North%20Africa/North%20Africa/Egypt/76_egypts_muslim_brothers_confrontation_or_integration.ashx.

[49] Myriam Benraad and Mohamed Abdelbaky, "Transition In Egypt: Radicals On The Rise?" Washington Institute for Near East Policy *Policywatch* 1588, September 24, 2009, http://www.washingtoninstitute.org/templateC05.php?CID=3126.

[50] Kristen Chick, "Egypt Election Routs Popular Muslim Brotherhood from Parliament," *Christian Science Monitor*, December 1, 2010, http://www.csmonitor.com/World/Middle-East/2010/1201/Egypt-election-routs-popular-Muslim-Brotherhood-from-parliament.

[51] Yasmine Fathi, "Muslim Brotherhood Expected To Win Legality, Lose Popularity," *Al-Ahram* (Cairo), February 20, 2011, http://english.ahram.org.eg/NewsContent/1/64/5956/Egypt/Politics-/Muslim-Brotherhood-expected-to-win-legality,-lose-.aspx; "Muslim Brotherhood To Form Party At Appropriate Time," *Al-Masry Al-Youm* (Cairo), February 19, 2011, http://www.almasryalyoum.com/en/news/muslim-brotherhood-form-party-appropriate-time; "Muslim Brotherhood Ready For Transition In Egypt," Press Trust of India, February 4, 2011, http://www.dnaindia.com/world/report_muslim-brotherhood-ready-for-transition-in-egypt_1503081.

[52] Daniel Byman, "Egypt 2012: What If the Muslim Brotherhood Comes to Power?" *Wall Street Journal,* February 4, 2011, http://blogs.wsj.com/ideas-market/2011/02/04/egypt-2012-what-if-the-muslim-brotherhood-comes-to-power/.

[53] Eli Lake, "Muslim Brotherhood Seeks End to Israel Treaty," *Washington Times*, February 3, 2011, http://www.washingtontimes.com/news/2011/feb/3/muslim-brotherhood-seeks-end-to-israel-treaty/.

[54] Rana Moussaoui, "Egypt's Muslim Brotherhood Splits Opinion," Agence France Presse, February 10, 2011, http://www.zawya.com/Story.cfm/sidANA20110210T132912ZRAI46; Rhonda Spivak, "Head Of Egypt Human Rights Group Fears Brotherhood Takeover," *Jerusalem Post*, February 14, 2011, http://www.jpost.com/MiddleEast/Article.aspx?id=208104; Mounir Adib, Mohamed Talaat Dawod and Hany ElWaziry, "Muslim Brotherhood: Copts And Women Unsuitable For Presidency," *Al-Masry Al-Youm* (Cairo), February 20, 2011, http://www.almasryalyoum.com/en/news/muslim-brotherhood-copts-and-women-unsuitable-presidency.

[55] "Egypt's Muslim Brotherhood Promotes Moderate Path," BBC, February 20, 2011, http://www.bbc.co.uk/news/world-middle-east-12504820.

[56] Kerry Picket, "Egyptian protester: We Don't Want Muslim Brotherhood to 'Hijack' our Protests," *Washington Times,* February 3, 2011, http://www.washingtontimes.com/blog/watercooler/2011/feb/3/egyptian-protester-we-dont-want-muslim-brotherhood/

Kerry "Phone Survey of Cairo and Alexandria," Pechter Middle Polls, February 5-8, 2011, http://www.washingtoninstitute.org/html/pdf/pollock-Egyptpoll.pdf.

HIZB UT-TAHRIR

*Banned throughout the Middle East, South Asia, and Central Asia as
well as in a few European states,[1] yet ostensibly nonviolent in its methods,
Hizb ut-Tahrir al-Islami (The Party of Islamic Liberation, or HuT) is a
global organization that defies easy categorization. It is not engaged in traditional religious missionary work and although it is heavily influenced by the
Leninist model, it is neither a conventional political party (it eschews political participation) nor a violent revolutionary organization or terrorist group
(it abstains from violence).[2] In many ways Hizb ut-Tahrir (HuT) operates in
the gray zone between politics, ideology, and violent action.*

HISTORY AND IDEOLOGY

HuT was established in Jordanian-occupied East Jerusalem in or around
1953 by Taqiuddin an-Nabkhani al-Filastyni (1909-1977), a member of the
Egyptian Muslim Brotherhood.[3] The group's platform and ideology are well-
defined. HuT rejects the modern political state. It disavows nationalism,
democracy, capitalism, and socialism as concepts alien to Islam. Instead, the
organization seeks to bring about a return to the Caliphate that ruled Muslims following the death of the Prophet Muhammad under the four "righteous caliphs."[4]

The modern caliph envisioned by an-Nabkhani in his day, and thus by HuT, controls the religion, army, economy, foreign policy and internal political system of the caliphate. He is accountable only to God. In fact, Hizb ut-Tahrir explicitly rejects democracy and favors *sharia* – Islamic law – as the law of the land. It is left up to the caliph and his deputies to interpret and apply it and thereby solve all social, economic, and ethnic problems that the *ummah* (Islamic community) may have. Arabic will be the state language. The role of women will be restricted to the home, though they will be allowed to liberally pursue education. The defense minister will be appointed by the caliph to prepare the people for and to wage war against non-believers, including the United States. Military conscription will be mandatory for all Muslim men over 15.[5]

What distinguishes HuT from its brethren in the Muslim Brotherhood is the group's different understanding of the relationship between piety and power. Where the Brothers accept the legitimacy of the state as a framework for transforming society, HuT rejects its legitimacy and instead focuses on the inward purification of souls in great numbers which will then lead inevitably to political revolution. As one expert has explained:

> Rather than slogging through a political process that risks debasing the Koran and perpetuating the *ummah's* subjugation to the West, Hizb ut-Tahrir aims at global, grassroots revolution, culminating in a sudden, millenarian victory…when Muslims have achieved a critical mass of Koranic rectitude.[6]

HuT's strategy to achieve this goal consists of three stages.[7] The first is to promote the adoption of HuT's version of Islam in individuals' lives. This stage is followed by HuT's "interaction" with the *ummah* in an effort to impose its principles as the only legitimate version of Islam, "stripped of all cultural accretions and purged of alien influences."[8] Finally, the ensuing grass-roots revolution will re-establish the caliphate.

The scenario for broadening the caliphate played out in HuT literature involves one or more Islamic countries coming under the organization's control, creating a base from which it will be able to convince others to join the fold—generating what is in essence a domino effect. Leaders of HuT—citing the lack of secular space for political opposition, increasing despair and a lack of economic opportunity—believe that much of the Muslim World is approaching a "boiling point," making it ready for an Islamist takeover.[9] The group seeks to take advantage of dispossessed populations to seize power in particular states such as those in Central Asia and Pakistan as a prelude to the establishment of a broader caliphate, removing wayward Muslim regimes and, eventually, overthrowing non-Muslim ones as well.

It is widely reported that HuT shuns violence in the pursuit of these goals. That is certainly true at the early stages in the organization's strategy, and while there is no evidence that the organization is responsible for terrorist or guerilla attacks, HuT's understanding of political violence is more nuanced than much current analysis of the group suggests. Emmanuel Karagiannis and Clark McCauley provide two useful ways of summarizing the ideological complexities of HuT's position on violent action: "The first is to say that they have been committed to non-violence for fifty years. The second is to say that they have been waiting fifty years for the right moment to begin violent struggle."[10]

These two perspectives may not be as different as they appear at first glance. Historically, few groups are unconditionally committed to nonviolence, and "Hizb ut-Tahrir is not exceptional but typical in this regard. Its commitment to nonviolent struggle is conditional and the condition sought is the declaration of *jihad* by legitimate authority,"[11] HuT also endorses defensive *jihads*, where Muslims are required to fight against an invader if attacked—a position that clearly has the potential to be interpreted very broadly and has been applied by the group to Coalition forces in Iraq and Afghanistan.[12] Moreover, the group was proscribed in Denmark after distributing pamphlets urging Muslims to "kill [Jews] wherever you find them, and turn them out from where they have turned you out."[13]

Even within Muslim majority countries, where the organization attempts to win over mass support in the hope that one day its adherents will rise up in peaceful demonstrations to overthrow the regimes they live under, HuT has developed the concept of *nusrah* (seeking outside assistance) from other groups such as the militaries of target states.[14] It might be argued that HuT's preferred method of political change to establish the Caliphate is in fact a *coup d'état* by the military that would have first embraced Islam as its guiding politico-religious principle. It is relevant here to note that HuT encouraged elements within the Jordanian armed forces to attempt just this in 1968 and 1969, in addition to the group's links to a failed 1974 coup attempt in Egypt.[15]

Ultimately, however, HuT's present abstention from direct violent action, particularly in Muslim-majority countries, is a function of the organization's three stage strategy. HuT does not currently use violence because it views itself as being in the second phase of its strategy – the second phase of its imitation of the Prophet Mohammed. From HuT's point of view, the justification for non-violence lies in the example of the Prophet, who criticized the pagan leaders of Mecca, gathered followers around him, and initially resisted the use of force to establish the Islamic state.[16] Indeed, according to one expert:

> The Party still thinks that it must follow the strategy of the Prophet: like Muhammad in Mecca, they must preach without violence. In practical terms this, it means that when HT achieves a large following for its ideology, they could overthrow... regimes through peaceful demonstrations. Also like Muhammad in his war against the Arab tribes in Mecca, they could get outside assistance or nusrah from the military to organize a coup.[17]

The adoption of violent methods for HuT in Muslim-majority countries at this point in its history, then, would be either a reinterpretation or abandonment of its ideology. Developments such as these certainly cannot be excluded, but they would risk ideological purity and credibility for uncertain gains. It must be recalled that HuT seeks to achieve a mass grassroots following through persuasion that will inevitably lead to regime change and the reestablishment of the caliphate rather than seizing the levers of power and forcing society to accept Islam.[18] However, HuT makes an important distinction between *jihad* sanctioned by the caliph on the one hand and violent resistance against foreign invaders such as in Afghanistan, Iraq, and Israel/Palestine on the other, in which immediate violent action to repel the invaders is justified.[19]

Even if HuT as an organization does not adopt violence as a means to achieve its goals, another source of concern is that the group may radicalize members who then go on in their individual capacities to conduct violent acts. Scholar Zeyno Baran perhaps put it best when she said that HuT's activities involve "more than mere expression of opinion but less than terrorism."[20] She famously asserted that "HuT is not itself a terrorist organization, but it can usefully be thought of as a conveyor belt for terrorists."[21] Shiv Malik points out that Khalid Sheikh Mohammed and Abu Musab al-Zarqawi, two major al-Qaeda figures, both had ties to HuT. Moreover, British intelligence officials discovered a cache of HuT literature in the home of Omar Sharif, the Briton who attempted to blow himself up in a Tel Aviv bar in 2003.[22]

Similarly, there is concern in many quarters about what is perceived to be HuT's disingenuous dual track strategy of grassroots activism amongst Western Muslims on the one hand and engagement with wider society in the West on the other. Houriya Ahmed and Hannah Stuart from the London-based Centre for Social Cohesion discuss HuT activism in Britain as consisting of two messages and two complementary aims: one for the UK's Muslim communities and one for the wider public – specifically intellectuals and opinion-formers such as journalists and politicians. Presenting itself as the vanguard of Islam, HTB works within the British Muslim communities to promote political identification with Muslims globally and discourage any other sense of personal loyalty. Within wider society, HTB works to mainstream HuT ideology, presenting Islamism, the Caliphate and their interpretation of shariah law as non-threatening – and viable – alternative to current political thinking.[23]

They add that, "[i]n order to mainstream HuT ideology amongst Western Muslim communities and avoid rejection by wider society, the party has downplayed its more intolerant beliefs and presents itself as defending 'true' Islam in the face of a perceived Western 'War on Islam.'"[24]

GLOBAL REACH

Whatever the concerns over and criticisms of HuT's goals and methods, it is increasingly clear that it is a movement with a significant following in many parts of the world. For many analysts, HuT is the most important Islamist group in Central Asia. It is certainly the largest and best-organized.[25] Some even claim that "of all the banned Islamist groups in the former Soviet Union, Hizb ut-Tahrir is the only one that can be called a mass organization."[26] It is also a popular organization among "young Muslims in Western Europe"[27] and national conferences in the U.S. and Canada in July 2009 indicate a resurgence of HuT activism there.[28] The group's major organizational center is said to be in London, where most of its literature is published and a good deal of its fundraising and training occurs,[29] though some claim that Ata Abu Rashta, HuT's suspected current global leader, is based in Lebanon.[30]

Relatively little is known about HuT's organizational structure, chain of command, or leadership. What is clear is that the organization is cell-based, and heavily influenced by the Marxist-Leninist revolutionary model that controls HuT's worldwide activities and drastically reduces the possibility of the penetration of outsiders into the leadership echelons of the group. The principal leader of HuT meets regularly with regional leaders who distribute literature and funding to district leaders, who in turn redistribute these items, as well as provide strategic direction during their monthly meetings to individual cells. For operational security, most cell members only know the other people in their cell and are kept in the dark about other cells operating locally, nationally, and regionally.[31] Indeed, Ahmed and Stuart claim that:

HuT's ideology and strategy are centralised. HuT global leadership issues strategy communiqués to the executive committees of national branches, which then interpret them into a localised strategic action plan... Whilst HuT core ideology stressed the indivisibility of the Muslim 'ummah' and rejects national identity, national strategies often reflect the ethnic origins of the various Muslim communities... National executives are encouraged to interpret strategy to best suit their localised needs.[32]

Because the group operates clandestinely in most parts of the world, its global membership numbers are unknown. Rough estimates of its strength in Central Asia alone range from 20,000 to 100,000.[33] Emmanuel Karagiannis estimates that there are around 30,000 members and many more sympathizers in the region,[34] with the majority in the Ferghana Valley in Uzbekistan and thousands of members in Tajikistan and Kyrgyzstan alongside "hundreds (perhaps thousands) in Kazakhstan and Russia, as well as Azerbaijan and the Ukraine."[35] The group's support base consists of college students, the unemployed, factory workers and teachers[36] but it also seems to be making particularly strong headway behind prison walls in the region[37] where between 7,000 and 8,000 of its members are thought to reside in Uzbekistan alone.[38]

HuT's growth in Central Asia has been significantly, though unintentionally, fueled by the repressive tactics adopted by the regimes there. With few exceptions, the states that emerged out of the Soviet Union smother, rather than engage, their political opposition. The anti-democratic policies adopted by these regimes unwittingly expand the influence of extremist groups like HuT and the Islamic Movement of Uzbekistan from the margins of national political discourse to its center. When there is no room for moderate and reasonable opposition, the only channel for change comes through radical elements.

South and Southeast Asia are also strongholds of HuT activism. The organization claims that it has recruited "tens of thousands" of members in Indonesia.[39] While these numbers are difficult to verify, a 2007 HuT conference there drew somewhere between 80,000 and 100,000 attendees from around the world.[40] HuT also holds regular public protests and demonstrations in Pakistan and Bangladesh. Although the level of popular support HuT receives is unclear, the organization's presence at universities "points to a deliberate strategy of targeting students."[41] The group also has a presence of unknown strength in, among other places, Syria, Iraq, Turkey, Palestine, Lebanon, Egypt, Tunisia, Pakistan, the U.S., Canada, the UK, Russia, and the Ukraine.

Much like its opaque membership, HuT's secrecy makes it difficult to investigate its sources of funding. However, it appears that money is raised in Europe, the Middle East, and Pakistan.[42] Members are also expected to contribute to the operational costs of the organization including such mundane outlays as printing leaflets.[43] Organizational costs for HuT remain relatively low because most members live in and operate out of their own homes and very few volunteers are paid.[44] However, a great deal of the organization's technology in Central Asia has been funded and imported from abroad, signifying both the international scope of the movement and potentially the complicity of at least some officials responsible for customs and border controls among local governments.[45]

RECENT ACTIVITY

Hizb ut-Tahrir had a busy year in 2009. It openly and actively participated in public debates and conferences in the UK, U.S., and Canada.[46] Its annual conference in the Palestinian Territories, however, was blocked by the Palestinian Authority[47] and the party claimed that "hundreds" of its activists were arrested in the West Bank in July 2009.[48] Elsewhere in the Levant it was reported that HuT joined forces with the Lebanese branch of the Muslim Brotherhood, Hamas, and Hezbollah to oppose attempts to resolve the Arab-Israeli conflict.[49] Moreover, HuT spent 2009 under close scrutiny in Britain. There has been talk in both the Labour and Conservative parties of banning the group since the July 7, 2005 bombings in London and a school run by the wife of the group's spokesman had its public funding suspended in November 2009.[50]

The organization also had several run-ins with the authorities around the world in 2009. HuT members continued to be arrested in large numbers throughout Central Asia in 2009 and in October, three suspected Hizb ut-Tahrir activists were detained in the Simferopol district of Ukraine's Autonomous Republic of Crimea.[51] Approximately 200 alleged HuT members were arrested in a wide-ranging counterterrorism operation across 23 provinces in Turkey in July 2009.[52] Turkish authorities initially claimed that two of the suspects have continuing contact with military officers suspected of involvement in the Ergenekon coup plot but no further information or evidence of the connection has been released.[53] Thirty-five HuT members and supporters, including a nuclear scientist, were arrested on October 17, 2009 in Pakistan under anti-terrorism legislation[54] while eight more alleged members were arrested in Karachi on March 8, 2010.[55] HuT also protested the Government of Pakistan's counterinsurgency offensive in the Swat Valley.[56] Thirty HuT members were arrested in September 2009 in Bangladesh[57] and the group was banned in the country a month later.[58] However, the group showed resilience when it organized a demonstration in February 2010 in Dhaka calling for the removal of the current government.[59] Meanwhile, arrests of alleged HuT members continue to be regular occurrences throughout Central Asia.[60]

ENDNOTES

[1]Hizb ut-Tahrir is banned in countries such as Bangladesh, Denmark, Germany, Jordan, Kazakhstan, Kyrgyzstan, Pakistan, Russia, Syria, Tajikistan, Turkey, Turkmenistan, and Uzbekistan, among others.

[2] International Crisis Group, "Understanding Islamism," Middle East/North Africa Report, number 37, March 2, 2005, 4fn11.

[3] Ariel Cohen, Testimony before the U.S. House of Representatives Committee on International Relations, Subcommittee on the Middle East and Central Asia, Washington, DC, October 29, 2003.

[4] Taqiuddin an-Nabkhani, *The Islamic State* (Lahore: Hizb ut-Tahrir, 1962).

[5] Tyler Rauert, "The Next Threat from Central Asia," *Journal of International Security Affairs* 9 (Fall 2005), 28.

[6] Matthew Herbert, "The Plasticity of the Islamist Activist: Notes from the Counterterrorism Literature," *Studies in Conflict and Terrorism* 32 (2009), 399.

[7] Olivier Roy, *Globalized Islam: The Search for a New Ummah* (New York: Columbia University Press, 2004), 248.

[8] Herbert, "The Plasticity of the Islamist Activist," 399.

[9] *The Methodology of Hizb ut-Tahrir for Change.*

[10] Emmanuel Karagiannis and Clark McCauley, "Hizb ut-Tahrir al-Islami: Evaluating the Threat Posed by a Radical Islamic Group That Remains Nonviolent," *Terrorism and Political Violence* 18 (2006), 328.

[11] Ibid.

[12] Rauert, "The Next Threat From Central Asia," 28; See also A. Elizabeth Jones, Testimony before the U.S. House of Representatives Committee on International Relations, Subcommittee on the Middle East and Central Asia, Washington, DC, October 29, 2003.

[13] Christian Caryl, "Reality Check: The Party's Not Over," *Foreign Policy*, December 22, 2009.

[14] "Radical Islam in Central Asia: Responding to Hizb ut-Tahrir," International Crisis Group Asia Report No. 58, June 30, 2003, 8.

[15] Suha Taji-Farouki, *A Fundamental Quest: Hizb ut-Tahrir and the Search for the Islamic Caliphate* (London: Grey Seal, 1996), 27, 168.

[16] Karagiannis and McCauley, "Hizb ut-Tahrir al-Islami," 325.

[17] Didier Chaudet, "Hizb ut-Tahrir: An Islamist Threat to Central Asia?" *Journal of Muslim Minority Affairs* 26, no. 1, April 2006, 117.

[18] Karagiannis and McCauley, "Hizb ut-Tahrir al-Islami," 325-6.

[19] Mahan Abedin, "Inside Hizb ut-Tahrir: An Interview with Jalaluddin Patel, Leader of the Hizb ut-Tahrir in the UK," Jamestown Foundation *Spotlight on Terror* 2, no. 8, August 11, 2004.

[20] Zeyno Baran, "Fighting the War of Ideas," *Foreign Affairs* 84, iss. 6, Nov/Dec 2005, 80.

[21] Ibid., 79.

[22] Caryl, "Reality Check: The Party's Not Over."

[23] Houriya Ahmed and Hannah Stuart, *Hizb ut-Tahrir: Ideology and Strategy* (London: Centre for Social Cohesion, November 2009), 69.

[24] Ibid., 7.

[25] "Central Asia: islamists in Prison," International Crisis Group Asia *Briefing* number 97, March 15, 2009, 3.

[26] Ibid., 3fn20.

[27] Jane's Terrorism and Insurgency Center, *Hizb ut-Tahrir*, October 26, 2009.

[28] See Daniela Feldman, "Islamic extremists hold open conference in Chicago," Jerusalem Post, July 22, 2009, 7; See also "Open House with Hizb ut-Tahrir," invitation from Hizb ut-Tahrir Canada, www.torontomuslims.com/events_display.asp?ID=9232.

[29] Cohen, Testimony before the U.S. House of Representatives Committee on International Relations, Subcommittee on the Middle East and Central Asia.

[30] Ahmed and Stuart, *Hizb ut-Tahrir: Ideology and Strategy*, 52.

[31] Jane's, *Hizb ut-Tahrir*.

[32] Ibid., 68.

[33] "Radical Islam in Central Asia: Responding to Hizb ut-Tahrir," 17.

[34] Karagiannis and McCauley, "Hizb ut-Tahrir al-Islami," 316.

[35] "Central Asia: Islamists in Prison," 3.

[36] Rashid, *Jihad: The Rise of Militant Islam in Central Asia*, (New York, NY: Penguin Books, 2002), 124.

[37] See "Central Asia: Islamists in Prison."

[38] Shiv Malik, "For Allah and the Caliphate," *New Statesman* 17, no. 824 (2004).

[39] Ahmed and Stuart, *Hizb ut-Tahrir: Ideology and Strategy*, 55.

[40] "Stadium Crowd Pushes for Islamist Dream," BBC, August 12, 2009, http://news.bbc.co.uk/2/hi/south_asia/6943070.stm; see also "At massive rally, Hizb ut-Tahrir calls for a global Muslim state," *Christian Science Monitor*, August 14, 2007.

[41] Ahmed and Stuart, *Hizb ut-Tahrir: Ideology and Strategy*, 57.

[42] Jane's, *Hizb ut-Tahrir*.

[43] Ibid.

[44] Ibidem.

[45] Rauert, "The Next Threat From Central Asia," 31.

[46] See Feldman, "Islamic extremists hold open conference in Chicago," 7; See also "Open House with Hizb ut-Tahrir."

[47] Palestinian Centre for Human Rights Press Release, "PCHR condemns ban on Hizb-Ut-Tahreer peaceful conference in Ramallah," July 5, 2009, http://www.pchrgaza.org/files/PressR/English/2009/85-2009.html.

[48] Ahmed and Stuart, *Hizb ut-Tahrir: Ideology and Strategy*, 51-2.

[49] Muslim World News (http://standpointmag.co.uk/node/2122)

[accessed 22 January 2010] English translation of "Meeting of Islamist leaders in Beirut to discuss 'the ways to oppose the forthcoming American plan for settlement,'" *Now Lebanon*, August 31, 2009 available at http://nowlebanon.com/Arabic/NewsArticleDetails. aspx?ID=111747.

[50] Andrew Gilligan, "Funds for 'extremist' schools suspended," *Sunday Telegraph* (London), November 1, 2009.

[51] Jane's, *Hizb ut-Tahrir.*

[52] "Turkey detains 'pan-Islamists,'" *Al-Jazeera* (Doha), July 24, 2009, http://www.thefreelibrary.com/Turkey+detains+'pan-Islamists'.-a0204390803; See also Lale Saribrahimoglu, "Turkish Counter-Terror Police Allege Hizb ut-Tahrir Link with Ergenekon," Jamestown Foundation, *Eurasia Daily Monitor* 6, iss. 147, July 31, 2009.

[53] Jane's, *Hizb ut-Tahrir.*

[54] "35 held activists of banned outfit booked under ATA," *The News* (Pakistan), October 18, 2009, http://www.thenews.com.pk/updates. asp?id=89380.

[55] "8 Hizb-ut-Tahrir suspects arrested in Karachi," Central Asia Online available at http://www.centralasiaonline.com/cocoon/caii/mobile/en_GB/features/caii/newsbriefs/2010/03/08/newsbrief-02 [last accessed March 11, 2010].

[56] Ahmed and Stuart, *Hizb ut-Tahrir: Ideology and Strategy*, 56.

[57] Ibid.

[58] "Bangladesh Islamist group banned," BBC, October 23, 2009, http://news.bbc.co.uk/2/hi/8321329.stm.

[59] "Hizb ut-Tahrir Bangladesh: Demonstration calling for the removal of Sheikh Hasina and her government, http://www.khilafah. com/index.php/activism/asia/8877-hizb-ut-tahrir-demonstration-in-dhaka-calling-for-the-removal-of-sheikh-hasina-and-her-government. [accessed 11 March 2010].

[60] See, for example, "12 Hizb ut-Tahrir members arrested in Tajikistan," Central Asia Online, available at http://www.central-asiaonline.com/cocoon/caii/xhtml/en_GB/newsbriefs/caii/news-briefs/2010/02/17/newsbrief-03 [last accessed March 11, 2010]; "Hizb ut Tahrir activist arrested in Osh region," Central Asia Online, available at http://www.centralasiaonline.com/cocoon/caii/xhtml/en_GB/newsbriefs/caii/newsbriefs/2010/01/30/newsbrief-06 [last accessed March 11, 2010]; "Kyrgyz police detain more Hizb ut-Tahrir activists," Central Asia Online, available at http://centralasiaonline.com/cocoon/caii/xhtml/en_GB/newsbriefs/caii/newsbriefs/2010/02/23/newsbrief-08 [last accessed March 11, 2010]; "Tajikistan jails 56 Muslim activists for extremist activities," RIA Novosti available at http://en.rian.ru/world/20100310/158149624.html [last accessed March 11, 2010].

TABLIGHI JAMAAT

Geographical Areas of Operation: East Asia, Eurasia, Europe, the Middle East and North Africa, South Asia, and Sub-Saharan Africa

Numerical Strength (Members): Estimated from 12 to 80 million

Leadership: Mawlana Sa'd al-Hasan

Religious Identification: Sunni Islam

(Quick Facts courtesy of the U.S. State Department's Country Reports on Terrorism)

Tablighi Jama`at, or "[Islamic] transmission group," is a vast, transnational Islamic propagation and re-pietization organization. As of the early 21st Century, it is estimated to be active in at least 165 nations. Its annual assembly in Tongi, Bangladesh, is larger than any other in the Islamic world except for the Hajj itself;[1] and estimates of TJ's membership range from 12 to 80 million.[2] Officially apolitical and preferring word-of-mouth instruction to public written or online communiqués, TJ has heretofore flown largely under the analytical radar, unlike other pan-Islamic groups such as Hizb al-Tahrir and the Muslim Brotherhood, which are much more political, higher-profile and overt. But TJ's global presence and growing influence in both Muslim and non-Muslim majority countries make it arguably the modern world's most dynamic Islamic group.

HISTORY AND IDEOLOGY

Tablighi Jama'at, or TJ, germinated in British-ruled India, emerging from the Islamic Deoband movement active in South Asia.[3] From its inception in 1867, the Deoband movement fused some aspects of Sufism with the study of the *hadith* and strict adherence to *sharia*, as well as advocating non-state-sponsored Islamic *da`wah* (missionary activity).[4] In the late 19th and early 20th centuries, the Muslim minority in British India felt itself caught between the Scylla of the resurgent Hindu majority and the Charybdis of the small but British-supported Christian missionary agenda.

TJ's founder, Mawlana Muhammad Ilyas (1885-1944), graduated from the central Deoband *madrassa* in 1910 and, while working among the Muslim masses of Mewat, India (just south of Delhi) came to question whether education alone could renew Islam.[5] He eventually decided that "only through physical movement away from one's place could one leave behind one's esteem for life and its comforts for the cause of God."[6] Other Muslim groups in the subcontinent, notably the Barelvis,[7] had previously developed the idea of itinerant missionary work—*tabligh*[8]—in order to counter Hindu (and Christian) conversions of Muslims, but it was Ilyas' genius to teach that *tabligh* should be the responsibility of each and every individual (male) Muslim.[9] He aimed to recapitulate the alleged piety and practice of Muhammad and his companions in the 7th century AD, and as such was concerned not just with Hindu or Christian inroads into the Muslim community but with stemming the rising tide of Westernization and secularization. Unlike other contemporary Islamic renewers, Ilyas did not believe that Islam could be reconciled with Western science, technology and political ideologies.[10]

Ilyas, in the mid-1920s, enjoined upon his followers the practice of *gasht*, "rounds" in Persian: going to those Muslims who lived near a mosque and summoning them to Koran study and prayer. Eventually (by the mid-1930s) a more detailed program of belief and praxis was promulgated by Ilyas; it included, above and beyond the five pillars of Islam,[11] and belief in the usual Islamic doctrinal staples,[12] the following:

- Islamic education (especially of children, at home),
- Modest Islamic dress and appearance (shaving the moustache and allowing the beard to grow long),
- Rejection of other religions,
- High regard for other Muslims and protecting their honor,
- Propagating Islam,
- Self-financing of *tabligh* trips,
- Lawful means of earning a living, and
- Strict avoidance of divisive and sectarian issues.[13]

The missionary methodology of TJ incursion into new territories is a fairly set one: an initial "probing mission" is followed by TJ entrenchment into several local mosques which are increasingly controlled by the organization and eventually either taken over by TJ or, barring that, supplanted by TJ-built or -controlled mosques.[14] From these mosques the TJ teams teach their beliefs and practices to local Muslims, approaching first local religious leaders, then intellectuals and professionals, then businessmen and, finally, the lower levels of society.[15]

There is a typology of Islamic renewal/reform movements as either 1) emulative (adopters of Western ideas); 2) assimilationist (attempting to reconcile Islamic and Western concepts and practices); or 3) rejectionist (allowing only strictly Islamic answers to the challenges of personal and collective life).[16] Tablighi Jama`at is clearly in the latter category, based on its promulgation of strict adherence to the Koran and *sharia*, as well as its emphasis on emulating the lifestyle of Islam's founder, Muhammad. However, while undeniably conservative, even puritanical, whether TJ serves as an incubator for *jihad* remains the subject of some debate.

The movement teaches *jihad* as personal purification rather than as holy warfare.[17] And because it does, it has met with the disapproval of Saudi clerics, with TJ missionaries banned from preaching in the Kingdom of Saudi Arabia and a number of online Wahhabi *fatwas* listing TJ as a "deviant" group, along with Shi`ites.[18] However, practical connections between TJ practitioners and acts of terror (such as the attacks in Dar es Salaam and Nairobi), as well as anecdotal evidence that Ilyas himself believed he was "preparing soldiers" for *jihad*,[19] paint a more complex—and threatening—picture of the organization.

The available data today indicates that TJ, at least in the preponderance of locations around the world where it is found, can be considered *ipso facto* a passive supporter of *jihadist* groups via its reinforcement of strict Islamic norms, intolerance of other religious traditions and unwavering commitment to Islamizing the entire planet. TJ is thus both like and unlike its major transnational Islamic rivals: Hizb al-Tahrir (HuT) (dedicated to re-establishing the Caliphate); the Muslim Brotherhood (focused on expanding *sharia's* scope in both the Muslim and non-Muslim world); and the Gülen Movement (devoted to re-establishing Turkish power in the Islamic, and greater, world in order to advance Islam). TJ is much less political than any of the above, and much more focused on personal Muslim piety. However, its eschewal of politics (at least publicly) has enabled TJ, in most venues, to escape suppression by wary government organs. Whether TJ ever decides to risk this virtual immunity from interdiction by transforming into an active supporter of *jihadist* movements remains to be seen.

GLOBAL REACH

Under Mawlana Yusuf (d. 1965), Ilyas' son, TJ expanded out of India and

Pakistan to much of the rest of the world, and expanded its mission from simply re-pietizing Muslims to making some efforts to convert non-Muslims to Islam.[20] Most of the Muslim-majority nations of the world saw the infusion of some TJ presence between the end of World War II and the 1960s, with the exception of Soviet Central Asia.[21] It would not be until the end of the Cold War, post-1991, that the "Stans" opened up to TJ teams. TJ has been perhaps most successful in Africa, where it is at work in at least 35 of the continent's 52 countries.[22]

Tiny Gambia, in West Africa (whose 1.5 million people are 90 percent Muslim), may very well be the hub of TJ activity in that part of the continent.[23] Present there since the 1960s, TJ did not gain much popularity until the 1990s, when its missionaries' knowledge of English (spoken prevalently in Gambia as well as in India and Pakistan) and the global Islamic resurgence made many Gambian Muslims, especially its youth, more receptive to the organization's agenda. Currently, some 13,000 Gambians are estimated to be involved with TJ, and the organization's growth is worrisome enough to some Muslims leaders, steeped as they are in West Africa's heavily Sufi tradition, that they have expressed fears of TJ coming to dominate the country.[24]

In 99-percent-Muslim Morocco, TJ was introduced in 1960 under the name *Jama`at al-Tabligh wa-al-Da`wah* (JTD), although it was not recognized by the government until 1975.[25] While working on convincing Moroccan Muslims to re-Islamize their lives, JTD also (perhaps in emulation of Christian missionary groups, before their recent repression in the country) makes hospital calls upon sick Muslims. But TJ's main focus is increasing ritualized conduct—persuading Moroccans to eat, drink, prepare for bed and sleep, go to the market and even bathe in proper ways emulating the Prophet Muhammad.

TJ has also committed a number of teams to Mali, Mauritania and Niger,[26] a three-country region of some 26 million people, the vast majority of them Muslim. In fact, the organization has become, arguably, one of the three most important foreign actors in the region (the others being al-Qaeda in the Islamic Maghreb, or AQIM, and the U.S. military). TJ has made a comeback from its low standing in the immediate aftermath of 9/11, when the South Asian nature of the group led many in the Maghreb region to shun them for fear of inciting American retaliation. In fact, the government of Mali extradited 25 TJ members not long after the 9/11 attacks.[27] Since then, however, TJ contacts have been made among some Touareg tribal leaders, who in turn have hastened to point out that the group's activities are totally unconnected to global *jihad*.[28]

South Africa would seem an unlikely part of Africa for TJ work, considering that 80 percent of the nation's 50 million people are Christian. But South Africa shares with India and Pakistan a legacy of British rule, and some two million of its people are of South Asian stock, of whom perhaps half are Muslim. TJ's "Sufi-lite" orientation and its Deoband origins give it legitimacy with many South African Muslims—although the more Salafi/Wahhabi groups dislike any hint of Sufism and denigrate TJ for "un-Islamic" practices such as asking for Muhammad's intercession and promoting the reading of books in tandem with the Koran. Many Muslims in South Africa, egged on by TJ, also became disenchanted with majority black (Christian) rule after rules were relaxed on abortion, prostitution and other "immoral" activities. All in all, the polarization of the Muslim community in Africa's southernmost country was exacerbated, if not caused, by TJ.[29]

Eastern Africa is the continent's main TJ stage, partly because of geographical proximity to the subcontinent but also because, like South Africa, there are substantial expatriate Indo-Pak communities there, particularly in Tanzania, Kenya and Uganda. Perhaps one-third of Tanzania's 44-million-person population is Muslim (but 90 percent or more on the islands of Zanzibar[30] and Pemba). Kenya is home to about four million Muslims (out of a population of almost 40 million, mostly Christian) and Uganda's 32-million-person population is also majority Christian, with some 12 percent of it Muslim. Uganda's Allied Democratic Force, a Muslim separatist group, is alleged to have recruited from TJ.[31] But TJ has been most visible in Tanzania, particularly on Zanzibar, where its message of "return to Islam" has been received as complementary to Wahhabi/Salafi ideology. These two strains of Islamic renewal have come together in the preaching of militant TJ members such as Zahor Issa Omar, who, from his base on Pemba, travels to mainland Tanzania, Kenya and Uganda to advocate *jihad*, reportedly supported by Saudi Wahhabi money and even *khutbah* ("sermon") outlines.[32] More traditionalist Tanzanian Muslim leaders consider TJ to be an intruder bringing a foreign brand of Islam, mainly because of the group's opposition to full-blown Sufism.[33] In fact, anecdotal claims that TJ serves as a conveyor belt, even indirectly, to Islamic terrorism,[34] do gain some empirical support by the fact that two of the al-Qaeda terrorists indicted in the 1998 bombings of the U.S. embassies in Dar es Salaam and Nairobi—Khalfan Khamis Mohammad and Ahmed Khalfan Ghailani—were Zanzibaris previously involved with TJ.[35]

There is conflicting data on the relationship between the neo-Wahhabi al-Shabaab militia which controls much of southern and central Somalia and TJ. In 2009, a story surfaced that al-Shabaab had attacked a TJ mosque, killing at least five of its members.[36] However, in mid-2010 Indian media cited at least one terrorism analyst who claimed that TJ "has been very active in

Somalia, including sending terror fighters to Al Shabaab."[37]

Aside from Africa, one of TJ's major theaters of operations has been Southeast Asia. TJ has been active in Indonesia since 1952, and in its far-eastern province of Irian Jaya (West Papua, the western half of the island of New Guinea) since 1988.[38] TJ has tried, with limited success, to exploit the Jakarta-supported transmigration of thousands of Muslims from the rest of Indonesia to heavily-Christian West Papua; as of 2009, only perhaps 1,000 Muslims had joined TJ there.[39] TJ teams are stymied by indigenous Papu customs (especially the affinity for pork) and the large Christian missionary presence.[40] TJ has ironically, and counterintutively, been more successful in majority-Buddhist Thailand.[41] In 2003, some 100,000 Muslims from Southeast and South Asia came to a mass TJ gathering at Tha Sala in Nakhon Si Thammarat province.[42] In two decades, TJ has made inroads not only among the five percent of the country's 66 million citizens who are Muslim, but even among Buddhists—one effective strategy has been to play up the Sufi, mystical side of TJ while also practicing asceticism similar to that of Buddhist monks. However, TJ activities have also polarized the Thai Muslim communities; many traditionalist Muslims quite dislike the long absence of husbands and fathers on TJ mission treks, while more modernist Muslims denigrate TJ members as "fanatic mullahs" who neglect their families and have given up on the world. However, TJ in Thailand gives every indication of being well on its way to creating an independent mosque network that can serve as an alternative to the existing national Muslim association created by the Thai government.

In TJ's subcontinental home of Pakistan, besides decades-old allegations that senior government and military leaders are members (and that CIA agents attempting to penetrate the group were actually converted to Islam),[43] more recent stories suggest that the Pakistani Taliban are forcing singers and actors to join TJ—indicating, if true, a troublesome intersection between South Asian Islamic militancy and ostensibly peaceful Islamic missionaries.[44]

In the West, there may be as many as 150,000 TJ members in Europe, mainly in the UK (where they tend to be of South Asian descent) and France and Spain (where TJ members from North Africa predominate).[45] TJ in the UK was behind the scuttled plans to build a mega-mosque in London near the site of the upcoming 2012 Olympics.[46]

In the United States, some analysts claim that there may be as many as 50,000 Muslims affiliated with TJ,[47] and that the influential Islamic Circle of North America (ICNA) cooperates with, and hosts, TJ teams and activities.[48] TJ's North American headquarters is alleged to be either at the al-Falah

Mosque in Queens, New York,[49] or at the Masjid al-Noor in Chicago.[50] It is also asserted that TJ receives funds from Saudi Arabia, and that a number of prominent American Muslims have been linked to TJ (including John Walker Lindh, the "Lackawanna Six" and José Padilla).[51]

RECENT ACTIVITY

Upon Mawlana Yusuf's death in 1965, Ilyas' grand-nephew Mawlana In`am al-Hasan assumed leadership of TJ, and subsequently directed the group's activities for the following three decades. Then, beginning in 1995, and for the next decade or so, the organization was supervised by a collective leadership based at Nizamuddin, New Delhi and consisting of Mawlana Sa`d al-Hasan (grandson of Yusuf), Zubayr al-Hasan (son of In`am) and Izhar al-Hasan (another relative of Ilyas').[52] In recent years, Mawlana Sa`d has moved to the fore, once again giving TJ a single spiritual leader.[53] Yet it is also noteworthy that the world's most famous TJ personality, officially, is not Sa`d but the group's *amir* next door in Pakistan, Hajji Muhammad Abd al-Wahhab—who, according to Oman's Royal Islamic Strategic Studies Centre, is the 16th most influential Muslim on the planet.[54]

Despite the fact that "the Tablighis have apparently moved from a fringe phenomenon to the mainstream of Muslim society in South Asia,"[55] they engender no small measure of opposition from other Muslims on their home ground. From one side, TJ is attacked by Barelvis, whose mystical Sufi leadership deems the group "a thinly disguised front for the Wahhabis"[56] and is not above orchestrating armed attacks on TJ members. Some Barelvi propagandists even accuse TJ of being a tool of the British, Americans and Indians, employed to drain Muslims of *jihadist* zeal.[57] From the other side, the Ahl-i Hadith groups charge TJ with abandoning the concrete concerns of the world for a vacuous mysticism.[58] And Jama`at-i Islami, the Islamic political organization established by Sayyid Abu ala `Ali Mawdudi (d. 1979), considers TJ a threat to its own powerful position in Pakistani society, and disparages TJ's alleged lukewarm attitude toward establishing a caliphate.[59] At least some Islamic groups outside of South Asia appear even more ill-disposed toward TJ, evidenced by the fact that in October 2010 Pakistani intelligence was reporting that "four foreign militants have been assigned by their commanders to assassinate two prominent leaders of Tablighi Jamaat."[60]

Finally, TJ does not always succeed in its attempts at winning foreign hearts and minds for strict Sunni Islam. In early 2010, almost a hundred members of the organization were arrested in Tajikistan and given lengthy jail sentences for running afoul of that country's laws against miscreant versions of Islam.[61] And in perhaps the most famous example of a TJ setback, the group's plans for the massive mosque in London are on hold, possibly never to be resurrected.[62]

ENDNOTES

[1]Yoginder Sikand, *The Origins and Development of the Tablighi Jama`at, 1920-2000: A Cross-Country Comparative Survey* (Hyderabad: Orient Longman, 2002), pp. 2-12.

[2] PEW Forum on Religion and Public Life, "Muslim Networks and Movements in Western Europe: Tablighi Jama`at," September 15, 2010, http://pewforum.org/Muslim/Muslim-Networks-and-Movements-in-Western-Europe-Tablighi-Jamaat.aspx.

[3] Sikand, *The Origins and Development of the Tablighi Jama`at, 1920-2000, 2-77;* See also Muhammad Khalid Masud, ed., *Travelers in Faith: Studies of the Tablighi Jama`at Movement as a Transnational Movement for Faith Renewal* (Leiden: Brill, 2000), esp. "Introduction" and Chapter One, "The Growth and Development of the Tablighi Jama`at in India."

[4] Ira Lapidus, *A History of Islamic Societies* (Cambridge: Cambridge University Press, 1988), 725-26.

[5] Masud, *Travelers in Faith*, 6.

[6] Ibid., 7.

[7] Founded by Ahmad Riza Khan Bareilly (1856-1921), the Ahl al-Sunnat ("Family of the Sunnah") movement—popularly known as Barelvis or Barelwis—advocated Islamic renewal much as did the Deobandis, although Barelvis were (and are) "more inclined toward the emotional or magical," according to Usha Sanyal, *Ahmad Riza Khan Barelwi: In the Path of the Prophet* (Oxford: Oneworld, 2005), 129.

[8] In Arabic-speaking Islam, the word usually employed for such work is *da`wah*; but in Urdu, in India and, later, Pakistan, *tabligh* ("transmission, communication, propaganda") came to be substituted.

[9] Sikand, *The Origins and Development of the Tablighi Jama`at*, 1920-2000, 48.

[10] Ibid., 66ff.

[11] Profession of faith ("there is no god but Allah and Muhammad is his messenger"), fasting during the daytime during Ramadan, praying at the appointed five daily times, *zakat* (tithing 2.5 percent) and going on the *Hajj* once in a lifetime.

[12] Such as the infallibility of the Koran, the existence of angels and djinn, the standard eschatological doctrines about the Mahdi, the Dajjal, and the apocalyptic struggles at the end of time.

[13] Masud, *Travelers in Faith*, 10-11.

[14] Farish A. Noor, "The Arrival and Spread of the *Tablighi Jama`at* in West Papua (Irian Jaya), Indonesia," S. Rajaratnam School of International Studies RSIS *Working Paper*, February 10, 2010, http://www.rsis.edu.sg/publications/WorkingPapers/WP191.pdf

[15] Masud, *Travelers in Faith*, 134-35.

[16] This paradigm is adapted from Albert M. Craig, et al., eds., *The*

Heritage of World Civilizations. Volume II: Since 1500. Seventh Edition (Upper Saddle River, NJ: Pearson Prentice-Hall, 2006), pp. 812-816.

[17] Barbara Metcalf, "'Traditionalist' Islamic Activism: Deoband, Tablighis, and Talibs," *Social Science Research Council/After September 11*, November 1, 2004, http://essays.ssrc.org/sept11/essays/metcalf.htm.

[18] Yoginder Sikand, "A Critique of the 'Tablighi-as-Terrorist Thesis,'" n.d., http://www.uvm.edu/~envprog/madrassah/TablighiCritique.htm.

[19] Masud, *Travelers in Faith*, 106.

[20] Ibid., 121.

[21] Ibidem, 125-130.

[22] As extracted from http://tablighijamaat.wordpress.com/2008/05/13/worldwide-tablighi-markaz-address/.

[23] Marloes Janson, "The Prophet's Path: Tablighi Jama`at in The Gambia," *Institute for the Study of Islam in the Modern World Review* 17 (Spring 2006), 44-45.

[24] Ibid., 45.

[25] Masud, *Travelers in Faith*, 161-173.

[26] Baz Lecocq and Paul Schrijver, "The War on Terror in a Haze of Dust: Potholes and Pitfalls on the Saharan Front," *Journal of Contemporary African Studies* 25, no. 1 (2007), 141-166.

[27] Ibid., 151.

[28] Ibidem, 155.

[29] Goolam Vahed, "Contesting Orthodoxy: the Tablighi-Sunni Conflict among South African Muslims in the 1970s and 1980s," *Journal of Muslim Minority Affairs* 23, no. 2 (October 2003), 313-334; See also Masud, *Travelers in Faith*, 206-221.

[30] Zanzibar was the power base of the Omani Sultans who had taken control of the coastal areas of East Africa and the lucrative Muslim slave trade in the late 17th century and in 1856 was made the capital of the Omani Sultanate there; as such Zanzibar has been, under German, British and then independent Tanzanian rule, a hotbed of Islamic political thought and aspirations.

[31] Gregory Pirio, *African Jihad: Bin Laden's Quest for the Horn of Africa* (Trenton, NJ: The Red Sea Press, 2007), 167ff.

[32] Ibid.

[33] For example, Maalim Mohammad Idriss has stated that TJ and Wahhabism both pervert Islam and wrongly undermine Sufi traditions and practices. Ibidem, 168.

[34] Fred Burton and Scott Stewart, "Tablighi Jamaat: An Indirect Line to Terrorism," STRATFOR, January 23, 2010, http://www.stratfor.com/weekly/tablighi_jamaat_indirect_line_terrorism.

[35] Pirio, *Radical Islam in the Greater Horn of Africa*, IAQ, Inc., February 2, 2005, http://www.dankalia.com/africa/0101205023.htm.

[36] "Somalia: 5 Pakistani Preachers Killed Outside Tawfiq Mosque,"

Huffington Post, August 12, 2009, http://www.huffingtonpost.com/2009/08/12/somalia-5-pakistani-preac_n_257257.html.

[37] "Indian Jihadis in Qaida's Somalia Arm?" *The Times of India*, August 23, 2010, http://timesofindia.indiatimes.com/india/Indian-jihadis-in-Qaidas-Somalia-arm-/articleshow/6399366.cms.

[38] Noor, "The Arrival and Spread of the *Tablighi Jama`at* in West Papua (Irian Jaya), Indonesia," 1-10.

[39] Ibid., 18.

[40] Ibidem, 14, 16, 22.

[41] Alexander Horstmann, "Inculturation of a Transnational Islamic Missionary Movement: Tablighi Jamaat al-Dawa and Muslim Society in Southern Thailand," *SOJOURN: Journal of Social Issues in Southeast Asia* 22, 1 (April 2007), 107-131, http://findarticles.com/p/articles/mi_hb3413/is_1_22/ai_n29344399/.

[42] Ibid.

[43] B. Raman, "Dagestan: Focus on Pakistan's Tablighi Jamaat," South Asia Analysis Group, September 15, 1999, http://www.southasiaanalysis.org/%5Cpapers%5Cpaper80.html.

[44] "Taliban Threatens Pakistani Singers and Actors with Death," *Telegraph* (London), March 15, 2009, http://www.telegraph.co.uk/news/worldnews/asia/pakistan/4992107/Taliban-threatens-Pakistani-singers-and-actors-with-death.html.

[45] Pew Forum, "Muslim Networks and Movements in Western Europe: Tablighi Jama`at."

[46] "Muslim Group Behind 'Mega-Mosque' Seeks to Convert All Britain," *Times of London*, September 10, 2007, http://www.timesonline.co.uk/tol/comment/faith/article2419524.ece.

[47] Burton and Stewart, "An Indirect Line."

[48] Alex Alexiev, "Tablighi Jamaat: Jihad's Stealthy Legions," *Middle East Quarterly* 12, no. 1 (Winter 2005), 3-11, http://www.meforum.org/686/tablighi-jamaat-jihads-stealthy-legions.

[49] Salah Uddin Shoaib Choudhury, "What Is Tablighi Jamaat," *Family Security Matters*, June 4, 2010, http://familysecuritymatters.org/publications/id.6384/pub_detail.asp

[50] Thomas Gugler, "Parrots of Paradise—Symbols of the Super Muslim: Sunnah, Sunnaization, and Self-Fashioning in the Islamic Missionary Movements Tablighi Jama`at, Da`wat-e Islami, and Sunni Da`wat-e Islami," July 2007, 1, http://www.zmo.de/mitarbeiter/gugler/parrots%20of%20paradise.pdf; See also "Fact Sheet on U.S. Treasury Endorsement of Sharia Compliant Finance," n.d., available at http://usastopshariah.wordpress.com/background/.

[51] Alexiev, "Tablighi Jamaat."

[52] Gugler, "Parrots of Paradise—Symbols of the Super Muslim," 1; Dietrich Reetz, "The 'Faith Bureaucracy' of the Tablighi Jama`at: An Insight into their System of Self-organization (*Intizam*)," in Gwilym

Beckerlegge, ed., *Colonialism, Modernity and Religious Ideologies: Religious Reform Movements in South Asia* (New Delhi: Oxford University Press, 2008), 98-124.

[53] Reetz, "The 'Faith Bureaucracy' of the Tablighi Jama`at," 109.

[54] Joseph Lumbard and Aref Ali Nayed, eds., *The 500 Most Influential Muslims 2010* (Amman, Jordan: Royal Islamic Strategic Studies Centre, 2010), 58-59.

[55] Ibid., 121.

[56] Yoginder Sikand, "The Tablighi Jamaat's Contested Claims to Islamicity," n.d., http://www.indianmuslimobserver.com/2010/06/issues-tablighi-jamaats-contested.html.

[57] Ibid.

[58] Ibidem.

[59] Ibidem.

[60] "Intelligence Report: Foreign Militants Tasked to Assassinate Tablighi Jamaat Leaders," *Middle East Media Research Institute*, October 29, 2010, http://www.thememriblog.org/urdupashtu/blog_personal/en/31633.htm.

[61] "Tajikistan: Jail Terms and Massive Fines—But for What Crimes?," FORUM 18 News Service, May 19, 2010, http://www.forum18.org/Archive.php?article_id=1446.

[62] James Delingpole, "London's Mega-Mosque Blocked for Now," *Human Events,* January 26, 2010, http://www.humanevents.com/article.php?id=35321.

CONTRIBUTORS

Afghanistan
Brian Williams
Dr. Williams is an Associate Professor in the Department of History at the University of Massachusetts, Dartmouth. His fields of teaching and research include conflict in contemporary Islamic Eurasia, and nationalism and Identity in the Caucasus/Central Asia.

David Cook
David Cook is associate professor of religious studies at Rice University specializing in Islam. He did his undergraduate degrees at the Hebrew University in Jerusalem, and received his Ph.D. from the University of Chicago in 2001. His areas of specialization include early Islamic history and development, Muslim apocalyptic literature and movements (classical and contemporary), radical Islam, historical astronomy and Judeo-Arabic literature. His first book, *Studies in Muslim Apocalyptic*, was published by Darwin Press in the series *Studies in Late Antiquity and Early Islam*. Two further books, *Understanding Jihad* (Berkeley: University of California Press) and *Contemporary Muslim Apocalyptic Literature* (Syracuse: Syracuse University Press) were published during 2005, and *Martyrdom in Islam* (Cambridge: Cambridge University Press 2007) as well as *Understanding and Addressing Suicide Attacks* (with Olivia Allison, Westport, Conn.: Praeger Security Press, 2007) have been completed recently. Cook is continuing to work on contemporary Muslim apocalyptic literature, with a focus upon Shi`ite materials, as well as preparing manuscripts on *jihadi* groups and Western African Muslim history.

Al-Qaeda
Raymond Ibrahim
Raymond Ibrahim is associate director of the Middle East Forum, author of *The Al Qaeda Reader* (Doubleday, 2007), and deputy publisher of *The Middle East Quarterly*. A widely published author on Islam, he regularly discusses that topic with the media, including *Fox News, C-SPAN, Reuters, Al-Jazeera, NPR, CBN*, and *PBS*. Mr. Ibrahim guest-lectures at the National Defense

Intelligence College (Washington, D.C.), briefs governmental agencies (such as U.S. Strategic Command), provides expert testimony for Islam related lawsuits, and has testified before Congress regarding the conceptual failures that dominate American discourse concerning Islam. He began his career as a reference assistant at the Library of Congress' Near East Section.

Albania
Christopher Deliso
Christopher Deliso is an American journalist and author concentrating on the Balkans. Over the past decade, Chris has established a dedicated presence in the Balkans, and published analytical articles on related topics in numerous relevant media outlets, such as UPI, the *Economist Intelligence Unit*, and *Jane's Islamic Affairs Analyst* and *Jane's Intelligence Digest*. Chris is also the founder and director of the Balkan-interest news and current affairs website, www.balkanalysis.com, and the author of *The Coming Balkan Caliphate: The Threat of Radical Islam to Europe and the West* (Praeger Security International, 2007).

Algeria
Yahia Zoubir
Yahia Zoubir is a tenured Professor of International Relations and International Management and is the Head of Research in Geopolitics at Euromed Marseille in Marseille, France. He has also held a tenured position at The Gavin School of International Management at Thunderbird in Glensdale, Arizona. Dr. Zoubir has been an international consultant for several major corporations including, Honeywell, Motorola, and Boeing. He received his Ph.D. and MA in International Relations from the American University in Washington DC. He is the author of the upcoming book, North Africa: Politics, Region, and the Limits of Transformation (Routledge).

Australia
Waleed Aly
Waleed Aly is a lecturer in the Global Terrorism Research Centre at Monash University in Melbourne, Australia. His research interests include homegrown radicalization and the relationship between identity politics and political violence.

Azerbaijan
Ariel Cohen
Ariel Cohen is a Senior Research Fellow at The Kathryn and Shelby Cul-

lom Davis Institute for International Studies at the Heritage Foundation. He received his Ph.D. from the Fletcher School of Law and Diplomacy at Tufts University in Massachusetts. Dr. Cohen is also a member of the Council of Foreign Relations, International Institute of Strategic Studies in London, and Association for the Study of Nationalities. His research interests include the economic development and political reform in the former Soviet Republics, and continuing conflicts in the Middle East. He has on multiple occasions testified on Russian and Eurasian politics, economics, and law before the U.S. Congress. Dr. Cohen has also published numerous pieces of writing.

Bahrain
Don Radlauer
Donal Radlauer is the foremost expert on the demographics of the victims from the phase of the Israeli-Palestinian Conflict that began in September of 2000. He is an Associate of the International Policy Institute for Counter-Terrorism (ICT) where he has published and lectured extensively on topics relating to terror finance, counter-terrorism, casualty statistics, asymmetric conflict, and radicalization via "virtual communities." Mr. Radlauer is the Lead Researcher for the ICT's "*Al-Aqsa Intifada*" Database Project where he developed the project's technological infrastructure and wrote the projects findings in the study "An Engineered Tragedy." Mr. Radlauer studied History and Sociology of Science at the University of Pennsylvania. He is also a director and co-founder of the Institute for the Study of Asymmetric Conflict.

Bangladesh
Zaglul Haider
Zaglul Haider is a professor of Political Science at the University of Rajshahi. He received his Ph.D from Clark Atlanta University in Atlanta, Georgia, and his MA in Political Science from the University of Dhaka. Dr. Haider has published several articles in European, North American and South Asian academic journals.

Bolivia
Douglas Farah
Douglas Farah is president of IBI Consultants LLC and a senior fellow at the International Assessment and Strategy Center. For twenty years, he was a foreign correspondent and investigative reporter at the *Washington Post*, where he won numerous awards for his work. In addition to his national security consulting work he is a regular lecturer at universities, government agencies and foreign policy groups. He has testified before Congress on numerous occasions, has written two books and numerous articles and monographs.

Canada

Micah Levinson

Micah Levinson is a Junior Fellow at the American Foreign Policy Council. Trained in government and political economy, he earned a B.A. from Harvard University and an M.A. from Washington University in St. Louis, Missouri. He also holds a certificate in counterterrorism from the Interdisciplinary Center in Herzliya, Israel. Micah's research focuses on revolutionary groups and the stability of authoritarian regimes, and he has published on these topics in Politics, Philosophy & Economics and has contributed to *The Political Economy of Democracy and Tyranny*, edited by Norman Schofield.

China

Joshua Eisenman

Joshua Eisenman is Senior Fellow in China Studies at the American Foreign Policy Council. A former professional policy analyst on the staff of the Congressionally-mandated U.S.-China Economic and Security Review Commission, he is currently a Ph.D. Candidate in the political science department at the University of California, Los Angeles. Mr. Eisenman received his MA in International Relations with specializations in China studies and international economics at Johns Hopkins University's Paul H. Nitze School of Advanced International Studies (SAIS) and a BA in East Asian Studies and Chinese language from The George Washington University. He speaks and reads Mandarin Chinese.

Denmark

Manni Crone

Manni Crone is a Danish translator and holds a Ph.D. in Political Science from the Institut d'études politiques de Paris and the DEA from l'École des Hautes Études en Sciences Sociales . She has translated, among other works, *Boris Vian* and *Francis Picabia* from French to Danish together with Asger Schnack. She is an assistant professor at the Department of Political Science at the University of Copenhagen, where she conducts research in Islam, secularism, and religious influence on policy formation.

Egypt

Myriam Benraad

Myriam Benraad is a research fellow in the Middle East and Mediterranean doctoral program of the Paris Institute of Political Studies (Sciences Po), and at the Center for International Studies and Research (CERI). She is also an Associate Fellow at the Washington Institute for Near East Policy in Washington, DC.

Ethiopia

J. Peter Pham

J. Peter Pham is Director of the Michael S. Ansari Africa Center at the Atlantic Council and Associate Professor of Justice Studies, Political Science, and African Studies at James Madison University. He is also Vice President of the Association for the Study of the Middle East and Africa (ASMEA) and Editor-in-Chief of its refereed *Journal of the Middle East and Africa*.

France

Russell Berman

Russell A. Berman is the Walter A. Haas Professor in the Humanities at Stanford University and a Senior Fellow at the Hoover Institution. His areas of specialization include modern European culture, trans-Atlantic relations, anti-Americanism and terrorism. Recent publications include *Fiction Sets You Free: Literature, Liberty and Western Culture* (Lincoln: University of Iowa Press, 2007), *Anti-Americanism in Europe: A Cultural Problem* (Stanford: Hoover Press, 2008) and *Freedom or Terror: Europe Faces Jihad* (Stanford: Hoover Press, 2010).

Germany

Clemens Heni

Clemens Heni is a political scientist and author. In 2011 he is the Founding Director of The Berlin International Center for the Study of Antisemitism (BICSA). His main fields of research are German history, anti-Semitism/anti-Zionism, and Islamism. In 2008-2009, Dr. Heni was a Post-Doctoral researcher at the Yale Initiative for the Interdisciplinary Study of Antisemitism (YIISA), Yale University. He has been published internationally, with articles in English and German. The author of two books on German anti-Semitism, his new book (due out in German in June 2011) is on *"Schadenfreude. Islamic Studies and antisemitism in Germany after 9/11."*

Hezbollah

Matthew Levitt

Matthew Levitt is a senior fellow and director of The Washington Institute's Stein Program on Counterterrorism and Intelligence, and an adjunct professor at Johns Hopkins University's Paul H. Nitze School of Advanced International Studies (SAIS). Previously, he served as deputy assistant secretary for intelligence and analysis at the U.S. Department of the Treasury and earlier still as an FBI counterterrorism analyst. He is the author of several books, including *Hamas: Politics, Charity and Terrorism in the Service of Jihad* (Yale

University Press, 2006) and the forthcoming *Hezbollah's Global Reach: The Worldwide Presence of Lebanon's Party of God.*

Hizb ut-Tahrir
Tyler Rauert
Tyler Rauert is a Professor of International Law and Political Violence at the Near East South Asia Center for Strategic Studies of the National Defense University. He focuses on the study of just war theory, the law of armed conflict, human rights, transnational organized crime, and security in the Middle East and South Asia. The views expressed herein do not represent those of the National Defense University, the Department of Defense, or any other branch of the U.S. government.

India
Ajai Sahni
Ajai Sahni is the founding member and Executive Director of the Institute for Conflict Management. His focus of study is on security issues in South Asia, and as the Executive Director of the Institute, he has acted as a consultant for various national and state governments in regards to internal security issues. Dr. Sahni is also the Editor of the South Asian Intelligence Review and the Executive Editor of the quarterly journal, *Faultlines: Writings on Conflict and Resolution.* He is a member of the Council for Security Cooperation in the Asia Pacific – India. He has written extensively on issues pertaining to conflict and development in South Asia. Dr. Sahni received his Ph.D. from Delhi University.

Indonesia
Joseph Chinyong Liow
Joseph Chinyong Liow is Associate Dean and Associate Professor at the S. Rajaratnam School of International Studies, Nanyang Technological University, Singapore. He is the author of *Piety and Politics: Islamism in Contemporary Malaysia* (New York: Oxford University Press, 2009) and *Islam, Education and Reform in Southern Thailand* (Singapore: ISEAS, 2009).

Iran, Islamic Republic of
Ilan Berman
Ilan Berman is Vice President of the American Foreign Policy Council in Washington, DC. An expert on regional security in the Middle East, Central Asia, and the Russian Federation, he has consulted for both the U.S. Central Intelligence Agency and the U.S. Department of Defense, and provided assistance on foreign policy and national security issues to a range of govern-

mental agencies and congressional offices. Mr. Berman is the author of *Tehran Rising: Iran's Challenge to the United States* (Rowman & Littlefield, 2005), co-editor of *Dismantling Tyranny: Transitioning Beyond Totalitarian Regimes* (Rowman & Littlefield, 2005), and editor of *Taking on Tehran: Strategies for Confronting the Islamic Republic* (Rowman & Littlefield, 2007). His latest book, *Winning the Long War: Retaking the Offensive Against Radical Islam*, was published by Rowman & Littlefield in 2009.

Iraq
Marisa Sullivan
As Deputy Director at the Institute for the Study of War (ISW), Marisa Cochrane Sullivan supervises the Iraq and Afghanistan Projects. Ms. Cochrane Sullivan also conducts research on Iraqi political dynamics, Shi'a militia groups, and the security environment in central and southern Iraq. Ms. Cochrane Sullivan has also authored numerous publications on these issues, including *Balancing Maliki* and *The Fragmentation of the Sadrist Trend*. Ms. Cochrane Sullivan holds a Bachelor's Degree in International Studies from Boston College, where she held a Presidential Scholarship and won the prestigious McCarthy Award for her scholarship in the Social Sciences. She has also studied at the London School of Economics and Political Science.

Hussain Abdul Hussain
Hussain Abdul-Hussain is an expert on the Middle East and the Washington correspondent of Kuwaiti daily Al Rai. Abdul-Hussain previously worked for the Congressionally-funded Arabic television channel *Alhurra*, and for Beirut's *Daily Star*. He has contributed articles to the *New York Times*, the *Washington Post*, the *Christian Science Monitor*, the *International Herald Tribune* and *USA Today*, and has appeared on both CNN and MSNBC. He appears regularly on Arabic satellite television channels. Abdul-Hussain is a graduate of the American University of Beirut.

Israel
Barak Seener
Barak Seener is a Research Fellow in Middle Eastern Studies at the Royal United Services Institute (RUSI). Prior to his time at RUSI, Seener was one of the founding members of the Henry Jackson Society in Westminster, and was the Society's Director for the Greater Middle East Section. As an expert on the Middle East and the Israel-Palestine controversy, he has appeared on multiple TV networks such as Al-Jazeera, the BBC, CNN, Bloomberg, etc... and has published extensively for the Hudson Institute, *Middle East Quarterly*, *Muslim World*, *Jerusalem Post*, etc... Mr. Seener holds a Master's degree in International Security and Global Governance from Birbeck College,

University of London and a BA in History and Politics from Queen Mary, University of London.

Italy
Lorenzo Vidino
Lorenzo Vidino is an academic and security expert, specializing in Islamism and political violence in North America and Europe. He is currently a visiting consultant for the RAND Corporation in Washington, DC, and he previously held fellowships at the Belfer Center for Science and International Affairs, Kennedy School of Government, Harvard University, the U.S. Institute of Peace, and the Fletcher School of Law and Diplomacy. Dr. Vidino is the author of two books, his latest being *The New Muslim Brotherhood in the West* (Colombia University Press, 2010) and *Al Qaeda in Europe: The New Battleground of International Jihad* (Prometheus, 2005). A native of Milan, Italy, he holds a law degree from the University of Milan Law School and a Ph.D. in International Relations from the Fletcher School Law and Diplomacy.

Jordan
Shmuel Bar
Dr. Bar is Director of Studies at the Institute of Policy and Strategy, Interdisciplinary Center Herzliya, Israel. He retired from the Israeli civil service in 2003 after 30 years as an intelligence analyst, during which he specialized in Jordanian, Palestinian, Iranian and Syrian affairs, and ideological and operational aspects of the *Jihadi*-Salafi movement and served in various senior positions in Israel and abroad. Dr. Bar holds a Ph.D. in History of the Middle East from Tel-Aviv University (1989), M.A. (Magna cum Laude) in History of the Middle East from Tel-Aviv University (1984) and a B.A from The Hebrew University of Jerusalem, 1974, in Jewish and Middle Eastern History. He has published numerous books and papers on Middle Eastern affairs, terrorism and radical Islam.

Kazakhstan
Ariel Cohen
Ariel Cohen is a Senior Research Fellow at The Kathryn and Shelby Cullom Davis Institute for International Studies at the Heritage Foundation. He received his Ph.D. from the Fletcher School of Law and Diplomacy at Tufts University in Massachusetts. Dr. Cohen is also a member of the Council of Foreign Relations, International Institute of Strategic Studies in London, and Association for the Study of Nationalities. His research interests include the economic development and political reform in the former Soviet Republics, and continuing conflicts in the Middle East. He has on multiple occasions

testified on Russian and Eurasian politics, economics, and law before the U.S. Congress. Dr. Cohen has also published numerous pieces of writing.

Kosovo
Christpher Deliso
Christopher Deliso is an American journalist and author concentrating on the Balkans. Over the past decade, Chris has established a dedicated presence in the Balkans, and published analytical articles on related topics in numerous relevant media outlets, such as UPI, the *Economist Intelligence Unit*, and *Jane's Islamic Affairs Analyst* and *Jane's Intelligence Digest*. Chris is also the founder and director of the Balkan-interest news and current affairs website, www.balkanalysis.com, and the author of *The Coming Balkan Caliphate: The Threat of Radical Islam to Europe and the West* (Praeger Security International, 2007).

Kuwait
Aviv Oreg
Aviv Oreg is a veteran officer of the Israeli intelligence community, mostly covering issues related to the "Global Jihad" phenomenon and its most dominant entity factor - the al-Qaeda organization. His last position was as head of the "Al Qaeda and Global Jihad" desk in the IDF's military intelligence. Since the summer of 2007, Mr. Oreg has served as the founding president of CeifiT, an investigative consulting firm composes of veterans of the Israeli intelligence community that offers comprehensive research, analysis and counseling services of the global *jihad* phenomenon.

Kyrgyzstan
Evgeuni Novikov
Evgueni Novikov is an expert with extensive on-the-ground experience in Islam and considerable practical experience in the Central Asia and Persian Gulf regions. Dr. Novikov was one of top experts on Islamic affairs for the Soviet government. He is the author of a number of articles and of several books, including *Gorbachev and the Collapse of the Soviet Communist Party: The Historical and Theoretical Background* (Peter Lang, 1994) and *Central Asian Responses to Radical Islam* (AFPC, 2006).

Orozbek Modaliev
Orozbek Moldaliev is one of the best-informed Central Asian experts on terrorism and radical Islam. Dr. Moldaliev is professor and head of the Department of World Politics and International Relations at the Diplomatic Academy of the Kyrgyz Republic. Both a faithful Muslim and an established

intellectual, he has published 36 books and articles on Islam, Islamic terrorism and problems of Central Asian national security.

Lashkar-e Taiba
Ashley Tellis
Ashley Tellis is a foremost expert in the fields of non-proliferation, South Asian strategic issues and U.S. Foreign Policy. Dr. Tellis is currently a senior associate at the Carnegie Endowment for International Peace, and has served as the senior adviser to the Undersecretary of State for Political Affairs in negotiating the civil nuclear agreement with India. Prior to his position at the Carnegie Endowment, he was commissioned into the U.S. Foreign service, where he served as senior advisor to the ambassador at the U.S. Embassy in New Delhi. Dr. Tellis is the author and co-author of several books, and has contributed greatly to many annual volumes and journals. Dr. Tellis holds a BA and MA from the University of Bombay and received a second MA and his Ph.D. from the University of Chicago.

Lebanon
Robert Rabil
Robert Rabil is the director of graduate studies and an associate professor of Middle Eastern Studies at the Florida Atlantic University's Department of Political Science. Dr. Rabil is an expert on Middle Eastern affairs, having written several books and multiple articles dealing with the Arab-Israeli Conflict, Radical Islam, Hezbollah, Lebanon, Israel, Iraq, and Syria. He served as chief of emergency of the Red Cross in Lebanon's Baabda ditsrict during the country's civil war. He also was project manager of Iraq Research and Documentation Project, a project affiliated with Harvard University and funded by the US State Department. Dr. Rabil holds a Master's degree in Government from the Harvard University Extension School and a Ph.D. in Near Eastern and Judaic Studies from Brandeis University.

Libya
Aviv Oreg
Aviv Oreg is a veteran officer of the Israeli intelligence community, mostly covering issues related to the "Global Jihad" phenomenon and its most dominant entity factor - the al-Qaeda organization. His last position was as head of the "Al Qaeda and Global Jihad" desk in the IDF's military intelligence. Since the summer of 2007, Mr. Oreg has served as the founding president of CeifiT, an investigative consulting firm composes of veterans of the Israeli intelligence community that offers comprehensive research, analysis and counseling services of the global *jihad* phenomenon.

Macedonia

Christopher Deliso

Christopher Deliso is an American journalist and author concentrating on the Balkans. Over the past decade, Chris has established a dedicated presence in the Balkans, and published analytical articles on related topics in numerous relevant media outlets, such as UPI, the *Economist Intelligence Unit*, and *Jane's Islamic Affairs Analyst* and *Jane's Intelligence Digest*. Chris is also the founder and director of the Balkan-interest news and current affairs website, www.balkanalysis.com, and the author of The Coming Balkan Caliphate: The Threat of Radical Islam to Europe and the West (Praeger Security International, 2007).

Malaysia

Joseph Chinyong Liow

Joseph Chinyong Liow is Associate Dean and Associate Professor at the S. Rajaratnam School of International Studies, Nanyang Technological University, Singapore. He is the author of *Piety and Politics: Islamism in Contemporary Malaysia* (New York: Oxford University Press, 2009) and Islam, Education and Reform in Southern Thailand (Singapore: ISEAS, 2009).

Maldives

Animesh Roul

Animesh Roul is the executive director of the New Delhi-based Society for the Study of Peace and Conflict. His areas of interest are terrorism, arms control and proliferation, armed conflict, and security developments in the South Asian region. Associated with a number of media and policy organizations in India and abroad, he has written articles in the Jamestown Foundation *Terrorism Monitor*, ISN *Security Watch*, *CBWMagazine*, *Open Democracy*, the *CTC Sentinel* and *NBR Analysis*. Roul is the recipient of MacArthur Foundation's Asia Security Initiative Blogger award for 2009 and 2010, and he also blogs frequently at the Counterterrorism Foundation's blog on South Asian terrorism issues.

Mali

Laura Grossman

Laura Grossman is a Research Analyst for the Foundation for Defense of Democracies' Iran Energy Project. She co-authored *Homegrown Terrorists in the U.S. and the U.K.* and *Terrorism in the West 2008* with Daveed Gartenstein-Ross, in addition to *Iran's Energy Partners and Iran's Chinese Energy Partners* with Mark Dubowitz. She holds a BA in History from the University of Michigan and an MS in Global Affairs from New York University.

Mauritania

Daniel Zisenwine

Daniel Zisenwine is the author of two books, *The Maghrib in the New Century* (University Press of Florida, 2007) and *The Emergence of Nationalist Politics in Morocco* (Tauris Academic Studies, 2010). Dr. Zisenwine is a Research Fellow at the Moshe Dayan Center for Middle Eastern and African Studies. He holds a Ph.D. from the Tel Aviv University.

Morocco

Marc Ginsberg

Marc Ginsberg served as U.S. Ambassador to Morocco under President Clinton, and before that as Deputy Senior Advisor to the President for Middle East Policy from 1979-1981. He is Senior Vice-President of APCO Worldwide and President of Layalina Productions, a producer of television series and documentaries for Middle East television networks.

Muslim Brotherhood

Myriam Benraad

Myriam Benraad is a research fellow in the Middle East and Mediterranean doctoral program of the Paris Institute of Political Studies (Sciences Po), and at the Center for International Studies and Research (CERI). She is also an Associate Fellow at the Washington Institute for Near East Policy in Washington, DC.

Netherlands

Ronald Sandee

Ronald Sandee has served as the director of analysis & research at the NEFA Foundation since June 2006. Previously, he worked as a senior analyst at the transnational affairs desk at the Dutch Ministry of Defense. He focuses his research on core al-Qaeda in the Afghanistan-Pakistan area, terrorism in Africa and radicalization in Europe and the U.S.

Nicaragua

Douglas Farah

Douglas Farah is president of IBI Consultants LLC and a senior fellow at the International Assessment and Strategy Center. For twenty years, he was a foreign correspondent and investigative reporter at the *Washington Post*, where he won numerous awards for his work. In addition to his national security consulting work he is a regular lecturer at universities, government agencies and foreign policy groups. He has testified before Congress on numerous occasions, has written two books and numerous articles and monographs.

Pakistan
Lisa Curtis
Lisa Curtis is a senior research fellow at the Heritage Foundation. She specializes in America's economic, security and political relationships with India, Pakistan, Afghanistan, and other South Asian countries. Curtis has testified before Congress on more than a dozen occasions on topics relating to India, Pakistan, radical Islamists, and America's image abroad. Prior to her work at the Heritage Foundation, Curtis was a member of the professional staff of the Senate Foreign Relations Committee, in charge of South Asian affairs for then chairman Sen. Richard Luger (R-Ind). Curtis also served abroad in the U.S. Foreign Service, where she was assigned to the U.S. embassies in Pakistan and India. She received her BA in Economics from the Indiana University.

Palestinian Authority
Raymond Ibrahim
Raymond Ibrahim is associate director of the Middle East Forum, author of *The Al Qaeda Reader* (Doubleday, 2007), and deputy publisher of *The Middle East Quarterly*. A widely published author on Islam, he regularly discusses that topic with the media, including *Fox News, C-SPAN, Reuters, Al-Jazeera, NPR, CBN,* and *PBS*. Mr. Ibrahim guest-lectures at the National Defense Intelligence College (Washington, D.C.), briefs governmental agencies (such as U.S. Strategic Command), provides expert testimony for Islam related lawsuits, and has testified before Congress regarding the conceptual failures that dominate American discourse concerning Islam. He began his career as a reference assistant at the Library of Congress' Near East Section.

Philippines
Zachary Abuza
Zachary Abuza is Professor of National Security Studies at the National War College and Professor of Political Science and International Relations at Simmons College. He is the author of four books on politics and security issues in Southeast Asia.

Qatar
Yael Shahar
Yael Shahar is the Director for the Database Project Institute for Counter-Terrorism at the IDC Herzliya. Ms. Shahar also heads the International Institute

for Counter-Terrorism's (ICT) OSINT project. She specializes in the study of technological trends as applied to terrorism and intelligence sharing. She is a dynamic speaker, and has lectured worldwide on topics related to trends in terrorism, non-conventional and techno-terrorism, threat assessment and asymmetric conflict. Ms. Shahar studied Physics and Philosophy of Science at the University of Texas and at the Hebrew University in Jerusalem. She has also served as a reservist in the IDF hostage rescue unit, and is a director and co-founder of the Institute for the Study of Asymmetric Conflict.

Russia
Gordon Hahn
Gordon Hahn is a Senior Researcher for the Center for Terrorism and Intelligence Studies (CETIS) and an academic fellow at Smolny College in St. Petersburg, Russia. He has taught extensively on the topics of Russian domestic and foreign policy at Stanford, St. Petersburg State (Russia), Boston, American, and San Jose State Universities. Dr. Hahn is the author of two books and is published in many Russian and English language scholarly journals. He specializes in Muslim politics and terrorism in Russia. Dr, Hahn received his BA and MA from Boston College, and his Ph.D. from Boston University.

Saudi Arabia
Steve Miller
Steve Miller is a Research Associate at the Foundation for Defense of Democracies (FDD). He is fluent in Arabic and as part of his research at FDD; he monitors and analyzes the Arabic language press. He also conducts research related to extremism, ideology, and online media in Saudi Arabia. Prior to his time at the FDD, Mr. Miller was a policy analyst at the Institute for Gulf Affairs in Washington, DC. He received his BA in Economics and Near Eastern Languages and Cultures, including classical Arabic from Indiana University.

Somalia
J. Peter Pham
J. Peter Pham is Director of the Michael S. Ansari Africa Center at the Atlantic Council and Associate Professor of Justice Studies, Political Science, and African Studies at James Madison University. He is also Vice President of the Association for the Study of the Middle East and Africa (ASMEA) and Editor-in-Chief of its refereed *Journal of the Middle East and Africa*.

South Africa
Laura Grossman

Laura Grossman is a Research Analyst for the Foundation for Defense of Democracies' Iran Energy Project. She co-authored *Homegrown Terrorists in the U.S. and the U.K.* and *Terrorism in the West 2008* with Daveed Gartenstein-Ross, in addition to *Iran's Energy Partners and Iran's Chinese Energy Partners* with Mark Dubowitz. She holds a BA in History from the University of Michigan and an MS in Global Affairs from New York University.

Spain
Rafael Bardaji
Rafael Bardaji is a member of the Atlantic Council's Strategic Advisors Group. He has published several books and multiple works for scholarly journals. He was the founder and Director of the Grupo de Estudios Estrategicos until 1996 when he served as the executive adviser to the Spanish Ministers of Defense Eduardo Serra and Federico Trillo. He is also a member of the IISS in London and the International Council of the Institute for Foreign Policy Analysis. Mr. Bardaji is a graduate in Political Sciences and Sociology from the Complutense University of Madrid.

Sudan
Mohamed-Ali Adraoui
Mohamed-Ali Adraoui is a researcher in the Institute of Political Studies in Paris. He is completing a Ph.D dissertation on Salafism in France and lectures in Political Science at Sciences Po Paris. He has written several articles and reports dealing with the topic of Islam and Islamism.

Syria
Matt Brodsky
Matt Brodsky is the Director of Policy for the Jewish Policy Center (JPC) and the editor for the JPC's journal, in*FOCUS Quarterly.* Prior to his work at the JPC, Mr. Brodsky was the Senior Geopolitical Analyst for IntelliWhiz LLC and a Legacy Heritage Fellow at the American Foreign Policy Council. He is an expert in Middle Eastern Affairs and Arab Politics, and has on multiple occasions has briefed and advised members of Congress, the Department of State, the Department of Defense and the National Security Council. Mr. Brodsky holds a MA in Middle East History from the Tel Aviv University.

Tablighi Jamaat
Timothy R. Furnish
Dr. Timothy R. Furnish works as an analyst and author specializing in Islamic eschatology, Mahdism and sects. He blogs on these topics at the History News Network as the Occidental Jihadist (http://hnn.us/blogs/78.html) and

on his own site www.mahdiwatch.org. His new book, *The Caliphate: Threat or Opportunity?*, is due out in 2011.

Tajikistan
Jonathan Lee
Jonathan Lee is a human terrain analyst for the U.S. government, and a former researcher at the American Foreign Policy Council. His views do not reflect those of the United States government or the Department of Defense.

Taliban
Matt DuPee
Matt DuPee has studied political and security events in Afghanistan since 1999. His articles have been published in a variety of publications, including the *CTC Sentinel, World Politics Review, Himal SouthAsian Magazine, Asia Times, The Center for Conflict and Peace Studies,* and others. He holds an M.A. in Regional Security Studies (South Asia) from the Naval Postgraduate School, Monterey, California, and continues his research on Afghanistan's narcotics, politics, security, geography and human terrain issues for the U.S. Department of Defense.

Thailand
Zachary Abuza
Zachary Abuza is Professor of National Security Studies at the National War College and Professor of Political Science and International Relations at Simmons College. He is the author of four books on politics and security issues in Southeast Asia.

Tunisia
Lawrence Velte
Lawrence Velte is an Associate Professor at the Near East South Asia Center for Strategic Studies at the National Defense University, focusing on the Maghreb and the Levant. He previously served as Deputy Chief of the Middle East Division, Joint Chiefs of Staff, and, as a U.S. Army officer, Middle East specialist, with tours of duty in Tunisia, Jerusalem, and Jordan.

Turkey
Okan Altiparmak
Okan Altiparmak is an international consultant on business and political matters located in Istanbul, Turkey. He is the founder of Nimbus Productions, which provides consultation and production services for film production and media companies filming or seeking guidance in Turkey.

Turkmenistan

Annette Bohr

Annette Bohr is an Associate Fellow of the Russia and Eurasia Programme at the Institute of International Affairs in London (Chatham House). She is the author or co-author of two monographs and numerous articles on Central Asian politics, contemporary history, and ethnic and language policies.

United Arab Emirates

Malcolm Peck

Malcolm Peck is a program officer at Meridian International Center in Washington, DC, and has taught at the University of Tennessee, Chattanooga. Dr. Peck was also a post-doctoral fellow at the Harvard University Center for Middle Eastern Studies and from 1970-1981 was the director of programs at the Middle East Institute. Dr. Peck is an expert on Gulf-Arabian Peninsula issues and has written several books and published numerous articles on the topic. He received an A.B. and A.M. from Harvard University, and a M.A., M.A.L.D., and Ph.D. from the Fletcher School of Law and Diplomacy.

United Kingdom

Alexander Meleagrou-Hitchens

Alexander Meleagrou-Hitchens is a Research Fellow at the International Centre for the Study of Radicalisation, King's College, London, where he is also a PhD candidate. His main area of study is Islamism in the West, and Salafi-Jihadist messaging in the English language.

United States

Ryan Evans

Ryan Evans is an Associate Fellow at the International Centre for the Study of Radicalisation and Political Violence, King's College London, where he previously worked as a project manager. In that capacity, he designed research projects and managed a U.S. government-funded study on the radicalization of Muslims in the West in collaboration with the National Consortium for the Study of Terrorism and Responses to Terrorism at the University of Maryland. From 2005 to 2008, he was a senior research analyst at the Washington-based Investigative Project on Terrorism.

Uzbekistan

Evgeuni Novikov

Evgueni Novikov is an expert with extensive on-the-ground experience in Islam and considerable practical experience in the Central Asia and Persian Gulf regions. Dr. Novikov was one of top experts on Islamic affairs for the Soviet government. He is the author of a number of articles and of several books, including *Gorbachev and the Collapse of the Soviet Communist Party: The Historical and Theoretical Background* (Peter Lang, 1994) and *Central Asian Responses to Radical Islam* (AFPC, 2006).

Orozbek Moldaiev
Orozbek Moldaliev is one of the best-informed Central Asian experts on terrorism and radical Islam. Dr. Moldaliev is professor and head of the Department of World Politics and International Relations at the Diplomatic Academy of the Kyrgyz Republic. Both a faithful Muslim and an established intellectual, he has published 36 books and articles on Islam, Islamic terrorism and problems of Central Asian national security.

Venezuela
Pearse Rafael Marschner
Pearse Rafael Marschner has spent five of the past seven years in the Middle East and has spent time in Latin America and the Caribbean. He is a student of Latin American and Middle Eastern synergies.

Yemen
Adam Seitz
Adam C. Seitz is the Senior Research Associate for Middle East Studies at Marine Corps University in Quantico, Virginia where he supports the University with his expertise on the Middle East, with a concentration on Iran and the Persian Gulf Region. Mr. Seitz is the co-author, with Anthony H. Cordesman (CSIS), of the book *Iranian Weapons of Mass Destruction: The Birth of a Regional Nuclear Arms Race?* (Praeger Security International, 2009). Mr. Seitz served in the U.S. Army as an Intelligence Analyst and is an Operation Iraqi Freedom Veteran, serving in Al-Anbar province in 2003 and 2004.